MW01630224

THE COMEDIES

The Complete Works of William Shakespeare

VOLUME I

* * * * *

The Comedies

Wordsworth Editions

The Complete Works of William Shakespeare
Volume I : The Comedies

First published in 2002
by Wordsworth Editions Limited
Cumberland House, Crib Street, Ware,
Hertfordshire SG12 9ET

ISBN 1 84022 037 6

Printed and bound in the United States of America

CONTENTS

THE PLAYS

THE PLAYS

THE COMEDY OF ERRORS

DRAMATIS PERSONAE

SOLINUS, *Duke of Ephesus.*
AEGEON, *a merchant of Syracuse.*
ANTIPHOLUS OF EPHESUS, ANTIPHOLUS OF SYRACUSE, *twin brothers and sons to Aegeon and Aemilia.*
DROMIO OF EPHESUS, DROMIO OF SYRACUSE, *twin brothers, and attendants on the two Antipholuses.*
BALTHAZAR, *a merchant.*
ANGELO, *a goldsmith.*
FIRST MERCHANT, *friend to Antipholus of Syracuse.*
SECOND MERCHANT, *to whom Angelo is a debtor.*
PINCH, *a schoolmaster.*

AEMILIA, *wife to Aegeon, an abbess at Ephesus.*
ADRIANA, *wife to Antipholus of Ephesus.*
LUCIANA, *her sister.*
LUCE, *servant to Adriana.*
A COURTEZAN.

GAOLER, OFFICERS, *and other* ATTENDANTS.

SCENE—*Ephesus.*

ACT I. SCENE I.

A hall in the DUKE'S *palace.*

Enter DUKE, AEGEON, GAOLER, OFFICERS, *and other* ATTENDANTS.

AEGEON.

PROCEED, Solinus, to procure my fall,
And by the doom of death end woes and all.

DUKE OF EPHESUS.

Merchant of Syracusa, plead no more;
I am not partial to infringe our laws:
The enmity and discord which of late
Sprung from the rancorous outrage of your duke
To merchants, our well-dealing countrymen,—
Who, wanting guilders to redeem their lives,
Have seal'd his rigorous statutes with their bloods,
Excludes all pity from our threat'ning looks.
For, since the mortal and intestine jars
'Twixt thy seditious countrymen and us,
It hath in solemn synods been decreed,
Both by the Syracusians and ourselves,
To admit no traffic to our adverse towns:
Nay, more, if any born at Ephesus
Be seen at Syracusian marts and fairs;
Again, if any Syracusian born
Come to the bay of Ephesus, he dies,
His goods confiscate to the duke's dispose;
Unless a thousand marks be levied,
To quit the penalty and to ransom him.
Thy substance, valued at the highest rate,
Cannot amount unto a hundred marks;
Therefore by law thou art condemn'd to die.

AEGEON.

Yet this my comfort,—when your words are done,
My woes end likewise with the evening sun.

DUKE OF EPHESUS.

Well, Syracusian, say, in brief, the cause
Why thou departed'st from thy native home,
And for what cause thou camest to Ephesus.

AEGEON.

A heavier task could not have been imposed
Than I to speak my griefs unspeakable:
Yet, that the world may witness that my end
Was wrought by nature, not by vile offence,
I'll utter what my sorrow gives me leave.
In Syracusa was I born; and wed
Unto a woman, happy but for me,
And by me too, had not our hap been bad.
With her I lived in joy; our wealth increased
By prosperous voyages I often made
To Epidamnum; till my factor's death,
And the great care of goods at random left,
Drew me from kind embracements of my spouse:
From whom my absence was not six months old,
Before herself—almost at fainting under
The pleasing punishment that women bear—
Had made provision for her following me,
And soon and safe arrived where I was.
There had she not been long but she became
A joyful mother of two goodly sons;
And, which was strange, the one so like the other
As could not be distinguish'd but by names.
That very hour, and in the self-same inn,
A meaner woman was delivered
Of such a burden, male twins, both alike:
Those, for their parents were exceeding poor,
I bought, and brought up to attend my sons.
My wife, not meanly proud of two such boys,
Made daily motions for our home return:
Unwilling I agreed. Alas, too soon
We came aboard!
A league from Epidamnum had we sail'd,
Before the always-wind-obeying deep
Gave any tragic instance of our harm:
But longer did we not retain much hope;
For what obscured light the heavens did grant
Did but convey unto our fearful minds
A doubtful warrant of immediate death;
Which though myself would gladly have embraced
Yet the incessant weepings of my wife,
Weeping before for what she saw must come,
And piteous plainings of the pretty babes,
That mourn'd for fashion, ignorant what to fear,
Forced me to seek delays for them and me.
And this it was,—for other means was none:—
The sailors sought for safety by our boat,
And left the ship, then sinking-ripe, to us:
My wife, more careful for the latter-born,
Had fasten'd him unto a small spare mast,
Such as seafaring men provide for storms;
To him one of the other twins was bound,
Whilst I had been like heedful of the other:
The children thus disposed, my wife and I,
Fixing our eyes on whom our care was fixt,
Fasten'd ourselves at either end the mast;
And floating straight, obedient to the stream,
Was carried towards Corinth, as we thought.
At length the sun, gazing upon the earth,

Dispersed those vapours that offended us;
And, by the benefit of his wished light,
The seas waxt calm, and we discovered
Two ships from far making amain to us,
Of Corinth that, of Epidaurus this:
But ere they came,—O, let me say no more!
Gather the sequel by that went before.

DUKE OF EPHESUS.

Nay, forward, old man; do not break off so;
For we may pity, though not pardon thee.

AEGEON.

O, had the gods done so, I had not now
Worthily term'd them merciless to us!
For, ere the ships could meet by twice five leagues,
We were encounter'd by a mighty rock;
Which being violently borne upon,
Our helpful ship was splitted in the midst;
So that, in this unjust divorce of us,
Fortune had left to both of us alike
What to delight in, what to sorrow for.
Her part, poor soul! seeming as burdened
With lesser weight, but not with lesser woe,
Was carried with more speed before the wind;
And in our sight they three were taken up
By fishermen of Corinth, as we thought.
At length, another ship had seized on us;
And, knowing whom it was their hap to save,
Gave healthful welcome to their shipwrackt guests;
And would have reft the fishers of their prey,
Had not their bark been very slow of sail,
And therefore homeward did they bend their course.—
Thus have you heard me sever'd from my bliss;
That by misfortunes was my life prolong'd,
To tell sad stories of my own mishaps.

DUKE OF EPHESUS.

And, for the sake of them thou sorrowest for,
Do me the favour to dilate at full
What have befall'n of them and thee till now.

AEGEON.

My youngest boy, and yet my eldest care,
At eighteen years became inquisitive
After his brother; and importuned me
That his attendant—so his case was like,
Reft of his brother, but retain'd his name—
Might bear him company in the quest of him:
Whom whilst I labour'd of a love to see,
I hazarded the loss of whom I loved
Five summers have I spent in furthest Greece,
Roaming clean through the bounds of Asia,
And, coasting homeward, came to Ephesus;
Hopeless to find, yet loth to leave unsought
Or that, or any place that harbours men.
But here must end the story of my life;
And happy were I in my timely death,
Could all my travels warrant me they live.

DUKE OF EPHESUS.

Hapless Aegeon, whom the fates have markt
To bear the extremity of dire mishap!
Now, trust me, were it not against our laws,
Against my crown, my oath, my dignity,—
Which princes, would they, may not disannul,—
My soul should sue as advocate for thee.
But, though thou art adjudged to the death,
And passed sentence may not be recall'd
But to our honour's great disparagement,
Yet will I favour thee in what I can.
Therefore, merchant, I'll limit thee this day
To seek thy life by beneficial help:
Try all the friends thou hast in Ephesus;
Beg thou, or borrow, to make up the sum,
And live; if no, then thou art doom'd to die.—
Gaoler, take him to thy custody.

GAOLER.

I will, my lord.

AEGEON.

Hopeless and helpless doth Aegeon wend,
But to procrastinate his lifeless end. [*Exeunt.*

SCENE II.

The Mart.

Enter ANTIPHOLUS OF SYRACUSE, DROMIO OF SYRACUSE, *and* FIRST MERCHANT.

FIRST MERCHANT.

THEREfore give out you are of Epidamnum,
Lest that your goods too soon be confiscate.
This very day a Syracusian merchant
Is apprehended for arrival here;
And, not being able to buy out his life,
According to the statute of the town,
Dies ere the weary sun set in the west.
There is your money that I had to keep.

ANTIPHOLUS OF SYRACUSE.

Go bear it to the Centaur, where we host,
And stay there, Dromio, till I come to thee.
Within this hour it will be dinner-time:
Till that, I'll view the manners of the town,
Peruse the traders, gaze upon the buildings,
And then return, and sleep within mine inn;
For with long travel I am stiff and weary.
Get thee away.

DROMIO OF SYRACUSE.

Many a man would take you at your word,
And go indeed, having so good a mean. [*Exit.*

ANTIPHOLUS OF SYRACUSE.

A trusty villain, sir; that very oft,
When I am dull with care and melancholy,
Lightens my humour with his merry jests.
What, will you walk with me about the town,
And then go to my inn, and dine with me?

FIRST MERCHANT.

I am invited, sir, to certain merchants,
Of whom I hope to make much benefit;
I crave your pardon. Soon at five o'clock,
Please you, I'll meet with you upon the mart,
And afterwards consort you till bed-time:
My present business calls me from you now.

ANTIPHOLUS OF SYRACUSE.

Farewell till then: I will go lose myself,
And wander up and down to view the city.

FIRST MERCHANT.

Sir, I commend you to your own content. [*Exit.*

ANTIPHOLUS OF SYRACUSE.

He that commends me to mine own content
Commends me to the thing I cannot get.
I to the world am like a drop of water,
That in the ocean seeks another drop;
Who, falling there to find his fellow forth,
Unseen, inquisitive, confounds himself:
So I, to find a mother and a brother,

In quest of them, unhappy, lose myself.—
Here comes the almanack of my true date.
Enter DROMIO OF EPHESUS.
What now? how chance thou art return'd so soon?

DROMIO OF EPHESUS.
Return'd so soon! rather approacht too late:
The capon burns, the pig falls from the spit;
The clock hath strucken twelve upon the bell,—
My mistress made it one upon my cheek:
She is so hot, because the meat is cold;
The meat is cold, because you come not home;
You come not home, because you have no stomach;
You have no stomach, having broke your fast;
But we, that know what 'tis to fast and pray,
Are penitent for your default to-day.

ANTIPHOLUS OF SYRACUSE.
Stop in your wind, sir: tell me this, I pray,—
Where have you left the money that I gave you?

DROMIO OF EPHESUS.
O,—sixpence, that I had o' Wednesday last
To pay the saddler for my mistress' crupper:—
The saddler had it, sir; I kept it not.

ANTIPHOLUS OF SYRACUSE.
I am not in a sportive humour now:
Tell me, and dally not, where is the money?
We being strangers here, how darest thou trust
So great a charge from thine own custody?

DROMIO OF EPHESUS.
I pray you, jest, sir, as you sit at dinner:
I from my mistress come to you in post;
If I return, I shall be post indeed,
For she will score your fault upon my pate.
Methinks your maw, like mine, should be your clock,
And strike you home without a messenger.

ANTIPHOLUS OF SYRACUSE.
Come, Dromio, come, these jests are out of season;
Reserve them till a merrier hour than this.
Where is the gold I gave in charge to thee?

DROMIO OF EPHESUS.
To me, sir! why, you gave no gold to me.

ANTIPHOLUS OF SYRACUSE.
Come on, sir knave, have done your foolishness,
And tell me how thou hast disposed thy charge.

DROMIO OF EPHESUS.
My charge was but to fetch you from the mart
Home to your house, the Phœnix, sir, to dinner:
My mistress and her sister stay for you.

ANTIPHOLUS OF SYRACUSE.
Now, as I am a Christian, answer me,
In what safe place you have bestow'd my money;
Or I shall break that merry sconce of yours,
That stands on tricks when I am undisposed:
Where is the thousand marks thou hadst of me?

DROMIO OF EPHESUS.
I have some marks of yours upon my pate,
Some of my mistress' marks upon my shoulders;
But not a thousand marks between you both.
If I should pay your worship those again,
Perchance you will not bear them patiently.

ANTIPHOLUS OF SYRACUSE.
Thy mistress' marks! what mistress, slave, hast thou?

DROMIO OF EPHESUS.
Your worship's wife, my mistress at the Phœnix;
She that doth fast till you come home to dinner,
And prays that you will hie you home to dinner.

ANTIPHOLUS OF SYRACUSE.
What, wilt thou flout me thus unto my face,
Being forbid? There, take you that, sir knave.
[*Beating him.*

DROMIO OF EPHESUS.
What mean you, sir? for God's sake, hold your hands!
Nay, an you will not, sir, I'll take my heels. [*Exit.*

ANTIPHOLUS OF SYRACUSE.
Upon my life, by some device or other
The villain is o'er-raught of all my money.
They say this town is full of cozenage;
As, nimble jugglers that deceive the eye,
Dark-working sorcerers that change the mind,
Soul-killing witches that deform the body,
Disguised cheaters, prating mountebanks,
And many such-like liberties of sin:
If it prove so, I will be gone the sooner.
I'll to the Centaur, to go seek this slave:
I greatly fear my money is not safe. [*Exit.*

ACT II. SCENE I.

Before the house of ANTIPHOLUS OF EPHESUS.

Enter ADRIANA *and* LUCIANA.

ADRIANA.
NEITHER my husband nor the slave return'd,
That in such haste I sent to seek his master!
Sure, Luciana, it is two o'clock.

LUCIANA.
Perhaps some merchant hath invited him,
And from the mart he's somewhere gone to dinner.
Good sister, let us dine, and never fret:
A man is master of his liberty:
Time is their master; and when they see time,
They'll go or come: if so, be patient, sister.

ADRIANA.
Why should their liberty than ours be more?

LUCIANA.
Because their business still lies out o' door.

ADRIANA.
Look, when I serve him so, he takes it ill.

LUCIANA.
O, know he is the bridle of your will.

ADRIANA.
There's none but asses will be bridled so.

LUCIANA.
Why, headstrong liberty is lasht with woe.
There's nothing situate under heaven's eye
But hath his bound, in earth, in sea, in sky:
The beasts, the fishes, and the winged fowls,
Are their males' subjects and at their controls:
Men, more divine, the masters of all these,
Lords of the wide world and wild wat'ry seas,
Indued with intellectual sense and souls,
Of more pre-eminence than fish and fowls,
Are masters to their females and their lords:
Then let your will attend on their accords.

ADRIANA.
This servitude makes you to keep unwed.

LUCIANA.
Not this, but troubles of the marriage-bed.

ADRIANA.
But, were you wedded, you would bear some sway.

LUCIANA.
Ere I learn love, I'll practise to obey.

ADRIANA.
How if your husband start some other where?

LUCIANA.
Till he come home again, I would forbear.

ADRIANA.
Patience unmoved! no marvel though she pause;
They can be meek that have no other cause.
A wretched soul, bruised with adversity,
We bid be quiet when we hear it cry;
But were we burden'd with like weight of pain,
As much, or more, we should ourselves complain:
So thou, that hast no unkind mate to grieve thee,
With urging helpless patience would relieve me;
But, if thou live to see like right bereft,
This fool-begg'd patience in thee will be left.

LUCIANA.
Well, I will marry one day, but to try.—
Here comes your man; now is your husband nigh.

Enter DROMIO OF EPHESUS.

ADRIANA.
Say, is your tardy master now at hand?

DROMIO OF EPHESUS.
Nay, he's at two hands with me, and that my two ears can witness.

ADRIANA.
Say, didst thou speak with him? know'st thou his mind?

DROMIO OF EPHESUS.
Ay, ay, he told his mind upon mine ear:
Beshrew his hand, I scarce could understand it.

LUCIANA.
Spake he so doubtfully, thou couldst not feel his meaning?

DROMIO OF EPHESUS.
Nay, he struck so plainly, I could too well feel his blows; and withal so doubtfully, that I could scarce understand them.

ADRIANA.
But say, I prithee, is he coming home?
It seems he hath great care to please his wife.

DROMIO OF EPHESUS.
Why, mistress, sure my master is horn-mad.

ADRIANA.
Horn-mad, thou villain!

DROMIO OF EPHESUS.
I mean not cuckold-mad;
But, sure, he is stark mad.
When I desired him to come home to dinner.
He ask'd me for a thousand marks in gold:
''Tis dinner-time,' quoth I; 'My gold,' quoth he:
'Your meat doth burn,' quoth I; 'My gold,' quoth he:
'Will you come home?' quoth I; 'My gold,' quoth he;
'Where is the thousand marks I gave thee, villain?'
'The pig,' quoth I, 'is burn'd;' 'My gold,' quoth he:
'My mistress, sir,' quoth I; 'Hang up thy mistress!
I know not thy mistress; out on thy mistress!'

LUCIANA.
Quoth who?

DROMIO OF EPHESUS.
Quoth my master:
'I know,' quoth he, 'no house, no wife, no mistress.'
So that my arrant, due unto my tongue,
I thank him, I bear home upon my shoulders;
For, in conclusion, he did beat me there.

ADRIANA.
Go back again, thou slave, and fetch him home.

DROMIO OF EPHESUS.
Go back again, and be new beaten home!
For God's sake, send some other messenger.

ADRIANA.
Back, slave, or I will break thy pate across.

DROMIO OF EPHESUS.
And he will bless that cross with other beating:
Between you I shall have a holy head.

ADRIANA.
Hence, prating peasant! fetch thy master home.

DROMIO OF EPHESUS.
Am I so round with you as you with me,
That like a football you do spurn me thus?
You spurn me hence, and he will spurn me hither:
If I last in this service, you must case me in leather. [*Exit.*

LUCIANA.
Fie, how impatience low'reth in your face!

ADRIANA.
His company must do his minions grace,
Whilst I at home starve for a merry look.
Hath homely age th' alluring beauty took
From my poor cheek? then he hath wasted it:
Are my discourses dull? barren my wit?
If voluble and sharp discourse be marr'd,
Unkindness blunts it more than marble hard:
Do their gay vestments his affections bait?
That's not my fault,—he's master of my state:
What ruins are in me that can be found
By him not ruin'd? then is he the ground
Of my defeatures. My decayed fair
A sunny look of his would soon repair:
But, too unruly deer, he breaks the pale,
And feeds from home; poor I am but his stale.

LUCIANA.
Self-harming jealousy,—fie, beat it hence!

ADRIANA.
Unfeeling fools can with such wrongs dispense.
I know his eye doth homage otherwhere;
Or else what lets it but he would be here?
Sister, you know he promised me a chain;—
Would that alone alone he would detain,
So he would keep fair quarter with his bed!
I see the jewel best enamelled
Will lose his beauty; and though gold bides still
The tester's touch, yet often-touching will
Wear gold: and so no man that hath a name,
But falsehood and corruption doth it shame.
Since that my beauty cannot please his eye,
I'll weep what's left away, and weeping die.

LUCIANA.
How many fond fools serve mad jealousy!
[*Exeunt.*

SCENE II.

The Mart.

Enter ANTIPHOLUS OF SYRACUSE.

ANTIPHOLUS OF SYRACUSE.

THE gold I gave to Dromio is laid up
Safe at the Centaur; and the heedful slave
Is wander'd forth, in care to seek me out.
By computation and mine host's report,
I could not speak with Dromio since at first
I sent him from the mart.—See, here he comes.

Enter DROMIO OF SYRACUSE.

How now, sir! is your merry humour alter'd?
As you love strokes, so jest with me again.
You know no Centaur? you received no gold?
Your mistress sent to have me home to dinner?
My house was at the Phœnix? Wast thou mad,
That thus so madly thou didst answer me?

DROMIO OF SYRACUSE.

What answer, sir? when spake I such a word?

ANTIPHOLUS OF SYRACUSE.

Even now, even here, not half an hour since.

DROMIO OF SYRACUSE.

I did not see you since you sent me hence,
Home to the Centaur, with the gold you gave me.

ANTIPHOLUS OF SYRACUSE.

Villain, thou didst deny the gold's receipt,
And told'st me of a mistress and a dinner;
For which, I hope, thou felt'st I was displeased.

DROMIO OF SYRACUSE.

I am glad to see you in this merry vein:
What means this jest? I pray you, master, tell me.

ANTIPHOLUS OF SYRACUSE.

Yea, dost thou jeer and flout me in the teeth?
Think'st thou I jest? Hold, take thou that, and that. [*Beats* DROMIO.

DROMIO OF SYRACUSE.

Hold, sir, for God's sake! now your jest is earnest:
Upon what bargain do you give it me?

ANTIPHOLUS OF SYRACUSE.

Because that I familiarly sometimes
Do use you for my fool, and chat with you,
Your sauciness will jet upon my love,
And make a common of my serious hours.
When the sun shines let foolish gnats make sport,
But creep in crannies when he hides his beams.
If you will jest with me, know my aspect,
And fashion your demeanour to my looks,
Or I will beat this method in your sconce.

DROMIO OF SYRACUSE.

Sconce call you it? so you would leave battering, I had rather have it a head: an you use these blows long, I must get a sconce for my head, and ensconce it too; or else I shall seek my wit in my shoulders. But, I pray, sir, why am I beaten?

ANTIPHOLUS OF SYRACUSE.

Dost thou not know?

DROMIO OF SYRACUSE.

Nothing, sir, but that I am beaten.

ANTIPHOLUS OF SYRACUSE.

Shall I tell you why?

DROMIO OF SYRACUSE.

Ay, sir, and wherefore; for they say every why hath a wherefore.

ANTIPHOLUS OF SYRACUSE.

Why, first,—for flouting me; and then, wherefore,—
For urging it the second time to me.

DROMIO OF SYRACUSE.

Was there ever any man thus beaten out of season,
When in the why and the wherefore is neither rime nor reason?
Well, sir, I thank you.

ANTIPHOLUS OF SYRACUSE.

Thank me, sir! for what?

DROMIO OF SYRACUSE.

Marry, sir, for this something that you gave me for nothing.

ANTIPHOLUS OF SYRACUSE.

I'll make you amends next, to give you nothing for something. But say, sir, is it dinner-time?

DROMIO OF SYRACUSE.

No, sir: I think the meat wants that I have.

ANTIPHOLUS OF SYRACUSE.

In good time, sir; what's that?

DROMIO OF SYRACUSE.

Basting.

ANTIPHOLUS OF SYRACUSE.

Well, sir, then 'twill be dry.

DROMIO OF SYRACUSE.

If it be, sir, I pray you, eat none of it.

ANTIPHOLUS OF SYRACUSE.

Your reason?

DROMIO OF SYRACUSE.

Lest it make you choleric, and purchase me another dry basting.

ANTIPHOLUS OF SYRACUSE.

Well, sir, learn to jest in good time: there's a time for all things.

DROMIO OF SYRACUSE.

I durst have denied that, before you were so choleric.

ANTIPHOLUS OF SYRACUSE.

By what rule, sir?

DROMIO OF SYRACUSE.

Marry, sir, by a rule as plain as the plain bald pate of father Time himself.

ANTIPHOLUS OF SYRACUSE.

Let's hear it.

DROMIO OF SYRACUSE.

There's no time for a man to recover his hair that grows bald by nature.

ANTIPHOLUS OF SYRACUSE.

May he not do it by fine and recovery?

DROMIO OF SYRACUSE.

Yes, to pay a fine for a periwig, and recover the lost hair of another man.

ANTIPHOLUS OF SYRACUSE.

Why is Time such a niggard of hair, being, as it is, so plentiful an excrement?

DROMIO OF SYRACUSE.

Because it is a blessing that he bestows on beasts: and what he hath scanted men in hair, he hath given them in wit.

ANTIPHOLUS OF SYRACUSE.

Why, but there's many a man hath more hair than wit.

DROMIO OF SYRACUSE.

Not a man of those but he hath the wit to lose his hair.

ANTIPHOLUS OF SYRACUSE.
Why, thou didst conclude hairy men plain-dealers without wit.

DROMIO OF SYRACUSE.
The plainer dealer, the sooner lost: yet he loseth it in a kind of jollity.

ANTIPHOLUS OF SYRACUSE.
For what reason?

DROMIO OF SYRACUSE.
For two; and sound ones too.

ANTIPHOLUS OF SYRACUSE.
Nay, not sound, I pray you.

DROMIO OF SYRACUSE.
Sure ones, then.

ANTIPHOLUS OF SYRACUSE.
Nay, not sure, in a thing falsing.

DROMIO OF SYRACUSE.
Certain ones, then.

ANTIPHOLUS OF SYRACUSE.
Name them.

DROMIO OF SYRACUSE.
The one, to save the money that he spends in tiring; the other, that at dinner they should not drop in his porridge.

ANTIPHOLUS OF SYRACUSE.
You would all this time have proved there is no time for all things.

DROMIO OF SYRACUSE.
Marry, and did, sir; namely, no time to recover hair lost by nature.

ANTIPHOLUS OF SYRACUSE.
But your reason was not substantial, why there is no time to recover.

DROMIO OF SYRACUSE.
Thus I mend it: Time himself is bald, and therefore to the world's end will have bald followers.

ANTIPHOLUS OF SYRACUSE.
I knew 'twould be a bald conclusion:
But, soft! who wafts us yonder?

Enter ADRIANA *and* LUCIANA.

ADRIANA.
Ay, ay, Antipholus, look strange and frown:
Some other mistress hath thy sweet aspects;
I am not Adriana nor thy wife.
The time was once when thou unurged wouldst vow
That never words were music to thine ear,
That never object pleasing in thine eye,
That never touch well-welcome to thy hand,
That never meat sweet-savour'd in thy taste,
Unless I spake, or look'd, or touch'd, or carved to thee.
How comes it now, my husband, O, how comes it,
That thou art then estranged from thyself?
Thyself I call it, being strange to me,
That, undividable, incorporate,
Am better than thy dear self's better part.
Ah, do not tear away thyself from me!
For know, my love, as easy mayst thou fall
A drop of water in the breaking gulf,
And take unmingled thence that drop again,
Without addition or diminishing,
As take from me thyself, and not me too.
How dearly would it touch thee to the quick,
Shouldst thou but hear I were licentious,
And that this body, consecrate to thee,
By ruffian lust should be contaminate!
Wouldst thou not spit at me and spurn at me,
And hurl the name of husband in my face,
And tear the stain'd skin off my harlot-brow,
And from my false hand cut the wedding-ring,
And break it with a deep-divorcing vow?
I know thou canst; and therefore see thou do it.
I am possest with an adulterate blot;
My blood is mingled with the grime of lust:
For if we two be one, and thou play false,
I do digest the poison of thy flesh,
Being strumpeted by thy contagion.
Keep, then, fair league and truce with thy true bed;
I live unstain'd, thou undishonoured.

ANTIPHOLUS OF SYRACUSE.
Plead you to me, fair dame? I know you not:
In Ephesus I am but two hours old,
As strange unto your town as to your talk;
Who, every word by all my wit being scann'd,
Want wit in all one word to understand.

LUCIANA.
Fie, brother! how the world is changed with you!
When were you wont to use my sister thus?
She sent for you by Dromio home to dinner.

ANTIPHOLUS OF SYRACUSE.
By Dromio!

DROMIO OF SYRACUSE.
By me!

ADRIANA.
By thee; and this thou didst return from him,—
That he did buffet thee, and, in his blows,
Denied my house for his, me for his wife.

ANTIPHOLUS OF SYRACUSE.
Did you converse, sir, with this gentlewoman?
What is the course and drift of your compact?

DROMIO OF SYRACUSE.
I, sir! I never saw her till this time.

ANTIPHOLUS OF SYRACUSE.
Villain, thou liest; for even her very words
Didst thou deliver to me on the mart.

DROMIO OF SYRACUSE.
I never spake with her in all my life.

ANTIPHOLUS OF SYRACUSE.
How can she thus, then, call us by our names,
Unless it be by inspiration?

ADRIANA.
How ill agrees it with your gravity
To counterfeit thus grossly with your slave,
Abetting him to thwart me in my mood!
Be it my wrong you are from me exempt,
But wrong not that wrong with a more contempt.
Come, I will fasten on this sleeve of thine:
Thou art an elm, my husband,—I a vine,
Whose weakness, married to thy stronger state,
Makes me with thy strength to communicate:
If aught possess thee from me, it is dross,
Usurping ivy, brier, or idle moss;
Who, all for want of pruning, with intrusion
Infect thy sap, and live on thy confusion.

ANTIPHOLUS OF SYRACUSE [*aside*].
To me she speaks; she moves me for her theme:
What, was I married to her in my dream?
Or sleep I now, and think I hear all this?
What error drives our eyes and ears amiss?

Until I know this sure uncertainty,
I'll entertain the offer'd fallacy.

LUCIANA.

Dromio, go bid the servants spread for dinner.

DROMIO OF SYRACUSE.

O, for my beads! I cross me for a sinner.
This is the fairy land;—O spite of spites!—
We talk with goblins, owls, and elvish sprites:
If we obey them not, this will ensue,—
They'll suck our breath, or pinch us black and blue.

LUCIANA.

Why pratest thou to thyself, and answer'st not?
Dromio, thou drone, thou snail, thou slug, thou sot!

DROMIO OF SYRACUSE.

I am transformed, master, am not I?

ANTIPHOLUS OF SYRACUSE.

I think thou art in mind, and so am I.

DROMIO OF SYRACUSE.

Nay, master, both in mind and in my shape.

ANTIPHOLUS OF SYRACUSE.

Thou hast thine own form.

DROMIO OF SYRACUSE.

No, I am an ape.

LUCIANA.

If thou art changed to aught, 'tis to an ass.

DROMIO OF SYRACUSE.

'Tis true; she rides me, and I long for grass.
'Tis so, I am an ass; else it could never be
But I should know her as well as she knows me.

ADRIANA.

Come, come, no longer will I be a fool,
To put the finger in the eye and weep,
Whilst man and master laugh my woes to scorn.—
Come, sir, to dinner.—Dromio, keep the gate.—
Husband, I'll dine above with you to-day,
And shrive you of a thousand idle pranks.—
Sirrah, if any ask you for your master,
Say he dines forth, and let no creature enter.—
Come, sister.—Dromio, play the porter well.

ANTIPHOLUS OF SYRACUSE [*aside*].

Am I in earth, in heaven, or in hell?
Sleeping or waking? mad or well-advised?
Known unto these, and to myself disguised!
I'll say as they say, and persever so,
And in this mist at all adventures go.

DROMIO OF SYRACUSE.

Master, shall I be porter at the gate?

ADRIANA.

Ay; and let none enter, lest I break your pate.

LUCIANA.

Come, come, Antipholus, we dine too late.

[*Exeunt.*

ACT III. SCENE I.

Before the house of ANTIPHOLUS OF EPHESUS.

Enter ANTIPHOLUS OF EPHESUS, DROMIO OF EPHESUS, ANGELO, *and* BALTHAZAR.

ANTIPHOLUS OF EPHESUS.

GOOD Signior Angelo, you must excuse us all;
My wife is shrewish when I keep not hours:
Say that I linger'd with you at your shop
To see the making of her carcanet,
And that to-morrow you will bring it home.
But here's a villain that would face me down
He met me on the mart, and that I beat him,
And charged him with a thousand marks in gold,
And that I did deny my wife and house.—
Thou drunkard, thou, what didst thou mean by this?

DROMIO OF EPHESUS.

Say what you will, sir, but I know what I know;
That you beat me at the mart, I have your hand to show:
If the skin were parchment, and the blows you gave were ink,
Your own handwriting would tell you what I think.

ANTIPHOLUS OF EPHESUS.

I think thou art an ass.

DROMIO OF EPHESUS.

Marry, so it doth appear
By the wrongs I suffer and the blows I bear.
I should kick, being kickt; and, being at that pass,
You would keep from my heels, and beware of an ass.

ANTIPHOLUS OF EPHESUS.

You're sad, Signior Balthazar: pray God our cheer
May answer my good will and your good welcome here!

BALTHAZAR.

I hold your dainties cheap, sir, and your welcome dear.

ANTIPHOLUS OF EPHESUS.

O, Signior Balthazar, either at flesh or fish,
A table full of welcome makes scarce one dainty dish.

BALTHAZAR.

Good meat, sir, is common; that every churl affords.

ANTIPHOLUS OF EPHESUS.

And welcome more common; for that's nothing but words.

BALTHAZAR.

Small cheer and great welcome makes a merry feast.

ANTIPHOLUS OF EPHESUS.

Ay, to a niggardly host and more sparing guest:
But though my cates be mean, take them in good part:
Better cheer may you have, but not with better heart.
But, soft! my door is lockt.—Go bid them let us in.

DROMIO OF EPHESUS.

Maud, Bridget, Marian, Cicely, Gillian, Ginn!

DROMIO OF SYRACUSE [*within*].

Mome, malt-horse, capon, coxcomb, idiot, patch!
Either get thee from the door, or sit down at the hatch.
Dost thou conjure for wenches, that thou call'st for such store,
When one is one too many? Go get thee from the door.

DROMIO OF EPHESUS.

What patch is made our porter?—My master stays in the street.

DROMIO OF SYRACUSE [*within*].
Let him walk from whence he came, lest he catch cold on's feet.

ANTIPHOLUS OF EPHESUS.
Who talks within there? ho, open the door!

DROMIO OF SYRACUSE [*within*].
Right, sir; I'll tell you when, an you'll tell me wherefore.

ANTIPHOLUS OF EPHESUS.
Wherefore! for my dinner: I have not dined to-day.

DROMIO OF SYRACUSE [*within*].
Nor to-day here you must not; come again when you may.

ANTIPHOLUS OF EPHESUS.
What art thou that keep'st me out from the house I owe?

DROMIO OF SYRACUSE [*within*].
The porter for this time, sir, and my name is Dromio.

DROMIO OF EPHESUS.
O villain, thou hast stol'n both mine office and my name!
The one ne'er got me credit, the other mickle blame.
If thou hadst been Dromio to-day in my place,
Thou wouldst have changed thy face for a name, or thy name for an ass.

LUCE [*within*].
What a coil is there, Dromio! who are those at the gate?

DROMIO OF EPHESUS.
Let my master in, Luce.

LUCE [*within*].
Faith, no; he comes too late;
And so tell your master.

DROMIO OF EPHESUS.
O Lord, I must laugh!—
Have at you with a proverb;—Shall I set in my staff?

LUCE [*within*].
Have at you with another; that's, —When? can you tell?

DROMIO OF SYRACUSE [*within*].
If thy name be call'd Luce,—Luce, thou hast answer'd him well.

ANTIPHOLUS OF EPHESUS.
Do you hear, you minion? you'll let us in, I hope?

LUCE [*within*].
I thought to have askt you.

DROMIO OF SYRACUSE [*within*].
And you said no.

DROMIO OF EPHESUS.
So, come, help:—well struck! there was blow for blow.

ANTIPHOLUS OF EPHESUS.
Thou baggage, let me in.

LUCE [*within*].
Can you tell for whose sake?

DROMIO OF EPHESUS.
Master, knock the door hard.

LUCE [*within*].
Let him knock till it ache.

ANTIPHOLUS OF EPHESUS.
You'll cry for this, minion, if I beat the door down.

LUCE [*within*].
What needs all that, and a pair of stocks in the town?

ADRIANA [*within*].
Who is that at the door that keeps all this noise?

DROMIO OF SYRACUSE [*within*].
By my troth, your town is troubled with unruly boys.

ANTIPHOLUS OF EPHESUS.
Are you there, wife? you might have come before.

ADRIANA [*within*].
Your wife, sir knave! go get you from the door.

DROMIO OF EPHESUS.
If you went in pain, master, this knave would go sore.

ANGELO.
Here is neither cheer, sir, nor welcome: we would fain have either.

BALTHAZAR.
In debating which was best, we shall part with neither.

DROMIO OF EPHESUS.
They stand at the door, master; bid them welcome hither.

ANTIPHOLUS OF EPHESUS.
There is something in the wind, that we cannot get in.

DROMIO OF EPHESUS.
You would say so, master, if your garments were thin.
Your cake there is warm within; you stand here in the cold:
It would make a man mad as a buck, to be so bought and sold.

ANTIPHOLUS OF EPHESUS.
Go fetch me something: I'll break ope the gate.

DROMIO OF SYRACUSE [*within*].
Break any breaking here, and I'll break your knave's pate.

DROMIO OF EPHESUS.
A man may break a word with you, sir; and words are but wind;
Ay, and break it in your face, so he break it not behind.

DROMIO OF SYRACUSE [*within*].
It seems thou want'st breaking: out upon thee, hind!

DROMIO OF EPHESUS.
Here's too much 'out upon thee!' I pray thee, let me in.

DROMIO OF SYRACUSE [*within*].
Ay, when fowls have no feathers, and fish have no fin.

ANTIPHOLUS OF EPHESUS.
Well, I'll break in:—go borrow me a crow.

DROMIO OF EPHESUS.
A crow without feather,—master, mean you so?
For a fish without a fin, there's a fowl without a feather:
If a crow help us in, sirrah, we'll pluck a crow together.

ANTIPHOLUS OF EPHESUS.
Go get thee gone; fetch me an iron crow.

BALTHAZAR.

Have patience, sir; O, let it not be so!
Herein you war against your reputation,
And draw within the compass of suspect
Th' unviolated honour of your wife.
Once this,—your long experience of her wisdom,
Her sober virtue, years, and modesty,
Plead on her part some cause to you unknown;
And doubt not, sir, but she will well excuse
Why at this time the doors are made against you.
Be ruled by me: depart in patience,
And let us to the Tiger all to dinner;
And about evening come yourself alone
To know the reason of this strange restraint.
If by strong hand you offer to break in
Now in the stirring passage of the day,
A vulgar comment will be made of it,
And that supposed by the common rout
Against your yet ungalled estimation,
That may with foul intrusion enter in,
And dwell upon your grave when you are dead;
For slander lives upon succession,
For ever housed where it gets possession.

ANTIPHOLUS OF EPHESUS.

You have prevail'd: I will depart in quiet,
And, in despite of mirth, mean to be merry.
I know a wench of excellent discourse,
Pretty and witty; wild, and yet, too, gentle:
There will we dine. This woman that I mean,
My wife—but, I protest, without desert—
Hath oftentimes upbraided me withal:
To her will we to dinner.—Get you home,
And fetch the chain; by this I know 'tis made:
Bring it, I pray you, to the Porpentine;
For there's the house: that chain will I bestow—
Be it for nothing but to spite my wife—
Upon mine hostess there: good sir, make haste.
Since mine own doors refuse to entertain me,
I'll knock elsewhere, to see if they'll disdain me.

ANGELO.

I'll meet you at that place some hour hence.

ANTIPHOLUS OF EPHESUS.

Do so. This jest shall cost me some expense.
[*Exeunt.*

SCENE II.

The same.

Enter LUCIANA *and* ANTIPHOLUS OF SYRACUSE.

LUCIANA.

AND may it be that you have quite forgot
A husband's office? shall, Antipholus,
Even in the spring of love, thy love-springs rot?
Shall love, in building, grow so ruinous?
If you did wed my sister for her wealth,
Then for her wealth's sake use her with more kindness:
Or if you like elsewhere, do it by stealth;
Muffle your false love with some show of blindness:
Let not my sister read it in your eye;
Be not thy tongue thy own shame's orator;
Look sweet, speak fair, become disloyalty;
Apparel vice like virtue's harbinger;
Bear a fair presence, though your heart be tainted;
Teach sin the carriage of a holy saint;
Be secret-false: what need she be acquainted?
What simple thief brags of his own attaint?
'Tis double wrong, to truant with your bed,
And let her read it in thy looks at board:
Shame hath a bastard fame, well managed;
Ill deeds is doubled with an evil word.
Alas, poor women! make us but believe,
Being compact of credit, that you love us;
Though others have the arm, show us the sleeve;
We in your motion turn, and you may move us.
Then, gentle brother, get you in again;
Comfort my sister, cheer her, call her wife:
'Tis holy sport, to be a little vain,
When the sweet breath of flattery conquers strife.

ANTIPHOLUS OF SYRACUSE.

Sweet mistress,—what your name is else, I know not,
Nor by what wonder you do hit of mine,—
Less in your knowledge and your grace you show not
Than our earth's wonder; more than earth divine.
Teach me, dear creature, how to think and speak;
Lay open to my earthy-gross conceit,
Smother'd in errors, feeble, shallow, weak,
The folded meaning of your words' deceit.
Against my soul's pure truth why labour you
To make it wander in an unknown field?
Are you a god? would you create me new?
Transform me, then, and to your power I'll yield.
But if that I am I, then well I know
Your weeping sister is no wife of mine,
Nor to her bed no homage do I owe:
Far more, far more to you do I decline.
O, train me not, sweet mermaid, with thy note,
To drown me in thy sister's flood of tears:
Sing, siren, for thyself, and I will dote:
Spread o'er the silver waves thy golden hairs,
And as a bed I'll take them, and there lie;
And, in that glorious supposition, think
He gains by death that hath such means to die:
Let Love, being light, be drowned if she sink!

LUCIANA.

What, are you mad, that you do reason so?

ANTIPHOLUS OF SYRACUSE.

Not mad, but mated; how, I do not know.

LUCIANA.

It is a fault that springeth from your eye.

ANTIPHOLUS OF SYRACUSE.

For gazing on your beams, fair sun, being by.

LUCIANA.

Gaze where you should, and that will clear your sight.

ANTIPHOLUS OF SYRACUSE.

As good to wink, sweet love, as look on night.

LUCIANA.

Why call you me love? call my sister so.

ANTIPHOLUS OF SYRACUSE.

Thy sister's sister.

LUCIANA.

That's my sister.

ANTIPHOLUS OF SYRACUSE.

No;
It is thyself, mine own self's better part,

Mine eye's clear eye, my dear heart's dearer heart,
My food, my fortune, and my sweet hope's aim,
My sole earth's heaven, and my heaven's claim.

LUCIANA.

All this my sister is, or else should be.

ANTIPHOLUS OF SYRACUSE.

Call thyself sister, sweet, for I aim thee.
Thee will I love, and with thee lead my life:
Thou hast no husband yet, nor I no wife.
Give me thy hand.

LUCIANA.

O, soft, sir! hold you still:
I'll fetch my sister, to get her good-will. [*Exit.*

Enter DROMIO OF SYRACUSE.

ANTIPHOLUS OF SYRACUSE.

Why, how now, Dromio! where runn'st thou so fast?

DROMIO OF SYRACUSE.

Do you know me, sir? am I Dromio? am I your man? am I myself?

ANTIPHOLUS OF SYRACUSE.

Thou art Dromio, thou art my man, thou art thyself.

DROMIO OF SYRACUSE.

I am an ass, I am a woman's man, and besides myself.

ANTIPHOLUS OF SYRACUSE.

What woman's man? and how besides thyself?

DROMIO OF SYRACUSE.

Marry, sir, besides myself, I am due to a woman; one that claims me, one that haunts me, one that will have me.

ANTIPHOLUS OF SYRACUSE.

What claim lays she to thee?

DROMIO OF SYRACUSE.

Marry, sir, such claim as you would lay to your horse; and she would have me as a beast: not that, I being a beast, she would have me; but that she, being a very beastly creature, lays claim to me.

ANTIPHOLUS OF SYRACUSE.

What is she?

DROMIO OF SYRACUSE.

A very reverend body; ay, such a one as a man may not speak of, without he say 'sir-reverence.' I have but lean luck in the match, and yet is she a wondrous fat marriage.

ANTIPHOLUS OF SYRACUSE.

How dost thou mean,—a fat marriage?

DROMIO OF SYRACUSE.

Marry, sir, she's the kitchen-wench, and all grease; and I know not what use to put her to, but to make a lamp of her, and run from her by her own light. I warrant, her rags, and the tallow in them, will burn a Poland winter: if she lives till doomsday, she'll burn a week longer than the whole world.

ANTIPHOLUS OF SYRACUSE.

What complexion is she of?

DROMIO OF SYRACUSE.

Swart, like my shoe, but her face nothing like so clean kept: for why? she sweats; a man may go over shoes in the grime of it.

ANTIPHOLUS OF SYRACUSE.

That's a fault that water will mend.

DROMIO OF SYRACUSE.

No, sir, 'tis in grain; Noah's flood could not do it.

ANTIPHOLUS OF SYRACUSE.

What's her name?

DROMIO OF SYRACUSE.

Nell, sir; but her name and three quarters, that's an ell and three quarters, will not measure her from hip to hip.

ANTIPHOLUS OF SYRACUSE.

Then she bears some breadth?

DROMIO OF SYRACUSE.

No longer from head to foot than from hip to hip: she is spherical, like a globe; I could find out countries in her.

ANTIPHOLUS OF SYRACUSE.

In what part of her body stands Ireland?

DROMIO OF SYRACUSE.

Marry, sir, in her buttocks: I found it out by the bogs.

ANTIPHOLUS OF SYRACUSE.

Where Scotland?

DROMIO OF SYRACUSE.

I found it by the barrenness; hard in the palm of the hand.

ANTIPHOLUS OF SYRACUSE.

Where France?

DROMIO OF SYRACUSE.

In her forehead; arm'd and reverted, making war against her heir.

ANTIPHOLUS OF SYRACUSE.

Where England?

DROMIO OF SYRACUSE.

I look'd for the chalky cliffs, but I could find no whiteness in them; but I guess it stood in her chin, by the salt rheum that ran between France and it.

ANTIPHOLUS OF SYRACUSE.

Where Spain?

DROMIO OF SYRACUSE.

Faith, I saw it not; but I felt it hot in her breath.

ANTIPHOLUS OF SYRACUSE.

Where America, the Indies?

DROMIO OF SYRACUSE.

O, sir, upon her nose, all o'er embellish'd with rubies, carbuncles, sapphires, declining their rich aspect to the hot breath of Spain; who sent whole armadoes of caracks to be ballast at her nose.

ANTIPHOLUS OF SYRACUSE.

Where stood Belgia, the Netherlands?

DROMIO OF SYRACUSE.

O, sir, I did not look so low. To conclude, this drudge, or diviner, laid claim to me; call'd me Dromio; swore I was assured to her; told me what privy marks I had about me, as, the mark of my shoulder, the mole in my neck, the great wart on my left arm, that I, amazed, ran from her as a witch:
And, I think, if my breast had not been made of faith, and my heart of steel,
She had transform'd me to a curtal dog, and made me turn i' th' wheel.

ANTIPHOLUS OF SYRACUSE.

Go hie thee presently post to the road:—
An if the wind blow any way from shore,
I will not harbour in this town to-night:—
If any bark put forth, come to the mart,
Where I will walk till thou return to me.
If every one knows us, and we know none,
'Tis time, I think, to trudge, pack, and be gone.

DROMIO OF SYRACUSE.
As from a bear a man would run for life,
So fly I from her that would be my wife. [*Exit.*

ANTIPHOLUS OF SYRACUSE.
There's none but witches do inhabit here;
And therefore 'tis high time that I were hence.
She that doth call me husband, even my soul
Doth for a wife abhor. But her fair sister,
Possest with such a gentle sovereign grace,
Of such enchanting presence and discourse,
Hath almost made me traitor to myself:
But, lest myself be guilty to self-wrong,
I'll stop mine ears against the mermaid's song.

Enter ANGELO *with the chain.*

ANGELO.
Master Antipholus,—

ANTIPHOLUS OF SYRACUSE.
Ay, that's my name.

ANGELO.
I know it well, sir:—lo, here's the chain.
I thought to have ta'en you at the Porpentine:
The chain unfinish'd made me stay thus long.

ANTIPHOLUS OF SYRACUSE.
What is your will that I shall do with this?

ANGELO.
What please yourself, sir: I have made it for you.

ANTIPHOLUS OF SYRACUSE.
Made it for me, sir! I bespoke it not.

ANGELO.
Not once, nor twice, but twenty times you have.
Go home with it, and please your wife withal;
And soon at supper-time I'll visit you,
And then receive my money for the chain.

ANTIPHOLUS OF SYRACUSE.
I pray you, sir, receive the money now,
For fear you ne'er see chain nor money more.

ANGELO.
You are a merry man, sir: fare you well. [*Exit.*

ANTIPHOLUS OF SYRACUSE.
What I should think of this, I cannot tell:
But this I think, there's no man is so vain
That would refuse so fair an offer'd chain.
I see a man here needs not live by shifts,
When in the streets he meets such golden gifts.
I'll to the mart, and there for Dromio stay:
If any ship put out, then straight away. [*Exit.*

ACT IV. SCENE I.

A public place.

Enter SECOND MERCHANT, ANGELO, *and an* OFFICER.

SECOND MERCHANT.
YOU know since Pentecost the sum is due,
And since I have not much importuned you;
Nor now I had not, but that I am bound
To Persia, and want guilders for my voyage:
Therefore make present satisfaction,
Or I'll attach you by this officer.

ANGELO.
Even just the sum that I do owe to you
Is growing to me by Antipholus;
And in the instant that I met with you
He had of me a chain: at five o'clock
I shall receive the money for the same.
Pleaseth you walk with me down to his house,
I will discharge my bond, and thank you too.

OFFICER.
That labour may you save: see where he comes.

Enter ANTIPHOLUS OF EPHESUS *and* DROMIO OF EPHESUS *from the* COURTEZAN'S.

ANTIPHOLUS OF EPHESUS.
While I go to the goldsmith's house, go thou
And buy a rope's-end: that will I bestow
Among my wife and her confederates
For locking me out of my doors by day.—
But, soft! I see the goldsmith.—Get thee gone;
Buy thou a rope, and bring it home to me.

DROMIO OF EPHESUS.
I buy a thousand pound a year! I buy a rope!
[*Exit.*

ANTIPHOLUS OF EPHESUS.
A man is well holp up that trusts to you:
You promised your presence and the chain;
But neither chain nor goldsmith came to me.
Belike you thought our love would last too long,
If it were chain'd together, and therefore came
not.

ANGELO.
Saving your merry humour, here's the note
How much your chain weighs to the utmost
carat,
The fineness of the gold, and chargeful fashion,
Which doth amount to three odd ducats more
Than I stand debted to this gentleman:
I pray you, see him presently discharged,
For he is bound to sea, and stays but for it.

ANTIPHOLUS OF EPHESUS.
I am not furnish'd with the present money;
Besides, I have some business in the town.
Good signior, take the stranger to my house,
And with you take the chain, and bid my wife
Disburse the sum on the receipt thereof:
Perchance I will be there as soon as you.

ANGELO.
Then you will bring the chain to her yourself?

ANTIPHOLUS OF EPHESUS.
No; bear it with you, lest I come not time enough.

ANGELO.
Well, sir, I will. Have you the chain about you?

ANTIPHOLUS OF EPHESUS.
An if I have not, sir, I hope you have;
Or else you may return without your money.

ANGELO.
Nay, come, I pray you, sir, give me the chain:
Both wind and tide stays for this gentleman,
And I, to blame, have held him here too long.

ANTIPHOLUS OF EPHESUS.
Good Lord, you use this dalliance to excuse
Your breach of promise to the Porpentine.
I should have chid you for not bringing it,
But, like a shrew, you first begin to brawl.

SECOND MERCHANT.
The hour steals on; I pray you, sir, dispatch.

ANGELO.
You hear how he importunes me;—the chain!—

ANTIPHOLUS OF EPHESUS.
Why, give it to my wife, and fetch your money.

ANGELO.
Come, come, you know I gave it you even now.
Either send the chain, or send me by some token.

ANTIPHOLUS OF EPHESUS.
Fie, now you run this humour out of breath.
Come, where's the chain? I pray you, let me see it.

SECOND MERCHANT.
My business cannot brook this dalliance.
Good sir, say whe'r you'll answer me or no:
If not, I'll leave him to the officer.

ANTIPHOLUS OF EPHESUS.
I answer you! what should I answer you?

ANGELO.
The money that you owe me for the chain.

ANTIPHOLUS OF EPHESUS.
I owe you none till I receive the chain.

ANGELO.
You know I gave it you half an hour since.

ANTIPHOLUS OF EPHESUS.
You gave me none: you wrong me much to say so.

ANGELO.
You wrong me more, sir, in denying it:
Consider how it stands upon my credit.

SECOND MERCHANT.
Well, officer, arrest him at my suit.

OFFICER.
I do;—
And charge you in the duke's name to obey me.

ANGELO.
This touches me in reputation.—
Either consent to pay this sum for me,
Or I attach you by this officer.

ANTIPHOLUS OF EPHESUS.
Consent to pay thee that I never had!
Arrest me, foolish fellow, if thou darest.

ANGELO.
Here is thy fee; arrest him, officer.—
I would not spare my brother in this case,
If he should scorn me so apparently.

OFFICER.
I do arrest you, sir: you hear the suit.

ANTIPHOLUS OF EPHESUS.
I do obey thee till I give thee bail.—
But, sirrah, you shall buy this sport as dear
As all the metal in your shop will answer.

ANGELO.
Sir, sir, I shall have law in Ephesus,
To your notorious shame I doubt it not.

Enter DROMIO OF SYRACUSE *from the Bay.*

DROMIO OF SYRACUSE.
Master, there's a bark of Epidamnum
That stays but till her owner comes aboard,
And then she bears away. Our fraughtage, sir,
I have convey'd aboard; and I have bought
The oil, the balsamum, and aqua-vitæ.
The ship is in her trim; the merry wind
Blows fair from land: they stay for naught at all
But for their owner, master, and yourself.

ANTIPHOLUS OF EPHESUS.
How now! a madman! Why, thou peevish sheep,
What ship of Epidamnum stays for me?

DROMIO OF SYRACUSE.
A ship you sent me to, to hire waftage.

ANTIPHOLUS OF EPHESUS.
Thou drunken slave, I sent thee for a rope,
And told thee to what purpose and what end.

DROMIO OF SYRACUSE.
You sent me for a rope's-end as soon:
You sent me to the bay, sir, for a bark.

ANTIPHOLUS OF EPHESUS.
I will debate this matter at more leisure,
And teach your ears to list me with more heed.
To Adriana, villain, hie thee straight:
Give her this key, and tell her, in the desk
That's cover'd o'er with Turkish tapestry
There is a purse of ducats; let her send it:
Tell her I am arrested in the street,
And that shall bail me: hie thee, slave, be gone.—
On, officer, to prison till it come.

[*Exeunt* SECOND MERCHANT, ANGELO, OFFICER, *and* ANTIPHOLUS OF EPHESUS.

DROMIO OF SYRACUSE.
To Adriana! that is where we dined,
Where Dowsabel did claim me for her husband:
She is too big, I hope, for me to compass.
Thither I must, although against my will,
For servants must their masters' minds fulfil.
[*Exit.*

SCENE II.

The house of ANTIPHOLUS OF EPHESUS.

Enter ADRIANA *and* LUCIANA.

ADRIANA.
AH, Luciana, did he tempt thee so?
Mightst thou perceive austerely in his eye
That he did plead in earnest, yea or no?
Look'd he or red or pale, or sad or merrily?
What observation madest thou, in this case,
Of his heart's meteors tilting in his face?

LUCIANA.
First he denied you had in him no right.

ADRIANA.
He meant he did me none; the more my spite.

LUCIANA.
Then swore he that he was a stranger here.

ADRIANA.
And true he swore, though yet forsworn he were.

LUCIANA.
Then pleaded I for you.

ADRIANA.
And what said he?

LUCIANA.
That love I begg'd for you he begg'd of me.

ADRIANA.
With what persuasion did he tempt thy love?

LUCIANA.
With words that in an honest suit might move.
First he did praise my beauty, then my speech.

ADRIANA.
Didst speak him fair?

LUCIANA.
Have patience, I beseech.

ADRIANA.
I cannot, nor I will not, hold me still;
My tongue, though not my heart, shall have his will.
He is deformed, crooked, old, and sere,
Ill-faced, worse-bodied, shapeless everywhere;
Vicious, ungentle, foolish, blunt, unkind;
Stigmatical in making, worse in mind.

LUCIANA.
Who would be jealous, then, of such a one?
No evil lost is wail'd when it is gone.

ADRIANA.

Ah, but I think him better than I say,
And yet would herein others' eyes were worse.
Far from her nest the lapwing cries away:
My heart prays for him, though my tongue do [curse.

Enter DROMIO OF SYRACUSE.

DROMIO OF SYRACUSE.

Here, go; the desk, the purse! sweet, now, make haste.

LUCIANA.

How hast thou lost thy breath?

DROMIO OF SYRACUSE.

By running fast.

ADRIANA.

Where is thy master, Dromio? is he well?

DROMIO OF SYRACUSE.

No, he's in Tartar limbo, worse than hell.
A devil in an everlasting garment hath him;
One whose hard heart is button'd up with steel;
A fiend, a fairy, pitiless and rough;
A wolf, nay, worse,—a fellow all in buff;
A back-friend, a shoulder-clapper, one that countermands
The passages of alleys, creeks, and narrow lands;
A hound that runs counter, and yet draws dry-foot well;
One that, before the judgement, carries poor souls to hell.

ADRIANA.

Why, man, what is the matter?

DROMIO OF SYRACUSE.

I do not know the matter: he is 'rested on the case.

ADRIANA.

What, is he arrested? tell me at whose suit.

DROMIO OF SYRACUSE.

I know not at whose suit he is arrested well;
But is in a suit of buff which 'rested him, that can I tell.
Will you send him, mistress, redemption, the money in his desk?

ADRIANA.

Go fetch it, sister.—This I wonder at,
[*Exit* LUCIANA.
That he, unknown to me, should be in debt.—
Tell me, was he arrested on a band?

DROMIO OF SYRACUSE.

Not on a band, but on a stronger thing,—
A chain, a chain:—do you not hear it ring?

ADRIANA.

What, the chain?

DROMIO OF SYRACUSE.

No, no, the bell:—'tis time that I were gone:
It was two ere I left him, and now the clock strikes one.

ADRIANA.

The hours come back! that did I never hear.

DROMIO OF SYRACUSE.

O, yes; if any hour meet a sergeant, 'a turns back for very fear.

ADRIANA.

As if Time were in debt! how fondly dost thou reason!

DROMIO OF SYRACUSE.

Time is a very bankrout, and owes more than he's worth to season.
Nay, he's a thief too: have you not heard men say,
That Time comes stealing on by night and day?
If Time be in debt and theft, and a sergeant in the way,
Hath he not reason to turn back an hour in a day?

Enter LUCIANA *with the purse.*

ADRIANA.

Go, Dromio; there's the money, bear it straight;
And bring thy master home immediately.—
Come, sister: I am prest down with conceit,—
Conceit, my comfort and my injury. [*Exeunt.*

SCENE III.

A public place.

Enter ANTIPHOLUS OF SYRACUSE.

ANTIPHOLUS OF SYRACUSE.

THERE'S not a man I meet but doth salute me
As if I were their well-acquainted friend;
And every one doth call me by my name.
Some tender money to me; some invite me;
Some other give me thanks for kindnesses;
Some offer me commodities to buy;—
Even now a tailor call'd me in his shop,
And show'd me silks that he had bought for me,
And therewithal took measure of my body.
Sure, these are but imaginary wiles,
And Lapland sorcerers inhabit here.

Enter DROMIO OF SYRACUSE.

DROMIO OF SYRACUSE.

Master, here's the gold you sent me for.—What, have you got rid of the picture of old Adam new-apparell'd?

ANTIPHOLUS OF SYRACUSE.

What gold is this? what Adam dost thou mean?

DROMIO OF SYRACUSE.

Not that Adam that kept the Paradise, but that Adam that keeps the prison: he that goes in the calf's skin that was kill'd for the Prodigal; he that came behind you, sir, like an evil angel, and bid you forsake your liberty.

ANTIPHOLUS OF SYRACUSE.

I understand thee not.

DROMIO OF SYRACUSE.

No? why, 'tis a plain case: he that went, like a base-viol, in a case of leather; the man, sir, that, when gentlemen are tired, gives them a sob, and 'rests them; he, sir, that takes pity on decay'd men, and gives them suits of durance; he that sets up his rest to do more exploits with his mace than a morris-pike.

ANTIPHOLUS OF SYRACUSE.

What, thou mean'st an officer?

DROMIO OF SYRACUSE.

Ay, sir, the sergeant of the band; he that brings any man to answer it that breaks his band; one that thinks a man always going to bed, and says, 'God give you good rest!'

ANTIPHOLUS OF SYRACUSE.

Well, sir, there rest in your foolery. Is there any ship puts forth to-night? may we be gone?

DROMIO OF SYRACUSE.

Why, sir, I brought you word an hour since, that the bark Expedition put forth to-night; and then were you hinder'd by the sergeant, to tarry for the hoy Delay. Here are the angels that you sent for to deliver you.

ANTIPHOLUS OF SYRACUSE.
The fellow is distract, and so am I;
And here we wander in illusions:
Some blessed power deliver us from hence!

Enter a COURTEZAN.

COURTEZAN.
Well met, well met, Master Antipholus.
I see, sir, you have found the goldsmith now:
Is that the chain you promised me to-day?

ANTIPHOLUS OF SYRACUSE.
Satan, avoid! I charge thee, tempt me not.

DROMIO OF SYRACUSE.
Master, is this Mistress Satan?

ANTIPHOLUS OF SYRACUSE.
It is the devil.

DROMIO OF SYRACUSE.
Nay, she is worse, she is the devil's dam; and here she comes in the habit of a light wench: and thereof comes that the wenches say, 'God damn me;' that's as much as to say, 'God make me a light wench.' It is written, they appear to men like angels of light: light is an effect of fire, and fire will burn; *ergo*, light wenches will burn. Come not near her.

COURTEZAN.
Your man and you are marvellous merry, sir.
Will you go with me? We'll mend our dinner here.

DROMIO OF SYRACUSE.
Master, if you do, expect spoon-meat; so bespeak a long spoon.

ANTIPHOLUS OF SYRACUSE.
Why, Dromio?

DROMIO OF SYRACUSE.
Marry, he must have a long spoon that must eat with the devil.

ANTIPHOLUS OF SYRACUSE.
Avoid, thou fiend! what tell'st thou me of supping?
Thou art, as you are all, a sorceress:
I conjure thee to leave me and be gone.

COURTEZAN.
Give me the ring of mine you had at dinner,
Or, for my diamond, the chain you promised;
And I'll be gone, sir, and not trouble you.

DROMIO OF SYRACUSE.
Some devils ask but the parings of one's nail,
A rush, a hair, a drop of blood, a pin,
A nut, a cherry-stone;
But she, more covetous, would have a chain.
Master, be wise: an if you give it her,
The devil will shake her chain, and fright us with it.

COURTEZAN.
I pray you, sir, my ring, or else the chain:
I hope you do not mean to cheat me so.

ANTIPHOLUS OF SYRACUSE.
Avaunt, thou witch!—Come, Dromio, let us go.

DROMIO OF SYRACUSE.
'Fly pride,' says the peacock: mistress, that you know.

[*Exeunt* ANTIPHOLUS OF SYRACUSE *and* DROMIO OF SYRACUSE.

COURTEZAN.
Now, out of doubt Antipholus is mad,
Else would he never so demean himself.
A ring he hath of mine worth forty ducats,
And for the same he promised me a chain:
Both one and other he denies me now.
The reason that I gather he is mad,—
Besides this present instance of his rage,—
Is a mad tale he told to-day at dinner,
Of his own doors being shut against his entrance.
Belike his wife, acquainted with his fits,
On purpose shut the doors against his way.
My way is now to hie home to his house,
And tell his wife that, being lunatic,
He rush'd into my house, and took perforce
My ring away. This course I fittest choose;
For forty ducats is too much to lose. [*Exit.*

SCENE IV.

A street.

Enter ANTIPHOLUS OF EPHESUS *and the* OFFICER.

ANTIPHOLUS OF EPHESUS.
FEAR me not, man; I will not break away:
I'll give thee, ere I leave thee, so much money,
To warrant thee, as I am 'rested for.
My wife is in a wayward mood to-day,
And will not lightly trust the messenger:
That I should be attach'd in Ephesus,
I tell you, 'twill sound harshly in her ears.—
Here comes my man; I think he brings the money.

Enter DROMIO OF EPHESUS *with a rope's-end.*

How now, sir! have you that I sent you for?

DROMIO OF EPHESUS.
Here's that, I warrant you, will pay them all.

ANTIPHOLUS OF EPHESUS.
But where's the money?

DROMIO OF EPHESUS.
Why, sir, I gave the money for the rope.

ANTIPHOLUS OF EPHESUS.
Five hundred ducats, villain, for a rope?

DROMIO OF EPHESUS.
I'll serve you, sir, five hundred at the rate.

ANTIPHOLUS OF EPHESUS.
To what end did I bid thee hie thee home?

DROMIO OF EPHESUS.
To a rope's-end, sir; and to that end am I return'd.

ANTIPHOLUS OF EPHESUS.
And to that end, sir, I will welcome you. [*Beating him.*

OFFICER.
Good sir, be patient.

DROMIO OF EPHESUS.
Nay, 'tis for me to be patient; I am in adversity.

OFFICER.
Good, now, hold thy tongue.

DROMIO OF EPHESUS.
Nay, rather persuade him to hold his hands.

ANTIPHOLUS OF EPHESUS.
Thou whoreson, senseless villain!

DROMIO OF EPHESUS.
I would I were senseless, sir, that I might not feel your blows.

ANTIPHOLUS OF EPHESUS.
Thou art sensible in nothing but blows, and so is an ass.

DROMIO OF EPHESUS.

I am an ass, indeed; you may prove it by my long ears.—I have served him from the hour of my nativity to this instant, and have nothing at his hands for my service but blows. When I am cold, he heats me with beating; when I am warm, he cools me with beating; I am waked with it when I sleep; raised with it when I sit; driven out of doors with it when I go from home; welcomed home with it when I return: nay, I bear it on my shoulders, as a beggar wont her brat; and, I think, when he hath lamed me, I shall beg with it from door to door.

ANTIPHOLUS OF EPHESUS.

Come, go along; my wife is coming yonder.

Enter ADRIANA, LUCIANA, *the* COURTEZAN, *and a schoolmaster call'd* PINCH.

DROMIO OF EPHESUS.

Mistress, *respice finem*, respect your end;—or rather, the prophecy like the parrot, 'Beware the rope's-end.'

ANTIPHOLUS OF EPHESUS.

Wilt thou still talk? [*Beating him.*

COURTEZAN.

How say you now? is not your husband mad?

ADRIANA.

His incivility confirms no less.—
Good Doctor Pinch, you are a conjurer;
Establish him in his true sense again,
And I will please you what you will demand.

LUCIANA.

Alas, how fiery and how sharp he looks!

COURTEZAN.

Mark how he trembles in his ecstasy!

PINCH.

Give me your hand, and let me feel your pulse.

ANTIPHOLUS OF EPHESUS.

There is my hand, and let it feel your ear.
[*Striking him.*

PINCH.

I charge thee, Satan, housed within this man,
To yield possession to my holy prayers,
And to thy state of darkness hie thee straight;
I conjure thee by all the saints in heaven!

ANTIPHOLUS OF EPHESUS.

Peace, doting wizard, peace! I am not mad.

ADRIANA.

O, that thou wert not, poor distressed soul!

ANTIPHOLUS OF EPHESUS.

You minion, you, are these your customers?
Did this companion with the saffron face
Revel and feast it at my house to-day,
Whilst upon me the guilty doors were shut,
And I denied to enter in my house?

ADRIANA.

O husband, God doth know you dined at home;
Where would you had remain'd until this time,
Free from these slanders and this open shame!

ANTIPHOLUS OF EPHESUS.

Dined at home!—Thou villain, what sayest thou?

DROMIO OF EPHESUS.

Sir, sooth to say, you did not dine at home.

ANTIPHOLUS OF EPHESUS.

Were not my doors lockt up, and I shut out?

DROMIO OF EPHESUS.

Perdy, your doors were lockt, and you shut out.

ANTIPHOLUS OF EPHESUS.

And did not she herself revile me there?

DROMIO OF EPHESUS.

Sans fable, she herself reviled you there.

ANTIPHOLUS OF EPHESUS.

Did not her kitchen-maid rail, taunt, and scorn [me?

DROMIO OF EPHESUS.

Certes, she did; the kitchen-vestal scorn'd ye.

ANTIPHOLUS OF EPHESUS.

And did not I in rage depart from thence?

DROMIO OF EPHESUS.

In verity you did;—my bones bear witness,
That since have felt the vigour of his rage.

ADRIANA.

Is't good to soothe him in these contraries?

PINCH.

It is no shame: the fellow finds his vein,
And, yielding to him, humours well his frenzy.

ANTIPHOLUS OF EPHESUS.

Thou hast suborn'd the goldsmith to arrest me.

ADRIANA.

Alas, I sent you money to redeem you,
By Dromio here, who came in haste for it.

DROMIO OF EPHESUS.

Money by me! heart and good-will you might;
But surely, master, not a rag of money.

ANTIPHOLUS OF EPHESUS.

Went'st not thou to her for a purse of ducats?

ADRIANA.

He came to me, and I deliver'd it.

LUCIANA.

And I am witness with her that she did.

DROMIO OF EPHESUS.

God and the rope-maker bear me witness
That I was sent for nothing but a rope!

PINCH [*aside to* ADRIANA].

Mistress, both man and master is possest;
I know it by their pale and deadly looks:
They must be bound, and laid in some dark room.

ANTIPHOLUS OF EPHESUS.

Say, wherefore didst thou lock me forth to-day—
And why dost thou deny the bag of gold?

ADRIANA.

I did not, gentle husband, lock thee forth.

DROMIO OF EPHESUS.

And, gentle master, I received no gold;
But I confess, sir, that we were lockt out.

ADRIANA.

Dissembling villain, thou speak'st false in both.

ANTIPHOLUS OF EPHESUS.

Dissembling harlot, thou art false in all;
And art confederate with a damned pack
To make a loathsome abject scorn of me:
But with these nails I'll pluck out those false eyes,
That would behold in me this shameful sport.

ADRIANA.

O, bind him, bind him! let him not come near me.

PINCH.

More company!—The fiend is strong within him.

LUCIANA.

Ay me, poor man, how pale and wan he looks!

Enter three or four, and offer to bind him; he strives.

ANTIPHOLUS OF EPHESUS.

What, will you murder me?—Thou gaoler, thou,
I am thy prisoner: wilt thou suffer them
To make a rescue?

OFFICER.
Masters, let him go:
He is my prisoner, and you shall not have him.

PINCH.
Go bind this man, for he is frantic too.
[*They bind* DROMIO OF EPHESUS.

ADRIANA.
What wilt thou do, thou peevish officer?
Hast thou delight to see a wretched man
Do outrage and displeasure to himself?

OFFICER.
He is my prisoner: if I let him go,
The debt he owes will be required of me.

ADRIANA.
I will discharge thee ere I go from thee:
Bear me forthwith unto his creditor,
And, knowing how the debt grows, I will pay it.—
Good master doctor, see him safe convey'd
Home to my house.—O most unhappy day!

ANTIPHOLUS OF EPHESUS.
O most unhappy strumpet!

DROMIO OF EPHESUS.
Master, I am here enter'd in bond for you.

ANTIPHOLUS OF EPHESUS.
Out on thee, villain! wherefore dost thou mad me?

DROMIO OF EPHESUS.
Will you be bound for nothing? be mad, good master; cry, 'The devil!'

LUCIANA.
God help, poor souls, how idly do they talk!

ADRIANA.
Go bear him hence.—Sister, go you with me.
[*Exeunt* PINCH *and* ASSISTANTS, *with* ANTIPHOLUS OF EPHESUS and DROMIO OF EPHESUS.
Say now whose suit is he arrested at?

OFFICER.
One Angelo, a goldsmith: do you know him?

ADRIANA.
I know the man. What is the sum he owes?

OFFICER.
Two hundred ducats.

ADRIANA.
Say, how grows it due?

OFFICER.
Due for a chain your husband had of him.

ADRIANA.
He did bespeak a chain for me, but had it not.

COURTEZAN.
Whenas your husband, all in rage, to-day
Came to my house, and took away my ring,—
The ring I saw upon his finger now,—
Straight after did I meet him with a chain.

ADRIANA.
It may be so, but I did never see it.—
Come, gaoler, bring me where the goldsmith is:
I long to know the truth hereof at large.

Enter ANTIPHOLUS OF SYRACUSE *with his rapier drawn, and* DROMIO OF SYRACUSE.

LUCIANA.
God, for thy mercy! they are loose again.

ADRIANA.
And come with naked swords. Let 's call more [help,
To have them bound again.

OFFICER.
Away! they'll kill us.
[*Exeunt* ADRIANA, *&c., as fast as may be, frighted.*

ANTIPHOLUS OF SYRACUSE.
I see these witches are afraid of swords.

DROMIO OF SYRACUSE.
She that would be your wife now ran from you.

ANTIPHOLUS OF SYRACUSE.
Come to the Centaur; fetch our stuff from thence:
I long that we were safe and sound aboard.

DROMIO OF SYRACUSE.
Faith, stay here this night; they will surely do us no harm: you saw they speak us fair, give us gold: methinks they are such a gentle nation, that, but for the mountain of mad flesh that claims marriage of me, I could find in my heart to stay here still, and turn witch.

ANTIPHOLUS OF SYRACUSE.
I will not stay to-night for all the town;
Therefore away, to get our stuff aboard. [*Exeunt.*

ACT V. SCENE I.

Before an abbey.

Enter SECOND MERCHANT *and* ANGELO.

ANGELO.
I AM sorry, sir, that I have hinder'd you;
But, I protest, he had the chain of me,
Though most dishonestly he doth deny it.

SECOND MERCHANT.
How is the man esteem'd here in the city?

ANGELO.
Of very reverend reputation, sir,
Of credit infinite, highly beloved,
Second to none that lives here in the city:
His word might bear my wealth at any time.

SECOND MERCHANT.
Speak softly: yonder, as I think, he walks.

Enter ANTIPHOLUS OF SYRACUSE *and* DROMIO OF SYRACUSE.

ANGELO.
'Tis so; and that self chain about his neck,
Which he forswore most monstrously to have.
Good sir, draw near to me, I'll speak to him.—
Signior Antipholus, I wonder much
That you would put me to this shame and trouble;
And, not without some scandal to yourself,
With circumstance and oaths so to deny
This chain, which now you wear so openly:
Beside the charge, the shame, imprisonment,
You have done wrong to this my honest friend;
Who, but for staying on our controversy,
Had hoisted sail and put to sea to-day:
This chain you had of me; can you deny it?

ANTIPHOLUS OF SYRACUSE.
I think I had; I never did deny it.

SECOND MERCHANT.
Yes, that you did, sir, and forswore it too.

ANTIPHOLUS OF SYRACUSE.
Who heard me to deny it or forswear it?

SECOND MERCHANT.
These ears of mine, thou know'st, did hear thee:
Fie on thee, wretch! 'tis pity that thou livest
To walk where any honest men resort.

ANTIPHOLUS OF SYRACUSE.
Thou art a villain to impeach me thus:
I'll prove mine honour and mine honesty
Against thee presently, if thou darest stand.

SECOND MERCHANT.
I dare, and do defy thee for a villain. [*They draw.*

Enter ADRIANA, LUCIANA, *the* COURTEZAN, *and others.*

ADRIANA.
Hold, hurt him not, for God's sake! he is mad.—
Some get within him, take his sword away:
Bind Dromio too, and bear them to my house.

DROMIO OF SYRACUSE.
Run, master, run; for God's sake, take a house!
This is some priory:—in, or we are spoil'd.

[*Exeunt* ANTIPHOLUS OF SYRACUSE *and* DROMIO OF SYRACUSE *to the abbey.*

Enter LADY ABBESS.

ABBESS.
Be quiet, people. Wherefore throng you hither?

ADRIANA.
To fetch my poor distracted husband hence.
Let us come in, that we may bind him fast,
And bear him home for his recovery.

ANGELO.
I knew he was not in his perfect wits.

SECOND MERCHANT.
I am sorry now that I did draw on him.

ABBESS.
How long hath this possession held the man?

ADRIANA.
This week he hath been heavy, sour, sad,
And much different from the man he was;
But till this afternoon his passion
Ne'er brake into extremity of rage.

ABBESS.
Hath he not lost much wealth by wrack of sea?
Buried some dear friend? Hath not else his eye
Stray'd his affection in unlawful love,—
A sin prevailing much in youthful men,
Who give their eyes the liberty of gazing?
Which of these sorrows is he subject to?

ADRIANA.
To none of these, except it be the last;
Namely, some love that drew him oft from home.

ABBESS.
You should for that have reprehended him.

ADRIANA.
Why, so I did.

ABBESS.
Ay, but not rough enough.

ADRIANA.
As roughly as my modesty would let me.

ABBESS.
Haply, in private.

ADRIANA.
And in assemblies too.

ABBESS.
Ay, but not enough.

ADRIANA.
It was the copy of our conference:
In bed, he slept not for my urging it;
At board, he fed not for my urging it;
Alone, it was the subject of my theme;
In company I often glanced it;
Still did I tell him it was vile and bad.

ABBESS.
And thereof came it that the man was mad:
The venom-clamours of a jealous woman
Poisons more deadly than a mad-dog's tooth.
It seems his sleeps were hinder'd by thy railing:
And thereof comes it that his head is light.
Thou say'st his meat was sauced with thy upbraidings:
Unquiet meals make ill digestions,—
Thereof the raging fire of fever bred;
And what's a fever but a fit of madness?
Thou say'st his sports were hinder'd by thy brawls:
Sweet recreation barr'd, what doth ensue
But moody and dull melancholy,
Kinsman to grim and comfortless despair;
And at her heels a huge infectious troop
Of pale distemperatures and foes to life?
In food, in sport, and life-preserving rest
To be disturb'd, would mad or man or beast:
The consequence is, then, thy jealous fits
Have scared thy husband from the use of wits.

LUCIANA.
She never reprehended him but mildly,
When he demean'd himself rough-rude and wildly.—
Why bear you these rebukes, and answer not?

ADRIANA.
She did betray me to my own reproof.—
Good people, enter, and lay hold on him.

ABBESS.
No, not a creature enters in my house.

ADRIANA.
Then let your servants bring my husband forth.

ABBESS.
Neither: he took this place for sanctuary,
And it shall privilege him from your hands
Till I have brought him to his wits again,
Or lose my labour in assaying it.

ADRIANA.
I will attend my husband, be his nurse,
Diet his sickness, for it is my office,
And will have no attorney but myself;
And therefore let me have him home with me.

ABBESS.
Be patient; for I will not let him stir
Till I have used the approved means I have,
With wholesome syrups, drugs, and holy prayers,
To make of him a formal man again:
It is a branch and parcel of mine oath,
A charitable duty of my order.
Therefore depart, and leave him here with me.

ADRIANA.
I will not hence, and leave my husband here:
And ill it doth beseem your holiness
To separate the husband and the wife.

ABBESS.
Be quiet, and depart: thou shalt not have him. [*Exit.*

LUCIANA.
Complain unto the duke of this indignity.

ADRIANA.
Come, go: I will fall prostrate at his feet,
And never rise until my tears and prayers
Have won his grace to come in person hither,
And take perforce my husband from the abbess.

SECOND MERCHANT.

By this, I think, the dial points at five:
Anon, I'm sure, the duke himself in person
Comes this way to the melancholy vale,
The place of death and sorry execution,
Behind the ditches of the abbey here.

ANGELO.

Upon what cause?

SECOND MERCHANT.

To see a reverend Syracusian merchant,
Who put unluckily into this bay
Against the laws and statutes of this town,
Beheaded publicly for his offence.

ANGELO.

See where they come: we will behold his death.

LUCIANA.

Kneel to the duke before he pass the abbey.

Enter DUKE, *attended;* AEGEON *bareheaded; with the* HEADSMAN *and other* OFFICERS.

DUKE.

Yet once again proclaim it publicly,
If any friend will pay the sum for him,
He shall not die, so much we tender him.

ADRIANA.

Justice, most sacred duke, against the abbess!

DUKE OF EPHESUS.

She is a virtuous and a reverend lady:
It cannot be that she hath done thee wrong.

ADRIANA.

May it please your grace, Antipholus my husband,—
Who I made lord of me and all I had,
At your important letters,—this ill day
A most outrageous fit of madness took him;
That desp'rately he hurried through the street,—
With him his bondman, all as mad as he,—
Doing displeasure to the citizens
By rushing in their houses, bearing thence
Rings, jewels, any thing his rage did like.
Once did I get him bound, and sent him home,
Whilst to take order for the wrongs I went,
That here and there his fury had committed.
Anon, I wot not by what strong escape
He broke from those that had the guard of him;
And both his mad attendant and himself,
Each one with ireful passion, with drawn swords,
Met us again, and, madly bent on us,
Chased us away; till, raising of more aid,
We came again to bind them. Then they fled
Into this abbey, whither we pursued them;
And here the abbess shuts the gates on us,
And will not suffer us to fetch him out,
Nor send him forth, that we may bear him hence.
Therefore, most gracious duke, with thy command
Let him be brought forth, and borne hence for help.

DUKE OF EPHESUS.

Long since thy husband served me in my wars;
And I to thee engaged a prince's word,
When thou didst make him master of thy bed,
To do him all the grace and good I could.—
Go, some of you, knock at the abbey-gate,
And bid the lady abbess come to me.—
I will determine this before I stir.

Enter a SERVANT.

SERVANT.

O mistress, mistress, shift and save yourself!
My master and his man are both broke loose,
Beaten the maids a-row, and bound the doctor,
Whose beard they have singed off with brands of fire;
And ever, as it blazed, they threw on him
Great pails of puddled mire to quench the hair:
My master preaches patience to him, and the while
His man with scissors nicks him like a fool;
And sure, unless you send some present help,
Between them they will kill the conjurer.

ADRIANA.

Peace, fool! thy master and his man are here;
And that is false thou dost report to us.

SERVANT.

Mistress, upon my life, I tell you true;
I have not breathed almost since I did see it.
He cries for you, and vows, if he can take you,
To scorch your face, and to disfigure you.
[*Cry within.*
Hark, hark! I hear him, mistress: fly, be gone!

DUKE OF EPHESUS.

Come, stand by me; fear nothing.—Guard with halberds!

ADRIANA.

Ay me, it is my husband! Witness you,
That he is borne about invisible:
Even now we housed him in the abbey here;
And now he's there, past thought of human reason.

Enter ANTIPHOLUS OF EPHESUS *and* DROMIO OF EPHESUS.

ANTIPHOLUS OF EPHESUS.

Justice, most gracious duke, O, grant me justice!
Even for the service that long since I did thee,
When I bestrid thee in the wars, and took
Deep scars to save thy life; even for the blood
That then I lost for thee, now grant me justice.

AEGEON.

Unless the fear of death doth make me dote,
I see my son Antipholus, and Dromio.

ANTIPHOLUS OF EPHESUS.

Justice, sweet prince, against that woman there!
She whom thou gavest to me to be my wife,
That hath abused and dishonour'd me
Even in the strength and height of injury:
Beyond imagination is the wrong
That she this day hath shameless thrown on me.

DUKE OF EPHESUS.

Discover how, and thou shalt find me just.

ANTIPHOLUS OF EPHESUS.

This day, great duke, she shut the doors upon me,
While she with harlots feasted in my house.

DUKE OF EPHESUS.

A grievous fault.—Say, woman, didst thou so?

ADRIANA.

No, my good lord: myself, he, and my sister,
To-day did dine together. So befall my soul
As this is false he burdens me withal!

LUCIANA.

Ne'er may I look on day, nor sleep on night,
But she tells to your highness simple truth!

ANGELO.

O perjured woman!—They are both forsworn:
In this the madman justly chargeth them.

ANTIPHOLUS OF EPHESUS.

My liege, I am advised what I say;
Neither disturb'd with the effect of wine,
Nor heady-rash, provoked with raging ire,
Albeit my wrongs might make one wiser mad.
This woman lockt me out this day from dinner:
That goldsmith there, were he not pack'd with
her,
Could witness it, for he was with me then;
Who parted with me to go fetch a chain,
Promising to bring it to the Porpentine,
Where Balthazar and I did dine together.
Our dinner done, and he not coming thither,
I went to seek him: in the street I met him,
And in his company that gentleman.
There did this perjured goldsmith swear me down
That I this day of him received the chain,
Which, God he knows, I saw not: for the which
He did arrest me with an officer.
I did obey; and sent my peasant home
For certain ducats: he with none return'd.
Then fairly I bespoke the officer
To go in person with me to my house.
By th' way we met
My wife, her sister, and a rabble more
Of vile confederates. Along with them
They brought one Pinch, a hungry lean-faced [villain,
A mere anatomy, a mountebank,
A threadbare juggler, and a fortune-teller,
A needy, hollow-eyed, sharp-looking wretch,
A living-dead man: this pernicious slave,
Forsooth, took on him as a conjurer;
And, gazing in mine eyes, feeling my pulse,
And with no face, as 'twere, outfacing me,
Cries out, I was possest. Then all together
They fell upon me, bound me, bore me thence,
And in a dark and dankish vault at home
There left me and my man, both bound together;
Till, gnawing with my teeth my bonds in sunder,
I gain'd my freedom, and immediately
Ran hither to your grace; whom I beseech
To give me ample satisfaction
For these deep shames and great indignities.

ANGELO.

My lord, in truth, thus far I witness with him,
That he dined not at home, but was lockt out.

DUKE OF EPHESUS.

But had he such a chain of thee or no?

ANGELO.

He had, my lord: and when he ran in here,
These people saw the chain about his neck.

SECOND MERCHANT.

Besides, I will be sworn these ears of mine
Heard you confess you had the chain of him,
After you first forswore it on the mart:
And thereupon I drew my sword on you;
And then you fled into this abbey here,
From whence, I think, you are come by miracle.

ANTIPHOLUS OF EPHESUS.

I never came within these abbey-walls;
Nor ever didst thou draw thy sword on me:
I never saw the chain, so help me heaven!
And this is false you burden me withal!

DUKE OF EPHESUS.

Why, what an intricate impeach is this!
I think you all have drunk of Circe's cup.
If here you housed him, here he would have
been;
If he were mad, he would not plead so coldly:—
You say he dined at home; the goldsmith here
Denies that saying.—Sirrah, what say you?

DROMIO OF EPHESUS.

Sir, he dined with her there, at the Porpentine.

COURTEZAN.

He did; and from my finger snatcht that ring.

ANTIPHOLUS OF EPHESUS.

'Tis true, my liege; this ring I had of her.

DUKE OF EPHESUS.

Saw'st thou him enter at the abbey here?

COURTEZAN.

As sure, my liege, as I do see your grace.

DUKE OF EPHESUS.

Why, this is strange.—Go call the abbess
hither.— [*Exit one to the* ABBESS.
I think you are all mated or stark mad.

AEGEON.

Most mighty duke, vouchsafe me speak a word:
Haply I see a friend will save my life,
And pay the sum that may deliver me.

DUKE OF EPHESUS.

Speak freely, Syracusian, what thou wilt.

AEGEON.

Is not your name, sir, call'd Antipholus?
And is not that your bondman Dromio?

DROMIO OF EPHESUS.

Within this hour I was his bondman, sir,
But he, I thank him, gnaw'd in two my cords:
Now am I Dromio, and his man unbound.

AEGEON.

I am sure you both of you remember me.

DROMIO OF EPHESUS.

Ourselves we do remember, sir, by you;
For lately we were bound, as you are now.
You are not Pinch's patient, are you, sir?

AEGEON.

Why look you strange on me? you know me
well.

ANTIPHOLUS OF EPHESUS.

I never saw you in my life till now.

AEGEON.

O, grief hath changed me since you saw me
last,
And careful hours with Time's deformed hand
Have written strange defeatures in my face:
But tell me yet, dost thou not know my voice?

ANTIPHOLUS OF EPHESUS.

Neither.

AEGEON.

Dromio, nor thou?

DROMIO OF EPHESUS.

No, trust me, sir, nor I.

AEGEON.

I am sure thou dost.

DROMIO OF EPHESUS.

Ay, sir, but I am sure I do not; and whatsoever a man denies, you are now bound to believe him.

AEGEON.

Not know my voice! O time's extremity,

Hast thou so crack'd and splitted my poor tongue
In seven short years, that here my only son
Knows not my feeble key of untuned cares?
Though now this grained face of mine be hid
In sap-consuming winter's drizzled snow,
And all the conduits of my blood froze up,
Yet hath my night of life some memory,
My wasting lamps some fading glimmer left,
My dull deaf ears a little use to hear:
All these old witnesses—I cannot err—
Tell me thou art my son Antipholus.

ANTIPHOLUS OF EPHESUS.

I never saw my father in my life.

AEGEON.

But seven years since, in Syracusa, boy,
Thou know'st we parted: but perhaps, my son,
Thou shamest to acknowledge me in misery.

ANTIPHOLUS OF EPHESUS.

The duke, and all that know me in the city,
Can witness with me that it is not so:
I ne'er saw Syracusa in my life.

DUKE OF EPHESUS.

I tell thee, Syracusian, twenty years
Have I been patron to Antipholus,
During which time he ne'er saw Syracusa:
I see thy age and dangers make thee dote.

Enter ABBESS, *with* ANTIPHOLUS OF SYRACUSE *and* DROMIO OF SYRACUSE.

ABBESS.

Most mighty duke, behold a man much wrong'd.
[*All gather to see them.*

ADRIANA.

I see two husbands, or mine eyes deceive me.

DUKE OF EPHESUS.

One of these men is Genius to the other;
And so of these. Which is the natural man,
And which the spirit? who deciphers them?

DROMIO OF SYRACUSE.

I, sir, am Dromio: command him away.

DROMIO OF EPHESUS.

I, sir, am Dromio: pray, let me stay.

ANTIPHOLUS OF SYRACUSE.

Aegeon art thou not? or else his ghost?

DROMIO OF SYRACUSE.

O, my old master! who hath bound him here?

ABBESS.

Whoever bound him, I will loose his bonds,
And gain a husband by his liberty.—
Speak, old Aegeon, if thou be'st the man
That hadst a wife once call'd Aemilia,
That bore thee at a burden two fair sons:
O, if thou be'st the same Aegeon, speak,
And speak unto the same Aemilia!

AEGEON.

If I dream not, thou art Aemilia:
If thou art she, tell me where is that son
That floated with thee on the fatal raft?

ABBESS.

By men of Epidamnum he and I
And the twin Dromio all were taken up;
But by and by rude fishermen of Corinth
By force took Dromio and my son from them,
And me they left with those of Epidamnum.
What then became of them I cannot tell;
I to this fortune that you see me in.

DUKE OF EPHESUS.

Why, here begins his morning story right:
These two Antipholus', these two so like,
And these two Dromios, one in semblance,—
Besides her urging of her wrack at sea,—
These are the parents to these children,
Which accidentally are met together.—
Antipholus, thou camest from Corinth first?

ANTIPHOLUS OF SYRACUSE.

No, sir, not I; I came from Syracuse.

DUKE OF EPHESUS.

Stay, stand apart; I know not which is which.

ANTIPHOLUS OF EPHESUS.

I came from Corinth, my most gracious lord,—

DROMIO OF EPHESUS.

And I with him.

ANTIPHOLUS OF EPHESUS.

Brought to this town by that most famous warrior,
Duke Menaphon, your most renowned uncle.

ADRIANA.

Which of you two did dine with me to-day?

ANTIPHOLUS OF SYRACUSE.

I, gentle mistress.

ADRIANA.

And are not you my husband?

ANTIPHOLUS OF EPHESUS.

No; I say nay to that.

ANTIPHOLUS OF SYRACUSE.

And so do I; yet did she call me so:
And this fair gentlewoman, her sister here,
Did call me brother.—[*to* LUCIANA] What I told you then,
I hope I shall have leisure to make good;
If this be not a dream I see and hear.

ANGELO.

That is the chain, sir, which you had of me.

ANTIPHOLUS OF SYRACUSE.

I think it be, sir; I deny it not.

ANTIPHOLUS OF EPHESUS.

And you, sir, for this chain arrested me.

ANGELO.

I think I did, sir; I deny it not.

ADRIANA.

I sent you money, sir, to be your bail,
By Dromio; but I think he brought it not.

DROMIO OF EPHESUS.

No, none by me.

ANTIPHOLUS OF SYRACUSE.

This purse of ducats I received from you,
And Dromio my man did bring them me.
I see we still did meet each other's man;
And I was ta'en for him, and he for me;
And thereupon these errors are arose.

ANTIPHOLUS OF EPHESUS.

These ducats pawn I for my father here.

DUKE OF EPHESUS.

It shall not need; thy father hath his life.

COURTEZAN.

Sir, I must have that diamond from you.

ANTIPHOLUS OF EPHESUS.

There, take it; and much thanks for my good cheer.

ABBESS.

Renowned duke, vouchsafe to take the pains
To go with us into the abbey here,

And hear at large discoursed all our fortunes;—
And all that are assembled in this place,
That by this sympathized one day's error
Have suffer'd wrong, go keep us company,
And we shall make full satisfaction.—
Thirty-three years have I but gone in travail
Of you, my sons; and, till this present hour,
My heavy burden ne'er delivered.—
The duke, my husband, and my children both,
And you the calendars of their nativity,
Go to a gossip's feast, and joy with me;
After so long grief, such felicity!

DUKE OF EPHESUS.

With all my heart, I'll gossip at this feast.

[*Exeunt* DUKE, ABBESS, AEGEON, COURTEZAN, SECOND MERCHANT, ANGELO, *and* ATTENDANTS.

DROMIO OF SYRACUSE.

Master, shall I fetch your stuff from shipboard?

ANTIPHOLUS OF EPHESUS.

Dromio, what stuff of mine hast thou embarkt?

DROMIO OF SYRACUSE.

Your goods that lay at host, sir, in the Centaur.

ANTIPHOLUS OF SYRACUSE.

He speaks to me.—I am your master, Dromio:
Come, go with us; we'll look to that anon:
Embrace thy brother there; rejoice with him.

[*Exeunt* ANTIPHOLUS OF SYRACUSE *and* ANTIPHOLUS OF EPHESUS, ADRIANA *and* LUCIANA.

DROMIO OF SYRACUSE.

There is a fat friend at your master's house,
That kitchen'd me for you to-day at dinner:
She now shall be my sister, not my wife.

DROMIO OF EPHESUS.

Methinks you are my glass, and not my brother:
I see by you I am a sweet-faced youth.
Will you walk in to see their gossiping?

DROMIO OF SYRACUSE.

Not I, sir; you are my elder.

DROMIO OF EPHESUS.

That's a question: how shall we try it?

DROMIO OF SYRACUSE.

We'll draw cuts for the senior: till then lead thou first.

DROMIO OF EPHESUS.

Nay, then, thus:—
We came into the world like brother and brother;
And now let's go hand in hand, not one before another.

[*Exeunt.*

THE TAMING OF THE SHREW

DRAMATIS PERSONAE

A LORD.
CHRISTOPHER SLY, *a tinker.*
HOSTESS, PAGE, PLAYERS, HUNTSMEN, *and* SERVANTS.
(Persons in the Induction.)

BAPTISTA, *a rich gentleman of Padua.*
VINCENTIO, *an old gentleman of Pisa.*
LUCENTIO, *son to Vincentio, in love with Bianca.*
PETRUCHIO, *a gentleman of Verona, a suitor to Katharina.*

GREMIO, HORTENSIO, *suitors to Bianca.*

TRANIO, BIONDELLO, *servants to Lucentio.*
GRUMIO, CURTIS, *servants to Petruchio.*
PEDANT.

KATHARINA *the shrew,* BIANCA, *daughters to Baptista.*
WIDOW.
TAILOR, HABERDASHER, *and* SERVANTS.

SCENE—*Padua, and sometimes in Petruchio's house in the country.*

INDUCTION. SCENE I.

Before an alehouse on a heath.

Enter HOSTESS *and* SLY.

CHRISTOPHER SLY.

I'LL pheeze you, in faith.

HOSTESS.

A pair of stocks, you rogue!

CHRISTOPHER SLY.

Y'are a baggage: the Slys are no rogues; look in the Chronicles; we came in with Richard Conqueror. Therefore, *paucas pallabris;* let the world slide: sessa!

HOSTESS.

You will not pay for the glasses you have burst?

CHRISTOPHER SLY.

No, not a denier. Go by, Jeronimy; go to thy cold bed, and warm thee.

HOSTESS.

I know my remedy; I must go fetch the third-borough. [*Exit.*

CHRISTOPHER SLY.

Third, or fourth, or fifth borough, I'll answer him by law: I'll not budge an inch, boy: let him come, and kindly.

[*Lies down on the ground and falls asleep.*

Horns winded. Enter a LORD *from hunting, with* HUNTSMEN *and* SERVANTS.

LORD.

Huntsman, I charge thee, tender well my hounds:
Brach Merriman, the poor cur is imbost;
And couple Clowder with the deep-mouth'd brach.
Saw'st thou not, boy, how Silver made it good
At the hedge-corner, in the coldest fault?
I would not lose the dog for twenty pound.

FIRST HUNTSMAN.

Why, Belman is as good as he, my lord;
He cried upon it at the merest loss,
And twice to-day pickt out the dullest scent:
Trust me, I take him for the better dog.

LORD.

Thou art a fool: if Echo were as fleet,
I would esteem him worth a dozen such.
But sup them well, and look unto them all:
To-morrow I intend to hunt again.

FIRST HUNTSMAN.

I will, my lord.

LORD.

What's here? one dead, or drunk? See, doth he breathe?

SECOND HUNTSMAN.

He breathes, my lord. Were he not warm'd with ale,
This were a bed but cold to sleep so soundly.

LORD.

O monstrous beast! how like a swine he lies!—
Grim death, how foul and loathsome is thine image!—
Sirs, I will practise on this drunken man.
What think you, if he were convey'd to bed,
Wrapt in sweet clothes, rings put upon his fingers,
A most delicious banquet by his bed,
And brave attendants near him when he wakes,—
Would not the beggar then forget himself?

FIRST HUNTSMAN.

Believe me, lord, I think he cannot choose.

SECOND HUNTSMAN.

It would seem strange unto him when he waked.

LORD.

Even as a flattering dream or worthless fancy.
Then take him up, and manage well the jest:—
Carry him gently to my fairest chamber,
And hang it round with all my wanton pictures:
Balm his foul head in warm distilled waters,
And burn sweet wood to make the lodging sweet:
Procure me music ready, when he wakes,
To make a dulcet and a heavenly sound;
And if he chance to speak, be ready straight
And with a low submissive reverence
Say 'What is it your honour will command?'
Let one attend him with a silver basin
Full of rose-water, and bestrew'd with flowers;
Another bear the ewer, the third a diaper,
And say 'Will't please your lordship cool your hands?'
Some one be ready with a costly suit,
And ask him what apparel he will wear;
Another tell him of his hounds and horse,
And that his lady mourns at his disease:

Persuade him that he hath been lunatic;
And when he says he is —, say that he dreams,
For he is nothing but a mighty lord.
This do, and do it kindly, gentle sirs:
It will be pastime passing excellent,
If it be husbanded with modesty.

FIRST HUNTSMAN.

My lord, I warrant you, we'll play our part,
As he shall think, by our true diligence,
He is no less than what we say he is.

LORD.

Take him up gently, and to bed with him;
And each one to his office when he wakes.
[SLY *is borne out. Sound trumpets.*
Sirrah, go see what trumpet 'tis that sounds:—
[*Exit* SERVANT.
Belike, some noble gentleman, that means,
Travelling some journey, to repose him here.—

Enter SERVANT.

How now! who is it?

SERVANT.

An it please your honour,
Players that offer service to your lordship.

LORD.

Bid them come near.

Enter PLAYERS.

Now, fellows, you are welcome.

PLAYERS.

We thank your honour.

LORD.

Do you intend to stay with me to-night?

SECOND PLAYER.

So please your lordship to accept our duty.

LORD.

With all my heart.—This fellow I remember,
Since once he play'd a farmer's eldest son:—
'Twas where you woo'd the gentlewoman so well:
I have forgot your name; but, sure, that part
Was aptly fitted, and naturally perform'd,

FIRST PLAYER.

I think 'twas Soto that your honour means.

LORD.

'Tis very true: thou didst it excellent.—
Well, you are come to me in happy time;
The rather for I have some sport in hand,
Wherein your cunning can assist me much.
There is a lord will hear you play to-night:
But I am doubtful of your modesties;
Lest, over-eying of his odd behaviour,—
For yet his honour never heard a play,—
You break into some merry passion,
And so offend him; for, I tell you, sirs,
If you should smile, he grows impatient.

FIRST PLAYER.

Fear not, my lord: we can contain ourselves,
Were he the veriest antick in the world.

LORD.

Go, sirrah, take them to the buttery,
And give them friendly welcome every one:
Let them want nothing that my house affords.
[*Exit one with the* PLAYERS.
Sirrah, go you to Barthol'mew my page,
[*to another* SERVANT.
And see him drest in all suits like a lady:
That done, conduct him to the drunkard's chamber;
And call him madam, do him obeisance.
Tell him from me,—as he will win my love,—
He bear himself with honourable action,
Such as he hath observed in noble ladies
Unto their lords, by them accomplished:
Such duty to the drunkard let him do,
With soft low tongue and lowly courtesy;
And say, 'What is't your honour will command,
Wherein your lady and your humble wife
May show her duty and make known her love?'
And then,—with kind embracements, tempting kisses,
And with declining head into his bosom,—
Bid him shed tears, as being overjoy'd
To see her noble lord restored to health,
Who for twice seven years hath esteemed him
No better than a poor and loathsome beggar:
And if the boy have not a woman's gift
To rain a shower of commanded tears,
An onion will do well for such a shift;
Which in a napkin being close convey'd,
Shall in despite enforce a watery eye.
See this dispatcht with all the haste thou canst:
Anon I'll give thee more instructions.
[*Exit* SERVANT.
I know the boy will well usurp the grace,
Voice, gait, and action of a gentlewoman:
I long to hear him call the drunkard husband;
And how my men will stay themselves from laughter
When they do homage to this simple peasant.
I'll in to counsel them; haply my presence
May well abate the over-merry spleen
Which otherwise would grow into extremes.
[*Exeunt.*

SCENE II.

A bedchamber in the LORD'S *house.*

Enter aloft the drunkard SLY, *with* ATTENDANTS; *some with apparel, basin, ewer, and other appurtenances; and* LORD.

CHRISTOPHER SLY.

FOR God's sake, a pot of small ale.

FIRST SERVANT.

Will't please your lordship drink a cup of sack?

SECOND SERVANT.

Will't please your honour taste of these conserves?

THIRD SERVANT.

What raiment will your honour wear to-day?

CHRISTOPHER SLY.

I am Christophero Sly; call not me honour nor lordship: I ne'er drank sack in my life; and if you give me any conserves, give me conserves of beef: ne'er ask me what raiment I'll wear; for I have no more doublets than backs, no more stockings than legs, nor no more shoes than feet,—nay, sometime more feet than shoes, or such shoes as my toes look through the overleather.

LORD.

Heaven cease this idle humour in your honour!
O, that a mighty man, of such descent,
Of such possessions, and so high esteem,
Should be infused with so foul a spirit!

CHRISTOPHER SLY.

What, would you make me mad? Am not I Christopher Sly, old Sly's son of Burton-heath;

by birth a pedlar, by education a card-maker, by transmutation a bear-herd, and now by present profession a tinker? Ask Marian Hacket, the fat ale-wife of Wincot, if she know me not: if she say I am not fourteen pence on the score for sheer ale, score me up for the lying'st knave in Christendom. What! I am not bestraught: here's—

FIRST SERVANT.

O, this it is that makes your lady mourn!

SECOND SERVANT.

O, this it is that makes your servants droop!

LORD.

Hence comes it that your kindred shuns your house,
As beaten hence by your strange lunacy.
O noble lord, bethink thee of thy birth;
Call home thy ancient thoughts from banishment,
And banish hence these abject lowly dreams.
Look how thy servants do attend on thee,
Each in his office ready at thy beck.
Wilt thou have music? hark! Apollo plays, [*Music.*
And twenty caged nightingales do sing:
Or wilt thou sleep? we'll have thee to a couch
Softer and sweeter than the lustful bed
On purpose trimm'd up for Semiramis.
Say thou wilt walk; we will bestrew the ground:
Or wilt thou ride? thy horses shall be trapt,
Their harness studded all with gold and pearl.
Dost thou love hawking? thou hast hawks will soar
Above the morning lark: or wilt thou hunt?
Thy hounds shall make the welkin answer them,
And fetch shrill echoes from the hollow earth.

FIRST SERVANT.

Say thou wilt course; thy greyhounds are as swift
As breathed stags, ay, fleeter than the roe.

SECOND SERVANT.

Dost thou love pictures? we will fetch thee straight
Adonis painted by a running brook,
And Cytherea all in sedges hid,
Which seem to move and wanton with her breath,
Even as the waving sedges play with wind.

LORD.

We'll show thee Io as she was a maid,
And how she was beguiled and surprised,
As lively painted as the deed was done.

THIRD SERVANT.

Or Daphne roaming through a thorny wood,
Scratching her legs, that one shall swear she bleeds;
And at that sight shall sad Apollo weep,
So workmanly the blood and tears are drawn.

LORD.

Thou art a lord, and nothing but a lord:
Thou hast a lady far more beautiful
Than any woman in this waning age.

FIRST SERVANT.

And, till the tears that she hath shed for thee,
Like envious floods, o'er-run her lovely face,
She was the fairest creature in the world;
And yet she is inferior to none.

CHRISTOPHER SLY.

Am I a lord? and have I such a lady?
Or do I dream? or have I dream'd till now?
I do not sleep: I see, I hear, I speak;
I smell sweet savours, and I feel soft things:—
Upon my life, I am a lord indeed;
And not a tinker, nor Christophero Sly.
Well, bring our lady hither to our sight;
And once again a pot o' th' smallest ale.

SECOND SERVANT.

Will't please your mightiness to wash your hands?
[SERVANTS *present a ewer, basin, and napkin.*
O, how we joy to see your wit restored!
O, that once more you knew but what you are!
These fifteen years you have been in a dream;
Or when you waked, so waked as if you slept.

CHRISTOPHER SLY.

These fifteen years! by my fay, a goodly nap.
But did I never speak of all that time?

FIRST SERVANT.

O, yes, my lord; but very idle words:
For though you lay here in this goodly chamber,
Yet would you say ye were beaten out of door;
And rail upon the hostess of the house;
And say, you would present her at the leet,
Because she brought stone jugs and no seal'd quarts:
Sometimes you would call out for Cicely Hacket.

CHRISTOPHER SLY.

Ay, the woman's maid of the house.

THIRD SERVANT.

Why, sir, you know no house, nor no such maid;
Nor no such men as you have reckon'd up,—
As Stephen Sly, and old John Naps of Greece,
And Peter Turf, and Henry Pimpernell;
And twenty more such names and men as these,
Which never were, nor no man ever saw.

CHRISTOPHER SLY.

Now, Lord be thanked for my good amends!

ALL.

Amen.

CHRISTOPHER SLY.

I thank thee: thou shalt not lose by it.

Enter the PAGE *as a lady, with* ATTENDANTS.

PAGE.

How fares my noble lord?

CHRISTOPHER SLY.

Marry, I fare well; for here is cheer enough.
Where is my wife?

PAGE.

Here, noble lord: what is thy will with her?

CHRISTOPHER SLY.

Are you my wife, and will not call me husband?
My men should call me lord: I am your goodman.

PAGE.

My husband and my lord, my lord and husband;
I am your wife in all obedience.

CHRISTOPHER SLY.

I know it well.—What must I call her?

LORD.

Madam.

CHRISTOPHER SLY.

Al'ce madam, or Joan madam?

LORD.

Madam, and nothing else: so lords call ladies.

CHRISTOPHER SLY.

Madam wife, they say that I have dream'd,
And slept above some fifteen year or more.

PAGE.

Ay, and the time seems thirty unto me,
Being all this time abandon'd from your bed.

CHRISTOPHER SLY.

'Tis much.—Servants, leave me and her alone.—
Madam, undress you, and come now to bed.

PAGE.

Thrice-noble lord, let me entreat of you
To pardon me yet for a night or two;
Or, if not so, until the sun be set:
For your physicians have expressly charged,
In peril to incur your former malady,
That I should yet absent me from your bed:
I hope this reason stands for my excuse.

CHRISTOPHER SLY.

Ay, it stands so that I may hardly tarry so long. But I would be loth to fall into my dreams again: I will therefore tarry, in despite of the flesh and the blood.

Enter a MESSENGER.

SERVANT.

Your honour's players, hearing your amendment,
Are come to play a pleasant comedy;
For so your doctors hold it very meet,
Seeing too much sadness hath congeal'd your blood,
And melancholy is the nurse of frenzy:
Therefore they thought it good you hear a play,
And frame your mind to mirth and merriment,
Which bars a thousand harms and lengthens life.

CHRISTOPHER SLY.

Marry, I will; let them play it. Is not a commonty a Christmas gambol or a tumbling-trick?

PAGE.

No, my good lord; it is more pleasing stuff.

CHRISTOPHER SLY.

What, household stuff?

PAGE.

It is a kind of history.

CHRISTOPHER SLY.

Well, we'll see't.—Come, madam wife, sit by my side, and let the world slip: we shall ne'er be younger.

ACT I. SCENE I.

Padua. A public place.

Flourish. Enter LUCENTIO *and his man* TRANIO.

LUCENTIO.

Tranio, since, for the great desire I had
To see fair Padua, nursery of arts,
I am arrived for fruitful Lombardy,
The pleasant garden of great Italy;
And, by my father's love and leave, am arm'd
With his good will, and thy good company,
My trusty servant, well approved in all;
Here let us breathe, and haply institute
A course of learning and ingenious studies.
Pisa, renowned for grave citizens,
Gave me my being and my father first,
A merchant of great traffic through the world,
Vincentio, come of the Bentivolii.
Lucentio his son, brought up in Florence,
It shall become, to serve all hopes conceived,
To deck his fortune with his virtuous deeds:
And therefore, Tranio, for the time I study,
Virtue, and that part of philosophy
Will I apply, that treats of happiness
By virtue specially to be achieved.
Tell me thy mind; for I have Pisa left,
And am to Padua come, as he that leaves
A shallow plash, to plunge him in the deep,
And with satiety seeks to quench his thirst.

TRANIO.

Mi perdonate, gentle master mine,
I am in all affected as yourself;
Glad that you thus continue your resolve
To suck the sweets of sweet philosophy.
Only, good master, while we do admire
This virtue and this moral discipline,
Let's be no stoics nor no stocks, I pray;
Or so devote to Aristotle's ethics,
As Ovid be an outcast quite abjured:
Balk logic with acquaintance that you have,
And practise rhetoric in your common talk;
Music and poesy use to quicken you;
The mathematics and the metaphysics,
Fall to them, as you find your stomach serves you;
No profit grows, where is no pleasure ta'en:
In brief, sir, study what you most affect.

LUCENTIO.

Gramercies, Tranio, well dost thou advise.
If, Biondello, thou wert come ashore,
We could at once put us in readiness;
And take a lodging, fit to entertain
Such friends as time in Padua shall beget.
But stay awhile: what company is this?

TRANIO.

Master, some show, to welcome us to town.

Enter BAPTISTA *with his two daughters,* KATHARINA *and* BIANCA; GREMIO, *a pantaloon; and* HORTENSIO, *suitor to* LIANCA. LUCENTIO *and* TRANIO *stand by.*

BAPTISTA.

Gentlemen, importune me no further,
For how I firmly am resolved you know;
That is, not to bestow my youngest daughter
Before I have a husband for the elder;
If either of you both love Katharina,
Because I know you well, and love you well,
Leave shall you have to court her at your pleasure.

GREMIO.

To cart her rather: she's too rough for me.—
There, there, Hortensio, will you any wife?

KATHARINA [*to* BAPTISTA].

I pray you, sir, is it your will
To make a stale of me among these mates?

HORTENSIO.

Mates, maid! how mean you that? no mates for you,
Unless you were of gentler, milder mould.

KATHARINA.

I'faith, sir, you shall never need to fear:
I wis it is not half way to her heart;
But if it were, doubt not her care should be
To comb your noddle with a three-legg'd stool,
And paint your face, and use you like a fool.

HORTENSIO.

From all such devils, good Lord, deliver us!

GREMIO.

And me too, good Lord!

TRANIO [*aside to* LUCENTIO].
Hush, master! here's some good pastime toward:
That wench is stark mad, or wonderful froward.

LUCENTIO [*aside to* TRANIO].
But in the other's silence do I see
Maid's mild behaviour and sobriety.
Peace, Tranio!

TRANIO [*aside to* LUCENTIO].
Well said, master; mum! and gaze your fill.

BAPTISTA.
Gentlemen, that I may soon make good
What I have said, Bianca, get you in:
And let it not displease thee, good Bianca;
For I will love thee ne'er the less, my girl.

KATHARINA.
A pretty peat! it is best put finger in the eye, an she knew why.

BIANCA.
Sister, content you in my discontent.—
Sir, to your pleasure humbly I subscribe:
My books and instruments shall be my company,
On them to look, and practise by myself.

LUCENTIO [*aside to* TRANIO].
Hark, Tranio! thou mayst hear Minerva speak.

HORTENSIO.
Signior Baptista, will you be so strange?
Sorry am I that our good will effects
Bianca's grief.

GREMIO.
Why, will you mew her up,
Signior Baptista, for this fiend of hell,
And make her bear the penance of her tongue?

BAPTISTA.
Gentlemen, content ye; I am resolved:—
Go in, Bianca:— [*Exit* BIANCA.
And for I know she taketh most delight
In music, instruments, and poetry,
Schoolmasters will I keep within my house,
Fit to instruct her youth. If you, Hortensio,
Or Signior Gremio, you, know any such,
Prefer them hither; for to cunning men
I will be very kind, and liberal
To mine own children in good bringing-up:
And so, farewell.—Katharina, you may stay;
For I have more to commune with Bianca. [*Exit.*

KATHARINA.
Why, and I trust I may go too, may I not? What, shall I be appointed hours; as though, belike, I knew not what to take, and what to leave, ha? [*Exit.*

GREMIO.
You may go to the devil's dam: your gifts are so good, here's none will hold you.—Our love is not so great, Hortensio, but we may blow our nails together, and fast it fairly out: our cake's dough on both sides. Farewell: yet, for the love I bear my sweet Bianca, if I can by any means light on a fit man to teach her that wherein she delights, I will wish him to her father.

HORTENSIO.
So will I, Signior Gremio: but a word, I pray. Though the nature of our quarrel yet never brookt parle, know now, upon advice, it toucheth us both,—that we may yet again have access to our fair mistress, and be happy rivals in Bianca's love,—to labour and effect one thing specially.

GREMIO.
What's that, I pray?

HORTENSIO.
Marry, sir, to get a husband for her sister.

GREMIO.
A husband! a devil.

HORTENSIO.
I say, a husband.

GREMIO.
I say, a devil. Think'st thou, Hortensio, though her father be very rich, any man is so very a fool to be married to hell?

HORTENSIO.
Tush, Gremio, though it pass your patience and mine to endure her loud alarums, why, man, there be good fellows in the world, an a man could light on them, would take her with all faults and money enough.

GREMIO.
I cannot tell; but I had as lief take her dowry with this condition,—to be whipt at the high-cross every morning.

HORTENSIO.
Faith, as you say, there's small choice in rotten apples. But, come; since this bar in law makes us friends, it shall be so far forth friendly maintain'd, till by helping Baptista's eldest daughter to a husband, we set his youngest free for a husband, and then have to't afresh.—Sweet Bianca!—Happy man be his dole! He that runs fastest gets the ring. How say you, Signior Gremio?

GREMIO.
I am agreed: and would I had given him the best horse in Padua to begin his wooing, that would thoroughly woo her, wed her, and bed her, and rid the house of her! Come on.
[*Exeunt* GREMIO *and* HORTENSIO.

TRANIO.
I pray, sir, tell me,—is it possible
That love should of a sudden take such hold?

LUCENTIO.
O Tranio, till I found it to be true,
I never thought it possible or likely;
But, see! while idly I stood looking on,
I found the effect of love in idleness:
And now in plainness do confess to thee,—
That art to me as secret and as dear
As Anna to the Queen of Carthage was,—
Tranio, I burn, I pine, I perish, Tranio,
If I achieve not this young modest girl.
Counsel me, Tranio, for I know thou canst;
Assist me, Tranio, for I know thou wilt.

TRANIO.
Master, it is no time to chide you now;
Affection is not rated from the heart:
If love have toucht you, naught remains but so,—
Redime te captum quam queas minimo.

LUCENTIO.
Gramercies, lad; go forward; this contents:
The rest will comfort, for thy counsel's sound.

TRANIO.
Master, you lookt so longly on the maid,
Perhaps you markt not what's the pith of all.

LUCENTIO.
O, yes, I saw sweet beauty in her face,
Such as the daughter of Agenor had,

That made great Jove to humble him to her hand,
When with his knees he kist the Cretan strand.

TRANIO.

Saw you no more? markt you not how her sister
Began to scold, and raise up such a storm,
That mortal ears might hardly endure the din?

LUCENTIO.

Tranio, I saw her coral lips to move,
And with her breath she did perfume the air:
Sacred and sweet was all I saw in her.

TRANIO.

Nay, then, 'tis time to stir him from his trance.—
I pray, awake, sir: if you love the maid,
Bend thoughts and wits to achieve her. Thus it stands:
Her elder sister is so curst and shrewd,
That, till the father rid his hands of her,
Master, your love must live a maid at home;
And therefore has he closely mew'd her up,
Because she will not be annoy'd with suitors.

LUCENTIO.

Ah, Tranio, what a cruel father's he!
But art thou not advised, he took some care
To get her cunning schoolmasters to instruct her?

TRANIO.

Ay, marry, am I, sir; and now 'tis plotted.

LUCENTIO.

I have it, Tranio.

TRANIO.

Master, for my hand,
Both our inventions meet and jump in one.

LUCENTIO.

Tell me thine first.

TRANIO.

You will be schoolmaster,
And undertake the teaching of the maid:
That's your device.

LUCENTIO.

It is: may it be done?

TRANIO.

Not possible; for who shall bear your part,
And be in Padua here Vincentio's son;
Keep house, and ply his book; welcome his friends;
Visit his countrymen, and banquet them?

LUCENTIO.

Basta; content thee; for I have it full.
We have not yet been seen in any house;
Nor can we be distinguisht by our faces
For man or master: then it follows thus;—
Thou shalt be master, Tranio, in my stead,
Keep house, and port, and servants, as I should:
I will some other be; some Florentine,
Some Neapolitan, or meaner man of Pisa.
'Tis hatcht, and shall be so:—Tranio, at once
Uncase thee; take my colour'd hat and cloak:
When Biondello comes, he waits on thee;
But I will charm him first to keep his tongue.

TRANIO.

So had you need. [*They exchange habits.*
In brief, sir, sith it your pleasure is,
And I am tied to be obedient,—
For so your father charged me at our parting;
'Be serviceable to my son,' quoth he,
Although I think 'twas in another sense,—
I am content to be Lucentio,
Because so well I love Lucentio.

LUCENTIO.

Tranio, be so, because Lucentio loves:
And let me be a slave, t'achieve that maid
Whose sudden sight hath thrall'd my wounded eye.—
Here comes the rogue.

Enter BIONDELLO.

Sirrah, where have you been?

BIONDELLO.

Where have I been! Nay, how now! where are you? Master, has my fellow Tranio stol'n your clothes? or you stol'n his? or both? pray, what's the news?

LUCENTIO.

Sirrah, come hither: 'tis no time to jest,
And therefore frame your manners to the time.
Your fellow Tranio here, to save my life,
Puts my apparel and my countenance on,
And I for my escape have put on his;
For in a quarrel, since I came ashore,
I kill'd a man, and fear I was descried:
Wait you on him, I charge you, as becomes,
While I make way from hence to save my life:
You understand me?

BIONDELLO.

I, sir! Ne'er a whit.

LUCENTIO.

And not a jot of Tranio in your mouth:
Tranio is changed into Lucentio.

BIONDELLO.

The better for him: would I were so too!

TRANIO.

So could I, faith, boy, to have the next wish after,
That Lucentio indeed had Baptista's youngest daughter.
But, sirrah,—not for my sake, but your master's,—I advise
You use your manners discreetly in all kind of companies:
When I am alone, why, then I am Tranio;
But in all places else your master Lucentio.

LUCENTIO.

Tranio, let's go:
One thing more rests, that thyself execute,—
To make one among these wooers: if thou ask me why,—
Sufficeth, my reasons are both good and weighty.
[*Exeunt.*

The Presenters above speak.

FIRST SERVANT.

My lord, you nod; you do not mind the play.

CHRISTOPHER SLY.

Yes, by Saint Anne, do I. A good matter, surely: comes there any more of it?

PAGE.

My lord, 'tis but begun.

CHRISTOPHER SLY.

'Tis a very excellent piece of work, madam lady; would 'twere done! [*They sit and mark.*

SCENE II.

The same. Before HORTENSIO'S *house.*

Enter PETRUCHIO *and his man* GRUMIO.

PETRUCHIO.

VERONA, for awhile I take my leave,
To see my friends in Padua; but, of all,
My best beloved and approved friend,

Hortensio; and I trow this is his house.—
Here, sirrah Grumio; knock, I say.

GRUMIO.

Knock, sir! whom should I knock? is there any man has rebused your worship?

PETRUCHIO.

Villain, I say, knock me here soundly.

GRUMIO.

Knock you here, sir! why, sir, what am I, sir, that I should knock you here, sir?

PETRUCHIO.

Villain, I say, knock me at this gate,
And rap me well, or I'll knock your knave's pate.

GRUMIO.

My master is grown quarrelsome.—I should knock you first,
And then I know after who comes by the worst.

PETRUCHIO.

Will it not be?
Faith, sirrah, an you'll not knock, I'll wring it;
I'll try how you can *sol, fa*, and sing it.
[*He wrings him by the ears.*

GRUMIO.

Help, masters, help! my master is mad.

PETRUCHIO.

Now, knock when I bid you, sirrah villain!

Enter HORTENSIO.

HORTENSIO.

How now! what's the matter?—My old friend Grumio! and my good friend Petruchio!—How do you all at Verona?

PETRUCHIO.

Signior Hortensio, come you to part the fray?
Con tutto il cuore ben trovato, may I say.

HORTENSIO.

Alla nostra casa ben venuto, molto honorato signor mio Petruchio.—
Rise, Grumio, rise: we will compound this quarrel.

GRUMIO [*rising*].

Nay, 'tis no matter, sir, what he 'leges in Latin.—If this be not a lawful cause for me to leave his service,—look you, sir,—he bid me knock him and rap him soundly, sir: well, was it fit for a servant to use his master so; being perhaps, for aught I see, two-and-thirty,—a pip out?
Whom would to God I had well knockt at first,
Then had not Grumio come by the worst.

PETRUCHIO.

A senseless villain!—Good Hortensio,
I bade the rascal knock upon your gate,
And could not get him for my heart to do it.

GRUMIO.

Knock at the gate!—O heavens! Spake you not these words plain,—'Sirrah, knock me here, rap me here, knock me well, and knock me soundly'? And come you now with—knocking at the gate?

PETRUCHIO.

Sirrah, be gone, or talk not, I advise you.

HORTENSIO.

Petruchio, patience; I am Grumio's pledge:
Why, this' a heavy chance 'twixt him and you,
Your ancient, trusty, pleasant servant Grumio.
And tell me now, sweet friend, what happy gale
Blows you to Padua here, from old Verona?

PETRUCHIO.

Such wind as scatters young men through the world,
To seek their fortunes further than at home,
Where small experience grows. But, in a few,
Signior Hortensio, thus it stands with me:—
Antonio, my father, is deceased;
And I have thrust myself into this maze,
Haply to wive and thrive as best I may:
Crowns in my purse I have, and goods at home,
And so am come abroad to see the world.

HORTENSIO.

Petruchio, shall I, then, come roundly to thee,
And wish thee to a shrewd ill-favour'd wife?
Thou'ldst thank me but a little for my counsel:
And yet I'll promise thee she shall be rich,
And very rich: but thou'rt too much my friend,
And I'll not wish thee to her.

PETRUCHIO.

Signior Hortensio, 'twixt such friends as we
Few words suffice; and therefore, if thou know
One rich enough to be Petruchio's wife,—
As wealth is burthen of my wooing dance,—
Be she as foul as was Florentius' love,
As old as Sibyl, and as curst and shrewd
As Socrates' Xantippe, or a worse,
She moves me not, or not removes, at least,
Affection's edge in me, were she as rough
As are the swelling Adriatic seas:
I come to wive it wealthily in Padua;
If wealthily, then happily in Padua.

GRUMIO.

Nay, look you, sir, he tells you flatly what his mind is: why, give him gold enough and marry him to a puppet or an aglet-baby; or an old trot with ne'er a tooth in her head, though she have as many diseases as two and fifty horses: why, nothing comes amiss, so money comes withal.

HORTENSIO.

Petruchio, since we are stept thus far in,
I will continue that I broacht in jest.
I can, Petruchio, help thee to a wife
With wealth enough, and young and beauteous;
Brought up as best becomes a gentlewoman:
Her only fault—and that is faults enough—
Is, that she is intolerable curst,
And shrewd, and froward; so beyond all measure,
That, were my state far worser than it is,
I would not wed her for a mine of gold.

PETRUCHIO.

Hortensio, peace! thou know'st not gold's effect:
Tell me her father's name, and 'tis enough;
For I will board her, though she chide as loud
As thunder when the clouds in autumn crack.

HORTENSIO.

Her father is Baptista Minola,
An affable and courteous gentleman:
Her name is Katharina Minola,
Renown'd in Padua for her scolding tongue.

PETRUCHIO.

I know her father, though I know not her:
And he knew my deceased father well.
I will not sleep, Hortensio, till I see her;
And therefore let me be thus bold with you
To give you over at this first encounter,
Unless you will accompany me thither.

GRUMIO.

I pray you, sir, let him go while the humour lasts. O' my word, an she knew him as well as I do, she would think scolding would do little good upon him: she may, perhaps, call him half a score knaves, or so: why, that's nothing; an he begin once, he'll rail in his rope-tricks. I'll tell you what, sir,—an she stand him but a little, he will throw a figure in her face, and so disfigure her with it, that she shall have no more eyes to see withal than a cat. You know him not, sir.

HORTENSIO.

Tarry, Petruchio, I must go with thee;
For in Baptista's keep my treasure is:
He hath the jewel of my life in hold,
His youngest daughter, beautiful Bianca;
And her withholds from me and other more,
Suitors to her and rivals in my love;
Supposing it a thing impossible,—
For those defects I have before rehearsed,—
That ever Katharina will be woo'd;
Therefore this order hath Baptista ta'en,
That none shall have access unto Bianca
Till Katharine the curst have got a husband.

GRUMIO.

Katharine the curst!
A title for a maid, of all titles the worst.

HORTENSIO.

Now shall my friend Petruchio do me grace;
And offer me, disguised in sober robes,
To old Baptista as a schoolmaster
Well seen in music, to instruct Bianca;
That so I may, by this device, at least
Have leave and leisure to make love to her,
And unsuspected court her by herself.

GRUMIO.

Here's no knavery! See, to beguile the old folks, how the young folks lay their heads together!

Enter GREMIO *and* LUCENTIO *disguised.*

Master, master, look about you: who goes there, ha?

HORTENSIO.

Peace, Grumio! it is the rival of my love.—
Petruchio, stand by awhile.

GRUMIO.

A proper stripling and an amorous!

[*They stand aside.*

GREMIO.

O, very well; I have perused the note.
Hark you, sir; I'll have them very fairly bound:
All books of love, see that at any hand;
And see you read no other lectures to her:
You understand me:—over and beside
Signior Baptista's liberality,
I'll mend it with a largess:—take your papers too,
And let me have them very well perfumed;
For she is sweeter than perfume itself,
To whom they go to. What will you read to her?

LUCENTIO.

Whate'er I read to her, I'll plead for you
As for my patron,—stand you so assured,—
As firmly as yourself were still in place:
Yea, and perhaps with more successful words
Than you, unless you were a scholar, sir.

GREMIO.

O this learning! what a thing it is!

GRUMIO.

O this woodcock! what an ass it is!

PETRUCHIO.

Peace, sirrah!

HORTENSIO.

Grumio, mum!—[*Coming forward*] God save you, Signior Gremio!

GREMIO.

And you are well met, Signior Hortensio.
Trow you whither I am going?—To Baptista Minola.
I promised to inquire carefully
About a schoolmaster for the fair Bianca:
And, by good fortune, I have lighted well
On this young man; for learning and behaviour
Fit for her turn; well read in poetry,
And other books,—good ones, I warrant ye.

HORTENSIO.

'Tis well: and I have met a gentleman
Hath promised me to help me to another,
A fine musician to instruct our mistress;
So shall I no whit be behind in duty
To fair Bianca, so beloved of me.

GREMIO.

Beloved of me,—and that my deeds shall prove.

GRUMIO [*aside*].

And that his bags shall prove.

HORTENSIO.

Gremio, 'tis now no time to vent our love:
Listen to me; and if you speak me fair,
I'll tell you news indifferent good for either.
Here is a gentleman, whom by chance I met,
Upon agreement from us to his liking,
Will undertake to woo curst Katharine,
Yea, and to marry her, if her dowry please.

GREMIO.

So said, so done, is well:—
Hortensio, have you told him all her faults?

PETRUCHIO.

I know she is an irksome brawling scold:
If that be all, masters, I hear no harm.

GREMIO.

No, say'st me so, friend? What countryman?

PETRUCHIO.

Born in Verona, old Antonio's son:
My father dead, my fortune lives for me;
And I do hope good days and long to see.

GREMIO.

O, sir, such a life, with such a wife, were strange!
But if you have a stomach, to't o' God's name:
You shall have me assisting you in all.
But will you woo this wild-cat?

PETRUCHIO.

Will I live?

GRUMIO.

Will he woo her? ay, or I'll hang her.

PETRUCHIO.

Why came I hither but to that intent?
Think you a little din can daunt mine ears?
Have I not in my time heard lions roar?
Have I not heard the sea, puft up with winds,
Rage like an angry boar chafed with sweat?
Have I not heard great ordnance in the field,
And heaven's artillery thunder in the skies?
Have I not in a pitched battle heard
Loud 'larums, neighing steeds, and trumpet's [clang?

And do you tell me of a woman's tongue,
That gives not half so great a blow to th'ear
As will a chestnut in a farmer's fire?
Tush, tush! fear boys with bugs.

GRUMIO.

For he fears none.

GREMIO.

Hortensio, hark:
This gentleman is happily arrived,
My mind presumes, for his own good and ours.

HORTENSIO.

I promised we would be contributors,
And bear his charge of wooing, whatsoe'er.

GREMIO.

And so we will,—provided that he win her.

GRUMIO.

I would I were as sure of a good dinner.

Enter TRANIO *brave, and* BIONDELLO.

TRANIO.

Gentlemen, God save you! If I may be bold,
Tell me, I beseech you, which is the readiest way
To the house of Signior Baptista Minola?

GREMIO.

He that has the two fair daughters,—is't he you mean?

TRANIO.

Even he.—Biondello,—

GREMIO.

Hark you, sir; you mean not her to—

TRANIO.

Perhaps, him and her, sir: what have you to do?

PETRUCHIO.

Not her that chides, sir, at any hand, I pray.

TRANIO.

I love no chiders, sir.—Biondello, let's away.

LUCENTIO [*aside*].

Well begun, Tranio.

HORTENSIO.

Sir, a word ere you go;—
Are you a suitor to the maid you talk of, yea or no?

TRANIO.

An if I be, sir, is it any offence?

GREMIO.

No; if without more words you will get you hence.

TRANIO.

Why, sir, I pray, are not the streets as free
For me as for you?

GREMIO.

But so is not she.

TRANIO.

For what reason, I beseech you?

GREMIO.

For this reason, if you'll know,—
That she's the choice love of Signior Gremio.

HORTENSIO.

That she's the chosen of Signior Hortensio.

TRANIO.

Softly, my masters! if you be gentlemen,
Do me this right,—hear me with patience.
Baptista is a noble gentleman,
To whom my father is not all unknown;
And, were his daughter fairer than she is,
She may more suitors have, and me for one.
Fair Leda's daughter had a thousand wooers;
Then well one more may fair Bianca have:
And so she shall; Lucentio shall make one,
Though Paris came in hope to speed alone.

GREMIO.

What, this gentleman will out-talk us all!

LUCENTIO.

Sir, give him head: I know he'll prove a jade.

PETRUCHIO.

Hortensio, to what end are all these words?

HORTENSIO.

Sir, let me be so bold as ask you,
Did you yet ever see Baptista's daughter?

TRANIO.

No, sir; but hear I do that he hath two;
The one as famous for a scolding tongue,
As is the other for beauteous modesty.

PETRUCHIO.

Sir, sir, the first's for me; let her go by.

GREMIO.

Yea, leave that labour to great Hercules;
And let it be more than Alcides' twelve.

PETRUCHIO.

Sir, understand you this of me, in sooth:
The youngest daughter, whom you hearken for,
Her father keeps from all access of suitors;
And will not promise her to any man
Until the elder sister first be wed:
The younger then is free, and not before.

TRANIO.

If it be so, sir, that you are the man
Must stead us all, and me amongst the rest;
And if you break the ice, and do this feat,
Achieve the elder, set the younger free
For our access,—whose hap shall be to have her
Will not so graceless be to be ingrate.

HORTENSIO.

Sir, you say well, and well you do conceive;
And since you do profess to be a suitor,
You must, as we do, gratify this gentleman,
To whom we all rest generally beholding.

TRANIO.

Sir, I shall not be slack: in sign whereof,
Please ye we may contrive this afternoon,
And quaff carouses to our mistress' health;
And do as adversaries do in law,—
Strive mightily, but eat and drink as friends.

GRUMIO *and* BIONDELLO.

O excellent motion! Fellows, let's be gone.

HORTENSIO.

The motion's good indeed, and be it so:—
Petruchio, I shall be your *ben venuto*. [*Exeunt.*

ACT II. SCENE I.

Padua. A room in BAPTISTA'S *house.*

Enter KATHARINA, *and* BIANCA *with her hands bound.*

BIANCA.

GOOD sister, wrong me not, nor wrong your self,
To make a bondmaid and a slave of me;
That I disdain: but for these other gauds,
Unbind my hands, I'll pull them off myself,
Yea, all my raiment, to my petticoat;
Or, what you will command me, will I do.
So well I know my duty to my elders.

KATHARINA.

Of all thy suitors, here I charge thee, tell
Whom thou lovest best: see thou dissemble not.

BIANCA.

Believe me, sister, of all the men alive,
I never yet beheld that special face
Which I could fancy more than any other.

KATHARINA.

Minion, thou liest: is't not Hortensio?

BIANCA.

If you affect him, sister, here I swear
I'll plead for you myself, but you shall have him.

KATHARINA.

O, then, belike you fancy riches more:
You will have Gremio to keep you fair.

BIANCA.

Is it for him you do envy me so?
Nay, then, you jest; and now I well perceive
You have but jested with me all this while:
I prithee, sister Kate, untie my hands.

KATHARINA.

If that be jest, then all the rest was so.
[*Strikes her.*

Enter BAPTISTA.

BAPTISTA.

Why, how now, dame! whence grows this insolence?—
Bianca, stand aside:—poor girl! she weeps:—
Go ply thy needle; meddle not with her.—
For shame, thou hilding of a devilish spirit,
Why dost thou wrong her that did ne'er wrong thee?
When did she cross thee with a bitter word?

KATHARINA.

Her silence flouts me, and I'll be revenged.
[*Flies after* BIANCA.

BAPTISTA [*holding her back*].

What, in my sight?—Bianca, get thee in.
[*Exit* BIANCA.

KATHARINA.

What, will you not suffer me? Nay, now I see
She is your treasure, she must have a husband;
I must dance barefoot on her wedding-day,
And, for your love to her, lead apes in hell.
Talk not to me: I will go sit and weep,
Till I can find occasion of revenge. [*Exit.*

BAPTISTA.

Was ever gentleman thus grieved as I?
But who comes here?

Enter GREMIO, *with* LUCENTIO *in the habit of a mean man;* PETRUCHIO, *with* HORTENSIO *as a musician; and* TRANIO, *with* BIONDELLO *bearing a lute and books.*

GREMIO.

Good morrow, neighbour Baptista.

BAPTISTA.

Good morrow, neighbour Gremio.—God save you, gentlemen!

PETRUCHIO.

And you, good sir! Pray, have you not a daughter
Call'd Katharina, fair and virtuous?

BAPTISTA.

I have a daughter, sir, call'd Katharina.

GREMIO.

You are too blunt: go to it orderly.

PETRUCHIO.

You wrong me, Signior Gremio: give me leave.—
I am a gentleman of Verona, sir,
That, hearing of her beauty and her wit,
Her affability and bashful modesty,
Her wondrous qualities and mild behaviour,
Am bold to show myself a forward guest
Within your house, to make mine eye the witness
Of that report which I so oft have heard.
And, for an entrance to my entertainment,
I do present you with a man of mine,
[*presenting* HORTENSIO.
Cunning in music and the mathematics,
To instruct her fully in those sciences,
Whereof I know she is not ignorant:
Accept of him, or else you do me wrong:
His name is Licio, born in Mantua.

BAPTISTA.

You're welcome, sir; and he, for your good sake.
But for my daughter Katharine,—this I know,
She is not for your turn, the more my grief.

PETRUCHIO.

I see you do not mean to part with her;
Or else you like not of my company.

BAPTISTA.

Mistake me not; I speak but as I find.
Whence are you, sir? what may I call your name?

PETRUCHIO.

Petruchio is my name; Antonio's son,
A man well known throughout all Italy.

BAPTISTA.

I knew him well: you are welcome for his sake.

GREMIO.

Saving your tale, Petruchio, I pray,
Let us, that are poor petitioners, speak too:
Baccare! you are marvellous forward.

PETRUCHIO.

O, pardon me, Signior Gremio; I would fain be doing.

GREMIO.

I doubt it not, sir; but you will curse your wooing.
Neighbour, this is a gift very grateful, I am sure of it. To express the like kindness myself, that have been more kindly beholding to you than any, I freely give unto you this young scholar [*presenting* LUCENTIO], that hath been long studying at Rheims; as cunning in Greek, Latin, and other languages, as the other in music and mathematics: his name is Cambio: pray, accept his service.

BAPTISTA.

A thousand thanks, Signior Gremio.—Welcome, good Cambio.—But, gentle sir [*to* TRANIO], methinks you walk like a stranger: may I be so bold to know the cause of your coming?

TRANIO.

Pardon me, sir, the boldness is mine own;
That, being a stranger in this city here,
Do make myself a suitor to your daughter,
Unto Bianca, fair and virtuous.
Nor is your firm resolve unknown to me,
In the preferment of the eldest sister.
This liberty is all that I request,—
That, upon knowledge of my parentage,
I may have welcome 'mongst the rest that woo,
And free access and favour as the rest:
And, toward the education of your daughters,

I here bestow a simple instrument,
And this small packet of Greek and Latin books:
If you accept them, then their worth is great.
Lucentio is my name.

BAPTISTA.

Of whence, I pray?

TRANIO.

Of Pisa, sir; son to Vincentio.

BAPTISTA.

A mighty man of Pisa; by report
I know him well: you are very welcome, sir.—
Take you [*to* HORTENSIO] the lute, and you [*to* LUCENTIO] the set of books;
You shall go see your pupils presently.—
Holla, within!

Enter a SERVANT.

Sirrah, lead these gentlemen
To my two daughters; and tell them both
These are their tutors: bid them use them well.

[*Exit* SERVANT, *with* HORTENSIO, LUCENTIO, *and* BIONDELLO.

We will go walk a little in the orchard,
And then to dinner. You are passing welcome,
And so I pray you all to think yourselves.

PETRUCHIO.

Signior Baptista, my business asketh haste,
And every day I cannot come to woo.
You knew my father well; and in him, me,
Left solely heir to all his lands and goods,
Which I have better'd rather than decreased:
Then tell me,—if I get your daughter's love,
What dowry shall I have with her to wife?

BAPTISTA.

After my death, the one half of my lands,
And in possession twenty thousand crowns.

PETRUCHIO.

And, for that dowry, I'll assure her of
Her widowhood, be it that she survive me,
In all my lands and leases whatsoever:
Let specialties be therefore drawn between us,
That covenants may be kept on either hand.

BAPTISTA.

Ay, when the special thing is well obtain'd,
That is, her love; for that is all in all.

PETRUCHIO.

Why, that is nothing; for I tell you, father,
I am as peremptory as she proud-minded;
And where two raging fires meet together,
They do consume the thing that feeds their fury:
Though little fire grows great with little wind,
Yet extreme gusts will blow out fire and all:
So I to her, and so she yields to me;
For I am rough, and woo not like a babe.

BAPTISTA.

Well mayst thou woo, and happy be thy speed!
But be thou arm'd for some unhappy words.

PETRUCHIO.

Ay, to the proof; as mountains are for winds,
That shakes not, though they blow perpetually.

Enter HORTENSIO, *with his head broke.*

BAPTISTA.

How now, my friend! why dost thou look so pale?

HORTENSIO.

For fear, I promise you, if I look pale.

BAPTISTA.

What, will my daughter prove a good musician?

HORTENSIO.

I think she'll sooner prove a soldier:
Iron may hold with her, but never lutes.

BAPTISTA.

Why, then thou canst not break her to the lute?

HORTENSIO.

Why, no; for she hath broke the lute to me.
I did but tell her she mistook her frets,
And bow'd her hand to teach her fingering;
When, with a most impatient devilish spirit,
'Frets call you these?' quoth she; 'I'll fume with them:'
And, with that word, she struck me on the head,
And through the instrument my pate made way;
And there I stood amazed for a while,
As on a pillory, looking through the lute;
While she did call me rascal fiddler
And twangling Jack, with twenty such vile terms,
As had she studied to misuse me so.

PETRUCHIO.

Now, by the world, it is a lusty wench;
I love her ten times more than e'er I did:
O, how I long to have some chat with her!

BAPTISTA.

Well, go with me, and be not so discomfited:
Proceed in practice with my younger daughter;
She's apt to learn, and thankful for good turns.—
Signior Petruchio, will you go with us,
Or shall I send my daughter Kate to you?

PETRUCHIO.

I pray you do; I will attend her here,—

[*Exeunt* BAPTISTA, GREMIO, TRANIO, *and* HORTENSIO.

And woo her with some spirit when she comes.
Say that she rail; why, then, I'll tell her plain,
She sings as sweetly as a nightingale:
Say that she frown; I'll say, she looks as clear
As morning roses newly washt with dew:
Say she be mute and will not speak a word;
Then I'll commend her volubility,
And say she uttereth piercing eloquence:
If she do bid me pack, I'll give her thanks,
As though she bid me stay by her a week:
If she deny to wed, I'll crave the day
When I shall ask the banns, and when be married.—
But here she comes; and now, Petruchio, speak.

Enter KATHARINA.

Good morrow, Kate; for that's your name, I hear.

KATHARINA.

Well have you heard, but something hard of hearing:
They call me Katharine that do talk of me.

PETRUCHIO.

You lie, in faith; for you are call'd plain Kate,
And bonny Kate, and sometimes Kate the curst;
But, Kate, the prettiest Kate in Christendom,
Kate of Kate-Hall, my super-dainty Kate,
For dainties are all cates,—and therefore, Kate,
Take this of me, Kate of my consolation;—
Hearing thy mildness praised in every town,
Thy virtues spoke of, and thy beauty sounded,
Yet not so deeply as to thee belongs,—
Myself am moved to woo thee for my wife.

KATHARINA.

Moved! in good time: let him that moved you hither

Remove you hence: I knew you at the first,
You were a moveable.

PETRUCHIO.
Why, what's a moveable?

KATHARINA.
A joint-stool.

PETRUCHIO.
Thou hast hit it: come, sit on me.

KATHARINA.
Asses are made to bear, and so are you.

PETRUCHIO.
Women are made to bear, and so are you.

KATHARINA.
No such jade as you, if me you mean.

PETRUCHIO.
Alas, good Kate! I will not burthen thee!
For, knowing thee to be but young and light—

KATHARINA.
Too light for such a swain as you to catch;
And yet as heavy as my weight should be.

PETRUCHIO.
Should be! should—buzz!

KATHARINA.
Well ta'en, and like a buzzard.

PETRUCHIO.
O slow-wing'd turtle! shall a buzzard take thee?

KATHARINA.
Ay, for a turtle,—as he takes a buzzard.

PETRUCHIO.
Come, come, you wasp; i'faith, you are too angry.

KATHARINA.
If I be waspish, best beware my sting.

PETRUCHIO.
My remedy is then, to pluck it out.

KATHARINA.
Ay, if the fool could find it where it lies.

PETRUCHIO.
Who knows not where a wasp does wear his sting?
In his tail.

KATHARINA.
In his tongue.

PETRUCHIO.
Whose tongue?

KATHARINA.
Yours, if you talk of tails: and so farewell.

PETRUCHIO.
What, with my tongue in your tail? nay, come again,
Good Kate; I am a gentleman.

KATHARINA.
That I'll try.
[*She strikes him.*

PETRUCHIO.
I swear I'll cuff you, if you strike again.

KATHARINA.
So may you lose your arms:
If you strike me, you are no gentleman;
And if no gentleman, why, then no arms.

PETRUCHIO.
A herald, Kate? O, put me in thy books!

KATHARINA.
What is your crest? a coxcomb?

PETRUCHIO.
A combless cock, so Kate will be my hen.

KATHARINA.
No cock of mine; you crow too like a craven.

PETRUCHIO.
Nay, come, Kate, come; you must not look so sour.

KATHARINA.
It is my fashion when I see a crab.

PETRUCHIO.
Why, here's no crab; and therefore look not sour.

KATHARINA.
There is, there is.

PETRUCHIO.
Then show it me.

KATHARINA.
Had I a glass, I would.

PETRUCHIO.
What, you mean my face?

KATHARINA.
Well aim'd of such a young one.

PETRUCHIO.
Now, by Saint George, I am too young for you.

KATHARINA.
Yet you are wither'd.

PETRUCHIO.
'Tis with cares.

KATHARINA.
I care not.

PETRUCHIO.
Nay, hear you, Kate: in sooth, you scape not so.

KATHARINA.
I chafe you, if I tarry: let me go.

PETRUCHIO.
No, not a whit: I find you passing gentle.
'Twas told me you were rough, and coy, and sullen,
And now I find report a very liar;
For thou art pleasant, gamesome, passing courteous;
But slow in speech, yet sweet as spring-time flowers:
Thou canst not frown, thou canst not look askance,
Nor bite the lip, as angry wenches will;
Nor hast thou pleasure to be cross in talk;
But thou with mildness entertain'st thy wooers,
With gentle conference, soft and affable.
Why does the world report that Kate doth limp?
O slanderous world! Kate, like the hazel-twig,
Is straight and slender; and as brown in hue
As hazel-nuts, and sweeter than the kernels.
O, let me see thee walk: thou dost not halt.

KATHARINA.
Go, fool, and whom thou keep'st command.

PETRUCHIO.
Did ever Dian so become a grove,
As Kate this chamber with her princely gait?
O, be thou Dian, and let her be Kate;
And then let Kate be chaste, and Dian sportful!

KATHARINA.
Where did you study all this goodly speech?

PETRUCHIO.
It is extempore, from my mother-wit.

KATHARINA.
A witty mother! witless else her son.

PETRUCHIO.
Am I not wise?

KATHARINA.
Yes; keep you warm.

PETRUCHIO.

Marry, so I mean, sweet Katharine, in thy bed:
And therefore, setting all this chat aside,
Thus in plain terms:—your father hath consented
That you shall be my wife; your dowry 'greed on;
And, will you, nill you, I will marry you.
Now, Kate, I am a husband for your turn;
For, by this light, whereby I see thy beauty,—
Thy beauty, that doth make me like thee well,—
Thou must be married to no man but me;
For I am he am born to tame you, Kate,
And bring you from a wild Kate to a Kate
Conformable, as other household Kates.
Here comes your father: never make denial;
I must and will have Katharine to my wife.

Enter BAPTISTA, GREMIO, *and* TRANIO.

BAPTISTA.

Now, Signior Petruchio, how speed you with
My daughter?

PETRUCHIO.

How but well, sir? how but well?
It were impossible I should speed amiss.

BAPTISTA.

Why, how now, daughter Katharine! in your dumps?

KATHARINA.

Call you me daughter? now, I promise you,
You have show'd a tender fatherly regard,
To wish me wed to one half lunatic;
A mad-cap ruffian and a swearing Jack,
That thinks with oaths to face the matter out.

PETRUCHIO.

Father, 'tis thus:—yourself and all the world,
That talkt of her, have talkt amiss of her:
If she be curst, it is for policy,
For she's not froward, but modest as the dove;
She is not hot, but temperate as the morn;
For patience she will prove a second Grissel,
And Roman Lucrece for her chastity:
And to conclude,—we have 'greed so well together,
That upon Sunday is the wedding day.

KATHARINA.

I'll see thee hang'd on Sunday first.

GREMIO.

Hark, Petruchio; she says, she'll see thee hang'd first.

TRANIO.

Is this your speeding? nay, then, good night our part!

PETRUCHIO.

Be patient, gentlemen; I choose her for myself:
If she and I be pleased, what's that to you?
'Tis bargain'd 'twixt us twain, being alone,
That she shall still be curst in company.
I tell you, 'tis incredible to believe
How much she loves me: O, the kindest Kate!—
She hung about my neck; and kiss on kiss
She vied so fast, protesting oath on oath,
That in a twink she won me to her love.
O, you are novices! 'tis a world to see,
How tame, when men and women are alone,
A meacock wretch can make the curstest shrew.—
Give me thy hand, Kate: I will unto Venice,
To buy apparel 'gainst the wedding-day.—
Provide the feast, father, and bid the guests;
I will be sure my Katharine shall be fine.

BAPTISTA.

I know not what to say: but give me your hands;
God send you joy, Petruchio! 'tis a match.

GREMIO *and* TRANIO.

Amen, say we: we will be witnesses.

PETRUCHIO.

Father, and wife, and gentlemen, adieu;
I will to Venice; Sunday comes apace:—
We will have rings, and things, and fine array;
And kiss me, Kate; we will be married o' Sunday.

[*Exeunt* PETRUCHIO *and* KATHARINA *severally*.

GREMIO.

Was ever match clapt up so suddenly?

BAPTISTA.

Faith, gentlemen, now I play a merchant's part,
And venture madly on a desperate mart.

TRANIO.

'Twas a commodity lay fretting by you:
'Twill bring you gain, or perish on the seas.

BAPTISTA.

The gain I seek is, quiet in the match.

GREMIO.

No doubt but he hath got a quiet catch.
But now, Baptista, to your younger daughter:
Now is the day we long have looked for:
I am your neighbour, and was suitor first.

TRANIO.

And I am one that love Bianca more
Than words can witness, or your thoughts can guess.

GREMIO.

Youngling, thou canst not love so dear as I.

TRANIO.

Greybeard, thy love doth freeze.

GREMIO.

But thine doth fry.
Skipper, stand back: 'tis age that nourisheth.

TRANIO.

But youth in ladies' eyes that flourisheth.

BAPTISTA.

Content you, gentlemen: I will compound this strife:
'Tis deeds must win the prize; and he, of both,
That can assure my daughter greatest dower
Shall have Bianca's love.—
Say, Signior Gremio, what can you assure her?

GREMIO.

First, as you know, my house within the city
Is richly furnished with plate and gold;
Basins and ewers, to lave her dainty hands;
My hangings all of Tyrian tapestry;
In ivory coffers I have stuft my crowns;
In cypress chests my arras-counterpoints,
Costly apparel, tents, and canopies,
Fine linen, Turkey cushions bost with pearl,
Valance of Venice gold in needlework;
Pewter and brass, and all things that belong
To house or housekeeping: then, at my farm
I have a hundred milch-kine to the pail,
Six score fat oxen standing in my stalls;
And all things answerable to this portion.
Myself am struck in years, I must confess;

And if I die to-morrow, this is hers,
If whilst I live she will be only mine.

TRANIO.

That 'only' came well in.—Sir, list to me:
I am my father's heir and only son:
If I may have your daughter to my wife,
I'll leave her houses three or four as good,
Within rich Pisa walls, as any one
Old Signior Gremio has in Padua;
Besides two thousand ducats by the year
Of fruitful land, all which shall be her jointure.—
What, have I pincht you, Signior Gremio?

GREMIO.

Two thousand ducats by the year of land!
My land amounts but to so much in all:
That she shall have: besides an argosy
That now is lying in Marseilles' road.—
What, have I choked you with an argosy?

TRANIO.

Gremio, 'tis known my father hath no less
Than three great argosies; besides two galliasses,
And twelve tight galleys; these I will assure her,
And twice as much, whate'er thou offer'st next.

GREMIO.

Nay, I have offer'd all,—I have no more;
And she can have no more than all I have:—
If you like me, she shall have me and mine.

TRANIO.

Why, then, the maid is mine from all the world,
By your firm promise: Gremio is out-vied.

BAPTISTA.

I must confess your offer is the best;
And, let your father make her the assurance,
She is your own; else, you must pardon me:
If you should die before him, where's her dower?

TRANIO.

That's but a cavil: he is old, I young.

GREMIO.

And may not young men die, as well as old?

BAPTISTA.

Well, gentlemen,
I am thus resolved:—on Sunday next you know
My daughter Katharine is to be married:
Now, on the Sunday following, shall Bianca
Be bride to you, if you make this assurance;
If not, to Signior Gremio:
And so, I take my leave, and thank you both.

GREMIO.

Adieu, good neighbour. [*Exit* BAPTISTA.
Now I fear thee not:
Sirrah young gamester, your father were a fool
To give thee all, and in his waning age
Set foot under thy table: tut, a toy!
An old Italian fox is not so kind, my boy. [*Exit.*

TRANIO.

A vengeance on your crafty wither'd hide!
Yet I have faced it with a card of ten.
'Tis in my head to do my master good:
I see no reason but supposed Lucentio
Must get a father, call'd—supposed Vincentio;
And that's a wonder: fathers commonly
Do get their children; but in this case of wooing,
A child shall get a sire, if I fail not of my cunning.
[*Exit.*

ACT III. SCENE I.

Padua. A room in BAPTISTA'S *house.*

Enter LUCENTIO, HORTENSIO, *and* BIANCA.

LUCENTIO.

Fiddler, forbear; you grow too forward, sir:
Have you so soon forgot the entertainment
Her sister Katharine welcomed you withal?

HORTENSIO.

But, wrangling pedant, this' the patroness
Of heavenly harmony:
Then give me leave to have prerogative;
And when in music we have spent an hour,
Your lecture shall have leisure for as much.

LUCENTIO.

Preposterous ass, that never read so far
To know the cause why music was ordain'd!
Was it not to refresh the mind of man
After his studies or his usual pain?
Then give me leave to read philosophy,
And while I pause, serve in your harmony.

HORTENSIO.

Sirrah, I will not bear these braves of thine.

BIANCA.

Why, gentlemen, you do me double wrong,
To strive for that which resteth in my choice:
I am no breeching scholar in the schools;
I'll not be tied to hours nor 'pointed times,
But learn my lessons as I please myself.
And, to cut off all strife, here sit we down:—
Take you your instrument, play you the whiles;
His lecture will be done ere you have tuned.

HORTENSIO.

You'll leave his lecture when I am in tune?
[*To* BIANCA. HORTENSIO *retires.*

LUCENTIO.

That will be never:—tune your instrument.

BIANCA.

Where left we last?

LUCENTIO.

Here, madam:— [*Reads.*
Hac ibat Simois; hic est Sigeia tellus;
Hic steterat Priami regia celsa senis.

BIANCA.

Conster them.

LUCENTIO.

Hac ibat, as I told you before,—*Simois*, I am Lucentio,—*hic est*, son unto Vincentio of Pisa,—*Sigeia tellus*, disguised thus to get your love;—*Hic steterat*, and that Lucentio that comes a-wooing,—*Priami*, is my man Tranio,—*regia*, bearing my port,—*celsa senis*, that we might beguile the old pantaloon.

HORTENSIO [*coming forward*].

Madam, my instrument's in tune.

BIANCA.

Let's hear. [HORTENSIO *plays.*
O, fie! the treble jars.

LUCENTIO.

Spit in the hole, man,
And tune again.

BIANCA.

Now let me see if I can conster it:—
Hac ibat Simois, I know you not,—*hic est Sigeia tellus*, I trust you not;—*Hic steterat Priami*, take

heed he hear us not,—*regia*, presume not,—*celsa senis*, despair not.

HORTENSIO.

Madam, 'tis now in tune.

LUCENTIO.

All but the base.

HORTENSIO.

The base is right; 'tis the base knave that jars.—
[*aside*] How fiery and forward our pedant is!
Now, for my life, the knave doth court my love:
Pedascule, I'll watch you better yet.

BIANCA.

In time I may believe, yet I mistrust.

LUCENTIO.

Mistrust it not; for, sure, Aeacides
Was Ajax,—call'd so from his grandfather.

BIANCA.

I must believe my master; else, I promise you,
I should be arguing still upon that doubt:
But let it rest.—Now, Licio, to you:—
Good masters, take it not unkindly, pray,
That I have been thus pleasant with you both.

HORTENSIO [*to* LUCENTIO].

You may go walk, and give me leave awhile:
My lessons make no music in three parts.

LUCENTIO.

Are you so formal, sir? well, I must wait,
[*aside*] And watch withal; for, but I be deceived,
Our fine musician groweth amorous.

HORTENSIO.

Madam, before you touch the instrument,
To learn the order of my fingering,
I must begin with rudiments of art;
To teach you gamut in a briefer sort,
More pleasant, pithy, and effectual,
Than hath been taught by any of my trade:
And there it is in writing, fairly drawn.

BIANCA.

Why, I am past my gamut long ago.

HORTENSIO.

Yet read the gamut of Hortensio.

BIANCA [*reads*].

'*Gamut* I am, the ground of all accord,
A re, to plead Hortensio's passion;
B mi, Bianca, take him for thy lord,
C fa ut, that loves with all affection:
D sol re, one cliff, two notes have I:
E la mi, show pity, or I die.'
Call you this gamut? tut, I like it not:
Old fashions please me best; I am not so nice,
To change true rules for old inventions.

Enter a SERVANT.

SERVANT.

Mistress, your father prays you leave your books,
And help to dress your sister's chamber up:
You know to-morrow is the wedding-day.

BIANCA.

Farewell, sweet masters, both; I must be gone.
[*Exeunt* BIANCA *and* SERVANT.

LUCENTIO.

Faith, mistress, then I have no cause to stay.
[*Exit.*

HORTENSIO.

But I have cause to pry into this pedant:
Methinks he looks as though he were in love:—
Yet if thy thoughts, Bianca, be so humble,
To cast thy wandering eyes on every stale,
Seize thee that list: if once I find thee ranging,
Hortensio will be quit with thee by changing.
[*Exit.*

SCENE II.

The same. Before BAPTISTA'S *house.*

Enter BAPTISTA, GREMIO, TRANIO, KATHARINA, BIANCA, LUCENTIO, *and others, with* ATTENDANTS.

BAPTISTA [*to* TRANIO].

SIGNIOR Lucentio, this is the 'pointed day
That Katharine and Petruchio should be married,
And yet we hear not of our son-in-law.
What will be said? what mockery will it be,
To want the bridegroom when the priest attends
To speak the ceremonial rites of marriage!
What says Lucentio to this shame of ours?

KATHARINA.

No shame but mine: I must, forsooth, be forced
To give my hand, opposed against my heart,
Unto a mad-brain rudesby, full of spleen;
Who woo'd in haste, and means to wed at leisure.
I told you, I, he was a frantic fool,
Hiding his bitter jests in blunt behaviour:
And, to be noted for a merry man,
He'll woo a thousand, 'point the day of marriage,
Make feasts, invite friends, and proclaim the banns;
Yet never means to wed where he hath woo'd.
Now must the world point at poor Katharine,
And say, 'Lo, there is mad Petruchio's wife,
If it would please him come and marry her!'

TRANIO.

Patience, good Katharine, and Baptista too.
Upon my life, Petruchio means but well,
Whatever fortune stays him from his word:
Though he be blunt, I know him passing wise;
Though he be merry, yet withal he's honest.

KATHARINA.

Would Katharine had never seen him, though!
[*Exit weeping, follow'd by* BIANCA *and others.*

BAPTISTA.

Go, girl; I cannot blame thee now to weep;
For such an injury would vex a saint,
Much more a shrew of thy impatient humour.

Enter BIONDELLO.

BIONDELLO.

Master, master! news, old news and such news as you never heard of!

BAPTISTA.

Is it new and old too? how may that be?

BIONDELLO.

Why, is it not news, to hear of Petruchio's coming?

BAPTISTA.

Is he come?

BIONDELLO.

Why, no, sir.

BAPTISTA.

What then?

BIONDELLO.

He is coming.

BAPTISTA.

When will he be here?

BIONDELLO.

When he stands where I am, and sees you there.

TRANIO.

But, say, what to thine old news?

BIONDELLO.

Why, Petruchio is coming, in a new hat and an old jerkin; a pair of old breeches, thrice turn'd; a pair of boots that have been candle-cases, one buckled, another laced; an old rusty sword ta'en out of the town-armoury, with a broken hilt, and chapeless; with two broken points: his horse hipt with an old mothy saddle, and stirrups of no kindred; besides, possest with the glanders, and like to mose in the chine; troubled with the lampass, infected with the fashions, full of windgalls, sped with spavins, ray'd with the yellows, past cure of the fives, stark spoil'd with the staggers, begnawn with the bots; sway'd in the back, and shoulder-shotten; near-legg'd before, and with a half-cheekt bit, and a headstall of sheep's leather, which, being restrain'd to keep him from stumbling, hath been often burst, and new-repair'd with knots; one girth six times pieced, and a woman's crupper of velure, which hath two letters for her name fairly set down in studs, and here and there pieced with packthread.

BAPTISTA.

Who comes with him?

BIONDELLO.

O, sir, his lackey, for all the world caparison'd like the horse; with a linen stock on one leg, and a kersey boot-hose on the other, garter'd with a red and blue list; an old hat, and *The Humour of Forty Fancies* prickt in't for a feather: a monster, a very monster in apparel; and not like a Christian footboy or a gentleman's lackey.

TRANIO.

'Tis some odd humour pricks him to this fashion;
Yet oftentimes he goes but mean-apparell'd.

BAPTISTA.

I am glad he's come, howsoe'er he comes.

BIONDELLO.

Why, sir, he comes not.

BAPTISTA.

Didst thou not say he comes?

BIONDELLO.

Who? that Petruchio came?

BAPTISTA.

Ay, that Petruchio came.

BIONDELLO.

No, sir; I say his horse comes, with him on his back.

BAPTISTA.

Why, that's all one.

BIONDELLO.

Nay, by Saint Jamy,
I hold you a penny,
A horse and a man
Is more than one,
And yet not many.

Enter PETRUCHIO *and* GRUMIO.

PETRUCHIO.

Come, where be these gallants? who's at home?

BAPTISTA.

You're welcome, sir.

PETRUCHIO.

And yet I come not well.

BAPTISTA.

And yet you halt not.

TRANIO.

Not so well apparell'd
As I wish you were.

PETRUCHIO.

Were it better, I should rush in thus.
But where is Kate? where is my lovely bride?—
How does my father?—Gentles, methinks you frown:
And wherefore gaze this goodly company,
As if they saw some wondrous monument,
Some comet or unusual prodigy?

BAPTISTA.

Why, sir, you know this is your wedding-day:
First we were sad, fearing you would not come;
Now sadder, that you come so unprovided.
Fie, doff this habit, shame to your estate,
An eye-sore to our solemn festival!

TRANIO.

And tell us, what occasion of import
Hath all so long detain'd you from your wife,
And sent you hither so unlike yourself?

PETRUCHIO.

Tedious it were to tell, and harsh to hear:
Sufficeth, I am come to keep my word,
Though in some part enforced to digress;
Which, at more leisure, I will so excuse
As you shall well be satisfied withal.
But where is Kate? I stay too long from her:
The morning wears, 'tis time we were at church.

TRANIO.

See not your bride in these unreverent robes:
Go to my chamber; put on clothes of mine.

PETRUCHIO.

Not I, believe me: thus I'll visit her.

BAPTISTA.

But thus, I trust, you will not marry her.

PETRUCHIO.

Good sooth, even thus; therefore ha' done with words:
To me she's married, not unto my clothes:
Could I repair what she will wear in me,
As I can change these poor accoutrements,
'Twere well for Kate, and better for myself.
But what a fool am I to chat with you,
When I should bid good morrow to my bride,
And seal the title with a lovely kiss!

[*Exeunt* PETRUCHIO *and* GRUMIO.

TRANIO.

He hath some meaning in his mad attire:
We will persuade him, be it possible,
To put on better ere he go to church.

BAPTISTA.

I'll after him, and see the event of this.

[*Exeunt* BAPTISTA, GREMIO, *and* ATTENDANTS.

TRANIO.

But, sir, to her love concerneth us to add
Her father's liking: which to bring to pass,
As I before imparted to your worship,
I am to get a man,—whate'er he be,
It skills not much, we'll fit him to our turn,—
And he shall be Vincentio of Pisa;
And make assurance here in Padua
Of greater sums than I have promised.

So shall you quietly enjoy your hope,
And marry sweet Bianca with consent.

LUCENTIO.

Were it not that my fellow-schoolmaster
Doth watch Bianca's steps so narrowly,
'Twere good, methinks, to steal our marriage;
Which once perform'd, let all the world say no,
I'll keep mine own, despite of all the world.

TRANIO.

That by degrees we mean to look into,
And watch our vantage in this business:
We'll over-reach the greybeard, Gremio,
The narrow-prying father, Minola,
The quaint musician, amorous Licio;
All for my master's sake, Lucentio.

Enter GREMIO.

Signior Gremio, came you from the church?

GREMIO.

As willingly as e'er I came from school.

TRANIO.

And is the bride and bridegroom coming home?

GREMIO.

A bridegroom say you? 'tis a groom indeed,
A grumbling groom, and that the girl shall find.

TRANIO.

Curster than she? why, 'tis impossible.

GREMIO.

Why, he's a devil, a devil, a very fiend.

TRANIO.

Why, she's a devil, a devil, the devil's dam.

GREMIO.

Tut, she's a lamb, a dove, a fool to him.
I'll tell you, Sir Lucentio: when the priest
Should ask, if Katharine should be his wife,
'Ay, by gogs-wouns,' quoth he; and swore so loud,
That, all amazed, the priest let fall the book;
And, as he stoopt again to pick it up,
The mad-brain'd bridegroom took him such a cuff,
That down fell priest and book, and book and priest:
'Now take them up,' quoth he, 'if any list.'

TRANIO.

What said the wench when he rose again?

GREMIO.

Trembled and shook; for why he stampt and swore,
As if the vicar meant to cozen him.
But after many ceremonies done,
He calls for wine: 'A health!' quoth he; as if
He had been aboard, carousing to his mates
After a storm; quaft off the muscadel,
And threw the sops all in the sexton's face;
Having no other reason
But that his beard grew thin and hungerly,
And seem'd to ask him sops as he was drinking.
This done, he took the bride about the neck,
And kist her lips with such a clamorous smack,
That, at the parting, all the church did echo:
And I, seeing this, came thence for very shame;
And after me, I know, the rout is coming.
Such a mad marriage never was before:—
Hark, hark! I hear the minstrels play.
[*Music plays.*

Enter PETRUCHIO, KATHARINA, BIANCA, BAPTISTA, GRUMIO; *with* HORTENSIO *and* TRAIN.

PETRUCHIO.

Gentlemen and friends, I thank you for your pains:
I know you think to dine with me to-day,
And have prepared great store of wedding cheer;
But so it is, my haste doth call me hence,
And therefore here I mean to take my leave.

BAPTISTA.

Is't possible you will away to-night?

PETRUCHIO.

I must away to-day, before night come:
Make it no wonder; if you knew my business,
You would entreat me rather go than stay.
And, honest company, I thank you all,
That have beheld me give away myself
To this most patient, sweet, and virtuous wife:
Dine with my father, drink a health to me;
For I must hence; and farewell to you all.

TRANIO.

Let us entreat you stay till after dinner.

PETRUCHIO.

It may not be.

GREMIO.

Let me entreat you.

PETRUCHIO.

It cannot be.

KATHARINA.

Let me entreat you.

PETRUCHIO.

I am content.

KATHARINA.

Are you content to stay?

PETRUCHIO.

I am content you shall entreat me stay;
But yet not stay, entreat me how you can.

KATHARINA.

Now, if you love me, stay.

PETRUCHIO.

Grumio, my horse.

GRUMIO.

Ay, sir, they be ready: the oats have eaten the horses.

KATHARINA.

Nay, then,
Do what thou canst, I will not go to-day;
No, nor to-morrow, not till I please myself.
The door is open, sir; there lies your way;
You may be jogging whiles your boots are green;
For me, I'll not be gone till I please myself:
'Tis like you'll prove a jolly surly groom,
That take it on you at the first so roundly.

PETRUCHIO.

O, Kate, content thee; prithee, be not angry.

KATHARINA.

I will be angry: what hast thou to do?—
Father, be quiet: he shall stay my leisure.

GREMIO.

Ay, marry, sir, now it begins to work.

KATHARINA.

Gentlemen, forward to the bridal dinner:
I see a woman may be made a fool,
If she had not a spirit to resist.

PETRUCHIO.

They shall go forward, Kate, at thy command.—

Obey the bride, you that attend on her;
Go to the feast, revel and domineer,
Carouse full measure to her maidenhead,
Be mad and merry,—or go hang yourselves:
But for my bonny Kate, she must with me.
Nay, look not big, nor stamp, nor stare, nor fret;
I will be master of what is mine own:
She is my goods, my chattels; she is my house,
My household-stuff, my field, my barn,
My horse, my ox, my ass, my anything;
And here she stands, touch her whoever dare;
I'll bring mine action on the proudest he
That stops my way in Padua.—Grumio,
Draw forth thy weapon, we are beset with thieves;
Rescue thy mistress, if thou be a man.— [Kate:
Fear not, sweet wench, they shall not touch thee,
I'll buckler thee against a million.

[*Exeunt* PETRUCHIO, KATHARINA, *and* GRUMIO.

BAPTISTA.

Nay, let them go, a couple of quiet ones.

GREMIO.

Went they not quickly, I should die with laughing.

TRANIO.

Of all mad matches never was the like.

LUCENTIO.

Mistress, what's your opinion of your sister?

BIANCA.

That, being mad herself, she's madly mated.

GREMIO.

I warrant him, Petruchio is Kated.

BAPTISTA.

Neighbours and friends, though bride and bride-
groom wants
For to supply the places at the table,
You know there wants no junkets at the feast.—
Lucentio, you shall supply the bridegroom's
place;
And let Bianca take her sister's room.

TRANIO.

Shall sweet Bianca practise how to bride it?

BAPTISTA.

She shall, Lucentio.—Come, gentlemen, let's go.

[*Exeunt.*

ACT IV. SCENE I.

PETRUCHIO'S *country house.*

Enter GRUMIO.

GRUMIO.

FIE, fie on all tired jades, on all mad masters, and all foul ways! Was ever man so beaten? was ever man so ray'd? was ever man so weary? I am sent before to make a fire, and they are coming after to warm them. Now, were not I a little pot, and soon hot, my very lips might freeze to my teeth, my tongue to the roof of my mouth, my heart in my belly, ere I should come by a fire to thaw me:—but I, with blowing the fire, shall warm myself; for, considering the weather, a taller man than I will take cold.—Holla, ho! Curtis!

Enter CURTIS.

CURTIS.

Who is that calls so coldly?

GRUMIO.

A piece of ice: if thou doubt it, thou mayst slide from my shoulder to my heel with no greater a run but my head and my neck. A fire, good Curtis.

CURTIS.

Is my master and his wife coming, Grumio?

GRUMIO.

O, ay, Curtis, ay: and therefore fire, fire; cast on no water.

CURTIS.

Is she so hot a shrew as she's reported?

GRUMIO.

She was, good Curtis, before this frost: but, thou know'st, winter tames man, woman and beast; for it hath tamed my old master, and my new mistress, and myself, fellow Curtis.

CURTIS.

Away, you three-inch fool! I am no beast.

GRUMIO.

Am I but three inches? why, thy horn is a foot; and so long am I at the least. But wilt thou make fire, or shall I complain on thee to our mistress, whose hand—she being now at hand—thou shalt soon feel, to thy cold comfort, for being slow in thy hot office?

CURTIS.

I prithee, good Grumio, tell me, how goes the world?

GRUMIO.

A cold world, Curtis, in every office but thine; and therefore fire: do thy duty, and have thy duty; for my master and mistress are almost frozen to death.

CURTIS.

There's fire ready; and therefore, good Grumio, the news?

GRUMIO.

Why, 'Jack, boy! ho, boy!' and as much news as wilt thou.

CURTIS.

Come, you are so full of cony-catching!—

GRUMIO.

Why, therefore fire; for I have caught extreme cold. Where's the cook? is supper ready, the house trimm'd, rushes strew'd, cobwebs swept; the serving-men in their new fustian, their white stockings, and every officer his wedding-garment on? Be the jacks fair within, the jills fair without, the carpets laid, and everything in order?

CURTIS.

All ready; and therefore, I pray thee, news?

GRUMIO.

First, know, my horse is tired; my master and mistress fallen out.

CURTIS.

How?

GRUMIO.

Out of their saddles into the dirt; and thereby hangs a tale.

CURTIS.

Let's ha't, good Grumio.

GRUMIO.

Lend thine ear.

CURTIS.

Here.

GRUMIO.

There. [*Striking him.*

CURTIS.

This is to feel a tale, not to hear a tale.

GRUMIO.

And therefore 'tis call'd a sensible tale: and this cuff was but to knock at your ear, and beseech listening. Now I begin: *Imprimis*, we came down a foul hill, my master riding behind my mistress:—

CURTIS.

Both of one horse?

GRUMIO.

What's that to thee?

CURTIS.

Why, a horse.

GRUMIO.

Tell thou the tale:—but hadst thou not crost me, thou shouldst have heard how her horse fell, and she under her horse; thou shouldst have heard, in how miry a place; how she was bemoil'd; how he left her with the horse upon her; how he beat me because her horse stumbled; how she waded through the dirt to pluck him off me; how he swore; how she pray'd—that never pray'd before; how I cried; how the horses ran away; how her bridle was burst; how I lost my crupper;—with many things of worthy memory, which now shall die in oblivion, and thou return unexperienced to thy grave.

CURTIS.

By this reckoning, he is more shrew than she.

GRUMIO.

Ay; and that thou and the proudest of you all shall find when he comes home. But what talk I of this?—Call forth Nathaniel, Joseph, Nicholas, Philip, Walter, Sugarsop, and the rest: let their heads be slickly comb'd, their blue coats brusht, and their garters of an indifferent knit: let them curtsy with their left legs; and not presume to touch a hair of my master's horse-tail till they kiss their hands. Are they all ready?

CURTIS.

They are.

GRUMIO.

Call them forth.

CURTIS.

Do you hear, ho? you must meet my master, to countenance my mistress!

GRUMIO.

Why, she hath a face of her own.

CURTIS.

Who knows not that?

GRUMIO.

Thou, it seems, that calls for company to countenance her.

CURTIS.

I call them forth to credit her.

GRUMIO.

Why, she comes to borrow nothing of them.

Enter four or five SERVING MEN.

NATHANIEL.

Welcome home, Grumio!

PHILIP.

How now, Grumio!

JOSEPH.

What, Grumio!

NICHOLAS.

Fellow Grumio!

NATHANIEL.

How now, old lad!

GRUMIO.

Welcome, you!—how now, you!—what, you!—fellow, you!—and thus much for greeting. Now, my spruce companions, is all ready, and all things neat?

NATHANIEL.

All things is ready. How near is our master?

GRUMIO.

E'en at hand, alighted by this; and therefore be not—Cock's passion, silence!—I hear my master.

Enter PETRUCHIO *and* KATHARINA.

PETRUCHIO.

Where be these knaves? What, no man at door
To hold my stirrup nor to take my horse!
Where is Nathaniel, Gregory, Philip?—

ALL SERVANTS.

Here, here, sir; here, sir.

PETRUCHIO.

Here, sir! here, sir! here, sir! here, sir!—
You logger-headed and unpolisht grooms!
What, no attendance? no regard? no duty?—
Where is the foolish knave I sent before?

GRUMIO.

Here, sir: as foolish as I was before.

PETRUCHIO.

You peasant swain! you whoreson malt-horse drudge!
Did I not bid thee meet me in the park,
And bring along these rascal knaves with thee?

GRUMIO.

Nathaniel's coat, sir, was not fully made,
And Gabriel's pumps were all unpinkt i' th' heel;
There was no link to colour Peter's hat,
And Walter's dagger was not come from sheathing:
There were none fine but Adam, Rafe, and Gregory;
The rest were ragged, old, and beggarly;
Yet, as they are, here are they come to meet you.

PETRUCHIO.

Go, rascals, go, and fetch my supper in.—
[*Exeunt* SERVANTS.
[*Sings*] Where is the life that late I led—
Where are those—Sit down, Kate, and welcome.—
Soud, soud, soud, soud!

Enter SERVANTS *with supper.*

Why, when, I say?—Nay, good sweet Kate, be merry.—
Off with my boots, you rogues! you villains, when?
[*Sings.*] It was the friar of orders grey,
As he forth walked on his way:—
Out, you rogue! you pluck my foot awry:
Take that, and mend the plucking off the other.—
[*Strikes him.*
Be merry, Kate.—Some water, here; what, ho!
Where's my spaniel Troilus?—Sirrah, get you hence,
And bid my cousin Ferdinand come hither:—
[*Exit* SERVANT.
One, Kate, that you must kiss, and be acquainted with.—
Where are my slippers?—Shall I have some water?

Enter one with water.

Come, Kate, and wash, and welcome heartily.—
You whoreson villain! will you let it fall?
[*Strikes him.*

KATHARINA.

Patience, I pray you; 'twas a fault unwilling.

PETRUCHIO.

A whoreson, beetle-headed, flap-ear'd knave!—
Come, Kate, sit down; I know you have a stomach.
Will you give thanks, sweet Kate; or else shall I?
What's this? mutton?

FIRST SERVANT.

Ay.

PETRUCHIO.

Who brought it?

PETER.

I.

PETRUCHIO.

'Tis burnt; and so is all the meat.
What dogs are these!—Where is the rascal cook?
How durst you, villains, bring it from the dresser,
And serve it thus to me that love it not?
There, take it to you, trenchers, cups, and all:
[*Throws the meat, &c., at them.*
You heedless joltheads and unmanner'd slaves!
What, do you grumble? I'll be with you straight.
[*Exeunt* SERVANTS.

KATHARINA.

I pray you, husband, be not so disquiet:
The meat was well, if you were so contented.

PETRUCHIO.

I tell thee, Kate, 'twas burnt and dried away;
And I expressly am forbid to touch it,
For it engenders choler, planteth anger;
And better 'twere that both of us did fast,—
Since, of ourselves, ourselves are choleric,—
Than feed it with such over-roasted flesh.
Be patient; to-morrow't shall be mended,
And, for this night, we'll fast for company:—
Come, I will bring thee to thy bridal chamber.
[*Exeunt.*

Enter SERVANTS *severally.*

NATHANIEL.

Peter, didst ever see the like?

PETER.

He kills her
In her own humour.

Enter CURTIS.

GRUMIO.

Where is he?

CURTIS.

In her chamber,
Making a sermon of continency to her;
And rails, and swears, and rates, that she, poor soul,
Knows not which way to stand, to look, to speak.
And sits as one new-risen from a dream.—
Away, away! for he is coming hither. [*Exeunt.*

Enter PETRUCHIO.

PETRUCHIO.

Thus have I politicly begun my reign,
And 'tis my hope to end successfully.
My falcon now is sharp, and passing empty;
And, till she stoop, she must not be full-gorged,
For then she never looks upon her lure.
Another way I have to man my haggard,
To make her come, and know her keeper's call,
That is, to watch her, as we watch these kites
That bate, and beat, and will not be obedient.
She eat no meat to-day, nor none shall eat;
Last night she slept not, nor to-night she shall not;
As with the meat, some undeserved fault
I'll find about the making of the bed;
And here I'll fling the pillow, there the bolster,
This way the coverlet, another way the sheets:—
Ay, and amid this hurly, I intend
That all is done in reverent care of her;
And, in conclusion, she shall watch all night:
And, if she chance to nod, I'll rail and brawl,
And with the clamour keep her still awake.
This is a way to kill a wife with kindness;
And thus I'll curb her mad and headstrong humour.—
He that knows better how to tame a shrew,
Now let him speak: 'tis charity to shew. [*Exit.*

SCENE II.

Padua. Before BAPTISTA'S *house.*

Enter TRANIO *and* HORTENSIO.

TRANIO.

IS'T possible, friend Licio, that Mistress Bianca
Doth fancy any other but Lucentio?
I tell you, sir, she bears me fair in hand.

HORTENSIO.

Sir, to satisfy you in what I have said,
Stand by, and mark the manner of his teaching.
[*They stand aside.*

Enter BIANCA *and* LUCENTIO.

LUCENTIO.

Now, mistress, profit you in what you read?

BIANCA.

What, master, read you? first resolve me that.

LUCENTIO.

I read that I profess, the Art to Love.

BIANCA.

And may you prove, sir, master of your art!

LUCENTIO.

While you, sweet dear, prove mistress of my heart! [*They retire.*

HORTENSIO.

Quick proceeders, marry! Now, tell me, I pray,
You that durst swear that your mistress Bianca
Loved none in the world so well as Lucentio,—

TRANIO.

O despiteful love! unconstant womankind!—
I tell thee, Licio, this is wonderful.

HORTENSIO.

Mistake no more: I am not Licio,
Nor a musician, as I seem to be;
But one that scorn to live in this disguise,
For such a one as leaves a gentleman,
And makes a god of such a cullion:
Know, sir, that I am call'd Hortensio.

TRANIO.

Signior Hortensio, I have often heard
Of your entire affection to Bianca;
And since mine eyes are witness of her lightness,
I will with you,—if you be so contented,—
Forswear Bianca and her love for ever.

HORTENSIO.

See, how they kiss and court!—Signior Lucentio,
Here is my hand, and here I firmly vow
Never to woo her more; but do forswear her,
As one unworthy all the former favours
That I have fondly flatter'd her withal.

TRANIO.

And here I take the like unfeigned oath,
Never to marry with her though she would
entreat:
Fie on her! see, how beastly she doth court him!

HORTENSIO.

Would all the world but he had quite forsworn!
For me, that I may surely keep mine oath,
I will be married to a wealthy widow,
Ere three days pass, which hath as long loved me
As I have loved this proud disdainful haggard.
And so farewell, Signior Lucentio.—
Kindness in women, not their beauteous looks,
Shall win my love:—and so, I take my leave,
In resolution as I swore before.

[*Exit* HORTENSIO; LUCENTIO *and* BIANCA *advance.*

TRANIO.

Mistress Bianca, bless you with such grace
As 'longeth to a lover's blessed case!
Nay, I have ta'en you napping, gentle love;
And have forsworn you, with Hortensio.

BIANCA.

Tranio, you jest: but have you both forsworn me?

TRANIO.

Mistress, we have.

LUCENTIO.

Then we are rid of Licio.

TRANIO.

I'faith, he'll have a lusty widow now,
That shall be woo'd and wedded in a day.

BIANCA.

God give him joy!

TRANIO.

Ay, and he'll tame her.

BIANCA.

He says so, Tranio.

TRANIO.

Faith, he is gone unto the taming-school.

BIANCA.

The taming-school! what, is there such a place?

TRANIO.

Ay, mistress, and Petruchio is the master;
That teacheth tricks eleven and twenty long,
To tame a shrew, and charm her chattering
tongue.

Enter BIONDELLO.

BIONDELLO.

O master, master, I have watcht so long
That I am dog-weary! but at last I spied
An ancient angel coming down the hill,
Will serve the turn.

TRANIO.

What is he, Biondello?

BIONDELLO.

Master, a mercatante, or a pedant,
I know not what; but formal in apparel,
In gait and countenance surly like a father.

LUCENTIO.

And what of him, Tranio?

TRANIO.

If he be credulous and trust my tale,
I'll make him glad to seem Vincentio;
And give assurance to Baptista Minola,
As if he were the right Vincentio.
Take in your love, and then let me alone.

[*Exeunt* LUCENTIO *and* BIANCA.

Enter a PEDANT.

PEDANT.

God save you, sir!

TRANIO.

And you, sir! you are welcome.
Travel you far on, or are you at the furthest?

PEDANT.

Sir, at the furthest for a week or two:
But then up further, and as far as Rome;
And so to Tripoli, if God lend me life.

TRANIO.

What countryman, I pray?

PEDANT.

Of Mantua.

TRANIO.

Of Mantua, sir?—marry, God forbid!
And come to Padua, careless of your life?

PEDANT.

My life, sir! how, I pray? for that goes hard.

TRANIO.

'Tis death for any one in Mantua
To come to Padua. Know you not the cause?
Your ships are stay'd at Venice; and the duke—
For private quarrel 'twixt your duke and him—
Hath publisht and proclaim'd it openly:
'Tis marvel, but that you are but newly come,
You might have heard it else proclaim'd about.

PEDANT.

Alas, sir, it is worse for me than so!
For I have bills for money by exchange
From Florence, and must here deliver them.

TRANIO.

Well, sir, to do you courtesy,
This will I do, and this I will advise you:—
First, tell me, have you ever been at Pisa?

PEDANT.

Ay, sir, in Pisa have I often been;
Pisa renowned for grave citizens.

TRANIO.

Among them know you one Vincentio?

PEDANT.

I know him not, but I have heard of him;
A merchant of incomparable wealth.

TRANIO.

He is my father, sir; and, sooth to say,
In countenance somewhat doth resemble you.

BIONDELLO [*aside*].

As much as an apple doth an oyster, and all one.

TRANIO.

To save your life in this extremity,
This favour will I do you for his sake;
And think it not the worst of all your fortunes
That you are like to Sir Vincentio.
His name and credit shall you undertake,
And in my house you shall be friendly lodged:—
Look that you take upon you as you should;
You understand me, sir:—so shall you stay
Till you have done your business in the city:
If this be courtesy, sir, accept of it.

PEDANT.

O, sir, I do; and will repute you ever
The patron of my life and liberty.

TRANIO.

Then go with me, to make the matter good.
This, by the way, I let you understand;—
My father is here lookt for every day,
To pass assurance of a dower in marriage
'Twixt me and one Baptista's daughter here:
In all these circumstances I'll instruct you:
Go with me, sir, to clothe you as becomes you.
[*Exeunt.*

SCENE III.

A room in PETRUCHIO'S *house.*

Enter KATHARINA *and* GRUMIO.

GRUMIO.

NO, no, forsooth; I dare not, for my life.

KATHARINA.

The more my wrong, the more his spite appears:
What, did he marry me to famish me?
Beggars, that come unto my father's door,
Upon entreaty have a present alms;
If not, elsewhere they meet with charity:
But I,—who never knew how to entreat,
Nor never needed that I should entreat,—
Am starved for meat, giddy for lack of sleep;
With oaths kept waking, and with brawling fed:
And that which spites me more than all these wants,
He does it under name of perfect love;
As who should say, if I should sleep or eat,
'Twere deadly sickness or else present death.—
I prithee go, and get me some repast;
I care not what, so it be wholesome food.

GRUMIO.

What say you to a neat's foot?

KATHARINA.

'Tis passing good: I prithee let me have it.

GRUMIO.

I fear it is too choleric a meat.
How say you to a fat tripe finely broil'd?

KATHARINA.

I like it well: good Grumio, fetch it me.

GRUMIO.

I cannot tell; I fear 'tis choleric.
What say you to a piece of beef and mustard?

KATHARINA.

A dish that I do love to feed upon.

GRUMIO.

Ay, but the mustard is too hot a little.

KATHARINA.

Why, then the beef, and let the mustard rest.

GRUMIO.

Nay, then I will not: you shall have the mustard,
Or else you get no beef of Grumio.

KATHARINA.

Then both, or one, or any thing thou wilt.

GRUMIO.

Why, then the mustard without the beef.

KATHARINA.

Go, get thee gone, thou false deluding slave,
[*Beats him.*
That feed'st me with the very name of meat:
Sorrow on thee, and all the pack of you,
That triumph thus upon my misery!
Go, get thee gone, I say.

Enter PETRUCHIO *and* HORTENSIO *with meat.*

PETRUCHIO.

How fares my Kate? What, sweeting, all amort?

HORTENSIO.

Mistress, what cheer?

KATHARINA.

Faith, as cold as can be.

PETRUCHIO.

Pluck up thy spirits, look cheerfully upon me.
Here, love; thou see'st how diligent I am
To dress thy meat myself, and bring it thee:
I am sure, sweet Kate, this kindness merits thanks.
What, not a word? Nay, then thou lovest it not;
And all my pains is sorted to no proof.—
Here, take away this dish.

KATHARINA.

I pray you, let it stand.

PETRUCHIO.

The poorest service is repaid with thanks;
And so shall mine, before you touch the meat.

KATHARINA.

I thank you, sir.

HORTENSIO.

Signior Petruchio, fie! you are to blame.—
Come, Mistress Kate, I'll bear you company.

PETRUCHIO [*aside to* HORTENSIO].

Eat it up all, Hortensio, if thou lovest me.—
[*to* KATHARINA] Much good do it unto thy gentle heart!
Kate, eat apace:—and now, my honey love,
Will we return unto thy father's house,
And revel it as bravely as the best,
With silken coats, and caps, and golden rings,
With ruffs, and cuffs, and farthingales, and things;
With scarfs, and fans, and double change of bravery,
With amber bracelets, beads, and all this knavery.
What, hast thou dined? The tailor stays thy leisure,
To deck thy body with his ruffling treasure.

Enter TAILOR.

Come, tailor, let us see these ornaments;
Lay forth the gown.

Enter HABERDASHER.

What news with you, sir?

HABERDASHER.

Here is the cap your worship did bespeak.

PETRUCHIO.

Why, this was moulded on a porringer;
A velvet dish:—fie, fie! 'tis lewd and filthy:
Why, 'tis a cockle or a walnut-shell,
A knack, a toy, a trick, a baby's cap:
Away with it! come, let me have a bigger.

KATHARINA.

I'll have no bigger: this doth fit the time,
And gentlewomen wear such caps as these.

PETRUCHIO.

When you are gentle, you shall have one too,
And not till then.

HORTENSIO [*aside*].

That will not be in haste.

KATHARINA.
Why, sir, I trust I may have leave to speak;
And speak I will; I am no child, no babe:
Your betters have endured me say my mind;
And if you cannot, best you stop your ears.
My tongue will tell the anger of my heart;
Or else my heart, concealing it, will break:
And rather than it shall, I will be free
Even to the uttermost, as I please, in words.

PETRUCHIO.
Why, thou say'st true: it is a paltry cap,
A custard-coffin, a bauble, a silken pie:
I love thee well, in that thou likest it not.

KATHARINA.
Love me or love me not, I like the cap;
And it I will have, or I will have none.

PETRUCHIO.
Thy gown? why, ay:—come, tailor, let us see't.
O, mercy, God! what masking stuff is here?
What's this? a sleeve? 'tis like a demi-cannon:
What, up and down, carved like an apple-tart?
Here's snip, and nip, and cut, and slish, and slash,
Like to a censer in a barber's shop:—
Why, what, o' devil's name, tailor, call'st thou this?

HORTENSIO [*aside*].
I see she's like to have neither cap nor gown.

TAILOR.
You bid me make it orderly and well,
According to the fashion and the time.

PETRUCHIO.
Marry, and did; but if you be remember'd,
I did not bid you mar it to the time.
Go, hop me over every kennel home,
For you shall hop without my custom, sir:
I'll none of it: hence! make your best of it.

KATHARINA.
I never saw a better-fashion'd gown,
More quaint, more pleasing, nor more commendable:
Belike you mean to make a puppet of me.

PETRUCHIO.
Why, true; he means to make a puppet of thee.

TAILOR.
She says your worship means to make a puppet of her.

PETRUCHIO.
O monstrous arrogance! Thou liest, thou thread, Thou thimble,
Thou yard, three-quarters, half-yard, quarter, nail!
Thou flea, thou nit, thou winter-cricket thou!—
Braved in mine own house with a skein of thread?
Away, thou rag, thou quantity, thou remnant;
Or I shall so be-mete thee with thy yard,
As thou shalt think on prating whilst thou livest!
I tell thee, I, that thou hast marr'd her gown.

TAILOR.
Your worship is deceived; the gown is made
Just as my master had direction:
Grumio gave order how it should be done.

GRUMIO.
I gave him no order; I gave him the stuff.

TAILOR.
But how did you desire it should be made?

GRUMIO.
Marry, sir, with needle and thread.

TAILOR.
But did you not request to have it cut?

GRUMIO.
Thou hast faced many things;—

TAILOR.
I have.

GRUMIO.
Face not me: thou hast braved many men; brave not me: I will neither be faced nor braved. I say unto thee, I bid thy master cut out the gown; but I did not bid him cut it to pieces: *ergo*, thou liest.

TAILOR.
Why, here is the note of the fashion to testify.

PETRUCHIO.
Read it.

GRUMIO.
The note lies in's throat, if he say I said so.

TAILOR [*reads*].
Imprimis, a loose-bodied gown:—

GRUMIO.
Master, if ever I said loose-bodied gown, sew me in the skirts of it, and beat me to death with a bottom of brown thread: I said a gown.

PETRUCHIO.
Proceed.

TAILOR [*reads*].
With a small compass cape:—

GRUMIO.
I confess the cape.

TAILOR [*reads*].
With a trunk sleeve:—

GRUMIO.
I confess two sleeves.

TAILOR [*reads*].
The sleeves curiously cut.

PETRUCHIO.
Ay, there's the villainy.

GRUMIO.
Error i' th' bill, sir; error i' th' bill.—I commanded the sleeves should be cut out, and sew'd up again; and that I'll prove upon thee, though thy little finger be arm'd in a thimble.

TAILOR.
This is true that I say; an I had thee in place where, thou shouldst know it.

GRUMIO.
I am for thee straight: take thou the bill, give me thy mete-yard, and spare not me.

HORTENSIO.
God-a-mercy, Grumio! then he shall have no odds.

PETRUCHIO.
Well, sir, in brief, the gown is not for me.

GRUMIO.
You are i' th' right, sir: 'tis for my mistress.

PETRUCHIO.
Go take it up unto thy master's use.

GRUMIO.
Villain, not for thy life: take up my mistress' gown for thy master's use!

PETRUCHIO.
Why, sir, what's your conceit in that?

GRUMIO.
O, sir, the conceit is deeper than you think for:
Take up my mistress' gown to his master's use!
O, fie, fie, fie!

PETRUCHIO [*aside to* HORTENSIO].
Hortensio, say thou wilt see the tailor paid.—
[*to* TAILOR] Go take it hence; be gone, and say no more.

HORTENSIO.
Tailor, I'll pay thee for thy gown to-morrow:
Take no unkindness of his hasty words:
Away! I say; commend me to thy master.
[*Exeunt* TAILOR *and* HABERDASHER.

PETRUCHIO.
Well, come, my Kate; we will unto your father's,
Even in these honest mean habiliments:
Our purses shall be proud, our garments poor;
For 'tis the mind that makes the body rich;
And as the sun breaks through the darkest clouds,
So honour peereth in the meanest habit.
What, is the jay more precious than the lark,
Because his feathers are more beautiful?
Or is the adder better than the eel,
Because his painted skin contents the eye?
O, no, good Kate; neither art thou the worse
For this poor furniture and mean array.
If thou account'st it shame, lay it on me;
And therefore frolic: we will hence forthwith,
To feast and sport us at thy father's house.—
Go call my men, and let us straight to him;
And bring our horses unto Long-lane end;
There will we mount, and thither walk on foot.—
Let's see; I think 'tis now some seven o'clock,
And well we may come there by dinner-time.

KATHARINA.
I dare assure you, sir, 'tis almost two;
And 'twill be supper-time ere you come there.

PETRUCHIO.
It shall be seven ere I go to horse:
Look, what I speak, or do, or think to do,
You are still crossing it.—Sirs, let't alone:
I will not go to-day; and ere I do,
It shall be what o'clock I say it is.

HORTENSIO.
Why, so! this gallant will command the sun!
[*Exeunt.*

SCENE IV.

Padua. Before BAPTISTA'S *house.*

Enter TRANIO, *and the* PEDANT *drest like* VINCENTIO.

TRANIO.
SIR, this is the house: please it you that I call?

PEDANT.
Ay, what else? and, but I be deceived,
Signior Baptista may remember me,
Near twenty years ago, in Genoa,
Where we were lodgers at the Pegasus.

TRANIO.
'Tis well; and hold your own, in any case,
With such austerity as 'longeth to a father.

PEDANT.
I warrant you. But, sir, here comes your boy;
'Twere good he were school'd.

Enter BIONDELLO.

TRANIO.
Fear you not him.—Sirrah Biondello,
Now do your duty throughly, I advise you:
Imagine 'twere the right Vincentio.

BIONDELLO.
Tut, fear not me.

TRANIO.
But hast thou done thy errand to Baptista?

BIONDELLO.
I told him that your father was at Venice;
And that you lookt for him this day in Padua.

TRANIO.
Thou'rt a tall fellow: hold thee that to drink.
Here comes Baptista:—set your countenance, sir.

Enter BAPTISTA *and* LUCENTIO.

Signior Baptista, you are happily met.—
[*to the* PEDANT] Sir, this is the gentleman I told you of:
I pray you, stand good father to me now,
Give me Bianca for my patrimony.

PEDANT.
Soft, son!—
Sir, by your leave: having come to Padua
To gather in some debts, my son Lucentio
Made me acquainted with a weighty cause
Of love between your daughter and himself:
And,—for the good report I hear of you,
And for the love he beareth to your daughter,
And she to him,—to stay him not too long,
I am content, in a good father's care,
To have him matcht; and, if you please to like
No worse than I, upon some agreement,
Me shall you find ready and willing
With one consent to have her so bestow'd;
For curious I cannot be with you,
Signior Baptista, of whom I hear so well.

BAPTISTA.
Sir, pardon me in what I have to say:
Your plainness and your shortness please me well.
Right true it is, your son Lucentio here
Doth love my daughter, and she loveth him,
Or both dissemble deeply their affections:
And therefore, if you say no more than this,
That like a father you will deal with him,
And pass my daughter a sufficient dower,
The match is made, and all is done:
Your son shall have my daughter with consent.

TRANIO.
I thank you, sir. Where, then, do you hold best
We be affied, and such assurance ta'en
As shall with either part's agreement stand?

BAPTISTA.
Not in my house, Lucentio; for, you know,
Pitchers have ears, and I have many servants:
Besides, old Gremio is hearkening still;
And happily we might be interrupted.

TRANIO.
Then at my lodging, an it like you:
There doth my father lie; and there, this night,
We'll pass the business privately and well.
Send for your daughter by your servant here;
My boy shall fetch the scrivener presently.
The worst is this,—that at so slender warning,
You are like to have a thin and slender pittance.

BAPTISTA.
It likes me well. Biondello, hie you home,
And bid Bianca make her ready straight;
And, if you will, tell what hath happened—
Lucentio's father is arrived in Padua,
And how she's like to be Lucentio's wife.

BIONDELLO.
I pray the gods she may with all my heart!
TRANIO.
Dally not with the gods, but get thee gone.—
[*Exit* BIONDELLO.
Signior Baptista, shall I lead the way?
Welcome! one mess is like to be your cheer:
Come, sir; we will better it in Pisa.
BAPTISTA.
I follow you.
[*Exeunt* TRANIO, PEDANT, *and* BAPTISTA.
Enter BIONDELLO.
BIONDELLO.
Cambio,—
LUCENTIO.
What say'st thou, Biondello?
BIONDELLO.
You saw my master wink and laugh upon you?
LUCENTIO.
Biondello, what of that?
BIONDELLO.
Faith, nothing; but 'has left me here behind, to expound the meaning or moral of his signs and tokens.
LUCENTIO.
I pray thee, moralize them.
BIONDELLO.
Then thus. Baptista is safe, talking with the deceiving father of a deceitful son.
LUCENTIO.
And what of him?
BIONDELLO.
His daughter is to be brought by you to the supper.
LUCENTIO.
And then?
BIONDELLO.
The old priest at Saint Luke's church is at your command at all hours.
LUCENTIO.
And what of all this?
BIONDELLO.
I cannot tell, except, while they are busied about a counterfeit assurance, take you assurance of her, *cum privilegio ad imprimendum solum:* to th' church;—take the priest, clerk, and some sufficient honest witnesses:
If this be not that you look for, I have no more to say,
But bid Bianca farewell for ever and a day.
[*Going.*
LUCENTIO.
Hear'st thou, Biondello?
BIONDELLO.
I cannot tarry: I knew a wench married in an afternoon as she went to the garden for parsley to stuff a rabbit; and so may you, sir: and so, adieu, sir. My master hath appointed me to go to Saint Luke's, to bid the priest be ready to come against you come with your appendix. [*Exit.*
LUCENTIO.
I may, and will, if she be so contented:
She will be pleased; then wherefore should I doubt?
Hap what hap may, I'll roundly go about her:
It shall go hard if Cambio go without her. [*Exit.*

SCENE V.

A public road.

Enter PETRUCHIO, KATHARINA, *and* HORTENSIO.

PETRUCHIO.
Come on, o' God's name; once more toward our father's.
Good Lord, how bright and goodly shines the moon!
KATHARINA.
The moon! the sun: it is not moonlight now.
PETRUCHIO.
I say it is the moon that shines so bright.
KATHARINA.
I know it is the sun that shines so bright.
PETRUCHIO.
Now, by my mother's son, and that's myself,
It shall be moon, or star, or what I list,
Or e'er I journey to your father's house.—
Go one, and fetch our horses back again.—
Evermore crost and crost; nothing but crost!
HORTENSIO [*aside to* KATHARINA].
Say as he says, or we shall never go.
KATHARINA.
Forward, I pray, since we have come so far,
And be it moon, or sun, or what you please:
An if you please to call it a rush-candle,
Henceforth I vow it shall be so for me.
PETRUCHIO.
I say it is the moon.
KATHARINA.
I know it is the moon.
PETRUCHIO.
Nay, then, you lie: it is the blessed sun.
KATHARINA.
Then, God be blest, it is the blessed sun:—
But sun it is not, when you say it is not;
And the moon changes, even as your mind.
What you will have it named, even that it is;
And so it shall be still for Katharine.
HORTENSIO [*aside*].
Petruchio, go thy ways; the field is won.
PETRUCHIO.
Well, forward, forward! thus the bowl should run,
And not unluckily against the bias.—
But, soft! what company is coming here?
Enter VINCENTIO.
[*to* VINCENTIO] Good morrow, gentle mistress: where away?—
Tell me, sweet Kate, and tell me truly too,
Hast thou beheld a fresher gentlewoman?
Such war of white and red within her cheeks!
What stars do spangle heaven with such beauty,
As those two eyes become that heavenly face?—
Fair lovely maid, once more good day to thee.—
Sweet Kate, embrace her for her beauty's sake.
HORTENSIO [*aside*].
A' will make the man mad, to make a woman of him.
KATHARINA.
Young budding virgin, fair and fresh and sweet,
Whither away; or where is thy abode?
Happy the parents of so fair a child;
Happier the man whom favourable stars
Allot thee for his lovely bedfellow!

PETRUCHIO.
Why, how now, Kate! I hope thou art not mad:
This is a man, old, wrinkled, faded, wither'd;
And not a maiden, as thou say'st he is.

KATHARINA.
Pardon, old father, my mistaking eyes,
That have been so bedazzled with the sun,
That every thing I look on seemeth green:
Now I perceive thou art a reverend father;
Pardon, I pray thee, for my mad mistaking.

PETRUCHIO.
Do, good old grandsire; and withal make known
Which way thou travellest; if along with us,
We shall be joyful of thy company.

VINCENTIO.
Fair sir, and you my merry mistress,
That with your strange encounter much amazed me,
My name is call'd Vincentio; my dwelling Pisa;
And bound I am to Padua; there to visit
A son of mine, which long I have not seen.

PETRUCHIO.
What is his name?

VINCENTIO.
Lucentio, gentle sir.

PETRUCHIO.
Happily met; the happier for thy son.
And now by law, as well as reverend age,
I may entitle thee my loving father:
The sister to my wife, this gentlewoman,
Thy son by this hath married. Wonder not,
Nor be not grieved: she is of good esteem,
Her dowry wealthy, and of worthy birth;
Beside, so qualified as may beseem
The spouse of any noble gentleman.
Let me embrace with old Vincentio:
And wander we to see thy honest son,
Who will of thy arrival be full joyous.

VINCENTIO.
But is this true? or is it else your pleasure,
Like pleasant travellers, to break a jest
Upon the company you overtake?

HORTENSIO.
I do assure thee, father, so it is.

PETRUCHIO.
Come, go along, and see the truth hereof;
For our first merriment hath made thee jealous.
[*Exeunt* PETRUCHIO, KATHARINA, *and* VINCENTIO.

HORTENSIO.
Well, Petruchio, this has put me in heart.
Have to my widow! and if she be froward,
Then hast thou taught Hortensio to be untoward.
[*Exit.*

ACT V. SCENE I.

Padua. Before LUCENTIO'S *house.*

Enter BIONDELLO, LUCENTIO, *and* BIANCA; GREMIO *is out before.*

BIONDELLO.
SOFTLY and swiftly, sir; for the priest is ready.

LUCENTIO.
I fly, Biondello: but they may chance to need thee at home; therefore leave us.

BIONDELLO.
Nay, faith, I'll see the church o' your back; and then come back to my master as soon as I can.
[*Exeunt* LUCENTIO, BIANCA, *and* BIONDELLO.

GREMIO.
I marvel Cambio comes not all this while.

Enter PETRUCHIO, KATHARINA, VINCENTIO, GRUMIO, *and* ATTENDANTS.

PETRUCHIO.
Sir, here's the door, this is Lucentio's house:
My father's bears more toward the market-place;
Thither must I; and here I leave you, sir.

VINCENTIO.
You shall not choose but drink before you go:
I think I shall command your welcome here.
And, by all likelihood, some cheer is toward.
[*Knocks.*

GREMIO.
They're busy within; you were best knock louder.

PEDANT *looks out of the window.*

PEDANT.
What's he that knocks as he would beat down the gate?

VINCENTIO.
Is Signior Lucentio within, sir?

PEDANT.
He's within, sir, but not to be spoken withal.

VINCENTIO.
What if a man bring him a hundred pound or two, to make merry withal?

PEDANT.
Keep your hundred pounds to yourself: he shall need none, so long as I live.

PETRUCHIO.
Nay, I told you your son was well beloved in Padua.—Do you hear, sir?—to leave frivolous circumstances,—I pray you, tell Signior Lucentio that his father is come from Pisa, and is here at the door to speak with him.

PEDANT.
Thou liest: his father is come from Pisa, and here looking out at the window.

VINCENTIO.
Art thou his father?

PEDANT.
Ay, sir; so his mother says, if I may believe her.

PETRUCHIO [*to* VINCENTIO].
Why, how now, gentleman! why, this is flat knavery, to take upon you another man's name.

PEDANT.
Lay hands on the villain: I believe a' means to cozen somebody in this city under my countenance.

Enter BIONDELLO.

BIONDELLO.
I have seen them in the church together: God send 'em good shipping!—But who is here? mine old master, Vincentio! now we are undone, and brought to nothing.

VINCENTIO.
Come hither, crack-hemp.

BIONDELLO.
I hope I may choose, sir.

VINCENTIO.
Come hither, you rogue. What, have you forgot me?

BIONDELLO.

Forgot you! no, sir: I could not forget you, for I never saw you before in all my life.

VINCENTIO.

What, you notorious villain, didst thou never see thy master's father, Vincentio?

BIONDELLO.

What, my old worshipful old master? yes, marry, sir: see where he looks out of the window.

VINCENTIO.

Is't so, indeed? [*He beats* BIONDELLO.

BIONDELLO.

Help, help, help! here's a madman will murder me. [*Exit.*

PEDANT.

Help, son! help, Signior Baptista!

PETRUCHIO.

Prithee, Kate, let's stand aside, and see the end of this controversy. [*They retire.*

Enter PEDANT *below;* BAPTISTA, TRANIO, *and* SERVANTS.

TRANIO.

Sir, what are you that offer to beat my servant?

VINCENTIO.

What am I, sir! nay, what are you, sir?—O immortal gods! O fine villain! A silken doublet! a velvet hose! a scarlet cloak! and a copatain hat!—O, I am undone! I am undone! while I play the good husband at home, my son and my servant spend all at the university.

TRANIO.

How now! what's the matter?

BAPTISTA.

What, is the man lunatic?

TRANIO.

Sir, you seem a sober ancient gentleman by your habit, but your words show you a madman. Why, sir, what 'cerns it you if I wear pearl and gold? I thank my good father, I am able to maintain it.

VINCENTIO.

Thy father! O villain! he is a sail-maker in Bergamo.

BAPTISTA.

You mistake, sir, you mistake, sir. Pray, what do you think is his name?

VINCENTIO.

His name! as if I knew not his name: I have brought him up ever since he was three years old, and his name is Tranio.

PEDANT.

Away, away, mad ass! his name is Lucentio; and he is mine only son, and heir to the lands of me, Signior Vincentio.

VINCENTIO.

Lucentio! O, he hath murder'd his master!—Lay hold on him, I charge you, in the duke's name.—O, my son, my son!—Tell me, thou villain, where is my son Lucentio?

TRANIO.

Call forth an officer.

SERVANT *brings in an* OFFICER.

Carry this mad knave to the gaol.—Father Baptista, I charge you see that he be forthcoming.

VINCENTIO.

Carry me to the gaol!

GREMIO.

Stay, officer: he shall not go to prison.

BAPTISTA.

Talk not, Signior Gremio: I say he shall go to prison.

GREMIO.

Take heed, Signior Baptista, lest you be cony-catcht in this business: I dare swear this is the right Vincentio.

PEDANT.

Swear, if thou darest.

GREMIO.

Nay, I dare not swear it.

TRANIO.

Then thou wert best say that I am not Lucentio.

GREMIO.

Yes, I know thee to be Signior Lucentio.

BAPTISTA.

Away with the dotard! to the gaol with him!

VINCENTIO.

Thus strangers may be haled and abused:—
O monstrous villainy!

Enter BIONDELLO, *with* LUCENTIO *and* BIANCA.

BIONDELLO.

O, we are spoil'd! and yonder he is: deny him, forswear him, or else we are all undone.

LUCENTIO.

Pardon, sweet father. [*Kneeling.*

VINCENTIO.

Lives my sweet son?

[*Exeunt* BIONDELLO, TRANIO, *and* PEDANT, *as fast as may be.*

BIANCA.

Pardon, dear father. [*Kneeling.*

BAPTISTA.

How hast thou offended?—
Where is Lucentio?

LUCENTIO.

Here's Lucentio,
Right son unto the right Vincentio;
That have by marriage made thy daughter mine,
While counterfeit supposes blear'd thine eyne.

GREMIO.

Here's packing, with a witness, to deceive us all!

VINCENTIO.

Where is that damned villain Tranio,
That faced and braved me in this matter so?

BAPTISTA.

Why, tell me, is not this my Cambio?

BIANCA.

Cambio is changed into Lucentio.

LUCENTIO.

Love wrought these miracles. Bianca's love
Made me exchange my state with Tranio,
While he did bear my countenance in the town,
And happily I have arrived at last
Unto the wished haven of my bliss.
What Tranio did, myself enforced him to;
Then pardon him, sweet father, for my sake.

VINCENTIO.

I'll slit the villain's nose, that would have sent me to the gaol.

BAPTISTA [*to* LUCENTIO].

But do you hear, sir? have you married my daughter without asking my good-will?

VINCENTIO.

Fear not, Baptista; we will content you, go to: but I will in, to be revenged for this villainy. [*Exit.*

BAPTISTA.

And I, to sound the depth of this knavery. [*Exit.*

LUCENTIO.

Look not pale, Bianca; thy father will not frown.

[*Exeunt* LUCENTIO *and* BIANCA.

GREMIO.

My cake is dough: but I'll in among the rest;
Out of hope of all, but my share of the feast. [*Exit.*

PETRUCHIO *and* KATHARINA *come forward.*

KATHARINA.

Husband, let's follow, to see the end of this ado.

PETRUCHIO.

First kiss me, Kate, and we will.

KATHARINA.

What, in the midst of the street?

PETRUCHIO.

What, art thou ashamed of me?

KATHARINA.

No, sir, God forbid; but ashamed to kiss.

PETRUCHIO.

Why, then, let's home again: come, sirrah, let's away.

KATHARINA.

Nay, I will give thee a kiss [*kisses him*]: now, pray thee, love, stay.

PETRUCHIO.

Is not this well?—Come, my sweet Kate:
Better once than never, for never too late. [*Exeunt.*

SCENE II.

A room in LUCENTIO'S *house.*

Enter BAPTISTA, VINCENTIO, GREMIO, *the* PEDANT, LUCENTIO, BIANCA, PETRUCHIO, KATHARINA, HORTENSIO *and* WIDOW, TRANIO, BIONDELLO *and* GRUMIO; *the* SERVINGMEN *with* TRANIO *bringing in a banquet.*

LUCENTIO.

AT last, though long, our jarring notes agree:
And time it is, when raging war is done,
To smile at scapes and perils overblown.
My fair Bianca, bid my father welcome,
While I with selfsame kindness welcome thine.
Brother Petruchio, sister Katharina,
And thou, Hortensio, with thy loving widow,—
Feast with the best, and welcome to my house:
My banquet is to close our stomachs up,
After our great good cheer. Pray you, sit down;
For now we sit to chat, as well as eat.

[*They sit at table.*

PETRUCHIO.

Nothing but sit and sit, and eat and eat!

BAPTISTA.

Padua affords this kindness, son Petruchio.

PETRUCHIO.

Padua affords nothing but what is kind.

HORTENSIO.

For both our sakes, I would that word were true.

PETRUCHIO.

Now, for my life, Hortensio fears his widow.

WIDOW.

Then never trust me, if I be afeard.

PETRUCHIO.

You are very sensible, and yet you miss my sense:
I mean, Hortensio is afeard of you.

WIDOW.

He that is giddy thinks the world turns round.

PETRUCHIO.

Roundly replied.

KATHARINA.

Mistress, how mean you that?

WIDOW.

Thus I conceive by him.

PETRUCHIO.

Conceives by me!—How likes Hortensio that?

HORTENSIO.

My widow says, thus she conceives her tale.

PETRUCHIO.

Very well mended.—Kiss him for that, good widow.

KATHARINA.

He that is giddy thinks the world turns round:—
I pray you, tell me what you meant by that.

WIDOW.

Your husband, being troubled with a shrew,
Measures my husband's sorrow by his woe:
And now you know my meaning.

KATHARINA.

A very mean meaning.

WIDOW.

Right, I mean you.

KATHARINA.

And I am mean, indeed, respecting you.

PETRUCHIO.

To her, Kate!

HORTENSIO.

To her, widow!

PETRUCHIO.

A hundred marks, my Kate does put her down.

HORTENSIO.

That's my office.

PETRUCHIO.

Spoke like an officer:—ha' to thee, lad.

[*Drinks to* HORTENSIO.

BAPTISTA.

How likes Gremio these quick-witted folks?

GREMIO.

Believe me, sir, they butt together well.

BIANCA.

Head and butt! an hasty-witted body
Would say your head and butt were head and horn.

VINCENTIO.

Ay, mistress bride, hath that awaken'd you?

BIANCA.

Ay, but not frighted me; therefore I'll sleep again.

PETRUCHIO.

Nay, that you shall not: since you have begun,
Have at you for a bitter jest or two!

BIANCA.

Am I your bird? I mean to shift my bush;
And then pursue me as you draw your bow.—
You are welcome all.

[*Exeunt* BIANCA, KATHARINA, *and* WIDOW.

PETRUCHIO.

She hath prevented me.—Here, Signior Tranio,
This bird you aim'd at, though you hit her not;
Therefore a health to all that shot and mist.

TRANIO.
O, sir, Lucentio slipt me like his greyhound,
Which runs himself, and catches for his master.

PETRUCHIO.
A good swift simile, but something currish.

TRANIO.
'Tis well, sir, that you hunted for yourself:
'Tis thought your deer does hold you at a bay.

BAPTISTA.
O, ho, Petruchio! Tranio hits you now.

LUCENTIO.
I thank thee for that gird, good Tranio.

HORTENSIO.
Confess, confess, hath he not hit you here?

PETRUCHIO.
A' has a little gall'd me, I confess;
And, as the jest did glance away from me,
'Tis ten to one it maim'd you two outright.

BAPTISTA.
Now, in good sadness, son Petruchio,
I think thou hast the veriest shrew of all.

PETRUCHIO.
Well, I say no: and therefore, for assurance,
Let's each one send unto his wife;
And he whose wife is most obedient
To come at first when he doth send for her,
Shall win the wager which we will propose.

HORTENSIO.
Content. What is the wager?

LUCENTIO.
Twenty crowns.

PETRUCHIO.
Twenty crowns!
I'll venture so much of my hawk or hound,
But twenty times so much upon my wife.

LUCENTIO.
A hundred, then.

HORTENSIO.
Content.

PETRUCHIO.
A match! 'tis done.

HORTENSIO.
Who shall begin?

LUCENTIO.
That will I.—
Go, Biondello, bid your mistress come to me.

BIONDELLO.
I go. [*Exit.*

BAPTISTA.
Son, I'll be your half, Bianca comes.

LUCENTIO.
I'll have no halves; I'll bear it all myself.

Enter BIONDELLO.

How now! what news?

BIONDELLO.
Sir, my mistress sends you word
That she is busy, and she cannot come.

PETRUCHIO.
How! she is busy, and she cannot come!
Is that an answer?

GREMIO.
Ay, and a kind one too:
Pray God, sir, your wife send you not a worse.

PETRUCHIO.
I hope, better.

HORTENSIO.
Sirrah Biondello, go and entreat my wife
To come to me forthwith. [*Exit* BIONDELLO.

PETRUCHIO.
O, ho! entreat her!
Nay, then she must needs come.

HORTENSIO.
I am afraid, sir,
Do what you can, yours will not be entreated.

Enter BIONDELLO.

Now, where's my wife?

BIONDELLO.
She says you have some goodly jest in hand:
She will not come; she bids you come to her.

PETRUCHIO.
Worse and worse; she will not come! O vile,
Intolerable, not to be endured!—
Sirrah Grumio, go to your mistress;
Say, I command her come to me.
[*Exit* GRUMIO.

HORTENSIO.
I know her answer.

PETRUCHIO.
What?

HORTENSIO.
She will not come.

PETRUCHIO.
The fouler fortune mine, and there an end.

BAPTISTA.
Now, by my holidame, here comes Katharina!

Enter KATHARINA.

KATHARINA.
What is your will, sir, that you send for me?

PETRUCHIO.
Where is your sister, and Hortensio's wife?

KATHARINA.
They sit conferring by the parlour fire.

PETRUCHIO.
Go fetch them hither: if they deny to come,
Swinge me them soundly forth unto their husbands:
Away, I say, and bring them hither straight.
[*Exit* KATHARINA.

LUCENTIO.
Here is a wonder, if you talk of a wonder.

HORTENSIO.
And so it is: I wonder what it bodes.

PETRUCHIO.
Marry, peace it bodes, and love, and quiet life,
An awful rule, and right supremacy,
And, to be short, what not that's sweet and happy?

BAPTISTA.
Now, fair befall thee, good Petruchio!
The wager thou hast won; and I will add
Unto their losses twenty thousand crowns;
Another dowry to another daughter,
For she is changed, as she had never been.

PETRUCHIO.
Nay, I will win my wager better yet,
And show more sign of her obedience,
Her new-built virtue and obedience.
See, where she comes, and brings your froward wives
As prisoners to her womanly persuasion.

Enter KATHARINA, *with* BIANCA *and* WIDOW.
Katharine, that cap of yours becomes you not:
Off with that bauble, throw it under foot.
[*She obeys.*

WIDOW.
Lord, let me never have a cause to sigh,
Till I be brought to such a silly pass!

BIANCA.
Fie, what a foolish duty call you this?

LUCENTIO.
I would your duty were as foolish too:
The wisdom of your duty, fair Bianca,
Hath cost me a hundred crowns since supper-time.

BIANCA.
The more fool you, for laying on my duty.

PETRUCHIO.
Katharine, I charge thee, tell these headstrong women
What duty they do owe their lords and husbands.

WIDOW.
Come, come, you're mocking: we will have no telling.

PETRUCHIO.
Come on, I say; and first begin with her.

WIDOW.
She shall not.

PETRUCHIO.
I say she shall:—and first begin with her.

KATHARINA.
Fie, fie! unknit that threatening unkind brow:
And dart not scornful glances from those eyes,
To wound thy lord, thy king, thy governor:
It blots thy beauty, as frosts do bite the meads;
Confounds thy fame, as whirlwinds shake fair buds;
And in no sense is meet or amiable.
A woman moved is like a fountain troubled,
Muddy, ill-seeming, thick, bereft of beauty;
And while it is so, none so dry or thirsty
Will deign to sip, or touch one drop of it.
Thy husband is thy lord, thy life, thy keeper,
Thy head, thy sovereign; one that cares for thee,
And for thy maintenance commits his body
To painful labour both by sea and land,
To watch the night in storms, the day in cold,
Whilst thou liest warm at home, secure and safe;
And craves no other tribute at thy hands
But love, fair looks, and true obedience,—
Too little payment for so great a debt.
Such duty as the subject owes the prince,
Even such a woman oweth to her husband;
And when she is froward, peevish, sullen, sour,
And not obedient to his honest will,
What is she but a foul contending rebel,
And graceless traitor to her loving lord?
I am ashamed that women are so simple
To offer war, where they should kneel for peace;
Or seek for rule, supremacy, and sway,
When they are bound to serve, love, and obey.
Why are our bodies soft and weak and smooth,
Unapt to toil and trouble in the world,
But that our soft conditions and our hearts
Should well agree with our external parts?
Come, come, you froward and unable worms!
My mind hath been as big as one of yours,
My heart as great; my reason, haply, more,
To bandy word for word and frown for frown:
But now I see our lances are but straws;
Our strength as weak, our weakness past compare,—
That seeming to be most, which we indeed least are.
Then vail your stomachs, for it is no boot,
And place your hands below your husband's foot:
In token of which duty, if he please,
My hand is ready, may it do him ease.

PETRUCHIO.
Why, there's a wench!—Come on, and kiss me, Kate.

LUCENTIO.
Well, go thy ways, old lad; for thou shalt ha't.

VINCENTIO.
'Tis a good hearing when children are toward.

LUCENTIO.
But a harsh hearing when women are froward.

PETRUCHIO.
Come, Kate, we'll to bed.—
We three are married, but you two are sped.
'Twas I won the wager, though you hit the white;
[*to* LUCENTIO.
And, being a winner, God give you good night!
[*Exeunt* PETRUCHIO *and* KATHARINA.

HORTENSIO.
Now, go thy ways; thou hast tamed a curst shrow.

LUCENTIO.
'Tis a wonder, by your leave, she will be tamed so.
[*Exeunt.*

THE TWO GENTLEMEN OF VERONA

DRAMATIS PERSONAE.

DUKE OF MILAN, *father to Silvia.*
VALENTINE, } *the two Gentlemen.*
PROTEUS, }
ANTONIO, *father to Proteus.*
THURIO, *a foolish rival to Valentine.*
EGLAMOUR, *agent for Silvia in her escape.*
SPEED, *a clownish servant to Valentine.*
LAUNCE, *the like to Proteus.*
PANTHINO, *servant to Antonio.*

HOST, *where Julia lodges.*
OUTLAWS, *with Valentine.*

JULIA, *beloved of Proteus.*
SILVIA, *beloved of Valentine.*
LUCETTA, *waiting-woman to Julia.*

SERVANTS, MUSICIANS.

SCENE—*Verona; Milan; the frontiers of Mantua.*

ACT I. SCENE I.

Verona. An open place.

Enter VALENTINE *and* PROTEUS.

VALENTINE.

CEASE to persuade, my loving Proteus:
Home-keeping youth have ever homely wits.
Were't not affection chains thy tender days
To the sweet glances of thy honour'd love,
I rather would entreat thy company
To see the wonders of the world abroad,
Than, living dully sluggardized at home,
Wear out thy youth with shapeless idleness.
But since thou lovest, love still, and thrive therein,
Even as I would, when I to love begin.

PROTEUS.

Wilt thou be gone? Sweet Valentine, adieu!
Think on thy Proteus, when thou haply see'st
Some rare note-worthy object in thy travel:
Wish me partaker in thy happiness,
When thou dost meet good hap; and in thy danger,
If ever danger do environ thee,
Commend thy grievance to my holy prayers,
For I will be thy beadsman, Valentine.

VALENTINE.

And on a love-book pray for my success?

PROTEUS.

Upon some book I love I'll pray for thee.

VALENTINE.

That's on some shallow story of deep love;
How young Leander cross'd the Hellespont.

PROTEUS.

That's a deep story of a deeper love;
For he was more than over shoes in love.

VALENTINE.

'Tis true; for you are over boots in love,
And yet you never swum the Hellespont.

PROTEUS.

Over the boots! nay, give me not the boots.

VALENTINE.

No, I will not, for it boots thee not.

PROTEUS.

What?

VALENTINE.

To be in love, where scorn is bought with groans;
Coy looks with heart-sore sighs; one fading moment's mirth
With twenty watchful, weary, tedious nights:
If haply won, perhaps a hapless gain;
If lost, why then a grievous labour won;
However, but a folly bought with wit,
Or else a wit by folly vanquished.

PROTEUS.

So, by your circumstance, you call me fool.

VALENTINE.

So, by your circumstance, I fear you'll prove.

PROTEUS.

'Tis love you cavil at: I am not Love.

VALENTINE.

Love is your master, for he masters you:
And he that is so yoked by a fool,
Methinks, should not be chronicled for wise.

PROTEUS.

Yet writers say, as in the sweetest bud
The eating canker dwells, so eating love
Inhabits in the finest wits of all.

VALENTINE.

And writers say, as the most forward bud
Is eaten by the canker ere it blow,
Even so by love the young and tender wit
Is turn'd to folly; blasting in the bud,
Losing his verdure even in the prime,
And all the fair effects of future hopes.
But wherefore waste I time to counsel thee,
That art a votary to fond desire?
Once more adieu! my father at the road
Expects my coming, there to see me shipp'd.

PROTEUS.

And thither will I bring thee, Valentine.

VALENTINE.

Sweet Proteus, no; now let us take our leave.
To Milan let me hear from thee by letters
Of thy success in love, and what news else
Betideth here in absence of thy friend;
And I likewise will visit thee with mine.

PROTEUS.

All happiness bechance to thee in Milan!

VALENTINE.

As much to you at home! and so, farewell. [*Exit.*

PROTEUS.

He after honour hunts, I after love:
He leaves his friends to dignify them more;
I leave myself, my friends, and all, for love.
Thou, Julia, thou hast metamorphosed me,—

LUCETTA.

Madam, it will not lie where it concerns,
Unless it have a false interpreter.

JULIA.

Some love of yours hath writ to you in rhyme.

LUCETTA.

That I might sing it, madam, to a tune.
Give me a note: your ladyship can set.

JULIA.

As little by such toys as may be possible.
Best sing it to the tune of *Light o' love.*

LUCETTA.

It is too heavy for so light a tune.

JULIA.

Heavy! belike it hath some burden, then?

LUCETTA.

Ay; and melodious were it, would you sing it.

JULIA.

And why not you?

LUCETTA.

I cannot reach so high.

JULIA.

Let's see your song [*Taking the letter*]. How now, minion!

LUCETTA.

Keep tune there still, so you will sing it out:
And yet methinks I do not like this tune.

JULIA.

You do not?

LUCETTA.

No, madam; 'tis too sharp.

JULIA.

You, minion, are too saucy.

LUCETTA.

Nay, now you are too flat,
And mar the concord with too harsh a descant:
There wanteth but a mean to fill your song.

JULIA.

The mean is drown'd with your unruly base.

LUCETTA.

Indeed, I bid the base for Proteus.

JULIA.

This babble shall not henceforth trouble me:—
Here is a coil with protestation!—
[*Tears the letter.*
Go get you gone, and let the papers lie:
You would be fingering them, to anger me.

LUCETTA.

She makes it strange; but she would be best pleased
To be so anger'd with another letter. [*Exit.*

JULIA.

Nay, would I were so anger'd with the same!
O hateful hands, to tear such loving words!
Injurious wasps, to feed on such sweet honey,
And kill the bees, that yield it, with your stings!
I'll kiss each several paper for amends.
Look, here is writ—'kind Julia:'—unkind Julia!
As in revenge of thy ingratitude,
I throw thy name against the bruising stones,
Trampling contemptuously on thy disdain.
And here is writ—'love-wounded Proteus:'—
Poor wounded name! my bosom, as a bed,
Shall lodge thee, till thy wound be throughly heal'd;
And thus I search it with a sovereign kiss.
But twice or thrice was 'Proteus' written down:—
Be calm, good wind, blow not a word away,
Till I have found each letter in the letter,
Except mine own name: that some whirlwind bear
Unto a ragged, fearful-hanging rock,
And throw it thence into the raging sea!—
Lo, here in one line is his name twice writ,—
'Poor forlorn Proteus, passionate Proteus,
To the sweet Julia:'—that I'll tear away;—
And yet I will not, sith so prettily
He couples it to his complaining names.
Thus will I fold them one upon another:
Now kiss, embrace, contend, do what you will.

Enter LUCETTA.

LUCETTA.

Madam,
Dinner is ready, and your father stays.

JULIA.

Well, let us go.

LUCETTA.

What, shall these papers lie like tell-tales here?

JULIA.

If you respect them, best to take them up.

LUCETTA.

Nay, I was taken up for laying them down:
Yet here they shall not lie, for catching cold.

JULIA.

I see you have a month's mind to them.

LUCETTA.

Ay, madam, you may say what sights you see;
I see things too, although you judge I wink.

JULIA.

Come, come; will't please you go? [*Exeunt.*

SCENE III.

The same. ANTONIO'S *house.*

Enter ANTONIO *and* PANTHINO.

ANTONIO.

Tell me, Panthino, what sad talk was that
Wherewith my brother held you in the cloister?

PANTHINO.

'Twas of his nephew Proteus, your son.

ANTONIO.

Why, what of him?

PANTHINO.

He wonder'd that your lordship
Would suffer him to spend his youth at home,
While other men, of slender reputation,
Put forth their sons to seek preferment out:
Some to the wars, to try their fortune there;
Some to discover islands far away;
Some to the studious universities.
For any or for all these exercises,
He said that Proteus your son was meet;
And did request me to importune you
To let him spend his time no more at home,
Which would be great impeachment to his age,
In having known no travel in his youth.

ANTONIO.

Nor need'st thou much importune me to that
Whereon this month I have been hammering.
I have consider'd well his loss of time,

And how he cannot be a perfect man,
Not being tried and tutor'd in the world:
Experience is by industry achieved,
And perfected by the swift course of time.
Then, tell me, whither were I best to send him?

PANTHINO.

I think your lordship is not ignorant
How his companion, youthful Valentine,
Attends the emperor in his royal court.

ANTONIO.

I know it well.

PANTHINO.

'Twere good, I think, your lordship sent him thither:
There shall he practise tilts and tournaments,
Hear sweet discourse, converse with noblemen,
And be in eye of every exercise
Worthy his youth and nobleness of birth.

ANTONIO.

I like thy counsel; well hast thou advised:
And that thou mayst perceive how well I like it,
The execution of it shall make known.
Even with the speediest expedition
I will dispatch him to the emperor's court.

PANTHINO.

To-morrow, may it please you, Don Alphonso,
With other gentlemen of good esteem,
Are journeying to salute the emperor,
And to commend their service to his will.

ANTONIO.

Good company; with them shall Proteus go:
And,—in good time:—now will we break with him.

Enter PROTEUS.

PROTEUS.

Sweet love! sweet lines! sweet life!
Here is her hand, the agent of her heart;
Here is her oath for love, her honour's pawn.
O, that our fathers would applaud our loves,
To seal our happiness with their consents!
O heavenly Julia!

ANTONIO.

How now! what letter are you reading there?

PROTEUS.

May 't please your lordship, 'tis a word or two
Of commendations sent from Valentine,
Deliver'd by a friend that came from him.

ANTONIO.

Lend me the letter; let me see what news.

PROTEUS.

There is no news, my lord; but that he writes
How happily he lives, how well beloved,
And daily graced by the emperor;
Wishing me with him, partner of his fortune.

ANTONIO.

And how stand you affected to his wish?

PROTEUS.

As one relying on your lordship's will,
And not depending on his friendly wish.

ANTONIO.

My will is something sorted with his wish.
Muse not that I thus suddenly proceed;
For what I will, I will, and there an end.
I am resolved that thou shalt spend some time
With Valentinus in the emperor's court:
What maintenance he from his friends receives,
Like exhibition thou shalt have from me.
To-morrow be in readiness to go:
Excuse it not, for I am peremptory.

PROTEUS.

My lord, I cannot be so soon provided:
Please you, deliberate a day or two.

ANTONIO.

Look, what thou want'st shall be sent after thee:
No more of stay; to-morrow thou must go.—
Come on, Panthino: you shall be employ'd
To hasten on his expedition.

[*Exeunt* ANTONIO *and* PANTHINO.

PROTEUS.

Thus have I shunn'd the fire for fear of burning,
And drench'd me in the sea, where I am drown'd.
I fear'd to show my father Julia's letter,
Lest he should take exceptions to my love;
And with the vantage of mine own excuse
Hath he excepted most against my love.
O, how this spring of love resembleth
The uncertain glory of an April day,
Which now shows all the beauty of the sun,
And by and by a cloud takes all away!

Enter PANTHINO.

PANTHINO.

Sir Proteus, your father calls for you:
He is in haste; therefore, I pray you, go.

PROTEUS.

Why, this it is,—my heart accords thereto,
And yet a thousand times it answers, No.

[*Exeunt.*

ACT II. SCENE I.

Milan. The DUKE'S *palace.*

Enter VALENTINE *and* SPEED.

SPEED.

SIR, your glove.

VALENTINE.

Not mine; my gloves are on.

SPEED.

Why, then, this may be yours, for this is but one.

VALENTINE.

Ha, let me see: ay, give it me, it's mine:—
Sweet ornament that decks a thing divine!
Ah, Silvia, Silvia!

SPEED.

Madam Silvia, Madam Silvia!

VALENTINE.

How now, sirrah!

SPEED.

She is not within hearing, sir.

VALENTINE.

Why, sir, who bade you call her?

SPEED.

Your worship, sir; or else I mistook.

VALENTINE.

Well, you'll still be too forward.

SPEED.

And yet I was last chidden for being too slow.

VALENTINE.

Go to, sir: tell me, do you know Madam Silvia?

SPEED.

She that your worship loves?

VALENTINE.

Why, how know you that I am in love?

SPEED.
Marry, by these special marks: first, you have learn'd, like Sir Proteus, to wreathe your arms, like a malecontent; to relish a love-song, like a robin-redbreast; to walk alone, like one that had the pestilence; to sigh, like a school-boy that had lost his A B C; to weep, like a young wench that had buried her grandam; to fast, like one that takes diet; to watch, like one that fears robbing; to speak puling, like a beggar at Hallowmas. You were wont, when you laugh'd, to crow like a cock; when you walk'd, to walk like one of the lions; when you fasted, it was presently after dinner; when you look'd sadly, it was for want of money: and now you are metamorphosed with a mistress, that, when I look on you, I can hardly think you my master.

VALENTINE.
Are all these things perceived in me?

SPEED.
They are all perceived without ye.

VALENTINE.
Without me! they cannot.

SPEED.
Without you! nay, that's certain, for, without you were so simple, none else would: but you are so without these follies, that these follies are within you, and shine through you like the water in an urinal, that not an eye that sees you but is a physician to comment on your malady.

VALENTINE.
But tell me, dost thou know my lady Silvia?

SPEED.
She that you gaze on so as she sits at supper?

VALENTINE.
Hast thou observed that? even she I mean.

SPEED.
Why, sir, I know her not.

VALENTINE.
Dost thou know her by my gazing on her, and yet know'st her not?

SPEED.
Is she not hard-favour'd, sir?

VALENTINE.
Not so fair, boy, as well-favour'd.

SPEED.
Sir, I know that well enough.

VALENTINE.
What dost thou know?

SPEED.
That she is not so fair as, of you, well favour'd.

VALENTINE.
I mean, that her beauty is exquisite, but her favour infinite.

SPEED.
That's because the one is painted, and the other out of all count.

VALENTINE.
How painted? and how out of count?

SPEED.
Marry, sir, so painted, to make her fair, that no man counts of her beauty.

VALENTINE.
How esteem'st thou me? I account of her beauty.

SPEED.
You never saw her since she was deform'd.

VALENTINE.
How long hath she been deform'd?

SPEED.
Ever since you loved her.

VALENTINE.
I have loved her ever since I saw her; and still I see her beautiful.

SPEED.
If you love her, you cannot see her.

VALENTINE.
Why?

SPEED.
Because Love is blind. O, that you had mine eyes; or your own eyes had the lights they were wont to have when you chid at Sir Proteus for going ungarter'd!

VALENTINE.
What should I see then?

SPEED.
Your own present folly, and her passing deformity: for he, being in love, could not see to garter his hose; and you, being in love, cannot see to put on your hose.

VALENTINE.
Belike, boy, then, you are in love; for last morning you could not see to wipe my shoes.

SPEED.
True, sir; I was in love with my bed: I thank you, you swinged me for my love, which makes me the bolder to chide you for yours.

VALENTINE.
In conclusion, I stand affected to her.

SPEED.
I would you were set; so your affection would cease.

VALENTINE.
Last night she enjoin'd me to write some lines to one she loves.

SPEED.
And have you?

VALENTINE.
I have.

SPEED.
Are they not lamely writ?

VALENTINE.
No, boy, but as well as I can do them.—Peace! here she comes.

SPEED [*aside*].
O excellent motion! O exceeding puppet! Now will he interpret to her.

Enter SILVIA.

VALENTINE.
Madam and mistress, a thousand good-morrows!

SPEED [*aside*].
O, give ye good even! here's a million of manners.

SILVIA.
Sir Valentine and servant, to you two thousand.

SPEED [*aside*].
He should give her interest, and she gives it him.

VALENTINE.
As you enjoin'd me, I have writ your letter
Unto the secret nameless friend of yours;
Which I was much unwilling to proceed in,
But for my duty to your ladyship.

SILVIA.
I thank you, gentle servant: 'tis very clerkly done.
VALENTINE.
Now trust me, madam, it came hardly off;
For, being ignorant to whom it goes,
I writ at random, very doubtfully.
SILVIA.
Perchance you think too much of so much pains?
VALENTINE.
No, madam; so it stead you, I will write,
Please you command, a thousand times as much:
And yet,—
SILVIA.
A pretty period! Well, I guess the sequel;
And yet I will not name it;—and yet I care not;—
And yet take this again;—and yet I thank you;
Meaning henceforth to trouble you no more.
SPEED [*aside*].
And yet you will; and yet another 'yet.'
VALENTINE.
What means your ladyship? do you not like it?
SILVIA.
Yes, yes; the lines are very quaintly writ:
But since unwillingly, take them again;
Nay, take them.
VALENTINE.
Madam, they are for you.
SILVIA.
Ay, ay, you writ them, sir, at my request;
But I will none of them; they are for you:
I would have had them writ more movingly.
VALENTINE.
Please you, I'll write your ladyship another.
SILVIA.
And when it's writ, for my sake read it over:
And if it please you, so; if not, why, so.
VALENTINE.
If it please me, madam! what then?
SILVIA.
Why, if it please you, take it for your labour:
And so, good morrow, servant. [*Exit.*
SPEED.
O jest unseen, inscrutable, invisible,
As a nose on a man's face, or a weathercock on a steeple!
My master sues to her; and she hath taught her suitor,
He being her pupil, to become her tutor.
O excellent device! was there ever heard a better,
That my master, being scribe, to himself should write the letter?
VALENTINE.
How now, sir! what are you reasoning with yourself?
SPEED.
Nay, I was rhyming: 'tis you that have the reason.
VALENTINE.
To do what?
SPEED.
To be a spokesman from Madam Silvia.
VALENTINE.
To whom?
SPEED.
To yourself: why, she woos you by a figure.
VALENTINE.
What figure?
SPEED.
By a letter, I should say.
VALENTINE.
Why, she hath not writ to me?
SPEED.
What need she, when she hath made you write to yourself? Why, do you not perceive the jest?
VALENTINE.
No, believe me.
SPEED.
No believing you, indeed, sir. But did you perceive her earnest?
VALENTINE.
She gave me none, except an angry word.
SPEED.
Why, she hath given you a letter.
VALENTINE.
That's the letter I writ to her friend.
SPEED.
And that letter hath she deliver'd, and there an end.
VALENTINE.
I would it were no worse.
SPEED.
I'll warrant you, 'tis as well:
For often have you writ to her; and she, in modesty,
Or else for want of idle time, could not again reply;
Or fearing else some messenger that might her mind discover,
Herself hath taught her love himself to write unto her lover.
All this I speak in print, for in print I found it.
Why muse you, sir? 'tis dinner-time.
VALENTINE.
I have dined.
SPEED.
Ay, but hearken, sir; though the chameleon Love can feed on the air, I am one that am nourish'd by my victuals, and would fain have meat. O, be not like your mistress; be moved, be moved. [*Exeunt.*

SCENE II.

Verona. JULIA'S *garden.*

Enter PROTEUS *and* JULIA.

PROTEUS.
HAVE patience, gentle Julia.
JULIA.
I must, where is no remedy.
PROTEUS.
When possibly I can, I will return.
JULIA.
If you turn not, you will return the sooner.
Keep this remembrance for thy Julia's sake.
[*Gives him a ring.*
PROTEUS.
Why, then, we'll make exchange; here, take you this. [*Gives her another.*
JULIA.
And seal the bargain with a holy kiss.
PROTEUS.
Here is my hand for my true constancy;
And when that hour o'erslips me in the day

Wherein I sigh not, Julia, for thy sake,
The next ensuing hour some foul mischance
Torment me for my love's forgetfulness!
My father stays my coming; answer not;
The tide is now:—nay, not thy tide of tears;
That tide will stay me longer than I should:
Julia, farewell! [*Exit* JULIA.
What, gone without a word?
Ay, so true love should do: it cannot speak;
For truth hath better deeds than words to grace
it.

Enter PANTHINO.

PANTHINO.

Sir Proteus, you are stay'd for.

PROTEUS.

Go; I come, I come:—
Alas, this parting strikes poor lovers dumb!
[*Exeunt.*

SCENE III.

The same. A street.

Enter LAUNCE, *leading his dog.*

LAUNCE.

NAY, 'twill be this hour ere I have done weeping; all the kind of the Launces have this very fault. I have received my proportion, like the prodigious son, and am going with Sir Proteus to the imperial's court. I think Crab my dog be the sourest-natured dog that lives: my mother weeping, my father wailing, my sister crying, our maid howling, our cat wringing her hands, and all our house in a great perplexity, yet did not this cruel-hearted cur shed one tear: he is a stone, a very pebble-stone, and has no more pity in him than a dog: a Jew would have wept to have seen our parting; why, my grandam, having no eyes, look you, wept herself blind at my parting. Nay, I'll show you the manner of it. This shoe is my father;—no, this left shoe is my father;—no, no, this left shoe is my mother;—nay, that cannot be so neither;—yes, it is so, it is so,—it hath the worser sole. This shoe, with the hole in it, is my mother, and this my father; a vengeance on't! there 'tis: now, sir, this staff is my sister; for, look you, she is as white as a lily, and as small as a wand: this hat is Nan, our maid: I am the dog;—no, the dog is himself, and I am the dog,—O, the dog is me, and I am myself; ay, so, so. Now come I to my father; 'Father, your blessing!' now should not the shoe speak a word for weeping: now should I kiss my father; well, he weeps on. Now come I to my mother;—O, that she could speak now like a wood woman!—well, I kiss her;—why, there 'tis; here's my mother's breath up and down. Now come I to my sister: mark the moan she makes. Now the dog all this while sheds not a tear, nor speaks a word: but see how I lay the dust with my tears.

Enter PANTHINO.

PANTHINO.

Launce, away, away, aboard! thy master is shipp'd, and thou art to post after with oars. What's the matter? why weep'st thou, man? Away, ass! you'll lose the tide, if you tarry any longer.

LAUNCE.

It is no matter if the tied were lost; for it is the unkindest tied that ever any man tied.

PANTHINO.

What's the unkindest tide?

LAUNCE.

Why, he that's tied here,—Crab, my dog.

PANTHINO.

Tut, man, I mean thou'lt lose the flood: and, in losing the flood, lose thy voyage; and, in losing thy voyage, lose thy master; and, in losing thy master, lose thy service; and, in losing thy service,—Why dost thou stop my mouth?

LAUNCE.

For fear thou shouldst lose thy tongue.

PANTHINO.

Where should I lose my tongue?

LAUNCE.

In thy tale.

PANTHINO.

In thy tail!

LAUNCE.

Lose the tide, and the voyage, and the master, and the service, and the tied! Why, man, if the river were dry, I am able to fill it with my tears; if the wind were down, I could drive the boat with my sighs.

PANTHINO.

Come, come away, man; I was sent to call thee.

LAUNCE.

Sir, call me what thou darest.

PANTHINO.

Wilt thou go?

LAUNCE.

Well, I will go. [*Exeunt.*

SCENE IV.

Milan. The DUKE'S *palace.*

Enter SILVIA, VALENTINE, THURIO, *and* SPEED.

SILVIA.

SERVANT,—

VALENTINE.

Mistress?

SPEED.

Master, Sir Thurio frowns on you.

VALENTINE.

Ay, boy, it's for love.

SPEED.

Not of you.

VALENTINE.

Of my mistress, then.

SPEED.

'Twere good you knock'd him.

SILVIA.

Servant, you are sad.

VALENTINE.

Indeed, madam, I seem so.

THURIO.

Seem you that you are not?

VALENTINE.

Haply I do.

THURIO.

So do counterfeits.

VALENTINE.

So do you.

THURIO.
What seem I that I am not?

VALENTINE.
Wise.

THURIO.
What instance of the contrary?

VALENTINE.
Your folly.

THURIO.
And how quote you my folly?

VALENTINE.
I quote it in your jerkin.

THURIO.
My jerkin is a doublet.

VALENTINE.
Well, then, I'll double your folly.

THURIO.
How!

SILVIA.
What, angry, Sir Thurio! do you change colour?

VALENTINE.
Give him leave, madam; he is a kind of chameleon.

THURIO.
That hath more mind to feed on your blood than live in your air.

VALENTINE.
You have said, sir.

THURIO.
Ay, sir, and done too, for this time.

VALENTINE.
I know it well, sir; you always end ere you begin.

SILVIA.
A fine volley of words, gentlemen, and quickly shot off.

VALENTINE.
'Tis indeed, madam; we thank the giver.

SILVIA.
Who is that, servant?

VALENTINE.
Yourself, sweet lady; for you gave the fire. Sir Thurio borrows his wit from your ladyship's looks, and spends what he borrows kindly in your company.

THURIO.
Sir, if you spend word for word with me, I shall make your wit bankrupt.

VALENTINE.
I know it well, sir; you have an exchequer of words, and, I think, no other treasure to give your followers,—for it appears, by their bare liveries, that they live by your bare words.

SILVIA.
No more, gentlemen, no more:—here comes my father.

Enter DUKE.

DUKE OF MILAN.
Now, daughter Silvia, you are hard beset.—
Sir Valentine, your father's in good health:
What say you to a letter from your friends
Of much good news?

VALENTINE.
My lord, I will be thankful
To any happy messenger from thence.

DUKE OF MILAN.
Know ye Don Antonio, your countryman?

VALENTINE.
Ay, my good lord, I know the gentleman
To be of worth and worthy estimation,
And not without desert so well reputed.

DUKE OF MILAN.
Hath he not a son?

VALENTINE.
Ay, my good lord; a son that well deserves
The honour and regard of such a father.

DUKE OF MILAN.
You know him well?

VALENTINE.
I know him as myself; for from our infancy
We have conversed and spent our hours together:
And though myself have been an idle truant,
Omitting the sweet benefit of time
To clothe mine age with angel-like perfection,
Yet hath Sir Proteus, for that's his name,
Made use and fair advantage of his days;
His years but young, but his experience old;
His head unmellow'd, but his judgment ripe;
And, in a word,—for far behind his worth
Comes all the praises that I now bestow,—
He is complete in feature and in mind,
With all good grace to grace a gentleman.

DUKE OF MILAN.
Beshrew me, sir, but if he make this good,
He is as worthy for an empress' love
As meet to be an emperor's counsellor.
Well, sir; this gentleman is come to me,
With commendation from great potentates;
And here he means to spend his time awhile:
I think 'tis no unwelcome news to you.

VALENTINE.
Should I have wish'd a thing, it had been he.

DUKE OF MILAN.
Welcome him, then, according to his worth;
Silvia, I speak to you; and you, Sir Thurio:—
For Valentine, I need not cite him to it:
I will send him hither to you presently. [*Exit.*

VALENTINE.
This is the gentleman I told your ladyship
Had come along with me, but that his mistress
Did hold his eyes lockt in her crystal looks.

SILVIA.
Belike that now she hath enfranchised them,
Upon some other pawn for fealty.

VALENTINE.
Nay, sure, I think she holds them prisoners still.

SILVIA.
Nay, then, he should be blind; and, being blind,
How could he see his way to seek out you?

VALENTINE.
Why, lady, Love hath twenty pair of eyes.

THURIO.
They say that Love hath not an eye at all.

VALENTINE.
To see such lovers, Thurio, as yourself:
Upon a homely object Love can wink.

SILVIA.
Have done, have done; here comes the gentleman.

Enter PROTEUS.

VALENTINE.
Welcome, dear Proteus!—Mistress, I beseech you,
Confirm his welcome with some special favour.

SILVIA.
His worth is warrant for his welcome hither,
If this be he you oft have wish'd to hear from.

VALENTINE.
Mistress, it is: sweet lady, entertain him
To be my fellow-servant to your ladyship.

SILVIA.
Too low a mistress for so high a servant.

PROTEUS.
Not so, sweet lady; but too mean a servant
To have a look of such a worthy mistress.

VALENTINE.
Leave off discourse of disability:—
Sweet lady, entertain him for your servant.

PROTEUS.
My duty will I boast of, nothing else.

SILVIA.
And duty never yet did want his meed:
Servant, you are welcome to a worthless mistress.

PROTEUS.
I'll die on him that says so, but yourself.

SILVIA.
That you are welcome?

PROTEUS.
That you are worthless.

Enter a SERVANT.

SERVANT.
Madam, my lord your father would speak with you.

SILVIA.
I wait upon his pleasure. [*Exit* SERVANT.
Come, Sir Thurio,
Go with me.—Once more, new servant, welcome:
I'll leave you to confer of home affairs;
When you have done, we look to hear from you.

PROTEUS.
We'll both attend upon your ladyship.

[*Exeunt* SILVIA *and* THURIO.

VALENTINE.
Now, tell me, how do all from whence you came?

PROTEUS.
Your friends are well, and have them much commended.

VALENTINE.
And how do yours?

PROTEUS.
I left them all in health.

VALENTINE.
How does your lady? and how thrives your love?

PROTEUS.
My tales of love were wont to weary you;
I know you joy not in a love-discourse.

VALENTINE.
Ay, Proteus, but that life is alter'd now.
I have done penance for contemning Love,
Whose high imperious thoughts have punish'd me
With bitter fasts, with penitential groans,
With nightly tears, and daily heart-sore sighs;
For, in revenge of my contempt of love,
Love hath chased sleep from my enthralled eyes,
And made them watchers of mine own heart's sorrow.
O gentle Proteus, Love's a mighty lord,
And hath so humbled me, as, I confess,
There is no woe to his correction,
Nor to his service no such joy on earth!
Now, no discourse, except it be of love;
Now can I break my fast, dine, sup, and sleep,
Upon the very naked name of love.

PROTEUS.
Enough; I read your fortune in your eye.
Was this the idol that you worship so?

VALENTINE.
Even she; and is she not a heavenly saint?

PROTEUS.
No; but she is an earthly paragon.

VALENTINE.
Call her divine.

PROTEUS.
I will not flatter her.

VALENTINE.
O, flatter me; for love delights in praises.

PROTEUS.
When I was sick, you gave me bitter pills;
And I must minister the like to you.

VALENTINE.
Then speak the truth by her: if not divine,
Yet let her be a principality,
Sovereign to all the creatures on the earth.

PROTEUS.
Except my mistress.

VALENTINE.
Sweet, except not any;
Except thou wilt except against my love.

PROTEUS.
Have I not reason to prefer mine own?

VALENTINE.
And I will help thee to prefer her too:
She shall be dignified with this high honour,—
To bear my lady's train, lest the base earth
Should from her vesture chance to steal a kiss,
And, of so great a favour growing proud,
Disdain to root the summer-swelling flower,
And make rough winter everlastingly.

PROTEUS.
Why, Valentine, what braggardism is this?

VALENTINE.
Pardon me, Proteus: all I can is nothing
To her, whose worth makes other worthies nothing;
She is alone.

PROTEUS.
Then let her alone.

VALENTINE.
Not for the world: why, man, she is mine own;
And I as rich in having such a jewel
As twenty seas, if all their sand were pearl,
The water nectar, and the rocks pure gold.
Forgive me, that I do not dream on thee,
Because thou see'st me dote upon my love.
My foolish rival, that her father likes
Only for his possessions are so huge,
Is gone with her along; and I must after,
For love, thou know'st, is full of jealousy.

PROTEUS.
But she loves you?

VALENTINE.
Ay, and we are betroth'd: nay, more, our marriage-hour,

With all the cunning manner of our flight,
Determined of; how I must climb her window,
The ladder made of cords; and all the means
Plotted and 'greed on for my happiness.
Good Proteus, go with me to my chamber,
In these affairs to aid me with thy counsel.

PROTEUS.

Go on before; I shall inquire you forth:
I must unto the road, to disembark
Some necessaries that I needs must use;
And then I'll presently attend you.

VALENTINE.

Will you make haste?

PROTEUS.

I will. [*Exeunt* VALENTINE *and* SPEED.
Even as one heat another heat expels,
Or as one nail by strength drives out another,
So the remembrance of my former love
Is by a newer object quite forgotten.
Is it mine eye, or Valentinus' praise,
Her true perfection, or my false transgression,
That makes me, reasonless, to reason thus?
She's fair; and so is Julia, that I love,—
That I did love, for now my love is thaw'd;
Which, like a waxen image 'gainst a fire,
Bears no impression of the thing it was.
Methinks my zeal to Valentine is cold,
And that I love him not as I was wont:
O, but I love his lady too-too much;
And that's the reason I love him so little.
How shall I dote on her with more advice,
That thus without advice begin to love her!
'Tis but her picture I have yet beheld,
And that hath dazzled my reason's light;
But when I look on her perfections,
There is no reason but I shall be blind.
If I can check my erring love, I will;
If not, to compass her I'll use my skill. [*Exit.*

SCENE V.

The same. A street.

Enter SPEED *and* LAUNCE *severally.*

SPEED.

LAUNCE! by mine honesty, welcome to Padua!

LAUNCE.

Forswear not thyself, sweet youth; for I am not welcome. I reckon this always—that a man is never undone till he be hang'd; nor never welcome to a place till some certain shot be paid, and the hostess say, 'Welcome.'

SPEED.

Come on, you madcap, I'll to the alehouse with you presently; where, for one shot of five pence, thou shalt have five thousand welcomes. But, sirrah, how did thy master part with Madam Julia?

LAUNCE.

Marry, after they closed in earnest, they parted very fairly in jest.

SPEED.

But shall she marry him?

LAUNCE.

No.

SPEED.

How, then? shall he marry her?

LAUNCE.

No, neither.

SPEED.

What, are they broken?

LAUNCE.

No, they are both as whole as a fish.

SPEED.

Why, then, how stands the matter with them?

LAUNCE.

Marry, thus; when it stands well with him, it stands well with her.

SPEED.

What an ass art thou! I understand thee not.

LAUNCE.

What a block art thou, that thou canst not! My staff understands me.

SPEED.

What thou say'st?

LAUNCE.

Ay, and what I do too: look thee, I'll but lean, and my staff understands me.

SPEED.

It stands under thee, indeed.

LAUNCE.

Why, stand-under and under-stand is all one.

SPEED.

But tell me true, will't be a match?

LAUNCE.

Ask my dog: if he say ay, it will; if he say no, it will; if he shake his tail and say nothing, it will.

SPEED.

The conclusion is, then, that it will.

LAUNCE.

Thou shalt never get such a secret from me but by a parable.

SPEED.

'Tis well that I get it so. But, Launce, how say'st thou, that my master is become a notable lover?

LAUNCE.

I never knew him otherwise.

SPEED.

Than how?

LAUNCE.

A notable lubber, as thou reportest him to be.

SPEED.

Why, thou whoreson ass, thou mistakest me.

LAUNCE.

Why, fool, I meant not thee; I meant thy master.

SPEED.

I tell thee, my master is become a hot lover.

LAUNCE.

Why, I tell thee, I care not though he burn himself in love. If thou wilt, go with me to the alehouse; if not, thou art an Hebrew, a Jew, and not worth the name of a Christian.

SPEED.

Why?

LAUNCE.

Because thou hast not so much charity in thee as to go to the ale with a Christian. Wilt thou go?

SPEED.

At thy service.

[*Exeunt.*

SCENE VI.

The same. The DUKE'S *palace.*

Enter PROTEUS.

PROTEUS.

TO leave my Julia, shall I be forsworn;
To love fair Silvia, shall I be forsworn;
To wrong my friend, I shall be much forsworn;
And even that power, which gave me first my oath,
Provokes me to this threefold perjury:
Love bade me swear, and Love bids me forswear:
O sweet-suggesting Love, if thou hast sinn'd,
Teach me, thy tempted subject, to excuse it!
At first I did adore a twinkling star,
But now I worship a celestial sun:
Unheedful vows may heedfully be broken;
And he wants wit that wants resolved will
To learn his wit t'exchange the bad for better.
Fie, fie, unreverend tongue! to call her bad,
Whose sovereignty so oft thou hast preferr'd
With twenty thousand soul-confirming oaths.
I cannot leave to love, and yet I do;
But there I leave to love where I should love.
Julia I lose, and Valentine I lose:
If I keep them, I needs must lose myself;
If I lose them, thus find I by their loss,—
For Valentine, myself; for Julia, Silvia.
I to myself am dearer than a friend,
For love is still most precious in itself;
And Silvia—witness Heaven, that made her fair!—
Shows Julia but a swarthy Ethiop.
I will forget that Julia is alive,
Rememb'ring that my love to her is dead;
And Valentine I'll hold an enemy,
Aiming at Silvia as a sweeter friend.
I cannot now prove constant to myself,
Without some treachery used to Valentine.
This night he meaneth with a corded ladder
To climb celestial Silvia's chamber-window;
Myself in counsel his competitor:
Now presently I'll give her father notice
Of their disguising and pretended flight;
Who, all enraged, will banish Valentine,
For Thurio, he intends, shall wed his daughter:
But, Valentine being gone, I'll quickly cross,
By some sly trick, blunt Thurio's dull proceeding.
Love, lend me wings to make my purpose swift,
As thou hast lent me wit to plot this drift! [*Exit.*

SCENE VII.

Verona. JULIA'S *house.*

Enter JULIA *and* LUCETTA.

JULIA.

COUNSEL, Lucetta; gentle girl, assist me;
And, even in kind love, I do conjure thee,—
Who art the table wherein all my thoughts
Are visibly character'd and engraved,—
To lesson me; and tell me some good mean,
How, with my honour, I may undertake
A journey to my loving Proteus.

LUCETTA.

Alas, the way is wearisome and long!

JULIA.

A true-devoted pilgrim is not weary
To measure kingdoms with his feeble steps;
Much less shall she that hath Love's wings to fly,
And when the flight is made to one so dear,
Of such divine perfection, as Sir Proteus.

LUCETTA.

Better forbear till Proteus make return.

JULIA.

O, know'st thou not, his looks are my soul's food?
Pity the dearth that I have pined in,
By longing for that food so long a time,
Didst thou but know the inly touch of love,
Thou wouldst as soon go kindle fire with snow
As seek to quench the fire of love with words.

LUCETTA.

I do not seek to quench your love's hot fire,
But qualify the fire's extreme rage,
Lest it should burn above the bounds of reason.

JULIA.

The more thou damm'st it up, the more it burns:
The current that with gentle murmur glides,
Thou know'st, being stopp'd, impatiently doth rage;
But when his fair course is not hindered,
He makes sweet music with th'enamell'd stones,
Giving a gentle kiss to every sedge
He overtaketh in his pilgrimage;
And so by many winding nooks he strays,
With willing sport, to the wide ocean.
Then let me go, and hinder not my course:
I'll be as patient as a gentle stream,
And make a pastime of each weary step,
Till the last step have brought me to my love;
And there I'll rest, as, after much turmoil,
A blessed soul doth in Elysium.

LUCETTA.

But in what habit will you go along?

JULIA.

Not like a woman; for I would prevent
The loose encounters of lascivious men;
Gentle Lucetta, fit me with such weeds
As may beseem some well-reputed page.

LUCETTA.

Why, then, your ladyship must cut your hair.

JULIA.

No, girl; I'll knit it up in silken strings,
With twenty odd-conceited true-love knots:
To be fantastic may become a youth
Of greater time than I shall show to be.

LUCETTA.

What fashion, madam, shall I make your breeches?

JULIA.

That fits as well as—'Tell me, good my lord,
What compass will you wear your farthingale?'
Why, even what fashion thou best likest, Lucetta.

LUCETTA.

You must needs have them with a codpiece, madam.

JULIA.

Out, out, Lucetta! that will be ill-favour'd.

LUCETTA.

A round hose, madam, now's not worth a pin,
Unless you have a codpiece to stick pins on.

JULIA.

Lucetta, as thou lovest me, let me have
What thou think'st meet, and is most mannerly.
But tell me, wench, how will the world repute me
For undertaking so unstaid a journey?
I fear me, it will make me scandalized.

LUCETTA.

If you think so, then stay at home, and go not.

JULIA.

Nay, that I will not.

LUCETTA.

Then never dream on infamy, but go.
If Proteus like your journey when you come,
No matter who's displeased when you are gone:
I fear me, he will scarce be pleased withal.

JULIA.

That is the least, Lucetta, of my fear:
A thousand oaths, an ocean of his tears,
And instances of infinite of love,
Warrant me welcome to my Proteus.

LUCETTA.

All these are servants to deceitful men.

JULIA.

Base men, that use them to so base effect!
But truer stars did govern Proteus' birth:
His words are bonds, his oaths are oracles;
His love sincere, his thoughts immaculate;
His tears pure messengers sent from his heart;
His heart as far from fraud as heaven from earth.

LUCETTA.

Pray heaven he prove so, when you come to him!

JULIA.

Now, as thou lovest me, do him not that wrong,
To bear a hard opinion of his truth:
Only deserve my love by loving him;
And presently go with me to my chamber,
To take a note of what I stand in need of,
To furnish me upon my longing journey.
All that is mine I leave at thy dispose,
My goods, my lands, my reputation;
Only, in lieu thereof, dispatch me hence.
Come, answer not, but to it presently;
I am impatient of my tarriance. [*Exeunt.*

ACT III. SCENE I.

Milan. An ante-room in the DUKE'S *palace.*

Enter DUKE, THURIO, *and* PROTEUS.

DUKE OF MILAN.

SIR THURIO, give us leave, I pray, awhile;
We have some secrets to confer about.
[*Exit* THURIO.
Now, tell me, Proteus, what's your will with me?

PROTEUS.

My gracious lord, that which I would discover
The law of friendship bids me to conceal;
But when I call to mind your gracious favours
Done to me, undeserving as I am,
My duty pricks me on to utter that
Which else no worldly good should draw from me.
Know, worthy prince, Sir Valentine, my friend,
This night intends to steal away your daughter;
Myself am one made privy to the plot.
I know you have determined to bestow her
On Thurio, whom your gentle daughter hates;
And should she thus be stol'n away from you,
It would be much vexation to your age.
Thus, for my duty's sake, I rather chose
To cross my friend in his intended drift
Than, by concealing it, heap on your head
A pack of sorrows, which would press you down,
Being unprevented, to your timeless grave.

DUKE OF MILAN.

Proteus, I thank thee for thine honest care;
Which to requite, command me while I live.
This love of theirs myself have often seen,
Haply when they have judged me fast asleep;
And oftentimes have purposed to forbid
Sir Valentine her company and my court:
But, fearing lest my jealous aim might err,
And so, unworthily, disgrace the man,—
A rashness that I ever yet have shunn'd,—
I gave him gentle looks; thereby to find
That which thyself hast now disclosed to me.
And, that thou mayst perceive my fear of this,
Knowing that tender youth is soon suggested,
I nightly lodge her in an upper tower,
The key whereof myself have ever kept;
And thence she cannot be convey'd away.

PROTEUS.

Know, noble lord, they have devised a mean
How he her chamber-window will ascend,
And with a corded ladder fetch her down;
For which the youthful lover now is gone,
And this way comes he with it presently;
Where, if it please you, you may intercept him.
But, good my lord, do it so cunningly
That my discovery be not aimed at;
For love of you, not hate unto my friend,
Hath made me publisher of this pretence.

DUKE OF MILAN.

Upon mine honour, he shall never know
That I had any light from thee of this.

PROTEUS.

Adieu, my lord; Sir Valentine is coming. [*Exit.*

Enter VALENTINE.

DUKE OF MILAN.

Sir Valentine, whither away so fast?

VALENTINE.

Please it your grace, there is a messenger
That stays to bear my letters to my friends,
And I am going to deliver them.

DUKE OF MILAN.

Be they of much import?

VALENTINE.

The tenour of them doth but signify
My health, and happy being at your court.

DUKE OF MILAN.

Nay, then, no matter; stay with me awhile;
I am to break with thee of some affairs
That touch me near, wherein thou must be secret.
'Tis not unknown to thee that I have sought
To match my friend Sir Thurio to my daughter.

VALENTINE.

I know it well, my lord; and, sure, the match
Were rich and honourable; besides, the gentleman
Is full of virtue, bounty, worth, and qualities
Beseeming such a wife as your fair daughter:
Cannot your grace win her to fancy him?

DUKE OF MILAN.

No, trust me; she is peevish, sullen, froward,
Proud, disobedient, stubborn, lacking duty;

Neither regarding that she is my child,
Nor fearing me as if I were her father:
And, may I say to thee, this pride of hers,
Upon advice, hath drawn my love from her;
And, where I thought the remnant of mine age
Should have been cherish'd by her child-like duty,
I now am full resolved to take a wife,
And turn her out to who will take her in:
Then let her beauty be her wedding-dower;
For me and my possessions she esteems not.

VALENTINE.

What would your grace have me to do in this?

DUKE OF MILAN.

There is a lady of Verona here
Whom I affect; but she is nice and coy,
And naught esteems my aged eloquence:
Now, therefore, would I have thee to my tutor,—
For long agone I have forgot to court;
Besides, the fashion of the time is changed,—
How, and which way, I may bestow myself,
To be regarded in her sun-bright eye.

VALENTINE.

Win her with gifts, if she respect not words:
Dumb jewels often, in their silent kind,
More than quick words, do move a woman's mind.

DUKE OF MILAN.

But she did scorn a present that I sent her.

VALENTINE.

A woman sometimes scorns what best contents her:
Send her another; never give her o'er;
For scorn at first makes after-love the more.
If she do frown, 'tis not in hate of you,
But rather to beget more love in you:
If she do chide, 'tis not to have you gone;
For why the fools are mad, if left alone.
Take no repulse, whatever she doth say;
For 'get you gone,' she doth not mean 'away!'
Flatter and praise, commend, extol their graces;
Though ne'er so black, say they have angels' faces.
That man that hath a tongue, I say, is no man,
If with his tongue he cannot win a woman.

DUKE OF MILAN.

But she I mean is promised by her friends
Unto a youthful gentleman of worth;
And kept severely from resort of men,
That no man hath access by day to her.

VALENTINE.

Why, then, I would resort to her by night.

DUKE OF MILAN.

Ay, but the doors be lockt, and keys kept safe,
That no man hath recourse to her by night.

VALENTINE.

What lets but one may enter at her window?

DUKE OF MILAN.

Her chamber is aloft, far from the ground,
And built so shelving, that one cannot climb it
Without apparent hazard of his life.

VALENTINE.

Why, then, a ladder, quaintly made of cords,
To cast up, with a pair of anchoring hooks,
Would serve to scale another Hero's tower,
So bold Leander would adventure it.

DUKE OF MILAN.

Now, as thou art a gentleman of blood,
Advise me where I may have such a ladder.

VALENTINE.

When would you use it? pray, sir, tell me that.

DUKE OF MILAN.

This very night; for Love is like a child,
That longs for every thing that he can come by.

VALENTINE.

By seven o'clock I'll get you such a ladder.

DUKE OF MILAN.

But, hark thee; I will go to her alone:
How shall I best convey the ladder thither?

VALENTINE.

It will be light, my lord, that you may bear it
Under a cloak that is of any length.

DUKE OF MILAN.

A cloak as long as thine will serve the turn?

VALENTINE.

Ay, my good lord.

DUKE OF MILAN.

Then let me see thy cloak:
I'll get me one of such another length.

VALENTINE.

Why, any cloak will serve the turn, my lord.

DUKE OF MILAN.

How shall I fashion me to wear a cloak?—
I pray thee, let me feel thy cloak upon me.—
What letter is this same? What's here?—'*To Silvia*'!
And here an engine fit for my proceeding!
I'll be so bold to break the seal for once. [*Reads.*
'My thoughts do harbour with my Silvia nightly;
And slaves they are to me, that send them flying:
O, could their master come and go as lightly,
Himself would lodge where senseless they are lying!
My herald thoughts in thy pure bosom rest them;
While I, their king, that thither them importune,
Do curse the grace that with such grace hath blest them,
Because myself do want my servants' fortune:
I curse myself, for they are sent by me,
That they should harbour where their lord would be.'
What's here?
'Silvia, this night I will enfranchise thee.'
'Tis so; and here's the ladder for the purpose.
Why, Phaethon,—for thou art Merops' son,—
Wilt thou aspire to guide the heavenly car,
And with thy daring folly burn the world?
Wilt thou reach stars, because they shine on thee?
Go, base intruder! overweening slave!
Bestow thy fawning smiles on equal mates;
And think my patience, more than thy desert,
Is privilege for thy departure hence:
Thank me for this, more than for all the favours
Which, all too much, I have bestow'd on thee.
But if thou linger in my territories
Longer than swiftest expedition

Will give thee time to leave our royal court,
By heaven, my wrath shall far exceed the love
I ever bore my daughter or thyself.
Be gone! I will not hear thy vain excuse;
But, as thou lovest thy life, make speed from hence. [*Exit* DUKE.

VALENTINE.

And why not death, rather than living torment?
To die, is to be banish'd from myself;
And Silvia is myself: banish'd from her,
Is self from self,—a deadly banishment!
What light is light, if Silvia be not seen?
What joy is joy, if Silvia be not by?
Unless it be to think that she is by,
And feed upon the shadow of perfection.
Except I be by Silvia in the night,
There is no music in the nightingale;
Unless I look on Silvia in the day,
There is no day for me to look upon:
She is my essence; and I leave to be,
If I be not by her fair influence
Foster'd, illumined, cherish'd, kept alive.
I fly not death, to fly his deadly doom:
Tarry I here, I but attend on death;
But, fly I hence, I fly away from life.

Enter PROTEUS *and* LAUNCE.

PROTEUS.

Run, boy, run, run, and seek him out.

LAUNCE.

So-ho, so-ho!

PROTEUS.

What see'st thou?

LAUNCE.

Him we go to find: there's not a hair on's head but 'tis a Valentine.

PROTEUS.

Valentine!

VALENTINE.

No.

PROTEUS.

Who then? his spirit?

VALENTINE.

Neither.

PROTEUS.

What then?

VALENTINE.

Nothing.

LAUNCE.

Can nothing speak? Master, shall I strike?

PROTEUS.

Who wouldst thou strike?

LAUNCE.

Nothing.

PROTEUS.

Villain, forbear.

LAUNCE.

Why, sir, I'll strike nothing: I pray you,—

PROTEUS.

Sirrah, I say, forbear.—Friend Valentine, a word.

VALENTINE.

My ears are stopt, and cannot hear good news,
So much of bad already hath possest them.

PROTEUS.

Then in dumb silence will I bury mine,
For they are harsh, untuneable, and bad.

VALENTINE.

Is Silvia dead?

PROTEUS.

No, Valentine.

VALENTINE.

No Valentine, indeed, for sacred Silvia!—
Hath she forsworn me?

PROTEUS.

No, Valentine.

VALENTINE.

No Valentine, if Silvia have forsworn me!—
What is your news?

LAUNCE.

Sir, there is a proclamation that you are vanish'd.

PROTEUS.

That thou art banished—O, that's the news!—
From hence, from Silvia, and from me thy friend.

VALENTINE.

O, I have fed upon this woe already,
And now excess of it will make me surfeit.
Doth Silvia know that I am banished?

PROTEUS.

Ay, ay; and she hath offer'd to the doom—
Which, unreversed, stands in effectual force—
A sea of melting pearl, which some call tears;
Those at her father's churlish feet she tender'd;
With them, upon her knees, her humble self;
Wringing her hands, whose whiteness so became them
As if but now they waxed pale for woe:
But neither bended knees, pure hands held up,
Sad sighs, deep groans, nor silver-shedding tears,
Could penetrate her uncompassionate sire;
But Valentine, if he be ta'en, must die.
Besides, her intercession chafed him so,
When she for thy repeal was suppliant,
That to close prison he commanded her,
With many bitter threats of biding there.

VALENTINE.

No more; unless the next word that thou speak'st
Have some malignant power upon my life:
If so, I pray thee, breathe it in mine ear,
As ending anthem of my endless dolour.

PROTEUS.

Cease to lament for that thou canst not help,
And study help for that which thou lament'st.
Time is the nurse and breeder of all good.
Here if thou stay, thou canst not see thy love;
Besides, thy staying will abridge thy life.
Hope is a lover's staff; walk hence with that,
And manage it against despairing thoughts.
Thy letters may be here, though thou art hence;
Which, being writ to me, shall be deliver'd
Even in the milk-white bosom of thy love.
The time now serves not to expostulate:
Come, I'll convey thee through the city-gate;
And, ere I part with thee, confer at large
Of all that may concern thy love-affairs.
As thou lovest Silvia, though not for thyself,
Regard thy danger, and along with me.

VALENTINE.

I pray thee, Launce, an if thou see'st my boy,
Bid him make haste, and meet me at the north-gate.

PROTEUS.

Go, sirrah, find him out.—Come, Valentine.

VALENTINE.

O my dear Silvia!—Hapless Valentine!

[*Exeunt* VALENTINE *and* PROTEUS.

LAUNCE.

I am but a fool, look you; and yet I have the wit to think my master is a kind of a knave; but that's all one, if he be but one knave. He lives not now that knows me to be in love; yet I am in love; but a team of horse shall not pluck that from me; nor who 'tis I love; and yet 'tis a woman; but what woman, I will not tell myself; and yet 'tis a milk-maid; yet 'tis not a maid, for she hath had gossips; yet 'tis a maid, for she is her master's maid, and serves for wages. She hath more qualities than a water-spaniel,—which is much in a bare Christian. [*Pulling out a paper*.] Here is the cate-log of her conditions. [*Reads*] 'Imprimis, She can fetch and carry.' Why, a horse can do no more: nay, a horse cannot fetch, but only carry; therefore is she better than a jade. 'Item, She can milk;' look you, a sweet virtue in a maid with clean hands.

Enter SPEED.

SPEED.

How now, Signior Launce! what news with your mastership?

LAUNCE.

With my master's ship? why, it is at sea.

SPEED.

Well, your old vice still; mistake the word. What news, then, in your paper?

LAUNCE.

The black'st news that ever thou heard'st.

SPEED.

Why, man, how black?

LAUNCE.

Why, as black as ink.

SPEED.

Let me read them.

LAUNCE.

Fie on thee, jolt-head! thou canst not read.

SPEED.

Thou liest; I can.

LAUNCE.

I will try thee. Tell me this: who begot thee?

SPEED.

Marry, the son of my grandfather.

LAUNCE.

O illiterate loiterer! it was the son of thy grandmother: this proves that thou canst not read.

SPEED.

Come, fool, come; try me in thy paper.

LAUNCE.

There; and Saint Nicholas be thy speed!

SPEED [*reads*].

'Imprimis, She can milk.'

LAUNCE.

Ay, that she can.

SPEED.

'Item, She brews good ale.'

LAUNCE.

And thereof comes the proverb,—Blessing of your heart, you brew good ale.

SPEED.

'Item, She can sew.'

LAUNCE.

That's as much as to say, Can she so?

SPEED.

'Item, She can knit.'

LAUNCE.

What need a man care for a stock with a wench, when she can knit him a stock?

SPEED.

'Item, She can wash and scour.'

LAUNCE.

A special virtue; for then she need not be wash'd and scour'd.

SPEED.

'Item, She can spin.'

LAUNCE.

Then may I set the world on wheels, when she can spin for her living.

SPEED.

'Item, She hath many nameless virtues.'

LAUNCE.

That's as much as to say, bastard virtues; that, indeed, know not their fathers, and therefore have no names.

SPEED.

'Here follow her vices.'

LAUNCE.

Close at the heels of her virtues.

SPEED.

'Item, She is not to be kiss'd fasting, in respect of her breath.'

LAUNCE.

Well, that fault may be mended with a breakfast. Read on.

SPEED.

'Item, She hath a sweet mouth.'

LAUNCE.

That makes amends for her sour breath.

SPEED.

'Item, She doth talk in her sleep.'

LAUNCE.

It's no matter for that, so she sleep not in her talk.

SPEED.

'Item, She is slow in words.'

LAUNCE.

O villain, that set this down among her vices! To be slow in words is a woman's only virtue: I pray thee, out with't, and place it for her chief virtue.

SPEED.

'Item, She is proud.'

LAUNCE.

Out with that too; it was Eve's legacy, and cannot be ta'en from her.

SPEED.

'Item, She hath no teeth.'

LAUNCE.

I care not for that neither, because I love crusts.

SPEED.

'Item, she is curst.'

LAUNCE.

Well, the best is, she hath no teeth to bite.

SPEED.

'Item, She will often praise her liquor.'

LAUNCE.

If her liquor be good, she shall: if she will not, I will; for good things should be praised.

SPEED.

'Item, She is too liberal.'

LAUNCE.

Of her tongue she cannot, for that's writ down she is slow of; of her purse she shall not, for that I'll keep shut: now, of another thing she may, and that cannot I help. Well, proceed.

SPEED.

'Item, She hath more hair than wit, and more faults than hairs, and more wealth than faults.'

LAUNCE.

Stop there; I'll have her: she was mine, and not mine, twice or thrice in that last article. Rehearse that once more.

SPEED.

'Item, She hath more hair than wit,'—

LAUNCE.

More hair than wit,—it may be: I'll prove it. The cover of the salt hides the salt, and therefore it is more than the salt; the hair that covers the wit is more than the wit, for the greater hides the less. What's next?

SPEED.

'And more faults than hairs,'—

LAUNCE.

That's monstrous: O, that that were out!

SPEED.

'And more wealth than faults.'

LAUNCE.

Why, that word makes the faults gracious. Well, I'll have her: and if it be a match, as nothing is impossible,—

SPEED.

What then?

LAUNCE.

Why, then will I tell thee—that thy master stays for thee at the north-gate.

SPEED.

For me!

LAUNCE.

For thee! ay; who art thou? he hath stay'd for a better man than thee.

SPEED.

And must I go to him?

LAUNCE.

Thou must run to him, for thou hast stay'd so long, that going will scarce serve the turn.

SPEED.

Why didst not tell me sooner? pox of your love-letters! [*Exit.*

LAUNCE.

Now will he be swinged for reading my letter,—an unmannerly slave, that will thrust himself into secrets! I'll after, to rejoice in the boy's correction. [*Exit.*

SCENE II.

The same. The DUKE'S *palace.*

Enter DUKE *and* THURIO.

DUKE OF MILAN.

Sir Thurio, fear not but that she will love you,
Now Valentine is banish'd from her sight.

THURIO.

Since his exile she hath despised me most,
Forsworn my company, and rail'd at me,
That I am desperate of obtaining her.

DUKE OF MILAN.

This weak impress of love is as a figure
Trenched in ice, which with an hour's heat
Dissolves to water, and doth lose his form.
A little time will melt her frozen thoughts,
And worthless Valentine shall be forgot.

Enter PROTEUS.

How now, Sir Proteus! Is your countryman,
According to our proclamation, gone?

PROTEUS.

Gone, my good lord.

DUKE OF MILAN.

My daughter takes his going grievously.

PROTEUS.

A little time, my lord, will kill that grief.

DUKE OF MILAN.

So I believe; but Thurio thinks not so.
Proteus, the good conceit I hold of thee—
For thou hast shown some sign of good desert—
Makes me the better to confer with thee.

PROTEUS.

Longer than I prove loyal to your grace
Let me not live to look upon your grace.

DUKE OF MILAN.

Thou know'st how willingly I would effect
The match between Sir Thurio and my daughter?

PROTEUS.

I do, my lord.

DUKE OF MILAN.

And also, I think, thou art not ignorant
How she opposes her against my will.

PROTEUS.

She did, my lord, when Valentine was here.

DUKE OF MILAN.

Ay, and perversely she persevers so.
What might we do to make the girl forget
The love of Valentine, and love Sir Thurio?

PROTEUS.

The best way is to slander Valentine
With falsehood, cowardice, and poor descent,—
Three things that women highly hold in hate.

DUKE OF MILAN.

Ay, but she'll think that it is spoke in hate.

PROTEUS.

Ay, if his enemy deliver it:
Therefore it must with circumstance be spoken
By one whom she esteemeth as his friend.

DUKE OF MILAN.

Then you must undertake to slander him.

PROTEUS.

And that, my lord, I shall be loth to do:
'Tis an ill office for a gentleman,
Especially against his very friend.

DUKE OF MILAN.

Where your good word cannot advantage him,
Your slander never can endamage him;
Therefore the office is indifferent,
Being entreated to it by your friend.

PROTEUS.

You have prevail'd, my lord: if I can do it
By aught that I can speak in his dispraise,
She shall not long continue love to him.
But say this weed her love from Valentine,
It follows not that she will love Sir Thurio.

THURIO.

Therefore, as you unwind her love from him,

Lest it should ravel and be good to none,
You must provide to bottom it on me;
Which must be done by praising me as much
As you in worth dispraise Sir Valentine.

DUKE OF MILAN.

And, Proteus, we dare trust you in this kind,
Because we know, on Valentine's report,
You are already Love's firm votary,
And cannot soon revolt and change your mind.
Upon this warrant shall you have access
Where you with Silvia may confer at large;
For she is lumpish, heavy, melancholy,
And, for your friend's sake, will be glad of you;
Where you may temper her, by your persuasion,
To hate young Valentine, and love my friend.

PROTEUS.

As much as I can do, I will effect:—
But you, Sir Thurio, are not sharp enough;
You must lay lime to tangle her desires
By wailful sonnets, whose composed rhymes
Should be full-fraught with serviceable vows.

DUKE OF MILAN.

Ay,
Much is the force of heaven-bred poesy.

PROTEUS.

Say, that upon the altar of her beauty
You sacrifice your tears, your sighs, your heart:
Write till your ink be dry, and with your tears
Moist it again, and frame some feeling line
That may discover such integrity:
For Orpheus' lute was strung with poets' sinews;
Whose golden touch could soften steel and stones,
Make tigers tame, and huge leviathans
Forsake unsounded deeps to dance on sands.
After your dire-lamenting elegies,
Visit by night your lady's chamber-window
With some sweet consort; to their instruments
Tune a deploring dump: the night's dead silence
Will well become such sweet-complaining grievance.
This, or else nothing, will inherit her.

DUKE OF MILAN.

This discipline shows thou hast been in love.

THURIO.

And thy advice this night I'll put in practice.
Therefore, sweet Proteus, my direction-giver,
Let us into the city presently
To sort some gentlemen well skill'd in music:
I have a sonnet that will serve the turn
To give the onset to thy good advice.

DUKE OF MILAN.

About it, gentlemen.

PROTEUS.

We'll wait upon your grace till after supper,
And afterward determine our proceedings.

DUKE OF MILAN.

Even now about it; I will pardon you. [*Exeunt.*

ACT IV. SCENE I.

A forest.

Enter certain OUTLAWS.

FIRST OUTLAW.

FELLOWS, stand fast; I see a passenger.

SECOND OUTLAW.

If there be ten, shrink not, but down with 'em.

Enter VALENTINE *and* SPEED.

THIRD OUTLAW.

Stand, sir, and throw us that you have about ye:
If not, we'll make you sit, and rifle you.

SPEED.

Sir, we are undone! these are the villains
That all the travellers do fear so much.

VALENTINE.

My friends,—

FIRST OUTLAW.

That's not so, sir,—we are your enemies.

SECOND OUTLAW.

Peace! we'll hear him.

THIRD OUTLAW.

Ay, by my beard, will we; for he is a proper man.

VALENTINE.

Then know that I have little wealth to lose;
A man I am cross'd with adversity:
My riches are these poor habiliments,
Of which if you should here disfurnish me,
You take the sum and substance that I have.

SECOND OUTLAW.

Whither travel you?

VALENTINE.

To Verona.

FIRST OUTLAW.

Whence came you?

VALENTINE.

From Milan.

THIRD OUTLAW.

Have you long sojourn'd there?

VALENTINE.

Some sixteen months; and longer might have stay'd,
If crooked fortune had not thwarted me.

FIRST OUTLAW.

What, were you banish'd thence?

VALENTINE.

I was.

SECOND OUTLAW.

For what offence?

VALENTINE.

For that which now torments me to rehearse:
I kill'd a man, whose death I much repent;
But yet I slew him manfully in fight,
Without false vantage or base treachery.

FIRST OUTLAW.

Why, ne'er repent it, if it were done so.
But were you banish'd for so small a fault?

VALENTINE.

I was, and held me glad of such a doom.

SECOND OUTLAW.

Have you the tongues?

VALENTINE.

My youthful travel therein made me happy,
Or else I often had been miserable.

THIRD OUTLAW.

By the bare scalp of Robin Hood's fat friar
This fellow were a king for our wild faction!

FIRST OUTLAW.

We'll have him:—sirs, a word.

SPEED.

Master, be one of them; it's an honourable kind of thievery.

VALENTINE.

Peace, villain!

SECOND OUTLAW.
Tell us this: have you any thing to take to?

VALENTINE.
Nothing but my fortune.

THIRD OUTLAW.
Know, then, that some of us are gentlemen,
Such as the fury of ungovern'd youth
Thrust from the company of awful men:
Myself was from Verona banished
For practising to steal away a lady,
An heir, and near allied unto the duke.

SECOND OUTLAW.
And I from Mantua, for a gentleman,
Who, in my mood, I stabb'd unto the heart.

FIRST OUTLAW.
And I for such-like petty crimes as these.
But to the purpose,—for we cite our faults,
That they may hold excused our lawless lives;
And partly, seeing you are beautified
With goodly shape, and by your own report
A linguist, and a man of such perfection
As we do in our quality much want,—

SECOND OUTLAW.
Indeed, because you are a banish'd man,
Therefore, above the rest, we parley to you:
Are you content to be our general?
To make a virtue of necessity,
And live, as we do, in this wilderness?

THIRD OUTLAW.
What say'st thou? wilt thou be of our consort?
Say ay, and be the captain of us all:
We'll do thee homage and be ruled by thee,
Love thee as our commander and our king.

FIRST OUTLAW.
But if thou scorn our courtesy, thou diest.

SECOND OUTLAW.
Thou shalt not live to brag what we have offer'd.

VALENTINE.
I take your offer, and will live with you,
Provided that you do no outrages
On silly women or poor passengers.

THIRD OUTLAW.
No, we detest such vile base practices.
Come, go with us, we'll bring thee to our crews,
And show thee all the treasure we have got;
Which, with ourselves, all rest at thy dispose.
[*Exeunt.*

SCENE II.

Milan. The court of the DUKE'S *palace.*

Enter PROTEUS.

PROTEUS.
ALREADY have I been false to Valentine,
And now I must be as unjust to Thurio.
Under the colour of commending him,
I have access my own love to prefer:
But Silvia is too fair, too true, too holy,
To be corrupted with my worthless gifts.
When I protest true loyalty to her,
She twits me with my falsehood to my friend;
When to her beauty I commend my vows,
She bids me think how I have been forsworn
In breaking faith with Julia whom I loved:
And notwithstanding all her sudden quips,
The least whereof would quell a lover's hope,
Yet, spaniel-like, the more she spurns my love,
The more it grows, and fawneth on her still.
But here comes Thurio: now must we to her window,
And give some evening music to her ear.

Enter THURIO *and* MUSICIANS.

THURIO.
How now, Sir Proteus! are you crept before us?

PROTEUS.
Ay, gentle Thurio; for you know that love
Will creep in service where it cannot go.

THURIO.
Ay, but I hope, sir, that you love not here.

PROTEUS.
Sir, but I do; or else I would be hence.

THURIO.
Who? Silvia?

PROTEUS.
Ay, Silvia,—for your sake.

THURIO.
I thank you for your own.—Now, gentlemen,
Let's tune, and to it lustily awhile.

Enter, at a distance, HOST, *and* JULIA *in boy's clothes.*

HOST.
Now, my young guest,—methinks you're allicholy: I pray you, why is it?

JULIA.
Marry, mine host, because I cannot be merry.

HOST.
Come, we'll have you merry: I'll bring you where you shall hear music, and see the gentleman that you ask'd for.

JULIA.
But shall I hear him speak?

HOST.
Ay, that you shall.

JULIA.
That will be music.
[*Music plays.*

HOST.
Hark, hark!

JULIA.
Is he among these?

HOST.
Ay: but, peace! let's hear 'em.

Song.

Who is Silvia? what is she,
  That all our swains commend her?
Holy, fair, and wise is she;
  The heaven such grace did lend her,
That she might admired be.

Is she kind as she is fair,—
  For beauty lives with kindness?
Love doth to her eyes repair,
  To help him of his blindness;
And, being help'd, inhabits there.

Then to Silvia let us sing,
  That Silvia is excelling;
She excels each mortal thing
  Upon the dull earth dwelling:
To her let us garlands bring.

HOST.

How now! are you sadder than you were before? How do you, man? the music likes you not.

JULIA.

You mistake; the musician likes me not.

HOST.

Why, my pretty youth?

JULIA.

He plays false, father.

HOST.

How? out of tune on the strings?

JULIA.

Not so; but yet so false that he grieves my very heart-strings.

HOST.

You have a quick ear.

JULIA.

Ay, I would I were deaf; it makes me have a slow heart.

HOST.

I perceive you delight not in music.

JULIA.

Not a whit, when it jars so.

HOST.

Hark, what fine change is in the music!

JULIA.

Ay, that change is the spite.

HOST.

You would have them always play but one thing?

JULIA.

I would always have one play but one thing.
But, host, doth this Sir Proteus that we talk on
Often resort unto this gentlewoman?

HOST.

I tell you what Launce, his man, told me,—he loved her out of all nick.

JULIA.

Where is Launce?

HOST.

Gone to seek his dog; which to-morrow, by his master's command, he must carry for a present to his lady.

JULIA.

Peace! stand aside: the company parts.

PROTEUS.

Sir Thurio, fear not you: I will so plead,
That you shall say my cunning drift excels.

THURIO.

Where meet we?

PROTEUS.

At Saint Gregory's well.

THURIO.

Farewell.

[*Exeunt* THURIO *and* MUSICIANS.

SILVIA *appears above, at her window.*

PROTEUS.

Madam, good even to your ladyship.

SILVIA.

I thank you for your music, gentlemen.
Who is that that spake?

PROTEUS.

One, lady, if you knew his pure heart's truth,
You would quickly learn to know him by his voice.

SILVIA.

Sir Proteus, as I take it.

PROTEUS.

Sir Proteus, gentle lady, and your servant.

SILVIA.

What is your will?

PROTEUS.

That I may compass yours.

SILVIA.

You have your wish; my will is even this,—
That presently you hie you home to bed.
Thou subtle, perjured, false, disloyal man!
Think'st thou I am so shallow, so conceitless,
To be seduced by thy flattery,
That hast deceived so many with thy vows?
Return, return, and make thy love amends.
For me,—by this pale queen of night I swear,
I am so far from granting thy request,
That I despise thee for thy wrongful suit;
And by and by intend to chide myself
Even for this time I spend in talking to thee.

PROTEUS.

I grant, sweet love, that I did love a lady;
But she is dead.

JULIA [*aside*].

'Twere false, if I should speak it;
For I am sure she is not buried.

SILVIA.

Say that she be; yet Valentine thy friend
Survives; to whom, thyself art witness,
I am betroth'd: and art thou not ashamed
To wrong him with thy importunacy?

PROTEUS.

I likewise hear that Valentine is dead.

SILVIA.

And so suppose am I; for in his grave
Assure thyself my love is buried.

PROTEUS.

Sweet lady, let me rake it from the earth.

SILVIA.

Go to thy lady's grave, and call hers thence;
Or, at the least, in hers sepulchre thine.

JULIA [*aside*].

He heard not that.

PROTEUS.

Madam, if your heart be so obdurate,
Vouchsafe me yet your picture for my love,
The picture that is hanging in your chamber;
To that I'll speak, to that I'll sigh and weep:
For since the substance of your perfect self
Is else devoted, I am but a shadow;
And to your shadow will I make true love.

JULIA [*aside*].

If 'twere a substance, you would, sure, deceive it,
And make it but a shadow, as I am.

SILVIA.

I am very loth to be your idol, sir;
But since your falsehood shall become you well
To worship shadows and adore false shapes,
Send to me in the morning, and I'll send it:
And so good rest.

PROTEUS.

As wretches have o'ernight
That wait for execution in the morn.

[*Exeunt* PROTEUS, *and* SILVIA *above.*

JULIA.

Host, will you go?

HOST.
By my halidom, I was fast asleep.

JULIA.
Pray you, where lies Sir Proteus?

HOST.
Marry, at my house. Trust me, I think 'tis almost day.

JULIA.
Not so; but it hath been the longest night
That e'er I watch'd, and the most heaviest.
[*Exeunt.*

SCENE III.

The same.

Enter EGLAMOUR.

EGLAMOUR.
THIS is the hour that Madam Silvia
Entreated me to call and know her mind:
There's some great matter she'ld employ me in.—
Madam, madam!

SILVIA *above, at her window.*

SILVIA.
Who calls?

EGLAMOUR.
Your servant and your friend;
One that attends your ladyship's command.

SILVIA.
Sir Eglamour, a thousand times good morrow.

EGLAMOUR.
As many, worthy lady, to yourself.
According to your ladyship's impose,
I am thus early come to know what service
It is your pleasure to command me in.

SILVIA.
O Eglamour, thou art a gentleman,
(Think not I flatter, for I swear I do not)
Valiant, wise, remorseful, well accomplish'd:
Thou art not ignorant what dear good will
I bear unto the banish'd Valentine;
Nor how my father would enforce me marry
Vain Thurio, whom my very soul abhors.
Thyself hast loved; and I have heard thee say
No grief did ever come so near thy heart
As when thy lady and thy true love died,
Upon whose grave thou vow'dst pure chastity.
Sir Eglamour, I would to Valentine,
To Mantua, where I hear he makes abode;
And, for the ways are dangerous to pass,
I do desire thy worthy company,
Upon whose faith and honour I repose.
Urge not my father's anger, Eglamour,
But think upon my grief,—a lady's grief,—
And on the justice of my flying hence,
To keep me from a most unholy match,
Which heaven and fortune still rewards with plagues.
I do desire thee, even from a heart
As full of sorrows as the sea of sands,
To bear me company, and go with me:
If not, to hide what I have said to thee,
That I may venture to depart alone.

EGLAMOUR.
Madam, I pity much your grievances;
Which since I know they virtuously are placed,
I give consent to go along with you;
Recking as little what betideth me
As much I wish all good befortune you.
When will you go?

SILVIA.
This evening coming.

EGLAMOUR.
Where shall I meet you?

SILVIA.
At Friar Patrick's cell,
Where I intend holy confession.

EGLAMOUR.
I will not fail your ladyship. Good morrow,
Gentle lady.

SILVIA.
Good morrow, kind Sir Eglamour.
[*Exeunt* EGLAMOUR, *and* SILVIA *above.*

SCENE IV.

The same.

Enter LAUNCE, *with his Dog.*

LAUNCE.
WHEN a man's servant shall play the cur with him, look you, it goes hard: one that I brought up of a puppy; one that I saved from drowning, when three or four of his blind brothers and sisters went to it! I have taught him, even as one would say precisely, 'Thus I would teach a dog.' I was sent to deliver him as a present to Mistress Silvia from my master; and I came no sooner into the dining-chamber, but he steps me to her trencher, and steals her capon's leg: O, 'tis a foul thing when a cur cannot keep himself in all companies! I would have, as one should say, one that takes upon him to be a dog indeed, to be, as it were, a dog at all things. If I had not had more wit than he, to take a fault upon me that he did, I think verily he had been hang'd for't; sure as I live, he had suffer'd for't: you shall judge. He thrusts me himself into the company of three or four gentlemanlike dogs, under the duke's table: he had not been there (bless the mark!) a pissing while, but all the chamber smelt him. 'Out with the dog,' says one; 'What cur is that?' says another; 'Whip him out,' says the third; 'Hang him up,' says the duke. I, having been acquainted with the smell before, knew it was Crab; and goes me to the fellow that whips the dogs: 'Friend,' quoth I, 'you mean to whip the dog?' 'Ay, marry, do I,' quoth he. 'You do him the more wrong,' quoth I; ''twas I did the thing you wot of.' He makes me no more ado, but whips me out of the chamber. How many masters would do this for his servant? Nay, I'll be sworn, I have sat in the stocks for puddings he hath stolen, otherwise he had been executed; I have stood on the pillory for geese he hath kill'd, otherwise he had suffer'd for't.—Thou think'st not of this now! Nay, I remember the trick you served me when I took my leave of Madam Silvia; did not I bid thee still mark me, and do as I do? when didst thou see me heave up my leg, and make water against a gentlewoman's farthingale? didst thou ever see me do such a trick?

Enter PROTEUS, *and* JULIA *in boy's clothes.*

PROTEUS.

Sebastian is thy name? I like thee well,
And will employ thee in some service presently.

JULIA.

In what you please: I will do what I can.

PROTEUS.

I hope thou wilt.—How now, you whoreson peasant!
Where have you been these two days loitering?

LAUNCE.

Marry, sir, I carried Mistress Silvia the dog you bade me.

PROTEUS.

And what says she to my little jewel?

LAUNCE.

Marry, she says your dog was a cur, and tells you currish thanks is good enough for such a present.

PROTEUS.

But she received my dog?

LAUNCE.

No, indeed, did she not: here have I brought him back again.

PROTEUS.

What, didst thou offer her this from me?

LAUNCE.

Ay, sir; the other squirrel was stolen from me by the hangman boys in the market-place: and then I offer'd her mine own,—who is a dog as big as ten of yours, and therefore the gift the greater.

PROTEUS.

Go get thee hence, and find my dog again,
Or ne'er return again into my sight.
Away, I say! stay'st thou to vex me here?
A slave, that still an end turns me to shame!
[*Exit* LAUNCE.
Sebastian, I have entertained thee,
Partly that I have need of such a youth,
That can with some discretion do my business,
For 'tis no trusting to yond foolish lout;
But chiefly for thy face and thy behaviour,
Which—if my augury deceive me not—
Witness good bringing up, fortune, and truth:
Therefore know thou, for this I entertain thee.
Go presently, and take this ring with thee,
Deliver it to Madam Silvia:
She loved me well deliver'd it to me.

JULIA.

It seems you loved not her, to leave her token.
She is dead, belike?

PROTEUS.

Not so; I think she lives.

JULIA.

Alas!

PROTEUS.

Why dost thou cry, 'Alas'?

JULIA.

I cannot choose
But pity her.

PROTEUS.

Wherefore shouldst thou pity her?

JULIA.

Because methinks that she loved you as well
As you do love your lady Silvia:
She dreams on him that has forgot her love;
You dote on her that cares not for your love.
'Tis pity love should be so contrary;
And thinking on it makes me cry, 'Alas!'

PROTEUS.

Well: give her that ring, and therewithal
This letter:—that's her chamber:—tell my lady
I claim the promise for her heavenly picture.
Your message done, hie home unto my chamber,
Where thou shalt find me, sad and solitary. [*Exit.*

JULIA.

How many women would do such a message?
Alas, poor Proteus! thou hast entertain'd
A fox to be the shepherd of thy lambs:—
Alas, poor fool! why do I pity him,
That with his very heart despiseth me?
Because he loves her, he despiseth me;
Because I love him, I must pity him.
This ring I gave him when he parted from me,
To bind him to remember my good will:
And now am I—unhappy messenger—
To plead for that which I would not obtain;
To carry that which I would have refused;
To praise his faith which I would have dispraised.
I am my master's true-confirmed love;
But cannot be true servant to my master,
Unless I prove false traitor to myself.
Yet will I woo for him; but yet so coldly
As, heaven it knows, I would not have him speed.

Enter SILVIA, *attended.*

Gentlewoman, good day! I pray you, be my mean
To bring me where to speak with Madam Silvia.

SILVIA.

What would you with her, if that I be she?

JULIA.

If you be she, I do entreat your patience
To hear me speak the message I am sent on.

SILVIA.

From whom?

JULIA.

From my master, Sir Proteus, madam.

SILVIA.

O,—he sends you for a picture?

JULIA.

Ay, madam.

SILVIA.

Ursula, bring my picture there.—
Go give your master this: tell him, from me,
One Julia, that his changing thoughts forget,
Would better fit his chamber than this shadow.

JULIA.

Madam, please you peruse this letter:—
Pardon me, madam; I have unadvised
Deliver'd you a paper that I should not:
This is the letter to your ladyship.

SILVIA.

I pray thee, let me look on that again.

JULIA.

It may not be; good madam, pardon me.

SILVIA.

There, hold:—
I will not look upon your master's lines:
I know they are stuft with protestations,
And full of new-found oaths; which he will break
As easily as I do tear his paper.

JULIA.

Madam, he sends your ladyship this ring.

SILVIA.
The more shame for him that he sends it me;
For I have heard him say a thousand times
His Julia gave it him at his departure.
Though his false finger have profaned the ring,
Mine shall not do his Julia so much wrong.

JULIA.
She thanks you.

SILVIA.
What say'st thou?

JULIA.
I thank you, madam, that you tender her.
Poor gentlewoman! my master wrongs her much.

SILVIA.
Dost thou know her?

JULIA.
Almost as well as I do know myself:
To think upon her woes I do protest
That I have wept a hundred several times.

SILVIA.
Belike she thinks that Proteus hath forsook her.

JULIA.
I think she doth; and that's her cause of sorrow.

SILVIA.
Is she not passing fair?

JULIA.
She hath been fairer, madam, than she is:
When she did think my master loved her well,
She, in my judgment, was as fair as you;
But since she did neglect her looking-glass,
And threw her sun-expelling mask away,
The air hath starved the roses in her cheeks,
And pinch'd the lily-tincture of her face,
That now she is become as black as I.

SILVIA.
How tall was she?

JULIA.
About my stature: for, at Pentecost,
When all our pageants of delight were play'd,
Our youth got me to play the woman's part,
And I was trimm'd in Madam Julia's gown;
Which served me as fit, by all men's judgments,
As if the garment had been made for me:
Therefore I know she is about my height.
And at that time I made her weep a-good,
For I did play a lamentable part;
Madam, 'twas Ariadne, passioning
For Theseus' perjury and unjust flight;
Which I so lively acted with my tears,
That my poor mistress, moved therewithal,
Wept bitterly; and, would I might be dead,
If I in thought felt not her very sorrow!

SILVIA.
She is beholding to thee, gentle youth.
Alas, poor lady, desolate and left!
I weep myself to think upon thy words.
Here, youth, there is my purse: I give thee this
For thy sweet mistress' sake, because thou lovest
her.
Farewell.

JULIA.
And she shall thank you for't, if e'er you know
her. [*Exit* SILVIA, *attended.*
A virtuous gentlewoman, mild and beautiful!
I hope my master's suit will be but cold,
Since she respects my mistress' love so much.
Alas, how love can trifle with itself!
Here is her picture: let me see; I think,
If I had such a tire, this face of mine
Were full as lovely as is this of hers:
And yet the painter flatter'd her a little,
Unless I flatter with myself too much.
Her hair is auburn, mine is perfect yellow:
If that be all the difference in his love,
I'll get me such a colour'd periwig.
Her eyes are grey as glass; and so are mine:
Ay, but her forehead's low, and mine's as high.
What should it be that he respects in her,
But I can make respective in myself,
If this fond Love were not a blinded god?
Come, shadow, come, and take this shadow up,
For 'tis thy rival. O thou senseless form,
Thou shalt be worshipp'd, kiss'd, loved and
adored!
And, were there sense in his idolatry,
My substance should be statue in thy stead.
I'll use thee kindly for thy mistress' sake,
That used me so; or else, by Jove I vow,
I should have scratch'd out your unseeing eyes,
To make my master out of love with thee! [*Exit.*

ACT V. SCENE I.

Milan. An abbey.

Enter EGLAMOUR.

EGLAMOUR.
THE sun begins to gild the western sky;
And now it is about the very hour
That Silvia, at Friar Patrick's cell, should meet
me.
She will not fail; for lovers break not hours,
Unless it be to come before their time;
So much they spur their expedition.
See where she comes.

Enter SILVIA.

Lady, a happy evening!

SILVIA.
Amen, amen! Go on, good Eglamour,
Out at the postern by the abbey-wall:
I fear I am attended by some spies.

EGLAMOUR.
Fear not: the forest is not three leagues off;
If we recover that, we are sure enough. [*Exeunt.*

SCENE II.

The same. The DUKE'S *palace.*

Enter THURIO, PROTEUS, *and* JULIA *in boy's clothes.*

THURIO.
SIR PROTEUS, what says Silvia to my suit?

PROTEUS.
O, sir, I find her milder than she was;
And yet she takes exceptions at your person.

THURIO.
What, that my leg is too long?

PROTEUS.
No; that it is too little.

THURIO.
I'll wear a boot, to make it somewhat rounder.

JULIA [*aside*].
But love will not be spurr'd to what it loathes.

THURIO.
What says she to my face?

PROTEUS.
She says it is a fair one.

THURIO.
Nay, then, the wanton lies; my face is black.

PROTEUS.
But pearls are fair; and the old saying is,
Black men are pearls in beauteous ladies' eyes.

JULIA [*aside*].
'Tis true, such pearls as put out ladies' eyes;
For I had rather wink than look on them.

THURIO.
How likes she my discourse?

PROTEUS.
Ill, when you talk of war.

THURIO.
But well, when I discourse of love and peace?

JULIA [*aside*].
But better, indeed, when you hold your peace.

THURIO.
What says she to my valour?

PROTEUS.
O, sir, she makes no doubt of that.

JULIA [*aside*].
She needs not, when she knows it cowardice.

THURIO.
What says she to my birth?

PROTEUS.
That you are well derived.

JULIA [*aside*].
True; from a gentleman to a fool.

THURIO.
Considers she my possessions?

PROTEUS.
O, ay; and pities them.

THURIO.
Wherefore?

JULIA [*aside*].
That such an ass should owe them.

PROTEUS.
That they are out by lease.

JULIA.
Here comes the duke.

Enter DUKE OF MILAN.

DUKE OF MILAN.
How now, Sir Proteus! how now, Thurio!
Which of you saw Sir Eglamour of late?

THURIO.
Not I.

PROTEUS.
Nor I.

DUKE OF MILAN.
Saw you my daughter?

PROTEUS.
Neither.

DUKE OF MILAN.
Why, then,
She's fled unto that peasant Valentine;
And Eglamour is in her company.
'Tis true; for Friar Laurence met them both,
As he in penance wander'd through the forest:
Him he knew well; and guess'd that it was she,
But, being mask'd, he was not sure of it:
Besides, she did intend confession
At Patrick's cell this even; and there she was not:
These likelihoods confirm her flight from hence.
Therefore, I pray you, stand not to discourse,
But mount you presently; and meet with me
Upon the rising of the mountain-foot
That leads toward Mantua, whither they are fled:
Dispatch, sweet gentlemen, and follow me. [*Exit.*

THURIO.
Why, this it is to be a peevish girl,
That flies her fortune when it follows her.
I'll after, more to be revenged on Eglamour
Than for the love of reckless Silvia. [*Exit.*

PROTEUS.
And I will follow, more for Silvia's love
Than hate of Eglamour, that goes with her. [*Exit.*

JULIA.
And I will follow, more to cross that love
Than hate for Silvia, that is gone for love. [*Exit.*

SCENE III.

The forest.

Enter OUTLAWS *with* SILVIA.

FIRST OUTLAW.
COME, come;
Be patient; we must bring you to our captain.

SILVIA.
A thousand more mischances than this one
Have learn'd me how to brook this patiently.

SECOND OUTLAW.
Come, bring her away.

FIRST OUTLAW.
Where is the gentleman that was with her?

THIRD OUTLAW.
Being nimble-footed, he hath outrun us,
But Moyses and Valerius follow him.
Go thou with her to the west end of the wood;
There is our captain: we'll follow him that's fled;
The thicket is beset, he cannot scape.

FIRST OUTLAW.
Come, I must bring you to our captain's cave:
Fear not; he bears an honourable mind,
And will not use a woman lawlessly.

SILVIA.
O Valentine, this I endure for thee! [*Exeunt.*

SCENE IV.

Another part of the forest.

Enter VALENTINE.

VALENTINE.
HOW use doth breed a habit in a man!
This shadowy desert, unfrequented woods,
I better brook than flourishing peopled towns:
Here can I sit alone, unseen of any,
And to the nightingale's complaining notes
Tune my distresses and record my woes.
O thou that dost inhabit in my breast,
Leave not the mansion so long tenantless,
Lest, growing ruinous, the building fall,
And leave no memory of what it was!
Repair me with thy presence, Silvia!
Thou gentle nymph, cherish thy forlorn swain!
[*Noise within.*

What halloing and what stir is this to-day?
These are my mates, that make their wills their law,
Have some unhappy passenger in chase:
They love me well; yet I have much to do
To keep them from uncivil outrages.—
Withdraw thee, Valentine: who's this comes here?
[*Retires.*

Enter PROTEUS, SILVIA, *and* JULIA *in boy's clothes.*

PROTEUS.

Madam, this service I have done for you,—
Though you respect not aught your servant doth,—
To hazard life, and rescue you from him
That would have forced your honour and your love:
Vouchsafe me, for my meed, but one fair look;
A smaller boon than this I cannot beg,
And less than this, I am sure, you cannot give.

VALENTINE [*aside*].

How like a dream is this I see and hear!
Love, lend me patience to forbear awhile.

SILVIA.

O miserable, unhappy that I am!

PROTEUS.

Unhappy were you, madam, ere I came;
But by my coming I have made you happy.

SILVIA.

By thy approach thou makest me most unhappy.

JULIA [*aside*].

And me, when he approacheth to your presence.

SILVIA.

Had I been seized by a hungry lion,
I would have been a breakfast to the beast,
Rather than have false Proteus rescue me.
O, Heaven be judge how I love Valentine,
Whose life's as tender to me as my soul;
And full as much—for more there cannot be—
I do detest false perjured Proteus!
Therefore be gone, solicit me no more.

PROTEUS.

What dangerous action, stood it next to death,
Would I not undergo for one calm look.
O, 'tis the curse in love, and still approved,
When women cannot love where they're beloved!

SILVIA.

When Proteus cannot love where he's beloved.
Read over Julia's heart, thy first best love,
For whose dear sake thou didst then rend thy faith
Into a thousand oaths; and all those oaths
Descended into perjury, to love me.
Thou hast no faith left now, unless thou'dst two,
And that's far worse than none; better have none
Than plural faith, which is too much by one:
Thou counterfeit to thy true friend!

PROTEUS.

In love
Who respects friend?

SILVIA.

All men but Proteus.

PROTEUS.

Nay, if the gentle spirit of moving words
Can no way change you to a milder form,
I'll woo you like a soldier, at arms' end,
And love you 'gainst the nature of love,—force ye.

SILVIA.

O heaven!

PROTEUS.

I'll force thee yield to my desire.

VALENTINE [*coming forward*].

Ruffian, let go that rude uncivil touch,—
Thou friend of an ill fashion!

PROTEUS.

Valentine!

VALENTINE.

Thou common friend, that's without faith or love,
For such is a friend now; treacherous man!
Thou hast beguiled my hopes; naught but mine eye
Could have persuaded me: now I dare not say
I have one friend alive; thou wouldst disprove me.
Who should be trusted now, when one's right hand
Is perjured to the bosom? Proteus,
I am sorry I must never trust thee more,
But count the world a stranger for thy sake.
The private wound is deepest: O time most accurst!
'Mongst all foes that a friend should be the worst!

PROTEUS.

My shame and guilt confounds me.
Forgive me, Valentine: if hearty sorrow
Be a sufficient ransom for offence,
I tender't here; I do as truly suffer
As e'er I did commit.

VALENTINE.

Then I am paid;
And once again I do receive thee honest.
Who by repentance is not satisfied
Is nor of heaven nor earth; for these are pleased;
By penitence th' Eternal wrath's appeased:
And, that my love may appear plain and free,
All that was mine in Silvia I give thee.

JULIA.

O me unhappy! [*Faints.*

PROTEUS.

Look to the boy.

VALENTINE.

Why, boy! why, wag! how now! what's the matter?
Look up; speak.

JULIA.

O good sir, my master charged me
To deliver a ring to Madam Silvia;
Which, out of my neglect, was never done.

PROTEUS.

Where is that ring, boy?

JULIA.

Here 'tis; this is it. [*Gives a ring.*

PROTEUS.

How! let me see:—
Why, this is the ring I gave to Julia.

JULIA.

O, cry you mercy, sir, I have mistook:
This is the ring you sent to Silvia.
[*Shows another ring.*

PROTEUS.

But how camest thou by this ring? At my depart
I gave this unto Julia.

JULIA.

And Julia herself did give it me;
And Julia herself hath brought it hither.

PROTEUS.

How! Julia!

JULIA.

Behold her that gave aim to all thy oaths,
And entertain'd 'em deeply in her heart:
How oft hast thou with perjury cleft the root!
O Proteus, let this habit make thee blush!
Be thou ashamed that I have took upon me
Such an immodest raiment,—if shame live
In a disguise of love:
It is the lesser blot, modesty finds,
Women to change their shapes than men their minds.

PROTEUS.

Than men their minds! 'tis true. O heaven, were man
But constant, he were perfect! that one error
Fills him with faults; makes him run through all th' sins:
Inconstancy falls off ere it begins.
What is in Silvia's face, but I may spy
More fresh in Julia's with a constant eye?

VALENTINE.

Come, come, a hand from either:
Let me be blest to make this happy close;
'Twere pity two such friends should be long foes.

PROTEUS.

Bear witness, Heaven, I have my wish for ever.

JULIA.

And I mine.

Enter OUTLAWS, *with* DUKE *and* THURIO.

OUTLAWS.

A prize, a prize, a prize!

VALENTINE.

Forbear, forbear, I say! it is my lord the duke.—
Your grace is welcome to a man disgraced,
Banished Valentine.

DUKE OF MILAN.

Sir Valentine!

THURIO.

Yonder is Silvia; and Silvia's mine.

VALENTINE.

Thurio, give back, or else embrace thy death;
Come not within the measure of my wrath:
Do not name Silvia thine; if once again,
Verona shall not hold thee. Here she stands:
Take but possession of her with a touch;—
I dare thee but to breathe upon my love.

THURIO.

Sir Valentine, I care not for her, I;
I hold him but a fool that will endanger
His body for a girl that loves him not:
I claim her not, and therefore she is thine.

DUKE OF MILAN.

The more degenerate and base art thou,
To make such means for her as thou hast done,
And leave her on such slight conditions.—
Now, by the honour of my ancestry,
I do applaud thy spirit, Valentine,
And think thee worthy of an empress' love:
Know, then, I here forget all former griefs,
Cancel all grudge, repeal thee home again,
Plead a new state in thy unrivall'd merit,
To which I thus subscribe,—Sir Valentine,
Thou art a gentleman, and well derived;
Take thou thy Silvia, for thou hast deserved her.

VALENTINE.

I thank your grace; the gift hath made me happy.
I now beseech you, for your daughter's sake,
To grant one boon that I shall ask of you.

DUKE OF MILAN.

I grant it, for thine own, whate'er it be.

VALENTINE.

These banish'd men, that I have kept withal,
Are men endued with worthy qualities:
Forgive them what they have committed here,
And let them be recall'd from their exile:
They are reformed, civil, full of good,
And fit for great employment, worthy lord.

DUKE OF MILAN.

Thou hast prevail'd; I pardon them and thee:
Dispose of them as thou know'st their deserts.—
Come, let us go: we will include all jars
With triumphs, mirth, and rare solemnity.

VALENTINE.

And, as we walk along, I dare be bold
With our discourse to make your grace to smile.
What think you of this page, my lord?

DUKE OF MILAN.

I think the boy hath grace in him; he blushes.

VALENTINE.

I warrant you, my lord, more grace than boy.

DUKE OF MILAN.

What mean you by that saying?

VALENTINE.

Please you, I'll tell you as we pass along,
That you will wonder what hath fortuned.
Come, Proteus; 'tis your penance but to hear
The story of your loves discovered:
That done, our day of marriage shall be yours;
One feast, one house, one mutual happiness.

[*Exeunt.*

LOVE'S LABOUR'S LOST

DRAMATIS PERSONAE

FERDINAND, *King of Navarre.*
BEROWNE, LONGAVILLE, DUMAINE, } *lords attending on the King.*
BOYET, MERCADÉ, } *lords attending on the Princes of France.*
DON ADRIANO DE ARMADO, *a fantastical Spaniard.*
SIR NATHANIEL, *a curate.*
HOLOFERNES, *a schoolmaster.*
DULL, *a constable.*
COSTARD, *a clown.*
MOTH, *page to Armado.*
A FORESTER.

PRINCESS OF FRANCE.
ROSALINE, MARIA, KATHERINE, } *ladies attending on the Princess.*
JAQUENETTA, *a country wench.*
LORDS, ATTENDANTS, *&c.*

SCENE—*Navarre.*

ACT I. SCENE I.

Navarre. A park with a palace in it.

Enter the KING, BEROWNE, LONGAVILLE, *and* DUMAINE.

KING.

LET fame, that all hunt after in their lives,
Live register'd upon our brazen tombs,
And then grace us in the disgrace of death;
When, spite of cormorant devouring Time,
Th'endeavour of this present breath may buy
That honour which shall bate his scythe's keen edge,
And make us heirs of all eternity.
Therefore, brave conquerors,—for so you are,
That war against your own affections,
And the huge army of the world's desires,—
Our late edict shall strongly stand in force:
Navarre shall be the wonder of the world;
Our court shall be a little Academe,
Still and contemplative in living art.
You three, Berowne, Dumaine, and Longaville,
Have sworn for three years' term to live with me
My fellow-scholars, and to keep those statutes
That are recorded in this schedule here:
Your oaths are pass'd; and now subscribe your names,
That his own hand may strike his honour down
That violates the smallest branch herein:
If you are arm'd to do as sworn to do,
Subscribe to your deep oaths, and keep it too.

LONGAVILLE.

I am resolv'd; 'tis but a three years' fast:
The mind shall banquet, though the body pine:
Fat paunches have lean pates; and dainty bits
Make rich the ribs, but bankrout quite the wits.

DUMAINE.

My loving lord, Dumaine is mortify'd:
The grosser manner of these world's delights
He throws upon the gross world's baser slaves:
To love, to wealth, to pomp, I pine and die;
With all these living in philosophy.

BEROWNE.

I can but say their protestation over;
So much, dear liege, I have already sworn,
That is, to live and study here three years.
But there are other strict observances:
As, not to see a woman in that term,—
Which I hope well is not enrolled there;
And one day in a week to touch no food,
And but one meal on every day beside,—
The which I hope is not enrolled there;
And then, to sleep but three hours in the night,
And not be seen to wink of all the day
(When I was wont to think no harm all night,
And make a dark night too of half the day),—
Which I hope well is not enrolled there:
O, these are barren tasks, too hard to keep,—
Not to see ladies, study, fast, not sleep!

KING.

Your oath is pass'd to pass away from these.

BEROWNE.

Let me say no, my liege, an if you please:
I only swore to study with your grace,
And stay here in your court for three years' space.

LONGAVILLE.

You swore to that, Berowne, and to the rest.

BEROWNE.

By yea and nay, sir, then I swore in jest.—
What is the end of study? let me know.

KING.

Why, that to know, which else we should not know.

BEROWNE.

Things hid and barr'd, you mean, from common sense?

KING.

Ay, that is study's god-like recompense.

BEROWNE.

Come on, then; I will swear to study so,
To know the thing I am forbid to know
As thus,—to study where I well may dine,
When I to feast expressly am forbid;
Or study where to meet some mistress fine,
When mistresses from common sense are hid;
Or, having sworn too hard-a-keeping oath
Study to break it, and not break my troth.
If study's gain be thus, and this be so,
Study knows that which yet it doth not know:
Swear me to this, and I will ne'er say no.

KING.

These be the stops that hinder study quite,
And train our intellects to vain delight.

BEROWNE.

Why, all delights are vain; but that most vain,
Which, with pain purchased, doth inherit pain:

As, painfully to pore upon a book
  To seek the light of truth; while truth the while
Doth falsely blind the eyesight of his look:
  Light, seeking light, doth light of light beguile:
So, ere you find where light in darkness lies,
Your light grows dark by losing of your eyes.
Study me how to please the eye indeed,
  By fixing it upon a fairer eye;
Who dazzling so, that eye shall be his heed,
  And give him light that it was blinded by.
Study is like the heaven's glorious sun,
  That will not be deep-search'd with saucy looks:
Small have continual plodders ever won,
  Save base authority from others' books.
These earthly godfathers of heaven's lights,
  That give a name to every fixed star,
Have no more profit of their shining nights
  Than those that walk and wot not what they
    are.
Too much to know, is to know naught but fame;
And every godfather can give a name.

KING.

How well he's read, to reason against reading!

DUMAINE.

Proceeded well, to stop all good proceeding!

LONGAVILLE.

He weeds the corn, and still lets grow the weeding.

BEROWNE.

The spring is near, when green geese are a-breed-
  ing.

DUMAINE.

How follows that?

BEROWNE.

Fit in his place and time.

DUMAINE.

In reason nothing.

BEROWNE.

Something, then, in rime.

KING.

Berowne is like an envious-sneaping frost,
  That bites the first-born infants of the spring.

BEROWNE.

Well, say I am; why should proud summer boast,
  Before the birds have any cause to sing?
Why should I joy in an abortive birth?
  At Christmas I no more desire a rose
Than wish a snow in May's new-fangled earth;
  But like of each thing that in season grows.
So you—to study now it is too late—
Climb o'er the house to unlock the little gate.

KING.

Well, sit you out: go home, Berowne: adieu.

BEROWNE.

No, my good lord; I have sworn to stay with
  you:
And though I have for barbarism spoke more
  Than for that angel knowledge you can say,
Yet confident I'll keep what I have swore,
  And bide the penance of each three years' day.
Give me the paper,—let me read the same;
And to the strict'st decrees I'll write my name.

KING.

How well this yielding rescues thee from shame!

BEROWNE [*reads*].

'Item, That no woman shall come within a mile of my court,'—Hath this been proclaim'd?

LONGAVILLE.

Four days ago.

BEROWNE.

Let's see the penalty.—[*reads*] 'on pain of losing her tongue.'—Who devised this penalty?

LONGAVILLE.

Marry, that did I.

BEROWNE.

Sweet lord, and why?

LONGAVILLE.

To fright them hence with that dread penalty.

BEROWNE.

A dangerous law against gentility!
  [*Reads*] 'Item, If any man be seen to talk with a woman within the term of three years, he shall endure such public shame as the rest of the court can possibly devise.'
This article, my liege, yourself must break;
  For well you know here comes in embassy
The French king's daughter with yourself to
    speak,—
  A maid of grace and complete majesty,—
About surrender-up of Aquitaine
  To her decrepit, sick, and bed-rid father:
Therefore this article is made in vain,
  Or vainly comes th'admired princess hither.

KING.

What say you, lords? why, this was quite forgot.

BEROWNE.

So study evermore is overshot:
While it doth study to have what it would,
It doth forget to do the thing it should;
And when it hath the thing it hunteth most,
'Tis won as towns with fire,—so won, so lost.

KING.

We must of force dispense with this decree;
She must lie here on mere necessity.

BEROWNE.

Necessity will make us all forsworn
  Three thousand times within this three years'
    space;
For every man with his affects is born,
  Not by might master'd, but by special grace:
If I break faith, this word shall speak for me,
I am forsworn on mere necessity.—
So to the laws at large I write my name:
[*Subscribes.*
  And he that breaks them in the least degree
Stands in attainder of eternal shame:
  Suggestions are to other as to me;
But I believe, although I seem so loth,
I am the last that will last keep his oath.
But is there no quick recreation granted?

KING.

Ay, that there is. Our court, you know, is haunted
  With a refined traveller of Spain;
A man in all the world's new fashion planted,
  That hath a mint of phrases in his brain;
One whom the music of his own vain tongue
  Doth ravish like enchanting harmony;
A man of complements, whom right and wrong
  Have chose as umpire of their mutiny:
This child of fancy, that Armado hight,
  For interim to our studies, shall relate,
In high-born words, the worth of many a
    knight

From tawny Spain, lost in the world's debate.
How you delight, my lords, I know not, I;
But, I protest, I love to hear him lie,
And I will use him for my minstrelsy.

BEROWNE.

Armado is a most illustrious wight,
A man of fire-new words, fashion's own knight.

LONGAVILLE.

Costard the swain and he shall be our sport;
And, so to study, three years is but short.

Enter DULL *with a letter, and* COSTARD.

DULL.

Which is the duke's own person?

BEROWNE.

This, fellow: what wouldst?

DULL.

I myself reprehend his own person, for I am his Grace's tharborough: but I would see his own person in flesh and blood.

BEROWNE.

This is he.

DULL.

Signior Arme—Arme—commends you. There's villainy abroad: this letter will tell you more.

COSTARD.

Sir, the contempts thereof are as touching me.

KING.

A letter from the magnificent Armado.

BEROWNE.

How low soever the matter, I hope in God for high words.

LONGAVILLE.

A high hope for a low having: God grant us patience!

BEROWNE.

To hear? or forbear laughing?

LONGAVILLE.

To hear meekly, sir, and to laugh moderately; or to forbear both.

BEROWNE.

Well, sir, be it as the style shall give us cause to climb in the merriness.

COSTARD.

The matter is to me, sir, as concerning Jaquenetta. The manner of it is, I was taken with the manner.

BEROWNE.

In what manner?

COSTARD.

In manner and form following, sir; all those three: I was seen with her in the manor-house, sitting with her upon the form, and taken following her into the park; which, put together, is in manner and form following. Now, sir, for the manner,—it is the manner of a man to speak to a woman: for the form,—in some form.

BEROWNE.

For the following, sir?

COSTARD.

As it shall follow in my correction: and God defend the right!

KING.

Will you hear this letter with attention?

BEROWNE.

As we would hear an oracle.

COSTARD.

Such is the simplicity of man to hearken after the flesh.

KING [*reads*].

Great deputy, the welkin's vicegerent, and sole dominator of Navarre, my soul's earth's god and body's fostering patron,—

COSTARD.

Not a word of Costard yet.

KING [*reads*].

So it is,—

COSTARD.

It may be so: but if he says it is so, he is, in telling true, but so—

KING.

Peace!

COSTARD.

Be to me, and every man that dares not fight!

KING.

No words!

COSTARD.

Of other men's secrets, I beseech you.

KING [*reads*].

So it is, besieged with sable-colour'd melancholy, I did commend the black-oppressing humour to the most wholesome physic of thy health-giving air; and, as I am a gentleman, betook myself to walk. The time when? About the sixth hour; when beasts most graze, birds best peck, and men sit down to that nourishment which is call'd supper; so much for the time when. Now for the ground which; which, I mean, I walkt upon: it is ycleped thy park. Then for the place where; where, I mean, I did encounter that obscene and most preposterous event, that draweth from my snow-white pen the ebon-colour'd ink, which here thou viewest, beholdest, surveyest, or seest: but to the place where,—it standeth north-north-east and by east from the west corner of thy curious-knotted garden: there did I see that low-spirited swain, that base minnow of thy mirth,—

COSTARD.

Me?

KING [*reads*].

that unletter'd small-knowing soul,—

COSTARD.

Me?

KING [*reads*].

that shallow vassal,—

COSTARD.

Still me?

KING [*reads*].

which, as I remember, hight Costard,—

COSTARD.

O, me!

KING [*reads*].

sorted and consorted, contrary to thy establish'd proclaim'd edict and continent canon, with—with,—O, with—but with this I passion to say wherewith,—

COSTARD.

With a wench.

KING [*reads*].

with a child of our grandmother Eve, a female; or, for thy more sweet understanding, a woman. Him I—as my ever-esteem'd duty pricks me on—have sent to thee, to receive the meed of punishment, by thy sweet Grace's officer, Antony Dull; a man of good repute, carriage, bearing, and estimation.

DULL.

Me, an't shall please you; I am Antony Dull.

KING [*reads*].

For Jaquenetta,—so is the weaker vessel call'd which I apprehended with the aforesaid swain,—I keep her as a vessel of thy law's fury; and shall, at the least of thy sweet notice, bring her to trial. Thine, in all compl̃ements of devoted and heart-burning heat of duty,

DON ADRIANO DE ARMADO.

BEROWNE.

This is not so well as I look't for, but the best that ever I heard.

KING.

Ay, the best for the worst.—But, sirrah, what say you to this?

COSTARD.

Sir, I confess the wench.

KING.

Did you hear the proclamation?

COSTARD.

I do confess much of the hearing it, but little of the marking of it.

KING.

It was proclaim'd a year's imprisonment, to be taken with a wench.

COSTARD.

I was taken with none, sir: I was taken with a damsel.

KING.

Well, it was proclaim'd damsel.

COSTARD.

This was no damsel neither, sir; she was a virgin.

KING.

It is so varied too; for it was proclaim'd virgin.

COSTARD.

If it were, I deny her virginity: I was taken with a maid.

KING.

This maid will not serve your turn, sir.

COSTARD.

This maid will serve my turn, sir.

KING.

Sir, I will pronounce your sentence: you shall fast a week with bran and water.

COSTARD.

I had rather pray a month with mutton and porridge.

KING.

And Don Armado shall be your keeper.—
My Lord Berowne, see him deliver'd o'er:—
And go we, lords, to put in practice that
Which each to other hath so strongly sworn.

[*Exeunt* KING, LONGAVILLE, *and* DUMAINE.

BEROWNE.

I'll lay my head to any good man's hat,
These oaths and laws will prove an idle scorn.—
Sirrah, come on.

COSTARD.

I suffer for the truth, sir; for true it is, I was taken with Jaquenetta, and Jaquenetta is a true girl; and therefore, Welcome the sour cup of prosperity! Affliction may one day smile again; and till then, Sit thee down, sorrow! [*Exeunt.*

SCENE II.

The same.

Enter ARMADO *and* MOTH, *his Page.*

ARMADO.

BOY, what sign is it when a man of great spirit grows melancholy?

MOTH.

A great sign, sir, that he will look sad.

ARMADO.

Why, sadness is one and the selfsame thing, dear imp.

MOTH.

No, no; O Lord, sir, no.

ARMADO.

How canst thou part sadness and melancholy, my tender juvenal?

MOTH.

By a familiar demonstration of the working, my tough signior.

ARMADO.

Why tough signior? why tough signior?

MOTH.

Why tender juvenal? why tender juvenal?

ARMADO.

I spoke it, tender juvenal, as a congruent epitheton appertaining to thy young days, which we may nominate tender.

MOTH.

And I, tough signior, as an appertinent title to your old time, which we may name tough.

ARMADO.

Pretty and apt.

MOTH.

How mean you, sir? I pretty, and my saying apt? or I apt, and my saying pretty?

ARMADO.

Thou pretty, because little.

MOTH.

Little pretty, because little. Wherefore apt?

ARMADO.

And therefore apt, because quick.

MOTH.

Speak you this in my praise, master?

ARMADO.

In thy condign praise.

MOTH.

I will praise an eel with the same praise.

ARMADO.

What, that an eel is ingenious?

MOTH.

That an eel is quick.

ARMADO.

I do say thou art quick in answers: thou heat'st my blood.

MOTH.

I am answered, sir.

ARMADO.

I love not to be crost.

MOTH [*aside*].

He speaks the mere contrary,—crosses love not him.

ARMADO.

I have promised to study three years with the duke.

MOTH.

You may do it in an hour, sir.

ARMADO.

Impossible.

MOTH.

How many is one thrice told?

ARMADO.

I am ill at reck'ning,—it fitteth the spirit of a tapster.

MOTH.

You are a gentleman and a gamester, sir.

ARMADO.

I confess both: they are both the varnish of a complete man.

MOTH.

Then, I am sure, you know how much the gross sum of deuce-ace amounts to.

ARMADO.

It doth amount to one more than two.

MOTH.

Which the base vulgar do call three.

ARMADO.

True.

MOTH.

Why, sir, is this such a piece of study? Now here's three studied, ere you'll thrice wink: and how easy it is to put years to the word three, and study three years in two words, the dancing horse will tell you.

ARMADO.

A most fine figure!

MOTH [*aside*].

To prove you a cipher.

ARMADO.

I will hereupon confess I am in love: and as it is base for a soldier to love, so am I in love with a base wench. If drawing my sword against the humour of affection would deliver me from the reprobate thought of it, I would take Desire prisoner, and ransom him to any French courtier for a new-devised courtesy. I think scorn to sigh: methinks I should outswear Cupid. Comfort me, boy: what great men have been in love?

MOTH.

Hercules, master.

ARMADO.

Most sweet Hercules!—More authority, dear boy, name more; and, sweet my child, let them be men of good repute and carriage.

MOTH.

Samson, master: he was a man of good carriage, great carriage,—for he carried the town-gates on his back like a porter: and he was in love.

ARMADO.

O well-knit Samson! strong-jointed Samson! I do excel thee in my rapier as much as thou didst me in carrying gates. I am in love too:—who was Samson's love, my dear Moth?

MOTH.

A woman, master.

ARMADO.

Of what complexion?

MOTH.

Of all the four, or the three, or the two; or one of the four.

ARMADO.

Tell me precisely of what complexion.

MOTH.

Of the sea-water green, sir.

ARMADO.

Is that one of the four complexions?

MOTH.

As I have read, sir; and the best of them too.

ARMADO.

Green, indeed, is the colour of lovers; but to have a love of that colour, methinks Samson had small reason for it. He surely affected her for her wit.

MOTH.

It was so, sir; for she had a green wit.

ARMADO.

My love is most immaculate white and red.

MOTH.

Most maculate thoughts, master, are maskt under such colours.

ARMADO.

Define, define, well-educated infant.

MOTH.

My father's wit and my mother's tongue assist me!

ARMADO.

Sweet invocation of a child; most pretty and pathetical!

MOTH.

If she be made of white and red,
  Her faults will ne'er be known;
For blushing cheeks by faults are bred,
  And fears by pale white shown:
Then if she fear, or be to blame,
  By this you shall not know;
For still her cheeks possess the same,
  Which native she doth owe.

A dangerous rime, master, against the reason of white and red.

ARMADO.

Is there not a ballad, boy, of the King and the Beggar?

MOTH.

The world was very guilty of such a ballad some three ages since: but, I think, now 'tis not to be found; or, if it were, it would neither serve for the writing nor the tune.

ARMADO.

I will have that subject newly writ o'er, that I may example my digression by some mighty precedent. Boy, I do love that country girl that I took in the park with the rational hind Costard: she deserves well.

MOTH [*aside*].

To be whipt; and yet a better love than my master.

ARMADO.

Sing, boy; my spirit grows heavy in love.

MOTH.

And that's great marvel, loving a light wench.

ARMADO.

I say, sing.

MOTH.

Forbear till this company be past.

Enter DULL, COSTARD, *and* JAQUENETTA.

DULL.

Sir, the duke's pleasure is, that you keep Costard safe: and you must let him take no delight nor no penance; but a' must fast three days a week. For this damsel, I must keep her at the park: she is allowed for the day-woman. Fare you well.

ARMADO.

I do betray myself with blushing.—Maid,—

JAQUENETTA.

Man.

ARMADO.

I will visit thee at the lodge.

JAQUENETTA.

That's hereby.

ARMADO.

I know where it is situate.

JAQUENETTA.

Lord, how wise you are!

ARMADO.

I will tell thee wonders.

JAQUENETTA.

With that face?

ARMADO.

I love thee.

JAQUENETTA.

So I heard you say.

ARMADO.

And so, farewell.

JAQUENETTA.

Fair weather after you!

DULL.

Come, Jaquenetta, away!

[*Exeunt* DULL *and* JAQUENETTA.

ARMADO.

Villain, thou shalt fast for thy offences ere thou be pardoned.

COSTARD.

Well, sir, I hope, when I do it, I shall do it on a full stomach.

ARMADO.

Thou shalt be heavily punished.

COSTARD.

I am more bound to you than your fellows, for they are but lightly rewarded.

ARMADO.

Take away this villain; shut him up.

MOTH.

Come, you transgressing slave; away!

COSTARD.

Let me not be pent up, sir: I will fast, being loose.

MOTH.

No, sir; that were fast and loose: thou shalt to prison.

COSTARD.

Well, if ever I do see the merry days of desolation that I have seen, some shall see—

MOTH.

What shall some see?

COSTARD.

Nay, nothing, Master Moth, but what they look upon. It is not for prisoners to be too silent in their words; and therefore I will say nothing: I thank God I have as little patience as another man; and therefore I can be quiet.

[*Exeunt* MOTH *and* COSTARD.

ARMADO.

I do affect the very ground, which is base, where her shoe, which is baser, guided by her foot, which is basest, doth tread. I shall be forsworn,—which is a great argument of falsehood,—if I love. And how can that be true love which is falsely attempted? Love is a familiar; Love is a devil: there is no evil angel but love. Yet was Samson so tempted,—and he had an excellent strength; yet was Solomon so seduced,—and he had a very good wit. Cupid's buttshaft is too hard for Hercules' club; and therefore too much odds for a Spaniard's rapier. The first and second cause will not serve my turn; the passado he respects not, the duello he regards not: his disgrace is to be called boy; but his glory is to subdue men. Adieu, valour! rust, rapier! be still, drum! for your manager is in love; yea, he loveth. Assist me some extemporal god of rime, for I am sure I shall turn sonnet. Devise, wit,—write, pen; for I am for whole volumes in folio.

ACT II. SCENE I.

The same.

Enter the PRINCESS OF FRANCE, ROSALINE, MARIA, KATHARINE, BOYET, LORDS, *and other* ATTENDANTS.

BOYET.

NOW, madam, summon up your dearest spirits:
Consider who the king your father sends;
To whom he sends; and what's his embassy:
Yourself, held precious in the world's esteem,
To parley with the sole inheritor
Of all perfections that a man may owe,
Matchless Navarre; the plea of no less weight
Than Aquitaine,—a dowry for a queen.
Be now as prodigal of all dear grace,
As Nature was in making graces dear,
When she did starve the general world beside,
And prodigally gave them all to you.

PRINCESS.

Good Lord Boyet, my beauty, though but mean,
Needs not the painted flourish of your praise:
Beauty is bought by judgement of the eye,
Not utter'd by base sale of chapmen's tongues:
I am less proud to hear you tell my worth
Than you much willing to be counted wise
In spending your wit in the praise of mine.
But now to task the tasker:—good Boyet,
You are not ignorant, all-telling fame
Doth noise abroad, Navarre hath made a vow,
Till painful study shall outwear three years,
No woman may approach his silent court:
Therefore to's seemeth it a needful course,
Before we enter his forbidden gates,
To know his pleasure; and in that behalf,
Bold of your worthiness, we single you
As our best-moving fair solicitor.
Tell him, the daughter of the King of France,
On serious business, craving quick dispatch,
Importunes personal conference with his Grace:
Haste, signify so much; while we attend,
Like humble-visaged suitors, his high will.

BOYET.

Proud of employment, willingly I go.

PRINCESS.

All pride is willing pride, and yours is so.

[*Exit* BOYET.

Who are the votaries, my loving lords,
That are vow-fellows with this virtuous duke?

FIRST LORD.

Lord Longaville is one.

PRINCESS.

Know you the man?

MARIA.

I know him, madam: at a marriage-feast,
Between Lord Perigort and the beauteous heir
Of Jaques Falconbridge, solemnized
In Normandy, saw I this Longaville:
A man of sovereign parts he is esteem'd;
Well-fitted in arts, glorious in arms:
Nothing becomes him ill that he would well.
The only soil of his fair virtue's gloss—
If virtue's gloss will stain with any soil—
Is a sharp wit match'd with too blunt a will;
Whose edge hath power to cut, whose will still wills
It should none spare that come within his power.

PRINCESS.

Some merry mocking lord, belike; is't so?

MARIA.

They say so most that most his humours know.

PRINCESS.

Such short-lived wits do wither as they grow.
Who are the rest?

KATHARINE.

The young Dumaine, a well-accomplisht youth,
Of all that virtue love for virtue loved:
Most power to do most harm, least knowing ill;
For he hath wit to make an ill shape good,
And shape to win grace, though he had no wit.
I saw him at the Duke Alençon's once;
And much too little of that good I saw
Is my report to his great worthiness.

ROSALINE.

Another of these students at that time
Was there with him: if I have heard a truth,
Berowne they call him; but a merrier man,
Within the limit of becoming mirth,
I never spent an hour's talk withal:
His eye begets occasion for his wit;
For every object that the one doth catch,
The other turns to a mirth-moving jest,
Which his fair tongue—conceit's expositor—
Delivers in such apt and gracious words,
That aged ears play truant at his tales,
And younger hearings are quite ravished;
So sweet and voluble is his discourse.

PRINCESS.

God bless my ladies! are they all in love,
That every one her own hath garnished
With such bedecking ornaments of praise?

FIRST LORD.

Here comes Boyet.

Enter BOYET.

PRINCESS.

Now, what admittance, lord?

BOYET.

Navarre had notice of your fair approach;
And he and his competitors in oath
Were all addrest to meet you, gentle lady,
Before I came. Marry, thus much I have learnt,—
He rather means to lodge you in the field,
Like one that comes here to besiege his court,
Than seek a dispensation for his oath,
To let you enter his unpeopled house.
Here comes Navarre. [*The Ladies mask.*

Enter KING, LONGAVILLE, DUMAINE, BEROWNE, *and* ATTENDANTS.

KING.

Fair princess, welcome to the court of Navarre.

PRINCESS.

'Fair' I give you back again; and 'welcome' I have not yet: the roof of this court is too high to be yours; and welcome to the wide fields too base to be mine.

KING.

You shall be welcome, madam, to my court.

PRINCESS.

I will be welcome, then: conduct me thither.

KING.

Hear me, dear lady,—I have sworn an oath.

PRINCESS.

Our Lady help my lord! he'll be forsworn.

KING.

Not for the world, fair madam, by my will.

PRINCESS.

Why, will shall break it; will, and nothing else.

KING.

Your ladyship is ignorant what it is.

PRINCESS.

Were my lord so, his ignorance were wise,
Where now his knowledge must prove ignorance.
I hear your grace hath sworn-out house-keeping:
'Tis deadly sin to keep that oath, my lord,
And sin to break it.
But pardon me, I am too sudden-bold:
To teach a teacher ill beseemeth me.
Vouchsafe to read the purpose of my coming.
And suddenly resolve me in my suit.
[*Gives a paper.*

KING.

Madam, I will, if suddenly I may.

PRINCESS.

You will the sooner, that I were away;
For you'll prove perjured, if you make me stay.

BEROWNE.

Did not I dance with you in Brabant once?

ROSALINE.

Did not I dance with you in Brabant once?

BEROWNE.

I know you did.

ROSALINE.

How needless was it, then, to ask the question!

BEROWNE.

You must not be so quick.

ROSALINE.

'Tis 'long of you that spur me with such questions.

BEROWNE.

Your wit's too hot, it speeds too fast, 'twill tire.

ROSALINE.

Not till it leave the rider in the mire.

BEROWNE.

What time o' day?

ROSALINE.

The hour that fools should ask.

BEROWNE.

Now fair befall your mask!

ROSALINE.

Fair fall the face it covers!

BEROWNE.
And send you many lovers!

ROSALINE.
Amen, so you be none.

BEROWNE.
Nay, then will I be gone.

KING.
Madam, your father here doth intimate
The payment of a hundred thousand crowns;
Being but th' one-half of an entire sum
Disbursed by my father in his wars.
But say that he or we—as neither have—
Received that sum, yet there remains unpaid
A hundred thousand more; in surety of the which,
One part of Aquitaine is bound to us,
Although not valued to the money's worth.
If, then, the king your father will restore
But that one-half which is unsatisfied,
We will give up our right in Aquitaine,
And hold fair friendship with his Majesty.
But that, it seems, he little purposeth,
For here he doth demand to have repaid
A hundred thousand crowns; and not demands,
On payment of a hundred thousand crowns,
To have his title live in Aquitaine,
Which we much rather had depart withal,
And have the money by our father lent,
Than Aquitaine so gelded as it is.
Dear princess, were not his requests so far
From reason's yielding, your fair self should make
A yielding, 'gainst some reason, in my breast,
And go well satisfied to France again.

PRINCESS.
You do the king my father too much wrong,
And wrong the reputation of your name,
In so unseeming to confess receipt
Of that which hath so faithfully been paid.

KING.
I do protest I never heard of it;
And if you prove it, I'll repay it back,
Or yield up Aquitaine.

PRINCESS.
We arrest your word.—
Boyet, you can produce acquittances
For such a sum from special officers
Of Charles his father.

KING.
Satisfy me so.

BOYET.
So please your grace, the packet is not come,
Where that and other specialties are bound:
To-morrow you shall have a sight of them.

KING.
It shall suffice me: at which interview
All liberal reason I will yield unto.
Meantime receive such welcome at my hand
As honour, without breach of honour, may
Make tender of to thy true worthiness:
You may not come, fair princess, in my gates;
But here without you shall be so received
As you shall deem yourself lodged in my heart,
Though so denied fair harbour in my house.
Your own good thoughts excuse me, and farewell:
To-morrow shall we visit you again.

PRINCESS.
Sweet health and fair desires consort your Grace!

KING.
Thy own wish wish I thee in every place!
[*Exit* KING *attended.*

BEROWNE.
Lady, I will commend you to mine own heart.

ROSALINE.
Pray you, do my commendations; I would be glad to see it.

BEROWNE.
I would you heard it groan.

ROSALINE.
Is the fool sick?

BEROWNE.
Sick at the heart.

ROSALINE.
Alack, let it blood.

BEROWNE.
Would that do it good?

ROSALINE.
My physic says ay.

BEROWNE.
Will you prick't with your eye?

ROSALINE.
No point, with my knife.

BEROWNE.
Now, God save thy life!

ROSALINE.
And yours from long living!

BEROWNE.
I cannot stay thanksgiving. [*Retiring.*

DUMAINE.
Sir, I pray you, a word: what lady is that same?

BOYET.
The heir of Alençon, Katharine her name.

DUMAINE.
A gallant lady. Monsieur, fare you well. [*Exit.*

LONGAVILLE.
I beseech you, a word: what is she in the white?

BOYET.
A woman sometimes, an you saw her in the light.

LONGAVILLE.
Perchance light in the light. I desire her name.

BOYET.
She hath but one for herself; to desire that were a shame.

LONGAVILLE.
Pray you, sir, whose daughter?

BOYET.
Her mother's, I have heard.

LONGAVILLE.
God's blessing on your beard!

BOYET.
Good sir, be not offended.
She is an heir of Falconbridge.

LONGAVILLE.
Nay, my choler is ended.
She is a most sweet lady.

BOYET.
Not unlike, sir, that may be.
[*Exit* LONGAVILLE.

BEROWNE.
What's her name in the cap?

BOYET.
Rosaline, by good hap.

BEROWNE.
Is she wedded or no?

BOYET.

To her will, sir, or so.

BEROWNE.

You are welcome, sir: adieu.

BOYET.

Farewell to me, sir, and welcome to you.

[*Exit* BEROWNE. *Ladies unmask.*

MARIA.

That last is Berowne, the merry madcap lord:
Not a word with him but a jest.

BOYET.

And every jest but a word.

PRINCESS.

It was well done of you to take him at his word.

BOYET.

I was as willing to grapple as he was to board.

MARIA.

Two hot sheeps, marry.

BOYET.

And wherefore not ships?
No sheep, sweet lamb, unless we feed on your lips.

MARIA.

You sheep, and I pasture: shall that finish the jest?

BOYET.

So you grant pasture for me. [*Offering to kiss her.*

MARIA.

Not so, gentle beast:
My lips are no common, though several they be.

BOYET.

Belonging to whom?

MARIA.

To my fortunes and me.

PRINCESS.

Good wits will be jangling; but, gentles, agree:
This civil war of wits were much better used
On Navarre and his book-men; for here 'tis abused.

BOYET.

If my observation,—which very seldom lies,—
By the heart's still rhetoric disclosed with eyes,
Deceive me not now, Navarre is infected.

PRINCESS.

With what?

BOYET.

With that which we lovers entitle affected.

PRINCESS.

Your reason?

BOYET.

Why, all his behaviours did make their retire
To the court of his eye, peeping thorough desire:
His heart, like an agate, with your print impress,
Proud with his form, in his eye pride exprest:
His tongue, all impatient to speak and not see,
Did stumble with haste in his eyesight to be;
All senses to that sense did make their repair,
To feel only looking on fairest of fair:
Methought all his senses were lockt in his eye,
As jewels in crystal for some prince to buy;
Who, tendering their own worth from where they were glass'd,
Did point you to buy them, along as you pass'd:
His face's own margent did cote such amazes,
That all eyes saw his eyes enchanted with gazes.
I'll give you Aquitaine, and all that is his,
An you give him for my sake but one loving kiss.

PRINCESS.

Come to our pavilion: Boyet is disposed.

BOYET.

But to speak that in words which his eye hath disclosed:
I only have made a mouth of his eye,
By adding a tongue which I know will not lie.

ROSALINE.

Thou art an old love-monger, and speakest skilfully.

MARIA.

He is Cupid's grandfather, and learns news of him.

ROSALINE.

Then was Venus like her mother; for her father is but grim.

BOYET.

Do you hear, my mad wenches?

MARIA.

No.

BOYET.

What then? do you see?

ROSALINE.

Ay, our way to be gone.

BOYET.

You are too hard for me.

[*Exeunt.*

ACT III. SCENE I.

The same.

Enter ARMADO *and* MOTH.

ARMADO.

WARBLE, child; make passionate my sense o' hearing.

MOTH.

Concolinel— [*Singing.*

ARMADO.

Sweet air!—Go, tenderness of years; take this key, give enlargement to the swain, bring him festinately hither: I must employ him in a letter to my love.

MOTH.

Master, will you win your love with a French brawl?

ARMADO.

How meanest thou? brawling in French?

MOTH.

No, my complete master: but to jig off a tune at the tongue's end, canary to it with your feet, humour it with turning up your eyelids; sigh a note and sing a note,—sometime through the throat, as if you swallow'd love with singing love,—sometime through the nose, as if you snuft up love by smelling love; with your hat penthouse-like, o'er the shop of your eyes; with your arms crossed on your thin-belly doublet, like a rabbit on a spit; or your hands in your pocket, like a man after the old painting; and keep not too long in one tune, but a snip and away. These are complements, these are humours; these betray nice wenches,—that would be betrayed without these; and make them men of note—do you note me?—that most are affected to these.

ARMADO.

How hast thou purchased this experience?

MOTH.

By my penny of observation.

ARMADO.

But O,—but O,—

MOTH.

'The hobby-horse is forgot.'

ARMADO.

Call'st thou my love hobby-horse?

MOTH.

No, master; the hobby-horse is but a colt, and your love perhaps a hackney. But have you forgot your love?

ARMADO.

Almost I had.

MOTH.

Negligent student! learn her by heart.

ARMADO.

By heart and in heart, boy.

MOTH.

And out of heart, master: all those three I will prove.

ARMADO.

What wilt thou prove?

MOTH.

A man, if I live;—and this, by, in, and without, upon the instant: by heart you love her, because your heart cannot come by her; in heart you love her, because your heart is in love with her; and out of heart you love her, being out of heart that you cannot enjoy her.

ARMADO.

I am all these three.

MOTH.

And three times as much more,—and yet nothing at all.

ARMADO.

Fetch hither the swain: he must carry me a letter.

MOTH.

A message well sympathized; a horse to be ambassador for an ass.

ARMADO.

Ha, ha! what sayest thou?

MOTH.

Marry, sir, you must send the ass upon the horse, for he is very slow-gaited. But I go.

ARMADO.

The way is but short: away!

MOTH.

As swift as lead, sir.

ARMADO.

Thy meaning, pretty ingenious?
Is not lead a metal heavy, dull, and slow?

MOTH.

Minime, honest master; or rather, master, no.

ARMADO.

I say lead is slow.

MOTH.

You are too swift, sir, to say so:
Is that lead slow which is fired from a gun?

ARMADO.

Sweet smoke of rhetoric!
He reputes me a cannon, and the bullet, that's he:—
I shoot thee at the swain.

MOTH.

Thump, then, and I flee.
[*Exit.*

ARMADO.

A most acute juvenal; voluble and free of grace!—
By thy favour, sweet welkin, I must sigh in thy face:—
Most rude melancholy, valour gives thee place.—
My herald is return'd.

Enter MOTH *with* COSTARD.

MOTH.

A wonder, master! here's a Costard broken in a shin.

ARMADO.

Some enigma, some riddle: come,—thy *l'envoy;*—begin.

COSTARD.

No egma, no riddle, no *l'envoy;* no salve in the mail, sir: O, sir, plantain, a plain plantain! no *l'envoy*, no *l'envoy;* no salve, sir, but a plantain!

ARMADO.

By virtue, thou enforcest laughter; thy silly thought, my spleen: the heaving of my lungs provokes me to ridiculous smiling,—O, pardon me, my stars! Doth the inconsiderate take salve for *l'envoy*, and the word *l'envoy* for a salve?

MOTH.

Do the wise think them other? is not *l'envoy* a salve?

ARMADO.

No, page: it is an epilogue or discourse, to make plain
Some obscure precedence that hath tofore been sain.
I will example it:
The fox, the ape, and the humble-bee,
Were still at odds, being but three.
There's the moral. Now the *l'envoy*.

MOTH.

I will add the *l'envoy*. Say the moral again.

ARMADO.

The fox, the ape, and the humble-bee,
Were still at odds, being but three.

MOTH.

Until the goose came out of door,
And stay'd the odds by adding four.
Now will I begin your moral, and do you follow with my *l'envoy*.
The fox, the ape, and the humble-bee,
Were still at odds, being but three.

ARMADO.

Until the goose came out of door,
Staying the odds by adding four.

MOTH.

A good *l'envoy*, ending in the goose: would you desire more?

COSTARD.

The boy hath sold him a bargain, a goose, that's flat.—
Sir, your pennyworth is good, an your goose be fat.—
To sell a bargain well is as cunning as fast and loose:
Let me see—a fat *l'envoy;* ay, that's a fat goose.

ARMADO.

Come hither, come hither. How did this argument begin?

MOTH.

By saying that a Costard was broken in a shin.
Then call'd you for the *l'envoy*.

COSTARD.

True, and I for a plaintain: thus came your argument in;
Then the boy's fat *l'envoy*, the goose that you bought;
And he ended the market.

ARMADO.

But tell me; how was there a Costard broken in a shin?

MOTH.

I will tell you sensibly.

COSTARD.

Thou hast no feeling of it, Moth: I will speak that *l'envoy:*

I, Costard, running out, that was safely within,
Fell over the threshold, and broke my shin.

ARMADO.

We will talk no more of this matter.

COSTARD.

Till there be more matter in the shin.

ARMADO.

Sirrah Costard, I will enfranchise thee.

COSTARD.

O, marry me to one Frances:—I smell some *l'envoy*, some goose, in this.

ARMADO.

By my sweet soul, I mean setting thee at liberty, enfreedoming thy person: thou wert immured, restrain'd, captivated, bound.

COSTARD.

True, true; and now you will be my purgation, and let me loose.

ARMADO.

I give thee thy liberty, set thee from durance; and, in lieu thereof, impose on thee nothing but this:—bear this significant [*giving a letter*] to the country maid Jaquenetta: there is remuneration [*giving money*]; for the best ward of mine honour is rewarding my dependents.—Moth, follow. [*Exit.*

MOTH.

Like the sequel, I.—Signior Costard, adieu.

COSTARD.

My sweet ounce of man's flesh! my incony Jew!— [*Exit* MOTH.

Now will I look to his remuneration. Remuneration! O, that's the Latin word for three farthings: three farthings — remuneration. — 'What's the price of this inkle?'—'A penny.'—'No, I'll give you a remuneration:' why, it carries it.—Remuneration!—why, it is a fairer name than French crown. I will never buy and sell out of this word.

Enter BEROWNE.

BEROWNE.

O, my good knave Costard! exceedingly well met.

COSTARD.

Pray you, sir, how much carnation ribbon may a man buy for a remuneration?

BEROWNE.

What is a remuneration?

COSTARD.

Marry, sir, halfpenny farthing.

BEROWNE.

O, why, then, three-farthing-worth of silk.

COSTARD.

I thank your worship: God be wi' you!

BEROWNE.

O, stay, slave; I must employ thee:
As thou wilt win my favour, good my knave,
Do one thing for me that I shall entreat.

COSTARD.

When would you have it done, sir?

BEROWNE.

O, this afternoon.

COSTARD.

Well, I will do it, sir: fare you well.

BEROWNE.

O, thou knowest not what it is.

COSTARD.

I shall know, sir, when I have done it.

BEROWNE.

Why, villain, thou must know first.

COSTARD.

I will come to your worship to-morrow morning.

BEROWNE.

It must be done this afternoon. Hark, slave, it is but this:—
The princess comes to hunt here in the park,
And in her train there is a gentle lady;
When tongues speak sweetly, then they name her name,
And Rosaline they call her: ask for her;
And to her white hand see thou do commend
This seal'd-up counsel. There's thy guerdon; go. [*Giving money.*

COSTARD.

Gardon,—O sweet gardon! better than remuneration; eleven-pence farthing better: most sweet gardon!—I will do it, sir, in print.—Gardon—remuneration. [*Exit.*

BEROWNE.

O,—and I, forsooth, in love! I, that have been love's whip;
A very beadle to a humorous sigh;
A critic, nay, a night-watch constable;
A domineering pedant o'er the boy,
Than whom no mortal so magnificent!
This wimpled, whining, purblind, wayward boy;
This signior-junior, giant-dwarf, Dan Cupid;
Regent of love-rimes, lord of folded arms,
Th'anointed sovereign of sighs and groans,
Liege of all loiterers and malecontents,
Dread prince of plackets, king of codpieces,
Sole imperator and great general
Of trotting paritors:—O my little heart!—
And I to be a corporal of his field,
And wear his colours like a tumbler's hoop!
What! I love! I sue! I seek a wife!
A woman, that is like a German clock,
Still a-repairing; ever out of frame;
And never going aright, being a watch,
But being watcht that it may still go right!
Nay, to be perjured, which is worst of all;
And, among three, to love the worst of all;
A whitely wanton with a velvet brow,
With two pitch-balls stuck in her face for eyes;
Ay, and, by heaven, one that will do the deed,
Though Argus were her eunuch and her guard:
And I to sigh for her! to watch for her!
To pray for her! Go to; it is a plague
That Cupid will impose for my neglect
Of his almighty dreadful little might.
Well, I will love, write, sigh, pray, sue, and groan:
Some men must love my lady, and some Joan. [*Exit.*

ACT IV. SCENE I.

The same.

Enter the PRINCESS, ROSALINE, MARIA, KATHARINE, BOYET, LORDS, ATTENDANTS, *and a* FORESTER.

PRINCESS.

WAS that the king, that spurr'd his horse so hard
Against the steep uprising of the hill?

BOYET.

I know not; but I think it was not he.

PRINCESS.

Whoe'er a' was, a' show'd a mounting mind.
Well, lords, to-day we shall have our dispatch:
On Saturday we will return to France.—
Then, forester, my friend, where is the bush
That we must stand and play the murderer in?

FORESTER.

Hereby, upon the edge of yonder coppice;
A stand where you may make the fairest shoot.

PRINCESS.

I thank my beauty, I am fair that shoot,
And thereupon thou speak'st the fairest shoot.

FORESTER.

Pardon me, madam, for I meant not so.

PRINCESS.

What, what? first praise me, and again say no?
O short-lived pride! Not fair? alack for woe!

FORESTER.

Yes, madam, fair.

PRINCESS.

Nay, never paint me now:
Where fair is not, praise cannot mend the brow.
Here, good my glass, take this for telling true:
[*Giving him money.*
Fair payment for foul words is more than due.

FORESTER.

Nothing but fair is that which you inherit.

PRINCESS.

See, see, my beauty will be saved by merit!
O heresy in fair, fit for these days!
A giving hand, though foul, shall have fair praise.—
But come, the bow:—now mercy goes to kill,
And shooting well is then accounted ill.
Thus will I save my credit in the shoot:
Not wounding, pity would not let me do't;
If wounding, then it was to show my skill,
That more for praise than purpose meant to kill.
And, out of question, so it is sometimes,—
Glory grows guilty of detested crimes,
When, for fame's sake, for praise, an outward part,
We bend to that the working of the heart;
As I for praise alone now seek to spill
The poor deer's blood, that my heart means no ill.

BOYET.

Do not curst wives hold that self-sovereignty
Only for praise' sake, when they strive to be
Lords o'er their lords?

PRINCESS.

Only for praise: and praise we may afford
To any lady that subdues a lord.

BOYET.

Here comes a member of the commonwealth.

Enter COSTARD.

COSTARD.

God dig-you-den all! Pray you, which is the head lady?

PRINCESS.

Thou shalt know her, fellow, by the rest that have no heads.

COSTARD.

Which is the greatest lady, the highest?

PRINCESS.

The thickest and the tallest.

COSTARD.

The thickest and the tallest! it is so; truth is truth.
An your waist, mistress, were as slender as my wit,
One o' these maids' girdles for your waist should be fit.
Are not you the chief woman? you are the thickest [here.

PRINCESS.

What's your will, sir? what's your will?

COSTARD.

I have a letter from Monsieur Berowne to one Lady Rosaline.

PRINCESS.

O, thy letter, thy letter! he's a good friend of mine:
Stand aside, good bearer.—Boyet, you can carve;
Break up this capon.

BOYET.

I am bound to serve.—
This letter is mistook, it importeth none here;
It is writ to Jaquenetta.

PRINCESS.

We will read it, I swear.
Break the neck of the wax, and every one give ear.

BOYET [*reads*].

By heaven, that thou art fair, is most infallible; true, that thou art beauteous; truth itself, that thou art lovely. More fairer than fair, beautiful than beauteous, truer than truth itself, have commiseration on thy heroical vassal! The magnanimous and most illustrate king Cophetua set eye upon the pernicious and indubitate beggar Zenelophon; and he it was that might rightly say, *Veni, vidi, vici;* which to annothanize in the vulgar,—O base and obscure vulgar!—*videlicet*, He came, saw, and overcame: he came, one; saw, two; overcame, three. Who came? the king: why did he come? to see: why did he see? to overcome: to whom came he? to the beggar: what saw he? the beggar: who overcame he? the beggar. The conclusion is victory: on whose side? the king's. The captive is enricht: on whose side? the beggar's. The catastrophe is a nuptial: on whose side? the king's,—no, on both in one, or one in both. I am the king; for so stands the comparison: thou the beggar; for so witnesseth thy lowliness. Shall I command thy love? I may: shall I enforce thy love? I could: shall I entreat thy love? I will. What shalt thou exchange for rags? robes; for tittles? titles; for thyself? me. Thus, expecting thy reply, I profane my lips on thy foot, my eyes on thy picture, and my heart on thy every part.—Thine, in the dearest design of industry, DON ADRIANO DE ARMADO.

Thus dost thou hear the Nemean lion roar
'Gainst thee, thou lamb, that standest as his prey.
Submissive fall his princely feet before,
And he from forage will incline to play:

But if thou strive, poor soul, what art thou then?
Food for his rage, repasture for his den.

PRINCESS.
What plume of feathers is he that indited this letter?
What vane? what weathercock? did you ever hear better?

BOYET.
I am much deceived but I remember the style.

PRINCESS.
Else your memory is bad, going o'er it erewhile.

BOYET.
This Armado is a Spaniard, that keeps here in court;
A phantasm, a Monarcho, and one that makes sport
To the prince and his book-mates.

PRINCESS.
Thou fellow, a word:
Who gave thee this letter?

COSTARD.
I told you; my lord.

PRINCESS.
To whom shouldst thou give it?

COSTARD.
From my lord to my lady.

PRINCESS.
From which lord to which lady?

COSTARD.
From my Lord Berowne, a good master of mine,
To a lady of France that he call'd Rosaline.

PRINCESS.
Thou hast mistaken his letter.—Come, lords, away.—
Here, sweet, put up this: 'twill be thine another day. [*Exit* PRINCESS *attended.*

BOYET.
Who is the suitor? who is the suitor?

ROSALINE.
Shall I teach you to know?

BOYET.
Ay, my continent of beauty.

ROSALINE.
Why, she that bears the bow.
Finely put off!

BOYET.
My lady goes to kill horns; but, if thou marry,
Hang me by the neck, if horns that year miscarry.
Finely put on!

ROSALINE.
Well, then, I am the shooter.

BOYET.
And who is your deer?

ROSALINE.
If we choose by the horns, yourself: come not near.
Finely put on, indeed!

MARIA.
You still wrangle with her, Boyet, and she strikes at the brow.

BOYET.
But she herself is hit lower: have I hit her now?

ROSALINE.
Shall I come upon thee with an old saying, that was a man when King Pepin of France was a little boy, as touching the hit it?

BOYET.
So I may answer thee with one as old, that was a woman when Queen Guinever of Britain was a little wench, as touching the hit it.

ROSALINE.
Thou canst not hit it, hit it, hit it,
Thou canst not hit it, my good man.

BOYET.
An I cannot, cannot, cannot,
An I cannot, another can.
[*Exeunt* ROSALINE *and* KATHARINE.

COSTARD.
By my troth, most pleasant: how both did fit it!

MARIA.
A mark marvellous well shot, for they both did hit it.

BOYET.
A mark! O, mark but that mark! A mark, says my lady!
Let the mark have a prick in't, to mete at, if it may be.

MARIA.
Wide o' th' bow-hand! i'faith, your hand is out.

COSTARD.
Indeed, a' must shoot nearer, or he'll ne'er hit the clout.

BOYET.
An if my hand be out, then belike your hand is in.

COSTARD.
Then will she get the upshoot by cleaving the pin.

MARIA.
Come, come, you talk greasily; your lips grow foul.

COSTARD.
She's too hard for you at pricks, sir: challenge her to bowl.

BOYET.
I fear too much rubbing. Good night, my good owl.
[*Exeunt* BOYET *and* MARIA.

COSTARD.
By my soul, a swain! a most simple clown!
Lord, Lord, how the ladies and I have put him down!
O' my troth, most sweet jests! most incony vulgar wit!
When it comes so smoothly off, so obscenely, as it were, so fit.
Armado o' th' one side;—O, a most dainty man!
To see him walk before a lady and to bear her fan!
To see him kiss his hand! and how most sweetly a' will swear!—
And his page o' t'other side, that handful of wit!
Ah, heavens, it is a most pathetical nit!
Sola, sola! [*Shout within. Exit* COSTARD, *running.*

SCENE II.

The same.

Enter HOLOFERNES, SIR NATHANIEL, *and* DULL.

SIR NATHANIEL.
VERY reverend sport, truly; and done in the testimony of a good conscience.

HOLOFERNES.
The deer was, as you know, *sanguis,*—in blood; ripe as a pomewater, who now hangeth like a jewel in the ear of *cœlo,*—the sky, the welkin, the heaven; and anon falleth like a crab on the face of *terra,*—the soil, the land, the earth.

SIR NATHANIEL.
Truly, Master Holofernes, the epithets are sweetly varied, like a scholar at the least: but, sir, I assure ye, it was a buck of the first head.

HOLOFERNES.

Sir Nathaniel, *haud credo.*

DULL.

'Twas not a *haud credo;* 'twas a pricket.

HOLOFERNES.

Most barbarous intimation! yet a kind of insinuation, as it were, *in via*, in way, of explication; *facere* as it were, replication, or, rather, *ostentare*, to show, as it were, his inclination,—after his undrest, unpolisht, uneducated, unpruned, untrain'd, or, rather, unletter'd, or, ratherest, unconfirm'd fashion,—to insert again my *haud credo* for a deer.

DULL.

I said the deer was not a *haud credo;* 'twas a pricket.

HOLOFERNES.

Twice-sod simplicity, *bis coctus!*
O thou monster Ignorance, how deformed dost thou look!

SIR NATHANIEL.

Sir, he hath never fed of the dainties that are bred in a book;
he hath not eat paper, as it were; he hath not drunk ink: his intellect is not replenisht; he is only an animal, only sensible in the duller parts:
And such barren plants are set before us, that we thankful should be—
Which we of taste and feeling are—for those parts that do fructify in us more than he.
For as it would ill become me to be vain, indiscreet, or a fool,
So, were there a patch set on learning, to see him in a school:
But, *omne bene*, say I; being of an old father's mind,—
'Many can brook the weather that love not the wind.'

DULL.

You two are book-men: can you tell by your wit
What was a month old at Cain's birth, that's not five weeks old as yet?

HOLOFERNES.

Dictynna, goodman Dull; Dictynna, goodman Dull.

DULL.

What is Dictynna?

SIR NATHANIEL.

A title to Phœbe, to Luna, to the moon.

HOLOFERNES.

The moon was a month old when Adam was no more,
And raught not to five weeks when he came to five-score.
Th'allusion holds in the exchange.

DULL.

'Tis true indeed; the collusion holds in the exchange.

HOLOFERNES.

God comfort thy capacity! I say, th'allusion holds in the exchange.

DULL.

And I say, the pollusion holds in the exchange; for the moon is never but a month old: and I say beside, that 'twas a pricket that the princess kill'd.

HOLOFERNES.

Sir Nathaniel, will you hear an extemporal epitaph on the death of the deer? and, to humour the ignorant, I have call'd the deer the princess kill'd a pricket.

SIR NATHANIEL.

Perge, good Master Holofernes, *perge;* so it shall please you to abrogate scurrility.

HOLOFERNES.

I will something affect the letter, for it argues facility.

The preyful princess pierced and prickt
a pretty pleasing pricket;
Some say a sore; but not a sore,
till now made sore with shooting.
The dogs did yell: put *l* to sore,
then sorel jumps from thicket;
Or pricket, sore, or else sorel;
the people fall a-hooting.
If sore be sore, then *l* to sore
makes fifty sores: O sore *l!*
Of one sore I an hundred make
by adding but one more *l.*

SIR NATHANIEL.

A rare talent!

DULL [*aside*].

If a talent be a claw, look how he claws him with a talent.

HOLOFERNES.

This is a gift that I have, simple, simple; a foolish extravagant spirit, full of forms, figures, shapes, objects, ideas, apprehensions, motions, revolutions: these are begot in the ventricle of memory, nourisht in the womb of *pia mater*, and deliver'd upon the mellowing of occasion. But the gift is good in those in whom it is acute, and I am thankful for it.

SIR NATHANIEL.

Sir, I praise the Lord for you: and so may my parishioners; for their sons are well tutor'd by you, and their daughters profit very greatly under you: you are a good member of the commonwealth.

HOLOFERNES.

Mehercle, if their sons be ingenious, they shall want no instruction; if their daughters be capable, I will put it to them: but, *vir sapit qui pauca loquitur.* A soul feminine saluteth us.

Enter JAQUENETTA *and* COSTARD.

JAQUENETTA.

God give you good morrow, master person.

HOLOFERNES.

Master person,—*quasi* pers-on. An if one should be pierced, which is the one?

COSTARD.

Marry, master schoolmaster, he that is likest to a hogshead.

HOLOFERNES.

Of piercing a hogshead! a good lustre of conceit in a turf of earth; fire enough for a flint, pearl enough for a swine: 'tis pretty; it is well.

JAQUENETTA.

Good master person, be so good as read me this letter: it was given me by Costard, and sent me from Don Armado: I beseech you, read it.

HOLOFERNES.

Fauste, precor, gelidâ quando pecus omne sub umbrâ Ruminat,—and so forth. Ah, good old Mantuan! I may speak of thee as the traveller doth of Venice;

——*Venetia, Venetia,*
Chi non te vede, non ti pretia.

Old Mantuan, old Mantuan! who understandeth thee not, loves thee not.—*Ut, re, sol, la, mi, fa.*—Under pardon, sir, what are the contents? or rather, as Horace says in his—What, my soul, verses?

SIR NATHANIEL.

Ay, sir, and very learned.

HOLOFERNES.

Let me hear a staff, a stanze, a verse; *lege, domine.*

SIR NATHANIEL [*reads*].

If love make me forsworn, how shall I swear to love?
Ah, never faith could hold, if not to beauty vow'd!
Though to myself forsworn, to thee I'll faithful prove;
Those thoughts to me were oaks, to thee like osiers bow'd.
Study his bias leaves, and makes his book thine eyes,
Where all those pleasures live that art would comprehend:
If knowledge be the mark, to know thee shall suffice;
Well learned is that tongue that well can thee commend;
All ignorant that soul that sees thee without wonder,—
Which is to me some praise that I thy parts admire:
Thy eye Jove's lightning bears, thy voice his dreadful thunder,
Which, not to anger bent, is music, and sweet fire.
Celestial as thou art, O, pardon love this wrong,
That sings heavens' praise with such an earthly tongue.

HOLOFERNES.

You find not the apostrophes, and so miss the accent: let me supervise the canzonet. Here are only numbers ratified; but, for the elegancy, facility, and golden cadence of poesy, *caret.* Ovidius Naso was the man: and why, indeed, Naso, but for smelling out the odoriferous flowers of fancy, the jerks of invention? *Imitari* is nothing: so doth the hound his master, the ape his keeper, the tired horse his rider.—But, damosella virgin, was this directed to you?

JAQUENETTA.

Ay, sir, from one Monsieur Berowne, one of the strange queen's lords.

HOLOFERNES.

I will overglance the superscript: 'To the snow-white hand of the most beauteous Lady Rosaline.' I will look again on the intellect of the letter, for the nomination of the party writing to the person written unto: 'Your ladyship's in all desired employment, Berowne.'—Sir Nathaniel, this Berowne is one of the votaries with the king; and here he hath framed a letter to a sequent of the stranger queen's, which accidentally, or by the way of progression, hath miscarried.—Trip and go, my sweet; deliver this paper into the royal hand of the king: it may concern much. Stay not thy compliment; I forgive thy duty: adieu.

JAQUENETTA.

Good Costard, go with me.—Sir, God save your life!

COSTARD.

Have with thee, my girl.

[*Exeunt* COSTARD *and* JAQUENETTA.

SIR NATHANIEL.

Sir, you have done this in the fear of God, very religiously; and, as a certain father saith—

HOLOFERNES.

Sir, tell not me of the father; I do fear colourable colours. But to return to the verses: did they please you, Sir Nathaniel?

SIR NATHANIEL.

Marvellous well for the pen.

HOLOFERNES.

I do dine to-day at the father's of a certain pupil of mine; where, if, before repast, it shall please you to gratify the table with a grace, I will, on my privilege I have with the parents of the foresaid child or pupil, undertake your *ben venuto;* where I will prove those verses to be very unlearned, neither savouring of poetry, wit, nor invention: I beseech your society.

SIR NATHANIEL.

And thank you too; for society, saith the text, is the happiness of life.

HOLOFERNES.

And, certes, the text most infallibly concludes it.—[*to* DULL] Sir, I do invite you too; you shall not say me nay: *pauca verba.* Away! the gentles are at their game, and we will to our recreation.

[*Exeunt.*

SCENE III.

The same.

Enter BEROWNE, *with a paper in his hand, alone.*

BEROWNE.

THE king he is hunting the deer; I am coursing myself: they have pitcht a toil; I am toiling in a pitch,—pitch that defiles: defile! a foul word. Well, Set thee down, sorrow! for so they say the fool said, and so say I, and I the fool: well proved, wit! By the Lord, this love is as mad as Ajax: it kills sheep; it kills me, I a sheep: well proved again o' my side! I will not love: if I do, hang me; i'faith, I will not. O, but her eye,—by this light, but for her eye, I would not love her; yes, for her two eyes. Well, I do nothing in the world but lie, and lie in my throat. By heaven, I do love: and it hath taught me to rime, and to be mallicholy; and here is part of my rime, and here my mallicholy. Well, she hath one o' my sonnets already: the clown bore it, the fool sent it, and the lady hath it: sweet clown, sweeter fool, sweetest lady! By the world, I would not care a pin, if the other three were in.—Here comes one with a paper: God give him grace to groan!

[*He stands aside.*

The KING *ent'reth.*

KING.

Ay me!

BEROWNE [*aside*].

Shot, by heaven!—Proceed, sweet Cupid: thou hast thumpt him with thy bird-bolt under the left pap.—In faith, secrets!

KING [*reads*].

'So sweet a kiss the golden sun gives not
To those fresh morning drops upon the rosè,
As thy eye-beams, when their fresh rays have smot
The night of dew that on my cheeks down flows:
Nor shines the silver moon one half so bright
Through the transparent bosom of the deep,
As doth thy face through tears of mine give light;
Thou shin'st in every tear that I do weep:
No drop but as a coach doth carry thee;
So ridest thou triumphing in my woe.
Do but behold the tears that swell in me,
And they thy glory through my grief will show:
But do not love thyself; then thou wilt keep
My tears for glasses, and still make me weep.
O queen of queens! how far dost thou excel,
No thought can think, nor tongue of mortal tell.'—
How shall she know my griefs? I'll drop the paper:—
Sweet leaves, shade folly.—Who is he comes here?
[*Steps aside.*
What, Longaville! and reading! listen, ear.

BEROWNE [*aside*].

Now, in thy likeness, one more fool appear!

Enter LONGAVILLE.

LONGAVILLE.

Ay me, I am forsworn!

BEROWNE [*aside*].

Why, he comes in like a perjure, wearing papers.

KING [*aside*].

In love, I hope: sweet fellowship in shame!

BEROWNE [*aside*].

One drunkard loves another of the name.

LONGAVILLE.

Am I the first that have been perjured so?

BEROWNE [*aside*].

I could put thee in comfort,—not by two that I know:
Thou makest the triumviry, the corner-cap of society,
The shape of Love's Tyburn that hangs up simplicity.

LONGAVILLE.

I fear these stubborn lines lack power to move:—
O sweet Maria, empress of my love!—
These numbers will I tear, and write in prose.

BEROWNE [*aside*].

O, rimes are guards on wanton Cupid's hose:
Disfigure not his shop.

LONGAVILLE.

This same shall go.—
[*Reads.*

Did not the heavenly rhetoric of thine eye,
'Gainst whom the world can not hold argument,
Persuade my heart to this false perjury?
Vows for thee broke deserve not punishment.
A woman I forswore; but I will prove,
Thou being a goddess, I forswore not thee:
My vow was earthly, thou a heavenly love;
Thy grace being gain'd cures all disgrace in me.
Vows are but breath, and breath a vapour is:
Then thou, fair sun, which on my earth dost shine,
Exhalest this vapour-vow; in thee it is:
If broken then, it is no fault of mine:
If by me broke, what fool is not so wise
To lose an oath to win a paradise?

BEROWNE [*aside*].

This is the liver-vein, which makes flesh a deity,
A green goose a goddess: pure, pure idolatry,
God amend us, God amend! we are much out o' th' way.

LONGAVILLE.

By whom shall I send this?—Company! stay.
[*Steps aside.*

BEROWNE [*aside*].

All hid, all hid, an old infant play.
Like a demigod here sit I in the sky,
And wretched fools' secrets heedfully o'er-eye.
More sacks to the mill! O heavens, I have my wish!

Enter DUMAINE.

Dumaine transform'd! four woodcocks in a dish!

DUMAINE.

O most divine Kate!

BEROWNE [*aside*].

O most profane coxcomb!

DUMAINE.

By heaven, the wonder in a mortal eye!

BEROWNE [*aside*].

By earth she is not, corporal: there you lie.

DUMAINE.

Her amber hairs for foul hath amber quoted.

BEROWNE [*aside*].

An amber-colour'd raven was well noted.

DUMAINE.

As upright as the cedar.

BEROWNE [*aside*].

Stoop, I say;
Her shoulder is with child.

DUMAINE.

As fair as day.

BEROWNE [*aside*].

Ay, as some days; but then no sun must shine.

DUMAINE.

O, that I had my wish!

LONGAVILLE [*aside*].

And I had mine!

KING [*aside*].

And I mine too, good Lord!

BEROWNE [*aside*].

Amen, so I had mine: is not that a good word?

DUMAINE.

I would forget her; but a fever she
Reigns in my blood, and will remember'd be.

BEROWNE [*aside*].

A fever in your blood! why, then incision
Would let her out in saucers: sweet misprision!

DUMAINE.

Once more I'll read the ode that I have writ.

BEROWNE [*aside*].

Once more I'll mark how love can vary wit.

DUMAINE [*reads*].

'On a day—alack the day!—
Love, whose month is ever May,
Spied a blossom passing fair
Playing in the wanton air:
Through the velvet leaves the wind,
All unseen, can passage find;

That the lover, sick to death,
Wisht himself the heaven's breath.
Air, quoth he, thy cheeks may blow;
Air, would I might triumph so!
But, alack, my hand is sworn
Ne'er to pluck thee from thy thorn;—
Vow, alack, for youth unmeet,
Youth so apt to pluck a sweet!
Do not call it sin in me,
That I am forsworn for thee;
Thou for whom Jove would swear
Juno but an Ethiop were;
And deny himself for Jove,
Turning mortal for thy love.'
This will I send, and something else more plain,
That shall express my true love's fasting pain.
O, would the king, Berowne, and Longaville,
Were lovers too! Ill, to example ill,
Would from my forehead wipe a perjured note;
For none offend where all alike do dote.

LONGAVILLE [*advancing*].
Dumaine, thy love is far from charity,
That in love's grief desir'st society:
You may look pale, but I should blush, I know,
To be o'erheard and taken napping so.

KING [*advancing*].
Come, sir, you blush: as his your case is such;
You chide at him, offending twice as much:
You do not love Maria? Longaville
Did never sonnet for her sake compile,
Nor never lay his wreathed arms athwart
His loving bosom, to keep down his heart!
I have been closely shrouded in this bush,
And markt you both, and for you both did blush:
I heard your guilty rimes, observed your fashion,
Saw sighs reek from you, noted well your passion:
Ay me! says one: O Jove! the other cries;
One her hairs were gold, crystal the other's eyes:
You would for paradise break faith and troth;
[*To* LONGAVILLE.
And Jove, for your love, would infringe an oath.
[*To* DUMAINE.
What will Berowne say when that he shall hear
A faith infringed, which such zeal did swear?
How will he scorn! how will he spend his wit!
How will he triumph, leap, and laugh at it!
For all the wealth that ever I did see,
I would not have him know so much by me.

BEROWNE.
Now step I forth to whip hypocrisy. [*Advancing*.
Ah, good my liege, I pray thee, pardon me!
Good heart, what grace hast thou, thus to reprove
These worms for loving, that art most in love?
Your eyes do make no coaches; in your tears
There is no certain princess that appears;
You'll not be perjured, 'tis a hateful thing;
Tush, none but minstrels like of sonneting!
But are you not ashamed? nay, are you not,
All three of you, to be thus much o'ershot?
You found his mote; the king your mote did see;
But I a beam do find in each of three.
O, what a scene of foolery have I seen,
Of sighs, of groans, of sorrow, and of teen!
O me, with what strict patience have I sat,
To see a king transformed to a gnat!
To see great Hercules whipping a gig,
And profound Solomon to tune a jig,
And Nestor play at push-pin with the boys,
And critic Timon laugh at idle toys!
Where lies thy grief, O tell me, good Dumaine?
And, gentle Longaville, where lies thy pain?
And where my liege's? all about the breast:—
A caudle, ho!

KING.
Too bitter is thy jest.
Are we betray'd thus to thy over-view?

BEROWNE.
Not you to me, but I betray'd by you:
I, that am honest; I, that hold it sin
To break the vow I am engaged in;
I am betray'd, by keeping company
With men like you, men of inconstancy.
When shall you see me write a thing in rime?
Or groan for Joan? or spend a minute's time
In pruning me? When shall you hear that I
Will praise a hand, a foot, a face, an eye,
A gait, a state, a brow, a breast, a waist,
A leg, a limb?—

KING.
Soft! whither away so fast?
A true man or a thief that gallops so?

BEROWNE.
I post from love: good lover, let me go.

Enter JAQUENETTA *and* COSTARD.

JAQUENETTA.
God bless the king!

KING.
What present hast thou there?

COSTARD.
Some certain treason.

KING.
What makes treason here?

COSTARD.
Nay, it makes nothing, sir.

KING.
If it mar nothing neither,
The treason and you go in peace away together.

JAQUENETTA.
I beseech your Grace, let this letter be read:
Our person misdoubts it; 'twas treason, he said.

KING.
Berowne, read it over.
[*Giving him the letter*.
Where hadst thou it?

JAQUENETTA.
Of Costard.

KING.
Where hadst thou it?

COSTARD.
Of Dun Adramadio, Dun Adramadio.
[BEROWNE *tears the letter*.

KING.
How now! what is in you? why dost thou tear it?

BEROWNE.
A toy, my liege, a toy: your Grace needs not fear it.

LONGAVILLE.
It did move him to passion, and therefore let's hear it.

DUMAINE.
It is Berowne's writing, and here is his name.
[*Picking up the pieces*.

BEROWNE [*to* COSTARD].

Ah, you whoreson loggerhead! you were born to do me shame.—
Guilty, my lord, guilty! I confess, I confess.

KING.

What?

BEROWNE.

That you three fools lackt me fool to make up the mess:
He, he, and you, and you, my liege, and I,
Are pick-purses in love, and we deserve to die.
O, dismiss this audience, and I shall tell you more.

DUMAINE.

Now the number is even.

BEROWNE.

True, true; we are four.
Will these turtles be gone?

KING.

Hence, sirs; away!

COSTARD.

Walk aside the true folk, and let the traitors stay.

[*Exeunt* COSTARD *and* JAQUENETTA.

BEROWNE.

Sweet lords, sweet lovers, O, let us embrace!
As true we are as flesh and blood can be:
The sea will ebb and flow, heaven show his face;
Young blood doth not obey an old decree:
We cannot cross the cause why we were born;
Therefore of all hands must we be forsworn.

KING.

What, did these rent lines show some love of thine?

BEROWNE.

Did they, quoth you? Who sees the heavenly Rosaline,
That, like a rude and savage man of Inde,
At the first opening of the gorgeous east,
Bows not his vassal head and strucken blind
Kisses the base ground with obedient breast?
What peremptory eagle-sighted eye
Dares look upon the heaven of her brow,
That is not blinded by her majesty?

KING.

What zeal, what fury hath inspired thee now?
My love, her mistress, is a gracious moon;
She an attending star, scarce seen a light.

BEROWNE.

My eyes are then no eyes, nor I Berowne:
O, but for my love, day would turn to night!
Of all complexions the cull'd sovereignty
Do meet, as at a fair, in her fair cheek,
Where several worthies make one dignity,
Where nothing wants that want itself doth seek.
Lend me the flourish of all gentle tongues,—
Fie, painted rhetoric! O, she needs it not:
To things of sale a seller's praise belongs,
She passes praise; then praise too short doth blot.
A wither'd hermit, five-score winters worn,
Might shake off fifty, looking in her eye:
Beauty doth varnish age, as if new-born,
And gives the crutch the cradle's infancy:
O, 'tis the sun that maketh all things shine.

KING.

By heaven, thy love is black as ebony.

BEROWNE.

Is ebony like her? O wood divine!
A wife of such wood were felicity.
O, who can give an oath? where is a book?
That I may swear beauty doth beauty lack,
If that she learn not of her eyè to look:
No face is fair that is not full so black.

KING.

O paradox! Black is the badge of hell,
The hue of dungeons and the stole of night;
And beauty's crest becomes the heavens well.

BEROWNE.

Devils soonest tempt, resembling spirits of light.
O, if in black my lady's brows be deckt,
It mourns that painting and usurping hair
Should ravish doters with a false aspect;
And therefore is she born to make black fair.
Her favour turns the fashion of the days,
For native blood is counted painting now;
And therefore red, that would avoid dispraise,
Paints itself black, to imitate her brow.

DUMAINE.

To look like her are chimney-sweepers black.

LONGAVILLE.

And since her time are colliers counted bright.

KING.

And Ethiopes of their sweet complexion crack.

DUMAINE.

Dark needs no candles now, for dark is light.

BEROWNE.

Your mistresses dare never come in rain,
For fear their colours should be washt away.

KING.

'Twere good, yours did; for, sir, to tell you plain,
I'll find a fairer face not washt to-day.

BEROWNE.

I'll prove her fair, or talk till doomsday here.

KING.

No devil will fright thee then so much as she.

DUMAINE.

I never knew man hold vile stuff so dear.

LONGAVILLE.

Look, here's thy love: my foot and her face see.

BEROWNE.

O, if the streets were paved with thine eyes,
Her feet were much too dainty for such tread!

DUMAINE.

O vile! then, as she goes, what upward lies
The street should see as she walkt overhead.

KING.

But what of this? are we not all in love?

BEROWNE.

Nothing so sure; and thereby all forsworn.

KING.

Then leave this chat; and, good Berowne, now prove
Our loving lawful, and our faith not torn.

DUMAINE.

Ay, marry, there; some flattery for this evil.

LONGAVILLE.

O, some authority how to proceed;
Some tricks, some quillets, how to cheat the devil.

DUMAINE.

Some salve for perjury.

BEROWNE.

'Tis more than need.
Have at you, then, affection's men-at-arms.
Consider what you first did swear unto,
To fast, to study, and to see no woman;

Flat treason 'gainst the kingly state of youth.
Say, can you fast? your stomachs are too young;
And abstinence engenders maladies.
And where that you have vow'd to study, lords,
In that each of you have forsworn his book,
Can you still dream and pore and thereon look?
For when would you, my lord, or you, or you,
Have found the ground of study's excellence
Without the beauty of a woman's face?
[From women's eyes this doctrine I derive;
They are the ground, the books, the academes
From whence doth spring the true Promethean fire.]
Why, universal plodding poisons up
The nimble spirits in the arteries,
As motion and long-during action tires
The sinewy vigour of the traveller.
Now, for not looking on a woman's face,
You have in that forsworn the use of eyes,
And study too, the causer of your vow;
For where is any author in the world
Teaches such beauty as a woman's eye?
Learning is but an adjunct to ourself
And where we are our learning likewise is:
Then when ourselves we see in ladies' eyes,
Do we not likewise see our learning there?
O, we have made a vow to study, lords,
And in that vow we have forsworn our books.
For when would you, my liege, or you, or you,
In leaden contemplation have found out
Such fiery numbers as the prompting eyes
Of beauty's tutors have enricht you with?
Other slow arts entirely keep the brain;
And therefore, finding barren practisers,
Scarce show a harvest of their heavy toil:
But love, first learned in a lady's eyes,
Lives not alone immured in the brain;
But, with the motion of all elements,
Courses as swift as thought in every power,
And gives to every power a double power,
Above their functions and their offices.
It adds a precious seeing to the eye;
A lover's eyes will gaze an eagle blind;
A lover's ear will hear the lowest sound,
When the suspicious head of theft is stopt:
Love's feeling is more soft and sensible
Than are the tender horns of cockled snails;
Love's tongue proves dainty Bacchus gross in taste:
For valour, is not Love a Hercules,
Still climbing trees in the Hesperides?
Subtle as Sphinx; as sweet and musical
As bright Apollo's lute, strung with his hair:
And when Love speaks, the voice of all the gods
Make heaven drowsy with the harmony.
Never durst poet touch a pen to write
Until his ink were temper'd with Love's sighs;
O, then his lines would ravish savage ears
And plant in tyrants mild humility.
From women's eyes this doctrine I derive:
They sparkle still the right Promethean fire;
They are the books, the arts, the academes,
That show, contain and nourish all the world:
Else none at all in aught proves excellent.
Then fools you were these women to forswear,
Or keeping what is sworn, you will prove fools.
For wisdom's sake, a word that all men love,
Or for love's sake, a word that loves all men,
Or for men's sake, the authors of these women,
Or women's sake, by whom we men are men,
Let us once lose our oaths to find ourselves,
Or else we lose ourselves to keep our oaths.
It is religion to be thus forsworn,
For charity itself fulfils the law,
And who can sever love from charity?

KING.
Saint Cupid, then! and, soldiers, to the field!

BEROWNE.
Advance your standards, and upon them, lords;
Pell-mell, down with them! but be first advised,
In conflict that you get the sun of them.

LONGAVILLE.
Now to plain-dealing; lay these glozes by:
Shall we resolve to woo these girls of France?

KING.
And win them too: therefore let us devise
Some entertainment for them in their tents.

BEROWNE.
First, from the park let us conduct them thither;
Then homeward every man attach the hand
Of his fair mistress: in the afternoon
We will with some strange pastime solace them,
Such as the shortness of the time can shape;
For revels, dances, masks and merry hours
Forerun fair Love, strewing her way with flowers.

KING.
Away, away! no time shall be omitted
That will betime, and may by us be fitted.

BEROWNE.
Allons! allons! Sow'd cockle reap'd no corn;
And justice always whirls in equal measure:
Light wenches may prove plagues to men forsworn;
If so, our copper buys no better treasure.
[Exeunt.

ACT V. SCENE I.

The same.

Enter HOLOFERNES, SIR NATHANIEL, *and* DULL.

HOLOFERNES.
SATIS *quod sufficit.*

SIR NATHANIEL.
I praise God for you, sir: your reasons at dinner have been sharp and sententious; pleasant without scurrility, witty without affection, audacious without impudency, learned without opinion, and strange without heresy. I did converse this quondam day with a companion of the king's, who is intituled, nominated, or call'd, Don Adriano de Armado.

HOLOFERNES.
Novi hominem tanquam te: his humour is lofty, his discourse peremptory, his tongue filed, his eye ambitious, his gait majestical, and his general behaviour vain, ridiculous, and thrasonical. He is too pickt, too spruce, too affected, too odd, as it were, too peregrinate, as I may call it.

SIR NATHANIEL.
A most singular and choice epithet.
[Draws out his table-book.

HOLOFERNES.
He draweth out the thread of his verbosity finer

than the staple of his argument. I abhor such fanatical phantasms, such insociable and point-device companions; such rackers of orthography, as to speak dout, fine, when he should say doubt; det, when he should pronounce debt,—d, e, b, t, not d, e, t: he clepeth a calf, cauf; half, hauf; neighbour *vocatur* nebour; neigh abbreviated ne. This is abhominable,—which he would call abbominable: it insinuateth me of insanie: *ne intelligis, domine?* to make frantic, lunatic.

SIR NATHANIEL.

Laus Deo, bone intelligo.

HOLOFERNES.

Bone?—*bone* for *bene!* Priscian a little scratcht, 'twill serve.

SIR NATHANIEL.

Videsne quis venit?

HOLOFERNES.

Video, et gaudeo.

Enter ARMADO, MOTH, *and* COSTARD.

ARMADO.

Chirrah! [*To* MOTH.

HOLOFERNES.

Quare chirrah, not sirrah?

ARMADO.

Men of peace, well encounter'd.

HOLOFERNES.

Most military sir, salutation.

MOTH [*aside to* COSTARD].

They have been at a great feast of languages, and stolen the scraps.

COSTARD.

O, they have lived long on the alms-basket of words. I marvel thy master hath not eaten thee for a word; for thou art not so long by the head as *honorificabilitudinitatibus;* thou art easier swallow'd than a flap-dragon.

MOTH.

Peace! the peal begins.

ARMADO [*to* HOLOFERNES].

Monsieur, are you not letter'd?

MOTH.

Yes, yes; he teaches boys the horn-book. What is a, b, spelt backward, with the horn on his head?

HOLOFERNES.

Ba, *pueritia,* with a horn added.

MOTH.

Ba, most silly sheep with a horn. You hear his learning.

HOLOFERNES.

Quis, quis, thou consonant?

MOTH.

The last of the five vowels, if You repeat them; or the fifth, if I.

HOLOFERNES.

I will repeat them,—a, e, i,—

MOTH.

The sheep: the other two concludes it,—o, u.

ARMADO.

Now, by the salt wave of the Mediterraneum, a sweet touch, a quick venue of wit! snip, snap, quick and home! it rejoiceth my intellect: true wit!

MOTH.

Offer'd by a child to an old man; which is wit-old.

HOLOFERNES.

What is the figure? what is the figure?

MOTH.

Horns.

HOLOFERNES.

Thou disputes like an infant: go, whip thy gig.

MOTH.

Lend me your horn to make one, and I will whip about your infamy *circum circa,*—a gig of a cuckold's horn.

COSTARD.

An I had but one penny in the world, thou shouldst have it to buy gingerbread: hold, there is the very remuneration I had of thy master, thou halfpenny purse of wit, thou pigeon-egg of discretion. O, an the heavens were so pleased that thou wert but my bastard, what a joyful father wouldst thou make me! Go to; thou hast it *ad dunghill,* at the fingers' ends, as they say.

HOLOFERNES.

O, I smell false Latin; dunghill for *unguem.*

ARMADO.

Arts-man, *præambula,* we will be singled from the barbarous. Do you not educate youth at the charge-house on the top of the mountain?

HOLOFERNES.

Or *mons,* the hill.

ARMADO.

At your sweet pleasure, for the mountain.

HOLOFERNES.

I do, sans question.

ARMADO.

Sir, it is the king's most sweet pleasure and affection to congratulate the princess at her pavilion in the posteriors of this day, which the rude multitude call the afternoon.

HOLOFERNES.

The posterior of the day, most generous sir, is liable, congruent and measurable for the afternoon: the word is well cull'd, chose, sweet and apt, I do assure you, sir, I do assure.

ARMADO.

Sir, the king is a noble gentleman, and my familiar, I do assure ye, very good friend: for what is inward between us, let it pass. I do beseech thee, remember thy courtesy; I beseech thee, apparel thy head: and among other importunate and most serious designs, and of great import indeed, too, but let that pass: for I must tell thee, it will please his Grace, by the world, sometime to lean upon my poor shoulder, and with his royal finger, thus, dally with my excrement, with my mustachio; but, sweet heart, let that pass. By the world, I recount no fable: some certain special honours it pleaseth his greatness to impart to Armado, a soldier, a man of travel, that hath seen the world; but let that pass. The very all of all is,—but, sweet heart, I do implore secrecy,—that the king would have me present the princess, sweet chuck, with some delightful ostentation, or show, or pageant, or antick, or firework. Now, understanding that the curate and your sweet self are good at such eruptions and sudden breaking out of mirth, as it were, I have acquainted you withal, to the end to crave your assistance.

HOLOFERNES.

Sir, you shall present before her the Nine Worthies. Sir Nathaniel, as concerning some entertainment of time, some show in the posterior of this day, to be render'd by our assistance, the king's command, and this most gallant, illustrate, and learned gentleman, before the princess; I say none so fit as to present the Nine Worthies.

SIR NATHANIEL.

Where will you find men worthy enough to present them?

HOLOFERNES.

Joshua, yourself; myself or this gallant gentleman, Judas Maccabæus; this swain, because of his great limb or joint, shall pass Pompey the Great; the page, Hercules,—

ARMADO.

Pardon, sir; error: he is not quantity enough for that Worthy's thumb: he is not so big as the end of his club.

HOLOFERNES.

Shall I have audience? he shall present Hercules in minority: his enter and exit shall be strangling a snake; and I will have an apology for that purpose.

MOTH.

An excellent device! so, if any of the audience hiss, you may cry, 'Well done, Hercules! now thou crushest the snake!' that is the way to make an offence gracious, though few have the grace to do it.

ARMADO.

For the rest of the Worthies?—

HOLOFERNES.

I will play three myself.

MOTH.

Thrice-worthy gentleman!

ARMADO.

Shall I tell you a thing?

HOLOFERNES.

We attend.

ARMADO.

We will have, if this fadge not, an antick. I beseech you, follow.

HOLOFERNES.

Via, goodman Dull! thou hast spoken no word all this while.

DULL.

Nor understood none neither, sir.

HOLOFERNES.

Allons! we will employ thee.

DULL.

I'll make one in a dance, or so; or I will play
On the tabor to the Worthies, and let them dance
the hay.

HOLOFERNES.

Most dull, honest Dull! To our sport, away!
[*Exeunt.*

SCENE II.

The same. Before the Princess's pavilion.

Enter the PRINCESS, KATHARINE, ROSALINE, *and* MARIA.

PRINCESS.

SWEET hearts, we shall be rich ere we depart,
If fairings come thus plentifully in:
A lady wall'd about with diamonds!
Look you what I have from the loving king.

ROSALINE.

Madam, came nothing else along with that?

PRINCESS.

Nothing but this! yes, as much love in rime
As would be cramm'd up in a sheet of paper,
Writ o' both sides the leaf, margent and all,
That he was fain to seal on Cupid's name.

ROSALINE.

That was the way to make his godhead wax,
For he hath been five thousand years a boy.

KATHARINE.

Ay, and a shrewd unhappy gallows too.

ROSALINE.

You'll ne'er be friends with him; a' kill'd your
sister.

KATHARINE.

He made her melancholy, sad, and heavy;
And so she died: had she been light, like you,
Of such a merry, nimble, stirring spirit,
She might ha' been a grandam ere she died:
And so may you; for a light heart lives long.

ROSALINE.

What's your dark meaning, mouse, of this light
word?

KATHARINE.

A light condition in a beauty dark.

ROSALINE.

We need more light to find your meaning out.

KATHARINE.

You'll mar the light by taking it in snuff;
Therefore I'll darkly end the argument.

ROSALINE.

Look, what you do, you do it still i' th' dark.

KATHARINE.

So do not you, for you are a light wench.

ROSALINE.

Indeed I weigh not you, and therefore light.

KATHARINE.

You weigh me not? O, that's you care not for me.

ROSALINE.

Great reason; for 'past cure is still past care.'

PRINCESS.

Well bandied both; a set of wit well play'd.
But, Rosaline, you have a favour too:
Who sent it? and what is it?

ROSALINE.

I would you knew:
An if my face were but as fair as yours,
My favour were as great; be witness this.
Nay, I have verses too, I thank Berowne:
The numbers true; and, were the numb'ring too,
I were the fairest goddess on the ground:
I am compared to twenty thousand fairs.
O, he hath drawn my picture in his letter!

PRINCESS.

Any thing like?

ROSALINE.

Much in the letters; nothing in the praise.

PRINCESS.

Beauteous as ink; a good conclusion.

KATHARINE.

Fair as a text B in a copy-book.

ROSALINE.

'Ware pencils, ho! let me not die your debtor,
My red dominical, my golden letter:
O that your face were not so full of O's!

PRINCESS.

A pox of that jest! and I beshrew all shrows.

But, Katharine, what was sent to you from fair
Dumaine?

KATHARINE.

Madam, this glove.

PRINCESS.

Did he not send you twain?

KATHARINE.

Yes, madam, and moreover
Some thousand verses of a faithful lover,
A huge translation of hypocrisy,
Vilely compiled, profound simplicity.

MARIA.

This and these pearls to me sent Longaville:
The letter is too long by half a mile.

PRINCESS.

I think no less. Dost thou not wish in heart
The chain were longer and the letter short?

MARIA.

Ay, or I would these hands might never part.

PRINCESS.

We are wise girls to mock our lovers so.

ROSALINE.

They are worse fools to purchase mocking so.
That same Berowne I'll torture ere I go:
O that I knew he were but in by th' week!
How I would make him fawn and beg and seek
And wait the season and observe the times,
And spend his prodigal wits in bootless rimes,
And shape his service wholly to my hests,
And make him proud to make me proud that jests!
So pertaunt-like would I o'ersway his state
That he should be my fool and I his fate.

PRINCESS.

None are so surely caught, when they are catcht,
As wit turn'd fool: folly, in wisdom hatcht,
Hath wisdom's warrant and the help of school
And wit's own grace to grace a learned fool.

ROSALINE.

The blood of youth burns not with such excess
As gravity's revolt to wantonness.

MARIA.

Folly in fools bears not so strong a note
As foolery in the wise, when wit doth dote;
Since all the power thereof it doth apply
To prove, by wit, worth in simplicity.

PRINCESS.

Here comes Boyet, and mirth is in his face.

Enter BOYET.

BOYET.

O, I am stabb'd with laughter! Where's her Grace?

PRINCESS.

Thy news, Boyet?

BOYET.

Prepare, madam, prepare!
Arm, wenches, arm! encounters mounted are
Against your peace: Love doth approach disguised,
Armed in arguments; you'll be surprised:
Muster your wits; stand in your own defence;
Or hide your heads like cowards, and fly hence.

PRINCESS.

Saint Denis to Saint Cupid! What are they
That charge their breath against us? say, scout, say.

BOYET.

Under the cool shade of a sycamore
I thought to close mine eyes some half an hour;
When, lo! to interrupt my purposed rest,
Toward that shade I might behold addrest
The king and his companions: warily
I stole into a neighbour thicket by,
And overheard what you shall overhear;
That, by and by, disguised they will be here.
Their herald is a pretty knavish page,
That well by heart hath conn'd his embassage:
Action and accent did they teach him there;
'Thus must thou speak,' and 'thus thy body bear':
And ever and anon they made a doubt
Presence majestical would put him out;
'For,' quoth the king, 'an angel shalt thou see;
Yet fear not thou, but speak audaciously.'
The boy replied, 'An angel is not evil;
I should have fear'd her had she been a devil.'
With that, all laught and clapt him on the
shoulder,
Making the bold wag by their praises bolder:
One rubb'd his elbow thus, and fleer'd and swore
A better speech was never spoke before;
Another, with his finger and his thumb,
Cried, 'Via! we will do't, come what will come;'
The third he caper'd, and cried, 'All goes well;'
The fourth turn'd on the toe, and down he fell.
With that, they all did tumble on the ground,
With such a zealous laughter, so profound,
That in this spleen ridiculous appears,
To check their folly, passion's solemn tears.

PRINCESS.

But what, but what, come they to visit us?

BOYET.

They do, they do; and are apparell'd thus,
Like Muscovites or Russians, as I guess.
Their purpose is to parle, to court and dance;
And every one his love-feat will advance
Unto his several mistress, which they'll know
By favours several which they did bestow.

PRINCESS.

And will they so? the gallants shall be taskt;
For, ladies, we will every one be maskt;
And not a man of them shall have the grace,
Despite of suit, to see a lady's face.
Hold, Rosaline, this favour thou shalt wear,
And then the king will court thee for his dear;
Hold, take thou this, my sweet, and give me thine,
So shall Berowne take me for Rosaline.
And change you favours too; so shall your loves
Woo contrary, deceived by these removes.

ROSALINE.

Come on, then; wear the favours most in sight.

KATHARINE.

But in this changing what is your intent?

PRINCESS.

The effect of my intent is to cross theirs:
They do it but in mocking merriment;
And mock for mock is only my intent.
Their several counsels they unbosom shall
To loves mistook, and so be mockt withal
Upon the next occasion that we meet,
With visages display'd, to talk and greet.

ROSALINE.

But shall we dance, if they desire us to't?

PRINCESS.

No, to the death, we will not move a foot;
Nor to their penn'd speech render we no grace,
But while 'tis spoke each turn away her face.

BOYET.
Why, that contempt will kill the speaker's heart,
And quite divorce his memory from his part.
PRINCESS.
Therefore I do it; and I make no doubt
The rest will ne'er come in, if he be out.
There's no such sport as sport by sport o'erthrown,
To make theirs ours and ours none but our own:
So shall we stay, mocking intended game,
And they, well mockt, depart away with shame.
[*Trumpets sound within.*
BOYET.
The trumpet sounds: be maskt; the maskers come.
[*The Ladies mask.*
Enter BLACKAMOORS *with music;* MOTH *with a speech; the* KING, BEROWNE, LONGAVILLE, *and* DUMAINE, *disguised as Russians.*
MOTH.
All hail, the richest beauties on the earth!—
BOYET.
Beauties no richer than rich taffeta.
MOTH.
A holy parcel of the fairest dames
[*The Ladies turn their backs to him.*
That ever turn'd their—backs—to mortal views!
BEROWNE [*aside to* MOTH].
Their eyes, villain, their eyes.
MOTH.
That ever turn'd their eyes to mortal views!—
Out—
BOYET.
True; out indeed.
MOTH.
Out of your favours, heavenly spirits, vouchsafe
Not to behold—
BEROWNE [*aside to* MOTH].
Once to behold, rogue.
MOTH.
Once to behold with your sun-beamed eyes,
——with your sun-beamed eyes—
BOYET.
They will not answer to that epithet;
You were best call it 'daughter-beamed eyes.'
MOTH.
They do not mark me, and that brings me out.
BEROWNE.
Is this your perfectness? be gone, you rogue!
[*Exit* MOTH.
ROSALINE.
What would these strangers? know their minds, Boyet:
If they do speak our language, 'tis our will
That some plain man recount their purposes:
Know what they would.
BOYET.
What would you with the princess?
BEROWNE.
Nothing but peace and gentle visitation.
ROSALINE.
What would they, say they?
BOYET.
Nothing but peace and gentle visitation.
ROSALINE.
Why, that they have; and bid them so be gone.
BOYET.
She says, you have it, and you may be gone.
KING.
Say to her, we have measured many miles
To tread a measure with her on this grass.
BOYET.
They say, that they have measured many a mile
To tread a measure with you on this grass.
ROSALINE.
It is not so. Ask them how many inches
Is in one mile: if they have measured many,
The measure then of one is easily told.
BOYET.
If to come hither you have measured miles,
And many miles, the princess bids you tell
How many inches doth fill up one mile.
BEROWNE.
Tell her, we measure them by weary steps.
BOYET.
She hears herself.
ROSALINE.
How many weary steps,
Of many weary miles you have o'ergone,
Are number'd in the travel of one mile?
BEROWNE.
We number nothing that we spend for you:
Our duty is so rich, so infinite,
That we may do it still without accompt.
Vouchsafe to show the sunshine of your face,
That we, like savages, may worship it.
ROSALINE.
My face is but a moon, and clouded too.
KING.
Blessed are clouds, to do as such clouds do!
Vouchsafe, bright moon, and these thy stars, to shine,
Those clouds removed, upon our watery eyne.
ROSALINE.
O vain petitioner! beg a greater matter;
Thou now requests but moonshine in the water.
KING.
Then, in our measure do but vouchsafe one change.
Thou bid'st me beg: this begging is not strange.
ROSALINE.
Play, music, then! Nay, you must do it soon.
[*Music plays.*
Not yet! no dance! Thus change I like the moon.
KING.
Will you not dance? How come you thus estranged?
ROSALINE.
You took the moon at full, but now she's changed.
KING.
Yet still she is the moon, and I the man.
The music plays; vouchsafe some motion to it.
ROSALINE.
Our ears vouchsafe it.
KING.
But your legs should do it.
ROSALINE.
Since you are strangers and come here by chance,
We'll not be nice: take hands. We will not dance.
KING.
Why take we hands, then?
ROSALINE.
Only to part friends:
Curtsey, sweet hearts; and so the measure ends.

KING.
More measure of this measure; be not nice.

ROSALINE.
We can afford no more at such a price.

KING.
Price you yourselves: what buys your company?

ROSALINE.
Your absence only.

KING.
That can never be.

ROSALINE.
Then cannot we be bought: and so, adieu;
Twice to your visor, and half once to you.

KING.
If you deny to dance, let's hold more chat.

ROSALINE.
In private, then.

KING.
I am best pleased with that.
[*They converse apart.*

BEROWNE.
White-handed mistress, one sweet word with thee.

PRINCESS.
Honey, and milk, and sugar; there is three.

BEROWNE.
Nay then, two treys, an if you grow so nice,
Metheglin, wort, and malmsey: well run, dice!
There's half-a-dozen sweets.

PRINCESS.
Seventh sweet, adieu:
Since you can cog, I'll play no more with you.

BEROWNE.
One word in secret.

PRINCESS.
Let it not be sweet.

BEROWNE.
Thou grievest my gall.

PRINCESS.
Gall! bitter.

BEROWNE.
Therefore meet.
[*They converse apart.*

DUMAINE.
Will you vouchsafe with me to change a word?

MARIA.
Name it.

DUMAINE.
Fair lady,—

MARIA.
Say you so? Fair lord,—
Take that for your fair lady.

DUMAINE.
Please it you,
As much in private, and I'll bid adieu.
[*They converse apart.*

KATHARINE.
What, was your visard made without a tongue?

LONGAVILLE.
I know the reason, lady, why you ask.

KATHARINE.
O for your reason! quickly, sir; I long.

LONGAVILLE.
You have a double tongue within your mask,
And would afford my speechless visard half.

KATHARINE.
Veal, quoth the Dutchman. Is not 'veal' a calf?

LONGAVILLE.
A calf, fair lady!

KATHARINE.
No, a fair lord calf.

LONGAVILLE.
Let's part the word.

KATHARINE.
No, I'll not be your half:
Take all, and wean it; it may prove an ox.

LONGAVILLE.
Look, how you butt yourself in these sharp mocks!
Will you give horns, chaste lady? do not so.

KATHARINE.
Then die a calf, before your horns do grow.

LONGAVILLE.
One word in private with you, ere I die.

KATHARINE.
Bleat softly then; the butcher hears you cry.
[*They converse apart.*

BOYET.
The tongues of mocking wenches are as keen
As is the razor's edge invisible,
Cutting a smaller hair than may be seen,
Above the sense of sense; so sensible
Seemeth their conference; their conceits have wings
Fleeter than arrows, bullets, wind, thought, swifter things.

ROSALINE.
Not one word more, my maids; break off, break off.

BEROWNE.
By heaven, all dry-beaten with pure scoff!

KING.
Farewell, mad wenches; you have simple wits.

PRINCESS.
Twenty adieus, my frozen Muscovits.
[*Exeunt* KING, LORDS, *and* BLACKAMOORS.
Are these the breed of wits so wonder'd at?

BOYET.
Tapers they are, with your sweet breaths puft out.

ROSALINE.
Well-liking wits they have; gross, gross; fat, fat.

PRINCESS.
O poverty in wit, kingly-poor flout!
Will they not, think you, hang themselves to-night?
Or ever, but in visards, show their faces?
This pert Berowne was out of countenance quite.

ROSALINE.
O, they were all in lamentable cases!
The king was weeping-ripe for a good word.

PRINCESS.
Berowne did swear himself out of all suit.

MARIA.
Dumaine was at my service, and his sword:
No point, quoth I; my servant straight was mute.

KATHARINE.
Lord Longaville said, I came o'er his heart;
And trow you what he call'd me?

PRINCESS.
Qualm, perhaps.

KATHARINE.
Yes, in good faith.

PRINCESS.
Go, sickness as thou art!

ROSALINE.
Well, better wits have worn plain statute-caps.
But will you hear? the king is my love sworn.

PRINCESS.
And quick Berowne hath plighted faith to me.
KATHARINE.
And Longaville was for my service born.
MARIA.
Dumaine is mine, as sure as bark on tree.
BOYET.
Madam, and pretty mistresses, give ear:
Immediately they will again be here
In their own shapes; for it can never be
They will digest this harsh indignity.
PRINCESS.
Will they return?
BOYET.
They will, they will, God knows.
And leap for joy, though they are lame with blows:
Therefore change favours; and, when they repair,
Blow like sweet roses in this summer air.
PRINCESS.
How blow? how blow? speak to be understood.
BOYET.
Fair ladies maskt are roses in their bud;
Dismaskt, their damask sweet commixture shown,
Are angels vailing clouds, or roses blown.
PRINCESS.
Avaunt, perplexity! What shall we do,
If they return in their own shapes to woo?
ROSALINE.
Good madam, if by me you'll be advised,
Let's mock them still, as well known as disguised:
Let us complain to them what fools were here,
Disguised like Muscovites, in shapeless gear;
And wonder what they were and to what end
Their shallow shows and prologue vilely penn'd,
And their rough carriage so ridiculous,
Should be presented at our tent to us.
BOYET.
Ladies, withdraw: the gallants are at hand.
PRINCESS.
Whip to our tents, as roes runs o'er land.
[*Exeunt* PRINCESS, ROSALINE, KATHARINE, *and* MARIA.
Enter the KING, BEROWNE, LONGAVILLE, *and* DUMAINE, *in their proper habits.*
KING.
Fair sir, God save you! Where's the princess?
BOYET.
Gone to her tent. Please it your majesty
Command me any service to her thither?
KING.
That she vouchsafe me audience for one word.
BOYET.
I will; and so will she, I know, my lord. [*Exit.*
BEROWNE.
This fellow pecks up wit as pigeons pease,
And utters it again when God doth please:
He is wit's pedlar, and retails his wares
At wakes and wassails, meetings, markets, fairs;
And we that sell by gross, the Lord doth know,
Have not the grace to grace it with such show.
This gallant pins the wenches on his sleeve;
Had he been Adam, he had tempted Eve;
A' can carve too, and lisp: why, this is he
That kist his hand away in courtesy;
This is the ape of form, monsieur the nice,
That, when he plays at tables, chides the dice
In honourable terms: nay, he can sing
A mean most meanly; and in ushering
Mend him who can: the ladies call him sweet;
The stairs, as he treads on them, kiss his feet:
This is the flower that smiles on every one,
To show his teeth as white as whales bone;
And consciences, that will not die in debt,
Pay him the due of honey-tongued Boyet.
KING.
A blister on his sweet tongue, with my heart,
That put Armado's page out of his part!
BEROWNE.
See where it comes! Behaviour, what wert thou
Till this madman show'd thee? and what art thou now?
Enter the PRINCESS, *usher'd by* BOYET; ROSALINE, MARIA, *and* KATHARINE.
KING.
All hail, sweet madam, and fair time of day!
PRINCESS.
'Fair' in 'all hail' is foul, as I conceive.
KING.
Construe my speeches better, if you may.
PRINCESS.
Then wish me better; I will give you leave.
KING.
We came to visit you, and purpose now
To lead you to our court; vouchsafe it then.
PRINCESS.
This field shall hold me; and so hold your vow:
Nor God, nor I, delights in perjured men.
KING.
Rebuke me not for that which you provoke:
The virtue of your eye must break my oath.
PRINCESS.
You nickname virtue; vice you should have spoke;
For virtue's office never breaks men's troth.
Now by my maiden honour, yet as pure
As the unsullied lily, I protest,
A world of torments though I should endure,
I would not yield to be your house's guest;
So much I hate a breaking cause to be
Of heavenly oaths, vow'd with integrity.
KING.
O, you have lived in desolation here,
Unseen, unvisited, much to our shame.
PRINCESS.
Not so, my lord; it is not so, I swear;
We have had pastimes here and pleasant game:
A mess of Russians left us but of late.
KING.
How, madam! Russians!
PRINCESS.
Ay, in truth, my lord;
Trim gallants, full of courtship and of state.
ROSALINE.
Madam, speak true. It is not so, my lord:
My lady, to the manner of the days,
In courtesy gives undeserving praise.
We four indeed confronted were with four
In Russian habit: here they stay'd an hour,
And talkt apace; and in that hour, my lord,
They did not bless us with one happy word.
I dare not call them fools; but this I think,
When they are thirsty, fools would fain have drink.

BEROWNE.
This jest is dry to me. Fair gentle sweet,
Your wits makes wise things foolish: when we greet,
With eyes best seeing, heaven's fiery eye,
By light we lose light: your capacity
Is of that nature that to your huge store
Wise things seem foolish and rich things but poor.

ROSALINE.
This proves you wise and rich, for in my eye,—

BEROWNE.
I am a fool, and full of poverty.

ROSALINE.
But that you take what doth to you belong,
It were a fault to snatch words from my tongue.

BEROWNE.
O, I am yours, and all that I possess!

ROSALINE.
All the fool mine?

BEROWNE.
I cannot give you less.

ROSALINE.
Which of the visards was it that you wore?

BEROWNE.
Where? when? what visard? why demand you this?

ROSALINE.
There, then, that visard; that superfluous case
That hid the worse and show'd the better face.

KING.
We are descried; they'll mock us now downright.

DUMAINE.
Let us confess and turn it to a jest.

PRINCESS.
Amazed, my lord? why looks your highness sad?

ROSALINE.
Help, hold his brows! he'll swound! Why look you pale?
Sea-sick, I think, coming from Muscovy.

BEROWNE.
Thus pour the stars down plagues for perjury.
Can any face of brass hold longer out?
Here stand I, lady: dart thy skill at me;
Bruise me with scorn, confound me with a flout;
Thrust thy sharp wit quite through my ignorance;
Cut me to pieces with thy keen conceit;
And I will wish thee never more to dance,
Nor never more in Russian habit wait.
O, never will I trust to speeches penn'd,
Nor to the motion of a schoolboy's tongue,
Nor never come in visard to my friend,
Nor woo in rime, like a blind harper's song!
Taffeta phrases, silken terms precise,
Three-piled hyperboles, spruce affectation,
Figures pedantical; these summer-flies
Have blown me full of maggot ostentation:
I do forswear them; and I here protest,
By this white glove,—how white the hand, God knows!—
Henceforth my wooing mind shall be exprest
In russet yeas and honest kersey noes:
And, to begin, wench,—so God help me, la!—
My love to thee is sound, sans crack or flaw.

ROSALINE.
Sans sans, I pray you.

BEROWNE.
Yet I have a trick
Of the old rage: bear with me, I am sick;
I'll leave it by degrees. Soft, let us see:
Write, 'Lord have mercy on us' on those three;
They are infected; in their hearts it lies;
They have the plague, and caught it of your eyes;
These lords are visited; you are not free,
For the Lord's tokens on you do I see.

PRINCESS.
No, they are free that gave these tokens to us.

BEROWNE.
Our states are forfeit: seek not to undo us.

ROSALINE.
It is not so; for how can this be true,
That you stand forfeit, being those that sue?

BEROWNE.
Peace! for I will not have to do with you.

ROSALINE.
Nor shall not, if I do as I intend.

BEROWNE.
Speak for yourselves; my wit is at an end.

KING.
Teach us, sweet madam, for our rude transgression
Some fair excuse.

PRINCESS.
The fairest is confession.
Were not you here but even now disguised?

KING.
Madam, I was.

PRINCESS.
And were you well advised?

KING.
I was, fair madam.

PRINCESS.
When you then were here,
What did you whisper in your lady's ear?

KING.
That more than all the world I did respect her.

PRINCESS.
When she shall challenge this, you will reject her.

KING.
Upon mine honour, no.

PRINCESS.
Peace, peace! forbear:
Your oath once broke, you force not to forswear.

KING.
Despise me, when I break this oath of mine.

PRINCESS.
I will: and therefore keep it. Rosaline,
What did the Russian whisper in your ear?

ROSALINE.
Madam, he swore that he did hold me dear
As precious eyesight, and did value me
Above this world; adding thereto, moreover,
That he would wed me, or else die my lover.

PRINCESS.
God give thee joy of him! the noble lord
Most honourably doth uphold his word.

KING.
What mean you, madam? by my life, my troth,
I never swore this lady such an oath.

ROSALINE.
By heaven, you did; and to confirm it plain,
You gave me this: but take it, sir, again.

KING.
My faith and this the princess I did give:
I knew her by this jewel on her sleeve.

PRINCESS.

Pardon me, sir, this jewel did she wear;
And Lord Berowne, I thank him, is my dear.
What, will you have me, or your pearl again?

BEROWNE.

Neither of either; I remit both twain.
I see the trick on't: here was a consent,
Knowing aforehand of our merriment,
To dash it like a Christmas comedy:
Some carry-tale, some please-man, some slight zany,
Some mumble-news, some trencher-knight, some Dick,
That smiles his cheek in years and knows the trick
To make my lady laugh when she's disposed,
Told our intents before; which once disclosed,
The ladies did change favours: and then we,
Following the signs, woo'd but the sign of she.
Now, to our perjury to add more terror,
We are again forsworn, in will and error.
Much upon this it is: and might not you [*to* BOYET.
Forestall our sport, to make us thus untrue?
Do not you know my lady's foot by th' squier,
And laugh upon the apple of her eye?
And stand between her back, sir, and the fire,
Holding a trencher, jesting merrily?
You put our page out: go, you are allow'd;
Die when you will, a smock shall be your shroud.
You leer upon me, do you? there's an eye
Wounds like a leaden sword.

BOYET.

Full merrily
Hath this brave manage, this career, been run.

BEROWNE.

Lo, he is tilting straight! Peace! I have done.

Enter COSTARD.

Welcome, pure wit! thou partest a fair fray.

COSTARD.

O Lord, sir, they would know
Whether the three Worthies shall come in or no.

BEROWNE.

What, are there but three?

COSTARD.

No, sir; but it is vara fine,
For every one pursents three.

BEROWNE.

And three times thrice is nine.

COSTARD.

Not so, sir; under correction, sir; I hope it is not so.
You cannot beg us, sir, I can assure you, sir; we know what we know:
I hope, sir, three times thrice, sir,—

BEROWNE.

—Is not nine.

COSTARD.

Under correction, sir, we know whereuntil it doth amount.

BEROWNE.

By Jove, I always took three threes for nine.

COSTARD.

O Lord, sir, it were pity you should get your living by reck'ning, sir.

BEROWNE.

How much is it?

COSTARD.

O Lord, sir, the parties themselves, the actors, sir, will show whereuntil it doth amount: for mine own part, I am, as they say, but to parfect one man in one poor man, Pompey the Great, sir.

BEROWNE.

Art thou one of the Worthies?

COSTARD.

It pleased them to think me worthy of Pompey the Great: for mine own part, I know not the degree of the Worthy, but I am to stand for him.

BEROWNE.

Go, bid them prepare.

COSTARD.

We will turn it finely off, sir; we will take some care. [*Exit.*

KING.

Berowne, they will shame us: let them not approach.

BEROWNE.

We are shame-proof, my lord: and 'tis some policy
To have one show worse than the king's and his company.

KING.

I say they shall not come.

PRINCESS.

Nay, my good lord, let me o'errule you now:
That sport best pleases that doth least know how:
Where zeal strives to content, and the contents
Dies in the zeal of that which it presents:
Their form confounded makes most form in mirth,
When great things labouring perish in their birth.

BEROWNE.

A right description of our sport, my lord.

Enter ARMADO.

ARMADO.

Anointed, I implore so much expense of thy royal sweet breath as will utter a brace of words.

[*Converses apart with the* KING, *and delivers him a paper.*

PRINCESS.

Doth this man serve God?

BEROWNE.

Why ask you?

PRINCESS.

A' speaks not like a man of God his making.

ARMADO.

That is all one, my fair, sweet, honey monarch; for, I protest, the schoolmaster is exceeding fantastical; too too vain, too too vain: but we will put it, as they say, to fortune de la guerra. I wish you the peace of mind, most royal couplement! [*Exit.*

KING.

Here is like to be a good presence of Worthies. He presents Hector of Troy; the swain, Pompey the Great; the parish curate, Alexander; Armado's page, Hercules; the pedant, Judas Maccabæus:
And if these four Worthies in their first show thrive,
These four will change habits, and present the other five.

BEROWNE.

There is five in the first show.

KING.

You are deceived; 'tis not so.

BEROWNE.

The pedant, the braggart, the hedge-priest, the fool and the boy:—

Abate throw at novum, and the whole world again
Cannot pick out five such, take each one in his vein.

KING.

The ship is under sail, and here she comes amain.

Enter COSTARD, *for* POMPEY.

COSTARD.

I Pompey am,—

BOYET.

You lie, you are not he.

COSTARD.

I Pompey am,—

BOYET.

With libbard's head on knee.

BEROWNE.

Well said, old mocker: I must needs be friends with thee.

COSTARD.

I Pompey am, Pompey surnamed the Big,—

DUMAINE.

The Great.

COSTARD.

It is 'Great,' sir:—
Pompey surnamed the Great;
That oft in field, with targe and shield, did make my foe to sweat:
And travelling along this coast, I here am come by chance,
And lay my arms before the legs of this sweet lass of France.
If your ladyship would say, 'Thanks, Pompey,' I had done.

PRINCESS.

Great thanks, great Pompey.

COSTARD.

'Tis not so much worth; but I hope I was perfect:
I made a little fault in 'Great.'

BEROWNE.

My hat to a halfpenny, Pompey proves the best Worthy.

Enter SIR NATHANIEL, *for* ALEXANDER.

SIR NATHANIEL.

When in the world I lived, I was the world's commander;
By east, west, north, and south, I spread my conquering might:
My scutcheon plain declares that I am Alisander,—

BOYET.

Your nose says, no, you are not; for it stands too right.

BEROWNE.

Your nose smells 'no' in this, most tender-smelling knight.

PRINCESS.

The conqueror is dismay'd. Proceed, good Alexander.

SIR NATHANIEL.

When in the world I lived, I was the world's commander.

BOYET.

Most true, 'tis right; you were so, Alisander.

BEROWNE.

Pompey the Great,—

COSTARD.

Your servant, and Costard.

BEROWNE.

Take away the conqueror, take away Alisander.

COSTARD [*to* SIR NATHANIEL].

O, sir, you have overthrown Alisander the conqueror! You will be scraped out of the painted cloth for this: your lion, that holds his poll-axe sitting on a close-stool, will be given to Ajax: he will be the ninth Worthy. A conqueror, and afeard to speak! run away for shame, Alisander. [SIR NATHANIEL *retires*.] There, an't shall please you; a foolish mild man; an honest man, look you, and soon dasht. He is a marvellous good neighbour, faith, and a very good bowler: but, for Alisander,—alas, you see how 'tis,—a little o'erparted. But there are Worthies a-coming will speak their mind in some other sort.

PRINCESS.

Stand aside, good Pompey.

Enter HOLOFERNES, *for* JUDAS; *and* MOTH, *for* HERCULES.

HOLOFERNES.

Great Hercules is presented by this imp,
Whose club kill'd Cerberus, that three-headed canis;
And when he was a babe, a child, a shrimp,
Thus did he strangle serpents in his manus.
Quoniam he seemeth in minority,
Ergo I come with this apology.
—Keep some state in thy exit, and vanish.
[MOTH *retires*.
Judas I am,—

DUMAINE.

A Judas!

HOLOFERNES.

Not Iscariot, sir.
Judas I am, ycliped Maccabæus.

DUMAINE.

Judas Maccabæus clipt is plain Judas.

BEROWNE.

A kissing traitor. How art thou proved Judas?

HOLOFERNES.

Judas I am,—

DUMAINE.

The more shame for you, Judas.

HOLOFERNES.

What mean you, sir?

BOYET.

To make Judas hang himself.

HOLOFERNES.

Begin, sir; you are my elder.

BEROWNE.

Well follow'd: Judas was hang'd on an elder.

HOLOFERNES.

I will not be put out of countenance.

BEROWNE.

Because thou hast no face.

HOLOFERNES.

What is this?

BOYET.

A cittern-head.

DUMAINE.

The head of a bodkin.

BEROWNE.

A Death's face in a ring.

LONGAVILLE.

The face of an old Roman coin, scarce seen.

BOYET.

The pommel of Cæsar's falchion.

DUMAINE.
The carved-bone face on a flask.
BEROWNE.
Saint George's half-cheek in a brooch.
DUMAINE.
Ay, and in a brooch of lead.
BEROWNE.
Ay, and worn in the cap of a tooth-drawer.
And now forward; for we have put thee in countenance.
HOLOFERNES.
You have put me out of countenance.
BEROWNE.
False; we have given thee faces.
HOLOFERNES.
But you have out-faced them all.
BEROWNE.
An thou wert a lion, we would do so.
BOYET.
Therefore, as he is an ass, let him go.
And so adieu, sweet Jude! nay, why dost thou stay?
DUMAINE.
For the latter end of his name.
BEROWNE.
For the ass to the Jude; give it him:—Jud-as, away!
HOLOFERNES.
This is not generous, not gentle, not humble.
BOYET.
A light for Monsieur Judas! it grows dark, he may stumble. [HOLOFERNES *retires.*
PRINCESS.
Alas, poor Maccabæus, how hath he been baited!
Enter ARMADO, *for* HECTOR.
BEROWNE.
Hide thy head, Achilles: here comes Hector in arms.
DUMAINE.
Though my mocks come home by me, I will now be merry.
KING.
Hector was but a Troyan in respect of this.
BOYET.
But is this Hector?
KING.
I think Hector was not so clean-timber'd.
LONGAVILLE.
His leg is too big for Hector's.
DUMAINE.
More calf, certain.
BOYET.
No; he is best indued in the small.
BEROWNE.
This cannot be Hector.
DUMAINE.
He's a god or a painter; for he makes faces.
ARMADO.
The armipotent Mars, of lances the almighty,
Gave Hector a gift,—
DUMAINE.
A gilt nutmeg.
BEROWNE.
A lemon.
LONGAVILLE.
Stuck with cloves.
DUMAINE.
No, cloven.

ARMADO.
Peace!—
The armipotent Mars, of lances the almighty,
Gave Hector a gift, the heir of Ilion;
A man so breathed, that certain he would fight; yea
From morn till night, out of his pavilion.
I am that flower,—
DUMAINE.
That mint.
LONGAVILLE.
That columbine.
ARMADO.
Sweet Lord Longaville, rein thy tongue.
LONGAVILLE.
I must rather give it the rein, for it runs against Hector.
DUMAINE.
Ay, and Hector's a greyhound.
ARMADO.
The sweet war-man is dead and rotten; sweet chucks, beat not the bones of the buried: when he breathed, he was a man. But I will forward with my device. [*To the* PRINCESS] Sweet royalty, bestow on me the sense of hearing.
[BEROWNE *steps forth.*
PRINCESS.
Speak, brave Hector: we are much delighted.
ARMADO.
I do adore thy sweet Grace's slipper.
BOYET [*aside to* DUMAINE].
Loves her by the foot.
DUMAINE [*aside to* BOYET].
He may not by the yard.
ARMADO.
This Hector far surmounted Hannibal,—
COSTARD.
The party is gone.
Fellow Hector, she is gone; she is two months on her way.
ARMADO.
What meanest thou?
COSTARD.
Faith, unless you play the honest Troyan, the poor wench is cast away; she's quick; the child brags in her belly already: 'tis yours.
ARMADO.
Dost thou infamonize me among potentates? thou shalt die.
COSTARD.
Then shall Hector be whipped for Jaquenetta that is quick by him and hang'd for Pompey that is dead by him.
DUMAINE.
Most rare Pompey!
BOYET.
Renowned Pompey!
BEROWNE.
Greater than great, great, great, great Pompey! Pompey the Huge!
DUMAINE.
Hector trembles.
BEROWNE.
Pompey is moved. More Ates, more Ates! stir them on! stir them on!
DUMAINE.
Hector will challenge him.

BEROWNE.

Ay, if a' have no more man's blood in's belly than will sup a flea.

ARMADO.

By the north pole, I do challenge thee.

COSTARD.

I will not fight with a pole, like a northern man: I'll slash; I'll do it by the sword. I bepray you, let me borrow my arms again.

DUMAINE.

Room for the incensed Worthies!

COSTARD.

I'll do it in my shirt.

DUMAINE.

Most resolute Pompey!

MOTH.

Master, let me take you a button-hole lower. Do you not see Pompey is uncasing for the combat? What mean you? You will lose your reputation.

ARMADO.

Gentlemen and soldiers, pardon me; I will not combat in my shirt.

DUMAINE.

You may not deny it: Pompey hath made the challenge.

ARMADO.

Sweet bloods, I both may and will.

BEROWNE.

What reason have you for't?

ARMADO.

The naked truth of it is, I have no shirt; I go woolward for penance.

BOYET

True, and it was enjoin'd him in Rome for want of linen: since when, I'll be sworn, he wore none but a dishclout of Jaquenetta's, and that a' wears next his heart for a favour.

Enter a Messenger, MONSIEUR MERCADÉ.

MERCADÉ.

God save you, madam!

PRINCESS.

Welcome, Mercadé;
But that thou interrupt'st our merriment.

MERCADÉ.

I am sorry, madam; for the news I bring
Is heavy in my tongue. The king your father—

PRINCESS.

Dead, for my life!

MERCADÉ.

Even so; my tale is told.

BEROWNE.

Worthies, away! the scene begins to cloud.

ARMADO.

For mine own part, I breathe free breath. I have seen the day of wrong through the little hole of discretion, and I will right myself like a soldier.

[*Exeunt* WORTHIES.

KING.

How fares your majesty?

PRINCESS.

Boyet, prepare; I will away to-night.

KING.

Madam, not so; I do beseech you, stay.

PRINCESS.

Prepare, I say, I thank you, gracious lords,
For all your fair endeavours; and entreat,
Out of a new-sad soul, that you vouchsafe
In your rich wisdom to excuse or hide
The liberal opposition of our spirits,
If over-boldly we have borne ourselves
In the converse of breath: your gentleness
Was guilty of it. Farewell, worthy lord!
A heavy heart bears not a humble tongue:
Excuse me so, coming too short of thanks
For my great suit so easily obtain'd.

KING.

The extreme pace of time extremely forms
All causes to the purpose of his speed,
And often at his very loose decides
That which long process could not arbitrate:
And though the mourning brow of progeny
Forbid the smiling courtesy of love
The holy suit which fain it would convince,
Yet, since love's argument was first on foot,
Let not the cloud of sorrow justle it
From what it purposed; since, to wail friends lost
Is not by much so wholesome-profitable
As to rejoice at friends but newly found.

PRINCESS.

I understand you not: my griefs are double.

BEROWNE.

Honest plain words best pierce the ear of grief;
And by these badges understand the king.
For your fair sakes have we neglected time,
Play'd foul play with our oaths: your beauty, ladies,
Hath much deform'd us, fashioning our humours
Even to the opposed end of our intents:
And what in us hath seem'd ridiculous,—
As love is full of unbefitting strains,
All wanton as a child, skipping and vain,
Form'd by the eye and therefore, like the eye,
Full of straying shapes, of habits, and of forms,
Varying in subjects as the eye doth roll
To every varied object in his glance:
Which parti-coated presence of loose love
Put on by us, if, in your heavenly eyes,
Have misbecomed our oaths and gravities,
Those heavenly eyes, that look into these faults,
Suggested us to make. Therefore, ladies,
Our love being yours, the error that love makes
Is likewise yours: we to ourselves prove false,
By being once false for ever to be true
To those that make us both,—fair ladies, you:
And even that falsehood, in itself a sin,
Thus purifies itself and turns to grace.

PRINCESS.

We have received your letters full of love;
Your favours, the ambassadors of love;
And, in our maiden council, rated them
At courtship, pleasant jest and courtesy,
As bombast and as lining to the time:
But more devout than this in our respects
Have we not been; and therefore met your loves
In their own fashion, like a merriment.

DUMAINE.

Our letters, madam, show'd much more than jest.

LONGAVILLE.

So did our looks.

ROSALINE.

We did not cote them so.

KING.
Now, at the latest minute of the hour,
Grant us your loves.

PRINCESS.
A time, methinks, too short
To make a world-without-end bargain in.
No, no, my lord, your Grace is perjured much,
Full of dear guiltiness; and therefore this:—
If for my love, as there is no such cause,
You will do aught, this shall you do for me:
Your oath I will not trust; but go with speed
To some forlorn and naked hermitage,
Remote from all the pleasures of the world;
There stay until the twelve celestial signs
Have brought about their annual reckoning.
If this austere insociable life
Change not your offer made in heat of blood;
If frosts and fasts, hard lodging and thin weeds
Nip not the gaudy blossoms of your love,
But that it bear this trial and last love;
Then, at the expiration of the year,
Come challenge me, challenge by these deserts,
And, by this virgin palm now kissing thine,
I will be thine; and till that instant shut
My woeful self up in a mourning house,
Raining the tears of lamentation
For the remembrance of my father's death.
If this thou do deny, let our hands part,
Neither intitled in the other's heart.

KING.
If this, or more than this, I would deny,
To flatter up these powers of mine with rest,
The sudden hand of death close up mine eye!
Hence hermit then, my heart is in thy breast.

[BEROWNE.
And what to me, my love? and what to me?

ROSALINE.
You must be purged too, your sins are rackt,
You are attaint with faults and perjury:
Therefore if you my favour mean to get,
A twelvemonth shall you spend, and never rest,
But seek the weary beds of people sick.]

DUMAINE.
But what to me, my love? but what to me?

KATHARINE.
A wife?—A beard, fair health, and honesty;
With three fold love I wish you all these three.

DUMAINE.
O, shall I say, I thank you, gentle wife?

KATHARINE.
Not so, my lord; a twelvemonth and a day
I'll mark no words that smooth-faced wooers say:
Come when the king doth to my lady come;
Then, if I have much love, I'll give you some.

DUMAINE.
I'll serve thee true and faithfully till then.

KATHARINE.
Yet swear not, lest ye be forsworn again.

LONGAVILLE.
What says Maria?

MARIA.
At the twelvemonth's end
I'll change my black gown for a faithful friend.

LONGAVILLE.
I'll stay with patience; but the time is long.

MARIA.
The liker you; few taller are so young.

BEROWNE.
Studies my lady? mistress, look on me;
Behold the window of my heart, mine eye,
What humble suit attends thy answer there:
Impose some service on me for thy love.

ROSALINE.
Oft have I heard of you, my Lord Berowne,
Before I saw you; and the world's large tongue
Proclaims you for a man replete with mocks,
Full of comparisons and wounding flouts,
Which you on all estates will execute
That lie within the mercy of your wit.
To weed this wormwood from your fruitful brain,
And therewithal to win me, if you please,
Without the which I am not to be won,
You shall this twelvemonth term from day to day
Visit the speechless sick and still converse
With groaning wretches; and your task shall be,
With all the fierce endeavour of your wit
To enforce the pained impotent to smile.

BEROWNE.
To move wild laughter in the throat of death?
It cannot be; it is impossible:
Mirth cannot move a soul in agony.

ROSALINE.
Why, that's the way to choke a gibing spirit,
Whose influence is begot of that loose grace
Which shallow laughing hearers give to fools:
A jest's prosperity lies in the ear
Of him that hears it, never in the tongue
Of him that makes it: then, if sickly ears,
Deaf'd with the clamours of their own dear groans,
Will hear your idle scorns, continue then,
And I will have you and that fault withal;
But if they will not, throw away that spirit,
And I shall find you empty of that fault,
Right joyful of your reformation.

BEROWNE.
A twelvemonth! well; befall what will befall,
I'll jest a twelvemonth in an hospital.

PRINCESS [*to the* KING].
Ay, sweet my lord; and so I take my leave.

KING.
No, madam; we will bring you on your way.

BEROWNE.
Our wooing doth not end like an old play;
Jack hath not Jill: these ladies' courtesy
Might well have made our sport a comedy.

KING.
Come, sir, it wants a twelvemonth and a day,
And then 'twill end.

BEROWNE.
That's too long for a play.

Enter ARMADO.

ARMADO.
Sweet Majesty, vouchsafe me,—

PRINCESS.
Was not that Hector?

DUMAINE.
The worthy knight of Troy.

ARMADO.
I will kiss thy royal finger, and take leave.
I am a votary; I have vow'd to Jaquenetta to hold the plough for her sweet love three years. But,

most esteem'd greatness, will you hear the dialogue that the two learned men have compiled in praise of the owl and the cuckoo? it should have follow'd in the end of our show.

KING.

Call them forth quickly; we will do so.

ARMADO.

Holla! approach.

Enter HOLOFERNES, SIR NATHANIEL, MOTH, COSTARD, *and others.*

This side is Hiems, Winter, this Ver, the Spring; the one maintain'd by the owl, the other by the cuckoo. Ver, begin.

The Song.

SPRING.

When daisies pied and violets blue,
  And lady-smocks all silver-white,
And cuckoo-buds of yellow hue
  Do paint the meadows with delight,
The cuckoo then on every tree
Mocks married men; for thus sings he,
  Cuckoo;
Cuckoo, cuckoo: O word of fear,
Unpleasing to a married ear!

When shepherds pipe on oaten straws
  And merry larks are ploughmen's clocks,
When turtles tread, and rooks, and daws,
  And maidens bleach their summer smocks,
The cuckoo then on every tree,
Mocks married men; for thus sings he,
  Cuckoo;
Cuckoo, cuckoo: O word of fear,
Unpleasing to a married ear!

WINTER.

When icicles hang by the wall,
  And Dick the shepherd blows his nail,
And Tom bears logs into the hall,
  And milk comes frozen home in pail,
When blood is nipt and ways be foul,
Then nightly sings the staring owl,
  Tu-whit;
Tu-who, a merry note,
While greasy Joan doth keel the pot.

When all aloud the wind doth blow,
  And coughing drowns the parson's saw,
And birds sit brooding in the snow,
  And Marian's nose looks red and raw,
When roasted crabs hiss in the bowl,
Then nightly sings the staring owl,
  Tu-whit;
Tu-who, a merry note,
While greasy Joan doth keel the pot.

ARMADO.

The words of Mercury are harsh after the songs of Apollo. You that way: we this way. [*Exeunt.*

A MIDSUMMER NIGHT'S DREAM

DRAMATIS PERSONAE

THESEUS, *Duke of Athens.*
EGEUS, *father to Hermia.*
LYSANDER, } *in love with Hermia.*
DEMETRIUS, }
PHILOSTRATE, *master of the revels to Theseus.*
QUINCE, *a carpenter.*
SNUG, *a joiner.*
BOTTOM, *a weaver.*
FLUTE, *a bellows-mender.*
SNOUT, *a tinker.*
STARVELING, *a tailor.*

HIPPOLYTA, *queen of the Amazons, betrothed to Theseus.*
HERMIA, *daughter to Egeus, in love with Lysander.*
HELENA, *in love with Demetrius.*

OBERON, *king of the fairies.*
TITANIA, *queen of the fairies.*
PUCK, *or Robin Goodfellow.*
PEAS-BLOSSOM, }
COBWEB, }
MOTH, } *fairies.*
MUSTARD-SEED, }

PYRAMUS, }
THISBE, }
WALL, } *characters in the interlude perform'd by the Clowns.*
MOONSHINE, }
LION, }

Other FAIRIES *attending their* KING *and* QUEEN.
ATTENDANTS *on* THESEUS *and* HIPPOLYTA.

SCENE—*Athens, and a wood near it.*

ACT I. SCENE I.

Athens. The palace of THESEUS.

Enter THESEUS, HIPPOLYTA, PHILOSTRATE, *and* ATTENDANTS.

THESEUS.
NOW, fair Hippolyta, our nuptial hour
Draws on apace; four happy days bring in
Another moon: but, O, methinks, how slow
This old moon wanes! she lingers my desires
Like to a step-dame, or a dowager,
Long withering out a young man's revenue.

HIPPOLYTA.
Four days will quickly steep themselves in night;
Four nights will quickly dream away the time;
And then the moon, like to a silver bow
New-bent in heaven, shall behold the night
Of our solemnities.

THESEUS.
Go, Philostrate,
Stir up the Athenian youth to merriments;
Awake the pert and nimble spirit of mirth:
Turn melancholy forth to funerals,—
The pale companion is not for our pomp.
[*Exit* PHILOSTRATE
Hippolyta, I woo'd thee with my sword,
And won thy love, doing thee injuries;
But I will wed thee in another key,
With pomp, with triumph, and with revelling.

Enter EGEUS *and his daughter* HERMIA, LYSANDER, *and* DEMETRIUS.

EGEUS.
Happy be Theseus, our renowned duke!

THESEUS.
Thanks, good Egeus: what's the news with thee?

EGEUS.
Full of vexation come I, with complaint
Against my child, my daughter Hermia.
Stand forth, Demetrius. My noble lord,
This man hath my consent to marry her.
Stand forth, Lysander: and, my gracious duke,
This hath bewitch'd the bosom of my child:—
Thou, thou, Lysander, thou hast given her rimes,
And interchanged love-tokens with my child:
Thou hast by moonlight at her window sung,
With feigning voice, verses of feigning love;
And stol'n the impression of her fantasy
With bracelets of thy hair, rings, gauds, conceits,
Knacks, trifles, nosegays, sweetmeats,—messengers
Of strong prevailment in unharden'd youth:
With cunning hast thou filch'd my daughter's heart;
Turn'd her obedience, which is due to me,
To stubborn harshness:—and, my gracious duke,
Be it so she will not here before your Grace
Consent to marry with Demetrius,
I beg the ancient privilege of Athens,—
As she is mine, I may dispose of her:
Which shall be either to this gentleman
Or to her death, according to our law
Immediately provided in that case.

THESEUS.
What say you, Hermia? be advised, fair maid:
To you your father should be as a god;
One that composed your beauties; yea, and one
To whom you are but as a form in wax,
By him imprinted, and within his power
To leave the figure, or disfigure it.
Demetrius is a worthy gentleman.

HERMIA.
So is Lysander.

THESEUS.
In himself he is;
But in this kind, wanting your father's voice,
The other must be held the worthier.

HERMIA.
I would my father lookt but with my eyes.

THESEUS.

Rather your eyes must with his judgement look.

HERMIA.

I do entreat your Grace to pardon me.
I know not by what power I am made bold,
Nor how it may concern my modesty,
In such a presence here to plead my thoughts;
But I beseech your Grace that I may know
The worst that may befall me in this case,
If I refuse to wed Demetrius.

THESEUS.

Either to die the death, or to abjure
For ever the society of men.
Therefore, fair Hermia, question your desires;
Know of your youth, examine well your blood,
Whether, if you yield not to your father's choice,
You can endure the livery of a nun;
For aye to be in shady cloister mew'd,
To live a barren sister all your life,
Chanting faint hymns to the cold fruitless moon.
Thrice-blessed they that master so their blood,
To undergo such maiden pilgrimage;
But earthlier-happy is the rose distill'd
Than that which, withering on the virgin thorn,
Grows, lives, and dies in single blessedness.

HERMIA.

So will I grow, so live, so die, my lord,
Ere I will yield my virgin patent up
Unto his lordship, whose unwished yoke
My soul consents not to give sovereignty.

THESEUS.

Take time to pause; and, by the next new moon,—
The sealing-day betwixt my love and me,
For everlasting bond of fellowship,—
Upon that day either prepare to die
For disobedience to your father's will,
Or else to wed Demetrius, as he would;
Or on Diana's altar to protest
For aye austerity and single life.

DEMETRIUS.

Relent, sweet Hermia:—and, Lysander, yield
Thy crazed title to my certain right.

LYSANDER.

You have her father's love, Demetrius;
Let me have Hermia's: do you marry him.

EGEUS.

Scornful Lysander! true, he hath my love,—
And what is mine my love shall render him;
And she is mine,—and all my right of her
I do estate unto Demetrius.

LYSANDER.

I am, my lord, as well derived as he,
As well possest; my love is more than his;
My fortunes every way as fairly rank'd,
If not with vantage, as Demetrius';
And, which is more than all these boasts can be,
I am beloved of beauteous Hermia:
Why should not I, then, prosecute my right?
Demetrius, I'll avouch it to his head,
Made love to Nedar's daughter, Helena,
And won her soul; and she, sweet lady, dotes,
Devoutly dotes, dotes in idolatry,
Upon this spotted and inconstant man.

THESEUS.

I must confess that I have heard so much,
And with Demetrius thought to have spoke thereof;
But, being over-full of self-affairs,
My mind did lose it. But, Demetrius, come;
And come, Egeus; you shall go with me,
I have some private schooling for you both.
For you, fair Hermia, look you arm yourself
To fit your fancies to your father's will;
Or else the law of Athens yields you up—
Which by no means we may extenuate—
To death, or to a vow of single life.
Come, my Hippolyta: what cheer, my love?
Demetrius, and Egeus, go along:
I must employ you in some business
Against our nuptial; and confer with you
Of something nearly that concerns yourselves.

EGEUS.

With duty and desire we follow you.

[*Exeunt* THESEUS, HIPPOLYTA, EGEUS, DEMETRIUS, *and* TRAIN.

LYSANDER.

How now, my love! why is your cheek so pale?
How chance the roses there do fade so fast?

HERMIA.

Belike for want of rain, which I could well
Beteem them from the tempest of my eyes.

LYSANDER.

Ay me! for aught that I could ever read,
Could ever hear by tale or history,
The course of true love never did run smooth;
But, either it was different in blood,—

HERMIA.

O cross! too high to be enthrall'd to low!

LYSANDER.

Or else misgraffed in respect of years,—

HERMIA.

O spite! too old to be engaged to young!

LYSANDER.

Or else it stood upon the choice of friends,—

HERMIA.

O hell! to choose love by another's eyes!

LYSANDER.

Or, if there were a sympathy in choice,
War, death, or sickness did lay siege to it,
Making it momentany as a sound,
Swift as a shadow, short as any dream;
Brief as the lightning in the collied night,
That, in a spleen, unfolds both heaven and earth,
And ere a man hath power to say, 'Behold!'
The jaws of darkness do devour it up:
So quick bright things come to confusion.

HERMIA.

If, then, true lovers have been ever crost,
It stands as an edict in destiny:
Then let us teach our trial patience,
Because it is a customary cross,
As due to love as thoughts, and dreams, and sighs,
Wishes, and tears, poor fancy's followers.

LYSANDER.

A good persuasion: therefore, hear me, Hermia.
I have a widow aunt, a dowager
Of great revenue, and she hath no child:
From Athens is her house remote seven leagues;
And she respects me as her only son.
There, gentle Hermia, may I marry thee;
And to that place the sharp Athenian law

Cannot pursue us. If thou lovest me, then,
Steal forth thy father's house to-morrow night;
And in the wood, a league without the town,
Where I did meet thee once with Helena,
To do observance to a morn of May,
There will I stay for thee.

HERMIA.

My good Lysander!
I swear to thee, by Cupid's strongest bow,
By his best arrow with the golden head,
By the simplicity of Venus' doves,
By that which knitteth souls and prospers loves,
And by that fire which burn'd the Carthage queen,
When the false Troyan under sail was seen;
By all the vows that ever men have broke,
In number more than ever women spoke;—
In that same place thou hast appointed me,
To-morrow truly will I meet with thee.

LYSANDER.

Keep promise, love. Look, here comes Helena.

Enter HELENA.

HERMIA.

God speed fair Helena! whither away?

HELENA.

Call you me fair? that fair again unsay.
Demetrius loves your fair: O happy fair!
Your eyes are lode-stars; and your tongue's sweet air
More tuneable than lark to shepherd's ear,
When wheat is green, when hawthorn buds appear.
Sickness is catching: O, were favour so,
Yours would I catch, fair Hermia! ere I go,
My hair should catch your hair, my eye your eye,
My tongue should catch your tongue's sweet melody.
Were the world mine, Demetrius being bated,
The rest I'ld give to be to you translated.
O, teach me how you look; and with what art
You sway the motion of Demetrius' heart!

HERMIA.

I frown upon him, yet he loves me still.

HELENA.

O, that your frowns would teach my smiles such skill!

HERMIA.

I give him curses, yet he gives me love.

HELENA.

O, that my prayers could such affection move!

HERMIA.

The more I hate, the more he follows me.

HELENA.

The more I love, the more he hateth me.

HERMIA.

His folly, Helena, is no fault of mine.

HELENA.

None, but your beauty: would that fault were mine!

HERMIA.

Take comfort: he no more shall see my face;
Lysander and myself will fly this place.
Before the time I did Lysander see,
Seem'd Athens as a paradise to me:
O, then, what graces in my love do dwell,
That he hath turn'd a heaven unto a hell!

LYSANDER.

Helen, to you our minds we will unfold:
To-morrow night, when Phœbe doth behold
Her silver visage in the watery glass,
Decking with liquid pearl the bladed grass,—
A time that lovers' flights doth still conceal,—
Through Athens' gates have we devised to steal.

HERMIA.

And in the wood, where often you and I
Upon faint primrose-beds were wont to lie,
Emptying our bosoms of their counsel sweet,
There my Lysander and myself shall meet;
And thence from Athens turn away our eyes,
To seek new friends and stranger companies.
Farewell, sweet playfellow: pray thou for us;
And good luck grant thee thy Demetrius!—
Keep word, Lysander: we must starve our sight
From lovers' food till morrow deep midnight.

LYSANDER.

I will, my Hermia. [*Exit* HERMIA.
Helena, adieu:
As you on him, Demetrius dote on you! [*Exit.*

HELENA.

How happy some o'er other-some can be!
Through Athens I am thought as fair as she.
But what of that? Demetrius thinks not so;
He will not know what all but he do know:
And as he errs, doting on Hermia's eyes,
So I, admiring of his qualities.
Things base and vile, holding no quantity,
Love can transpose to form and dignity:
Love looks not with the eyes, but with the mind;
And therefore is wing'd Cupid painted blind:
Nor hath love's mind of any judgement taste;
Wings, and no eyes, figure unheedy haste:
And therefore is Love said to be a child,
Because in choice he is so oft beguiled.
As waggish boys in game themselves forswear,
So the boy Love is perjured every where:
For ere Demetrius lookt on Hermia's eyne,
He hail'd down oaths that he was only mine;
And when this hail some heat from Hermia felt,
So he dissolved, and showers of oaths did melt.
I will go tell him of fair Hermia's flight:
Then to the wood will he to-morrow night
Pursue her; and for this intelligence
If I have thanks, it is a dear expense:
But herein mean I to enrich my pain,
To have his sight thither and back again. [*Exit.*

SCENE II.

The same. A room in QUINCE'S *house.*

Enter QUINCE *the Carpenter*, SNUG *the Joiner*, BOTTOM *the Weaver*, FLUTE *the Bellows-mender*, SNOUT *the Tinker*, *and* STARVELING *the Tailor*.

QUINCE.

IS all our company here?

BOTTOM.

You were best to call them generally, man by man, according to the scrip.

QUINCE.

Here is the scroll of every man's name, which is thought fit, through all Athens, to play in our interlude before the duke and the duchess on his wedding-day at night.

BOTTOM.

First, good Peter Quince, say what the play treats on; then read the names of the actors; and so grow to a point.

QUINCE.

Marry, our play is *The most lamentable comedy and most cruel death of Pyramus and Thisby.*

BOTTOM.

A very good piece of work, I assure you, and a merry.—Now, good Peter Quince, call forth your actors by the scroll.—Masters, spread yourselves.

QUINCE.

Answer as I call you.—Nick Bottom the weaver.

BOTTOM.

Ready. Name what part I am for, and proceed.

QUINCE.

You, Nick Bottom, are set down for Pyramus.

BOTTOM.

What is Pyramus? a lover, or a tyrant?

QUINCE.

A lover, that kills himself most gallant for love.

BOTTOM.

That will ask some tears in the true performing of it: if I do it, let the audience look to their eyes; I will move storms, I will condole in some measure. To the rest: yet my chief humour is for a tyrant: I could play Ercles rarely, or a part to tear a cat in, to make all split.

The raging rocks
And shivering shocks
Shall break the locks
Of prison-gates;
And Phibbus' car
Shall shine from far,
And make and mar
The foolish Fates.

This was lofty!—Now name the rest of the players.—This is Ercles' vein, a tyrant's vein;—a lover is more condoling.

QUINCE.

Francis Flute the bellows-mender.

FLUTE.

Here, Peter Quince.

QUINCE.

You must take Thisby on you.

FLUTE.

What is Thisby? a wandering knight?

QUINCE.

It is the lady that Pyramus must love.

FLUTE.

Nay, faith, let not me play a woman; I have a beard coming.

QUINCE.

That's all one: you shall play it in a mask, and you may speak as small as you will.

BOTTOM.

An I may hide my face, let me play Thisby too: I'll speak in a monstrous little voice;—'Thisne, Thisne,'—'Ah, Pyramus, my lover dear! thy Thisby dear, and lady dear!'

QUINCE.

No, no; you must play Pyramus:—and, Flute, you Thisby.

BOTTOM.

Well, proceed.

QUINCE.

Robin Starveling the tailor.

STARVELING.

Here, Peter Quince.

QUINCE.

Robin Starveling, you must play Thisby's mother. —Tom Snout the tinker.

SNOUT.

Here, Peter Quince.

QUINCE.

You, Pyramus' father; myself, Thisby's father;— Snug the joiner, you, the lion's part:—and, I hope, here is a play fitted.

SNUG.

Have you the lion's part written? pray you, if it be, give it me, for I am slow of study.

QUINCE.

You may do it extempore, for it is nothing but roaring.

BOTTOM.

Let me play the lion too: I will roar, that I will do any man's heart good to hear me; I will roar, that I will make the duke say, 'Let him roar again, let him roar again.'

QUINCE.

An you should do it too terribly, you would fright the duchess and the ladies, that they would shriek; and that were enough to hang us all.

ALL.

That would hang us, every mother's son.

BOTTOM.

I grant you, friends, if you should fright the ladies out of their wits, they would have no more discretion but to hang us: but I will aggravate my voice so, that I will roar you as gently as any sucking dove; I will roar you an 'twere any nightingale.

QUINCE.

You can play no part but Pyramus; for Pyramus is a sweet-faced man; a proper man as one shall see in a summer's day; a most lovely, gentleman-like man: therefore you must needs play Pyramus.

BOTTOM.

Well, I will undertake it. What beard were I best to play it in?

QUINCE.

Why, what you will.

BOTTOM.

I will discharge it in either your straw-colour beard, your orange-tawny beard, your purple-in-grain beard, or your French-crown-colour beard, your perfect yellow.

QUINCE.

Some of your French crowns have no hair at all, and then you will play barefaced.—But, masters, here are your parts: and I am to entreat you, request you, and desire you, to con them by to-morrow night; and meet me in the palace-wood, a mile without the town, by moonlight: there will we rehearse, for if we meet in the city, we shall be dogg'd with company, and our devices known. In the mean time I will draw a bill of properties, such as our play wants. I pray you, fail me not.

BOTTOM.

We will meet; and there we may rehearse most obscenely and courageously.

QUINCE.

Take pains; be perfit: adieu. At the duke's oak we meet.

BOTTOM.

Enough; hold, or cut bow-strings. [*Exeunt.*

ACT II. SCENE I.

A wood near Athens.

Enter a FAIRY *at one door and* PUCK *at another.*

PUCK.

HOW now, spirit! whither wander you?

FAIRY.

Over hill, over dale,
 Thorough bush, thorough brier,
Over park, over pale,
 Thorough flood, thorough fire,
I do wander every where,
Swifter than the moon's sphere;
And I serve the fairy queen,
To dew her orbs upon the green.
The cowslips tall her pensioners be:
In their gold coats spots you see;
Those be rubies, fairy favours,
In those freckles live their savours:
I must go seek some dewdrops here,
And hang a pearl in every cowslip's ear,
Farewell, thou lob of spirits; I'll be gone:
Our queen and all her elves come here anon.

PUCK.

The king doth keep his revels here to-night:
Take heed the queen come not within his sight;
For Oberon is passing fell and wrath,
Because that she, as her attendant, hath
A lovely boy, stol'n from an Indian king;
She never had so sweet a changeling:
And jealous Oberon would have the child
Knight of his train, to trace the forests wild;
But she perforce withholds the loved boy,
Crowns him with flowers, and makes him all her joy:
And now they never meet in grove or green,
By fountain clear or spangled starlight sheen,
But they do square, that all their elves, for fear,
Creep into acorn-cups, and hide them there.

FAIRY.

Either I mistake your shape and making quite,
Or else you are that shrewd and knavish sprite
Call'd Robin Goodfellow: are you not he
That frights the maidens of the villagery;
Skim milk, and sometimes labour in the quern,
And bootless make the breathless housewife churn;
And sometime make the drink to bear no barm;
Mislead night-wanderers, laughing at their harm?
Those that Hobgoblin call you, and sweet Puck,
You do their work, and they shall have good luck:
Are not you he?

PUCK.

 Thou speak'st aright;
I am that merry wanderer of the night,
I jest to Oberon, and make him smile,
When I a fat and bean-fed horse beguile,
Neighing in likeness of a filly foal:
And sometime lurk I in a gossip's bowl,
In very likeness of a roasted crab;
And when she drinks, against her lips I bob,
And on her wither'd dewlap pour the ale.
The wisest aunt, telling the saddest tale,
Sometime for three-foot stool mistaketh me;
Then slip I from her bum, down topples she,
And 'tailor' cries, and falls into a cough;
And then the whole quire hold their hips and loff,
And waxen in their mirth, and neeze, and swear
A merrier hour was never wasted there.—
But room, fairy! here comes Oberon.

FAIRY.

And here my mistress,—Would that he were gone!

Enter OBERON, *at one door, with his* TRAIN, *and* TITANIA, *at another, with hers.*

OBERON.

Ill met by moonlight, proud Titania.

TITANIA.

What, jealous Oberon!—Fairies, skip hence:
I have forsworn his bed and company.

OBERON.

Tarry, rash wanton: am not I thy lord?

TITANIA.

Then I must be thy lady: but I know
When thou hast stol'n away from fairy-land,
And in the shape of Corin sat all day,
Playing on pipes of corn, and versing love
To amorous Phyllida. Why art thou here,
Come from the furthest steep of India,
But that, forsooth, the bouncing Amazon,
Your buskin'd mistress and your warrior love,
To Theseus must be wedded? and you come
To give their bed joy and prosperity.

OBERON.

How canst thou thus, for shame, Titania,
Glance at my credit with Hippolyta,
Knowing I know thy love to Theseus?
Didst thou not lead him through the glimmering night
From Perigenia, whom he ravished?
And make him with fair Aegle break his faith,
With Ariadne and Antiopa?

TITANIA.

These are the forgeries of jealousy:
And never, since the middle summer's spring,
Met we on hill, in dale, forest, or mead,
By paved fountain or by rushy brook,
Or in the beached margent of the sea,
To dance our ringlets to the whistling wind,
But with thy brawls thou hast disturb'd our sport.
Therefore the winds, piping to us in vain,
As in revenge, have suck'd up from the sea
Contagious fogs; which falling in the land,
Hath every pelting river made so proud,
That they have overborne their continents:
The ox hath therefore stretch'd his yoke in vain,
The ploughman lost his sweat; and the green corn
Hath rotted ere his youth attain'd a beard:
The fold stands empty in the drowned field,
And crows are fatted with the murrion flock;
The nine-men's-morris is fill'd up with mud;
And the quaint mazes in the wanton green,

QUINCE.

Odours, odours.

BOTTOM.

——odours savours sweet:
So hath thy breath, my dearest Thisby dear.—
But hark, a voice! stay thou but here awhile,
And by and by I will to thee appear. [*Exit.*

PUCK [*Aside*].

A stranger Pyramus than e'er play'd here. [*Exit.*

FLUTE.

Must I speak now?

QUINCE.

Ay, marry, must you; for you must understand he goes but to see a noise that he heard, and is to come again.

FLUTE.

Most radiant Pyramus, most lily-white of hue,
Of colour like the red rose on triumphant brier,
Most brisky juvenal, and eke most lovely Jew,
As true as truest horse, that yet would never tire,
I'll meet thee, Pyramus, at Ninny's tomb.

QUINCE.

'Ninus' tomb,' man:—why, you must not speak that yet; that you answer to Pyramus: you speak all your part at once, cues and all.—Pyramus enter: your cue is past; it is, 'never tire.'

FLUTE.

O,—As true as truest horse, that yet would never tire.

Enter PUCK, *and* BOTTOM *with an ass-head.*

BOTTOM.

If I were fair, Thisby, I were only thine:—

QUINCE.

O monstrous! O strange! we are haunted.—
Pray, masters! fly, masters!—Help!

[*Exit with* SNUG, FLUTE, SNOUT, *and* STARVELING.

PUCK.

I'll follow you, I'll lead you about a round,
Through bog, through bush, through brake, through brier:
Sometime a horse I'll be, sometime a hound,
A hog, a headless bear, sometime a fire;
And neigh, and bark, and grunt, and roar, and burn,
Like horse, hound, hog, bear, fire, at every turn. [*Exit.*

BOTTOM.

Why do they run away? this is a knavery of them to make me afeard.

Enter SNOUT.

SNOUT.

O Bottom, thou art changed! what do I see on thee?

BOTTOM.

What do you see? you see an ass-head of your own, do you? [*Exit* SNOUT.

Enter QUINCE.

QUINCE.

Bless thee, Bottom! bless thee! thou art translated. [*Exit.*

BOTTOM.

I see their knavery: this is to make an ass of me; to fright me, if they could. But I will not stir from this place, do what they can: I will walk up and down here, and I will sing, that they shall hear I am not afraid. [*Sings.*

The ousel-cock so black of hue,
With orange-tawny bill,
The throstle with his note so true,
The wren with little quill:—

TITANIA [*awaking*].

What angel wakes me from my flowery bed?

BOTTOM [*sings*].

The finch, the sparrow, and the lark,
The plain-song cuckoo gray,
Whose note full many a man doth mark,
And dares not answer nay;—

for, indeed, who would set his wit to so foolish a bird? who would give a bird the lie, though he cry 'cuckoo' never so?

TITANIA.

I pray thee, gentle mortal, sing again:
Mine ear is much enamour'd of thy note;
So is mine eye enthralled to thy shape;
And thy fair virtue's force perforce doth move me,
On the first view, to say, to swear, I love thee.

BOTTOM.

Methinks, mistress, you should have little reason for that: and yet, to say the truth, reason and love keep little company together now-a-days;—the more the pity that some honest neighbours will not make them friends. Nay, I can gleek upon occasion.

TITANIA.

Thou art as wise as thou art beautiful.

BOTTOM.

Not so, neither: but if I had wit enough to get out of this wood, I have enough to serve mine own turn.

TITANIA.

Out of this wood do not desire to go:
Thou shalt remain here, whether thou wilt or no.
I am a spirit of no common rate,—
The summer still doth tend upon my state;
And I do love thee: therefore, go with me;
I'll give thee fairies to attend on thee;
And they shall fetch thee jewels from the deep,
And sing, while thou on pressed flowers dost sleep:
And I will purge thy mortal grossness so,
That thou shalt like an airy spirit go.—
Peas-blossom! Cobweb! Moth! and Mustard-seed!

Enter four FAIRIES.

FIRST FAIRY.

Ready.

SECOND FAIRY.

And I.

THIRD FAIRY.

And I.

FOURTH FAIRY.

And I.

ALL.

Where shall we go?

TITANIA.

Be kind and courteous to this gentleman,—
Hop in his walks, and gambol in his eyes;
Feed him with apricocks and dewberries,

With purple grapes, green figs, and mulberries;
The honey-bags steal from the humble-bees,
And for night-tapers crop their waxen thighs,
And light them at the fiery glow-worm's eyes,
To have my love to bed and to arise;
And pluck the wings from painted butterflies
To fan the moonbeams from his sleeping eyes:
Nod to him, elves, and do him courtesies.

FIRST FAIRY.

Hail, mortal!

SECOND FAIRY.

Hail!

THIRD FAIRY.

Hail!

FOURTH FAIRY.

Hail!

BOTTOM.

I cry your worships mercy heartily.—I beseech your worship's name.

COBWEB.

Cobweb.

BOTTOM.

I shall desire you of more acquaintance, good Master Cobweb: if I cut my finger, I shall make bold with you.—Your name, honest gentleman?

PEAS-BLOSSOM.

Peas-blossom.

BOTTOM.

I pray you, commend me to Mistress Squash, your mother, and to Master Peascod, your father. Good Master Peas-blossom, I shall desire you of more acquaintance too.—Your name, I beseech you, sir?

MUSTARD-SEED.

Mustard-seed.

BOTTOM.

Good Master Mustard-seed, I know your patience well: that same cowardly, giant-like ox-beef hath devour'd many a gentleman of your house: I promise you your kindred hath made my eyes water ere now. I desire you more acquaintance, good Master Mustard-seed.

TITANIA.

Come, wait upon him; lead him to my bower.
The moon methinks looks with a watery eye;
And when she weeps, weeps every little flower,
Lamenting some enforced chastity.
Tie up my love's tongue, bring him silently.
[*Exeunt.*

SCENE II.

Another part of the wood.

Enter OBERON.

OBERON.

I WONDER if Titania be awaked;
Then, what it was that next came in her eye,
Which she must dote on in extremity.—
Here comes my messenger.

Enter PUCK.

How now, mad spirit!
What night-rule now about this haunted grove?

PUCK.

My mistress with a monster is in love.
Near to her close and consecrated bower,
While she was in her dull and sleeping hour,
A crew of patches, rude mechanicals,
That work for bread upon Athenian stalls,
Were met together to rehearse a play,
Intended for great Theseus' nuptial day.
The shallowest thickskin of that barren sort,
Who Pyramus presented in their sport,
Forsook his scene, and enter'd in a brake:
When I did him at this advantage take,
An ass's nowl I fixed on his head:
Anon his Thisbe must be answered,
And forth my mimic comes. When they him spy,
As wild geese that the creeping fowler eye,
Or russet-pated choughs, many in sort,
Rising and cawing at the gun's report,
Sever themselves, and madly sweep the sky,
So, at his sight, away his fellows fly;
And, at our stamp, here o'er and o'er one falls;
He murder cries, and help from Athens calls.
Their sense thus weak, lost with their fears thus strong,
Made senseless things begin to do them wrong;
For briers and thorns at their apparel snatch;
Some, sleeves,—some, hats;—from yielders all things catch.
I led them on in this distracted fear,
And left sweet Pyramus translated there:
When in that moment,—so it came to pass,—
Titania waked, and straightway loved an ass.

OBERON.

This falls out better than I could devise.
But hast thou yet latcht the Athenian's eyes
With the love-juice, as I did bid thee do?

PUCK.

I took him sleeping,—that is finisht too,—
And the Athenian woman by his side;
That, when he waked, of force she must be eyed.

Enter HERMIA *and* DEMETRIUS.

OBERON.

Stand close: this is the same Athenian.

PUCK.

This is the woman, but not this the man.

DEMETRIUS.

O, why rebuke you him that loves you so?
Lay breath so bitter on your bitter foe.

HERMIA.

Now I but chide; but I should use thee worse,
For thou, I fear, hast given me cause to curse.
If thou hast slain Lysander in his sleep,
Being o'er shoes in blood, plunge in the deep,
And kill me too.
The sun was not so true unto the day
As he to me: would he have stol'n away
From sleeping Hermia? I'll believe as soon
This whole earth may be bored; and that the moon
May through the centre creep, and so displease
Her brother's noontide with th' Antipodes.
It cannot be but thou hast murder'd him;
So should a murderer look,—so dead, so grim.

DEMETRIUS.

So should the murder'd look; and so should I,
Pierced through the heart with your stern cruelty:
Yet you, the murderer, look as bright, as clear,
As yonder Venus in her glimmering sphere.

HERMIA.

What's this to my Lysander? where is he?
Ah, good Demetrius, wilt thou give him me?

DEMETRIUS.

I had rather give his carcass to my hounds.

HERMIA.

Out, dog! out, cur! thou drivest me past the bounds
Of maiden's patience. Hast thou slain him, then?
Henceforth be never number'd among men!
O, once tell true, tell true, even for my sake!
Durst thou have lookt upon him being awake,
And hast thou kill'd him sleeping? O brave touch!
Could not a worm, an adder, do so much?
An adder did it; for with doubler tongue
Than thine, thou serpent, never adder stung.

DEMETRIUS.

You spend your passion on a misprised mood:
I am not guilty of Lysander's blood;
Nor is he dead, for aught that I can tell.

HERMIA.

I pray thee, tell me, then, that he is well.

DEMETRIUS.

An if I could, what should I get therefore?

HERMIA.

A privilege, never to see me more:—
And from thy hated presence part I so:
See me no more, whether he be dead or no. [*Exit.*

DEMETRIUS.

There is no following her in this fierce vein:
Here therefore for a while I will remain.
So sorrow's heaviness doth heavier grow
For debt that bankrout sleep doth sorrow owe;
Which now in some slight measure it will pay,
If for his tender here I make some stay.
[*Lies down and sleeps.*

OBERON.

What hast thou done? thou hast mistaken quite,
And laid the love-juice on some true-love's sight:
Of thy misprision must perforce ensue
Some true-love turn'd, and not a false turn'd true.

PUCK.

Then fate o'er-rules; that, one man holding troth,
A million fail, confounding oath on oath.

OBERON.

About the wood go swifter than the wind,
And Helena of Athens look thou find:
All fancy-sick she is, and pale of cheer
With sighs of love, that costs the fresh blood dear:
By some illusion see thou bring her here:
I'll charm his eyes against she do appear.

PUCK.

I go, I go; look how I go,—
Swifter than arrow from the Tartar's bow. [*Exit.*

OBERON.

Flower of this purple dye,
Hit with Cupid's archery,
[*Squeezes the flower on* DEMETRIUS'S *eyelids.*
Sink in apple of his eye!
When his love he doth espy,
Let her shine as gloriously
As the Venus of the sky.—
When thou wakest, if she be by,
Beg of her for remedy.

Enter PUCK.

PUCK.

Captain of our fairy band,
Helena is here at hand;
And the youth, mistook by me,
Pleading for a lover's fee.
Shall we their fond pageant see?
Lord, what fools these mortals be!

OBERON.

Stand aside: the noise they make
Will cause Demetrius to awake.

PUCK.

Then will two at once woo one,—
That must needs be sport alone;
And those things do best please me
That befall preposterously.

Enter HELENA *and* LYSANDER.

LYSANDER.

Why should you think that I should woo in scorn?
Scorn and derision never come in tears:
Look, when I vow, I weep; and vows so born,
In their nativity all truth appears.
How can these things in me seem scorn to you,
Bearing the badge of faith, to prove them true?

HELENA.

You do advance your cunning more and more.
When truth kills truth, O devilish-holy fray!
These vows are Hermia's: will you give her o'er?
Weigh oath with oath, and you will nothing weigh:
Your vows to her and me, put in two scales,
Will even weigh; and both as light as tales.

LYSANDER.

I had no judgement when to her I swore.

HELENA.

Nor none, in my mind, now you give her o'er.

LYSANDER.

Demetrius loves her, and he loves not you.

DEMETRIUS [*awaking*].

O Helen, goddess, nymph, perfect, divine!
To what, my love, shall I compare thine eyne?
Crystal is muddy. O, how ripe in show
Thy lips, those kissing cherries, tempting grow!
That pure congealed white, high Taurus' snow,
Fann'd with the eastern wind, turns to a crow
When thou hold'st up thy hand: O, let me kiss
This princess of pure white, this seal of bliss!

HELENA.

O spite! O hell! I see you all are bent
To set against me for your merriment:
If you were civil and knew courtesy,
You would not do me thus much injury.
Can you not hate me, as I know you do,
But you must join in souls to mock me too?
If you were men, as men you are in show,
You would not use a gentle lady so;
To vow, and swear, and superpraise my parts,
When I am sure you hate me with your hearts.
You both are rivals, and love Hermia;
And now both rivals, to mock Helena:
A trim exploit, a manly enterprise,
To conjure tears up in a poor maid's eyes
With your derision! none of noble sort
Would so offend a virgin, and extort
A pour soul's patience, all to make you sport.

LYSANDER.

You are unkind, Demetrius; be not so;
For you love Hermia;—this you know I know:
And here, with all good will, with all my heart,
In Hermia's love I yield you up my part;
And yours of Helena to me bequeath,
Whom I do love, and will do to my death.

HELENA.

Never did mockers waste more idle breath.

DEMETRIUS.

Lysander, keep thy Hermia; I will none:
If e'er I loved her, all that love is gone.
My heart to her but as guest-wise sojourn'd,
And now to Helen is it home return'd,
There to remain.

LYSANDER.

Helen, it is not so.

DEMETRIUS.

Disparage not the faith thou dost not know,
Lest, to thy peril, thou aby it dear.—
Look, where thy love comes; yonder is thy dear.

Enter HERMIA.

HERMIA.

Dark night, that from the eye his function takes,
The ear more quick of apprehension makes;
Wherein it doth impair the seeing sense,
It pays the hearing double recompense.—
Thou art not by mine eye, Lysander, found;
Mine ear, I thank it, brought me to thy sound.
But why unkindly didst thou leave me so?

LYSANDER.

Why should he stay, whom love doth press to go?

HERMIA.

What love could press Lysander from my side?

LYSANDER.

Lysander's love, that would not let him bide,—
Fair Helena; who more engilds the night
Than all yon fiery O's and eyes of light.
Why seek'st thou me? could not this make thee know,
The hate I bear thee made me leave thee so?

HERMIA.

You speak not as you think: it cannot be.

HELENA.

Lo, she is one of this confederacy!
Now I perceive they have conjoin'd all three
To fashion this false sport in spite of me.
Injurious Hermia! most ungrateful maid!
Have you conspired, have you with these contrived
To bait me with this foul derision?
Is all the counsel that we two have shared,
The sisters' vows, the hours that we have spent,
When we have chid the hasty-footed time
For parting us,—O, and is all forgot?
All school-days' friendship, childhood innocence?
We, Hermia, like two artificial gods,
Have with our neelds created both one flower,
Both on one sampler, sitting on one cushion,
Both warbling of one song, both in one key;
As if our hands, our sides, voices, and minds,
Had been incorporate. So we grew together,
Like to a double cherry, seeming parted,
But yet an union in partition;
Two lovely berries moulded on one stem;
So, with two seeming bodies, but one heart;
Two of the first, like coats in heraldry,
Due but to one, and crowned with one crest.
And will you rent our ancient love asunder,
To join with men in scorning your poor friend?
It is not friendly, 'tis not maidenly:
Our sex, as well as I, may chide you for it,
Though I alone do feel the injury.

HERMIA.

I am amazed at your passionate words.
I scorn you not: it seems that you scorn me.

HELENA.

Have you not set Lysander, as in scorn,
To follow me, and praise my eyes and face?
And made your other love, Demetrius—
Who even but now did spurn me with his foot—
To call me goddess, nymph, divine, and rare,
Precious, celestial? Wherefore speaks he this
To her he hates? and wherefore doth Lysander
Deny your love, so rich within his soul,
And tender me, forsooth, affection,
But by your setting on, by your consent?
What though I be not so in grace as you,
So hung upon with love, so fortunate;
But miserable most, to love unloved?
This you should pity rather than despise.

HERMIA.

I understand not what you mean by this.

HELENA.

Ay, do, persever, counterfeit sad looks;
Make mouths upon me when I turn my back;
Wink each at other; hold the sweet jest up:
This sport, well carried, shall be chronicled.
If you have any pity, grace, or manners,
You would not make me such an argument.
But, fare ye well: 'tis partly mine own fault;
Which death or absence soon shall remedy.

LYSANDER.

Stay, gentle Helena; hear my excuse:
My love, my life, my soul, fair Helena!

HELENA.

O excellent!

HERMIA.

Sweet, do not scorn her so.

DEMETRIUS!

If she cannot entreat, I can compel.

LYSANDER.

Thou canst compel no more than she entreat:
Thy threats have no more strength than her weak prayers.—
Helen, I love thee; by my life, I do:
I swear by that which I will lose for thee,
To prove him false that says I love thee not.

DEMETRIUS.

I say I love thee more than he can do.

LYSANDER.

If thou say so, withdraw, and prove it too.

DEMETRIUS.

Quick, come!

HERMIA.

Lysander, whereto tends all this?

LYSANDER.

Away, you Ethiop!

DEMETRIUS.

No, no, sir;
Seem to break loose, take on as you would follow,
But yet come not: you are a tame man, go!

LYSANDER.

Hang off, thou cat, thou burr! vile thing, let loose,
Or I will shake thee from me like a serpent!

HERMIA.

Why are you grown so rude? what change is this,
Sweet love?

LYSANDER.

Thy love! out, tawny Tartar, out!
Out, loathed medicine! O hated potion, hence!

HERMIA.

Do you not jest?

HELENA.

Yes, sooth; and so do you.

LYSANDER.

Demetrius, I will keep my word with thee.

DEMETRIUS.

I would I had your bond, for I perceive
A weak bond holds you: I'll not trust your word.

LYSANDER.

What, should I hurt her, strike her, kill her dead?
Although I hate her, I'll not harm her so.

HERMIA.

What, can you do me greater harm than hate?
Hate me! wherefore? O me! what news, my love?
Am not I Hermia? are not you Lysander?
I am as fair now as I was erewhile.
Since night you loved me; yet since night you left me:
Why, then you left me,—O, the gods forbid!—
In earnest, shall I say?

LYSANDER.

Ay, by my life;
And never did desire to see thee more.
Therefore be out of hope, of question, doubt;
Be certain, nothing truer; 'tis no jest
That I do hate thee, and love Helena.

HERMIA.

O me!—you juggler! you canker-blossom!
You thief of love! what, have you come by night
And stol'n my love's heart from him?

HELENA.

Fine, i'faith!
Have you no modesty, no maiden shame,
No touch of bashfulness? What, will you tear
Impatient answers from my gentle tongue?
Fie, fie! you counterfeit, you puppet, you!

HERMIA.

Puppet! why, so; ay, that way goes the game.
Now I perceive that she hath made compare
Between our statures; she hath urged her height;
And with her personage, her tall personage,
Her height, forsooth, she hath prevail'd with him.
And are you grown so high in his esteem,
Because I am so dwarfish and so low?
How low am I, thou painted maypole? speak;
How low am I? I am not yet so low
But that my nails can reach unto thine eyes.

HELENA.

I pray you, though you mock me, gentlemen,
Let her not hurt me: I was never curst;
I have no gift at all in shrewishness;
I am a right maid for my cowardice:
Let her not strike me. You perhaps may think,
Because she is something lower than myself,
That I can match her.

HERMIA.

Lower! hark, again.

HELENA.

Good Hermia, do not be so bitter with me.
I evermore did love you, Hermia,
Did ever keep your counsels, never wrong'd you;
Save that, in love unto Demetrius,
I told him of your stealth unto this wood,
He follow'd you; for love I follow'd him;
But he hath chid me hence, and threaten'd me
To strike me, spurn me, nay, to kill me too:
And now, so you will let me quiet go,
To Athens will I bear my folly back,
And follow you no further: let me go:
You see how simple and how fond I am.

HERMIA.

Why, get you gone: who is't that hinders you?

HELENA.

A foolish heart, that I leave here behind.

HERMIA.

What, with Lysander?

HELENA.

With Demetrius.

LYSANDER.

Be not afraid; she shall not harm thee, Helena.

DEMETRIUS.

No, sir, she shall not, though you take her part.

HELENA.

O, when she's angry, she is keen and shrewd!
She was a vixen when she went to school;
And though she be but little, she is fierce.

HERMIA.

Little again! nothing but low and little!—
Why will you suffer her to flout me thus?
Let me come to her.

LYSANDER.

Get you gone, you dwarf;
You minimus, of hind'ring knot-grass made;
You bead, you acorn.

DEMETRIUS.

You are too officious
In her behalf that scorns your services.
Let her alone: speak not of Helena;
Take not her part; for, if thou dost intend
Never so little show of love to her,
Thou shalt aby it.

LYSANDER.

Now she holds me not;
Now follow, if thou darest, to try whose right,
Of thine or mine, is most in Helena.

DEMETRIUS.

Follow! nay, I'll go with thee, cheek by jole.

[*Exeunt* LYSANDER *and* DEMETRIUS.

HERMIA.

You, mistress, all this coil is 'long of you:
Nay, go not back.

HELENA.

I will not trust you, I,
Nor longer stay in your curst company,
Your hands than mine are quicker for a fray;
My legs are longer though, to run away. [*Exit.*

HERMIA.

I am amazed, and know not what to say. [*Exit.*

OBERON.

This is thy negligence: still thou mistakest,
Or else committ'st thy knaveries wilfully.

PUCK.

Believe me, king of shadows, I mistook.
Did not you tell me I should know the man
By the Athenian garments he had on?
And so far blameless proves my enterprise,
That I have 'nointed an Athenian's eyes;
And so far am I glad it so did sort,
As this their jangling I esteem a sport.

OBERON.

Thou see'st these lovers seek a place to fight:
Hie therefore, Robin, overcast the night;
The starry welkin cover thou anon
With drooping fog, as black as Acheron;
And lead these testy rivals so astray,
As one come not within another's way.
Like to Lysander sometime frame thy tongue,
Then stir Demetrius up with bitter wrong;
And sometime rail thou like Demetrius;
And from each other look thou lead them thus,
Till o'er their brows death-counterfeiting sleep
With leaden legs and batty wings doth creep:
Then crush this herb into Lysander's eye;
Whose liquor hath this virtuous property,
To take from thence all error with his might,
And make his eyeballs roll with wonted sight.
When they next wake, all this derision
Shall seem a dream and fruitless vision;
And back to Athens shall the lovers wend,
With league whose date till death shall never end.
Whiles I in this affair do thee employ,
I'll to my queen and beg her Indian boy;
And then I will her charmed eye release
From monster's view, and all things shall be peace.

PUCK.

My fairy lord, this must be done with haste,
For Night's swift dragons cut the clouds full fast,
And yonder shines Aurora's harbinger;
At whose approach, ghosts, wandering here and there,
Troop home to churchyards: damned spirits all,
That in crossways and floods have burial,
Already to their wormy beds are gone;
For fear lest day should look their shames upon,
They wilfully themselves exile from light,
And must for aye consort with black-brow'd night.

OBERON.

But we are spirits of another sort:
I with the Morning's love have oft made sport;
And, like a forester, the groves may tread,
Even till the eastern gate, all fiery-red,
Opening on Neptune, with fair blessed beams
Turns into yellow gold his salt green streams.
But, notwithstanding, haste; make no delay:
We may effect this business yet ere day. [*Exit.*

PUCK.

Up and down, up and down,
I will lead them up and down:
I am fear'd in field and town:
Goblin, lead them up and down.
Here comes one.

Enter LYSANDER.

LYSANDER.

Where art thou, proud Demetrius? speak thou now.

PUCK.

Here, villain; drawn and ready. Where art thou?

LYSANDER.

I will be with thee straight.

PUCK.

Follow me, then,
To plainer ground.

[*Exit* LYSANDER, *as following the voice.*

Enter DEMETRIUS.

DEMETRIUS.

Lysander! speak agen:
Thou runaway, thou coward, art thou fled?
Speak! in some bush? where dost thou hide thy head?

PUCK.

Thou coward, art thou bragging to the stars,
Telling the bushes that thou look'st for wars,
And wilt not come? Come, recreant; come, thou child;
I'll whip thee with a rod: he is defiled
That draws a sword on thee.

DEMETRIUS.

Yea, art thou there?

PUCK.

Follow my voice: we'll try no manhood here.
[*Exeunt.*

Enter LYSANDER.

LYSANDER.

He goes before me and still dares me on:
When I come where he calls, then he is gone.
The villain is much lighter-heel'd than I:
I follow'd fast, but faster he did fly;
That fall'n am I in dark uneven way,
And here will rest me. [*Lies down.*] Come, thou gentle day!
For if but once thou show me thy gray light,
I'll find Demetrius, and revenge this spite.
[*Sleeps.*

Enter PUCK *and* DEMETRIUS.

PUCK.

Ho, ho, ho! Coward, why comest thou not?

DEMETRIUS.

Abide me, if thou darest; for well I wot
Thou runn'st before me, shifting every place,
And darest not stand, nor look me in the face.
Where art thou now?

PUCK.

Come hither: I am here.

DEMETRIUS.

Nay, then, thou mock'st me. Thou shalt buy this dear,
If ever I thy face by daylight see:
Now, go thy way. Faintness constraineth me
To measure out my length on this cold bed.
By day's approach look to be visited.
[*Lies down and sleeps.*

Enter HELENA.

HELENA.

O weary night, O long and tedious night,
Abate thy hours! Shine comforts from the east,
That I may back to Athens by daylight,
From these that my poor company detest:
And sleep, that sometime shuts up sorrow's eye,
Steal me awhile from mine own company.
[*Lies down and sleeps.*

PUCK.

Yet but three? Come one more;
Two of both kinds makes up four.
Here she comes, curst and sad:—
Cupid is a knavish lad,
Thus to make poor females mad.

Enter HERMIA.

HERMIA.

Never so weary, never so in woe;
Bedabbled with the dew, and torn with briers;
I can no further crawl, no further go;
My legs can keep no pace with my desires.
Here will I rest me till the break of day.
Heavens shield Lysander, if they mean a fray!
[*Lies down and sleeps.*

PUCK.

On the ground
Sleep sound:
I'll apply
To your eye,
Gentle lover, remedy.
[*Squeezing the herb on* LYSANDER'S *eye-lids.*
When thou wakest,
Thou takest
True delight
In the sight
Of thy former lady's eye:
And the country proverb known,
That every man should take his own,
In your waking shall be shown:
Jack shall have Jill;
Naught shall go ill;
The man shall have his mare again, and all shall be well. [*Exit.*

ACT IV. SCENE I.

The wood. LYSANDER, DEMETRIUS, HELENA, *and* HERMIA, *lying asleep.*

Enter TITANIA *and* BOTTOM; PEAS-BLOSSOM, COBWEB, MOTH, MUSTARD-SEED, *and other* FAIRIES *attending;* OBERON *behind unseen.*

TITANIA.

COME, sit thee down upon this flowery bed,
While I thy amiable cheeks do coy,
And stick musk-roses in thy sleek smooth head,
And kiss thy fair large ears, my gentle joy.

BOTTOM.

Where's Peas-blossom?

PEAS-BLOSSOM.

Ready.

BOTTOM.

Scratch my head, Peas-blossom.—Where's Monsieur Cobweb?

COBWEB.

Ready.

BOTTOM.

Monsieur Cobweb, good monsieur, get your weapons in your hand, and kill me a red-hipt humble-bee on the top of a thistle; and, good monsieur, bring me the honey-bag. Do not fret yourself too much in the action, monsieur; and, good monsieur, have a care the honey-bag break not; I would be loth to have you overflown with a honey-bag, signior.—Where's Monsieur Mustard-seed?

MUSTARD-SEED.

Ready.

BOTTOM.

Give me your neif, Monsieur Mustard-seed. Pray you, leave your courtesy, good monsieur.

MUSTARD-SEED.

What's your will?

BOTTOM.

Nothing, good monsieur, but to help Cavalery Peas-blossom to scratch. I must to the barber's, monsieur; for methinks I am marvellous hairy about the face; and I am such a tender ass, if my hair do but tickle me, I must scratch.

TITANIA.

What, wilt thou hear some music, my sweet love?

BOTTOM.

I have a reasonable good ear in music: let's have the tongs and bones. [*Tongs. Rural music.*

TITANIA.

Or say, sweet love, what thou desirest to eat.

BOTTOM.

Truly, a peck of provender: I could munch your good dry oats. Methinks I have a great desire to a bottle of hay: good hay, sweet hay hath no fellow.

TITANIA.

I have a venturous fairy that shall seek
The squirrel's hoard, and fetch thee hence new nuts.

BOTTOM.

I had rather have a handful or two of dried peas. But, I pray you, let none of your people stir me: I have an exposition of sleep come upon me.

TITANIA.

Sleep thou, and I will wind thee in my arms.—
Fairies, be gone, and be all ways away.—
[*Exeunt* FAIRIES.
So doth the woodbine the sweet honeysuckle
Gently entwist; the female ivy so
Enrings the barky fingers of the elm.
O, how I love thee! how I dote on thee!
[*They sleep.*

Enter PUCK.

OBERON [*advancing*].

Welcome, good Robin. See'st thou this sweet sight?
Her dotage now I do begin to pity:
For, meeting her of late behind the wood,
Seeking sweet favours for this hateful fool,
I did upbraid her, and fall out with her;
For she his hairy temples then had rounded
With coronet of fresh and fragrant flowers;
And that same dew, which sometime on the buds
Was wont to swell, like round and orient pearls,
Stood now within the pretty flowerets' eyes,
Like tears, that did their own disgrace bewail.
When I had at my pleasure taunted her,
And she in mild terms begg'd my patience,
I then did ask of her her changeling child;
Which straight she gave me, and her fairy sent
To bear him to my bower in fairy-land.
And now I have the boy, I will undo
This hateful imperfection of her eyes:
And, gentle Puck, take this transformed scalp

From off the head of this Athenian swain;
That he, awaking when the other do,
May all to Athens back again repair,
And think no more of this night's accidents,
But as the fierce vexation of a dream.
But first I will release the fairy queen.
Be as thou wast wont to be;
[*Touching her eyes with an herb.*
See as thou wast wont to see:
Dian's bud o'er Cupid's flower
Hath such force and blessed power.
Now, my Titania: wake you, my sweet queen.

TITANIA.

My Oberon! what visions have I seen!
Methought I was enamour'd of an ass.

OBERON.

There lies your love.

TITANIA.

How came these things to pass?
O, how mine eyes do loathe his visage now!

OBERON.

Silence awhile.—Robin, take off this head.—
Titania, music call; and strike more dead
Than common sleep of all these five the sense.

TITANIA.

Music, ho! music, such as charmeth sleep!
[*Music, still.*

PUCK.

Now, when thou wakest, with thine own fool's eyes peep.

OBERON.

Sound, music!—Come, my queen, take hands with me,
And rock the ground whereon these sleepers be.
Now thou and I are new in amity,
And will to-morrow midnight solemnly
Dance in Duke Theseus' house triumphantly,
And bless it to all fair prosperity:
There shall the pairs of faithful lovers be
Wedded, with Theseus, all in jollity.

PUCK.

Fairy king, attend, and mark:
I do hear the morning lark.

OBERON.

Then, my queen, in silence sad,
Trip we after the night's shade:
We the globe can compass soon,
Swifter than the wandering moon.

TITANIA.

Come, my lord; and in our flight,
Tell me how it came this night
That I sleeping here was found
With these mortals on the ground.
[*Exeunt. Wind horns.*

Enter THESEUS, HIPPOLYTA, EGEUS, *and* TRAIN.

THESEUS.

Go, one of you, find out the forester;
For now our observation is perform'd;
And since we have the vaward of the day,
My love shall hear the music of my hounds:
Uncouple in the western valley; go:—
Dispatch, I say, and find the forester.—
[*Exit an* ATTENDANT.
We will, fair queen, up to the mountain's top,
And mark the musical confusion
Of hounds and echo in conjunction.

HIPPOLYTA.

I was with Hercules and Cadmus once,
When in a wood of Crete they bay'd the bear
With hounds of Sparta: never did I hear
Such gallant chiding; for, besides the groves,
The skies, the fountains, every region near
Seem all one mutual cry: I never heard
So musical a discord, such sweet thunder.

THESEUS.

My hounds are bred out of the Spartan kind,
So flew'd, so sanded; and their heads are hung
With ears that sweep away the morning dew;
Crook-knee'd, and dew-lapt like Thessalian bulls;
Slow in pursuit, but matcht in mouth like bells,
Each under each. A cry more tuneable
Was never holla'd to, nor cheer'd with horn,
In Crete, in Sparta, nor in Thessaly:
Judge when you hear.—But, soft! what nymphs are these?

EGEUS.

My lord, this is my daughter here asleep
And this, Lysander; this Demetrius is;
This Helena, old Nedar's Helena:
I wonder of their being here together.

THESEUS.

No doubt they rose up early to observe
The rites of May; and, hearing our intent,
Came here in grace of our solemnity.—
But speak, Egeus; is not this the day
That Hermia should give answer of her choice?

EGEUS.

It is, my lord.

THESEUS.

Go, bid the huntsmen wake them with their horns.
[*Horns, and they wake. Shout within, and they all start up.*
Good morrow, friends.—Saint Valentine is past:
Begin these wood-birds but to couple now?

LYSANDER.

Pardon, my lord.

THESEUS.

I pray you all, stand up.
I know you two are rival enemies:
How comes this gentle concord in the world,
That hatred is so far from jealousy,
To sleep by hate, and fear no enmity?

LYSANDER.

My lord, I shall reply amazedly,
Half sleep, half waking: but as yet, I swear,
I cannot truly say how I came here;
But, as I think,—for truly would I speak,
And now I do bethink me, so it is,—
I came with Hermia hither: our intent
Was to be gone from Athens, where we might,
Without the peril of the Athenian law,—

EGEUS.

Enough, enough, my lord; you have enough:
I beg the law, the law, upon his head.—
They would have stol'n away; they would, Demetrius,
Thereby to have defeated you and me,
You of your wife, and me of my consent,—
Of my consent that she should be your wife.

DEMETRIUS.

My lord, fair Helen told me of their stealth,
Of this their purpose hither to this wood;
And I in fury hither follow'd them,
Fair Helena in fancy following me.
But, my good lord, I wot not by what power,—
But by some power it is,—my love to Hermia,
Melted as the snow, seems to me now
As the remembrance of an idle gaud,
Which in my childhood I did dote upon;
And all the faith, the virtue of my heart,
The object, and the pleasure of mine eye,
Is only Helena. To her, my lord,
Was I betroth'd ere I saw Hermia:
But, like in sickness, did I loathe this food;
But, as in health, come to my natural taste,
Now do I wish it, love it, long for it,
And will for evermore be true to it.

THESEUS.

Fair lovers, you are fortunately met:
Of this discourse we more will hear anon.—
Egeus, I will overbear your will;
For in the temple, by and by, with us
These couples shall eternally be knit:
And, for the morning now is something worn,
Our purposed hunting shall be set aside.
Away with us to Athens! three and three,
We'll hold a feast in great solemnity.
Come, Hippolyta.

[*Exeunt* THESEUS, HIPPOLYTA, EGEUS, *and* TRAIN.

DEMETRIUS.

These things seem small and undistinguishable,
Like far-off mountains turned into clouds.

HERMIA.

Methinks I see these things with parted eye,
When everything seems double.

HELENA.

So methinks:
And I have found Demetrius like a gemel,
Mine own, and not mine own.

DEMETRIUS.

Are you sure
That we are awake? It seems to me
That yet we sleep, we dream.—Do not you think
The duke was here, and bid us follow him?

HERMIA.

Yea; and my father.

HELENA.

And Hippolyta.

LYSANDER.

And he did bid us follow to the temple.

DEMETRIUS.

Why, then, we are awake: let's follow him;
And, by the way, let us recount our dreams.

[*Exeunt.*

BOTTOM [*awaking*].

When my cue comes, call me, and I will answer: —my next is, 'Most fair Pyramus,'——Heigh-ho! —Peter Quince! Flute the bellows-mender! Snout the tinker! Starveling!—God's my life, stol'n hence, and left me asleep! I have had a most rare vision. I have had a dream,—past the wit of man to say what dream it was: man is but an ass, if he go about to expound this dream. Methought I was—there is no man can tell what. Methought I was, and methought I had,—but man is but a patcht fool, if he will offer to say what methought I had. The eye of man hath not heard, the ear of man hath not seen, man's hand is not able to taste, his tongue to conceive, nor his heart to report, what my dream was. I will get Peter Quince to write a ballet of this dream: it shall be called Bottom's Dream, because it hath no bottom; and I will sing it in the latter end of a play before the duke: peradventure, to make it the more gracious, I shall sing it at her death. [*Exit.*

SCENE II.

Athens. A room in QUINCE'S *house.*

Enter QUINCE, FLUTE, SNOUT, *and* STARVELING.

QUINCE.

HAVE you sent to Bottom's house? is he come home yet?

STARVELING.

He cannot be heard of. Out of doubt he is transported.

FLUTE.

If he come not, then the play is marr'd: it goes not forward, doth it?

QUINCE.

It is not possible: you have not a man in all Athens able to discharge Pyramus but he.

FLUTE.

No, he hath simply the best wit of any handicraft man in Athens.

QUINCE.

Yea, and the best person too; and he is a very paramour for a sweet voice.

FLUTE.

You must say paragon: a paramour is, God bless us, a thing of naught.

Enter SNUG.

SNUG.

Masters, the duke is coming from the temple, and there is two or three lords and ladies more married: if our sport had gone forward, we had all been made men.

FLUTE.

O sweet bully Bottom! Thus hath he lost sixpence a day during his life; he could not have scaped sixpence a day: an the duke had not given him sixpence a day for playing Pyramus, I'll be hang'd; he would have deserved it: sixpence a day in Pyramus, or nothing.

Enter BOTTOM.

BOTTOM.

Where are these lads? where are these hearts?

QUINCE.

Bottom!—O most courageous day! O most happy hour!

BOTTOM.

Masters, I am to discourse wonders: but ask me not what; for if I tell you, I am no true Athenian. I will tell you everything, right as it fell out.

QUINCE.

Let us hear, sweet Bottom.

BOTTOM.

Not a word of me. All that I will tell you is, that the duke hath dined. Get your apparel together, good strings to your beards, new ribbons to your pumps; meet presently at the palace; every man look o'er his part; for the short and the long is, our play is preferr'd. In any case, let Thisby have clean linen; and let not him that plays the lion pare his nails, for they shall hang out for the lion's claws. And, most dear actors, eat no onions nor garlic, for we are to utter sweet breath; and I do not doubt but to hear them say it is a sweet comedy. No more words: away! go; away!

[*Exeunt.*

ACT V. SCENE I.

Athens. An apartment in the palace of THESEUS.

Enter THESEUS, HIPPOLYTA, PHILOSTRATE, LORDS, *and* ATTENDANTS.

HIPPOLYTA.

'TIS strange, my Theseus, that these lovers speak of.

THESEUS.

More strange than true: I never may believe
These antick fables nor these fairy toys.
Lovers and madmen have such seething brains,
Such shaping fantasies, that apprehend
More than cool reason ever comprehends.
The lunatic, the lover, and the poet
Are of imagination all compact:—
One sees more devils than vast hell can hold,—
That is, the madman: the lover, all as frantic,
Sees Helen's beauty in a brow of Egypt:
The poet's eye, in a fine frenzy rolling,
Doth glance from heaven to earth, from earth to heaven;
And, as imagination bodies forth
The forms of things unknown, the poet's pen
Turns them to shapes, and gives to airy nothing
A local habitation and a name.
Such tricks hath strong imagination,
That, if it would but apprehend some joy,
It comprehends some bringer of that joy;
Or in the night, imagining some fear,
How easy is a bush supposed a bear!

HIPPOLYTA.

But all the story of the night told over,
And all their minds transfigured so together,
More witnesseth than fancy's images,
And grows to something of great constancy;
But, howsoever, strange and admirable.

THESEUS.

Here come the lovers, full of joy and mirth.

Enter LYSANDER, DEMETRIUS, HERMIA, *and* HELENA.

Joy, gentle friends! joy and fresh days of love
Accompany your hearts!

LYSANDER.

More than to us
Wait in your royal walks, your board, your bed!

THESEUS.

Come now; what masks, what dances shall we have,
To wear away this long age of three hours
Between our after-supper and bed-time?
Where is our usual manager of mirth?
What revels are in hand? Is there no play,
To ease the anguish of a torturing hour?
Call Philostrate.

PHILOSTRATE.

Here, mighty Theseus.

THESEUS.

Say, what abridgement have you for this evening?
What mask? what music? How shall we beguile
The lazy time, if not with some delight?

PHILOSTRATE.

There is a brief how many sports are ripe:
Make choice of which your highness will see first.
[*Giving a paper.*

THESEUS [*reads*].

'The battle with the Centaurs, to be sung
By an Athenian eunuch to the harp.'
We'll none of that: that have I told my love,
In glory of my kinsman Hercules.—
[*Reads*] 'The riot of the tipsy Bacchanals,
Tearing the Thracian singer in their rage.'
That is an old device; and it was play'd
When I from Thebes came last a conqueror.—
[*Reads*] 'The thrice-three Muses mourning for the death
Of Learning, late deceased in beggary.'
That is some satire, keen and critical,
Not sorting with a nuptial ceremony.—
[*Reads*] 'A tedious brief scene of young Pyramus
And his love Thisbe; very tragical mirth.'
Merry and tragical! tedious and brief!
That is, hot ice and wondrous strange snow.
How shall we find the concord of this discord?

PHILOSTRATE.

A play there is, my lord, some ten words long,
Which is as brief as I have known a play;
But by ten words, by lord, it is too long,
Which makes it tedious; for in all the play
There is not one word apt, one player fitted:
And tragical, my noble lord, it is;
For Pyramus therein doth kill himself.
Which, when I saw rehearsed, I must confess,
Made mine eyes water; but more merry tears
The passion of loud laughter never shed.

THESEUS.

What are they that do play it?

PHILOSTRATE.

Hard-handed men, that work in Athens here,
Which never labour'd in their minds till now;
And now have toil'd their unbreathed memories
With this same play, against your nuptial.

THESEUS.

And we will hear it.

PHILOSTRATE.

No, my noble lord;
It is not for you: I have heard it over,
And it is nothing, nothing in the world;
Unless you can find sport in their intents,
Extremely stretcht and conn'd with cruel pain,
To do you service.

THESEUS.

I will hear that play;
For never any thing can be amiss,
When simpleness and duty tender it.
Go, bring them in:—and take your places, ladies.
[*Exit* PHILOSTRATE.

HIPPOLYTA.

I love not to see wretchedness o'ercharged,
And duty in his service perishing.

THESEUS.

Why, gentle sweet, you shall see no such thing.

HIPPOLYTA.

He says they can do nothing in this kind.

THESEUS.

The kinder we, to give them thanks for nothing.
Our sport shall be to take what they mistake:
And what poor duty cannot do,
Noble respect takes it in might, not merit.
Where I have come, great clerks have purposed
To greet me with premeditated welcomes;
Where I have seen them shiver and look pale,
Make periods in the midst of sentences,
Throttle their practised accent in their fears,
And, in conclusion, dumbly have broke off,
Not paying me a welcome. Trust me, sweet,
Out of this silence yet I pickt a welcome;
And in the modesty of fearful duty
I read as much as from the rattling tongue
Of saucy and audacious eloquence.
Love, therefore, and tongue-tied simplicity
In least speak most, to my capacity.

Enter PHILOSTRATE.

PHILOSTRATE.

So please your grace, the Prologue is addrest.

THESEUS.

Let him approach. [*Flourish of trumpets.*

Enter the PROLOGUE.

PROLOGUE.

If we offend, it is with our good will.
  That you should think, we come not to offend,
But with good will. To show our simple skill,
  That is the true beginning of our end.
Consider, then, we come but in despite.
  We do not come as minding to content you,
Our true intent is. All for your delight,
  We are not here. That you should here repent you,
The actors are at hand; and, by their show,
You shall know all that you are like to know.

THESEUS.

This fellow doth not stand upon points.

LYSANDER.

He hath rid his prologue like a rough colt; he knows not the stop. A good moral, my lord: it is not enough to speak, but to speak true.

HIPPOLYTA.

Indeed he hath play'd on his prologue like a child on a recorder; a sound, but not in government.

THESEUS.

His speech was like a tangled chain; nothing impair'd, but all disorder'd. Who is next?

Enter PYRAMUS *and* THISBE, WALL, MOONSHINE, *and* LION.

PROLOGUE.

Gentles, perchance you wonder at this show;
  But wonder on, till truth make all things plain.
This man is Pyramus, if you would know;
  This beauteous lady, Thisbe is certain.
This man, with lime and rough-cast, doth present
  Wall, that vile Wall which did these lovers sunder;
And through Wall's chink, poor souls, they are content
  To whisper; at the which let no man wonder.
This man, with lantern, dog, and bush of thorn,
  Presenteth Moonshine; for, if you will know
By moonshine did these lovers think no scorn
  To meet at Ninus' tomb, there, there to woo.
This grisly beast, which by name Lion hight,
The trusty Thisbe, coming first by night,
Did scare away, or rather did affright;
And, as she fled, her mantle she did fall,
  Which Lion vile with bloody mouth did stain.
Anon comes Pyramus, sweet youth and tall,
  And finds his trusty Thisbe's mantle slain:
Whereat, with blade, with bloody blameful blade,
  He bravely broacht his boiling bloody breast;
And Thisbe, tarrying in mulberry shade,
  His dagger drew, and died. For all the rest,
Let Lion, Moonshine, Wall, and lovers twain,
At large discourse, while here they do remain.

[*Exeunt* PROLOGUE, PYRAMUS, THISBE, LION, *and* MOONSHINE.

THESEUS.

I wonder if the lion be to speak.

DEMETRIUS.

No wonder, my lord: one lion may, when many asses do.

WALL.

In this same interlude it doth befall
That I, one Snout by name, present a wall;
And such a wall, as I would have you think,
That had in it a crannied hole or chink,
Through which the lovers, Pyramus and Thisbe,
Did whisper often very secretly.
This loam, this rough-cast, and this stone, doth show
That I am that same wall; the truth is so:
And this the cranny is, right and sinister,
Through which the fearful lovers are to whisper.

THESEUS.

Would you desire lime and hair to speak better?

DEMETRIUS.

It is the wittiest partition that ever I heard discourse, my lord.

THESEUS.

Pyramus draws near the wall: silence!

Enter PYRAMUS.

PYRAMUS

O grim-lookt night! O night with hue so black!
  O night, which ever art when day is not!
O night, O night! alack, alack, alack,
  I fear my Thisbe's promise is forgot!—
And thou, O wall, O sweet, O lovely wall,
  That stand'st between her father's ground and mine!
Thou wall, O wall, O sweet and lovely wall,
  Show me thy chink, to blink through with mine eyne! [WALL *holds up his fingers.*
Thanks, courteous wall: Jove shield thee well for this!
  But what see I? No Thisbe do I see.
O wicked wall, through whom I see no bliss!
  Cursed be thy stones for thus deceiving me!'

THESEUS.

The wall, methinks, being sensible, should curse again.

BOTTOM.

No, in truth, sir, he should not. 'Deceiving me' is Thisbe's cue: she is to enter now, and I am to spy her through the wall. You shall see, it will fall pat as I told you.—Yonder she comes.

Enter THISBE.

THISBE.

O wall, full often hast thou heard my moans,
For parting my fair Pyramus and me!
My cherry lips have often kist thy stones,
Thy stones with lime and hair knit up in thee.

PYRAMUS.

I see a voice: now will I to the chink,
To spy an I can hear my Thisbe's face.—
Thisbe!

THISBE.

My love! thou art my love, I think.

PYRAMUS.

Think what thou wilt, I am thy lover's grace;
And, like Limander, am I trusty still.

THISBE.

And I like Helen, till the Fates me kill.

PYRAMUS.

Not Shafalus to Procrus was so true.

THISBE.

As Shafalus to Procrus, I to you.

PYRAMUS.

O, kiss me through the hole of this vile wall!

THISBE.

I kiss the wall's hole, not your lips at all.

PYRAMUS.

Wilt thou at Ninny's tomb meet me straightway?

THISBE.

'Tide life, 'tide death, I come without delay.
[*Exeunt* PYRAMUS *and* THISBE.

WALL.

Thus have I, wall, my part discharged so;
And, being done, thus wall away doth go. [*Exit.*

THESEUS.

Now is the mural down between the two neighbours.

DEMETRIUS.

No remedy, my lord, when walls are so wilful to hear without warning.

HIPPOLYTA.

This is the silliest stuff that e'er I heard.

THESEUS.

The best in this kind are but shadows; and the worst are no worse, if imagination amend them.

HIPPOLYTA.

It must be your imagination then, and not theirs.

THESEUS.

If we imagine no worse of them than they of themselves, they may pass for excellent men.—Here come two noble beasts in, a moon and a lion.

Enter LION *and* MOONSHINE.

LION.

You, ladies, you, whose gentle hearts do fear,
The smallest monstrous mouse that creeps on floor,
May now perchance both quake and tremble here,
When lion rough in wildest rage doth roar.
Then know that I one Snug the joiner am,
No lion fell, nor else no lion's dam;
For, if I should as lion come in strife
Into this place, 'twere pity on my life.

THESEUS.

A very gentle beast, and of a good conscience.

DEMETRIUS.

The very best at a beast, my lord, that e'er I saw.

LYSANDER.

This lion is a very fox for his valour.

THESEUS.

True; and a goose for his discretion.

DEMETRIUS.

Not so, my lord; for his valour cannot carry his discretion; and the fox carries the goose.

THESEUS.

His discretion, I am sure, cannot carry his valour; for the goose carries not the fox. It is well: leave it to his discretion, and let us listen to the moon.

MOONSHINE.

This lantern doth the horned moon present;—

DEMETRIUS.

He should have worn the horns on his head.

THESEUS.

He is no crescent, and his horns are invisible within the circumference.

MOONSHINE.

This lantern doth the horned moon present;
Myself the man-i-th'-moon do seem to be.

THESEUS.

This is the greatest error of all the rest: the man should be put into the lantern. How is it else the man-i'-th'-moon?

DEMETRIUS.

He dares not come there for the candle; for, you see, it is already in snuff.

HIPPOLYTA.

I am a-weary of this moon: would he would change!

THESEUS.

It appears, by his small light of discretion, that he is in the wane; but yet, in courtesy, in all reason, we must stay the time.

LYSANDER.

Proceed, moon.

MOONSHINE.

All that I have to say is, to tell you that the lantern is the moon; I, the man-i'-th'-moon; this thorn-bush, my thorn-bush; and this dog, my dog.

DEMETRIUS.

Why, all these should be in the lantern; for all these are in the moon. But, silence! here comes Thisbe.

Enter THISBE.

THISBE.

This is old Ninny's tomb. Where is my love?

LION.

O—— [*The* LION *roars;* THISBE *runs off.*

DEMETRIUS.

Well roar'd, lion.

THESEUS.

Well run, Thisbe.

HIPPOLYTA.

Well shone, moon.—Truly, the moon shines with a good grace.

[*The* LION *tears* THISBE'S *mantle, and exit.*

THESEUS.

Well moused, lion.

DEMETRIUS.

And then came Pyramus.

LYSANDER.

And so the lion vanisht.

Enter PYRAMUS.

PYRAMUS.

Sweet moon, I thank thee for thy sunny beams;
I thank thee, moon, for shining now so bright;
For, by thy gracious, golden, glittering streams,
I trust to taste of truest Thisbe's sight.
But stay,—O spite!—
But mark, poor knight,
What dreadful dole is here!
Eyes, do you see?
How can it be?
O dainty duck! O dear!
Thy mantle good,
What, stain'd with blood?
Approach, ye Furies fell!
O Fates, come, come,
Cut thread and thrum;
Quail, crush, conclude, and quell!

THESEUS.

This passion, and the death of a dear friend, would go near to make a man look sad.

HIPPOLYTA.

Beshrew my heart, but I pity the man.

PYRAMUS.

O, wherefore, Nature, didst thou lions frame?
Since lion vile hath here deflower'd my dear:
Which is—no, no—which was the fairest dame
That lived, that loved, that liked, that lookt with cheer.
Come, tears, confound;
Out, sword, and wound
The pap of Pyramus,—
Ay, that left pap,
Where heart doth hop:—
[*Stabs himself.*
Thus die I, thus, thus, thus.
Now am I dead,
Now am I fled;
My soul is in the sky:
Tongue, lose thy light;
Moon, take thy flight:—
[*Exit* MOONSHINE.
Now die, die, die, die, die. [*Dies.*

DEMETRIUS.

No die, but an ace, for him; for he is but one.

LYSANDER.

Less than an ace, man; for he is dead; he is nothing.

THESEUS.

With the help of a surgeon he might yet recover; and prove an ass.

HIPPOLYTA.

How chance Moonshine is gone before Thisbe comes back to find her lover?

THESEUS.

She will find him by starlight.—Here she comes, and her passion ends the play.

Enter THISBE.

HIPPOLYTA.

Methinks she should not use a long one for such a Pyramus: I hope she will be brief.

DEMETRIUS.

A mote will turn the balance, which Pyramus, which Thisbe, is the better; he for a man, God warrant us,—she for a woman, God bless us.

LYSANDER.

She hath spied him already with those sweet eyes.

DEMETRIUS.

And thus she moans, *videlicet*:

THISBE.

Asleep, my love?
What, dead, my dove?
O Pyramus, arise!
Speak, speak. Quite dumb?
Dead, dead? A tomb
Must cover thy sweet eyes.
These lily lips,
This cherry nose,
These yellow cowslip cheeks,
Are gone, are gone:
Lovers, make moan:
His eyes were green as leeks.
O Sisters Three,
Come, come to me,
With hands as pale as milk;
Lay them in gore,
Since you have shore
With shears his thread of silk.
Tongue, not a word:
Come, trusty sword;
Come, blade, my breast imbrue;
[*Stabs herself.*
And, farewell, friends,—
Thus Thisbe ends,—
Adieu, adieu, adieu. [*Dies.*

THESEUS.

Moonshine and Lion are left to bury the dead.

DEMETRIUS.

Ay, and Wall too.

BOTTOM.

No, I assure you; the wall is down that parted their fathers. Will it please you to see the epilogue, or to hear a Bergomask dance between two of our company?

THESEUS.

No epilogue, I pray you; for your play needs no excuse. Never excuse; for when the players are all dead, there need none to be blamed. Marry, if he that writ it had play'd Pyramus and hang'd himself in Thisbe's garter, it would have been a fine tragedy: and so it is, truly; and very notably discharged. But, come, your Bergomask: let your epilogue alone. [*A dance.*

The iron tongue of midnight hath told twelve:—
Lovers, to bed; 'tis almost fairy-time.
I fear we shall out-sleep the coming morn,
As much as we this night have overwatcht.
This palpable-gross play hath well beguiled
The heavy gait of night.—Sweet friends, to bed.—
A fortnight hold we this solemnity
In nightly revels and new jollity.

[*Exeunt.*

Enter PUCK.

PUCK.

Now the hungry lion roars,
  And the wolf behowls the moon;
Whilst the heavy ploughman snores,
  All with weary task fordone.
Now the wasted brands do glow,
  Whilst the screech-owl, screeching loud
Puts the wretch that lies in woe
  In remembrance of a shroud.
Now it is the time of night,
  That the graves, all gaping wide,
Every one lets forth his sprite,
  In the church-way paths to glide:
And we fairies, that do run
  By the triple Hecate's team
From the presence of the sun,
  Following darkness like a dream,
Now are frolic: not a mouse
Shall disturb this hallow'd house:
I am sent, with broom, before,
To sweep the dust behind the door.

Enter OBERON *and* TITANIA, *with their* TRAIN.

OBERON.

Through the house give glimmering light,
  By the dead and drowsy fire;
Every elf and fairy sprite
  Hop as light as bird from brier;
And this ditty, after me,
Sing, and dance it trippingly.

TITANIA.

First, rehearse your song by rote,
To each word a warbling note:
Hand in hand, with fairy grace,
Will we sing, and bless this place.

[*Song and dance.*

OBERON.

Now, until the break of day,
Through this house each fairy stray.
To the best bride-bed will we,
Which by us shall blessed be;
And the issue there create
Ever shall be fortunate.
So shall all the couples three
Ever true in loving be;
And the blots of Nature's hand
Shall not in their issue stand;
Never mole, hare-lip, nor scar,
Nor mark prodigious, such as are
Despised in nativity,
Shall upon their children be.
With this field-dew consecrate,
Every fairy take his gait;
And each several chamber bless,
Through this palace, with sweet peace:
Ever shall in safety rest,
And the owner of it blest.
  Trip away;
  Make no stay;
Meet me all by break of day.

[*Exeunt* OBERON, TITANIA, *and* TRAIN.

PUCK.

If we shadows have offended,
Think but this, and all is mended,—
That you have but slumber'd here,
While these visions did appear.
And this weak and idle theme,
No more yielding but a dream,
Gentles, do not reprehend:
If you pardon, we will mend.
And, as I am an honest Puck,
If we have unearned luck
Now to 'scape the serpent's tongue,
We will make amends ere long;
Else the Puck a liar call:
So, good night unto you all.
Give me your hands, if we be friends,
And Robin shall restore amends. [*Exit.*

THE MERCHANT OF VENICE

DRAMATIS PERSONAE

DUKE OF VENICE.
PRINCE OF MOROCCO, PRINCE OF ARRAGON, } *suitors to Portia.*
ANTONIO, *a merchant of Venice.*
BASSANIO, *his kinsman and friend.*
SOLANIO, SALARINO, GRATIANO, } *friends to Antonio and Bassanio.*
LORENZO, *in love with Jessica.*
SHYLOCK, *a rich Jew.*
TUBAL, *a Jew, his friend.*
LAUNCELOT GOBBO, *a clown, servant to Shylock.*
OLD GOBBO, *father to Launcelot.*

LEONARDO, *servant to Bassanio.*
BALTHAZAR, STEPHANO, } *servants to Portia.*

PORTIA, *a rich heiress.*
NERISSA, *her waiting-maid.*
JESSICA, *daughter to Shylock.*

MAGNIFICOES OF VENICE, OFFICERS OF THE COURT OF JUSTICE, GAOLER, SERVANTS, *and other* ATTENDANTS.

SCENE—*Partly at Venice, and partly at Belmont, the seat of Portia, on the Continent.*

ACT I. SCENE I.

Venice. A street.

Enter ANTONIO, SALARINO, *and* SOLANIO.

ANTONIO.

In sooth, I know not why I am so sad:
It wearies me; you say it wearies you;
But how I caught it, found it, or came by it,
What stuff 'tis made of, whereof it is born,
I am to learn;
And such a want-wit sadness makes of me,
That I have much ado to know myself.

SALARINO.

Your mind is tossing on the ocean;
There, where your argosies with portly sail,—
Like signiors and rich burghers of the flood,
Or, as it were, the pageants of the sea,—
Do overpeer the petty traffickers,
That curtsey to them, do them reverence,
As they fly by them with their woven wings.

SOLANIO.

Believe me, sir, had I such venture forth,
The better part of my affections would
Be with my hopes abroad. I should be still
Plucking the grass, to know where sits the wind;
Peering in maps for ports, and piers, and roads;
And every object that might make me fear
Misfortune to my ventures, out of doubt
Would make me sad.

SALARINO.

My wind, cooling my broth.
Would blow me to an ague, when I thought
What harm a wind too great might do at sea.
I should not see the sandy hour-glass run,
But I should think of shallows and of flats;
And see my wealthy Andrew dockt in sand,
Vailing her high-top lower than her ribs,
To kiss her burial. Should I go to church,
And see the holy edifice of stone,
And not bethink me straight of dangerous rocks,
Which touching but my gentle vessel's side,
Would scatter all her spices on the stream;
Enrobe the roaring waters with my silks;
And, in a word, but even now worth this,
And now worth nothing? Shall I have the thought
To think on this; and shall I lack the thought,
That such a thing bechanced would make me sad?
But tell not me; I know Antonio
Is sad to think upon his merchandise.

ANTONIO.

Believe me, no: I thank my fortune for it,
My ventures are not in one bottom trusted,
Nor to one place; nor is my whole estate
Upon the fortune of this present year:
Therefore my merchandise makes me not sad.

SALARINO.

Why, then you are in love.

ANTONIO.

Fie, fie!

SALARINO.

Not in love neither? Then let's say you're sad,
Because you are not merry: and 'twere as easy
For you to laugh, and leap, and say you are merry,
Because you are not sad. Now, by two-headed Janus,
Nature hath framed strange fellows in her time:
Some that will evermore peep through their eyes,
And laugh, like parrots, at a bag-piper;
And other of such vinegar aspect,
That they'll not show their teeth in way of smile,
Though Nestor swear the jest be laughable.

SOLANIO.

Here comes Bassanio, your most noble kinsman,
Gratiano, and Lorenzo. Fare ye well:
We leave you now with better company.

SALARINO.

I would have stay'd till I had made you merry,
If worthier friends had not prevented me.

ANTONIO.

Your worth is very dear in my regard.
I take it, your own business calls on you,
And you embrace th' occasion to depart.

Enter BASSANIO, LORENZO, *and* GRATIANO.

SALARINO.

Good morrow, my good lords.

BASSANIO.

Good signiors both, when shall we laugh? say, when?
You grow exceeding strange: must it be so?

SALARINO.

We'll make our leisures to attend on yours.

[*Exeunt* SALARINO *and* SOLANIO.

LORENZO.

My Lord Bassanio, since you have found Antonio,
We two will leave you: but, at dinner-time,
I pray you, have in mind where we must meet.

BASSANIO.

I will not fail you.

GRATIANO.

You look not well, Signior Antonio;
You have too much respect upon the world:
They lose it that do buy it with much care:
Believe me, you are marvellously changed.

ANTONIO.

I hold the world but as the world, Gratiano;
A stage, where every man must play a part,
And mine a sad one.

GRATIANO.

Let me play the fool:
With mirth and laughter let old wrinkles come;
And let my liver rather heat with wine
Than my heart cool with mortifying groans.
Why should a man, whose blood is warm within,
Sit like his grandsire cut in alabaster?
Sleep when he wakes? and creep into the jaundice
By being peevish? I tell thee what, Antonio,—
I love thee, and it is my love that speaks,—
There are a sort of men, whose visages
Do cream and mantle like a standing pond;
And do a wilful stillness entertain,
With purpose to be drest in an opinion
Of wisdom, gravity, profound conceit;
As who should say, 'I am Sir Oracle,
And when I ope my lips, let no dog bark!'
O my Antonio, I do know of these,
That therefore only are reputed wise
For saying nothing; when, I am very sure,
If they should speak, would almost damn those ears,
Which, hearing them, would call their brothers fools.
I'll tell thee more of this another time:
But fish not, with this melancholy bait,
For this fool-gudgeon, this opinion.—
Come, good Lorenzo.—Fare yé well awhile:
I'll end my exhortation after dinner.

LORENZO.

Well, we will leave you, then, till dinner-time:
I must be one of these same dumb wise men,
For Gratiano never lets me speak.

GRATIANO.

Well, keep me company but two years moe,
Thou shalt not know the sound of thine own tongue.

ANTONIO.

Farewell: I'll grow a talker for this gear.

GRATIANO.

Thanks, i'faith; for silence is only commendable
In a neat's tongue dried, and a maid not vendible.

[*Exeunt* GRATIANO *and* LORENZO.

ANTONIO.

Is that any thing now?

BASSANIO.

Gratiano speaks an infinite deal of nothing, more than any man in all Venice. His reasons are as two grains of wheat hid in two bushels of chaff: you shall seek all day ere you find them; and when you have them, they are not worth the search.

ANTONIO.

Well; tell me now, what lady is the same
To whom you swore a secret pilgrimage,
That you to-day promised to tell me of?

BASSANIO.

'Tis not unknown to you, Antonio,
How much I have disabled mine estate,
By something showing a more swelling port
Than my faint means would grant continuance:
Nor do I now make moan to be abridged
From such a noble rate; but my chief care
Is, to come fairly off from the great debts,
Wherein my time, something too prodigal,
Hath left me gaged. To you, Antonio,
I owe the most, in money and in love;
And from your love I have a warranty
To unburden all my plots and purposes
How to get clear of all the debts I owe.

ANTONIO.

I pray you, good Bassanio, let me know it;
And if it stand, as you yourself still do,
Within the eye of honour, be assured
My purse, my person, my extremest means,
Lie all unlockt to your occasions.

BASSANIO.

In my school-days, when I had lost one shaft,
I shot his fellow of the selfsame flight
The selfsame way with more advised watch,
To find the other forth; and by advent'ring both,
I oft found both: I urge this childhood proof,
Because what follows is pure innocence.
I owe you much; and, like a wilful youth,
That which I owe is lost: but if you please
To shoot another arrow that self way
Which you did shoot the first, I do not doubt,
As I will watch the aim, or to find both,
Or bring your latter hazard back again,
And thankfully rest debtor for the first.

ANTONIO.

You know me well; and herein spend but time
To wind about my love with circumstance;
And out of doubt you do me now more wrong
In making question of my uttermost,
Than if you had made waste of all I have:
Then do but say to me what I should do,
That in your knowledge may by me be done,
And I am prest unto it: therefore, speak.

BASSANIO.

In Belmont is a lady richly left;
And she is fair, and, fairer than that word,
Of wondrous virtues: sometimes from her eyes
I did receive fair speechless messages:
Her name is Portia; nothing undervalued
To Cato's daughter, Brutus' Portia:
Nor is the wide world ignorant of her worth;
For the four winds blow in from every coast
Renowned suitors: and her sunny locks
Hang on her temples like a golden fleece;

Which makes her seat of Belmont Colchos' strond,
And many Jasons come in quest of her.
O my Antonio, had I but the means
To hold a rival place with one of them,
I have a mind presages me such thrift,
That I should questionless be fortunate!

ANTONIO.

Thou know'st that all my fortunes are at sea;
Neither have I money, nor commodity
To raise a present sum: therefore, go forth;
Try what my credit can in Venice do:
That shall be rackt, even to the uttermost,
To furnish thee to Belmont, to fair Portia.
Go, presently inquire, and so will I,
Where money is; and I no question make,
To have it of my trust, or for my sake. [*Exeunt.*

SCENE II.

Belmont. A room in PORTIA'S *house.*

Enter PORTIA *and* NERISSA.

PORTIA.

BY my troth, Nerissa, my little body is aweary of this great world.

NERISSA.

You would be, sweet madam, if your miseries were in the same abundance as your good fortunes are: and yet, for aught I see, they are as sick that surfeit with too much, as they that starve with nothing. It is no mean happiness, therefore, to be seated in the mean: superfluity comes sooner by white hairs; but competency lives longer.

PORTIA.

Good sentences, and well pronounced.

NERISSA.

They would be better, if well follow'd.

PORTIA.

If to do were as easy as to know what were good to do, chapels had been churches, and poor men's cottages princes' palaces. It is a good divine that follows his own instructions: I can easier teach twenty what were good to be done, than be one of the twenty to follow mine own teaching. The brain may devise laws for the blood; but a hot temper leaps o'er a cold decree: such a hare is madness the youth, to skip o'er the meshes of good-counsel the cripple. But this reasoning is not in the fashion to choose me a husband:—O me, the word 'choose'! I may neither choose who I would, nor refuse who I dislike; so is the will of a living daughter curb'd by the will of a dead father.—Is it not hard, Nerissa, that I cannot choose one, nor refuse none?

NERISSA.

Your father was ever virtuous; and holy men, at their death, have good inspirations: therefore, the lottery, that he hath devised in these three chests of gold, silver, and lead,—whereof who chooses his meaning chooses you,—will, no doubt, never be chosen by any rightly, but one who shall rightly love. But what warmth is there in your affection towards any of these princely suitors that are already come?

PORTIA.

I pray thee, over-name them; and as thou namest them, I will describe them; and, according to my description, level at my affection.

NERISSA.

First, there is the Neapolitan prince.

PORTIA.

Ay, that's a colt indeed, for he doth nothing but talk of his horse; and he makes it a great appropriation to his own good parts, that he can shoe him himself. I am much afeard my lady his mother play'd false with a smith.

NERISSA.

Then there is the County Palatine.

PORTIA.

He doth nothing but frown; as who should say, 'An you will not have me, choose:' he hears merry tales, and smiles not: I fear he will prove the weeping philosopher when he grows old, being so full of unmannerly sadness in his youth. I had rather be married to a Death's-head with a bone in his mouth than to either of these:—God defend me from these two!

NERISSA.

How say you by the French lord, Monsieur Le Bon?

PORTIA.

God made him, and therefore let him pass for a man. In truth, I know it is a sin to be a mocker: but, he!—why, he hath a horse better than the Neapolitan's; a better bad habit of frowning than the Count Palatine: he is every man in no man; if a throstle sing, he falls straight a-capering; he will fence with his own shadow: if I should marry him, I should marry twenty husbands. If he would despise me, I would forgive him; for if he love me to madness, I shall never requite him.

NERISSA.

What say you, then, to Falconbridge, the young baron of England?

PORTIA.

You know I say nothing to him: for he understands not me, nor I him: he hath neither Latin, French, nor Italian; and you will come into the court and swear that I have a poor pennyworth in the English. He is a proper man's picture; but, alas, who can converse with a dumb-show? How oddly he is suited! I think he bought his doublet in Italy, his round hose in France, his bonnet in Germany, and his behaviour every where.

NERISSA.

What think you of the Scottish lord, his neighbour?

PORTIA.

That he hath a neighbourly charity in him; for he borrow'd a box of the ear of the Englishman, and swore he would pay him again when he was able: I think the Frenchman became his surety, and seal'd under for another.

NERISSA.

How like you the young German, the Duke of Saxony's nephew?

PORTIA.

Very vilely in the morning, when he is sober; and most vilely in the afternoon, when he is drunk: when he is best, he is a little worse than a man; and when he is worst, he is little better than a beast. An the worst fall that ever fell, I hope I shall make shift to go without him.

NERISSA.
If he should offer to choose, and choose the right casket, you should refuse to perform your father's will, if you should refuse to accept him.

PORTIA.
Therefore, for fear of the worst, I pray thee, set a deep glass of Rhenish wine on the contrary casket; for, if the devil be within, and that temptation without, I know he will choose it. I will do any thing, Nerissa, ere I will be married to a sponge.

NERISSA.
You need not fear, lady, the having any of these lords: they have acquainted me with their determinations; which is, indeed, to return to their home, and to trouble you with no more suit, unless you may be won by some other sort than your father's imposition, depending on the caskets.

PORTIA.
If I live to be as old as Sibylla, I will die as chaste as Diana, unless I be obtain'd by the manner of my father's will. I am glad this parcel of wooers are so reasonable; for there is not one among them but I dote on his very absence; and I pray God grant them a fair departure.

NERISSA.
Do you not remember, lady, in your father's time, a Venetian, a scholar and a soldier, that came hither in company of the Marquis of Montferrat?

PORTIA.
Yes, yes, it was Bassanio: as I think, so was he call'd.

NERISSA.
True, madam: he, of all the men that ever my foolish eyes lookt upon, was the best deserving a fair lady.

PORTIA.
I remember him well; and I remember him worthy of thy praise.

Enter a SERVANT.

How now! what news?

SERVANT.
The four strangers seek for you, madam, to take their leave: and there is a forerunner come from a fifth, the Prince of Morocco; who brings word, the prince his master will be here to-night.

PORTIA.
If a could bid the fifth welcome with so good a heart as I can bid the other four farewell, I should be glad of his approach: if he have the condition of a saint and the complexion of a devil, I had rather he should shrive me than wive me.
Come, Nerissa.—Sirrah, go before.—
Whiles we shut the gates upon one wooer, another knocks at the door. [*Exeunt.*

SCENE III.

Venice. A public place.

Enter BASSANIO *with* SHYLOCK *the Jew.*

SHYLOCK.
THREE thousand ducats,—well.

BASSANIO.
Ay, sir, for three months.

SHYLOCK.
For three months,—well.

BASSANIO.
For the which, as I told you, Antonio shall be bound.

SHYLOCK.
Antonio shall become bound,—well.

BASSANIO.
May you stead me? will you pleasure me? shall I know your answer?

SHYLOCK.
Three thousand ducats for three months, and Antonio bound.

BASSANIO.
Your answer to that.

SHYLOCK.
Antonio is a good man.

BASSANIO.
Have you heard any imputation to the contrary?

SHYLOCK.
Ho, no, no, no, no;—my meaning, in saying he is a good man is to have you understand me that he is sufficient. Yet his means are in supposition: he hath an argosy bound to Tripolis, another to the Indies; I understand, moreover, upon the Rialto, he hath a third at Mexico, a fourth for England,—and other ventures he hath, squander'd abroad. But ships are but boards, sailors but men: there be land-rats and water-rats, water-thieves and land-thieves, I mean pirates; and then there is the peril of waters, winds, and rocks. The man is, notwithstanding, sufficient:—three thousand ducats:—I think I may take his bond.

BASSANIO.
Be assured you may.

SHYLOCK.
I will be assured I may; and, that I may be assured, I will bethink me. May I speak with Antonio?

BASSANIO.
If it please you to dine with us.

SHYLOCK.
Yes, to smell pork; to eat of the habitation which your prophet the Nazarite conjured the devil into. I will buy with you, sell with you, talk with you, walk with you, and so following; but I will not eat with you, drink with you, nor pray with you. What news on the Rialto?—Who is he comes here?

Enter ANTONIO.

BASSANIO.
This is Signior Antonio.

SHYLOCK [*aside*].
How like a fawning publican he looks!
I hate him for he is a Christian!
But more, for that, in low simplicity,
He lends out money gratis, and brings down
The rate of usance here with us in Venice.
If I can catch him once upon the hip,
I will feed fat the ancient grudge I bear him.
He hates our sacred nation; and he rails,
Even there where merchants most do congregate,
On me, my bargains, and my well-won thrift,
Which he calls interest. Cursed be my tribe,
If I forgive him!

BASSANIO.

Shylock, do you hear?

SHYLOCK.

I am debating of my present store;
And, by the near guess of my memory,
I cannot instantly raise up the gross
Of full three thousand ducats. What of that?
Tubal, a wealthy Hebrew of my tribe,
Will furnish me. But soft! how many months
Do you desire?—Rest you fair, good signior;
[*to* ANTONIO.
Your worship was the last man in our mouths.

ANTONIO.

Shylock, although I neither lend nor borrow
By taking nor by giving of excess,
Yet, to supply the ripe wants of my friend,
I'll break a custom.—Is he yet possest
How much ye would?

SHYLOCK.

Ay, ay, three thousand ducats.

ANTONIO.

And for three months.

SHYLOCK.

I had forgot,—three months, you told me so.
Well, then, your bond; and let me see,—but hear you;
Methought you said you neither lend nor borrow
Upon advantage.

ANTONIO.

I do never use it.

SHYLOCK.

When Jacob grazed his uncle Laban's sheep,—
This Jacob from our holy Abram was
(As his wise mother wrought in his behalf)
The third possessor; ay, he was the third,—

ANTONIO.

And what of him? did he take interest?

SHYLOCK.

No, not take interest; not as you would say,
Directly interest: mark what Jacob did.
When Laban and himself were compromised
That all the eanlings which were streakt and pied
Should fall as Jacob's hire, the ewes, being rank,
In th' end of autumn turned to the rams;
And when the work of generation was
Between these woolly breeders in the act,
The skilful shepherd peel'd me certain wands,
And, in the doing of the deed of kind,
He stuck them up before the fulsome ewes,
Who, then conceiving, did in eaning time
Fall parti-colour'd lambs, and those were Jacob's.
This was a way to thrive, and he was blest:
And thrift is blessing, if men steal it not.

ANTONIO.

This was a venture, sir, that Jacob served for;
A thing not in his power to bring to pass,
But sway'd and fashion'd by the hand of heaven.
Was this inserted to make interest good?
Or is your gold and silver ewes and rams?

SHYLOCK.

I cannot tell: I make it breed as fast:—
But note me, signior.

ANTONIO.

Mark you this, Bassanio,
The devil can cite Scripture for his purpose.
An evil soul, producing holy witness,
Is like a villain with a smiling cheek;
A goodly apple rotten at the heart:
O, what a goodly outside falsehood hath!

SHYLOCK.

Three thousand ducats,—'tis a good round sum.
Three months from twelve,—then, let me see, the rate—

ANTONIO.

Well, Shylock, shall we be beholden to you?

SHYLOCK.

Signior Antonio, many a time and oft,
In the Rialto, you have rated me
About my moneys and my usances:
Still have I borne it with a patient shrug;
For sufferance is the badge of all our tribe:
You call me misbeliever, cut-throat dog,
And spit upon my Jewish gaberdine,
And all for use of that which is mine own.
Well, then, it now appears you need my help:
Go to, then; you come to me, and you say,
'Shylock, we would have moneys:'—you say so;
You, that did void your rheum upon my beard,
And foot me as you spurn a stranger cur
Over your threshold: moneys is your suit.
What should I say to you? Should I not say,
'Hath a dog money? is it possible
A cur can lend three thousand ducats?' or
Shall I bend low, and in a bondman's key,
With bated breath and whispering humbleness,
Say this,—
'Fair sir, you spit on me on Wednesday last;
You spurn'd me such a day; another time
You call'd me dog; and for these courtesies
I'll lend you thus much moneys'?

ANTONIO.

I am as like to call thee so again,
To spit on thee again, to spurn thee too.
If thou wilt lend this money, lend it not
As to thy friends—for when did friendship take
A breed for barren metal of his friend?—
But lend it rather to thine enemy;
Who if he break, thou mayst with better face
Exact the penalty.

SHYLOCK.

Why, look you, how you storm!
I would be friends with you, and have your love,
Forget the shames that you have stain'd me with,
Supply your present wants, and take no doit
Of usance for my moneys,
And you'll not hear me: this is kind I offer.

BASSANIO.

This were kindness.

SHYLOCK.

This kindness will I show:—
Go with me to a notary, seal me there
Your single bond; and, in a merry sport,
If you repay me not on such a day,
In such a place, such sum or sums as are
Exprest in the condition, let the forfeit
Be nominated for an equal pound
Of your fair flesh, to be cut off and taken
In what part of your body pleaseth me.

ANTONIO.

Content, i'faith: I'll seal to such a bond,
And say there is much kindness in the Jew.

BASSANIO.
You shall not seal to such a bond for me:
I'll rather dwell in my necessity.

ANTONIO.
Why, fear not, man; I will not forfeit it:
Within these two months, that's a month before
This bond expires, I do expect return
Of thrice three times the value of this bond.

SHYLOCK.
O father Abram, what these Christians are,
Whose own hard dealings teaches them suspect
The thoughts of others!—Pray you, tell me this;
If he should break his day, what should I gain
By the exaction of the forfeiture?
A pound of man's flesh taken from a man
Is not so estimable, profitable neither,
As flesh of muttons, beefs, or goats. I say,
To buy his favour, I extend this friendship:
If he will take it, so; if not, adieu;
And, for my love, I pray you wrong me not.

ANTONIO.
Yes, Shylock, I will seal unto this bond.

SHYLOCK.
Then meet me forthwith at the notary's,—
Give him direction for this merry bond;
And I will go and purse the ducats straight;
See to my house, left in the fearful guard
Of an unthrifty knave; and presently
I will be with you.

ANTONIO.
Hie thee, gentle Jew.
[*Exit* SHYLOCK.
The Hebrew will turn Christian: he grows kind.

BASSANIO.
I like not fair terms and a villain's mind.

ANTONIO.
Come on: in this there can be no dismay;
My ships come home a month before the day.
[*Exeunt.*

ACT II. SCENE I.

Belmont. A room in PORTIA'S *house.*

Enter the PRINCE OF MOROCCO, *a tawny Moor all in white, and three or four* FOLLOWERS *accordingly, with* PORTIA, NERISSA, *and their* TRAIN. *Flourish of cornets.*

PRINCE OF MOROCCO.
MISLIKE me not for my complexion,
The shadow'd livery of the burnisht sun,
To whom I am a neighbour and near bred.
Bring me the fairest creature northward born,
Where Phœbus' fire scarce thaws the icicles,
And let us make incision for your love,
To prove whose blood is reddest, his or mine.
I tell thee, lady, this aspect of mine
Hath fear'd the valiant: by my love, I swear
The best-regarded virgins of our clime
Hath loved it too: I would not change this hue,
Except to steal your thoughts, my gentle queen.

PORTIA.
In terms of choice I am not solely led
By nice direction of a maiden's eyes;
Besides, the lottery of my destiny
Bars me the right of voluntary choosing:
But, if my father had not scanted me,
And hedg'd me by his will, to yield myself
His wife who wins me by that means I told you,
Yourself, renowned prince, then stood as fair
As any comer I have lookt on yet
For my affection.

PRINCE OF MOROCCO.
Even for that I thank you:
Therefore, I pray you, lead me to the caskets,
To try my fortune. By this scimitar,
That slew the Sophy and a Persian prince
That won three fields of Sultan Solyman,
I would outstare the sternest eyes that look,
Outbrave the heart most daring on the earth,
Pluck the young sucking-cubs from the she-bear,
Yea, mock the lion when he roars for prey,
To win thee, lady. But, alas the while!
If Hercules and Lichas play at dice
Which is the better man, the greater throw
May turn by fortune from the weaker hand:
So is Alcides beaten by his page;
And so may I, blind Fortune leading me,
Miss that which one unworthier may attain,
And die with grieving.

PORTIA.
You must take your chance;
And either not attempt to choose at all,
Or swear before you choose,—if you choose wrong,
Never to speak to lady afterward
In way of marriage: therefore be advised.

PRINCE OF MOROCCO.
Nor will not. Come, bring me unto my chance.

PORTIA.
First, forward to the temple: after dinner
Your hazard shall be made.

PRINCE OF MOROCCO.
Good fortune, then!
To make me blest or cursed'st among men.
[*Cornets, and exeunt.*

SCENE II.

Venice. A street.

Enter LAUNCELOT *the Clown, alone.*

LAUNCELOT GOBBO.
CERTAINLY my conscience will serve me to run from this Jew my master. The fiend is at mine elbow, and tempts me, saying to me, 'Gobbo, Launcelot Gobbo, good Launcelot,' or 'good Gobbo,' or 'good Launcelot Gobbo, use your legs, take the start, run away.' My conscience says, 'No; take heed, honest Launcelot; take heed, honest Gobbo,' or, as aforesaid, 'honest Launcelot Gobbo; do not run; scorn running with thy heels.' Well, the most courageous fiend bids me pack: '*Via!*' says the fiend, 'away!' says the fiend; 'for the heavens, rouse up a brave mind,' says the fiend, 'and run.' Well, my conscience, hanging about the neck of my heart, says very wisely to me, 'My honest friend Launcelot, being an honest man's son,'—or rather an honest woman's son;—for, indeed, my father did something smack, something grow to,—he had a kind of taste;—well, my conscience says, 'Launcelot, budge not.' 'Budge,' says the fiend. 'Budge not,' says my conscience. 'Conscience,' say I, 'you counsel well;

'fiend,' say I, 'you counsel well:' to be ruled by my conscience, I should stay with the Jew my master, who—God bless the mark!—is a kind of devil; and, to run away from the Jew, I should be ruled by the fiend, who, saving your reverence, is the devil himself. Certainly the Jew is the very devil incarnal; and, in my conscience, my conscience is but a kind of hard conscience, to offer to counsel me to stay with the Jew. The fiend gives the more friendly counsel: I will run, fiend; my heels are at your command; I will run.

Enter OLD GOBBO, *with a basket.*

OLD GOBBO.

Master young man, you, I pray you, which is the way to master Jew's?

LAUNCELOT GOBBO [*aside*].

O heavens, this is my true-begotten father! who, being more than sand-blind, high-gravel-blind, knows me not:—I will try confusions with him.

OLD GOBBO.

Master young gentleman, I pray you, which is the way to master Jew's?

LAUNCELOT GOBBO.

Turn up on your right hand at the next turning, but, at the next turning of all, on your left; marry, at the very next turning, turn of no hand, but turn down indirectly to the Jew's house.

OLD GOBBO.

By God's sonties, 'twill be a hard way to hit. Can you tell me whether one Launcelot, that dwells with him, dwell with him or no?

LAUNCELOT GOBBO.

Talk you of young Master Launcelot?—[*aside*] Mark me now; now will I raise the waters.—Talk you of young Master Launcelot?

OLD GOBBO.

No master, sir, but a poor man's son: his father, though I say it, is an honest exceeding poor man, and, God be thankt, well to live.

LAUNCELOT GOBBO.

Well, let his father be what a' will, we talk of young Master Launcelot.

OLD GOBBO.

Your worship's friend, and Launcelot, sir.

LAUNCELOT GOBBO.

But, I pray you, *ergo*, old man, *ergo*, I beseech you, talk you of young Master Launcelot?

OLD GOBBO.

Of Launcelot, an't please your mastership.

LAUNCELOT GOBBO.

Ergo, Master Launcelot. Talk not of Master Launcelot, father; for the young gentleman—according to Fates and Destinies, and such odd sayings, the Sisters Three, and such branches of learning—is, indeed, deceased; or, as you would say in plain terms, gone to heaven.

OLD GOBBO.

Marry, God forbid! the boy was the very staff of my age, my very prop.

LAUNCELOT GOBBO.

Do I look like a cudgel or a hovel-post, a staff, or a prop?—Do you know me, father?

OLD GOBBO.

Alack the day, I know you not, young gentleman: but, I pray you, tell me, is my boy—God rest his soul!—alive or dead?

LAUNCELOT GOBBO.

Do you not know me, father?

OLD GOBBO.

Alack, sir, I am sand-blind; I know you not.

LAUNCELOT GOBBO.

Nay, indeed, if you had your eyes, you might fail of the knowing me: it is a wise father that knows his own child. Well, old man, I will tell you news of your son: give me your blessing [*kneels*]: truth will come to light; murder cannot be hid long,—a man's son may; but, in the end, truth will out.

OLD GOBBO.

Pray you, sir, stand up: I am sure you are not Launcelot, my boy.

LAUNCELOT GOBBO.

Pray you, let's have no more fooling about it, but give me your blessing: I am Launcelot, your boy that was, your son that is, your child that shall be.

OLD GOBBO.

I cannot think you are my son.

LAUNCELOT GOBBO.

I know not what I shall think of that: but I am Launcelot, the Jew's man; and I am sure Margery your wife is my mother.

OLD GOBBO.

Her name is Margery, indeed: I'll be sworn, if thou be Launcelot, thou art mine own flesh and blood. Lord worshipt might he be! what a beard hast thou got! thou hast got more hair on thy chin than Dobbin my fill-horse has on his tail.

LAUNCELOT GOBBO [*rising*].

It should seem, then, that Dobbin's tail grows backward; I am sure he had more hair of his tail than I have of my face when I last saw him.

OLD GOBBO.

Lord, how art thou changed! How dost thou and thy master agree? I have brought him a present. How 'gree you now?

LAUNCELOT GOBBO.

Well, well: but, for mine own part, as I have set up my rest to run away, so I will not rest till I have run some ground. My master's a very Jew: give him a present! give him a halter: I am famisht in his service; you may tell every finger I have with my ribs. Father, I am glad you are come: give me your present to one Master Bassanio, who, indeed, gives rare new liveries: if I serve not him, I will run as far as God has any ground.—O rare fortune! here comes the man:—to him, father; for I am a Jew, if I serve the Jew any longer.

Enter BASSANIO, *with* LEONARDO *and a* FOLLOWER *or two.*

BASSANIO.

You may do so;—but let it be so hasted, that supper be ready at the furthest by five of the clock. See these letters deliver'd; put the liveries to making; and desire Gratiano to come anon to my lodging. [*Exit a* SERVANT.

LAUNCELOT GOBBO.

To him, father.

OLD GOBBO.

God bless your worship!

BASSANIO.

Gramercy: wouldst thou aught with me?

OLD GOBBO.
Here's my son, sir, a poor boy,—

LAUNCELOT GOBBO.
Not a poor boy, sir, but the rich Jew's man; that would, sir,—as my father shall specify,—

OLD GOBBO.
He hath a great infection, sir, as one would say, to serve,—

LAUNCELOT GOBBO.
Indeed, the short and the long is, I serve the Jew, and have a desire,—as my father shall specify,—

OLD GOBBO.
His master and he—saving your worship's reverence—are scarce cater-cousins,—

LAUNCELOT GOBBO.
To be brief, the very truth is, that the Jew having done me wrong, doth cause me,—as my father, being, I hope, an old man, shall frutify unto you,—

OLD GOBBO.
I have here a dish of doves that I would bestow upon your worship; and my suit is,—

LAUNCELOT GOBBO.
In very brief, the suit is impertinent to myself, as your worship shall know by this honest old man; and, though I say it, though old man, yet poor man, my father.

BASSANIO.
One speak for both.—What would you?

LAUNCELOT GOBBO.
Serve you, sir.

OLD GOBBO.
That is the very defect of the matter, sir.

BASSANIO.
I know thee well; thou hast obtain'd thy suit:
Shylock thy master spoke with me this day,
And hath preferr'd thee,—if it be preferment
To leave a rich Jew's service, to become
The follower of so poor a gentleman.

LAUNCELOT GOBBO.
The old proverb is very well parted between my master Shylock and you, sir: you have the grace of God, sir, and he hath enough.

BASSANIO.
Thou speak'st it well.—Go, father, with thy
 son.—
Take leave of thy old master, and inquire
My lodging out.—Give him a livery
More guarded than his fellows': see it done.

LAUNCELOT GOBBO.
Father, in.—I cannot get a service, no;—I have ne'er a tongue in my head.—Well [*looking on his palm*], if any man in Italy have a fairer table, which doth offer to swear upon a book, I shall have good fortune!—Go to, here's a simple line of life! here's a small trifle of wives! alas, fifteen wives is nothing! eleven widows and nine maids is a simple coming-in for one man; and then to scape drowning thrice, and to be in peril of my life with the edge of a feather-bed,—here are simple scapes! Well, if Fortune be a woman, she's a good wench for this gear.—Father, come; I'll take my leave of the Jew in the twinkling of an eye. [*Exeunt* LAUNCELOT *and* OLD GOBBO.

BASSANIO.
I pray thee, good Leonardo, think on this:
These things being bought and orderly bestow'd,
Return in haste, for I do feast to-night
My best-esteem'd acquaintance: hie thee, go.

LEONARDO.
My best endeavours shall be done herein.

Enter GRATIANO.

GRATIANO.
Where's your master?

LEONARDO.
Yonder, sir, he walks. [*Exit.*

GRATIANO.
Signior Bassanio,—

BASSANIO.
Gratiano!

GRATIANO.
I have a suit to you.

BASSANIO.
You have obtain'd it.

GRATIANO.
You must not deny me: I must go with you to Belmont.

BASSANIO.
Why, then you must. But hear thee, Gratiano:
Thou art too wild, too rude, and bold of voice,—
Parts that become thee happily enough,
And in such eyes as ours appear not faults;
But where thou art not known, why, there they
 show
Something too liberal. Prithee, take pain
To allay with some cold drops of modesty
Thy skipping spirit; lest, through thy wild be-
 haviour,
I be misconstred in the place I go to,
And lose my hopes.

GRATIANO.
Signior Bassanio, hear me:
If I do not put on a sober habit,
Talk with respect, and swear but now and then,
Wear prayer-books in my pocket, look demurely;
Nay, more, while grace is saying, hood mine eyes
Thus with my hat, and sigh, and say amen;
Use all the observance of civility,
Like one well studied in a sad ostent
To please his grandam,—never trust me more.

BASSANIO.
Well, we shall see your bearing.

GRATIANO.
Nay, but I bar to-night: you shall not gauge me
By what we do to-night.

BASSANIO.
No, that were pity:
I would entreat you rather to put on
Your boldest suit of mirth, for we have friends
That purpose merriment. But fare ye well:
I have some business.

GRATIANO.
And I must to Lorenzo and the rest:
But we will visit you at supper-time. [*Exeunt.*

SCENE III.

The same. A room in SHYLOCK'S *house.*

Enter JESSICA AND LAUNCELOT.

JESSICA.
I AM sorry thou wilt leave my father so:
Our house is hell: and thou, a merry devil,
Didst rob it of some taste of tediousness.

But fare thee well; there is a ducat for thee:
And, Launcelot, soon at supper shalt thou see
Lorenzo, who is thy new master's guest:
Give him this letter; do it secretly;—
And so farewell: I would not have my father
See me in talk with thee.

LAUNCELOT GOBBO.

Adieu; tears exhibit my tongue. Most beautiful pagan, most sweet Jew! if a Christian did not play the knave and get thee, I am much deceived. But, adieu: these foolish drops do something drown my manly spirit: adieu.

JESSICA.

Farewell, good Launcelot.— [*Exit* LAUNCELOT.
Alack, what heinous sin is it in me
To be ashamed to be my father's child!
But though I am a daughter to his blood,
I am not to his manners. O Lorenzo,
If thou keep promise, I shall end this strife,—
Become a Christian, and thy loving wife! [*Exit.*

SCENE IV.

The same. A street.

Enter GRATIANO, LORENZO, SALARINO, *and* SOLANIO.

LORENZO.

NAY, we will slink away in supper-time,
Disguise us at my lodging, and return
All in an hour.

GRATIANO.

We have not made good preparation.

SALARINO.

We have not spoke us yet of torch-bearers.

SOLANIO.

'Tis vile, unless it may be quaintly order'd,
And better in my mind not undertook.

LORENZO.

'Tis now but four o'clock: we have two hours
To furnish us.

Enter LAUNCELOT, *with a letter.*

Friend Launcelot, what's the news?

LAUNCELOT GOBBO.

An it shall please you to break up this, it shall seem to signify.

LORENZO.

I know the hand: in faith, 'tis a fair hand;
And whiter than the paper it writ on
Is the fair hand that writ.

GRATIANO.

Love-news, in faith.

LAUNCELOT GOBBO.

By your leave, sir.

LORENZO.

Whither goest thou?

LAUNCELOT GOBBO.

Marry, sir, to bid my old master the Jew to sup to-night with my new master the Christian.

LORENZO.

Hold here, take this [*gives money*]:—tell gentle Jessica
I will not fail her; speak it privately; go.—
[*Exit* LAUNCELOT.
Gentlemen, will you prepare you for this mask to-night?
I am provided of a torch-bearer.

SALARINO.

Ay, marry, I'll be gone about it straight.

SOLANIO.

And so will I.

LORENZO.

Meet me and Gratiano
At Gratiano's lodging some hour hence.

SALARINO.

'Tis good we do so.

[*Exeunt* SALARINO *and* SOLANIO.

GRATIANO.

Was not that letter from fair Jessica?

LORENZO.

I must needs tell thee all. She hath directed
How I shall take her from her father's house;
What gold and jewels she is furnisht with;
What page's suit she hath in readiness.
If e'er the Jew her father come to heaven,
It will be for his gentle daughter's sake:
And never dare misfortune cross her foot,
Unless she do it under this excuse,—
That she is issue to a faithless Jew.
Come, go with me: peruse this as thou goest:
Fair Jessica shall be my torch-bearer. [*Exeunt.*

SCENE V.

The same. Before SHYLOCK'S *house.*

Enter SHYLOCK *and* LAUNCELOT.

SHYLOCK.

WELL, thou shalt see, thy eyes shall be thy judge,
The difference of old Shylock and Bassanio:—
What, Jessica!—thou shalt not gormandize,
As thou hast done with me;—what, Jessica!—
And sleep and snore, and rend apparel out;—
Why, Jessica, I say!

LAUNCELOT GOBBO.

Why, Jessica!

SHYLOCK.

Who bids thee call? I do not bid thee call.

LAUNCELOT GOBBO.

Your worship was wont to tell me that I could do nothing without bidding.

Enter JESSICA.

JESSICA.

Call you? what is your will?

SHYLOCK.

I am bid forth to supper, Jessica:
There are my keys.—But wherefore should I go?
I am not bid for love; they flatter me:
But yet I'll go in hate, to feed upon
The prodigal Christian.—Jessica, my girl,
Look to my house.—I am right loth to go:
There is some ill a-brewing towards my rest,
For I did dream of money-bags to-night.

LAUNCELOT GOBBO.

I beseech you, sir, go: my young master doth expect your reproach.

SHYLOCK.

So do I his.

LAUNCELOT GOBBO.

And they have conspired together,—I will not say you shall see a mask; but if you do, then it was not for nothing that my nose fell a-bleeding on Black-Monday last at six o'clock i' th' morning, falling out that year on Ash-Wednesday was four year, in th' afternoon.

SHYLOCK.

What, are there masks?—Hear you me, Jessica:
Lock up my doors; and when you hear the drum,
And the vile squealing of the wry-neckt fife,
Clamber not you up to the casements then,
Nor thrust your head into the public street,
To gaze on Christian fools with varnisht faces;
But stop my house's ears, I mean my casements:
Let not the sound of shallow foppery enter
My sober house.—By Jacob's staff, I swear
I have no mind of feasting forth to-night:
But I will go.—Go you before me, sirrah;
Say I will come.

LAUNCELOT GOBBO.

I will go before, sir.—
Mistress, look out at window for all this;
There will come a Christian by
Will be worth a Jewess' eye. [*Exit.*

SHYLOCK.

What says that fool of Hagar's offspring, ha?

JESSICA.

His words were, 'Farewell, mistress;' nothing else.

SHYLOCK.

The patch is kind enough; but a huge feeder,
Snail-slow in profit, and he sleeps by day
More than the wild-cat: drones hive not with me;
Therefore I part with him; and part with him
To one that I would have him help to waste
His borrow'd purse.—Well, Jessica, go in:
Perhaps I will return immediately:
Do as I bid you; shut doors after you:
Fast bind, fast find,—
A proverb never stale in thrifty mind. [*Exit.*

JESSICA.

Farewell; and if my fortune be not crost,
I have a father, you a daughter, lost. [*Exit.*

Enter the Maskers GRATIANO *and* SALARINO.

GRATIANO.

This is the pent-house under which Lorenzo
Desired us to make stand.

SALARINO.

His hour is almost past.

GRATIANO.

And it is marvel he out-dwells his hour,
For lovers ever run before the clock.

SALARINO.

O, ten times faster Venus' pigeons fly
To seal love's bonds new-made than they are wont
To keep obliged faith unforfeited!

GRATIANO.

That ever holds: who riseth from a feast
With that keen appetite that he sits down?
Where is the horse that doth untread again
His tedious measures with the unbated fire
That he did pace them first? All things that are,
Are with more spirit chased than enjoy'd.
How like a younker or a prodigal
The scarfed bark puts from her native bay,
Hugg'd and embraced by the strumpet wind!
How like a prodigal doth she return,
With over-weather'd ribs, and ragged sails,
Lean, rent, and beggar'd by the strumpet wind!

SALARINO.

Here comes Lorenzo:—more of this hereafter.

Enter LORENZO.

LORENZO.

Sweet friends, your patience for my long abode;
Not I, but my affairs, have made you wait:
When you shall please to play the thieves for wives,
I'll watch as long for you then.—Approach;
Here dwells my father Jew.—Ho! who's within?

Enter JESSICA, *above, in boy's clothes.*

JESSICA.

Who are you? Tell me, for more certainty,
Albeit I'll swear that I do know your tongue.

LORENZO.

Lorenzo, and thy love.

JESSICA.

Lorenzo, certain; and my love, indeed,—
For who love I so much? And now who knows
But you, Lorenzo, whether I am yours?

LORENZO.

Heaven and thy thoughts are witness that thou art.

JESSICA.

Here, catch this casket; it is worth the pains.
I am glad 'tis night, you do not look on me,
For I am much ashamed of my exchange:
But love is blind, and lovers cannot see
The pretty follies that themselves commit;
For if they could, Cupid himself would blush
To see me thus transformed to a boy.

LORENZO.

Descend, for you must be my torch-bearer.

JESSICA.

What, must I hold a candle to my shames?
They in themselves, good sooth, are too-too light.
Why, 'tis an office of discovery, love;
And I should be obscured.

LORENZO.

So are you, sweet,
Even in the lovely garnish of a boy.
But come at once;
For the close night doth play the runaway,
And we are stay'd for at Bassanio's feast.

JESSICA.

I will make fast the doors, and gild myself
With some moe ducats, and be with you straight.
[*Exit above.*

GRATIANO.

Now, by my hood, a Gentile, and no Jew.

LORENZO.

Beshrew me but I love her heartily;
For she is wise, if I can judge of her;
And fair she is, if that mine eyes be true;
And true she is, as she hath proved herself;
And therefore, like herself, wise, fair, and true,
Shall she be placed in my constant soul.

Enter JESSICA, *below.*

What, art thou come?—On, gentlemen; away!
Our masking mates by this time for us stay.

[*Exit with* JESSICA *and* SALARINO.

Enter ANTONIO.

ANTONIO.

Who's there?

GRATIANO.

Signior Antonio!

ANTONIO.

Fie, fie, Gratiano! where are all the rest?
'Tis nine o'clock; our friends all stay for you.
No mask to-night: the wind is come about;
Bassanio presently will go aboard:
I have sent twenty out to seek for you.

GRATIANO.

I am glad on't: I desire no more delight
Than to be under sail and gone to-night. [*Exeunt.*

SCENE VI.

Belmont. A room in PORTIA'S *house.*

Enter PORTIA, *with the* PRINCE OF MOROCCO, *and their* TRAINS. *Flourish cornets.*

PORTIA.

GO draw aside the curtains, and discover
The several caskets to this noble prince.—
Now make your choice.

PRINCE OF MOROCCO.

The first, of gold, which this inscription bears,—
'Who chooseth me shall gain what many men desire;'
The second, silver, which this promise carries,—
'Who chooseth me shall get as much as he deserves;'
This third, dull lead, with warning all as blunt,—
'Who chooseth me must give and hazard all he hath.'—
How shall I know if I do choose the right?

PORTIA.

The one of them contains my picture, prince:
If you choose that, then I am yours withal.

PRINCE OF MOROCCO.

Some god direct my judgement! Let me see;
I will survey the inscriptions back again.
What says this leaden casket?
'Who chooseth me must give and hazard all he hath.'
Must give,—for what? for lead? hazard for lead?
This casket threatens: men that hazard all
Do it in hope of fair advantages:
A golden mind stoops not to shows of dross;
I'll then nor give nor hazard aught for lead.
What says the silver, with her virgin hue?
'Who chooseth me shall get as much as he deserves.'
As much as he deserves!—Pause there, Morocco,
And weigh thy value with an even hand:
If thou be'st rated by thy estimation,
Thou dost deserve enough; and yet enough
May not extend so far as to the lady:
And yet to be afeard of my deserving,
Were but a weak disabling of myself.
As much as I deserve!—Why, that's the lady:
I do in birth deserve her, and in fortunes,
In graces, and in qualities of breeding;
But more than these, in love I do deserve.
What if I stray'd no further, but chose here?—
Let's see once more this saying graved in gold:
'Who chooseth me shall gain what many men desire.'
Why, that's the lady; all the world desires her;
From the four corners of the earth they come,
To kiss this shrine, this mortal-breathing saint:
The Hyrcanian deserts and the vasty wilds
Of wide Arabia are as throughfares now
For princes to come view fair Portia:
The watery kingdom, whose ambitious head
Spits in the face of heaven, is no bar
To stop the foreign spirits; but they come,
As o'er a brook, to see fair Portia.
One of these three contains her heavenly picture.
Is't like that lead contains her? 'Twere damnation
To think so base a thought: it were too gross
To rib her cerecloth in the obscure grave.
Or shall I think in silver she's immured,
Being ten times undervalued to tried gold?
O sinful thought! Never so rich a gem
Was set in worse than gold. They have in England
A coin that bears the figure of an angel
Stamped in gold,—but that's insculpt upon;
But here an angel in a golden bed
Lies all within.—Deliver me the key:
Here do I choose, and thrive I as I may!

PORTIA.

There, take it, prince; and if my form lie there,
Then I am yours. [*He opens the golden casket.*

PRINCE OF MOROCCO.

O hell! what have we here?
A carrion Death, within whose empty eye
There is a written scroll! I'll read the writing.

All that glisters is not gold,—
Often have you heard that told:
Many a man his life hath sold
But my outside to behold:
Gilded tombs do worms infold.
Had you been as wise as bold,
Young in limbs, in judgement old,
Your answer had not been inscroll'd:
Fare you well; your suit is cold.

Cold, indeed; and labour lost:
Then, farewell, heat; and welcome, frost!—
Portia, adieu. I have too grieved a heart
To take a tedious leave: thus losers part.
[*Exit with his* TRAIN. *Cornets.*

PORTIA.

A gentle riddance.—Draw the curtains, go.—
Let all of his complexion choose me so. [*Exeunt.*

SCENE VII.

Venice. A street.

Enter SALARINO *and* SOLANIO.

SALARINO.

WHY, man, I saw Bassanio under sail:
With him is Gratiano gone along;
And in their ship I am sure Lorenzo is not.

SOLANIO.

The villain Jew with outcries raised the duke;
Who went with him to search Bassanio's ship.

SALARINO.

He came too late, the ship was under sail:
But there the duke was given to understand
That in a gondola were seen together
Lorenzo and his amorous Jessica:
Besides, Antonio certified the duke
They were not with Bassanio in his ship.

SOLANIO.

I never heard a passion so confused,
So strange, outrageous, and so variable,

As the dog Jew did utter in the streets:
'My daughter!—O my ducats!—O my daughter!
Fled with a Christian!—O my Christian ducats!—
Justice! the law! my ducats, and my daughter!
A sealed bag, two sealed bags of ducats,
Of double ducats, stol'n from me by my daughter!
And jewels,—two stones, two rich and precious stones,
Stol'n by my daughter!—Justice! find the girl!
She hath the stones upon her, and the ducats!'

SALARINO.

Why, all the boys in Venice follow him,
Crying,—his stones, his daughter, and his ducats.

SOLANIO.

Let good Antonio look he keep his day,
Or he shall pay for this.

SALARINO.

Marry, well remember'd,
I reason'd with a Frenchman yesterday,
Who told me,—in the narrow seas that part
The French and English, there miscarried
A vessel of our country richly fraught:
I thought upon Antonio when he told me;
And wisht in silence that it were not his.

SOLANIO.

You were best to tell Antonio what you hear;
Yet do not suddenly, for it may grieve him.

SALARINO.

A kinder gentleman treads not the earth.
I saw Bassanio and Antonio part:
Bassanio told him he would make some speed
Of his return: he answer'd, 'Do not so,—
Slubber not business for my sake, Bassanio,
But stay the very riping of the time;
And for the Jew's bond which he hath of me,
Let it not enter in your mind of love:
Be merry; and employ your chiefest thoughts
To courtship, and such fair ostents of love
As shall conveniently become you there:'
And even there, his eye being big with tears,
Turning his face, he put his hand behind him,
And with affection wondrous sensible
He wrung Bassanio's hand; and so they parted.

SOLANIO.

I think he only loves the world for him.
I pray thee, let us go and find him out,
And quicken his embraced heaviness
With some delight or other.

SALARINO.

Do we so. [*Exeunt.*

SCENE VIII.

Belmont. A room in PORTIA'S *house.*

Enter NERISSA *and a* SERVITOR.

NERISSA.

QUICK, quick, I pray thee; draw the curtain straight:
The Prince of Arragon hath ta'en his oath,
And comes to his election presently.

Enter PRINCE OF ARRAGON, *his* TRAIN, *and* PORTIA. *Flourish cornets.*

PORTIA.

Behold, there stand the caskets, noble prince:
If you choose that wherein I am contain'd,
Straight shall our nuptial rites be solemnized:
But if you fail, without more speech, my lord,
You must be gone from hence immediately.

PRINCE OF ARRAGON.

I am enjoin'd by oath to observe three things:—
First, never to unfold to any one
Which casket 'twas I chose; next, if I fail
Of the right casket, never in my life
To woo a maid in way of marriage; lastly,
If I do fail in fortune of my choice,
Immediately to leave you and be gone.

PORTIA.

To these injunctions every one doth swear
That comes to hazard for my worthless self.

PRINCE OF ARRAGON.

And so have I addrest me. Fortune now
To my heart's hope!—Gold, silver, and base lead.
'Who chooseth me must give and hazard all he hath.'
You shall look fairer, ere I give or hazard.
What says the golden chest? ha! let me see:
'Who chooseth me shall gain what many men desire.'
What many men desire!—that many may be meant
By the fool multitude, that choose by show,
Not learning more than the fond eye doth teach;
Which pries not to th' interior, but, like the martlet,
Builds in the weather on the outward wall,
Even in the force and road of casualty.
I will not choose what many men desire,
Because I will not jump with common spirits,
And rank me with the barbarous multitudes.
Why, then to thee, thou silver treasure-house;
Tell me once more what title thou dost bear:
'Who chooseth me shall get as much as he deserves:'
And well said too; for who shall go about
To cozen fortune, and be honourable
Without the stamp of merit? Let none presume
To wear an undeserved dignity.
O, that estates, degrees, and offices,
Were not derived corruptly! and that clear honour
Were purchased by the merit of the wearer!
How many then should cover that stand bare!
How many be commanded that command!
How much low peasantry would then be glean'd
From the true seed of honour! and how much honour
Pickt from the chaff and ruin of the times,
To be new-varnisht! Well, but to my choice:
'Who chooseth me shall get as much as he deserves.'
I will assume desert.—Give me a key for this,
And instantly unlock my fortunes here.
[*He opens the silver casket.*

PORTIA [*aside*].

Too long a pause for that which you find here.

PRINCE OF ARRAGON.

What's here? the portrait of a blinking idiot,
Presenting me a schedule! I will read it.
How much unlike art thou to Portia!
How much unlike my hopes and my deservings!
'Who chooseth me shall have as much as he deserves.'

Did I deserve no more than a fool's head?
Is that my prize? are my deserts no better?

PORTIA.

To offend, and judge, are distinct offices,
And of opposed natures.

PRINCE OF ARRAGON.

What is here?

The fire seven times tried this:
Seven times tried that judgement is,
That did never choose amiss.
Some there be that shadows kiss;
Such have but a shadow's bliss.
There be fools alive, I wis,
Silver'd o'er; and so was this.
Take what wife you will to bed,
I will ever be your head:
So be gone; you are sped.

Still more fool I shall appear
By the time I linger here:
With one fool's head I came to woo,
But I go away with two.—
Sweet, adieu. I'll keep my oath,
Patiently to bear my wroth.
[*Exit with his* TRAIN.

PORTIA.

Thus hath the candle singed the moth.
O, these deliberate fools! when they do choose,
They have the wisdom by their wit to lose.

NERISSA.

The ancient saying is no heresy,—
Hanging and wiving goes by destiny.

PORTIA.

Come, draw the curtain, Nerissa.

Enter a SERVANT.

SERVANT.

Where is my lady?

PORTIA.

Here: what would my lord?

SERVANT.

Madam, there is alighted at your gate
A young Venetian, one that comes before
To signify th' approaching of his lord;
From whom he bringeth sensible regreets,
To wit, besides commends and courteous breath,
Gifts of rich value. Yet I have not seen
So likely an ambassador of love:
A day in April never came so sweet,
To show how costly summer was at hand,
As this fore-spurrer comes before his lord.

PORTIA.

No more, I pray thee: I am half afeard
Thou wilt say anon he is some kin to thee,
Thou spend'st such high-day wit in praising [him.—
Come, come, Nerissa; for I long to see
Quick Cupid's post that comes so mannerly.

NERISSA.

Bassanio, lord Love, if thy will it be! [*Exeunt.*

ACT III. SCENE I.

Venice. A street.

Enter SOLANIO *and* SALARINO.

SOLANIO.

NOW, what news on the Rialto?

SOLANIO.

Why, yet it lives there uncheckt, that Antonio hath a ship of rich lading wrackt on the narrow seas; the Goodwins, I think they call the place; a very dangerous flat and fatal, where the carcasses of many a tall ship lie buried, as they say, if my gossip Report be an honest woman of her word.

SOLANIO.

I would she were as lying a gossip in that as ever knapt ginger, or made her neighbours believe she wept for the death of a third husband. But it is true,—without any slips of prolixity, or crossing the plain highway of talk,—that the good Antonio, the honest Antonio,——O, that I had a title good enough to keep his name company!—

SALARINO.

Come, the full stop.

SOLANIO.

Ha,—what sayest thou?—Why, the end is, he hath lost a ship.

SALARINO.

I would it might prove the end of his losses.

SOLANIO.

Let me say amen betimes, lest the devil cross my prayer,—for here he comes in the likeness of a Jew.

Enter SHYLOCK.

How now, Shylock! what news among the merchants?

SHYLOCK.

You knew, none so well, none so well as you, of my daughter's flight.

SALARINO.

That's certain: I, for my part, knew the tailor that made the wings she flew withal.

SOLANIO.

And Shylock, for his own part, knew the bird was fledged; and then it is the complexion of them all to leave the dam.

SHYLOCK.

She is damn'd for it.

SALARINO.

That's certain, if the devil may be her judge.

SHYLOCK.

My own flesh and blood to rebel!

SOLANIO.

Out upon it, old carrion! rebels it at these years?

SHYLOCK.

I say my daughter is my flesh and blood.

SALARINO.

There is more difference between thy flesh and hers than between jet and ivory; more between your bloods than there is between red wine and rhenish.—But tell us, do you hear whether Antonio have had any loss at sea or no?

SHYLOCK.

There I have another bad match: a bankrout, a prodigal, who dare scarce show his head on the Rialto;—a beggar, that was used to come so smug upon the mart;—let him look to his bond; he was wont to call me usurer;—let him look to his bond: he was wont to lend money for a Christian courtesy:—let him look to his bond.

SALARINO.

Why, I am sure, if he forfeit, thou wilt not take his flesh: what's that good for?

SHYLOCK.

To bait fish withal: if it will feed nothing else, it will feed my revenge. He hath disgraced me, and hinder'd me half a million; laught at my losses, mockt at my gains, scorn'd my nation, thwarted my bargains, cooled my friends, heated mine enemies: and what's his reason? I am a Jew. Hath not a Jew eyes? hath not a Jew hands, organs, dimensions, senses, affections, passions? fed with the same food, hurt with the same weapons, subject to the same diseases, heal'd by the same means, warm'd and cool'd by the same winter and summer, as a Christian is? If you prick us, do we not bleed? if you tickle us, do we not laugh? if you poison us, do we not die? and if you wrong us, shall we not revenge? if we are like you in the rest, we will resemble you in that. If a Jew wrong a Christian, what is his humility? revenge: if a Christian wrong a Jew, what should his sufferance be by Christian example? why, revenge. The villainy you teach me, I will execute; and it shall go hard but I will better the instruction.

Enter a SERVANT *from* ANTONIO.

SERVANT.

Gentlemen, my master Antonio is at his house, and desires to speak with you both.

SALARINO.

We have been up and down to seek him.

SOLANIO.

Here comes another of the tribe: a third cannot be matcht, unless the devil himself turn Jew.

[*Exeunt* SOLANIO, SALARINO, *and* SERVANT.

Enter TUBAL.

SHYLOCK.

How now, Tubal! what news from Genoa? hast thou found my daughter?

TUBAL.

I often came where I did hear of her, but cannot find her.

SHYLOCK.

Why, there, there, there, there! a diamond gone, cost me two thousand ducats in Frankfort! The curse never fell upon our nation till now; I never felt it till now:—two thousand ducats in that; and other precious, precious jewels.—I would my daughter were dead at my foot, and the jewels in her ear! would she were hearsed at my foot, and the ducats in her coffin! No news of them?—Why, so:—and I know not what's spent in the search: why, thou, loss upon loss! the thief gone with so much, and so much to find the thief; and no satisfaction, no revenge: nor no ill luck stirring but what lights on my shoulders; no sighs but of my breathing; no tears but of my shedding.

TUBAL.

Yes, other men have ill luck too: Antonio, as I heard in Genoa,—

SHYLOCK.

What, what, what? ill luck, ill luck?

TUBAL.

Hath an argosy cast away, coming from Tripolis.

SHYLOCK.

I thank God, I thank God!—Is't true, is't true?

TUBAL.

I spoke with some of the sailors that escaped the wrack.

SHYLOCK.

I thank thee, good Tubal:—good news, good news! ha, ha!—where? in Genoa?

TUBAL.

Your daughter spent in Genoa, as I heard, one night fourscore ducats.

SHYLOCK.

Thou stick'st a dagger in me:—I shall never see my gold again: fourscore ducats at a sitting! fourscore ducats!

TUBAL.

There came divers of Antonio's creditors in my company to Venice, that swear he cannot choose but break.

SHYLOCK.

I am very glad of it:—I'll plague him; I'll torture him:—I am glad on't.

TUBAL.

One of them show'd me a ring that he had of your daughter for a monkey.

SHYLOCK.

Out upon her! Thou torturest me, Tubal: it was my turquoise; I had it of Leah when I was a bachelor: I would not have given it for a wilderness of monkeys.

TUBAL.

But Antonio is certainly undone.

SHYLOCK.

Nay, that's true, that's very true. Go, Tubal, fee me an officer; bespeak him a fortnight before. I will have the heart of him, if he forfeit; for, were he out of Venice, I can make what merchandise I will. Go, Tubal, and meet me at our synagogue; go, good Tubal; at our synagogue, Tubal.

[*Exeunt.*

SCENE II.

Belmont. A room in PORTIA'S *house.*

Enter BASSANIO, PORTIA, GRATIANO, NERISSA, *and all their* TRAIN.

PORTIA.

I PRAY you, tarry: pause a day or two
Before you hazard; for, in choosing wrong,
I lose your company: therefore, forbear awhile.
There's something tells me—but it is not love—
I would not lose you; and you know yourself,
Hate counsels not in such a quality.
But lest you should not understand me well,—
And yet a maiden hath no tongue but thought,—
I would detain you here some month or two
Before you venture for me. I could teach you
How to choose right, but then I am forsworn;
So will I never be: so may you miss me;
But if you do, you'll make me wish a sin,
That I had been forsworn. Beshrew your eyes,
They have o'erlookt me, and divided me;
One half of me is yours, the other half yours,—
Mine own, I would say; but if mine, then yours,
And so all yours! O, these naughty times
Put bars between the owners and their rights!
And so, though yours, not yours.—Prove it so,
Let fortune go to hell for it,—not I.
I speak too long; but 'tis to peize the time,
To eke it, and to draw it out in length,
To stay you from election.

BASSIANO.

Let me choose;
For, as I am, I live upon the rack.

PORTIA.

Upon the rack, Bassanio! then confess
What treason there is mingled with your love.

BASSANIO.

None but that ugly treason of mistrust,
Which makes me fear the enjoying of my love:
There may as well be amity and league
'Tween snow and fire, as treason and my love.

PORTIA.

Ay, but I fear you speak upon the rack,
Where men enforced do speak any thing.

BASSANIO.

Promise me life, and I'll confess the truth.

PORTIA.

Well then, confess, and live.

BASSANIO.

'Confess,' and 'love,'
Had been the very sum of my confession:
O happy torment, when my torturer
Doth teach me answers for deliverance!
But let me to my fortune and the caskets.

PORTIA.

Away, then! I am lockt in one of them:
If you do love me, you will find me out.—
Nerissa, and the rest, stand all aloof.—
Let music sound while he doth make his choice;
Then, if he lose, he makes a swan-like end,
Fading in music: that the comparison [stream
May stand more proper, my eye shall be the
And watery death-bed for him. He may win;
And what is music then? then music is
Even as the flourish when true subjects bow
To a new-crowned monarch: such it is
As are those dulcet sounds in break of day
That creep into the dreaming bridegroom's ear,
And summon him to marriage.—Now he goes,
With no less presence, but with much more love,
Than young Alcides, when he did redeem
The virgin tribute paid by howling Troy
To the sea-monster: I stand for sacrifice;
The rest aloof are the Dardanian wives,
With bleared visages, come forth to view
The issue of th' exploit. Go, Hercules!
Live thou, I live:—with much much more dismay
I view the fight than thou that makest the fray.

Here music.—A Song, the whilst BASSANIO *comments on the caskets to himself.*

Tell me where is fancy bred,
Or in the heart or in the head?
How begot, how nourished?
Reply, reply.
It is engender'd in the eyes,
With gazing fed; and fancy dies
In the cradle where it lies.
Let us all ring fancy's knell;
I'll begin it,—Ding, dong, bell.

All. Ding, dong, bell.

BASSANIO.

So may the outward shows be least themselves:
The world is still deceived with ornament.
In law, what plea so tainted and corrupt,
But, being season'd with a gracious voice,
Obscures the show of evil? In religion,
What damned error, but some sober brow
Will bless it, and approve it with a text,
Hiding the grossness with fair ornament?
There is no vice so simple, but assumes
Some mark of virtue on his outward parts:
How many cowards, whose hearts are all as false
As stairs of sand, wear yet upon their chins
The beards of Hercules and frowning Mars;
Who, inward searcht, have livers white as milk;
And these assume but valour's excrement
To render them redoubted! Look on beauty,
And you shall see 'tis purchased by the weight;
Which therein works a miracle in nature,
Making them lightest that wear most of it:
So are those crisped snaky golden locks,
Which make such wanton gambols with the wind,
Upon supposed fairness, often known
To be the dowry of a second head,
The skull that bred them in the sepulchre.
Thus ornament is but the guiled shore
To a most dangerous sea; the beauteous scarf
Veiling an Indian beauty; in a word,
The seeming truth which cunning times put on
To entrap the wisest. Therefore, thou gaudy gold,
Hard food for Midas, I will none of thee;
Nor none of thee, thou stale and common drudge
'Tween man and man: but thou, thou meagre lead, [aught,
Which rather threatenest than dost promise
Thy paleness moves me more than eloquence;
And here choose I:—joy be the consequence!

PORTIA [*aside*].

How all the other passions fleet to air,—
As doubtful thoughts, and rash-embraced despair,
And shuddering fear, and green-eyed jealousy!
O love, be moderate; allay thy ecstasy;
In measure rain thy joy; scant this excess!
I feel too much thy blessing : make it less,
For fear I surfeit!

BASSANIO.

What find I here?
[*Opening the leaden casket.*
Fair Portia's counterfeit! What demi-god
Hath come so near creation? Move these eyes?
Or whether, riding on the balls of mine,
Seem they in motion? Here are sever'd lips,
Parted with sugar breath: so sweet a bar
Should sunder such sweet friends. Here in her hairs
The painter plays the spider; and hath woven
A golden mesh t'entrap the hearts of men,
Faster than gnats in cobwebs: but her eyes,—
How could he see to do them? having made one,
Methinks it should have power to steal both his,
And leave itself unfurnisht. Yet look, how far
The substance of my praise doth wrong this shadow
In underprizing it, so far this shadow
Doth limp behind the substance.—Here's the scroll,
The continent and summary of my fortune.

You that choose not by the view,
Chance as fair, and choose as true!
Since this fortune falls to you,
Be content, and seek no new.
If you be well pleased with this,

And hold your fortune for your bliss,
Turn you where your lady is,
And claim her with a loving kiss.

A gentle scroll.—Fair lady, by your leave;
[*Kissing her.*
I come by note, to give and to receive.
Like one of two contending in a prize,
That thinks he hath done well in people's eyes,
Hearing applause and universal shout,
Giddy in spirit, still gazing in a doubt
Whether those peals of praise be his or no;
So, thrice-fair lady, stand I, even so;
As doubtful whether what I see be true,
Until confirm'd, sign'd, ratified by you.

PORTIA.

You see me, Lord Bassanio, where I stand,
Such as I am: though for myself alone
I would not be ambitious in my wish,
To wish myself much better; yet for you
I would be trebled twenty times myself;
A thousand times more fair, ten thousand times more rich;
That, only to stand high in your account,
I might in virtues, beauties, livings, friends,
Exceed account: but the full sum of me
Is sum of nothing; which, to term in gross,
Is an unlesson'd girl, unschool'd, unpractised:
Happy in this, she is not yet so old
But she may learn; happier than this,
She is not bred so dull but she can learn;
Happiest of all is that her gentle spirit
Commits itself to yours to be directed,
As from her lord, her governor, her king.
Myself and what is mine to you and yours
Is now converted: but now I was the lord
Of this fair mansion, master of my servants,
Queen o'er myself; and even now, but now,
This house, these servants, and this same myself,
Are yours, my lord: I give them with this ring;
Which when you part from, lose, or give away,
Let it presage the ruin of your love,
And be my vantage to exclaim on you.

BASSANIO.

Madam, you have bereft me of all words,
Only my blood speaks to you in my veins:
And there is such confusion in my powers,
As, after some oration fairly spoke
By a beloved prince, there doth appear
Among the buzzing pleased multitude;
Where every something, being blent together,
Turns to a wild of nothing, save of joy,
Exprest and not exprest. But when this ring
Parts from this finger, then parts life from hence:
O, then be bold to say Bassanio's dead!

NERISSA.

My lord and lady, it is now our time,
That have stood by, and seen our wishes prosper,
To cry, good joy:—good joy, my lord and lady!

GRATIANO.

My Lord Bassanio and my gentle lady,
I wish you all the joy that you can wish;
For I am sure you can wish none from me:
And, when your honours mean to solemnize
The bargain of your faith, I do beseech you,
Even at that time I may be married too.

BASSANIO.

With all my heart, so thou canst get a wife.

GRATIANO.

I thank your lordship, you have got me one.
My eyes, my lord, can look as swift as yours:
You saw the mistress, I beheld the maid;
You loved, I loved; for intermission
No more pertains to me, my lord, than you.
Your fortune stood upon the caskets there;
And so did mine too, as the matter falls;
For wooing here, until I sweat again,
And swearing, till my very roof was dry
With oaths of love, at last,—if promise last,—
I got a promise of this fair one here,
To have her love, provided that your fortune
Achieved her mistress.

PORTIA.

Is this true, Nerissa?

NERISSA.

Madam, it is, so you stand pleased withal.

BASSANIO.

And do you, Gratiano, mean good faith?

GRATIANO.

Yes, faith, my lord.

BASSANIO.

Our feast shall be much honour'd in your marriage.

GRATIANO.

We'll play with them the first boy for a thousand ducats.

NERISSA.

What, and stake down?

GRATIANO.

No; we shall ne'er win at that sport, and stake down.—
But who comes here? Lorenzo and his infidel?
What, and my old Venetian friend Solanio?

Enter LORENZO, JESSICA, *and* SOLANIO.

BASSANIO.

Lorenzo and Solanio, welcome hither;
If that the youth of my new interest here
Have power to bid you welcome.—By your leave,
I bid my very friends and countrymen,
Sweet Portia, welcome.

PORTIA.

So do I, my lord;
They are entirely welcome.

LORENZO.

I thank your honour.—For my part, my lord,
My purpose was not to have seen you here;
But meeting with Solanio by the way,
He did entreat me, past all saying nay,
To come with him along.

SOLANIO.

I did, my lord;
And I have reason for't. Signior Antonio
Commends him to you. [*Gives* BASSANIO *a letter.*

BASSANIO.

Ere I ope his letter,
I pray you, tell me how my good friend doth.

SOLANIO.

Not sick, my lord, unless it be in mind;
Not well, unless in mind: his letter there
Will show you his estate.
[BASSANIO *reads the letter.*

GRATIANO.

Nerissa, cheer yon stranger; bid her welcome.—
Your hand, Solanio: what's the news from Venice?
How doth that royal merchant, good Antonio?
I know he will be glad of our success;
We are the Jasons, we have won the fleece.

SOLANIO.

I would you had won the fleece that he hath lost!

PORTIA.

There are some shrewd contents in yon same paper,
That steals the colour from Bassanio's cheek:
Some dear friend dead; else nothing in the world
Could turn so much the constitution
Of any constant man. What, worse and worse!—
With leave, Bassanio; I am half yourself,
And I must freely have the half of any thing
That this same paper brings you.

BASSANIO.

O sweet Portia,
Here are a few of the unpleasant'st words
That ever blotted paper! Gentle lady,
When I did first impart my love to you,
I freely told you, all the wealth I had
Ran in my veins,—I was a gentleman;
And then I told you true: and yet, dear lady,
Rating myself at nothing, you shall see
How much I was a braggart. When I told you
My state was nothing, I should then have told you
That I was worse than nothing; for, indeed,
I have engaged myself to a dear friend,
Engaged my friend to his mere enemy,
To feed my means. Here is a letter, lady,—
The paper as the body of my friend,
And every word in it a gaping wound,
Issuing life-blood.—But is it true, Solanio?
Have all his ventures fail'd? What, not one hit?
From Tripolis, from Mexico, and England,
From Lisbon, Barbary, and India?
And not one vessel scape the dreadful touch
Of merchant-marring rocks?

SOLANIO.

Not one, my lord.
Besides, it should appear, that if he had
The present money to discharge the Jew,
He would not take it. Never did I know
A creature, that did bear the shape of man,
So keen and greedy to confound a man;
He plies the duke at morning and at night;
And doth impeach the freedom of the state,
If they deny him justice: twenty merchants,
The duke himself, and the magnificoes
Of greatest port, have all persuaded with him;
But none can drive him from the envious plea
Of forfeiture, of justice, and his bond.

JESSICA.

When I was with him, I have heard him swear,
To Tubal and to Chus, his countrymen,
That he would rather have Antonio's flesh
Than twenty times the value of the sum
That he did owe him: and I know, my lord,
If law, authority, and power deny not,
It will go hard with poor Antonio.

PORTIA.

Is it your dear friend that is thus in trouble?

BASSANIO.

The dearest friend to me, the kindest man,
The best-condition'd and unwearied spirit
In doing courtesies; and one in whom
The ancient Roman honour more appears
Than any that draws breath in Italy.

PORTIA.

What sum owes he the Jew?

BASSANIO.

For me three thousand ducats.

PORTIA.

What, no more?
Pay him six thousand, and deface the bond;
Double six thousand, and then treble that,
Before a friend of this description
Shall lose a hair through Bassanio's fault.
First go with me to church and call me wife,
And then away to Venice to your friend;
For never shall you lie by Portia's side
With an unquiet soul. You shall have gold
To pay the petty debt twenty times over:
When it is paid, bring your true friend along.
My maid Nerissa and myself meantime
Will live as maids and widows. Come, away!
For you shall hence upon your wedding-day:
Bid your friends welcome, show a merry cheer:
Since you are dear-bought, I will love you dear.—
But let me hear the letter of your friend.

BASSANIO [*reads*].

Sweet Bassanio, my ships have all miscarried, my creditors grow cruel, my estate is very low, my bond to the Jew is forfeit; and since in paying it, it is impossible I should live, all debts are clear'd between you and I, if I might but see you at my death. Notwithstanding, use your pleasure: if your love do not persuade you to come, let not my letter.

PORTIA.

O love, dispatch all business, and be gone!

BASSANIO.

Since I have your good leave to go away,
I will make haste: but, till I come again,
No bed shall e'er be guilty of my stay,
No rest be interposer 'twixt us twain. [*Exeunt.*

SCENE III.

Venice. A street.

Enter SHYLOCK, SALARINO, ANTONIO, *and* GAOLER.

SHYLOCK.

GAOLER, look to him:—tell not me of mercy;—
This is the fool that lent out money gratis:—
Gaoler, look to him.

ANTONIO.

Hear me yet, good Shylock.

SHYLOCK.

I'll have my bond; speak not against my bond:
I have sworn an oath that I will have my bond.
Thou call'dst me dog before thou hadst a cause;
But, since I am a dog, beware my fangs:
The duke shall grant me justice.—I do wonder,
Thou naughty gaoler, that thou art so fond
To come abroad with him at his request.

ANTONIO.

I pray thee, hear me speak.

SHYLOCK.

I'll have my bond; I will not hear thee speak:
I'll have my bond; and therefore speak no more.
I'll not be made a soft and dull-eyed fool,
To shake the head, relent, and sigh, and yield
To Christian intercessors. Follow not;
I'll have no speaking: I will have my bond. [*Exit.*

SALARINO.

It is the most impenetrable cur
That ever kept with men.

ANTONIO.

Let him alone:
I'll follow him no more with bootless prayers.
He seeks my life; his reason well I know:
I oft deliver'd from his forfeitures
Many that have at times made moan to me;
Therefore he hates me.

SALARINO.

I am sure the duke
Will never grant this forfeiture to hold.

ANTONIO.

The duke cannot deny the course of law;
For the commodity that strangers have
With us in Venice, if it be denied,
Will much impeach the justice of the state;
Since that the trade and profit of the city
Consisteth of all nations. Therefore, go:
These griefs and losses have so bated me,
That I shall hardly spare a pound of flesh
To-morrow to my bloody creditor.—
Well, gaoler, on.—Pray God, Bassanio come
To see me pay his debt,—and then I care not!
[*Exeunt.*

SCENE IV.

Belmont. A room in PORTIA'S *house.*

Enter PORTIA, NERISSA, LORENZO, JESSICA, *and* BALTHAZAR, *a man of* PORTIA'S.

LORENZO.

MADAM, although I speak it in your presence,
You have a noble and a true conceit
Of god-like amity; which appears most strongly
In bearing thus the absence of your lord.
But if you knew to whom you show this honour,
How true a gentleman you send relief,
How dear a lover of my lord your husband,
I know you would be prouder of the work
Than customary bounty can enforce you.

PORTIA.

I never did repent for doing good,
Nor shall not now: for in companions
That do converse and waste the time together,
Whose souls do bear an egal yoke of love,
There must be needs a like proportion
Of lineaments, of manners, and of spirit;
Which makes me think that this Antonio,
Being the bosom lover of my lord,
Must needs be like my lord. If it be so,
How little is the cost I have bestow'd
In purchasing the semblance of my soul
From out the state of hellish cruelty!
This comes too near the praising of myself;
Therefore no more of it: hear other things.—
Lorenzo, I commit into your hands
The husbandry and manage of my house
Until my lord's return: for mine own part,
I have toward heaven breathed a secret vow
To live in prayer and contemplation,
Only attended by Nerissa here,
Until her husband and my lord's return:
There is a monastery two miles off;
And there will we abide. I do desire you
Not to deny this imposition;
The which my love and some necessity
Now lays upon you.

LORENZO.

Madam, with all my heart;
I shall obey you in all fair commands.

PORTIA.

My people do already know my mind,
And will acknowledge you and Jessica
In place of Lord Bassanio and myself.
So fare you well, till we shall meet again.

LORENZO.

Fair thoughts and happy hours attend on you!

JESSICA.

I wish your ladyship all heart's content.

PORTIA.

I thank you for your wish, and am well pleased
To wish it back on you: fare you well, Jessica.
[*Exeunt* JESSICA *and* LORENZO.
Now, Balthazar,
As I have ever found thee honest-true,
So let me find thee still. Take this same letter,
And use thou all the endeavour of a man
In speed to Padua: see thou render this
Into my cousin's hand, Doctor Bellario;
And, look, what notes and garments he doth give thee,
Bring them, I pray thee, with imagined speed
Unto the tranect, to the common ferry
Which trades to Venice. Waste no time in words,
But get thee gone: I shall be there before thee.

BALTHAZAR.

Madam, I go with all convenient speed. [*Exit.*

PORTIA.

Come on, Nerissa; I have work in hand
That you yet know not of: we'll see our husbands
Before they think of us.

NERISSA.

Shall they see us?

PORTIA.

They shall, Nerissa; but in such a habit,
That they shall think we are accomplished
With that we lack. I'll hold thee any wager,
When we are both accoutred like young men,
I'll prove the prettier fellow of the two,
And wear my dagger with the braver grace;
And speak between the change of man and boy
With a reed voice; and turn two mincing steps
Into a manly stride; and speak of frays,
Like a fine-bragging youth; and tell quaint lies,
How honourable ladies sought my love,
Which I denying, they fell sick and died;—
I could not do withal;—then I'll repent,
And wish, for all that, that I had not kill'd them:
And twenty of these puny lies I'll tell;
That men shall swear I have discontinued school
Above a twelvemonth:—I have within my mind

A thousand raw tricks of these bragging Jacks,
Which I will practise.

NERISSA.

Why, shall we turn to men?

PORTIA.

Fie, what a question's that,
If thou wert near a lewd interpreter!
But come, I'll tell thee all my whole device
When I am in my coach, which stays for us
At the park-gate; and therefore haste away,
For we must measure twenty miles to-day.
[*Exeunt.*

SCENE V.

The same. A garden.

Enter LAUNCELOT *and* JESSICA.

LAUNCELOT.

YES, truly; for, look you, the sins of the father are to be laid upon the children: therefore, I promise ye, I fear you. I was always plain with you, and so now I speak my agitation of the matter: therefore be o' good cheer; for, truly, I think you are damn'd. There is but one hope in it that can do you any good; and that is but a kind of bastard hope neither.

JESSICA.

And what hope is that, I pray thee?

LAUNCELOT.

Marry, you may partly hope that your father got you not,—that you are not the Jew's daughter.

JESSICA.

That were a kind of bastard hope, indeed: so the sins of my mother should be visited upon me.

LAUNCELOT.

Truly, then, I fear you are damn'd both by father and mother: thus when I shun Scylla, your father, I fall into Charybdis, your mother: well, you are gone both ways.

JESSICA.

I shall be saved by my husband; he hath made me a Christian.

LAUNCELOT.

Truly, the more to blame he: we were Christians enow before; e'en as many as could well live, one by another. This making of Christians will raise the price of hogs: if we grow all to be pork-eaters, we shall not shortly have a rasher on the coals for money.

JESSICA.

I'll tell my husband, Launcelot, what you say: here he comes.

Enter LORENZO.

LORENZO.

I shall grow jealous of you shortly, Launcelot, if you thus get my wife into corners.

JESSICA.

Nay, you need not fear us, Lorenzo: Launcelot and I are out. He tells me flatly, there's no mercy for me in heaven, because I am a Jew's daughter: and he says, you are no good member of the commonwealth; for, in converting Jews to Christians, you raise the price of pork.

LORENZO.

I shall answer that better to the commonwealth than you can the getting up of the negro's belly: the Moor's with child by you, Launcelot.

LAUNCELOT.

It is much that the Moor should be more than reason: but if she be less than an honest woman, she is indeed more than I took her for.

LORENZO.

How every fool can play upon the word! I think the best grace of wit will shortly turn into silence, and discourse grow commendable in none only but parrots.—Go in, sirrah; bid them prepare for dinner.

LAUNCELOT.

That's done, sir; they have all stomachs.

LORENZO.

Goodly Lord, what a wit-snapper are you! then bid them prepare dinner.

LAUNCELOT.

That is done too, sir; only 'cover' is the word.

LORENZO.

Will you cover, then, sir?

LAUNCELOT.

Not so, sir, neither; I know my duty.

LORENZO.

Yet more quarrelling with occasion! Wilt thou show the whole wealth of thy wit in an instant? I pray thee, understand a plain man in his plain meaning: go to thy fellows, bid them cover the table, serve in the meat, and we will come in to dinner.

LAUNCELOT.

For the table, sir, it shall be served in; for the meat, sir, it shall be cover'd; for your coming in to dinner, sir, why, let it be as humours and conceits shall govern. [*Exit.*

LORENZO.

O dear discretion, how his words are suited!
The fool hath planted in his memory
An army of good words; and I do know
A many fools, that stand in better place,
Garnisht like him, that for a tricksy word
Defy the matter.—How cheer'st thou, Jessica?
And now, good sweet, say thy opinion,—
How dost thou like the Lord Bassanio's wife?

JESSICA.

Past all expressing. It is very meet
The Lord Bassanio live an upright life;
For, having such a blessing in his lady,
He finds the joys of heaven here on earth;
And if on earth he do not mean it, then
In reason he should never come to heaven.
Why, if two gods should play some heavenly match,
And on the wager lay two earthly women,
And Portia one, there must be something else
Pawn'd with the other; for the poor rude world
Hath not her fellow.

LORENZO.

Even such a husband
Hast thou of me as she is for a wife.

JESSICA.

Nay, but ask my opinion too of that.

LORENZO.

I will anon: first, let us go to dinner.

JESSICA.

Nay, let me praise you while I have a stomach.

LORENZO.

No, prithee, let it serve for table-talk;
Then, howsoe'er thou speak'st, 'mong other things
I shall digest it.

JESSICA.

Well, I'll set you forth. [*Exeunt.*

ACT IV. SCENE I.

Venice. A court of justice.

Enter the DUKE, *the* MAGNIFICOES, ANTONIO, BASSANIO, GRATIANO, SOLANIO, SALARINO, *and others.*

DUKE OF VENICE.

WHAT, is Antonio here?

ANTONIO.

Ready, so please your Grace.

DUKE OF VENICE.

I am sorry for thee: thou art come to answer
A stony adversary, an inhuman wretch
Uncapable of pity, void and empty
From any dram of mercy.

ANTONIO.

I have heard
Your Grace hath ta'en great pains to qualify
His rigorous course; but since he stands obdurate,
And that no lawful means can carry me
Out of his envy's reach, I do oppose
My patience to his fury; and am arm'd
To suffer, with a quietness of spirit,
The very tyranny and rage of his.

DUKE OF VENICE.

Go one, and call the Jew into the court.

SOLANIO.

He's ready at the door: he comes, my lord.

Enter SHYLOCK.

DUKE OF VENICE.

Make room, and let him stand before our face.—
Shylock, the world thinks, and I think so too,
That thou but lead'st this fashion of thy malice
To the last hour of act; and then 'tis thought
Thou'lt show thy mercy and remorse more strange
Than is thy strange apparent cruelty;
And where thou now exact'st the penalty,—
Which is a pound of this poor merchant's flesh,—
Thou wilt not only loose the forfeiture,
But, toucht with human gentleness and love,
Forgive a moiety of the principal;
Glancing an eye of pity on his losses,
That have of late so huddled on his back,
Enow to press a royal merchant down,
And pluck commiseration of his state
From brassy bosoms and rough hearts of flint,
From stubborn Turks and Tartars, never train'd
To offices of tender courtesy.
We all expect a gentle answer, Jew.

SHYLOCK.

I have possest your Grace of what I purpose;
And by our holy Sabbath have I sworn
To have the due and forfeit of my bond:
If you deny it, let the danger light
Upon your charter and your city's freedom.
You'll ask me, why I rather choose to have
A weight of carrion-flesh than to receive
Three thousand ducats: I'll not answer that;
But say it is my humour: is it answer'd?
What if my house be troubled with a rat,
And I be pleased to give ten thousand ducats
To have it baned! What, are you answer'd yet?
Some men there are love not a gaping pig;
Some, that are mad if they behold a cat;
And others, when the bag-pipe sings i' th' nose,
Cannot contain their urine: for affection,
Mistress of passion, sways it to the mood
Of what it likes or loathes. Now, for your answer:
As there is no firm reason to be render'd,
Why he cannot abide a gaping pig;
Why he, a harmless necessary cat;
Why he, a woollen bag-pipe,—but of force
Must yield to such inevitable shame
As to offend himself, being offended;
So can I give no reason, nor I will not,
More than a lodged hate and a certain loathing
I bear Antonio, that I follow thus
A losing suit against him. Are you answer'd?

BASSANIO.

This is no answer, thou unfeeling man,
To excuse the current of thy cruelty.

SHYLOCK.

I am not bound to please thee with my answer.

BASSANIO.

Do all men kill the things they do not love?

SHYLOCK.

Hates any man the thing he would not kill?

BASSANIO.

Every offence is not a hate at first.

SHYLOCK.

What, would'st thou have a serpent sting thee twice?

ANTONIO.

I pray you, think you question with the Jew:
You may as well go stand upon the beach,
And bid the main flood bate his usual height;
You may as well use question with the wolf,
Why he hath made the ewe bleat for the lamb;
You may as well forbid the mountain pines
To wag their high tops, and to make no noise,
When they are fretten with the gusts of heaven;
You may as well do any thing most hard,
As seek to soften that,—than which what's harder?—
His Jewish heart:—therefore, I do beseech you,
Make no more offers, use no further means,
But, with all brief and plain conveniency,
Let me have judgement, and the Jew his will.

BASSANIO.

For thy three thousand ducats here is six.

SHYLOCK.

If every ducat in six thousand ducats
Were in six parts, and every part a ducat,
I would not draw them,—I would have my bond.

DUKE OF VENICE.

How shalt thou hope for mercy, rendering none?

SHYLOCK.

What judgement shall I dread, doing no wrong?
You have among you many a purchased slave,
Which, like your asses and your dogs and mules
You use in abject and in slavish parts,
Because you bought them:—shall I say to you,
Let them be free, marry them to your heirs?

Why sweat they under burdens? let their beds
Be made as soft as yours, and let their palates
Be season'd with such viands? You will answer,
The slaves are ours:—so do I answer you:
The pound of flesh, which I demand of him,
Is dearly bought, 'tis mine, and I will have it.
If you deny me, fie upon your law!
There is no force in the decrees of Venice.
I stand for judgment: answer,—shall I have it?

DUKE OF VENICE.

Upon my power I may dismiss this court,
Unless Bellario, a learned doctor,
Whom I have sent for to determine this,
Come here to-day.

SOLANIO.

My lord, here stays without
A messenger with letters from the doctor,
New come from Padua.

DUKE OF VENICE.

Bring us the letters; call the messenger.

BASSANIO.

Good cheer, Antonio! What, man, courage yet!
The Jew shall have my flesh, blood, bones, and all,
Ere thou shalt lose for me one drop of blood.

ANTONIO.

I am a tainted wether of the flock,
Meetest for death: the weakest kind of fruit
Drops earliest to the ground; and so let me:
You cannot better be employ'd, Bassanio,
Than to live still, and write mine epitaph.

Enter NERISSA, *dressed like a lawyer's clerk.*

DUKE OF VENICE.

Came you from Padua, from Bellario?

NERISSA.

From both, my lord. Bellario greets your Grace.
[*Presents a letter.*

BASSANIO.

Why dost thou whet thy knife so earnestly?

SHYLOCK.

To cut the forfeiture from that bankrout there.

GRATIANO.

Not on thy sole, but on thy soul, harsh Jew,
Thou makest thy knife keen; but no metal can,
No, not the hangman's axe, bear half the keenness
Of thy sharp envy. Can no prayers pierce thee?

SHYLOCK.

No, none that thou hast wit enough to make.

GRATIANO.

O, be thou damn'd, inexecrable dog!
And for thy life let justice be accused.
Thou almost makest me waver in my faith,
To hold opinion with Pythagoras,
That souls of animals infuse themselves
Into the trunks of men: thy currish spirit
Govern'd a wolf, who, hang'd for human slaughter,
Even from the gallows did his fell soul fleet,
And, whilst thou lay'st in thy unhallow'd dam,
Infused itself in thee; for thy desires
Are wolvish, bloody, starved, and ravenous.

SHYLOCK.

Till thou canst rail the seal from off my bond,
Thou but offend'st thy lungs to speak so loud:
Repair thy wit, good youth, or it will fall
To cureless ruin.—I stand here for law.

DUKE OF VENICE.

This letter from Bellario doth commend
A young and learned doctor to our court.—
Where is he?

NERISSA.

He attendeth here hard by,
To know your answer, whether you'll admit him.

DUKE OF VENICE.

With all my heart.—Some three or four of you
Go give him courteous conduct to this place.—
Meantime the court shall hear Bellario's letter.

CLERK [*reads*].

Your Grace shall understand, that at the receipt of your letter I am very sick: but in the instant that your messenger came, in loving visitation was with me a young doctor of Rome; his name is Balthazar. I acquainted him with the cause in controversy between the Jew and Antonio the merchant: we turn'd o'er many books together: he is furnisht with my opinion; which, better'd with his own learning,—the greatness whereof I cannot enough commend,—comes with him, at my importunity, to fill up your Grace's request in my stead. I beseech you, let his lack of years be no impediment to let him lack a reverend estimation; for I never knew so young a body with so old a head. I leave him to your gracious acceptance, whose trial shall better publish his commendation.

DUKE OF VENICE.

You hear the learn'd Bellario, what he writes:
And here, I take it, is the doctor come.

Enter PORTIA *for* BALTHAZAR.

Give me your hand. Come you from old Bellario?

PORTIA.

I did, my lord.

DUKE OF VENICE.

You are welcome: take your place.
Are you acquainted with the difference
That holds this present question in the court?

PORTIA.

I am informed throughly of the cause.—
Which is the merchant here, and which the Jew?

DUKE OF VENICE.

Antonio and old Shylock, both stand forth.

PORTIA.

Is your name Shylock?

SHYLOCK.

Shylock is my name.

PORTIA.

Of a strange nature is the suit you follow;
Yet in such rule, that the Venetian law
Cannot impugn you as you do proceed.—
You stand within his danger, do you not?

ANTONIO.

Ay, so he says.

PORTIA.

Do you confess the bond?

ANTONIO.

I do.

PORTIA.

Then must the Jew be merciful.

SHYLOCK.

On what compulsion must I? tell me that.

PORTIA.

The quality of mercy is not strain'd,—
It droppeth as the gentle rain from heaven

Upon the place beneath: it is twice blest,—
It blesseth him that gives, and him that takes:
'Tis mightiest in the mightiest: it becomes
The throned monarch better than his crown;
His sceptre shows the force of temporal power,
The attribute to awe and majesty,
Wherein doth sit the dread and fear of kings;
But mercy is above this sceptred sway,—
It is enthroned in the hearts of kings,
It is an attribute to God himself;
And earthly power doth then show likest God's
When mercy seasons justice. Therefore, Jew,
Though justice be thy plea, consider this,—
That, in the course of justice, none of us
Should see salvation: we do pray for mercy;
And that same prayer doth teach us all to render
The deeds of mercy. I have spoke thus much
To mitigate the justice of thy plea;
Which if thou follow, this strict court of Venice
Must needs give sentence 'gainst the merchant
there.

SHYLOCK.

My deeds upon my head! I crave the law,
The penalty and forfeit of my bond.

PORTIA.

Is he not able to discharge the money?

BASSANIO.

Yes, here I tender it for him in the court;
Yea, thrice the sum: if that will not suffice,
I will be bound to pay it ten times o'er,
On forfeit of my hands, my head, my heart:
If this will not suffice, it must appear
That malice bears down truth. And I beseech you,
Wrest once the law to your authority:
To do a great right, do a little wrong;
And curb this cruel devil of his will.

PORTIA.

It must not be; there is no power in Venice
Can alter a decree established:
'Twill be recorded for a precedent;
And many an error, by the same example,
Will rush into the state: it cannot be.

SHYLOCK.

A Daniel come to judgement! yea, a Daniel!—
O wise young judge, how I do honour thee!

PORTIA.

I pray you, let me look upon the bond.

SHYLOCK.

Here 'tis, most reverend doctor, here it is.

PORTIA.

Shylock, there's thrice thy money offer'd thee.

SHYLOCK.

An oath, an oath, I have an oath in heaven:
Shall I lay perjury upon my soul?
No, not for Venice.

PORTIA.

Why, this bond is forfeit;
And lawfully by this the Jew may claim
A pound of flesh, to be by him cut off
Nearest the merchant's heart.—Be merciful:
Take thrice thy money; bid me tear the bond.

SHYLOCK.

When it is paid according to the tenour.—
It doth appear you are a worthy judge;
You know the law, your exposition
Hath been most sound: I charge you by the law,
Whereof you are a well-deserving pillar,
Proceed to judgement: by my soul I swear
There is no power in the tongue of man
To alter me: I stay here on my bond.

ANTONIO.

Most heartily I do beseech the court
To give the judgement.

PORTIA.

Why then, thus it is:—
You must prepare your bosom for his knife.

SHYLOCK.

O noble judge! O excellent young man!

PORTIA.

For the intent and purpose of the law
Hath full relation to the penalty,
Which here appeareth due upon the bond.

SHYLOCK.

'Tis very true: O wise and upright judge!
How much more elder art thou than thy looks!

PORTIA.

Therefore lay bare your bosom.

SHYLOCK.

Ay, his breast:
So says the bond:—doth it not, noble judge?—
Nearest his heart: those are the very words.

PORTIA.

It is so. Are there balance here to weigh
The flesh?

SHYLOCK.

I have them ready.

PORTIA.

Have by some surgeon, Shylock, on your charge,
To stop his wounds, lest he do bleed to death.

SHYLOCK.

Is it so nominated in the bond?

PORTIA.

It is not so exprest: but what of that?
'Twere good you do so much for charity.

SHYLOCK.

I cannot find it; 'tis not in the bond.

PORTIA.

You, merchant, have you any thing to say?

ANTONIO.

But little: I am arm'd and well prepared.—
Give me your hand, Bassanio: fare you well!
Grieve not that I am fall'n to this for you;
For herein Fortune shows herself more kind
Than is her custom: it is still her use
To let the wretched man outlive his wealth,
To view with hollow eye and wrinkled brow
An age of poverty; from which lingering penance
Of such a misery doth she cut me off.
Commend me to your honourable wife:
Tell her the process of Antonio's end;
Say how I loved you, speak me fair in death;
And, when the tale is told, bid her be judge
Whether Bassanio had not once a love.
Repent but you that you shall lose your friend,
And he repents not that he pays your debt;
For, if the Jew do cut but deep enough,
I'll pay it presently with all my heart.

BASSANIO.

Antonio, I am married to a wife
Which is as dear to me as life itself;
But life itself, my wife, and all the world,
Are not with me esteem'd above thy life:

I would lose all, ay, sacrifice them all
Here to this devil, to deliver you.

PORTIA.
Your wife would give you little thanks for that,
If she were by, to hear you make the offer.

GRATIANO.
I have a wife, whom, I protest, I love:
I would she were in heaven, so she could
Entreat some power to change this currish Jew.

NERISSA.
'Tis well you offer it behind her back;
The wish would make else an unquiet house.

SHYLOCK [*aside*].
These be the Christian husbands! I have a daughter;
Would any of the stock of Barabbas
Had been her husband rather than a Christian!—
We trifle time: I pray thee, pursue sentence.

PORTIA.
A pound of that same merchant's flesh is thine:
The court awards it, and the law doth give it.

SHYLOCK.
Most rightful judge!

PORTIA.
And you must cut this flesh from off his breast:
The law allows it, and the court awards it.

SHYLOCK.
Most learned judge!—A sentence! come, prepare!

PORTIA.
Tarry a little; there is something else.
This bond doth give thee here no jot of blood,—
The words expressly are, 'a pound of flesh':
Take then thy bond, take thou thy pound of flesh;
But, in the cutting it, if thou dost shed
One drop of Christian blood, thy lands and goods
Are, by the laws of Venice, confiscate
Unto the state of Venice.

GRATIANO.
O upright judge!—Mark, Jew:—O learned judge!

SHYLOCK.
Is that the law?

PORTIA.
Thyself shalt see the act:
For, as thou urgest justice, be assured
Thou shalt have justice, more than thou desirest.

GRATIANO.
O learned judge!—Mark, Jew:—a learned judge!

SHYLOCK.
I take his offer, then;— pay the bond thrice,
And let the Christian go.

BASSANIO.
Here is the money.

PORTIA.
Soft!
The Jew shall have all justice;—soft! no haste:—
He shall have nothing but the penalty.

GRATIANO.
O Jew! an upright judge, a learned judge!

PORTIA.
Therefore prepare thee to cut off the flesh.
Shed thou no blood; nor cut thou less nor more
But just a pound of flesh: if thou cutt'st more
Or less than a just pound,—be it but so much
As makes it light or heavy in the substance,
Or the division of the twentieth part
Of one poor scruple, nay, if the scale do turn
But in the estimation of a hair,—
Thou diest, and all thy goods are confiscate.

GRATIANO.
A second Daniel, a Daniel, Jew!
Now, infidel, I have you on the hip.

PORTIA.
Why doth the Jew pause? take thy forfeiture.

SHYLOCK.
Give me my principal, and let me go.

BASSANIO.
I have it ready for thee; here it is.

PORTIA.
He hath refused it in the open court:
He shall have merely justice and his bond.

GRATIANO.
A Daniel, still say I, a second Daniel!—
I thank thee, Jew, for teaching me that word.

SHYLOCK.
Shall I not have barely my principal?

PORTIA.
Thou shalt have nothing but the forfeiture,
To be so taken at thy peril, Jew.

SHYLOCK.
Why, then the devil give him good of it!
I'll stay no longer question.

PORTIA.
Tarry, Jew:
The law hath yet another hold on you.
It is enacted in the laws of Venice,—
If it be proved against an alien
That by direct or indirect attempts
He seek the life of any citizen,
The party 'gainst the which he doth contrive
Shall seize one half his goods; the other half
Comes to the privy coffer of the state;
And the offender's life lies in the mercy
Of the duke only, 'gainst all other voice.
In which predicament, I say, thou stand'st;
For it appears, by manifest proceeding,
That indirectly, and directly too,
Thou hast contrived against the very life
Of the defendant; and thou hast incurr'd
The danger formerly by me rehearsed.
Down, therefore, and beg mercy of the duke.

GRATIANO.
Beg that thou mayst have leave to hang thyself:
And yet, thy wealth being forfeit to the state,
Thou hast not left the value of a cord;
Therefore thou must be hang'd at the state's charge.

DUKE OF VENICE.
That thou shalt see the difference of our spirits,
I pardon thee thy life before thou ask it:
For half thy wealth, it is Antonio's;
The other half comes to the general state,
Which humbleness may drive unto a fine.

PORTIA.
Ay, for the state,—not for Antonio.

SHYLOCK.
Nay, take my life and all; pardon not that:
You take my house, when you do take the prop
That doth sustain my house; you take my life,
When you do take the means whereby I live.

PORTIA.
What mercy can you render him, Antonio?

GRATIANO.
A halter gratis; nothing else, for God's sake.

ANTONIO.

So please my lord the duke and all the court
To quit the fine for one half of his goods,
I am content; so he will let me have
The other half in use, to render it,
Upon his death, unto the gentleman
That lately stole his daughter:
Two things provided more,—that, for this favour,
He presently become a Christian;
The other, that he do record a gift,
Here in the court, of all he dies possest,
Unto his son Lorenzo and his daughter.

DUKE OF VENICE.

He shall do this; or else I do recant
The pardon that I late pronounced here.

PORTIA.

Art thou contented, Jew? what dost thou say?

SHYLOCK.

I am content.

PORTIA.

Clerk, draw a deed of gift.

SHYLOCK.

I pray you, give me leave to go from hence;
I am not well: send the deed after me,
And I will sign it.

DUKE OF VENICE.

Get thee gone, but do it.

GRATIANO.

In christening shalt thou have two godfathers:
Had I been judge, thou shouldst have had ten more,
To bring thee to the gallows, not the font.

[*Exit* SHYLOCK.

DUKE OF VENICE.

Sir, I entreat you home with me to dinner.

PORTIA.

I humbly do desire your Grace of pardon:
I must away this night toward Padua,
And it is meet I presently set forth.

DUKE OF VENICE.

I am sorry that your leisure serves you not.—
Antonio, gratify this gentleman;
For, in my mind, you are much bound to him.

[*Exeunt* DUKE *and his* TRAIN.

BASSANIO.

Most worthy gentleman, I and my friend
Have by your wisdom been this day acquitted
Of grievous penalties; in lieu whereof
Three thousand ducats, due unto the Jew,
We freely cope your courteous pains withal.

ANTONIO.

And stand indebted, over and above,
In love and service to you evermore.

PORTIA.

He is well paid that is well satisfied;
And I, delivering you, am satisfied,
And therein do account myself well paid:
My mind was never yet more mercenary.
I pray you, know me when we meet again:
I wish you well, and so I take my leave.

BASSANIO.

Dear sir, of force I must attempt you further:
Take some remembrance of us, as a tribute,
Not as a fee: grant me two things, I pray you,—
Not to deny me, and to pardon me.

PORTIA.

You press me far, and therefore I will yield.
[*to* ANTONIO] Give me your gloves, I'll wear them for your sake;
[*to* BASSANIO] And, for your love, I'll take this ring from you:—
Do not draw back your hand; I'll take no more;
And you in love shall not deny me this.

BASSANIO.

This ring, good sir,—alas, it is a trifle!
I will not shame myself to give you this.

PORTIA.

I will have nothing else but only this;
And now methinks I have a mind to it.

BASSANIO.

There's more depends on this than on the value,
The dearest ring in Venice will I give you,
And find it out by proclamation:
Only for this, I pray you, pardon me.

PORTIA.

I see, sir, you are liberal in offers:
You taught me first to beg; and now methinks
You teach me how a beggar should be answer'd.

BASSANIO.

Good sir, this ring was given me by my wife;
And, when she put it on, she made me vow
That I should neither sell nor give nor lose it.

PORTIA.

That 'scuse serves many men to save their gifts.
An if your wife be not a mad-woman,
And know how well I have deserved this ring,
She would not hold out enemy for ever
For giving it to me. Well, peace be with you!

[*Exeunt* PORTIA *and* NERISSA.

ANTONIO.

My Lord Bassanio, let him have the ring:
Let his deservings, and my love withal,
Be valued 'gainst your wife's commandment.

BASSANIO.

Go, Gratiano, run and overtake him;
Give him this ring; and bring him, if thou canst,
Unto Antonio's house:—away! make haste.

[*Exit* GRATIANO.

Come, you and I will thither presently;
And in the morning early will we both
Fly toward Belmont: come, Antonio. [*Exeunt.*

SCENE II.

The same. A street.

Enter PORTIA *and* NERISSA.

PORTIA.

INQUIRE the Jew's house out, give him this deed,
And let him sign it: we'll away to-night,
And be a day before our husbands home:
This deed will be well welcome to Lorenzo.

Enter GRATIANO.

GRATIANO.

Fair sir, you are well o'erta'en:
My Lord Bassanio, upon more advice,
Hath sent you here this ring; and doth entreat
Your company at dinner.

PORTIA.

That cannot be:
His ring I do accept most thankfully;

And so, I pray you, tell him: furthermore,
I pray you, show my youth old Shylock's house.

GRATIANO.

That will I do.

NERISSA.

Sir, I would speak with you.—
[*to* PORTIA] I'll see if I can get my husband's ring,
Which I did make him swear to keep for ever.

PORTIA [*to* NERISSA].

Thou mayst, I warrant. We shall have old swearing
That they did give the rings away to men;
But we'll outface them, and outswear them too.—
Away! make haste: thou know'st where I will tarry.

NERISSA.

Come, good sir, will you show me to this house?
[*Exeunt.*

ACT V. SCENE I.

Belmont. Avenue to PORTIA'S *house.*

Enter LORENZO *and* JESSICA.

LORENZO.

THE moon shines bright:—in such a night as this,
When the sweet wind did gently kiss the trees,
And they did make no noise,—in such a night
Troilus methinks mounted the Troyan walls,
And sigh'd his soul toward the Grecian tents,
Where Cressid lay that night.

JESSICA.

In such a night
Did Thisbe fearfully o'ertrip the dew,
And saw the lion's shadow ere himself,
And ran dismay'd away.

LORENZO.

In such a night
Stood Dido with a willow in her hand
Upon the wild sea-banks, and waft her love
To come again to Carthage.

JESSICA.

In such a night
Medea gather'd the enchanted herbs
That did renew old Aeson.

LORENZO.

In such a night
Did Jessica steal from the wealthy Jew,
And with an unthrift love did run from Venice
As far as Belmont.

JESSICA.

In such a night
Did young Lorenzo swear he loved her well,
Stealing her soul with many vows of faith,
And ne'er a true one.

LORENZO.

In such a night
Did pretty Jessica, like a little shrew,
Slander her love, and he forgave it her.

JESSICA.

I would out-night you, did no body come:
But, hark, I hear the footing of a man.

Enter STEPHANO.

LORENZO.

Who comes so fast in silence of the night?

STEPHANO.

A friend.

LORENZO.

A friend! what friend? your name, I pray you, friend?

STEPHANO.

Stephano is my name; and I bring word
My mistress will before the break of day
Be here at Belmont: she doth stray about
By holy crosses, where she kneels and prays
For happy wedlock hours.

LORENZO.

Who comes with her?

STEPHANO.

None but a holy hermit and her maid.
I pray you, is my master yet return'd?

LORENZO.

He is not, nor we have not heard from him.—
But go we in, I pray thee, Jessica,
And ceremoniously let us prepare
Some welcome for the mistress of the house.

Enter LAUNCELOT.

LAUNCELOT GOBBO.

Sola, sola! wo ha, ho! sola, sola!

LORENZO.

Who calls?

LAUNCELOT GOBBO.

Sola!—did you see Master Lorenzo? Master Lorenzo!—sola, sola!

LORENZO.

Leave hollaing, man:—here.

LAUNCELOT GOBBO.

Sola!—where? where?

LORENZO.

Here.

LAUNCELOT GOBBO.

Tell him there's a post come from my master, with his horn full of good news: my master will be here ere morning. [*Exit.*

LORENZO.

Sweet soul, let's in, and there expect their coming.
And yet no matter:—why should we go in ?—
My friend Stephano, signify, I pray you,
Within the house, your mistress is at hand;
And bring your music forth into the air.
[*Exit* STEPHANO.
How sweet the moonlight sleeps upon this bank!
Here will we sit, and let the sounds of music
Creep in our ears: soft stillness and the night
Become the touches of sweet harmony.
Sit, Jessica. Look, how the floor of heaven
Is thick inlaid with patines of bright gold:
There's not the smallest orb which thou behold'st
But in his motion like an angel sings,
Still quiring to the young-eyed cherubins,—
Such harmony is in immortal souls;
But whilst this muddy vesture of decay
Doth grossly close it in, we cannot hear it.

Enter MUSICIANS.

Come, ho, and wake Diana with a hymn!
With sweetest touches pierce your mistress' ear,
And draw her home with music. [*Music plays.*

JESSICA.

I am never merry when I hear sweet music.

LORENZO.

The reason is, your spirits are attentive:
For do but note a wild and wanton herd,
Or race of youthful and unhandled colts,
Fetching mad bounds, bellowing, and neighing loud,
Which is the hot condition of their blood;
If they but hear perchance a trumpet sound,
Or any air of music touch their ears,
You shall perceive them make a mutual stand,
Their savage eyes turn'd to a modest gaze,
By the sweet power of music: therefore the poet
Did feign that Orpheus drew trees, stones, and floods;
Since naught so stockish, hard, and full of rage,
But music for the time doth change his nature.
The man that hath no music in himself,
Nor is not moved with concord of sweet sounds,
Is fit for treasons, stratagems, and spoils;
The motions of his spirit are dull as night,
And his affections dark as Erebus:
Let no such man be trusted.—Mark the music.

Enter PORTIA *and* NERISSA.

PORTIA.

That light we see is burning in my hall.
How far that little candle throws his beams!
So shines a good deed in a naughty world.

NERISSA.

When the moon shone, we did not see the candle.

PORTIA.

So doth the greater glory dim the less:
A substitute shines brightly as a king,
Until a king be by; and then his state
Empties itself, as doth an inland brook
Into the main of waters.—Music! hark!

NERISSA.

It is your music, madam, of the house.

PORTIA.

Nothing is good, I see, without respect:
Methinks it sounds much sweeter than by day.

NERISSA.

Silence bestows that virtue on it, madam.

PORTIA.

The crow doth sing as sweetly as the lark,
When neither is attended; and I think
The nightingale, if she should sing by day,
When every goose is cackling, would be thought
No better a musician than the wren.
How many things by season season'd are
To their right praise and true perfection!—
Peace, ho! the moon sleeps with Endymion,
And would not be awaked. [*Music ceases.*

LORENZO.

That is the voice,
Or I am much deceived, of Portia.

PORTIA.

He knows me, as the blind man knows the cuckoo,
By the bad voice.

LORENZO.

Dear lady, welcome home.

PORTIA.

We have been praying for our husbands' health,
Which speed, we hope, the better for our words.
Are they return'd?

LORENZO.

Madam, they are not yet;
But there is come a messenger before,
To signify their coming.

PORTIA.

Go in, Nerissa;
Give orders to my servants that they take
No note at all of our being absent hence;—
Nor you, Lorenzo;—Jessica, nor you
[*A tucket sounds.*

LORENZO.

Your husband is at hand; I hear his trumpet:
We are no tell-tales, madam; fear you not.

PORTIA.

This night methinks is but the daylight sick;
It looks a little paler: 'tis a day,
Such as the day is when the sun is hid.

Enter BASSANIO, ANTONIO, GRATIANO, *and their* FOLLOWERS.

BASSANIO.

We should hold day with the Antipodes,
If you would walk in absence of the sun.

PORTIA.

Let me give light, but let me not be light;
For a light wife doth make a heavy husband,
And never be Bassanio so for me:
But God sort all!—You're welcome home, my lord.

BASSANIO.

I thank you, madam. Give welcome to my friend:
This is the man, this is Antonio,
To whom I am so infinitely bound.

PORTIA.

You should in all sense be much bound to him,
For, as I hear, he was much bound for you.

ANTONIO.

No more than I am well acquitted of.

PORTIA.

Sir, you are very welcome to our house:
It must appear in other ways than words,
Therefore I scant this breathing courtesy.

GRATIANO [*to* NERISSA].

By yonder moon I swear you do me wrong;
In faith, I gave it to the judge's clerk:
Would he were gelt that had it, for my part,
Since you do take it, love, so much at heart.

PORTIA.

A quarrel, ho, already! what's the matter?

GRATIANO.

About a hoop of gold, a paltry ring
That she did give to me; whose posy was
For all the world like cutler's poetry
Upon a knife, 'Love me, and leave me not.'

NERISSA.

What talk you of the posy or the value?
You swore to me, when I did give it you,
That you would wear it till your hour of death;
And that it should lie with you in your grave:
Though not for me, yet for your vehement oaths,
You should have been respective, and have kept it.
Gave it a judge's clerk! no, God's my judge,
The clerk will ne'er wear hair on's face that had it.

GRATIANO.

He will, an if he live to be a man.

NERISSA.

Ay, if a woman live to be a man.

GRATIANO.

Now, by this hand, I gave it to a youth,—
A kind of boy; a little scrubbed boy,

No higher than thyself, the judge's clerk;
A prating boy, that begg'd it as a fee:
I could not for my heart deny it him.

PORTIA.

You were to blame,—I must be plain with you,—
To part so slightly with your wife's first gift;
A thing stuck on with oaths upon your finger,
And so riveted with faith unto your flesh.
I gave my love a ring, and made him swear
Never to part with it; and here he stands,—
I dare be sworn for him, he would not leave it,
Nor pluck it from his finger, for the wealth
That the world masters. Now, in faith, Gratiano,
You give your wife too unkind a cause of grief:
An 'twere to me, I should be mad at it.

BASSANIO [*aside*].

Why, I were best to cut my left hand off,
And swear I lost the ring defending it.

GRATIANO.

My Lord Bassanio gave his ring away
Unto the judge that begg'd it, and indeed
Deserved it too; and then the boy, his clerk,
That took some pains in writing, he begg'd mine:
And neither man nor master would take aught
But the two rings.

PORTIA.

What ring gave you, my lord?
Not that, I hope, which you received of me.

BASSANIO.

If I could add a lie unto a fault,
I would deny it; but you see my finger
Hath not the ring upon it,—it is gone.

PORTIA.

Even so void is your false heart of truth.
By heaven, I will ne'er come in your bed
Until I see the ring.

NERISSA.

Nor I in yours
Till I again see mine.

BASSANIO.

Sweet Portia,
If you did know to whom I gave the ring,
If you did know for whom I gave the ring,
And would conceive for what I gave the ring,
And how unwillingly I left the ring,
When naught would be accepted but the ring,
You would abate the strength of your displeasure.

PORTIA.

If you had known the virtue of the ring,
Or half her worthiness that gave the ring,
Or your own honour to contain the ring,
You would not then have parted with the ring.
What man is there so much unreasonable,
If you had pleased to have defended it
With any terms of zeal, wanted the modesty
To urge the thing held as a ceremony?
Nerissa teaches me what to believe:
I'll die for't but some woman had the ring.

BASSANIO.

No, by my honour, madam, by my soul,
No woman had it, but a civil doctor,
Which did refuse three thousand ducats of me,
And begg'd the ring; the which I did deny him,
And suffer'd him to go displeased away;
Even he that did uphold the very life
Of my dear friend. What should I say, sweet lady?
I was enforced to send it after him:
I was beset with shame and courtesy;
My honour would not let ingratitude
So much besmear it. Pardon me, good lady;
For, by these blessed candles of the night,
Had you been there, I think, you would have begg'd
The ring of me to give the worthy doctor.

PORTIA.

Let not that doctor e'er come near my house:
Since he hath got the jewel that I loved,
And that which you did swear to keep for me,
I will become as liberal as you;
I'll not deny him any thing I have,
No, not my body nor my husband's bed:
Know him I shall, I am well sure of it:
Lie not a night from home; watch me like Argus:
If you do not, if I be left alone,
Now, by mine honour, which is yet mine own,
I'll have that doctor for my bedfellow.

NERISSA.

And I his clerk; therefore be well advised
How you do leave me to mine own protection.

GRATIANO.

Well, do you so: let not me take him, then;
For if I do, I'll mar the young clerk's pen.

ANTONIO.

I am the unhappy subject of these quarrels.

PORTIA.

Sir, grieve not you; you are welcome notwithstanding.

BASSANIO.

Portia, forgive me this enforced wrong;
And, in the hearing of these many friends,
I swear to thee, even by thine own fair eyes,
Wherein I see myself,—

PORTIA.

Mark you but that!
In both my eyes he doubly sees himself;
In each eye, one:—swear by your double self,
And there's an oath of credit.

BASSANIO.

Nay, but hear me:
Pardon this fault, and by my soul I swear
I never more will break an oath with thee.

ANTONIO.

I once did lend my body for his wealth;
Which, but for him that had your husband's ring,
Had quite miscarried: I dare be bound again,
My soul upon the forfeit, that your lord
Will never more break faith advisedly.

PORTIA.

Then you shall be his surety. Give him this;
And bid him keep it better than the other.

ANTONIO.

Here, Lord Bassanio; swear to keep this ring.

BASSANIO.

By heaven, it is the same I gave the doctor!

PORTIA.

I had it of him: pardon me, Bassanio;
For, by this ring, the doctor lay with me.

NERISSA.

And pardon me, my gentle Gratiano;
For that same scrubbed boy, the doctor's clerk,
In lieu of this, last night did lie with me.

GRATIANO.
Why, this is like the mending of highways
In summer, where the ways are fair enough:
What, are we cuckolds ere we have deserved it?

PORTIA.
Speak not so grossly.—You are all amazed:
Here is a letter, read it at your leisure;
It comes from Padua, from Bellario:
There you shall find that Portia was the doctor;
Nerissa there her clerk: Lorenzo here
Shall witness I set forth as soon as you,
And even but now return'd; I have not yet
Enter'd my house.—Antonio, you are welcome;
And I have better news in store for you
Than you expect: unseal this letter soon;
There you shall find three of your argosies
Are richly come to harbour suddenly:
You shall not know by what strange accident
I chanced on this letter.

ANTONIO.
I am dumb.

BASSANIO.
Were you the doctor, and I knew you not?

GRATIANO.
Were you the clerk that is to make me cuckold?

NERISSA.
Ay, but the clerk that never means to do it,
Unless he live until he be a man.

BASSANIO.
Sweet doctor, you shall be my bedfellow:
When I am absent, then lie with my wife.

ANTONIO.
Sweet lady, you have given me life and living;
For here I read for certain that my ships
Are safely come to road.

PORTIA.
How now, Lorenzo!
My clerk hath some good comforts too for you.

NERISSA.
Ay, and I'll give them him without a fee.—
There do I give to you and Jessica,
From the rich Jew, a special deed of gift,
After his death, of all he dies possest of.

LORENZO.
Fair ladies, you drop manna in the way
Of starved people.

PORTIA.
It is almost morning,
And yet I am sure you are not satisfied
Of these events at full. Let us go in;
And charge us there upon inter'gatories,
And we will answer all things faithfully.

GRATIANO.
Let it be so: the first inter'gatory
That my Nerissa shall be sworn on is,
Whether till the next night she had rather
stay,
Or go to bed now, being two hours to day:
But were the day come, I should wish it dark,
That I were couching with the doctor's clerk.
Well, while I live I'll fear no other thing
So sore as keeping safe Nerissa's ring. [*Exeunt.*

THE MERRY WIVES OF WINDSOR

DRAMATIS PERSONAE

SIR JOHN FALSTAFF.
FENTON, *a gentleman.*
SHALLOW, *a country justice.*
SLENDER, *cousin to Shallow.*
FORD, } *two gentlemen dwelling at Windsor.*
PAGE, }
WILLIAM PAGE, *a boy, son to Page.*
SIR HUGH EVANS, *a Welsh parson.*
DOCTOR CAIUS, *a French physician.*
HOST OF THE GARTER INN.
BARDOLPH, }
PISTOL, } *followers of Falstaff.*
NYM, }
ROBIN, *page to Falstaff.*
SIMPLE, *servant to Slender.*
RUGBY, *servant to Doctor Caius.*

MISTRESS FORD.
MISTRESS PAGE.
ANNE PAGE, *her daughter.*
MISTRESS QUICKLY, *servant to Doctor Caius.*

SERVANTS *to Page, Ford, &c.*

SCENE—*Windsor, and the neighbourhood.*

ACT I. SCENE I.

Windsor. Before PAGE'S *house.*

Enter JUSTICE SHALLOW, SLENDER, *and* SIR HUGH EVANS.

SHALLOW.

SIR HUGH, persuade me not; I will make a Star-Chamber matter of it: if he were twenty Sir John Falstaffs, he shall not abuse Robert Shallow, esquire.

SLENDER.

In the county of Gloster, justice of peace and *coram.*

SHALLOW.

Ay, cousin Slender, and *cust-alorum.*

SLENDER.

Ay, and *rato-lorum* too; and a gentleman born, master parson; who writes himself *armigero,*—in any bill, warrant, quittance, or obligation, *armigero.*

SHALLOW.

Ay, that I do; and have done any time these three hundred years.

SLENDER.

All his successors gone before him hath done't; and all his ancestors that come after him may: they may give the dozen white luces in their coat.

SHALLOW.

It is an old coat.

SIR HUGH EVANS.

The dozen white louses do become an old coat well; it agrees well, passant; it is a familiar beast to man, and signifies—love.

SHALLOW.

The luce is the fresh fish; the salt fish is an old coat.

SLENDER.

I may quarter, coz?

SHALLOW.

You may, by marrying.

SIR HUGH EVANS.

It is marring indeed, if he quarter it.

SHALLOW.

Not a whit.

SIR HUGH EVANS.

Yes, py'r lady; if he has a quarter of your coat, there is but three skirts for yourself, in my simple conjectures: but that is all one. If Sir John Falstaff have committed disparagements unto you, I am of the church, and will be glad to do my benevolence to make atonements and compremises between you.

SHALLOW.

The Council shall hear it; it is a riot.

SIR HUGH EVANS.

It is not meet the Council hear a riot; there is no fear of Got in a riot: the Council, look you, shall desire to hear the fear of Got, and not to hear a riot; take your vizaments in that.

SHALLOW.

Ha! o' my life, if I were young again, the sword should end it.

SIR HUGH EVANS.

It is petter that friends is the sword, and end it: and there is also another device in my prain, which peradventure prings goot discretions with it:—there is Anne Page, which is daughter to Master George Page, which is pretty virginity.

SLENDER.

Mistress Anne Page! She has brown hair, and speaks small like a woman.

SIR HUGH EVANS.

It is that fery person for all the orld, as just as you will desire; and seven hundred pounds of moneys, and gold, and silver, is her grandsire upon his death's-bed (Got deliver to a joyful resurrections!) give, when she is able to overtake seventeen years old. It were a goot motion if we leave our pribbles and prabbles, and desire a marriage between Master Abraham and Mistress Anne Page.

SHALLOW.

Did her grandsire leave her seven hundred pound?

SIR HUGH EVANS.

Ay, and her father is make her a petter penny.

SHALLOW.

I know the young gentlewoman; she has good gifts.

SIR HUGH EVANS.
Seven hundred pounds and possibilities is goot gifts.

SHALLOW.
Well, let us see honest Master Page. Is Falstaff there?

SIR HUGH EVANS.
Shall I tell you a lie? I do despise a liar as I do despise one that is false, or as I despise one that is not true. The knight, Sir John, is there; and, I beseech you, be ruled by your well-willers. I will peat the door for Master Page. [*Knocks.*] What, ho! Got pless your house here!

PAGE [*within*].
Who's there?

SIR HUGH EVANS.
Here is Got's plessing, and your friend, and Justice Shallow; and here young Master Slender, that peradventures shall tell you another tale, if matters grow to your likings.

Enter PAGE.

PAGE.
I am glad to see your worships well. I thank you for my venison, Master Shallow.

SHALLOW.
Master Page, I am glad to see you: much good do it your good heart! I wish'd your venison better; it was ill kill'd.—How doth good Mistress Page?—and I thank you always with my heart, la; with my heart.

PAGE.
Sir, I thank you.

SHALLOW.
Sir, I thank you; by yea and no, I do.

PAGE.
I am glad to see you, good Master Slender.

SLENDER.
How does your fallow greyhound, sir? I heard say he was outrun on Cotsall.

PAGE.
It could not be judged, sir.

SLENDER.
You'll not confess, you'll not confess.

SHALLOW.
That he will not.—'Tis your fault, 'tis your fault:—'tis a good dog.

PAGE.
A cur, sir.

SHALLOW.
Sir, he's a good dog, and a fair dog: can there be more said? he is good and fair.—Is Sir John Falstaff here?

PAGE.
Sir, he is within; and I would I could do a good office between you.

SIR HUGH EVANS.
It is spoke as a Christians ought to speak.

SHALLOW.
He hath wrong'd me, Master Page.

PAGE.
Sir, he doth in some sort confess it.

SHALLOW.
If it be confess'd, it is not redress'd: is not that so, Master Page? He hath wrong'd me; indeed he hath;—at a word, he hath;—believe me; Robert Shallow, esquire, saith he is wrong'd.

PAGE.
Here comes Sir John.

Enter SIR JOHN FALSTAFF, BARDOLPH, NYM, *and* PISTOL.

SIR JOHN FALSTAFF.
Now, Master Shallow,—you'll complain of me to the king?

SHALLOW.
Knight, you have beaten my men, killed my deer, and broke open my lodge.

SIR JOHN FALSTAFF.
But not kiss'd your keeper's daughter?

SHALLOW.
Tut, a pin! this shall be answer'd.

SIR JOHN FALSTAFF.
I will answer it straight; I have done all this:—that is now answer'd.

SHALLOW.
The Council shall know this.

SIR JOHN FALSTAFF.
'Twere better for you if it were known in counsel: you'll be laugh'd at.

SIR HUGH EVANS.
Pauca verba, Sir John, goot worts.

SIR JOHN FALSTAFF.
Good worts! good cabbage.—Slender, I broke your head: what matter have you against me?

SLENDER.
Marry, sir, I have matter in my head against you: and against your cony-catching rascals, Bardolph, Nym, and Pistol; they carried me to the tavern and made me drunk, and afterward picked my pocket.

BARDOLPH.
You Banbury cheese!

SLENDER.
Ay, it is no matter.

PISTOL.
How now, Mephostophilus!

SLENDER.
Ay, it is no matter.

NYM.
Slice, I say! *pauca, pauca;* slice! that's my humour.

SLENDER.
Where's Simple, my man?—can you tell, cousin?

SIR HUGH EVANS.
Peace, I pray you.—Now let us understand. There is three umpires in this matter, as I understand; that is, Master Page, *fidelicet* Master Page; and there is myself, *fidelicet* myself; and the three party is, lastly and finally, mine host of the Garter.

PAGE.
We three, to hear it and end it between them.

SIR HUGH EVANS.
Fery goot: I will make a prief of it in my note-book; and we will afterwards ork upon the cause with as great discreetly as we can.

SIR JOHN FALSTAFF.
Pistol,—

PISTOL.
He hears with ears.

SIR HUGH EVANS.
The tevil and his tam! what phrase is this, 'He hears with ear'? why, it is affectations.

SIR JOHN FALSTAFF.
Pistol, did you pick Master Slender's purse?

SLENDER.

Ay, by these gloves, did he—or I would I might never come in mine own great chamber again else—of seven groats in mill-sixpences, and two Edward shovel-boards, that cost me two shilling and two pence a-piece of Yead Miller, by these gloves.

SIR JOHN FALSTAFF.

Is this true, Pistol?

SIR HUGH EVANS.

No; it is false, if it is a pick-purse.

PISTOL.

Ha, thou mountain-foreigner!—Sir John and master mine,
I combat challenge of this latten bilbo.—
Word of denial in thy labras here;
Word of denial:—froth and scum, thou liest!

SLENDER.

By these gloves, then, 'twas he.

NYM.

Be avised, sir, and pass good humours: I will say 'marry trap' with you, if you run the nuthook's humour on me; that is the very note of it.

SLENDER.

By this hat, then, he in the red face had it; for though I cannot remember what I did when you made me drunk, yet I am not altogether an ass.

SIR JOHN FALSTAFF.

What say you, Scarlet and John?

BARDOLPH.

Why, sir, for my part, I say the gentleman had drunk himself out of his five sentences,—

SIR HUGH EVANS.

It is his five senses: fie, what the ignorance is!

BARDOLPH.

And being fap, sir, was, as they say, cashiered; and so conclusions passed the careires.

SLENDER.

Ay, you spake in Latin then too; but 'tis no matter: I'll ne'er be drunk whilst I live again, but in honest, civil, godly company, for this trick: if I be drunk, I'll be drunk with those that have the fear of God, and not with drunken knaves.

SIR HUGH EVANS.

So Got udge me, that is a virtuous mind.

SIR JOHN FALSTAFF.

You hear all these matters denied, gentlemen; you hear it.

Enter ANNE PAGE, *with wine;* MISTRESS FORD *and* MISTRESS PAGE.

PAGE.

Nay, daughter, carry the wine in; we'll drink within. [*Exit* ANNE PAGE.

SLENDER.

O heaven! this is Mistress Anne Page.

PAGE.

How now, Mistress Ford!

SIR JOHN FALSTAFF.

Mistress Ford, by my troth, you are very well met: by your leave, good mistress. [*Kisses her.*

PAGE.

Wife, bid these gentlemen welcome,—Come, we have a hot venison-pasty to dinner: come, gentlemen, I hope we shall drink down all unkindness.

[*Exeunt all except* SHALLOW, SLENDER, *and* EVANS.

SLENDER.

I had rather than forty shillings I had my Book of Songs and Sonnets here.

Enter SIMPLE.

How now, Simple! where have you been? I must wait on myself, must I? You have not the Book of Riddles about you, have you?

SIMPLE.

Book of Riddles! why, did you not lend it to Alice Shortcake upon All-hallowmas last, a fortnight afore Michaelmas?

SHALLOW.

Come, coz; come, coz; we stay for you. A word with you, coz; marry, this, coz;—there is, as 'twere, a tender, a kind of tender, made afar off by Sir Hugh here. Do you understand me?

SLENDER.

Ay, sir, you shall find me reasonable; if it be so, I shall do that that is reason.

SHALLOW.

Nay, but understand me.

SLENDER.

So I do, sir.

SIR HUGH EVANS.

Give ear to his motions, Master Slender: I will description the matter to you, if you be capacity of it.

SLENDER.

Nay, I will do as my cousin Shallow says: I pray you, pardon me; he's a justice of peace in his country, simple though I stand here.

SIR HUGH EVANS.

But that is not the question: the question is concerning your marriage.

SHALLOW.

Ay, there's the point, sir.

SIR HUGH EVANS.

Marry, is it; the very point of it; to Mistress Anne Page.

SLENDER.

Why, if it be so, I will marry her upon any reasonable demands.

SIR HUGH EVANS.

But can you affection the oman? Let us command to know that of your mouth or of your lips; for divers philosophers hold that the lips is parcel of the mouth. Therefore, precisely, can you carry your good will to the maid?

SHALLOW.

Cousin Abraham Slender, can you love her?

SLENDER.

I hope, sir, I will do as it shall become one that would do reason.

SIR HUGH EVANS.

Nay, Got's lords and his ladies, you must speak positable, if you can carry her your desires towards her.

SHALLOW.

That you must. Will you, upon good dowry, marry her?

SLENDER.

I will do a greater thing than that, upon your request, cousin, in any reason.

SHALLOW.

Nay. conceive me, conceive me, sweet coz: what I do is to pleasure you, coz. Can you love the maid?

SLENDER.
I will marry her, sir, at your request: but if there be no great love in the beginning, yet heaven may decrease it upon better acquaintance, when we are married and have more occasion to know one another; I hope, upon familiarity will grow more contempt: but if you say, 'marry her,' I will marry her; that I am freely dissolved, and dissolutely.

SIR HUGH EVANS.
It is a fery discretion answer; save the faul is in the ort 'dissolutely:' the ort is, according to our meaning, 'resolutely:'—his meaning is goot.

SHALLOW.
Ay, I think my cousin meant well.

SLENDER.
Ay, or else I would I might be hang'd, la.

SHALLOW.
Here comes fair Mistress Anne.

Enter ANNE PAGE.

Would I were young for your sake, Mistress Anne!

ANNE PAGE.
The dinner is on the table; my father desires your worships' company.

SHALLOW.
I will wait on him, fair Mistress Anne.

SIR HUGH EVANS.
Od's plessed will! I will not be absence at the grace. [*Exeunt* SHALLOW *and* EVANS.

ANNE PAGE.
Will't please your worship to come in, sir?

SLENDER.
No, I thank you, forsooth, heartily; I am very well.

ANNE PAGE.
The dinner attends you, sir.

SLENDER.
I am not a-hungry, I thank you, forsooth.—Go, sirrah, for all you are my man, go wait upon my cousin Shallow. [*Exit* SIMPLE.] A justice of peace sometime may be beholding to his friend for a man.—I keep but three men and a boy yet, till my mother be dead: but what though? yet I live like a poor gentleman born.

ANNE PAGE.
I may not go in without your worship: they will not sit till you come.

SLENDER.
I'faith, I'll eat nothing; I thank you as much as though I did.

ANNE PAGE.
I pray you, sir, walk in.

SLENDER.
I had rather walk here, I thank you. I bruised my shin th'other day with playing at sword and dagger with a master of fence,—three veneys for a dish of stew'd prunes; and, by my troth, I cannot abide the smell of hot meat since.—Why do your dogs bark so? be there bears i'th'town?

ANNE PAGE.
I think there are, sir; I heard them talk'd of.

SLENDER.
I love the sport well; but I shall as soon quarrel at it as any man in England. You are afraid, if you see the bear loose, are you not?

ANNE PAGE.
Ay, indeed, sir.

SLENDER.
That's meat and drink to me, now. I have seen Sackerson loose twenty times, and have taken him by the chain; but, I warrant you, the women have so cried and shriek'd at it, that it pass'd:—but women, indeed, cannot abide 'em; they are very ill-favour'd rough things.

Enter PAGE.

PAGE.
Come, gentle Master Slender, come; we stay for you.

SLENDER.
I'll eat nothing, I thank you, sir.

PAGE.
By cock and pie, you shall not choose, sir: come, come.

SLENDER.
Nay, pray you, lead the way.

PAGE.
Come on, sir.

SLENDER.
Mistress Anne, yourself shall go first.

ANNE PAGE.
Not I, sir; pray you, keep on.

SLENDER.
Truly, I will not go first; truly, la; I will not do you that wrong.

ANNE PAGE.
I pray you, sir.

SLENDER.
I'll rather be unmannerly than troublesome. You do yourself wrong, indeed, la. [*Exeunt.*

SCENE II.

The same.

Enter SIR HUGH EVANS *and* SIMPLE.

SIR HUGH EVANS.
GO your ways, and ask of Doctor Caius' house which is the way: and there dwells one Mistress Quickly, which is in the manner of his nurse, or his try nurse, or his cook, or his laundry, his washer, and his wringer.

SIMPLE.
Well, sir.

SIR HUGH EVANS.
Nay, it is petter yet.—Give her this letter; for it is a oman that altogether's acquaintance with Mistress Anne Page: and the letter is, to desire and require her to solicit your master's desires to Mistress Anne Page. I pray you, be gone: I will make an end of my dinner; there's pippins and seese to come. [*Exeunt.*

SCENE III.

A room in the Garter Inn.

Enter FALSTAFF, HOST, BARDOLPH, NYM, PISTOL, *and* ROBIN.

SIR JOHN FALSTAFF.
MINE host of the Garter,—

HOST.
What says my bully-rook? speak scholarly and wisely.

SIR JOHN FALSTAFF.

Truly, mine host, I must turn away some of my followers.

HOST.

Discard, bully Hercules; cashier: let them wag; trot, trot.

SIR JOHN FALSTAFF.

I sit at ten pounds a-week.

HOST.

Thou'rt an emperor, Cæsar, Keisar, and Pheezar. I will entertain Bardolph; he shall draw, he shall tap: said I well, bully Hector?

SIR JOHN FALSTAFF.

Do so, good mine host.

HOST.

I have spoke; let him follow.—Let me see thee froth and lime: I am at a word; follow. [*Exit.*

SIR JOHN FALSTAFF.

Bardolph, follow him. A tapster is a good trade: an old cloak makes a new jerkin; a wither'd serving-man a fresh tapster. Go; adieu.

BARDOLPH.

It is a life that I have desired: I will thrive.

PISTOL.

O base Hungarian wight! wilt thou the spigot
wield? [*Exit* BARDOLPH.

NYM.

He was gotten in drink: is not the humour conceited? His mind is not heroic, and there's the humour of it.

SIR JOHN FALSTAFF.

I am glad I am so acquit of this tinder-box: his thefts were too open; his filching was like an unskilful singer,—he kept not time.

NYM.

The good humour is to steal at a minim's rest.

PISTOL.

'Convey' the wise it call. 'Steal'! foh! a fico for the phrase!

SIR JOHN FALSTAFF.

Well, sirs, I am almost out at heels.

PISTOL.

Why, then, let kibes ensue.

SIR JOHN FALSTAFF.

There is no remedy; I must cony-catch; I must shift.

PISTOL.

Young ravens must have food.

SIR JOHN FALSTAFF.

Which of you know Ford of this town?

PISTOL.

I ken the wight: he is of substance good.

SIR JOHN FALSTAFF.

My honest lads, I will tell you what I am about.

PISTOL.

Two yards, and more.

SIR JOHN FALSTAFF.

No quips now, Pistol:—indeed, I am in the waist two yards about; but I am now about no waste; I am about thrift. Briefly, I do mean to make love to Ford's wife: I spy entertainment in her; she discourses, she carves, she gives the leer of invitation: I can construe the action of her familiar style; and the hardest voice of her behaviour, to be English'd rightly, is, 'I am Sir John Falstaff's.'

PISTOL.

He hath studied her well, and translated her well,—out of honesty into English.

NYM.

The anchor is deep: will that humour pass?

SIR JOHN FALSTAFF.

Now, the report goes she has all the rule of her husband's purse:—he hath a legion of angels.

PISTOL.

As many devils entertain; and, 'To her, boy,' say I.

NYM.

The humour rises; it is good: humour me the angels.

SIR JOHN FALSTAFF.

I have writ me here a letter to her: and here another to Page's wife, who even now gave me good eyes too, examined my parts with most judicious œilliades; sometimes the beam of her view gilded my foot, sometimes my portly belly.

PISTOL.

Then did the sun on dunghill shine.

NYM.

I thank thee for that humour.

SIR JOHN FALSTAFF.

O, she did so course o'er my exteriors with such a greedy intention, that the appetite of her eye did seem to scorch me up like a burning-glass! Here's another letter to her: she bears the purse too; she is a region in Guiana, all gold and bounty. I will be cheaters to them both, and they shall be exchequers to me; they shall be my East and West Indies, and I will trade to them both. Go bear thou this letter to Mistress Page; and thou this to Mistress Ford: we will thrive, lads, we will thrive.

PISTOL.

Shall I Sir Pandarus of Troy become,
And by my side wear steel? then, Lucifer take all!

NYM.

I will run no base humour: here, take the humour-letter: I will keep the haviour of reputation.

SIR JOHN FALSTAFF [*to* ROBIN].

Hold, sirrah, bear you these letters tightly;
Sail like my pinnace to these golden shores.—
Rogues, hence, avaunt! vanish like hailstones, go;
Trudge, plod away o'th'hoof; seek shelter, pack!
Falstaff will learn the humour of the age,
French thrift, you rogues; myself and skirted page.
[*Exeunt* FALSTAFF *and* ROBIN.

PISTOL.

Let vultures gripe thy guts! for gourd and fullam
holds,
And high and low beguiles the rich and poor:
Tester I'll have in pouch when thou shalt lack,
Base Phrygian Turk!

NYM.

I have operations in my head, which be humours of revenge.

PISTOL.

Wilt thou revenge?

NYM.

By welkin and her star!

PISTOL.

With wit or steel?

NYM.

With both the humours, I:
I will discuss the humour of this love to Page.

PISTOL.

And I to Ford shall eke unfold
How Falstaff, varlet vile,
His dove will prove, his gold will hold,
And his soft couch defile.

NYM.

My humour shall not cool: I will incense Page to deal with poison; I will possess him with yellowness, for the revolt of mien is dangerous: that is my true humour.

PISTOL.

Thou art the Mars of malecontents: I second thee; troop on. [*Exeunt.*

SCENE IV.

A room in DOCTOR CAIUS'S *house.*

Enter MISTRESS QUICKLY *and* SIMPLE.

MISTRESS QUICKLY.

WHAT, John Rugby!

Enter RUGBY.

I pray thee, go to the casement, and see if you can see my master, Master Doctor Caius, coming. If he do, i'faith, and find any body in the house, here will be an old abusing of God's patience and the king's English.

RUGBY.

I'll go watch.

MISTRESS QUICKLY.

Go; and we'll have a posset for't soon at night, in faith, at the latter end of a sea-coal fire. [*Exit* RUGBY.] An honest, willing, kind fellow, as ever servant shall come in house withal; and, I warrant you, no tell-tale nor no breed-bate: his worst fault is, that he is given to prayer; he is something peevish that way: but nobody but has his fault;—but let that pass.—Peter Simple you say your name is?

SIMPLE.

Ay, for fault of a better.

MISTRESS QUICKLY.

And Master Slender's your master?

SIMPLE.

Ay, forsooth.

MISTRESS QUICKLY.

Does he not wear a great round beard, like a glover's paring-knife?

SIMPLE.

No, forsooth: he hath but a little wee face, with a little yellow beard,—a Cain-colour'd beard.

MISTRESS QUICKLY.

A softly-sprighted man, is he not?

SIMPLE.

Ay, forsooth: but he is as tall a man of his hands as any is between this and his head; he hath fought with a warrener.

MISTRESS QUICKLY.

How say you?—O, I should remember him: does he not hold up his head, as it were, and strut in his gait?

SIMPLE.

Yes, indeed, does he.

MISTRESS QUICKLY.

Well, heaven send Anne Page no worse fortune! Tell Master Parson Evans I will do what I can for your master: Anne is a good girl, and I wish—

Enter RUGBY.

RUGBY.

Out, alas! here comes my master.

MISTRESS QUICKLY.

We shall all be shent. [*Exit* RUGBY.]—Run in here, good young man; go into this closet:—he will not stay long. [*Shuts* SIMPLE *in the closet.*]—What, John Rugby! John! what, John, I say! Go, John, go inquire for my master; I doubt he be not well, that he comes not home. [*Sings.*

And down, down, adown-a, &c.

Enter DOCTOR CAIUS.

DOCTOR CAIUS.

Vat is you sing? I do not like dese toys. Pray you, go and vetch me in my closet *un boitier vert,*—a box, a green-a box: do intend vat I speak? a green-a box.

MISTRESS QUICKLY.

Ay, forsooth; I'll fetch it you.—[*aside*] I am glad he went not in himself: if he had found the young man, he would have been horn-mad.

DOCTOR CAIUS.

Fe, fe, fe, fe! ma foi, il fait fort chaud. Je m'en vais à la cour,—la grande affaire.

MISTRESS QUICKLY.

Is it this, sir?

DOCTOR CAIUS.

Oui; mette le au mon pocket: *dépêche,* quickly.—Vere is dat knave Rugby?

MISTRESS QUICKLY.

What, John Rugby! John!

Enter RUGBY.

RUGBY.

Here, sir.

DOCTOR CAIUS.

You are John Rugby, and you are Jack Rugby. Come, take-a your rapier, and come after my heel to de court.

RUGBY.

'Tis ready, sir, here in the porch.

DOCTOR CAIUS.

By my trot, I tarry too long.—Od's me! *Qu'ai-j'oublié!* dere is some simples in my closet, dat I vill not for de varld I shall leave behind.

MISTRESS QUICKLY.

Ay me, he'll find the young man there, and be mad!

DOCTOR CAIUS.

O diable, diable! vat is in my closet? Villain! *larron!* [*Pulling* SIMPLE *out.*]—Rugby, my rapier!

MISTRESS QUICKLY.

Good master, be content.

DOCTOR CAIUS.

Verefore shall I be content-a?

MISTRESS QUICKLY.

The young man is an honest man.

DOCTOR CAIUS.

Vat shall de honest man do in my closet? dere is no honest man dat shall come in my closet.

MISTRESS QUICKLY.

I beseech you, be not so phlegmatic. Hear the truth of it: he came of an errand to me from Parson Hugh.

DOCTOR CAIUS.

Vell.

SIMPLE.

Ay, forsooth; to desire her to—

MISTRESS QUICKLY.

Peace, I pray you.

DOCTOR CAIUS.

Peace-a your tongue.—Speak-a your tale.

SIMPLE.

To desire this honest gentlewoman, your maid, to speak a good word to Mistress Anne Page for my master in the way of marriage.

MISTRESS QUICKLY.

This is all, indeed, la; but I'll ne'er put my finger in the fire, and need not.

DOCTOR CAIUS.

Sir Hugh send-a you?—Rugby, *baille* me some paper.—Tarry you a little-a while. [*Writes.*

MISTRESS QUICKLY.

I am glad he is so quiet: if he had been throughly moved, you should have heard him so loud and so melancholy.—But notwithstanding, man, I'll do you your master what good I can: and the very yea and the no is, the French doctor, my master, —I may call him my master, look you, for I keep his house; and I wash, wring, brew, bake, scour, dress meat and drink, make the beds, and do all myself,—

SIMPLE.

'Tis a great charge to come under one body's hand.

MISTRESS QUICKLY.

Are you avised o' that? you shall find it a great charge: and to be up early and down late;—but notwithstanding, to tell you in your ear,—I would have no words of it,—my master himself is in love with Mistress Anne Page: but notwithstanding that, I know Anne's mind,—that's neither here nor there.

DOCTOR CAIUS.

You jack'nape,—give-a dis letter to Sir Hugh; by gar, it is a shallenge: I vill cut his troat in de park; and I vill teach a scurvy jack-a-nape priest to meddle or make:—you may be gone; it is not good you tarry here:—by gar, I vill cut all his two stones; by gar, he shall not have a stone to trow at his dog. [*Exit* SIMPLE.

MISTRESS QUICKLY.

Alas, he speaks but for his friend.

DOCTOR CAIUS.

It is no matter-a ver dat:—do not you tell-a me dat I shall have Anne Page for myself?—by gar, I vill kill de Jack priest; and I have appointed mine host of de Jarteer to measure our weapon:—by gar, I vill myself have Anne Page.

MISTRESS QUICKLY.

Sir, the maid loves you, and all shall be well. We must give folks leave to prate: what, the good-jer!

DOCTOR CAIUS.

Rugby, come to de court vit me.—By gar, if I have not Anne Page, I shall turn your head out of my door.—Follow my heels, Rugby.

[*Exeunt* CAIUS *and* RUGBY.

MISTRESS QUICKLY.

You shall have An fool's-head of your own. No, I know Anne's mind for that: never a woman in Windsor knows more of Anne's mind than I do; nor can do more than I do with her, I thank heaven.

FENTON [*within*].

Who's within there? ho!

MISTRESS QUICKLY.

Who's there, I trow? Come near the house, I pray you.

Enter FENTON.

FENTON.

How now, good woman! how dost thou?

MISTRESS QUICKLY.

The better that it pleases your good worship to ask.

FENTON.

What news? how does pretty Mistress Anne?

MISTRESS QUICKLY.

In truth, sir, and she is pretty, and honest, and gentle; and one that is your friend, I can tell you that by the way; I praise heaven for it.

FENTON.

Shall I do any good, think'st thou? shall I not lose my suit?

MISTRESS QUICKLY.

Troth, sir, all is in his hands above: but notwithstanding, Master Fenton, I'll be sworn on a book, she loves you.—Have not your worship a wart above your eye?

FENTON.

Yes, marry, have I; what of that?

MISTRESS QUICKLY.

Well, thereby hangs a tale:—good faith, it is such another Nan;—but, I detest, an honest maid as ever broke bread:—we had an hour's talk of that wart:—I shall never laugh but in that maid's company!—But, indeed, she is given too much to allicholy and musing: but for you—well, go to.

FENTON.

Well, I shall see her to-day. Hold, there's money for thee; let me have thy voice in my behalf: if thou see'st her before me, commend me.

MISTRESS QUICKLY.

Will I? i'faith, that we will; and I will tell your worship more of the wart the next time we have confidence; and of other wooers.

FENTON.

Well, farewell; I am in great haste now.

MISTRESS QUICKLY.

Farewell to your worship. [*Exit* FENTON.] Truly, an honest gentleman: but Anne loves him not; for I know Anne's mind as well as another does. —Out upon't! what have I forgot? [*Exit.*

ACT II. SCENE I.

Before PAGE'S *house.*

Enter MISTRESS PAGE, *with a letter.*

MISTRESS PAGE.

WHAT, have I scaped love-letters in the holiday-time of my beauty, and am I now a subject for them? Let me see. [*Reads.*

Ask me no reason why I love you; for though Love use Reason for his physician, he admits him not for his counsellor. You are not young, no more am I; go to, then, there's sympathy: you are merry, so am I; ha, ha! then there's more sympathy: you love sack, and so do I; would you desire better sympathy? Let it suffice thee, Mistress Page,—at the least, if the love of soldier can suffice,—that I love thee. I will not say, pity me,—'tis not a soldier-like phrase; but I say, love me. By me,

Thine own true knig ht,
By day or night,
Or any kind of light,
With all his might
For thee to fight, JOHN FALSTAFF.

What a Herod of Jewry is this!—O wicked, wicked world!—one that is well-nigh worn to pieces with age to show himself a young gallant! What an unweigh'd behaviour hath this Flemish drunkard pick'd—with the devil's name—out of my conversation, that he dares in this manner assay me? Why, he hath not been thrice in my company!—What should I say to him?—I was then frugal of my mirth:—Heaven forgive me!—Why, I'll exhibit a bill in the parliament for the putting-down of fat men. How shall I be revenged on him? for revenged I will be, as sure as his guts are made of puddings.

Enter MISTRESS FORD.

MISTRESS FORD.

Mistress Page! trust me, I was going to your house.

MISTRESS PAGE.

And, trust me, I was coming to you. You look very ill.

MISTRESS FORD.

Nay, I'll ne'er believe that; I have to show to the contrary.

MISTRESS PAGE.

Faith, but you do, in my mind.

MISTRESS FORD.

Well, I do, then; yet, I say, I could show you to the contrary. O Mistress Page, give me some counsel!

MISTRESS PAGE.

What's the matter, woman?

MISTRESS FORD.

O woman, if it were not for one trifling respect, I could come to such honour!

MISTRESS PAGE.

Hang the trifle, woman! take the honour. What is it?—dispense with trifles;—what is it?

MISTRESS FORD.

If I would but go to hell for an eternal moment or so, I could be knighted.

MISTRESS PAGE.

What? thou liest!—Sir Alice Ford! These knights will hack; and so thou shouldst not alter the article of thy gentry.

MISTRESS FORD.

We burn daylight:—here, read, read; perceive how I might be knighted.—I shall think the worse of fat men, as long as I have an eye to make difference of men's liking: and yet he would not swear; praised women's modesty; and gave such orderly and well-behaved reproof to all uncomeliness, that I would have sworn his disposition would have gone to the truth of his words; but they do no more adhere and keep place together than the Hundredth Psalm to the tune of *Green sleeves*. What tempest, I trow, threw this whale, with so many tuns of oil in his belly, ashore at Windsor? How shall I be revenged on him? I think the best way were to entertain him with hope, till the wicked fire of lust have melted him in his own grease.—Did you ever hear the like?

MISTRESS PAGE.

Letter for letter, but that the name of Page and Ford differs!—To thy great comfort in this mystery of ill opinions, here's the twin-brother of thy letter: but let thine inherit first; for, I protest, mine never shall. I warrant he hath a thousand of these letters, writ with blank space for different names,—sure, more,—and these are of the second edition: he will print them, out of doubt; for he cares not what he puts into the press, when he would put us two. I had rather be a giantess, and lie under Mount Pelion. Well, I will find you twenty lascivious turtles, ere one chaste man.

MISTRESS FORD.

Why, this is the very same; the very hand, the very words. What doth he think of us?

MISTRESS PAGE.

Nay, I know not: it makes me almost ready to wrangle with mine own honesty. I'll entertain myself like one that I am not acquainted withal; for, sure, unless he know some strain in me, that I know not myself, he would never have boarded me in this fury.

MISTRESS FORD.

Boarding, call you it? I'll be sure to keep him above deck.

MISTRESS PAGE.

So will I: if he come under my hatches, I'll never to sea again. Let's be revenged on him: let's appoint him a meeting; give him a show of comfort in his suit; and lead him on with a fine-baited delay, till he hath pawn'd his horses to mine host of the Garter.

MISTRESS FORD.

Nay, I will consent to act any villainy against him, that may not sully the chariness of our honesty. O, that my husband saw this letter! it would give eternal food to his jealousy.

MISTRESS PAGE.

Why, look where he comes;—and my good man, too: he's as far from jealousy as I am from giving him cause; and that, I hope, is an unmeasurable distance.

MISTRESS FORD.

You are the happier woman.

MISTRESS PAGE.

Let's consult together against this greasy knight. Come hither. [*They retire.*

Enter FORD, PISTOL, PAGE, *and* NYM.

FORD.

Well, I hope it be not so.

PISTOL.

Hope is a curtal dog in some affairs:
Sir John affects thy wife.

FORD.

Why, sir, my wife is not young.

PISTOL.

He woos both high and low, both rich and poor,
Both young and old, one with another, Ford;
He loves the gallimaufry: Ford, perpend.

FORD.

Love my wife!

PISTOL.

With liver burning hot. Prevent, or go thou,
Like Sir Actæon he, with Ringwood at thy heels:—
O, odious is the name!

FORD.

What name, sir?

PISTOL.

The horn, I say. Farewell.
Take heed; have open eye; for thieves do foot by night:
Take heed, ere summer comes, or cuckoo-birds do sing.—
Away, Sir Corporal Nym!—
Believe it, Page; he speaks sense. [*Exit.*

FORD.

I will be patient; I will find out this.

NYM [*to* PAGE].

And this is true; I like not the humour of lying. He hath wrong'd me in some humours: I should have borne the humour'd letter to her; but I have a sword, and it shall bite upon my necessity. He loves your wife; there's the short and the long. My name is Corporal Nym; I speak, and I avouch 'tis true: my name is Nym, and Falstaff loves your wife.—Adieu. I love not the humour of bread and cheese; and there's the humour of it. Adieu. [*Exit.*

PAGE.

'The humour of it,' quoth a'! here's a fellow frights humour out of his wits.

FORD.

I will seek out Falstaff.

PAGE.

I never heard such a drawling, affecting rogue.

FORD.

If I do find it:—well.

PAGE.

I will not believe such a Cataian, though the priest o'th'town commended him for a true man.

FORD.

'Twas a good sensible fellow:—well.

[MISTRESS PAGE *and* MISTRESS FORD *come forward.*

PAGE.

How now, Meg!

MISTRESS PAGE.

Whither go you, George?—Hark you.

MISTRESS FORD.

How now, sweet Frank! why art thou melancholy?

FORD.

I melancholy! I am not melancholy.—Get you home, go.

MISTRESS FORD.

Faith, thou hast some crotchets in thy head now. —Will you go, Mistress Page?

MISTRESS PAGE.

Have with you.—You'll come to dinner, George? —[*Aside to* MISTRESS FORD] Look who comes yonder: she shall be our messenger to this paltry knight.

MISTRESS FORD [*aside to* MISTRESS PAGE].

Trust me, I thought on her: she'll fit it.

Enter MISTRESS QUICKLY.

MISTRESS PAGE.

You are come to see my daughter Anne?

MISTRESS QUICKLY.

Ay, forsooth; and, I pray, how does good Mistress Anne?

MISTRESS PAGE.

Go in with us and see: we have an hour's talk with you.

[*Exeunt* MISTRESS PAGE, MISTRESS FORD, *and* MISTRESS QUICKLY.

PAGE.

How now, Master Ford!

FORD.

You heard what this knave told me, did you not?

PAGE.

Yes: and you heard what the other told me?

FORD.

Do you think there is truth in them?

PAGE.

Hang 'em, slaves! I do not think the knight would offer it: but these that accuse him in his intent towards our wives are a yoke of his discarded men; very rogues, now they be out of service.

FORD.

Were they his men?

PAGE.

Marry, were they.

FORD.

I like it never the better for that.—Does he lie at the Garter?

PAGE.

Ay, marry, does he. If he should intend this voyage toward my wife, I would turn her loose to him; and what he gets more of her than sharp words, let it lie on my head.

FORD.

I do not misdoubt my wife; but I would be loth to turn them together. A man may be too confident: I would have nothing lie on my head: I cannot be thus satisfied.

PAGE.

Look where my ranting host of the Garter comes: there is either liquor in his pate, or money in his purse, when he looks so merrily.

Enter HOST.

How now, mine host!

HOST.

How now, bully-rook! thou'rt a gentleman.— Cavalero-justice, I say!

Enter SHALLOW.

SHALLOW.

I follow, mine host, I follow.—Good even and twenty, good Master Page! Master Page, will you go with us? we have sport in hand.

HOST.

Tell him, cavalero-justice; tell him, bully-rook.

SHALLOW.

Sir, there is a fray to be fought between Sir Hugh the Welsh priest and Caius the French doctor.

FORD.

Good mine host o'th'Garter, a word with you.

HOST.

What say'st thou, my bully-rook?

[*They go aside.*

SHALLOW [*to* PAGE].

Will you go with us to behold it? My merry host hath had the measuring of their weapons; and, I think, hath appointed them contrary places; for, believe me, I hear the parson is no jester. Hark, I will tell you what our sport shall be.

[*They go aside.*

HOST.

Hast thou no suit against my knight, my guest-cavalier?

FORD.

None, I protest: but I'll give you a pottle of burnt sack to give me recourse to him, and tell him my name is Brook, only for a jest.

HOST.

My hand, bully; thou shalt have egress and regress;—said I well?—and thy name shall be Brook. It is a merry knight.—Will you go, mynheers?

SHALLOW.

Have with you, mine host.

PAGE.

I have heard the Frenchman hath good skill in his rapier.

SHALLOW.

Tut, sir, I could have told you more. In these times you stand on distance, your passes, stoccadoes, and I know not what: 'tis the heart, Master Page; 'tis here, 'tis here. I have seen the time, with my long sword I would have made you four tall fellows skip like rats.

HOST.

Here, boys, here, here! shall we wag?

PAGE.

Have with you.—I had rather hear them scold than fight. [*Exeunt* HOST, SHALLOW, *and* PAGE.

FORD.

Though Page be a secure fool, and stands so firmly on his wife's frailty, yet I cannot put off my opinion so easily: she was in his company at Page's house; and what they made there, I know not. Well, I will look further into't: and I have a disguise to sound Falstaff. If I find her honest, I lose not my labour, if she be otherwise, 'tis labour well bestow'd. [*Exit.*

SCENE II.

A room in the Garter Inn.

Enter FALSTAFF *and* PISTOL.

SIR JOHN FALSTAFF.

I WILL not lend thee a penny.

PISTOL.

Why, then the world's mine oyster,
Which I with sword will open.—
I will retort the sum in equipage.

SIR JOHN FALSTAFF.

Not a penny. I have been content, sir, you should lay my countenance to pawn: I have grated upon my good friends for three reprieves for you and your coach-fellow Nym; or else you had look'd through the grate, like a geminy of baboons. I am damn'd in hell for swearing to gentlemen my friends you were good soldiers and tall fellows; and when Mistress Bridget lost the handle of her fan, I took't upon mine honour thou hadst it not.

PISTOL.

Didst not thou share? hadst thou not fifteen
pence?

SIR JOHN FALSTAFF.

Reason, you rogue, reason: think'st thou I'll endanger my soul gratis? At a word, hang no more about me, I am no gibbet for you:—go:—a short knife and a throng;—to your manor of Pickt-hatch, go.—You'll not bear a letter for me, you rogue!—you stand upon your honour!—Why, thou unconfinable baseness, it is as much as I can do to keep the terms of my honour precise; I, I, I myself sometimes, leaving the fear of God on the left hand, and hiding mine honour in my necessity, am fain to shuffle, to hedge, and to lurch; and yet you, rogue, will ensconce your rags, your cat-a-mountain looks, your red-lattice phrases, and your bold-beating oaths, under the shelter of your honour! You will not do it, you!

PISTOL.

I do relent:—what would thou more of man?

SIR JOHN FALSTAFF.

Well, go to, away, no more!

Enter ROBIN.

ROBIN.

Sir, here's a woman would speak with you.

SIR JOHN FALSTAFF.

Let her approach.

Enter MISTRESS QUICKLY.

MISTRESS QUICKLY.

Give your worship good morrow.

SIR JOHN FALSTAFF.

Good morrow, good wife.

MISTRESS QUICKLY.

Not so, an't please your worship.

SIR JOHN FALSTAFF.

Good maid, then.

MISTRESS QUICKLY.

I'll be sworn;
As my mother was, the first hour I was born.

SIR JOHN FALSTAFF.

I do believe the swearer. What with me?

MISTRESS QUICKLY.

Shall I vouchsafe your worship a word or two?

SIR JOHN FALSTAFF.

Two thousand, fair woman: and I'll vouchsafe thee the hearing.

MISTRESS QUICKLY.

There is one Mistress Ford, sir:—I pray, come a little nearer this ways:—I myself dwell with Master Doctor Caius,—

SIR JOHN FALSTAFF.

Well, on: Mistress Ford, you say,—

MISTRESS QUICKLY.

Your worship says very true:—I pray your worship, come a little nearer this ways.

SIR JOHN FALSTAFF.

I warrant thee, nobody hears;—mine own people, mine own people.

MISTRESS QUICKLY.

Are they so? God bless them, and make them his servants!

SIR JOHN FALSTAFF.

Well, Mistress Ford;—what of her?

MISTRESS QUICKLY.

Why, sir, she's a good creature.—Lord, Lord! your worship's a wanton! Well, heaven forgive you, and all of us, I pray!—

SIR JOHN FALSTAFF.

Mistress Ford;—come, Mistress Ford,—

MISTRESS QUICKLY.

Marry, this is the short and the long of it; you have brought her into such a canaries as 'tis wonderful. The best courtier of them all, when the court lay at Windsor, could never have brought her to such a canary. Yet there has been knights, and lords, and gentlemen, with their coaches; I warrant you, coach after coach, letter after letter, gift after gift; smelling so sweetly—all musk—and so rushling, I warrant you, in silk and gold; and in such alligant terms; and in such wine and sugar of the best and the fairest, that would have won any woman's heart; and, I warrant you, they could never get an eye-wink of her:—I had myself twenty angels given me this morning; but I defy all angels—in any such sort, as they say—but in the way of honesty:—and, I warrant you, they could never get her so much as sip on a cup with the proudest of them all: and yet there has been earls, nay, which is more, pensioners; but, I warrant you, all is one with her.

SIR JOHN FALSTAFF.

But what says she to me? be brief, my good she-Mercury.

MISTRESS QUICKLY.

Marry, she hath received your letter; for the which she thanks you a thousand times: and she gives you to notify, that her husband will be absence from his house between ten and eleven.

SIR JOHN FALSTAFF.

Ten and eleven?

MISTRESS QUICKLY.

Ay, forsooth; and then you may come and see the picture, she says, that you wot of;—Master Ford, her husband, will be from home. Alas, the sweet woman leads an ill life with him! he's a very jealousy man: she leads a very frampold life with him, good heart.

SIR JOHN FALSTAFF.

Ten and eleven:—woman, commend me to her; I will not fail her.

MISTRESS QUICKLY.

Why, you say well. But I have another messenger to your worship. Mistress Page hath her hearty commendations to you, too:—and let me tell you in your ear, she's as fartuous a civil modest wife, and one, I tell you, that will not miss you morning nor evening prayer, as any is in Windsor, whoe'er be the other:—and she bade me tell your worship that her husband is seldom from home; but, she hopes, there will come a time. I never knew a woman so dote upon a man: surely, I think you have charms, la; yes, in truth.

SIR JOHN FALSTAFF.

Not I, I assure thee: setting the attraction of my good parts aside, I have no other charms.

MISTRESS QUICKLY.

Blessing on your heart for't!

SIR JOHN FALSTAFF.

But, I pray thee, tell me this,—has Ford's wife and Page's wife acquainted each other how they love me?

MISTRESS QUICKLY.

That were a jest indeed!—they have not so little grace, I hope:—that were a trick indeed!—But Mistress Page would desire you to send her your little page, of all loves: her husband has a marvellous infection to the little page; and, truly, Master Page is an honest man. Never a wife in Windsor leads a better life than she does: do what she will, say what she will, take all, pay all, go to bed when she list, rise when she list, all is as she will: and, truly, she deserves it; for if there be a kind woman in Windsor, she is one. You must send her your page; no remedy.

SIR JOHN FALSTAFF.

Why, I will.

MISTRESS QUICKLY.

Nay, but do so, then: and, look you, he may come and go between you both; and, in any case, have a nay-word, that you may know one another's mind, and the boy never need to understand any thing; for 'tis not good that children should know any wickedness: old folks, you know, have discretion, as they say, and know the world.

SIR JOHN FALSTAFF.

Fare thee well: commend me to them both: there's my purse; I am yet thy debtor.—Boy, go along with this woman. [*Exeunt* MISTRESS QUICKLY *and* ROBIN.]—This news distracts me!

PISTOL.

This punk is one of Cupid's carriers:—
Clap on more sails; pursue; up with your fights;
Give fire; she is my prize, or ocean whelm them
all! [*Exit.*

SIR JOHN FALSTAFF.

Say'st thou so, old Jack? go thy ways: I'll make more of thy old body than I have done. Will they yet look after thee? Wilt thou, after the expense of so much money, be now a gainer? Good body, I thank thee. Let them say 'tis grossly done; so it be fairly done, no matter.

Enter BARDOLPH, *with a cup of sack.*

BARDOLPH.

Sir John, there's one Master Brook below would fain speak with you, and be acquainted with you; and hath sent your worship a morning's draught of sack.

SIR JOHN FALSTAFF.

Brook is his name?

BARDOLPH.

Ay, sir.

SIR JOHN FALSTAFF.

Call him in. [*Exit* BARDOLPH.] Such Brooks are welcome to me, that o'erflow such liquor.—Ah, ha! Mistress Ford and Mistress Page, have I encompass'd you? go to; *via!*

Enter BARDOLPH, *with* FORD *disguised.*

FORD.

'Bless you, sir!

SIR JOHN FALSTAFF.

And you, sir! Would you speak with me?

FORD.

I make bold to press with so little preparation upon you.

SIR JOHN FALSTAFF.

You're welcome. What's your will?—Give us leave, drawer. [*Exit* BARDOLPH.

FORD.

Sir, I am a gentleman that have spent much; my name is Brook.

SIR JOHN FALSTAFF.

Good Master Brook, I desire more acquaintance of you.

FORD.

Good Sir John, I sue for yours: not to charge you; for I must let you understand I think myself in better plight for a lender than you are: the which hath something embolden'd me to this unseason'd intrusion; for they say, if money go before, all ways do lie open.

SIR JOHN FALSTAFF.

Money is a good soldier, sir, and will on.

FORD.

Troth, and I have a bag of money here troubles me: if you will help to bear it, Sir John, take all, or half, for easing me of the carriage.

SIR JOHN FALSTAFF.

Sir, I know not how I may deserve to be your porter.

FORD.

I will tell you, sir, if you will give me the hearing.

SIR JOHN FALSTAFF.

Speak, good Master Brook: I shall be glad to be your servant.

FORD.

Sir, I hear you are a scholar,—I will be brief with you;—and you have been a man long known to me, though I had never so good means, as desire, to make myself acquainted with you. I shall discover a thing to you, wherein I must very much lay open mine own imperfection: but, good Sir John, as you have one eye upon my follies, as you hear them unfolded, turn another into the register of your own; that I may pass with a reproof the easier, sith you yourself know how easy it is to be such an offender.

SIR JOHN FALSTAFF.

Very well, sir; proceed.

FORD.

There is a gentlewoman in this town, her husband's name is Ford.

SIR JOHN FALSTAFF.

Well, sir.

FORD.

I have long loved her, and, I protest to you, bestow'd much on her: follow'd her with a doting observance; engross'd opportunities to meet her; fee'd every slight occasion that could but niggardly give me sight of her; not only bought many presents to give her, but have given largely to many to know what she would have given; briefly, I have pursued her as love hath pursued me; which hath been on the wing of all occasions. But whatsoever I have merited, either in my mind or in my means, meed, I am sure, I have received none; unless experience be a jewel: that I have purchased at an infinite rate; and that hath taught me to say this:

Love like a shadow flies when substance love pursues;
Pursuing that that flies, and flying what pursues.

SIR JOHN FALSTAFF.

Have you received no promise of satisfaction at her hands?

FORD.

Never.

SIR JOHN FALSTAFF.

Have you importuned her to such a purpose?

FORD.

Never.

SIR JOHN FALSTAFF.

Of what quality was your love, then?

FORD.

Like a fair house built on another man's ground; so that I have lost my edifice by mistaking the place where I erected it.

SIR JOHN FALSTAFF.

To what purpose have you unfolded this to me?

FORD.

When I have told you that, I have told you all. Some say, that though she appear honest to me, yet in other places she enlargeth her mirth so far that there is shrewd construction made of her. Now, Sir John, here is the heart of my purpose: you are a gentleman of excellent breeding, admirable discourse, of great admittance, authentic in your place and person, generally allow'd for your many war-like, court-like, and learned preparations,—

SIR JOHN FALSTAFF.

O, sir!

FORD.

Believe it, for you know it.—There is money; spend it, spend it; spend more; spend all I have; only give me so much of your time in exchange of it, as to lay an amiable siege to the honesty of this Ford's wife: use your art of wooing; win her to consent to you: if any man may, you may as soon as any.

SIR JOHN FALSTAFF.

Would it apply well to the vehemency of your affection, that I should win what you would enjoy? Methinks you prescribe to yourself very preposterously.

FORD.

O, understand my drift. She dwells so securely on the excellency of her honour, that the folly of my soul dares not present itself: she is too bright to be look'd against. Now, could I come to her with any detection in my hand, my desires had instance and argument to commend themselves: I could drive her then from the ward of her purity, her reputation, her marriage-vow, and a thousand other her defences, which now are too-too strongly embattled against me. What say you to't, Sir John?

SIR JOHN FALSTAFF.

Master Brook, I will first make bold with your money; next, give me your hand; and last, as I am a gentleman, you shall, if you will, enjoy Ford's wife.

FORD.

O good sir!

SIR JOHN FALSTAFF.

Master Brook, I say you shall.

FORD.

Want no money, Sir John; you shall want none.

SIR JOHN FALSTAFF.

Want no Mistress Ford, Master Brook; you shall want none. I shall be with her—I may tell you—by her own appointment; even as you came in to me, her assistant, or go-between, parted from me:

I say I shall be with her between ten and eleven; for at that time the jealous rascally knave her husband will be forth. Come you to me at night; you shall know how I speed.

FORD.

I am blest in your acquaintance. Do you know Ford, sir?

SIR JOHN FALSTAFF.

Hang him, poor cuckoldy knave! I know him not:—yet I wrong him to call him poor; they say the jealous wittolly knave hath masses of money; for the which his wife seems to me well-favour'd. I will use her as the key of the cuckoldly rogue's coffer; and there's my harvest-home.

FORD.

I would you knew Ford, sir, that you might avoid him, if you saw him.

SIR JOHN FALSTAFF.

Hang him, mechanical salt-butter rogue! I will stare him out of his wits; I will awe him with my cudgel,—it shall hang like a meteor o'er the cuckold's horns. Master Brook, thou shalt know I will predominate over the peasant, and thou shalt lie with his wife.—Come to me soon at night:—Ford's a knave, and I will aggravate his style; thou, Master Brook, shalt know him for knave and cuckold:—come to me soon at night. [*Exit.*

FORD.

What a damn'd Epicurean rascal is this!—My heart is ready to crack with impatience.—Who says this is improvident jealousy? my wife hath sent to him, the hour is fixt, the match is made. Would any man have thought this?—See the hell of having a false woman! My bed shall be abused, my coffers ransack'd, my reputation gnawn at; and I shall not only receive this villainous wrong, but stand under the adoption of abominable terms, and by him that does me this wrong. Terms! names!—Amaimon sounds well; Lucifer, well; Barbason, well; yet they are devils' additions, the names of fiends: but cuckold! wittol!—Cuckold! the devil himself hath not such a name. Page is an ass, a secure ass: he will trust his wife; he will not be jealous. I will rather trust a Fleming with my butter, Parson Hugh the Welshman with my cheese, an Irishman with my aqua-vitæ bottle, or a thief to walk my ambling gelding, than my wife with herself: then she plots, then she ruminates, then she devises; and what they think in their hearts they may effect, they will break their hearts but they will effect. Heaven be praised for my jealousy!—Eleven o'clock the hour:—I will prevent this, detect my wife, be revenged on Falstaff, and laugh at Page. I will about it; better three hours too soon than a minute too late, Fie, fie, fie! cuckold! cuckold! cuckold! [*Exit.*

SCENE III.

A field near Windsor.

Enter CAIUS *and* RUGBY.

DOCTOR CAIUS.

JACK RUGBY,—

RUGBY.

Sir?

DOCTOR CAIUS.

Vat is de clock, Jack?

RUGBY.

'Tis past the hour, sir, that Sir Hugh promised to meet.

DOCTOR CAIUS.

By gar, he has save his soul, dat he is no come; he has pray his Pible vell, dat he is no come: by gar, Jack Rugby, he is dead already, if he be come.

RUGBY.

He is wise, sir; he knew your worship would kill him, if he came.

DOCTOR CAIUS.

By gar, de herring is no dead so as I vill kill him. Take your rapier, Jack; I vill tell you how I vill kill him.

RUGBY.

Alas, sir, I cannot fence.

DOCTOR CAIUS.

Villainy, take your rapier.

RUGBY.

Forbear; here's company.

Enter HOST, SHALLOW, SLENDER, *and* PAGE.

HOST.

'Bless thee, bully doctor!

SHALLOW.

'Save you, Master Doctor Caius!

PAGE.

Now, good master doctor!

SLENDER.

'Give you good morrow, sir.

DOCTOR CAIUS.

Vat be all you, one, two, tree, four, come for?

HOST.

To see thee fight, to see thee foin, to see thee traverse; to see thee here, to see thee there; to see thee pass thy punto, thy stock, thy reverse, thy distance, thy montant. Is he dead, my Ethiopian? is he dead, my Francisco? ha, bully! What says my Aesculapius? my Galen? my heart of elder? ha! is he dead, bully-stale? is he dead?

DOCTOR CAIUS.

By gar, he is de coward Jack priest of de vorld; he is not show his face.

HOST.

Thou art a Castilian, King Urinal! Hector of Greece, my boy!

DOCTOR CAIUS.

I pray you, bear vitness that me have stay six or seven, two, tree hours for him, and he is no come.

SHALLOW.

He is the wiser man, master doctor: he is a curer of souls, and you a curer of bodies; if you should fight, you go against the hair of your professions.—Is it not true, Master Page?

PAGE.

Master Shallow, you have yourself been a great fighter, though now a man of peace.

SHALLOW.

Bodikins, Master Page, though I now be old, and of the peace, if I see a sword out, my finger itches to make one. Though we are justices, and doctors, and churchmen, Master Page, we have some salt of our youth in us; we are the sons of women, Master Page.

PAGE.
'Tis true, Master Shallow.

SHALLOW.
It will be found so, Master Page.—Master Doctor Caius, I am come to fetch you home. I am sworn of the peace: you have show'd yourself a wise physician, and Sir Hugh hath shown himself a wise and patient churchman. You must go with me, master doctor.

HOST.
Pardon, guest-justice.—A word, Monsieur Mock-water.

DOCTOR CAIUS.
Mock-vater! vat is dat?

HOST.
Mock-water, in our English tongue, is valour, bully.

DOCTOR CAIUS.
By gar, den, I have as mush mock-water as de Englishman.—Scurvy jack-dog priest! by gar, me vill cut his ears.

HOST.
He will clapper-claw thee tightly, bully.

DOCTOR CAIUS.
Clapper-de-claw! vat is dat?

HOST.
That is, he will make thee amends.

DOCTOR CAIUS.
By gar, me do look he shall clapper-de-claw me; for, by gar, me vill have it.

HOST.
And I will provoke him to't, or let him wag.

DOCTOR CAIUS.
Me tank you for dat.

HOST.
And, moreover, bully,—But first, master guest, and Master Page, and eke Cavalero Slender, go you through the town to Frogmore. [*Aside to them.*

PAGE.
Sir Hugh is there, is he?

HOST.
He is there: see what humour he is in; and I will bring the doctor about by the fields. Will it do well?

SHALLOW.
We will do it.

PAGE, SHALLOW, *and* SLENDER.
Adieu, good master doctor.

[*Exeunt* PAGE, SHALLOW, *and* SLENDER.

DOCTOR CAIUS.
By gar, me vill kill de priest; for he speak for a jack-an-ape to Anne Page.

HOST.
Let him die: sheathe thy impatience, throw cold water on thy choler: go about the fields with me through Frogmore: I will bring thee where Mistress Anne Page is, at a farm-house a-feasting; and thou shalt woo her. Cried I aim? said I well?

DOCTOR CAIUS.
By gar, me dank you vor dat: by gar, I love you; and I shall procure-a you de good guest, de earl, de knight, de lords, de gentlemen, my patients.

HOST.
For the which I will be thy adversary toward Anne Page. Said I well?

DOCTOR CAIUS.
By gar, 'tis good; vell said.

HOST.
Let us wag, then.

DOCTOR CAIUS.
Come at my heels, Jack Rugby. [*Exeunt.*

ACT III. SCENE I.

A field near Frogmore.

Enter SIR HUGH EVANS *and* SIMPLE.

SIR HUGH EVANS.
I PRAY you now, good Master Slender's serving-man, and friend Simple by your name, which way have you look'd for Master Caius, that calls himself doctor of physic?

SIMPLE.
Marry, sir, the pittie-ward, the park-ward, every way; old Windsor way, and every way but the town way.

SIR HUGH EVANS.
I most fehemently desire you you will also look that way.

SIMPLE.
I will, sir. [*Retires.*

SIR HUGH EVANS.
Pless my soul, how full of cholers I am, and trempling of mind!—I shall be glad if he have deceived me:—how melancholies I am!—I will knog his urinals about his knave's costard when I have goot opportunities for the ork:—Pless my soul!— [*Sings*

To shallow rivers, to whose falls
Melodious birds sing madrigals;
There will we make our peds of roses,
And a thousand fragrant posies.
To shallow—

Mercy on me! I have a great dispositions to cry.— [*Sings.*

Melodious birds sing madrigals;—
Whenas I sat in Pabylon,—
And a thousand vagram posies.
To shallow, &c.

SIMPLE [*coming forward*].
Yonder he is coming, this way, Sir Hugh.

SIR HUGH EVANS.
He's welcome. [*Sings.*

To shallow rivers, to whose falls—

Heaven prosper the right!—What weapons is he?

SIMPLE.
No weapons, sir. There comes my master, Master Shallow, and another gentleman, from Frogmore, over the stile, this way.

SIR HUGH EVANS.
Pray you, give me my gown; or else keep it in your arms.

Enter PAGE, SHALLOW, *and* SLENDER.

SHALLOW.
How now, master parson! Good morrow, good Sir Hugh. Keep a gamester from the dice, and a good student from his book, and it is wonderful.

SLENDER [*aside*].
Ah, sweet Anne Page!

PAGE.
'Save you, good Sir Hugh!

SIR HUGH EVANS.

'Pless you from his mercy sake, all of you!

SHALLOW.

What, the sword and the word! do you study them both, master parson?

PAGE.

And youthful still, in your doublet and hose this raw rheumatic day?

SIR HUGH EVANS.

There is reasons and causes for it.

PAGE.

We are come to you to do a good office, master parson.

SIR HUGH EVANS.

Fery well: what is it?

PAGE.

Yonder is a most reverend gentleman, who, belike having received wrong by some person, is at most odds with his own gravity and patience that ever you saw.

SHALLOW.

I have lived fourscore years and upward; I never heard a man of his place, gravity, and learning, so wide of his own respect.

SIR HUGH EVANS.

What is he?

PAGE.

I think you know him; Master Doctor Caius, the renown'd French physician.

SIR HUGH EVANS.

Got's will, and his passion of my heart! I had as lief you would tell me of a mess of porridge.

PAGE.

Why?

SIR HUGH EVANS.

He has no more knowledge in Hibbocrates and Galen,—and he is a knave besides; a cowardly knave as you would desires to be acquainted withal.

PAGE.

I warrant you, he's the man should fight with him.

SLENDER [*aside*].

O sweet Anne Page!

SHALLOW.

It appears so, by his weapons.—Keep them asunder:—here comes Doctor Caius.

Enter HOST, CAIUS, *and* RUGBY.

PAGE.

Nay, good master parson, keep in your weapon.

SHALLOW.

So do you, good master doctor.

HOST.

Disarm them, and let them question: let them keep their limbs whole, and hack our English.

DOCTOR CAIUS.

I pray you, let-a me speak a word vit your ear. Verefore vill you not meet-a me?

SIR HUGH EVANS [*aside to* CAIUS].

Pray you, use your patience: in goot time.

DOCTOR CAIUS.

By gar, you are de coward, de Jack dog, John ape.

SIR HUGH EVANS [*aside to* CAIUS].

Pray you, let us not be laughing-stogs to other men's humours; I desire you in friendship, and I will one way or other make you amends.—[*aloud*] I will knog your urinals about your knave's cogscomb for missing your meetings and appointments.

DOCTOR CAIUS.

Diable!—Jack Rugby,—mine host de Jarteer,—have I not stay for him to kill him? have I not, at de place I did appoint?

SIR HUGH EVANS.

As I am a Christians soul, now, look you, this is the place appointed: I'll be judgement by mine host of the Garter.

HOST.

Peace, I say, Gallia and Guallia, French and Welsh, soul-curer and body-curer!

DOCTOR CAIUS.

Ay, dat is very good; excellent.

HOST.

Peace, I say! hear mine host of the Garter. Am I politic? am I subtle? am I a Machivell? Shall I lose my doctor? no; he gives me the potions and the motions. Shall I lose my parson, my priest, my Sir Hugh? no; he gives me the proverbs and the noverbs.—Give me thy hand, terrestrial; so. —Give me thy hand, celestial; so.—Boys of art, I have deceived you both; I have directed you to wrong places: your hearts are mighty, your skins are whole, and let burnt sack be the issue.—Come, lay their swords to pawn.—Follow me, lads of peace; follow, follow, follow.

SHALLOW.

Trust me, a mad host.—Follow, gentlemen, follow.

SLENDER [*aside*].

O sweet Anne Page!

[*Exeunt* SHALLOW, SLENDER, PAGE, *and* HOST.

DOCTOR CAIUS.

Ha, do I perceive dat? have you make-a de sot of us, ha, ha?

SIR HUGH EVANS.

This is well; he has made us his vlouting stog.—I desire you that we may be friends; and let us knog our prains together to be revenge on this same scall, scurvy, cogging companion; the host of the Garter.

DOCTOR CAIUS.

By gar, vit all my heart. He promise to bring me vere is Anne Page; by gar, he deceive me too.

SIR HUGH EVANS.

Well, I will smite his noddles. Pray you, follow.

[*Exeunt.*

SCENE II.

The street, in Windsor.

Enter MISTRESS PAGE *and* ROBIN.

MISTRESS PAGE.

NAY, keep your way, little gallant; you were wont to be a follower, but now you are a leader. Whether had you rather lead mine eyes, or eye your master's heels?

ROBIN.

I had rather, forsooth, go before you like a man than follow him like a dwarf.

MISTRESS PAGE.

O, you are a flattering boy: now I see you'll be a courtier.

Enter FORD.

FORD.

Well met, Mistress Page. Whither go you?

MISTRESS PAGE.

Truly, sir, to see your wife. Is she at home?

FORD.

Ay, and as idle as she may hang together, for want of company. I think, if your husbands were dead, you two would marry.

MISTRESS PAGE.

Be sure of that,—two other husbands.

FORD.

Where had you this pretty weathercock?

MISTRESS PAGE.

I cannot tell what the dickens his name is my husband had him of.—What do you call your knight's name, sirrah?

ROBIN.

Sir John Falstaff.

FORD.

Sir John Falstaff!

MISTRESS PAGE.

He, he; I can never hit on's name.—There is such a league between my good man and he!—Is your wife at home indeed?

FORD.

Indeed she is.

MISTRESS PAGE.

By your leave, sir: I am sick till I see her.

[*Exeunt* MISTRESS PAGE *and* ROBIN.

FORD.

Has Page any brains? hath he any eyes? hath he any thinking? Sure, they sleep; he hath no use of them. Why, this boy will carry a letter twenty mile, as easy as a cannon will shoot point-blank twelve score. He pieces out his wife's inclination; he gives her folly motion and advantage: and now she's going to my wife, and Falstaff's boy with her:—a man may hear this shower sing in the wind:—and Falstaff's boy with her!—Good plots!—they are laid; and our revolted wives share damnation together. Well; I will take him, then torture my wife, pluck the borrow'd veil of modesty from the so seeming Mistress Page, divulge Page himself for a secure and wilful Actæon; and to these violent proceedings all my neighbours shall cry aim. [*Clock strikes.*] The clock gives me my cue, and my assurance bids me search: there I shall find Falstaff: I shall be rather praised for this than mock'd; for it is as positive as the earth is firm that Falstaff is there: I will go.

Enter PAGE, SHALLOW, SLENDER, HOST, SIR HUGH EVANS, CAIUS, *and* RUGBY.

SHALLOW, PAGE, &c.

Well met, Master Ford.

FORD.

Trust me, a good knot: I have good cheer at home; and I pray you all, go with me.

SHALLOW.

I must excuse myself, Master Ford.

SLENDER.

And so must I, sir: we have appointed to dine with Mistress Anne, and I would not break with her for more money than I'll speak of.

SHALLOW.

We have linger'd about a match between Anne Page and my cousin Slender, and this day we shall have our answer.

SLENDER.

I hope I have your good will, father Page.

PAGE.

You have, Master Slender; I stand wholly for you:—but my wife, master doctor, is for you altogether.

DOCTOR CAIUS.

Ay, by gar; and de maid is love-a me; my nursh-a Quickly tell me so mush.

HOST.

What say you to young Master Fenton? he capers, he dances, he has eyes of youth, he writes verses, he speaks holiday, he smells April and May: he will carry't, he will carry't; 'tis in his buttons; he will carry't.

PAGE.

Not by my consent, I promise you. The gentleman is of no having: he kept company with the wild prince and Pointz; he is of too high a region; he knows too much. No, he shall not knit a knot in his fortunes with the finger of my substance: if he take her, let him take her simply; the wealth I have waits on my consent, and my consent goes not that way.

FORD.

I beseech you heartily, some of you go home with me to dinner: besides your cheer, you shall have sport; I will show you a monster.—Master doctor, you shall go;—so shall you, Master Page;—and you, Sir Hugh.

SHALLOW.

Well, fare you well: we shall have the freer wooing at Master Page's.

[*Exeunt* SHALLOW *and* SLENDER.

DOCTOR CAIUS.

Go home, John Rugby; I come anon.

[*Exit* RUGBY.

HOST.

Farewell, my hearts: I will to my honest knight Falstaff, and drink canary with him. [*Exit.*

FORD [*aside*].

I think I shall drink in pipe-wine first with him; I'll make him dance.—Will you go, gentles?

ALL.

Have with you to see this monster. [*Exeunt.*

SCENE III.

A room in FORD'S *house.*

Enter MISTRESS FORD *and* MISTRESS PAGE.

MISTRESS FORD.

WHAT, John! What, Robert!

MISTRESS PAGE.

Quickly, quickly:—is the buck-basket—

MISTRESS FORD.

I warrant.—What, Robin, I say!

Enter SERVANTS *with a basket.*

MISTRESS PAGE.

Come, come, come.

MISTRESS FORD.

Here, set it down.

MISTRESS PAGE.

Give your men the charge: we must be brief.

MISTRESS FORD.

Marry, as I told you before, John and Robert, be ready here hard by in the brew-house; and when I suddenly call you, come forth, and, without any pause or staggering, take this basket on your shoulders: that done, trudge with it in all haste, and carry it among the whitsters in Datchet-mead, and there empty it in the muddy ditch close by the Thames side.

MISTRESS PAGE.

You will do it?

MISTRESS FORD.

I ha' told them over and over; they lack no direction.—Be gone, and come when you are called. [*Exeunt* SERVANTS.

MISTRESS PAGE.

Here comes little Robin.

Enter ROBIN.

MISTRESS FORD.

How now, my eyas-musket! what news with you?

ROBIN.

My master, Sir John, is come in at your back-door, Mistress Ford, and requests your company.

MISTRESS PAGE.

You little Jack-a-Lent, have you been true to us?

ROBIN.

Ay, I'll be sworn. My master knows not of your being here, and hath threaten'd to put me into everlasting liberty, if I tell you of it; for he swears he'll turn me away.

MISTRESS PAGE.

Thou'rt a good boy: this secrecy of thine shall be a tailor to thee, and shall make thee a new doublet and hose.—I'll go hide me.

MISTRESS FORD.

Do so.—Go tell thy master I am alone.—Mistress Page, remember you your cue. [*Exit* ROBIN.

MISTRESS PAGE.

I warrant thee; if I do not act it, hiss me. [*Exit.*

MISTRESS FORD.

Go to, then: we'll use this unwholesome humidity, this gross watery pumpion; we'll teach him to know turtles from jays.

Enter FALSTAFF.

SIR JOHN FALSTAFF.

Have I caught thee, my heavenly jewel? Why, now let me die, for I have lived long enough; this is the period of my ambition: O this blessed hour!

MISTRESS FORD.

O sweet Sir John!

SIR JOHN FALSTAFF.

Mistress Ford, I cannot cog, I cannot prate, Mistress Ford. Now shall I sin in my wish,—I would thy husband were dead; I'll speak it before the best lord,—I would make thee my lady.

MISTRESS FORD.

I your lady, Sir John! alas, I should be a pitiful lady!

SIR JOHN FALSTAFF.

Let the court of France show me such another. I see how thine eye would emulate the diamond: thou hast the right arch'd beauty of the brow that becomes the ship-tire, the tire-valiant, or any tire of Venetian admittance.

MISTRESS FORD.

A plain kerchief, Sir John: my brows become nothing else; nor that well neither.

SIR JOHN FALSTAFF.

By the Lord, thou art a traitor to say so: thou wouldst make an absolute courtier; and the firm fixture of thy foot would give an excellent motion to thy gait in a semi-circled farthingale. I see what thou wert, if Fortune thy foe were not, Nature thy friend. Come, thou canst not hide it.

MISTRESS FORD.

Believe me, there's no such thing in me.

SIR JOHN FALSTAFF.

What made me love thee? let that persuade thee there's something extraordinary in thee. Come, I cannot cog, and say thou art this and that, like a many of these lisping hawthorn-buds, that come like women in men's apparel, and smell like Bucklersbury in simple-time; I cannot: but I love thee; none but thee; and thou deservest it.

MISTRESS FORD.

Do not betray me, sir. I fear you love Mistress Page.

SIR JOHN FALSTAFF.

Thou mightst as well say I love to walk by the Counter-gate, which is as hateful to me as the reek of a lime-kiln.

MISTRESS FORD.

Well, heaven knows how I love you; and you shall one day find it.

SIR JOHN FALSTAFF.

Keep in that mind; I'll deserve it.

MISTRESS FORD.

Nay, I must tell you, so you do; or else I could not be in that mind.

ROBIN [*within*].

Mistress Ford, Mistress Ford! here's Mistress Page at the door, sweating, and blowing, and looking wildly, and would needs speak with you presently.

SIR JOHN FALSTAFF.

She shall not see me: I will ensconce me behind the arras.

MISTRESS FORD.

Pray you, do so: she's a very tattling woman.

[FALSTAFF *hides himself behind the arras.*

Enter MISTRESS PAGE *and* ROBIN.

What's the matter? how now!

MISTRESS PAGE.

O Mistress Ford, what have you done? You're shamed, you're overthrown, you're undone for ever!

MISTRESS FORD.

What's the matter, good Mistress Page?

MISTRESS PAGE.

O well-a-day, Mistress Ford! having an honest man to your husband, to give him such cause of suspicion!

MISTRESS FORD.

What cause of suspicion?

MISTRESS PAGE.

What cause of suspicion! Out upon you! how am I mistook in you!

MISTRESS FORD.

Why, alas, what's the matter?

MISTRESS PAGE.

Your husband's coming hither, woman, with all the officers in Windsor, to search for a gentleman that he says is here now in the house, by your consent, to take an ill advantage of his absence: you are undone.

MISTRESS FORD.

'Tis not so, I hope.

MISTRESS PAGE.

Pray heaven it be not so, that you have such a man here! but 'tis most certain your husband's coming, with half Windsor at his heels, to search for such a one. I come before to tell you. If you know yourself clear, why, I am glad of it; but if you have a friend here, convey, convey him out. Be not amazed; call all your senses to you; defend your reputation, or bid farewell to your good life for ever.

MISTRESS FORD.

What shall I do?—There is a gentleman my dear friend; and I fear not mine own shame so much as his peril! I had rather than a thousand pound he were out of the house.

MISTRESS PAGE.

For shame! never stand 'you had rather' and 'you had rather:' your husband's here at hand; bethink you of some conveyance: in the house you cannot hide him.—O, how have you deceived me!—Look, here is a basket: if he be of any reasonable stature, he may creep in here; and throw foul linen upon him, as if it were going to bucking: or, —it is whiting-time,—send him by your two men to Datchet-mead.

MISTRESS FORD.

He's too big to go in there. What shall I do?

Enter FALSTAFF.

SIR JOHN FALSTAFF.

Let me see't, let me see't, O, let me see't!—I'll in, I'll in:—follow your friend's counsel:—I'll in.

MISTRESS PAGE.

What, Sir John Falstaff! Are these your letters, knight?

SIR JOHN FALSTAFF [*aside to* MISTRESS PAGE].

I love thee, and none but thee:—[*aloud*] help me away: let me creep in here. I'll never—

[*Goes into the basket; they cover him with foul linen.*

MISTRESS PAGE.

Help to cover your master, boy.—Call your men, Mistress Ford.—You dissembling knight!

[*Exit* ROBIN.

MISTRESS FORD.

What, John! Robert! John!

Enter SERVANTS.

Go take up these clothes here quickly:—where's the cowl-staff? look, how you drumble!—carry them to the laundress in Datchet-mead; quickly, come.

Enter FORD, PAGE, CAIUS, *and* SIR HUGH EVANS.

FORD.

Pray you, come near: if I suspect without cause, why then make sport at me; then let me be your jest; I deserve it.—How now! whither bear you this?

SERVANTS.

To the laundress, forsooth.

MISTRESS FORD.

Why, what have you to do whither they bear it? You were best meddle with buck-washing.

FORD.

Buck!—I would I could wash myself of the buck! —Buck, buck, buck! Ay, buck; I warrant you, buck; and of the season too, it shall appear. [*Exeunt* SERVANTS *with the basket.*]—Gentlemen, I have dream'd to-night; I'll tell you my dream. Here, here, here be my keys: ascend my chambers; search, seek, find out: I'll warrant we'll unkennel the fox.—Let me stop this way first [*Locks the door*].—So, now uncape.

PAGE.

Good Master Ford, be contented: you wrong yourself too much.

FORD.

True, Master Page.—Up, gentlemen; you shall see sport anon: follow me, gentlemen. [*Exit.*

SIR HUGH EVANS.

This is fery fantastical humours and jealousies.

DOCTOR CAIUS.

By gar, 'tis no de fashion of France; it is not jealous in France.

PAGE.

Nay, follow him, gentlemen; see the issue of his search.

[*Exeunt* PAGE, CAIUS, *and* EVANS.

MISTRESS PAGE.

Is there not a double excellency in this?

MISTRESS FORD.

I know not which pleases me better, that my husband is deceived, or Sir John.

MISTRESS PAGE.

What a taking was he in when your husband asked what was in the basket!

MISTRESS FORD.

I am half afraid he will have need of washing; so throwing him into the water will do him a benefit.

MISTRESS PAGE.

Hang him, dishonest rascal! I would all of the same strain were in the same distress.

MISTRESS FORD.

I think my husband hath some special suspicion of Falstaff's being here; for I never saw him so gross in his jealousy till now.

MISTRESS PAGE.

I will lay a plot to try that; and we will yet have more tricks with Falstaff; his dissolute disease will scarce obey this medicine.

MISTRESS FORD.

Shall we send that foolish carrion Mistress Quickly to him, and excuse his throwing into the water; and give him another hope, to betray him to another punishment?

MISTRESS PAGE.

We will do it: let him be sent for to-morrow eight o'clock, to have amends.

Enter FORD, PAGE, CAIUS, *and* SIR HUGH EVANS.

FORD.

I cannot find him: may be the knave bragg'd of that he could not compass.

MISTRESS PAGE [*aside to* MISTRESS FORD].
Heard you that?

MISTRESS FORD [*aside to* MISTRESS PAGE].
Ay, ay, peace.—You use me well, Master Ford, do you?

FORD.
Ay, I do so.

MISTRESS FORD.
Heaven make you better than your thoughts!

FORD.
Amen!

MISTRESS PAGE.
You do yourself mighty wrong, Master Ford.

FORD.
Ay, ay; I must bear it.

SIR HUGH EVANS.
If there be any pody in the house, and in the chambers, and in the coffers, and in the presses, heaven forgive my sins at the day of judgment!

DOCTOR CAIUS.
By gar, nor I too: dere is no bodies.

PAGE.
Fie, fie, Master Ford! are you not ashamed? What spirit, what devil suggests this imagination? I would not ha' your distemper in this kind for the wealth of Windsor Castle.

FORD.
'Tis my fault, Master Page: I suffer for it.

SIR HUGH EVANS.
You suffer for a pad conscience: your wife is as honest a omans as I will desires among five thousand, and five hundred too.

DOCTOR CAIUS.
By gar, I see 'tis an honest woman.

FORD.
Well;—I promised you a dinner:—come, come, walk in the Park: I pray you, pardon me; I will hereafter make known to you why I have done this.—Come, wife;—come, Mistress Page.—I pray you, pardon me; pray heartily, pardon me.

PAGE.
Let's go in, gentleman; but, trust me, we'll mock him. I do invite you to-morrow morning to my house to breakfast; after, we'll a-birding together; I have a fine hawk for the bush. Shall it be so?

FORD.
Any thing.

SIR HUGH EVANS.
If there is one, I shall make two in the company.

DOCTOR CAIUS.
If dere be one or two, I shall make-a de turd.

SIR HUGH EVANS.
In your teeth: for shame!

FORD.
Pray you, go, Master Page.

SIR HUGH EVANS.
I pray you now, remembrance to-morrow on the lousy knave, mine host.

DOCTOR CAIUS.
Dat is good; by gar, vit all my heart.

SIR HUGH EVANS.
A lousy knave, to have his gibes and his mockeries! [*Exeunt.*

SCENE IV.

A room in PAGE'S *house.*

Enter FENTON *and* ANNE PAGE.

FENTON.
I SEE I cannot get thy father's love;
Therefore no more turn me to him, sweet Nan.

ANNE PAGE.
Alas, how then?

FENTON.
Why, thou must be thyself.
He doth object I am too great of birth;
And that, my state being gall'd with my expense,
I seek to heal it only by his wealth:
Besides these, other bars he lays before me,—
My riots past, my wild societies;
And tells me 'tis a thing impossible
I should love thee but as a property.

ANNE PAGE.
May be he tells you true.

FENTON.
No, heaven so speed me in my time to come!
Albeit, I will confess, thy father's wealth
Was the first motive that I woo'd thee, Anne:
Yet, wooing thee, I found thee of more value
Than stamps in gold or sums in sealed bags;
And 'tis the very riches of thyself
That now I aim at.

ANNE PAGE.
Gentle Master Fenton,
Yet seek my father's love; still seek it, sir:
If opportunity and humblest suit
Cannot attain it, why, then—Hark you hither.
[*They converse apart.*

Enter SHALLOW, SLENDER, *and* MISTRESS QUICKLY.

SHALLOW.
Break their talk, Mistress Quickly: my kinsman shall speak for himself.

SLENDER.
I'll make a shaft or a bolt on't: slid, 'tis but venturing.

SHALLOW.
Be not dismay'd.

SLENDER.
No, she shall not dismay me: I care not for that,—but that I am afeard.

MISTRESS QUICKLY.
Hark ye: Master Slender would speak a word with you.

ANNE PAGE.
I come to him.—[*aside*] This is my father's choice.
O, what a world of vile ill-favour'd faults
Looks handsome in three hundred pounds a-year!

MISTRESS QUICKLY.
And how does good Master Fenton? Pray you, a word with you.

SHALLOW.
She's coming; to her, coz. O boy, thou hadst a father!

SLENDER.
I had a father, Mistress Anne;—my uncle can tell you good jests of him.—Pray you, uncle, tell Mistress Anne the jest, how my father stole two geese out of a pen, good uncle.

SHALLOW.

Mistress Anne, my cousin loves you.

SLENDER.

Ay, that I do; as well as I love any woman in Glostershire.

SHALLOW.

He will maintain you like a gentlewoman.

SLENDER.

Ay, that I will, come cut and long-tail, under the degree of a squire.

SHALLOW.

He will make you a hundred and fifty pounds jointure.

ANNE PAGE.

Good Master Shallow, let him woo for himself.

SHALLOW.

Marry, I thank you for it; I thank you for that good comfort.—She calls you, coz: I'll leave you.

ANNE PAGE.

Now, Master Slender,—

SLENDER.

Now, good Mistress Anne,—

ANNE PAGE.

What is your will ?

SLENDER.

My will! od's heartlings, that's a pretty jest indeed! I ne'er made my will yet, I thank heaven; I am not such a sickly creature, I give heaven praise.

ANNE PAGE.

I mean, Master Slender, what would you with me?

SLENDER.

Truly, for mine own part, I would little or nothing with you. Your father and my uncle hath made motions: if it be my luck, so; if not, happy man be his dole! They can tell you how things go better than I can: you may ask your father; here he comes.

Enter PAGE *and* MISTRESS PAGE.

PAGE.

Now, Master Slender:—love him, daughter Anne.—
Why, how now! what does Master Fenton here?
You wrong me, sir, thus still to haunt my house:
I told you, sir, my daughter is disposed of.

FENTON.

Nay, Master Page, be not impatient.

MISTRESS PAGE.

Good Master Fenton, come not to my child.

PAGE.

She is no match for you.

FENTON.

Sir, will you hear me?

PAGE.

No, good Master Fenton.—
Come, Master Shallow; come, son Slender; in.—
Knowing my mind, you wrong me, Master Fenton.

[*Exeunt* PAGE, SHALLOW, *and* SLENDER.

MISTRESS QUICKLY.

Speak to Mistress Page.

FENTON.

Good Mistress Page, for that I love your daughter
In such a righteous fashion as I do,
Perforce, against all checks, rebukes, and manners,
I must advance the colours of my love,
And not retire: let me have your good will.

ANNE PAGE.

Good mother, do not marry me to yond fool.

MISTRESS PAGE.

I mean it not; I seek you a better husband.

MISTRESS QUICKLY.

That's my master, master doctor.

ANNE PAGE.

Alas, I had rather be set quick i'th'earth,
And bowl'd to death with turnips!

MISTRESS PAGE.

Come, trouble not yourself.—Good Master Fenton,
I will not be your friend nor enemy:
My daughter will I question how she loves you,
And as I find her, so am I affected.
Till then farewell, sir: she must needs go in;
Her father will be angry.

FENTON.

Farewell, gentle mistress.—Farewell, Nan.

[*Exeunt* MISTRESS PAGE *and* ANNE PAGE.

MISTRESS QUICKLY.

This is my doing now:—'Nay,' said I, 'will you cast away your child on a fool and a physician? Look on Master Fenton:'—this is my doing.

FENTON.

I thank thee; and I pray thee, once to-night
Give my sweet Nan this ring: there's for thy pains.

MISTRESS QUICKLY.

Now heaven send thee good fortune! [*Exit* FENTON.] A kind heart he hath: a woman would run through fire and water for such a kind heart. But yet I would my master had Mistress Anne; or I would Master Slender had her; or, in sooth, I would Master Fenton had her: I will do what I can for them all three; for so I have promised, and I'll be as good as my word; but speciously for Master Fenton. Well, I must of another errand to Sir John Falstaff from my two mistresses: what a beast am I to slack it! [*Exit.*

SCENE V.

A room in the Garter Inn.

Enter FALSTAFF *and* BARDOLPH.

SIR JOHN FALSTAFF.

BARDOLPH, I say,—

BARDOLPH.

Here, sir.

SIR JOHN FALSTAFF.

Go fetch me a quart of sack; put a toast in't. [*Exit* BARDOLPH.] Have I lived to be carried in a basket, like a barrow of butcher's offal, and to be thrown in the Thames? Well, if I be served such another trick, I'll have my brains ta'en out, and butter'd, and give them to a dog for a new-year's gift. The rogues slighted me into the river with as little remorse as they would have drown'd a bitch's blind puppies, fifteen i'th'litter: and you may know by my size that I have a kind of alacrity in sinking; if the bottom were as deep as hell, I should down. I had been drown'd, but that the shore was shelvy and shallow,—a death that I abhor; for the water swells a man; and what a thing should I have been when I had been swell'd! I should have been a mountain of mummy.

Enter BARDOLPH *with sack.*

BARDOLPH.

Here's Mistress Quickly, sir, to speak with you.

SIR JOHN FALSTAFF.

Come, let me pour in some sack to the Thames water; for my belly's as cold as if I had swallow'd snowballs for pills to cool the reins. Call her in.

BARDOLPH.

Come in, woman!

Enter MISTRESS QUICKLY.

MISTRESS QUICKLY.

By your leave; I cry you mercy:—give your worship good morrow.

SIR JOHN FALSTAFF.

Take away these chalices. Go brew me a pottle of sack finely.

BARDOLPH.

With eggs, sir?

SIR JOHN FALSTAFF.

Simple of itself; I'll no pullet-sperm in my brewage. [*Exit* BARDOLPH.] How now!

MISTRESS QUICKLY.

Marry, sir, I come to your worship from Mistress Ford.

SIR JOHN FALSTAFF.

Mistress Ford! I have had ford enough; I was thrown into the ford; I have my belly full of ford.

MISTRESS QUICKLY.

Alas the day! good heart, that was not her fault: she does so take on with her men; they mistook their erection.

SIR JOHN FALSTAFF.

So did I mine, to build upon a foolish woman's promise.

MISTRESS QUICKLY.

Well, she laments, sir, for it, that it would yearn your heart to see it. Her husband goes this morning a-birding; she desires you once more to come to her between eight and nine: I must carry her word quickly: she'll make you amends, I warrant you.

SIR JOHN FALSTAFF.

Well, I will visit her: tell her so; and bid her think what a man is: let her consider his frailty, and then judge of my merit.

MISTRESS QUICKLY.

I will tell her.

SIR JOHN FALSTAFF.

Do so. Between nine and ten, say'st thou?

MISTRESS QUICKLY.

Eight and nine, sir.

SIR JOHN FALSTAFF.

Well, be gone: I will not miss her.

MISTRESS QUICKLY.

Peace be with you, sir. [*Exit.*

SIR JOHN FALSTAFF.

I marvel I hear not of Master Brook; he sent me word to stay within: I like his money well.—O, here he comes.

Enter FORD *disguised.*

FORD.

Bless you, sir!

SIR JOHN FALSTAFF.

Now, Master Brook,—you come to know what hath pass'd between me and Ford's wife?

FORD.

That, indeed, Sir John, is my business.

SIR JOHN FALSTAFF.

Master Brook, I will not lie to you: I was at her house the hour she appointed me.

FORD.

And how sped you, sir?

SIR JOHN FALSTAFF.

Very ill-favour'dly, Master Brook.

FORD.

How so, sir? Did she change her determination?

SIR JOHN FALSTAFF.

No, Master Brook; but the peaking cornuto her husband, Master Brook, dwelling in a continual 'larum of jealousy, comes me in the instant of our encounter, after we had embraced, kiss'd, protested, and, as it were, spoke the prologue of our comedy; and at his heels a rabble of his companions, thither provoked and instigated by his distemper, and, forsooth, to search his house for his wife's love.

FORD.

What, while you were there?

SIR JOHN FALSTAFF.

While I was there.

FORD.

And did he search for you, and could not find you?

SIR JOHN FALSTAFF.

You shall hear. As good luck would have it, comes in one Mistress Page; gives intelligence of Ford's approach; and, in her invention and Ford's wife's distraction, they convey'd me into a buck-basket.

FORD.

A buck-basket!

SIR JOHN FALSTAFF.

By the Lord, a buck-basket!—ramm'd me in with foul shirts and smocks, socks, foul stockings, greasy napkins; that, Master Brook, there was the rankest compound of villainous smell that ever offended nostril.

FORD.

And how long lay you there?

SIR JOHN FALSTAFF.

Nay, you shall hear, Master Brook, what I have suffer'd to bring this woman to evil for your good. Being thus cramm'd in the basket, a couple of Ford's knaves, his hinds, were call'd forth by their mistress to carry me in the name of foul clothes to Datchet-lane: they took me on their shoulders; met the jealous knave their master in the door, who asked them once or twice what they had in their basket: I quaked for fear, lest the lunatic knave would have search'd it; but fate, ordaining he should be a cuckold, held his hand. Well: on went he for a search, and away went I for foul clothes. But mark the sequel, Master Brook: I suffer'd the pangs of three several deaths; first, an intolerable fright, to be detected with a jealous rotten bell-wether; next, to be compass'd, like a good bilbo, in the circumference of a peck, hilt to point, heel to head; and then, to be stopt in, like a strong distillation, with stinking clothes that fretted in their own grease: think of that,—a man of my kidney,—think of that,—that am as subject to heat as butter; a man of continual dissolution and thaw;—it was a miracle to scape suffocation. And in the height of this bath, when I was more than half stew'd in grease, like a Dutch dish, to be thrown into the Thames, and cool'd, glowing hot, in that surge, like a horse-shoe; think of that,—hissing hot,—think of that, Master Brook.

FORD.

In good sadness, sir, I am sorry that for my sake you have suffer'd all this. My suit, then, is desperate; you'll undertake her no more?

SIR JOHN FALSTAFF.

Master Brook, I will be thrown into Etna, as I have been into Thames, ere I will leave her thus. Her husband is this morning gone a-birding: I have received from her another embassy of meeting; 'twixt eight and nine is the hour, Master Brook.

FORD.

'Tis past eight already, sir.

SIR JOHN FALSTAFF.

Is it? I will then address me to my appointment. Come to me at your convenient leisure, and you shall know how I speed; and the conclusion shall be crown'd with your enjoying her. Adieu. You shall have her, Master Brook; Master Brook, you shall cuckold Ford. [*Exit.*

FORD.

Hum,—ha! is this a vision? is this a dream? do I sleep? Master Ford, awake! awake, Master Ford! there's a hole made in your best coat, Master Ford. This 'tis to be married! this 'tis to have linen and buck-baskets!—Well, I will proclaim myself what I am: I will now take the lecher; he is at my house; he cannot scape me; 'tis impossible he should; he cannot creep into a halfpenny purse, nor into a pepper-box: but, lest the devil that guides him should aid him, I will search impossible places. Though what I am I cannot avoid, yet to be what I would not shall not make me tame: if I have horns to make one mad, let the proverb go with me,—I'll be horn-mad. [*Exit.*

ACT IV. SCENE I.

The street.

Enter MISTRESS PAGE, MISTRESS QUICKLY, *and* WILLIAM.

MISTRESS PAGE.

Is he at Master Ford's already, think'st thou?

MISTRESS QUICKLY.

Sure he is by this, or will be presently: but, truly, he is very courageous mad about his throwing into the water. Mistress Ford desires you to come suddenly.

MISTRESS PAGE.

I'll be with her by and by; I'll but bring my young man here to school. Look, where his master comes: 'tis a playing-day, I see.

Enter SIR HUGH EVANS.

How now, Sir Hugh! no school to-day?

SIR HUGH EVANS.

No; Master Slender is let the boys leave to play.

MISTRESS QUICKLY.

Blessing of his heart!

MISTRESS PAGE.

Sir Hugh, my husband says my son profits nothing in the world at his book. I pray you, ask him some questions in his accidence.

SIR HUGH EVANS.

Come hither, William; hold up your head; come.

MISTRESS PAGE.

Come on, sirrah; hold up your head; answer your master, be not afraid.

SIR HUGH EVANS.

William, how many numbers is in nouns?

WILLIAM PAGE.

Two.

MISTRESS QUICKLY.

Truly, I thought there had been one number more, because they say, Od's-nouns.

SIR HUGH EVANS.

Peace your tattlings.—What is *fair*, William?

WILLIAM PAGE.

Pulcher.

MISTRESS QUICKLY.

Polecats! there are fairer things than polecats, sure.

SIR HUGH EVANS.

You are a very simplicity oman: I pray you, peace.—What is *lapis*, William?

WILLIAM PAGE.

A stone.

SIR HUGH EVANS.

And what is a stone, William?

WILLIAM PAGE.

A pebble.

SIR HUGH EVANS.

No, it is *lapis:* I pray you, remember in your prain.

WILLIAM PAGE.

Lapis.

SIR HUGH EVANS.

That is a good William. What is he, William, that does lend articles?

WILLIAM PAGE.

Articles are borrowed of the pronoun, and be thus declined, *Singulariter, nominativo, hic, hæc, hoc.*

SIR HUGH EVANS.

Nominativo, hig, hag, hog;—pray you, mark: *genitivo, hujus.* Well, what is your accusative case?

WILLIAM PAGE.

Accusativo, hinc.

SIR HUGH EVANS.

I pray you, have your remembrance, child; *accusativo, hung, hang, hog.*

MISTRESS QUICKLY.

Hang-hog is Latin for bacon, I warrant you.

SIR HUGH EVANS.

Leave your prabbles, oman.—What is the focative case, William?

WILLIAM PAGE.

O,—vocativo, O.

SIR HUGH EVANS.

Remember, William; focative is *caret.*

MISTRESS QUICKLY.

And that's a good root.

SIR HUGH EVANS.

Oman, forbear.

MISTRESS PAGE.

Peace!

SIR HUGH EVANS.
What is your genitive case plural, William?

WILLIAM PAGE.
Genitive case!

SIR HUGH EVANS.
Ay.

WILLIAM PAGE.
Genitivo,—horum, harum, horum.

MISTRESS QUICKLY.
Vengeance of Jenny's case! fie on her!—never name her, child, if she be a whore.

SIR HUGH EVANS.
For shame, oman.

MISTRESS QUICKLY.
You do ill to teach the child such words:—he teaches him to hick and to hack, which they'll do fast enough of themselves, and to call whorum:—fie upon you!

SIR HUGH EVANS.
Oman, art thou lunatics? hast thou no understandings for thy cases, and the numbers of the genders? Thou art as foolish Christian creatures as I would desires.

MISTRESS PAGE.
Prithee, hold thy peace.

SIR HUGH EVANS.
Show me now, William, some declensions of your pronouns.

WILLIAM PAGE.
Forsooth, I have forgot.

SIR HUGH EVANS.
It is *qui, quæ, quod:* if you forget your *quies*, your *quæs*, and your *quods*, you must be preeches. Go your ways, and play; go.

MISTRESS PAGE.
He is a better scholar than I thought he was.

SIR HUGH EVANS.
He is a good sprag memory. Farewell, Mistress Page.

MISTRESS PAGE.
Adieu, good Sir Hugh. [*Exit* EVANS.]—Get you home, boy.—Come, we stay too long. [*Exeunt.*

SCENE II.

A room in FORD'S *house.*

Enter FALSTAFF *and* MISTRESS FORD.

SIR JOHN FALSTAFF.
MISTRESS FORD, your sorrow hath eaten up my sufferance. I see you are obsequious in your love, and I profess requital to a hair's breadth; not only, Mistress Ford, in the simple office of love, but in all the accoutrement, complement, and ceremony of it. But are you sure of your husband now?

MISTRESS FORD.
He's a-birding, sweet Sir John.

MISTRESS PAGE [*within*].
What, ho, gossip Ford! what, ho!

MISTRESS FORD.
Step into the chamber, Sir John.
[*Exit* FALSTAFF.

Enter MISTRESS PAGE.

MISTRESS PAGE.
How now, sweetheart! who's at home besides yourself?

MISTRESS FORD.
Why, none but mine own people.

MISTRESS PAGE.
Indeed!

MISTRESS FORD.
No, certainly.—[*Aside to her*] Speak louder.

MISTRESS PAGE.
Truly, I am so glad you have nobody here.

MISTRESS FORD.
Why?

MISTRESS PAGE.
Why, woman, your husband is in his old lunes again: he so takes on yonder with my husband; so rails against all married mankind; so curses all Eve's daughters, of what complexion soever; and so buffets himself on the forehead, crying, 'Peer out, peer out!' that any madness I ever yet beheld seem'd but tameness, civility, and patience, to this his distemper he is in now: I am glad the fat knight is not here.

MISTRESS FORD.
Why, does he talk of him?

MISTRESS PAGE.
Of none but him; and swears he was carried out, the last time he search'd for him, in a basket; protests to my husband he is now here; and hath drawn him and the rest of their company from their sport, to make another experiment of his suspicion: but I am glad the knight is not here; now he shall see his own foolery.

MISTRESS FORD.
How near is he, Mistress Page?

MISTRESS PAGE.
Hard by; at street end; he will be here anon.

MISTRESS FORD.
I am undone!—the knight is here.

MISTRESS PAGE.
Why, then, you are utterly shamed, and he's but a dead man. What a woman are you!—Away with him, away with him! better shame than murder.

MISTRESS FORD.
Which way should he go? how should I bestow him? Shall I put him into the basket again?

Enter FALSTAFF.

SIR JOHN FALSTAFF.
No, I'll come no more i'th'basket. May I not go out ere he come?

MISTRESS PAGE.
Alas, three of Master Ford's brothers watch the door with pistols, that none shall issue out; otherwise you might slip away ere he came. But what make you here?

SIR JOHN FALSTAFF.
What shall I do?—I'll creep up into the chimney.

MISTRESS FORD.
There they always use to discharge their birding-pieces.

MISTRESS PAGE.
Creep into the kiln-hole.

SIR JOHN FALSTAFF.
Where is it?

MISTRESS FORD.
He will seek there, on my word. Neither press, coffer, chest, trunk, well, vault, but he hath an abstract for the remembrance of such places, and

goes to them by his note: there is no hiding you in the house.

SIR JOHN FALSTAFF.

I'll go out, then.

MISTRESS PAGE.

If you go out in your own semblance, you die, Sir John. Unless you go out disguised,—

MISTRESS FORD.

How might we disguise him?

MISTRESS PAGE.

Alas the day, I know not! There is no woman's gown big enough for him; otherwise he might put on a hat, a muffler, and a kerchief, and so escape.

SIR JOHN FALSTAFF.

Good hearts, devise something: any extremity rather than a mischief.

MISTRESS FORD.

My maid's aunt, the fat woman of Brainford, has a gown above.

MISTRESS PAGE.

On my word, it will serve him; she's as big as he is: and there's her thrumm'd hat, and her muffler too.—Run up, Sir John.

MISTRESS FORD.

Go, go, sweet Sir John: Mistress Page and I will look some linen for your head.

MISTRESS PAGE.

Quick, quick! we'll come dress you straight: put on the gown the while. [*Exit* FALSTAFF.

MISTRESS FORD.

I would my husband would meet him in this shape: he cannot abide the old woman of Brainford; he swears she's a witch; forbade her my house, and hath threaten'd to beat her.

MISTRESS PAGE.

Heaven guide him to thy husband's cudgel, and the devil guide his cudgel afterwards!

MISTRESS FORD.

But is my husband coming?

MISTRESS PAGE.

Ay, in good sadness, is he; and talks of the basket too, howsoever he hath had intelligence.

MISTRESS FORD.

We'll try that; for I'll appoint my men to carry the basket again, to meet him at the door with it, as they did last time.

MISTRESS PAGE.

Nay, but he'll be here presently: let's go dress him like the witch of Brainford.

MISTRESS FORD.

I'll first direct my men what they shall do with the basket. Go up; I'll bring linen for him straight. [*Exit.*

MISTRESS PAGE.

Hang him, dishonest varlet! we cannot misuse him enough.
We'll leave a proof, by that which we will do,
Wives may be merry, and yet honest too:
We do not act that often jest and laugh;
'Tis old, but true,—Still swine eats all the draff.
[*Exit.*

Enter MISTRESS FORD *with two* SERVANTS.

MISTRESS FORD.

Go, sirs, take the basket again on your shoulders: your master is hard at door; if he bid you set it down, obey him: quickly, dispatch. [*Exit.*

FIRST SERVANT.

Come, come, take it up.

SECOND SERVANT.

Pray heaven it be not full of knight again.

FIRST SERVANT.

I hope not; I had as lief bear so much lead.

Enter FORD, PAGE, SHALLOW, CAIUS, *and* SIR HUGH EVANS.

FORD.

Ay, but if it prove true, Master Page, have you any way then to unfool me again?—Set down the basket, villain!—Somebody call my wife.—You, youth in a basket, come out here!—O you pandarly rascals! there's a knot, a ging, a pack, a conspiracy against me: now shall the devil be shamed.—What, wife, I say! come, come forth! behold what honest clothes you send forth to bleaching!

MISTRESS PAGE.

Why, this passes! Master Ford, you are not to go loose any longer; you must be pinion'd.

SIR HUGH EVANS.

Why, this is lunatics! this is mad as a mad dog!

SHALLOW.

Indeed, Master Ford, this is not well; indeed.

FORD.

So say I too, sir.

Enter MISTRESS FORD.

Come hither, Mistress Ford; Mistress Ford, the honest woman, the modest wife, the virtuous creature, that hath the jealous fool to her husband! —I suspect without cause, mistress, do I?

MISTRESS FORD.

Heaven be my witness you do, if you suspect me in any dishonesty.

FORD.

Well said, brazen-face! hold it out.—Come forth, sirrah! [*Pulling the clothes out of the basket.*

PAGE.

This passes!

MISTRESS FORD.

Are you not ashamed? let the clothes alone.

FORD.

I shall find you anon.

SIR HUGH EVANS.

'Tis unreasonable! Will you take up your wife's clothes? Come away.

FORD.

Empty the basket, I say!

MISTRESS FORD.

Why, man, why,—

FORD.

Master Page, as I am a man, there was one convey'd out of my house yesterday in this basket: why may not he be there again? In my house I am sure he is: my intelligence is true; my jealousy is reasonable.—Pluck me out all the linen.

MISTRESS FORD.

If you find a man there, he shall die a flea's death.

PAGE.

Here's no man.

SHALLOW.

By my fidelity, this is not well, Master Ford; this wrongs you.

SIR HUGH EVANS.

Master Ford, you must pray, and not follow the imaginations of your own heart: this is jealousies.

FORD.

Well, he's not here I seek for.

PAGE.

No, nor nowhere else but in your brain.

FORD.

Help to search my house this one time. If I find not what I seek, show no colour for my extremity; let me for ever be your table-sport; let them say of me, 'As jealous as Ford, that search'd a hollow walnut for his wife's leman.' Satisfy me once more; once more search with me.

MISTRESS FORD.

What, ho, Mistress Page! come you and the old woman down; my husband will come into the chamber.

FORD.

Old woman! what old woman's that?

MISTRESS FORD.

Why it is my maid's aunt of Brainford.

FORD.

A witch, a quean, an old cozening quean! Have I not forbid her my house? She comes of errands, does she? We are simple men; we do not know what's brought to pass under the profession of fortune-telling. She works by charms, by spells, by th'figure; and such daubery as this is beyond our element; we know nothing.—Come down, you witch, you hag, you; come down, I say!

MISTRESS FORD.

Nay, good, sweet husband,—Good gentlemen, let him not strike the old woman.

Enter FALSTAFF *in woman's clothes, led by* MISTRESS PAGE.

MISTRESS PAGE.

Come, Mother Prat; come, give me your hand.

FORD.

I'll prat her.—[*Beating him*] Out of my door, you witch, you rag, you baggage, you polecat, you ronyon! out, out! I'll conjure you, I'll fortune-tell you. [*Exit* FALSTAFF.

MISTRESS PAGE.

Are you not ashamed? I think you have kill'd the poor woman.

MISTRESS FORD.

Nay, he will do it.—'Tis a goodly credit for you.

FORD.

Hang her, witch!

SIR HUGH EVANS.

By yea and no, I think the oman is a witch indeed: I like not when a oman has a great peard: I spy a great peard under her muffler.

FORD.

Will you follow, gentlemen? I beseech you, follow; see but the issue of my jealousy: if I cry out thus upon no trail, never trust me when I open again.

PAGE.

Let's obey his humour a little further: come, gentlemen.

[*Exeunt* FORD, PAGE, SHALLOW, CAIUS, *and* EVANS.

MISTRESS PAGE.

Trust me, he beat him most pitifully.

MISTRESS FORD.

Nay, by th'mass, that he did not; he beat him most unpitifully methought.

MISTRESS PAGE.

I'll have the cudgel hallow'd, and hung o'er the altar; it hath done meritorious service.

MISTRESS FORD.

What think you? may we, with the warrant of womanhood and the witness of a good conscience, pursue him with any further revenge?

MISTRESS PAGE.

The spirit of wantonness is, sure, scared out of him: if the devil have him not in fee-simple, with fine and recovery, he will never, I think, in the way of waste, attempt us again.

MISTRESS FORD.

Shall we tell our husbands how we have served him?

MISTRESS PAGE.

Yes, by all means; if it be but to scrape the figures out of your husband's brains. If they can find in their hearts the poor unvirtuous fat knight shall be any further afflicted, we two will still be the ministers.

MISTRESS FORD.

I'll warrant they'll have him publicly shamed: and methinks there would be no period to the jest, should he not be publicly shamed.

MISTRESS PAGE.

Come, to the forge with it, then; shape it: I would not have things cool. [*Exeunt.*

SCENE III.

A room in the Garter Inn.

Enter HOST *and* BARDOLPH.

BARDOLPH.

SIR, the Germans desire to have three of your horses: the duke himself will be to-morrow at court, and they are going to meet him.

HOST.

What duke should that be comes so secretly? I hear not of him in the court. Let me speak with the gentlemen: they speak English?

BARDOLPH.

Ay, sir; I'll call them to you.

HOST.

They shall have my horses; but I'll make them pay; I'll sauce them: they have had my house a week at command; I have turn'd away my other guests: they must come off; I'll sauce them. Come. [*Exeunt.*

SCENE IV.

A room in FORD'S *house.*

Enter PAGE, FORD, MISTRESS PAGE, MISTRESS FORD, *and* SIR HUGH EVANS.

SIR HUGH EVANS.

'TIS one of the best discretions of a oman as ever I did look upon.

PAGE.

And did he send you both these letters at an instant?

MISTRESS PAGE.

Within a quarter of an hour.

FORD.

Pardon me, wife. Henceforth do what thou wilt;
I rather will suspect the sun with cold

Than thee with wantonness: now doth thy honour stand,
In him that was of late an heretic,
As firm as faith.

PAGE.
'Tis well, 'tis well; no more:
Be not as extreme in submission
As in offence.
But let our plot go forward: let our wives
Yet once again, to make us public sport,
Appoint a meeting with this old fat fellow,
Where we may take him, and disgrace him for it.

FORD.
There is no better way than that they spoke of.

PAGE.
How! to send him word they'll meet him in the Park at midnight? Fie, fie! he'll never come.

SIR HUGH EVANS.
You say he has been thrown in the rivers; and has been grievously peaten, as an old oman: methinks there should be terrors in him that he should not come; methinks his flesh is punish'd, he shall have no desires.

PAGE.
So think I too.

MISTRESS FORD.
Devise but how you'll use him when he comes,
And let us two devise to bring him thither.

MISTRESS PAGE.
There is an old tale goes that Herne the Hunter,
Sometime a keeper here in Windsor forest,
Doth all the winter-time, at still midnight,
Walk round about an oak, with great ragg'd horns;
And there he blasts the tree, and takes the cattle,
And makes milch-kine yield blood, and shakes a chain
In a most hideous and dreadful manner:
You have heard of such a spirit; and well you know
The superstitious idle-headed eld
Received, and did deliver to our age,
This tale of Herne the hunter for a truth.

PAGE.
Why, yet there want not many that do fear
In deep of night to walk by this Herne's oak:
But what of this?

MISTRESS FORD.
Marry, this is our device;
That Falstaff at that oak shall meet with us,
Disguised like Herne, with huge horns on his head.

PAGE.
Well, let it not be doubted but he'll come:
And in this shape when you have brought him thither,
What shall be done with him? what is your plot?

MISTRESS PAGE.
That likewise have we thought upon, and thus:
Nan Page my daughter, and my little son,
And three or four more of their growth, we'll dress
Like urchins, ouphs, and fairies, green and white,
With rounds of waxen tapers on their heads,
And rattles in their hands: upon a sudden,
As Falstaff, she, and I, are newly met,
Let them from forth a sawpit rush at once
With some diffused song: upon their sight,
We two in great amazedness will fly:
Then let them all encircle him about,
And, fairy-like, to-pinch the unclean knight;
And ask him why, that hour of fairy revel,
In their so sacred paths he dares to tread
In shape profane.

MISTRESS FORD.
And till he tell the truth,
Let the supposed fairies pinch him sound,
And burn him with their tapers.

MISTRESS PAGE.
The truth being known,
We'll all present ourselves, dis-horn the spirit,
And mock him home to Windsor.

FORD.
The children must
Be practised well to this, or they'll ne'er do't.

SIR HUGH EVANS.
I will teach the children their behaviours; and I will be like a jack-an-apes also, to burn the knight with my taber.

FORD.
That will be excellent. I'll go buy them vizards.

MISTRESS PAGE.
My Nan shall be the queen of all the fairies,
Finely attired in a robe of white.

PAGE.
That silk will I go buy:—[*aside*] and in that time
Shall Master Slender steal my Nan away,
And marry her at Eton.—Go send to Falstaff straight.

FORD.
Nay, I'll to him again in name of Brook:
He'll tell me all his purpose: sure, he'll come.

MISTRESS PAGE.
Fear not you that. Go get us properties
And tricking for our fairies.

SIR HUGH EVANS.
Let us about it: it is admirable pleasures and fery honest knaveries.

[*Exeunt* PAGE, FORD, *and* EVANS.

MISTRESS PAGE.
Go, Mistress Ford,
Send quickly to Sir John, to know his mind.

[*Exit* MISTRESS FORD.

I'll to the doctor: he hath my good will,
And none but he, to marry with Nan Page.
That Slender, though well landed, is an idiot;
And he my husband best of all affects.
The doctor is well money'd, and his friends
Potent at court: he, none but he, shall have her,
Though twenty thousand worthier come to crave her.

[*Exit.*

SCENE V.

A room in the Garter Inn.

Enter HOST *and* SIMPLE.

HOST.
WHAT wouldst thou have, boor? what, thick-skin? speak, breathe, discuss; brief, short, quick, snap.

SIMPLE.
Marry, sir, I come to speak with Sir John Falstaff from Master Slender.

HOST.

There's his chamber, his house, his castle, his standing-bed, and truckle-bed; 'tis painted about with the story of the Prodigal, fresh and new. Go knock and call; he'll speak like an Anthropophaginian unto thee: knock, I say.

SIMPLE.

There's an old woman, a fat woman, gone up into his chamber: I'll be so bold as stay, sir, till she come down; I come to speak with her, indeed.

HOST.

Ha! a fat woman! the knight may be robb'd: I'll call.—Bully knight! bully Sir John! speak from thy lungs military: art thou there? it is thine host, thine Ephesian, calls.

SIR JOHN FALSTAFF [*above*].

How now, mine host!

HOST.

Here's a Bohemian-Tartar tarries the coming down of thy fat woman. Let her descend, bully, let her descend; my chambers are honourable: fie! privacy? fie!

Enter FALSTAFF.

SIR JOHN FALSTAFF.

There was, mine host, an old fat woman even now with me; but she's gone.

SIMPLE.

Pray you, sir, was't not the wise-woman of Brainford?

SIR JOHN FALSTAFF.

Ay, marry, was it, mussel-shell: what would you with her?

SIMPLE.

My master, sir, Master Slender, sent to her, seeing her go through the streets, to know, sir, whether one Nym, sir, that beguiled him of a chain, had the chain or no.

SIR JOHN FALSTAFF.

I spake with the old woman about it.

SIMPLE.

And what says she, I pray, sir?

SIR JOHN FALSTAFF.

Marry, she says that the very same man that beguiled Master Slender of his chain cozen'd him of it.

SIMPLE.

I would I could have spoken with the woman herself; I had other things to have spoken with her too from him.

SIR JOHN FALSTAFF.

What are they? let us know.

HOST.

Ay, come; quick.

SIMPLE.

I may not conceal them, sir.

HOST.

Conceal them, or thou diest.

SIMPLE.

Why, sir, they were nothing but about Mistress Anne Page; to know if it were my master's fortune to have her or no.

SIR JOHN FALSTAFF.

'Tis, 'tis his fortune.

SIMPLE.

What, sir?

SIR JOHN FALSTAFF.

To have her,—or no. Go; say the woman told me so.

SIMPLE.

May I be bold to say so, sir?

SIR JOHN FALSTAFF.

Ay, sir Tike!—who more bold?

SIMPLE.

I thank your worship: I shall make my master glad with these tidings. [*Exit.*

HOST.

Thou art clerkly, thou art clerkly, Sir John. Was there a wise woman with thee?

SIR JOHN FALSTAFF.

Ay, that there was, mine host; one that hath taught me more wit than ever I learn'd before in my life; and I paid nothing for it neither, but was paid for my learning.

Enter BARDOLPH.

BARDOLPH.

Out, alas, sir! cozenage, mere cozenage!

HOST.

Where be my horses? speak well of them, varletto.

BARDOLPH.

Run away with the cozeners: for so soon as I came beyond Eton, they threw me off, from behind one of them, in a slough of mire; and set spurs and away, like three German devils, three Dr. Faustuses.

HOST.

They are gone but to meet the duke, villain: do not say they be fled; Germans are honest men.

Enter SIR HUGH EVANS.

SIR HUGH EVANS.

Where is mine host?

HOST.

What is the matter, sir?

SIR HUGH EVANS.

Have a care of your entertainments: there is a friend of mine come to town, tells me there is three cozen-germans that has cozen'd all the hosts of Readins, of Maidenhead, of Colebrook, of horses and money. I tell you for good will, look you: you are wise, and full of gibes and vlouting-stogs, and 'tis not convenient you should be cozen'd. Fare you well. [*Exit.*

Enter DOCTOR CAIUS.

DOCTOR CAIUS.

Vere is mine host de Jarteer?

HOST.

Here, master doctor, in perplexity and doubtful dilemma.

DOCTOR CAIUS.

I cannot tell vat is dat: but it is tell-a me dat you make grand preparation for a duke de Jamany: by my trot, dere is no duke dat de court is know to come. I tell you for good vill: adieu. [*Exit.*

HOST.

Hue and cry, villain, go!—Assist me, knight.—I am undone!—Fly, run, hue and cry, villain!—I am undone! [*Exeunt* HOST *and* BARDOLPH.

SIR JOHN FALSTAFF.

I would all the world might be cozen'd; for I have been cozen'd and beaten too. If it should come to the ear of the court, how I have been transform'd, and how my transformation hath been wash'd and cudgell'd, they would melt me out of my fat drop by drop, and liquor fishermen's boots with me: I warrant they would whip me with their fine wits till I were as crest-fallen as a dried pear. I never prosper'd since I forswore myself at primero. Well, if my wind were but long enough to say my prayers, I would repent.

Enter MISTRESS QUICKLY.

Now, whence come you?

MISTRESS QUICKLY.

From the two parties, forsooth.

SIR JOHN FALSTAFF.

The devil take one party, and his dam the other! and so they shall be both bestow'd. I have suffer'd more for their sakes, more than the villainous inconstancy of man's disposition is able to bear.

MISTRESS QUICKLY.

And have not they suffer'd? Yes, I warrant; speciously one of them; Mistress Ford, good heart, is beaten black and blue, that you cannot see a white spot about her.

SIR JOHN FALSTAFF.

What tell'st thou me of black and blue? I was beaten myself into all the colours of the rainbow; and I was like to be apprehended for the witch of Brainford: but that my admirable dexterity of wit, my counterfeiting the action of an old woman, deliver'd me, the knave constable had set me i' th' stocks, i' th' common stocks, for a witch.

MISTRESS QUICKLY.

Sir, let me speak with you in your chamber: you shall hear how things go; and, I warrant, to your content. Here is a letter will say somewhat. Good hearts, what ado here is to bring you together! Sure, one of you does not serve heaven well, that you are so cross'd.

SIR JOHN FALSTAFF.

Come up into my chamber. [*Exeunt.*

SCENE VI.

Another room in the Garter Inn.

Enter FENTON *and* HOST.

HOST.

MASTER FENTON, talk not to me; my mind is heavy: I will give over all.

FENTON.

Yet hear me speak. Assist me in my purpose,
And, as I am a gentleman, I'll give thee
A hundred pound in gold more than your loss.

HOST.

I will hear you, Master Fenton; and I will at the least keep your counsel.

FENTON.

From time to time I have acquainted you
With the dear love I bear to fair Anne Page;
Who mutually hath answer'd my affection,
So far forth as herself might be her chooser,
Even to my wish: I have a letter from her
Of such contents as you will wonder at;
The mirth whereof so larded with my matter,
That neither singly can be manifested
Without the show of both;—wherein fat Falstaff
Hath a great scene: the image of the jest
I'll show you here at large. Hark, good mine host.
To-night at Herne's oak, just 'twixt twelve and one,
Must my sweet Nan present the Fairy Queen;
The purpose why, is here: in which disguise,
While other jests are something rank on foot,
Her father hath commanded her to slip
Away with Slender, and with him at Eton
Immediately to marry: she hath consented:
Now, sir,
Her mother, even strong against that match,
And firm for Doctor Caius, hath appointed
That he shall likewise shuffle her away,
While other sports are tasking of their minds,
And at the deanery, where a priest attends,
Straight marry her: to this her mother's plot
She, seemingly obedient, likewise hath
Made promise to the doctor.—Now, thus it rests:
Her father means she shall be all in white;
And in that habit, when Slender sees his time
To take her by the hand, and bid her go,
She shall go with him: her mother hath intended,
The better to denote her to the doctor,—
For they must all be mask'd and vizarded,—
That quaint in green she shall be loose enrobed,
With ribands pendent, flaring 'bout her head;
And when the doctor spies his vantage ripe,
To pinch her by the hand, and, on that token,
The maid hath given consent to go with him.

HOST.

Which means she to deceive, father or mother?

FENTON.

Both, my good host, to go along with me:
And here it rests,—that you'll procure the vicar
To stay for me at church 'twixt twelve and one,
And, in the lawful name of marrying,
To give our hearts united ceremony.

HOST.

Well, husband your device; I'll to the vicar:
Bring you the maid, you shall not lack a priest.

FENTON.

So shall I evermore be bound to thee;
Besides, I'll make a present recompense. [*Exeunt.*

ACT V. SCENE I.

A room in the Garter Inn.

Enter FALSTAFF *and* MISTRESS QUICKLY.

SIR JOHN FALSTAFF.

PRITHEE, no more prattling; go:—I'll hold. This is the third time; I hope good luck lies in odd numbers. Away! go. They say there is divinity in odd numbers, either in nativity, chance, or death. Away!

MISTRESS QUICKLY.

I'll provide you a chain; and I'll do what I can to get you a pair of horns.

SIR JOHN FALSTAFF.

Away, I say; time wears: hold up your head, and mince. [*Exit* MISTRESS QUICKLY.

Enter FORD *disguised.*

How now, Master Brook! Master Brook, the matter will be known to-night, or never. Be you in the Park about midnight, at Herne's oak, and you shall see wonders.

FORD.

Went you not to her yesterday, sir, as you told me you had appointed?

SIR JOHN FALSTAFF.

I went to her, Master Brook, as you see, like a poor old man: but I came from her, Master Brook, like a poor old woman. That same knave Ford, her husband, hath the finest mad devil of jealousy in him, Master Brook, that ever govern'd frenzy:—I will tell you:—he beat me grievously, in the shape of a woman; for in the shape of man, Master Brook, I fear not Goliath with a weaver's beam; because I know also life is a shuttle. I am in haste; go along with me: I'll tell you all, Master Brook. Since I pluck'd geese, play'd truant, and whipp'd top, I knew not what 'twas to be beaten till lately. Follow me: I'll tell you strange things of this knave Ford; on whom to-night I will be revenged, and I will deliver his wife into your hand. Follow:—strange things in hand, Master Brook:—follow. [*Exeunt.*

SCENE II.

Windsor Park.

Enter PAGE, SHALLOW, *and* SLENDER.

PAGE.

COME, come; we'll couch i'th'castle-ditch till we see the light of our fairies.—Remember, son Slender, my daughter.

SLENDER.

Ay, forsooth; I have spoke with her, and we have a nay-word how to know one another: I come to her in white, and cry 'mum;' she cries 'budget;' and by that we know one another.

SHALLOW.

That's good too; but what needs either your 'mum' or her 'budget'? the white will decipher her well enough.—It hath struck ten o'clock.

PAGE.

The night is dark; light and spirits will become it well. Heaven prosper our sport! No man means evil but the devil, and we shall know him by his horns. Let's away; follow me. [*Exeunt.*

SCENE III.

A street leading to the Park.

Enter MISTRESS PAGE, MISTRESS FORD, *and* DOCTOR CAIUS.

MISTRESS PAGE.

MASTER doctor, my daughter is in green: when you see your time, take her by the hand, away with her to the deanery, and dispatch it quickly. Go before into the Park: we two must go together.

DOCTOR CAIUS.

I know vat I have to do. Adieu.

MISTRESS PAGE.

Fare you well, sir. [*Exit* CAIUS.]—My husband will not rejoice so much at the abuse of Falstaff as he will chafe at the doctor's marrying my daughter: but 'tis no matter; better a little chiding than a great deal of heart-break.

MISTRESS FORD.

Where is Nan now and her troop of fairies? and the Welsh devil Hugh?

MISTRESS PAGE.

They are all couch'd in a pit hard by Herne's oak, with obscured lights; which, at the very instant of Falstaff's and our meeting, they will at once display to the night.

MISTRESS FORD.

That cannot choose but amaze him.

MISTRESS PAGE.

If he be not amazed, he will be mock'd; if he be amazed, he will every way be mock'd.

MISTRESS FORD.

We'll betray him finely.

MISTRESS PAGE.

Against such lewdsters and their lechery
Those that betray them do no treachery.

MISTRESS FORD.

The hour draws on. To the oak, to the oak! [*Exeunt.*

SCENE IV.

Windsor Park.

Enter SIR HUGH EVANS *disguised as a Satyr, with* ANNE PAGE *and others as Fairies.*

SIR HUGH EVANS.

TRIB, trib, fairies; come; and remember your parts: be pold, I pray you; follow me into the pit; and when I give the watch-ords, do as I pid you: come, come; trib, trib. [*Exeunt.*

SCENE V.

Another part of the Park.

Enter FALSTAFF, *with a buck's head upon him.*

SIR JOHN FALSTAFF.

THE Windsor bell hath struck twelve; the minute draws on. Now, the hot-blooded gods assist me!—Remember, Jove, thou wast a bull for thy Europa; love set on thy horns:—O powerful love! that, in some respects, makes a beast a man; in some other, a man a beast.—You were also, Jupiter, a swan for the love of Leda:—O omnipotent love! how near the god drew to the complexion of a goose!—A fault done first in the form of a beast;—O Jove, a beastly fault! and then another fault in the semblance of a fowl;—think on't, Jove; a foul fault! When gods have hot backs, what shall poor men do? For me, I am here a Windsor stag; and the fattest, I think, i'th'forest.—Send me a cool rut-time, Jove, or who can blame me to piss my tallow?—Who comes here? my doe?

Enter MISTRESS FORD *and* MISTRESS PAGE.

MISTRESS FORD.

Sir John! art thou there, my deer? my male deer?

SIR JOHN FALSTAFF.

My doe with the black scut!—Let the sky rain potatoes; let it thunder to the tune of *Green sleeves*, hail kissing-comfits, and snow eryngoes; let there come a tempest of provocation, I will shelter me here. [*Embracing her.*

MISTRESS FORD.

Mistress Page is come with me, sweetheart.

SIR JOHN FALSTAFF.

Divide me like a bribe-buck, each a haunch: I will keep my sides to myself, my shoulders for the fellow of this walk, and my horns I bequeath your husbands. Am I a woodman, ha? Speak I like Herne the hunter?—Why, now is Cupid a child of conscience; he makes restitution. As I am a true spirit, welcome! [*Noise of horns within.*

MISTRESS PAGE.

Alas, what noise?

MISTRESS FORD.

Heaven forgive our sins!

SIR JOHN FALSTAFF.

What should this be?

MISTRESS FORD *and* MISTRESS PAGE.

Away, away! [*They run off.*

SIR JOHN FALSTAFF.

I think the devil will not have me damn'd, lest the oil that's in me should set hell on fire; he would never else cross me thus.

Enter SIR HUGH EVANS *as a Satyr,* PISTOL *as Hobgoblin,* ANNE PAGE *as Fairy Queen, and others as fairies.*

ANNE PAGE.

Fairies, black, gray, green, and white,
You moonshine revellers, and shades of night,
You orphan heirs of fixed destiny,
Attend your office and your quality.—
Crier Hobgoblin, make the fairy oyes.

PISTOL.

Elves, list your names; silence, you airy toys.
Cricket, to Windsor chimneys shalt thou leap:
Where fires thou find'st unraked and hearths unswept,
There pinch the maids as blue as bilberry:
Our radiant queen hates sluts and sluttery.

SIR JOHN FALSTAFF.

They are fairies; he that speaks to them shall die:
I'll wink and couch: no man their works must eye. [*Lies down upon his face.*

SIR HUGH EVANS.

Where's Pead?—Go you, and where you find a maid
That, ere she sleep, has thrice her prayers said,
Raise up the organs of her fantasy,
Sleep she as sound as careless infancy:
But those as sleep and think not on their sins,
Pinch them, arms, legs, backs, shoulders, sides, and shins.

ANNE PAGE.

About, about;
Search Windsor Castle, elves, within and out:
Strew good luck, ouphs, on every sacred room;
That it may stand till the perpetual doom,
In site as wholesome as in state 'tis fit,
Worthy the owner, and the owner it.
The several chairs of order look you scour
With juice of balm and every precious flower:
Each fair instalment, coat, and several crest,
With loyal blazon, evermore be blest!
And nightly, meadow-fairies, look you sing,
Like to the Garter's compass, in a ring:
Th' expressure that it bears, green let it be,
More fertile-fresh than all the field to see;
And *Honi soit qui mal y pense* write
In emerald tufts, flowers purple, blue, and white;
Like sapphire, pearl, and rich embroidery,
Buckled below fair knighthood's bending knee:—
Fairies use flowers for their charactery.
Away; disperse: but till 'tis one o'clock,
Our dance of custom round about the oak
Of Herne the hunter let us not forget.

SIR HUGH EVANS.

Pray you, lock hand in hand; yourselves in order set;
And twenty glow-worms shall our lanterns be,
To guide our measure round about the tree.—
But stay; I smell a man of middle-earth.

SIR JOHN FALSTAFF.

Heavens defend me from that Welsh fairy, lest he transform me to a piece of cheese!

PISTOL.

Vile worm, thou wast o'erlook'd even in thy birth.

ANNE PAGE.

With trial-fire touch me his finger-end:
If he be chaste, the flame will back descend,
And turn him to no pain; but if he start,
It is the flesh of a corrupted heart.

PISTOL.

A trial, come.

SIR HUGH EVANS.

Come, will this wood take fire?

[*They put the tapers to his fingers and he starts.*

SIR JOHN FALSTAFF.

O, O, O!

ANNE PAGE.

Corrupt, corrupt, and tainted in desire!—
About him, fairies; sing a scornful rhyme;
And, as you trip, still pinch him to your time.

SIR HUGH EVANS.

It is right; indeed he is full of lecheries and iniquity.

Song.

Fie on sinful fantasy!
Fie on lust and luxury!
Lust is but a bloody fire,
Kindled with unchaste desire,
Fed in heart; whose flames aspire,
As thoughts do blow them, higher and higher.
Pinch him, fairies, mutually;
Pinch him for his villainy;
Pinch him, and burn him, and turn him about,
Till candles and starlight and moonshine be out.

Here they pinch him and sing about him, and the DOCTOR *comes one way, and steals away a Boy in green;* SLENDER *another way, and takes off a Boy in white; and* FENTON *steals* ANNE PAGE. *A noise of hunting is made within. All the Fairies run away.* FALSTAFF *pulls off his buck's head, and rises.*

Enter PAGE, FORD, MISTRESS PAGE, *and* MISTRESS FORD.

PAGE.

Nay, do not fly; I think we have watch'd you now:
Will none but Herne the hunter serve your turn?

MISTRESS PAGE.

I pray you, come, hold up the jest no higher.—
Now, good Sir John, how like you Windsor wives?—
See you these, husband? do not these fair yokes
Become the forest better than the town?

FORD.

Now, sir, who's a cuckold now?—Master Brook, Falstaff's a knave, a cuckoldly knave; here are his horns, Master Brook: and, Master Brook, he hath enjoy'd nothing of Ford's but his buck-basket, his cudgel, and twenty pounds of money, which must be paid to Master Brook; his horses are arrested for it, Master Brook.

MISTRESS FORD.

Sir John, we have had ill luck; we could never meet. I will never take you for my love again; but I will always count you my deer.

SIR JOHN FALSTAFF.

I do begin to perceive that I am made an ass.

FORD.

Ay, and an ox too: both the proofs are extant.

SIR JOHN FALSTAFF.

And these are not fairies? I was three or four times in the thought they were not fairies: and yet the guiltiness of my mind, the sudden surprise of my powers, drove the grossness of the foppery into a received belief, in despite of the teeth of all rhyme and reason, that they were fairies. See now how wit may be made a Jack-a-Lent, when 'tis upon ill employment!

SIR HUGH EVANS.

Sir John Falstaff, serve Got, and leave your desires, and fairies will not pinse you.

FORD.

Well said, fairy Hugh.

SIR HUGH EVANS.

And leave you your jealousies too, I pray you.

FORD.

I will never mistrust my wife again, till thou art able to woo her in good English.

SIR JOHN FALSTAFF.

Have I laid my brain in the sun, and dried it, that it wants matter to prevent so gross o'er-reaching as this? Am I ridden with a Welsh goat too? shall I have a coxcomb of frize? 'Tis time I were choked with a piece of toasted cheese.

SIR HUGH EVANS.

Seese is not to give putter; your pelly is all putter.

SIR JOHN FALSTAFF.

'Seese' and 'putter'! have I lived to stand at the taunt of one that makes fritters of English? This is enough to be the decay of lust and late-walking through the realm.

MISTRESS PAGE.

Why, Sir John, do you think, though we would have thrust virtue out of our hearts by the head and shoulders, and have given ourselves without scruple to hell, that ever the devil could have made you our delight?

FORD.

What, a hodge-pudding? a bag of flax?

MISTRESS PAGE.

A puff'd man?

FORD.

Old, cold, wither'd, and of intolerable entrails?

FORD.

And one that is as slanderous as Satan?

PAGE.

And as poor as Job?

FORD.

And as wicked as his wife?

SIR HUGH EVANS.

And given to fornications, and to taverns, and sack, and wine, and metheglins, and to drinkings, and swearings and starings, pribbles and prabbles?

SIR JOHN FALSTAFF.

Well, I am your theme: you have the start of me; I am dejected; I am not able to answer the Welsh flannel; ignorance itself is a plummet o'er me: use me as you will.

FORD.

Marry, sir, we'll bring you to Windsor, to one Master Brook, that you have cozen'd of money, to whom you should have been a pandar: over and above that you have suffer'd, I think to repay that money will be a biting affliction.

MISTRESS FORD.

Nay, husband, let that go to make amends;
Forgive that sum, and so we'll all be friends.

FORD.

Well, here is my hand; all's forgiven at last.

PAGE.

Yet be cheerful, knight: thou shalt eat a posset to-night at my house; where I will desire thee to laugh at my wife, that now laughs at thee: tell her Master Slender hath married her daughter.

MISTRESS PAGE [*aside*].

Doctors doubt that: if Anne Page be my daughter, she is, by this, Doctor Caius' wife.

Enter SLENDER.

SLENDER.

Whoa, ho! ho, father Page!

PAGE.

Son, how now! how now, son! have you dispatch'd?

SLENDER.

Dispatch'd!—I'll make the best in Glostershire know on't; would I were hang'd, la, else!

PAGE.

Of what, son?

SLENDER.

I came yonder at Eton to marry Mistress Anne Page, and she's a great lubberly boy. If it had not been i'th'church, I would have swinged him, or he should have swinged me. If I did not think it had been Anne Page, would I might never stir!—and 'tis a postmaster's boy.

PAGE.

Upon my life, then, you took the wrong.

SLENDER.

What need you tell me that? I think so, when I took a boy for a girl. If I had been married to him, for all he was in woman's apparel, I would not have had him.

PAGE.

Why, this is your own folly. Did not I tell you how you should know my daughter by her garments?

SLENDER.

I went to her in white, and cried 'mum,' and she cried 'budget,' as Anne and I had appointed; and yet it was not Anne, but a postmaster's boy.

SIR HUGH EVANS.

Jeshu, Master Slender! cannot you see but marry boys?

PAGE.

O, I am vext at heart! what shall I do?

MISTRESS PAGE.

Good George, be not angry: I knew of your purpose; turn'd my daughter into green; and, indeed, she is now with the doctor at the deanery, and there married.

Enter CAIUS.

DOCTOR CAIUS.

Vere is Mistress Page? By gar, I am cozen'd: I ha' married *un garçon*, a boy; *un paysan*, by gar, a boy; it is not Anne Page: by gar, I am cozen'd.

MISTRESS PAGE.

Why, did you take her in green?

DOCTOR CAIUS.

Ay, by gar, and 'tis a boy: by gar, I'll raise all Windsor. [*Exit.*

FORD.

This is strange. Who hath got the right Anne?

PAGE.

My heart misgives me:—here comes Master Fenton.

Enter FENTON *and* ANNE PAGE.

How now, Master Fenton!

ANNE PAGE.

Pardon, good father!—good my mother, pardon!

PAGE.

Now, mistress,—how chance you went not with Master Slender?

MISTRESS PAGE.

Why went you not with master doctor, maid?

FENTON.

You do amaze her: hear the truth of it.
You would have married her most shamefully,
Where there was no proportion held in love.
The truth is, she and I, long since contracted,
Are now so sure that nothing can dissolve us.
Th' offence is holy that she hath committed,
And this deceit loses the name of craft,
Of disobedience, or unduteous title,
Since therein she doth evitate and shun
A thousand irreligious cursed hours,
Which forced marriage would have brought upon her.

FORD.

Stand not amazed: here is no remedy:
In love the heavens themselves do guide the state;
Money buys lands, and wives are sold by fate.

SIR JOHN FALSTAFF.

I am glad, though you have ta'en a special stand to strike at me, that your arrow hath glanced.

PAGE.

Well, what remedy?—Fenton, heaven give thee joy!—
What cannot be eschew'd must be embraced.

SIR JOHN FALSTAFF.

When night-dogs run, all sorts of deer are chased.

SIR HUGH EVANS.

I will also dance and eat plums at your weddings.

MISTRESS PAGE.

Well, I will muse no further.—Master Fenton,
Heaven give you many, many merry days!—
Good husband, let us every one go home,
And laugh this sport o'er by a country fire;
Sir John and all.

FORD.

Let it be so.—Sir John,
To Master Brook you yet shall hold your word;
For he to-night shall lie with Mistress Ford.
[*Exeunt.*

MUCH ADO ABOUT NOTHING

DRAMATIS PERSONAE

DON PEDRO, *prince of Arragon.*
DON JOHN, *his bastard brother.*
CLAUDIO, *a young lord of Florence.*
BENEDICK, *a young lord of Padua.*
LEONATO, *governor of Messina.*
ANTONIO, *his brother.*
BALTHAZAR, *attendant on Don Pedro.*
BORACHIO, CONRADE, *followers of Don John.*
FRIAR FRANCIS.
DOGBERRY, *a constable.*
VERGES, *a headborough.*
A SEXTON.
A BOY.
HERO, *daughter to Leonato.*
BEATRICE, *niece to Leonato.*
MARGARET, URSULA, *gentlewomen attending on Hero.*

MESSENGERS, WATCH, ATTENDANTS, &c.

SCENE—*Messina.*

ACT I. SCENE I.

Before LEONATO'S *house.*

Enter LEONATO, HERO, *and* BEATRICE, *with a* MESSENGER.

LEONATO.
I LEARN in this letter that Don Pedro of Arragon comes this night to Messina.

MESSENGER.
He is very near by this: he was not three leagues off when I left him.

LEONATO.
How many gentlemen have you lost in this action?

MESSENGER.
But few of any sort, and none of name.

LEONATO.
A victory is twice itself when the achiever brings home full numbers. I find here that Don Pedro hath bestow'd much honour on a young Florentine called Claudio.

MESSENGER.
Much deserved on his part, and equally remember'd by Don Pedro. He hath borne himself beyond the promise of his age; doing, in the figure of a lamb, the feats of a lion: he hath, indeed, better better'd expectation than you must expect of me to tell you how.

LEONATO.
He hath an uncle here in Messina will be very much glad of it.

MESSENGER.
I have already deliver'd him letters, and there appears much joy in him; even so much, that joy could not show itself modest enough without a badge of bitterness.

LEONATO.
Did he break out into tears?

MESSENGER.
In great measure.

LEONATO.
A kind overflow of kindness: there are no faces truer than those that are so wash'd. How much better is it to weep at joy than to joy at weeping!

BEATRICE.
I pray you, is Signior Mountanto return'd from the wars or no?

MESSENGER.
I know none of that name, lady: there was none such in the army of any sort.

LEONATO.
What is he that you ask for, niece?

HERO.
My cousin means Signior Benedick of Padua.

MESSENGER.
O, he's return'd; and as pleasant as ever he was.

BEATRICE.
He set up his bills here in Messina, and challenged Cupid at the flight; and my uncle's fool, reading the challenge, subscribed for Cupid, and challenged him at the birdbolt.—I pray you, how many hath he kill'd and eaten in these wars? But how many hath he kill'd? for, indeed, I promised to eat all of his killing.

LEONATO.
Faith, niece, you tax Signior Benedick too much; but he'll be meet with you, I doubt it not.

MESSENGER.
He hath done good service, lady, in these wars.

BEATRICE.
You had musty victual, and he hath holp to eat it: he's a very valiant trencher-man; he hath an excellent stomach.

MESSENGER.
And a good soldier too, lady.

BEATRICE.
And a good soldier to a lady:—but what is he to a lord?

MESSENGER.
A lord to a lord, a man to a man; stuft with all honourable virtues.

BEATRICE.
It is so, indeed; he is no less than a stuft man: but for the stuffing,—well, we are all mortal.

LEONATO.
You must not, sir, mistake my niece. There is a kind of merry war betwixt Signior Benedick and her: they never meet but there's a skirmish of wit between them.

BEATRICE.
Alas, he gets nothing by that! In our last conflict four of his five wits went halting off, and now is the whole man govern'd with one: so that if he

have wit enough to keep himself warm, let him bear it for a difference between himself and his horse; for it is all the wealth that he hath left, to be known a reasonable creature.—Who is his companion now? He hath every month a new sworn brother.

MESSENGER.

Is't possible?

BEATRICE.

Very easily possible: he wears his faith but as the fashion of his hat; it ever changes with the next block.

MESSENGER.

I see, lady, the gentleman is not in your books.

BEATRICE.

No; an he were, I would burn my study. But, I pray you, who is his companion? Is there no young squarer now that will make a voyage with him to the devil?

MESSENGER.

He is most in the company of the right noble Claudio.

BEATRICE.

O Lord, he will hang upon him like a disease: he is sooner caught than the pestilence, and the taker runs presently mad. God help the noble Claudio! if he have caught the Benedick, it will cost him a thousand pound ere a' be cured.

MESSENGER.

I will hold friends with you, lady.

BEATRICE.

Do, good friend.

LEONATO.

You will never run mad, niece.

BEATRICE.

No, not till a hot January.

MESSENGER.

Don Pedro is approach'd.

Enter DON PEDRO, DON JOHN, CLAUDIO, BENEDICK, *and* BALTHAZAR.

DON PEDRO.

Good Signior Leonato, you are come to meet your trouble: the fashion of the world is to avoid cost, and you encounter it.

LEONATO.

Never came trouble to my house in the likeness of your grace: for trouble being gone, comfort should remain; but when you depart from me, sorrow abides, and happiness takes his leave.

DON PEDRO.

You embrace your charge too willingly.—I think this is your daughter.

LEONATO.

Her mother hath many times told me so.

BENEDICK.

Were you in doubt, sir, that you askt her?

LEONATO.

Signior Benedick, no; for then were you a child.

DON PEDRO.

You have it full, Benedick: we may guess by this what you are, being a man.—Truly, the lady fathers herself.—Be happy, lady; for you are like an honourable father.

BENEDICK.

If Signior Leonato be her father, she would not have his head on her shoulders for all Messina, as like him as she is.

BEATRICE.

I wonder that you will still be talking, Signior Benedick: nobody marks you.

BENEDICK.

What, my dear Lady Disdain! are you yet living?

BEATRICE.

Is it possible disdain should die while she hath such meet food to feed it as Signior Benedick? Courtesy itself must convert to disdain, if you come in her presence.

BENEDICK.

Then is courtesy a turncoat.—But it is certain I am loved of all ladies, only you excepted: and I would I could find it in my heart that I had not a hard heart; for, truly, I love none.

BEATRICE.

A dear happiness to women: they would else have been troubled with a pernicious suitor. I thank God and my cold blood, I am of your humour for that: I had rather hear my dog bark at a crow than a man swear he loves me.

BENEDICK.

God keep your ladyship still in that mind! so some gentleman or other shall scape a predestinate scratcht face.

BEATRICE.

Scratching could not make it worse, an 'twere such a face as yours were.

BENEDICK.

Well, you are a rare parrot-teacher.

BEATRICE.

A bird of my tongue is better than a beast of yours.

BENEDICK.

I would my horse had the speed of your tongue, and so good a continuer. But keep your way, i' God's name; I have done.

BEATRICE.

You always end with a jade's trick: I know you of old.

DON PEDRO.

This is the sum of all: Leonato,—Signior Claudio and Signior Benedick,—my dear friend Leonato hath invited you all. I tell him we shall stay here at the least a month; and he heartily prays some occasion may detain us longer: I dare swear he is no hypocrite, but prays from his heart.

LEONATO.

If you swear, my lord, you shall not be forsworn. —Let me bid you welcome, my lord: being reconciled to the prince your brother, I owe you all duty.

DON JOHN.

I thank you: I am not of many words, but I thank you.

LEONATO.

Please it your Grace lead on?

DON PEDRO.

Your hand, Leonato; we will go together.

[*Exeunt all except* BENEDICK *and* CLAUDIO.

CLAUDIO.

Benedick, didst thou note the daughter of Signior Leonato?

BENEDICK.

I noted her not; but I lookt on her.

CLAUDIO.

Is she not a modest young lady?

BENEDICK.

Do you question me, as an honest man should do, for my simple true judgement, or would you have me speak after my custom, as being a profest tyrant to their sex?

CLAUDIO.

No; I pray thee speak in sober judgement.

BENEDICK.

Why, i'faith, methinks she's too low for a high praise, too brown for a fair praise, and too little for a great praise: only this commendation I can afford her,—that were she other than she is, she were unhandsome; and being no other but as she is, I do not like her.

CLAUDIO.

Thou think'st I am in sport: I pray thee tell me truly how thou likest her.

BENEDICK.

Would you buy her, that you inquire after her?

CLAUDIO.

Can the world buy such a jewel?

BENEDICK.

Yea, and a case to put it into. But speak you this with a sad brow? or do you play the flouting Jack, to tell us Cupid is a good hare-finder, and Vulcan a rare carpenter? Come, in what key shall a man take you, to go in the song?

CLAUDIO.

In mine eye she is the sweetest lady that ever I lookt on.

BENEDICK.

I can see yet without spectacles, and I see no such matter: there's her cousin, an she were not possest with a fury, exceeds her as much in beauty as the first of May doth the last of December. But I hope you have no intent to turn husband, have you?

CLAUDIO.

I would scarce trust myself, though I had sworn the contrary, if Hero would be my wife.

BENEDICK.

Is't come to this? In faith, hath not the world one man but he will wear his cap with suspicion? Shall I never see a bachelor of threescore again? Go to, i'faith; an thou wilt needs thrust thy neck into a yoke, wear the print of it, and sigh away Sundays. Look; Don Pedro is return'd to seek you.

Enter DON PEDRO.

DON PEDRO.

What secret hath held you here, that you follow'd not to Leonato's?

BENEDICK.

I would your Grace would constrain me to tell.

DON PEDRO.

I charge thee on thy allegiance.

BENEDICK.

You hear, Count Claudio: I can be secret as a dumb man, I would have you think so; but on my allegiance,—mark you this, on my allegiance.—He is in love. With who?—now that is your Grace's part.—Mark how short his answer is;—With Hero, Leonato's short daughter.

CLAUDIO.

If this were so, so were it utter'd.

BENEDICK.

Like the old tale, my lord: 'it is not so, nor 'twas not so; but indeed, God forbid it should be so.'

CLAUDIO.

If my passion change not shortly, God forbid it should be otherwise.

DON PEDRO.

Amen, if you love her; for the lady is very well worthy.

CLAUDIO.

You speak this to fetch me in, my lord.

DON PEDRO.

By my troth, I speak my thought.

CLAUDIO.

And, in faith, my lord, I spoke mine.

BENEDICK.

And, by my two faiths and troths, my lord, I spoke mine.

CLAUDIO.

That I love her, I feel.

DON PEDRO.

That she is worthy, I know.

BENEDICK.

That I neither feel how she should be loved, nor know how she should be worthy, is the opinion that fire cannot melt out of me: I will die in it at the stake.

DON PEDRO.

Thou wast ever an obstinate heretic in the despite of beauty.

CLAUDIO.

And never could maintain his part but in the force of his will.

BENEDICK.

That a woman conceived me, I thank her; that she brought me up, I likewise give her most humble thanks: but that I will have a recheat winded in my forehead, or hang my bugle in an invisible baldrick, all women shall pardon me. Because I will not do them the wrong to mistrust any, I will do myself the right to trust none; and the fine is (for the which I may go the finer), I will live a bachelor.

DON PEDRO.

I shall see thee, ere I die, look pale with love.

BENEDICK.

With anger, with sickness, or with hunger, my lord; not with love: prove that ever I lose more blood with love than I will get again with drinking, pick out mine eyes with a ballet-maker's pen, and hang me up at the door of a brothel-house for the sign of blind Cupid.

DON PEDRO.

Well, if ever thou dost fall from this faith, thou wilt prove a notable argument.

BENEDICK.

If I do, hang me in a bottle like a cat, and shoot at me; and he that hits me, let him be clapt on the shoulder, and called Adam.

DON PEDRO.

Well, as time shall try:

'In time the savage bull doth bear the yoke.'

BENEDICK.

The savage bull may; but if ever the sensible Benedick bear it, pluck off the bull's horns, and set them in my forehead; and let me be vilely painted; and in such great letters as they write, 'Here is good horse to hire,' let them signify under my sign, 'Here you may see Benedick the married man.'

CLAUDIO.

If this should ever happen, thou wouldst be horn-mad.

DON PEDRO.

Nay, if Cupid have not spent all his quiver in Venice, thou wilt quake for this shortly.

BENEDICK.

I look for an earthquake too, then.

DON PEDRO.

Well, you will temporize with the hours. In the meantime, good Signior Benedick, repair to Leonato's: commend me to him, and tell him I will not fail him at supper; for indeed he hath made great preparation.

BENEDICK.

I have almost matter enough in me for such an embassage; and so I commit you,—

CLAUDIO.

To the tuition of God: From my house (if I had it),—

DON PEDRO.

The sixth of July: Your loving friend, Benedick.

BENEDICK.

Nay, mock not, mock not. The body of your discourse is sometime guarded with fragments, and the guards are but slightly basted on neither: ere you flout old ends any further, examine your conscience: and so I leave you. [*Exit.*

CLAUDIO.

My liege, your highness now may do me good.

DON PEDRO.

My love is thine to teach: teach it but how,
And thou shalt see how apt it is to learn
Any hard lesson that may do thee good.

CLAUDIO.

Hath Leonato any son, my lord?

DON PEDRO.

No child but Hero; she's his only heir.
Dost thou affect her, Claudio?

CLAUDIO.

O, my lord,
When you went onward on this ended action,
I lookt upon her with a soldier's eye,
That liked, but had a rougher task in hand
Than to drive liking to the name of love:
But now I am return'd, and that war-thoughts
Have left their places vacant, in their rooms
Come thronging soft and delicate desires,
All prompting me how fair young Hero is,
Saying, I liked her ere I went to wars.

DON PEDRO.

Thou wilt be like a lover presently
And tire the hearer with a book of words.
If thou dost love fair Hero, cherish it;
And I will break with her and with her father,
And thou shalt have her. Was't not to this end
That thou began'st to twist so fine a story?

CLAUDIO.

How sweetly you do minister to love,
That know love's grief by his complexion!
But lest my liking might too sudden seem,
I would have salved it with a longer treatise.

DON PEDRO.

What need the bridge much broader than the flood?
The fairest grant is the necessity.
Look, what will serve is fit: 'tis once, thou lovest;
And I will fit thee with the remedy.
I know we shall have revelling to-night:
I will assume thy part in some disguise,
And tell fair Hero I am Claudio;
And in her bosom I'll unclasp my heart,
And take her hearing prisoner with the force
And strong encounter of my amorous tale:
Then after to her father will I break;
And the conclusion is, she shall be thine.
In practice let us put it presently. [*Exeunt.*

SCENE II.

A room in LEONATO'S *house.*

Enter, severally, LEONATO *and* ANTONIO.

LEONATO.

HOW now, brother! Where is my cousin, your son? hath he provided this music?

ANTONIO.

He is very busy about it. But, brother, I can tell you strange news, that you yet dreamt not of.

LEONATO.

Are they good?

ANTONIO.

As the event stamps them: but they have a good cover; they show well outward. The prince and Count Claudio, walking in a thick-pleacht alley in my orchard, were thus much overheard by a man of mine: the prince discover'd to Claudio that he loved my niece your daughter, and meant to acknowledge it this night in a dance; and if he found her accordant, he meant to take the present time by the top, and instantly break with you of it.

LEONATO.

Hath the fellow any wit that told you this?

ANTONIO.

A good sharp fellow: I will send for him; and question him yourself.

LEONATO.

No, no; we will hold it as a dream till it appear itself: but I will acquaint my daughter withal, that she may be the better prepared for an answer, if peradventure this be true. Go you and tell her of it.—[*Exit* ANTONIO.—*Several persons cross the stage.*] Cousins, you know what you have to do.—O, I cry you mercy, friend; go you with me, and I will use your skill.—Good cousin, have a care this busy time. [*Exit.*

SCENE III.

Another room in LEONATO'S *house.*

Enter DON JOHN *and* CONRADE.

CONRADE.

WHAT the good-year, my lord! why are you thus out of measure sad?

DON JOHN.

There is no measure in the occasion that breeds it; therefore the sadness is without limit.

CONRADE.

You should hear reason.

DON JOHN.

And when I have heard it, what blessing bringeth it?

CONRADE.

If not a present remedy, yet a patient sufferance.

DON JOHN.

I wonder that thou, being (as thou say'st thou art) born under Saturn, goest about to apply a moral medicine to a mortifying mischief. I cannot hide what I am: I must be sad when I have cause, and smile at no man's jests; eat when I have stomach, and wait for no man's leisure; sleep when I am drowsy, and tend on no man's business; laugh when I am merry, and claw no man in his humour.

CONRADE.

Yea, but you must not make the full show of this till you may do it without controlment. You have of late stood out against your brother, and he hath ta'en you newly into his grace; where it is impossible you should take true root but by the fair weather that you make yourself: it is needful that you frame the season for your own harvest.

DON JOHN.

I had rather be a canker in a hedge than a rose in his grace; and it better fits my blood to be disdain'd of all than to fashion a carriage to rob love from any: in this, though I cannot be said to be a flattering honest man, it must not be denied but I am a plain-dealing villain. I am trusted with a muzzle, and enfranchised with a clog; therefore I have decreed not to sing in my cage. If I had my mouth, I would bite; if I had my liberty, I would do my liking: in the mean time let me be that I am, and seek not to alter me.

CONRADE.

Can you make no use of your discontent?

DON JOHN.

I make all use of it, for I use it only.—Who comes here?

Enter BORACHIO.

What news, Borachio?

BORACHIO.

I came yonder from a great supper: the prince your brother is royally entertain'd by Leonato; and I can give you intelligence of an intended marriage.

DON JOHN.

Will it serve for any model to build mischief on? What is he for a fool that betroths himself to unquietness?

BORACHIO.

Marry, it is your brother's right hand.

DON JOHN.

Who, the most exquisite Claudio?

BORACHIO.

Even he.

DON JOHN.

A proper squire! And who, and who? which way looks he?

BORACHIO.

Marry, on Hero, the daughter and heir of Leonato.

DON JOHN.

A very forward March-chick! How came you to this?

BORACHIO.

Being entertain'd for a perfumer, as I was smoking a musty room, comes me the prince and Claudio, hand in hand, in sad conference: I whipt me behind the arras; and there heard it agreed upon, that the prince should woo Hero for himself, and having obtain'd her, give her to Count Claudio.

DON JOHN.

Come, come, let us thither: this may prove food to my displeasure. That young start-up hath all the glory of my overthrow: if I can cross him any way, I bless myself every way. You are both sure, and will assist me?

CONRADE.

To the death, my lord.

DON JOHN.

Let us to the great supper: their cheer is the greater that I am subdued. Would the cook were of my mind!—Shall we go prove what's to be done?

BORACHIO.

We'll wait upon your lordship. [*Exeunt.*

ACT II. SCENE I.

A hall in LEONATO'S *house.*

Enter LEONATO, ANTONIO, HERO, BEATRICE, *and others.*

LEONATO.

WAS not Count John here at supper?

ANTONIO.

I saw him not.

BEATRICE.

How tartly that gentleman looks! I never can see him but I am heart-burn'd an hour after.

HERO.

He is of a very melancholy disposition.

BEATRICE.

He were an excellent man that were made just in the midway between him and Benedick: the one is too like an image, and says nothing; and the other too like my lady's eldest son, evermore tattling.

LEONATO.

Then half Signior Benedick's tongue in Count John's mouth, and half Count John's melancholy in Signior Benedick's face,—

BEATRICE.

With a good leg and a good foot, uncle, and money enough in his purse, such a man would win any woman in the world,—if a' could get her good-will.

LEONATO.

By my troth, niece, thou wilt never get thee a husband, if thou be so shrewd of thy tongue.

ANTONIO.

In faith, she's too curst.

BEATRICE.

Too curst is more than curst: I shall lessen God's sending that way; for it is said, 'God sends a curst cow short horns;' but to a cow too curst he sends none.

LEONATO.

So, by being too curst, God will send you no horns.

BEATRICE.

Just, if he send me no husband; for the which blessing I am at him upon my knees every morning and evening. Lord, I could not endure a husband with a beard on his face: I had rather lie in the woollen.

LEONATO.

You may light on a husband that hath no beard.

BEATRICE.

What should I do with him? dress him in my apparel, and make him my waiting-gentlewoman? He that hath a beard is more than a youth; and he that hath no beard is less than a man: and he that is more than a youth is not for me; and he that is less than a man, I am not for him: therefore I will even take sixpence in earnest of the bear-ward, and lead his apes into hell.

LEONATO.

Well, then, go you into hell?

BEATRICE.

No; but to the gate; and there will the devil meet me, like an old cuckold, with horns on his head, and say, 'Get you to heaven, Beatrice, get you to heaven; here's no place for you maids:' so deliver I up my apes, and away to Saint Peter for the heavens; he shows me where the bachelors sit, and there live we as merry as the day is long.

ANTONIO.

Well, niece [*to* HERO], I trust you will be ruled by your father.

BEATRICE.

Yes, faith; it is my cousin's duty to make curtsey, and say, 'Father, as it please you:'—but yet for all that, cousin, let him be a handsome fellow, or else make another curtsey, and say, 'Father, as it please me.'

LEONATO.

Well, niece, I hope to see you one day fitted with a husband.

BEATRICE.

Not till God make men of some other metal than earth. Would it not grieve a woman to be over-master'd with a piece of valiant dust? to make an account of her life to a clod of wayward marl? No, uncle, I'll none: Adam's sons are my brethren; and, truly, I hold it a sin to match in my kindred.

LEONATO.

Daughter, remember what I told you: if the prince do solicit you in that kind, you know your answer.

BEATRICE.

The fault will be in the music, cousin, if you be not wooed in good time: if the prince be too important, tell him there is measure in every thing, and so dance out the answer. For, hear me, Hero:—wooing, wedding, and repenting, is as a Scotch jig, a measure, and a cinque-pace: the first suit is hot and hasty, like a Scotch jig, and full as fantastical; the wedding, mannerly-modest, as a measure, full of state and ancientry; and then comes repentance, and, with his bad legs, falls into the cinque-pace faster and faster, till he sink into his grave.

LEONATO.

Cousin, you apprehend passing shrewdly.

BEATRICE.

I have a good eye, uncle; I can see a church by daylight.

LEONATO.

The revellers are ent'ring, brother: make good room.

Enter DON PEDRO, CLAUDIO, BENEDICK, BALTHAZAR, DON JOHN, BORACHIO, MARGARET, URSULA, *and others, maskt; with a drum.*

DON PEDRO.

Lady, will you walk about with your friend?

HERO.

So you walk softly, and look sweetly, and say nothing, I am yours for the walk; and especially when I walk away.

DON PEDRO.

With me in your company?

HERO.

I may say so, when I please.

DON PEDRO.

And when please you to say so?

HERO.

When I like your favour; for God defend the lute should be like the case!

DON PEDRO.

My visor is Philemon's roof; within the house is Jove.

HERO.

Why, then, your visor should be thatcht.

DON PEDRO.

Speak low, if you speak love.

[*Takes her aside.*

BALTHAZAR.

Well, I would you did like me.

MARGARET.

So would not I, for your own sake; for I have many ill qualities.

BALTHAZAR.

Which is one?

MARGARET.

I say my prayers aloud.

BALTHAZAR.

I love you the better: the hearers may cry, Amen.

MARGARET.

God match me with a good dancer!

BALTHAZAR.

Amen.

MARGARET.

And God keep him out of my sight when the dance is done!—Answer, clerk.

BALTHAZAR.

No more words: the clerk is answer'd.

URSULA.

I know you well enough; you are Signior Antonio.

ANTONIO.

At a word, I am not.

URSULA.

I know you by the waggling of your head.

ANTONIO.

To tell you true, I counterfeit him.

URSULA.

You could never do him so ill-well, unless you were the very man. Here's his dry hand up and down: you are he, you are he.

ANTONIO.

At a word, I am not.

URSULA.

Come, come, do you think I do not know you by your excellent wit? can virtue hide itself? Go to, mum, you are he: graces will appear, and there's an end.

BEATRICE.

Will you not tell me who told you so?

BENEDICK.

No, you shall pardon me.

BEATRICE.

Nor will you not tell me who you are?

BENEDICK.

Not now.

BEATRICE.

That I was disdainful, and that I had my good wit out of the *Hundred Merry Tales:*—well, this was Signior Benedick that said so.

BENEDICK.

What's he?

BEATRICE.

I am sure you know him well enough.

BENEDICK.

Not I, believe me.

BEATRICE.

Did he never make you laugh?

BENEDICK.

I pray you, what is he?

BEATRICE.

Why, he is the prince's jester: a very dull fool; only his gift is in devising impossible slanders: none but libertines delight in him; and the commendation is not in his wit, but in his villainy; for he both pleases men and angers them, and then they laugh at him and beat him. I am sure he is in the fleet: I would he had boarded me.

BENEDICK.

When I know the gentleman, I'll tell him what you say.

BEATRICE.

Do, do: he'll but break a comparison or two on me; which, peradventure, not markt, or not laugh'd at, strikes him into melancholy; and then there's a partridge wing saved, for the fool will eat no supper that night. [*Music within.*] We must follow the leaders.

BENEDICK.

In every good thing.

BEATRICE.

Nay, if they lead to any ill, I will leave them at the next turning.

[*Music. Dance. Then exeunt all except* DON JOHN, BORACHIO, *and* CLAUDIO.

DON JOHN.

Sure my brother is amorous on Hero, and hath withdrawn her father to break with him about it. The ladies follow her, and but one visor remains.

BORACHIO.

And that is Claudio: I know him by his bearing.

DON JOHN.

Are not you Signior Benedick?

CLAUDIO.

You know me well; I am he.

DON JOHN.

Signior, you are very near my brother in his love: he is enamour'd on Hero; I pray you, dissuade him from her, she is no equal for his birth: you may do the part of an honest man in it.

CLAUDIO.

How know you he loves her?

DON JOHN.

I heard him swear his affection.

BORACHIO.

So did I too; and he swore he would marry her to-night.

DON JOHN.

Come, let us to the banquet.

[*Exeunt* DON JOHN *and* BORACHIO.

CLAUDIO.

Thus answer I in name of Benedick,
But hear these ill news with the ears of Claudio.
'Tis certain so;—the prince wooes for himself.
Friendship is constant in all other things
Save in the office and affairs of love:
Therefore all hearts in love use their own tongues;
Let every eye negotiate for itself,
And trust no agent: for beauty is a witch,
Against whose charms faith melteth into blood.
This is an accident of hourly proof,
Which I mistrusted not. Farewell, therefore, Hero!

Enter BENEDICK.

BENEDICK.

Count Claudio?

CLAUDIO.

Yea, the same.

BENEDICK.

Come, will you go with me?

CLAUDIO.

Whither?

BENEDICK.

Even to the next willow, about your own business, county. What fashion will you wear the garland of? about your neck, like an usurer's chain? or under your arm, like a lieutenant's scarf? You must wear it one way, for the prince hath got your Hero.

CLAUDIO.

I wish him joy of her.

BENEDICK.

Why, that's spoken like an honest drovier: so they sell bullocks. But did you think the prince would have served you thus?

CLAUDIO.

I pray you, leave me.

BENEDICK.

Ho! now you strike like the blind man: 'twas the boy that stole your meat, and you'll beat the post.

CLAUDIO.

If it will not be, I'll leave you. [*Exit.*

BENEDICK.

Alas, poor hurt fowl! now will he creep into sedges.—But, that my Lady Beatrice should know me, and not know me! The prince's fool!—Ha! it may be I go under that title because I am merry.—Yea, but so I am apt to do myself wrong; I am not so reputed: it is the base thought, bitter disposition, of Beatrice that puts the world into her person, and so gives me out. Well, I'll be revenged as I may.

Enter DON PEDRO.

DON PEDRO.

Now, signior, where's the count? did you see him?

BENEDICK.

Troth, my lord, I have play'd the part of Lady Fame. I found him here as melancholy as a lodge in a warren: I told him, and I think I told him true, that your grace had got the good-will of this young lady; and I offer'd him my company to a willow-tree, either to make him a garland, as being forsaken, or to bind him up a rod, as being worthy to be whipt.

DON PEDRO.

To be whipt! What's his fault?

BENEDICK.

The flat transgression of a school-boy, who, being overjoy'd with finding a bird's-nest, shows it his companion, and he steals it.

DON PEDRO.

Wilt thou make a trust a transgression? The transgression is in the stealer.

BENEDICK.

Yet it had not been amiss the rod had been made, and the garland too; for the garland he might have worn himself, and the rod he might have bestow'd on you, who, as I take it, have stolen his bird's-nest.

DON PEDRO.

I will but teach them to sing, and restore them to the owner.

BENEDICK.

If their singing answer your saying, by my faith, you say honestly.

DON PEDRO.

The Lady Beatrice hath a quarrel to you: the gentleman that danced with her told her she is much wrong'd by you.

BENEDICK.

O, she misused me past the endurance of a block! an oak but with one green leaf on it would have answer'd her; my very visor began to assume life and scold with her. She told me,—not thinking I had been myself,—that I was the prince's jester, and that I was duller than a great thaw; huddling jest upon jest with such impossible conveyance upon me that I stood like a man at a mark, with a whole army shooting at me. She speaks poniards, and every word stabs: if her breath were as terrible as her terminations, there were no living near her; she would infect to the north star. I would not marry her, though she were endow'd with all that Adam had left him before he transgrest: she would have made Hercules have turn'd spit, yea, and have cleft his club to make the fire too. Come, talk not of her: you shall find her the infernal Ate in good apparel. I would to God some scholar would conjure her; for certainly, while she is here, a man may live as quiet in hell as in a sanctuary; and people sin upon purpose, because they would go thither; so, indeed, all disquiet, horror, and perturbation follow her.

DON PEDRO.

Look, here she comes.

Enter CLAUDIO, BEATRICE, HERO, & LEONATO.

BENEDICK.

Will your grace command me any service to the world's end? I will go on the slightest errand now to the Antipodes that you can devise to send me on; I will fetch you a toothpicker now from the furthest inch of Asia; bring you the length of Prester John's foot; fetch you a hair off the great Cham's beard; do you any embassage to the Pigmies;—rather than hold three words' conference with this harpy. You have no employment for me?

DON PEDRO.

None, but to desire your good company.

BENEDICK.

O God, sir, here's a dish I love not: I cannot endure my Lady Tongue. [*Exit.*

DON PEDRO.

Come, lady, come; you have lost the heart of Signior Benedick.

BEATRICE.

Indeed, my lord, he lent it me awhile; and I gave him use for it,—a double heart for his single one: marry, once before he won it of me with false dice, therefore your grace may well say I have lost it.

DON PEDRO.

You have put him down, lady, you have put him down.

BEATRICE.

So I would not he should do me, my lord, lest I should prove the mother of fools.—I have brought Count Claudio, whom you sent me to seek.

DON PEDRO.

Why, how now, count! wherefore are you sad?

CLAUDIO.

Not sad, my lord.

DON PEDRO.

How then? sick?

CLAUDIO.

Neither, my lord.

BEATRICE.

The count is neither sad, nor sick, nor merry, nor well; but civil, count,—civil as an orange, and something of that jealous complexion.

DON PEDRO.

I'faith, lady, I think your blazon to be true; though, I'll be sworn, if he be so, his conceit is false.—Here, Claudio, I have woo'd in thy name, and fair Hero is won: I have broke with her father, and, his good-will obtain'd, name the day of marriage, and God give thee joy!

LEONATO.

Count, take of me my daughter, and with her my fortunes: his grace hath made the match, and all grace say Amen to it!

BEATRICE.

Speak, count, 'tis your cue.

CLAUDIO.

Silence is the perfectest herald of joy: I were but little happy, if I could say how much.—Lady, as you are mine, I am yours: I give away myself for you, and dote upon the exchange.

BEATRICE.

Speak, cousin; or, if you cannot, stop his mouth with a kiss, and let not him speak neither.

DON PEDRO.

In faith, lady, you have a merry heart.

BEATRICE.

Yea, my lord; I thank it, poor fool, it keeps on the windy side of care.—My cousin tells him in his ear that he is in her heart.

CLAUDIO.

And so she doth, cousin.

BEATRICE.

Good Lord, for alliance!—Thus goes every one to the world but I, and I am sun-burn'd; I may sit in a corner, and cry heigh-ho for a husband!

DON PEDRO.

Lady Beatrice, I will get you one.

BEATRICE.

I would rather have one of your father's getting. Hath your grace ne'er a brother like you? Your father got excellent husbands, if a maid could come by them.

DON PEDRO.

Will you have me, lady?

BEATRICE.

No, my lord, unless I might have another for working-days: your grace is too costly to wear every day. But, I beseech your grace, pardon me: I was born to speak all mirth and no matter.

DON PEDRO.

Your silence most offends me, and to be merry best becomes you; for, out of question, you were born in a merry hour.

BEATRICE.

No, sure, my lord, my mother cried; but then there was a star danced, and under that was I born.—Cousins, God give you joy!

LEONATO.

Niece, will you look to those things I told you of?

BEATRICE.

I cry you mercy, uncle.—By your grace's pardon. [*Exit.*

DON PEDRO.

By my troth, a pleasant-spirited lady.

LEONATO.

There's little of the melancholy element in her, my lord: she is never sad but when she sleeps; and not ever sad then; for I have heard my daughter say, she hath often dreamt of unhappiness, and waked herself with laughing.

DON PEDRO.

She cannot endure to hear tell of a husband.

LEONATO.

O, by no means: she mocks all her wooers out of suit.

DON PEDRO.

She were an excellent wife for Benedick.

LEONATO.

O Lord, my lord, if they were but a week married, they would talk themselves mad!

DON PEDRO.

County Claudio, when mean you to go to church?

CLAUDIO.

To-morrow, my lord: time goes on crutches till love have all his rites.

LEONATO.

Not till Monday, my dear son, which is hence a just seven-night; and a time too brief, too, to have all things answer my mind.

DON PEDRO.

Come, you shake the head at so long a breathing: but, I warrant thee, Claudio, the time shall not go dully by us. I will, in the interim, undertake one of Hercules' labours; which is, to bring Signior Benedick and the Lady Beatrice into a mountain of affection the one with the other. I would fain have it a match; and I doubt not but to fashion it, if you three will but minister such assistance as I shall give you direction.

LEONATO.

My lord, I am for you, though it cost me ten nights' watchings.

CLAUDIO.

And I, my lord.

DON PEDRO.

And you too, gentle Hero?

HERO.

I will do any modest office, my lord, to help my cousin to a good husband.

DON PEDRO.

And Benedick is not the unhopefullest husband that I know. Thus far can I praise him; he is of a noble strain, of approved valour, and confirm'd honesty. I will teach you how to humour your cousin, that she shall fall in love with Benedick;—and I, with your two helps, will so practise on Benedick, that, in despite of his quick wit and his queasy stomach, he shall fall in love with Beatrice. If we can do this, Cupid is no longer an archer: his glory shall be ours, for we are the only love-gods. Go in with me, and I will tell you my drift. [*Exeunt.*

SCENE II.

Another room in LEONATO'S *house.*

Enter DON JOHN *and* BORACHIO.

DON JOHN.

It is so; the Count Claudio shall marry the daughter of Leonato.

BORACHIO.

Yea, my lord; but I can cross it.

DON JOHN.

Any bar, any cross, any impediment will be medicinable to me: I am sick in displeasure to him; and whatsoever comes athwart his affection ranges evenly with mine. How canst thou cross this marriage?

BORACHIO.

Not honestly, my lord; but so covertly that no dishonesty shall appear in me.

DON JOHN.

Show me briefly how.

BORACHIO.

I think I told your lordship, a year since, how much I am in the favour of Margaret, the waiting-gentlewoman to Hero.

DON JOHN.

I remember.

BORACHIO.

I can, at any unseasonable instant of the night, appoint her to look out at her lady's chamber-window.

DON JOHN.

What life is in that, to be the death of this marriage?

BORACHIO.

The poison of that lies in you to temper. Go you to the prince your brother; spare not to tell him that he hath wrong'd his honour in marrying the renown'd Claudio (whose estimation do you mightily hold up) to a contaminated stale, such a one as Hero.

DON JOHN.

What proof shall I make of that?

BORACHIO.

Proof enough to misuse the prince, to vex Claudio, to undo Hero, and kill Leonato. Look you for any other issue?

DON JOHN.

Only to despite them, I will endeavour any thing.

BORACHIO.

Go, then; find me a meet hour to draw Don Pedro and the Count Claudio alone: tell them that you know that Hero loves me; intend a kind of zeal both to the prince and Claudio, as,—in love of your brother's honour, who hath made this match, and his friend's reputation, who is thus like to be cozen'd with the semblance of a maid,—that you have discover'd thus. They will scarcely believe this without trial: offer them instances; which shall bear no less likelihood than to see me at her chamber-window; hear me call Margaret, Hero; hear Margaret term me Claudio; and bring them to see this the very night before the intended wedding,—for in the mean time I will so fashion the matter that Hero shall be absent, and there shall appear such seeming truth of Hero's disloyalty, that jealousy shall be call'd assurance, and all the preparation overthrown.

DON JOHN.

Grow this to what adverse issue it can, I will put it in practice. Be cunning in the working this, and thy fee is a thousand ducats.

BORACHIO.

Be you constant in the accusation, and my cunning shall not shame me.

DON JOHN.

I will presently go learn their day of marriage.

[*Exeunt.*

SCENE III.

LEONATO'S *orchard.*

Enter BENEDICK *alone.*

BENEDICK.

BOY,—

Enter BOY.

BOY.

Signior?

BENEDICK.

In my chamber-window lies a book: bring it hither to me in the orchard.

BOY.

I am here already, sir.

BENEDICK.

I know that; but I would have thee hence, and here again. [*Exit* BOY.]—I do much wonder that one man, seeing how much another man is a fool when he dedicates his behaviours to love, will, after he hath laught at such shallow follies in others, become the argument of his own scorn by falling in love: and such a man is Claudio. I have known when there was no music with him but the drum and the fife; and now had he rather hear the tabor and the pipe: I have known when he would have walkt ten mile a-foot to see a good armour; and now will he lie ten nights awake, carving the fashion of a new doublet. He was wont to speak plain and to the purpose, like an honest man and a soldier; and now is he turn'd orthography; his words are a very fantastical banquet,—just so many strange dishes. May I be so converted, and see with these eyes? I cannot tell; I think not: I will not be sworn but love may transform me to an oyster; but I'll take my oath on it, till he have made an oyster of me, he shall never make me such a fool. One woman is fair,—yet I am well; another is wise,—yet I am well; another virtuous,—yet I am well: but till all graces be in one woman, one woman shall not come in my grace. Rich she shall be, that's certain; wise, or I'll none; virtuous, or I'll never cheapen her; fair, or I'll never look on her; mild or come not near me; noble, or not I for an angel; of good discourse, an excellent musician, and her hair shall be of what colour it please God.—Ha, the prince and Monsieur Love! I will hide me in the arbour. [*Withdraws into the arbour.*

Enter DON PEDRO, CLAUDIO, LEONATO, BALTHAZAR, *and* MUSICIANS.

DON PEDRO.

Come, shall we hear this music?

CLAUDIO.

Yea, my good lord.—How still the evening is,
As husht on purpose to grace harmony!

DON PEDRO.

See you where Benedick hath hid himself?

CLAUDIO.

O, very well, my lord: the music ended,
We'll fit the kid-fox with a pennyworth.

DON PEDRO.

Come, Balthazar, we'll hear that song again.

BALTHAZAR.

O, good my lord, tax not so bad a voice
To slander music any more than once.

DON PEDRO.

It is the witness still of excellency
To put a strange face on his own perfection:—
I pray thee, sing, and let me woo no more.

BALTHAZAR.

Because you talk of wooing, I will sing;
Since many a wooer doth commence his suit
To her he thinks not worthy; yet he wooes,
Yet will he swear he loves.

DON PEDRO.

Nay, pray thee, come;
Or, if thou wilt hold longer argument,
Do it in notes.

BALTHAZAR.

Note this before my notes,—
There's not a note of mine that's worth the noting.

DON PEDRO.

Why, these are very crotchets that he speaks;
Note notes, forsooth, and nothing! [*Music.*

BENEDICK [*aside*].

Now, 'Divine air!' now is his soul ravisht!—Is it not strange that sheeps' guts should hale souls out of men's bodies?—Well, a horn for my money, when all's done.

BALTHAZAR *sings.*

Sigh no more, ladies, sigh no more,
Men were deceivers ever;
One foot in sea, and one on shore;
To one thing constant never:
Then sigh not so,
But let them go,
And be you blithe and bonny;
Converting all your sounds of woe
Into Hey nonny, nonny.

Sing no more ditties, sing no moe
Of dumps so dull and heavy;
The fraud of men was ever so,
Since summer first was leavy.
Then sigh not so, &c.

DON PEDRO.

By my troth, a good song.

BALTHAZAR.

And an ill singer, my lord.

DON PEDRO.

Ha, no, no, faith; thou sing'st well enough for a shift.

BENEDICK [*aside*].

An he had been a dog that should have howl'd thus, they would have hang'd him: and I pray God his bad voice bode no mischief! I had as lief have heard the night-raven, come what plague could have come after it.

DON PEDRO.

Yea, marry, dost thou hear, Balthazar? I pray thee, get us some excellent music; for to-morrow night we would have it at the Lady Hero's chamber-window.

BALTHAZAR.

The best I can, my lord.

DON PEDRO.

Do so: farewell. [*Exeunt* BALTHAZAR *and* MUSICIANS.]—Come hither, Leonato. What was it you told me of to-day,—that your niece Beatrice was in love with Signior Benedick?

CLAUDIO.

O, ay:—stalk on, stalk on; the fowl sits [*aside to* PEDRO].—I did never think that lady would have loved any man.

LEONATO.

No, nor I neither; but most wonderful that she should so dote on Signior Benedick, whom she hath in all outward behaviours seem'd ever to abhor.

BENEDICK [*aside*].

Is't possible? Sits the wind in that corner?

LEONATO.

By my troth, my lord, I cannot tell what to think of it: but that she loves him with an enraged affection,—it is past the infinite of thought.

DON PEDRO.

May be she doth but counterfeit.

CLAUDIO.

Faith, like enough.

LEONATO.

O God, counterfeit! There was never counterfeit of passion came so near the life of passion as she discovers it.

DON PEDRO.

Why, what effects of passion shows she?

CLAUDIO [*aside*].

Bait the hook well; this fish will bite.

LEONATO.

What effects, my lord!—She will sit you,—you heard my daughter tell you how.

CLAUDIO.

She did, indeed.

DON PEDRO.

How, how, I pray you? You amaze me: I would have thought her spirit had been invincible against all assaults of affection.

LEONATO.

I would have sworn it had, my lord; especially against Benedick.

BENEDICK [*aside*].

I should think this a gull, but that the white-bearded fellow speaks it: knavery cannot, sure, hide himself in such reverence.

CLAUDIO [*aside*].

He hath ta'en th'infection: hold it up.

DON PEDRO.

Hath she made her affection known to Benedick?

LEONATO.

No; and swears she never will: that's her torment.

CLAUDIO.

'Tis true, indeed; so your daughter says: 'Shall I,' says she, 'that have so oft encounter'd him with scorn, write to him that I love him?'

LEONATO.

This says she now when she is beginning to write to him; for she'll be up twenty times a night; and there will she sit in her smock till she have writ a sheet of paper:—my daughter tells us all.

CLAUDIO.

Now you talk of a sheet of paper, I remember a pretty jest your daughter told us of.

LEONATO.

O,—when she had writ it, and was reading it over, she found Benedick and Beatrice between the sheet?—

CLAUDIO.

That.

LEONATO.

O, she tore the letter into a thousand halfpence; rail'd at herself, that she should be so immodest to write to one that she knew would flout her: 'I measure him,' says she, 'by my own spirit; for I should flout him, if he writ to me; yea, though I love him, I should.'

CLAUDIO.

Then down upon her knees she falls, weeps, sobs, beats her heart, tears her hair, prays, curses;—'O sweet Benedick! God give me patience!'

LEONATO.

She doth indeed; my daughter says so: and the ecstasy hath so much overborne her, that my daughter is sometime afeard she will do a desperate outrage to herself: it is very true.

DON PEDRO.

It were good that Benedick knew of it by some other, if she will not discover it.

CLAUDIO.

To what end? He would but make a sport of it, and torment the poor lady worse.

DON PEDRO.
An he should, it were an alms to hang him. She's an excellent-sweet lady; and, out of all suspicion, she is virtuous.

CLAUDIO.
And she is exceeding wise

DON PEDRO.
In everything but in loving Benedick.

LEONATO.
O, my lord, wisdom and blood combating in so tender a body, we have ten proofs to one that blood hath the victory. I am sorry for her, as I have just cause, being her uncle and her guardian.

DON PEDRO.
I would she had bestow'd this dotage on me: I would have daff'd all other respects, and made her half myself. I pray you, tell Benedick of it, and hear what he will say.

LEONATO.
Were it good, think you?

CLAUDIO.
Hero thinks surely she will die; for she says she will die, if he love her not; and she will die, ere she make her love known; and she will die, if he woo her, rather than she will bate one breath of her accustom'd crossness.

DON PEDRO.
She doth well: if she should make tender of her love, 'tis very possible he'll scorn it; for the man, as you know all, hath a contemptible spirit.

CLAUDIO.
He is a very proper man.

DON PEDRO.
He hath indeed a good outward happiness.

CLAUDIO.
'Fore God, and in my mind, very wise.

DON PEDRO.
He doth indeed show some sparks that are like wit.

LEONATO.
And I take him to be valiant.

DON PEDRO.
As Hector, I assure you: and in the managing of quarrels you may say he is wise; for either he avoids them with great discretion, or undertakes them with a most Christian-like fear.

LEONATO.
If he do fear God, a' must necessarily keep the peace: if he break the peace, he ought to enter into a quarrel with fear and trembling.

DON PEDRO.
And so will he do; for the man doth fear God, howsoever it seems not in him by some large jests he will make. Well, I am sorry for your niece. Shall we go seek Benedick, and tell him of her love?

CLAUDIO.
Never tell him, my lord: let her wear it out with good counsel.

LEONATO.
Nay, that's impossible: she may wear her heart out first.

DON PEDRO.
Well, we will hear further of it by your daughter: let it cool the while. I love Benedick well; and I could wish he would modestly examine himself, to see how much he is unworthy so good a lady.

LEONATO.
My lord, will you walk? dinner is ready.

CLAUDIO [*aside*].
If he do not dote on her upon this, I will never trust my expectation.

DON PEDRO [*aside*].
Let there be the same net spread for her: and that must your daughter and her gentlewomen carry. The sport will be, when they hold one an opinion of another's dotage, and no such matter: that's the scene that I would see, which will be merely a dumb-show. Let us send her to call him in to dinner.

[*Exeunt* DON PEDRO, CLAUDIO, *and* LEONATO.

BENEDICK [*coming forward*].
This can be no trick: the conference was sadly borne. They have the truth of this from Hero. They seem to pity the lady: it seems her affections have their full bent. Love me! why, it must be requited. I hear how I am censured: they say I will bear myself proudly, if I perceive the love come from her; they say too that she will rather die than give any sign of affection.—I did never think to marry:—I must not seem proud:—happy are they that hear their detractions, and can put them to mending. They say the lady is fair,—'tis a truth, I can bear them witness; and virtuous,—'tis so, I cannot reprove it; and wise, but for loving me,—by my troth, it is no addition to her wit, nor no great argument of her folly, for I will be horribly in love with her. I may chance have some odd quirks and remnants of wit broken on me, because I have rail'd so long against marriage: but doth not the appetite alter? a man loves the meat in his youth that he cannot endure in his age. Shall quips and sentences, and these paper-bullets of the brain, awe a man from the career of his humour? no, the world must be peopled. When I said I would die a bachelor, I did not think I should live till I were married.—Here comes Beatrice. By this day, she's a fair lady: I do spy some marks of love in her.

Enter BEATRICE.

BEATRICE.
Against my will I am sent to bid you come in to dinner.

BENEDICK.
Fair Beatrice, I thank you for your pains.

BEATRICE.
I took no more pains for those thanks than you take pains to thank me: if it had been painful, I would not have come.

BENEDICK.
You take pleasure, then, in the message?

BEATRICE.
Yea, just so much as you may take upon a knife's point, and choke a daw withal.—You have no stomach, signior: fare you well. [*Exit.*

BENEDICK.
Ha! 'Against my will I am sent to bid you come in to dinner,'—there's a double meaning in that. 'I took no more pains for those thanks than you took pains to thank me,'—that's as much as to say,

Any pains that I take for you is as easy as thanks. —If I do not take pity of her, I am a villain; if I do not love her, I am a Jew. I will go get her picture. [*Exit.*

ACT III. SCENE I.

LEONATO'S *orchard.*

Enter HERO *and two gentlewomen,* MARGARET *and* URSULA.

HERO.

GOOD Margaret, run thee to the parlour;
There shalt thou find my cousin Beatrice
Proposing with the prince and Claudio:
Whisper her ear, and tell her, I and Ursula
Walk in the orchard, and our whole discourse
Is all of her; say that thou overheard'st us;
And bid her steal into the pleached bower,
Where honeysuckles, ripen'd by the sun,
Forbid the sun to enter;—like favourites,
Made proud by princes, that advance their pride
Against that power that bred it:—there will she hide her,
To listen our purpose. This is thy office:
Bear thee well in it, and leave us alone.

MARGARET.

I'll make her come, I warrant you, presently. [*Exit.*

HERO.

Now, Ursula, when Beatrice doth come,
As we do trace this alley up and down,
Our talk must only be of Benedick.
When I do name him, let it be thy part
To praise him more than ever man did merit:
My talk to thee must be, how Benedick
Is sick in love with Beatrice. Of this matter
Is little Cupid's crafty arrow made,
That only wounds by hearsay. Now begin;

Enter BEATRICE, *behind.*

For look where Beatrice, like a lapwing, runs
Close by the ground, to hear our conference.

URSULA.

The pleasant'st angling is to see the fish
Cut with her golden oars the silver stream,
And greedily devour the treacherous bait:
So angle we for Beatrice; who even now
Is couched in the woodbine coverture.
Fear you not my part of the dialogue.

HERO.

Then go we near her, that her ear lose nothing
Of the false-sweet bait that we lay for it.—
[*They advance to the bower.*
No, truly, Ursula, she's too disdainful;
I know her spirits are as coy and wild
As haggards of the rock.

URSULA.

But are you sure
That Benedick loves Beatrice so entirely?

HERO.

So says the prince and my new-trothed lord.

URSULA.

And did they bid you tell her of it, madam?

HERO.

They did entreat me to acquaint her of it;
But I persuaded them, if they loved Benedick,
To wish him wrestle with affection,
And never to let Beatrice know of it.

URSULA.

Why did you so? Doth not the gentleman
Deserve as full as fortunate a bed
As ever Beatrice shall couch upon?

HERO.

O god of love! I know he doth deserve
As much as may be yielded to a man:
But Nature never framed a woman's heart
Of prouder stuff than that of Beatrice;
Disdain and scorn ride sparkling in her eyes,
Misprising what they look on; and her wit
Values itself so highly, that to her
All matter else seems weak: she cannot love,
Nor take no shape nor project of affection,
She is so self-endear'd.

URSULA.

Sure, I think so;
And therefore certainly it were not good
She knew his love, lest she make sport at it.

HERO.

Why, you speak truth. I never yet saw man,
How wise, how noble, young, how rarely-featured,
But she would spell him backward: if fair-faced,
She'd swear the gentleman should be her sister;
If black, why, Nature, drawing of an antic,
Made a foul blot; if tall, a lance ill-headed;
If low, an agate very vilely cut;
If speaking, why, a vane blown with all winds;
If silent, why, a block moved with none.
So turns she every man the wrong side out;
And never gives to truth and virtue that
Which simpleness and merit purchaseth.

URSULA.

Sure, sure, such carping is not commendable.

HERO.

No, not to be so odd, and from all fashions,
As Beatrice is, cannot be commendable:
But who dare tell her so? If I should speak,
She would mock me into air; O, she would laugh me
Out of myself, press me to death with wit!
Therefore let Benedick, like cover'd fire,
Consume away in sighs, waste inwardly:
It were a better death than die with mocks,
Which is as bad as die with tickling.

URSULA.

Yet tell her of it: hear what she will say.

HERO.

No; rather I will go to Benedick,
And counsel him to fight against his passion.
And, truly, I'll devise some honest slanders
To stain my cousin with: one doth not know
How much an ill word may empoison liking.

URSULA.

O, do not do your cousin such a wrong!
She cannot be so much without true judgement
(Having so swift and excellent a wit
As she is prized to have) as to refuse
So rare a gentleman as Signior Benedick.

HERO.

He is the only man of Italy,
Always excepted my dear Claudio.

URSULA.

I pray you, be not angry with me, madam,
Speaking my fancy: Signior Benedick,

For shape, for bearing, argument, and valour,
Goes foremost in report through Italy.

HERO.

Indeed, he hath an excellent good name.

URSULA.

His excellence did earn it, ere he had it.—
When are you married, madam?

HERO.

Why, every day, to-morrow. Come, go in:
I'll show thee some attires; and have thy counsel
Which is the best to furnish me to-morrow.

URSULA [*aside*].

She's limed, I warrant you: we have caught her, madam.

HERO [*aside*].

If it prove so, then loving goes by haps:
Some Cupid kills with arrows, some with traps.
[*Exeunt* HERO *and* URSULA.

BEATRICE [*coming forward*].

What fire is in mine ears? Can this be true?
Stand I condemn'd for pride and scorn so much?
Contempt, farewell! and maiden pride, adieu!
No glory lives behind the back of such.
And, Benedick, love on; I will requite thee,
Taming my wild heart to thy loving hand:
If thou dost love, my kindness shall incite thee
To bind our loves up in a holy band;
For others say, thou dost deserve, and I
Believe it better than reportingly. [*Exit.*

SCENE II.

A room in LEONATO'S *house.*

Enter DON PEDRO, CLAUDIO, BENEDICK, *and* LEONATO.

DON PEDRO.

I DO but stay till your marriage be consummate, and then go I toward Arragon.

CLAUDIO.

I'll bring you thither, my lord, if you'll vouchsafe me.

DON PEDRO.

Nay, that would be as great a soil in the new gloss of your marriage, as to show a child his new coat, and forbid him to wear it. I will only be bold with Benedick for his company; for, from the crown of his head to the sole of his foot, he is all mirth: he hath twice or thrice cut Cupid's bow-string, and the little hangman dare not shoot at him; he hath a heart as sound as a bell, and his tongue is the clapper,—for what his heart thinks, his tongue speaks.

BENEDICK.

Gallants, I am not as I have been.

LEONATO.

So say I: methinks you are sadder.

CLAUDIO.

I hope he be in love.

DON PEDRO.

Hang him, truant! there's no true drop of blood in him, to be truly toucht with love: if he be sad, he wants money.

BENEDICK.

I have the toothache.

DON PEDRO.

Draw it.

BENEDICK.

Hang it!

CLAUDIO.

You must hang it first, and draw it afterwards.

DON PEDRO.

What! sigh for the toothache?

LEONATO.

Where is but a humour or a worm?

BENEDICK.

Well, every one can master a grief but he that has it.

CLAUDIO.

Yet say I he is in love.

DON PEDRO.

There is no appearance of fancy in him, unless it be a fancy that he hath to strange disguises; as, to be a Dutchman to-day, a Frenchman to-morrow; or in the shape of two countries at once, as, a German from the waist downward, all slops, and a Spaniard from the hip upward, no doublet. Unless he have a fancy to this foolery, as it appears he hath, he is no fool for fancy, as you would have it appear he is.

CLAUDIO.

If he be not in love with some woman, there is no believing old signs: a' brushes his hat o' mornings; what should that bode?

DON PEDRO.

Hath any man seen him at the barber's?

CLAUDIO.

No, but the barber's man hath been seen with him; and the old ornament of his cheek hath already stuft tennis-balls.

LEONATO.

Indeed, he looks younger than he did, by the loss of a beard.

DON PEDRO.

Nay, a' rubs himself with civet: can you smell him out by that?

CLAUDIO.

That's as much as to say, the sweet youth's in love.

DON PEDRO.

The greatest note of it is his melancholy.

CLAUDIO.

And when was he wont to wash his face?

DON PEDRO.

Yea, or to paint himself? for the which, I hear what they say of him.

CLAUDIO.

Nay, but his jesting spirit; which is now crept into a lute-string, and new-govern'd by stops.

DON PEDRO.

Indeed, that tells a heavy tale for him. Conclude, conclude he is in love.

CLAUDIO.

Nay, but I know who loves him.

DON PEDRO.

That would I know too: I warrant, one that knows him not.

CLAUDIO.

Yes, and his ill conditions; and, in despite of all, dies for him.

DON PEDRO.

She shall be buried with her face upwards.

BENEDICK.

Yet is this no charm for the toothache.—Old signior, walk aside with me: I have studied eight or nine wise words to speak to you, which these hobby-horses must not hear.

[*Exeunt* BENEDICK *and* LEONATO.

DON PEDRO.

For my life, to break with him about Beatrice.

CLAUDIO.

'Tis even so. Hero and Margaret have by this play'd their parts with Beatrice; and then the two bears will not bite one another when they meet.

Enter DON JOHN.

DON JOHN.

My lord and brother, God save you!

DON PEDRO.

Good den, brother.

DON JOHN.

If your leisure served, I would speak with you.

DON PEDRO.

In private?

DON JOHN.

If it please you: yet Count Claudio may hear: for what I would speak of concerns him.

DON PEDRO.

What's the matter?

DON JOHN [*to* CLAUDIO].

Means your lordship to be married to-morrow?

DON PEDRO.

You know he does.

DON JOHN.

I know not that, when he knows what I know.

CLAUDIO.

If there be any impediment, I pray you discover it.

DON JOHN.

You may think I love you not: let that appear hereafter, and aim better at me by that I now will manifest. For my brother, I think he holds you well; and in dearness of heart hath holp to effect your ensuing marriage,—surely suit ill spent and labour ill bestow'd.

DON PEDRO.

Why, what's the matter?

DON JOHN.

I came hither to tell you; and, circumstances shorten'd (for she hath been too long a talking of), the lady is disloyal.

CLAUDIO.

Who, Hero?

DON JOHN.

Even she; Leonato's Hero, your Hero, every man's Hero.

CLAUDIO.

Disloyal!

DON JOHN.

The word is too good to paint out her wickedness; I could say she were worse: think you of a worse title, and I will fit her to it. Wonder not till further warrant: go but with me to-night, you shall see her chamber-window enter'd, even the night before her wedding-day: if you love her then, to-morrow wed her; but it would better fit your honour to change your mind.

CLAUDIO.

May this be so?

DON PEDRO.

I will not think it.

DON JOHN.

If you dare not trust that you see, confess not that you know: if you will follow me, I will show you enough; and when you have seen more, and heard more, proceed accordingly.

CLAUDIO.

If I see anything to-night why I should not marry her to-morrow, in the congregation, where I should wed her, there will I shame her.

DON PEDRO.

And, as I woo'd for thee to obtain her, I will join thee to disgrace her.

DON JOHN.

I will disparage her no further till you are my witnesses: bear it coldly but till midnight, and let the issue show itself.

DON PEDRO.

O day untowardly turn'd!

CLAUDIO.

O mischief strangely thwarting!

DON JOHN.

O plague right well prevented! so will you say when you have seen the sequel. [*Exeunt.*

SCENE III.

A street.

Enter DOGBERRY *and his compartner* VERGES, *with the* WATCH.

DOGBERRY.

ARE you good men and true?

VERGES.

Yea, or else it were pity but they should suffer salvation, body and soul.

DOGBERRY.

Nay, that were a punishment too good for them, if they should have any allegiance in them, being chosen for the prince's watch.

VERGES.

Well, give them their charge, neighbour Dogberry.

DOGBERRY.

First, who think you the most desartless man to be constable?

FIRST WATCHMAN.

Hugh Oatcake, sir, or George Seacoal; for they can write and read.

DOGBERRY.

Come hither, neighbour Seacoal. God hath blest you with a good name; to be a well-favour'd man is the gift of fortune; but to write and read comes by nature.

SECOND WATCHMAN.

Both which, master constable,—

DOGBERRY.

You have: I knew it would be your answer. Well, for your favour, sir, why, give God thanks, and make no boast of it; and for your writing and reading, let that appear when there is no need of such vanity. You are thought here to be the most senseless and fit man for the constable of the watch, therefore bear you the lantern. This is your charge:—you shall comprehend all vagrom men; you are to bid any man stand, in the prince's name.

SECOND WATCHMAN.

How if a' will not stand?

DOGBERRY.

Why, then, take no note of him, but let him go; and presently call the rest of the watch together, and thank God you are rid of a knave.

VERGES.

If he will not stand when he is bidden, he is none of the prince's subjects.

DOGBERRY.

True, and they are to meddle with none but the prince's subjects.—You shall also make no noise in the streets; for for the watch to babble and talk is most tolerable and not to be endured.

SECOND WATCHMAN.

We will rather sleep than talk: we know what belongs to a watch.

DOGBERRY.

Why, you speak like an ancient and most quiet watchman; for I cannot see how sleeping should offend: only, have a care that your bills be not stolen.—Well, you are to call at all the alehouses, and bid those that are drunk get them to bed.

SECOND WATCHMAN.

How if they will not?

DOGBERRY.

Why, then, let them alone till they are sober: if they make you not then the better answer, you may say they are not the men you took them for.

SECOND WATCHMAN.

Well, sir.

DOGBERRY.

If you meet a thief, you may suspect him, by virtue of your office, to be no true man; and, for such kind of men, the less you meddle or make with them, why, the more is for your honesty.

SECOND WATCHMAN.

If we know him to be a thief, shall we not lay hands on him?

DOGBERRY.

Truly, by your office, you may; but I think they that touch pitch will be defiled: the most peaceable way for you, if you do take a thief, is to let him show himself what he is, and steal out of your company.

VERGES.

You have been always call'd a merciful man, partner.

DOGBERRY.

Truly, I would not hang a dog by my will, much more a man who hath any honesty in him.

VERGES.

If you hear a child cry in the night, you must call to the nurse and bid her still it.

SECOND WATCHMAN.

How if the nurse be asleep and will not hear us?

DOGBERRY.

Why, then, depart in peace, and let the child wake her with crying; for the ewe that will not hear her lamb when it baes will never answer a calf when he bleats.

VERGES.

'Tis very true.

DOGBERRY.

This is the end of the charge:—you, constable, are to present the prince's own person: if you meet the prince in the night, you may stay him.

VERGES.

Nay, by'r lady, that I think a' cannot.

DOGBERRY.

Five shillings to one on't, with any man that knows the statues, he may stay him: marry, not without the prince be willing; for, indeed, the watch ought to offend no man; and it is an offence to stay a man against his will.

VERGES.

By'r lady, I think it be so.

DOGBERRY.

Ha, ah-ha! Well, masters, good night: an there be any matter of weight chances, call up me: keep your fellows' counsels and your own; and good night.—Come, neighbour.

FIRST WATCHMAN.

Well, masters, we hear our charge: let us go sit here upon the church-bench till two, and then all to bed.

DOGBERRY.

One word more, honest neighbours. I pray you, watch about Signior Leonato's door; for the wedding being there to-morrow, there is a great coil to-night. Adieu: be vigitant, I beseech you.

[*Exeunt* DOGBERRY *and* VERGES.

Enter BORACHIO *and* CONRADE.

BORACHIO.

What, Conrade!—

FIRST WATCHMAN [*aside*].

Peace! stir not.

BORACHIO.

Conrade, I say!—

CONRADE.

Here, man; I am at thy elbow.

BORACHIO.

Mass, and my elbow itcht; I thought there would a scab follow.

CONRADE.

I will owe thee an answer for that: and now forward with thy tale.

BORACHIO.

Stand thee close, then, under this pent-house, for it drizzles rain; and I will, like a true drunkard, utter all to thee.

FIRST WATCHMAN [*aside*].

Some treason, masters: yet stand close.

BORACHIO.

Therefore know I have earn'd of Don John a thousand ducats.

CONRADE.

Is it possible that any villainy should be so dear?

BORACHIO.

Thou shouldst rather ask, if it were possible any villainy should be so rich; for when rich villains have need of poor ones, poor ones may make what price they will.

CONRADE.

I wonder at it.

BORACHIO.

That shows thou art unconfirm'd. Thou knowest that the fashion of a doublet, or a hat, or a cloak, is nothing to a man.

CONRADE.

Yes, it is apparel.

BORACHIO.
I mean, the fashion.

CONRADE.
Yes, the fashion is the fashion.

BORACHIO.
Tush! I may as well say the fool's the fool. But seest thou not what a deform'd thief this fashion is?

FIRST WATCHMAN [*aside*].
I know that Deform'd; a' has been a vile thief this seven year; a' goes up and down like a gentleman: I remember his name.

BORACHIO.
Didst thou not hear somebody?

CONRADE.
No; 'twas the vane on the house.

BORACHIO.
Seest thou not, I say, what a deform'd thief this fashion is? how giddily 'a turns about all the hot bloods between fourteen and five-and-thirty? sometimes fashioning them like Pharaoh's soldiers in the reechy painting, sometime like god Bel's priests in the old church-window, sometime like the shaven Hercules in the smircht worm-eaten tapestry, where his codpiece seems as massy as his club?

CONRADE.
All this I see; and I see that the fashion wears out more apparel than the man. But art not thou thyself giddy with the fashion too, that thou hast shifted out of thy tale into telling me of the fashion?

BORACHIO.
Not so, neither: but know that I have to-night woo'd Margaret, the Lady Hero's gentlewoman, by the name of Hero: she leans me out at her mistress' chamber-window, bids me a thousand times good night,—I tell this tale vilely:—I should first tell thee how the prince, Claudio, and my master, planted and placed and possest by my master Don John, saw afar off in the orchard this amiable encounter.

CONRADE.
And thought they Margaret was Hero?

BORACHIO.
Two of them did, the prince and Claudio; but the devil my master knew she was Margaret; and partly by his oaths, which first possest them, partly by the dark night, which did deceive them, but chiefly by my villainy, which did confirm any slander that Don John had made, away went Claudio enraged; swore he would meet her, as he was appointed, next morning at the temple, and there, before the whole congregation, shame her with what he saw o'ernight, and send her home again without a husband.

FIRST WATCHMAN.
We charge you, in the prince's name, stand!

SECOND WATCHMAN.
Call up the right master constable. We have here recover'd the most dangerous piece of lechery that ever was known in the commonwealth.

FIRST WATCHMAN.
And one Deform'd is one of them: I know him; a' wears a lock.

CONRADE.
Masters, masters,—

SECOND WATCHMAN.
You'll be made bring Deform'd forth, I warrant you.

CONRADE.
Masters,—

FIRST WATCHMAN.
Never speak: we charge you let us obey you to go with us.

BORACHIO.
We are like to prove a goodly commodity, being taken up of these men's bills.

CONRADE.
A commodity in question, I warrant you.—Come, we'll obey you. [*Exeunt.*

SCENE IV.

A room in LEONATO'S *house.*

Enter HERO, MARGARET, *and* URSULA.

HERO.
GOOD Ursula, wake my cousin Beatrice, and desire her to rise.

URSULA.
I will, lady.

HERO.
And bid her come hither.

URSULA.
Well. [*Exit.*

MARGARET.
Troth, I think your other rabato were better.

HERO.
No, pray thee, good Meg, I'll wear this.

MARGARET.
By my troth, 's not so good; and I warrant your cousin will say so.

HERO.
My cousin's a fool, and thou art another: I'll wear none but this.

MARGARET.
I like the new tire within excellently, if the hair were a thought browner; and your gown's a most rare fashion, i'faith. I saw the Duchess of Milan's gown that they praise so.

HERO.
O, that exceeds, they say.

MARGARET.
By my troth, 's but a night-gown in respect of yours,—cloth-o'-gold, and cuts, and laced with silver, set with pearls, down sleeves, side sleeves, and skirts round underborne with a bluish tinsel: but for a fine, quaint, graceful, and excellent fashion, yours is worth ten on't.

HERO.
God give me joy to wear it! for my heart is exceeding heavy.

MARGARET.
'Twill be heavier soon by the weight of a man.

HERO.
Fie upon thee! art not ashamed?

MARGARET.
Of what, lady? of speaking honourably? Is not marriage honourable in a beggar? Is not your lord honourable without marriage? I think you would have me say, 'saving your reverence, a husband'; an bad thinking do not wrest true speaking, I'll offend nobody: is there any harm in 'the heavier

for a husband'? None, I think, an it be the right husband and the right wife; otherwise 'tis light, and not heavy: ask my Lady Beatrice else; here she comes.

Enter BEATRICE.

HERO.

Good morrow, coz.

BEATRICE.

Good morrow, sweet Hero.

HERO.

Why, how now! do you speak in the sick tune?

BEATRICE.

I am out of all other tune, methinks.

MARGARET.

Clap's into *Light o' love*; that goes without a burden: do you sing it, and I'll dance it.

BEATRICE.

Ye light o' love, with your heels!—then, if your husband have stables enough, you'll see he shall lack no barns.

MARGARET.

O illegitimate construction! I scorn that with my heels.

BEATRICE.

'Tis almost five o'clock, cousin; 'tis time you were ready.—By my troth, I am exceeding ill:—heigh-ho!

MARGARET.

For a hawk, a horse, or a husband?

BEATRICE.

For the letter that begins them all, H.

MARGARET.

Well, an you be not turn'd Turk, there's no more sailing by the star.

BEATRICE.

What means the fool, trow?

MARGARET.

Nothing I; but God send every one their heart's desire!

HERO.

These gloves the Count sent me; they are an excellent perfume.

BEATRICE.

I am stuft, cousin; I cannot smell.

MARGARET.

A maid, and stuft! there's goodly catching of cold.

BEATRICE.

O, God help me! God help me! how long have you profest apprehension?

MARGARET.

Ever since you left it. Doth not my wit become me rarely?

BEATRICE.

It is not seen enough; you should wear it in your cap.—By my troth, I am sick.

MARGARET.

Get you some of this distill'd Carduus Benedictus, and lay it to your heart: it is the only thing for a qualm.

HERO.

There thou prick'st her with a thistle.

BEATRICE.

Benedictus! why Benedictus? you have some moral in this Benedictus.

MARGARET.

Moral! no, by my troth, I have no moral meaning; I meant, plain holy-thistle. You may think perchance that I think you are in love: nay, by'r lady, I am not such a fool to think what I list; nor I list not to think what I can; nor, indeed, I cannot think, if I would think my heart out of thinking, that you are in love, or that you will be in love, or that you can be in love. Yet Benedick was such another, and now is he become a man: he swore he would never marry; and yet now, in despite of his heart, he eats his meat without grudging: and how you may be converted, I know not; but methinks you look with your eyes as other women do.

BEATRICE.

What pace is this that thy tongue keeps?

MARGARET.

Not a false gallop.

Enter URSULA.

URSULA.

Madam, withdraw: the prince, the count, Signior Benedick, Don John, and all the gallants of the town, are come to fetch you to church.

HERO.

Help to dress me, good coz, good Meg, good Ursula. [*Exeunt.*

SCENE V.

Another room in LEONATO'S *house.*

Enter LEONATO, *with the* CONSTABLE DOGBERRY *and the* HEADBOROUGH VERGES.

LEONATO.

WHAT would you with me, honest neighbour?

DOGBERRY.

Marry, sir, I would have some confidence with you that decerns you nearly.

LEONATO.

Brief, I pray you; for you see it is a busy time with me.

DOGBERRY.

Marry, this it is, sir,—

VERGES.

Yes, in truth it is, sir.

LEONATO.

What is it, my good friends?

DOGBERRY.

Goodman Verges, sir, speaks a little off the matter: an old man, sir, and his wits are not so blunt as, God help, I would desire they were; but, in faith, honest as the skin between his brows.

VERGES.

Yes, I thank God I am as honest as any man living that is an old man and no honester than I.

DOGBERRY.

Comparisons are odorous: *palabras*, neighbour Verges.

LEONATO.

Neighbours, you are tedious.

DOGBERRY.

It pleases your worship to say so, but we are the poor duke's officers; but truly, for mine own part, if I were as tedious as a king, I could find in my heart to bestow it all of your worship.

LEONATO.

All thy tediousness on me, ha!

DOGBERRY.

Yea, an 'twere a thousand pound more than 'tis;

for I hear as good exclamation on your worship as of any man in the city; and though I be but a poor man, I am glad to hear it.

VERGES.

And so am I.

LEONATO.

I would fain know what you have to say.

VERGES.

Marry, sir, our watch to-night, excepting your worship's presence, ha' ta'en a couple of as arrant knaves as any in Messina.

DOGBERRY.

A good old man, sir; he will be talking: as they say, When the age is in, the wit is out: God help us! it is a world to see!—Well said, i'faith, neighbour Verges:—well, God's a good man; an two men ride of a horse, one must ride behind.—An honest soul, i'faith, sir; by my troth, he is, as ever broke bread: but God is to be worshipt: all men are not alike,—alas, good neighbour!

LEONATO.

Indeed, neighbour, he comes too short of you.

DOGBERRY.

Gifts that God gives.

LEONATO.

I must leave you.

DOGBERRY.

One word, sir: our watch, sir, have indeed comprehended two aspicious persons, and we would have them this morning examined before your worship.

LEONATO.

Take their examination yourself, and bring it me: I am now in great haste, as it may appear unto you.

DOGBERRY.

It shall be suffigance.

LEONATO.

Drink some wine ere you go: fare you well.

Enter a MESSENGER.

MESSENGER.

My lord, they stay for you to give your daughter to her husband.

LEONATO.

I'll wait upon them: I am ready.

[*Exeunt* LEONATO *and* MESSENGER.

DOGBERRY.

Go, good partner, go, get you to Francis Seacoal; bid him bring his pen and inkhorn to the gaol: we are now to examination these men.

VERGES.

And we must do it wisely.

DOGBERRY.

We will spare for no wit, I warrant you; here's that shall drive some of them to a non-come; only get the learned writer to set down our excommunication, and meet me at the gaol. [*Exeunt.*

ACT IV. SCENE I.

A church.

Enter DON PEDRO, DON JOHN, LEONATO, FRIAR FRANCIS, CLAUDIO, BENEDICK, HERO, BEATRICE, *and* ATTENDANTS.

LEONATO.

COME, Friar Francis, be brief; only to the plain form of marriage, and you shall recount their particular duties afterwards.

FRIAR FRANCIS.

You come hither, my lord, to marry this lady?

CLAUDIO.

No.

LEONATO.

To be married to her:—friar, you come to marry her.

FRIAR FRANCIS.

Lady, you come hither to be married to this count?

HERO.

I do.

FRIAR FRANCIS.

If either of you know any inward impediment why you should not be conjoin'd, I charge you, on your souls, to utter it.

CLAUDIO.

Know you any, Hero?

HERO.

None, my lord.

FRIAR FRANCIS.

Know you any, count?

LEONATO.

I dare make his answer,—none.

CLAUDIO.

O, what men dare do! what men may do! what men daily do, not knowing what they do!

BENEDICK.

How now! interjections? Why, then, some be of laughing, as, Ah, ha, he!

CLAUDIO.

Stand thee by, friar.—Father, by your leave:
Will you with free and unconstrained soul
Give me this maid, your daughter?

LEONATO.

As freely, son, as God did give her me.

CLAUDIO.

And what have I to give you back, whose worth
May counterpoise this rich and precious gift?

DON PEDRO.

Nothing, unless you render her again.

CLAUDIO.

Sweet prince, you learn me noble thankfulness.—
There, Leonato, take her back again:
Give not this rotten orange to your friend;
She's but the sign and semblance of her honour.—
Behold how like a maid she blushes here!
O, what authority and show of truth
Can cunning sin cover itself withal!
Comes not that blood as modest evidence
To witness simple virtue? Would you not swear,
All you that see her, that she were a maid,
By these exterior shows? But she is none:
She knows the heat of a luxurious bed;
Her blush is guiltiness, not modesty.

LEONATO.

What do you mean, my lord?

CLAUDIO.

Not to be married, not to knit my soul
To an approved wanton.

LEONATO.

Dear my lord, if you, in your own proof,
Have vanquisht the resistance of her youth,
And made defeat of her virginity,—

CLAUDIO.

I know what you would say: if I have known her,
You will say she did embrace me as a husband,
And so extenuate the 'forehand sin:
No, Leonato,
I never tempted her with word too large;
But, as a brother to his sister, show'd
Bashful sincerity and comely love.

HERO.

And seem'd I ever otherwise to you?

CLAUDIO.

Out on thee, seeming! I will write against it:
You seem to me as Dian in her orb,
As chaste as is the bud ere it be blown;
But you are more intemperate in your blood
Than Venus, or those pamper'd animals
That rage in savage sensuality.

HERO.

Is my lord well, that he doth speak so wide?

CLAUDIO.

Sweet prince, why speak not you?

DON PEDRO.

What should I speak?
I stand dishonour'd, that have gone about
To link my dear friend to a common stale.

LEONATO.

Are these things spoken? or do I but dream?

DON JOHN.

Sir, they are spoken, and these things are true.

BENEDICK.

This looks not like a nuptial.

HERO.

True!—O God!

CLAUDIO.

Leonato, stand I here?
Is this the prince? is this the prince's brother?
Is this face Hero's? are our eyes our own?

LEONATO.

All this is so: but what of this, my lord?

CLAUDIO.

Let me but move one question to your daughter;
And, by that fatherly and kindly power
That you have in her, bid her answer truly.

LEONATO.

I charge thee do so, as thou art my child.

HERO.

O, God defend me! how am I beset!—
What kind of catechising call you this?

CLAUDIO.

To make you answer truly to your name.

HERO.

Is it not Hero? Who can blot that name
With any just reproach?

CLAUDIO.

Marry, that can Hero;
Hero itself can blot out Hero's virtue.
What man was he talkt with you yesternight
Out at your window betwixt twelve and one?
Now, if you are a maid, answer to this.

HERO.

I talkt with no man at that hour, my lord.

DON PEDRO.

Why, then are you no maiden.—Leonato,
I am sorry you must hear: upon mine honour,
Myself, my brother, and this grieved count
Did see her, hear her, at that hour last night
Talk with a ruffian at her chamber-window;
Who hath indeed, most like a liberal villain,
Confest the vile encounters they have had
A thousand times in secret.

DON JOHN.

Fie, fie! they are not to be named, my lord,
Not to be spoke of;
There is not chastity enough in language,
Without offence to utter them.—Thus, pretty lady,
I am sorry for thy much misgovernment.

CLAUDIO.

O Hero, what a Hero hadst thou been,
If half thy outward graces had been placed
About thy thoughts and counsels of thy heart!
But fare thee well, most foul, most fair! farewell,
Thou pure impiety and impious purity!
For thee I'll lock up all the gates of love,
And on my eyelids shall conjecture hang,
To turn all beauty into thoughts of harm,
And never shall it more be gracious.

LEONATO.

Hath no man's dagger here a point for me?
[HERO *swoons.*

BEATRICE.

Why, how now, cousin! wherefore sink you down?

DON JOHN.

Come, let us go. These things, come thus to light,
Smother her spirits up.
[*Exeunt* DON PEDRO, DON JOHN, CLAUDIO, *and* ATTENDANTS.

BENEDICK.

How doth the lady?

BEATRICE.

Dead, I think:—help, uncle:—
Hero! why, Hero!—uncle!—Signior Benedick!—friar!

LEONATO.

O Fate, take not away thy heavy hand!
Death is the fairest cover for her shame
That may be wisht for.

BEATRICE.

How now, cousin Hero!

FRIAR FRANCIS.

Have comfort, lady.

LEONATO.

Dost thou look up?

FRIAR FRANCIS.

Yea, wherefore should she not?

LEONATO.

Wherefore! Why, doth not every earthly thing
Cry shame upon her? Could she here deny
The story that is printed in her blood?—
Do not live, Hero; do not ope thine eyes:
For, did I think thou wouldst not quickly die,
Thought I thy spirits were stronger than thy shames,
Myself would, on the rearward of reproaches,
Strike at thy life. Grieved I, I had but one?
Chid I for that at frugal nature's frame?
O, one too much by thee! Why had I one?
Why ever wast thou lovely in my eyes?
Why had I not with charitable hand
Took up a beggar's issue at my gates,
Who smirched thus and mired with infamy,
I might have said, 'No part of it is mine;

This shame derives itself from unknown loins'?
But mine, and mine I loved, and mine I praised,
And mine that I was proud on; mine so much
That I myself was to myself not mine,
Valuing of her; why, she—O, she is fall'n
Into a pit of ink, that the wide sea
Hath drops too few to wash her clean again,
And salt too little which may season give
To her foul-tainted flesh!

BENEDICK.
Sir, sir, be patient.
For my part, I am so attired in wonder,
I know not what to say.

BEATRICE.
O, on my soul, my cousin is belied!

BENEDICK.
Lady, were you her bedfellow last night?

BEATRICE.
No, truly, not; although, until last night,
I have this twelvemonth been her bedfellow.

LEONATO.
Confirm'd, confirm'd! O, that is stronger made
Which was before barr'd up with ribs of iron!
Would the two princes lie? and Claudio lie,
Who loved her so, that, speaking of her foulness,
Washt it with tears? Hence from her! let her die.

FRIAR FRANCIS.
Hear me a little;
For I have only been silent so long,
And given way unto this course of fortune,
By noting of the lady: I have markt
A thousand blushing apparitions
To start into her face; a thousand innocent shames
In angel whiteness beat away those blushes;
And in her eye there hath appear'd a fire,
To burn the errors that these princes hold
Against her maiden truth. Call me a fool;
Trust not my reading nor my observations,
Which with experimental seal doth warrant
The tenour of my book; trust not my age,
My reverence, calling, nor divinity,
If this sweet lady lie not guiltless here
Under some biting error.

LEONATO.
Friar, it cannot be.
Thou see'st that all the grace that she hath left
Is that she will not add to her damnation
A sin of perjury; she not denies it:
Why seek'st thou, then, to cover with excuse
That which appears in proper nakedness?

FRIAR FRANCIS.
Lady, what man is he you are accused of?

HERO.
They know that do accuse me; I know none:
If I know more of any man alive
Than that which maiden modesty doth warrant,
Let all my sins lack mercy!—O my father,
Prove you that any man with me conversed
At hours unmeet, or that I yesternight
Maintain'd the change of words with any creature,
Refuse me, hate me, torture me to death!

FRIAR FRANCIS.
There is some strange misprision in the princes.

BENEDICK.
Two of them have the very bent of honour;
And if their wisdoms be misled in this,
The practice of it lives in John the bastard,
Whose spirits toil in frame of villainies.

LEONATO.
I know not. If they speak but truth of her,
These hands shall tear her; if they wrong her honour,
The proudest of them shall well hear of it.
Time hath not yet so dried this blood of mine,
Nor age so eat up my invention,
Nor fortune made such havoc of my means,
Nor my bad life reft me so much of friends,
But they shall find, awaked in such a kind,
Both strength of limb and policy of mind,
Ability in means and choice of friends,
To quit me of them throughly.

FRIAR FRANCIS.
Pause awhile,
And let my counsel sway you in this case.
Your daughter here the princes left for dead,
Let her awhile be secretly kept in,
And publish it that she is dead indeed;
Maintain a mourning ostentation,
And on your family's old monument
Hang mournful epitaphs, and do all rites
That appertain unto a burial.

LEONATO.
What shall become of this? what will this do?

FRIAR FRANCIS.
Marry, this, well carried, shall on her behalf
Change slander to remorse;—that is some good:
But not for that dream I on this strange course,
But on this travail look for greater birth.
She dying, as it must be so maintain'd,
Upon the instant that she was accused,
Shall be lamented, pitied, and excused
Of every hearer: for it so falls out,
That what we have we prize not to the worth
Whiles we enjoy it; but being lackt and lost,
Why, then we rack the value, then we find
The virtue that possession would not show us
Whiles it was ours. So will it fare with Claudio:
When he shall hear she died upon his words,
Th'idea of her life shall sweetly creep
Into his study of imagination;
And every lovely organ of her life
Shall come apparell'd in more precious habit,
More moving-delicate and full of life,
Into the eye and prospect of his soul,
Than when she lived indeed; then shall he mourn
(If ever love had interest in his liver),
And wish he had not so accused her,—
No, though he thought his accusation true.
Let this be so, and doubt not but success
Will fashion the event in better shape
Than I can lay it down in likelihood.
But if all aim but this be levell'd false,
The supposition of the lady's death
Will quench the wonder of her infamy:
And if it sort not well, you may conceal her
(As best befits her wounded reputation)
In some reclusive and religious life,
Out of all eyes, tongues, minds, and injuries.

BENEDICK.

Signior Leonato, let the friar advise you:
And though you know my inwardness and love
Is very much unto the prince and Claudio,
Yet, by mine honour, I will deal in this
As secretly and justly as your soul
Should with your body.

LEONATO.

Being that I flow in grief,
The smallest twine may lead me.

FRIAR FRANCIS.

'Tis well consented: presently away; [cure.—
For to strange sores strangely they strain the
Come, lady, die to live: this wedding-day [endure.
Perhaps is but prolong'd: have patience and

[*Exeunt* FRIAR FRANCIS, HERO, *and* LEONATO.

BENEDICK.

Lady Beatrice, have you wept all this while?

BEATRICE.

Yea, and I will weep a while longer.

BENEDICK.

I will not desire that.

BEATRICE.

You have no reason; I do it freely.

BENEDICK.

Surely I do believe your fair cousin is wrong'd.

BEATRICE.

Ah, how much might the man deserve of me that would right her!

BENEDICK.

Is there any way to show such friendship?

BEATRICE.

A very even way, but no such friend.

BENEDICK.

May a man do it?

BEATRICE.

It is a man's office, but not yours.

BENEDICK.

I do love nothing in the world so well as you: is not that strange?

BEATRICE.

As strange as the thing I know not. It were as possible for me to say I loved nothing so well as you: but believe me not; and yet I lie not; I confess nothing, nor I deny nothing.—I am sorry for my cousin.

BENEDICK.

By my sword, Beatrice, thou lovest me.

BEATRICE.

Do not swear by it, and eat it.

BENEDICK.

I will swear by it that you love me; and I will make him eat it that says I love not you.

BEATRICE.

Will you not eat your word?

BENEDICK.

With no sauce that can be devised to it. I protest I love thee.

BEATRICE.

Why, then, God forgive me!

BENEDICK.

What offence, sweet Beatrice?

BEATRICE.

You have stay'd me in a happy hour: I was about to protest I loved you.

BENEDICK.

And do it with all thy heart.

BEATRICE.

I love you with so much of my heart, that none is left to protest.

BENEDICK.

Come, bid me do any thing for thee.

BEATRICE.

Kill Claudio.

BENEDICK.

Ha! not for the wide world.

BEATRICE.

You kill me to deny it. Farewell.

BENEDICK.

Tarry, sweet Beatrice.

BEATRICE.

I am gone, though I am here:—there is no love in you:—nay, I pray you, let me go.

BENEDICK.

Beatrice,—

BEATRICE.

In faith, I will go.

BENEDICK.

We'll be friends first.

BEATRICE.

You dare easier be friends with me than fight with mine enemy.

BENEDICK.

Is Claudio thine enemy?

BEATRICE.

Is he not approved in the height a villain, that hath slander'd, scorn'd, dishonour'd my kinswoman?—O that I were a man!—What, bear her in hand until they come to take hands; and then, with public accusation, uncover'd slander, unmitigated rancour,—O God, that I were a man! I would eat his heart in the market-place.

BENEDICK.

Hear me, Beatrice,—

BEATRICE.

Talk with a man out at a window!—a proper saying!

BENEDICK.

Nay, but, Beatrice,—

BEATRICE.

Sweet Hero!—she is wrong'd, she is slander'd, she is undone.

BENEDICK.

Beat—

BEATRICE.

Princes and counties! Surely, a princely testimony, a goodly count, Count Comfect; a sweet gallant, surely! O that I were a man for his sake! or that I had any friend would be a man for my sake! But manhood is melted into curtsies, valour into compliment, and men are only turn'd into tongue, and trim ones too: he is now as valiant as Hercules that only tells a lie, and swears it.—I cannot be a man with wishing, therefore I will die a woman with grieving.

BENEDICK.

Tarry, good Beatrice. By this hand, I love thee.

BEATRICE.

Use it for my love some other way than swearing by it.

BENEDICK.

Think you in your soul the Count Claudio hath wrong'd Hero?

BEATRICE.

Yea, as sure as I have a thought or a soul.

BENEDICK.

Enough, I am engaged; I will challenge him. I will kiss your hand, and so I leave you. By this hand, Claudio shall render me a dear account. As you hear of me, so think of me. Go, comfort your cousin: I must say she is dead: and so, farewell. [*Exeunt.*

SCENE II.

A prison.

Enter DOGBERRY *and* VERGES, *and* SEXTON, *in gowns; and the* WATCH, *with* CONRADE *and* BORACHIO.

DOGBERRY.

Is our whole dissembly appear'd?

VERGES.

O, a stool and a cushion for the sexton.

SEXTON.

Which be the malefactors?

DOGBERRY.

Marry, that am I and my partner.

VERGES.

Nay, that's certain; we have the exhibition to examine.

SEXTON.

But which are the offenders that are to be examined? let them come before master constable.

DOGBERRY.

Yea, marry, let them come before me.—What is your name, friend?

BORACHIO.

Borachio.

DOGBERRY.

Pray, write down—Borachio.—Yours, sirrah?

CONRADE.

I am a gentleman, sir, and my name is Conrade.

DOGBERRY.

Write down—master gentleman Conrade.—Masters, do you serve God?

CONRADE *and* BORACHIO.

Yea, sir, we hope.

DOGBERRY.

Write down—that they hope they serve God:—and write God first; for God defend but God should go before such villains!—Masters, it is proved already that you are little better than false knaves; and it will go near to be thought so shortly. How answer you for yourselves?

CONRADE.

Marry, sir, we say we are none.

DOGBERRY.

A marvellous witty fellow, I assure you; but I will go about with him.—Come you hither, sirrah: a word in your ear, sir; I say to you, it is thought you are false knaves.

BORACHIO.

Sir, I say to you we are none.

DOGBERRY.

Well, stand aside.—'Fore God, they are both in a tale. Have you writ down—that they are none?

SEXTON.

Master constable, you go not the way to examine: you must call forth the watch that are their accusers.

DOGBERRY.

Yea, marry, that's the eftest way.—Let the watch come forth.—Masters, I charge you, in the prince's name, accuse these men.

FIRST WATCHMAN.

This man said, sir, that Don John, the prince's brother, was a villain.

DOGBERRY.

Write down—Prince John a villain.—Why, this is flat perjury, to call a prince's brother villain.

BORACHIO.

Master constable,—

DOGBERRY.

Pray thee, fellow, peace: I do not like thy look, I promise thee.

SEXTON.

What heard you him say else?

SECOND WATCHMAN.

Marry, that he had received a thousand ducats of Don John for accusing the Lady Hero wrongfully.

DOGBERRY.

Flat burglary as ever was committed.

VERGES.

Yea, by th'mass, that it is.

SEXTON.

What else, fellow?

FIRST WATCHMAN.

And that Count Claudio did mean, upon his words, to disgrace Hero before the whole assembly, and not marry her.

DOGBERRY.

O villain! thou wilt be condemn'd into everlasting redemption for this.

SEXTON.

What else?

SECOND WATCHMAN.

This is all.

SEXTON.

And this is more, masters, than you can deny. Prince John is this morning secretly stolen away; Hero was in this manner accused, in this very manner refused, and upon the grief of this suddenly died.—Master constable, let these men be bound, and brought to Leonato's: I will go before and show him their examination. [*Exit.*

DOGBERRY.

Come, let them be opinion'd.

VERGES.

Let them be in the hands—

CONRADE.

Off, coxcomb!

DOGBERRY.

God's my life, where's the sexton? let him write down—the prince's officer, coxcomb.—Come, bind them.—Thou naughty varlet!

CONRADE.

Away! you are an ass, you are an ass.

DOGBERRY.

Dost thou not suspect my place? dost thou not suspect my years?—O that he were here to write me down an ass!—but, masters, remember that I am an ass; though it be not written down, yet forget not that I am an ass.—No, thou villain, thou art full of piety, as shall be proved upon thee by good witness. I am a wise fellow; and, which is more, an officer; and, which is more, a householder; and, which is more, as pretty a piece of flesh as any in Messina; and one that knows the law, go to; and a rich fellow enough, go to; find a fellow that hath had losses; and one that hath two gowns, and every thing handsome about him.—Bring him away.—O that I had been writ down an ass!

[*Exeunt.*

ACT V. SCENE I.

Before LEONATO'S *house.*

Enter LEONATO *and his brother* ANTONIO.

ANTONIO.

If you go on thus, you will kill yourself;
And 'tis not wisdom thus to second grief
Against yourself.

LEONATO.

I pray thee, cease thy counsel,
Which falls into mine ears as profitless
As water in a sieve: give not me counsel;
Nor let no comforter delight mine ear
But such a one whose wrongs do suit with mine.
Bring me a father that so loved his child,
Whose joy of her is overwhelm'd like mine,
And bid him speak of patience;
Measure his woe the length and breadth of mine,
And let it answer every strain for strain,
As thus for thus, and such a grief for such,
In every lineament, branch, shape, and form:
If such a one will smile, and stroke his beard,
Bid sorrow wag, cry 'hem!' when he should groan,
Patch grief with proverbs, make misfortune drunk
With candle-wasters,—bring him yet to me,
And I of him will gather patience.
But there is no such man: for, brother, men
Can counsel and speak comfort to that grief
Which they themselves not feel; but, tasting it,
Their counsel turns to passion, which before
Would give preceptial medicine to rage,
Fetter strong madness in a silken thread,
Charm ache with air, and agony with words:
No, no, 'tis all men's office to speak patience
To those that wring under the load of sorrow,
But no man's virtue nor sufficiency
To be so moral when he shall endure
The like himself. Therefore give me no counsel:
My griefs cry louder than advertisement.

ANTONIO.

Therein do men from children nothing differ.

LEONATO.

I pray thee, peace,—I will be flesh and blood;
For there was never yet philosopher
That could endure the toothache patiently,
However they have writ the style of gods,
And made a push at chance and sufferance.

ANTONIO.

Yet bend not all the harm upon yourself;
Make those that do offend you suffer too.

LEONATO.

There thou speak'st reason: nay, I will do so.
My soul doth tell me Hero is belied;
And that shall Claudio know; so shall the prince,
And all of them that thus dishonour her.

ANTONIO.

Here comes the prince and Claudio hastily.

Enter DON PEDRO *and* CLAUDIO.

DON PEDRO.

Good den, good den.

CLAUDIO.

Good day to both of you.

LEONATO.

Hear you, my lords,—

DON PEDRO.

We have some haste, Leonato.

LEONATO.

Some haste, my lord!—well, fare you well, my lord:—
Are you so hasty now?—well, all is one.

DON PEDRO.

Nay, do not quarrel with us, good old man.

ANTONIO.

If he could right himself with quarrelling,
Some of us would lie low.

CLAUDIO.

Who wrongs him?

LEONATO.

Marry, thou dost wrong me; thou dissembler, thou:—
Nay, never lay thy hand upon thy sword;
I fear thee not.

CLAUDIO.

Marry, beshrew my hand,
If it should give your age such cause of fear:
In faith, my hand meant nothing to my sword.

LEONATO.

Tush, tush, man; never fleer and jest at me:
I speak not like a dotard nor a fool,
As, under privilege of age, to brag
What I have done, being young, or what would do,
Were I not old. Know, Claudio, to thy head,
Thou hast so wrong'd mine innocent child and me,
That I am forced to lay my reverence by,
And, with grey hairs and bruise of many days,
Do challenge thee to trial of a man.
I say thou hast belied mine innocent child;
Thy slander hath gone through and through her heart,
And she lies buried with her ancestors,—
O, in a tomb where never scandal slept,
Save this of hers, framed by thy villainy!

CLAUDIO.

My villainy!

LEONATO.

Thine, Claudio; thine, I say.

DON PEDRO.

You say not right, old man.

LEONATO.

My lord, my lord,
I'll prove it on his body, if he dare,
Despite his nice fence and his active practice,
His May of youth and bloom of lustihood.

CLAUDIO.

Away! I will not have to do with you.

LEONATO.

Canst thou so daff me? Thou hast kill'd my child:
If thou kill'st me, boy, thou shalt kill a man.

ANTONIO.

He shall kill two of us, and men indeed:
But that's no matter; let him kill one first;—
Win me and wear me,—let him answer me.—
Come, follow me, boy; come, sir boy, come, follow me:
Sir boy, I'll whip you from your foining fence;
Nay, as I am a gentleman, I will.

LEONATO.

Brother,—

ANTONIO.

Content yourself. God knows I loved my niece;
And she is dead, slander'd to death by villains,
That dare as well answer a man indeed
As I dare take a serpent by the tongue;
Boys, apes, braggarts, Jacks, milksops!

LEONATO.

Brother Antony,—

ANTONIO.

Hold you content. What, man! I know them, yea,
And what they weigh, even to the utmost scruple,—
Scrambling, out-facing, fashion-mong'ring boys,
That lie, and cog, and flout, deprave, and slander,
Go antickly, show outward hideousness,
And speak off half a dozen dangerous words,
How they might hurt their enemies, if they durst;
And this is all.

LEONATO.

But, brother Antony,—

ANTONIO.

Come, 'tis no matter:
Do not you meddle; let me deal in this.

DON PEDRO.

Gentlemen both, we will not wake your patience.
My heart is sorry for your daughter's death:
But, on my honour, she was charged with nothing
But what was true, and very full of proof.

LEONATO.

My lord, my lord,—

DON PEDRO.

I will not hear you.

LEONATO.

No?—
Come, brother, away.—I will be heard.

ANTONIO.

And shall,
Or some of us will smart for't.

[*Exeunt* LEONATO *and* ANTONIO.

DON PEDRO.

See, see; here comes the man we went to seek.

Enter BENEDICT.

CLAUDIO.

Now, signior, what news?

BENEDICK.

Good day, my lord.

DON PEDRO.

Welcome, signior: you are almost come to part almost a fray.

CLAUDIO.

We had like to have had our two noses snapt off with two old men without teeth.

DON PEDRO.

Leonato and his brother. What think'st thou? Had we fought, I doubt we should have been too young for them.

BENEDICK.

In a false quarrel there is no true valour. I came to seek you both.

CLAUDIO.

We have been up and down to seek thee; for we are high-proof melancholy, and would fain have it beaten away. Wilt thou use thy wit?

BENEDICK.

It is in my scabbard: shall I draw it?

DON PEDRO.

Dost thou wear thy wit by thy side?

CLAUDIO.

Never any did so, though very many have been beside their wit.—I will bid thee draw, as we do the minstrels; draw, to pleasure us.

DON PEDRO.

As I am an honest man, he looks pale.—Art thou sick, or angry?

CLAUDIO.

What, courage, man! What though care kill'd a cat, thou hast mettle enough in thee to kill care.

BENEDICK.

Sir, I shall meet your wit in the career, an you charge it against me. I pray you choose another subject.

CLAUDIO.

Nay, then, give him another staff: this last was broke cross.

DON PEDRO.

By this light, he changes more and more: I think he be angry indeed.

CLAUDIO.

If he be, he knows how to turn his girdle.

BENEDICK.

Shall I speak a word in your ear?

CLAUDIO.

God bless me from a challenge!

BENEDICK.

You are a villain;—I jest not:—I will make it good how you dare, with what you dare, and when you dare.—Do me right, or I will protest your cowardice. You have kill'd a sweet lady, and her death shall fall heavy on you. Let me hear from you.

CLAUDIO.

Well, I will meet you, so I may have good cheer.

DON PEDRO.

What, a feast? a feast?

CLAUDIO.

I'faith, I thank him; he hath bid me to a calf's-head and a capon; the which if I do not carve most curiously, say my knife's naught.—Shall I not find a woodcock too?

BENEDICT.

Sir, your wit ambles well; it goes easily.

DON PEDRO.

I'll tell thee how Beatrice praised thy wit the other day. I said, thou hadst a fine wit: 'True,' says she, 'a fine little one.' 'No,' said I, 'a great wit:' 'Right,' says she, 'a great gross one.' 'Nay,' said I, 'a good wit:' 'Just,' said she, 'it hurts nobody.' 'Nay,' said I, 'the gentleman is wise:' 'Certain,' said she, 'a wise gentleman.' 'Nay,' said I, 'he hath the tongues:' 'That I believe,' said she, 'for he swore a thing to me on Monday night, which he forswore on Tuesday morning; there's a double tongue; there's two tongues.' Thus did she, an hour together, trans-shape thy particular virtues: yet at last she concluded with a sigh, thou wast the properest man in Italy.

CLAUDIO.

For the which she wept heartily, and said she cared not.

DON PEDRO.

Yea, that she did; but yet, for all that, an if she did not hate him deadly, she would love him dearly:—the old man's daughter told us all.

CLAUDIO.

All, all; and, moreover, God saw him when he was hid in the garden.

DON PEDRO.

But when shall we set the savage bull's horns on the sensible Benedick's head?

CLAUDIO.

Yea, and text underneath, 'Here dwells Benedick, the married man'?

BENEDICK.

Fare you well, boy: you know my mind. I will leave you now to your gossip-like humour: you break jests as braggarts do their blades, which, God be thank'd, hurt not.—My lord, for your many courtesies I thank you: I must discontinue your company: your brother the bastard is fled from Messina: you have among you kill'd a sweet and innocent lady. For my Lord Lackbeard there, he and I shall meet: and till then peace be with him. [*Exit.*

DON PEDRO.

He is in earnest.

CLAUDIO.

In most profound earnest; and, I'll warrant you, for the love of Beatrice.

DON PEDRO.

And hath challenged thee.

CLAUDIO.

Most sincerely.

DON PEDRO.

What a pretty thing man is when he goes in his doublet and hose, and leaves off his wit!

CLAUDIO.

He is then a giant to an ape: but then is an ape a doctor to such a man.

DON PEDRO.

But, soft you, let me be: pluck up, my heart, and be sad! Did he not say, my brother was fled?

Enter DOGBERRY *and* VERGES, *and the* WATCH, *with* CONRADE *and* BORACHIO.

DOGBERRY.

Come, you, sir: if justice cannot tame you, she shall ne'er weigh more reasons in her balance: nay, an you be a cursing hypocrite once, you must be lookt to.

DON PEDRO.

How now! two of my brother's men bound! Borachio one!

CLAUDIO.

Hearken after their offence, my lord.

DON PEDRO.

Officers, what offence have these men done?

DOGBERRY.

Marry, sir, they have committed false report; moreover, they have spoken untruths; secondarily, they are slanders; sixth and lastly, they have belied a lady; thirdly, thay have verified unjust things; and, to conclude, they are lying knaves.

DON PEDRO.

First, I ask thee what they have done; thirdly, I ask thee what's their offence; sixth and lastly, why they are committed: and, to conclude, what you lay to their charge.

CLAUDIO.

Rightly reason'd, and in his own division; and, by my troth, there's one meaning well suited.

DON PEDRO.

Who have you offended, masters, that you are thus bound to your answer? this learned constable is too cunning to be understood: what's your offence?

BORACHIO.

Sweet prince, let me go no further to mine answer: do you hear me, and let this count kill me. I have deceived even your very eyes: what your wisdoms could not discover, these shallow fools have brought to light; who, in the night, overheard me confessing to this man, how Don John your brother incensed me to slander the Lady Hero; how you were brought into the orchard, and saw me court Margaret in Hero's garments; how you disgraced her, when you should marry her: my villainy they have upon record; which I had rather seal with my death than repeat over to my shame. The lady is dead upon mine and my master's false accusation; and, briefly, I desire nothing but the reward of a villain.

DON PEDRO.

Runs not this speech like iron through your
blood?

CLAUDIO.

I have drunk poison whiles he utter'd it.

DON PEDRO.

But did my brother set thee on to this?

BORACHIO.

Yea, and paid me richly for the practice of it.

DON PEDRO.

He is composed and framed of treachery:
And fled he is upon this villainy.

CLAUDIO.

Sweet Hero! now thy image doth appear
In the rare semblance that I loved it first.

DOGBERRY.

Come, bring away the plaintiffs: by this time our sexton hath reform'd Signior Leonato of the matter: and, masters, do not forget to specify, when time and place shall serve, that I am an ass.

VERGES.

Here, here comes master Signior Leonato, and the sexton too.

Enter LEONATO *and* ANTONIO, *with the* SEXTON.

LEONATO.

Which is the villain? let me see his eyes,
That, when I note another man like him,
I may avoid him: which of these is he?

BORACHIO.

If you would know your wronger, look on me.

LEONATO.

Art thou the slave that with thy breath hast kill'd
Mine innocent child?

BORACHIO.

Yea, even I alone.

LEONATO.

No, not so, villain; thou beliest thyself:
Here stand a pair of honourable men,
A third is fled, that had a hand in it.—
I thank you, princes, for my daughter's death:
Record it with your high and worthy deeds;
'Twas bravely done, if you bethink you of it.

CLAUDIO.

I know not how to pray your patience;
Yet I must speak. Choose your revenge yourself;
Impose me to what penance your invention
Can lay upon my sin: yet sinn'd I not
But in mistaking.

DON PEDRO.

By my soul, nor I:
And yet, to satisfy this good old man,
I would bend under any heavy weight
That he'll enjoin me to.

LEONATO.

I cannot bid you bid my daughter live,—
That were impossible: but, I pray you both,
Possess the people in Messina here
How innocent she died; and if your love
Can labour aught in sad invention,
Hang her an epitaph upon her tomb,
And sing it to her bones,—sing it to-night:—
To-morrow morning come you to my house;
And since you could not be my son-in-law,
Be yet my nephew: my brother hath a daughter,
Almost the copy of my child that's dead,
And she alone is heir to both of us:
Give her the right you should have given her cousin,
And so dies my revenge.

CLAUDIO.

O noble sir,
Your over-kindness doth wring tears from me!
I do embrace your offer; and dispose
For henceforth of poor Claudio.

LEONATO.

To-morrow, then, I will expect your coming;
To-night I take my leave.—This naughty man
Shall face to face be brought to Margaret,
Who I believe was packt in all this wrong,
Hired to it by your brother.

BORACHIO.

No, by my soul, she was not;
Nor knew not what she did when she spoke to me;
But always hath been just and virtuous
In any thing that I do know by her.

DOGBERRY.

Moreover, sir (which indeed is not under white and black), this plaintiff here, the offender, did call me ass: I beseech you, let it be remember'd in his punishment. And also, the watch heard them talk of one Deform'd: they say he wears a key in his ear, and a lock hanging by it; and borrows money in God's name,—the which he hath used so long and never paid, that now men grow hard-hearted, and will lend nothing for God's sake: pray you, examine him upon that point.

LEONATO.

I thank thee for thy care and honest pains.

DOGBERRY.

Your worship speaks like a most thankful and reverend youth; and I praise God for you.

LEONATO.

There's for thy pains.

DOGBERRY.

God save the foundation!

LEONATO.

Go, I discharge thee of thy prisoner, and I thank thee.

DOGBERRY.

I leave an arrant knave with your worship; which I beseech your worship to correct yourself, for the example of others. God keep your worship! I wish your worship well; God restore you to health! I humbly give you leave to depart; and if a merry meeting may be wisht, God prohibit it! —Come, neighbour.

[*Exeunt* DOGBERRY *and* VERGES.

LEONATO.

Until to-morrow morning, lords, farewell.

ANTONIO.

Farewell, my lords: we look for you to-morrow.

DON PEDRO.

We will not fail.

CLAUDIO.

To-night I'll mourn with Hero.

[*Exeunt* DON PEDRO *and* CLAUDIO.

LEONATO [*to the* WATCH].

Bring you these fellows on. We'll talk with Margaret,
How her acquaintance grew with this lewd fellow.

[*Exeunt severally.*

SCENE II.

LEONATO'S *garden.*

Enter, severally, BENEDICK *and* MARGARET.

BENEDICK.

PRAY thee, sweet Mistress Margaret, deserve well at my hands by helping me to the speech of Beatrice.

MARGARET.

Will you, then, write me a sonnet in praise of my beauty?

BENEDICK.

In so high a style, Margaret, that no man living shall come over it; for, in most comely truth, thou deservest it.

MARGARET.

To have no man come over me! why, shall I always keep below stairs?

BENEDICK.

Thy wit is as quick as the greyhound's mouth,—it catches.

MARGARET.

And yours as blunt as the fencer's foils, which hit, but hurt not.

BENEDICK.

A most manly wit, Margaret; it will not hurt a woman: and so, I pray thee, call Beatrice: I give thee the bucklers.

MARGARET.

Give us the swords; we have bucklers of our own.

BENEDICK.

If you use them, Margaret, you must put in the pikes with a vice; and they are dangerous weapons for maids.

MARGARET.

Well, I will call Beatrice to you, who I think hath legs.

BENEDICK.

And therefore will come. [*Exit* MARGARET.

[*He sings.*

The god of love,
That sits above,
And knows me, and knows me,
How pitiful I deserve,—

I mean in singing; but in loving,—Leander the good swimmer, Troilus the first employer of pandars, and a whole book full of these quondam carpet-mongers, whose names yet run smoothly in the even road of a blank verse,—why, they were never so truly turn'd over and over as my poor self in love. Marry, I cannot show it in rime; I have tried: I can find out no rime to 'lady' but 'baby,'—an innocent rime; for 'scorn,' 'horn,'—a hard rime; for 'school,' 'fool,'—a babbling rime; very ominous endings: no, I was not born under a riming planet, nor I cannot woo in festival terms.

Enter BEATRICE.

Sweet Beatrice, wouldst thou come when I call'd thee?

BEATRICE.

Yea, signior, and depart when you bid me.

BENEDICK.

O, stay but till then!

BEATRICE.

'Then' is spoken; fare you well now:—and yet, ere I go, let me go with that I came; which is, with knowing what hath past between you and Claudio.

BENEDICK.

Only foul words; and thereupon I will kiss thee.

BEATRICE.

Foul words is but foul wind, and foul wind is but foul breath, and foul breath is noisome; therefore I will depart unkist.

BENEDICK.

Thou hast frighted the word out of his right sense, so forcible is thy wit. But I must tell thee plainly, Claudio undergoes my challenge; and either I must shortly hear from him, or I will subscribe him a coward. And, I pray thee now, tell me for which of my bad parts didst thou first fall in love with me?

BEATRICE.

For them all together; which maintain'd so politic a state of evil, that they will not admit any good part to intermingle with them. But for which of my good parts did you first suffer love for me?

BENEDICK.

Suffer love,—a good epithet! I do suffer love indeed, for I love thee against my will.

BEATRICE.

In spite of your heart, I think; alas, poor heart! If you spite it for my sake, I will spite it for yours; for I will never love that which my friend hates.

BENEDICK.

Thou and I are too wise to woo peaceably.

BEATRICE.

It appears not in this confession: there's not one wise man among twenty that will praise himself.

BENEDICK.

An old, an old instance, Beatrice, that lived in the time of good neighbours. If a man do not erect in this age his own tomb ere he dies, he shall live no longer in monument than the bell rings and the widow weeps.

BEATRICE.

And how long is that, think you?

BENEDICK.

Question:—why, an hour in clamour, and a quarter in rheum: therefore is it most expedient for the wise, if Don Worm, his conscience, find no impediment to the contrary, to be the trumpet of his own virtues, as I am to myself. So much for praising myself, who, I myself will bear witness, is praiseworthy: and now tell me, how doth your cousin?

BEATRICE.

Very ill.

BENEDICK.

And how do you?

BEATRICE.

Very ill too.

BENEDICK.

Serve God, love me, and mend. There will I leave you too, for here comes one in haste.

Enter URSULA.

URSULA.

Madam, you must come to your uncle. Yonder's old coil at home: it is proved my Lady Hero hath been falsely accused, the prince and Claudio mightily abused; and Don John is the author of all, who is fled and gone. Will you come presently?

BEATRICE.

Will you go hear this news, signior?

BENEDICK.

I will live in thy heart, die in thy lap, and be buried in thy eyes; and moreover I will go with thee to thy uncle's. [*Exeunt.*

SCENE III.

A church.

Enter DON PEDRO, CLAUDIO, *and three or four with tapers.*

CLAUDIO.

IS this the monument of Leonato?

ATTENDANT.

It is, my lord.

CLAUDIO [*reads from a scroll*].

Done to death by slanderous tongues
Was the Hero that here lies;
Death, in guerdon of her wrongs,
Gives her fame which never dies.
So the life that died with shame
Lives in death with glorious fame.
Hang thou there upon the tomb,
Praising her when I am dumb.—

Now, music, sound, and sing your solemn hymn.

Song.

Pardon, goddess of the night,
Those that slew thy virgin knight;
For the which, with songs of woe,
Round about her tomb they go.
Midnight, assist our moan;
Help us to sigh and groan,
Heavily, heavily;
Graves, yawn, and yield your dead,
Till death be uttered,
Heavily, heavily.

CLAUDIO.

Now, unto thy bones good night!—
Yearly will I do this rite.

DON PEDRO.

Good morrow, masters; put your torches out:
The wolves have prey'd; and look, the gentle day,
Before the wheels of Phœbus, round about
Dapples the drowsy east with spots of grey.
Thanks to you all, and leave us: fare you well.

CLAUDIO.

Good morrow, masters: each his several way.

DON PEDRO.

Come, let us hence, and put on other weeds;
And then to Leonato's we will go.

CLAUDIO.

And Hymen now with luckier issue speed's
Than this for whom we render'd up this woe!
[*Exeunt.*

SCENE IV.

A room in LEONATO'S *house.*

Enter LEONATO, ANTONIO, BENEDICK, BEATRICE, MARGARET, URSULA, FRIAR FRANCIS, *and* HERO.

FRIAR FRANCIS.

DID I not tell you she was innocent?

LEONATO.

So are the prince and Claudio, who accused her
Upon the error that you heard debated:
But Margaret was in some fault for this,
Although against her will, as it appears
In the true course of all the question.

ANTONIO.

Well, I am glad that all things sort so well.

BENEDICK.

And so am I, being else by faith enforced
To call young Claudio to a reckoning for it.

LEONATO.

Well, daughter, and you gentlewomen all,
Withdraw into a chamber by yourselves,
And when I send for you, come hither maskt:
The prince and Claudio promised by this hour
To visit me.—You know your office, brother:
[*Exeunt* LADIES.
You must be father to your brother's daughter,
And give her to young Claudio.

ANTONIO.

Which I will do with confirm'd countenance.

BENEDICK.

Friar, I must entreat your pains, I think.

FRIAR FRANCIS.

To do what, signior?

BENEDICK.

To bind me, or undo me; one of them.—
Signior Leonato, truth it is, good signior,
Your niece regards me with an eye of favour.

LEONATO.

That eye my daughter lent her: 'tis most true.

BENEDICK.

And I do with an eye of love requite her.

LEONATO.

The sight whereof I think you had from me,
From Claudio, and the prince: but what's your will?

BENEDICK.

Your answer, sir, is enigmatical:
But, for my will, my will is, your good-will
May stand with ours, this day to be conjoin'd
In the state of honourable marriage:—
In which, good friar, I shall desire your help.

LEONATO.

My heart is with your liking.

FRIAR FRANCIS.

And my help.—
Here comes the prince and Claudio.

Enter DON PEDRO *and* CLAUDIO, *with* ATTENDANTS.

DON PEDRO.

Good morrow to this fair assembly.

LEONATO.

Good morrow, prince; good morrow, Claudio:
We here attend you. Are you yet determined
To-day to marry with my brother's daughter?

CLAUDIO.

I'll hold my mind, were she an Ethiop.

LEONATO.

Call her forth, brother; here's the friar ready.
[*Exit* ANTONIO.

DON PEDRO.

Good morrow, Benedick. Why, what's the matter,
That you have such a February face,
So full of frost, of storm, and cloudiness?

CLAUDIO.

I think he thinks upon the savage bull.—
Tush, fear not, man; we'll tip thy horns with gold,
And all Europa shall rejoice at thee;
As once Europa did at lusty Jove,
When he would play the noble beast in love.

BENEDICK.

Bull Jove, sir, had an amiable low;
And some such strange bull leapt your father's cow,
And got a calf in that same noble feat
Much like to you, for you have just his bleat.

CLAUDIO.

For this I owe you: here come other reck'nings.

Enter ANTONIO, *with the* LADIES *maskt.*

Which is the lady I must seize upon?

ANTONIO.

This same is she, and I do give you her.

CLAUDIO.

Why, then she's mine.—Sweet, let me see your face.

LEONATO.

No, that you shall not, till you take her hand
Before this friar, and swear to marry her.

CLAUDIO.

Give me your hand before this holy friar:
I am your husband, if you like of me.

HERO.

And when I lived, I was your other wife:
[*Unmasking.*
And when you loved, you were my other husband.

CLAUDIO.

Another Hero!

HERO.

Nothing certainer:
One Hero died defiled; but I do live,
And surely as I live, I am a maid.

DON PEDRO.

The former Hero! Hero that is dead!

LEONATO.

She died, my lord, but whiles her slander lived.

FRIAR FRANCIS.

All this amazement can I qualify;
When after that the holy rites are ended,
I'll tell you largely of fair Hero's death:
Meantime let wonder seem familiar,
And to the chapel let us presently.

BENEDICK.

Soft and fair, friar.—Which is Beatrice?

BEATRICE [*unmasking*].

I answer to that name. What is your will?

BENEDICK.

Do not you love me?

BEATRICE.

Why, no; no more than reason.

BENEDICK.

Why, then your uncle, and the prince, and Claudio
Have been deceived; for they swore you did.

BEATRICE.

Do not you love me?

BENEDICK.

Troth, no; no more than reason.

BEATRICE.

Why, then my cousin, Margaret, and Ursula
Are much deceived; for they did swear you did.

BENEDICK.

They swore that you were almost sick for me.

BEATRICE.

They swore that you were well-nigh dead for me.

BENEDICK.

'Tis no such matter.—Then you do not love me?

BEATRICE.

No, truly, but in friendly recompense.

LEONATO.

Come, cousin, I am sure you love the gentleman.

CLAUDIO.

And I'll be sworn upon't that he loves her;
For here's a paper, written in his hand,
A halting sonnet of his own pure brain,
Fashion'd to Beatrice.

HERO.

And here's another,
Writ in my cousin's hand, stol'n from her pocket,
Containing her affection unto Benedick.

BENEDICK.

A miracle! here's our own hands against our hearts.—Come, I will have thee; but, by this light, I take thee for pity.

BEATRICE.

I would not deny you;—but, by this good day, I yield upon great persuasion; and partly to save your life, for I was told you were in a consumption.

BENEDICK.

Peace! I will stop your mouth. [*Kissing her.*

DON PEDRO.

How dost thou, Benedick, the married man?

BENEDICK.

I'll tell thee what, prince; a college of wit-crackers cannot flout me out of my humour. Dost thou think I care for a satire or an epigram? No: if a man will be beaten with brains, a' shall wear nothing handsome about him. In brief, since I do purpose to marry, I will think nothing to any purpose that the world can say against it; and therefore never flout at me for what I have said against it; for man is a giddy thing, and this is my conclusion.—For thy part, Claudio, I did think to have beaten thee; but in that thou art like to be my kinsman, live unbruised, and love my cousin.

CLAUDIO.

I had well hoped thou wouldst have denied Beatrice, that I might have cudgell'd thee out of thy single life, to make thee a double-dealer; which, out of question, thou wilt be, if my cousin do not look exceeding narrowly to thee.

BENEDICK.

Come, come, we are friends.—Let's have a dance ere we are married, that we may lighten our own hearts and our wives' heels.

LEONATO.

We'll have dancing afterward.

BENEDICK.

First, of my word; therefore play, music!—Prince, thou art sad; get thee a wife, get thee a wife: there is no staff more reverend than one tipt with horn.

Enter a MESSENGER.

MESSENGER.

My lord, your brother John is ta'en in flight,
And brought with armed men back to Messina.

BENEDICK.

Think not on him till to-morrow: I'll devise thee brave punishments for him.—Strike up, pipers!
[*Dance. Exeunt.*

AS YOU LIKE IT

DRAMATIS PERSONAE

DUKE, *living in banishment.*
FREDERICK, *his brother, and usurper of his dominions.*
AMIENS, } *lords attending on the banisht Duke.*
JAQUES, }
LE BEAU, *a courtier attending on Frederick.*
CHARLES, *wrestler to Frederick.*
OLIVER, }
JAQUES, } *sons of Sir Rowland de Boys.*
ORLANDO, }
ADAM, } *servants to Oliver.*
DENIS, }
TOUCHSTONE, *a clown.*
SIR OLIVER MARTEXT, *a vicar.*
CORIN, } *shepherds.*
SILVIUS, }
WILLIAM, *a country fellow, in love with Audrey.*
A person representing HYMEN.

ROSALIND, *daughter to the banisht Duke.*
CELIA, *daughter to Frederick.*
PHEBE, *a shepherdess.*
AUDREY, *a country wench.*

LORDS, PAGES, *and* ATTENDANTS, *&c.*

SCENE—*Oliver's house; Duke Frederick's court; and the Forest of Arden.*

ACT I. SCENE I.

Orchard of OLIVER'S *house.*

Enter ORLANDO *and* ADAM.

ORLANDO.

As I remember, Adam, it was upon this fashion bequeath'd me by will but poor a thousand crowns, and, as thou say'st, charged my brother, on his blessing, to breed me well: and there begins my sadness. My brother Jacques he keeps at school, and report speaks goldenly of his profit: for my part, he keeps me rustically at home, or, to speak more properly, stays me here at home unkept; for call you that keeping for a gentleman of my birth, that differs not from the stalling of an ox? His horses are bred better; for, besides that they are fair with their feeding, they are taught their manage, and to that end riders dearly hired: but I, his brother, gain nothing under him but growth; for the which his animals on his dunghills are as much bound to him as I. Besides this nothing that he so plentifully gives me, the something that nature gave me his countenance seems to take from me: he lets me feed with his hinds, bars me the place of a brother, and, as much as in him lies, mines my gentility with my education. This is it, Adam, that grieves me; and the spirit of my father, which I think is within me, begins to mutiny against this servitude: I will no longer endure it, though yet I know no wise remedy how to avoid it.

ADAM.

Yonder comes my master, your brother.

ORLANDO.

Go apart, Adam, and thou shalt hear how he will shake me up.

Enter OLIVER.

OLIVER.

Now, sir! what make you here?

ORLANDO.

Nothing: I am not taught to make anything.

OLIVER.

What mar you then, sir?

ORLANDO.

Marry, sir, I am helping you to mar that which God made, a poor unworthy brother of yours, with idleness.

OLIVER.

Marry, sir, be better employ'd, and be naught awhile.

ORLANDO.

Shall I keep your hogs, and eat husks with them? What prodigal's portion have I spent that I should come to such penury?

OLIVER.

Know you where you are, sir?

ORLANDO.

O, sir, very well: here in your orchard.

OLIVER.

Know you before whom, sir?

ORLANDO.

Ay, better than him I am before knows me. I know you are my eldest brother; and, in the gentle condition of blood, you should so know me. The courtesy of nations allows you my better, in that you are the first-born; but the same tradition takes not away my blood, were there twenty brothers betwixt us: I have as much of my father in me as you; albeit, I confess, your coming before me is nearer to his reverence.

OLIVER.

What, boy!

ORLANDO.

Come, come, elder brother, you are too young in this.

OLIVER.

Wilt thou lay hands on me, villain?

ORLANDO.

I am no villain; I am the youngest son of Sir Rowland de Boys; he was my father, and he is thrice a villain that says such a father begot villains. Wert thou not my brother, I would not take this hand from thy throat till this other had pull'd out thy tongue for saying so; thou hast rail'd on thyself.

ADAM.

Sweet masters, be patient: for your father's remembrance, be at accord.

OLIVER.

Let me go, I say.

ORLANDO.

I will not, till I please: you shall hear me. My father charged you in his will to give me good education: you have train'd me like a peasant, obscuring and hiding from me all gentleman-like qualities. The spirit of my father grows strong in me, and I will no longer endure it: therefore allow me such exercises as may become a gentleman, or give me the poor allottery my father left me by testament; with that I will go buy my fortunes.

OLIVER.

And what wilt thou do? beg, when that is spent? Well, sir, get you in: I will not long be troubled with you; you shall have some part of your will: I pray you, leave me.

ORLANDO.

I will no further offend you than becomes me for my good.

OLIVER.

Get you with him, you old dog.

ADAM.

Is 'old dog' my reward? Most true, I have lost my teeth in your service.—God be with my old master! he would not have spoke such a word.

[*Exeunt* ORLANDO *and* ADAM.

OLIVER.

Is it even so? begin you to grow upon me? I will physic your rankness, and yet give no thousand crowns neither.—Holla, Denis!

Enter DENIS.

DENIS.

Calls your worship?

OLIVER.

Was not Charles, the duke's wrestler, here to speak with me?

DENIS.

So please you, he is here at the door, and importunes access to you.

OLIVER.

Call him in. [*Exit* DENIS.] 'Twill be a good way; and to-morrow the wrestling is.

Enter CHARLES.

CHARLES.

Good morrow to your worship.

OLIVER.

Good morrow, Monsieur Charles.—What's the new news at the new court?

CHARLES.

There's no news at the court, sir, but the old news: that is, the old duke is banisht by his younger brother the new duke; and three or four loving lords have put themselves into voluntary exile with him, whose lands and revenues enrich the new duke; therefore he gives them good leave to wander.

OLIVER.

Can you tell if Rosalind, the duke's daughter, be banisht with her father?

CHARLES.

O, no; for the duke's daughter, her cousin, so loves her, being ever from their cradles bred together, that she would have follow'd her exile, or have died to stay behind her. She is at the court, and no less beloved of her uncle than his own daughter; and never two ladies loved as they do.

OLIVER.

Where will the old duke live?

CHARLES.

They say he is already in the forest of Arden, and a many merry men with him; and there they live like the old Robin Hood of England: they say many young gentlemen flock to him every day, and fleet the time carelessly, as they did in the golden world.

OLIVER.

What, you wrestle to-morrow before the new duke?

CHARLES.

Marry, do I, sir; and I came to acquaint you with a matter. I am given, sir, secretly to understand that your younger brother Orlando hath a disposition to come in disguised against me to try a fall. To-morrow, sir, I wrestle for my credit; and he that escapes me without some broken limb shall acquit him well. Your brother is but young and tender; and, for your love, I would be loth to foil him, as I must, for my own honour, if he come in: therefore, out of my love to you, I came hither to acquaint you withal, that either you might stay him from his intendment or brook such disgrace well as he shall run into, in that it is a thing of his own search and altogether against my will.

OLIVER.

Charles, I thank thee for thy love to me, which thou shalt find I will most kindly requite. I had myself notice of my brother's purpose herein, and have by underhand means labour'd to dissuade him from it; but he is resolute. I'll tell thee, Charles: it is the stubbornest young fellow of France; full of ambition, an envious emulator of every man's good parts, a secret and villainous contriver against me his natural brother: therefore use thy discretion; I had as lief thou didst break his neck as his finger. And thou wert best look to't; for if thou dost him any slight disgrace, or if he do not mightily grace himself on thee, he will practise against thee by poison, entrap thee by some treacherous device, and never leave thee till he hath ta'en thy life by some indirect means or other; for, I assure thee, and almost with tears I speak it, there is not one so young and so villainous this day living. I speak but brotherly of him; but should I anatomize him to thee as he is, I must blush and weep, and thou must look pale and wonder.

CHARLES.

I am heartily glad I came hither to you. If he come to-morrow, I'll give him his payment: if ever he go alone again, I'll never wrestle for prize more: and so, God keep your worship!

OLIVER.

Farewell, good Charles. [*Exit* CHARLES.] Now will I stir this gamester: I hope I shall see an end of him; for my soul, yet I know not why, hates nothing more than he. Yet he's gentle; never school'd, and yet learned; full of noble device; of all sorts enchantingly beloved; and, indeed, so much in the heart of the world, and especially of my own people, who best know him, that I am altogether misprised: but it shall not be so long;

this wrestler shall clear all: nothing remains but that I kindle the boy thither; which now I'll go about. [*Exit.*

SCENE II.

Lawn before the DUKE'S *palace.*

Enter ROSALIND *and* CELIA.

CELIA.

I PRAY thee, Rosalind, sweet my coz, be merry.

ROSALIND.

Dear Celia, I show more mirth than I am mistress of; and would you yet I were merrier? Unless you could teach me to forget a banisht father, you must not learn me how to remember any extraordinary pleasure.

CELIA.

Herein I see thou lovest me not with the full weight that I love thee. If my uncle, thy banisht father, had banisht thy uncle, the duke my father, so thou hadst been still with me, I could have taught my love to take thy father for mine: so wouldst thou, if the truth of thy love to me were so righteously temper'd as mine is to thee.

ROSALIND.

Well, I will forget the condition of my estate, to rejoice in yours.

CELIA.

You know my father hath no child but I, nor none is like to have: and, truly, when he dies, thou shalt be his heir; for what he hath taken away from thy father perforce, I will render thee again in affection; by mine honour, I will; and when I break that oath, let me turn monster: therefore, my sweet Rose, my dear Rose, be merry.

ROSALIND.

From henceforth I will, coz, and devise sports. Let me see; what think you of falling in love?

CELIA.

Marry, I prithee, do, to make sport withal: but love no man in good earnest; nor no further in sport neither than with safety of a pure blush thou mayst in honour come off again.

ROSALIND.

What shall be our sport, then?

CELIA.

Let us sit and mock the good housewife Fortune from her wheel, that her gifts may henceforth be bestow'd equally.

ROSALIND.

I would we could do so; for her benefits are mightily misplaced; and the bountiful blind woman doth most mistake in her gifts to women.

CELIA.

'Tis true; for those that she makes fair, she scarce makes honest; and those that she makes honest, she makes very ill-favour'dly.

ROSALIND.

Nay, now thou goest from Fortune's office to Nature's: Fortune reigns in gifts of the world, not in the lineaments of Nature.

Enter TOUCHSTONE.

CELIA.

No? when Nature hath made a fair creature, may she not by Fortune fall into the fire? Though Nature hath given us wit to flout at Fortune, hath not Fortune sent in this fool to cut off the argument?

ROSALIND.

Indeed, there is Fortune too hard for Nature, when Fortune makes Nature's natural the cutter-off of Nature's wit.

CELIA.

Peradventure this is not Fortune's work neither, but Nature's; who perceiveth our natural wits too dull to reason of such goddesses and hath sent this natural for our whetstone; for always the dulness of the fool is the whetstone of the wits.—How now, wit! whither wander you?

TOUCHSTONE.

Mistress, you must come away to your father.

CELIA.

Were you made the messenger?

TOUCHSTONE.

No, by mine honour; but I was bid to come for you.

ROSALIND.

Where learn'd you that oath, fool?

TOUCHSTONE.

Of a certain knight that swore by his honour they were good pancakes, and swore by his honour the mustard was naught: now I'll stand to it, the pancakes were naught, and the mustard was good; and yet was not the knight forsworn.

CELIA.

How prove you that, in the great heap of your knowledge?

ROSALIND.

Ay, marry, now unmuzzle your wisdom.

TOUCHSTONE.

Stand you both forth now: stroke your chins, and swear by your beards that I am a knave.

CELIA.

By our beards, if we had them, thou art.

TOUCHSTONE.

By my knavery, if I had it, then I were; but if you swear by that that is not, you are not forsworn: no more was this knight, swearing by his honour, for he never had any; or if he had, he had sworn it away before ever he saw those pancakes or that mustard.

CELIA.

Prithee, who is't that thou mean'st?

TOUCHSTONE.

One that old Frederick, your father, loves.

CELIA.

My father's love is enough to honour him enough: speak no more of him; you'll be whipt for taxation one of these days.

TOUCHSTONE.

The more pity, that fools may not speak wisely what wise men do foolishly.

CELIA.

By my troth, thou sayest true; for since the little wit that fools have was silenced, the little foolery that wise men have makes a great show.—Here comes Monsieur Le Beau.

ROSALIND.

With his mouth full of news.

CELIA.

Which he will put on us, as pigeons feed their young.

ROSALIND.

Then shall we be news-cramm'd.

CELIA.

All the better; we shall be the more marketable.

Enter LE BEAU.

Bon jour, Monsieur Le Beau: what's the news?

LE BEAU.

Fair princess, you have lost much good sport.

CELIA.

Sport! of what colour!

LE BEAU.

What colour, madam! how shall I answer you?

ROSALIND.

As wit and fortune will.

TOUCHSTONE.

Or as the Destinies decrees.

CELIA.

Well said: that was laid on with a trowel.

TOUCHSTONE.

Nay, if I keep not my rank,—

ROSALIND.

Thou losest thy old smell.

LE BEAU.

You amaze me, ladies: I would have told you of good wrestling, which you have lost the sight of.

ROSALIND.

Yet tell us the manner of the wrestling.

LE BEAU.

I will tell you the beginning; and, if it please your ladyships, you may see the end; for the best is yet to do; and here, where you are, they are coming to perform it.

CELIA.

Well,—the beginning, that is dead and buried.

LE BEAU.

There comes an old man and his three sons,—

CELIA.

I could match this beginning with an old tale.

LE BEAU.

Three proper young men, of excellent growth and presence.

ROSALIND.

With bills on their necks, 'Be it known unto all men by these presents.'

LE BEAU.

The eldest of the three wrestled with Charles, the duke's wrestler; which Charles in a moment threw him, and broke three of his ribs, that there is little hope of life in him: so he served the second, and so the third. Yonder they lie; the poor old man, their father, making such pitiful dole over them, that all the beholders take his part with weeping.

ROSALIND.

Alas!

TOUCHSTONE.

But what is the sport, monsieur, that the ladies have lost?

LE BEAU.

Why, this that I speak of.

TOUCHSTONE.

Thus men may grow wiser every day! it is the first time that ever I heard breaking of ribs was sport for ladies.

CELIA.

Or I, I promise thee.

ROSALIND.

But is there any else longs to see this broken music in his sides? is there yet another dotes upon rib-breaking?—Shall we see this wrestling, cousin?

LE BEAU.

You must, if you stay here; for here is the place appointed for the wrestling, and they are ready to perform it.

CELIA.

Yonder, sure, they are coming: let us now stay and see it.

Flourish. Enter DUKE FREDERICK, LORDS, ORLANDO, CHARLES, *and* ATTENDANTS.

DUKE FREDERICK.

Come on: since the youth will not be entreated, his own peril on his forwardness.

ROSALIND.

Is yonder the man?

LE BEAU.

Even he, madam.

CELIA.

Alas, he is too young! yet he looks successfully.

DUKE FREDERICK.

How now, daughter, and cousin! are you crept hither to see the wrestling?

ROSALIND.

Ay, my liege, so please you give us leave.

DUKE FREDERICK.

You will take little delight in it, I can tell you, there is such odds in the men. In pity of the challenger's youth, I would fain dissuade him, but he will not be entreated. Speak to him, ladies; see if you can move him.

CELIA.

Call him hither, good Monsieur Le Beau.

DUKE FREDERICK.

Do so: I'll not be by.

LE BEAU.

Monsieur the challenger, the princess calls for you.

ORLANDO.

I attend them with all respect and duty.

ROSALIND.

Young man, have you challenged Charles the wrestler?

ORLANDO.

No, fair princess; he is the general challenger: I come but in, as others do, to try with him the strength of my youth.

CELIA.

Young gentleman, your spirits are too bold for your years. You have seen cruel proof of this man's strength: if you saw yourself with your eyes, or knew yourself with your judgement, the fear of your adventure would counsel you to a more equal enterprise. We pray you, for your own sake, to embrace your own safety, and give over this attempt.

ROSALIND.

Do, young sir; your reputation shall not therefore be misprised: we will make it our suit to the duke that the wrestling might not go forward.

ORLANDO.

I beseech you, punish me not with your hard thoughts: wherein I confess me much guilty, to deny so fair and excellent ladies any thing. But let your fair eyes and gentle wishes go with me to my trial; wherein if I be foil'd, there is but one shamed that was never gracious; if kill'd, but one dead that is willing to be so: I shall do my friends no wrong, for I have none to lament me; the world no injury, for in it I have nothing; only in the world I fill up a place, which may be better supplied when I have made it empty.

ROSALIND.

The little strength that I have, I would it were with you.

CELIA.

And mine, to eke out hers.

ROSALIND.

Fare you well: pray heaven I be deceived in you!

CELIA.

Your heart's desires be with you!

CHARLES.

Come, where is this young gallant that is so desirous to lie with his mother earth?

ORLANDO.

Ready, sir; but his will hath in it a more modest working.

DUKE FREDERICK.

You shall try but one fall.

CHARLES.

No, I warrant your grace, you shall not entreat him to a second, that have so mightily persuaded him from a first.

ORLANDO.

An you mean to mock me after, you should not have mockt me before: but come your ways.

ROSALIND.

Now Hercules be thy speed, young man!

CELIA.

I would I were invisible, to catch the strong fellow by the leg. [*Wrestle.*

ROSALIND.

O excellent young man!

CELIA.

If I had a thunderbolt in mine eye, I can tell who should down. [*Shout.* CHARLES *is thrown.*

DUKE FREDERICK.

No more, no more.

ORLANDO.

Yes, I beseech your Grace: I am not yet well breath'd.

DUKE FREDERICK.

How dost thou, Charles?

LE BEAU.

He cannot speak, my lord.

DUKE FREDERICK.

Bear him away. What is thy name, young man?

ORLANDO.

Orlando, my liege; the youngest son of Sir Rowland de Boys.

DUKE FREDERICK.

I would thou hadst been son to some man else:
The world esteem'd thy father honourable,
But I did find him still mine enemy:
Thou shouldst have better pleased me with this deed,
Hadst thou descended from another house.
But fare thee well; thou art a gallant youth:
I would thou hadst told me of another father.

[*Exeunt* DUKE FREDERICK, TRAIN, *and* LE BEAU.

CELIA.

Were I my father, coz, would I do this?

ORLANDO.

I am more proud to be Sir Rowland's son,
His youngest son;—and would not change that calling,
To be adopted heir to Frederick.

ROSALIND.

My father loved Sir Rowland as his soul,
And all the world was of my father's mind:
Had I before known this young man his son,
I should have given him tears unto entreaties,
Ere he should thus have ventured.

CELIA.

Gentle cousin,
Let us go thank him and encourage him:
My father's rough and envious disposition
Sticks me at heart.—Sir, you have well deserved:
If you do keep your promises in love
But justly, as you have exceeded all promise,
Your mistress shall be happy.

ROSALIND.

Gentleman,
[*Giving him a chain from her neck.*
Wear this for me, one out of suits with fortune,
That would give more, but that her hand lacks means.
—Shall we go, coz?

CELIA.

Ay.—Fare you well, fair gentleman.

ORLANDO.

Can I not say, I thank you? My better parts
Are all thrown down, and that which here stands up
Is but a quintain, a mere lifeless block.

ROSALIND.

He calls us back: my pride fell with my fortunes;
I'll ask him what he would.—Did you call, sir?—
Sir, you have wrestled well, and overthrown
More than your enemies.

CELIA.

Will you go, coz?

ROSALIND.

Have with you.—Fare you well.

[*Exeunt* ROSALIND *and* CELIA.

ORLANDO.

What passion hangs these weights upon my tongue?
I cannot speak to her, yet she urged conference.
O poor Orlando, thou art overthrown!
Or Charles or something weaker masters thee.

Enter LE BEAU.

LE BEAU

Good sir, I do in friendship counsel you
To leave this place. Albeit you have deserved
High commendation, true applause and love,
Yet such is now the duke's condition
That he misconsters all that you have done.
The duke is humorous: what he is, indeed,
More suits you to conceive than I to speak of.

ORLANDO.

I thank you, sir: and, pray you, tell me this,—
Which of the two was daughter of the duke,
That here was at the wrestling?

LE BEAU.

Neither his daughter, if we judge by manners;
But yet, indeed, the smaller is his daughter:

The other is daughter to the banisht duke,
And here detain'd by her usurping uncle,
To keep his daughter company: whose loves
Are dearer than the natural bond of sisters.
But I can tell you that of late this duke
Hath ta'en displeasure 'gainst his gentle niece,
Grounded upon no other argument
But that the people praise her for her virtues
And pity her for her good father's sake;
And, on my life, his malice 'gainst the lady
Will suddenly break forth.—Sir, fare you well:
Hereafter, in a better world than this,
I shall desire more love and knowledge of you.

ORLANDO.

I rest much bounden to you: fare you well.
[*Exit* LE BEAU.

Thus must I from the smoke into the smother;
From tyrant duke unto a tyrant brother:—
But heavenly Rosalind! [*Exit.*

SCENE III.

A room in the palace.

Enter CELIA *and* ROSALIND.

WHY, cousin; why, Rosalind;—Cupid have mercy!—not a word?

ROSALIND.

Not one to throw at a dog.

CELIA.

No, thy words are too precious to be cast away upon curs; throw some of them at me; come, lame me with reasons.

ROSALIND.

Then there were two cousins laid up; when the one should be lamed with reasons, and the other mad without any.

CELIA.

But is all this for your father?

ROSALIND.

No, some of it is for my father's child. O, how full of briers is this working-day world!

CELIA.

They are but burs, cousin, thrown upon thee in holiday foolery: if we walk not in the trodden paths, our very petticoats will catch them.

ROSALIND.

I could shake them off my coat: these burs are in my heart.

CELIA.

Hem them away.

ROSALIND.

I would try, if I could cry 'hem,' and have him.

CELIA.

Come, come, wrestle with thy affections.

ROSALIND.

O, they take the part of a better wrestler than myself!

CELIA.

O, a good wish upon you! you will try in time, in despite of a fall.—But, turning these jests out of service, let us talk in good earnest: is it possible, on such a sudden, you should fall into so strong a liking with old Sir Rowland's youngest son?

ROSALIND.

The duke my father loved his father dearly.

CELIA.

Doth it therefore ensue that you should love his son dearly? By this kind of chase, I should hate him, for my father hated his father dearly; yet I hate not Orlando.

ROSALIND.

No, faith, hate him not, for my sake.

CELIA.

Why should I? doth he not deserve well?

ROSALIND.

Let me love him for that; and do you love him because I do.—Look, here comes the duke.

CELIA.

With his eyes full of anger.

Enter DUKE FREDERICK, *with* LORDS.

DUKE FREDERICK.

Mistress, dispatch you with your safest haste,
And get you from our court.

ROSALIND.

Me, uncle?

DUKE FREDERICK.

You, cousin:
Within these ten days if that thou be'st found
So near our public court as twenty miles,
Thou diest for it.

ROSALIND.

I do beseech your Grace,
Let me the knowledge of my fault bear with me:
If with myself I hold intelligence,
Or have acquaintance with mine own desires;
If that I do not dream, or be not frantic,
As I do trust I am not,—then, dear uncle,
Never so much as in a thought unborn
Did I offend your highness.

DUKE FREDERICK.

Thus do all traitors:
If their purgation did consist in words,
They are as innocent as grace itself:
Let it suffice thee that I trust thee not.

ROSALIND.

Yet your mistrust cannot make me a traitor:
Tell me whereon the likelihood depends.

DUKE FREDERICK.

Thou art thy father's daughter; there's enough.

ROSALIND.

So was I when your highness took his dukedom;
So was I when your highness banisht him:
Treason is not inherited, my lord;
Or, if we did derive it from our friends,
What's that to me? my father was no traitor:
Then, good my liege, mistake me not so much
To think my poverty is treacherous.

CELIA.

Dear sovereign, hear me speak.

DUKE FREDERICK.

Ay, Celia; we stay'd her for your sake,
Else had she with her father ranged along.

CELIA.

I did not then entreat to have her stay;
It was your pleasure and your own remorse:
I was too young that time to value her;
But now I know her: if she be a traitor,
Why, so am I; we still have slept together,
Rose at an instant, learn'd, play'd, eat together;
And wheresoe'er we went, like Juno's swans,
Still we went coupled and inseparable.

DUKE FREDERICK.

She is too subtle for thee; and her smoothness,
Her very silence and her patience
Speak to the people, and they pity her.
Thou art a fool: she robs thee of thy name;
And thou wilt show more bright and seem more virtuous
When she is gone. Then open not thy lips:
Firm and irrevocable is my doom
Which I have pass'd upon her;—she is banisht.

CELIA.

Pronounce that sentence then on me, my liege:
I cannot live out of her company.

DUKE FREDERICK.

You are a fool.—You, niece, provide yourself:
If you outstay the time, upon mine honour,
And in the greatness of my word, you die.

[*Exeunt* DUKE FREDERICK *and* LORDS.

CELIA.

O my poor Rosalind! whither wilt thou go?
Wilt thou change fathers? I will give thee mine.
I charge thee, be not thou more grieved than I am.

ROSALIND.

I have more cause.

CELIA.

Thou hast not, cousin;
Prithee, be cheerful: know'st thou not, the duke
Hath banisht me, his daughter?

ROSALIND.

That he hath not.

CELIA.

No, hath not? Rosalind lacks then the love
Which teacheth me that thou and I am one:
Shall we be sunder'd? shall we part, sweet girl?
No: let my father seek another heir.
Therefore devise with me how we may fly,
Whither to go and what to bear with us:
And do not seek to take the charge upon you,
To bear your griefs yourself and leave me out:
For, by this heaven, now at our sorrows pale,
Say what thou canst, I'll go along with thee.

ROSALIND.

Why, whither shall we go?

CELIA.

To seek my uncle in the forest of Arden.

ROSALIND.

Alas, what danger will it be to us,
Maids as we are, to travel forth so far!
Beauty provoketh thieves sooner than gold.

CELIA.

I'll put myself in poor and mean attire,
And with a kind of umber smirch my face;
The like do you: so shall we pass along
And never stir assailants.

ROSALIND.

Were it not better,
Because that I am more than common tall,
That I did suit me all points like a man?
A gallant curtle-axe upon my thigh,
A boar-spear in my hand; and—in my heart
Lie there what hidden woman's fear there will—
We'll have a swashing and a martial outside;
As many other mannish cowards have
That do outface it with their semblances.

CELIA.

What shall I call thee when thou art a man?

ROSALIND.

I'll have no worse a name than Jove's own page;
And therefore look you call me Ganymede.
But what will you be call'd?

CELIA.

Something that hath a reference to my state;
No longer Celia, but Aliena.

ROSALIND.

But, cousin, what if we assay'd to steal
The clownish fool out of your father's court?
Would he not be a comfort to our travel?

CELIA.

He'll go along o'er the wide world with me;
Leave me alone to woo him. Let's away,
And get our jewels and our wealth together;
Devise the fittest time and safest way
To hide us from pursuit that will be made
After my flight. Now go we in content,
To liberty, and not to banishment. [*Exeunt.*

ACT II. SCENE I.

The Forest of Arden.

Enter DUKE SENIOR, AMIENS, *and two or three* LORDS, *like foresters.*

DUKE SENIOR.

Now, my co-mates and brothers in exile,
Hath not old custom made this life more sweet
Than that of painted pomp? Are not these woods
More free from peril than the envious court?
Here feel we but the penalty of Adam,
The seasons' difference; as the icy fang
And churlish chiding of the winter's wind,
Which, when it bites and blows upon my body,
Even till I shrink with cold, I smile, and say
'This is no flattery; these are counsellors
That feelingly persuade me what I am.'
Sweet are the uses of adversity;
Which, like the toad, ugly and venomous,
Wears yet a precious jewel in his head;
And this our life, exempt from public haunt,
Finds tongues in trees, books in the running brooks,
Sermons in stones, and good in every thing:
I would not change it.

AMIENS.

Happy is your Grace,
That can translate the stubbornness of fortune
Into so quiet and so sweet a style.

DUKE SENIOR.

Come, shall we go and kill us venison?
And yet it irks me the poor dappled fools,
Being native burghers of this desert city,
Should in their own confines with forked heads
Have their round haunches gored.

FIRST LORD.

Indeed, my lord,
The melancholy Jaques grieves at that;
And, in that kind, swears you do more usurp
Than doth your brother that hath banisht you.
To-day my Lord of Amiens and myself
Did steal behind him, as he lay along
Under an oak, whose antique root peeps out
Upon the brook that brawls along this wood:

To the which place a poor sequester'd stag,
That from the hunter's aim had ta'en a hurt,
Did come to languish; and, indeed, my lord,
The wretched animal heaved forth such groans,
That their discharge did stretch his leathern coat
Almost to bursting; and the big round tears
Coursed one another down his innocent nose
In piteous chase: and thus the hairy fool,
Much marked of the melancholy Jaques,
Stood on th'extremest verge of the swift brook,
Augmenting it with tears.

DUKE SENIOR.
But what said Jaques?
Did he not moralise this spectacle?

FIRST LORD.
O, yes, into a thousand similes.
First, for his weeping into the needless stream;
'Poor deer,' quoth he, 'thou makest a testament
As worldlings do, giving thy sum of more
To that which had too much:' then, being there alone,
Left and abandon'd of his velvet friends;
''Tis right,' quoth he; 'thus misery doth part
The flux of company:' anon, a careless herd,
Full of the pasture, jumps along by him,
And never stays to greet him; 'Ay,' quoth Jaques,
'Sweep on, you fat and greasy citizens;
'Tis just the fashion: wherefore do you look
Upon that poor and broken bankrupt there?'
Thus most invectively he pierceth through
The body of the country, city, court,
Yea, and of this our life: swearing that we
Are mere usurpers, tyrants, and what's worse,
To fright the animals, and to kill them up,
In their assign'd and native dwelling-place.

DUKE SENIOR.
And did you leave him in this contemplation?

SECOND LORD.
We did, my lord, weeping and commenting
Upon the sobbing deer.

DUKE SENIOR.
Show me the place:
I love to cope him in these sullen fits,
For then he's full of matter.

FIRST LORD.
I'll bring you to him straight. [*Exeunt.*

SCENE II.

A room in the palace.

Enter DUKE FREDERICK, *with* LORDS.

DUKE FREDERICK.
CAN it be possible that no man saw them?
It cannot be: some villains of my court
Are of consent and sufferance in this.

FIRST LORD.
I cannot hear of any that did see her.
The ladies, her attendants of her chamber,
Saw her a-bed; and, in the morning early,
They found the bed untreasured of their mistress.

SECOND LORD.
My lord, the roynish clown, at whom so oft
Your Grace was wont to laugh, is also missing.
Hesperia, the princess' gentlewoman,
Confesses that she secretly o'erheard
Your daughter and her cousin much commend
The parts and graces of the wrestler
That did but lately foil the sinewy Charles;
And she believes, wherever they are gone,
That youth is surely in their company.

DUKE FREDERICK.
Send to his brother's; fetch that gallant hither:
If he be absent, bring his brother to me;
I'll make him find him: do this suddenly;
And let not search and inquisition quail
To bring again these foolish runaways. [*Exeunt.*

SCENE III.

Before OLIVER'S *house.*

Enter ORLANDO *and* ADAM, *meeting.*

ORLANDO.
WHO'S there?

ADAM.
What, my young master? O my gentle master!
O my sweet master! O you memory
Of old Sir Rowland! why, what make you here?
Why are you virtuous? why do people love you?
And wherefore are you gentle, strong, and valiant?
Why would you be so fond to overcome
The bony priser of the humorous duke?
Your praise is come too swiftly home before you.
Know you not, master, to some kind of men
Their graces serve them but as enemies?
No more do yours: your virtues, gentle master,
Are sanctified and holy traitors to you.
O, what a world is this, when what is comely
Envenoms him that bears it!

ORLANDO.
Why, what's the matter?

ADAM.
O, unhappy youth!
Come not within these doors; within this roof
The enemy of all your graces lives:
Your brother—no, no brother; yet the son—
Yet not the son, I will not call him son
Of him I was about to call his father—
Hath heard your praises; and this night he means
To burn the lodging where you use to lie,
And you within it: if he fail of that,
He will have other means to cut you off:
I overheard him and his practices.
This is no place; this house is but a butchery:
Abhor it, fear it, do not enter it.

ORLANDO.
Why, whither, Adam, wouldst thou have me go?

ADAM.
No matter whither, so you come not here.

ORLANDO.
What, wouldst thou have me go and beg my food?
Or with a base and boisterous sword enforce
A thievish living on the common road?
This I must do, or know not what to do:
Yet this I will not do, do how I can;
I rather will subject me to the malice
Of a diverted blood and bloody brother.

ADAM.
But do not so. I have five hundred crowns,
The thrifty hire I saved under your father,

Which I did store to be my foster-nurse
When service should in my old limbs lie lame
And unregarded age in corners thrown:
Take that; and He that doth the ravens feed,
Yea, providently caters for the sparrow,
Be comfort to my age! Here is the gold;
All this I give you. Let me be your servant:
Though I look old, yet I am strong and lusty:
For in my youth I never did apply
Hot and rebellious liquors in my blood,
Nor did not with unbashful forehead woo
The means of weakness and debility;
Therefore my age is as a lusty winter,
Frosty, but kindly: let me go with you;
I'll do the service of a younger man
In all your business and necessities.

ORLANDO.

O good old man, how well in thee appears
The constant service of the antique world,
When service sweat for duty, not for meed!
Thou art not for the fashion of these times,
Where none will sweat but for promotion,
And having that, do choke their service up
Even with the having: it is not so with thee.
But, poor old man, thou prunest a rotten tree,
That cannot so much as a blossom yield
In lieu of all thy pains and husbandry.
But come thy ways: we'll go along together;
And ere we have thy youthful wages spent,
We'll light upon some settled low content.

ADAM.

Master, go on, and I will follow thee,
To the last gasp, with truth and loyalty.
From seventeen years till now almost fourscore
Here lived I, but now live here no more.
At seventeen years many their fortunes seek;
But at fourscore it is too late a week:
Yet fortune cannot recompense me better
Than to die well and not my master's debtor.
[*Exeunt.*

SCENE IV.

The Forest of Arden.

Enter ROSALIND *for* GANYMEDE, CELIA *for* ALIENA, *and* TOUCHSTONE.

ROSALIND.

O JUPITER, how weary are my spirits!

TOUCHSTONE.

I care not for my spirits, if my legs were not weary.

ROSALIND.

I could find in my heart to disgrace my man's apparel and to cry like a woman; but I must comfort the weaker vessel, as doublet and hose ought to show itself courageous to petticoat: therefore, courage, good Aliena!

CELIA.

I pray you, bear with me; I cannot go no further.

TOUCHSTONE.

For my part, I had rather bear with you than bear you; yet I should bear no cross, if I did bear you, for I think you have no money in your purse.

ROSALIND.

Well, this is the forest of Arden.

TOUCHSTONE.

Ay, now am I in Arden; the more fool I; when I was at home, I was in a better place: but travellers must be content.

ROSALIND.

Ay, be so, good Touchstone.

Enter CORIN *and* SILVIUS.

Look you, who comes here; a young man and an old in solemn talk.

CORIN.

That is the way to make her scorn you still.

SILVIUS.

O Corin, that thou knew'st how I do love her!

CORIN.

I partly guess; for I have loved ere now.

SILVIUS.

No, Corin, being old, thou canst not guess;
Though in thy youth thou wast as true a lover
As ever sigh'd upon a midnight pillow:
But if thy love were ever like to mine,—
As sure I think did never man love so,—
How many actions most ridiculous
Hast thou been drawn to by thy fantasy?

CORIN.

Into a thousand that I have forgotten.

SILVIUS.

O, thou didst then never love so heartily!
If thou remember'st not the slightest folly
That ever love did make thee run into,
Thou hast not loved:
Or if thou hast not sat as I do now,
Wearing thy hearer in thy mistress' praise,
Thou hast not loved:
Or if thou hast not broke from company
Abruptly, as my passion now makes me,
Thou hast not loved.
O Phebe, Phebe, Phebe! [*Exit.*

ROSALIND.

Alas, poor shepherd! searching of thy wound, I have by hard adventure found mine own.

TOUCHSTONE.

And I mine. I remember, when I was in love I broke my sword upon a stone, and bid him take that for coming a-night to Jane Smile: and I remember the kissing of her batlet, and the cow's dugs that her pretty chopt hands had milkt: and I remember the wooing of a peascod instead of her; from whom I took two cods, and, giving her them again, said with weeping tears, 'Wear these for my sake.' We that are true lovers run into strange capers; but as all is mortal in nature, so is all nature in love mortal in folly.

ROSALIND.

Thou speak'st wiser than thou art ware of.

TOUCHSTONE.

Nay, I shall ne'er be ware of mine own wit till I break my shins against it.

ROSALIND.

Jove, Jove! this shepherd's passion
Is much upon my fashion.

TOUCHSTONE.

And mine; but it grows something stale with me.

CELIA.

I pray you, one of you question yond man,
If he for gold will give us any food:
I faint almost to death.

TOUCHSTONE.
Holla, you clown!

ROSALIND.
Peace, fool: he's not thy kinsman.

CORIN.
Who calls?

TOUCHSTONE.
Your betters, sir.

CORIN.
Else are they very wretched.

ROSALIND.
Peace, I say.—Good even to you, friend.

CORIN.
And to you, gentle sir, and to you all.

ROSALIND.
I prithee, shepherd, if that love or gold
Can in this desert place buy entertainment,
Bring us where we may rest ourselves and feed:
Here's a young maid with travel much oppress'd,
And faints for succour.

CORIN.
Fair sir, I pity her,
And wish, for her sake more than for mine own,
My fortunes were more able to relieve her;
But I am shepherd to another man
And do not shear the fleeces that I graze:
My master is of churlish disposition,
And little recks to find the way to heaven
By doing deeds of hospitality:
Besides, his cote, his flocks, and bounds of feed,
Are now on sale; and at our sheepcote now,
By reason of his absence, there is nothing
That you will feed on; but what is, come see,
And in my voice most welcome shall you be.

ROSALIND.
What is he that shall buy his flock and pasture?

CORIN.
That young swain that you saw here but erewhile,
That little cares for buying any thing.

ROSALIND.
I pray thee, if it stand with honesty,
Buy thou the cottage, pasture, and the flock,
And thou shalt have to pay for it of us.

CELIA.
And we will mend thy wages. I like this place,
And willingly could waste my time in it.

CORIN.
Assuredly the thing is to be sold:
Go with me: if you like, upon report,
The soil, the profit, and this kind of life,
I will your very faithful feeder be,
And buy it with your gold right suddenly.
[*Exeunt.*

SCENE V.

The forest.

Enter AMIENS, JAQUES, *and others.*

AMIENS [*sings*].
UNDER the greenwood tree
Who loves to lie with me,
And turn his merry note
Unto the sweet bird's throat,
Come hither, come hither, come hither:
Here shall he see
No enemy
But winter and rough weather.

JAQUES.
More, more, I prithee, more.

AMIENS.
It will make you melancholy, Monsieur Jaques.

JAQUES.
I thank it. More, I prithee, more. I can suck melancholy out of a song, as a weasel sucks eggs. More, I prithee, more.

AMIENS.
My voice is ragged: I know I cannot please you.

JAQUES.
I do not desire you to please me; I do desire you to sing. Come, more; another stanzo: call you 'em stanzos?

AMIENS.
What you will, Monsieur Jaques.

JAQUES.
Nay, I care not for their names; they owe me nothing. Will you sing?

AMIENS.
More at your request than to please myself.

JAQUES.
Well, then, if ever I thank any man, I'll thank you: but that they call compliment is like th' encounter of two dog-apes; and when a man thanks me heartily, methinks I have given him a penny and he renders me the beggarly thanks. Come, sing; and you that will not, hold your tongues.

AMIENS.
Well, I'll end the song.—Sirs, cover the while; the duke will drink under this tree.—He hath been all this day to look you.

JAQUES.
And I have been all this day to avoid him. He is too disputable for my company: I think of as many matters as he; but I give heaven thanks, and make no boast of them. Come, warble, come.

Song.
Who doth ambition shun [*All together here.*
And loves to live i'th'sun,
Seeking the food he eats
And pleased with what he gets,
Come hither, come hither, come hither:
Here shall he see
No enemy
But winter and rough weather.

JAQUES.
I'll give you a verse to this note, that I made yesterday in despite of my invention.

AMIENS.
And I'll sing it.

JAQUES.
Thus it goes:—
If it do come to pass
That any man turn ass,
Leaving his wealth and ease,
A stubborn will to please,
Ducdame, ducdame, ducdame:
Here shall he see
Gross fools as he,
An if he will come to me.

AMIENS.
What's that 'ducdame'?

JAQUES.

'Tis a Greek invocation, to call fools into a circle. I'll go sleep, if I can; if I cannot, I'll rail against all the first-born of Egypt.

AMIENS.

And I'll go seek the duke: his banquet is prepared. [*Exeunt severally.*

SCENE VI.

The forest.

Enter ORLANDO *and* ADAM.

ADAM.

DEAR master, I can go no further: O, I die for food! Here lie I down, and measure out my grave. Farewell, kind master.

ORLANDO.

Why, how now, Adam! no greater heart in thee? Live a little; comfort a little; cheer thyself a little. If this uncouth forest yield any thing savage, I will either be food for it or bring it for food to thee. Thy conceit is nearer death than thy powers. For my sake be comfortable; hold death awhile at the arm's end: I will here be with thee presently; and if I bring thee not something to eat, I will give thee leave to die: but if thou diest before I come, thou art a mocker of my labour. Well said! thou look'st cheerly; and I'll be with thee quickly. Yet thou liest in the bleak air: come, I will bear thee to some shelter; and thou shalt not die for lack of a dinner, if there live any thing in this desert. Cheerly, good Adam! [*Exeunt.*

SCENE VII.

The forest. A table set out.

Enter DUKE SENIOR, AMIENS, *and* LORDS *like* OUTLAWS.

DUKE SENIOR.

I THINK he be transform'd into a beast;
For I can no where find him like a man.

FIRST LORD.

My lord, he is but even now gone hence:
Here was he merry, hearing of a song.

DUKE SENIOR.

If he, compact of jars, grow musical,
We shall have shortly discord in the spheres.
Go, seek him: tell him I would speak with him.

Enter JAQUES.

FIRST LORD.

He saves my labour by his own approach.

DUKE SENIOR.

Why, how now, monsieur! what a life is this,
That your poor friends must woo your company!
What, you look merrily!

JAQUES.

A fool, a fool! I met a fool i'th'forest,
A motley fool; a miserable world!
As I do live by food, I met a fool;
Who laid him down and baskt him in the sun,
And rail'd on Lady Fortune in good terms,
In good set terms, and yet a motley fool.
'Good morrow, fool,' quoth I. 'No, sir,' quoth he,
'Call me not fool till heaven hath sent me fortune:'
And then he drew a dial from his poke,
And, looking on it with lack-lustre eye,
Says very wisely, 'It is ten o'clock:
Thus we may see,' quoth he, 'how the world wags:
'Tis but an hour ago since it was nine,
And after one hour more 'twill be eleven;
And so, from hour to hour, we ripe and ripe,
And then, from hour to hour, we rot and rot;
And thereby hangs a tale.' When I did hear
The motley fool thus moral on the time,
My lungs began to crow like chanticleer,
That fools should be so deep-contemplative;
And I did laugh sans intermission
An hour by his dial. O noble fool!
A worthy fool! Motley's the only wear.

DUKE SENIOR.

What fool is this?

JAQUES.

O worthy fool! One that hath been a courtier;
And says, if ladies be but young and fair,
They have the gift to know it: and in his brain,—
Which is as dry as the remainder biscuit
After a voyage,—he hath strange places cramm'd
With observation, the which he vents
In mangled forms.—O, that I were a fool!
I am ambitious for a motley coat.

DUKE SENIOR.

Thou shalt have one.

JAQUES.

It is my only suit;
Provided that you weed your better judgements
Of all opinion that grows rank in them
That I am wise. I must have liberty
Withal, as large a charter as the wind,
To blow on whom I please; for so fools have:
And they that are most galled with my folly,
They most must laugh. And why, sir, must they so?
The 'why' is plain as way to parish church:
He that a fool doth very wisely hit
Doth very foolishly, although he smart,
Not to seem senseless of the bob: if not,
The wise man's folly is anatomized
Even by the squandering glances of the fool.
Invest me in my motley; give me leave
To speak my mind, and I will through and through
Cleanse the foul body of th'infected world,
If they will patiently receive my medicine.

DUKE SENIOR.

Fie on thee! I can tell what thou wouldst do.

JAQUES.

What, for a counter, would I do but good?

DUKE SENIOR.

Most mischievous foul sin, in chiding sin:
For thou thyself hast been a libertine,
As sensual as the brutish sting itself;
And all th'imbossed sores and headed evils,
That thou with license of free foot hast caught,
Wouldst thou disgorge into the general world.

JAQUES.

Why, who cries out on pride,
That can therein tax any private party?
Doth it not flow as hugely as the sea,
Till that the weary very means do ebb?
What woman in the city do I name,
When that I say the city-woman bears
The cost of princes on unworthy shoulders?

Who can come in and say that I mean her,
When such a one as she such is her neighbour?
Or what is he of basest function,
That says his bravery is not on my cost,
Thinking that I mean him, but therein suits
His folly to the mettle of my speech?
There then; how then? what then? Let me see wherein
My tongue hath wrong'd him: if it do him right,
Then he hath wrong'd himself; if he be free,
Why, then my taxing like a wild-goose flies,
Unclaim'd of any man.—But who comes here?

Enter ORLANDO, *with his sword drawn.*

ORLANDO.
Forbear, and eat no more!

JAQUES.
Why, I have eat none yet.

ORLANDO.
Nor shalt not, till necessity be served.

JAQUES.
Of what kind should this cock come of?

DUKE SENIOR.
Art thou thus bolden'd, man, by thy distress,
Or else a rude despiser of good manners,
That in civility thou seem'st so empty?

ORLANDO.
You touch'd my vein at first: the thorny point
Of bare distress hath ta'en from me the show
Of smooth civility: yet am I inland bred,
And know some nurture. But forbear, I say:
He dies that touches any of this fruit
Till I and my affairs are answered.

JAQUES.
An you will not be answer'd with reason, I must die.

DUKE SENIOR.
What would you have? Your gentleness shall force
More than your force move us to gentleness.

ORLANDO.
I almost die for food; and let me have it.

DUKE SENIOR.
Sit down and feed, and welcome to our table.

ORLANDO.
Speak you so gently? Pardon me, I pray you:
I thought that all things had been savage here;
And therefore put I on the countenance
Of stern commandment. But whate'er you are,
That in this desert inaccessible,
Under the shade of melancholy boughs,
Lose and neglect the creeping hours of time;
If ever you have lookt on better days,
If ever been where bells have knoll'd to church,
If ever sat at any good man's feast,
If ever from your eyelids wiped a tear,
And know what 'tis to pity and be pitied,—
Let gentleness my strong enforcement be:
In the which hope I blush, and hide my sword.

DUKE SENIOR.
True is it that we have seen better days,
And have with holy bell been knoll'd to church,
And sat at good men's feasts, and wiped our eyes
Of drops that sacred pity hath engender'd:
And therefore sit you down in gentleness,
And take upon command what help we have,
That to your wanting may be minister'd.

ORLANDO.
Then but forbear your food a little while,
Whiles, like a doe, I go to find my fawn,
And give it food. There is an old poor man,
Who after me hath many a weary step
Limpt in pure love: till he be first sufficed,—
Opprest with two weak evils, age and hunger,—
I will not touch a bit.

DUKE SENIOR.
Go find him out,
And we will nothing waste till you return.

ORLANDO.
I thank ye; and be blest for your good comfort!
[*Exit.*

DUKE SENIOR.
Thou seest we are not all alone unhappy:
This wide and universal theatre
Presents more woeful pageants than the scene
Wherein we play in.

JAQUES.
All the world's a stage,
And all the men and women merely players:
They have their exits and their entrances;
And one man in his time plays many parts,
His acts being seven ages. As, first the infant,
Mewling and puking in the nurse's arms.
And then the whining schoolboy, with his satchel
And shining morning face, creeping like snail
Unwillingly to school. And then the lover,
Sighing like furnace, with a woeful ballad
Made to his mistress' eyebrow. Then the soldier,
Full of strange oaths, and bearded like the pard,
Jealous in honour, sudden and quick in quarrel,
Seeking the bubble reputation
Even in the cannon's mouth. And then the justice,
In fair round belly with good capon lined,
With eyes severe and beard of formal cut,
Full of wise saws and modern instances;
And so he plays his part. The sixth age shifts
Into the lean and slipper'd pantaloon,
With spectacles on nose and pouch on side;
His youthful hose, well saved, a world too wide
For his shrunk shank; and his big manly voice,
Turning again toward childish treble, pipes
And whistles in his sound. Last scene of all,
That ends this strange eventful history,
Is second childishness and mere oblivion,
Sans teeth, sans eyes, sans taste, sans every thing.

Enter ORLANDO, *with* ADAM.

DUKE SENIOR.
Welcome. Set down your venerable burthen,
And let him feed.

ORLANDO.
I thank you most for him.

ADAM.
So had you need:—
I scarce can speak to thank you for myself.

DUKE SENIOR.
Welcome; fall to: I will not trouble you
As yet, to question you about your fortunes.—
Give us some music; and, good cousin, sing.

AMIENS.
Blow, blow, thou winter wind,
Thou art not so unkind
As man's ingratitude;

Thy tooth is not so keen,
Because thou art not seen,
Although thy breath be rude.
Heigh-ho! sing, heigh-ho! unto the green holly:
Most friendship is feigning, most loving mere folly:
Then, heigh-ho, the holly!
This life is most jolly.

Freeze, freeze, thou bitter sky,
That dost not bite so nigh
As benefits forgot:
Though thou the waters warp,
Thy sting is not so sharp
As friend remember'd not.
Heigh-ho! sing, heigh-ho! etc.

DUKE SENIOR.

If that you were the good Sir Rowland's son,
As you have whisper'd faithfully you were,
And as mine eye doth his effigies witness
Most truly limn'd and living in your face,—
Be truly welcome hither: I am the duke,
That lovèd your father: the residue of your fortune,
Go to my cave and tell me. Good old man,
Thou art right welcome as thy master is.—
Support him by the arm.—Give me your hand,
And let me all your fortunes understand. [*Exeunt.*

ACT III. SCENE I.

A room in the palace.

Enter DUKE FREDERICK, LORDS, *and* OLIVER.

DUKE FREDERICK.

NOT see him since? Sir, sir, that cannot be:
But were I not the better part made mercy,
I should not seek an absent argument
Of my revenge, thou present. But look to it:
Find out thy brother, wheresoe'er he is;
Seek him with candle; bring him dead or living
Within this twelvemonth, or turn thou no more
To seek a living in our territory.
Thy lands, and all things that thou dost call thine
Worth seizure, do we seize into our hands,
Till thou canst quit thee by thy brother's mouth
Of what we think against thee.

OLIVER.

O, that your highness knew my heart in this!
I never loved my brother in my life.

DUKE FREDERICK.

More villain thou.—Well, push him out of doors;
And let my officers of such a nature
Make an extent upon his house and lands:
Do this expediently, and turn him going.
[*Exeunt.*

SCENE II.

The forest.

Enter ORLANDO, *with a paper.*

ORLANDO.

HANG there, my verse, in witness of my love:
And thou, thrice-crowned queen of night, survey
With thy chaste eye, from thy pale sphere above,
Thy huntress' name, that my full life doth sway.
O Rosalind! these trees shall be my books,
And in their barks my thoughts I'll character;
That every eye, which in this forest looks,
Shall see thy virtue witness'd every where.
Run, run, Orlando; carve on every tree
The fair, the chaste, and unexpressive she. [*Exit.*

Enter CORIN *and* TOUCHSTONE.

CORIN.

And how like you this shepherd's life, Master Touchstone?

TOUCHSTONE.

Truly, shepherd, in respect of itself, it is a good life; but in respect that it is a shepherd's life, it is naught. In respect that it is solitary, I like it very well; but in respect that it is private, it is a very vile life. Now, in respect it is in the fields, it pleaseth me well; but in respect it is not in the court, it is tedious. As it is a spare life, look you, it fits my humour well; but as there is no more plenty in it, it goes much against my stomach. Hast any philosophy in thee, shepherd?

CORIN.

No more but that I know the more one sickens the worse at ease he is; and that he that wants money, means, and content, is without three good friends; that the property of rain is to wet, and fire to burn; that good pasture makes fat sheep; and that a great cause of the night is lack of the sun; that he that hath learn'd no wit by nature nor art may complain of good breeding, or comes of a very dull kindred.

TOUCHSTONE.

Such a one is a natural philosopher. Wast ever in court, shepherd?

CORIN.

No, truly.

TOUCHSTONE.

Then thou art damn'd.

CORIN.

Nay, I hope,—

TOUCHSTONE.

Truly, thou art damn'd; like an ill-roasted egg, all on one side.

CORIN.

For not being at court? Your reason.

TOUCHSTONE.

Why, if thou never wast at court, thou never saw'st good manners; if thou never saw'st good manners, then thy manners must be wicked; and wickedness is sin, and sin is damnation. Thou art in a parlous state, shepherd.

CORIN.

Not a whit, Touchstone: those that are good manners at the court, are as ridiculous in the country as the behaviour of the country is most mockable at the court. You told me you salute not at the court, but you kiss your hands: that courtesy would be uncleanly, if courtiers were shepherds.

TOUCHSTONE.

Instance, briefly; come, instance.

CORIN.

Why, we are still handling our ewes; and their fells, you know, are greasy.

TOUCHSTONE.

Why, do not your courtier's hands sweat? and is not the grease of a mutton as wholesome as the sweat of a man? Shallow, shallow. A better instance, I say; come.

CORIN.

Besides, our hands are hard.

TOUCHSTONE.

Your lips will feel them the sooner. Shallow again. A more sounder instance, come.

CORIN.

And they are often tarr'd over with the surgery of our sheep; and would you have us kiss tar? The courtier's hands are perfumed with civet.

TOUCHSTONE.

Most shallow man! thou worms-meat, in respect of a good piece of flesh, indeed!—Learn of the wise, and perpend: civet is of a baser birth than tar,—the very uncleanly flux of a cat. Mend the instance, shepherd.

CORIN.

You have too courtly a wit for me: I'll rest.

TOUCHSTONE.

Wilt thou rest damn'd? God help thee, shallow man! God make incision in thee! thou art raw.

CORIN.

Sir, I am a true labourer: I earn that I eat, get that I wear; owe no man hate, envy no man's happiness; glad of other men's good, content with my harm; and the greatest of my pride is, to see my ewes graze and my lambs suck.

TOUCHSTONE.

That is another simple sin in you; to bring the ewes and the rams together, and to offer to get your living by the copulation of cattle; to be bawd to a bell-wether; and to betray a she-lamb of a twelvemonth to a crooked-pated, old, cuckoldly ram, out of all reasonable match. If thou be'st not damn'd for this, the devil himself will have no shepherds; I cannot see else how thou shouldst scape.

CORIN.

Here comes young Master Ganymede, my new mistress's brother.

Enter ROSALIND, *with a paper, reading.*

ROSALIND.

From the east to western Ind,
No jewel is like Rosalind.
Her worth, being mounted on the wind,
Through all the world bears Rosalind.
All the pictures fairest lined
Are but black to Rosalind.
Let no face be kept in mind
But the fair of Rosalind.

TOUCHSTONE.

I'll rime you so eight years together, dinners and suppers and sleeping-hours excepted: it is the right butter-women's rank to market.

ROSALIND.

Out, fool!

TOUCHSTONE.

For a taste:

If a hart do lack a hind,
Let him seek out Rosalind.
If the cat will after kind,
So be sure will Rosalind.
Winter garments must be lined,
So must slender Rosalind.
They that reap must sheaf and bind;
Then to cart with Rosalind.
Sweetest nut hath sourest rind,
Such a nut is Rosalind.
He that sweetest rose will find,
Must find love's prick and Rosalind.

This is the very false gallop of verses: why do you infect yourself with them?

ROSALIND.

Peace, you dull fool! I found them on a tree.

TOUCHSTONE.

Truly, the tree yields bad fruit.

ROSALIND.

I'll graff it with you, and then I shall graff it with a medlar: then it will be the earliest fruit i'th'country; for you'll be rotten ere you be half ripe, and that's the right virtue of the medlar.

TOUCHSTONE.

You have said; but whether wisely or no, let the forest judge.

Enter CELIA, *with a writing.*

ROSALIND.

Peace!
Here comes my sister, reading: stand aside.

CELIA [*reads*].

Why should this a desert be?
  For it is unpeopled? No;
Tongues I'll hang on every tree,
  That shall civil sayings show:
Some, how brief the life of man
  Runs his erring pilgrimage,
That the stretching of a span
  Buckles in his sum of age;
Some, of violated vows
  'Twixt the souls of friend and friend:
But upon the fairest boughs,
  Or at every sentence end,
Will I Rosalinda write;
  Teaching all that read to know
The quintessence of every sprite
  Heaven would in little show.
Therefore Heaven Nature charged
  That one body should be fill'd
With all graces wide-enlarged:
  Nature presently distill'd
Helen's cheek, but not her heart;
  Cleopatra's majesty;
Atalanta's better part;
  Sad Lucretia's modesty.
Thus Rosalind of many parts
  By heavenly synod was devised;
Of many faces, eyes, and hearts,
  To have the touches dearest prized.
Heaven would that she these gifts should have,
And I to live and die her slave.

ROSALIND.

O most gentle pulpiter!—what tedious homily of love have you wearied your parishioners withal, and never cried, 'Have patience, good people!'

CELIA.

How now! back, friends:—shepherd, go off a little:—go with him, sirrah.

TOUCHSTONE.

Come, shepherd, let us make an honourable retreat; though not with bag and baggage, yet with scrip and scrippage.

[*Exeunt* CORIN *and* TOUCHSTONE.

CELIA.

Didst thou hear these verses?

ROSALIND.

O, yes, I heard them all, and more too; for some of them had in them more feet than the verses would bear.

CELIA.

That's no matter: the feet might bear the verses.

ROSALIND.

Ay, but the feet were lame, and could not bear themselves without the verse, and therefore stood lamely in the verse.

CELIA.

But didst thou hear without wondering how thy name should be hang'd and carved upon these trees?

ROSALIND.

I was seven of the nine days out of the wonder before you came; for look here what I found on a palm-tree:—I was never so berimed since Pythagoras' time, that I was an Irish rat, which I can hardly remember.

CELIA.

Trow you who hath done this?

ROSALIND.

Is it a man?

CELIA.

And a chain, that you once wore, about his neck. Change you colour?

ROSALIND.

I prithee, who?

CELIA.

O Lord, Lord! it is a hard matter for friends to meet; but mountains may be removed with earthquakes, and so encounter.

ROSALIND.

Nay, but who is it?

CELIA.

Is it possible?

ROSALIND.

Nay, I prithee now with most petitionary vehemence, tell me who it is.

CELIA.

O wonderful, wonderful, and most wonderful wonderful! and yet again wonderful, and after that, out of all whooping!

ROSALIND.

Good my complexion! dost thou think, though I am caparison'd like a man, I have a doublet and hose in my disposition? One inch of delay more is a South-sea of discovery; I prithee, tell me who is it quickly, and speak apace. I would thou couldst stammer, that thou mightest pour this conceal'd man out of thy mouth, as wine comes out of a narrow-mouth'd bottle,—either too much at once, or none at all. I prithee, take the cork out of thy mouth, that I may drink thy tidings.

CELIA.

So you may put a man in your belly.

ROSALIND.

Is he of God's making? What manner of man? Is his head worth a hat, or his chin worth a beard?

CELIA.

Nay, he hath but a little beard.

ROSALIND.

Why, God will send more, if the man will be thankful: let me stay the growth of his beard, if thou delay me not the knowledge of his chin.

CELIA.

It is young Orlando, that tript up the wrestler's heels and your heart both in an instant.

ROSALIND.

Nay, but the devil take mocking: speak, sad brow and true maid.

CELIA.

I'faith, coz, 'tis he.

ROSALIND.

Orlando?

CELIA.

Orlando.

ROSALIND.

Alas the day! what shall I do with my doublet and hose?—What did he when thou saw'st him? What said he? How lookt he? Wherein went he? What makes he here? Did he ask for me? Where remains he? How parted he with thee? and when shalt thou see him again? Answer me in one word.

CELIA.

You must borrow me Gargantua's mouth first: 'tis a word too great for any mouth of this age's size. To say ay and no to these particulars is more than to answer in a catechism.

ROSALIND.

But doth he know that I am in this forest, and in man's apparel? Looks he as freshly as he did the day he wrestled?

CELIA.

It is as easy to count atomies as to resolve the propositions of a lover:—but take a taste of my finding him, and relish it with good observance. I found him under a tree, like a dropt acorn.

ROSALIND.

It may well be call'd Jove's tree, when it drops forth such fruit.

CELIA.

Give me audience, good madam.

ROSALIND.

Proceed.

CELIA.

There lay he, stretcht along, like a wounded knight.

ROSALIND.

Though it be pity to see such a sight, it well becomes the ground.

CELIA.

Cry, holla! to thy tongue, I prithee; it curvets unseasonably. He was furnisht like a hunter.

ROSALIND.

O, ominous, he comes to kill my heart.

CELIA.

I would sing my song without a burthen: thou bring'st me out of tune.

ROSALIND.
Do you not know I am a woman? when I think, I must speak. Sweet, say on.

CELIA.
You bring me out.—Soft! comes he not here?

ROSALIND.
'Tis he: slink by, and note him.

[CELIA *and* ROSALIND *retire.*

Enter ORLANDO *and* JAQUES.

JAQUES.
I thank you for your company; but, good faith, I had as lief have been myself alone.

ORLANDO.
And so had I; but yet, for fashion sake,
I thank you too for your society.

JAQUES.
God b'wi'you! let's meet as little as we can.

ORLANDO.
I do desire we may be better strangers.

JAQUES.
I pray you, mar no more trees with writing love-songs in their barks.

ORLANDO.
I pray you, mar no moe of my verses with reading them ill-favour'dly.

JAQUES.
Rosalind is your love's name?

ORLANDO.
Yes, just.

JAQUES.
I do not like her name.

ORLANDO.
There was no thought of pleasing you when she was christen'd.

JAQUES.
What stature is she of?

ORLANDO.
Just as high as my heart.

JAQUES.
You are full of pretty answers. Have you not been acquainted with goldsmiths' wives, and conn'd them out of rings?

ORLANDO.
Not so; but I answer you right painted cloth, from whence you have studied your questions.

JAQUES.
You have a nimble wit: I think 'twas made of Atalanta's heels. Will you sit down with me? and we two will rail against our mistress the world and all our misery.

ORLANDO.
I will chide no breather in the world but myself, against whom I know most faults.

JAQUES.
The worst fault you have is to be in love.

ORLANDO.
'Tis a fault I will not change for your best virtue. I am weary of you.

JAQUES.
By my troth, I was seeking for a fool when I found you.

ORLANDO.
He is drown'd in the brook: look but in, and you shall see him.

JAQUES.
There I shall see mine own figure.

ORLANDO.
Which I take to be either a fool or a cipher.

JAQUES.
I'll tarry no longer with you: farewell, good Signior Love.

ORLANDO.
I am glad of your departure: adieu, good Monsieur Melancholy.

[*Exit* JAQUES. CELIA *and* ROSALIND *come forward.*

ROSALIND [*aside to* CELIA].
I will speak to him like a saucy lackey, and under that habit play the knave with him.—Do you hear, forester?

ORLANDO.
Very well: what would you?

ROSALIND.
I pray you, what is't o'clock?

ORLANDO.
You should ask me, what time o'day: there's no clock in the forest.

ROSALIND.
Then there is no true lover in the forest; else sighing every minute, and groaning every hour, would detect the lazy foot of Time as well as a clock.

ORLANDO.
And why not the swift foot of Time? had not that been as proper?

ROSALIND.
By no means, sir. Time travels in divers paces with divers persons: I'll tell you who Time ambles withal, who Time trots withal, who Time gallops withal, and who he stands still withal.

ORLANDO.
I prithee, who doth he trot withal?

ROSALIND.
Marry, he trots hard with a young maid between the contract of her marriage and the day it is solemnized: if the interim be but a se'nnight, Time's pace is so hard that it seems the length of seven year.

ORLANDO.
Who ambles Time withal?

ROSALIND.
With a priest that lacks Latin, and a rich man that hath not the gout; for the one sleeps easily, because he cannot study; and the other lives merrily, because he feels no pain: the one lacking the burthen of lean and wasteful learning; the other knowing no burthen of heavy tedious penury: these Time ambles withal.

ORLANDO.
Who doth he gallop withal?

ROSALIND.
With a thief to the gallows; for though he go as softly as foot can fall, he thinks himself too soon there.

ORLANDO.
Who stays it still withal?

ROSALIND.
With lawyers in the vacation; for they sleep between term and term, and then they perceive not how Time moves.

ORLANDO.
Where dwell you, pretty youth?

ROSALIND.

With this shepherdess, my sister; here in the skirts of the forest, like fringe upon a petticoat.

ORLANDO.

Are you native of this place?

ROSALIND.

As the cony, that you see dwell where she is kindled.

ORLANDO.

Your accent is something finer than you could purchase in so removed a dwelling.

ROSALIND.

I have been told so of many: but indeed an old religious uncle of mine taught me to speak, who was in his youth an inland man; one that knew courtship too well, for there he fell in love. I have heard him read many lectures against it; and I thank God I am not a woman, to be toucht with so many giddy offences as he hath generally taxt their whole sex withal.

ORLANDO.

Can you remember any of the principal evils that he laid to the charge of women?

ROSALIND.

There were none principal: they were all like one another as half-pence are; every one fault seeming monstrous till his fellow-fault came to match it.

ORLANDO.

I prithee, recount some of them.

ROSALIND.

No, I will not cast away my physic but on those that are sick. There is a man haunts the forest, that abuses our young plants with carving Rosalind on their barks; hangs odes upon hawthorns, and elegies on brambles; all, forsooth, deifying the name of Rosalind: if I could meet that fancy-monger, I would give him some good counsel, for he seems to have the quotidian of love upon him.

ORLANDO.

I am he that is so love-shaked: I pray you, tell me your remedy.

ROSALIND.

There is none of my uncle's marks upon you: he taught me how to know a man in love; in which cage of rushes I am sure you are not prisoner.

ORLANDO.

What were his marks?

ROSALIND.

A lean cheek,—which you have not; a blue eye and sunken,—which you have not; an unquestionable spirit,—which you have not; a beard neglected,—which you have not;—but I pardon you for that; for simply your having in beard is a younger brother's revenue:—then your hose should be ungarter'd, your bonnet unbanded, your sleeve unbutton'd, your shoe untied, and every thing about you demonstrating a careless desolation;—but you are no such man,—you are rather point-devise in your accoutrements, as loving yourself than seeming the lover of any other.

ORLANDO.

Fair youth, I would I could make thee believe I love.

ROSALIND.

Me believe it! you may as soon make her that you love believe it; which, I warrant, she is apter to do than to confess she does: that is one of the points in the which women still give the lie to their consciences. But, in good sooth, are you he that hangs the verses on the trees, wherein Rosalind is so admired?

ORLANDO.

I swear to thee, youth, by the white hand of Rosalind, I am that he, that unfortunate he.

ROSALIND.

But are you so much in love as your rimes speak?

ORLANDO.

Neither rime nor reason can express how much.

ROSALIND.

Love is merely a madness; and, I tell you, deserves as well a dark house and a whip as madmen do: and the reason why they are not so punisht and cured is, that the lunacy is so ordinary, that the whippers are in love too. Yet I profess curing it by counsel.

ORLANDO.

Did you ever cure any so?

ROSALIND.

Yes, one; and in this manner. He was to imagine me his love, his mistress; and I set him every day to woo me: at which time would I, being but a moonish youth, grieve, be effeminate, changeable, longing, and liking; proud, fantastical, apish, shallow, inconstant, full of tears, full of smiles; for every passion something, and for no passion truly any thing, as boys and women are for the most part cattle of this colour: would now like him, now loathe him; then entertain him, then forswear him; now weep for him, then spit at him; that I drave my suitor from his mad humour of love to a loving humour of madness; which was, to forswear the full stream of the world, and to live in a nook merely monastic. And thus I cured him; and this way will I take upon me to wash your liver as clean as a sound sheep's heart, that there shall not be one spot of love in't.

ORLANDO.

I would not be cured, youth.

ROSALIND.

I would cure you, if you would but call me Rosalind, and come every day to my cote and woo me.

ORLANDO.

Now, by the faith of my love, I will: tell me where it is.

ROSALIND.

Go with me to it, and I'll show it you: and, by the way, you shall tell me where in the forest you live. Will you go?

ORLANDO.

With all my heart, good youth.

ROSALIND.

Nay, you must call me Rosalind.—Come, sister, will you go? *[Exeunt.*

SCENE III.

The forest.

Enter TOUCHSTONE *and* AUDREY; JAQUES *behind.*

TOUCHSTONE.

COME apace, good Audrey: I will fetch up your goats, Audrey. And how, Audrey? am I the man yet? doth my simple feature content you?

AUDREY.

Your features! Lord warrant us! what features?

TOUCHSTONE.

I am here with thee and thy goats, as the most capricious poet, honest Ovid, was among the Goths.

JAQUES [*aside*].

O knowledge ill-inhabited,—worse than Jove in a thatcht house!

TOUCHSTONE.

When a man's verses cannot be understood, nor a man's good wit seconded with the forward child Understanding, it strikes a man more dead than a great reckoning in a little room.—Truly, I would the gods had made thee poetical.

AUDREY.

I do not know what 'poetical' is: is it honest in deed and word? is it a true thing?

TOUCHSTONE.

No, truly; for the truest poetry is the most feigning; and lovers are given to poetry; and what they swear in poetry may be said as lovers they do feign.

AUDREY.

Do you wish, then, that the gods had made me poetical?

TOUCHSTONE.

I do, truly; for thou swear'st to me thou art honest: now, if thou wert a poet, I might have some hope thou didst feign.

AUDREY.

Would you not have me honest?

TOUCHSTONE.

No, truly, unless thou wert hard-favour'd; for honesty coupled to beauty is to have honey a sauce to sugar.

JAQUES [*aside*].

A material fool!

AUDREY.

Well, I am not fair; and therefore I pray the gods make me honest.

TOUCHSTONE.

Truly, and to cast away honesty upon a foul slut, were to put good meat into an unclean dish.

AUDREY.

I am not a slut, though I thank the gods I am foul.

TOUCHSTONE.

Well, praised be the gods for thy foulness! sluttishness may come hereafter. But be it as it may be, I will marry thee: and to that end I have been with Sir Oliver Martext, the vicar of the next village; who hath promised to meet me in this place of the forest, and to couple us.

JAQUES [*aside*].

I would fain see this meeting.

AUDREY.

Well, the gods give us joy!

TOUCHSTONE.

Amen. A man may, if he were of a fearful heart, stagger in this attempt; for here we have no temple but the wood, no assembly but horn-beasts. But what though? Courage! As horns are odious, they are necessary. It is said, 'Many a man knows no end of his goods:' right; many a man has good horns, and knows no end of them. Well, that is the dowry of his wife; 'tis none of his own getting. Horns? even so; poor men alone? No, no; the noblest deer hath them as huge as the rascal. Is the single man therefore blessed? No: as a wall'd town is more worthier than a village, so is the forehead of a married man more honourable than the bare brow of a bachelor; and by how much defence is better than no skill, by so much is a horn more precious than to want.—Here comes Sir Oliver.

Enter SIR OLIVER MARTEXT.

Sir Oliver Martext, you are well met: will you dispatch us here under this tree, or shall we go with you to your chapel?

SIR OLIVER MARTEXT.

Is there none here to give the woman?

TOUCHSTONE.

I will not take her on gift of any man.

SIR OLIVER MARTEXT.

Truly, she must be given, or the marriage is not lawful.

JAQUES [*coming forward*].

Proceed, proceed: I'll give her.

TOUCHSTONE.

Good even, good Master What-ye-call't: how do you, sir? You are very well met: God ild you for your last company: I am very glad to see you:—even a toy in hand here, sir:—nay, pray be cover'd.

JAQUES.

Will you be married, motley?

TOUCHSTONE.

As the ox hath his bow, sir, the horse his curb, and the falcon her bells, so man hath his desires; and as pigeons bill, so wedlock would be nibbling.

JAQUES.

And will you, being a man of your breeding, be married under a bush like a beggar? Get you to church and have a good priest that can tell you what marriage is: this fellow will but join you together as they join wainscot; then one of you will prove a shrunk panel, and like green timber warp, warp.

TOUCHSTONE [*aside*].

I am not in the mind but I were better to be married of him than of another: for he is not like to marry me well; and not being well married, it will be a good excuse for me hereafter to leave my wife.

JAQUES.

Go thou with me, and let me counsel thee.

TOUCHSTONE.

Come, sweet Audrey:
We must be married, or we must live in baw-
dry.—
Farewell, good Master Oliver:—not,
O sweet Oliver,
O brave Oliver,
Leave me not behind thee;—
but,
Wind away,
Be gone, I say,
I will not to wedding with thee.

[*Exeunt* JAQUES, TOUCHSTONE, *and* AUDREY.

SIR OLIVER MARTEXT.

'Tis no matter: ne'er a fantastical knave of them all shall flout me out of my calling. [*Exit.*

SCENE IV.

The forest.

Enter ROSALIND *and* CELIA.

ROSALIND.

NEVER talk to me; I will weep.

CELIA.

Do, I prithee; but yet have the grace to consider that tears do not become a man.

ROSALIND.

But have I not cause to weep?

CELIA.

As good cause as one would desire: therefore weep.

ROSALIND.

His very hair is of the dissembling colour.

CELIA.

Something browner than Judas's: marry, his kisses are Judas's own children.

ROSALIND.

I'faith, his hair is of a good colour.

CELIA.

An excellent colour: your chestnut was ever the only colour.

ROSALIND.

And his kissing is as full of sanctity as the touch of holy bread.

CELIA.

He hath bought a pair of cast lips of Diana: a nun of winter's sisterhood kisses not more religiously; the very ice of chastity is in them.

ROSALIND.

But why did he swear he would come this morning, and comes not?

CELIA.

Nay, certainly, there is no truth in him.

ROSALIND.

Do you think so?

CELIA.

Yes; I think he is not a pick-purse nor a horse-stealer; but for his verity in love, I do think him as concave as a cover'd goblet or a worm-eaten nut.

ROSALIND.

Not true in love?

CELIA.

Yes, when he is in; but I think he is not in.

ROSALIND.

You have heard him swear downright he was.

CELIA.

'Was' is not 'is:' besides, the oath of a lover is no stronger than the word of a tapster; they are both the confirmers of false reckonings. He attends here in the forest on the duke your father.

ROSALIND.

I met the duke yesterday, and had much question with him: he askt me, of what parentage I was; I told him, of as good as he; so he laught, and let me go. But what talk we of fathers, when there is such a man as Orlando?

CELIA.

O, that's a brave man! he writes brave verses, speaks brave words, swears brave oaths, and breaks them bravely, quite traverse, athwart the heart of his lover; as a puisny tilter, that spurs his horse but on one side, breaks his staff like a noble goose: but all's brave that youth mounts and folly guides.—Who comes here?

Enter CORIN.

CORIN.

Mistress and master, you have oft inquired
After the shepherd that complain'd of love,
Who you saw sitting by me on the turf,
Praising the proud disdainful shepherdess
That was his mistress.

CELIA.

Well, and what of him?

CORIN.

If you will see a pageant truly play'd,
Between the pale complexion of true love
And the red glow of scorn and proud disdain,
Go hence a little, and I shall conduct you,
If you will mark it.

ROSALIND.

O, come, let us remove:
The sight of lovers feedeth those in love.—
Bring us to this sight, and you shall say
I'll prove a busy actor in their play. [*Exeunt.*

SCENE V.

The forest.

Enter SILVIUS *and* PHEBE.

SILVIUS.

SWEET Phebe, do not scorn me; do not, Phebe:
Say that you love me not; but say not so
In bitterness. The common executioner,
Whose heart th'accustom'd sight of death makes hard,
Falls not the axe upon the humbled neck
But first begs pardon: will you sterner be
Than he that dies and lives by bloody drops?

Enter ROSALIND *and* CELIA; CORIN *behind.*

PHEBE.

I would not be thy executioner:
I fly thee, for I would not injure thee.
Thou tell'st me there is murder in mine eye:
'Tis pretty, sure, and very probable,
That eyes—that are the frail'st and softest things,
Who shut their coward gates on atomies—
Should be call'd tyrants, butchers, murderers!
Now I do frown on thee with all my heart;
And, if mine eyes can wound, now let them kill thee:
Now counterfeit to swoon; why, now fall down;
Or, if thou canst not, O, for shame, for shame,
Lie not, to say mine eyes are murderers!
Now show the wound mine eye hath made in thee:
Scratch thee but with a pin, and there remains
Some scar of it; lean but upon a rush,
The cicatrice and capable impressure
Thy palm some moment keeps: but now mine eyes,
Which I have darted at thee, hurt thee not;
Nor, I am sure, there is no force in eyes
That can do hurt.

SILVIUS.

O dear Phebe,
If ever—as that ever may be near—
You meet in some fresh cheek the power of fancy,
Then shall you know the wounds invisible
That love's keen arrows make.

PHEBE.

But, till that time,
Come not thou near me: and, when that time comes,
Afflict me with thy mocks, pity me not;
As, till that time, I shall not pity thee.

ROSALIND [*coming forward*].

And why, I pray you? Who might be your mother,
That you insult, exult, and all at once,
Over the wretched? What though you have no beauty,—
As, by my faith, I see no more in you
Than without candle may go dark to bed,—
Must you be therefore proud and pitiless?
Why, what means this? Why do you look on me?
I see no more in you than in the ordinary
Of nature's sale-work:—'Od's my little life,
I think she means to tangle my eyes too!—
No, faith, proud mistress, hope not after it:
'Tis not your inky brows, your black-silk hair,
Your bugle eyeballs, nor your cheek of cream,
That can entame my spirits to your worship.—
You foolish shepherd, wherefore do you follow her,
Like foggy south, puffing with wind and rain?
You are a thousand times a properer man
Than she a woman: 'tis such fools as you
That makes the world full of ill-favour'd children:
'Tis not her glass, but you, that flatters her;
And out of you she sees herself more proper
Than any of her lineaments can show her.—
But, mistress, know yourself: down on your knees,
And thank heaven, fasting, for a good man's love:
For I must tell you friendly in your ear,—
Sell when you can: you are not for all markets:
Cry the man mercy; love him; take his offer:
Foul is most foul, being foul to be a scoffer.—
So, take her to thee, shepherd:—fare you well.

PHEBE.

Sweet youth, I pray you, chide a year together:
I had rather hear you chide than this man woo.

ROSALIND.

He's fall'n in love with her foulness, and she'll fall in love with my anger:—if it be so, as fast as she answers thee with frowning looks, I'll sauce her with bitter words.—Why look you so upon me?

PHEBE.

For no ill will I bear you.

ROSALIND.

I pray you, do not fall in love with me,
For I am falser than vows made in wine:
Besides, I like you not.—If you will know my house,
'Tis at the tuft of olives here hard by.—
Will you go, sister?—Shepherd, ply her hard.—
Come, sister.—Shepherdess, look on him better,
And be not proud: though all the world could see,
None could be so abused in sight as he.—
Come, to our flock.

[*Exeunt* ROSALIND, CELIA, *and* CORIN.

PHEBE.

Dead shepherd, now I find thy saw of might,—
'Who ever loved that loved not at first sight?'

SILVIUS.

Sweet Phebe,—

PHEBE.

Ha, what say'st thou, Silvius?

SILVIUS.

Sweet Phebe, pity me.

PHEBE.

Why, I am sorry for thee, gentle Silvius.

SILVIUS.

Wherever sorrow is, relief would be:
If you do sorrow at my grief in love,
By giving love, your sorrow and my grief
Were both extermined.

PHEBE.

Thou hast my love: is not that neighbourly?

SILVIUS.

I would have you.

PHEBE.

Why, that were covetousness.
Silvius, the time was, that I hated thee;
And yet it is not that I bear thee love:
But since that thou canst talk of love so well,
Thy company, which erst was irksome to me,
I will endure; and I'll employ thee too:
But do not look for further recompense
Than thine own gladness that thou art employ'd.

SILVIUS.

So holy and so perfect is my love,
And I in such a poverty of grace,
That I shall think it a most plenteous crop
To glean the broken ears after the man
That the main harvest reaps: loose now and then
A scatter'd smile, and that I'll live upon.

PHEBE.

Know'st thou the youth that spoke to me erewhile?

SILVIUS.

Not very well, but I have met him oft;
And he hath bought the cottage and the bounds
That the old carlot once was master of.

PHEBE.

Think not I love him, though I ask for him;
'Tis but a peevish boy:—yet he talks well;—
But what care I for words? yet words do well,
When he that speaks them pleases those that hear.
It is a pretty youth:—not very pretty:—
But, sure, he's proud; and yet his pride becomes him:
He'll make a proper man: the best thing in him
Is his complexion; and faster than his tongue
Did make offence, his eye did heal it up.
He is not very tall; yet for his years he's tall:
His leg is but so-so; and yet 'tis well:
There was a pretty redness in his lip,
A little riper and more lusty red
Than that mixt in his cheek; 'twas just the difference
Betwixt the constant red and mingled damask.
There be some women, Silvius, had they markt him
In parcels as I did, would have gone near
To fall in love with him: but, for my part,
I love him not, nor hate him not; and yet
I have more cause to hate him than to love him:
For what had he to do to chide at me?
He said mine eyes were black, and my hair black;
And, now I am remember'd, scorn'd at me:
I marvel why I answer'd not again:

But that's all one; omittance is no quittance.
I'll write to him a very taunting letter,
And thou shalt bear it; wilt thou, Silvius?

SILVIUS.

Phebe, with all my heart.

PHEBE.

I'll write it straight;
The matter's in my head and in my heart:
I will be bitter with him and passing short.
Go with me, Silvius. [*Exeunt.*

ACT IV. SCENE I.

The forest.

Enter ROSALIND, CELIA, *and* JAQUES.

JAQUES.

I PRITHEE, pretty youth, let me be better acquainted with thee.

ROSALIND.

They say you are a melancholy fellow.

JAQUES.

I am so; I do love it better than laughing.

ROSALIND.

Those that are in extremity of either are abominable fellows, and betray themselves to every modern censure worse than drunkards.

JAQUES.

Why, 'tis good to be sad and say nothing.

ROSALIND.

Why, then 'tis good to be a post.

JAQUES.

I have neither the scholar's melancholy, which is emulation; nor the musician's, which is fantastical; nor the courtier's, which is proud; nor the soldier's, which is ambitious; nor the lawyer's, which is politic; nor the lady's, which is nice; nor the lover's, which is all these;—but it is a melancholy of mine own, compounded of many simples, extracted from many objects, and, indeed, the sundry contemplation of my travels, which, by often rumination, wraps me in a most humorous sadness.

ROSALIND.

A traveller! By my faith, you have great reason to be sad: I fear you have sold your own lands, to see other men's; then, to have seen much, and to have nothing, is to have rich eyes and poor hands.

JAQUES.

Yes, I have gain'd my experience.

ROSALIND.

And your experience makes you sad: I had rather have a fool to make me merry than experience to make me sad; and to travel for it too!

Enter ORLANDO.

ORLANDO.

Good day and happiness, dear Rosalind!

JAQUES.

Nay, then, God b'wi'you, an you talk in blank verse! [*Exit.*

ROSALIND.

Farewell, Monsieur Traveller: look you lisp, and wear strange suits; disable all the benefits of your own country; be out of love with your nativity, and almost chide God for making you that countenance you are; or I will scarce think you have swam in a gondola. Why, how now, Orlando! where have you been all this while? You a lover! —An you serve me such another trick, never come in my sight more.

ORLANDO.

My fair Rosalind, I come within an hour of my promise.

ROSALIND.

Break an hour's promise in love! He that will divide a minute into a thousand parts, and break but a part of the thousandth part of a minute in the affairs of love, it may be said of him, that Cupid hath clapt him o'th'shoulder, but I'll warrant him heart-whole.

ORLANDO.

Pardon me, dear Rosalind.

ROSALIND.

Nay, an you be so tardy, come no more in my sight: I had as lief be woo'd of a snail.

ORLANDO.

Of a snail!

ROSALIND.

Ay, of a snail; for though he comes slowly, he carries his house on his head,—a better jointure, I think, than you make a woman: besides, he brings his destiny with him.

ORLANDO.

What's that?

ROSALIND.

Why, horns; which such as you are fain to be beholding to your wives for: but he comes arm'd in his fortune, and prevents the slander of his wife.

ORLANDO.

Virtue is no horn-maker; and my Rosalind is virtuous.

ROSALIND.

And I am your Rosalind.

CELIA.

It pleases him to call you so; but he hath a Rosalind of a better leer than you.

ROSALIND.

Come, woo me, woo me; for now I am in a holiday humour, and like enough to consent.—What would you say to me now, an I were your very very Rosalind?

ORLANDO.

I would kiss before I spoke.

ROSALIND.

Nay, you were better speak first; and when you were gravell'd for lack of matter, you might take occasion to kiss. Very good orators, when they are out, they will spit; and for lovers, lacking (God warn us!) matter, the cleanliest shift is to kiss.

ORLANDO.

How if the kiss be denied?

ROSALIND.

Then she puts you to entreaty, and there begins new matter.

ORLANDO.

Who could be out, being before his beloved mistress?

ROSALIND.

Marry, that should you, if I were your mistress; or I should think my honesty ranker than my wit.

ORLANDO.

What, of my suit?

ROSALIND.

Not out of your apparel, and yet out of your suit. Am not I your Rosalind?

ORLANDO.

I take some joy to say you are, because I would be talking of her.

ROSALIND.

Well, in her person, I say,—I will not have you.

ORLANDO.

Then, in mine own person, I die.

ROSALIND.

No, faith, die by attorney. The poor world is almost six thousand years old, and in all this time there was not any man died in his own person, *videlicet*, in a love-cause. Troilus had his brains dasht out with a Grecian club; yet he did what he could to die before; and he is one of the patterns of love. Leander, he would have lived many a fair year, though Hero had turn'd nun, if it had not been for a hot midsummer night; for, good youth, he went but forth to wash him in the Hellespont, and, being taken with the cramp, was drown'd: and the foolish chroniclers of that age found it was —Hero of Sestos. But these are all lies: men have died from time to time, and worms have eaten them, but not for love.

ORLANDO.

I would not have my right Rosalind of this mind; for, I protest, her frown might kill me.

ROSALIND.

By this hand, it will not kill a fly. But come, now I will be your Rosalind in a more coming-on disposition; and ask me what you will, I will grant it.

ORLANDO.

Then love me, Rosalind.

ROSALIND.

Yes, faith, will I, Fridays and Saturdays and all.

ORLANDO.

And wilt thou have me?

ROSALIND.

Ay, and twenty such.

ORLANDO.

What sayest thou?

ROSALIND.

Are you not good?

ORLANDO.

I hope so.

ROSALIND.

Why, then, can one desire too much of a good thing?—Come, sister, you shall be the priest, and marry us.—Give me your hand, Orlando.—What do you say, sister?

ORLANDO.

Pray thee, marry us.

CELIA.

I cannot say the words.

ROSALIND.

You must begin,—'Will you, Orlando,'—

CELIA.

Go to.—Will you, Orlando, have to wife this Rosalind?

ORLANDO.

I will.

ROSALIND.

Ay, but when?

ORLANDO.

Why now; as fast as she can marry us.

ROSALIND.

Then you must say,—'I take thee, Rosalind, for wife.'

ORLANDO.

I take thee, Rosalind, for wife.

ROSALIND.

I might ask you for your commission; but,—I do take thee, Orlando, for my husband:—there's a girl goes before the priest; and, certainly, a woman's thought runs before her actions.

ORLANDO.

So do all thoughts,—they are wing'd.

ROSALIND.

Now tell me how long you would have her, after you have possest her.

ORLANDO.

For ever and a day.

ROSALIND.

Say a day, without the ever. No, no, Orlando; men are April when they woo, December when they wed: maids are May when they are maids, but the sky changes when they are wives. I will be more jealous of thee than a Barbary cock-pigeon over his hen; more clamorous than a parrot against rain; more new-fangled than an ape; more giddy in my desires than a monkey: I will weep for nothing, like Diana in the fountain, and I will do that when you are disposed to be merry; I will laugh like a hyen, and that when thou art inclined to weep.

ORLANDO.

But will my Rosalind do so?

ROSALIND.

By my life, she will do as I do.

ORLANDO.

O, but she is wise.

ROSALIND.

Or else she could not have the wit to do this: the wiser, the waywarder: make the doors upon a woman's wit, and it will out at the casement; shut that, and 'twill out at the key-hole; stop that, 'twill fly with the smoke out at the chimney.

ORLANDO.

A man that had a wife with such a wit, he might say,—'Wit, whither wilt?'

ROSALIND.

Nay, you might keep that check for it till you met your wife's wit going to your neighbour's bed.

ORLANDO.

And what wit could wit have to excuse that?

ROSALIND.

Marry, to say,—she came to seek you there. You shall never take her without her answer, unless you take her without her tongue. O, that woman that cannot make her fault her husband's occasion, let her never nurse her child herself, for she will breed it like a fool!

ORLANDO.

For these two hours, Rosalind, I will leave thee.

ROSALIND.

Alas, dear love, I cannot lack thee two hours!

ORLANDO.

I must attend the duke at dinner: by two o'clock I will be with thee again.

ROSALIND.

Ay, go your ways, go your ways;—I knew what you would prove: my friends told me as much, and I thought no less:—that flattering tongue of yours won me:—'tis but one cast away, and so,—come, death!—Two o'clock is your hour?

ORLANDO.

Ay, sweet Rosalind.

ROSALIND.

By my troth, and in good earnest, and so God mend me, and by all pretty oaths that are not dangerous, if you break one jot of your promise, or come one minute behind your hour, I will think you the most pathetical break-promise, and the most hollow lover, and the most unworthy of her you call Rosalind, that may be chosen out of the gross band of the unfaithful: therefore beware my censure, and keep your promise.

ORLANDO.

With no less religion than if thou wert indeed my Rosalind: so, adieu.

ROSALIND.

Well, Time is the old justice that examines all such offenders, and let Time try: adieu.

[*Exit* ORLANDO.

CELIA.

You have simply misused our sex in your love-prate: we must have your doublet and hose pluckt over your head, and show the world what the bird hath done to her own nest.

ROSALIND.

O coz, coz, coz, my pretty little coz, that thou didst know how many fathom deep I am in love! But it cannot be sounded: my affection hath an unknown bottom, like the bay of Portugal.

CELIA.

Or rather, bottomless; that as fast as you pour affection in, it runs out.

ROSALIND.

No, that same wicked bastard of Venus, that was begot of thought, conceived of spleen, and born of madness; that blind rascally boy, that abuses every one's eyes, because his own are out, let him be judge how deep I am in love:—I'll tell thee, Aliena, I cannot be out of the sight of Orlando; I'll go find a shadow, and sigh till he come.

CELIA.

And I'll sleep. [*Exeunt.*

SCENE II.

The forest.

Enter JAQUES, LORDS, *and* FORESTERS.

JAQUES.

WHICH is he that kill'd the deer?

A LORD.

Sir, it was I.

JAQUES.

Let's present him to the duke, like a Roman conqueror; and it would do well to set the deer's horns upon his head, for a branch of victory.—Have you no song, forester, for this purpose?

FORESTER.

Yes, sir.

JAQUES.

Sing it: 'tis no matter how it be in tune, so it make noise enough.

Song.

What shall he have that kill'd the deer?
His leather skin and horns to wear.
Then sing him home!
[*The rest shall bear this burthen.*
Take thou no scorn to wear the horn;
It was a crest ere thou wast born;
Thy father's father wore it,
And thy father bore it:
The horn, the horn, the lusty horn
Is not a thing to laugh to scorn. [*Exeunt.*

SCENE III.

The forest.

Enter ROSALIND AND CELIA.

ROSALIND.

HOW, say you now? Is it not past two o'clock? and here much Orlando!

CELIA.

I warrant you, with pure love and troubled brain, he hath ta'en his bow and arrows, and is gone forth—to sleep. Look, who comes here.

Enter SILVIUS.

SILVIUS.

My errand is to you, fair youth;—
My gentle Phebe bid me give you this:
[*gives a letter.*
I know not the contents; but, as I guess
By the stern brow and waspish action
Which she did use as she was writing of it,
It bears an angry tenour: pardon me,
I am but as a guiltless messenger.

ROSALIND.

Patience herself would startle at this letter,
And play the swaggerer; bear this, bear all:
She says I am not fair; that I lack manners;
She calls me proud; and that she could not love me,
Were man as rare as phœnix. 'Od's my will!
Her love is not the hare that I do hunt:
Why writes she so to me?—Well, shepherd, well,
This is a letter of your own device.

SILVIUS.

No, I protest, I know not the contents:
Phebe did write it.

ROSALIND.

Come, come, you are a fool,
And turn'd into the extremity of love.
I saw her hand: she has a leathern hand,
A freestone-colour'd hand; I verily did think
That her old gloves were on, but 'twas her hands:
She has a housewife's hand; but that's no matter:
I say, she never did invent this letter;
This is a man's invention, and his hand.

SILVIUS.

Sure, it is hers.

ROSALIND.

Why, 'tis a boisterous and a cruel style,
A style for challengers; why, she defies me,
Like Turk to Christian: women's gentle brain
Could not drop forth such giant-rude invention,

Such Ethiop words, blacker in their effect
Than in their countenance.—Will you hear the letter?

SILVIUS.

So please you, for I never heard it yet;
Yet heard too much of Phebe's cruelty.

ROSALIND.

She Phebes me: mark how the tyrant writes.
[*Reads*] Art thou god to shepherd turn'd,
That a maiden's heart hath burn'd?—
Can a woman rail thus?

SILVIUS.

Call you this railing?

ROSALIND [*reads*].

Why, thy godhead laid apart,
Warr'st thou with a woman's heart?—
Did you ever hear such railing?—
Whiles the eye of man did woo me,
That could do no vengeance to me.—
Meaning me a beast.—
If the scorn of your bright eyne
Have power to raise such love in mine,
Alack, in me what strange effect
Would they work in mild aspect!
Whiles you chid me, I did love;
How, then, might your prayers move!
He that brings this love to thee
Little knows this love in me:
And by him seal up thy mind;
Whether that thy youth and kind
Will the faithful offer take
Of me, and all that I can make;
Or else by him my love deny,
And then I'll study how to die.

SILVIUS.

Call you this chiding?

CELIA.

Alas, poor shepherd!

ROSALIND.

Do you pity him? no, he deserves no pity. Wilt thou love such a woman? What, to make thee an instrument, and play false strains upon thee! not to be endured! Well, go your way to her, for I see love hath made thee a tame snake, and say this to her:—that if she love me, I charge her to love thee; if she will not, I will never have her, unless thou entreat for her.—If you be a true lover, hence, and not a word; for here comes more company. [*Exit* SILVIUS.

Enter OLIVER.

OLIVER.

Good morrow, fair ones: pray you, if you know,
Where in the purlieus of this forest stands
A sheep-cote fenced about with olive-trees?

CELIA.

West of this place, down in the neighbour bottom:
The rank of osiers, by the murmuring stream,
Left on your right hand, brings you to the place.
But at this hour the house doth keep itself;
There's none within.

OLIVER.

If that an eye may profit by a tongue,
Then should I know you by description;
Such garments and such years:—'The boy is fair,
Of female favour, and bestows himself
Like a ripe sister: the woman low,
And browner than her brother.' Are not you
The owners of the house I did inquire for?

CELIA.

It is no boast, being askt, to say we are.

OLIVER.

Orlando doth commend him to you both;
And to that youth he calls his Rosalind
He sends this bloody napkin;—are you he?

ROSALIND.

I am: what must we understand by this?

OLIVER.

Some of my shame; if you will know of me
What man I am, and how, and why, and where
This handkercher was stain'd.

CELIA.

I pray you, tell it.

OLIVER.

When last the young Orlando parted from you,
He left a promise to return again
Within an hour; and, pacing through the forest,
Chewing the food of sweet and bitter fancy,
Lo, what befell! he threw his eye aside,
And, mark, what object did present itself:
Under an oak, whose boughs were moss'd with age,
And high top bald with dry antiquity,
A wretched ragged man, o'ergrown with hair,
Lay sleeping on his back: about his neck
A green and gilded snake had wreath'd itself,
Who with her head, nimble in threats, approacht
The opening of his mouth; but suddenly,
Seeing Orlando, it unlinkt itself,
And with indented glides did slip away
Into a bush: under which bush's shade
A lioness, with udders all drawn dry,
Lay couching, head on ground, with catlike watch,
When that the sleeping man should stir; for 'tis
The royal disposition of that beast
To prey on nothing that doth seem as dead:
This seen, Orlando did approach the man,
And found it was his brother, his elder brother.

CELIA.

O, I have heard him speak of that same brother;
And he did render him the most unnatural
That lived 'mongst men.

OLIVER.

And well he might so do,
For well I know he was unnatural.

ROSALIND.

But, to Orlando:—did he leave him there,
Food to the suckt and hungry lioness?

OLIVER.

Twice did he turn his back, and purposed so;
But kindness, nobler ever than revenge,
And nature, stronger than his just occasion,
Made him give battle to the lioness,
Who quickly fell before him: in which hurtling
From miserable slumber I awaked.

CELIA.

Are you his brother?

ROSALIND.

Was't you he rescued?

CELIA.

Was't you that did so oft contrive to kill him?

OLIVER.

'Twas I: but 'tis not I: I do not shame
To tell you what I was, since my conversion
So sweetly tastes, being the thing I am.

ROSALIND.

But, for the bloody napkin?—

OLIVER.

By and by.
When from the first to last, betwixt us two,
Tears our recountments had most kindly bathed,
As how I came into that desert place;—
In brief, he led me to the gentle duke,
Who gave me fresh array and entertainment,
Committing me unto my brother's love;
Who led me instantly unto his cave,
There stript himself, and here upon his arm
The lioness had torn some flesh away,
Which all this while had bled; and now he fainted,
And cried, in fainting, upon Rosalind.
Brief, I recover'd him, bound up his wound;
And, after some small space, being strong at heart,
He sent me hither, stranger as I am,
To tell this story, that you might excuse
His broken promise, and to give this napkin,
Dyed in his blood, unto the shepherd youth
That he in sport doth call his Rosalind.

CELIA.

Why, how now, Ganymede! sweet Ganymede!
[ROSALIND *faints.*

OLIVER.

Many will swoon when they do look on blood.

CELIA.

There is more in it.—Cousin Ganymede!

OLIVER.

Look, he recovers.

ROSALIND.

I would I were at home.

CELIA.

We'll lead you thither.—
I pray you, will you take him by the arm?

OLIVER.

Be of good cheer, youth:—you a man? you lack a man's heart.

ROSALIND.

I do so, I confess it! Ah, sirrah, a body would think this was well counterfeited! I pray you, tell your brother how well I counterfeited.—Heigh-ho!

OLIVER.

This was not counterfeit: there is too great testimony in your complexion, that it was a passion of earnest.

ROSALIND.

Counterfeit, I assure you.

OLIVER.

Well, then, take a good heart, and counterfeit to be a man.

ROSALIND.

So I do: but, i'faith, I should have been a woman by right.

CELIA.

Come, you look paler and paler: pray you, draw homewards.—Good sir, go with us.

OLIVER.

That will I, for I must bear answer back
How you excuse my brother, Rosalind.

ROSALIND.

I shall devise something: but, I pray you, commend my counterfeiting to him:—will you go?
[*Exeunt.*

ACT V. SCENE I.

The forest.

Enter TOUCHSTONE *and* AUDREY.

TOUCHSTONE.

We shall find a time, Audrey; patience, gentle Audrey.

AUDREY.

Faith, the priest was good enough, for all the old gentleman's saying.

TOUCHSTONE.

A most wicked Sir Oliver, Audrey, a most vile Martext. But, Audrey, there is a youth here in the forest lays claim to you.

AUDREY.

Ay, I know who 'tis: he hath no interest in me in the world: here comes the man you mean.

TOUCHSTONE.

It is meat and drink to me to see a clown: by my troth, we that have good wits have much to answer for; we shall be flouting; we cannot hold.

Enter WILLIAM.

WILLIAM.

Good even, Audrey.

AUDREY.

God ye good even, William.

WILLIAM.

And good even to you, sir.

TOUCHSTONE.

Good even, gentle friend. Cover thy head, cover thy head; nay, prithee, be cover'd. How old are you, friend?

WILLIAM.

Five and twenty, sir.

TOUCHSTONE.

A ripe age. Is thy name William?

WILLIAM.

William, sir.

TOUCHSTONE.

A fair name. Wast born i'th'forest here?

WILLIAM.

Ay, sir, I thank God.

TOUCHSTONE.

Thank God;—a good answer. Art rich?

WILLIAM.

Faith, sir, so-so.

TOUCHSTONE.

So-so is good, very good, very excellent good:—and yet it is not; it is but so-so. Art thou wise?

WILLIAM.

Ay, sir, I have a pretty wit.

TOUCHSTONE.

Why, thou say'st well. I do now remember a saying, 'The fool doth think he is wise; but the wise man knows himself to be a fool.' The heathen philosopher, when he had a desire to eat a grape, would open his lips when he put it into his mouth; meaning thereby, that grapes were made to eat, and lips to open. You do love this maid?

WILLIAM.

I do, sir.

TOUCHSTONE.

Give me your hand. Art thou learned?

WILLIAM.

No, sir.

TOUCHSTONE.

Then learn this of me:—to have, is to have; for it is a figure in rhetoric, that drink, being pour'd out of a cup into a glass, by filling the one doth empty the other; for all your writers do consent that *ipse* is he: now, you are not *ipse*, for I am he.

WILLIAM.

Which he, sir?

TOUCHSTONE.

He, sir, that must marry this woman. Therefore, you clown, abandon,—which is in the vulgar leave,—the society,—which in the boorish is company,—of this female,—which in the common is woman; which together is, abandon the society of this female, or, clown, thou perishest; or, to thy better understanding, diest; or (to wit) I kill thee, make thee away, translate thy life into death, thy liberty into bondage: I will deal in poison with thee, or in bastinado, or in steel; I will bandy with thee in faction; I will o'er-run thee with policy; I will kill thee a hundred and fifty ways: therefore tremble, and depart.

AUDREY.

Do, good William.

WILLIAM.

God rest you merry, sir. [*Exit.*

Enter CORIN.

CORIN.

Our master and mistress seek you; come, away, away!

TOUCHSTONE.

Trip, Audrey, trip, Audrey.—I attend, I attend. [*Exeunt.*

SCENE II.

The forest.

Enter ORLANDO *and* OLIVER.

ORLANDO.

IS'T possible that, on so little acquaintance, you should like her? that, but seeing, you should love her? and, loving, woo? and, wooing, she should grant? and will you persever to enjoy her?

OLIVER.

Neither call the giddiness of it in question, the poverty of her, the small acquaintance, my sudden wooing, nor her sudden consenting; but say with me, I love Aliena; say with her, that she loves me; consent with both, that we may enjoy each other: it shall be to your good; for my father's house, and all the revenue that was old Sir Rowland's, will I estate upon you, and here live and die a shepherd.

ORLANDO.

You have my consent. Let your wedding be to-morrow: thither will I invite the duke, and all's contented followers. Go you and prepare Aliena; for, look you, here comes my Rosalind.

Enter ROSALIND.

ROSALIND.

God save you, brother.

OLIVER.

And you, fair sister. [*Exit.*

ROSALIND.

O, my dear Orlando, how it grieves me to see thee wear thy heart in a scarf!

ORLANDO.

It is my arm.

ROSALIND.

I thought thy heart had been wounded with the claws of a lion.

ORLANDO.

Wounded it is, but with the eyes of a lady.

ROSALIND.

Did your brother tell you how I counterfeited to swoon when he show'd me your handkercher?

ORLANDO.

Ay, and greater wonders than that.

ROSALIND.

O, I know where you are:—nay, 'tis true: there was never any thing so sudden, but the fight of two rams, and Cæsar's thrasonical brag of—'I came, saw, and overcame:' for your brother and my sister no sooner met, but they lookt; no sooner lookt, but they loved; no sooner loved, but they sigh'd; no sooner sigh'd, but they askt one another the reason; no sooner knew the reason, but they sought the remedy: and in these degrees have they made a pair of stairs to marriage, which they will climb incontinent, or else be incontinent before marriage: they are in the very wrath of love, and they will together; clubs cannot part them.

ORLANDO.

They shall be married to-morrow; and I will bid the duke to the nuptial. But, O, how bitter a thing it is to look into happiness through another man's eyes! By so much the more shall I to-morrow be at the height of heart-heaviness, by how much I shall think my brother happy in having what he wishes for.

ROSALIND.

Why, then, to-morrow I cannot serve your turn for Rosalind?

ORLANDO.

I can live no longer by thinking.

ROSALIND.

I will weary you, then, no longer with idle talking. Know of me, then—for now I speak to some purpose,—that I know you are a gentleman of good conceit: I speak not this, that you should bear a good opinion of my knowledge, insomuch I say I know you are; neither do I labour for a greater esteem than may in some little measure draw a belief from you, to do yourself good, and not to grace me. Believe, then, if you please, that I can do strange things: I have, since I was three year old, conversed with a magician, most profound in his art, and yet not damnable. If you do love Rosalind so near the heart as your gesture cries it out, when your brother marries Aliena, shall you marry her: I know into what straits of fortune she is driven; and it is not impossible to me, if it appear not inconvenient to you, to set her before your eyes to-morrow human as she is, and without any danger.

ORLANDO.

Speak'st thou in sober meanings?

ROSALIND.

By my life I do; which I tender dearly, though I say I am a magician. Therefore, put you in your best array, bid your friends; for if you will be married to-morrow,you shall; and to Rosalind, if you will.—Look, here comes a lover of mine, and a lover of hers.

Enter SILVIUS *and* PHEBE.

PHEBE.

Youth, you have done me much ungentleness,
To show the letter that I writ to you.

ROSALIND.

I care not, if I have: it is my study
To seem despiteful and ungentle to you:
You are there follow'd by a faithful shepherd;
Look upon him, love him; he worships you.

PHEBE.

Good shepherd, tell this youth what 'tis to love.

SILVIUS.

It is to be all made of sighs and tears;—
And so am I for Phebe.

PHEBE.

And I for Ganymede.

ORLANDO.

And I for Rosalind.

ROSALIND.

And I for no woman.

SILVIUS.

It is to be all made of faith and service;—
And so am I for Phebe.

PHEBE.

And I for Ganymede.

ORLANDO.

And I for Rosalind.

ROSALIND.

And I for no woman.

SILVIUS.

It is to be all made of fantasy,
All made of passion, and all made of wishes;
All adoration, duty, and observance,
All humbleness, all patience, and impatience,
All purity, all trial, all deservings;—
And so am I for Phebe.

PHEBE.

And so am I for Ganymede.

ORLANDO.

And so am I for Rosalind.

ROSALIND.

And so am I for no woman.

PHEBE [*to* ROSALIND].

If this be so, why blame you me to love you?

SILVIUS [*to* PHEBE].

If this be so, why blame you me to love you?

ORLANDO.

If this be so, why blame you me to love you?

ROSALIND.

Who do you speak to,—'Why blame you me to love you?'

ORLANDO.

To her that is not here, not doth not hear.

ROSALIND.

Pray you, no more of this; 'tis like the howling of Irish wolves against the moon.—I will help you [*to* SILVIUS], if I can:—I would love you [*to* PHEBE], if I could.—To-morrow meet me all together.—I will marry you [*to* PHEBE], if ever I marry woman, and I'll be married to-morrow;—I will satisfy you [*to* ORLANDO], if ever I satisfy man and you shall be married to-morrow:—I will content you [*to* SILVIUS], if what pleases you contents you, and you shall be married to-morrow.—As you [*to* ORLANDO] love Rosalind, meet:—as you [*to* SILVIUS] love Phebe, meet: and as I love no woman, I'll meet.—So, fare you well: I have left you commands.

SILVIUS.

I'll not fail, if I live.

PHEBE.

Nor I.

ORLANDO.

Nor I. [*Exeunt.*

SCENE III.

The forest.

Enter TOUCHSTONE *and* AUDREY.

TOUCHSTONE.

TO-MORROW is the joyful day, Audrey; to-morrow will we be married.

AUDREY.

I do desire it with all my heart; and I hope it is no dishonest desire, to desire to be a woman of the world. Here come two of the banisht duke's pages.

Enter two PAGES.

FIRST PAGE.

Well met, honest gentleman.

TOUCHSTONE.

By my troth, well met. Come, sit, sit, and a song.

SECOND PAGE.

We are for you: sit i'th'middle.

FIRST PAGE.

Shall we clap into't roundly, without hawking, or spitting, or saying we are hoarse, which are the only prologues to a bad voice?

SECOND PAGE.

I'faith, i'faith; and both in a tune, like two gipsies on a horse.

Song.

It was a lover and his lass,
With a hey, and a ho, and a hey nonino,
That o'er the green corn-field did pass
In spring-time, the only pretty ring-time,
When birds do sing, hey ding a ding, ding:
Sweet lovers love the spring.

Between the acres of the rye,
With a hey, and a ho, and a hey nonino,
These pretty country-folks would lie
In spring-time, &c.

This carol they began that hour,
With a hey, and a ho, and a hey nonino,
How that a life was but a flower
In spring-time, &c.

And therefore take the present time,
With a hey, and a ho, and a hey nonino;
For love is crowned with the prime
In spring-time, &c.

TOUCHSTONE.

Truly, young gentlemen, though there was no great matter in the ditty, yet the note was very untuneable.

FIRST PAGE.

You are deceived, sir: we kept time, we lost not our time.

TOUCHSTONE.

By my troth, yes; I count it but time lost to hear such a foolish song. God b'wi'you; and God mend your voices!—Come, Audrey. [*Exeunt.*

SCENE IV.

The forest.

Enter DUKE SENIOR, AMIENS, JAQUES, ORLANDO, OLIVER, *and* CELIA.

DUKE SENIOR.

DOST thou believe, Orlando, that the boy
Can do all this that he hath promised?

ORLANDO.

I sometimes do believe, and sometimes do not;
As those that fear,—they hope, and know they fear.

Enter ROSALIND, SILVIUS, *and* PHEBE.

ROSALIND.

Patience once more, whiles our compact is urged;—
You say, if I bring in your Rosalind, [*to the* DUKE.
You will bestow her on Orlando here?

DUKE SENIOR.

That would I, had I kingdoms to give with her.

ROSALIND [*to* ORLANDO].

And you say, you will have her, when I bring her?

ORLANDO.

That would I, were I of all kingdoms king.

ROSALIND [*to* PHEBE].

You say, you'll marry me, if I be willing?

PHEBE.

That will I, should I die the hour after.

ROSALIND.

But if you do refuse to marry me,
You'll give yourself to this most faithful shepherd?

PHEBE.

So is the bargain.

ROSALIND [*to* SILVIUS].

You say, that you'll have Phebe, if she will?

SILVIUS.

Though to have her and death were both one thing.

ROSALIND.

I have promised to make this matter even.
Keep you your word, O duke, to give your daughter;—
You yours, Orlando, to receive his daughter:—
Keep your word, Phebe, that you'll marry me,
Or else, refusing me, to wed this shepherd:—
Keep your word, Silvius, that you'll marry her,
If she refuse me:—and from hence I go,
To make these doubts all even.

[*Exeunt* ROSALIND *and* CELIA.

DUKE SENIOR.

I do remember in this shepherd boy
Some lively touches of my daughter's favour.

ORLANDO.

My lord, the first time that I ever saw him
Methought he was a brother to your daughter:
But, my good lord, this boy is forest-born,
And hath been tutor'd in the rudiments
Of many desperate studies by his uncle,
Whom he reports to be a great magician,
Obscured in the circle of this forest.

JAQUES.

There is, sure, another flood toward, and these couples are coming to the ark. Here comes a pair of very strange beasts, which in all tongues are call'd fools.

Enter TOUCHSTONE *and* AUDREY.

TOUCHSTONE.

Salutation and greeting to you all!

JAQUES.

Good my lord, bid him welcome: this is the motley-minded gentleman that I have so often met in the forest: he hath been a courtier, he swears.

TOUCHSTONE.

If any man doubt that, let him put me to my purgation. I have trod a measure; I have flatter'd a lady; I have been politic with my friend, smooth with mine enemy; I have undone three tailors; I have had four quarrels, and like to have fought one.

JAQUES.

And how was that ta'en up?

TOUCHSTONE.

Faith, we met, and found the quarrel was upon the seventh cause.

JAQUES.

How seventh cause?—Good my lord, like this fellow.

DUKE SENIOR.

I like him very well.

TOUCHSTONE.

God ild you, sir; I desire you of the like. I press in here, sir, amongst the rest of the country copulatives, to swear and to forswear; according as marriage binds and blood breaks:—a poor virgin, sir, an ill-favour'd thing, sir, but mine own; a poor humour of mine, sir, to take that that no man else will: rich honesty dwells like a miser, sir, in a poor house; as your pearl in your foul oyster.

DUKE SENIOR.

By my faith, he is very swift and sententious.

TOUCHSTONE.

According to the fool's bolt, sir, and such dulcet diseases.

JAQUES.

But, for the seventh cause; how did you find the quarrel on the seventh cause?

TOUCHSTONE.

Upon a lie seven times removed:—bear your body more seeming, Audrey:—as thus, sir. I did dislike the cut of a certain courtier's beard: he sent me word, if I said his beard was not cut well, he was in the mind it was: this is call'd the Retort Courteous. If I sent him word again it was not well cut, he would send me word he cut it to please himself: this is call'd the Quip Modest. If again it was not well cut, he disabled my judgement: this is call'd the Reply Churlish. If again it was not well cut, he would answer I spake not true: this is call'd the Reproof Valiant. If again it was not well cut, he would say I lie: this is call'd the Countercheck Quarrelsome: and so to the Lie Circumstantial and the Lie Direct.

JAQUES.

And how oft did you say his beard was not well cut?

TOUCHSTONE.

I durst go no further than the Lie Circumstantial, nor he durst not give me the Lie Direct; and so we measured swords, and parted.

JAQUES.

Can you nominate in order now the degrees of the lie?

TOUCHSTONE.

O sir, we quarrel in print, by the book; as you have books for good manners: I will name you the degrees. The first, the Retort Courteous; the second, the Quip Modest; the third, the Reply Churlish; the fourth, the Reproof Valiant; the fifth, the Countercheck Quarrelsome; the sixth, the Lie with Circumstance; the seventh, the Lie Direct. All these you may avoid, but the Lie Direct; and you may avoid that too with an 'if.' I knew when seven justices could not take up a quarrel; but when the parties were met themselves, one of them thought but of an 'if,' as, 'If you said so, then I said so;' and they shook hands, and swore brothers. Your 'if' is the only peacemaker; much virtue in 'if.'

JAQUES.

Is not this a rare fellow, my lord? he's as good at any thing, and yet a fool.

DUKE SENIOR.

He uses his folly like a stalking-horse, and under the presentation of that he shoots his wit.

Enter HYMEN *leading* ROSALIND *in woman's clothes, and* CELIA.
Still music.

HYMEN.

Then is there mirth in heaven,
When earthly things made even
Atone together.
Good duke, receive thy daughter:
Hymen from heaven brought her,
Yea, brought her hither,
That thou mightst join her hand with his
Whose heart within her bosom is.

ROSALIND [*to* DUKE SENIOR].

To you I give myself, for I am yours.—
[*to* ORLANDO]. To you I give myself, for I am yours.

DUKE SENIOR.

If there be truth in sight, you are my daughter.

ORLANDO.

If there be truth in sight, you are my Rosalind.

PHEBE.

If sight and shape be true,
Why, then,—my love adieu!

ROSALIND [*to* DUKE SENIOR].

I'll have no father, if you be not he:—
[*to* ORLANDO]. I'll have no husband, if you be not he:—
[*to* PHEBE]. Nor ne'er wed woman, if you be not she.

HYMEN.

Peace, ho! I bar confusion:
'Tis I must make conclusion
Of these most strange events:
Here's eight that must take hands
To join in Hymen's bands,
If truth holds true contents.
You and you no cross shall part:—
[*to* ORLANDO *and* ROSALIND.
You and you are heart in heart:—
[*to* OLIVER *and* CELIA.
You to his love must accord, [*to* PHEBE.
Or have a woman to your lord:—
You and you are sure together,
[*to* TOUCHSTONE *and* AUDREY.
As the winter to foul weather.
Whiles a wedlock-hymn we sing,
Feed yourselves with questioning;
That reason wonder may diminish,
How thus we met, and these things finish.

Song.

Wedding is great Juno's crown:
O blessed bond of board and bed!
'Tis Hymen peoples every town;
High wedlock, then, be honoured:
Honour, high honour, and renown,
To Hymen, god of every town!

DUKE SENIOR.

O my dear niece, welcome thou art to me,
Even daughter-welcome, in no less degree!

PHEBE [*to* SILVIUS].

I will not eat my word, now thou art mine;
Thy faith my fancy to thee doth combine.

Enter JAQUES DE BOYS.

JAQUES DE BOYS.

Let me have audience for a word or two:
I am the second son of old Sir Rowland,
That bring these tidings to this fair assembly.—
Duke Frederick, hearing how that every day
Men of great worth resorted to this forest,
Addrest a mighty power; which were on foot,
In his own conduct, purposely to take
His brother here, and put him to the sword:
And to the skirts of this wild wood he came;
Where meeting with an old religious man,
After some question with him, was converted
Both from his enterprise and from the world;
His crown bequeathing to his banisht brother,
And all their lands restored to them again
That were with him exiled. This to be true,
I do engage my life.

DUKE SENIOR.

Welcome, young man;
Thou offer'st fairly to thy brothers' wedding:
To one, his lands withheld; and to the other,
A land itself at large, a potent dukedom.
First, in this forest, let us do those ends
That here were well begun and well begot:
And after, every of this happy number,
That have endured shrewd days and nights with us,

Shall share the good of our returned fortune,
According to the measure of their states.
Meantime forget this new-fall'n dignity,
And fall into our rustic revelry.—
Play, music!—and you, brides and bridegrooms all,
With measure heap'd in joy, to th'measures fall.

JAQUES.

Sir, by your patience.—If I heard you rightly,
The duke hath put on a religious life,
And thrown into neglect the pompous court?

JAQUES DE BOYS.

He hath.

JAQUES.

To him will I: out of these convertites
There is much matter to be heard and learn'd.—
You [*to* DUKE SENIOR] to your former honour I bequeath;
Your patience and your virtue well deserve it:—
You [*to* ORLANDO] to a love that your true faith doth merit:—
You [*to* OLIVER] to your land, and love, and great allies:—
You [*to* SILVIUS] to a long and well-deserved bed:—
And you [*to* TOUCHSTONE] to wrangling; for thy loving voyage
Is but for two months victuall'd.—So, to your pleasures:
I am for other than for dancing measures.

DUKE SENIOR.

Stay, Jaques, stay.

JAQUES.

To see no pastime I:—what you would have
I'll stay to know at your abandon'd cave. [*Exit.*

DUKE SENIOR.

Proceed, proceed: we will begin these rites,
As we do trust they'll end, in true delights.
[*A dance.*

EPILOGUE.

ROSALIND.

IT is not the fashion to see the lady the epilogue; but it is no more unhandsome than to see the lord the prologue. If it be true that good wine needs no bush, 'tis true that a good play needs no epilogue: yet to good wine they do use good bushes; and good plays prove the better by the help of good epilogues. What a case am I in, then, that am neither a good epilogue, nor cannot insinuate with you in the behalf of a good play! I am not furnisht like a beggar, therefore to beg will not become me: my way is, to conjure you; and I'll begin with the women. I charge you, O women, for the love you bear to men, to like as much of this play as please you: and I charge you, O men, for the love you bear to women (as I perceive by your simpering, none of you hates them), that between you and the women the play may please. If I were a woman, I would kiss as many of you as had beards that pleased me, complexions that liked me, and breaths that I defied not: and, I am sure, as many as have good beards, or good faces, or sweet breaths, will, for my kind offer, when I make curtsy, bid me farewell. [*Exeunt.*

TWELFTH NIGHT; OR, WHAT YOU WILL

DRAMATIS PERSONAE

ORSINO, *Duke of Illyria.*
SEBASTIAN, *a young gentleman.*
ANTONIO, *a sea captain, friend to Sebastian.*
A SEA CAPTAIN, *friend to Viola.*
VALENTINE, } *gentlemen attending on the Duke.*
CURIO, }
SIR TOBY BELCH, *uncle to Olivia.*
SIR ANDREW AGUECHEEK.
MALVOLIO, *steward to Olivia.*
FABIAN, } *servants to Olivia.*
CLOWN, }
OLIVIA.
VIOLA, *sister to Sebastian.*
MARIA, *Olivia's woman.*

LORDS, *a* PRIEST, SAILORS, OFFICERS, MUSICIANS, *and* ATTENDANTS.

SCENE—*A city in Illyria, and the sea-coast near it.*

ACT I. SCENE I.

The DUKE'S *palace.*

Enter DUKE, LORDS, *and* CURIO; MUSICIANS *attending.*

DUKE OF ILLYRIA.

If music be the food of love, play on;
Give me excess of it, that, surfeiting,
The appetite may sicken, and so die.—
That strain again!—it had a dying fall:
O, it came o'er my ear like the sweet sound,
That breathes upon a bank of violets,
Stealing and giving odour!—Enough; no more;
'Tis not so sweet now as it was before.
O spirit of love, how quick and fresh art thou!
That, notwithstanding thy capacity
Receiveth as the sea, naught enters there,
Of what validity and pitch soe'er,
But falls into abatement and low price,
Even in a minute! so full of shapes is fancy,
That it alone is high-fantastical.

CURIO.

Will you go hunt, my lord?

DUKE OF ILLYRIA.

What, Curio?

CURIO.

The hart.

DUKE OF ILLYRIA.

Why, so I do, the noblest that I have:
O, when mine eyes did see Olivia first,
Methought she purged the air of pestilence!
That instant was I turn'd into a hart;
And my desires, like fell and cruel hounds,
E'er since pursue me.

Enter VALENTINE.

How now! what news from her?

VALENTINE.

So please my lord, I might not be admitted;
But from her handmaid do return this answer:
The element itself, till seven years hence,
Shall not behold her face at ample view;
But, like a cloistress, she will veiled walk,
And water once a day her chamber round
With eye-offending brine: all this to season
A brother's dead love, which she would keep fresh
And lasting in her sad remembrance.

DUKE OF ILLYRIA.

O, she that hath a heart of that fine frame
To pay this debt of love but to a brother,
How will she love, when the rich golden shaft
Hath kill'd the flock of all affections else
That live in her; when liver, brain, and heart,
These sovereign thrones, are all supplied, and fill'd
Her sweet perfections with one self king!—
Away before me to sweet beds of flowers:
Love-thoughts lie rich when canopied with bowers. [*Exeunt.*

SCENE II.

The sea-coast.

Enter VIOLA, CAPTAIN, *and* SAILORS.

VIOLA.

What country, friends, is this?

CAPTAIN.

This is Illyria, lady.

VIOLA.

And what should I do in Illyria?
My brother he is in Elysium.
Perchance he is not drown'd:—what think you, sailors?

CAPTAIN.

It is perchance that you yourself were saved.

VIOLA.

O my poor brother! and so perchance may he be.

CAPTAIN.

True, madam; and, to comfort you with chance,
Assure yourself, after our ship did split,
When you, and those poor number saved with you,
Hung on our driving boat, I saw your brother,
Most provident in peril, bind himself—
Courage and hope both teaching him the practice—
To a strong mast that lived upon the sea;
Where, like Arion on the dolphin's back,
I saw him hold acquaintance with the waves
So long as I could see.

VIOLA.

For saying so, there's gold:
Mine own escape unfoldeth to my hope,
Whereto thy speech serves for authority,
The like of him. Know'st thou this country?

CAPTAIN.

Ay, madam, well; for I was bred and born
Not three hours' travel from this very place.

VIOLA.

Who governs here?

CAPTAIN.

A noble duke, in nature as in name.

VIOLA.

What is his name?

CAPTAIN.

Orsino.

VIOLA.

Orsino! I have heard my father name him:
He was a bachelor then.

CAPTAIN.

And so is now, or was so very late;
For but a month ago I went from hence,
And then 'twas fresh in murmur,—as, you know,
What great ones do, the less will prattle of,—
That he did seek the love of fair Olivia.

VIOLA.

What's she?

CAPTAIN.

A virtuous maid, the daughter of a count
That died some twelvemonth since; then leaving her
In the protection of his son, her brother,
Who shortly also died: for whose dear loss,
They say, she hath abjured the company
And sight of men.

VIOLA.

O, that I served that lady,
And might not be deliver'd to the world,
Till I had made mine own occasion mellow,
What my estate is!

CAPTAIN.

That were hard to compass;
Because she will admit no kind of suit,
No, not the duke's.

VIOLA.

There is a fair behaviour in thee, captain;
And though that nature with a beauteous wall
Doth oft close in pollution, yet of thee
I will believe thou hast a mind that suits
With this thy fair and outward character.
I prithee,—and I'll pay thee bounteously,—
Conceal me what I am; and be my aid
For such disguise as haply shall become
The form of my intent. I'll serve this duke:
Thou shalt present me as an eunuch to him:
It may be worth thy pains; for I can sing,
And speak to him in many sorts of music,
That will allow me very worth his service.
What else may hap, to time I will commit;
Only shape thou thy silence to my wit.

CAPTAIN.

Be you his eunuch, and your mute I'll be:
When my tongue blabs, then let mine eyes not see.

VIOLA.

I thank thee: lead me on. [*Exeunt.*

SCENE III.

Olivia's house.

Enter SIR TOBY BELCH *and* MARIA.

SIR TOBY BELCH.

WHAT a plague means my niece, to take the death of her brother thus? I am sure care's an enemy to life.

MARIA.

By my troth, Sir Toby, you must come in earlier o'nights: your cousin, my lady, takes great exceptions to your ill hours.

SIR TOBY BELCH.

Why, let her except before excepted.

MARIA.

Ay, but you must confine yourself within the modest limits of order.

SIR TOBY BELCH.

Confine! I'll confine myself no finer than I am: these clothes are good enough to drink in; and so be these boots too,—an they be not, let them hang themselves in their own straps.

MARIA.

That quaffing and drinking will undo you: I heard my lady talk of it yesterday; and of a foolish knight that you brought in one night here to be her wooer.

SIR TOBY BELCH.

Who, Sir Andrew Aguecheek?

MARIA.

Ay, he.

SIR TOBY BELCH.

He's as tall a man as any's in Illyria.

MARIA.

What's that to th'purpose?

SIR TOBY BELCH.

Why, he has three thousand ducats a year.

MARIA.

Ay, but he'll have but a year in all these ducats: he's a very fool and a prodigal.

SIR TOBY BELCH.

Fie, that you'll say so! he plays o'th'viol-de-gamboys, and speaks three or four languages word for word without book, and hath all the good gifts of nature.

MARIA.

He hath, indeed, almost natural: for, besides that he's a fool, he's a great quarreller; and, but that he hath the gift of a coward to allay the gust he hath in quarrelling, 'tis thought among the prudent he would quickly have the gift of a grave.

SIR TOBY BELCH.

By this hand, they are scoundrels and substractors that say so of him. Who are they?

MARIA.

They that add, moreover, he's drunk nightly in your company.

SIR TOBY BELCH.

With drinking healths to my niece: I'll drink to her as long as there is a passage in my throat and drink in Illyria: he's a coward and a coistrel that will not drink to my niece till his brains turn o'th'toe like a parish-top. What, wench! *Castiliano volto;* for here comes Sir Andrew Agueface.

Enter SIR ANDREW AGUECHEEK.

SIR ANDREW AGUECHEEK.

Sir Toby Belch,—how now, Sir Toby Belch!

SIR TOBY BELCH.

Sweet Sir Andrew!

SIR ANDREW AGUECHEEK.

Bless you, fair shrew.

MARIA.

And you too, sir.

SIR TOBY BELCH.

Accost, Sir Andrew, accost.

SIR ANDREW AGUECHEEK.

What's that?

SIR TOBY BELCH.

My niece's chambermaid.

SIR ANDREW AGUECHEEK.

Good Mistress Accost, I desire better acquaintance.

MARIA.

My name is Mary, sir.

SIR ANDREW AGUECHEEK.

Good Mistress Mary Accost,—

SIR TOBY BELCH.

You mistake, knight: 'accost' is front her, board her, woo her, assail her.

SIR ANDREW AGUECHEEK.

By my troth, I would not undertake her in this company. Is that the meaning of 'accost'?

MARIA.

Fare you well, gentlemen.

SIR TOBY BELCH.

An thou let part so, Sir Andrew, would thou mightst never draw sword again.

SIR ANDREW AGUECHEEK.

An you part so, mistress, I would I might never draw sword again. Fair lady, do you think you have fools in hand?

MARIA.

Sir, I have not you by th'hand.

SIR ANDREW AGUECHEEK.

Marry, but you shall have; and here's my hand.

MARIA.

Now, sir, thought is free: I pray you, bring your hand to th'buttery-bar, and let it drink.

SIR ANDREW AGUECHEEK.

Wherefore, sweet-heart? what's your metaphor?

MARIA.

It's dry, sir.

SIR ANDREW AGUECHEEK.

Why, I think so: I am not such an ass but I can keep my hand dry. But what's your jest?

MARIA.

A dry jest, sir.

SIR ANDREW AGUECHEEK.

Are you full of them?

MARIA.

Ay, sir, I have them at my fingers' ends: marry, now I let go your hand, I am barren. [*Exit.*

SIR TOBY BELCH.

O knight, thou lack'st a cup of canary: when did I see thee so put down?

SIR ANDREW AGUECHEEK.

Never in your life, I think; unless you see canary put me down. Methinks sometimes I have no more wit than a Christian or an ordinary man has: but I am a great eater of beef, and I believe that does harm to my wit.

SIR TOBY BELCH.

No question.

SIR ANDREW AGUECHEEK.

An I thought that, I'ld forswear it. I'll ride home to-morrow, Sir Toby.

SIR TOBY BELCH.

Pourquoi, my dear knight?

SIR ANDREW AGUECHEEK.

What is *pourquoi?* do or not do? I would I had bestow'd that time in the tongues that I have in fencing, dancing, and bear-baiting: O, had I but follow'd the arts!

SIR TOBY BELCH.

Then hadst thou had an excellent head of hair.

SIR ANDREW AGUECHEEK.

Why, would that have mended my hair?

SIR TOBY BELCH.

Past question; for thou seest it will not curl by nature.

SIR ANDREW AGUECHEEK.

But it becomes me well enough, does't not?

SIR TOBY BELCH.

Excellent; it hangs like flax on a distaff; and I hope to see a housewife take thee between her legs and spin it off.

SIR ANDREW AGUECHEEK.

Faith, I'll home to-morrow, Sir Toby: your niece will not be seen; or if she be, it's four to one she'll none of me: the count himself here hard by woos her.

SIR TOBY BELCH.

She'll none o'th'count: she'll not match above her degree, neither in estate, years, nor wit; I have heard her swear't. Tut, there's life in't, man.

SIR ANDREW AGUECHEEK.

I'll stay a month longer. I am a fellow o'th' strangest mind i'th'world; I delight in masks and revels sometimes altogether.

SIR TOBY BELCH.

Art thou good at these kickshawses, knight?

SIR ANDREW AGUECHEEK.

As any man in Illyria, whatsoever he be, under the degree of my betters; and yet I will not compare with a nobleman.

SIR TOBY BELCH.

What is thy excellence in a galliard, knight?

SIR ANDREW AGUECHEEK.

Faith, I can cut a caper.

SIR TOBY BELCH.

And I can cut the mutton to't.

SIR ANDREW AGUECHEEK.

And I think I have the back-trick simply as strong as any man in Illyria.

SIR TOBY BELCH.

Wherefore are these things hid? wherefore have these gifts a curtain before 'em? are they like to take dust, like Mistress Mall's picture? why dost thou not go to church in a galliard, and come home in a coranto? My very walk should be a jig; I would not so much as make water but in a sink-a-pace. What dost thou mean? is it a world to hide virtues in? I did think, by the excellent constitution of thy leg, it was form'd under the star of a galliard.

SIR ANDREW AGUECHEEK.
Ay, 'tis strong, and it does indifferent well in a flame-colour'd stock. Shall we set about some revels?

SIR TOBY BELCH.
What shall we do else? were we not born under Taurus?

SIR ANDREW AGUECHEEK.
Taurus! that's sides and heart.

SIR TOBY BELCH.
No, sir; it is legs and thighs. Let me see thee caper [SIR ANDREW *dances*]: ha! higher: ha, ha! excellent! [*Exeunt.*

SCENE IV.

The Duke's palace.

Enter VALENTINE, *and* VIOLA *in man's attire.*

VALENTINE.
If the duke continue these favours towards you, Cesario, you are like to be much advanced: he hath known you but three days, and already you are no stranger.

VIOLA.
You either fear his humour or my negligence, that you call in question the continuance of his love: is he inconstant, sir, in his favours?

VALENTINE.
No, believe me.

VIOLA.
I thank you. Here comes the count.

Enter DUKE, CURIO, *and* ATTENDANTS.

DUKE OF ILLYRIA.
Who saw Cesario, ho?

VIOLA.
On your attendance, my lord; here.

DUKE OF ILLYRIA.
Stand you awhile aloof.—Cesario,
Thou know'st no less but all; I have unclaspt
To thee the book even of my secret soul:
Therefore, good youth, address thy gait unto her,
Be not denied access, stand at her doors,
And tell them, there thy fixed foot shall grow
Till thou have audience.

VIOLA.
Sure, my noble lord,
If she be so abandon'd to her sorrow
As it is spoke, she never will admit me.

DUKE OF ILLYRIA.
Be clamorous, and leap all civil bounds,
Rather than make unprofited return.

VIOLA.
Say I do speak with her, my lord, what then?

DUKE OF ILLYRIA.
O, then unfold the passion of my love,
Surprise her with discourse of my dear faith!
It shall become thee well to act my woes;
She will attend it better in thy youth
Than in a nuncio of more grave aspect.

VIOLA.
I think not so, my lord.

DUKE OF ILLYRIA.
Dear lad, believe it;
For they shall yet belie thy happy years,
That say thou art a man: Diana's lip
Is not more smooth and rubious; thy small pipe
Is as the maiden's organ, shrill and sound;
And all is semblative a woman's part.
I know thy constellation is right apt
For this affair:—some four or five attend him;
All, if you will; for I myself am best
When least in company:—prosper well in this,
And thou shalt live as freely as thy lord,
To call his fortunes thine.

VIOLA.
I'll do my best
To woo your lady:—[*aside*] yet, a barful strife!
Whoe'er I woo, myself would be his wife.
[*Exeunt.*

SCENE V.

OLIVIA'S *house.*

Enter MARIA *and* CLOWN.

MARIA.
Nay, either tell me where thou hast been, or I will not open my lips so wide as a bristle may enter in way of thy excuse: my lady will hang thee for thy absence.

CLOWN.
Let her hang me: he that is well hang'd in this world need to fear no colours.

MARIA.
Make that good.

CLOWN.
He shall see none to fear.

MARIA.
A good lenten answer: I can tell thee where that saying was born, of,—I fear no colours.

CLOWN.
Where, good Mistress Mary?

MARIA.
In the wars; and that may you be bold to say in your foolery.

CLOWN.
Well, God give them wisdom that have it; and those that are fools, let them use their talents.

MARIA.
Yet you will be hang'd for being so long absent; or, to be turn'd away,—is not that as good as a hanging to you?

CLOWN.
Many a good hanging prevents a bad marriage; and, for turning away, let summer bear it out.

MARIA.
You are resolute, then?

CLOWN.
Not so, neither; but I am resolved on two points.

MARIA.
That if one break, the other will hold; or, if both break, your gaskins fall.

CLOWN.
Apt, in good faith; very apt. Well, go thy way; if Sir Toby would leave drinking, thou wert as witty a piece of Eve's flesh as any in Illyria.

MARIA.
Peace, you rogue, no more o'that. Here comes my lady: make your excuse wisely, you were best.
[*Exit.*

CLOWN.
Wit, an't be thy will, put me into good fooling! Those wits, that think they have thee, do very oft

prove fools; and I, that am sure I lack thee, may pass for a wise man: for what says Quinapalus? 'Better a witty fool than a foolish wit.'

Enter LADY OLIVIA *with* MALVOLIO.

God bless thee, lady!

OLIVIA.

Take the fool away.

CLOWN.

Do you not hear, fellows? Take away the lady.

OLIVIA.

Go to, y'are a dry fool: I'll no more of you: besides, you grow dishonest.

CLOWN.

Two faults, madonna, that drink and good counsel will amend: for give the dry fool drink, then is the fool not dry: bid the dishonest man mend himself; if he mend, he is no longer dishonest: if he cannot, let the botcher mend him: any thing that's mended is but patcht: virtue that transgresses is but patcht with sin; and sin that amends is but patcht with virtue: if that this simple syllogism will serve, so; if it will not, what remedy? As there is no true cuckold but calamity, so beauty's a flower.—The lady bade take away the fool; therefore, I say again, take her away.

OLIVIA.

Sir, I bade them take away you.

CLOWN.

Misprision in the highest degree!—Lady, *cucullus non facit monachum;* that's as much to say as, I wear not motley in my brain. Good madonna, give me leave to prove you a fool.

OLIVIA.

Can you do it?

CLOWN.

Dexteriously, good madonna.

OLIVIA.

Make your proof.

CLOWN.

I must catechize you for it, madonna: good my mouse of virtue, answer me.

OLIVIA.

Well, sir, for want of other idleness, I'll bide your proof.

CLOWN.

Good madonna, why mourn'st thou?

OLIVIA.

Good fool, for my brother's death.

CLOWN.

I think his soul is in hell, madonna.

OLIVIA.

I know his soul is in heaven, fool.

CLOWN.

The more fool, madonna, to mourn for your brother's soul being in heaven.—Take away the fool, gentlemen.

OLIVIA.

What think you of this fool, Malvolio? doth he not mend?

MALVOLIO.

Yes, and shall do till the pangs of death shake him: infirmity, that decays the wise, doth ever make the better fool.

CLOWN.

God send you, sir, a speedy infirmity, for the better increasing your folly! Sir Toby will be sworn that I am no fox; but he will not pass his word for twopence that you are no fool.

OLIVIA.

How say you to that, Malvolio?

MALVOLIO.

I marvel your ladyship takes delight in such a barren rascal: I saw him put down the other day with an ordinary fool, that has no more brain than a stone. Look you now, he's out of his guard already; unless you laugh and minister occasion to him, he is gagg'd. I protest, I take these wise men, that crow so at these set kind of fools, no better than the fools' zanies.

OLIVIA.

O, you are sick of self-love, Malvolio, and taste with a distemper'd appetite. To be generous, guiltless, and of free disposition, is to take those things for bird-bolts that you deem cannon-bullets: there is no slander in an allow'd fool, though he do nothing but rail; nor no railing in a known discreet man, though he do nothing but reprove.

CLOWN.

Now Mercury endue thee with leasing, for thou speak'st well of fools!

Enter MARIA.

MARIA.

Madam, there is at the gate a young gentleman much desires to speak with you.

OLIVIA.

From the Count Orsino, is it?

MARIA.

I know not, madam: 'tis a fair young man, and well attended.

OLIVIA.

Who of my people hold him in delay?

MARIA.

Sir Toby, madam, your kinsman.

OLIVIA.

Fetch him off, I pray you; he speaks nothing but madman: fie on him! [*Exit* MARIA.] Go you, Malvolio: if it be a suit from the count, I am sick, or not at home; what you will, to dismiss it. [*Exit* MALVOLIO.] Now you see, sir, how your fooling grows old, and people dislike it.

CLOWN.

Thou hast spoke for us, madonna, as if thy eldest son should be a fool; whose skull Jove cram with brains! for—here he comes—one of thy kin has a most weak *pia mater*.

Enter SIR TOBY.

OLIVIA.

By mine honour, half drunk.—What is he at the gate, cousin?

SIR TOBY BELCH.

A gentleman.

OLIVIA.

A gentleman! what gentleman?

SIR TOBY BELCH.

'Tis a gentleman here—a plague o'these pickle-herring!—How now, sot!

CLOWN.

Good Sir Toby!—

OLIVIA.

Cousin, cousin, how have you come so early by this lethargy?

SIR TOBY BELCH.

Lechery! I defy lechery. There's one at the gate.

OLIVIA.

Ay, marry, what is he?

SIR TOBY BELCH.

Let him be the devil, an he will, I care not: give me faith, say I. Well, it's all one. [*Exit.*

OLIVIA.

What's a drunken man like, fool?

CLOWN.

Like a drown'd man, a fool, and a madman: one draught above heat makes him a fool; the second mads him; and a third drowns him.

OLIVIA.

Go thou and seek the crowner, and let him sit o' my coz; for he's in the third degree of drink,—he's drown'd: go, look after him.

CLOWN.

He is but mad yet, madonna; and the fool shall look to the madman. [*Exit.*

Enter MALVOLIO.

MALVOLIO.

Madam, yond young fellow swears he will speak with you. I told him you were sick; he takes on him to understand so much, and therefore comes to speak with you: I told him you were asleep; he seems to have a foreknowledge of that too, and therefore comes to speak with you. What is to be said to him, lady? he's fortified against any denial.

OLIVIA.

Tell him he shall not speak with me.

MALVOLIO.

Has been told so; and he says, he'll stand at your door like a sheriff's post, and be the supporter to a bench, but he'll speak with you.

OLIVIA.

What kind o'man is he?

MALVOLIO.

Why, of mankind.

OLIVIA.

What manner of man?

MALVOLIO.

Of very ill manner; he'll speak with you, will you or no.

OLIVIA.

Of what personage and years is he?

MALVOLIO.

Not yet old enough for a man, nor young enough for a boy; as a squash is before 'tis a peascod, or a codling when 'tis almost an apple: 'tis with him e'en standing water, between boy and man. He is very well-favour'd, and he speaks very shrewishly; one would think his mother's milk were scarce out of him.

OLIVIA.

Let him approach: call in my gentlewoman.

MALVOLIO.

Gentlewoman, my lady calls. [*Exit.*

Enter MARIA.

OLIVIA.

Give me my veil: come, throw it o'er my face. We'll once more hear Orsino's embassy.

Enter VIOLA.

VIOLA.

The honourable lady of the house, which is she?

OLIVIA.

Speak to me; I shall answer for her. Your will?

VIOLA.

Most radiant, exquisite, and unmatchable beauty, —I pray you, tell me if this be the lady of the house, for I never saw her: I would be loth to cast away my speech; for, besides that it is excellently well penn'd, I have taken great pains to con it. Good beauties, let me sustain no scorn; I am very comptible, even to the least sinister usage.

OLIVIA.

Whence came you, sir?

VIOLA.

I can say little more than I have studied, and that question's out of my part. Good gentle one, give me modest assurance if you be the lady of the house, that I may proceed in my speech.

OLIVIA.

Are you a comedian?

VIOLA.

No, my profound heart: and yet, by the very fangs of malice I swear I am not that I play. Are you the lady of the house?

OLIVIA.

If I do not usurp myself, I am.

VIOLA.

Most certain, if you are she, you do usurp yourself; for, what is yours to bestow is not yours to reserve. But this is from my commission: I will on with my speech in your praise, and then show you the heart of my message.

OLIVIA.

Come to what is important in't: I forgive you the praise.

VIOLA.

Alas, I took great pains to study it, and 'tis poetical.

OLIVIA.

It is the more like to be feign'd: I pray you, keep it in. I heard you were saucy at my gates; and allow'd your approach rather to wonder at you than to hear you. If you be mad, be gone; if you have reason, be brief: 'tis not that time of moon with me to make one in so skipping a dialogue.

MALVOLIO.

Will you hoist sail, sir? here lies your way.

VIOLA.

No, good swabber; I am to hull here a little longer. Some mollification for your giant, sweet lady. Tell me your mind: I am a messenger.

OLIVIA.

Sure, you have some hideous matter to deliver, when the courtesy of it is so fearful. Speak your office.

VIOLA.

It alone concerns your ear. I bring no overture of war, no taxation of homage: I hold the olive in my hand; my words are as full of peace as matter.

OLIVIA.

Yet you began rudely. What are you? what would you?

VIOLA.

The rudeness that hath appear'd in me have I learn'd from my entertainment. What I am, and what I would, are as secret as maidenhead: to your ears, divinity; to any other's, profanation.

OLIVIA.

Give us the place alone: we will hear this divinity. [*Exit* MARIA.] Now, sir, what is your text?

VIOLA.

Most sweet lady,—

OLIVIA.

A comfortable doctrine, and much may be said of it. Where lies your text?

VIOLA.

In Orsino's bosom.

OLIVIA.

In his bosom! In what chapter of his bosom?

VIOLA.

To answer by the method, in the first of his heart.

OLIVIA.

O, I have read it: it is heresy. Have you no more to say?

VIOLA.

Good madam, let me see your face.

OLIVIA.

Have you any commission from your lord to negotiate with my face? You are now out of your text: but we will draw the curtain, and show you the picture. Look you, sir, such a one I was, this presents: is't not well done? [*Unveiling.*

VIOLA.

Excellently done, if God did all.

OLIVIA.

'Tis in grain, sir; 'twill endure wind and weather.

VIOLA.

'Tis beauty truly blent, whose red and white
Nature's own sweet and cunning hand laid on:
Lady, you are the cruell'st she alive,
If you will lead these graces to the grave,
And leave the world no copy.

OLIVIA.

O, sir, I will not be so hard-hearted; I will give out divers schedules of my beauty: it shall be inventoried, and every particle and utensil labell'd to my will:—as, item, two lips, indifferent red; item, two gray eyes, with lids to them; item, one neck, one chin, and so forth. Were you sent hither to 'praise me?

VIOLA.

I see you what you are,—you are too proud;
But, if you were the devil, you are fair.
My lord and master loves you: O, such love
Could be but recompensed, though you were crown'd
The nonpareil of beauty!

OLIVIA.

How does he love me?

VIOLA.

With adorations, with fertile tears,
With groans that thunder love, with sighs of fire.

OLIVIA.

Your lord does know my mind; I cannot love him:
Yet I suppose him virtuous, know him noble,
Of great estate, of fresh and stainless youth;
In voices well divulged, free, learn'd, and valiant;
And, in dimension and the shape of nature,
A gracious person: but yet I cannot love him;
He might have took his answer long ago.

VIOLA.

If I did love you in my master's flame,
With such a suffering, such a deadly life,
In your denial I would find no sense;
I would not understand it.

OLIVIA.

Why, what would you?

VIOLA.

Make me a willow cabin at your gate,
And call upon my soul within the house;
Write loyal cantons of contemned love,
And sing them loud even in the dead of night;
Holla your name to the reverberate hills,
And make the babbling gossip of the air
Cry out, 'Olivia!' O, you should not rest
Between the elements of air and earth,
But you should pity me!

OLIVIA.

You might do much. What is your parentage?

VIOLA.

Above my fortunes, yet my state is well:
I am a gentleman.

OLIVIA.

Get you to your lord;
I cannot love him: let him send no more;
Unless, perchance, you come to me again,
To tell me how he takes it. Fare you well:
I thank you for your pains: spend this for me.

VIOLA.

I am no fee'd post, lady; keep your purse:
My master, not myself, lacks recompense.
Love make his heart of flint, that you shall love;
And let your fervour, like my master's, be
Placed in contempt! Farewell, fair cruelty. [*Exit.*

OLIVIA.

'What is your parentage?'
'Above my fortunes, yet my state is well:
I am a gentleman.' I'll be sworn thou art;
Thy tongue, thy face, thy limbs, actions, and spirit,
Do give thee fivefold blazon:—not too fast;—
Soft, soft!—
Unless the master were the man.—How now!
Even so quickly may one catch the plague?
Methinks I feel this youth's perfections
With an invisible and subtle stealth
To creep in at mine eyes. Well, let it be.—
What, ho, Malvolio!

Enter MALVOLIO.

MALVOLIO.

Here, madam, at your service.

OLIVIA.

Run after that same peevish messenger,
The county's man: he left this ring behind him,
Would I or not: tell him I'll none of it.
Desire him not to flatter with his lord,
Nor hold him up with hopes; I am not for him:
If that the youth will come this way to-morrow,
I'll give him reasons for't. Hie thee, Malvolio.

MALVOLIO.

Madam, I will. [*Exit.*

OLIVIA.

I do I know not what; and fear to find
Mine eye too great a flatterer for my mind.
Fate, show thy force: ourselves we do not owe;
What is decreed must be,—and be this so! [*Exit.*

ACT II. SCENE I.

The sea-coast.

Enter ANTONIO *and* SEBASTIAN.

ANTONIO.

WILL you stay no longer? nor will you not that I go with you?

SEBASTIAN.

By your patience, no. My stars shine darkly over me: the malignancy of my fate might perhaps distemper yours; therefore I shall crave of you your leave that I may bear my evils alone: it were a bad recompense for your love, to lay any of them on you.

ANTONIO.

Let me yet know of you whither you are bound.

SEBASTIAN.

No, sooth, sir: my determinate voyage is mere extravagancy. But I perceive in you so excellent a touch of modesty, that you will not extort from me what I am willing to keep in; therefore it charges me in manners the rather to express myself. You must know of me, then, Antonio, my name is Sebastian, which I call'd Roderigo. My father was that Sebastian of Messaline, whom I know you have heard of. He left behind him myself and a sister, both born in an hour: if the heavens had been pleased, would we had so ended! but you, sir, alter'd that; for some hour before you took me from the breach of the sea was my sister drown'd.

ANTONIO.

Alas the day!

SEBASTIAN.

A lady, sir, though it was said she much resembled me, was yet of many accounted beautiful: but, though I could not, with such estimable wonder, overfar believe that, yet thus far I will boldly publish her,—she bore a mind that envy could not but call fair. She is drown'd already, sir, with salt water, though I seem to drown her remembrance again with more.

ANTONIO.

Pardon me, sir, your bad entertainment.

SEBASTIAN.

O good Antonio, forgive me your trouble!

ANTONIO.

If you will not murder me for my love, let me be your servant.

SEBASTIAN.

If you will not undo what you have done, that is, kill him whom you have recover'd, desire it not. Fare ye well at once: my bosom is full of kindness; and I am yet so near the manners of my mother, that, upon the least occasion more, mine eyes will tell tales of me. I am bound to the Count Orsino's court: farewell. [*Exit.*

ANTONIO.

The gentleness of all the gods go with thee!
I have many enemies in Orsino's court,
Else would I very shortly see thee there:
But, come what may, I do adore thee so,
That danger shall seem sport, and I will go. [*Exit.*

SCENE II.

A street.

Enter VIOLA, MALVOLIO *following.*

MALVOLIO.

WERE not you even now with the Countess Olivia?

VIOLA.

Even now, sir; on a moderate pace I have since arrived but hither.

MALVOLIO.

She returns this ring to you, sir: you might have saved me my pains, to have taken it away yourself. She adds, moreover, that you should put your lord into a desperate assurance she will none of him: and one thing more, that you be never so hardy to come again in his affairs, unless it be to report your lord's taking of this. Receive it so.

VIOLA.

She took no ring of me;—I'll none of it.

MALVOLIO.

Come, sir, you peevishly threw it to her; and her will is, it should be so return'd: if it be worth stooping for, there it lies in your eye; if not, be it his that finds it. [*Exit.*

VIOLA.

I left no ring with her: what means this lady?
Fortune forbid, my outside have not charm'd her!
She made good view of me; indeed, so much,
That, sure, methought, her eyes had lost her tongue,
For she did speak in starts distractedly.
She loves me, sure; the cunning of her passion
Invites me in this churlish messenger.
None of my lord's ring! why, he sent her none.
I am the man: if it be so, as 'tis,
Poor lady, she were better love a dream.
Disguise, I see, thou art a wickedness,
Wherein the pregnant enemy does much.
How easy is it for the proper-false
In women's waxen hearts to set their forms!
Alas, our frailty is the cause, not we!
For such as we are made of, such we be.
How will this fadge? my master loves her dearly;
And I, poor monster, fond as much on him;
And she, mistaken, seems to dote on me.
What will become of this? As I am man,
My state is desperate for my master's love;
As I am woman,—now, alas the day!—
What thriftless sighs shall poor Olivia breathe!
O Time, thou must untangle this, not I;
It is too hard a knot for me t'untie! [*Exit.*

SCENE III.

Olivia's house.

Enter SIR TOBY *and* SIR ANDREW.

SIR TOBY BELCH.

APPROACH, Sir Andrew: not to be a-bed after midnight is to be up betimes; and *diluculo surgere*, thou know'st,—

SIR ANDREW AGUECHEEK.

Nay, by my troth, I know not: but I know, to be up late is to be up late.

SIR TOBY BELCH.
A false conclusion: I hate it as an unfill'd can. To be up after midnight, and to go to bed then, is early: so that to go to bed after midnight is to go to bed betimes. Does not our life consist of the four elements?

SIR ANDREW AGUECHEEK.
Faith, so they say; but, I think, it rather consists of eating and drinking.

SIR TOBY BELCH.
Th'art a scholar: let us therefore eat and drink.— Marian, I say! a stoup of wine!

SIR ANDREW AGUECHEEK.
Here comes the fool, i'faith.

Enter CLOWN.

CLOWN.
How now, my hearts! did you never see the picture of We Three?

SIR TOBY BELCH.
Welcome, ass. Now let's have a catch.

SIR ANDREW AGUECHEEK.
By my troth, the fool has an excellent breast. I had rather than forty shillings I had such a leg, and so sweet a breath to sing, as the fool has. In sooth, thou wast in very gracious fooling last night, when thou spokest of Pigrogromitus, of the Vapians passing the equinoctial of Queubus: 'twas very good, i'faith. I sent thee sixpence for thy leman: hadst it?

CLOWN.
I did impeticos thy gratillity; for Malvolio's nose is no whipstock; my lady has a white hand, and the Myrmidons are no bottle-ale houses.

SIR ANDREW AGUECHEEK.
Excellent! why, this is the best fooling, when all is done. Now, a song.

SIR TOBY BELCH.
Come on; there is sixpence for you: let's have a song.

SIR ANDREW AGUECHEEK.
There's a testril of me too; if one knight give a—

CLOWN.
Would you have a love-song, or a song of good life?

SIR TOBY BELCH.
A love-song, a love-song.

SIR ANDREW AGUECHEEK.
Ay, ay: I care not for good life.

CLOWN [*sings*].
O mistress mine, where are you roaming?
O, stay and hear; your true-love's coming,
  That can sing both high and low:
Trip no further, pretty sweeting;
Journeys end in lovers' meeting,
  Every wise man's son doth know.

SIR ANDREW AGUECHEEK.
Excellent good, i'faith.

SIR TOBY BELCH.
Good, good.

CLOWN.
What is love? 'tis not hereafter;
Present mirth hath present laughter;
  What's to come is still unsure:
In delay there lies no plenty;
Then come kiss me, sweet-and-twenty,
  Youth's a stuff will not endure.

SIR ANDREW AGUECHEEK.
A mellifluous voice, as I am true knight.

SIR TOBY BELCH.
A contagious breath.

SIR ANDREW AGUECHEEK.
Very sweet and contagious, i'faith.

SIR TOBY BELCH.
To hear by the nose, it is dulcet in contagion. But shall we make the welkin dance indeed? shall we rouse the night-owl in a catch that will draw three souls out of one weaver? shall we do that?

SIR ANDREW AGUECHEEK.
An you love me, let's do't: I am dog at a catch.

CLOWN.
By'r lady, sir, and some dogs will catch well.

SIR ANDREW AGUECHEEK.
Most certain. Let our catch be, 'Thou knave.'

CLOWN.
'Hold thy peace, thou knave,' knight? I shall be constrain'd in't to call thee knave, knight.

SIR ANDREW AGUECHEEK.
'Tis not the first time I have constrain'd one to call me knave. Begin, fool: it begins, 'Hold thy peace.'

CLOWN.
I shall never begin, if I hold my peace.

SIR ANDREW AGUECHEEK.
Good, i'faith. Come, begin. [*Catch sung.*

Enter MARIA.

MARIA.
What a caterwauling do you keep here! If my lady have not call'd up her steward Malvolio, and bid him turn you out of doors, never trust me.

SIR TOBY BELCH.
My lady's a Cataian, we are politicians, Malvolio's a Peg-a-Ramsey, and 'Three merry men be we.' Am not I consanguineous? am I not of her blood? Tilly-vally, lady! [*Sings*] 'There dwelt a man in Babylon, lady, lady!'

CLOWN.
Beshrew me, the knight's in admirable fooling.

SIR ANDREW AGUECHEEK.
Ay, he does well enough if he be disposed, and so do I too: he does it with a better grace, but I do it more natural.

SIR TOBY BELCH.
'O, the twelfth day of December,—'

MARIA.
For the love o' God, peace!

Enter MALVOLIO.

MALVOLIO.
My masters, are you mad? or what are you? Have you no wit, manners, nor honesty, but to gabble like tinkers at this time of night? Do ye make an ale-house of my lady's house, that ye squeak out your cosiers' catches without any mitigation or remorse of voice? Is there no respect of place, persons, nor time, in you?

SIR TOBY BELCH.
We did keep time, sir, in our catches. Sneck-up!

MALVOLIO.
Sir Toby, I must be round with you. My lady bade me tell you, that, though she harbours you as her kinsman, she's nothing allied to your disorders. If you can separate yourself and your misdemeanours, you are welcome to the house; if not,

an it would please you to take leave of her, she is very willing to bid you farewell.

SIR TOBY BELCH.

'Farewell, dear heart, since I must needs be gone.'

MARIA.

Nay, good Sir Toby.

CLOWN.

'His eyes do show his days are almost done.'

MALVOLIO.

Is't even so?

SIR TOBY BELCH.

'But I will never die.'

CLOWN.

Sir Toby, there you lie.

MALVOLIO.

This is much credit to you.

SIR TOBY BELCH.

'Shall I bid him go?'

CLOWN.

'What an if you do?'

SIR TOBY BELCH.

'Shall I bid him go, and spare not?'

CLOWN.

'O, no, no, no, no, you dare not.'

SIR TOBY BELCH.

Out o'time, sir? ye lie.—Art any more than a steward? Dost thou think, because thou art virtuous, there shall be no more cakes and ale?

CLOWN.

Yes, by Saint Anne; and ginger shall be hot i'th' mouth too.

SIR TOBY BELCH.

Th'art i'th'right.—Go, sir, rub your chain with crumbs.—A stoup of wine, Maria!

MALVOLIO.

Mistress Mary, if you prized my lady's favour at any thing more than contempt, you would not give means for this uncivil rule: she shall know of it, by this hand. [*Exit.*

MARIA.

Go shake your ears.

SIR ANDREW AGUECHEEK.

'Twere as good a deed as to drink when a man's a-hungry, to challenge him the field, and then to break promise with him, and make a fool of him.

SIR TOBY BELCH.

Do't, knight: I'll write thee a challenge; or I'll deliver thy indignation to him by word of mouth.

MARIA.

Sweet Sir Toby, be patient for to-night; since the youth of the count's was to-day with my lady, she is much out of quiet. For Monsieur Malvolio, let me alone with him: if I do not gull him into a nayword, and make him a common recreation, do not think I have wit enough to lie straight in my bed: I know I can do it.

SIR TOBY BELCH.

Possess us, possess us; tell us something of him.

MARIA.

Marry, sir, sometimes he is a kind of puritan.

SIR ANDREW AGUECHEEK.

O, if I thought that, I'ld beat him like a dog!

SIR TOBY BELCH.

What, for being a puritan? thy exquisite reason, dear knight?

SIR ANDREW AGUECHEEK.

I have no exquisite reason for't, but I have reason good enough.

MARIA.

The devil a puritan that he is, or any thing constantly, but a time-pleaser; an affection'd ass, that cons state without book, and utters it by great swarths: the best persuaded of himself, so cramm'd, as he thinks, with excellencies, that it is his grounds of faith that all that look on him love him; and on that vice in him will my revenge find notable cause to work.

SIR TOBY BELCH.

What wilt thou do?

MARIA.

I will drop in his way some obscure epistles of love; wherein, by the colour of his beard, the shape of his leg, the manner of his gait, the expressure of his eye, forehead, and complexion, he shall find himself most feelingly personated: I can write very like my lady, your niece; on a forgotten matter we can hardly make distinction of our hands.

SIR TOBY BELCH.

Excellent! I smell a device.

SIR ANDREW AGUECHEEK.

I have't in my nose too.

SIR TOBY BELCH.

He shall think, by the letters that thou wilt drop, that they come from my niece, and that she's in love with him.

MARIA.

My purpose is, indeed, a horse of that colour.

SIR TOBY BELCH.

And your horse now would make him an ass.

MARIA.

Ass, I doubt not.

SIR ANDREW AGUECHEEK.

O, 'twill be admirable!

MARIA.

Sport royal, I warrant you: I know my physic will work with him. I will plant you two, and let the fool make a third, where he shall find the letter: observe his construction of it. For this night, to bed, and dream on the event. Farewell.

SIR TOBY BELCH.

Good night, Penthesilea. [*Exit* MARIA.

SIR ANDREW AGUECHEEK.

Before me, she's a good wench.

SIR TOBY BELCH.

She's a beagle, true-bred, and one that adores me: what o'that?

SIR ANDREW AGUECHEEK.

I was adored once too.

SIR TOBY BELCH.

Let's to bed, knight.—Thou hadst need send for more money.

SIR ANDREW AGUECHEEK.

If I cannot recover your niece, I am a foul way out.

SIR TOBY BELCH.

Send for money, knight: if thou hast her not i'th' end, call me cut.

SIR ANDREW AGUECHEEK.

If I do not, never trust me, take it how you will.

SIR TOBY BELCH.

Come, come; I'll go burn some sack; 'tis too late to go to bed now: come, knight; come, knight. [*Exeunt.*

SCENE IV.

The DUKE'S *palace.*

Enter DUKE, VIOLA, CURIO, *and others.*

DUKE OF ILLYRIA.

GIVE me some music:—now, good morrow, friends:—
Now, good Cesario, but that piece of song,
That old and antique song we heard last night:
Methought it did relieve my passion much,
More than light airs and recollected terms
Of these most brisk and giddy-paced times:—
Come, but one verse.

CURIO.

He is not here, so please your lordship, that should sing it.

DUKE OF ILLYRIA.

Who was it?

CURIO.

Feste, the jester, my lord; a fool that the Lady Olivia's father took much delight in: he is about the house.

DUKE OF ILLYRIA.

Seek him out: and play the tune the while.
[*Exit* CURIO. *Music plays.*
Come hither, boy: if ever thou shalt love,
In the sweet pangs of it remember me;
For such as I am all true lovers are,
Unstaid and skittish in all motions else,
Save in the constant image of the creature
That is beloved.—How dost thou like this tune?

VIOLA.

It gives a very echo to the seat
Where Love is throned.

DUKE OF ILLYRIA.

Thou dost speak masterly:
My life upon't, young though thou art, thine eye
Hath stay'd upon some favour that it loves;—
Hath it not, boy?

VIOLA.

A little, by your favour.

DUKE OF ILLYRIA.

What kind of woman is't?

VIOLA.

Of your complexion.

DUKE OF ILLYRIA.

She is not worth thee, then. What years, i'faith?

VIOLA.

About your years, my lord.

DUKE OF ILLYRIA.

Too old, by heaven: let still the woman take
An elder than herself; so wears she to him,
So sways she level in her husband's heart:
For, boy, however we do praise ourselves,
Our fancies are more giddy and unfirm,
More longing, wavering, sooner lost and worn,
Than women's are.

VIOLA.

I think it well, my lord.

DUKE OF ILLYRIA.

Then let thy love be younger than thyself,
Or thy affection cannot hold the bent;
For women are as roses, whose fair flower
Being once display'd, doth fall that very hour.

VIOLA.

And so they are: alas, that they are so,—
To die, even when they to perfection grow!

Enter CURIO *and* CLOWN.

DUKE OF ILLYRIA.

O, fellow, come, the song we had last night.—
Mark it, Cesario; it is old and plain:
The spinsters and the knitters in the sun,
And the free maids that weave their thread with bones,
Do use to chant it: it is silly sooth,
And dallies with the innocence of love,
Like the old age.

CLOWN.

Are you ready, sir?

DUKE OF ILLYRIA.

Ay; prithee, sing. [*Music.*

CLOWN.

Come away, come away, death,
And in sad cypress let me be laid;
Fly away, fly away, breath;
I am slain by a fair cruel maid.
My shroud of white, stuck all with yew,
O, prepare it!
My part of death, no one so true
Did share it.

Not a flower, not a flower sweet,
On my black coffin let there be strown;
Not a friend, not a friend greet
My poor corpse, where my bones shall be thrown:
A thousand thousand sighs to save,
Lay me, O, where
Sad true lover never find my grave,
To weep there!

DUKE OF ILLYRIA.

There's for thy pains.

CLOWN.

No pains, sir; I take pleasure in singing, sir.

DUKE OF ILLYRIA.

I'll pay thy pleasure, then.

CLOWN.

Truly, sir, and pleasure will be paid, one time or another.

DUKE OF ILLYRIA.

Give me now leave to leave thee.

CLOWN.

Now, the melancholy god protect thee; and the tailor make thy doublet of changeable taffeta, for thy mind is a very opal! I would have men of such constancy put to sea, that their business might be every thing, and their intent every where; for that's it that always makes a good voyage of nothing. Farewell. [*Exit.*

DUKE OF ILLYRIA.

Let all the rest give place.
[*Exeunt* CURIO *and* ATTENDANTS.
Once more, Cesario,
Get thee to yond same sovereign cruelty:
Tell her, my love, more noble than the world,
Prizes not quantity of dirty lands;
The parts that Fortune hath bestow'd upon her,
Tell her, I hold as giddily as Fortune;

But 'tis that miracle and queen of gems,
That nature pranks her in, attracts my soul.

VIOLA.

But if she cannot love you, sir?

DUKE OF ILLYRIA.

I cannot be so answer'd.

VIOLA.

Sooth, but you must.
Say that some lady—as, perhaps, there is—
Hath for your love as great a pang of heart
As you have for Olivia: you cannot love her;
You tell her so; must she not, then, be answer'd?

DUKE OF ILLYRIA.

There is no woman's sides
Can bide the beating of so strong a passion
As love doth give my heart; no woman's heart
So big, to hold so much; they lack retention.
Alas, their love may be call'd appetite,—
No motion of the liver, but the palate,—
That suffer surfeit, cloyment, and revolt;
But mine is all as hungry as the sea,
And can digest as much: make no compare
Between that love a woman can bear me
And that I owe Olivia.

VIOLA.

Ay, but I know,—

DUKE OF ILLYRIA.

What dost thou know?

VIOLA.

Too well what love women to men may owe:
In faith, they are as true of heart as we.
My father had a daughter loved a man,
As it might be, perhaps, were I a woman,
I should your lordship.

DUKE OF ILLYRIA.

And what's her history?

VIOLA.

A blank, my lord. She never told her love,
But let concealment, like a worm i'th'bud,
Feed on her damask cheek: she pined in thought;
And, with a green and yellow melancholy,
She sat like Patience on a monument,
Smiling at grief. Was not this love indeed?
We men may say more, swear more: but, indeed,
Our shows are more than will; for still we prove
Much in our vows, but little in our love.

DUKE OF ILLYRIA.

But died thy sister of her love, my boy?

VIOLA.

I am all the daughters of my father's house,
And all the brothers too;—and yet I know not.—
Sir, shall I to this lady?

DUKE OF ILLYRIA.

Ay, that's the theme.
To her in haste; give her this jewel; say,
My love can give no place, bide no denay.

[*Exeunt*.

SCENE V.

OLIVIA'S *garden*.

Enter SIR TOBY, SIR ANDREW, *and* FABIAN.

SIR TOBY BELCH.

Come thy ways, Signior Fabian.

FABIAN.

Nay, I'll come: if I lose a scruple of this sport, let me be boil'd to death with melancholy.

SIR TOBY BELCH.

Wouldst thou not be glad to have the niggardly rascally sheep-biter come by some notable shame?

FABIAN.

I would exult, man: you know he brought me out o'favour with my lady about a bear-baiting here.

SIR TOBY BELCH.

To anger him, we'll have the bear again; and we will fool him black and blue:—shall we not, Sir Andrew?

SIR ANDREW AGUECHEEK.

An we do not, it is pity of our lives.

SIR TOBY BELCH.

Here comes the little villain.

Enter MARIA.

How now, my metal of India!

MARIA.

Get ye all three into the box-tree: Malvolio's coming down this walk: he has been yonder i'the sun practising behaviour to his own shadow this half-hour: observe him, for the love of mockery; for I know this letter will make a contemplative idiot of him. Close, in the name of jesting! Lie thou there [*throws down a letter*]; for here comes the trout that must be caught with tickling. [*Exit*.

Enter MALVOLIO.

MALVOLIO.

'Tis but fortune; all is fortune. Maria once told me she did affect me: and I have heard herself come thus near, that, should she fancy, it should be one of my complexion. Besides, she uses me with a more exalted respect than any one else that follows her. What should I think on't?

SIR TOBY BELCH.

Here's an overweening rogue!

FABIAN.

O, peace! Contemplation makes a rare turkey-cock of him: how he jets under his advanced plumes!

SIR ANDREW AGUECHEEK.

'Slight, I could so beat the rogue!

SIR TOBY BELCH.

Peace, I say.

MALVOLIO.

To be Count Malvolio,—

SIR TOBY BELCH.

Ah, rogue!

SIR ANDREW AGUECHEEK.

Pistol him, pistol him.

SIR TOBY BELCH.

Peace, peace!

MALVOLIO.

There is example for't; the lady of the Strachy married the yeoman of the wardrobe.

SIR ANDREW AGUECHEEK.

Fie on him, Jezebel!

FABIAN.

O, peace! now he's deeply in: look how imagination blows him.

MALVOLIO.

Having been three months married to her, sitting in my state,—

SIR TOBY BELCH.

O, for a stone-bow, to hit him in the eye!

MALVOLIO.

Calling my officers about me, in my brancht velvet gown; having come from a day-bed, where I have left Olivia sleeping,—

SIR TOBY BELCH.

Fire and brimstone!

FABIAN.

O, peace, peace!

MALVOLIO.

And then to have the humour of state; and after a demure travel of regard,—telling them I know my place, as I would they should do theirs,—to ask for my kinsman Toby,—

SIR TOBY BELCH.

Bolts and shackles!

FABIAN.

O, peace, peace, peace! now, now.

MALVOLIO.

Seven of my people, with an obedient start, make out for him: I frown the while; and perchance wind up my watch, or play with some rich jewel. Toby approaches; court'sies there to me,—

SIR TOBY BELCH.

Shall this fellow live?

FABIAN.

Though our silence be drawn from us with cars, yet peace.

MALVOLIO.

I extend my hand to him thus, quenching my familiar smile with an austere regard of control,—

SIR TOBY BELCH.

And does not Toby take you a blow o'the lips, then?

MALVOLIO.

Saying, 'Cousin Toby, my fortunes having cast me on your niece, give me this prerogative of speech,'—

SIR TOBY BELCH.

What, what?

MALVOLIO.

'You must amend your drunkenness.'

SIR TOBY BELCH.

Out, scab!

FABIAN.

Nay, patience, or we break the sinews of our plot.

MALVOLIO.

'Besides, you waste the treasure of your time with a foolish knight,'—

SIR ANDREW AGUECHEEK.

That's me, I warrant you.

MALVOLIO.

'One Sir Andrew,'—

SIR ANDREW AGUECHEEK.

I knew 'twas I; for many do call me fool.

MALVOLIO.

What employment have we here?

[*Taking up the letter.*

FABIAN.

Now is the woodcock near the gin.

SIR TOBY BELCH.

O, peace! and the spirit of humours intimate reading aloud to him!

MALVOLIO.

By my life, this is my lady's hand: these be her very C's, her U's, and her T's; and thus makes she her great P's. It is, in contempt of question, her hand.

SIR ANDREW AGUECHEEK.

Her C's, her U's, and her T's: why that?

MALVOLIO [*reads*].

To the unknown beloved, this, and my good wishes: her very phrases!—By your leave, wax.—Soft!—and the impressure her Lucrece, with which she uses to seal: 'tis my lady. To whom should this be?

FABIAN.

This wins him, liver and all.

MALVOLIO [*reads*].

Jove knows I love:
But who?
Lips, do not move;
No man must know.

'No man must know.'—What follows? the numbers alter'd!—'No man must know:'—if this should be thee, Malvolio?

SIR TOBY BELCH.

Marry, hang thee, brock!

MALVOLIO [*reads*].

I may command where I adore;
But silence, like a Lucrece knife,
With bloodless stroke my heart doth gore:
M, O, A, I, doth sway my life.

FABIAN.

A fustian riddle!

SIR TOBY BELCH.

Excellent wench, say I.

MALVOLIO.

'M, O, A, I, doth sway my life.'—Nay, but first, let me see,—let me see,—let me see.

FABIAN.

What dish o'poison has she drest him!

SIR TOBY BELCH.

And with what wing the staniel checks at it!

MALVOLIO.

'I may command where I adore.' Why, she may command me: I serve her; she is my lady. Why, this is evident to any formal capacity; there is no obstruction in this:—and the end,—what should that alphabetical position portend? if I could make that resemble something in me,—Softly!—M, O, A, I,—

SIR TOBY BELCH.

O, ay, make up that:—he is now at a cold scent.

FABIAN.

Sowter will cry upon't, for all this, though it be as rank as a fox.

MALVOLIO.

M,—Malvolio;—M,—why, that begins my name.

FABIAN.

Did not I say he would work it out? the cur is excellent at faults.

MALVOLIO.

M,—but then there is no consonancy in the sequel; that suffers under probation: A should follow, but O does.

FABIAN.

And O shall end, I hope.

SIR TOBY BELCH.

Ay, or I'll cudgel him, and make him cry O!

MALVOLIO.

And then I comes behind.

FABIAN.

Ay, an you had any eye behind you, you might see more detraction at your heels than fortunes before you.

MALVOLIO.

M, O, A, I;—this simulation is not as the former:—and yet, to crush this a little, it would bow to me, for every one of these letters are in my name. Soft! here follows prose.—[*reads*] If this fall into thy hand, revolve. In my stars I am above thee; but be not afraid of greatness: some are born great, some achieve greatness, and some have greatness thrust upon 'em. Thy Fates open their hands; let thy blood and spirit embrace them: and, to inure thyself to what thou art like to be, cast thy humble slough, and appear fresh. Be opposite with a kinsman, surly with servants; let thy tongue tang arguments of state; put thyself into the trick of singularity: she thus advises thee that sighs for thee. Remember who commended thy yellow stockings, and wisht to see thee ever cross-garter'd: I say, remember. Go to, thou art made, if thou desirest to be so; if not, let me see thee a steward still, the fellow of servants, and not worthy to touch Fortune's fingers. Farewell. She that would alter services with thee,

THE FORTUNATE-UNHAPPY.

Daylight and champain discovers not more: this is open. I will be proud, I will read politic authors, I will baffle Sir Toby, I will wash off gross acquaintance, I will be point-devise the very man. I do not now fool myself, to let imagination jade me; for every reason excites to this, that my lady loves me. She did commend my yellow stockings of late, she did praise my leg being cross-garter'd; and in this she manifests herself to my love, and, with a kind of injunction, drives me to these habits of her liking. I thank my stars, I am happy. I will be strange, stout, in yellow stockings, and cross-garter'd, even with the swiftness of putting on. Jove and my stars be praised!—Here is yet a postscript. [*reads*] 'Thou canst not choose but know who I am. If thou entertain'st my love, let it appear in thy smiling: thy smiles become thee well; therefore in my presence still smile, dear my sweet, I prithee.' Jove, I thank thee.—I will smile; I will do every thing that thou wilt have me. [*Exit.*

FABIAN.

I will not give my part of this sport for a pension of thousands to be paid from the Sophy.

SIR TOBY BELCH.

I could marry this wench for this device,—

SIR ANDREW AGUECHEEK.

So could I too.

SIR TOBY BELCH.

And ask no other dowry with her but such another jest.

SIR ANDREW AGUECHEEK.

Nor I neither.

FABIAN.

Here comes my noble gull-catcher.

Enter MARIA.

SIR TOBY BELCH.

Wilt thou set thy foot o'my neck?

SIR ANDREW AGUECHEEK.

Or o'mine either?

SIR TOBY BELCH.

Shall I play my freedom at tray-trip, and become thy bond-slave?

SIR ANDREW AGUECHEEK.

I'faith, or I either?

SIR TOBY BELCH.

Why, thou hast put him in such a dream, that, when the image of it leaves him, he must run mad.

MARIA.

Nay, but say true; does it work upon him?

SIR TOBY BELCH.

Like aqua-vitæ with a midwife.

MARIA.

If you will then see the fruits of the sport, mark his first approach before my lady: he will come to her in yellow stockings, and 'tis a colour she abhors, and cross-garter'd, a fashion she detests; and he will smile upon her, which will now be so unsuitable to her disposition, being addicted to a melancholy as she is, that it cannot but turn him into a notable contempt. If you will see it, follow me.

SIR TOBY BELCH.

To the gates of Tartar, thou most excellent devil of wit!

SIR ANDREW AGUECHEEK.

I'll make one too. [*Exeunt.*

ACT III. SCENE I.

OLIVIA'S *garden.*

Enter VIOLA, *and* CLOWN *with a tabor.*

VIOLA.

SAVE thee, friend, and thy music! dost thou live by thy tabor?

CLOWN.

No, sir, I live by the church.

VIOLA.

Art thou a churchman?

CLOWN.

No such matter, sir: I do live by the church; for I do live at my house, and my house doth stand by the church.

VIOLA.

So thou mayst say, the king lies by a beggar, if a beggar dwell near him; or, the church stands by thy tabor, if thy tabor stand by the church.

CLOWN.

You have said, sir.—To see this age!—A sentence is but a cheveril glove to a good wit: how quickly the wrong side may be turn'd outward!

VIOLA.

Nay, that's certain; they that dally nicely with words may quickly make them wanton.

CLOWN.

I would, therefore, my sister had had no name, sir.

VIOLA.

Why, man?

CLOWN.

Why, sir, her name's a word; and to dally with that word might make my sister wanton. But, indeed, words are very rascals, since bonds disgraced them.

VIOLA.

Thy reason, man?

CLOWN.

Troth, sir, I can yield you none without words; and words are grown so false, I am loth to prove reason with them.

VIOLA.

I warrant thou art a merry fellow, and carest for nothing.

CLOWN.

Not so, sir; I do care for something; but in my conscience, sir, I do not care for you: if that be to care for nothing, sir, I would it would make you invisible.

VIOLA.

Art not thou the Lady Olivia's fool?

CLOWN.

No, indeed, sir; the Lady Olivia has no folly: she will keep no fool, sir, till she be married; and fools are as like husbands as pilchers are to herrings,—the husband's the bigger: I am, indeed, not her fool, but her corrupter of words.

VIOLA.

I saw thee late at the Count Orsino's.

CLOWN.

Foolery, sir, does walk about the orb like the sun, it shines every where. I would be sorry, sir, but the fool should be as oft with your master as with my mistress: I think I saw your wisdom there.

VIOLA.

Nay, an thou pass upon me, I'll no more with thee. Hold, there's expenses for thee.

CLOWN.

Now Jove, in his next commodity of hair, send thee a beard!

VIOLA.

By my troth, I'll tell thee, I am almost sick for one; though I would not have it grow on my chin. Is thy lady within?

CLOWN.

Would not a pair of these have bred, sir?

VIOLA.

Yes, being kept together and put to use.

CLOWN.

I would play Lord Pandarus of Phrygia, sir, to bring a Cressida to this Troilus.

VIOLA.

I understand you, sir; 'tis well begg'd.

CLOWN.

The matter, I hope, is not great, sir, begging but a beggar: Cressida was a beggar. My lady is within, sir. I will conster to them whence you come; who you are, and what you would, are out of my welkin,—I might say element, but the word is over-worn. [*Exit.*

VIOLA.

This fellow is wise enough to play the fool;
And to do that well craves a kind of wit:
He must observe their mood on whom he jests,
The quality of persons, and the time;
Not, like the haggard, check at every feather
That comes before his eye. This is a practice
As full of labour as a wise man's art:
For folly, that he wisely shows, is fit;
But wise men, folly-fall'n, quite taint their wit.

Enter SIR TOBY *and* SIR ANDREW.

SIR TOBY BELCH.

Save you, gentleman!

VIOLA.

And you, sir.

SIR ANDREW AGUECHEEK.

Dieu vous garde, monsieur.

VIOLA.

Et vous aussi; votre serviteur.

SIR ANDREW AGUECHEEK.

I hope, sir, you are; and I am yours.

SIR TOBY BELCH.

Will you encounter the house? my niece is desirous you should enter, if your trade be to her.

VIOLA.

I am bound to your niece, sir; I mean, she is the list of my voyage.

SIR TOBY BELCH.

Taste your legs, sir; put them to motion.

VIOLA.

My legs do better understand me, sir, than I understand what you mean by bidding me taste my legs.

SIR TOBY BELCH.

I mean, to go, sir, to enter.

VIOLA.

I will answer you with gait and entrance:—but we are prevented.

Enter OLIVIA *and* MARIA.

Most excellent accomplisht lady, the heavens rain odours on you!

SIR ANDREW AGUECHEEK [*aside*].

That youth's a rare courtier: 'Rain odours:'—well.

VIOLA.

My matter hath no voice, lady, but to your own most pregnant and vouchsafed ear.

SIR ANDREW AGUECHEEK [*aside*].

'Odours,' 'pregnant,' and 'vouchsafed:'—I'll get 'em all three all ready.

OLIVIA.

Let the garden-door be shut, and leave me to my hearing. [*Exeunt* SIR TOBY, SIR ANDREW, *and* MARIA.] Give me your hand, sir.

VIOLA.

My duty, madam, and most humble service.

OLIVIA.

What is your name?

VIOLA.

Cesario is your servant's name, fair princess.

OLIVIA.

My servant, sir! 'Twas never merry world
Since lowly feigning was call'd compliment:
Y'are servant to the Count Orsino, youth.

VIOLA.

And he is yours, and his must needs be yours:
Your servant's servant is your servant, madam.

OLIVIA.

For him, I think not on him: for his thoughts,
Would they were blanks, rather than fill'd with me!

VIOLA.

Madam, I come to whet your gentle thoughts
On his behalf:—

OLIVIA.

O, by your leave, I pray you,—
I bade you never speak again of him:

But, would you undertake another suit,
I had rather hear you to solicit that
Than music from the spheres.

VIOLA.

Dear lady,—

OLIVIA.

Give me leave, beseech you. I did send,
After the last enchantment you did here,
A ring in chase of you: so did I abuse
Myself, my servant, and, I fear me, you:
Under your hard construction must I sit,
To force that on you, in a shameful cunning,
Which you knew none of yours: what might you think?
Have you not set mine honour at the stake,
And baited it with all th'unmuzzled thoughts
That tyrannous heart can think? To one of your receiving
Enough is shown: a cypress, not a bosom,
Hides my poor heart. So, let me hear you speak.

VIOLA.

I pity you.

OLIVIA.

That's a degree to love.

VIOLA.

No, not a grise; for 'tis a vulgar proof,
That very oft we pity enemies.

OLIVIA.

Why, then, methinks 'tis time to smile again.
O world, how apt the poor are to be proud!
If one should be a prey, how much the better
To fall before the lion than the wolf!
[*Clock strikes.*
The clock upbraids me with the waste of time.—
Be not afraid, good youth, I will not have you:
And yet, when wit and youth is come to harvest,
Your wife is like to reap a proper man:
There lies your way, due west.

VIOLA.

Then westward-ho!—
Grace and good disposition attend your ladyship!
You'll nothing, madam, to my lord by me?

OLIVIA.

Stay:
I prithee, tell me what thou think'st of me.

VIOLA.

That you do think you are not what you are.

OLIVIA.

If I think so, I think the same of you.

VIOLA.

Then think you right: I am not what I am.

OLIVIA.

I would you were as I would have you be!

VIOLA.

Would it be better, madam, than I am,
I wish it might; for now I am your fool.

OLIVIA.

O, what a deal of scorn looks beautiful
In the contempt and anger of his lip!
A murderous guilt shows not itself more soon
Than love that would seem hid: love's night is noon.
Cesario, by the roses of the spring,
By maidhood, honour, truth, and every thing,
I love thee so, that, maugre all thy pride,
Nor wit nor reason can my passion hide.
Do not extort thy reasons from this clause,
For that I woo, thou therefore hast no cause;
But, rather, reason thus with reason fetter,—
Love sought is good, but given unsought is better.

VIOLA.

By innocence I swear, and by my youth,
I have one heart, one bosom, and one truth,—
And that no woman has; nor never none
Shall mistress be of it, save I alone.
And so adieu, good madam: never more
Will I my master's tears to you deplore.

OLIVIA.

Yet come again; for thou perhaps mayst move
That heart, which now abhors, to like his love.
[*Exeunt.*

SCENE II.

OLIVIA'S *house.*

Enter SIR TOBY, SIR ANDREW, *and* FABIAN.

SIR ANDREW AGUECHEEK.

NO, faith, I'll not stay a jot longer.

SIR TOBY BELCH.

Thy reason, dear venom; give thy reason.

FABIAN.

You must needs yield your reason, Sir Andrew.

SIR ANDREW AGUECHEEK.

Marry, I saw your niece do more favours to the count's serving-man than ever she bestow'd upon me; I saw't i'th'orchard.

SIR TOBY BELCH.

Did she see thee the while, old boy? tell me that.

SIR ANDREW AGUECHEEK.

As plain as I see you now.

FABIAN.

This was a great argument of love in her toward you.

SIR ANDREW AGUECHEEK.

'Slight, will you make an ass o'me?

FABIAN.

I will prove it legitimate, sir, upon the oaths of judgement and reason.

SIR TOBY BELCH.

And they have been grand-jurymen since before Noah was a sailor.

FABIAN.

She did show favour to the youth in your sight only to exasperate you, to awake your dormouse valour, to put fire in your heart, and brimstone in your liver. You should then have accosted her; and with some excellent jests, fire-new from the mint, you should have bang'd the youth into dumbness. This was lookt for at your hand, and this was balkt: the double gilt of this opportunity you let time wash off, and you are now sail'd into the north of my lady's opinion; where you will hang like an icicle on a Dutchman's beard, unless you do redeem it by some laudable attempt either of valour or policy.

SIR ANDREW AGUECHEEK.

An't be any way, it must be with valour; for policy I hate: I had as lief be a Brownist as a politician.

SIR TOBY BELCH.

Why, then, build me thy fortunes upon the basis of valour. Challenge me the count's youth to fight with him; hurt him in eleven places: my niece shall take note of it; and assure thyself, there is no love-broker in the world can more prevail in man's commendation with woman than report of valour.

FABIAN.

There is no way but this, Sir Andrew.

SIR ANDREW AGUECHEEK.

Will either of you bear me a challenge to him?

SIR TOBY BELCH.

Go, write it in a martial hand; be curst and brief; it is no matter how witty, so it be eloquent and full of invention: taunt him with the license of ink: if thou 'thou'st' him some thrice, it shall not be amiss; and as many lies as will lie in thy sheet of paper, although the sheet were big enough for the bed of Ware in England, set 'em down: go, about it. Let there be gall enough in thy ink, though thou write with a goose-pen, no matter: about it.

SIR ANDREW AGUECHEEK.

Where shall I find you?

SIR TOBY BELCH.

We'll call thee at the *cubiculo:* go.

[*Exit* SIR ANDREW.

FABIAN.

This is a dear manakin to you, Sir Toby.

SIR TOBY BELCH.

I have been dear to him, lad,—some two thousand strong, or so.

FABIAN.

We shall have a rare letter from him: but you'll not deliver't?

SIR TOBY BELCH.

Never trust me, then; and by all means stir on the youth to an answer. I think oxen and wainropes cannot hale them together. For Andrew, if he were open'd, and you find so much blood in his liver as will clog the foot of a flea, I'll eat the rest of th'anatomy.

FABIAN.

And his opposite, the youth, bears in his visage no great presage of cruelty.

SIR TOBY BELCH.

Look, where the youngest wren of nine comes.

Enter MARIA.

MARIA.

If you desire the spleen, and will laugh yourselves into stitches, follow me. Yond gull Malvolio is turn'd heathen, a very renegado; for there is no Christian, that means to be saved by believing rightly, can ever believe such impossible passages of grossness. He's in yellow stockings.

SIR TOBY BELCH.

And cross-garter'd?

MARIA.

Most villainously; like a pedant that keeps a school i'th'church.—I have dogg'd him, like his murderer. He does obey every point of the letter that I dropt to betray him: he does smile his face into more lines than is in the new map, with the augmentation of the Indies: you have not seen such a thing as 'tis; I can hardly forbear hurling things at him. I know my lady will strike him: if she do, he'll smile, and take't for a great favour.

SIR TOBY BELCH.

Come, bring us, bring us where he is. [*Exeunt.*

SCENE III.

A street.

Enter SEBASTIAN *and* ANTONIO.

SEBASTIAN.

I WOULD not, by my will, have troubled you;
But, since you make your pleasure of your pains,
I will no further chide you.

ANTONIO.

I could not stay behind you: my desire,
More sharp than filed steel, did spur me forth;
And not all love to see you,—though so much
As might have drawn me to a longer voyage,—
But jealousy what might befall your travel,
Being skilless in these parts; which to a stranger,
Unguided and unfriended, often prove
Rough and unhospitable: my willing love,
The rather by these arguments of fear,
Set forth in your pursuit.

SEBASTIAN.

My kind Antonio,
I can no other answer make, but thanks,
And thanks, and ever; oft good turns
Are shuffled off with such uncurrent pay:
But, were my worth, as is my conscience, firm,
You should find better dealing. What's to do?
Shall we go see the reliques of this town?

ANTONIO.

To-morrow, sir; best first go see your lodging.

SEBASTIAN.

I am not weary, and 'tis long to night:
I pray you, let us satisfy our eyes
With the memorials and the things of fame
That do renown this city.

ANTONIO.

Would you'ld pardon me;
I do not without danger walk these streets:
Once, in a sea-fight, 'gainst the count his galleys
I did some service; of such note, indeed,
That, were I ta'en here, it would scarce be answer'd.

SEBASTIAN.

Belike you slew great number of his people?

ANTONIO.

Th'offence is not of such a bloody nature;
Albeit the quality of the time and quarrel
Might well have given us bloody argument.
It might have since been answer'd in repaying
What we took from them; which, for traffic's sake,
Most of our city did: only myself stood out;
For which, if I be lapsed in this place,
I shall pay dear.

SEBASTIAN.

Do not, then, walk too open.

ANTONIO.

It doth not fit me. Hold, sir, here's my purse.
In the south suburbs, at the Elephant,
Is best to lodge: I will bespeak our diet,
Whiles you beguile the time and feed your knowledge
With viewing of the town: there shall you have me.

SEBASTIAN.

Why I your purse?

ANTONIO.

Haply your eye shall light upon some toy
You have desire to purchase; and your store,
I think, is not for idle markets, sir.

SEBASTIAN.
I'll be your purse-bearer, and leave you for
An hour.

ANTONIO.
To th'Elephant.

SEBASTIAN.
I do remember.
[*Exeunt*.

SCENE IV.

OLIVIA'S *garden*.

Enter OLIVIA *and* MARIA.

OLIVIA.
I HAVE sent after him: he says he'll come;—
How shall I feast him? what bestow of him?
For youth is bought more oft than begg'd or borrow'd.
I speak too loud.—
Where is Malvolio?—he is sad and civil,
And suits well for a servant with my fortunes:—
Where is Malvolio?

MARIA.
He's coming, madam; but in very strange manner. He is, sure, possest, madam.

OLIVIA.
Why, what's the matter? does he rave?

MARIA.
No, madam, he does nothing but smile: your ladyship were best to have some guard about you, if he come; for, sure, the man is tainted in's wits.

OLIVIA.
Go call him hither. [*Exit* MARIA.] I am as mad as he,
If sad and merry madness equal be.

Enter MARIA, *with* MALVOLIO.

How now, Malvolio!

MALVOLIO.
Sweet lady, ho, ho. [*Smiles fantastically*.

OLIVIA.
Smilest thou?
I sent for thee upon a sad occasion.

MALVOLIO.
Sad, lady! I could be sad: this does make some obstruction in the blood, this cross-gartering; but what of that? if it please the eye of one, it is with me as the very true sonnet is, 'Please one, and please all.'

OLIVIA.
Why, how dost thou, man? what is the matter with thee?

MALVOLIO.
Not black in my mind, though yellow in my legs. It did come to his hands, and commands shall be executed: I think we do know the sweet Roman hand.

OLIVIA.
Wilt thou go to bed, Malvolio?

MALVOLIO.
To bed! ay, sweet-heart; and I'll come to thee.

OLIVIA.
God comfort thee! Why dost thou smile so, and kiss thy hand so oft?

MARIA.
How do you, Malvolio?

MALVOLIO.
At your request! yes: nightingales answer daws.

MARIA.
Why appear you with this ridiculous boldness before my lady?

MALVOLIO.
'Be not afraid of greatness:'—'twas well writ.

OLIVIA.
What mean'st thou by that, Malvolio?

MALVOLIO.
'Some are born great,'—

OLIVIA.
Ha!

MALVOLIO.
'Some achieve greatness,'—

OLIVIA.
What say'st thou?

MALVOLIO.
'And some have greatness thrust upon them.'

OLIVIA.
Heaven restore thee!

MALVOLIO.
'Remember who commended thy yellow stockings,'—

OLIVIA.
Thy yellow stockings!

MALVOLIO.
'And wisht to see thee cross-garter'd.'

OLIVIA.
Cross-garter'd!

MALVOLIO.
Go to, thou art made, if thou desirest to be so;'—

OLIVIA.
Am I made?

MALVOLIO.
'If not, let me see thee a servant still.'

OLIVIA.
Why, this is very midsummer madness.

Enter a SERVANT.

SERVANT.
Madam, the young gentleman of the Count Orsino's is return'd: I could hardly entreat him back: he attends your ladyship's pleasure.

OLIVIA.
I'll come to him. [*Exit* SERVANT.] Good Maria, let this fellow be lookt to. Where's my cousin Toby? Let some of my people have a special care of him: I would not have him miscarry for the half of my dowry. [*Exeunt* OLIVIA *and* MARIA.

MALVOLIO.
O, ho! do you come near me now? no worse man than Sir Toby to look to me? This concurs directly with the letter: she sends him on purpose, that I may appear stubborn to him; for she incites me to that in the letter. 'Cast thy humble slough,' says she; 'be opposite with a kinsman, surly with servants; let thy tongue tang with arguments of state; put thyself into the trick of singularity;'—and, consequently, sets down the manner how; as, a sad face, a reverend carriage, a slow tongue, in the habit of some sir of note, and so forth. I have limed her; but it is Joves's doing, and Jove make me thankful! And, when she went away now, 'Let this fellow be lookt to:' fellow! not Malvolio, nor after my degree, but fellow. Why, every thing adheres together, that no dram of a scruple, no scruple of a scruple, no obstacle, no incredulous or unsafe circumstance—What can be said?

Nothing, that can be, can come between me and the full prospect of my hopes. Well, Jove, not I, is the doer of this, and he is to be thankt.

Enter MARIA *with* SIR TOBY *and* FABIAN.

SIR TOBY BELCH.

Which way is he, in the name of sanctity? If all the devils of hell be drawn in little, and Legion himself possest him, yet I'll speak to him.

FABIAN.

Here he is, here he is.—How is't with you, sir? how is't with you, man?

MALVOLIO.

Go off; I discard you: let me enjoy my private: go off.

MARIA.

Lo, how hollow the fiend speaks within him; did not I tell you?—Sir Toby, my lady prays you to have a care of him.

MALVOLIO.

Ah, ha! does she so?

SIR TOBY BELCH.

Go to, go to; peace, peace; we must deal gently with him: let me alone.—How do you, Malvolio? how is't with you? What, man! defy the devil: consider, he's an enemy to mankind.

MALVOLIO.

Do you know what you say?

MARIA.

La you, an you speak ill of the devil, how he takes it at heart! Pray God, he be not bewitcht!

FABIAN.

Carry his water to th'wise woman.

MARIA.

Marry, and it shall be done to-morrow morning, if I live. My lady would not lose him for more than I'll say.

MALVOLIO.

How now, mistress!

MARIA.

O Lord!

SIR TOBY BELCH.

Prithee, hold thy peace; this is not the way: do you not see you move him? let me alone with him.

FABIAN.

No way but gentleness; gently, gently: the fiend is rough, and will not be roughly used.

SIR TOBY BELCH.

Why, how now, my bawcock! how dost thou, chuck?

MALVOLIO.

Sir!

SIR TOBY BELCH.

Ay, Biddy, come with me. What, man! 'tis not for gravity to play at cherry-pit with Satan: hang him, foul collier!

MARIA.

Get him to say his prayers; good Sir Toby, get him to pray.

MALVOLIO.

My prayers, minx!

MARIA.

No, I warrant you, he will not hear of godliness.

MALVOLIO.

Go, hang yourselves all! you are idle shallow things: I am not of your element: you shall know more hereafter. [*Exit.*

SIR TOBY BELCH.

Is't possible?

FABIAN.

If this were play'd upon a stage now, I could condemn it as an improbable fiction.

SIR TOBY BELCH.

His very genius hath taken the infection of the device, man.

MARIA.

Nay, pursue him now, lest the device take air, and taint.

FABIAN.

Why, we shall make him mad indeed.

MARIA.

The house will be the quieter.

SIR TOBY BELCH.

Come, we'll have him in a dark room and bound. My niece is already in the belief that he's mad; we may carry it thus, for our pleasure and his penance, till our very pastime, tired out of breath, prompt us to have mercy on him: at which time we will bring the device to the bar, and crown thee for a finder of madmen.—But see, but see.

FABIAN.

More matter for a May morning.

Enter SIR ANDREW.

SIR ANDREW AGUECHEEK.

Here's the challenge, read it: I warrant there's vinegar and pepper in't.

FABIAN.

Is't so saucy?

SIR ANDREW AGUECHEEK.

Ay, is't, I warrant him: do but read.

SIR TOBY BELCH.

Give me. [*reads*] Youth, whatsoever thou art, thou art but a scurvy fellow.

FABIAN.

Good, and valiant.

SIR TOBY BELCH [*reads*].

Wonder not, nor admire not in thy mind, why I do call thee so, for I will show thee no reason for't.

FABIAN.

A good note: that keeps you from the blow of the law.

SIR TOBY BELCH [*reads*].

Thou comest to the Lady Olivia, and in my sight she uses thee kindly: but thou liest in thy throat; that is not the matter I challenge thee for.

FABIAN.

Very brief, and to exceeding good sense—less.

SIR TOBY BELCH [*reads*].

I will waylay thee going home; where if it be thy chance to kill me,—

FABIAN.

Good.

SIR TOBY BELCH [*reads*].

Thou kill'st me like a rogue and a villain.

FABIAN.

Still you keep o'th'windy side of the law: good.

SIR TOBY BELCH [*reads*].

Fare thee well; and God have mercy upon one of our souls! He may have mercy upon mine; but my hope is better, and so look to thyself. Thy friend, as thou usest him, and thy sworn enemy,

ANDREW AGUECHEEK.

If this letter move him not, his legs cannot: I'll give't him.

MARIA.

You may have very fit occasion for't: he is now in some commerce with my lady, and will by and by depart.

SIR TOBY BELCH.

Go, Sir Andrew; scout me for him at the corner of the orchard, like a bum-baily: so soon as ever thou seest him, draw; and, as thou draw'st, swear horrible; for it comes to pass oft, that a terrible oath, with a swaggering accent sharply twang'd off, gives manhood more approbation then ever proof itself would have earn'd him. Away!

SIR ANDREW AGUECHEEK.

Nay, let me alone for swearing. [*Exit.*

SIR TOBY BELCH.

Now will not I deliver his letter: for the behaviour of the young gentleman gives him out to be of good capacity and breeding: his employment between his lord and my niece confirms no less: therefore this letter, being so excellently ignorant, will breed no terror in the youth: he will find it comes from a clodpole. But, sir, I will deliver his challenge by word of mouth; set upon Aguecheek a notable report of valour; and drive the gentleman—as I know his youth will aptly receive it—into a most hideous opinion of his rage, skill, fury, and impetuosity. This will so fright them both, that they will kill one another by the look, like cockatrices.

FABIAN.

Here he comes with your niece: give them way till he take leave, and presently after him.

SIR TOBY BELCH.

I will meditate the while upon some horrid message for a challenge.

[*Exeunt* SIR TOBY, FABIAN, *and* MARIA.

Enter OLIVIA, *with* VIOLA.

OLIVIA.

I have said too much unto a heart of stone,
And laid mine honour too unchary out:
There's something in me that reproves my fault;
But such a headstrong potent fault it is,
That it but mocks reproof.

VIOLA.

With the same 'haviour that your passion bears,
Goes on my master's griefs.

OLIVIA.

Here, wear this jewel for me, 'tis my picture:
Refuse it not: it hath no tongue to vex you:
And, I beseech you, come again to-morrow.
What shall you ask of me that I'll deny,
That honour saved may upon asking give?

VIOLA.

Nothing but this,—your true love for my master.

OLIVIA.

How with mine honour may I give him that
Which I have given to you?

VIOLA.

I will acquit you.

OLIVIA.

Well, come again to-morrow; fare thee well:
A fiend like thee might bear my soul to hell.

[*Exit.*

Enter SIR TOBY *and* FABIAN.

SIR TOBY BELCH.

Gentleman, God save thee!

VIOLA.

And you, sir.

SIR TOBY BELCH.

That defence thou hast, betake thee to't: of what nature the wrongs are thou hast done him, I know not: but thy intercepter, full of despite, bloody as the hunter, attends thee at the orchard-end: dismount thy tuck, be yare in thy preparation; for thy assailant is quick, skilful, and deadly.

VIOLA.

You mistake, sir; I am sure no man hath any quarrel to me: my remembrance is very free and clear from any image of offence done to any man.

SIR TOBY BELCH.

You'll find it otherwise, I assure you: therefore, if you hold your life at any price, betake you to your guard; for your opposite hath in him what youth, strength, skill, and wrath can furnish man withal.

VIOLA.

I pray you, sir, what is he?

SIR TOBY BELCH.

He is knight, dubb'd with unhatcht rapier and on carpet consideration; but he is a devil in private brawl: souls and bodies hath he divorced three; and his incensement at this moment is so implacable, that satisfaction can be none but by pangs of death and sepulchre: hob-nob is his word; give't or take't.

VIOLA.

I will return again into the house, and desire some conduct of the lady. I am no fighter. I have heard of some kind of men that put quarrels purposely on others, to taste their valour; belike this is a man of that quirk.

SIR TOBY BELCH.

Sir, no; his indignation derives itself out of a very competent injury: therefore, get you on, and give him his desire. Back you shall not to the house, unless you undertake that with me which with as much safety you might answer him: therefore, on, or strip your sword stark naked; for meddle you must, that's certain, or forswear to wear iron about you.

VIOLA.

This is as uncivil as strange. I beseech you, do me this courteous office, as to know of the knight what my offence to him is: it is something of my negligence, nothing of my purpose.

SIR TOBY BELCH.

I will do so.—Signior Fabian, stay you by this gentleman till my return. [*Exit.*

VIOLA.

Pray you, sir, do you know of this matter?

FABIAN.

I know the knight is incensed against you, even to a mortal arbitrement; but nothing of the circumstance more.

VIOLA.

I beseech you, what manner of man is he?

FABIAN.

Nothing of that wonderful promise, to read him by his form, as you are like to find him in the proof of his valour. He is, indeed, sir, the most skilful, bloody, and fatal opposite that you could possibly have found in any part of Illyria. Will you walk towards him? I will make your peace with him, if I can.

VIOLA.

I shall be much bound to you for't: I am one that had rather go with sir priest than sir knight: I care not who knows so much of my mettle. [*Exeunt.*

Enter SIR TOBY *and* SIR ANDREW.

SIR TOBY BELCH.

Why, man, he's a very devil; I have not seen such a firago. I had a pass with him, rapier, scabbard, and all, and he gives me the stuck-in with such a mortal motion, that it is inevitable; and on the answer, he pays you as surely as your feet hit the ground they step on: they say he has been fencer to the Sophy.

SIR ANDREW AGUECHEEK.

Pox on't, I'll not meddle with him.

SIR TOBY BELCH.

Ay, but he will not now be pacified: Fabian can scarce hold him yonder.

SIR ANDREW AGUECHEEK.

Plague on't, an I thought he had been valiant and so cunning in fence, I'ld have seen him damn'd ere I'ld have challenged him. Let him let the matter slip, and I'll give him my horse, gray Capulet.

SIR TOBY BELCH.

I'll make the motion: stand here, make a good show on't: this shall end without the perdition of souls.—[*aside*] Marry, I'll ride your horse as well as I ride you.

Enter FABIAN *and* VIOLA.

[*to* FABIAN] I have his horse to take up the quarrel: I have persuaded him the youth's a devil.

FABIAN.

He is as horribly conceited of him; and pants and looks pale, as if a bear were at his heels.

SIR TOBY BELCH [*to* VIOLA].

There's no remedy, sir; he will fight with you for's oath-sake: marry, he hath better bethought him of his quarrel, and he finds that now scarce to be worth talking of: therefore draw, for the supportance of his vow; he protests he will not hurt you.

VIOLA [*aside*].

Pray God defend me! A little thing would make me tell them how much I lack of a man.

FABIAN.

Give ground, if you see him furious.

SIR TOBY BELCH.

Come, Sir Andrew, there's no remedy; the gentleman will, for his honour's sake, have one bout with you; he cannot by the duello avoid it: but he has promised me, as he is a gentleman and a soldier, he will not hurt you. Come on, to't.

SIR ANDREW AGUECHEEK.

Pray God, he keep his oath! [*Draws.*

VIOLA.

I do assure you, 'tis against my will. [*Draws.*

Enter ANTONIO.

ANTONIO.

Put up your sword. If this young gentleman
Have done offence, I take the fault on me:
If you offend him, I for him defy you.

SIR TOBY BELCH.

You, sir! why, what are you?

ANTONIO [*drawing*].

One, sir, that for his love dares yet do more
Than you have heard him brag to you he will.

SIR TOBY BELCH.

Nay, if you be an undertaker, I am for you. [*Draws.*

FABIAN.

O good Sir Toby, hold! here come the officers.

SIR TOBY BELCH [*to* ANTONIO].

I'll be with you anon.

VIOLA [*to* SIR ANDREW].

Pray, sir, put your sword up, if you please.

SIR ANDREW AGUECHEEK.

Marry, will I, sir; and, for that I promised you, I'll be as good as my word: he will bear you easily, and reins well.

Enter OFFICERS.

FIRST OFFICER.

This is the man; do thy office,

SECOND OFFICER.

Antonio, I arrest thee at the suit of Count Orsino.

ANTONIO.

You do mistake me, sir.

FIRST OFFICER.

No, sir, no jot; I know your favour well,
Though now you have no sea-cap on your head.—
Take him away: he knows I know him well.

ANTONIO.

I must obey. [*to* VIOLA] This comes with seeking you:
But there's no remedy; I shall answer it.
What will you do, now my necessity
Makes me to ask you for my purse? It grieves me
Much more for what I cannot do for you
Than what befalls myself. You stand amazed;
But be of comfort.

SECOND OFFICER.

Come sir, away.

ANTONIO.

I must entreat of you some of that money.

VIOLA.

What money, sir?
For the fair kindness you have show'd me here,
And, part, being prompted by your present trouble,
Out of my lean and low ability
I'll lend you something: my having is not much;
I'll make division of my present with you:
Hold, there's half my coffer.

ANTONIO.

Will you deny me now?
Is't possible that my deserts to you
Can lack persuasion? Do not tempt my misery,
Lest that it make me so unsound a man
As to upbraid you with those kindnesses
That I have done for you.

VIOLA.

I know of none;
Nor know I you by voice or any feature:
I hate ingratitude more in a man
Than lying, vainness, babbling, drunkenness,
Or any taint of vice whose strong corruption
Inhabits our frail blood.

ANTONIO.

O heavens themselves!

SECOND OFFICER.

Come, sir, I pray you, go.

ANTONIO.

Let me speak a little. This youth that you see here
I snatcht one half out of the jaws of death,
Relieved him with such sanctity of love,
And to his image, which methought did promise
Most venerable worth, did I devotion.

FIRST OFFICER.

What's that to us? The time goes by: away!

ANTONIO.

But, O, how vile an idol proves this god!
Thou hast, Sebastian, done good feature shame.
In nature there's no blemish but the mind;
None can be call'd deform'd but the unkind:
Virtue is beauty: but the beauteous evil
Are empty trunks, o'erflourisht by the devil.

FIRST OFFICER.

The man grows mad: away with him!—come, come, sir.

ANTONIO.

Lead me on. [*Exit with* OFFICERS.

VIOLA.

Methinks his words do from such passion fly,
That he believes himself: so do not I.
Prove true, imagination, O, prove true,
That I, dear brother, be now ta'en for you!

SIR TOBY BELCH.

Come hither, knight; come hither, Fabian: we'll whisper o'er a couplet or two of most sage saws.

VIOLA.

He named Sebastian: I my brother know
Yet living in my glass; even such, and so,
In favour was my brother; and he went
Still in this fashion, colour, ornament,—
For him I imitate: O, if it prove,
Tempests are kind, and salt waves fresh in love!
[*Exit.*

SIR TOBY BELCH.

A very dishonest paltry boy, and more a coward than a hare: his dishonesty appears in leaving his friend here in necessity, and denying him; and for his cowardship, ask Fabian.

FABIAN.

A coward, a most devout coward, religious in it.

SIR ANDREW AGUECHEEK.

'Slid, I'll after him again, and beat him.

SIR TOBY BELCH.

Do; cuff him soundly, but never draw thy sword.

SIR ANDREW AGUECHEEK.

An I do not,— [*Exit.*

FABIAN.

Come, let's see the event.

SIR TOBY BELCH.

I dare lay any money 'twill be nothing yet.
[*Exeunt.*

ACT IV. SCENE I.

Before OLIVIA'S *house.*

Enter SEBASTIAN *and* CLOWN.

CLOWN.

WILL you make me believe that I am not sent for you?

SEBASTIAN.

Go to, go to, thou art a foolish fellow:
Let me be clear of thee.

CLOWN.

Well held out, i'faith! No, I do not know you; nor I am not sent to you by my lady, to bid you come speak with her; nor your name is not Master Cesario; nor this is not my nose neither. Nothing that is so is so.

SEBASTIAN.

I prithee, vent thy folly somewhere else;
Thou know'st not me.

CLOWN.

Vent my folly! he has heard that word of some great man, and now applies it to a fool: vent my folly! I am afraid this great lubber, the world, will prove a cockney.—I prithee, now, ungird thy strangeness, and tell me what I shall vent to my lady: shall I vent to her that thou art coming?

SEBASTIAN.

I prithee, foolish Greek, depart from me:
There's money for thee: if you tarry longer,
I shall give worse payment.

CLOWN.

By my troth, thou hast an open hand.—These wise men, that give fools money, get themselves a good report after fourteen years' purchase.

Enter SIR ANDREW.

SIR ANDREW AGUECHEEK.

Now, sir, have I met you again? there's for you.
[*Striking* SEBASTIAN.

SEBASTIAN.

Why, there's for thee, and there, and there!
[*Beating* SIR ANDREW.
Are all the people mad?

Enter SIR TOBY *and* FABIAN.

SIR TOBY BELCH.

Hold, sir, or I'll throw your dagger o'er the house.

CLOWN.

This will I tell my lady straight: I would not be in some of your coats for twopence. [*Exit.*

SIR TOBY BELCH.

Come on, sir; hold.

SIR ANDREW AGUECHEEK.

Nay, let him alone: I'll go another way to work with him; I'll have an action of battery against him, if there be any law in Illyria: though I struck him first, yet it's no matter for that.

SEBASTIAN.

Let go thy hand.

SIR TOBY BELCH.

Come, sir, I will not let you go. Come, my young soldier, put up your iron: you are well flesht; come on.

SEBASTIAN.

I will be free from thee. What wouldst thou now?
If thou darest tempt me further, draw thy sword.
[*Draws.*

SIR TOBY BELCH.

What, what? Nay, then I must have an ounce or two of this malapert blood from you. [*Draws.*

Enter OLIVIA.

OLIVIA.

Hold, Toby; on thy life, I charge thee, hold!

SIR TOBY BELCH.

Madam!

OLIVIA.

Will it be ever thus? Ungracious wretch,
Fit for the mountains and the barbarous caves,

Where manners ne'er were preacht! out of my sight!—
Be not offended, dear Cesario.—
Rudesby, be gone!

[*Exeunt* SIR TOBY, SIR ANDREW, *and* FABIAN.

I prithee, gentle friend,
Let thy fair wisdom, not thy passion, sway
In this uncivil and unjust extent
Against thy peace. Go with me to my house;
And hear thou there how many fruitless pranks
This ruffian hath botcht up, that thou thereby
Mayst smile at this: thou shalt not choose but go:
Do not deny. Beshrew his soul for me,
He started one poor heart of mine in thee.

SEBASTIAN.

What relish is in this? how runs the stream?
Or I am mad, or else this is a dream:
Let fancy still my sense in Lethe steep;
If it be thus to dream, still let me sleep!

OLIVIA.

Nay, come, I prithee: would thou'ldst be ruled by me!

SEBASTIAN.

Madam, I will.

OLIVIA.

O, say so, and so be ! [*Exeunt.*

SCENE II.

OLIVIA'S *house.*

Enter MARIA *and* CLOWN.

MARIA.

NAY, I prithee, put on this gown and this beard; make him believe thou art Sir Topas the curate: do it quickly; I'll call Sir Toby the whilst. [*Exit.*

CLOWN.

Well, I'll put it on, and I will dissemble myself in't; and I would I were the first that ever dissembled in such a gown. I am not tall enough to become the function well; nor lean enough to be thought a good student: but to be said an honest man and a good housekeeper, goes as fairly as to say a careful man and a great scholar. The competitors enter.

Enter SIR TOBY *and* MARIA.

SIR TOBY BELCH.

Jove bless thee, master parson.

CLOWN.

Bonos dies, Sir Toby: for, as the old hermit of Prague, that never saw pen and ink, very wittily said to a niece of King Gorboduc, 'That that is is;' so I, being master parson, am master parson; for, what is that but that, and is but is?

SIR TOBY BELCH.

To him, Sir Topas.

CLOWN.

What, ho, I say,—peace in this prison!

SIR TOBY BELCH.

The knave counterfeits well; a good knave.

MALVOLIO [*within*].

Who calls there?

CLOWN.

Sir Topas the curate, who comes to visit Malvolio the lunatic.

MALVOLIO.

Sir Topas, Sir Topas, good Sir Topas, go to my lady.

CLOWN.

Out, hyperbolical fiend! how vexest thou this man! talkest thou nothing but of ladies?

SIR TOBY BELCH.

Well said, master parson.

MALVOLIO.

Sir Topas, never was man thus wrong'd: good Sir Topas, do not think I am mad: they have laid me here in hideous darkness.

CLOWN.

Fie, thou dishonest Satan! I call thee by the most modest terms; for I am one of those gentle ones that will use the devil himself with courtesy: say'st thou that house is dark?

MALVOLIO.

As hell, Sir Topas.

CLOWN.

Why, it hath bay windows transparent as barricadoes, and the clearstories toward the south-north are as lustrous as ebony; and yet complainest thou of obstruction?

MALVOLIO.

I am not mad, Sir Topas: I say to you, this house is dark.

CLOWN.

Madman, thou errest: I say, there is no darkness but ignorance; in which thou art more puzzled than the Egyptians in their fog.

MALVOLIO.

I say, this house is as dark as ignorance, though ignorance were as dark as hell; and I say, there was never man thus abused. I am no more mad than you are: make the trial of it in any constant question.

CLOWN.

What is the opinion of Pythagoras concerning wildfowl?

MALVOLIO.

That the soul of our grandam might haply inhabit a bird.

CLOWN.

What think'st thou of his opinion?

MALVOLIO.

I think nobly of the soul, and no way approve his opinion.

CLOWN.

Fare thee well. Remain thou still in darkness: thou shalt hold the opinion of Pythagoras ere I will allow of thy wits; and fear to kill a woodcock, lest thou dispossess the soul of thy grandam. Fare thee well.

MALVOLIO.

Sir Topas, Sir Topas,—

SIR TOBY BELCH.

My most exquisite Sir Topas!

CLOWN.

Nay, I am for all waters.

MARIA.

Thou mightst have done this without thy beard and gown: he sees thee not.

SIR TOBY BELCH.

To him in thine own voice, and bring me word how thou find'st him: I would we were well rid of this knavery. If he may be conveniently deliver'd, I would he were; for I am now so far in offence with my niece, that I cannot pursue with any safety this sport to the upshot. Come by and by to my chamber. [*Exeunt* SIR TOBY *and* MARIA.

CLOWN [*singing*].

Hey, Robin, jolly Robin,
Tell me how thy lady does.

MALVOLIO.

Fool,—

CLOWN.

'My lady is unkind, perdy.'

MALVOLIO.

Fool,—

CLOWN.

'Alas, why is she so?'

MALVOLIO.

Fool, I say,—

CLOWN.

'She loves another'—Who calls, ha?

MALVOLIO.

Good fool, as ever thou wilt deserve well at my hand, help me to a candle, and pen, ink, and paper: as I am a gentleman, I will live to be thankful to thee for't.

CLOWN.

Master Malvolio!

MALVOLIO.

Ay, good fool.

CLOWN.

Alas, sir, how fell you besides your five wits?

MALVOLIO.

Fool, there was never man so notoriously abused: I am as well in my wits, fool, as thou art.

CLOWN.

But as well? then you are mad indeed, if you be no better in your wits than a fool.

MALVOLIO.

They have here propertied me; keep me in darkness, send ministers to me, asses, and do all they can to face me out of my wits.

CLOWN.

Advise you what you say; the minister is here.—Malvolio, Malvolio, thy wits the heavens restore! endeavour thyself to sleep, and leave thy vain bibble-babble.

MALVOLIO.

Sir Topas,—

CLOWN.

Maintain no words with him, good fellow.—Who, I, sir? not I, sir. God b'wi'you, good Sir Topas! —Marry, amen.—I will, sir, I will.

MALVOLIO.

Fool, fool, fool, I say,—

CLOWN.

Alas, sir, be patient. What say you, sir? I am shent for speaking to you.

MALVOLIO.

Good fool, help me to some light and some paper: I tell thee, I am as well in my wits as any man in Illyria.

CLOWN.

Well-a-day, that you were, sir!

MALVOLIO.

By this hand, I am. Good fool, some ink, paper, and light; and convey what I will set down to my lady: it shall advantage thee more than ever the bearing of letter did.

CLOWN.

I will help you to't. But tell me true, are you not mad indeed? or do you but counterfeit?

MALVOLIO.

Believe me, I am not; I tell thee true.

CLOWN.

Nay, I'll ne'er believe a madman till I see his brains. I will fetch you light, and paper, and ink.

MALVOLIO.

Fool, I'll requite it in the highest degree: I prithee, be gone.

CLOWN [*singing*].

I am gone, sir;
And anon, sir,
I'll be with you again,
In a trice,
Like to the old Vice,
Your need to sustain;
Who, with dagger of lath,
In his rage and his wrath,
Cries, ah, ha! to the devil:
Like a mad lad,
Pare thy nails, dad;
Adieu, goodman devil. [*Exit.*

SCENE III.

OLIVIA'S *garden.*

Enter SEBASTIAN.

SEBASTIAN.

THIS is the air; that is the glorious sun;
This pearl she gave me, I do feel't and see't:
And though 'tis wonder that enwraps me thus,
Yet 'tis not madness. Where's Antonio, then?
I could not find him at the Elephant:
Yet there he was; and there I found this credit,
That he did range the town to seek me out.
His counsel now might do me golden service;
For though my soul disputes well with my sense,
That this may be some error, but no madness,
Yet doth this accident and flood of fortune
So far exceed all instance, all discourse,
That I am ready to distrust mine eyes,
And wrangle with my reason, that persuades me
To any other trust but that I am mad
Or else the lady's mad; yet, if 'twere so,
She could not sway her house, command her followers,
Take and give back affairs, and their dispatch,
With such a smooth, discreet, and stable bearing,
As I perceive she does: there's something in't
That is deceivable. But here the lady comes.

Enter OLIVIA *and a* PRIEST.

OLIVIA.

Blame not this haste of mine. If you mean well,
Now go with me and with his holy man
Into the chantry by: there, before him,
And underneath that consecrated roof,
Plight me the full assurance of your faith;
That my most jealous and too doubtful soul
May live at peace: he shall conceal it,
Whiles you are willing it shall come to note,
What time we will our celebration keep
According to my birth.—What do you say?

SEBASTIAN.

I'll follow this good man, and go with you;
And, having sworn truth, ever will be true.

OLIVIA.

Then lead the way, good father; and heavens so shine,
That they may fairly note this act of mine!
[*Exeunt.*

ACT V. SCENE I.

Before OLIVIA'S *house.*

Enter CLOWN *and* FABIAN.

FABIAN.

NOW, as thou lovest me, let me see his letter.

CLOWN.

Good Master Fabian, grant me another request.

FABIAN.

Any thing.

CLOWN.

Do not desire to see this letter.

FABIAN.

This is, to give a dog, and in recompense desire my dog again.

Enter DUKE, VIOLA, CURIO, *and* ATTENDANTS.

DUKE OF ILLYRIA.

Belong you to the Lady Olivia, friends?

CLOWN.

Ay, sir; we are some of her trappings.

DUKE OF ILLYRIA.

I know thee well: how dost thou, my good fellow?

CLOWN.

Truly, sir, the better for my foes, and the worse for my friends.

DUKE OF ILLYRIA.

Just the contrary; the better for thy friends.

CLOWN.

No, sir, the worse.

DUKE OF ILLYRIA.

How can that be?

CLOWN.

Marry, sir, they praise me, and make an ass of me; now my foes tell me plainly I am an ass: so that by my foes, sir, I profit in the knowledge of myself; and by my friends I am abused: so that, conclusions to be as kisses, if your four negatives make your two affirmatives, why, then, the worse for my friends, and the better for my foes.

DUKE OF ILLYRIA.

Why, this is excellent.

CLOWN.

By my troth, sir, no; though it please you to be one of my friends.

DUKE OF ILLYRIA.

Thou shalt not be the worse for me: there's gold.
[*Gives money.*

CLOWN.

But that it would be double-dealing, sir, I would you could make it another.

DUKE OF ILLYRIA.

O, you give me ill counsel.

CLOWN.

Put your grace in your pocket, sir, for this once, and let your flesh and blood obey it.

DUKE OF ILLYRIA.

Well, I will be so much a sinner to be a double-dealer: there's another. [*Gives money.*

CLOWN.

Primo, secundo, tertio, is a good play; and the old saying is, the third pays for all: the *triplex,* sir, is a good tripping measure; or the bells of Saint Bennet, sir, may put you in mind,—one, two, three.

DUKE OF ILLYRIA.

You can fool no more money out of me at this throw: if you will let your lady know I am here to speak with her, and bring her along with you, it may awake my bounty further.

CLOWN.

Marry, sir, lullaby to your bounty till I come again. I go, sir; but I would not have you to think that my desire of having is the sin of covetousness: but, as you say, sir, let your bounty take a nap, I will awake it anon. [*Exit.*

VIOLA.

Here comes the man, sir, that did rescue me.

Enter OFFICERS, *with* ANTONIO.

DUKE OF ILLYRIA.

That face of his I do remember well;
Yet, when I saw it last, it was besmear'd
As black as Vulcan in the smoke of war:
A bawbling vessel was he captain of,
For shallow draught and bulk unprizable;
With which such scatheful grapple did he make
With the most noble bottom of our fleet,
That very envy and the tongue of loss
Cried fame and honour on him.—What's the matter?

FIRST OFFICER.

Orsino, this is that Antonio
That took the Phœnix and her fraught from Candy;
And this is he that did the Tiger board,
When your young nephew Titus lost his leg:
Here in the streets, desperate of shame and state,
In private brabble did we apprehend him.

VIOLA.

He did me kindness, sir; drew on my side;
But, in conclusion, put strange speech upon me,—
I know not what 'twas but distraction.

DUKE OF ILLYRIA.

Notable pirate! thou salt-water thief!
What foolish boldness brought thee to their mercies,
Whom thou, in terms so bloody and so dear,
Hast made thine enemies?

ANTONIO.

Orsino, noble sir,
Be pleased that I shake off these names you give me:
Antonio never yet was thief or pirate,
Though, I confess, on base and ground enough,
Orsino's enemy. A witchcraft drew me hither:
That most ingrateful boy there by your side,
From the rude sea's enraged and foamy mouth
Did I redeem; a wreck past hope he was:
His life I gave him, and did thereto add
My love, without retention or restraint,
All his in dedication; for his sake
Did I expose myself, pure for his love,

Into the danger of this adverse town;
Drew to defend him when he was beset:
Where being apprehended, his false cunning,
Not meaning to partake with me in danger,
Taught him to face me out of his acquaintance,
And grew a twenty-years-removed thing
While one would wink; denied me mine own purse,
Which I had recommended to his use
Not half an hour before.

VIOLA.

How can this be?

DUKE OF ILLYRIA.

When came he to this town?

ANTONIO.

To-day, my lord: and for three months before—
No interim, not a minute's vacancy—
Both day and night did we keep company.

DUKE OF ILLYRIA.

Here comes the countess: now heaven walks on earth.—
But for thee, fellow; fellow, thy words are madness:
Three months this youth hath tended upon me;
But more of that anon. Take him aside.

Enter OLIVIA *and* ATTENDANTS.

OLIVIA.

What would my lord, but that he may not have,
Wherein Olivia may seem serviceable?—
Cesario, you do not keep promise with me.

VIOLA.

Madam!

DUKE OF ILLYRIA.

Gracious Olivia,—

OLIVIA.

What do you say, Cesario? Good my lord,—

VIOLA.

My lord would speak; my duty hushes me.

OLIVIA.

If it be aught to the old tune, my lord,
It is as fat and fulsome to mine ear
As howling after music.

DUKE OF ILLYRIA.

Still so cruel?

OLIVIA.

Still so constant, lord.

DUKE OF ILLYRIA.

What, to perverseness? you uncivil lady,
To whose ingrate and unauspicious altars
My soul the faithfull'st offerings hath breathed out
That e'er devotion tender'd! What shall I do?

OLIVIA.

Even what it please my lord, that shall become him.

DUKE OF ILLYRIA.

Why should I not, had I the heart to do it,
Like to th'Egyptian thief at point of death,
Kill what I love? a savage jealousy
That sometimes savours nobly.—But hear me this:
Since you to non-regardance cast my faith,
And that I partly know the instrument
That screws me from my true place in your favour,
Live you, the marble-breasted tyrant, still;
But this your minion, whom I know you love,
And whom, by heaven I swear, I tender dearly,
Him will I tear out of that cruel eye,
Where he sits crowned in his master's spite.—
Come, boy, with me; my thoughts are ripe in mischief:
I'll sacrifice the lamb that I do love,
To spite a raven's heart within a dove.

VIOLA.

And I, most jocund, apt, and willingly,
To do you rest, a thousand deaths would die.

OLIVIA.

Where goes Cesario?

VIOLA.

After him I love
More than I love these eyes, more than my life,
More, by all mores, than e'er I shall love wife.
If I do feign, you witnesses above
Punish my life for tainting of my love!

OLIVIA.

Ay me, detested! how am I beguiled!

VIOLA.

Who does beguile you? who does do you wrong?

OLIVIA.

Hast thou forgot thyself? is it so long?
Call forth the holy father. [*Exit an* ATTENDANT.

DUKE OF ILLYRIA.

Come, away! [*to* VIOLA.

OLIVIA.

Whither, my lord?—Cesario, husband, stay.

DUKE OF ILLYRIA.

Husband!

OLIVIA.

Ay, husband: can he that deny?

DUKE OF ILLYRIA.

Her husband, sirrah!

VIOLA.

No, my lord, not I.

OLIVIA.

Alas, it is the baseness of thy fear
That makes thee strangle thy propriety:
Fear not, Cesario, take thy fortunes up;
Be that thou know'st thou art, and then thou art
As great as that thou fear'st.

Enter ATTENDANT, *with* PRIEST.

O, welcome, father!
Father, I charge thee, by thy reverence,
Here to unfold—though lately we intended
To keep in darkness what occasion now
Reveals before 'tis ripe—what thou dost know
Hath newly past between this youth and me.

PRIEST.

A contract of eternal bond of love,
Confirm'd by mutual joinder of your hands,
Attested by the holy close of lips,
Strengthen'd by interchangement of your rings;
And all the ceremony of this compact
Seal'd in my function, by my testimony:
Since when, my watch hath told me, toward my grave
I have travell'd but two hours.

DUKE OF ILLYRIA.

O thou dissembling cub! what wilt thou be
When time hath sow'd a grizzle on thy case?
Or will not else thy craft so quickly grow,
That thine own trip shall be thine overthrow?
Farewell, and take her; but direct thy feet
Where thou and I henceforth may never meet.

VIOLA.

My lord, I do protest,—

OLIVIA.

O, do not swear!
Hold little faith, though thou hast too much fear.

Enter SIR ANDREW.

SIR ANDREW AGUECHEEK.

For the love of God, a surgeon! send one presently to Sir Toby.

OLIVIA.

What's the matter?

SIR ANDREW AGUECHEEK.

'Has broke my head across, and has given Sir Toby a bloody coxcomb too: for the love of God, your help! I had rather than forty pound I were at home.

OLIVIA.

Who has done this, Sir Andrew?

SIR ANDREW AGUECHEEK.

The count's gentleman, one Cesario: we took him for a coward, but he's the very devil incardinate.

DUKE OF ILLYRIA.

My gentleman Cesario?

SIR ANDREW AGUECHEEK.

'Od's lifelings, here he is!—You broke my head for nothing; and that that I did, I was set on to do't by Sir Toby.

VIOLA.

Why do you speak to me? I never hurt you:
You drew your sword upon me without cause;
But I bespake you fair, and hurt you not.

SIR ANDREW AGUECHEEK.

If a bloody coxcomb be a hurt, you have hurt me: I think you set nothing by a bloody coxcomb.—Here comes Sir Toby halting; you shall hear more: but if he had not been in drink, he would have tickled you othergates than he did.

Enter SIR TOBY *and* CLOWN.

DUKE OF ILLYRIA.

How now, gentleman! how is't with you?

SIR TOBY BELCH.

That's all one: has hurt me, and there's the end on't.—Sot, didst see Dick surgeon, sot?

CLOWN.

O, he's drunk, Sir Toby, an hour agone; his eyes were set at eight i'th'morning.

SIR TOBY BELCH.

Then he's a rogue and a passy-measures pavin: I hate a drunken rogue.

OLIVIA.

Away with him! Who hath made this havoc with them?

SIR ANDREW AGUECHEEK.

I'll help you, Sir Toby, because we'll be drest together.

SIR TOBY BELCH.

Will you help? an ass-head and a coxcomb and a knave, a thin-faced knave, a gull?

OLIVIA.

Get him to bed, and let his hurt be lookt to.

[*Exeunt* CLOWN, FABIAN, SIR TOBY, *and* SIR ANDREW.

Enter SEBASTIAN.

SEBASTIAN.

I am sorry, madam, I have hurt your kinsman;
But, had it been the brother of my blood,
I must have done no less with wit and safety.
You throw a strange regard upon me, and by that
I do perceive it hath offended you:
Pardon me, sweet one, even for the vows
We made each other but so late ago.

DUKE OF ILLYRIA.

One face, one voice, one habit, and two persons,—
A natural perspective, that is and is not!

SEBASTIAN.

Antonio, O my dear Antonio!
How have the hours rackt and tortured me,
Since I have lost thee!

ANTONIO.

Sebastian are you?

SEBASTIAN.

Fear'st thou that, Antonio?

ANTONIO.

How have you made division of yourself?
An apple, cleft in two, is not more twin
Than these two creatures. Which is Sebastian?

OLIVIA.

Most wonderful!

SEBASTIAN.

Do I stand there? I never had a brother;
Nor can there be that deity in my nature,
Of here and every where. I had a sister,
Whom the blind waves and surges have devour'd.—
Of charity, what kin are you to me? [*to* VIOLA.
What countryman? what name? what parentage?

VIOLA.

Of Messaline: Sebastian was my father;
Such a Sebastian was my brother too,
So went he suited to his watery tomb:
If spirits can assume both form and suit,
You come to fright us.

SEBASTIAN.

A spirit I am indeed;
But am in that dimension grossly clad,
Which from the womb I did participate.
Were you a woman, as the rest goes even,
I should my tears let fall upon your cheek,
And say, 'Thrice-welcome, drowned Viola!'

VIOLA.

My father had a mole upon his brow,—

SEBASTIAN.

And so had mine.

VIOLA.

And died that day when Viola from her birth
Had number'd thirteen years.

SEBASTIAN.

O, that record is lively in my soul!
He finished, indeed, his mortal act
That day that made my sister thirteen years.

VIOLA.

If nothing lets to make us happy both
But this my masculine usurpt attire,
Do not embrace me till each circumstance
Of place, time, fortune, do cohere and jump,
That I am Viola: which to confirm,
I'll bring you to a captain in this town,
Where lie my maiden weeds; by whose gentle help
I was preserved to serve this noble count.
All the occurrence of my fortune since
Hath been between this lady and this lord.

SEBASTIAN [*to* OLIVIA].

So comes it, lady, you have been mistook:
But nature to her bias drew in that.
You would have been contracted to a maid;
Nor are you therein, by my life, deceived,—
You are betrothed both to a maid and man.

DUKE OF ILLYRIA.

Be not amazed; right noble is his blood.—
If this be so, as yet the glass seems true,
I shall have share in this most happy wrack.—
[*to* VIOLA] Boy, thou hast said to me a thousand times
Thou never shouldst love woman like to me.

VIOLA.

And all those sayings will I over-swear;
And all those swearings keep as true in soul
As doth that orbed continent the fire
That severs day from night.

DUKE OF ILLYRIA.

Give me thy hand;
And let me see thee in thy woman's weeds.

VIOLA.

The captain that did bring me first on shore
Hath my maid's garments: he, upon some action,
Is now in durance, at Malvolio's suit,
A gentleman and follower of my lady's.

OLIVIA.

He shall enlarge him:—fetch Malvolio hither:—
And yet, alas, now I remember me,
They say, poor gentlemen, he's much distract.

Enter CLOWN *with a letter, and* FABIAN.

A most extracting frenzy of mine own
From my remembrance clearly banisht his.—
How does he, sirrah?

CLOWN.

Truly, madam, he holds Beelzebub at the stave's end as well as a man in his case may do: has here writ a letter to you; I should have given't you to-day morning, but as a madman's epistles are no gospels, so it skills not much when they are deliver'd.

OLIVIA.

Open't, and read it.

CLOWN.

Look, then, to be well edified when the fool delivers the madman. [*reads*] By the Lord, madam,—

OLIVIA.

How now! art thou mad?

CLOWN.

No, madam, I do but read madness: an your ladyship will have it as it ought to be, you must allow *vox*.

OLIVIA.

Prithee, read i'thy right wits.

CLOWN.

So I do, madonna; but to read his right wits is to read thus: therefore perpend, my princess, and give ear.

OLIVIA.

Read it you, sirrah. [*to* FABIAN.

FABIAN [*reads*].

By the Lord, madam, you wrong me, and the world shall know it: though you have put me into darkness, and given your drunken cousin rule over me, yet have I the benefit of my senses as well as your ladyship. I have your own letter that induced me to the semblance I put on; with the which I doubt not but to do myself much right, or you much shame. Think of me as you please. I leave my duty a little unthought of, and speak out of my injury.

THE MADLY-USED MALVOLIO.

OLIVIA.

Did he write this?

CLOWN.

Ay, madam.

DUKE OF ILLYRIA.

This savours not much of distraction.

OLIVIA.

See him deliver'd, Fabian; bring him hither.
[*Exit* FABIAN.
My lord, so please you, these things further thought on,
To think me as well a sister as a wife,
One day shall crown th'alliance on't, so please you,
Here at my house, and at my proper cost.

DUKE OF ILLYRIA.

Madam, I am most apt t'embrace your offer.—
[*to* VIOLA] Your master quits you; and, for your service done him,
So much against the mettle of your sex,
So far beneath your soft and tender breeding,
And since you call'd me master for so long,
Here is my hand: you shall from this time be
Your master's mistress.

OLIVIA.

A sister!—you are she.

Enter FABIAN, *with* MALVOLIO.

DUKE OF ILLYRIA.

Is this the madman?

OLIVIA.

Ay, my lord, this same.—
How now, Malvolio!

MALVOLIO!

Madam, you have done me wrong,
Notorious wrong.

OLIVIA.

Have I, Malvolio? no.

MALVOLIO.

Lady, you have. Pray you, peruse that letter:
You must not now deny it is your hand,—
Write from it, if you can, in hand or phrase;
Or say 'tis not your seal, not your invention:
You can say none of this: well, grant it, then,
And tell me, in the modesty of honour,
Why you have given me such clear lights of favour,
Bade me come smiling and cross-garter'd to you,
To put on yellow stockings, and to frown
Upon Sir Toby and the lighter people;
And, acting this in an obedient hope,
Why have you suffer'd me to be imprison'd,
Kept in a dark house, visited by the priest,
And made the most notorious geck and gull
That e'er invention play'd on? tell me why.

OLIVIA.

Alas, Malvolio, this is not my writing,
Though, I confess, much like the character:
But, out of question, 'tis Maria's hand.
And now I do bethink me, it was she

First told me thou wast mad: thou camest in smiling,
And in such forms which here were presupposed
Upon thee in the letter. Prithee, be content:
This practice hath most shrewdly past upon thee;
But, when we know the grounds and authors of it,
Thou shalt be both the plaintiff and the judge
Of thine own cause.

FABIAN.

Good madam, hear me speak:
And let no quarrel nor no brawl to come
Taint the condition of this present hour,
Which I have wonder'd at. In hope it shall not,
Most freely I confess, myself and Toby
Set this device against Malvolio here,
Upon some stubborn and uncourteous parts
We had conceived in him: Maria writ
The letter at Sir Toby's great importance;
In recompense whereof he hath married her.
How with a sportful malice it was follow'd,
May rather pluck on laughter than revenge;
If that the injuries be justly weigh'd
That have on both sides past.

OLIVIA.

Alas, poor fool, how have they baffled thee!

CLOWN.

Why, 'some are born great, some achieve greatness, and some have greatness thrown upon them.' I was one, sir, in this interlude,—one Sir Topas, sir; but that's all one.—'By the Lord, fool, I am not mad;'—but do you remember? 'Madam, why laugh you at such a barren rascal? an you smile not, he's gagg'd:' and thus the whirligig of time brings in his revenges.

MALVOLIO.

I'll be revenged on the whole pack of you. [*Exit.*

OLIVIA.

He hath been most notoriously abused.

DUKE OF ILLYRIA.

Pursue him, and entreat him to a peace:—
He hath not told us of the captain yet:
When that is known, and golden time convents,
A solemn combination shall be made
Of our dear souls. Meantime, sweet sister,
We will not part from hence.—Cesario, come;
For so you shall be, while you are a man;
But when in other habits you are seen,
Orsino's mistress and his fancy's queen.

[*Exeunt all, except* CLOWN.

CLOWN [*sings*].

When that I was and a little tiny boy,
With hey, ho, the wind and the rain,
A foolish thing was but a toy,
For the rain it raineth every day.

But when I came to man's estate,
With hey, ho, the wind and the rain,
'Gainst knaves and thieves men shut their gate,
For the rain it raineth every day.

But when I came, alas! to wive,
With hey, ho, the wind and the rain,
By swaggering could I never thrive,
For the rain it raineth every day.

But when I came unto my beds,
With hey, ho, the wind and the rain,
With toss-pots still had drunken heads,
For the rain it raineth every day.

A great while ago the world begun,
With hey, ho, the wind and the rain:—
But that's all one, our play is done,
And we'll strive to please you every day.

[*Exit.*

TROILUS AND CRESSIDA

DRAMATIS PERSONAE

PRIAM, *King of Troy.*
HECTOR, TROILUS, PARIS, DEIPHOBUS, HELENUS, *his sons.*
MARGARELON, *a bastard son of Priam.*
AENEAS, ANTENOR, *Trojan commanders.*
CALCHAS, *a Trojan priest, taking part with the Greeks.*
PANDARUS, *uncle to Cressida.*
AGAMEMNON, *the Grecian general.*
MENELAUS, *his brother.*
ACHILLES, AJAX, ULYSSES, *Grecian commanders.*
NESTOR, DIOMEDES, PATROCLUS, *Grecian commanders.*
THERSITES, *a deform'd and scurrilous Grecian.*
ALEXANDER, *servant to Cressida.*
SERVANT *to Troilus.*
SERVANT *to Paris.*
SERVANT *to Diomedes.*

HELEN, *wife to Menelaus.*
ANDROMACHE, *wife to Hector.*
CASSANDRA, *daughter of Priam; a prophetess.*
CRESSIDA, *daughter of Calchas.*

TROJAN *and* GREEK SOLDIERS, *and* ATTENDANTS.

SCENE—*Troy, and the Grecian camp before it.*

PROLOGUE.

In Troy, there lies the scene. From isles of Greece
The princes orgulous, their high blood chafed,
Have to the port of Athens sent their ships,
Fraught with the ministers and instruments
Of cruel war: sixty and nine, that wore
Their crownets regal, from th'Athenian bay
Put forth toward Phrygia: and their vow is made
To ransack Troy; within whose strong immures
The ravisht Helen, Menelaus' queen,
With wanton Paris sleeps; and that's the quarrel.
To Tenedos they come;
And the deep-drawing barks do there disgorge
Their warlike fraughtage: now on Dardan plains
The fresh and yet unbruised Greeks do pitch
Their brave pavilions: Priam's six-gated city,
Dardan, and Tymbria, Helias, Chetas, Troien,
And Antenorides, with massy staples,
And corresponsive and fulfilling bolts,
Sperr up the sons of Troy.
Now expectation, tickling skittish spirits,
On one and other side, Trojan and Greek,
Sets all on hazard: and hither am I come
A prologue arm'd,—but not in confidence
Of author's pen or actor's voice; but suited
In like conditions as our argument,—
To tell you, fair beholders, that our play
Leaps o'er the vaunt and firstlings of those broils,
Beginning in the middle; starting thence away
To what may be digested in a play.
Like, or find fault; do as your pleasures are;
Now good or bad, 'tis but the chance of war.

ACT I. SCENE I.

Troy. Before PRIAM'S *palace.*

Enter PANDARUS *and* TROILUS.

TROILUS.
Call here my varlet; I'll unarm again:
Why should I war without the walls of Troy,
That find such cruel battle here within?
Each Trojan that is master of his heart,
Let him to field; Troilus, alas, hath none!

PANDARUS.
Will this gear ne'er be mended?

TROILUS.
The Greeks are strong, and skilful to their strength,
Fierce to their skill, and to their fierceness valiant;
But I am weaker than a woman's tear,
Tamer than sleep, fonder than ignorance,
Less valiant than the virgin in the night,
And skilless as unpractised infancy.

PANDARUS.
Well, I have told you enough of this: for my part, I'll not meddle nor make no further. He that will have a cake out of the wheat must needs tarry the grinding.

TROILUS.
Have I not tarried?

PANDARUS.
Ay, the grinding; but you must tarry the bolting.

TROILUS.
Have I not tarried?

PANDARUS.
Ay, the bolting; but you must tarry the leavening.

TROILUS.
Still have I tarried.

PANDARUS.
Ay, to the leavening; but here's yet in the word 'hereafter' the kneading, the making of the cake, the heating of the oven, and the baking; nay, you must stay the cooling too, or you may chance to burn your lips.

TROILUS.
Patience herself, what goddess e'er she be,
Doth lesser blench at sufferance than I do.
At Priam's royal table do I sit;
And when fair Cressid comes into my thoughts,—
So, traitor!—'when she comes!'—When is she thence?

PANDARUS.
Well, she lookt yesternight fairer than ever I saw her look, or any woman else.

TROILUS.

I was about to tell thee,—when my heart,
As wedged with a sigh, would rive in twain;
Lest Hector or my father should perceive me,—
I have—as when the sun doth light a storm—
Buried this sigh in wrinkle of a smile:
But sorrow, that is coucht in seeming gladness,
Is like that mirth fate turns to sudden sadness.

PANDARUS.

An her hair were not somewhat darker than Helen's,—well, go to,—there were no more comparison between the women,—but, for my part, she is my kinswoman; I would not, as they term it, praise her,—but I would somebody had heard her talk yesterday, as I did. I will not dispraise your sister Cassandra's wit; but—

TROILUS.

O Pandarus! I tell thee, Pandarus,—
When I do tell thee, there my hopes lie drown'd,
Reply not in how many fadoms deep
They lie indrencht. I tell thee, I am mad
In Cressid's love: thou answer'st, 'she is fair;'
Pour'st in the open ulcer of my heart
Her eyes, her hair, her cheek, her gait, her voice;
Handlest in thy discourse, O, that her hand,
In whose comparison all whites are ink,
Writing their own reproach; to whose soft seizure
The cygnet's down is harsh, and spirit of sense
Hard as the palm of ploughman!—this thou tell'st me,
As true thou tell'st me, when I say I love her;
But, saying thus, instead of oil and balm,
Thou lay'st in every gash that love hath given me
The knife that made it.

PANDARUS.

I speak no more than truth.

TROILUS.

Thou dost not speak so much.

PANDARUS.

Faith, I'll not meddle in't. Let her be as she is: if she be fair, 'tis the better for her; an she be not, she has the mends in her own hands.

TROILUS.

Good Pandarus,—how now, Pandarus!

PANDARUS.

I have had my labour for my travail; ill-thought on of her, and ill-thought on of you: gone between and between, but small thanks for my labour.

TROILUS.

What, art thou angry, Pandarus? what, with me?

PANDARUS.

Because she's kin to me, therefore she's not so fair as Helen: an she were not kin to me, she would be as fair on Friday as Helen is on Sunday. But what care I? I care not an she were a black-a-moor; 'tis all one to me.

TROILUS.

Say I she is not fair?

PANDARUS.

I do not care whether you do or no. She's a fool to stay behind her father; let her to the Greeks; and so I'll tell her the next time I see her: for my part, I'll meddle nor make no more i'th'matter.

TROILUS.

Pandarus,—

PANDARUS.

Not I.

TROILUS.

Sweet Pandarus,—

PANDARUS.

Pray you, speak no more to me: I will leave all as I found it, and there an end.

[*Exit* PANDARUS. *Sound alarum.*

TROILUS.

Peace, you ungracious clamours! peace, rude sounds!
Fools on both sides! Helen must needs be fair,
When with your blood you daily paint her thus.
I cannot fight upon this argument;
It is too starved a subject for my sword.
But Pandarus,—O gods, how do you plague me!
I cannot come to Cressid but by Pandar;
And he's as tetchy to be woo'd to woo,
As she is stubborn-chaste against all suit.
Tell me, Apollo, for thy Daphne's love,
What Cressid is, what Pandar, and what we?
Her bed is India; there she lies, a pearl:
Between our Ilium and where she resides,
Let it be call'd the wild and wandering flood.
Ourself the merchant; and this sailing Pandar,
Our doubtful hope, our convoy, and our bark.

Alarum. Enter AENEAS.

AENEAS.

How now, Prince Troilus! wherefore not a-field?

TROILUS.

Because not there: this woman's answer sorts,
For womanish it is to be from thence.
What news, Aeneas, from the field to-day?

AENEAS.

That Paris is returned home, and hurt.

TROILUS.

By whom, Aeneas?

AENEAS.

Troilus, by Menelaus.

TROILUS.

Let Paris bleed; 'tis but a scar to scorn;
Paris is gored with Menelaus' horn. [*Alarum.*

AENEAS.

Hark, what good sport is out of town to-day!

TROILUS.

Better at home, if 'would I might' were 'may.'—
But to the sport abroad:—are you bound thither?

AENEAS.

In all swift haste.

TROILUS.

Come, go we, then, together. [*Exeunt.*

SCENE II.

The same. A street.

Enter CRESSIDA *and* ALEXANDER *her* MAN.

CRESSIDA.

WHO were those went by?

ALEXANDER.

Queen Hecuba and Helen.

CRESSIDA.

And whither go they?

ALEXANDER.

Up to the eastern tower,
Whose height commands as subject all the vale,

To see the battle. Hector, whose patience
Is, as a virtue, fixt, to-day was moved:
He chid Andromache, and struck his armourer;
And, like as there were husbandry in war,
Before the sun rose, he was harnest light,
And to the field goes he; where every flower
Did, as a prophet, weep what it foresaw
In Hector's wrath.

CRESSIDA.

What was his cause of anger?

ALEXANDER.

The noise goes, this: there is among the Greeks
A lord of Trojan blood, nephew to Hector;
They call him Ajax.

CRESSIDA.

Good; and what of him?

ALEXANDER.

They say he is a very man *per se*,
And stands alone.

CRESSIDA.

So do all men,—unless they are drunk, sick, or have no legs.

ALEXANDER.

This man, lady, hath robb'd many beasts of their particular additions; he is as valiant as the lion, churlish as the bear, slow as the elephant: a man into whom nature hath so crowded humours, that his valour is crusht into folly, his folly sauced with discretion: there is no man hath a virtue that he hath not a glimpse of; nor any man an attaint but he carries some stain of it: he is melancholy without cause, and merry against the hair: he hath the joints of every thing; but every thing so out of joint, that he is a gouty Briareus, many hands and no use; or purblind Argus, all eyes and no sight.

CRESSIDA.

But how should this man, that makes me smile, make Hector angry?

ALEXANDER.

They say he yesterday coped Hector in the battle, and struck him down; the disdain and shame whereof hath ever since kept Hector fasting and waking.

CRESSIDA.

Who comes here?

ALEXANDER.

Madam, your uncle Pandarus.

Enter PANDARUS.

CRESSIDA.

Hector's a gallant man.

ALEXANDER.

As may be in the world, lady.

PANDARUS.

What's that? what's that?

CRESSIDA.

Good morrow, uncle Pandarus.

PANDARUS.

Good morrow, cousin Cressid: what do you talk of?—Good morrow, Alexander.—How do you, cousin? When were you at Ilium?

CRESSIDA.

This morning, uncle.

PANDARUS.

What were you talking of when I came? Was Hector arm'd and gone, ere ye came to Ilium? Helen was not up, was she?

CRESSIDA.

Hector was gone; but Helen was not up.

PANDARUS.

E'en so: Hector was stirring early.

CRESSIDA.

That were we talking of, and of his anger.

PANDARUS.

Was he angry?

CRESSIDA.

So he says here.

PANDARUS.

True, he was so; I know the cause too; he'll lay about him to-day, I can tell them that: and there's Troilus will not come far behind him; let them take heed of Troilus, I can tell them that too.

CRESSIDA.

What, is he angry too?

PANDARUS.

Who, Troilus? Troilus is the better man of the two.

CRESSIDA.

O Jupiter! there's no comparison.

PANDARUS.

What, not between Troilus and Hector? Do you know a man if you see him?

CRESSIDA.

Ay, if I ever saw him before, and knew him.

PANDARUS.

Well, I say Troilus is Troilus.

CRESSIDA.

Then you say as I say; for, I am sure, he is not Hector.

PANDARUS.

No, nor Hector is not Troilus in some degrees.

CRESSIDA.

'Tis just to each of them; he is himself.

PANDARUS.

Himself! Alas, poor Troilus! I would he were,—

CRESSIDA.

So he is.

PANDARUS.

Condition, I had gone barefoot to India.

CRESSIDA.

He is not Hector.

PANDARUS.

Himself! no, he's not himself:—would a' were himself! Well, the gods are above; time must friend or end: well, Troilus, well,—I would my heart were in her body!—No, Hector is not a better man than Troilus.

CRESSIDA.

Excuse me.

PANDARUS.

He is elder.

CRESSIDA.

Pardon me, pardon me.

PANDARUS.

Th'other's not come to't; you shall tell me another tale, when th'other's come to't. Hector shall not have his wit this year,—

CRESSIDA.

He shall not need it, if he have his own.

PANDARUS.

Nor his qualities,—

CRESSIDA.

No matter.

PANDARUS.
Nor his beauty.

CRESSIDA.
'Twould not become him,—his own's better.

PANDARUS.
You have no judgement, niece: Helen herself swore th'other day, that Troilus, for a brown favour—for so 'tis, I must confess,—not brown neither,—

CRESSIDA.
No, but brown.

PANDARUS.
Faith, to say truth, brown and not brown.

CRESSIDA.
To say the truth, true and not true.

PANDARUS.
She praised his complexion above Paris.

CRESSIDA.
Why, Paris hath colour enough.

PANDARUS.
So he has.

CRESSIDA.
Then Troilus should have too much: if she praised him above, his complexion is higher than his; he having colour enough, and the other higher, is too flaming a praise for a good complexion. I had as lief Helen's golden tongue had commended Troilus for a copper nose.

PANDARUS.
I swear to you, I think Helen loves him better than Paris.

CRESSIDA.
Then she's a merry Greek indeed.

PANDARUS.
Nay, I am sure she does. She came to him th' other day into the compast window,—and, you know, he has not past three or four hairs on his chin—

CRESSIDA.
Indeed, a tapster's arithmetic may soon bring his particulars therein to a total.

PANDARUS.
Why, he is very young: and yet will he, within three pound, lift as much as his brother Hector.

CRESSIDA.
Is he so young a man, and so old a lifter?

PANDARUS.
But, to prove to you that Helen loves him,—she came, and puts me her white hand to his cloven chin—

CRESSIDA.
Juno have mercy! how came it cloven?

PANDARUS.
Why, you know, 'tis dimpled: I think his smiling becomes him better than any man in all Phrygia.

CRESSIDA.
O, he smiles valiantly.

PANDARUS.
Does he not?

CRESSIDA.
O yes, an 'twere a cloud in autumn.

PANDARUS.
Why, go to, then:—but to prove to you that Helen loves Troilus,—

CRESSIDA.
Troilus will stand to the proof, if you'll prove it so.

PANDARUS.
Troilus! why, he esteems her no more than I esteem an addle egg.

CRESSIDA.
If you love an addle egg as well as you love an idle head, you would eat chickens i'th'shell.

PANDARUS.
I cannot choose but laugh, to think how she tickled his chin;—indeed, she has a marvellous white hand, I must needs confess,—

CRESSIDA.
Without the rack.

PANDARUS.
And she takes upon her to spy a white hair on his chin.

CRESSIDA.
Alas, poor chin! many a wart is richer.

PANDARUS.
But there was such laughing!—Queen Hecuba laught, that her eyes ran o'er,—

CRESSIDA.
With mill-stones.

PANDARUS.
And Cassandra laught,—

CRESSIDA.
But there was more temperate fire under the pot of her eyes:—did her eyes run o'er too?

PANDARUS.
And Hector laught.

CRESSIDA.
At what was all this laughing?

PANDARUS.
Marry, at the white hair that Helen spied on Troilus' chin.

CRESSIDA.
An't had been a green hair, I should have laught too.

PANDARUS.
They laught not so much at the hair as at his pretty answer.

CRESSIDA.
What was his answer?

PANDARUS.
Quoth she, 'Here's but one and fifty hairs on your chin, and one of them is white.'

CRESSIDA.
This is her question.

PANDARUS.
That's true; make no question of that. 'One and fifty hairs,' quoth he, 'and one white: that white hair is my father, and all the rest are his sons.' 'Jupiter!' quoth she, 'which of these hairs is Paris my husband?' 'The forkt one,' quoth he; 'pluck't out, and give it him.' But there was such laughing! and Helen so blusht, and Paris so chafed, and all the rest so laught, that it past.

CRESSIDA.
So let it now; for it has been a great while going by.

PANDARUS.
Well, cousin, I told you a thing yesterday; think on't.

CRESSIDA.
So I do.

PANDARUS.
I'll be sworn 'tis true; he will weep you, an 'twere a man born in April.

CRESSIDA.

And I'll spring up in his tears, an 'twere a nettle against May. [*A retreat sounded.*

PANDARUS.

Hark! they are coming from the field: shall we stand up here, and see them as they pass toward Ilium? good niece, do,—sweet niece Cressida.

CRESSIDA.

At your pleasure.

PANDARUS.

Here, here, here's an excellent place; here we may see most bravely: I'll tell you them all by their names as they pass by; but mark Troilus above the rest.

CRESSIDA.

Speak not so loud.

AENEAS *passes.*

PANDARUS.

That's Aeneas: is not that a brave man? he's one of the flowers of Troy, I can tell you: but mark Troilus; you shall see anon.

ANTENOR *passes.*

CRESSIDA.

Who's that?

PANDARUS.

That's Antenor: he has a shrewd wit, I can tell you; and he's a man good enough: he's one o'th' soundest judgements in Troy, whosoever, and a proper man of person.—When comes Troilus?—I'll show you Troilus anon: if he see me, you shall see him nod at me.

CRESSIDA.

Will he give you the nod?

PANDARUS.

You shall see.

CRESSIDA.

If he do, the rich shall have more.

HECTOR *passes.*

PANDARUS.

That's Hector, that, that, look you, that; there's a fellow!—Go thy way, Hector!—There's a brave man, niece.—O brave Hector!—Look how he looks! there's a countenance! is't not a brave man?

CRESSIDA.

O, a brave man!

PANDARUS.

Is a' not? it does a man's heart good:—look you what hacks are on his helmet! look you yonder, do you see? look you there: there's no jesting; there's laying on, take't off who will, as they say: there be hacks!

CRESSIDA.

Be those with swords?

PANDARUS.

Swords! any thing, he cares not; an the devil come to him, it's all one: by God's lid, it does one's heart good.—Yonder comes Paris, yonder comes Paris:

PARIS *passes.*

look ye yonder, niece; is't not a gallant man too, is't not?—Why, this is brave now.—Who said he came hurt home to-day? he's not hurt: why, this will do Helen's heart good now, ha!—Would I could see Troilus now!—You shall see Troilus anon.

HELENUS *passes.*

CRESSIDA.

Who's that?

PANDARUS.

That's Helenus:—I marvel where Troilus is:—that's Helenus:—I think he went not forth to-day:—that's Helenus.

CRESSIDA.

Can Helenus fight, uncle?

PANDARUS.

Helenus! no; yes, he'll fight indifferent well.—I marvel where Troilus is.—Hark! do you not hear the people cry 'Troilus'?—Helenus is a priest.

CRESSIDA.

What sneaking fellow comes yonder?

TROILUS *passes.*

PANDARUS.

Where? yonder? that's Deiphobus': tis Troilus! there's a man, niece! Hem! Brave Troilus! the prince of chivalry!

CRESSIDA.

Peace, for shame, peace!

PANDARUS.

Mark him; note him:—O brave Troilus!—look well upon him, niece: look you how his sword is bloodied, and his helm more hackt than Hector's; and how he looks, and how he goes!—O admirable youth! he ne'er saw three-and-twenty.—Go thy way, Troilus, go thy way!—Had I a sister were a grace, or a daughter a goddess, he should take his choice. O admirable man! Paris?—Paris is dirt to him; and, I warrant, Helen, to change, would give an eye to boot.

CRESSIDA.

Here come more.

COMMON SOLDIERS *pass.*

PANDARUS.

Asses, fools, dolts! chaff and bran, chaff and bran! porridge after meat!—I could live and die i'th' eyes of Troilus.—Ne'er look, ne'er look; the eagles are gone: crows and daws, crows and daws!—I had rather be such a man as Troilus than Agamemnon and all Greece.

CRESSIDA.

There is among the Greeks Achilles,—a better man than Troilus.

PANDARUS.

Achilles! a drayman, a porter, a very camel.

CRESSIDA.

Well, well.

PANDARUS.

Well, well!—Why, have you any discretion? have you any eyes? do you know what a man is? Is not birth, beauty, good shape, discourse, manhood, learning, gentleness, virtue, youth, liberality, and such like, the spice and salt that season a man?

CRESSIDA.

Ay, a minced man: and then to be baked with no date in the pie,—for then the man's date's out.

PANDARUS.

You are such a woman! one knows not at what ward you lie.

CRESSIDA.

Upon my back, to defend my belly; upon my wit, to defend my wiles; upon my secrecy, to defend mine honesty; my mask, to defend my beauty;

and you, to defend all these: and at all these wards I lie, at a thousand watches.

PANDARUS.

Say one of your watches.

CRESSIDA.

Nay, I'll watch you for that; and that's one of the chiefest of them too: if I cannot ward what I would not have hit, I can watch you for telling how I took the blow; unless it swell past hiding, and then it's past watching.

PANDARUS.

You are such another!

Enter TROILUS' BOY.

BOY.

Sir, my lord would instantly speak with you.

PANDARUS.

Where?

BOY.

At your own house; there he unarms him.

PANDARUS.

Good boy, tell him I come. [*Exit* BOY.] I doubt he be hurt.—Fare ye well, good niece.

CRESSIDA.

Adieu, uncle.

PANDARUS.

I'll be with you, niece, by and by.

CRESSIDA.

To bring, uncle.

PANDARUS.

Ay, a token from Troilus.

CRESSIDA.

By the same token—you are a bawd.

[*Exit* PANDARUS.

Words, vows, gifts, tears, and love's full sacrifice,
He offers in another's enterprise:
But more in Troilus thousand-fold I see
Than in the glass of Pandar's praise may be;
Yet hold I off. Women are angels, wooing:
Things won are done: joy's soul lies in the doing:
That she beloved knows naught that knows not this,—
Men prize the thing ungain'd more than it is:
That she was never yet that ever knew
Love got so sweet as when desire did sue:
Therefore this maxim out of love, I teach,—
Achievement is command; ungain'd, beseech:
Then, though my heart's content firm love doth bear,
Nothing of that shall from mine eyes appear.

[*Exeunt.*

SCENE III.

The Grecian camp. Before AGAMEMNON'S *tent.*

Sennet. Enter AGAMEMNON, NESTOR, ULYSSES, MENELAUS, *with others.*

AGAMEMNON.

PRINCES,
What grief hath set the jaundice on your cheeks?
The ample proposition that hope makes
In all designs begun on earth below
Fails in the promised largeness: checks and disasters
Grow in the veins of actions highest rear'd;
As knots, by the conflux of meeting sap,
Infect the sound pine, and divert his grain
Tortive and errant from his course of growth.
Nor, princes, is it matter new to us,
That we come short of our suppose so far,
That, after seven years' siege, yet Troy walls stand;
Sith every action that hath gone before,
Whereof we have record, trial did draw
Bias and thwart, not answering the aim,
And that unbodied figure of the thought
That gave't surmised shape. Why, then, you princes,
Do you with cheeks abasht behold our works,
And call them shames, which are, indeed, naught else
But the protractive trials of great Jove
To find persistive constancy in men?
The fineness of which metal is not found
In fortune's love; for then the bold and coward,
The wise and fool, the artist and unread,
The hard and soft, seem all affined and kin:
But, in the wind and tempest of her frown,
Distinction, with a broad and powerful fan,
Puffing at all, winnows the light away;
And what hath mass or matter, by itself
Lies rich in virtue and unmingled.

NESTOR.

With due observance of thy godlike seat,
Great Agamemnon, Nestor shall apply
Thy latest words. In the reproof of chance
Lies the true proof of men: the sea being smooth,
How many shallow bauble boats dare sail
Upon her patient breast, making their way
With those of nobler bulk!
But let the ruffian Boreas once enrage
The gentle Thetis, and, anon, behold
The strong-ribb'd bark through liquid mountains cut,
Bounding between the two moist elements,
Like Perseus' horse: where's then the saucy boat,
Whose weak untimber'd sides but even now
Co-rivall'd greatness? either to harbour fled,
Or made a toast for Neptune. Even so
Doth valour's show and valour's worth divide
In storms of fortune: for in her ray and brightness
The herd hath more annoyance by the breese
Than by the tiger; but when the splitting wind
Makes flexible the knees of knotted oaks,
And flies fled under shade, why, then the thing of courage,
As roused with rage, with rage doth sympathize,
And with an accent tuned in selfsame key
Returns to chiding fortune.

ULYSSES.

Agamemnon,—
Thou great commander, nerve and bone of Greece,
Heart of our numbers, soul and only spirit,
In whom the tempers and the minds of all
Should be shut up,—hear what Ulysses speaks.
Besides the applause and approbation
The which—[*to* AGAMEMNON] most mighty for thy place and sway,—
[*to* NESTOR] And thou most reverend for thy stretcht-out life—

I give to both your speeches,—which were such
As Agamemnon and the hand of Greece
Should hold up high in brass; and such again
As venerable Nestor, hatcht in silver,
Should with a bond of air—strong as the axletree
On which heaven rides—knit all the Greekish ears
To his experienced tongue,—yet let it please
both,
Though great and wise, to hear Ulysses speak.

AGAMEMNON.

Speak, Prince of Ithaca; and be't of less expect
That matter needless, of importless burden,
Divide thy lips, than we are confident,
When rank Thersites opes his mastic jaws,
We shall hear music, wit, and oracle.

ULYSSES.

Troy, yet upon his basis, had been down,
And the great Hector's sword had lackt a master,
But for these instances.
The specialty of rule hath been neglected:
And, look, how many Grecian tents do stand
Hollow upon this plain, so many hollow factions.
When that the general is not like the hive,
To whom the foragers shall all repair,
What honey is expected? Degree being vizarded,
Th'unworthiest shows as fairly in the mask.
The heavens themselves, the planets, and this
centre,
Observe degree, priority, and place,
Insisture, course, proportion, season, form,
Office, and custom, in all line of order:
And therefore is the glorious planet Sol
In noble eminence enthroned and sphered
Amidst the other; whose med'cinable eye
Corrects the ill aspects of planets evil,
And posts, like the commandment of a king,
Sans check, to good and bad: but when the
planets,
In evil mixture, to disorder wander,
What plagues, and what portents, what mutiny,
What raging of the sea, shaking of earth,
Commotion in the winds, frights, changes, hor-
rors,
Divert and crack, rend and deracinate
The unity and married calm of states
Quite from their fixure! O, when degree is
shaked,
Which is the ladder to all high designs,
The enterprise is sick! How could communities,
Degrees in schools, and brotherhoods in cities,
Peaceful commerce from dividable shores,
The primogenity and due of birth,
Prerogative of age, crowns, sceptres, laurels,
But by degree, stand in authentic place?
Take but degree away, untune that string,
And, hark, what discord follows! each thing meets
In mere oppugnancy: the bounded waters
Should lift their bosoms higher than the shores,
And make a sop of all this solid globe:
Strength should be lord of imbecility,
And the rude son should strike his father dead:
Force should be right; or rather, right and
wrong—
Between whose endless jar justice resides—
Should lose their names, and so should justice
too.
Then every thing includes itself in power,
Power into will, will into appetite;
And appetite, an universal wolf,
So doubly seconded with will and power,
Must make perforce an universal prey,
And last eat up himself. Great Agamemnon,
This chaos, when degree is suffocate,
Follows the choking.
And this neglection of degree it is
That by a pace goes backward, with a purpose
It hath to climb. The general's disdain'd
By him one step below; he, by the next;
That next, by him beneath: so every step,
Exampled by the first pace that is sick
Of his superior, grows to an envious fever
Of pale and bloodless emulation:
And 'tis this fever that keeps Troy on foot,
Not her own sinews. To end a tale of length,
Troy in our weakness stands, not in her strength.

NESTOR.

Mose wisely hath Ulysses here discover'd
The fever whereof all our power is sick.

AGAMEMNON.

The nature of the sickness found, Ulysses,
What is the remedy?

ULYSSES.

The great Achilles,—whom opinion crowns
The sinew and the forehand of our host,—
Having his ear full of his airy fame,
Grows dainty of his worth, and in his tent
Lies mocking our designs: with him, Patroclus,
Upon a lazy bed, the livelong day
Breaks scurril jests;
And with ridiculous and awkward action—
Which, slanderer, he imitation calls—
He pageants us. Sometime, great Agamemnon,
Thy topless deputation he puts on;
And, like a strutting player,—whose conceit
Lies in his hamstring, and doth think it rich
To hear the wooden dialogue and sound
'Twixt his stretcht footing and the scaffoldage,—
Such to-be-pitied and o'er-wrested seeming
He acts thy greatness in: and when he speaks,
'Tis like a chime a-mending; with terms un-
squared,
Which, from the tongue of roaring Typhon dropt,
Would seem hyperboles. At this fusty stuff
The large Achilles, on his prest bed lolling,
From his deep chest laughs out a loud applause;
Cries, 'Excellent! 'tis Agamemnon just.
Now play me Nestor; hem, and stroke thy beard,
As he being drest to some oration.'
That's done;—as near as the extremest ends
Of parallels; as like as Vulcan and his wife:
Yet god Achilles still cries, 'Excellent!
'Tis Nestor right. Now play him me, Patroclus,
Arming to answer in a night-alarm.'
And then, forsooth, the faint defects of age
Must be the scene of mirth; to cough and spit,
And, with a palsy fumbling on his gorget,
Shake in and out the rivet:—and at this sport
Sir Valour dies; cries, 'O, enough, Patroclus;
Or give me ribs of steel! I shall split all
In pleasure of my spleen.' And in this fashion,
All our abilities, gifts, natures, shapes,
Severals and generals of grace exact,

Achievements, plots, orders, preventions,
Excitements to the field, or speech for truce,
Success or loss, what is or is not, serves
As stuff for these two to make paradoxes.

NESTOR.

And in the imitation of these twain—
Who, as Ulysses says, opinion crowns
With an imperial voice—many are infect.
Ajax is grown self-will'd; and bears his head
In such a rein, in full as proud a pace
As broad Achilles; keeps his tent like him;
Makes factious feasts; rails on our state of war,
Bold as an oracle; and sets Thersites—
A slave whose gall coins slanders like a mint—
To match us in comparisons with dirt,
To weaken and discredit our exposure,
How rank soever rounded in with danger.

ULYSSES.

They tax our policy, and call it cowardice;
Count wisdom as no member of the war;
Forestall prescience, and esteem no act
But that of hand: the still and mental parts,
That do contrive how many hands shall strike,
When fitness calls them on; and know, by measure
Of their observant toil, the enemies' weight,—
Why, this hath not a finger's dignity:
They call this bed-work, mappery, closet-war;
So that the ram that batters down the wall,
For the great swing and rudeness of his poise,
They place before his hand that made the engine,
Or those that with the fineness of their souls
By reason guide his execution.

NESTOR.

Let this be granted, and Achilles' horse
Makes many Thetis' sons. [*Tucket.*

AGAMEMNON.

What trumpet? look, Menelaus.

MENELAUS.

From Troy.

Enter AENEAS.

AGAMEMNON.

What would you 'fore our tent?

AENEAS.

Is this great Agamemnon's tent, I pray you?

AGAMEMNON.

Even this.

AENEAS.

May one, that is a herald and a prince,
Do a fair message to his kingly ears?

AGAMEMNON.

With surety stronger than Achilles' arm
'Fore all the Greekish heads, which with one voice
Call Agamemnon head and general.

AENEAS.

Fair leave and large security. How may
A stranger to those most imperial looks
Know them from eyes of other mortals?

AGAMEMNON.

How?

AENEAS.

Ay;
I ask, that I might waken reverence,
And bid the cheek be ready with a blush
Modest as morning when she coldly eyes
The youthful Phœbus:
Which is that god in office, guiding men?
Which is the high and mighty Agamemnon?

AGAMEMNON.

This Trojan scorns us; or the men of Troy
Are ceremonious courtiers.

AENEAS.

Courtiers as free, as debonair, unarm'd,
As bending angels; that's their fame in peace:
But when they would seem soldiers, they have galls,
Good arms, strong joints, true swords; and, Jove's accord,
Nothing so full of heart. But peace, Aeneas,
Peace, Trojan; lay thy finger on thy lips!
The worthiness of praise distains his worth,
If that the praised himself bring the praise forth:
But what the repining enemy commends,
That breath fame blows; that praise, sole purè, transcends.

AGAMEMNON.

Sir, you of Troy, call you yourself Aeneas?

AENEAS.

Ay, Greek, that is my name.

AGAMEMNON.

What's your affair, I pray you?

AENEAS.

Sir, pardon; 'tis for Agamemnon's ears.

AGAMEMNON.

He hears naught privately that comes from Troy.

AENEAS.

Nor I from Troy come not to whisper him:
I bring a trumpet to awake his ear;
To set his sense on the attentive bent,
And then to speak.

AGAMEMNON.

Speak frankly as the wind;
It is not Agamemnon's sleeping hour:
That thou shalt know, Trojan, he is awake,
He tells thee so himself.

AENEAS.

Trumpet, blow loud,
Send thy brass voice through all these lazy tents;
And every Greek of mettle, let him know,
What Troy means fairly shall be spoke aloud.
[*Trumpet sounds.*
We have, great Agamemnon, here in Troy
A prince call'd Hector,—Priam is his father,—
Who in this dull and long-continued truce
Is rusty grown: he bade me take a trumpet,
And to this purpose speak. Kings, princes, lords!
If there be one among the fair'st of Greece
That holds his honour higher than his ease;
That seeks his praise more than he fears his peril;
That knows his valour, and knows not his fear;
That loves his mistress more than in confession
With truant vows to her own lips he loves,
And dare avow her beauty and her worth
In other arms than hers,—to him this challenge.
Hector, in view of Trojans and of Greeks,
Shall make it good, or do his best to do it,
He hath a lady, wiser, fairer, truer,
Than ever Greek did compass in his arms;
And will to-morrow with his trumpet call
Midway between your tents and walls of Troy,
To rouse a Grecian that is true in love:

If any come, Hector shall honour him;
If none, he'll say in Troy when he retires,
The Grecian dames are sunburnt, and not worth
The splinter of a lance. Even so much.

AGAMEMNON.

This shall be told our lovers, Lord Aeneas;
If none of them have soul in such a kind,
We left them all at home: but we are soldiers;
And may that soldier a mere recreant prove,
That means not, hath not, or is not in love!
If then one is, or hath, or means to be,
That one meets Hector; if none else, I am he.

NESTOR.

Tell him of Nestor, one that was a man
When Hector's grandsire suckt: he is old now;
But if there be not in our Grecian host
One noble man that hath one spark of fire,
To answer for his love, tell him from me,—
I'll hide my silver beard in a gold beaver,
And in my vantbrace put this wither'd brawn;
And, meeting him, will tell him that my lady
Was fairer than his grandam, and as chaste
As may be in the world; his youth in flood,
I'll prove this truth with my three drops of blood.

AENEAS.

Now heavens forbid such scarcity of youth!

ULYSSES.

Amen.

AGAMEMNON.

Fair Lord Aeneas, let me touch your hand;
To our pavilion shall I lead you, sir.
Achilles shall have word of this intent;
So shall each lord of Greece, from tent to tent:
Yourself shall feast with us before you go,
And find the welcome of a noble foe.

[*Exeunt all but* ULYSSES *and* NESTOR.

ULYSSES.

Nestor,—

NESTOR.

What says Ulysses?

ULYSSES.

I have a young conception in my brain;
Be you my time to bring it to some shape.

NESTOR.

What is't?

ULYSSES.

This 'tis:—
Blunt wedges rive hard knots: the seeded pride
That hath to this maturity blown up
In rank Achilles must or now be cropt,
Or, shedding, breed a nursery of like evil,
To overbulk us all.

NESTOR.

Well, and how?

ULYSSES.

This challenge that the gallant Hector sends,
However it is spread in general name,
Relates in purpose only to Achilles.

NESTOR.

The purpose is perspicuous even as substance
Whose grossness little characters sum up:
And, in the publication, make no strain,
But that Achilles, were his brain as barren
As banks of Libya,—though, Apollo knows,
'Tis dry enough,—will, with great speed of judgement,
Ay, with celerity, find Hector's purpose
Pointing on him.

ULYSSES.

And wake him to the answer, think you?

NESTOR.

Yes,
It is most meet: who may you else oppose,
That can from Hector bring his honour off,
If not Achilles? Though't be a sportful combat,
Yet in the trial much opinion dwells;
For here the Trojans taste our dear'st repute
With their finest palate: and trust to me, Ulysses,
Our imputation shall be oddly poised
In this wild action; for the success,
Although particular, shall give a scantling
Of good or bad unto the general;
And in such indexes, although small pricks
To their subsequent volumes, there is seen
The baby figure of the giant mass
Of things to come at large. It is supposed,
He that meets Hector issues from our choice:
And choice, being mutual act of all our souls,
Makes merit her election; and doth boil,
As 'twere from forth us all, a man distill'd
Out of our virtues; who miscarrying,
What heart receives from hence the conquering part,
To steel a strong opinion of themselves?
Which entertain'd, limbs are his instruments,
In no less working than are swords and bows
Directive by the limbs.

ULYSSES.

Give pardon to my speech;—
Therefore 'tis meet Achilles meet not Hector.
Let us, like merchants, show our foulest wares,
And think, perchance, they'll sell; if not,
The lustre of the better yet to show,
Shall show the better. Do not, then, consent
That ever Hector and Achilles meet;
For both our honour and our shame in this
Are dogg'd with two strange followers.

NESTOR.

I see them not with my old eyes: what are they?

ULYSSES.

What glory our Achilles shares from Hector,
Were he not proud, we all should share with him:
But he already is too insolent;
And we were better parch in Afric sun
Than in the pride and salt scorn of his eyes,
Should he scape Hector fair: if he were foil'd,
Why, then we did our main opinion crush
In taint of our best man. No, make a lottery;
And, by device, let blockish Ajax draw
The sort of fight with Hector: among ourselves
Give him allowance as the worthier man;
For that will physic the great Myrmidon
Who broils in loud applause, and make him fall
His crest that prouder than blue Iris bends.
If the dull brainless Ajax come safe off,
We'll dress him up in voices: if he fail,
Yet go we under our opinion still
That we have better men. But, hit or miss,
Our project's life this shape of sense assumes,—
Ajax employ'd plucks down Achilles' plumes.

NESTOR.

Ulysses,
Now I begin to relish thy advice;

And I will give a taste of it forthwith
To Agamemnon: go we to him straight.
Two curs shall tame each other: pride alone
Must tarre the mastiffs on, as 'twere their bone.
[*Exeunt.*

ACT II. SCENE I.

A part of the Grecian camp.

Enter AJAX *and* THERSITES.

AJAX.

THERSITES,—

THERSITES.

Agamemnon,—how if he had boils,—full, all over, generally?—

AJAX.

Thersites,—

THERSITES.

And those boils did run?—Say so,—did not the general run then? were not that a botchy core?—

AJAX.

Dog,—

THERSITES.

Then would come some matter from him; I see none now.

AJAX.

Thou bitch-woif's son, canst thou not hear? Feel, then. [*Strikes him.*

THERSITES.

The plague of Greece upon thee, thou mongrel beef-witted lord!

AJAX.

Speak, then, thou vinewedst leaven, speak: I will beat thee into handsomeness.

THERSITES.

I shall sooner rail thee into wit and holiness: but, I think, thy horse will sooner con an oration than thou learn a prayer without book. Thou canst strike, canst thou? a red murrain o' thy jade's tricks!

AJAX.

Toadstool, learn me the proclamation.

THERSITES.

Dost thou think I have no sense, thou strikest me thus?

AJAX.

The proclamation!

THERSITES.

Thou art proclaim'd a fool, I think.

AJAX.

Do not, porpentine, do not: my fingers itch.

THERSITES.

I would thou didst itch from head to foot, and I had the scratching of thee; I would make thee the loathsom'st scab in Greece. When thou art forth in the incursions, thou strikest as slow as another.

AJAX.

I say, the proclamation!

THERSITES.

Thou grumblest and railest every hour on Achilles; and thou art as full of envy at his greatness as Cerberus is at Proserpina's beauty, ay, that thou bark'st at him.

AJAX.

Mistress Thersites!

THERSITES.

Thou shouldst strike him.

AJAX.

Cobloaf!

THERSITES.

He would pun thee into shivers with his fist, as a sailor breaks a biscuit.

AJAX.

You whoreson cur! [*Beating him.*

THERSITES.

Do, do.

AJAX.

Thou stool for a witch!

THERSITES.

Ay, do, do; thou sodden-witted lord! thou hast no more brain than I have in mine elbows; an assinego may tutor thee: thou scurvy-valiant ass! thou art here but to thrash Trojans; and thou art bought and sold among those of any wit, like a barbarian slave. If thou use to beat me, I will begin at thy heel, and tell what thou art by inches, thou thing of no bowels, thou!

AJAX.

You dog!

THERSITES.

You scurvy lord!

AJAX.

You cur! [*Beating him.*

THERSITES.

Mars his idiot! do, rudeness, do, camel; do, do.

Enter ACHILLES *and* PATROCLUS.

ACHILLES.

Why, how now, Ajax! wherefore do you thus?—
How now, Thersites! what's the matter, man?

THERSITES.

You see him there, do you?

ACHILLES.

Ay, what's the matter?

THERSITES.

Nay, look upon him.

ACHILLES.

So I do: what's the matter?

THERSITES.

Nay, but regard him well.

ACHILLES.

Well! why, so I do.

THERSITES.

But yet you look not well upon him; for, whosoever you take him to be, he is Ajax.

ACHILLES.

I know that, fool.

THERSITES.

Ay, but that fool knows not himself.

AJAX.

Therefore I beat thee.

THERSITES.

Lo, lo, lo, lo, what modicums of wit he utters! his evasions have ears thus long. I have bobb'd his brain more than he has beat my bones: I will buy nine sparrows for a penny, and his *pia mater* is not worth the ninth part of a sparrow. This lord, Achilles, Ajax,—who wears his wit in his belly, and his guts in his head,—I'll tell you what I say of him.

ACHILLES.

What?

THERSITES.
I say, this Ajax—
[AJAX *offers to beat him,* ACHILLES *interposes.*

ACHILLES.
Nay, good Ajax.

THERSITES.
Has not so much wit—

ACHILLES.
Nay, I must hold you.

THERSITES.
As will stop the eye of Helen's needle, for whom he comes to fight.

ACHILLES.
Peace, fool!

THERSITES.
I would have peace and quietness, but the fool will not: he there; that he; look you there.

AJAX.
O thou damn'd cur! I shall—

ACHILLES.
Will you set your wit to a fool's?

THERSITES.
No, I warrant you; for a fool's will shame it.

PATROCLUS.
Good words, Thersites.

ACHILLES.
What's the quarrel?

AJAX.
I bade the vile owl go learn me the tenour of the proclamation, and he rails upon me.

THERSITES.
I serve thee not.

AJAX.
Well, go to, go to.

THERSITES.
I serve here voluntary.

ACHILLES.
Your last service was sufferance, 'twas not voluntary,—no man is beaten voluntary: Ajax was here the voluntary, and you as under an impress.

THERSITES.
E'en so; a great deal of your wit, too, lies in your sinews, or else there be liars. Hector shall have a great catch, if he knock out either of your brains: a' were as good crack a fusty nut with no kernel.

ACHILLES.
What, with me too, Thersites?

THERSITES.
There's Ulysses and old Nestor—whose wit was mouldy ere your grandsires had nails on their toes—yoke you like draught-oxen, and make you plough up the wars.

ACHILLES.
What, what?

THERSITES.
Yes, good sooth: to, Achilles! to, Ajax! to!

AJAX.
I shall cut out your tongue.

THERSITES.
'Tis no matter; I shall speak as much as thou afterwards.

PATROCLUS.
No more words, Thersites; peace!

THERSITES.
I will hold my peace when Achilles' brach bids me, shall I?

ACHILLES.
There's for you, Patroclus.

THERSITES.
I will see you hang'd, like clotpoles, ere I come any more to your tents: I will keep where there is wit stirring, and leave the faction of fools. [*Exit.*

PATROCLUS.
A good riddance.

ACHILLES.
Marry, this, sir, is proclaim'd through all our
host:—
That Hector, by the fifth hour of the sun,
Will, with a trumpet, 'twixt our tents and Troy,
To-morrow morning call some knight to arms
That hath a stomach; and such a one that dare
Maintain—I know not what; 'tis trash. Farewell.

AJAX.
Farewell. Who shall answer him?

ACHILLES.
I know not,—'tis put to lottery; otherwise
He knew his man.
[*Exeunt* ACHILLES *and* PATROCLUS.

AJAX.
O, meaning you.—I will go learn more of it.
[*Exit.*

SCENE II.

Troy. PRIAM'S *palace.*

Enter PRIAM, HECTOR, TROILUS, PARIS, *and* HELENUS.

PRIAM.
After so many hours, lives, speeches spent,
Thus once again says Nestor from the
Greeks:—
'Deliver Helen, and all damage else—
As honour, loss of time, travail, expense,
Wounds, friends, and what else dear that is con-
sumed
In hot digestion of this cormorant war—
Shall be struck off:'—Hector, what say you to't?

HECTOR.
Though no man lesser fears the Greeks than I
As far as toucheth my particular,
Yet, dread Priam,
There is no lady of more softer bowels,
More spongy to suck in the sense of fear,
More ready to cry out 'Who knows what follows?'
Than Hector is: the wound of peace is surety,
Surety secure; but modest doubt is call'd
The beacon of the wise, the tent that searches
To th'bottom of the worst. Let Helen go:
Since the first sword was drawn about this ques-
tion,
Every tithe soul, 'mongst many thousand dismes,
Hath been as dear as Helen,—I mean, of ours:
If we have lost so many tenths of ours,
To guard a thing not ours nor worth to us,
Had it our name, the value of one ten,—
What merit's in that reason which denies
The yielding of her up?

TROILUS.
Fie, fie, my brother!
Weigh you the worth and honour of a king,
So great as our dread father, in a scale
Of common ounces? will you with counters sum

The past-proportion of his infinite?
And buckle in a waist most fathomless
With spans and inches so diminutive
As fears and reasons? fie, for godly shame!

HELENUS.

No marvel, though you bite so sharp at reasons,
You are so empty of them. Should not our father
Bear the great sway of his affairs with reasons,
Because your speech hath none that tells him so?

TROILUS.

You are for dreams and slumbers, brother priest;
You fur your gloves with reason. Here are your reasons:
You know an enemy intends you harm;
You know a sword employ'd is perilous,
And reason flies the object of all harm:
Who marvels, then, when Helenus beholds
A Grecian and his sword, if he do set
The very wings of reason to his heels,
And fly like chidden Mercury from Jove,
Or like a star disorb'd? Nay, if we talk of reason,
Let's shut our gates, and sleep: manhood and honour
Should have hare-hearts, would they but fat their thoughts
With this cramm'd reason: reason and respect
Make livers pale, and lustihood deject.

HECTOR.

Brother, she is not worth what she doth cost
The holding.

TROILUS.

What is aught, but as 'tis valued?

HECTOR.

But value dwells not in particular will;
It holds his estimate and dignity
As well therein 'tis precious of itself
As in the prizer: 'tis mad idolatry
To make the service greater than the god;
And the will dotes, that is attributive
To what infectiously itself affects,
Without some image of th'affected merit.

TROILUS.

I take to-day a wife, and my election
Is led on in the conduct of my will;
My will enkindled by mine eyes and ears,
Two traded pilots 'twixt the dangerous shores
Of will and judgement: how may I avoid,
Although my will distaste what it elected,
The wife I chose? there can be no evasion
To blench from this, and to stand firm by honour:
We turn not back the silks upon the merchant
When we have soil'd them; nor the remainder viands
We do not throw in unrespective sieve
Because we now are full. It was thought meet
Paris should do some vengeance on the Greeks:
Your breath of full consent bellied his sails;
The seas and winds, old wranglers, took a truce,
And did him service: he toucht the ports desired;
And, for an old aunt whom the Greeks held captive,
He brought a Grecian queen, whose youth and freshness
Wrinkles Apollo's, and makes stale the morning.
Why keep we her? the Grecians keep our aunt:
Is she worth keeping? why, she is a pearl,
Whose price hath launcht above a thousand ships,
And turn'd crown'd kings to merchants.
If you'll avouch 'twas wisdom Paris went,—
As you must needs, for you all cried, 'Go, go;'
If you'll confess he brought home noble prize,—
As you must needs, for you all clapt your hands,
And cried, 'Inestimable!'—why do you now
The issue of your proper wisdoms rate,
And do a deed that fortune never did,—
Beggar the estimation which you prized
Richer than sea and land? O, theft most base,
That we have stoln what we do fear to keep!
But, thieves, unworthy of a thing so stoln,
That in their country did them that disgrace
We fear to warrant in our native place!

CASSANDRA [*within*].

Cry, Trojans, cry!

PRIAM.

What noise? what shriek is this?

TROILUS.

'Tis our mad sister, I do know her voice.

CASSANDRA [*within*].

Cry, Trojans!

HECTOR.

It is Cassandra.

Enter CASSANDRA, *raving, with her hair about her ears.*

CASSANDRA.

Cry, Trojans, cry! lend me ten thousand eyes,
And I will fill them with prophetic tears.

HECTOR.

Peace, sister, peace!

CASSANDRA.

Virgins and boys, mid-age and wrinkled eld,
Soft infancy, that nothing canst but cry,
Add to my clamours! let us pay betimes
A moiety of that mass of moan to come.
Cry, Trojans, cry! practise your eyes with tears!
Troy must not be, nor goodly Ilion stand;
Our firebrand brother, Paris, burns us all.
Cry, Trojans, cry! a Helen and a woe!
Cry, cry! Troy burns, or else let Helen go. [*Exit.*

HECTOR.

Now, youthful Troilus, do not these high strains
Of divination in our sister work
Some touches of remorse? or is your blood
So madly hot, that no discourse of reason,
Nor fear of bad success in a bad cause,
Can qualify the same?

TROILUS.

Why, brother Hector,
We may not think the justness of each act
Such and no other than event doth form it;
Nor once deject the courage of our minds,
Because Cassandra's mad: her brain-sick raptures
Cannot distaste the goodness of a quarrel
Which hath our several honours all engaged
To make it gracious. For my private part,
I am no more toucht than all Priam's sons:
And Jove forbid there should be done amongst us
Such things as might offend the weakest spleen
To fight for and maintain!

PARIS.

Else might the world convince of levity
As well my undertakings as your counsels:

But I attest the gods, your full consent
Gave wings to my propension, and cut off
All fears attending on so dire a project.
For what, alas, can these my single arms?
What propugnation is in one man's valour,
To stand the push and enmity of those
This quarrel would excite? Yet, I protest,
Were I alone to pass the difficulties,
And had as ample power as I have will,
Paris should ne'er retract what he hath done,
Nor faint in the pursuit.

PRIAM.

Paris, you speak
Like one besotted on your sweet delights:
You have the honey still, but these the gall;
So to be valiant is no praise at all.

PARIS.

Sir, I propose not merely to myself
The pleasures such a beauty brings with it;
But I would have the soil of her fair rape
Wiped off, in honourable keeping her.
What treason were it to the ransackt queen,
Disgrace to your great worths, and shame to me,
Now to deliver her possession up
On terms of base compulsion! Can it be
That so degenerate a strain as this
Should once set footing in your generous bosoms?
There's not the meanest spirit on our party
Without a heart to dare, or sword to draw,
When Helen is defended; nor none so noble
Whose life were ill bestow'd, or death unfamed,
Where Helen is the subject: then, I say,
Well may we fight for her, whom, we know well,
The world's large spaces cannot parallel.

HECTOR.

Paris and Troilus, you have both said well;
And on the cause and question now in hand
Have glozed, but superficially; not much
Unlike young men, whom Aristotle thought
Unfit to hear moral philosophy:
The reasons you allege do more conduce
To the hot passion of distemper'd blood
Than to make up a free determination
'Twixt right and wrong; for pleasure and revenge
Have ears more deaf than adders to the voice
Of any true decision. Nature craves
All dues be render'd to their owners: now,
What nearer debt in all humanity
Than wife is to the husband? If this law
Of nature be corrupted through affection,
And that great minds, of partial indulgence
To their benumbed wills, resist the same,
There is a law in each well-order'd nation
To curb those raging appetites that are
Most disobedient and refractory.
If Helen, then, be wife to Sparta's king,—
As it is known she is,—these moral laws
Of nature and of nations speak aloud
To have her back return'd: thus to persist
In doing wrong extenuates not wrong,
But makes it much more heavy. Hector's opinion
Is this, in way of truth: yet, ne'ertheless,
My spritely brethren, I propend to you
In resolution to keep Helen still;
For 'tis a cause that hath no mean dependance
Upon our joint and several dignities.

TROILUS.

Why, there you toucht the life of our design:
Were it not glory that we more affected
Than the performance of our heaving spleens,
I would not wish a drop of Trojan blood
Spent more in her defence. But, worthy Hector,
She is a theme of honour and renown;
A spur to valiant and magnanimous deeds;
Whose present courage may beat down our foes,
And fame in time to come canonize us:
For, I presume, brave Hector would not lose
So rich advantage of a promised glory,
As smiles upon the forehead of this action,
For the wide world's revenue.

HECTOR.

I am yours,
You valiant offspring of great Priamus.—
I have a roisting challenge sent amongst
The dull and factious nobles of the Greeks
Will strike amazement to their drowsy spirits:
I was advertised their great general slept,
Whilst emulation in the army crept:
This, I presume, will wake him. [*Exeunt.*

SCENE III.

The Grecian camp. Before ACHILLES' *tent.*

Enter THERSITES.

THERSITES.

HOW now, Thersites! what, lost in the labyrinth of thy fury! Shall the elephant Ajax carry it thus? he beats me, and I rail at him: O, worthy satisfaction! would it were otherwise; that I could beat him, whilst he rail'd at me: 'sfoot, I'll learn to conjure and raise devils, but I'll see some issue of my spiteful execrations. Then there's Achilles,—a rare enginer. If Troy be not taken till these two undermine it, the walls will stand till they fall of themselves. O thou great thunder-darter of Olympus, forget that thou art Jove, the king of gods; and, Mercury, lose all the serpentine craft of thy caduceus; if ye take not that little little less-than-little wit from them that they have! which short-arm'd ignorance itself knows is so abundant scarce, it will not in circumvention deliver a fly from a spider, without drawing their massy irons and cutting the web. After this, the vengeance on the whole camp! or, rather, the Neapolitan bone-ache! for that, methinks, is the curse dependant on those that war for a placket. I have said my prayers; and devil Envy say Amen.—What, ho! my Lord Achilles!

Enter PATROCLUS.

PATROCLUS.

Who's there? Thersites! Good Thersites, come in and rail.

THERSITES.

If I could ha' remember'd a gilt counterfeit, thou wouldst not have slipt out of my contemplation: but it is no matter; thyself upon thyself! The common curse of mankind, folly and ignorance, be thine in great revenue! heaven bless thee from a tutor, and discipline come not near thee! Let thy blood be thy direction till thy death! then if she that lays thee out says thou art a fair corse, I'll be sworn and sworn upon't she never shrouded any but lazars. Amen.—Where's Achilles?

PATROCLUS.

What, art thou devout? wast thou in prayer?

THERSITES.

Ay; the heavens hear me!

Enter ACHILLES.

ACHILLES.

Who's there?

PATROCLUS.

Thersites, my lord.

ACHILLES.

Where, where?—Art thou come? why, my cheese, my digestion, why hast thou not served thyself in to my table so many meals? Come,—what's Agamemnon?

THERSITES.

Thy commander, Achilles.—Then tell me, Patroclus, what's Achilles?

PATROCLUS.

Thy lord, Thersites: then tell me, I pray thee, what's thyself?

THERSITES.

Thy knower, Patroclus: then tell me, Patroclus, what art thou?

PATROCLUS.

Thou mayst tell that know'st.

ACHILLES.

O, tell, tell.

THERSITES.

I'll decline the whole question. Agamemnon commands Achilles; Achilles is my lord; I am Patroclus' knower; and Patroclus is a fool.

PATROCLUS.

You rascal!

THERSITES.

Peace, fool! I have not done.

ACHILLES.

He is a privileged man.—Proceed, Thersites.

THERSITES.

Agamemnon is a fool; Achilles is a fool; Thersites is a fool; and, as aforesaid, Patroclus is a fool.

ACHILLES.

Derive this; come.

THERSITES.

Agamemnon is a fool to offer to command Achilles; Achilles is a fool to be commanded of Agamemnon; Thersites is a fool to serve such a fool; and Patroclus is a fool positive.

PATROCLUS.

Why am I a fool?

THERSITES.

Make that demand to the Creator. It suffices me thou art.—Look you, who comes here?

ACHILLES.

Patroclus, I'll speak with nobody.—Come in with me, Thersites. [*Exit.*

THERSITES.

Here is such patchery, such juggling, and such knavery! all the argument is a cuckold and a whore; a good quarrel to draw emulous factions and bleed to death upon. Now, the dry serpigo on the subject! and war and lechery confound all! [*Exit.*

Enter AGAMEMNON, ULYSSES, NESTOR, DIOMEDES, *and* AJAX.

AGAMEMNON.

Where is Achilles?

PATROCLUS.

Within his tent: but ill-disposed, my lord.

AGAMEMNON.

Let it be known to him that we are here.
He shent our messengers; and we lay by
Our appertainments, visiting of him:
Let him be told so; lest perchance he think
We dare not move the question of our place,
Or know not what we are.

PATROCLUS.

I shall say so to him. [*Exit.*

ULYSSES.

We saw him at the opening of his tent:
He is not sick.

AJAX.

Yes, lion-sick, sick of proud heart: you may call it melancholy, if you will favour the man; but, by my head, 'tis pride: but why, why? let him show us the cause.—A word, my lord.

[*Takes* AGAMEMNON *aside.*

NESTOR.

What moves Ajax thus to bay at him?

ULYSSES.

Achilles hath inveigled his fool from him.

NESTOR.

Who, Thersites?

ULYSSES.

He.

NESTOR.

Then will Ajax lack matter, if he have lost his argument.

ULYSSES.

No, you see, he is his argument that has his argument,—Achilles.

NESTOR.

All the better; their fraction is more our wish than their faction: but it was a strong composure a fool could disunite.

ULYSSES.

The amity that wisdom knits not, folly may easily untie.—Here comes Patroclus.

NESTOR.

No Achilles with him.

ULYSSES.

The elephant hath joints, but none for courtesy: his legs are legs for necessity, not for flexure.

Enter PATROCLUS.

PATROCLUS.

Achilles bids me say, he is much sorry,
If any thing more than your sport and pleasure
Did move your greatness and this noble state
To call upon him; he hopes it is no other
But for your health and your digestion sake,—
An after-dinner's breath.

AGAMEMNON.

Hear you, Patroclus:—
We are too well acquainted with these answers:
But his evasion, wing'd thus swift with scorn,
Cannot outfly our apprehensions.
Much attribute he hath; and much the reason
Why we ascribe it to him: yet all his virtues,
Not virtuously on his own part beheld,

Do in our eyes begin to lose their gloss;
Yea, like fair fruit in an unwholesome dish,
Are like to rot untasted. Go and tell him,
We come to speak with him; and you shall not sin,
If you do say we think him over-proud
And under-honest; in self-assumption greater
Than in the note of judgement; and worthier than himself
Here tend the savage strangeness he puts on,
Disguise the holy strength of their command,
And underwrite in an observing kind
His humorous predominance; yea, watch
His pettish lunes, his ebbs, his flows, as if
The passage and whole carriage of this action
Rode on his tide. Go tell him this; and add,
That if he overhold his price so much,
We'll none of him; but let him, like an engine
Not portable, lie under this report,—
'Bring action hither, this cannot go to war:
A stirring dwarf we do allowance give
Before a sleeping giant:'—tell him so.

PATROCLUS.

I shall; and bring his answer presently. [*Exit.*

AGAMEMNON.

In second voice we'll not be satisfied;
We come to speak with him.—Ulysses, enter you.
[*Exit* ULYSSES.

AJAX.

What is he more than another?

AGAMEMNON.

No more than what he thinks he is.

AJAX.

Is he so much? Do you not think he thinks himself a better man than I am?

AGAMEMNON.

No question.

AJAX.

Will you subscribe his thought, and say he is?

AGAMEMNON.

No, noble Ajax; you are as strong, as valiant, as wise, no less noble, much more gentle, and altogether more tractable.

AJAX.

Why should a man be proud? How doth pride grow? I know not what pride is.

AGAMEMNON.

Your mind is the clearer, Ajax, and your virtues the fairer. He that is proud eats up himself; pride is his own glass, his own trumpet, his own chronicle; and whatever praises itself but in the deed, devours the deed in the praise.

AJAX.

I do hate a proud man, as I hate the engendering of toads.

NESTOR [*aside*].

Yet he loves himself: is't not strange?

Enter ULYSSES.

ULYSSES.

Achilles will not to the field to-morrow.

AGAMEMNON.

What's his excuse?

ULYSSES.

He doth rely on none;
But carries on the stream of his dispose,
Without observance or respect of any,
In will peculiar and in self-admission.

AGAMEMNON.

Why will he not, upon our fair request,
Untent his person, and share the air with us?

ULYSSES.

Things small as nothing, for request's sake only,
He makes important: possest he is with greatness;
And speaks not to himself, but with a pride
That quarrels at self-breath: imagined worth
Holds in his blood such swoln and hot discourse,
That 'twixt his mental and his active parts
Kingdom'd Achilles in commotion rages,
And batters down himself: what should I say?
He is so plaguy proud, that the death-tokens of it
Cry 'No recovery.'

AGAMEMNON.

Let Ajax go to him.—
Dear lord, go you and greet him in his tent:
'Tis said he holds you well; and will be led,
At your request, a little from himself.

ULYSSES.

O Agamemnon, let it not be so!
We'll consecrate the steps that Ajax makes
When they go from Achilles: shall the proud lord,
That bastes his arrogance with his own seam,
And never suffers matter of the world
Enter his thoughts, save such as doth revolve
And ruminate himself,—shall he be worshipt
Of that we hold an idol more than he?
No, this thrice-worthy and right-valiant lord
Must not so stale his palm, nobly acquired;
Nor, by my will, assubjugate his merit,
As amply titled as Achilles is,
By going to Achilles:
That were to enlard his fat-already pride,
And add more coals to Cancer when he burns
With entertaining great Hyperion.
This lord go to him! Jupiter forbid;
And say in thunder, 'Achilles go to him.'

NESTOR [*aside*].

O, this is well; he rubs the vein of him.

DIOMEDES [*aside*].

And how his silence drinks up this applause!

AJAX.

If I go to him, with my armed fist
I'll pash him o'er the face.

AGAMEMNON.

O, no, you shall not go.

AJAX.

An a' be proud with me, I'll pheeze his pride:
Let me go to him.

ULYSSES.

Not for the worth that hangs upon our quarrel.

AJAX.

A paltry, insolent fellow!

NESTOR [*aside*].

How he describes himself!

AJAX.

Can he not be sociable?

ULYSSES [*aside*].

The raven chides blackness.

AJAX.

I'll let his humours blood.

AGAMEMNON [*aside*].

He will be the physician that should be the patient.

AJAX.
An all men were o' my mind,—

ULYSSES [*aside*].
Wit would be out of fashion.

AJAX.
A' should not bear it so, a' should eat swords first: shall pride carry it?

NESTOR [*aside*].
An 'twould, you'ld carry half.

ULYSSES [*aside*].
A' would have ten shares.

AJAX.
I will knead him; I'll make him supple.

NESTOR [*aside*].
He's not yet through warm: force him with praises: pour in, pour in; his ambition is dry.

ULYSSES [*to* AGAMEMNON].
My lord, you feed too much on this dislike.

NESTOR.
Our noble general, do not do so.

DIOMEDES.
You must prepare to fight without Achilles.

ULYSSES.
Why, 'tis this naming of him does him harm.
Here is a man—but 'tis before his face;
I will be silent.

NESTOR.
Wherefore should you so?
He is not emulous, as Achilles is.

ULYSSES.
Know the whole world, he is as valiant.

AJAX.
A whoreson dog, that shall palter thus with us!
Would he were a Trojan!

NESTOR.
What a vice were it in Ajax now,—

ULYSSES.
If he were proud,—

DIOMEDES.
Or covetous of praise,—

ULYSSES.
Ay, or surly borne,—

DIOMEDES.
Or strange, or self-affected!

ULYSSES.
Thank the heavens, lord, thou art of sweet composure;
Praise him that got thee, she that gave thee suck:
Famed be thy tutor, and thy parts of nature
Thrice-famed, beyond all erudition:
But he that disciplined thy arms to fight,
Let Mars divide eternity in twain,
And give him half: and, for thy vigour,
Bull-bearing Milo his addition yield
To sinewy Ajax. I will not praise thy wisdom,
Which, like a bourn, a pale, a shore, confines
Thy spacious and dilated parts: here's Nestor,—
Instructed by the antiquary times,
He must, he is, he cannot but be wise:—
But pardon, father Nestor, were your days
As green as Ajax', and your brain so temper'd,
You should not have the eminence of him,
But be as Ajax.

AJAX.
Shall I call you father?

NESTOR.
Ay, my good son.

DIOMEDES.
Be ruled by him, Lord Ajax.

ULYSSES.
There is no tarrying here; the hart Achilles
Keeps thicket. Please it our great general
To call together all his state of war;
Fresh kings are come to Troy: to-morrow
We must with all our main of power stand fast:
And here's a lord,—come knights from east to west,
And cull their flower, Ajax shall cope the best.

AGAMEMNON.
Go we to council. Let Achilles sleep:
Light boats sail swift, though greater hulks draw deep. [*Exeunt*.

ACT III. SCENE I.

Troy. PRIAM'S *palace.*

Enter PANDARUS *and a* SERVANT.

PANDARUS.
FRIEND, you,—pray you, a word: do not you follow the young Lord Paris?

SERVANT.
Ay, sir, when he goes before me.

PANDARUS.
You depend upon him, I mean?

SERVANT.
Sir, I do depend upon the Lord.

PANDARUS.
You depend upon a noble gentleman; I must needs praise him.

SERVANT.
The Lord be praised!

PANDARUS.
You know me, do you not?

SERVANT.
Faith, sir, superficially.

PANDARUS.
Friend, know me better; I am the Lord Pandarus.

SERVANT.
I hope I shall know your honour better.

PANDARUS.
I do desire it.

SERVANT.
You are in the state of grace.

PANDARUS.
Grace! not so, friend; honour and lordship are my titles. [*Music sounds within.*]—What music is this?

SERVANT.
I do but partly know, sir: it is music in parts.

PANDARUS.
Know you the musicians?

SERVANT.
Wholly, sir.

PANDARUS.
Who play they to?

SERVANT.
To the hearers, sir.

PANDARUS.
At whose pleasure, friend?

SERVANT.
At mine, sir, and theirs that love music.

PANDARUS.
Command, I mean, friend.

SERVANT.
Who shall I command, sir?

PANDARUS.
Friend, we understand not one another: I am too courtly, and thou art too cunning. At whose request do these men play?

SERVANT.
That's to't, indeed, sir: marry, sir, at the request of Paris my lord, who's there in person; with him, the mortal Venus, the heart-blood of beauty, love's invisible soul,—

PANDARUS.
Who, my cousin Cressida?

SERVANT.
No, sir, Helen: could you not find out that by her attributes?

PANDARUS.
It should seem, fellow, that thou hast not seen the Lady Cressida. I come to speak with Paris from the Prince Troilus: I will make a complimental assault upon him, for my business seethes.

SERVANT.
Sodden business! there's a stew'd phrase indeed!

Enter PARIS *and* HELEN, *attended.*

PANDARUS.
Fair be to you, my lord, and to all this fair company! fair desires, in all fair measure, fairly guide them!—especially to you, fair queen! fair thoughts be your fair pillow!

HELEN.
Dear lord, you are full of fair words.

PANDARUS.
You speak your fair pleasure, sweet queen.—Fair prince, here is good broken music.

PARIS.
You have broke it, cousin: and, by my life, you shall make it whole again; you shall piece it out with a piece of your performance.—Nell, he is full of harmony.

PANDARUS.
Truly, lady, no.

HELEN.
O, sir,—

PANDARUS.
Rude, in sooth; in good sooth, very rude.

PARIS.
Well said, my lord! well, you say so in fits.

PANDARUS.
I have business to my lord, dear queen.—My lord, will you vouchsafe me a word?

HELEN.
Nay, this shall not hedge us out: we'll hear you sing, certainly.

PANDARUS.
Well, sweet queen, you are pleasant with me.—But, marry, thus, my lord,—My dear lord, and most esteem'd friend, your brother Troilus,—

HELEN.
My Lord Pandarus; honey-sweet lord,—

PANDARUS.
Go to, sweet queen, go to:—commends himself most affectionately to you,—

HELEN.
You shall not bob us out of our melody: if you do, our melancholy upon your head!

PANDARUS.
Sweet queen, sweet queen; that's a sweet queen, i'faith,—

HELEN.
And to make a sweet lady sad is a sour offence.

Nay, that shall not serve your turn; that shall it not, in truth, la. Nay, I care not for such words; no, no.

PANDARUS.
And, my lord, he desires you, that if the king call for him at supper, you will make his excuse.

HELEN.
My Lord Pandarus,—

PANDARUS.
What says my sweet queen,—my very very sweet queen?

PARIS.
What exploit's in hand? where sups he to-night?

HELEN.
Nay, but, my lord,—

PANDARUS.
What says my sweet queen?—My cousin will fall out with you. You must not know where he sups.

PARIS.
I'll lay my life, with my disposer Cressida.

PANDARUS.
No, no, no such matter; you are wide: come, your disposer is sick.

PARIS.
Well, I'll make excuse.

PANDARUS.
Ay, good my lord. Why should you say Cressida? no, your poor disposer's sick.

PARIS.
I spy.

PANDARUS.
You spy! what do you spy?—Come, give me an instrument.—Now, sweet queen.

HELEN.
Why, this is kindly done.

PANDARUS.
My niece is horribly in love with a thing you have, sweet queen.

HELEN.
She shall have it, my lord, if it be not my lord Paris.

PANDARUS.
He! no, she'll none of him; they two are twain.

HELEN.
Falling in, after falling out, may make them three.

PANDARUS.
Come, come, I'll hear no more of this; I'll sing you a song now.

HELEN.
Ay, ay, prithee now. By my troth, sweet lord, thou hast a fine forehead.

PANDARUS.
Ay, you may, you may.

HELEN.
Let thy song be love: this love will undo us all. O Cupid, Cupid, Cupid!

PANDARUS.
Love! ay, that it shall, i'faith.

PARIS.

Ay, good now, love, love, nothing but love.

PANDARUS.

In good troth, it begins so. [*Sings.*

Love, love, nothing but love, still more!
For, O, love's bow
Shoots buck and doe:
The shaft confounds,
Not that it wounds,
But tickles still the sore.
These lovers cry—Oh! oh! they die!
Yet that which seems the wound to kill
Doth turn oh! oh! to ha! ha! he!
So dying love lives still:
Oh! oh! a while, but ha! ha! ha!
Oh! oh! groans out for ha! ha! ha!
Heigh-ho!

HELEN.

In love, i'faith, to the very tip of the nose.

PARIS.

He eats nothing but doves, love; and that breeds hot blood, and hot blood begets hot thoughts, and hot thoughts beget hot deeds, and hot deeds is love.

PANDARUS.

Is this the generation of love? hot blood, hot thoughts, and hot deeds? Why, they are vipers: is love a generation of vipers?—Sweet lord, who's a-field to-day?

PARIS.

Hector, Deiphobus, Helenus, Antenor, and all the gallantry of Troy: I would fain have arm'd to-day, but my Nell would not have it so. How chance my brother Troilus went not?

HELEN.

He hangs the lip at something:—you know all, Lord Pandarus.

PANDARUS.

Not I, honey-sweet queen.—I long to hear how they sped to-day.—You'll remember your brother's excuse?

PARIS.

To a hair.

PANDARUS.

Farewell, sweet queen.

HELEN.

Commend me to your niece.

PANDARUS.

I will, sweet queen. [*Exit.*

[*Sound a retreat.*

PARIS.

They're come from field: let us to Priam's hall,
To greet the warriors. Sweet Helen, I must woo you
To help unarm our Hector: his stubborn buckles,
With these your white enchanting fingers toucht,
Shall more obey than to the edge of steel
Or force of Greekish sinews; you shall do more
Than all the island kings,—disarm great Hector.

HELEN.

'Twill make us proud to be his servant, Paris;
Yea, what he shall receive of us in duty
Gives us more palm in beauty than we have,
Yea, overshines ourself.

PARIS.

Sweet, above thought I love thee. [*Exeunt.*

SCENE II.

PANDARUS' *orchard.*

Enter PANDARUS *and* TROILUS' BOY, *meeting.*

PANDARUS.

How now! where's thy master? at my cousin Cressida's?

BOY.

No, sir; he stays for you to conduct him thither.

PANDARUS.

O, here he comes.

Enter TROILUS.

How now, how now!

TROILUS.

Sirrah, walk off. [*Exit* BOY.

PANDARUS.

Have you seen my cousin?

TROILUS.

No, Pandarus: I stalk about her door,
Like a strange soul upon the Stygian banks
Staying for waftage. O, be thou my Charon,
And give me swift transportance to those fields
Where I may wallow in the lily-beds
Proposed for the deserver! O gentle Pandarus,
From Cupid's shoulder pluck his painted wings,
And fly with me to Cressid!

PANDARUS.

Walk here i'th'orchard, I'll bring her straight. [*Exit.*

TROILUS.

I am giddy; expectation whirls me round.
Th'imaginary relish is so sweet
That it enchants my sense: what will it be,
When that the watery palate tastes indeed
Love's thrice-repured nectar? death, I fear me;
Swooning destruction; or some joy too fine,
Too subtle-potent, tuned too sharp in sweetness,
For the capacity of my ruder powers:
I fear it much; and I do fear besides,
That I shall lose distinction in my joys;
As doth a battle, when they charge on heaps
The enemy flying.

Enter PANDARUS.

PANDARUS.

She's making her ready, she'll come straight: you must be witty now. She does so blush, and fetches her wind so short, as if she were fray'd with a sprite: I'll fetch her. It is the prettiest villain: she fetches her breath as short as a new-ta'en sparrow. [*Exit.*

TROILUS.

Even such a passion doth embrace my bosom:
My heart beats thicker than a feverous pulse;
And all my powers do their bestowing lose,
Like vassalage at unawares encountering
The eye of majesty.

Enter PANDARUS *with* CRESSIDA.

PANDARUS.

Come, come, what need you blush? shame's a baby.—Here she is now: swear the oaths now to her that you have sworn to me.—What, are you gone again? you must be watcht ere you be made tame, must you? Come your ways, come your ways: an you draw backward, we'll put you i'th' fills. Why do you not speak to her? Come, draw this curtain, and let's see your picture. Alas the day, how loth you are to offend daylight! an 'twere dark, you'ld close sooner. So, so; rub on, and kiss the mistress. How now! a kiss in fee-farm! build there, carpenter; the air is sweet. Nay, you shall fight your hearts out ere I part you. The falcon as the tercel, for all the ducks i'th'river: go to, go to.

TROILUS.

You have bereft me of all words, lady.

PANDARUS.

Words pay no debts, give her deeds: but she'll bereave you o'th'deeds too, if she call your activity in question. What, billing again? Here's —'In witness whereof the parties interchangeably'—Come in, come in: I'll go get a fire. [*Exit.*

CRESSIDA.

Will you walk in, my lord?

TROILUS.

O Cressida, how often have I wisht me thus!

CRESSIDA.

Wisht, my lord!—The gods grant—O my lord!

TROILUS.

What should they grant? what makes this pretty abruption? What too curious dreg espies my sweet lady in the fountain of our love?

CRESSIDA.

More dregs than water, if my fears have eyes.

TROILUS.

Fears make devils of cherubins; they never see truly.

CRESSIDA.

Blind fear, that seeing reason leads, finds safer footing than blind reason stumbling without fear: to fear the worst oft cures the worst.

TROILUS.

O, let my lady apprehend no fear: in all Cupid's pageant there is presented no monster.

CRESSIDA.

Nor nothing monstrous neither?

TROILUS.

Nothing, but our undertakings; when we vow to weep seas, live in fire, eat rocks, tame tigers; thinking it harder for our mistress to devise imposition enough than for us to undergo any difficulty imposed. This is the monstruosity in love, lady,—that the will is infinite, and the execution confined; that the desire is boundless, and the act a slave to limit.

CRESSIDA.

They say, all lovers swear more performance than they are able, and yet reserve an ability that they never perform; vowing more than the perfection of ten, and discharging less than the tenth part of one. They that have the voice of lions and the act of hares, are they not monsters?

TROILUS.

Are there such? such are not we: praise us as we are tasted, allow us as we prove; our head shall go bare till merit crown it: no perfection in reversion shall have a praise in present: we will not name desert before his birth; and, being born, his addition shall be humble. Few words to fair faith: Troilus shall be such to Cressid as what envy can say worst shall be a mock for his truth, and what truth can speak truest not truer than Troilus.

CRESSIDA.

Will you walk in, my lord?

Enter PANDARUS.

PANDARUS.

What, blushing still? have you not done talking yet?

CRESSIDA.

Well, uncle, what folly I commit, I dedicate to you.

PANDARUS.

I thank you for that: if my lord get a boy of you, you'll give him me. Be true to my lord: if he flinch, chide me for it.

TROILUS.

You know now your hostages; your uncle's word and my firm faith.

PANDARUS.

Nay, I'll give my word for her too: our kindred, though they be long ere they are wooed, they are constant being won: they are burs, I can tell you; they'll stick where they are thrown.

CRESSIDA.

Boldness comes to me now, and brings me heart:—
Prince Troilus, I have loved you night and day
For many weary months.

TROILUS.

Why was my Cressid, then, so hard to win?

CRESSIDA.

Hard to seem won: but I was won, my lord,
With the first glance that ever—pardon me—
If I confess much, you will play the tyrant.
I love you now; but not, till now, so much
But I might master it:—in faith, I lie;
My thoughts were like unbridled children, grown
Too headstrong for their mother:—see, we fools!
Why have I blabb'd? who shall be true to us
When we are so unsecret to ourselves?—
But, though I loved you well, I woo'd you not;
And yet, good faith, I wisht myself a man,
Or that we women had men's privilege
Of speaking first. Sweet, bid me hold my tongue;
For, in this rapture, I shall surely speak
The thing I shall repent. See, see, your silence,
Cunning in dumbness, from my weakness draws
My very soul of counsel!—stop my mouth.

TROILUS.

And shall, albeit sweet music issues thence.
[*Kisses her.*

PANDARUS.

Pretty, i'faith.

CRESSIDA.

My lord, I do beseech you, pardon me;
'Twas not my purpose thus to beg a kiss:
I am ashamed;—O heavens! what have I done?
For this time will I take my leave, my lord.

TROILUS.

Your leave, sweet Cressid!

PANDARUS.

Leave! an you take leave till to-morrow morning,—

CRESSIDA.

Pray you, content you.

TROILUS.

What offends you, lady?

CRESSIDA.

Sir, mine own company.

TROILUS.

You cannot shun
Yourself.

CRESSIDA.

Let me go and try:
I have a kind of self resides with you;
But an unkind self, that itself will leave,
To be another's fool. I would be gone:—
Where is my wit? I know not what I speak.

TROILUS.

Well know they what they speak that speak so wisely.

CRESSIDA.

Perchance, my lord, I show'd more craft than love;
And fell so roundly to a large confession,
To angle for your thoughts: but you are wise;
Or else you love not; for to be wise and love
Exceeds man's might; that dwells with gods above.

TROILUS.

O, that I thought it could be in a woman—
As, if it can, I will presume in you—
To feed for aye her lamp and flames of love;
To keep her constancy in plight and youth,
Outliving beauty's outward, with a mind
That doth renew swifter than blood decays!
Or, that persuasion could but thus convince me,—
That my integrity and truth to you
Might be affronted with the match and weight
Of such a winnow'd purity in love;
How were I then uplifted! but, alas!
I am as true as truth's simplicity,
And simpler than the infancy of truth.

CRESSIDA.

In that I'll war with you.

TROILUS.

O virtuous fight,
When right with right wars who shall be most right!
True swains in love shall, in the world to come,
Approve their truths by Troilus: when their rimes,
Full of protest, of oath, and big compare,
Want similes, truth tired with iteration,—
As true as steel, as plantage to the moon,
As sun to day, as turtle to her mate,
As iron to adamant, as earth to th'centre,—
Yet, after all comparisons of truth,
As truth's authentic author to be cited,
'As true as Troilus' shall crown up the verse,
And sanctify the numbers.

CRESSIDA.

Prophet may you be!
If I be false, or swerve a hair from truth,
When time is old and hath forgot itself,
When waterdrops have worn the stones of Troy,
And blind oblivion swallow'd cities up,
And mighty states characterless are grated
To dusty nothing; yet let memory,
From false to false, among false maids in love,
Upbraid my falsehood! when they've said 'as false
As air, as water, wind, or sandy earth,
As fox to lamb, or wolf to heifer's calf,
Pard to the hind, or stepdame to her son,'—
'Yea,' let them say, to stick the heart of falsehood
'As false as Cressid.'

PANDARUS.

Go to, a bargain made: seal it, seal it; I'll be the witness. Here I hold your hand; here my cousin's. If ever you prove false one to another, since I have taken such pains to bring you together, let all pitiful goers-between be call'd to the world's end after my name; call them all Pandars; let all inconstant men be Troiluses, all false women Cressids, and all brokers-between Pandars! say, amen.

TROILUS.

Amen.

CRESSIDA.

Amen.

PANDARUS.

Amen. Whereupon I will show you a chamber with a bed; which bed, because it shall not speak of your pretty encounters, press it to death: away!
And Cupid grant all tongue-tied maidens here
Bed, chamber, Pandar to provide this gear!

[*Exeunt.*

SCENE III.

The Grecian camp.

Flourish. Enter AGAMEMNON, ULYSSES, DIOMEDES, NESTOR, AJAX, MENELAUS, *and* CALCHAS.

CALCHAS.

NOW, princes, for the service I have done you,
Th'advantage of the time prompts me aloud
To call for recompense. Appear it to your mind
That, through the sight I bear in things to love,
I have abandon'd Troy, left my possession,
Incurr'd a traitor's name; exposed myself,
From certain and possest conveniences,
To doubtful fortunes; sequest'ring from me all
That time, acquaintance, custom, and condition,
Made tame and most familiar to my nature;
And here, to do you service, am become
As new into the world, strange, unacquainted:
I do beseech you, as in way of taste,
To give me now a little benefit,
Out of those many register'd in promise,
Which, you say, live to come in my behalf.

AGAMEMNON.

What wouldst thou of us, Trojan? make demand.

CALCHAS.

You have a Trojan prisoner, call'd Antenor,
Yesterday took: Troy holds him very dear.
Oft have you—often have you thanks therefore—
Desired my Cressid in right great exchange,
Whom Troy hath still denied: but this Antenor,
I know, is such a wrest in their affairs,
That their negotiations all must slack,
Wanting his manage; and they will almost
Give us a prince of blood, a son of Priam,
In change of him: let him be sent, great princes,
And he shall buy my daughter; and her presence
Shall quite strike off all service I have done,
In most accepted pay.

AGAMEMNON.

Let Diomedes bear him,
And bring us Cressid hither: Calchas shall have

What he requests of us.—Good Diomed,
Furnish you fairly for this interchange:
Withal, bring word if Hector will to-morrow
Be answer'd in his challenge: Ajax is ready.

DIOMEDES.

This shall I undertake; and 'tis a burden
Which I am proud to bear.

[*Exeunt* DIOMEDES *and* CALCHAS.

Enter ACHILLES *and* PATROCLUS, *before their tent.*

ULYSSES.

Achilles stands i'th'entrance of his tent:—
Please it our general to pass strangely by him,
As if he were forgot; and, princes all,
Lay negligent and loose regard upon him:
I will come last. 'Tis like he'll question me
Why such unplausive eyes are bent on him:
If so, I have derision medicinable,
To use between your strangeness and his pride,
Which his own will shall have desire to drink:
It may do good: pride hath no other glass
To show itself but pride; for supple knees
Feed arrogance, and are the proud man's fees.

AGAMEMNON.

We'll execute your purpose, and put on
A form of strangeness as we pass along:—
So do each lord; and either greet him not,
Or else disdainfully, which shall shake him more
Than if not lookt on. I will lead the way.

ACHILLES.

What, comes the general to speak with me?
You know my mind, I'll fight no more 'gainst Troy.

AGAMEMNON.

What says Achilles? would he aught with us?

NESTOR.

Would you, my lord, aught with the general?

ACHILLES.

No.

NESTOR.

Nothing, my lord.

AGAMEMNON.

The better.

[*Exeunt* AGAMEMNON *and* NESTOR.

ACHILLES.

Good day, good day.

MENELAUS.

How do you? how do you? [*Exit.*

ACHILLES.

What, does the cuckold scorn me?

AJAX.

How now, Patroclus!

ACHILLES.

Good morrow, Ajax.

AJAX.

Ha!

ACHILLES.

Good morrow.

AJAX.

Ay, and good next day too. [*Exit.*

ACHILLES.

What mean these fellows? Know they not Achilles?

PATROCLUS.

They pass by strangely: they were used to bend,
To send their smiles before them to Achilles;
To come as humbly as they use to creep
To holy altars.

ACHILLES.

What, am I poor of late?
'Tis certain, greatness, once faln out with fortune,
Must fall out with men too: what the declined is,
He shall as soon read in the eyes of others
As feel in his own fall; for men, like butterflies,
Show not their mealy wings but to the summer;
And not a man, for being simply man,
Hath any honour, but honour for those honours
That are without him, as place, riches, favour,
Prizes of accident as oft as merit:
Which when they fall, as being slippery standers,
The love that lean'd on them as slippery too,
Do one pluck down another, and together
Die in the fall. But 'tis not so with me:
Fortune and I are friends: I do enjoy
At ample point all that I did possess,
Save these men's looks; who do, methinks, find out
Something not worth in me such rich beholding
As they have often given. Here is Ulysses:
I'll interrupt his reading.—
How now, Ulysses!

ULYSSES.

Now, great Thetis' son!

ACHILLES.

What are you reading?

ULYSSES.

A strange fellow here
Writes me, 'That man—how dearly ever parted,
How much in having, or without or in—
Cannot make boast to have that which he hath,
Nor feels not what he owes, but by reflection;
As when his virtues shining upon others
Heat them, and they retort that heat again
To the first giver.'

ACHILLES.

This is not strange, Ulysses.
The beauty that is borne here in the face
The bearer knows not, but commends itself
To others' eyes: nor doth the eye itself,
That most pure spirit of sense, behold itself,
Not going from itself; but eye to eye opposed
Salutes each other with each other's form:
For speculation turns not to itself,
Till it hath travell'd, and is mirror'd there
Where it may see itself. This is not strange at all.

ULYSSES.

I do not strain at the position,—
It is familiar,—but at the author's drift;
Who, in his circumstance, expressly proves
That no man is the lord of any thing,
Though in and of him there be much consisting,
Till he communicate his parts to others;
Nor doth he of himself know them for aught
Till he behold them formed in th'applause
Where they're extended; who, like an arch, reverb'rates
The voice again; or, like a gate of steel
Fronting the sun, receives and renders back
His figure and his heat. I was much rapt in this;
And apprehended here immediately
The unknown Ajax.
Heavens, what a man is there! a very horse;

That has he knows not what. Nature, what things there are,
Most abject in regard, and dear in use!
What things again most dear in the esteem,
And poor in worth! Now shall we see to-morrow—
An act that very chance doth throw upon him—
Ajax renown'd. O heavens, what some men do,
While some men leave to do!
How some men creep in skittish Fortune's hall,
Whiles others play the idiots in her eyes!
How one man eats into another's pride,
While pride is fasting in his wantonness!
To see these Grecian lords!—why, even already
They clap the lubber Ajax on the shoulder,
As if his foot were on brave Hector's breast,
And great Troy shrieking.

ACHILLES.

I do believe it; for they past by me
As misers do by beggars,—neither gave to me
Good word nor look: what, are my deeds forgot?

ULYSSES.

Time hath, my lord, a wallet at his back,
Wherein he puts alms for oblivion,
A great-sized monster of ingratitudes:
Those scraps are good deeds past; which are devour'd
As fast as they are made, forgot as soon
As done: perseverance, dear my lord,
Keeps honour bright: to have done, is to hang
Quite out of fashion, like a rusty mail
In monumental mockery. Take the instant way;
For honour travels in a strait so narrow,
Where one but goes abreast: keep, then, the path;
For emulation hath a thousand sons,
That one by one pursue: if you give way,
Or hedge aside from the direct forthright,
Like to an enter'd tide, they all rush by,
And leave you hindmost;
Or, like a gallant horse faln in first rank,
Lie there for pavement to the abject rear,
O'er-run and trampled on: then what they do in present,
Though less than yours in past, must o'ertop yours;
For time is like a fashionable host,
That slightly shakes his parting guest by th'hand,
And with his arms outstretcht, as he would fly,
Grasps-in the comer: welcome ever smiles,
And farewell goes out sighing. O, let not virtue seek
Remuneration for the thing it was;
For beauty, wit,
High birth, vigour of bone, desert in service,
Love, friendship, charity, are subjects all
To envious and calumniating time.
One touch of nature makes the whole world kin,—
That all, with one consent, praise new-born gawds,
Though they are made and moulded of things past,
And give to dust, that is a little gilt,
More laud than gilt o'er-dusted.
The present eye praises the present object:
Then marvel not, thou great and complete man,
That all the Greeks begin to worship Ajax;
Since things in motion sooner catch the eye
Than what not stirs. The cry went once on thee,
And still it might, and yet it may again,
If thou wouldst not entomb thyself alive,
And case thy reputation in thy tent;
Whose glorious deeds, but in these fields of late,
Made emulous missions 'mongst the gods themselves,
And drave great Mars to faction.

ACHILLES.

Of this my privacy
I have strong reasons.

ULYSSES.

But 'gainst your privacy
The reasons are more potent and heroical:
'Tis known, Achilles, that you are in love
With one of Priam's daughters.

ACHILLES.

Ha! known!

ULYSSES.

Is that a wonder?
The providence that's in a watchful state
Knows almost every grain of Pluto's gold;
Finds bottom in th'uncomprehensive deeps;
Keeps place with thought, and almost, like the gods,
Does thoughts unveil in their dumb cradles.
There is a mystery—with whom relation
Durst never meddle—in the soul of state;
Which hath an operation more divine
Than breath or pen can give expressure to:
All the commerce that you have had with Troy
As perfectly is ours as yours, my lord;
And better would it fit Achilles much
To throw down Hector than Polyxena:
But it must grieve young Pyrrhus now at home,
When fame shall in our islands sound her trump,
And all the Greekish girls shall tripping sing,
'Great Hector's sister did Achilles win;
But our great Ajax bravely beat down him.'
Farewell, my lord: I as your lover speak;
The fool slides o'er the ice that you should break.
[*Exit.*

PATROCLUS.

To this effect, Achilles, have I moved you:
A woman impudent and mannish grown
Is not more loath'd than an effeminate man
In time of action. I stand condemn'd for this;
They think, my little stomach to the war,
And your great love to me, restrains you thus:
Sweet, rouse yourself; and the weak wanton Cupid
Shall from your neck unloose his amorous fold,
And, like a dew-drop from the lion's mane,
Be shook to air.

ACHILLES.

Shall Ajax fight with Hector?

PATROCLUS.

Ay, and perhaps receive much honour by him.

ACHILLES.

I see my reputation is at stake;
My fame is shrewdly gored.

PATROCLUS.

O, then, beware;
Those wounds heal ill that men do give themselves:
Omission to do what is necessary
Seals a commission to a blank of danger;

And danger, like an ague, subtly taints
Even then when we sit idly in the sun.

ACHILLES.

Go call Thersites hither, sweet Patroclus:
I'll send the fool to Ajax, and desire him
T'invite the Trojan lords after the combat
To see us here unarm'd: I have a woman's longing,
An appetite that I am sick withal,
To see great Hector in his weeds of peace;
To talk with him, and to behold his visage,
Even to my full of view.—A labour saved!

Enter THERSITES.

THERSITES.

A wonder!

ACHILLES.

What?

THERSITES.

Ajax goes up and down the field, asking for himself.

ACHILLES.

How so?

THERSITES.

He must fight singly to-morrow with Hector; and is so prophetically proud of an heroical cudgelling that he raves in saying nothing.

ACHILLES.

How can that be?

THERSITES.

Why, he stalks up and down like a peacock,—a stride and a stand: ruminates like an hostess that hath no arithmetic but her brain to set down her reckoning: bites his lip with a politic regard, as who should say 'There were wit in this head, an 'twould out;' and so there is; but it lies as coldly in him as fire in a flint, which will not show without knocking. The man's undone for ever; for if Hector break not his neck i'th'combat, he'll break't himself in vainglory. He knows not me: I said, 'Good morrow, Ajax;' and he replies, 'Thanks, Agamemnon.' What think you of this man, that takes me for the general? He's grown a very land-fish, languageless, a monster. A plague of opinion! a man may wear it on both sides, like a leather jerkin.

ACHILLES.

Thou must be my ambassador to him, Thersites.

THERSITES.

Who, I? why, he'll answer nobody; he professes not answering: speaking is for beggars; he wears his tongue in's arms. I will put on his presence: let Patroclus make demands to me, you shall see the pageant of Ajax.

ACHILLES.

To him, Patroclus: tell him,—I humbly desire the valiant Ajax to invite the most valorous Hector to come unarm'd to my tent; and to procure safe-conduct for his person of the magnanimous and most illustrious six-or-seven-times-honour'd captain-general of the Grecian army, Agamemnon, et cetera. Do this.

PATROCLUS.

Jove bless great Ajax!

THERSITES.

Hum!

PATROCLUS.

I come from the worthy Achilles,—

THERSITES.

Ha!

PATROCLUS.

Who most humbly desires you to invite Hector to his tent,—

THERSITES.

Hum!

PATROCLUS.

And to procure safe-conduct from Agamemnon.

THERSITES.

Agamemnon!

PATROCLUS.

Ay, my lord.

THERSITES.

Ha!

PATROCLUS.

What say you to't?

THERSITES.

God b'wi'you, with all my heart.

PATROCLUS.

Your answer, sir.

THERSITES.

If to-morrow be a fair day, by eleven o'clock it will go one way or other: howsoever, he shall pay for me ere he has me.

PATROCLUS.

Your answer, sir.

THERSITES.

Fare you well, with all my heart.

ACHILLES.

Why, but he is not in this tune, is he?

THERSITES.

No, but he's out o' tune thus. What music will be in him when Hector has knockt out his brains, I know not; but, I am sure, none,—unless the fiddler Apollo get his sinews to make catlings on.

ACHILLES.

Come, thou shalt bear a letter to him straight.

THERSITES.

Let me bear another to his horse; for that's the more capable creature.

ACHILLES.

My mind is troubled, like a fountain stirr'd;
And I myself see not the bottom of it.

[*Exeunt* ACHILLES *and* PATROCLUS.

THERSITES.

Would the fountain of your mind were clear again, that I might water an ass at it! I had rather be a tick in a sheep than such a valiant ignorance.

[*Exit.*

ACT IV. SCENE I.

Troy. A street.

Enter, at one door, AENEAS, *and* SERVANT *with a torch; at another,* PARIS, DEIPHOBUS, ANTENOR, DIOMEDES *the Grecian, and others, with torches.*

PARIS.

SEE, ho! who is that there?

DEIPHOBUS.

It is the Lord Aeneas.

AENEAS.

Is the prince there in person?—
Had I so good occasion to lie long

As you, Prince Paris, nothing but heavenly business
Should rob my bed-mate of my company.

DIOMEDES.

That's my mind too.—Good morrow, Lord Aeneas.

PARIS.

A valiant Greek, Aeneas,—take his hand,—
Witness the process of your speech, wherein
You told how Diomed, a whole week by days,
Did haunt you in the field.

AENEAS.

Health to you, valiant sir,
During all question of the gentle truce;
But when I meet you arm'd, as black defiance
As heart can think or courage execute.

DIOMEDES.

The one and other Diomed embraces.
Our bloods are now in calm; and, so long, health;
But when contention and occasion meet,
By Jove, I'll play the hunter for thy life
With all my force, pursuit, and policy.

AENEAS.

And thou shalt hunt a lion, that will fly
With his face backward.—In humane gentleness,
Welcome to Troy! now, by Anchises' life,
Welcome, indeed! By Venus' hand I swear
No man alive can love in such a sort
The thing he means to kill more excellently.

DIOMEDES.

We sympathize:—Jove, let Aeneas live,
If to my sword his fate be not the glory,
A thousand complete courses of the sun!
But, in mine emulous honour, let him die,
With every joint a wound, and that to-morrow!

AENEAS.

We know each other well.

DIOMEDES.

We do; and long to know each other worse.

PARIS.

This is the most despiteful gentle greeting,
The noblest hateful love, that e'er I heard of.—
What business, lord, so early?

AENEAS.

I was sent for to the king; but why, I know not.

PARIS.

His purpose meets you: 'twas to bring this Greek
To Calchas' house; and there to render him,
For the enfreed Antenor, the fair Cressid:
Let's have your company; or, if you please,
Haste there before us: I constantly do think—
Or, rather, call my thought a certain knowledge—
My brother Troilus lodges there to-night:
Rouse him, and give him note of our approach,
With the whole quality wherefore: I fear
We shall be much unwelcome.

AENEAS.

That I assure you:
Troilus had rather Troy were borne to Greece
Than Cressid borne from Troy.

PARIS.

There is no help;
The bitter disposition of the time
Will have it so. On, lord; we'll follow you.

AENEAS.

Good morrow, all. [*Exit with* SERVANT.

PARIS.

And tell me, noble Diomed,—faith, tell me true,
Even in the soul of sound good-fellowship,—
Who, in your thoughts, merits fair Helen best,
Myself or Menelaus?

DIOMEDES.

Both alike:
He merits well to have her, that doth seek her,
Not making any scruple of her soilure,
With such a hell of pain and world of charge;
And you as well to keep her, that defend her,
Not palating the taste of her dishonour,
With such a costly loss of wealth and friends:
He, like a puling cuckold, would drink up
The lees and dregs of a flat tamed piece;
You, like a lecher, out of whorish loins
Are pleased to breed out your inheritors:
Both merits poised, each weighs nor less nor more;
But he as he, the heavier for a whore.

PARIS.

You are too bitter to your countrywoman.

DIOMEDES.

She's bitter to her country: hear me, Paris:—
For every false drop in her bawdy veins
A Grecian's life hath sunk; for every scruple
Of her contaminated carrion weight
A Trojan hath been slain; since she could speak,
She hath not given so many good words breath
As for her Greeks and Trojans suffer'd death.

PARIS.

Fair Diomed, you do as chapmen do,
Dispraise the thing that you desire to buy:
But we in silence hold this virtue well,—
We'll not commend what we intend not sell.
Here lies our way. [*Exeunt.*

SCENE II.

Court of PANDARUS' *house.*

Enter TROILUS *and* CRESSIDA.

TROILUS.

Dear, trouble not yourself: the morn is cold.

CRESSIDA.

Then, sweet my lord, I'll call mine uncle down;
He shall unbolt the gates.

TROILUS.

Trouble him not;
To bed, to bed: sleep kill those pretty eyes,
And give as soft attachment to thy senses
As infants' empty of all thought!

CRESSIDA.

Good morrow, then.

TROILUS.

I prithee now, to bed.

CRESSIDA.

Are you a-weary of me?

TROILUS.

O Cressida! but that the busy day,
Waked by the lark, hath roused the ribald crows,
And dreaming night will hide our joys no longer,
I would not from thee.

CRESSIDA.

Night hath been too brief.

TROILUS.

Beshrew the witch! with venomous wights she stays
As tediously as hell; but flies the grasps of love
With wings more momentary-swift than thought.
You will catch cold, and curse me.

CRESSIDA.

Prithee, tarry;—
You men will never tarry.—
O foolish Cressid!—I might have still held off,
And then you would have tarried.—Hark! there's one up.

PANDARUS [*within*].

What, 's all the doors open here?

TROILUS.

It is your uncle.

CRESSIDA.

A pestilence on him! now will he be mocking:
I shall have such a life!

Enter PANDARUS.

PANDARUS.

How now, how now! how go maidenheads?—
Here, you maid! where's my cousin Cressid?

CRESSIDA.

Go hang yourself, you naughty mocking uncle!
You bring me to do—and then you flout me too.

PANDARUS.

To do what? to do what?—let her say what:—what have I brought you to do?

CRESSIDA.

Come, come, beshrew your heart! you'll ne'er be good,
Nor suffer others.

PANDARUS.

Ha, ha! Alas, poor wretch! ah, poor capocchia! hast not slept to-night? would he not—a naughty man—let it sleep? a bugbear take him!

CRESSIDA.

Did not I tell you?—would he were knockt i'th' head!— [*One knocks.*
Who's that at door? good uncle, go and see.—
My lord, come you again into my chamber:
You smile and mock me, as if I meant naughtily.

TROILUS.

Ha, ha!

CRESSIDA.

Come, you are deceived, I think of no such thing.— [*Knock.*
How earnestly they knock!—Pray you, come in:
I would not for half Troy have you seen here.

[*Exeunt* TROILUS *and* CRESSIDA.

PANDARUS.

Who's there? what's the matter? will you beat down the door? How now! what's the matter?

Enter AENEAS.

AENEAS.

Good morrow, lord, good morrow.

PANDARUS.

Who's there? my Lord Aeneas! By my troth,
I knew you not: what news with you so early?

AENEAS.

Is not Prince Troilus here?

PANDARUS.

Here! what should he do here?

AENEAS.

Come, he is here, my lord; do not deny him:
It doth import him much to speak with me.

PANDARUS.

Is he here, say you? 'tis more than I know, I'll be sworn:—for my own part, I came in late. What should he do here?

AENEAS.

Who!—nay, then:—come, come, you'll do him wrong ere you're ware: you'll be so true to him to be false to him: do not you know of him, but yet go fetch him hither; go.

Enter TROILUS.

TROILUS.

How now! what's the matter?

AENEAS.

My lord, I scarce have leisure to salute you,
My matter is so rash: there is at hand
Paris your brother, and Deiphobus,
The Grecian Diomed, and our Antenor
Deliver'd to us; and for him forthwith,
Ere the first sacrifice, within this hour,
We must give up to Diomedes' hand
The Lady Cressida.

TROILUS.

Is it so concluded?

AENEAS.

By Priam and the general state of Troy:
They are at hand, and ready to effect it.

TROILUS.

How my achievements mock me!—
I will go meet them: and, my Lord Aeneas,
We met by chance; you did not find me here.

AENEAS.

Good, good, my lord; the secrets of nature
Have not more gift in taciturnity.

[*Exeunt* TROILUS *and* AENEAS.

PANDARUS.

Is't possible? no sooner got but lost? The devil take Antenor! the young prince will go mad: a plague upon Antenor! I would they had broke's neck!

Enter CRESSIDA.

CRESSIDA.

How now! what's the matter? who was here?

PANDARUS.

Ah, ah!

CRESSIDA.

Why sigh you so profoundly? where's my lord? gone! Tell me, sweet uncle, what's the matter?

PANDARUS.

Would I were as deep under the earth as I am above!

CRESSIDA.

O the gods!—what's the matter?

PANDARUS.

Prithee, get thee in: would thou hadst ne'er been born! I knew thou wouldst be his death:—O, poor gentleman!—A plague upon Antenor!

CRESSIDA.

Good uncle, I beseech you, on my knees I beseech you, what's the matter?

PANDARUS.

Thou must be gone, wench, thou must be gone; thou art changed for Antenor: thou must to thy father, and be gone from Troilus: 'twill be his death; 'twill be his bane; he cannot bear it.

CRESSIDA.

O you immortal gods!—I will not go.

PANDARUS.

Thou must.

CRESSIDA.

I will not, uncle: I have forgot my father;
I know no touch of consanguinity;
No kin, no love, no blood, no soul so near me
As the sweet Troilus.—O you gods divine,
Make Cressid's name the very crown of falsehood,
If ever she leave Troilus! Time, force, and death,
Do to this body what extremes you can;
But the strong base and building of my love
Is as the very centre of the earth,
Drawing all things to it.—I'll go in and weep,—

PANDARUS.

Do, do.

CRESSIDA.

Tear my bright hair, and scratch my praised cheeks;
Crack my clear voice with sobs, and break my heart
With sounding 'Troilus.' I will not go from Troy.
[*Exeunt.*

SCENE III.

Before PANDARUS' *house.*

Enter PARIS, TROILUS, AENEAS, DEIPHOBUS, ANTENOR, *and* DIOMEDES.

PARIS.

It is great morning; and the hour prefixt
Of her delivery to this valiant Greek
Comes fast upon:—good my brother Troilus,
Tell you the lady what she is to do,
And haste her to the purpose.

TROILUS.

Walk into her house;
I'll bring her to the Grecian presently:
And to his hand when I deliver her,
Think it an altar, and thy brother Troilus
A priest, there offering to it his own heart. [*Exit.*

PARIS.

I know what 'tis to love;
And would, as I shall pity, I could help!—
Please you walk in, my lords. [*Exeunt.*

SCENE IV.

A room in PANDARUS' *house.*

Enter PANDARUS *and* CRESSIDA.

PANDARUS.

Be moderate, be moderate.

CRESSIDA.

Why tell you me of moderation?
The grief is fine, full, perfect, that I taste,
And violenteth in a sense as strong
As that which causeth it: how can I moderate it?
If I could temporize with my affection,
Or brew it to a weak and colder palate,
The like allayment could I give my grief:
My love admits no qualifying dross;
No more my grief, in such a precious loss.

PANDARUS.

Here, here, here he comes.

Enter TROILUS.

Ah, sweet ducks!

CRESSIDA.

O Troilus! Troilus! [*Embracing him.*

PANDARUS.

What a pair of spectacles is here! Let me embrace too. 'O heart,' as the goodly saying is,

'——O heart, O heavy heart,
Why sigh'st thou without breaking?'

where he answers again,

'Because thou canst not ease thy smart
By friendship nor by speaking.'

There was never a truer rime. Let us cast away nothing, for we may live to have need of such a verse: we see it, we see it.—How now, lambs!

TROILUS.

Cressid, I love thee in so strain'd a purity,
That the blest gods, as angry with my fancy,
More bright in zeal than the devotion which
Cold lips blow to their deities, take thee from me.

CRESSIDA.

Have the gods envy?

PANDARUS.

Ay, ay, ay, ay; 'tis too plain a case.

CRESSIDA.

And is it true that I must go from Troy?

TROILUS.

A hateful truth.

CRESSIDA.

What, and from Troilus too?

TROILUS.

From Troy and Troilus.

CRESSIDA.

Is it possible?

TROILUS.

And suddenly; where injury of chance
Puts back leave-taking, justles roughly by
All time of pause, rudely beguiles our lips
Of all rejoindure, forcibly prevents
Our lockt embrasures, strangles our dear vows
Even in the birth of our own labouring breath:
We two, that with so many thousand sighs
Did buy each other, must poorly sell ourselves
With the rude brevity and discharge of one.
Injurious time now, with a robber's haste,
Crams his rich thievery up, he knows not how:
As many farewells as be stars in heaven,
With distinct breath and consign'd kisses to them,
He fumbles up into a loose adieu;
And scants us with a single famisht kiss,
Distasted with the salt of broken tears.

AENEAS [*within*].

My lord, is the lady ready?

TROILUS.

Hark! you are call'd: some say the Genius so
Cries 'Come!' to him that instantly must die.—
Bid them have patience; she shall come anon.

PANDARUS.

Where are my tears? rain, to lay this wind, or my heart will be blown up by the root. [*Exit.*

CRESSIDA.

I must, then, to the Grecians?

TROILUS.

No remedy.

CRESSIDA.
A woful Cressid 'mongst the merry Greeks!
When shall we see again?

TROILUS.
Hear me, my love: be thou but true of heart,—

CRESSIDA.
I true! how now! what wicked deem is this?

TROILUS.
Nay, we must use expostulation kindly,
For it is parting from us:
I speak not 'be thou true,' as fearing thee;
For I will throw my glove to Death himself,
That there's no maculation in thy heart:
But 'be thou true,' say I, to fashion in
My sequent protestation; be thou true,
And I will see thee.

CRESSIDA.
O, you shall be exposed, my lord, to dangers
As infinite as imminent! but I'll be true.

TROILUS.
And I'll grow friend with danger. Wear this sleeve.

CRESSIDA.
And you this glove. When shall I see you?

TROILUS.
I will corrupt the Grecian sentinels,
To give thee nightly visitation.
But yet, be true.

CRESSIDA.
O heavens!—'be true' again!

TROILUS.
Hear why I speak it, love:
The Grecian youths are full of quality;
They're loving, well composed with gifts of nature,
And swelling o'er with arts and exercise:
How novelty may move, and parts with person,
Alas, a kind of godly jealousy—
Which, I beseech you, call a virtuous sin—
Makes me afeard.

CRESSIDA.
O heavens! you love me not.

TROILUS.
Die I a villain, then!
In this I do not call your faith in question
So mainly as my merit: I cannot sing,
Nor heel the high lavolt, nor sweeten talk,
Nor play at subtle games; fair virtues all,
To which the Grecians are most prompt and pregnant:
But I can tell, that in each grace of these
There lurks a still and dumb-discoursive devil
That tempts most cunningly: but be not tempted.

CRESSIDA.
Do you think I will?

TROILUS.
No.
But something may be done that we will not:
And sometimes we are devils to ourselves,
When we will tempt the frailty of our powers,
Presuming on their changeful potency.

AENEAS [*within*].
Nay, good my lord,—

TROILUS.
Come, kiss; and let us part.

PARIS [*within*].
Brother Troilus!

TROILUS.
Good brother, come you hither;
And bring Aeneas and the Grecian with you.

CRESSIDA.
My lord, will you be true?

TROILUS.
Who, I? alas, it is my vice, my fault:
Whiles others fish with craft for great opinion,
I with great truth catch mere simplicity;
Whilst some with cunning gild their copper crowns,
With truth and plainness I do wear mine bare.
Fear not my truth: the moral of my wit
Is 'plain and true;' there's all the reach of it.

Enter AENEAS, PARIS, ANTENOR, DEIPHOBUS, *and* DIOMEDES.

Welcome, Sir Diomed! here is the lady
Which for Antenor we deliver you:
At the port, lord, I'll give her to thy hand;
And by the way possess thee what she is.
Entreat her fair; and, by my soul, fair Greek,
If e'er thou stand at mercy of my sword,
Name Cressid, and thy life shall be as safe
As Priam is in Ilion.

DIOMEDES.
Fair Lady Cressid,
So please you, save the thanks this prince expects:
The lustre in your eye, heaven in your cheek,
Pleads your fair usage; and to Diomed
You shall be mistress, and command him wholly.

TROILUS.
Grecian, thou dost not use me courteously,
To shame the zeal of my petition to thee
In praising her: I tell thee, lord of Greece,
She is as far high-soaring o'er thy praises
As thou unworthy to be call'd her servant.
I charge thee use her well, even for my charge;
For, by the dreadful Pluto, if thou dost not,
Though the great bulk Achilles be thy guard,
I'll cut thy throat.

DIOMEDES.
O, be not moved, Prince Troilus:
Let me be privileged by my place and message
To be a speaker free; when I am hence,
I'll answer to my lust: and know you, lord,
I'll nothing do on charge: to her own worth
She shall be prized; but that you say, 'Be't so,'
I'll speak it in my spirit and honour, 'No.'

TROILUS.
Come, to the port.—I'll tell thee, Diomed,
This brave shall oft make thee to hide thy head.—
Lady, give me your hand; and, as we walk,
To our own selves bend we our needful talk.

[*Exeunt* TROILUS, CRESSIDA, *and* DIOMEDES. *Sound trumpet.*

PARIS.
Hark! Hector's trumpet.

AENEAS.
How have we spent this morning!
The prince must think me tardy and remiss,
That swore to ride before him to the field.

PARIS.
'Tis Troilus' fault: come, come, to field with him.

DEIPHOBUS.
Let us make ready straight.

AENEAS.
Yea, with a bridegroom's fresh alacrity,
Let us address to tend on Hector's heels:
The glory of our Troy doth this day lie
On his fair worth and single chivalry. [*Exeunt.*

SCENE V.

The Grecian camp. Lists set out.

Enter AJAX, *arm'd;* AGAMEMNON, ACHILLES, PATROCLUS, MENELAUS, ULYSSES, NESTOR, *and others.*

AGAMEMNON.
Here art thou in appointment fresh and fair,
Anticipating time with starting courage.
Give with thy trumpet a loud note to Troy,
Thou dreadful Ajax; that the appalled air
May pierce the head of the great combatant,
And hale him hither.

AJAX.
Thou, trumpet, there's my purse.
Now crack thy lungs, and split thy brazen pipe:
Blow, villain, till thy sphered bias cheek
Outswell the colic of puft Aquilon:
Come, stretch thy chest, and let thy eyes spout blood;
Thou blow'st for Hector. [*Trumpet sounds.*

ULYSSES.
No trumpet answers.

ACHILLES.
'Tis but early days.

AGAMEMNON.
Is not yond Diomed, with Calchas' daughter?

ULYSSES.
'Tis he, I ken the manner of his gait;
He rises on the toe: that spirit of his
In aspiration lifts him from the earth.

Enter DIOMEDES *with* CRESSIDA.

AGAMEMNON.
Is this the Lady Cressid?

DIOMEDES.
Even she.

AGAMEMNON.
Most dearly welcome to the Greeks, sweet lady.
[*Kisses her.*

NESTOR.
Our general doth salute you with a kiss.

ULYSSES.
Yet is the kindness but particular;
'Twere better she were kist in general.

NESTOR.
And very courtly counsel: I'll begin.—
[*Kisses her.*
So much for Nestor.

ACHILLES.
I'll take that winter from your lips, fair lady:
[*Kisses her.*
Achilles bids you welcome.

MENELAUS.
I had good argument for kissing once.

PATROCLUS.
But that's no argument for kissing now;
For thus popt Paris in his hardiment,
And parted thus you and your argument.
[*Kisses her.*

ULYSSES.
O deadly gall, and theme of all our scorns!
For which we lose our heads to gild his horns.

PATROCLUS.
The first was Menelaus' kiss;—this, mine:
[*Kisses her again.*
Patroclus kisses you.

MENELAUS.
O, this is trim!

PATROCLUS.
Paris and I kiss evermore for him.

MENELAUS.
I'll have my kiss, sir.—Lady, by your leave.

CRESSIDA.
In kissing, do you render or receive?

MENELAUS.
Both take and give.

CRESSIDA.
I'll make my match to live,
The kiss you take is better than you give;
Therefore no kiss.

MENELAUS.
I'll give you boot, I'll give you three for one.

CRESSIDA.
You're an odd man; give even, or give none.

MENELAUS.
An odd man, lady! every man is odd.

CRESSIDA.
No, Paris is not; for you know 'tis true
That you are odd, and he is even with you.

MENELAUS.
You fillip me o' th' head.

CRESSIDA.
No, I'll be sworn.

ULYSSES.
It were no match, your nail against his horn.—
May I, sweet lady, beg a kiss of you?

CRESSIDA.
You may.

ULYSSES.
I do desire it.

CRESSIDA.
Why, beg, then.

ULYSSES.
Why, then, for Venus' sake, give me a kiss,
When Helen is a maid again, and his.

CRESSIDA.
I am your debtor, claim it when 'tis due.

ULYSSES.
Never's my day, and then a kiss of you.

DIOMEDES.
Lady, a word:—I'll bring you to your father.
[*Exit with* CRESSIDA.

NESTOR.
A woman of quick sense.

ULYSSES.
Fie, fie upon her!
There's language in her eye, her cheek, her lip,
Nay, her foot speaks; her wanton spirits look out
At every joint and motive of her body.
O, these encounterers, so glib of tongue,
That give a coasting welcome ere it comes,
And wide unclasp the tables of their thoughts
To every ticklish reader! set them down
For sluttish spoils of opportunity
And daughters of the game. [*Trumpet within.*

ALL.

The Trojans' trumpet.

AGAMEMNON.

Yonder comes the troop.

Flourish. Enter all of Troy; HECTOR, AENEAS, TROILUS, *and* ATTENDANTS.

AENEAS.

Hail, all the state of Greece! what shall be done
To him that victory commands? or do you purpose
A victor shall be known? will you the knights
Shall to the edge of all extremity
Pursue each other; or shall be divided
By any voice or order of the field?
Hector bade ask.

AGAMEMNON.

Which way would Hector have it?

AENEAS.

He cares not; he'll obey conditions.

ACHILLES.

'Tis done like Hector; but securely done,
A little proudly, and great deal misprizing
The knight opposed.

AENEAS.

If not Achilles, sir,
What is your name?

ACHILLES.

If not Achilles, nothing.

AENEAS.

Therefore Achilles: but whate'er, know this:—
In the extremity of great and little,
Valour and pride excel themselves in Hector;
The one almost as infinite as all,
The other blank as nothing. Weigh him well,
And that which looks like pride is courtesy.
This Ajax is half made of Hector's blood:
In love whereof half Hector stays at home;
Half heart, half hand, half Hector comes to seek
This blended knight, half Trojan and half Greek.

ACHILLES.

A maiden battle, then?—O, I perceive you.

Enter DIOMEDES.

AGAMEMNON.

Here is Sir Diomed.—Go, gentle knight,
Stand by our Ajax: as you and Lord Aeneas
Consent upon the order of their fight,
So be it; either to the uttermost,
Or else a breath: the combatants being kin
Half stints their strife before their strokes begin.

[AJAX *and* HECTOR *enter the lists.*

ULYSSES.

They are opposed already.

AGAMEMNON.

What Trojan is that same that looks so heavy?

ULYSSES.

The youngest son of Priam, a true knight;
Not yet mature, yet matchless: firm of word;
Speaking in deeds, and deedless in his tongue;
Not soon provoked, nor being provoked soon calm'd:
His heart and hand both open and both free;
For what he has he gives, what thinks he shows;
Yet gives he not till judgement guide his bounty,
Nor dignifies an impair thought with breath:
Manly as Hector, but more dangerous;
For Hector, in his blaze of wrath, subscribes
To tender objects; but he, in heat of action,
Is more vindicative than jealous love:
They call him Troilus; and on him erect
A second hope, as fairly built as Hector.
Thus says Aeneas; one that knows the youth
Even to his inches, and with private soul
Did in great Ilion thus translate him to me.

[*Alarum.* HECTOR *and* AJAX *fight.*

AGAMEMNON.

They are in action.

NESTOR.

Now, Ajax, hold thine own!

TROILUS.

Hector, thou sleep'st;
Awake thee!

AGAMEMNON.

His blows are well disposed:—there, Ajax!

DIOMEDES.

You must no more. [*Trumpets cease.*

AENEAS.

Princes, enough, so please you.

AJAX.

I am not warm yet; let us fight again.

DIOMEDES.

As Hector pleases.

HECTOR.

Why, then will I no more:—
Thou art, great lord, my father's sister's son,
A cousin-german to great Priam's seed;
The obligation of our blood forbids
A gory emulation 'twixt us twain:
Were thy commixtion Greek and Trojan so
That thou couldst say, 'This hand is Grecian all,
And this is Trojan; the sinews of this leg
All Greek, and this all Troy; my mother's blood
Runs on the dexter cheek, and this sinister
Bounds in my father's;' by Jove multipotent,
Thou shouldst not bear from me a Greekish member
Wherein my sword had not impressure made
Of our rank feud: but the just gods gainsay
That any drop thou borrow'dst from thy mother,
My sacred aunt, should by my mortal sword
Be drained! Let me embrace thee, Ajax:
By him that thunders, thou hast lusty arms;
Hector would have them fall upon him thus:
Cousin, all honour to thee!

AJAX.

I thank thee, Hector:
Thou art too gentle and too free a man:
I came to kill thee, cousin, and bear hence
A great addition earned in thy death.

HECTOR.

Not Neoptolemus so mirable—
On whose bright crest Fame with her loud'st oyes
Cries 'This is he'—could promise to himself
A thought of added honour torn from Hector.

AENEAS.

There is expectance here from both the sides,
What further you will do.

HECTOR.

We'll answer it;
The issue is embracement:—Ajax, farewell.

AJAX.

If I might in entreaties find success—
As seld I have the chance—I would desire
My famous cousin to our Grecian tents.

DIOMEDES.

'Tis Agamemnon's wish; and great Achilles
Doth long to see unarm'd the valiant Hector.

HECTOR.

Aeneas, call my brother Troilus to me:
And signify this loving interview
To the expecters of our Trojan part;
Desire them home.—Give me thy hand, my cousin;
I will go eat with thee, and see your knights.

AGAMEMNON *and the rest come forward.*

AJAX.

Great Agamemnon comes to meet us here.

HECTOR.

The worthiest of them tell me name by name;
But for Achilles, mine own searching eyes
Shall find him by his large and portly size.

AGAMEMNON.

Worthy of arms! as welcome as to one
That would be rid of such an enemy;
But that's no welcome: understand more clear,
What's past and what's to come is strew'd with husks
And formless ruin of oblivion;
But in this extant moment, faith and troth,
Strain'd purely from all hollow bias-drawing,
Bids thee, with most divine integrity,
From heart of very heart, great Hector, welcome.

HECTOR.

I thank thee, most imperious Agamemnon.

AGAMEMNON [*to* TROILUS].

My well-famed lord of Troy, no less to you.

MENELAUS.

Let me confirm my princely brother's greeting;—
You brace of warlike brothers, welcome hither.

HECTOR.

Who must we answer?

AENEAS.

The noble Menelaus.

HECTOR.

O, you, my lord? by Mars his gauntlet, thanks!
Mock not, that I affect th'untraded oath;
Your *quondam* wife swears still by Venus' glove:
She's well, but bade me not commend her to you.

MENELAUS.

Name her not now, sir; she's a deadly theme.

HECTOR.

O, pardon; I offend.

NESTOR.

I have, thou gallant Trojan, seen thee oft,
Labouring for destiny, make cruel way
Through ranks of Greekish youth; and I have seen thee,
As hot as Perseus, spur thy Phrygian steed,
Despising many forfeits and subduements,
When thou hast hung thy advanced sword i'th'air,
Not letting it decline on the declined;
That I have said to some my standers-by,
'Lo, Jupiter is yonder, dealing life!'
And I have seen thee pause and take thy breath,
When that a ring of Greeks have hemm'd thee in,
Like an Olympian wrestling: this have I seen;
But this thy countenance, still lockt in steel,
I never saw till now. I knew thy grandsire,
And once fought with him: he was a soldier good;
But, by great Mars, the captain of us all,
Never like thee. Let an old man embrace thee;
And, worthy warrior, welcome to our tents.

AENEAS.

'Tis the old Nestor.

HECTOR.

Let me embrace thee, good old chronicle,
That hast so long walkt hand in hand with time:—
Most reverend Nestor, I am glad to clasp thee.

NESTOR.

I would my arms could match thee in contention,
As they contend with thee in courtesy.

HECTOR.

I would they could.

NESTOR.

Ha!
By this white beard, I'ld fight with thee to-morrow:—
Well, welcome, welcome!—I have seen the time—

ULYSSES.

I wonder now how yonder city stands
When we have here her base and pillar by us.

HECTOR.

I know your favour, Lord Ulysses, well.
Ah, sir, there's many a Greek and Trojan dead,
Since first I saw yourself and Diomed
In Ilion, on your Greekish embassy.

ULYSSES.

Sir, I foretold you then what would ensue:
My prophecy is but half his journey yet;
For yonder walls, that pertly front your town,
Yond towers, whose wanton tops do buss the clouds,
Must kiss their own feet.

HECTOR.

I must not believe you:
There they stand yet; and modestly I think,
The fall of every Phrygian stone will cost
A drop of Grecian blood: the end crowns all;
And that old common arbitrator, Time,
Will one day end it.

ULYSSES.

So to him we leave it.
Most gentle and most valiant Hector, welcome:
After the general, I beseech you next
To feast with me, and see me at my tent.

ACHILLES.

I shall forestall thee, Lord Ulysses, thou!—
Now, Hector, I have fed mine eyes on thee;
I have with exact view perused thee, Hector,
And quoted joint by joint.

HECTOR.

Is this Achilles?

ACHILLES.

I am Achilles.

HECTOR.

Stand fair, I pray thee: let me look on thee.

ACHILLES.

Behold thy fill.

HECTOR.

Nay, I have done already.

ACHILLES.

Thou art too brief: I will the second time,
As I would buy thee, view thee limb by limb.

HECTOR.

O, like a book of sport thou'lt read me o'er;
But there's more in me than thou understand'st.
Why dost thou so oppress me with thine eye?

ACHILLES.
Tell me, you heavens, in which part of his body
Shall I destroy him? whether there, or there, or there?
That I may give the local wound a name,
And make distinct the very breach whereout
Hector's great spirit flew: answer me, heavens!

HECTOR.
It would discredit the blest gods, proud man,
To answer such a question: stand again:
Think'st thou to catch my life so pleasantly
As to prenominate in nice conjecture
Where thou wilt hit me dead?

ACHILLES.
I tell thee, yea.

HECTOR.
Wert thou the oracle to tell me so,
I'ld not believe thee. Henceforth guard thee well;
For I'll not kill thee there, not there, nor there;
But, by the forge that stithied Mars his helm,
I'll kill thee every where, yea, o'er and o'er.—
You wisest Grecians, pardon me this brag,
His insolence draws folly from my lips;
But I'll endeavour deeds to match these words,
Or may I never—

AJAX.
Do not chafe thee, cousin:—
And you, Achilles, let these threats alone,
Till accident or purpose bring you to't:
You may have every day enough of Hector,
If you have stomach; the general state, I fear,
Can scarce entreat you to be odd with him.

HECTOR.
I pray you, let us see you in the field:
We have had pelting wars, since you refused
The Grecians' cause.

ACHILLES.
Dost thou entreat me, Hector?
To-morrow do I meet thee, fell as death;
To-night all friends.

HECTOR.
Thy hand upon that match.

AGAMEMNON.
First, all you peers of Greece, go to my tent;
There in the full convive we: afterwards,
As Hector's leisure and your bounties shall
Concur together, severally entreat him.—
Beat loud the tabourines, let the trumpets blow,
That this great soldier may his welcome know.
[*Exeunt all but* TROILUS *and* ULYSSES.

TROILUS.
My Lord Ulysses, tell me, I beseech you,
In what place of the field doth Calchas keep?

ULYSSES.
At Menelaus' tent, most princely Troilus:
There Diomed doth feast with him to-night;
Who neither looks upon the heaven nor earth,
But gives all gaze and bent of amorous view
On the fair Cressid.

TROILUS.
Shall I, sweet lord, be bound to you so much,
After we part from Agamemnon's tent,
To bring me thither?

ULYSSES.
You shall command me, sir.
As gentle tell me, of what honour was
This Cressida in Troy? Had she no lover there
That wails her absence?

TROILUS.
O, sir, to such as boasting show their scars
A mock is due. Will you walk on, my lord?
She was beloved, she loved; she is, and doth:
But still sweet love is food for fortune's tooth.
[*Exeunt.*

ACT V. SCENE I.

The Grecian camp. Before ACHILLES' *tent.*

Enter ACHILLES *and* PATROCLUS.

ACHILLES.
I'LL heat his blood with Greekish wine to-night,
Which with my scimitar I'll cool to-morrow.—
Patroclus, let us feast him to the height.

PATROCLUS.
Here comes Thersites.

Enter THERSITES.

ACHILLES.
How now, thou core of envy!
Thou crusty batch of nature, what's the news?

THERSITES.
Why, thou picture of what thou seem'st, and idol of idiot-worshippers, here's a letter for thee.

ACHILLES.
From whence, fragment?

THERSITES.
Why, thou full dish of fool, from Troy.

PATROCLUS.
Who keeps the tent now?

THERSITES.
The surgeon's box, or the patient's wound.

PATROCLUS.
Well said, adversity! and what need these tricks?

THERSITES.
Prithee, be silent, boy; I profit not by thy talk: thou art thought to be Achilles' male varlet.

PATROCLUS.
Male varlet, you rogue! what's that?

THERSITES.
Why, his masculine whore. Now, the rotten diseases of the south, the guts-griping, ruptures, catarrhs, loads o'gravel i'th'back, lethargies, cold palsies, raw eyes, dirt-rotten livers, wheezing lungs, bladders full of imposthume, sciaticas, limekilns i'th'palm, incurable bone-ache, and the rivell'd fee-simple of the tetter, take and take again such preposterous discoveries!

PATROCLUS.
Why, thou damnable box of envy, thou, what mean'st thou to curse thus?

THERSITES.
Do I curse thee?

PATROCLUS.
Why, no, you ruinous butt; you whoreson indistinguishable cur, no.

THERSITES.
No! why art thou, then, exasperate, thou idle immaterial skein of sleave-silk, thou green sarcenet flap for a sore eye, thou tassel of a prodigal's purse, thou? Ah, how the poor world is pester'd with such waterflies,—diminutives of nature!

PATROCLUS.
Out, gall!

THERSITES.

Finch-egg!

ACHILLES.

My sweet Patroclus, I am thwarted quite
From my great purpose in to-morrow's battle.
Here is a letter from Queen Hecuba;
A token from her daughter, my fair love;
Both taxing me and gaging me to keep
An oath that I have sworn. I will not break it:
Fall Greeks; fail fame; honour or go or stay;
My major vow lies here, this I'll obey.—
Come, come, Thersites, help to trim my tent;
This night in banqueting must all be spent.—
Away, Patroclus!

[*Exeunt* ACHILLES *and* PATROCLUS.

THERSITES.

With too much blood and too little brain, these two may run mad; but, if with too much brain and too little blood they do, I'll be a curer of madmen. Here's Agamemnon,—an honest fellow enough, and one that loves quails: but he has not so much brain as ear-wax: and the goodly transformation of Jupiter there, his brother, the bull,—the primitive statue, and oblique memorial of cuckolds; a thrifty shoeing-horn in a chain, hanging at his brother's leg,—to what form, but that he is, should wit larded with malice, and malice forced with wit, turn him to? To an ass, were nothing; he is both ass and ox: to an ox, were nothing; he is both ox and ass. To be a dog, a mule, a cat, a fitchew, a toad, a lizard, an owl, a puttock, or a herring without a roe, I would not care; but to be Menelaus!—I would conspire against destiny. Ask me not what I would be, if I were not Thersites; for I care not to be the louse of a lazar, so I were not Menelaus.—Hoyday! spirits and fires!

Enter HECTOR, TROILUS, AJAX, AGAMEMNON, ULYSSES, NESTOR, MENELAUS, DIOMEDES, *with lights.*

AGAMEMNON.

We go wrong, we go wrong.

AJAX.

No, yonder 'tis;
There, where we see the lights.

HECTOR.

I trouble you.

AJAX.

No, not a whit.

ULYSSES.

Here comes himself to guide you.

Enter ACHILLES.

ACHILLES.

Welcome, brave Hector; welcome, princes all.

AGAMEMNON.

So now, fair Prince of Troy, I bid good night.
Ajax commands the guard to tend on you.

HECTOR.

Thanks and good night to the Greeks' general.

MENELAUS.

Good night, my lord.

HECTOR.

Good night, sweet Lord Menelaus.

THERSITES.

Sweet draught: sweet, quoth a'! sweet sink, sweet sewer.

ACHILLES.

Good night and welcome, both at once, to those
That go or tarry.

AGAMEMNON.

Good night.

[*Exeunt* AGAMEMNON *and* MENELAUS.

ACHILLES.

Old Nestor tarries; and you too, Diomed,
Keep Hector company an hour or two.

DIOMEDES.

I cannot, lord; I have important business,
The tide whereof is now.—Good night, great Hector.

HECTOR.

Give me your hand.

ULYSSES [*aside to* TROILUS].

Follow his torch; he goes to Calchas' tent:
I'll keep you company.

TROILUS [*aside to* ULYSSES].

Sweet sir, you honour me.

HECTOR.

And so, good night.

[*Exit* DIOMEDES; ULYSSES *and* TROILUS *following.*

ACHILLES.

Come, come, enter my tent.

[*Exeunt* ACHILLES, HECTOR, AJAX, *and* NESTOR.

THERSITES.

That same Diomed's a false-hearted rogue, a most unjust knave; I will no more trust him when he leers than I will a serpent when he hisses: he will spend his mouth, and promise, like Brabbler the hound; but when he performs, astronomers foretell it; it is prodigious, there will come some change; the sun borrows of the moon, when Diomed keeps his word. I will rather leave to see Hector than not to dog him: they say he keeps a Trojan drab, and uses the traitor Calchas' tent: I'll after.—Nothing but lechery! all incontinent varlets! [*Exit.*

SCENE II.

The same. Before CALCHAS' *tent.*

Enter DIOMEDES.

DIOMEDES.

WHAT, are you up here, ho? speak.

CALCHAS [*within*].

Who calls?

DIOMEDES.

Diomed.—Calchas, I think. Where's your daughter?

CALCHAS [*within*].

She comes to you.

Enter TROILUS *and* ULYSSES, *at a distance; after them* THERSITES.

ULYSSES.

Stand where the torch may not discover us.

Enter CRESSIDA.

TROILUS.

Cressid comes forth to him.

DIOMEDES.

How now, my charge!

CRESSIDA.

Now, my sweet guardian!—Hark, a word with you.

[*Whispers.*

TROILUS.

Yea, so familiar!

ULYSSES.

She will sing any man at first sight.

THERSITES.

And any man may sing her, if he can take her cliff: she's noted.

DIOMEDES.

Will you remember?

CRESSIDA.

Remember! yes.

DIOMEDES.

Nay, but do, then;
And let your mind be coupled with your words.

TROILUS.

What should she remember?

ULYSSES.

List.

CRESSIDA.

Sweet honey Greek, tempt me no more to folly.

THERSITES.

Roguery!

DIOMEDES.

Nay, then,—

CRESSIDA.

I'll tell you what,—

DIOMEDES.

Foh, foh! come, tell a pin: you are forsworn.

CRESSIDA.

In faith, I cannot: what would you have me do?

THERSITES.

A juggling trick,—to be secretly open.

DIOMEDES.

What did you swear you would bestow on me?

CRESSIDA.

I prithee, do not hold me to mine oath;
Bid me do any thing but that, sweet Greek.

DIOMEDES.

Good night.

TROILUS.

Hold, patience!

ULYSSES.

How now, Trojan!

CRESSIDA.

Diomed,—

DIOMEDES.

No, no, good night: I'll be your fool no more.

TROILUS.

Thy better must.

CRESSIDA.

Hark, one word in your ear.

TROILUS.

O plague and madness!

ULYSSES.

You are moved, prince; let us depart, I pray you,
Lest your displeasure should enlarge itself
To wrathful terms: this place is dangerous;
The time right deadly; I beseech you, go.

TROILUS.

Behold, I pray you!

ULYSSES.

Nay, good my lord, go off:
You flow to great distraction; come, my lord.

TROILUS.

I pray thee, stay.

ULYSSES.

You have not patience; come.

TROILUS.

I pray you, stay; by hell and all hell's torments,
I will not speak a word!

DIOMEDES.

And so, good night.

CRESSIDA.

Nay, but you part in anger.

TROILUS.

Doth that grieve thee?
O wither'd truth!

ULYSSES.

Why, how now, lord!

TROILUS.

By Jove,
I will be patient.

CRESSIDA.

Guardian!—why, Greek!

DIOMEDES.

Foh, foh! adieu; you palter.

CRESSIDA.

In faith, I do not: come hither once again.

ULYSSES.

You shake, my lord, at something: will you go?
You will break out.

TROILUS.

She strokes his cheek!

ULYSSES.

Come, come.

TROILUS.

Nay, stay; by Jove, I will not speak a word:
There is between my will and all offences
A guard of patience:—stay a little while.

THERSITES.

How the devil luxury, with his fat rump and potato-finger, tickles these together! Fry, lechery, fry!

DIOMEDES.

But will you, then?

CRESSIDA.

In faith, I will, la; never trust me else.

DIOMEDES.

Give me some token for the surety of it.

CRESSIDA.

I'll fetch you one. [*Exit.*

ULYSSES.

You have sworn patience.

TROILUS.

Fear me not, sweet lord;
I will not be myself, nor have cognition
Of what I feel: I am all patience.

Enter CRESSIDA.

THERSITES.

Now the pledge; now, now, now!

CRESSIDA.

Here, Diomed, keep this sleeve.

TROILUS.

O beauty! where is thy faith?

ULYSSES.

My lord,—

TROILUS.

I will be patient; outwardly I will.

CRESSIDA.

You look upon that sleeve; behold it well.—
He loved me—O false wench!—Give't me again.

DIOMEDES.
Whose was't?

CRESSIDA.
It is no matter, now I have't again.
I will not meet with you to-morrow night:
I prithee, Diomed, visit me no more.

THERSITES.
Now she sharpens:—well said, whetstone!

DIOMEDES.
I shall have it.

CRESSIDA.
What, this?

DIOMEDES.
Ay, that.

CRESSIDA.
O, all you gods!—O pretty, pretty pledge!
Thy master now lies thinking in his bed
Of thee and me: and sighs, and takes my glove,
And gives memorial dainty kisses to it,
As I kiss thee.—Nay, do not snatch it from me;
He that takes that doth take my heart withal.

DIOMEDES.
I had your heart before, this follows it.

TROILUS.
I did swear patience.

CRESSIDA.
You shall not have it, Diomed; faith, you shall not;
I'll give you something else.

DIOMEDES.
I will have this: whose was it?

CRESSIDA.
It is no matter.

DIOMEDES.
Come, tell me whose it was.

CRESSIDA.
'Twas one's that loved me better than you will.
But, now you have it, take it.

DIOMEDES.
Whose was it?

CRESSIDA.
By all Diana's waiting-women yond,
And by herself, I will not tell you whose.

DIOMEDES.
To-morrow will I wear it on my helm;
And grieve his spirit that dares not challenge it.

TROILUS.
Wert thou the devil, and worest it on thy horn,
It should be challenged.

CRESSIDA.
Well, well, 'tis done, 'tis past;—and yet it is not;
I will not keep my word,

DIOMEDES.
Why, then, farewell;
Thou never shalt mock Diomed again.

CRESSIDA.
You shall not go:—one cannot speak a word,
But it straight starts you.

DIOMEDES.
I do not like this fooling.

THERSITES.
Nor I, by Pluto: but that that likes not you pleases me best.

DIOMEDES.
What, shall I come? the hour?

CRESSIDA.
Ay, come:—O Jove!—do come:—I shall be plagued.

DIOMEDES.
Farewell till then.

CRESSIDA.
Good night: I prithee, come.
Exit DIOMEDES.
Troilus, farewell! one eye yet looks on thee;
But with my heart the other eye doth see.
Ah, poor our sex! this fault in us I find,
The error of our eye directs our mind:
What error leads must err; O, then conclude
Minds sway'd by eyes are full of turpitude. [*Exit.*

THERSITES.
A proof of strength she could not publish more,
Unless she said 'My mind is now turn'd whore.'

ULYSSES.
All's done, my lord.

TROILUS.
It is.

ULYSSES.
Why stay we, then?

TROILUS.
To make a recordation to my soul
Of every syllable that here was spoke.
But if I tell how these two did co-act,
Shall I not lie in publishing a truth?
Sith yet there is a credence in my heart,
An esperance so obstinately strong,
That doth invert th'attest of eyes and ears;
As if those organs had deceptious functions,
Created only to calumniate.
Was Cressid here?

ULYSSES.
I cannot conjure, Trojan.

TROILUS.
She was not, sure.

ULYSSES.
Most sure she was.

TROILUS.
Why, my negation hath no taste of madness.

ULYSSES.
Nor mine, my lord: Cressid was here but now.

TROILUS.
Let it not be believed for womanhood!
Think, we had mothers; do not give advantage
To stubborn critics,—apt, without a theme,
For depravation,—to square the general sex
By Cressid's rule: rather think this not Cressid.

ULYSSES.
What hath she done, prince, that can soil our mothers?

TROILUS.
Nothing at all, unless that this were she.

THERSITES.
Will he swagger himself out on's own eyes?

TROILUS.
This she? no, this is Diomed's Cressida:
If beauty have a soul, this is not she;
If souls guide vows, if vows be sanctimonies,
If sanctimony be the gods' delight,
If there be rule in unity itself,
This is not she. O madness of discourse,
That cause sets up with and against itself!
Bi-fold authority! where reason can revolt

Without perdition, and loss assume all reason
Without revolt: this is, and is not, Cressid!
Within my soul there doth conduce a fight
Of this strange nature, that a thing inseparate
Divides more wider than the sky and earth;
And yet the spacious breadth of this division
Admits no orifex for a point, as subtle
As Ariachne's broken woof, to enter.
Instance, O instance! strong as Pluto's gates;
Cressid is mine, tied with the bonds of heaven:
Instance, O instance! strong as heaven itself;
The bonds of heaven are slipt, dissolved, and loosed;
And with another knot, five-finger-tied,
The fractions of her faith, orts of her love,
The fragments, scraps, the bits, and greasy relics
Of her o'er-eaten faith, are bound to Diomed.

ULYSSES.

May worthy Troilus be half attacht
With that which here his passion doth express?

TROILUS.

Ay, Greek, and that shall be divulged well
In characters as red as Mars his heart
Inflamed with Venus; never did young man fancy
With so eternal and so fixt a soul.
Hark, Greek:—as much as I do Cressid love,
So much by weight hate I her Diomed:
That sleeve is mine that he'll bear on his helm;
Were it a casque composed by Vulcan's skill,
My sword should bite it: not the dreadful spout,
Which shipmen do the hurricano call,
Constringed in mass by the almighty sun,
Shall dizzy with more clamour Neptune's ear
In his descent than shall my prompted sword
Falling on Diomed.

THERSITES.

He'll tickle it for his concupy.

TROILUS.

O Cressid! O false Cressid! false, false, false!
Let all untruths stand by thy stained name,
And they'll seem glorious.

ULYSSES.

O, contain yourself;
Your passion draws ears hither.

Enter AENEAS.

AENEAS.

I have been seeking you this hour, my lord:
Hector, by this, is arming him in Troy;
Ajax, your guard, stays to conduct you home.

TROILUS.

Have with you, prince.—My courteous lord, adieu.—
Farewell, revolted fair!—and, Diomed,
Stand fast, and wear a castle on thy head!

ULYSSES.

I'll bring you to the gates.

TROILUS.

Accept distracted thanks.

[*Exeunt* TROILUS, AENEAS, *and* ULYSSES.

THERSITES.

Would I could meet that rogue Diomed! I would croak like a raven; I would bode, I would bode. Patroclus will give me any thing for the intelligence of this whore: the parrot will not do more for an almond than he for a commodious drab. Lechery, lechery; still, wars and lechery; nothing else holds fashion: a burning devil take them!

[*Exit.*

SCENE III.

Troy. Before PRIAM'S *palace.*

Enter HECTOR *and* ANDROMACHE.

ANDROMACHE.

WHEN was my lord so much ungently temper'd,
To stop his ears against admonishment?
Unarm, unarm, and do not fight to-day.

HECTOR.

You train me to offend you; get you in:
By all the everlasting gods, I'll go!

ANDROMACHE.

My dreams will, sure, prove ominous to the day.

HECTOR.

No more, I say.

Enter CASSANDRA.

CASSANDRA.

Where is my brother Hector?

ANDROMACHE.

Here, sister; arm'd, and bloody in intent.
Consort with me in loud and dear petition,
Pursue we him on knees; for I have dream'd
Of bloody turbulence, and this whole night
Hath nothing been but shapes and forms of slaughter.

CASSANDRA.

O, 'tis true.

HECTOR.

Ho! bid my trumpet sound!

CASSANDRA.

No notes of sally, for the heavens, sweet brother.

HECTOR.

Be gone, I say: the gods have heard me swear.

CASSANDRA.

The gods are deaf to hot and peevish vows:
They are polluted offerings, more abhorr'd
Than spotted livers in the sacrifice.

ANDROMACHE.

O, be persuaded! do not count it holy
To hurt by being just: it is as lawful,
For we would give much, to use violent thefts,
And rob in the behalf of charity.

CASSANDRA.

It is the purpose that makes strong the vow;
But vows to every purpose must not hold:
Unarm, sweet Hector.

HECTOR.

Hold you still, I say;
Mine honour keeps the weather of my fate:
Life every man holds dear; but the brave man
Holds honour far more precious-dear than life.

Enter TROILUS.

How now, young man! mean'st thou to fight to-day?

ANDROMACHE.

Cassandra, call my father to persuade.

[*Exit* CASSANDRA.

HECTOR.

No, faith, young Troilus; doff thy harness, youth;
I am to-day i'th'vein of chivalry:

Let grow thy sinews till their knots be strong,
And tempt not yet the brushes of the war.
Unarm thee, go; and doubt thou not, brave boy,
I'll stand to-day for thee, and me, and Troy.

TROILUS.

Brother, you have a vice of mercy in you,
Which better fits a lion than a man.

HECTOR.

What vice is that, good Troilus? chide me for it.

TROILUS.

When many times the captive Grecian falls,
Even in the fan and wind of your fair sword,
You bid them rise, and live.

HECTOR.

O, 'tis fair play.

TROILUS.

Fool's play, by heaven, Hector.

HECTOR.

How now! how now!

TROILUS.

For th'love of all the gods,
Let's leave the hermit pity with our mothers;
And when we have our armours buckled on,
The venom'd vengeance ride upon our swords,
Spur them to ruthful work, rein them from ruth.

HECTOR.

Fie, savage, fie!

TROILUS.

Hector, then 'tis wars.

HECTOR.

Troilus, I would not have you fight to-day.

TROILUS.

Who should withhold me?
Not fate, obedience, nor the hand of Mars
Beckoning with fiery truncheon my retire;
Not Priamus and Hecuba on knees,
Their eyes o'ergalled with recourse of tears;
Nor you, my brother, with your true sword drawn,
Opposed to hinder me, should stop my way,
But by my ruin.

Enter CASSANDRA *with* PRIAM.

CASSANDRA.

Lay hold upon him, Priam, hold him fast:
He is thy crutch; now if thou lose thy stay,
Thou on him leaning, and all Troy on thee,
Fall all together.

PRIAM.

Come, Hector, come, go back:
Thy wife hath dream'd; thy mother hath had visions;
Cassandra doth foresee; and I myself
Am like a prophet suddenly enrapt,
To tell thee that this day is ominous:
Therefore, come back.

HECTOR.

Aeneas is a-field;
And I do stand engaged to many Greeks,
Even in the faith of valour, to appear
This morning to them.

PRIAM.

Ay, but thou shalt not go.

HECTOR.

I must not break my faith.
You know me dutiful; therefore, dear sir,
Let me not shame respect; but give me leave
To take that course by your consent and voice,
Which you do here forbid me, royal Priam.

CASSANDRA.

O Priam, yield not to him!

ANDROMACHE.

Do not, dear father.

HECTOR.

Andromache, I am offended with you:
Upon the love you bear me, get you in.

[*Exit* ANDROMACHE.

TROILUS.

This foolish, dreaming, superstitious girl
Makes all these bodements.

CASSANDRA.

O, farewell, dear Hector!
Look, how thou diest! look, how thy eye turns pale!
Look, how thy wounds do bleed at many vents!
Hark, how Troy roars! how Hecuba cries out!
How poor Andromache shrills her dolours forth!
Behold distraction, frenzy, and amazement,
Like witless antics, one another meet,
And all cry 'Hector! Hector's dead!' O Hector!

TROILUS.

Away! away!

CASSANDRA.

Farewell:—yet, soft!—Hector, I take my leave:
Thou dost thyself and all our Troy deceive.

[*Exit.*

HECTOR.

You are amazed, my liege, at her exclaim:
Go in, and cheer the town: we'll forth, and fight;
Do deeds worth praise, and tell you them at night.

PRIAM.

Farewell: the gods with safety stand about thee!

[*Exeunt severally* PRIAM *and* HECTOR. *Alarum.*

TROILUS.

They are at it, hark!—Proud Diomed, believe,
I come to lose my arm, or win my sleeve.

Enter PANDARUS.

PANDARUS.

Do you hear, my lord? do you hear?

TROILUS.

What now?

PANDARUS.

Here's a letter come from yond poor girl.

TROILUS.

Let me read.

PANDARUS.

A whoreson tisick, a whoreson rascally tisick so troubles me, and the foolish fortune of this girl; and what one thing, what another, that I shall leave you one o'th's days: and I have a rheum in mine eyes too; and such an ache in my bones, that, unless a man were curst, I cannot tell what to think on't.—What says she there?

TROILUS.

Words, words, mere words, no matter from the heart;
Th'effect doth operate another way.—

[*Tearing the letter.*

Go, wind, to wind, there turn and change together.—
My love with words and errors still she feeds;
But edifies another with her deeds.

[*Exeunt severally.*

SCENE IV.

Plains between Troy and the Grecian camp.

Alarums: excursions. Enter THERSITES.

THERSITES.

NOW they are clapper-clawing one another; I'll go look on. That dissembling abominable varlet, Diomed, has got that same scurvy doting foolish young knave's sleeve of Troy there in his helm: I would fain see them meet; that that same young Trojan ass, that loves the whore there, might send that Greekish whore-masterly villain, with the sleeve, back to the dissembling luxurious drab of a sleeveless errand. O'th't'other side, the policy of those crafty swearing rascals—that stale old mouse-eaten dry cheese, Nestor, and that same-dog-fox, Ulysses—is not proved worth a blackberry:—they set me up, in policy, that mongrel cur, Ajax, against that dog of as bad a kind, Achilles: and now is the cur Ajax prouder than the cur Achilles, and will not arm to-day; whereupon the Grecians begin to proclaim barbarism, and policy grows into an ill opinion.—Soft! here comes sleeve, and t'other.

Enter DIOMEDES *and* TROILUS.

TROILUS.

Fly not: for shouldst thou take the river Styx,
I would swim after.

DIOMEDES.

Thou dost miscall retire:
I do not fly; but advantageous care
Withdrew me from the odds of multitude:
Have at thee!

THERSITES.

Hold thy whore, Grecian! now for thy whore, Trojan!—now the sleeve! now the sleeve!

[*Exeunt* TROILUS *and* DIOMEDES, *fighting*.

Enter HECTOR.

HECTOR.

What art thou, Greek? art thou for Hector's match?
Art thou of blood and honour?

THERSITES.

No, no,—I am a rascal; a scurvy railing knave; a very filthy rogue.

HECTOR.

I do believe thee;—live. [*Exit*.

THERSITES.

God-a-mercy, that thou wilt believe me; but a plague break thy neck for frighting me!—What's become of the wenching rogues? I think they have swallow'd one another: I would laugh at that miracle:—yet, in a sort, lechery eats itself. I'll seek them. [*Exit*.

SCENE V.

Another part of the plains.

Enter DIOMEDES *and* SERVANT.

DIOMEDES.

GO, go, my servant, take thou Troilus' horse;
Present the fair steed to my lady Cressid:
Fellow, commend my service to her beauty;
Tell her I have chastised the amorous Trojan,
And am her knight by proof.

SERVANT.

I go, my lord. [*Exit*.

Enter AGAMEMNON.

AGAMEMNON.

Renew, renew! The fierce Polydamas
Hath beat down Menon: bastard Margarelon
Hath Doreus prisoner,
And stands colossus-wise, waving his beam,
Upon the pashed corses of the kings
Epistrophus and Cedius: Polyxenes is slain;
Amphimachus and Thoas deadly hurt;
Patroclus ta'en or slain; and Palamedes
Sore hurt and bruised: the dreadful Sagittary
Appals our numbers:—haste we, Diomed,
To reinforcement, or we perish all.

Enter NESTOR.

NESTOR.

Go, bear Patroclus' body to Achilles;
And bid the snail-paced Ajax arm for shame.—
There is a thousand Hectors in the field:
Now here he fights on Galathe his horse,
And there lacks work; anon he's there afoot,
And there they fly or die, like scaled sculls
Before the belching whale; then is he yonder,
And there the strawy Greeks, ripe for his edge,
Fall down before him, like the mower's swath:
Here, there, and every where, he leaves and takes;
Dexterity so obeying appetite,
That what he will he does; and does so much,
That proof is call'd impossibility.

Enter ULYSSES.

ULYSSES.

O, courage, courage, princes! great Achilles
Is arming, weeping, cursing, vowing vengeance:
Patroclus' wounds have roused his drowsy blood,
Together with his mangled Myrmidons,
That noseless, handless, hackt and chipt, come to him,
Crying on Hector. Ajax hath lost a friend,
And foams at mouth, and he is arm'd and at it,
Roaring for Troilus; who hath done to-day
Mad and fantastic execution;
Engaging and redeeming of himself,
With such a careless force and forceless care,
As if that luck, in very spite of cunning,
Bade him win all.

Enter AJAX.

AJAX.

Troilus! thou coward Troilus! [*Exit*.

DIOMEDES.

Ay, there, there.

NESTOR.

So, so, we draw together.

Enter ACHILLES.

ACHILLES.

Where is this Hector?—
Come, come, thou boy-queller, show thy face;
Know what it is to meet Achilles angry:—
Hector! where's Hector? I will none but Hector.
[*Exeunt*.

SCENE VI.

Another part of the plains.

Enter AJAX.

AJAX.

TROILUS, thou coward Troilus, show thy head!

Enter DIOMEDES.

DIOMEDES.

Troilus, I say! where's Troilus?

AJAX.

What wouldst thou?

DIOMEDES.

I would correct him.

AJAX.

Were I the general, thou shouldst have my office
Ere that correction.—Troilus, I say! what, Troilus!

Enter TROILUS.

TROILUS.

O traitor Diomed!—turn thy false face, thou traitor,
And pay thy life thou owest me for my horse!

DIOMEDES.

Ha, art thou there?

AJAX.

I'll fight with him alone: stand, Diomed.

DIOMEDES.

He is my prize; I will not look upon.

TROILUS.

Come, both you cogging Greeks; have at you both!
[*Exeunt, fighting.*

Enter HECTOR.

HECTOR.

Yea, Troilus? O, well fought, my youngest brother!

Enter ACHILLES.

ACHILLES.

Now do I see thee, ha!—have at thee, Hector!

HECTOR.

Pause, if thou wilt.

ACHILLES.

I do disdain thy courtesy, proud Trojan:
Be happy that my arms are out of use:
My rest and negligence befriend thee now,
But thou anon shalt hear of me again;
Till when, go seek thy fortune. [*Exit.*

HECTOR.

Fare thee well:—
I would have been much more a fresher man,
Had I expected thee.

Enter TROILUS.

How now, my brother!

TROILUS.

Ajax hath ta'en Aeneas: shall it be?
No, by the flame of yonder glorious heaven,
He shall not carry him; I'll be ta'en too,
Or bring him off:—fate, hear me what I say!
I reck not though I end my life to-day. [*Exit.*

Enter one in sumptuous armour.

HECTOR.

Stand, stand, thou Greek; thou art a goodly mark:—
No? wilt thou not?—I like thy armour well;
I'll frush it, and unlock the rivets all,
But I'll be master of it:—wilt thou not, beast, abide?
Why then, fly on, I'll hunt thee for thy hide.
[*Exeunt.*

SCENE VII.

Another part of the plains.

Enter ACHILLES *with* MYRMIDONS.

ACHILLES.

COME here about me, you my Myrmidons;
Mark what I say. Attend me where I wheel:
Strike not a stroke, but keep yourselves in breath:
And when I have the bloody Hector found,
Empale him with your weapons round about;
In fellest manner execute your arms.
Follow me, sirs, and my proceedings eye:—
It is decreed Hector the great must die. [*Exeunt.*

Enter MENELAUS *and* PARIS, *fighting; then* THERSITES.

THERSITES.

The cuckold and the cuckold-maker are at it.—Now, bull! now, dog! 'Loo, Paris, 'loo! now my double-henn'd sparrow! 'loo, Paris, 'loo!—The bull has the game:—ware horns, ho!

[*Exeunt* PARIS *and* MENELAUS.

Enter MARGARELON.

MARGARELON.

Turn, slave, and fight.

THERSITES.

What art thou?

MARGARELON.

A bastard son of Priam's.

THERSITES.

I am a bastard too; I love bastards: I am a bastard begot, bastard instructed, bastard in mind, bastard in valour, in every thing illegitimate. One bear will not bite another, and wherefore should one bastard? Take heed, the quarrel's most ominous to us: if the son of a whore fight for a whore, he tempts judgement: farewell, bastard. [*Exit.*

MARGARELON.

The devil take thee, coward! [*Exit.*

SCENE VIII.

Another part of the plains.

Enter HECTOR.

HECTOR.

MOST putrefied core, so fair without,
Thy goodly armour thus hath cost thy life.
Now is my day's work done; I'll take good breath:
Rest, sword; thou hast thy fill of blood and death.
[*Puts off his helmet, and hangs his shield behind him.*

Enter ACHILLES *and* MYRMIDONS.

ACHILLES.

Look, Hector, how the sun begins to set;
How ugly night comes breathing at his heels:
Even with the vail and darkening of the sun,
To close the day up, Hector's life is done.

HECTOR.

I am unarm'd; forgo this vantage, Greek.

ACHILLES.

Strike, fellows, strike; this is the man I seek.
[HECTOR *falls.*
So, Ilion, fall thou next! now, Troy, sink down!
Here lies thy heart, thy sinews, and thy bone.—
On, Myrmidons; and cry you all amain,
'Achilles hath the mighty Hector slain.'—
[*A retreat sounded.*
Hark! a retire upon our Grecian part.

MYRMIDONS.

The Trojan trumpets sound the like, my lord.

ACHILLES.

The dragon wing of night o'erspreads the earth,
And, stickler-like, the armies separates.
My half-supt sword, that frankly would have fed,

Pleased with this dainty bait, thus goes to bed.
[*Sheathes his sword.*
Come, tie his body to my horse's tail;
Along the field I will the Trojan trail. [*Exeunt.*

SCENE IX.

Another part of the plains.

Enter AGAMEMNON, AJAX, MENELAUS, NESTOR, DIOMEDES, *and the rest, marching. Shouts within.*

AGAMEMNON.

Hark! hark! what shout is that?

NESTOR.

Peace, drums!

[*within*] Achilles! Achilles! Hector's slain! Achilles!

DIOMEDES.

The bruit is, Hector's slain, and by Achilles.

AJAX.

If it be so, yet bragless let it be;
Great Hector was a man as good as he.

AGAMEMNON.

March patiently along:—let one be sent
To pray Achilles see us at our tent.—
If in his death the gods have us befriended,
Great Troy is ours, and our sharp wars are ended.
[*Exeunt, marching.*

SCENE X.

Another part of the plains.

Enter AENEAS, PARIS, ANTENOR, *and* DEIPHOBUS.

AENEAS.

Stand, ho! yet are we masters of the field:
Never go home; here starve we out the night.

Enter TROILUS.

TROILUS.

Hector is slain.

ALL.

Hector!—the gods forbid!

TROILUS.

He's dead; and at the murderer's horse's tail,
In beastly sort, dragg'd through the shameful field.—
Frown on, you heavens, effect your rage with speed!
Sit, gods, upon your thrones, and smile at Troy!
I say, at once let your brief plagues be mercy,
And linger not our sure destructions on!

AENEAS.

My lord, you do discomfort all the host.

TROILUS.

You understand me not that tell me so:
I do not speak of flight, of fear, of death;
But dare all imminence that gods and men
Address their dangers in. Hector is gone:
Who shall tell Priam so, or Hecuba?
Let him that will a screech-owl aye be call'd,
Go into Troy, and say there 'Hector's dead:'
There is a word will Priam turn to stone;
Make wells and Niobes of the maids and wives,
Cold statues of the youth; and, in a word,
Scare Troy out of itself. But, march away:
Hector is dead; there is no more to say.
Stay yet.—You vile abominable tents,
Thus proudly pight upon our Phrygian plains,
Let Titan rise as early as he dare,
I'll through and through you!—and, thou great-sized coward,
No space of earth shall sunder our two hates:
I'll haunt thee like a wicked conscience still,
That mouldeth goblins swift as frenzy's thoughts.—
Strike a free march to Troy!—with comfort go:
Hope of revenge shall hide our inward woe.
[*Exeunt* AENEAS *and* TROJANS.

As TROILUS *is going out, enter, from the other side,* PANDARUS.

PANDARUS.

But hear you, hear you!

TROILUS.

Hence, broker-lackey! ignomy and shame
Pursue thy life, and live aye with thy name! [*Exit.*

PANDARUS.

A goodly medicine for my aching bones!—O world! world! world! thus is the poor agent despised! O traders and bawds, how earnestly are you set a-work, and how ill requited! why should our endeavour be so loved, and the performance so loathed? what verse for it? what instance for it?—Let me see:—

Full merrily the humble-bee doth sing,
Till he hath lost his honey and his sting;
And being once subdued in armed tail,
Sweet honey and sweet notes together fail.—

Good traders in the flesh, set this in your painted cloths.
As many as be here of Pandar's hall,
Your eyes, half out, weep out at Pandar's fall;
Or if you cannot weep, yet give some groans,
Though not for me, yet for your aching bones.
Brethren and sisters of the hold-door trade,
Some two months hence my will shall here be made:
It should be now, but that my fear is this,—
Some galled goose of Winchester would hiss:
Till then I'll sweat, and seek about for eases;
And at that time bequeath you my diseases. [*Exit.*

MEASURE FOR MEASURE

DRAMATIS PERSONAE

VINCENTIO, *the Duke.*
ANGELO, *the Deputy.*
ESCALUS, *an ancient Lord.*
CLAUDIO, *a young Gentleman.*
LUCIO, *a Fantastic.*
TWO OTHER LIKE GENTLEMEN.
PROVOST.
THOMAS, } *Two Friars.*
PETER, }
A JUSTICE.
VARRIUS.
ELBOW, *a simple Constable.*
FROTH, *a foolish Gentleman.*
POMPEY, *servant to Mistress Overdone.*
ABHORSON, *an Executioner.*
BARNARDINE, *a dissolute Prisoner.*

ISABELLA, *sister to Claudio.*
MARIANA, *betrothed to Angelo.*
JULIET, *beloved of Claudio.*
FRANCISCA, *a Nun.*
MISTRESS OVERDONE, *a Bawd.*

LORDS, OFFICERS, CITIZENS, BOY, *and* ATTENDANTS.

SCENE—*Vienna.*

ACT I. SCENE I.

An apartment in the DUKE'S *palace.*

Enter DUKE, ESCALUS, LORDS, & ATTENDANTS.

DUKE.

Escalus,—

ESCALUS.

My lord?

DUKE.

Of government the properties to unfold,
Would seem in me t'affect speech and discourse;
Since I am put to know that your own science
Exceeds, in that, the lists of all advice
My strength can give you: then no more remains
But that to your sufficiency . . . . .
. . . . as your worth is able,
And let them work. The nature of our people,
Our city's institutions, and the terms
For common justice, you're as pregnant in
As art and practice has enriched any
That we remember. There is our commission,
From which we would not have you warp.—Call hither,
I say, bid come before us Angelo.

[*Exit an* ATTENDANT.

What figure of us think you he will bear?
For, you must know, we have with special soul
Elected him our absence to supply;
Lent him our terror, dress'd him with our love,
And given his deputation all the organs
Of our own power: what think you of it?

ESCALUS.

If any in Vienna be of worth
To undergo such ample grace and honour,
It is Lord Angelo.

DUKE.

Look where he comes.

Enter ANGELO.

ANGELO.

Always obedient to your grace's will,
I come to know your pleasure.

DUKE.

Angelo,
There is a kind of character in thy life,
That to th'observer doth thy history
Fully unfold. Thyself and thy belongings
Are not thine own so proper, as to waste
Thyself upon thy virtues, they on thee.
Heaven doth with us as we with torches do,
Not light them for themselves; for if our virtues
Did not go forth of us, 'twere all alike
As if we had them not. Spirits are not finely touch'd
But to fine issues; nor Nature never lends
The smallest scruple of her excellence
But, like a thrifty goddess, she determines
Herself the glory of a creditor,
Both thanks and use. But I do bend my speech
To one that can my part in him advertise;
Hold, therefore, Angelo:—
In our remove be thou at full ourself;
Mortality and mercy in Vienna
Live in thy tongue and heart: old Escalus,
Though first in question, is thy secondary:—
Take thy commission.

ANGELO.

Now, good my lord,
Let there be some more test made of my metal,
Before so noble and so great a figure
Be stamp'd upon it.

DUKE.

No more evasion:
We have with a leaven'd and prepared choice
Proceeded to you; therefore take your honours.
Our haste from hence is of so quick condition,
That it prefers itself and leaves unquestion'd
Matters of needful value. We shall write to you,
As time and our concernings shall importune,
How it goes with us; and do look to know
What doth befall you here. So, fare you well:
To th'hopeful execution do I leave you
Of your commissions.

ANGELO.

Yet, give leave, my lord,
That we may bring you something on the way.

DUKE.

My haste may not admit it;
Nor need you, on mine honour, have to do
With any scruple: your scope is as mine own,
So to enforce or qualify the laws
As to your soul seems good. Give me your hand:
I'll privily away. I love the people,

But do not like to stage me to their eyes:
Though it do well, I do not relish well
Their loud applause and Aves vehement;
Nor do I think the man of safe discretion
That does affect it. Once more, fare you well.

ANGELO.

The heavens give safety to your purposes!—

ESCALUS.

Lead forth and bring you back in happiness!

DUKE.

I thank you. Fare you well. [*Exit.*

ESCALUS.

I shall desire you, sir, to give me leave
To have free speech with you; and it concerns me
To look into the bottom of my place:
A power I have, but of what strength and nature
I am not yet instructed.

ANGELO.

'Tis so with me. Let us withdraw together,
And we may soon our satisfaction have
Touching that point.

ESCALUS.

I'll wait upon your honour.
[*Exeunt.*

SCENE II.

A street.

Enter LUCIO *and two other* GENTLEMEN.

LUCIO.

If the duke, with the other dukes, come not to composition with the King of Hungary, why, then, all the dukes fall upon the king.

FIRST GENTLEMAN.

Heaven grant us its peace, but not the King of Hungary's!

SECOND GENTLEMAN.

Amen.

LUCIO.

Thou concludest like the sanctimonious pirate, that went to sea with the Ten Commandments, but scraped one out of the table.

SECOND GENTLEMAN.

'Thou shalt not steal'?

LUCIO.

Ay, that he razed.

FIRST GENTLEMAN.

Why, 'twas a commandment to command the captain and all the rest from their functions: they put forth to steal. There's not a soldier of us all, that, in the thanksgiving before meat, do relish the petition well that prays for peace.

SECOND GENTLEMAN.

I never heard any soldier dislike it.

LUCIO.

I believe thee; for I think thou never wast where grace was said.

SECOND GENTLEMAN.

No? a dozen times at least.

FIRST GENTLEMAN.

What, in metre?

LUCIO.

In any proportion or in any language.

FIRST GENTLEMAN.

I think, or in any religion.

LUCIO.

Ay, why not? Grace is grace, despite of all controversy: as, for example,—thou thyself art a wicked villain, despite of all grace.

FIRST GENTLEMAN.

Well, there went but a pair of shears between us.

LUCIO.

I grant; as there may between the lists and the velvet. Thou art the list.

FIRST GENTLEMAN.

And thou the velvet: thou art good velvet; thou'rt a three-piled piece, I warrant thee: I had as lief be a list of an English kersey, as be piled, as thou art piled, for a French velvet. Do I speak feelingly now?

LUCIO.

I think thou dost; and, indeed, with most painful feeling of thy speech, I will, out of thine own confession, learn to begin thy health; but, whilst I live, forget to drink after thee.

FIRST GENTLEMAN.

I think I have done myself wrong, have I not?

SECOND GENTLEMAN.

Yes, that thou hast, whether thou art tainted or free.

LUCIO.

Behold, behold, where Madam Mitigation comes!

FIRST GENTLEMAN.

I have purchased as many diseases under her roof as come to—

SECOND GENTLEMAN.

To what, I pray?

FIRST GENTLEMAN.

Judge.

SECOND GENTLEMAN.

To three thousand dolours a year.

FIRST GENTLEMAN.

Ay, and more.

LUCIO.

A French crown more.

FIRST GENTLEMAN.

Thou art always figuring diseases in me; but thou art full of error,—I am sound.

LUCIO.

Nay, not as one would say, healthy; but so sound as things that are hollow: thy bones are hollow; impiety has made a feast of thee.

Enter MISTRESS OVERDONE.

FIRST GENTLEMAN.

How now! which of your hips has the most profound sciatica?

MISTRESS OVERDONE.

Well, well; there's one yonder arrested and carried to prison was worth five thousand of you all.

SECOND GENTLEMAN.

Who's that, I pray thee?

MISTRESS OVERDONE.

Marry, sir, that's Claudio, Signior Claudio.

FIRST GENTLEMAN.

Claudio to prison! 'tis not so.

MISTRESS OVERDONE.

Nay, but I know 'tis so: I saw him arrested; saw him carried away; and, which is more, within these three days his head to be chopp'd off.

LUCIO.
But, after all this fooling, I would not have it so. Art thou sure of this?

MISTRESS OVERDONE.
I am too sure of it: and it is for getting Madam Julietta with child.

LUCIO.
Believe me, this may be: he promised to meet me two hours since, and he was ever precise in promise-keeping.

SECOND GENTLEMAN.
Besides, you know, it draws something near to the speech we had to such a purpose.

FIRST GENTLEMAN.
But, most of all, agreeing with the proclamation.

LUCIO.
Away! let's go learn the truth of it.
[*Exeunt* LUCIO *and* GENTLEMEN.

MISTRESS OVERDONE.
Thus, what with the war, what with the sweat, what with the gallows, and what with poverty, I am custom-shrunk.

Enter POMPEY.

How now! What's the news with you?

POMPEY.
Yonder man is carried to prison.

MISTRESS OVERDONE.
Well: what has he done?

POMPEY.
A woman.

MISTRESS OVERDONE.
But what's his offence?

POMPEY.
Groping for trouts in a peculiar river.

MISTRESS OVERDONE.
What, is there a maid with child by him?

POMPEY.
No, but there's a woman with maid by him. You have not heard of the proclamation, have you?

MISTRESS OVERDONE.
What proclamation, man?

POMPEY.
All houses in the suburbs of Vienna must be pluck'd down.

MISTRESS OVERDONE.
And what shall become of those in the city?

POMPEY.
They shall stand for seed: they had gone down too, but that a wise burgher put in for them.

MISTRESS OVERDONE.
But shall all our houses of resort in the suburbs be pull'd down?

POMPEY.
To the ground, mistress.

MISTRESS OVERDONE.
Why, here's a change indeed in the commonwealth! What shall become of me?

POMPEY.
Come; fear not you: good counsellors lack no clients: though you change your place, you need not change your trade; I'll be your tapster still. Courage! there will be pity taken on you: you that have worn your eyes almost out in the service, you will be consider'd.

MISTRESS OVERDONE.
What's to do here, Thomas Tapster? let's withdraw.

POMPEY.
Here comes Signior Claudio, led by the provost to prison; and there's Madam Juliet. [*Exeunt.*

Enter PROVOST, CLAUDIO, JULIET, *and* OFFICERS.

CLAUDIO.
Fellow, why dost thou show me thus to th'world?
Bear me to prison, where I am committed.

PROVOST.
I do it not in evil disposition,
But from Lord Angelo by special charge.

CLAUDIO.
Thus can the demigod Authority
Make us pay down for our offence by weight.—
The words of heaven;—on whom it will, it will;
On whom it will not, so; yet still 'tis just.

Enter LUCIO *and two* GENTLEMEN.

LUCIO.
Why, how now, Claudio! whence comes this restraint?

CLAUDIO.
From too much liberty, my Lucio, liberty:
As surfeit is the father of much fast,
So every scope by the immoderate use
Turns to restraint. Our natures do pursue,
Like rats that ravin down their proper bane,
A thirsty evil; and when we drink we die.

LUCIO.
If I could speak so wisely under an arrest, I would send for certain of my creditors: and yet, to say the truth, I had as lief have the foppery of freedom as the morality of imprisonment.—What's thy offence, Claudio?

CLAUDIO.
What but to speak of would offend again.

LUCIO.
What, is't murder?

CLAUDIO.
No.

LUCIO.
Lechery?

CLAUDIO.
Call it so.

PROVOST.
Away, sir! you must go.

CLAUDIO.
One word, good friend.—Lucio, a word with you.
[*Takes him aside.*

LUCIO.
A hundred, if they'll do you any good.—
Is lechery so look'd after?

CLAUDIO.
Thus stands it with me:—upon a true contract
I got possession of Julietta's bed:
You know the lady; she is fast my wife,
Save that we do the denunciation lack
Of outward order: this we came not to,
Only for propagation of a dower
Remaining in the coffer of her friends;
From whom we thought it meet to hide our love
Till time had made them for us. But it chances
The stealth of our most mutual entertainment
With character too gross is writ on Juliet.

LUCIO.
With child, perhaps?
CLAUDIO.
Unhappily, even so.
And the new deputy now for the duke,—
Whether it be the fault and glimpse of newness,
Or whether that the body public be
A horse whereon the governor doth ride,
Who, newly in the seat, that it may know
He can command, lets it straight feel the spur;
Whether the tyranny be in his place,
Or in his eminence that fills it up,
I stagger in:—but this new governor
Awakes me all the enrolled penalties
Which have, like unscour'd armour, hung by the wall
So long, that nineteen zodiacs have gone round,
And none of them been worn; and, for a name,
Now puts the drowsy and neglected act
Freshly on me:—'tis surely for a name.
LUCIO.
I warrant it is: and thy head stands so tickle on thy shoulders, that a milkmaid, if she be in love, may sigh it off. Send after the duke, and appeal to him.
CLAUDIO.
I have done so, but he's not to be found.
I prithee, Lucio, do me this kind service:—
This day my sister should the cloister enter.
And there receive her approbation:
Acquaint her with the danger of my state;
Implore her, in my voice, that she make friends
To the strict deputy; bid herself assay him:
I have great hope in that; for in her youth
There is a prone and speechless dialect,
Such as move men; beside, she hath prosperous art
When she will play with reason and discourse,
And well she can persuade.
LUCIO.
I pray she may; as well for the encouragement of the like, which else would stand under grievous imposition, as for the enjoying of thy life, who I would be sorry should be thus foolishly lost at a game of tick-tack. I'll to her.
CLAUDIO.
I thank you, good friend Lucio.
LUCIO.
Within two hours.
CLAUDIO.
Come, officer, away! [*Exeunt.*

SCENE III.

A monastery.

Enter DUKE *and* FRIAR THOMAS.

DUKE.
NO, holy father; throw away that thought;
Believe not that the dribbling dart of love
Can pierce a complete bosom. Why I desire thee
To give me secret harbour, hath a purpose
More grave and wrinkled than the aims and ends
Of burning youth.
FRIAR THOMAS.
May your grace speak of it?
DUKE.
My holy sir, none better knows than you
How I have ever loved the life removed;
And held in idle price to haunt assemblies,
Where youth, and cost, and witless bravery keeps.
I have deliver'd to Lord Angelo—
A man of stricture and firm abstinence—
My absolute power and place here in Vienna,
And he supposes me travell'd to Poland;
For so I have strew'd it in the common ear,
And so it is received. Now, pious sir,
You will demand of me why I do this?
FRIAR THOMAS.
Gladly, my lord.
DUKE.
We have strict statutes and most biting laws,—
The needful bits and curbs to headstrong wills,—
Which for this fourteen years we have let slip;
Even like an o'ergrown lion in a cave,
That goes not out to prey. Now, as fond fathers,
Having bound up the threat'ning twigs of birch,
Only to stick it in their children's sight
For terror, not to use, in time the rod
Becomes more mock'd than fear'd; so our decrees,
Dead to infliction, to themselves are dead;
And liberty plucks justice by the nose;
The baby beats the nurse, and quite athwart
Goes all decorum.
FRIAR THOMAS.
It rested in your grace
To unloose this tied-up justice when you pleased:
And it in you more dreadful would have seem'd
Than in Lord Angelo.
DUKE.
I do fear, too dreadful:
Sith 'twas my fault to give the people scope,
'Twould be my tyranny to strike and gall them
For what I bid them do: for we bid this be done,
When evil deeds have their permissive pass,
And not the punishment. Therefore, indeed, my father,
I have on Angelo imposed the office,
Who may, in th'ambush of my name, strike home;
And yet my nature never in the fight
To do it slander. And to behold his sway,
I will, as 'twere a brother of your order,
Visit both prince and people: therefore, I prithee,
Supply me with the habit, and instruct me
How I may formally in person bear me
Like a true friar. Moe reasons for this action
At our more leisure shall I render you;
Only, this one:—Lord Angelo is precise;
Stands at a guard with envy; scarce confesses
That his blood flows, or that his appetite
Is more to bread than stone: hence shall we see,
If power change purpose, what our seemers be.
[*Exeunt.*

SCENE IV.

A nunnery.

Enter ISABELLA *and* FRANCISCA, *a* NUN.

ISABELLA.
AND have you nuns no further privileges?
FRANCISCA.
Are not these large enough?
ISABELLA.
Yes, truly: I speak not as desiring more;

But rather wishing a more strict restraint
Upon the sisterhood, the votarists of Saint Clare.

LUCIO [*within*].
Ho! Peace be in this place!

ISABELLA.
Who's that which calls?

FRANCISCA.
It is a man's voice. Gentle Isabella,
Turn you the key, and know his business of him;
You may, I may not; you are yet unsworn.
When you have vow'd, you must not speak with men
But in the presence of the prioress:
Then, if you speak, you must not show your face;
Or, if you show your face, you must not speak.
He calls again; I pray you, answer him. [*Exit.*

ISABELLA.
Peace and prosperity! Who is't that calls?

Enter LUCIO.

LUCIO.
Hail, virgin, if you be, as those cheek-roses
Proclaim you are no less! Can you so stead me
As bring me to the sight of Isabella,
A novice of this place, and the fair sister
To her unhappy brother Claudio?

ISABELLA.
Why 'her unhappy brother'? let me ask;
The rather, for I now must make you know
I am that Isabella and his sister.

LUCIO.
Gentle and fair, your brother kindly greets you:
Not to be weary with you, he's in prison.

ISABELLA.
Woe me! for what?

LUCIO.
For that which, if myself might be his judge,
He should receive his punishment in thanks:
He hath got his friend with child.

ISABELLA.
Sir, make me not your story.

LUCIO.
'Tis true.
I would not—though 'tis my familiar sin
With maids to seem the lapwing, and to jest,
Tongue far from heart—play with all virgins so:
I hold you as a thing ensky'd and sainted;
By your renouncement, an immortal spirit;
And to be talk'd with in sincerity,
As with a saint.

ISABELLA.
You do blaspheme the good in mocking me.

LUCIO.
Do not believe it. Fewness and truth, 'tis thus:—
Your brother and his lover have embraced:
As those that feed grow full; as blossoming-time,
That from the seedness the bare fallow brings
To teeming foison; even so her plenteous womb
Expresseth his full tilth and husbandry.

ISABELLA.
Some one with child by him?—My cousin Juliet?

LUCIO.
Is she your cousin?

ISABELLA.
Adoptedly; as school-maids change their names
By vain, though apt, affection.

LUCIO.
She it is.

ISABELLA.
O, let him marry her.

LUCIO.
This is the point.
The duke is very strangely gone from hence;
Bore many gentlemen, myself being one,
In hand, and hope of action: but we do learn
By those that know the very nerves of state,
His givings-out were of an infinite distance
From his true-meant design. Upon his place,
And with full line of his authority,
Governs Lord Angelo; a man whose blood
Is very snow-broth; one who never feels
The wanton stings and motions of the sense,
But doth rebate and blunt his natural edge
With profits of the mind, study and fast.
He—to give fear to use and liberty,
Which have for long run by the hideous law,
As mice by lions—hath pick'd out an act,
Under whose heavy sense your brother's life
Falls into forfeit: he arrests him on it;
And follows close the rigour of the statute,
To make him an example. All hope is gone,
Unless you have the grace by your fair prayer
To soften Angelo: and that's my pith
Of business 'twixt you and your poor brother.

ISABELLA.
Doth he so seek his life?

LUCIO.
Has censured him
Already; and, as I hear, the provost hath
A warrant for his execution.

ISABELLA.
Alas, what poor ability's in me
To do him good!

LUCIO.
Assay the power you have.

ISABELLA.
My power! Alas, I doubt,—

LUCIO.
Our doubts are traitors,
And make us lose the good we oft might win
By fearing to attempt. Go to Lord Angelo,
And let him learn to know, when maidens sue,
Men give like gods; but when they weep and kneel,
All their petitions are as freely theirs
As they themselves would owe them.

ISABELLA.
I'll see what I can do.

LUCIO.
But speedily.

ISABELLA.
I will about it straight;
No longer staying but to give the mother
Notice of my affair. I humbly thank you:
Commend me to my brother: soon at night
I'll send him certain word of my success.

LUCIO.
I take my leave of you.

ISABELLA.
Good sir, adieu. [*Exeunt.*

ACT II. SCENE I.

A hall in ANGELO'S *house.*

Enter ANGELO, ESCALUS, *a* JUSTICE, PROVOST, OFFICERS, *and other* ATTENDANTS.

ANGELO.

We must not make a scarecrow of the law,
Setting it up to fear the birds of prey,
And let it keep one shape, till custom make it
Their perch, and not their terror.

ESCALUS.

Ay, but yet
Let us be keen, and rather cut a little,
Than fall, and bruise to death. Alas, this gentleman,
Whom I would save, had a most noble father!
Let but your honour know,—
Whom I believe to be most strait in virtue,—
That, in the working of your own affections,
Had time cohered with place, or place with wishing,
Or that the resolute acting of your blood
Could have attain'd th'effect of your own purpose,
Whether you had not sometime in your life
Err'd in this point which now you censure him,
And pull'd the law upon you.

ANGELO.

'Tis one thing to be tempted, Escalus,
Another thing to fall. I not deny,
The jury, passing on the prisoner's life,
May in the sworn twelve have a thief or two
Guiltier than him they try. What's open made to justice,
That justice seizes: what know the laws
That thieves do pass on thieves? 'Tis very pregnant,
The jewel that we find, we stoop and take't,
Because we see it; but what we do not see
We tread upon, and never think of it.
You may not so extenuate his offence
For I have had such faults; but rather tell me,
When I, that censure him, do so offend,
Let mine own judgement pattern out my death,
And nothing come in partial. Sir, he must die.

ESCALUS.

Be it as your wisdom will.

ANGELO.

Where is the provost?

PROVOST.

Here, if it like your honour.

ANGELO.

See that Claudio
Be executed by nine to-morrow morning:
Bring him his confessor, let him be prepared;
For that's the utmost of his pilgrimage.

[*Exit* PROVOST.

ESCALUS [*aside*].

Well, heaven forgive him! and forgive us all!
Some rise by sin, and some by virtue fall;
Some run from brakes of vice, and answer none;
And some condemned for a fault alone.

Enter ELBOW, *and* OFFICERS *with* FROTH *and* POMPEY.

ELBOW.

Come, bring them away: if these be good people in a commonweal that do nothing but use their abuses in common houses, I know no law: bring them away.

ANGELO.

How now, sir! What's your name? and what's the matter?

ELBOW.

If it please your honour, I am the poor duke's constable, and my name is Elbow: I do lean upon justice, sir, and do bring in here before your good honour two notorious benefactors.

ANGELO.

Benefactors! Well; what benefactors are they? are they not malefactors?

ELBOW.

If it please your honour, I know not well what they are: but precise villains they are, that I am sure of; and void of all profanation in the world that good Christians ought to have.

ESCALUS.

This comes off well; here's a wise officer.

ANGELO.

Go to:—what quality are they of? Elbow is your name? why dost thou not speak, Elbow?

POMPEY.

He cannot, sir; he's out at elbow.

ANGELO.

What are you, sir?

ELBOW.

He, sir! a tapster, sir; parcel-bawd; one that serves a bad woman; whose house, sir, was, as they say, pluck'd down in the suburbs; and now she professes a hot-house, which, I think, is a very ill house too.

ESCALUS.

How know you that?

ELBOW.

My wife, sir, whom I detest before heaven and your honour,—

ESCALUS.

How! thy wife!

ELBOW.

Ay, sir;—whom, I thank heaven, is an honest woman,—

ESCALUS.

Dost thou detest her therefore?

ELBOW.

I say, sir, I will detest myself also, as well as she, that this house, if it be not a bawd's house, it is pity of her life, for it is a naughty house.

ESCALUS.

How dost thou know that, constable?

ELBOW.

Marry, sir, by my wife; who, if she had been a woman cardinally given, might have been accused in fornication, adultery, and all uncleanliness there.

ESCALUS.

By the woman's means?

ELBOW.

Ay, sir, by Mistress Overdone's means: but as she spit in his face, so she defied him.

POMPEY.

Sir, if it please your honour, this is not so.

ELBOW.

Prove it before these varlets here, thou honourable man; prove it.

ESCALUS [*to* ANGELO].
Do you hear how he misplaces?

POMPEY.
Sir, she came in great with child; and longing—saving your honour's reverence—for stew'd prunes. Sir, we had but two in the house, which at that very distant time stood, as it were, in a fruit-dish, a dish of some three-pence;—your honours have seen such dishes; they are not China dishes, but very good dishes,—

ESCALUS.
Go to, go to: no matter for the dish, sir.

POMPEY.
No, indeed, sir, not of a pin; you are therein in the right:—but to the point. As I say, this Mistress Elbow, being, as I say, with child, and being great-bellied, and longing, as I said, for prunes; and having but two in the dish, as I said, Master Froth here, this very man, having eaten the rest, as I said, and, as I say, paying for them very honestly;—for, as you know, Master Froth, I could not give you three-pence again,—

FROTH.
No, indeed.

POMPEY.
Very well;—you being then, if you be remember'd, cracking the stones of the aforesaid prunes,—

FROTH.
Ay, so I did indeed.

POMPEY.
Why, very well;—I telling you then, if you be remember'd, that such a one and such a one were past cure of the thing you wot of, unless they kept very good diet, as I told you,—

FROTH.
All this is true.

POMPEY.
Why, very well, then,—

ESCALUS.
Come, you are a tedious fool: to the purpose. What was done to Elbow's wife, that he hath cause to complain of? Come me to what was done to her.

POMPEY.
Sir, your honour cannot come to that yet.

ESCALUS.
No, sir, nor I mean it not.

POMPEY.
Sir, but you shall come to it, by your honour's leave. And, I beseech you, look into Master Froth here, sir; a man of fourscore pound a year; whose father died at Hallowmas:—was't not at Hallowmas, Master Froth?—

FROTH.
All-hallond eve.

POMPEY.
Why, very well; I hope here be truths. He, sir, sitting, as I say, in a lower chair, sir;—'twas in the Bunch of Grapes, where, indeed, you have a delight to sit, have you not?—

FROTH.
I have so; because it is an open room, and good for winter.

POMPEY.
Why, very well, then; I hope here be truths.

ANGELO.
This will last out a night in Russia,
When nights are longest there: I'll take my leave,
And leave you to the hearing of the cause;
Hoping you'll find good cause to whip them all.

ESCALUS.
I think no less. Good morrow to your lordship.
[*Exit* ANGELO.
Now, sir, come on: what was done to Elbow's wife, once more?

POMPEY.
Once, sir! there was nothing done to her once.

ELBOW.
I beseech you, sir, ask him what this man did to my wife.

POMPEY.
I beseech your honour, ask me.

ESCALUS.
Well, sir; what did this gentleman to her?

POMPEY.
I beseech you, sir, look in this gentleman's face.—Good Master Froth, look upon his honour; 'tis for a good purpose.—Doth your honour mark his face?

ESCALUS.
Ay, sir, very well.

POMPEY.
Nay, I beseech you, mark it well.

ESCALUS.
Well, I do so.

POMPEY.
Doth your honour see any harm in his face?

ESCALUS.
Why, no.

POMPEY.
I'll be supposed upon a book, his face is the worst thing about him. Good, then; if his face be the worst thing about him, how could Master Froth do the constable's wife any harm? I would know that of your honour.

ESCALUS.
He's in the right.—Constable, what say you to it?

ELBOW.
First, an it like you, the house is a respected house; next, this is a respected fellow; and his mistress is a respected woman.

POMPEY.
By this hand, sir, his wife is a more respected person than any of us all.

ELBOW.
Varlet, thou liest; thou liest, wicked varlet! the time is yet to come, that she was ever respected with man, woman, or child.

POMPEY.
Sir, she was respected with him before he married with her.

ESCALUS.
Which is the wiser here? Justice or Iniquity?—Is this true?

ELBOW.
O thou caitiff! O thou varlet! O thou wicked Hannibal! I respected with her before I was married to her!—If ever I was respected with her, or she with me, let not your worship think me the poor duke's officer.—Prove this, thou wicked Hannibal, or I'll have mine action of battery on thee.

ESCALUS.
If he took you a box o'th'ear, you might have your action of slander too.

ELBOW.
Marry, I thank your good worship for it.—What is't your worship's pleasure I shall do with this wicked caitiff?

ESCALUS.
Truly, officer, because he hath some offences in him that thou wouldst discover if thou couldst, let him continue in his courses till thou know'st what they are.

ELBOW.
Marry, I thank your worship for it.—Thou seest, thou wicked varlet, now, what's come upon thee: thou art to continue now, thou varlet; thou art to continue.

ESCALUS [*to* FROTH].
Where were you born, friend?

FROTH.
Here in Vienna, sir.

ESCALUS.
Are you of fourscore pounds a year?

FROTH.
Yes, an't please you, sir.

ESCALUS.
So.—[*to* POMPEY] What trade are you of, sir?

POMPEY.
A tapster; a poor widow's tapster.

ESCALUS.
Your mistress' name?

POMPEY.
Mistress Overdone.

ESCALUS.
Hath she had any more than one husband?

POMPEY.
Nine, sir; Overdone by the last.

ESCALUS.
Nine!—Come hither to me, Master Froth. Master Froth, I would not have you acquainted with tapsters: they will draw you, Master Froth, and you will hang them. Get you gone, and let me hear no more of you.

FROTH.
I thank your worship. For mine own part, I never come into any room in a taphouse, but I am drawn in.

ESCALUS.
Well, no more of it, Master Froth: farewell. [*Exit* FROTH.] Come you hither to me, master tapster. What's your name, master tapster?

POMPEY.
Pompey.

ESCALUS.
What else?

POMPEY.
Bum, sir.

ESCALUS.
Troth, and your bum is the greatest thing about you; so that, in the beastliest sense, you are Pompey the Great. Pompey, you are partly a bawd, Pompey, howsoever you colour it in being a tapster. Are you not? come, tell me true: it shall be the better for you.

POMPEY.
Truly, sir, I am a poor fellow that would live.

ESCALUS.
How would you live, Pompey? by being a bawd? What do you think of the trade, Pompey? is it a lawful trade?

POMPEY.
If the law would allow it, sir.

ESCALUS.
But the law will not allow it, Pompey; nor it shall not be allow'd in Vienna.

POMPEY.
Does your worship mean to geld and splay all the youth of the city?

ESCALUS.
No, Pompey.

POMPEY.
Truly, sir, in my poor opinion, they will to't, then. If your worship will take order for the drabs and the knaves, you need not to fear the bawds.

ESCALUS.
There is pretty orders beginning, I can tell you: it is but heading and hanging.

POMPEY.
If you head and hang all that offend that way but for ten year together, you'll be glad to give out a commission for more heads: if this law hold in Vienna ten year, I'll rent the fairest house in it after three-pence a bay: if you live to see this come to pass, say Pompey told you so.

ESCALUS.
Thank you, good Pompey; and, in requital of your prophecy, hark you:—I advise you, let me not find you before me again upon any complaint whatsoever; no, not for dwelling where you do: if I do, Pompey, I shall beat you to your tent, and prove a shrewd Cæsar to you; in plain dealing, Pompey, I shall have you whipt: so, for this time, Pompey, fare you well.

POMPEY.
I thank your worship for your good counsel.—[*aside*] But I shall follow it as the flesh and fortune shall better determine.
Whip me! No, no; let carman whip his jade:
The valiant's heart's not whipt out of his trade.
[*Exit.*

ESCALUS.
Come hither to me, Master Elbow; come hither, master constable. How long have you been in this place of constable?

ELBOW.
Seven year and a half, sir.

ESCALUS.
I thought, by your readiness in the office, you had continued in it some time. You say, seven years together?

ELBOW.
And a half, sir.

ESCALUS.
Alas, it hath been great pains to you! They do you wrong to put you so oft upon't: are there not men in your ward sufficient to serve it?

ELBOW.
Faith, sir, few of any wit in such matters: as they are chosen, they are glad to choose me for them; I do it for some piece of money, and go through with all.

ESCALUS.
Look you bring me in the names of some six or seven, the most sufficient of your parish.

ELBOW.
To your worship's house, sir?

ESCALUS.
To my house. Fare you well. [*Exit* ELBOW.
What's o'clock, think you?

JUSTICE.
Eleven, sir.

ESCALUS.
I pray you home to dinner with me.

JUSTICE.
I humbly thank you.

ESCALUS.
It grieves me for the death of Claudio;
But there's no remedy.

JUSTICE.
Lord Angelo is severe.

ESCALUS.
It is but needful:
Mercy is not itself, that oft looks so;
Pardon is still the nurse of second woe:
But yet,—poor Claudio!—There is no remedy.—
Come, sir. [*Exeunt.*

SCENE II.

Another room in the same.

Enter PROVOST *and a* SERVANT.

SERVANT.
HE'S hearing of a cause; he will come straight:
I'll tell him of you.

PROVOST.
Pray you, do. [*Exit* SERVANT.] I'll know
His pleasure; may be he will relent. Alas,
He hath but as offended in a dream!
All sects, all ages smack of this vice; and he
To die for't!

Enter ANGELO.

ANGELO.
Now, what's the matter, provost?

PROVOST.
Is it your will Claudio shall die to-morrow?

ANGELO.
Did not I tell thee yea? hadst thou not order?
Why dost thou ask again?

PROVOST.
Lest I might be too rash:
Under your good correction, I have seen,
When, after execution, judgement hath
Repented o'er his doom.

ANGELO.
Go to; let that be mine:
Do you your office, or give up your place,
And you shall well be spared.

PROVOST.
I crave your honour's pardon.—
What shall be done, sir, with the groaning Juliet?
She's very near her hour.

ANGELO.
Dispose of her
To some more fitter place; and that with speed.

Enter SERVANT.

SERVANT.
Here is the sister of the man condemn'd
Desires access to you.

ANGELO.
Hath he a sister?

PROVOST.
Ay, my good lord; a very virtuous maid,
And to be shortly of a sisterhood,
If not already.

ANGELO.
Well, let her be admitted. [*Exit* SERVANT.
See you the fornicatress be removed:
Let her have needful, but not lavish, means;
There shall be order for't.

Enter ISABELLA *and* LUCIO.

PROVOST.
'Save your honour!

ANGELO.
Stay a little while.—[*to* ISABELLA.] You're welcome: what's your will?

ISABELLA.
I am a woeful suitor to your honour,
Please but your honour hear me.

ANGELO.
Well; what's your suit?

ISABELLA.
There is a vice that most I do abhor,
And most desire should meet the blow of justice;
For which I would not plead, but that I must;
For which I must not plead, but that I am
At war 'twixt *will* and *will not*.

ANGELO.
Well; the matter?

ISABELLA.
I have a brother is condemn'd to die:
I do beseech you, let it be his fault,
And not my brother.

PROVOST [*aside*].
Heaven give thee moving graces!

ANGELO.
Condemn the fault, and not the actor of it?
Why, every fault's condemn'd ere it be done:
Mine were the very cipher of a function,
To fine the faults, whose fine stands in record,
And let go by the actor.

ISABELLA.
O just but severe law!
I had a brother, then.—Heaven keep your honour!

LUCIO [*aside to* ISABELLA].
Give't not o'er so: to him again, entreat him;
Kneel down before him, hang upon his gown:
You are too cold; if you should need a pin,
You could not with more tame a tongue desire it:
To him, I say.

ISABELLA.
Must he needs die?

ANGELO.
Maiden, no remedy.

ISABELLA.
Yes; I do think that you might pardon him,
And neither heaven nor man grieve at the mercy.

ANGELO.
I will not do't.

ISABELLA.
But can you, if you would?

ANGELO.
Look, what I will not, that I cannot do.

ISABELLA.
But might you do't, and do the world no wrong,

If so your heart were touch'd with that remorse
As mine is to him.

ANGELO.

He's sentenced; 'tis too late.

LUCIO [*aside to* ISABELLA].

You are too cold.

ISABELLA.

Too late! why, no; I, that do speak a word,
May call it back again. Well, believe this,
No ceremony that to great ones 'longs,
Not the king's crown nor the deputed sword,
The marshal's truncheon nor the judge's robe,
Become them with one half so good a grace
As mercy does.
If he had been as you, and you as he,
You would have slipp'd like him; but he, like you,
Would not have been so stern.

ANGELO.

Pray you, be gone.

ISABELLA.

I would to heaven I had your potency,
And you were Isabel! should it then be thus?
No; I would tell what 'twere to be a judge,
And what a prisoner.

LUCIO [*aside to* ISABELLA].

Ay, touch him; there's the vein.

ANGELO.

Your brother is a forfeit of the law,
And you but waste your words.

ISABELLA.

Alas, alas!
Why, all the souls that were were forfeit once;
And He that might the vantage best have took
Found out the remedy. How would you be,
If He, which is the top of judgement, should
But judge you as you are? O, think on that;
And mercy then will breathe within your lips,
Like man new-made.

ANGELO.

Be you content, fair maid;
It is the law, not I, condemn your brother:
Were he my kinsman, brother, or my son,
It should be thus with him:—he must die to-morrow.

ISABELLA.

To-morrow! O, that's sudden! Spare him, spare him!—
He's not prepared for death. Even for our kitchens
We kill the fowl of season: shall we serve heaven
With less respect than we do minister
To our gross selves? Good, good my lord, bethink you;
Who is it that hath died for this offence?
There's many have committed it.

LUCIO [*aside to* ISABELLA].

Ay, well said.

ANGELO.

The law hath not been dead, though it hath slept:
Those many had not dared to do that evil,
If that the first that did th'edict infringe
Had answer'd for his deed: now 'tis awake,
Takes note of what is done; and, like a prophet,
Looks in a glass, that shows what future evils,—
Either new, or by remissness new-conceived,
And so in progress to be hatch'd and born,—
Are now to have no successive degrees,
But, ere they live, to end.

ISABELLA.

Yet show some pity.

ANGELO.

I show it most of all when I show justice;
For then I pity those I do not know,
Which a dismiss'd offence would after gall;
And do him right that, answering one foul wrong,
Lives not to act another. Be satisfied;
Your brother dies to-morrow; be content.

ISABELLA.

So you must be the first that gives this sentence,
And he that suffers. O, it is excellent
To have a giant's strength; but it is tyrannous
To use it like a giant.

LUCIO [*aside to* ISABELLA].

That's well said.

ISABELLA.

Could great men thunder
As Jove himself does, Jove would ne'er be quiet,
For every pelting, petty officer
Would use his heaven for thunder. Nothing but thunder!
Merciful Heaven,
Thou rather with thy sharp and sulphurous bolt
Splitt'st the unwedgeable and gnarled oak
Than the soft myrtle: but man, proud man,
Drest in a little brief authority,—
Most ignorant of what he's most assured,
His glassy essence,—like an angry ape,
Plays such fantastic tricks before high heaven
As make the angels weep; who, with our spleens,
Would all themselves laugh mortal.

LUCIO [*aside to* ISABELLA].

O, to him, to him, wench! he will relent;
He's coming; I perceive't.

PROVOST [*aside*].

Pray heaven she win him!

ISABELLA.

We cannot weigh our brother with ourself:
Great men may jest with saints; 'tis wit in them,
But in the less foul profanation.

LUCIO [*aside to* ISABELLA].

Thou'rt i'the right, girl; more o' that.

ISABELLA.

That in the captain's but a choleric word,
Which in the soldier is flat blasphemy.

LUCIO [*aside to* ISABELLA].

Art avised o' that? more on't.

ANGELO.

Why do you put these sayings upon me?

ISABELLA.

Because authority, though it err like others,
Hath yet a kind of medicine in itself,
That skins the vice o'the top. Go to your bosom;
Knock there, and ask your heart what it doth know
That's like my brother's fault: if it confess
A natural guiltiness such as is his,
Let it not sound a thought upon your tongue
Against my brother's life.

ANGELO [*aside*].

She speaks, and 'tis
Such sense, that my sense breeds with't.—Fare you well.

ISABELLA.
Gentle my lord, turn back.
ANGELO.
I will bethink me: come again to-morrow.
ISABELLA.
Hark how I'll bribe you: good my lord, turn back.
ANGELO.
How! bribe me!
ISABELLA.
Ay, with such gifts that heaven shall share with you.
LUCIO [*aside to* ISABELLA].
You had marr'd all else.
ISABELLA.
Not with fond shekels of the tested gold,
Or stones, whose rates are either rich or poor
As fancy values them; but with true prayers,
That shall be up at heaven and enter there
Ere sun-rise,—prayers from preserved souls,
From fasting maids, whose minds are dedicate
To nothing temporal.
ANGELO.
Well; come to me to-morrow.
LUCIO [*aside to* ISABELLA].
Go to; 'tis well; away!
ISABELLA.
Heaven keep your honour safe!
ANGELO [*aside*].
Amen; for I
Am that way going to temptation,
Where prayers cross.
ISABELLA.
At what hour to-morrow
Shall I attend your lordship?
ANGELO.
At any time 'fore noon?
ISABELLA.
Save you honour!
[*Exeunt* ISABELLA, LUCIO, *and* PROVOST.
ANGELO.
From thee,—even from thy virtue!—
What's this, what's this? Is this her fault or mine?
The tempter or the tempted, who sins most, ha?
Not she; nor doth she tempt: but it is I
That, lying by the violet in the sun,
Do as the carrion does, not as the flower,
Corrupt with virtuous season. Can it be
That modesty may more betray our sense
Than woman's lightness? Having waste ground enough,
Shall we desire to raze the sanctuary,
And pitch our evils there? O, fie, fie, fie!
What dost thou, or what art thou, Angelo?
Dost thou desire her foully for those things
That make her good? O, let her brother live:
Thieves for their robbery have authority
When judges steal themselves. What, do I love her,
That I desire to hear her speak again,
And feast upon her eyes? What is't I dream on?
O cunning enemy, that, to catch a saint,
With saints dost bait thy hook! Most dangerous
Is that temptation that doth goad us on
To sin in loving virtue: never could the strumpet,
With all her double vigour, art and nature,
Once stir my temper; but this virtuous maid
Subdues me quite:—ever till now,
When men were fond, I smiled, and wonder'd how. [*Exit.*

SCENE III.

A prison.

Enter, severally, DUKE *disguised as a friar, and* PROVOST.

DUKE.
HAIL to you, provost!—so I think you are.
PROVOST.
I am the provost. What's your will, good friar?
DUKE.
Bound by my charity and my blest order,
I come to visit the afflicted spirits
Here in the prison. Do me the common right
To let me see them, and to make me know
The nature of their crimes, that I may minister
To them accordingly.
PROVOST.
I would do more than that, if more were needful.
Look, here comes one,—a gentlewoman of mine,
Who, falling in the flaws of her own youth,
Hath blister'd her report: she is with child;
And he that got it, sentenced,— a young man
More fit to do another such offence
Than die for this.
Enter JULIET.
DUKE.
When must he die?
PROVOST.
As I do think, to-morrow.—
[*to* JULIET.] I have provided for you: stay awhile,
And you shall be conducted.
DUKE.
Repent you, fair one, of the sin you carry?
JULIET.
I do; and bear the shame most patiently.
DUKE.
I'll teach you how you shall arraign your conscience,
And try your penitence, if it be sound,
Or hollowly put on.
JULIET.
I'll gladly learn.
DUKE.
Love you the man that wrong'd you?
JULIET.
Yes, as I love the woman that wrong'd him.
DUKE.
So, then, it seems your most offenceful act
Was mutually committed?
JULIET.
Mutually.
DUKE.
Then was your sin of heavier kind than his.
JULIET.
I do confess it, and repent it, father.
DUKE.
'Tis meet so, daughter: but lest you do repent,
As that the sin hath brought you to this shame,—
Which sorrow is always toward ourselves, not heaven,
Showing we would not spare heaven as we love it,
But as we stand in fear,—

JULIET.

I do repent me, as it is an evil,
And take the shame with joy.

DUKE.

There rest.
Your partner, as I hear, must die to-morrow,
And I am going with instruction to him.
Grace go with you! *Benedicite!* [*Exit.*

JULIET.

Must die to-morrow! O injurious law,
That respites me a life, whose very comfort
Is still a dying horror!

PROVOST.

'Tis pity of him. [*Exeunt.*

SCENE IV.

ANGELO'S *house.*

Enter ANGELO.

ANGELO.

When I would pray and think, I think and pray
To several subjects. Heaven hath my empty words;
Whilst my invention, hearing not my tongue,
Anchors on Isabel: Heaven in my mouth,
As if I did but only chew his name;
And in my heart the strong and swelling evil
Of my conception. The state, whereon I studied,
Is like a good thing, being often read,
Grown sear'd and tedious; yea, my gravity,
Wherein—let no man hear me—I take pride,
Could I with boot change for an idle plume,
Which the air beats for vain. O place, O form,
How often dost thou with thy case, thy habit,
Wrench awe from fools, and tie the wiser souls
To thy false seeming! Blood, thou art blood:
Let's write good angel on the devil's horn,
'Tis not the devil's crest.

Enter SERVANT.

How now! who's there?

SERVANT.

One Isabel, a sister,
Desires access to you.

ANGELO.

Teach her the way.
[*Exit* SERVANT.
O heavens!
Why does my blood thus muster to my heart,
Making both it unable for itself,
And dispossessing all my other parts
Of necessary fitness?
So play the foolish throngs with one that swoons;
Come all to help him, and so stop the air
By which he should revive: and even so
The general, subject to a well-wish'd king,
Quit their own part, and in obsequious fondness
Crowd to his presence, where their untaught love
Must needs appear offence.

Enter ISABELLA.

How now, fair maid!

ISABELLA.

I am come to know your pleasure.

ANGELO.

That you might know it, would much better please me
Than to demand what 'tis. Your brother cannot live.

ISABELLA.

Even so.—Heaven keep your honour! [*Retiring.*

ANGELO.

Yet may he live awhile; and, it may be,
As long as you or I: yet he must die.

ISABELLA.

Under your sentence?

ANGELO.

Yea.

ISABELLA.

When, I beseech you? that in his reprieve,
Longer or shorter, he may be so fitted
That his soul sicken not.

ANGELO.

Ha! fie, these filthy vices! It were as good
To pardon him that hath from nature stol'n
A man already made, as to remit
Their saucy sweetness that do coin heaven's image
In stamps that are forbid: 'tis all as easy
Falsely to take away a life true made,
As to put metal in restrained means
To make a false one.

ISABELLA.

'Tis set down so in heaven, but not in earth.

ANGELO.

Say you so? then I shall pose you quickly.
Which had you rather,—that the most just law
Now took your brother's life; or, to redeem him,
Give up your body to such sweet uncleanness
As she that he hath stain'd?

ISABELLA.

Sir, believe this,
I had rather give my body than my soul.

ANGELO.

I talk not of your soul: our compell'd sins
Stand more for number than accompt.

ISABELLA.

How say you?

ANGELO.

Nay, I'll not warrant that; for I can speak
Against the thing I say. Answer to this:—
I, now the voice of the recorded law,
Pronounce a sentence on your brother's life:
Might there not be a charity in sin
To save this brother's life?

ISABELLA.

Please you to do't,
I'll take it as a peril to my soul,
It is no sin at all, but charity.

ANGELO.

Pleased you to do't at peril of your soul,
Were equal poise of sin and charity.

ISABELLA.

That I do beg his life, if it be sin,
Heaven let me bear it! you granting of my suit,
If that be sin, I'll make it my morn-prayer
To have it added to the faults of mine,
And nothing of your answer.

ANGELO.

Nay, but hear me.
Your sense pursues not mine: either you are ignorant,
Or seem so, craftily; and that's not good.

ISABELLA.

Let me be ignorant, and in nothing good,
But graciously to know I am no better.

ANGELO.

Thus wisdom wishes to appear most bright
When it doth tax itself; as these black masks
Proclaim an enshield beauty ten times louder
Than beauty could, display'd.—But mark me;
To be received plain, I'll speak more gross:
Your brother is to die.

ISABELLA.

So.

ANGELO.

And his offence is so, as it appears,
Accountant to the law upon that pain.

ISABELLA.

True.

ANGELO.

Admit no other way to save his life,—
As I subscribe not that, nor any other,
But in the toss of question,—that you, his sister,
Finding yourself desired of such a person,
Whose credit with the judge, or own great place,
Could fetch your brother from the manacles
Of the all-bridling law; and that there were
No earthly mean to save him, but that either
You must lay down the treasures of your body
To this supposed, or else to let him suffer;
What would you do?

ISABELLA.

As much for my poor brother as myself:
That is, were I under the terms of death,
Th'impression of keen whips I'ld wear as rubies,
And strip myself to death, as to a bed
That longing have been sick for, ere I'ld yield
My body up to shame.

ANGELO.

Then must
Your brother die.

ISABELLA.

And 'twere the cheaper way:
Better it were a brother died at once,
Than that a sister, by redeeming him,
Should die for ever.

ANGELO.

Were not you, then, as cruel as the sentence
That you have slander'd so?

ISABELLA.

Ignomy in ransom, and free pardon,
Are of two houses: lawful mercy
Is nothing kin to foul redemption.

ANGELO.

You seem'd of late to make the law a tyrant;
And rather proved the sliding of your brother
A merriment than a vice.

ISABELLA.

O, pardon me, my lord; it oft falls out,
To have what we would have, we speak not what we [mean:
I something do excuse the thing I hate,
For his advantage that I dearly love.

ANGELO.

We are all frail.

ISABELLA.

Else let my brother die,
If not a feodary, but only he,
Owe and succeed this weakness.

ANGELO.

Nay, women are frail too.

ISABELLA.

Ay, as the glasses where they view themselves;
Which are as easy broke as they make forms.
Women!—Help heaven! men their creation mar
In profiting by them. Nay, call us ten times frail;
For we are soft as our complexions are,
And credulous to false prints.

ANGELO.

I think it well:
And from this testimony of your own sex,—
Since, I suppose, we are made to be no stronger
Than faults may shake our frames,—let me be bold;—
I do arrest your words. Be that you are,
That is, a woman; if you be more, you're none;
If you be one,—as you are well exprest
By all external warrants,—show it now,
By putting on the destined livery.

ISABELLA.

I have no tongue but one: gentle my lord,
Let me entreat you speak the former language.

ANGELO.

Plainly conceive, I love you.

ISABELLA.

My brother did love Juliet; and you tell me
That he shall die for't.

ANGELO.

He shall not, Isabel, if you give me love.

ISABELLA.

I know your virtue hath a licence in't,
Which seems a little fouler than it is,
To pluck on others.

ANGELO.

Believe me, on mine honour,
My words express my purpose.

ISABELLA.

Ha! little honour to be much believed,
And most pernicious purpose!—Seeming, seeming!—
I will proclaim thee, Angelo; look for't:
Sign me a present pardon for my brother,
Or with an outstretch'd throat I'll tell the world
Aloud what man thou art.

ANGELO.

Who will believe thee, Isabel?
My unsoil'd name, th'austereness of my life,
My vouch against you, and my place i'the state,
Will so your accusation overweigh,
That you shall stifle in your own report,
And smell of calumny. I have begun;
And now I give my sensual race the rein:
Fit thy consent to my sharp appetite;
Lay by all nicety and prolixious blushes,
That banish what they sue for; redeem thy brother
By yielding up thy body to my will;
Or else he must not only die the death,
But thy unkindness shall his death draw out
To lingering sufferance. Answer me to-morrow,
Or, by the affection that now guides me most,
I'll prove a tyrant to him. As for you,
Say what you can, my false o'erweighs your true.
[*Exit.*

ISABELLA.

To whom should I complain? Did I tell this,
Who would believe me? O perilous mouths,
That bear in them one and the self-same tongue,
Either of condemnation or approof;
Bidding the law make court'sy to their will;
Hooking both right and wrong to the appetite,
To follow as it draws! I'll to my brother:
Though he hath fall'n by prompture of the blood,
Yet hath he in him such a mind of honour,
That, had he twenty heads to tender down
On twenty bloody blocks, he'ld yield them up,
Before his sister should her body stoop
To such abhorred pollution.
Then, Isabel, live chaste, and, brother, die:
More than our brother is our chastity.
I'll tell him yet of Angelo's request,
And fit his mind to death, for his soul's rest.
[*Exit.*

ACT III. SCENE I.

The prison.

Enter DUKE *disguised as before*, CLAUDIO, *and* PROVOST.

DUKE.

So, then, you hope of pardon from Lord Angelo?

CLAUDIO.

The miserable have no other medicine
But only hope:
I have hope to live, and am prepared to die.

DUKE.

Be absolute for death; either death or life
Shall thereby be the sweeter. Reason thus with life:—
If I do lose thee, I do lose a thing
That none but fools would keep: a breath thou art,
Servile to all the skyey influences
That do this habitation, where thou keep'st,
Hourly afflict: merely, thou art death's fool;
For him thou labour'st by thy flight to shun,
And yet runn'st toward him still. Thou art not noble;
For all th'accommodations that thou bear'st
Are nursed by baseness. Thou'rt by no means valiant;
For thou dost fear the soft and tender fork
Of a poor worm. Thy best of rest is sleep,
And that thou oft provokest; yet grossly fear'st
Thy death, which is no more. Thou art not thyself;
For thou exists on many a thousand grains
That issue out of dust. Happy thou art not;
For what thou hast not, still thou strivest to get,
And what thou hast, forgett'st. Thou art not certain;
For thy complexion shifts to strange affects,
After the moon. If thou art rich, thou'rt poor;
For, like an ass whose back with ingots bows,
Thou bear'st thy heavy riches but a journey,
And death unloads thee. Friend hast thou none;
For thine own bowels, which do call thee sire,
The mere effusions of thy proper loins,
Do curse the gout, serpigo, and the rheum,
For ending thee no sooner. Thou hast nor youth nor age,
But, as it were, an after-dinner's sleep,
Dreaming on both; for all thy blessed youth
Becomes as aged, and doth beg the alms
Of palsied eld; and when thou art old and rich,
Thou hast neither heat, affection, limb, nor beauty,
To make thy riches pleasant. What's yet in this
That bears the name of life? Yet in this life
Lie hid moe thousand deaths: yet death we fear,
That makes these odds all even.

CLAUDIO.

I humbly thank you.
To sue to live, I find I seek to die;
And, seeking death, find life: let it come on.

ISABELLA [*within*].

What, ho! Peace here; grace and good company!

PROVOST.

Who's there? come in: the wish deserves a welcome.

DUKE.

Dear sir, ere long I'll visit you again.

CLAUDIO.

Most holy sir, I thank you.

Enter ISABELLA.

ISABELLA.

My business is a word or two with Claudio.

PROVOST.

And very welcome.—Look, signior, here's your sister.

DUKE.

Provost, a word with you.

PROVOST.

As many as you please.

DUKE.

Bring me to hear them speak, where I may be conceal'd. [*Exeunt* DUKE *and* PROVOST.

CLAUDIO.

Now, sister, what's the comfort?

ISABELLA.

Why,
As all comforts are; most good, most good indeed.
Lord Angelo, having affairs to heaven,
Intends you for his swift ambassador,
Where you shall be an everlasting leiger:
Therefore your best appointment make with speed;
To-morrow you set on.

CLAUDIO.

Is there no remedy?

ISABELLA.

None, but such remedy as, to save a head,
To cleave a heart in twain.

CLAUDIO.

But is there any?

ISABELLA.

Yes, brother, you may live:
There is a devilish mercy in the judge,
If you'll implore it, that will free your life,
But fetter you till death.

CLAUDIO.

Perpetual durance?

ISABELLA.

Ay, just; perpetual durance,—a restraint,
Though all the world's vastidity you had,
To a determined scope.

CLAUDIO.
But in what nature?
ISABELLA.
In such a one as, you consenting to't,
Would bark your honour from that trunk you bear,
And leave you naked.
CLAUDIO.
Let me know the point.
ISABELLA.
O, I do fear thee, Claudio; and I quake,
Lest thou a feverous life shouldst entertain,
And six or seven winters more respect
Than a perpetual honour. Darest thou die?
The sense of death is most in apprehension;
And the poor beetle that we tread upon,
In corporal sufferance finds a pang as great
As when a giant dies.
CLAUDIO.
Why give you me this shame?
Think you I can a resolution fetch
From flowery tenderness? If I must die,
I will encounter darkness as a bride,
And hug it in mine arms.
ISABELLA.
There spake my brother; there my father's grave
Did utter forth a voice! Yes, thou must die:
Thou art too noble to conserve a life
In base appliances. This outward-sainted deputy—
Whose settled visage and deliberate word
Nips youth i'the head, and follies doth emmew
As falcon doth the fowl—is yet a devil;
His filth within being cast, he would appear
A pond as deep as hell.
CLAUDIO.
The priestly Angelo?
ISABELLA.
O, 'tis the cunning livery of hell,
The damned'st body to invest and cover
In priestly guards! Dost thou think, Claudio?—
If I would yield him my virginity,
Thou mightst be freed.
CLAUDIO.
O heavens! it cannot be.
ISABELLA.
Yes, he would give't thee, from this rank offence,
So to offend him still. This night's the time
That I should do what I abhor to name,
Or else thou diest to-morrow.
CLAUDIO.
Thou shalt not do't.
ISABELLA.
O, were it but my life,
I'd throw it down for your deliverance
As frankly as a pin.
CLAUDIO.
Thanks, dear Isabel.
ISABELLA.
Be ready, Claudio, for your death to-morrow.
CLAUDIO.
Yes.—Has he affections in him,
That thus can make him bite the law by the nose,
When he would force it? Sure, it is no sin;
Or of the deadly seven it is the least.
ISABELLA.
Which is the least?
CLAUDIO.
If it were damnable, he being so wise,
Why would he for the momentary trick
Be perdurably fined?—O Isobel!
ISABELLA.
What says my brother?
CLAUDIO.
Death is a fearful thing.
ISABELLA.
And shamed life a hateful.
CLAUDIO.
Ay, but to die, and go we know not where;
To lie in cold obstruction, and to rot;
This sensible warm motion to become
A kneaded clod; and the delighted spirit
To bathe in fiery floods, or to reside
In thrilling region of thick-ribbed ice;
To be imprison'd in the viewless winds,
And blown with restless violence round about
The pendent world; or to be worse than worst
Of those that lawless and incertain thought
Imagine howling!—'tis too horrible!
The weariest and most loathed worldly life
That age, ache, penury, and imprisonment
Can lay on nature, is a paradise
To what we fear of death.
ISABELLA.
Alas, alas!
CLAUDIO.
Sweet sister, let me live:
What sin you do to save a brother's life,
Nature dispenses with the deed so far
That it becomes a virtue.
ISABELLA.
O you beast!
O faithless coward! O dishonest wretch!
Wilt thou be made a man out of my vice?
Is't not a kind of incest, to take life
From thine own sister's shame? What should I think?
Heaven shield my mother play'd my father fair?
For such a warped slip of wilderness
Ne'er issued from his blood. Take my defiance;
Die, perish! might but my bending down
Reprieve thee from thy fate, it should proceed:
I'll pray a thousand prayers for thy death,—
No word to save thee.
CLAUDIO.
Nay, hear me, Isabel.
ISABELLA.
O, fie, fie, fie!
Thy sin's not accidental, but a trade.
Mercy to thee would prove itself a bawd:
'Tis best that thou diest quickly. [*Going*.
CLAUDIO.
O, hear me, Isabella!
Enter DUKE.
DUKE.
Vouchsafe a word, young sister, but one word.
ISABELLA.
What is your will?
DUKE.
Might you dispense with your leisure, I would by and by have some speech with you: the satisfaction I would require is likewise your own benefit.

ISABELLA.

I have no superfluous leisure; my stay must be stolen out of other affairs; but I will attend you awhile.

DUKE.

Son, I have overheard what hath pass'd between you and your sister. Angelo had never the purpose to corrupt her; only he hath made an assay of her virtue to practise his judgement with the disposition of natures: she, having the truth of honour in her, hath made him that gracious denial which he is most glad to receive. I am confessor to Angelo, and I know this to be true; therefore prepare yourself to death: do not satisfy your resolution with hopes that are fallible: to-morrow you must die; go to your knees, and make ready.

CLAUDIO.

Let me ask my sister pardon. I am so out of love with life, that I will sue to be rid of it.

DUKE.

Hold you there: farewell. [*Exit* CLAUDIO.] Provost, a word with you!

Enter PROVOST.

PROVOST.

What's your will, father?

DUKE.

That now you are come, you will be gone. Leave me awhile with the maid: my mind promises with my habit no loss shall touch her by my company.

PROVOST.

In good time. [*Exit.*

DUKE.

The hand that hath made you fair hath made you good: the goodness that is cheap in beauty makes beauty brief in goodness; but grace, being the soul of your complexion, shall keep the body of it ever fair. The assault that Angelo hath made to you, fortune hath convey'd to my understanding; and, but that frailty hath examples for his falling, I should wonder at Angelo. How will you do to content this substitute, and to save your brother?

ISABELLA.

I am now going to resolve him, I had rather my brother die by the law than my son should be unlawfully born. But, O, how much is the good duke deceived in Angelo! If ever he [illegible]rn, and I can speak to him, I will open my li[illegible] in vain, or discover his government.

DUKE.

That shall not be much amiss: yet, as the matter now stands, he will avoid your accusation,—he made trial of you only. Therefore fasten your ear on my advisings: to the love I have in doing good a remedy presents itself. I do make myself believe that you may most uprighteously do a poor wrong'd lady a merited benefit; redeem your brother from the angry law; do no stain to your own gracious person; and much please the absent duke, if peradventure he shall ever return to have hearing of this business.

ISABELLA.

Let me hear you speak further. I have spirit to do any thing that appears not foul in the truth of my spirit.

DUKE.

Virtue is bold, and goodness never fearful. Have you not heard speak of Mariana, the sister of Frederick the great soldier who miscarried at sea?

ISABELLA.

I have heard of the lady, and good words went with her name.

DUKE.

She should this Angelo have married; was affianced to her by oath, and the nuptial appointed: between which time of the contract and limit of the solemnity, her brother Frederick was wrackt at sea, having in that perish'd vessel the dowry of his sister. But mark how heavily this befell to the poor gentlewoman: there she lost a noble and renown'd brother, in his love toward her ever most kind and natural; with him, the portion and sinew of her fortune, her marriage-dowry; with both, her combinate husband, this well-seeming Angelo.

ISABELLA.

Can this be so? did Angelo so leave her?

DUKE.

Left her in her tears, and dried not one of them with his comfort; swallow'd his vows whole, pretending in her discoveries of dishonour: in few, bestow'd her on her own lamentation, which she yet wears for his sake; and he, a marble to her tears, is wash'd with them, but relents not.

ISABELLA.

What a merit were it in death to take this poor maid from the world! What corruption in this life, that it will let this man live!—But how out of this can she avail?

DUKE.

It is a rupture that you may easily heal: and the cure of it not only saves your brother, but keeps you from dishonour in doing it.

ISABELLA.

Show me how, good father.

DUKE.

This forenamed maid hath yet in her the continuance of her first affection: his unjust unkindness, that in all reason should have quench'd her love, hath, like an impediment in the current, made it more violent and unruly. Go you to Angelo; answer his requiring with a plausible obedience; agree with his demands to the point; only refer yourself to this advantage,—first, that your stay with him may not be long; that the time may have all shadow and silence in it; and the place answer to convenience. This being granted in course—and now follows all—we shall advise this wrong'd maid to stead up your appointment, go in your place; if the encounter acknowledge itself hereafter, it may compel him to her recompense: and here, by this, is your brother saved, your honour untainted, the poor Mariana advantaged, and the corrupt deputy scaled. The maid will I frame and make fit for his attempt. If you think well to carry this as you may, the doubleness of the benefit defends the deceit from reproof. What think you of it?

ISABELLA.

The image of it gives me content already; and I trust it will grow to a most prosperous perfection.

DUKE.

It lies much in your holding up. Haste you speedily to Angelo: if for this night he entreat you to his bed, give him promise of satisfaction. I will presently to Saint Luke's: there, at the moated grange, resides this dejected Mariana. At that place call upon me; and dispatch with Angelo, that it may be quickly.

ISABELLA.

I thank you for this comfort. Fare you well, good father. [*Exeunt.*

SCENE II.

The street before the prison.

Enter DUKE *disguised as before; to him,* ELBOW *and* OFFICERS *with* POMPEY.

ELBOW.

NAY, if there be no remedy for it, but that you will needs buy and sell men and women like beasts, we shall have all the world drink brown and white bastard.

DUKE.

O heavens! what stuff is here?

POMPEY.

'Twas never merry world since, of two usuries, the merriest was put down, and the worser allowed by order of law a furr'd gown to keep him warm; and furr'd with fox and lamb-skins too, to signify, that craft, being richer than innocency, stands for the facing.

ELBOW.

Come your way, sir.—'Bless you, good father friar.

DUKE.

And you, good brother father. What offence hath this man made you, sir?

ELBOW.

Marry, sir, he hath offended the law: and, sir, we take him to be a thief too, sir; for we have found upon him, sir, a strange picklock, which we have sent to the deputy.

DUKE.

Fie, sirrah! a bawd, a wicked bawd!
The evil that thou causest to be done,
That is thy means to live. Do thou but think
What 'tis to cram a maw or clothe a back
From such a filthy vice: say to thyself,—
From their abominable and beastly touches
I drink, I eat, array myself, and live.
Canst thou believe thy living is a life,
So stinkingly depending? Go mend, go mend.

POMPEY.

Indeed, it does stink in some sort, sir; but yet, sir, I would prove—

DUKE.

Nay, if the devil have given thee proofs for sin,
Thou wilt prove his.—Take him to prison, officer:
Correction and instruction must both work
Ere this rude beast will profit.

ELBOW.

He must before the deputy, sir; he has given him warning: the deputy cannot abide a whoremaster: if he be a whoremonger, and comes before him, he were as good go a mile on his errand.

DUKE.

That we were all, as some would seem to be,
From our faults, or faults from seeming, free!

ELBOW.

His neck will come to your waist,—a cord, sir.

POMPEY.

I spy comfort; I cry, bail! Here's a gentleman and a friend of mine.

Enter LUCIO.

LUCIO.

How now, noble Pompey! What, at the wheels of Cæsar! art thou led in triumph? What, is there none of Pygmalion's images, newly-made woman, to be had now, for putting the hand in the pocket and extracting it clutch'd? What reply, ha? What say'st thou to this tune, matter, and method? Is't not drown'd i'the last rain, ha? What say'st thou, Trot? Is the world as it was, man? Which is the way? Is it sad, and few words? or how? The trick of it?

DUKE.

Still thus, and thus; still worse!

LUCIO.

How doth my dear morsel, thy mistress? Procures she still, ha?

POMPEY.

Troth, sir, she hath eaten up all her beef, and she is herself in the tub.

LUCIO.

Why, 'tis good; it is the right of it; it must be so: ever your fresh whore and your powder'd bawd: an unshunn'd consequence; it must be so. Art going to prison, Pompey?

POMPEY.

Yes, faith, sir.

LUCIO.

Why, 'tis not amiss, Pompey. Farewell: go, say I sent thee thither. For debt, Pompey? or how?

ELBOW.

For being a bawd, for being a bawd.

LUCIO.

Well, then, imprison him: if imprisonment be the due of a bawd, why, 'tis his right: bawd is he doubtless, and of antiquity too; bawd-born.—Farewell, good Pompey. Commend me to the prison, Pompey: you will turn good husband now, Pompey; you will keep the house.

POMPEY.

I hope, sir, your good worship will be my bail.

LUCIO.

No, indeed, will I not, Pompey; it is not the wear. I will pray, Pompey, to increase your bondage: if you take it not patiently, why, your mettle is the more. Adieu, trusty Pompey.—Bless you, friar.

DUKE.

And you.

LUCIO.

Does Bridget paint still, Pompey, ha?

ELBOW.

Come your ways, sir; come.

POMPEY.

You will not bail me, then, sir?

LUCIO.

Then, Pompey, nor now.—What news abroad, friar, what news?

ELBOW.
Come your ways, sir; come.

LUCIO.
Go,—to kennel, Pompey, go. [*Exeunt* ELBOW *and* OFFICERS *with* POMPEY.] What news, friar, of the duke?

DUKE.
I know none. Can you tell me of any?

LUCIO.
Some say he is with the Emperor of Russia; other some, he is in Rome: but where is he, think you?

DUKE.
I know not where; but wheresoever, I wish him well.

LUCIO.
It was a mad fantastical trick of him to steal from the state, and usurp the beggary he was never born to. Lord Angelo dukes it well in his absence; he puts transgression to't.

DUKE.
He does well in't.

LUCIO.
A little more lenity to lechery would do no harm in him: something too crabb'd that way, friar.

DUKE.
It is too general a vice, and severity must cure it.

LUCIO.
Yes, in good sooth, the vice is of a great kindred; it is well allied; but it is impossible to extirp it quite, friar, till eating and drinking be put down. They say this Angelo was not made by man and woman, after the downright way of creation: is it true, think you?

DUKE.
How should he be made, then?

LUCIO.
Some report a sea-maid spawn'd him; some, that he was begot between two stock-fishes. But it is certain that, when he makes water, his urine is congeal'd ice; that I know to be true: and he is a motion ungenerative; that's infallible.

DUKE.
You are pleasant, sir, and speak apace.

LUCIO.
Why, what a ruthless thing is this in him, for the rebellion of a codpiece to take away the life of a man! Would the duke that is absent have done this? Ere he would have hang'd a man for the getting a hundred bastards, he would have paid for the nursing a thousand: he had some feeling of the sport; he knew the service, and that instructed him to mercy.

DUKE.
I never heard the absent duke much detected for women; he was not inclined that way.

LUCIO.
O, sir, you are deceived.

DUKE.
'Tis not possible.

LUCIO.
Who, not the duke? yes, your beggar of fifty; and his use was to put a ducat in her clack-dish: the duke had crotchets in him. He would be drunk too; that let me inform you.

DUKE.
You do him wrong, surely.

LUCIO.
Sir, I was an inward of his. A sly fellow was the duke: and I believe I know the cause of his withdrawing.

DUKE.
What, I prithee, might be the cause?

LUCIO.
No,—pardon; 'tis a secret must be lockt within the teeth and the lips: but this I can let you understand,—the greater file of the subject held the duke to be wise.

DUKE.
Wise! why, no question but he was.

LUCIO.
A very superficial, ignorant, unweighing fellow.

DUKE.
Either this is envy in you, folly, or mistaking: the very stream of his life and the business he hath helm'd must, upon a warranted need, give him a better proclamation. Let him be but testimonied in his own bringings-forth, and he shall appear to the envious a scholar, a statesman, and a soldier. Therefore you speak unskilfully; or if your knowledge be more, it is much darken'd in your malice.

LUCIO.
Sir, I know him, and I love him.

DUKE.
Love talks with better knowledge, and knowledge with dearer love.

LUCIO.
Come, sir, I know what I know.

DUKE.
I can hardly believe that, since you know not what you speak. But, if ever the duke return,—as our prayers are he may,—let me desire you to make your answer before him. If it be honest you have spoke, you have courage to maintain it: I am bound to call upon you; and, I pray you, your name?

LUCIO.
Sir, my name is Lucio; well known to the duke.

DUKE.
He shall know you better, sir, if I may live to report you.

LUCIO.
I fear you not.

DUKE.
O, you hope the duke will return no more; or you imagine me too unhurtful an opposite. But, indeed, I can do you little harm; you'll forswear this again.

LUCIO.
I'll be hang'd first: thou art deceived in me, friar. But no more of this. Canst thou tell if Claudio die to-morrow or no?

DUKE.
Why should he die, sir?

LUCIO.
Why, for filling a bottle with a tun-dish. I would the duke we talk of were return'd again: this ungenitured agent will unpeople the province with continency; sparrows must not build in his house-eaves, because they are lecherous. The duke yet would have dark deeds darkly answer'd; he would never bring them to light: would he were re-

turn'd! Marry, this Claudio is condemn'd for untrussing. Farewell, good friar: I prithee, pray for me. The duke, I say to thee again, would eat mutton on Fridays. He's now past it; yet, and I say to thee, he would mouth with a beggar, though she smelt brown bread and garlick: say that I said so. Farewell. [*Exit.*

DUKE.

No might nor greatness in mortality
Can censure scape; back-wounding calumny
The whitest virtue strikes. What king so strong
Can tie the gall up in the slanderous tongue?—
But who comes here?

Enter ESCALUS, PROVOST, *and* OFFICERS *with* MISTRESS OVERDONE.

ESCALUS.

Go; away with her to prison!

MISTRESS OVERDONE.

Good my lord, be good to me; your honour is accounted a merciful man; good my lord.

ESCALUS.

Double and treble admonition, and still forfeit in the same kind? This would make mercy swear and play the tyrant.

PROVOST.

A bawd of eleven years' continuance, may it please your honour.

MISTRESS OVERDONE.

My lord, this is one Lucio's information against me. Mistress Kate Keep-down was with child by him in the duke's time; he promised her marriage: his child is a year and a quarter old, come Philip and Jacob: I have kept it myself; and see how he goes about to abuse me!

ESCALUS.

That fellow is a fellow of much license:—let him be call'd before us.—Away with her to prison!—Go to; no more words. [*Exeunt* OFFICERS *with* MISTRESS OVERDONE.] Provost, my brother Angelo will not be alter'd; Claudio must die to-morrow: let him be furnish'd with divines, and have all charitable preparation. If my brother wrought by my pity, it should not be so with him.

PROVOST.

So please you, this friar hath been with him, and advised him for the entertainment of death.

ESCALUS.

Good even, good father.

DUKE.

Bliss and goodness on you!

ESCALUS.

Of whence are you?

DUKE.

Not of this country, though my chance is now
To use it for my time: I am a brother
Of gracious order, late come from the See
In special business from his holiness.

ESCALUS.

What news abroad i'the world?

DUKE.

None, but that there is so great a fever on goodness, that the dissolution of it must cure it: novelty is only in request; and it is as dangerous to be aged in any kind of course, as it is virtuous to be constant in any undertaking: there is scarce truth enough alive to make societies secure; but security enough to make fellowships accurst: —much upon this riddle runs the wisdom of the world. This news is old enough, yet it is every day's news. I pray you, sir, of what disposition was the duke?

ESCALUS.

One that, above all other strifes, contended especially to know himself.

DUKE.

What pleasure was he given to?

ESCALUS.

Rather rejoicing to see another merry, than merry at any thing which profest to make him rejoice: a gentleman of all temperance. But leave we him to his events, with a prayer they may prove prosperous; and let me desire to know how you find Claudio prepared. I am made to understand that you have lent him visitation.

DUKE.

He professes to have received no sinister measure from his judge, but most willingly humbles himself to the determination of justice: yet had he framed to himself, by the instruction of his frailty, many deceiving promises of life; which I, by my good leisure, have discredited to him, and now is he resolved to die.

ESCALUS.

You have paid the heavens your function, and the prisoner the very debt of your calling. I have labour'd for the poor gentleman to the extremest shore of my modesty: but my brother justice have I found so severe, that he hath forced me to tell him he is indeed Justice.

DUKE.

If his own life answer the straitness of his proceeding, it shall become him well; wherein if he chance to fail, he hath sentenced himself.

ESCALUS.

I am going to visit the prisoner. Fare you well.

DUKE.

Peace be with you!

[*Exeunt* ESCALUS *and* PROVOST.

He who the sword of heaven will bear
Should be as holy as severe;
Pattern in himself to know,
Grace to stand, and virtue go;
More nor less to others paying
Than by self-offences weighing.
Shame to him whose cruel striking
Kills for faults of his own liking!
Twice treble shame on Angelo,
To weed my vice, and let his grow!
O, what may man within him hide,
Though angel on the outward side!
How may likeness wade in crimes,
Making practice on the times,
To draw with idle spiders' strings
Most ponderous and substantial things!
Craft against vice I must apply:
With Angelo to-night shall lie
His old betrothed but despised;
So disguise shall, by the disguised,
Pay with falsehood false exacting,
And perform an old contracting. [*Exit.*

ACT IV. SCENE I.

The Moated Grange.

Enter MARIANA; *a* BOY *singing.*

Song.

TAKE, O take those lips away,
That so sweetly were forsworn;
And those eyes, the break of day,
Lights that do mislead the morn:
But my kisses bring again, bring again;
Seals of love, but seal'd in vain, seal'd in vain.

MARIANA.

Break off thy song, and haste thee quick away:
Here comes a man of comfort, whose advice
Hath often still'd my brawling discontent.
[*Exit* BOY.

Enter DUKE *disguised as before.*

I cry you mercy, sir; and well could wish
You had not found me here so musical:
Let me excuse me, and believe me so,—
My mirth it much displeased, but pleased my woe.

DUKE.

'Tis good; though music oft hath such a charm
To make bad good, and good provoke to harm.—
I pray you, tell me, hath anybody inquired for me here to-day? much upon this time have I promised here to meet.

MARIANA.

You have not been inquired after: I have sat here all day.

DUKE.

I do constantly believe you.—The time is come even now. I shall crave your forbearance a little: may be I will call upon you anon, for some advantage to yourself.

MARIANA.

I am always bound to you. [*Exit.*

Enter ISABELLA.

DUKE.

Very well met, and welcome.
What is the news from this good deputy?

ISABELLA.

He hath a garden circummured with brick,
Whose western side is with a vineyard back'd;
And to that vineyard is a planched gate,
That makes his opening with this bigger key:
This other doth command a little door
Which from the vineyard to the garden leads;
There have I made my promise
Upon the heavy middle of the night
To call upon him.

DUKE.

But shall you on your knowledge find this way?

ISABELLA.

I have ta'en a due and wary note upon't:
With whispering and most guilty diligence,
In action all of precept, he did show me
The way twice o'er.

DUKE.

Are there no other tokens
Between you 'greed concerning her observance?

ISABELLA.

No, none, but only a repair i'the dark;
And that I have possest him my most stay
Can be but brief; for I have made him know
I have a servant comes with me along,
That stays upon me; whose persuasion is
I come about my brother.

DUKE.

'Tis well borne up.
I have not yet made known to Mariana
A word of this.—What, ho! within! come forth!

Enter MARIANA.

I pray you, be acquainted with this maid;
She comes to do you good.

ISABELLA.

I do desire the like.

DUKE.

Do you persuade yourself that I respect you?

MARIANA.

Good friar, I know you do, and have found it.

DUKE.

Take, then, this your companion by the hand,
Who hath a story ready for your ear.
I shall attend your leisure: but make haste;
The vaporous night approaches.

MARIANA.

Will't please you walk aside?
[*Exeunt* MARIANA *and* ISABELLA.

DUKE.

O place and greatness, millions of false eyes
Are stuck upon thee! volumes of report
Run with these false and most contrarious quests
Upon thy doings! thousand escapes of wit
Make thee the father of their idle dream,
And rack thee in their fancies!

Enter MARIANA *and* ISABELLA.

Welcome! How agreed?

ISABELLA.

She'll take the enterprise upon her, father,
If you advise it.

DUKE.

It is not my consent,
But my entreaty too.

ISABELLA.

Little have you to say
When you depart from him, but, soft and low,
'Remember now my brother.'

MARIANA.

Fear me not.

DUKE.

Nor, gentle daughter, fear you not at all.
He is your husband on a pre-contract:
To bring you thus together, 'tis no sin,
Sith that the justice of your title to him
Doth flourish the deceit. Come, let us go:
Our corn's to reap, for yet our tilth's to sow.
[*Exeunt.*

SCENE II.

The prison.

Enter PROVOST *and* POMPEY.

PROVOST.

COME hither, sirrah. Can you cut off a man's head?

POMPEY.

If the man be a bachelor, sir, I can; but if he be a married man, he's his wife's head, and I can never cut off a woman's head.

PROVOST.

Come, sir, leave me your snatches, and yield me a direct answer. To-morrow morning are to die

Claudio and Barnardine. Here is in our prison a common executioner, who in his office lacks a helper: if you will take it on you to assist him, it shall redeem you from your gyves; if not, you shall have your full time of imprisonment, and your deliverance with an unpitied whipping, for you have been a notorious bawd.

POMPEY.

Sir, I have been an unlawful bawd time out of mind; but yet I will be content to be a lawful hangman. I would be glad to receive some instruction from my fellow partner.

PROVOST.

What, ho, Abhorson! Where's Abhorson, there?

Enter ABHORSON.

ABHORSON.

Do you call, sir?

PROVOST.

Sirrah, here's a fellow will help you to-morrow in your execution. If you think it meet, compound with him by the year, and let him abide here with you; if not, use him for the present, and dismiss him. He cannot plead his estimation with you; he hath been a bawd.

ABHORSON.

A bawd, sir! fie upon him! he will discredit our mystery.

PROVOST.

Go to, sir; you weigh equally; a feather will turn the scale. [*Exit.*

POMPEY.

Pray, sir, by your good favour,—for surely, sir, a good favour you have, but that you have a hanging look,—do you call, sir, your occupation a mystery?

ABHORSON.

Ay, sir; a mystery.

POMPEY.

Painting, sir, I have heard say, is a mystery; and your whores, sir, being members of my occupation, using painting, do prove my occupation a mystery: but what mystery there should be in hanging, if I should be hang'd, I cannot imagine.

ABHORSON.

Sir, it is a mystery.

POMPEY.

Proof?

ABHORSON.

Every true man's apparel fits your thief: if it be too little for your thief, your true man thinks it big enough; if it be too big for your thief, your thief thinks it little enough: so every true man's apparel fits your thief.

Enter PROVOST.

PROVOST.

Are you agreed?

POMPEY.

Sir, I will serve him; for I do find your hangman is a more penitent trade than your bawd,—he doth oftener ask forgiveness.

PROVOST.

You, sirrah, provide your block and your axe to-morrow four o'clock.

ABHORSON.

Come on, bawd; I will instruct thee in my trade; follow.

POMPEY.

I do desire to learn, sir: and I hope, if you have occasion to use me for your own turn, you shall find me yare; for, truly, sir, for your kindness I owe you a good turn.

PROVOST.

Call hither Barnardine and Claudio:
[*Exeunt* POMPEY *and* ABHORSON.
Th'one has my pity; not a jot the other,
Being a murderer, though he were my brother.

Enter CLAUDIO.

Look, here's the warrant, Claudio, for thy death:
'Tis now dead midnight, and by eight to-morrow
Thou must be made immortal. Where's Barnardine?

CLAUDIO.

As fast lockt up in sleep as guiltless labour,
When it lies starkly in the traveller's bones:
He will not wake.

PROVOST.

Who can do good on him?
Well, go, prepare thyself. [*Knocking within.*] But, hark, what noise?—
Heaven give your spirits comfort! [*Exit* CLAUDIO.] By and by!—
I hope it is some pardon or reprieve
For the most gentle Claudio.

Enter DUKE *disguised as before.*

Welcome, father.

DUKE.

The best and wholesom'st spirits of the night
Envelop you, good provost! Who call'd here of late?

PROVOST.

None, since the curfew rung.

DUKE.

Not Isabel?

PROVOST.

No.

DUKE.

They will, then, ere't be long.

PROVOST.

What comfort is for Claudio?

DUKE.

There's some in hope.

PROVOST.

It is a bitter deputy.

DUKE.

Not so, not so; his life is parallel'd
Even with the stroke and line of his great justice:
He doth with holy abstinence subdue
That in himself which he spurs on his power
To qualify in others: were he meal'd with that
Which he corrects, then were he tyrannous;
But this being so, he's just. [*Knocking within.*
Now are they come.
[*Exit* PROVOST.
This is a gentle provost: seldom, when
The steeled gaoler is the friend of men.
[*Knocking within.*
How now! what noise? That spirit's possest with haste
That wounds th'unresisting postern with these strokes.

Enter PROVOST.

PROVOST.

There he must stay until the officer
Arise to let him in: he is call'd up.

DUKE.

Have you no countermand for Claudio yet,
But he must die to-morrow?

PROVOST.

None, sir, none.

DUKE.

As near the dawning, provost, as it is,
You shall hear more ere morning.

PROVOST.

Happily
You something know; yet I believe there comes
No countermand; no such example have we:
Besides, upon the very siege of justice
Lord Angelo hath to the public ear
Profest the contrary.

Enter a MESSENGER.

This is his lordship's man.

DUKE.

And here comes Claudio's pardon.

MESSENGER [*giving a paper*].

My lord hath sent you this note; and by me this further charge,—that you swerve not from the smallest article of it, neither in time, matter, or other circumstance. Good morrow; for, as I take it, it is almost day.

PROVOST.

I shall obey him. [*Exit* MESSENGER.

DUKE [*aside*].

This is his pardon, purchased by such sin
For which the pardoner himself is in.
Hence hath offence his quick celerity,
When it is borne in high authority:
When vice makes mercy, mercy's so extended,
That for the fault's love is th'offender friended.—
Now, sir, what news?

PROVOST.

I told you: Lord Angelo, belike thinking me remiss in mine office, awakens me with this unwonted putting-on; methinks strangely, for he hath not used it before.

DUKE.

Pray you, let's hear.

PROVOST [*reads*].

Whatsoever you may hear to the contrary, let Claudio be executed by four of the clock; and in the afternoon Barnardine: for my better satisfaction, let me have Claudio's head sent me by five. Let this be duly perform'd; with a thought that more depends on it than we must yet deliver. Thus fail not to do your office, as you will answer it at your peril.
What say you to this, sir?

DUKE.

What is that Barnardine who is to be executed in th'afternoon?

PROVOST.

A Bohemian born, but here nursed up and bred; one that is a prisoner nine years old.

DUKE.

How came it that the absent duke had not either deliver'd him to his liberty or executed him? I have heard it was ever his manner to do so.

PROVOST.

His friends still wrought reprieves for him: and, indeed, his fact, till now in the government of Lord Angelo, came not to an undoubtful proof.

DUKE.

It is now apparent?

PROVOST.

Most manifest, and not denied by himself.

DUKE.

Hath he borne himself penitently in prison? How seems he to be touch'd?

PROVOST.

A man that apprehends death no more dreadfully but as a drunken sleep; careless, reckless, and fearless of what's past, present, or to come; insensible of mortality, and desperately mortal.

DUKE.

He wants advice.

PROVOST.

He will hear none: he hath evermore had the liberty of the prison; give him leave to escape hence, he would not: drunk many times a day, if not many days entirely drunk. We have very oft awaked him, as if to carry him to execution, and show'd him a seeming warrant for it: it hath not moved him at all.

DUKE.

More of him anon. There is written in your brow, provost, honesty and constancy: if I read it not truly, my ancient skill beguiles me; but, in the boldness of my cunning, I will lay myself in hazard. Claudio, whom here you have warrant to execute, is no greater forfeit to the law than Angelo, who hath sentenced him. To make you understand this in a manifested effect, I crave but four days' respite; for the which you are to do me both a present and a dangerous courtesy.

PROVOST.

Pray, sir, in what?

DUKE.

In the delaying death.

PROVOST.

Alack, how may I do it,—having the hour limited, and an express command, under penalty, to deliver his head in the view of Angelo? I may make my case as Claudio's, to cross this in the smallest.

DUKE.

By the vow of mine order I warrant you, if my instructions may be your guide. Let this Barnadine be this morning executed, and his head borne to Angelo.

PROVOST.

Angelo hath seen them both, and will discover the favour.

DUKE.

O, death's a great disguiser; and you may add to it. Shave the head and tie the beard; and say it was the desire of the penitent to be so bared before his death: you know the course is common. If any thing fall to you upon this, more than thanks and good fortune, by the saint whom I profess, I will plead against it with my life.

PROVOST.

Pardon me, good father; it is against my oath.

DUKE.

Were you sworn to the duke, or to the deputy?

PROVOST.

To him, and to his substitutes.

DUKE.

You will think you have made no offence, if the duke avouch the justice of your dealing?

PROVOST.

But what likelihood is in that?

DUKE.

Not a resemblance, but a certainty. Yet since I see you fearful that neither my coat, integrity, nor persuasion can with ease attempt you, I will go further than I meant, to pluck all fears out of you. Look you, sir, here is the hand and seal of the duke: you know the character, I doubt not; and the signet is not strange to you.

PROVOST.

I know them both.

DUKE.

The contents of this is the return of the duke; you shall anon over-read it at your pleasure; where you shall find, within these two days he will be here. This is a thing that Angelo knows not; for he this very day receives letters of strange tenour; perchance of the duke's death; perchance entering into some monastery; but, by chance, nothing of what is writ. Look, th'unfolding star calls up the shepherd. Put not yourself into amazement how these things should be: all difficulties are but easy when they are known. Call your executioner, and off with Barnardine's head: I will give him a present shrift, and advise him for a better place. Yet you are amazed; but this shall absolutely resolve you. Come away; it is almost clear dawn.

[*Exeunt.*

SCENE III.

Another room in the same.

Enter POMPEY.

POMPEY.

I AM as well acquainted here as I was in our house of profession: one would think it were Mistress Overdone's own house, for here be many of her old customers. First, here's young Master Rash; he's in for a commodity of brown paper and old ginger, nine-score and seventeen pounds; of which he made five marks, ready money; marry, then ginger was not much in request, for the old women were all dead. Then is there here one Master Caper, at the suit of Master Three-pile the mercer, for some four suits of peach-colour'd satin, which now peaches him a beggar. Then have we here young Dizzy, and young Master Deep-vow, and Master Copper-spur, and Master Starve-lackey, the rapier-and-dagger-man, and young Drop-heir that kill'd lusty Pudding, and Master Forthright the tilter, and brave Master Shoe-tie the great traveller, and wild Half-can that stabb'd Pots, and, I think, forty more, all great doers in our trade, and are now 'for the Lord's sake.'

Enter ABHORSON.

ABHORSON.

Sirrah, bring Barnardine hither.

POMPEY.

Master Barnardine! you must rise and be hang'd, Master Barnardine!

ABHORSON.

What, ho, Barnardine!

BARNARDINE [*within*].

A pox o' your throats! Who makes that noise there? Who are you?

POMPEY.

Your friends, sir; the hangman. You must be so good, sir, to rise and be put to death.

BARNARDINE [*within*].

Away, you rogue, away! I am sleepy.

ABHORSON.

Tell him he must awake, and that quickly too.

POMPEY.

Pray, Master Barnardine, awake till you are executed, and sleep afterwards.

ABHORSON.

Go in to him, and fetch him out.

POMPEY.

He is coming, sir, he is coming; I hear his straw rustle.

ABHORSON.

Is the axe upon the block, sirrah?

POMPEY.

Very ready, sir.

Enter BARNARDINE.

BARNARDINE.

How now, Abhorson! what's the news with you?

ABHORSON.

Truly, sir, I would desire you to clap into your prayers; for, look you, the warrant's come.

BARNARDINE.

You rogue, I have been drinking all night; I am not fitted for't.

POMPEY.

O, the better, sir; for he that drinks all night, and is hang'd betimes in the morning, may sleep the sounder all the next day.

ABHORSON.

Look you, sir; here comes your ghostly father: do we jest now, think you?

Enter DUKE *disguised as before.*

DUKE.

Sir, induced by my charity, and hearing how hastily you are to depart, I am come to advise you, comfort you, and pray with you.

BARNARDINE.

Friar, not I: I have been drinking hard all night, and I will have more time to prepare me, or they shall beat out my brains with billets: I will not consent to die this day, that's certain.

DUKE.

O, sir, you must: and therefore I beseech you
Look forward on the journey you shall go.

BARNARDINE.

I swear I will not die to-day for any man's persuasion.

DUKE.

But hear you,—

BARNARDINE.

Not a word: if you have anything to say to me, come to my ward; from thence will not I to-day.

[*Exit.*

DUKE.

Unfit to live or die: O gravel heart!—
After him, fellows; bring him to the block.

[*Exeunt* ABHORSON *and* POMPEY.

Enter PROVOST.

PROVOST.

Now, sir, how do you find the prisoner?

DUKE.

A creature unprepared, unmeet for death;
And to transport him in the mind he is
Were damnable.

PROVOST.

Here in the prison, father,
There died this morning of a cruel fever
One Ragozine, a most notorious pirate,
A man of Claudio's years; his beard and head
Just of his colour. What if we do omit
This reprobate till he were well inclined;
And satisfy the deputy with the visage
Of Ragozine, more like to Claudio?

DUKE.

O, 'tis an accident that heaven provides!
Dispatch it presently; the hour draws on
Prefixt by Angelo: see this be done,
And sent according to command; whiles I
Persuade this rude wretch willingly to die.

PROVOST.

This shall be done, good father, presently.
But Barnardine must die this afternoon:
And how shall we continue Claudio,
To save me from the danger that might come
If he were known alive?

DUKE.

Let this be done,—put them in secret holds,
Both Barnardine and Claudio:
Ere twice the sun hath made his journal greeting
To th'under generation, you shall find
Your safety manifested.

PROVOST.

I am your free dependant.

DUKE.

Quick, dispatch,
And send the head to Angelo. [*Exit* PROVOST.
Now will I write letters to Angelo,—
The provost, he shall bear them,—whose contents
Shall witness to him I am near at home,
And that, by great injunctions, I am bound
To enter publicly: him I'll desire
To meet me at the consecrated fount,
A league below the city; and from thence,
By cold gradation and well-balanced form,
We shall proceed with Angelo.

Enter PROVOST *with* RAGOZINE'S *head*.

PROVOST.

Here is the head; I'll carry it myself.

DUKE.

Convenient is it. Make a swift return;
For I would commune with you of such things
That want no ear but yours.

PROVOST.

I'll make all speed. [*Exit*.

ISABELLA [*within*].

Peace, ho, be here!

DUKE.

The tongue of Isabel. She's come to know
If yet her brother's pardon be come hither:
But I will keep her ignorant of her good,
To make her heavenly comforts of despair,
When it is least expected.

Enter ISABELLA.

ISABELLA.

Ho, by your leave!

DUKE.

Good morning to you, fair and gracious daughter.

ISABELLA.

The better, given by so holy a man.
Hath yet the deputy sent my brother's pardon?

DUKE.

He hath released him, Isabel, from the world:
His head is off, and sent to Angelo.

ISABELLA.

Nay, but it is not so.

DUKE.

It is no other: show your wisdom, daughter,
In your close patience.

ISABELLA.

O, I will to him and pluck out his eyes!

DUKE.

You shall not be admitted to his sight.

ISABELLA.

Unhappy Claudio! wretched Isabel!
Injurious world! most damned Angelo!

DUKE.

This nor hurts him nor profits you a jot;
Forbear it therefore; give your cause to heaven.
Mark what I say, which you shall find
By every syllable a faithful verity:
The duke comes home to-morrow;—nay, dry your eyes;
One of our covent, and his confessor,
Gives me this instance: already he hath carried
Notice to Escalus and Angelo;
Who do prepare to meet him at the gates,
There to give up their power. If you can, pace your wisdom
In that good path that I would wish it go;
And you shall have your bosom on this wretch,
Grace of the duke, revenges to your heart,
And general honour.

ISABELLA.

I am directed by you.

DUKE.

This letter, then, to Friar Peter give;
'Tis that he sent me of the duke's return:
Say, by this token, I desire his company
At Mariana's house to-night. Her cause and yours
I'll perfect him withal; and he shall bring you
Before the duke; and to the head of Angelo
Accuse him home and home. For my poor self,
I am combined by a sacred vow,
And shall be absent. Wend you with this letter:
Command these fretting waters from your eyes
With a light heart; trust not my holy order,
If I pervert your course.—Who's here?

Enter LUCIO.

LUCIO.

Good even, friar: where's the provost?

DUKE.

Not within, sir.

LUCIO.

O pretty Isabella, I am pale at mine heart to see thine eyes so red: thou must be patient. I am fain to dine and sup with water and bran; I dare not for my head fill my belly; one fruitful meal would set me to't. But they say the duke will be here to-morrow. By my troth, Isabel, I loved thy brother: if the old fantastical duke of dark corners had been at home, he had lived. [*Exit* ISABELLA.

DUKE.

Sir, the duke is marvellous little beholding to your reports; but the best is, he lives not in them.

LUCIO.

Friar, thou know'st not the duke so well as I do: he's a better woodman than thou takest him for.

DUKE.

Well, you'll answer this one day. Fare ye well.

LUCIO.

Nay, tarry; I'll go along with thee: I can tell thee pretty tales of the duke.

DUKE.

You have told me too many of him already, sir, if they be true; if not true, none were enough.

LUCIO.

I was once before him for getting a wench with child.

DUKE.

Did you such a thing?

LUCIO.

Yes, marry, did I: but I was fain to forswear it; they would else have married me to the rotten medlar.

DUKE.

Sir, your company is fairer than honest. Rest you well.

LUCIO.

By my troth, I'll go with thee to the lane's end: if bawdy talk offend you, we'll have very little of it. Nay, friar, I am a kind of burr; I shall stick. [*Exeunt.*

SCENE IV.

ANGELO'S *house.*

Enter ANGELO *and* ESCALUS.

ESCALUS.

EVERY letter he hath writ hath disvouch'd other.

ANGELO.

In most uneven and distracted manner. His actions show much like to madness: pray heaven his wisdom be not tainted! And why meet him at the gates, and redeliver our authorities there?

ESCALUS.

I guess not.

ANGELO.

And why should we proclaim it in an hour before his entering, that if any crave redress of injustice, they should exhibit their petitions in the street?

ESCALUS.

He shows his reason for that;—to have a dispatch of complaints, and to deliver us from devices hereafter, which shall then have no power to stand against us.

ANGELO.

Well, I beseech you, let it be proclaim'd:
Betimes i'the morn I'll call you at your house:
Give notice to such men of sort and suit
As are to meet him.

ESCALUS.

I shall, sir. Fare you well.

ANGELO.

Good night. [*Exit* ESCALUS.
This deed unshapes me quite, makes me unpregnant,
And dull to all proceedings. A deflower'd maid!
And by an eminent body that enforced
The law against it! But that her tender shame
Will not proclaim against her maiden loss,
How might she tongue me! Yet reason dares her no;
For my authority bears a credent bulk,
That no particular scandal once can touch
But it confounds the breather. He should have lived,
Save that his riotous youth, with dangerous sense,
Might in the times to come have ta'en revenge,
By so receiving a dishonour'd life
With ransom of such shame. Would yet he had lived!
Alack, when once our grace we have forgot,
Nothing goes right,—we would, and we would not! [*Exit.*

SCENE V.

Fields without the town.

Enter DUKE *in his own habit, and* FRIAR PETER.

DUKE.

THESE letters at fit time deliver me: [*Giving letters.*
The provost knows our purpose and our plot.
The matter being afoot, keep your instruction,
And hold you ever to our special drift;
Though sometimes you do blench from this to that,
As cause doth minister. Go call at Flavius' house,
And tell him where I stay: give the like notice
To Valentinus, Rowland, and to Crassus,
And bid them bring the trumpets to the gate;
But send me Flavius first.

FRIAR PETER.

It shall be speeded well. [*Exit.*

Enter VARRIUS.

DUKE.

I thank thee, Varrius; thou hast made good haste:
Come, we will walk. There's other of our friends
Will greet us here anon, my gentle Varrius. [*Exeunt.*

SCENE VI.

Street near the city-gate.

Enter ISABELLA *and* MARIANA.

ISABELLA.

TO speak so indirectly I am loth:
I would say the truth; but to accuse him so,
That is your part: yet I am advised to do it;
He says, to vailful purpose.

MARIANA.

Be ruled by him.

ISABELLA.

Besides, he tells me that, if peradventure
He speak against me on the adverse side,
I should not think it strange; for 'tis a physic
That's bitter to sweet end.

MARIANA.

I would Friar Peter,—

ISABELLA.

O, peace! the friar is come.

Enter FRIAR PETER.

FRIAR PETER.

Come, I have found you out a stand most fit,
Where you may have such vantage on the duke,
He shall not pass you. Twice have the trumpets sounded;
The generous and gravest citizens
Have hent the gates, and very near upon
The duke is ent'ring: therefore, hence, away!

[*Exeunt.*

ACT V. SCENE I.

A public place near the city-gate.

MARIANA *veiled,* ISABELLA, *and* FRIAR PETER *at their stand. Enter at opposite doors,* DUKE *in his own habit,* VARRIUS, LORDS; ANGELO, ESCALUS, LUCIO, PROVOST, OFFICERS, *and* CITIZENS.

DUKE.

My very worthy cousin, fairly met:—
Our old and faithful friend, we are glad to see you.

ANGELO *and* ESCALUS.

Happy return be to your royal grace!

DUKE.

Many and hearty thankings to you both.
We have made inquiry of you; and we hear
Such goodness of your justice, that our soul
Cannot but yield you forth to public thanks,
Forerunning more requital.

ANGELO.

You make my bonds still greater.

DUKE.

O, your desert speaks loud; and I should wrong it,
To lock it in the wards of covert bosom,
When it deserves, with characters of brass,
A forted residence 'gainst the tooth of time
And razure of oblivion. Give me your hand,
And let the subject see, to make them know
That outward courtesies would fain proclaim
Favours that keep within.—Come, Escalus;
You must walk by us on our other hand:—
And good supporters are you.

FRIAR PETER *and* ISABELLA *come forward.*

FRIAR PETER.

Now is your time: speak loud, and kneel before him.

ISABELLA.

Justice, O royal duke! Vail your regard
Upon a wrong'd, I would fain have said, a maid!
O worthy prince, dishonour not your eye
By throwing it on any other object
Till you have heard me in my true complaint,
And given me justice, justice, justice, justice!

DUKE.

Relate your wrongs; in what? by whom? be brief.
Here is Lord Angelo shall give you justice.
Reveal yourself to him.

ISABELLA.

O worthy duke,
You bid me seek redemption of the devil:
Hear me yourself; for that which I must speak
Must either punish me, not being believed,
Or wring redress from you: hear me, O, hear me, here!

ANGELO.

My lord, her wits, I fear me, are not firm:
She hath been a suitor to me for her brother
Cut off by course of justice,—

ISABELLA.

By course of justice!

ANGELO.

And she will speak most bitterly and strange.

ISABELLA.

Most strange, but yet most truly, will I speak:
That Angelo's forsworn; is it not strange?
That Angelo's a murderer; is't not strange?
That Angelo is an adulterous thief,
An hypocrite, a virgin-violator;
Is it not strange and strange?

DUKE.

Nay, it is ten times strange.

ISABELLA.

It is not truer he is Angelo
Than this is all as true as it is strange:
Nay, it is ten times true; for truth is truth
To th'end of reck'ning.

DUKE.

Away with her!—Poor soul,
She speaks this in th'infirmity of sense.

ISABELLA.

O prince, I conjure thee, as thou believest
There is another comfort than this world,
That thou neglect me not, with that opinion
That I am touch'd with madness! Make not impossible
That which but seems unlike: 'tis not impossible
But one, the wicked'st caitiff on the ground,
May seem as shy, as grave, as just, as absolute
As Angelo; even so may Angelo,
In all his dressings, characts, titles, forms,
Be an arch-villain; believe it, royal prince:
If he be less, he's nothing; but he's more,
Had I more name for badness.

DUKE.

By mine honesty,
If she be mad,—as I believe no other,—
Her madness hath the oddest frame of sense,
Such a dependency of thing on thing,
As e'er I heard in madness.

ISABELLA.

O gracious duke,
Harp not on that; nor do not banish reason
For inequality; but let your reason serve
To make the truth appear where it seems hid,
And hide the false seems true.

DUKE.

Many that are not mad
Have, sure, more lack of reason.—What would you say?

ISABELLA.

I am the sister of one Claudio,
Condemn'd upon the act of fornication
To lose his head; condemn'd by Angelo:
I, in probation of a sisterhood,
Was sent to by my brother; one Lucio
As then the messenger,—

LUCIO.

That's I, an't like your grace:
I came to her from Claudio, and desired her

To try her gracious fortune with Lord Angelo
For her poor brother's pardon.

ISABELLA.
That's he indeed.

DUKE.
You were not bid to speak.

LUCIO.
No, my good lord;
Nor wish'd to hold my peace.

DUKE.
I wish you now, then;
Pray you, take note of it: and when you have
A business for yourself, pray heaven you then
Be perfect.

LUCIO.
I warrant your honour.

DUKE.
The warrant's for yourself; take heed to't.

ISABELLA.
This gentleman told somewhat of my tale,—

LUCIO.
Right.

DUKE.
It may be right; but you are i'the wrong
To speak before your time.—Proceed.

ISABELLA.
I went
To this pernicious caitiff deputy,—

DUKE.
That's somewhat madly spoken.

ISABELLA.
Pardon it;
The phrase is to the matter.

DUKE.
Mended again. The matter;—proceed.

ISABELLA.
In brief,—to set the needless process by,
How I persuaded, how I pray'd, and kneel'd,
How he refell'd me, and how I replied,—
For this was of much length,—the vile conclusion
I now begin with grief and shame to utter;
He would not, but by gift of my chaste body
To his concupiscible intemperate lust,
Release my brother; and, after much debatement,
My sisterly remorse confutes mine honour,
And I did yield to him; but the next morn betimes,
His purpose surfeiting, he sends a warrant
For my poor brother's head.

DUKE.
This is most likely!

ISABELLA.
O, that it were as like as it is true!

DUKE.
By heaven, fond wretch, thou know'st not what thou speak'st.
Or else thou art suborn'd against his honour
In hateful practice. First, his integrity
Stands without blemish. Next, it imports no reason
That with such vehemency he should pursue
Faults proper to himself: if he had so offended,
He would have weigh'd thy brother by himself,
And not have cut him off. Some one hath set you on:
Confess the truth, and say by whose advice
Thou camest here to complain.

ISABELLA.
And is this all?
Then, O you blessed ministers above,
Keep me in patience, and with ripen'd time
Unfold the evil which is here wrapt up
In countenance!—Heaven shield your grace from woe,
As I, thus wrong'd, hence unbelieved go!

DUKE.
I know you'ld fain be gone.—An officer!
To prison with her!—Shall we thus permit
A blasting and a scandalous breath to fall
On him so near us? This needs must be a practice.—
Who knew of your intent and coming hither?

ISABELLA.
One that I would were here, Friar Lodowick.

DUKE.
A ghostly father, belike.—Who knows that Lodowick?

LUCIO.
My lord, I know him; 'tis a meddling friar;
I do not like the man: had he been lay, my lord,
For certain words he spake against your grace
In your retirement, I had swinged him soundly.

DUKE.
Words against me! this' a good friar, belike!
And to set on this wretched woman here
Against our substitute!—Let this friar be found.

LUCIO.
But yesternight, my lord, she and that friar,
I saw them at the prison: a saucy friar,
A very scurvy fellow.

FRIAR PETER.
Bless'd be your royal grace!
I have stood by, my lord, and I have heard
Your royal ear abused. First, hath this woman
Most wrongfully accused your substitute,
Who is as free from touch or soil with her
As she from one ungot.

DUKE.
We did believe no less.
Know you that Friar Lodowick that she speaks of?

FRIAR PETER.
I know him for a man divine and holy;
Not scurvy, nor a temporary meddler,
As he's reported by this gentleman;
And, on my trust, a man that never yet
Did, as he vouches, misreport your grace.

LUCIO.
My lord, most villainously; believe it.

FRIAR PETER.
Well, he in time may come to clear himself;
But at this instant he is sick, my lord,
Of a strange fever. Upon his mere request,—
Being come to knowledge that there was complaint
Intended 'gainst Lord Angelo,—came I hither,
To speak, as from his mouth, what he doth know
Is true and false; and what he, with his oath
And all probation, will make up full clear,
Whensoever he's convented. First, for this woman,—
To justify this worthy nobleman,
So vulgarly and personally accused,—
Her shall you hear disproved to her eyes,
Till she herself confess it.

DUKE.

Good friar, let's hear it.

[*ISABELLA is carried off guarded; and MARIANA comes forward.*

Do you not smile at this, Lord Angelo?—
O heaven, the vanity of wretched fools!—
Give us some seats.—Come, cousin Angelo;
In this I'll be impartial; be you judge
Of your own cause.—Is this the witness, friar?
First, let her show her face, and after speak.

MARIANA.

Pardon, my lord; I will not show my face
Until my husband bid me.

DUKE.

What, are you married?

MARIANA.

No, my lord.

DUKE.

Are you a maid?

MARIANA.

No, my lord.

DUKE.

A widow, then?

MARIANA.

Neither, my lord.

DUKE.

Why, you are nothing, then:—neither maid, widow, nor wife?

LUCIO.

My lord, she may be a punk; for many of them are neither maid, widow, nor wife.

DUKE.

Silence that fellow: I would he had some cause
To prattle for himself.

LUCIO.

Well, my lord.

MARIANA.

My lord, I do confess I ne'er was married;
And I confess, besides, I am no maid:
I've known my husband: yet my husband knows [not
That ever he knew me.

LUCIO.

He was drunk, then, my lord: it can be no better.

DUKE.

For the benefit of silence, would thou wert so too!

LUCIO.

Well, my lord.

DUKE.

This is no witness for Lord Angelo.

MARIANA.

Now I come to't, my lord:
She that accuses him of fornication,
In self-same manner doth accuse my husband;
And charges him, my lord, with such a time
When I'll depose I had him in mine arms
With all th'effect of love.

ANGELO.

Charges she moe than me?

MARIANA.

Not that I know.

DUKE.

No? you say your husband.

MARIANA.

Why, just, my lord, and that is Angelo,
Who thinks he knows that he ne'er knew my body,
But knows he thinks that he knows Isabel's.

ANGELO.

This is a strange abuse.—Let's see thy face.

MARIANA.

My husband bids me; now I will unmask.
This is that face, thou cruel Angelo, [*Unveiling.*
Which once thou sworest was worth the looking on;
This is the hand which, with a vow'd contract,
Was fast belockt in thine; this is the body
That took away the match from Isabel,
And did supply thee at thy garden-house
In her imagined person.

DUKE.

Know you this woman?

LUCIO.

Carnally, she says.

DUKE.

Sirrah, no more!

LUCIO.

Enough, my lord.

ANGELO.

My lord, I must confess I know this woman:
And five years since there was some speech of marriage
Betwixt myself and her; which was broke off,
Partly for that her promised proportions
Came short of composition; but in chief
For that her reputation was disvalued
In levity: since which time of five years
I never spake with her, saw her, nor heard from her,
Upon my faith and honour.

MARIANA.

Noble prince,
As there comes light from heaven and words from breath,
As there is sense in truth and truth in virtue,
I am affianced this man's wife as strongly
As words could make up vows: and, my good lord,
But Tuesday night last gone, in's garden-house,
He knew me as a wife. As this is true,
Let me in safety raise me from my knees;
Or else for ever be confixed here,
A marble monument!

ANGELO.

I did but smile till now;
Now, good my lord, give me the scope of justice;
My patience here is touch'd. I do perceive
These poor informal women are no more
But instruments of some more mightier member
That sets them on: let me have way, my lord,
To find this practice out.

DUKE.

Ay, with my heart;
And punish them to your height of pleasure.—
Thou foolish friar; and thou pernicious woman,
Compact with her that's gone, think'st thou thy oaths,
Though they would swear down each particular saint,
Were testimonies against his worth and credit,
That's seal'd in approbation?—You, Lord Escalus,
Sit with my cousin; lend him your kind pains
To find out this abuse, whence 'tis derived.—
There is another friar that set them on;
Let him be sent for.

FRIAR PETER.
Would he were here, my lord! for he, indeed,
Hath set the women on to this complaint:
Your provost knows the place where he abides,
And he may fetch him.

DUKE.
Go do it instantly. [*Exit* PROVOST.
And you, my noble and well-warranted cousin,
Whom it concerns to hear this matter forth,
Do with your injuries as seems you best,
In any chastisement: I for a while will leave you;
But stir not till you have well determined
Upon these slanderers.

ESCALUS.
My lord, we'll do it throughly. [*Exit* DUKE.
Signior Lucio, did not you say you knew that Friar Lodowick to be a dishonest person?

LUCIO.
Cucullus non facit monachum: honest in nothing but in his clothes; and one that hath spoke most villainous speeches of the duke.

ESCALUS.
We shall entreat you to abide here till he come, and enforce them against him: we shall find this friar a notable fellow.

LUCIO.
As any in Vienna, on my word.

ESCALUS.
Call that same Isabel here once again: I would speak with her. [*Exit an* ATTENDANT.]—Pray you, my lord, give me leave to question; you shall see how I'll handle her.

LUCIO.
Not better than he, by her own report.

ESCALUS.
Say you?

LUCIO.
Marry, sir, I think, if you handled her privately, she would sooner confess: perchance, publicly, she'll be ashamed.

ESCALUS.
I will go darkly to work with her.

LUCIO.
That's the way; for women are light at midnight.

Enter OFFICERS *with* ISABELLA.

ESCALUS [*to* ISABELLA].
Come on, mistress: here's a gentlewoman denies all that you have said.

LUCIO.
My lord, here comes the rascal I spoke of; here with the provost.

ESCALUS.
In very good time:—speak not you to him till we call upon you.

LUCIO.
Mum.

Enter DUKE *disguised as a friar, and* PROVOST.

ESCALUS.
Come, sir: did you set these women on to slander Lord Angelo? they have confess'd you did.

DUKE.
'Tis false.

ESCALUS.
How! know you where you are?

DUKE.
Respect to your great place! and let the devil
Be sometime honour'd for his burning throne!—
Where is the duke? 'tis he should hear me speak.

ESCALUS.
The duke's in us; and we will hear you speak:
Look you speak justly.

DUKE.
Boldly, at least.—But, O, poor souls,
Come you to seek the lamb here of the fox?
Good night to your redress! Is the duke gone?
Then is your cause gone too. The duke's unjust,
Thus to retort your manifest appeal,
And put your trial in the villain's mouth
Which here you come to accuse.

LUCIO.
This is the rascal; this is he I spoke of

ESCALUS.
Why, thou unreverend and unhallow'd friar,
Is't not enough thou hast suborn'd these women
To accuse this worthy man, but, in foul mouth,
And in the witness of his proper ear,
To call him villain? and then to glance from him
To th'duke himself, to tax him with injustice?—
Take him hence; to th'rack with him!—We'll touse you
Joint by joint, but we will know his purpose.—
What, 'unjust'?

DUKE.
Be not so hot; the duke
Dare no more stretch this finger of mine than he
Dare rack his own: his subject am I not,
Nor here provincial. My business in this state
Made me a looker-on here in Vienna,
Where I have seen corruption boil and bubble
Till it o'er-run the stew; laws for all faults,
But faults so countenanced, that the strong statutes
Stand like the forfeits in a barber's shop,
As much in mock as mark.

ESCALUS.
Slander to th'state!—Away with him to prison!

ANGELO.
What can you vouch against him, Signior Lucio?
Is this the man that you did tell us of?

LUCIO.
'Tis he, my lord.—Come hither, goodman bald-pate: do you know me?

DUKE.
I remember you, sir, by the sound of your voice: I met you at the prison, in the absence of the duke.

LUCIO.
O, did you so? And do you remember what you said of the duke?

DUKE.
Most notedly, sir.

LUCIO.
Do you so, sir? And was the duke a fleshmonger, a fool, and a coward, as you then reported him to be?

DUKE.
You must, sir, change persons with me, ere you make that my report; you, indeed, spoke so of him; and much more, much worse.

LUCIO.
O thou damnable fellow! Did not I pluck thee by the nose for thy speeches?

DUKE.
I protest I love the duke as I love myself.

ANGELO.

Hark, how the villain would close now, after his treasonable abuses!

ESCALUS.

Such a fellow is not to be talk'd withal.—Away with him to prison!—Where is the provost?—Away with him to prison! lay bolts enough upon him: let him speak no more.—Away with those giglots too, and with the other confederate companion!

DUKE [*to the* PROVOST].

Stay, sir; stay awhile;

ANGELO.

What, resists he?—Help him, Lucio.

LUCIO.

Come, sir; come, sir; come sir, foh, sir! Why, you bald-pated, lying rascal, you must be hooded, must you? Show your knave's visage, with a pox to you! show your sheep-biting face, and be hang'd an hour! Will't not off?

[*Pulls off the friar's hood, and discovers the* DUKE.

DUKE.

Thou art the first knave that e'er madest a duke.—
First, provost, let me bail these gentle three.—
[*to* LUCIO] Sneak not away, sir; for the friar and you
Must have a word anon.—Lay hold on him.

LUCIO.

This may prove worse than hanging.

DUKE [*to* ESCALUS].

What you have spoke I pardon: sit you down:
We'll borrow place of him.—[*to* ANGELO] Sir, by your leave.
Hast thou or word, or wit, or impudence,
That yet can do thee office? If thou hast,
Rely upon it till my tale be heard,
And hold no longer out.

ANGELO.

O my dread lord,
I should be guiltier than my guiltiness,
To think I can be undiscernible,
When I perceive your grace, like power divine,
Hath look'd upon my passes. Then, good prince,
No longer session hold upon my shame,
But let my trial be mine own confession:
Immediate sentence then, and sequent death,
Is all the grace I beg.

DUKE.

Come hither, Mariana.—
Say, wast thou e'er contracted to this woman?

ANGELO.

I was, my lord.

DUKE.

Go take her hence, and marry her instantly.—
Do you the office, friar; which consummate,
Return him here again.—Go with him, provost.

[*Exeunt* ANGELO, MARIANA, FRIAR PETER, *and* PROVOST.

ESCALUS.

My lord, I am more amazed at his dishonour
Than at the strangeness of it.

DUKE.

Come hither, Isabel.
Your friar is now your prince: as I was then
Advertising and holy to your business,
Not changing heart with habit, I am still
Attorney'd at your service.

ISABELLA.

O, give me pardon,
That I, your vassal, have employ'd and pain'd
Your unknown sovereignty!

DUKE.

You are pardon'd, Isabel:
And now, dear maid, be you as free to us.
Your brother's death, I know, sits at your heart;
And you may marvel why I obscured myself,
Labouring to save his life, and would not rather
Make rash remonstrance of my hidden power
Than let him so be lost. O most kind maid,
It was the swift celerity of his death,
Which I did think with slower foot came on,
That brain'd my purpose:—but peace be with him!
That life is better life, past fearing death,
Than that which lives to fear: make it your comfort,
So happy is your brother.

ISABELLA.

I do, my lord.

Enter ANGELO, MARIANA, FRIAR PETER, *and* PROVOST.

DUKE.

For this new-married man, approaching here,
Whose salt imagination yet hath wrong'd
Your well-defended honour, you must pardon
For Mariana's sake: but as he adjudged your brother,—
Being criminal, in double violation
Of sacred chastity, and of promise-breach
Thereon dependent, for your brother's life,—
The very mercy of the law cries out
Most audible, even from his proper tongue,
'An Angelo for Claudio, death for death!'
Haste still pays haste, and leisure answers leisure;
Like doth quit like, and *Measure* still *for Measure*.
Then, Angelo, thy fault thus manifested,—
Which, though thou wouldst deny, denies thee vantage,—
We do condemn thee to the very block
Where Claudio stoop'd to death, and with like haste.—
Away with him!

MARIANA.

O my most gracious lord,
I hope you will not mock me with a husband.

DUKE.

It is your husband mock'd you with a husband.
Consenting to the safeguard of your honour,
I thought your marriage fit; else imputation,
For that he knew you, might reproach your life,
And choke your good to come; for his possessions,
Although by confiscation they are ours,
We do instate and widow you withal,
To buy you a better husband.

MARIANA.

O my dear lord,
I crave no other, nor no better man.

DUKE.

Never crave him; we are definitive.

MARIANA.

Gentle my liege,— [*Kneeling.*

DUKE.

You do but lose your labour.—
Away with him to death!—[*to* LUCIO] Now, sir, to you.

MARIANA.

O my good lord!—Sweet Isabel, take my part;
Lend me your knees, and all my life to come
I'll lend you all my life to do you service.

DUKE.

Against all sense you do importune her:
Should she kneel down in mercy of this fact,
Her brother's ghost his paved bed would break,
And take her hence in horror.

MARIANA.

Isabel,
Sweet Isabel, do yet but kneel by me;
Hold up your hands, say nothing,—I'll speak all.
They say, best men are moulded out of faults;
And, for the most, become much more the better
For being a little bad: so may my husband.
O Isabel, will you not lend a knee?

DUKE.

He dies for Claudio's death.

ISABELLA.

Most bounteous sir, [*Kneeling.*
Look, if it please you, on this man condemn'd,
As if my brother lived: I partly think
A due sincerity govern'd his deeds,
Till he did look on me: since it is so,
Let him not die. My brother had but justice,
In that he did the thing for which he died:
For Angelo,
His act did not o'ertake his bad intent;
And must be buried but as an intent
That perish'd by the way: thoughts are no subjects,
Intents but merely thoughts.

MARIANA.

Merely, my lord.

DUKE.

Your suit's unprofitable; stand up, I say.—
I have bethought me of another fault.—
Provost, how came it Claudio was beheaded
At an unusual hour?

PROVOST.

It was commanded so.

DUKE.

Had you a special warrant for the deed?

PROVOST.

No, my good lord; it was by private message.

DUKE.

For which I do discharge you of your office:
Give up your keys.

PROVOST.

Pardon me, noble lord:
I thought it was a fault, but knew it not;
Yet did repent me, after more advice:
For testimony whereof, one in the prison,
That should by private order else have died,
I have reserved alive.

DUKE.

What's he?

PROVOST.

His name is Barnardine.

DUKE.

I would thou hadst done so by Claudio.—
Go fetch him hither; let me look upon him.
[*Exit* PROVOST.

ESCALUS.

I am sorry, one so learned and so wise
As you, Lord Angelo, have still appear'd,
Should slip so grossly, both in the heat of blood,
And lack of temper'd judgement afterward.

ANGELO.

I am sorry that such sorrow I procure:
And so deep sticks it in my penitent heart,
That I crave death more willingly than mercy;
'Tis my deserving, and I do entreat it.

Enter PROVOST, *with* BARNARDINE, CLAUDIO *muffled, and* JULIET.

DUKE.

Which is that Barnardine?

PROVOST.

This, my lord.

DUKE.

There was a friar told me of this man.—
Sirrah, thou art said to have a stubborn soul,
That apprehends no further than this world,
And squarest thy life according. Thou'rt condemn'd:
But, for those earthly faults, I quit them all;
And pray thee take this mercy to provide
For better times to come.—Friar, advise him;
I leave him to your hand.—What muffled fellow's that?

PROVOST.

This is another prisoner that I saved,
Who should have died when Claudio lost his head;
As like almost to Claudio as himself.
[*Unmuffles* CLAUDIO.

DUKE [*to* ISABELLA].

If he be like your brother, for his sake
Is he pardon'd; and, for your lovely sake,
Give me your hand, and say you will be mine,
He is my brother too: but fitter time for that.
By this Lord Angelo perceives he's safe;
Methinks I see a quick'ning in his eye.—
Well, Angelo, your evil quits you well:
Look that you love your wife; her worth worth yours.—
I find an apt remission in myself;
And yet here's one in place I cannot pardon.—
[*to* LUCIO] You, sirrah, that knew me for a fool, a coward,
One all of luxury, an ass, a madman;
Wherein have I so deserved of you,
That you extol me thus?

LUCIO.

Faith, my lord, I spoke it but according to the trick. If you will hang me for it, you may; but I had rather it would please you I might be whipt.

DUKE.

Whipt first, sir, and hang'd after.—
Proclaim it, provost, round about the city,
If any woman wrong'd by this lewd fellow,—
As I have heard him swear himself there's one
Whom he begot with child,—let her appear,
And he shall marry her: the nuptial finish'd,
Let him be whipt and hang'd.

LUCIO.

I beseech your highness, do not marry me to a whore! Your highness said even now, I made you a duke: good my lord, do not recompense me in making me a cuckold.

DUKE.

Upon mine honour, thou shalt marry her.
Thy slanders I forgive; and therewithal
Remit thy other forfeits.—Take him to prison;
And see our pleasure herein executed.

LUCIO.

Marrying a punk, my lord, is pressing to death, whipping, and hanging.

DUKE.

Slandering a prince deserves it.—

[*Exeunt* OFFICERS *with* LUCIO.

She, Claudio, that you wrong'd, look you restore.—
Joy to you, Mariana!—Love her, Angelo:
I have confess'd her, and I know her virtue.—
Thanks, good friend Escalus, for thy much goodness:
There's more behind that is more gratulate.—
Thanks, provost, for thy care and secrecy:
We shall employ thee in a worthier place.—
Forgive him, Angelo, that brought you home
The head of Ragozine for Claudio's:
Th'offence pardons itself.—Dear Isabel,
I have a motion much imports your good;
Whereto if you'll a willing ear incline,
What's mine is yours, and what is yours is mine.—
So, bring us to our palace; where we'll show
What's yet behind, that's meet you all should know.

[*Exeunt.*

ALL'S WELL THAT ENDS WELL

DRAMATIS PERSONAE

KING OF FRANCE.
DUKE OF FLORENCE.
BERTRAM, *Count of Rousillon.*
LAFEU, *an old lord.*
PAROLLES, *a follower of Bertram.*
Several young French LORDS, *who serve with Bertram in the Florentine war.*
STEWARD, } *servants to the Countess of Rousillon.*
LAVACHE, *a Clown,* }
A PAGE.

COUNTESS OF ROUSILLON, *mother to Bertram.*
HELENA, *a gentlewoman protected by the Countess.*
A WIDOW *of Florence.*
DIANA, *her daughter.*
VIOLENTA, } *neighbours and friends to the Widow.*
MARIANA, }

LORDS ATTENDING ON THE KING; OFFICERS, SOLDIERS, *&c.*, FRENCH AND FLORENTINE.

SCENE—*Rousillon; Paris; Florence; Marseilles.*

ACT I. SCENE I.

Rousillon. A hall in the house of the COUNTESS.

Enter BERTRAM, *the* COUNTESS OF ROUSILLON, HELENA, *and* LAFEU, *all in black.*

COUNTESS.

IN delivering my son from me, I bury a second husband.

BERTRAM.

And I, in going, madam, weep o'er my father's death anew; but I must attend his majesty's command, to whom I am now in ward, evermore in subjection.

LAFEU.

You shall find of the king a husband, madam;—you, sir, a father: he that so generally is at all times good, must of necessity hold his virtue to you; whose worthiness would stir it up where it wanted, rather than lack it where there is such abundance.

COUNTESS.

What hope is there of his majesty's amendment?

LAFEU.

He hath abandon'd his physicians, madam; under whose practices he hath persecuted time with hope; and finds no other advantage in the process but only the losing of hope by time.

COUNTESS.

This young gentlewoman had a father,—O, that 'had'! how sad a passage 'tis!—whose skill was almost as great as his honesty; had it stretcht so far, would have made nature immortal, and death should have play for lack of work. Would, for the king's sake, he were living! I think it would be the death of the king's disease.

LAFEU.

How call'd you the man you speak of, madam?

COUNTESS.

He was famous, sir, in his profession, and it was his great right to be so,—Gerard de Narbon.

LAFEU.

He was excellent indeed, madam: the king very lately spoke of him admiringly and mourningly: he was skilful enough to have lived still, if knowledge could be set up against mortality.

BERTRAM.

What is it, my good lord, the king languishes of?

LAFEU.

A fistula, my lord.

BERTRAM.

I heard not of it before.

LAFEU.

I would it were not notorious.—Was this gentlewoman the daughter of Gerard de Narbon?

COUNTESS.

His sole child, my lord; and bequeath'd to my overlooking. I have those hopes of her good that her education promises: her dispositions she inherits, which makes fair gifts fairer; for where an unclean mind carries virtuous qualities, there commendations go with pity,—they are virtues and traitors too: in her they are the better for their simpleness; she derives her honesty, and achieves her goodness.

LAFEU.

Your commendations, madam, get from her tears.

COUNTESS.

'Tis the best brine a maiden can season her praise in. The remembrance of her father never approaches her heart but the tyranny of her sorrows takes all livelihood from her cheek.—No more of this, Helena,—go to, no more; lest it be rather thought you affect a sorrow than to have—

HELENA.

I do affect a sorrow, indeed; but I have it too.

LAFEU.

Moderate lamentation is the right of the dead; excessive grief the enemy of the living.

COUNTESS.

If the living be enemy to the grief, the excess makes it soon mortal.

LAFEU.

How understand we that?

BERTRAM.

Madam, I desire your holy wishes.

COUNTESS.

Be thou blest, Bertram! and succeed thy father
In manners, as in shape! thy blood and virtue
Contend for empire in thee, and thy goodness
Share with thy birthright! Love all, trust a few,
Do wrong to none; be able for thine enemy
Rather in power than use, and keep thy friend
Under thy own life's key; be checkt for silence,
But never taxt for speech. What heaven more will,
That thee may furnish, and my prayers pluck down,
Fall on thy head!—Farewell, my lord:

'Tis an unseason'd courtier; good my lord,
Advise him.

LAFEU.

He cannot want the best
That shall attend his love.

COUNTESS.

Heaven bless him!—Farewell, Bertram. [*Exit.*

BERTRAM [*to* HELENA].

The best wishes that can be forged in your thoughts be servants to you! Be comfortable to my mother, your mistress, and make much of her.

LAFEU.

Farewell, pretty lady: you must hold the credit of your father. [*Exeunt* BERTRAM *and* LAFEU.

HELENA.

O, were that all! I think not on my father;
And these great tears grace his remembrance more
Than those I shed for him. What was he like?
I have forgot him: my imagination
Carries no favour in't but Bertram's.
I am undone: there is no living, none,
If Bertram be away. 'Twere all one
That I should love a bright particular star
And think to wed it, he is so above me:
In his bright radiance and collateral light
Must I be comforted, not in his sphere.
The ambition in my love thus plagues itself:
The hind that would be mated by the lion
Must die for love. 'Twas pretty, though a plague,
To see him every hour; to sit and draw
His arched brows, his hawking eye, his curls,
In our heart's table,—heart too capable
Of every line and trick of his sweet favour:
But now he's gone, and my idolatrous fancy
Must sanctify his reliques.—Who comes here?
One that goes with him: I love him for his sake;
And yet I know him a notorious liar,
Think him a great way fool, solely a coward;
Yet these fixt evils sit so fit in him,
That they take place, when virtue's steely bones
Look bleak i'th'cold wind: withal, full oft we see
Cold wisdom waiting on superfluous folly.

Enter PAROLLES.

PAROLLES.

Save you, fair queen!

HELENA.

And you, monarch!

PAROLLES.

No.

HELENA.

And no.

PAROLLES.

Are you meditating on virginity?

HELENA.

Ay. You have some stain of soldier in you: let me ask you a question. Man is enemy to virginity; how may we barricado it against him?

PAROLLES.

Keep him out.

HELENA.

But he assails; and our virginity, though valiant in the defence, yet is weak: unfold to us some warlike resistance.

PAROLLES.

There is none: man, sitting down before you, will undermine you, and blow you up.

HELENA.

Bless our poor virginity from underminers and blowers-up!—Is there no military policy, how virgins might blow up men?

PAROLLES.

Virginity being blown down, man will quicklier be blown up: marry, in blowing him down again, with the breach yourselves made, you lose your city. It is not politic in the commonwealth of nature to preserve virginity. Loss of virginity is rational increase; and there was never virgin got till virginity was first lost. That you were made of, is metal to make virgins. Virginity, by being once lost, may be ten times found; by being ever kept, it is ever lost: 'tis too cold a companion; away with't!

HELENA.

I will stand for't a little, though therefore I die a virgin.

PAROLLES.

There's little can be said in't; 'tis against the rule of nature. To speak on the part of virginity, is to accuse your mothers; which is most infallible disobedience. He that hangs himself is a virgin: virginity murders itself; and should be buried in highways, out of all sanctified limit, as a desperate offendress against nature. Virginity breeds mites, much like a cheese; consumes itself to the very paring, and so dies with feeding his own stomach. Besides, virginity is peevish, proud, idle, made of self-love, which is the most inhibited sin in the canon. Keep it not; you cannot choose but lose by't: out with't! within ten year it will make itself ten, which is a goodly increase; and the principal itself not much the worse: away with't!

HELENA.

How might one do, sir, to lose it to her own liking?

PAROLLES.

Let me see: marry, ill, to like him that ne'er it likes. 'Tis a commodity will lose the gloss with lying; the longer kept, the less worth: off with't while 'tis vendible; answer the time of request. Virginity, like an old courtier, wears her cap out of fashion; richly suited, but unsuitable: just like the brooch and the toothpick, which wear not now. Your date is better in your pie and your porridge than in your cheek: and your virginity, your old virginity, is like one of our French wither'd pears,—it looks ill, it eats dryly; marry, 'tis a wither'd pear; it was formerly better; marry, yet, 'tis a wither'd pear: will you any thing with it?

HELENA.

Not my virginity yet. . . .
There shall your master have a thousand loves,
A mother, and a mistress, and a friend,
A phœnix, captain, and an enemy,
A guide, a goddess, and a sovereign,
A counsellor, a traitress, and a dear;
His humble ambition, proud humility,
His jarring concord, and his discord dulcet,
His faith, his sweet disaster; with a world
Of pretty, fond, adoptious christendoms,
That blinking Cupid gossips. Now shall he—
I know not what he shall:—God send him well!—
The court's a learning-place;—and he is one—

PAROLLES.
What one, i'faith?

HELENA.
That I wish well.—'Tis pity—

PAROLLES.
What's pity?

HELENA.
That wishing well had not a body in't,
Which might be felt; that we, the poorer born,
Whose baser stars do shut us up in wishes,
Might with effects of them follow our friends,
And show what we alone must think; which never
Returns us thanks.

Enter a PAGE.

PAGE.
Monsieur Parolles, my lord calls for you. [*Exit.*

PAROLLES.
Little Helen, farewell: if I can remember thee, I will think of thee at court.

HELENA.
Monsieur Parolles, you were born under a charitable star.

PAROLLES.
Under Mars, I.

HELENA.
I especially think, under Mars.

PAROLLES.
Why under Mars?

HELENA.
The wars have so kept you under, that you must needs be born under Mars.

PAROLLES.
When he was predominant.

HELENA.
When he was retrograde, I think, rather.

PAROLLES.
Why think you so?

HELENA.
You go so much backward when you fight.

PAROLLES.
That's for advantage.

HELENA.
So is running away, when fear proposes the safety: but the composition, that your valour and fear makes in you, is a virtue of a good wing, and I like the wear well.

PAROLLES.
I am so full of businesses, I cannot answer thee acutely. I will return perfect courtier; in the which, my instruction shall serve to naturalize thee, so thou wilt be capable of a courtier's counsel, and understand what advice shall thrust upon thee; else thou diest in thine unthankfulness, and thine ignorance makes thee away: farewell. When thou hast leisure, say thy prayers; when thou hast none, remember thy friends: get thee a good husband, and use him as he uses thee: so, farewell. [*Exit.*

HELENA.
Our remedies oft in ourselves do lie,
Which we ascribe to heaven: the fated sky
Gives us free scope; only doth backward pull
Our slow designs when we ourselves are dull.
What power is it which mounts my love so high;
That makes me see, and cannot feed mine eye?
The mightiest space in fortune nature brings
To join like likes and kiss like native things.
Impossible be strange attempts to those
That weigh their pains in sense; and do suppose
What hath not been can't be: who ever strove
To show her merit, that did miss her love?
The king's disease,—my project may deceive me,
But my intents are fixt, and will not leave me.
[*Exit.*

SCENE II.

Paris. A room in the KING'S *palace.*

Flourish of cornets. Enter the KING OF FRANCE *with letters, and divers* ATTENDANTS.

KING.
THE Florentines and Senoys are by th' ears;
Have fought with equal fortune, and continue
A braving war.

FIRST LORD.
So 'tis reported, sir.

KING.
Nay, 'tis most credible; we here receive it
A certainty, voucht from our cousin Austria,
With caution, that the Florentine will move us
For speedy aid; wherein our dearest friend
Prejudicates the business, and would seem
To have us make denial.

FIRST LORD.
His love and wisdom,
Approved so to your majesty, may plead
For amplest credence.

KING.
He hath arm'd our answer,
And Florence is denied before he comes:
Yet, for our gentlemen that mean to see
The Tuscan service, freely have they leave
To stand on either part.

SECOND LORD.
It well may serve
A nursery to our gentry, who are sick
For breathing and exploit.

KING.
What's he comes here?

Enter BERTRAM, LAFEU, *and* PAROLLES.

FIRST LORD.
It is the Count Rousillon, my good lord,
Young Bertram.

KING.
Youth, thou bear'st thy father's face;
Frank nature, rather curious than in haste,
Hath well composed thee. Thy father's moral parts
Mayst thou inherit too! Welcome to Paris.

BERTRAM.
My thanks and duty are your majesty's.

KING.
I would I had that corporal soundness now
As when thy father and myself in friendship
First tried our soldiership! He did look far
Into the service of the time, and was
Discipled of the bravest: he lasted long;
But on us both did haggish age steal on,
And wore us out of act. It much repairs me
To talk of your good father. In his youth
He had the wit, which I can well observe
To-day in our young lords; but they may jest,
Till their own scorn return to them unnoted,

Ere they can hide their levity in honour
So like a courtier: contempt nor bitterness
Were in his pride, or sharpness; if they were,
His equal had awaked them; and his honour,
Clock to itself, knew the true minute when
Exception bid him speak, and at this time
His tongue obey'd his hand: who were below him
He used as creatures of another place;
And bow'd his eminent top to their low ranks,
Making them proud of his humility,
In their poor praise he humbled. Such a man
Might be a copy to these younger times;
Which, follow'd well, would demonstrate them now
But goers backward.

BERTRAM.

His good remembrance, sir,
Lies richer in your thoughts than on his tomb;
So in approof lives not his epitaph
As in your royal speech.

KING.

Would I were with him! He would always say,—
Methinks I hear him now; his plausive words
He scatter'd not in ears, but grafted them,
To grow there, and to bear,—'Let me not live,'—
Thus his good melancholy oft began,
On the catastrophe and heel of pastime,
When it was out,—'Let me not live,' quoth he,
'After my flame lacks oil, to be the snuff
Of younger spirits, whose apprehensive senses
All but new things disdain; whose judgements are
Mere fathers of their garments; whose constancies
Expire before their fashions:'—this he wisht:
I, after him, do after him wish too,
Since I nor wax nor honey can bring home,
I quickly were dissolved from my hive,
To give some labourer room.

SECOND LORD.

You are loved, sir;
They that least lend it you shall lack you first.

KING.

I fill a place, I know't.—How long is't, count,
Since the physician at your father's died?
He was much famed.

BERTRAM.

Some six months since, my lord.

KING.

If he were living, I would try him yet;—
Lend me an arm;—the rest have worn me out
With several applications:—nature and sickness
Debate it at their leisure. Welcome, count;
My son's no dearer.

BERTRAM.

Thank your majesty.

[*Exeunt. Flourish.*

SCENE III.

Rousillon. A room in the house of the COUNTESS.

Enter COUNTESS, STEWARD, *and* CLOWN.

COUNTESS.

I WILL now hear: what say you of this gentlewoman?

STEWARD.

Madam, the care I have had to even your content, I wish might be found in the calendar of my past endeavours; for then we wound our modesty, and make foul the clearness of our deservings, when of ourselves we publish them.

COUNTESS.

What does this knave here? Get you gone, sirrah: the complaints I have heard of you I do not all believe: 'tis my slowness that I do not; for I know you lack not folly to commit them, and have ability enough to make such knaveries yours.

CLOWN.

'Tis not unknown to you, madam, I am a poor fellow.

COUNTESS.

Well, sir.

CLOWN.

No, madam, 'tis not so well that I am poor; though many of the rich are damn'd: but, if I may have your ladyship's good-will to go to the world, Isbel your woman and I will do as we may.

COUNTESS.

Wilt thou needs be a beggar?

CLOWN.

I do beg your good-will in this case.

COUNTESS.

In what case?

CLOWN.

In Isbel's case and mine own. Service is no heritage: and I think I shall never have the blessing of God till I have issue o' my body; for they say barns are blessings.

COUNTESS.

Tell me thy reason why thou wilt marry.

CLOWN.

My poor body, madam, requires it: I am driven on by the flesh; and he must needs go that the devil drives.

COUNTESS.

Is this all your worship's reason?

CLOWN.

Faith, madam, I have other holy reasons, such as they are.

COUNTESS.

May the world know them?

CLOWN.

I have been, madam, a wicked creature, as you and all flesh and blood are; and, indeed, I do marry that I may repent.

COUNTESS.

Thy marriage,—sooner than thy wickedness.

CLOWN.

I am out o' friends, madam; and I hope to have friends for my wife's sake.

COUNTESS.

Such friends are thine enemies, knave.

CLOWN.

Y'are shallow, madam; e'en great friends; for the knaves come to do that for me, which I am a-weary of. He that ears my land spares my team, and gives me leave to in the crop; if I be his cuckold, he's my drudge: he that comforts my wife is the cherisher of my flesh and blood; he that cherishes my flesh and blood loves my flesh and blood; he that loves my flesh and blood is my friend: *ergo*, he that kisses my wife is my friend. If men could be contented to be what they are, there were no fear in marriage; for young Charbon the puritan and old Poysam the papist, howsome'er their hearts are sever'd in religion, their heads are both one,—they may jowl horns together, like any deer i'th'herd.

COUNTESS.

Wilt thou ever be a foul-mouth'd and calumnious knave?

CLOWN.

A prophet I, madam; and I speak the truth the next way:

For I the ballad will repeat,
Which men full true shall find;
Your marriage comes by destiny,
Your cuckoo sings by kind.

COUNTESS.

Get you gone, sir; I'll talk with you more anon.

STEWARD.

May it please you, madam, that he bid Helen come to you: of her I am to speak.

COUNTESS.

Sirrah, tell my gentlewoman I would speak with her; Helen I mean.

CLOWN.

Was this fair face the cause, quoth she,
Why the Grecians sacked Troy?
Fond done, done fond,
Was this King Priam's joy?
With that she sighed as she stood,
With that she sighed as she stood,
And gave this sentence then;
Among nine bad if one be good,
Among nine bad if one be good,
There's yet one good in ten.

COUNTESS.

What, one good in ten? you corrupt the song, sirrah.

CLOWN.

One good woman in ten, madam; which is a purifying o'th'song: would God would serve the world so all the year! we'ld find no fault with the tithe-woman, if I were the parson: one in ten, quoth a'! an we might have a good woman born but 'fore every blazing star, or at an earthquake, 'twould mend the lottery well: a man may draw his heart out, ere a' pluck one.

COUNTESS.

You'll begone, sir knave, and do as I command you?

CLOWN.

That man should be at woman's command, and yet no hurt done!—Though honesty be no puritan, yet it will do no hurt; it will wear the surplice of humility over the black gown of a big heart.—I am going, forsooth: the business is for Helen to come hither. [*Exit.*

COUNTESS.

Well, now.

STEWARD.

I know, madam, you love your gentlewoman entirely.

COUNTESS.

Faith, I do: her father bequeath'd her to me; and she herself, without other advantage, may lawfully make title to as much love as she finds: there is more owing her than is paid; and more shall be paid her than she'll demand.

STEWARD.

Madam, I was very late more near her than I think she wisht me: alone she was, and did communicate to herself her own words to her own ears; she thought, I dare vow for her, they toucht not any stranger sense. Her matter was, she loved your son: Fortune, she said, was no goddess, that had put such difference betwixt their two estates; Love no god, that would not extend his might, only where qualities were level; Dian no queen of virgins, that would suffer her poor knight surprised, without rescue in the first assault, or ransom afterward. This she deliver'd in the most bitter touch of sorrow that e'er I heard virgin exclaim in: which I held my duty speedily to acquaint you withal; sithence, in the loss that may happen, it concerns you something to know it.

COUNTESS.

You have discharged this honestly; keep it to yourself: many likelihoods inform'd me of this before, which hung so tottering in the balance, that I could neither believe nor misdoubt. Pray you, leave me: stall this in your bosom, and I thank you for your honest care: I will speak with you further anon. [*Exit* STEWARD.

Even so it was with me when I was young:
If we are nature's, these are ours; this thorn
Doth to our rose of youth rightly belong;
Our blood to us, this to our blood is born;
It is the show and seal of nature's truth,
Where love's strong passion is imprest in youth:
By our remembrances of days foregone,
Such were our faults; nor then we thought them none.

Enter HELENA.

Her eye is sick on't: I observe her now.

HELENA.

What is your pleasure, madam?

COUNTESS.

You know, Helen,
I am a mother to you.

HELENA.

Mine honourable mistress.

COUNTESS.

Nay, a mother:
Why not a mother? When I said a mother,
Methought you saw a serpent: what's in 'mother,'
That you start at it? I say, I am your mother;
And put you in the catalogue of those
That were enwombed mine: 'tis often seen
Adoption strives with nature; and choice breeds
A native slip to us from foreign seeds:
You ne'er opprest me with a mother's groan,
Yet I express to you a mother's care:—
God's mercy, maiden! does it curd thy blood,
To say, I am thy mother? What's the matter,
That this distemper'd messenger of wet,
The many-colour'd Iris, rounds thine eye?
Why,—that you are my daughter?

HELENA.

That I am not.

COUNTESS.

I say, I am your mother.

HELENA.

Pardon, madam;
The Count Rousillon cannot be my brother:

I am from humble, he from honour'd name;
No note upon my parents, his all noble:
My master, my dear lord he is; and I
His servant live, and will his vassal die:
He must not be my brother.

COUNTESS.
Nor I your mother?

HELENA.
You are my mother, madam; would you were—
So that my lord your son were not my brother—
Indeed my mother!—or were you both our mothers,
I care no more for than I do for heaven,
So I were not his sister. Can't no other,
But I your daughter, he must be my brother?

COUNTESS.
Yes, Helen, you might be my daughter-in-law:
God shield, you mean it not! 'daughter' and 'mother'
So strive upon your pulse. What, pale again?
My fear hath catcht your fondness: now I see
The mystery of your loneliness, and find
Your salt tears' head: now to all sense 'tis gross
You love my son; invention is ashamed,
Against the proclamation of thy passion,
To say thou dost not: therefore tell me true;
But tell me then, 'tis so;—for, look, thy cheeks
Confess it, th'one to th'other; and thine eyes
See it so grossly shown in thy behaviours,
That in their kind they speak it: only sin
And hellish obstinacy tie thy tongue,
That truth should be suspected. Speak, is't so?
If it be so, you have wound a goodly clew;
If it be not, forswear't: howe'er, I charge thee,
As heaven shall work in me for thine avail,
To tell me truly.

HELENA.
Good madam, pardon me!

COUNTESS.
Do you love my son?

HELENA.
Your pardon, noble mistress!

COUNTESS.
Love you my son?

HELENA.
Do not you love him, madam?

COUNTESS.
Go not about; my love hath in't a bond,
Whereof the world takes note: come, come, disclose
The state of your affection; for your passions
Have to the full appeacht.

HELENA.
Then, I confess,
Here on my knee, before high heaven and you,
That before you, and next unto high heaven,
I love your son:—
My friends were poor, but honest; so's my love:
Be not offended; for it hurts not him,
That he is loved of me: I follow him not
By any token of presumptuous suit;
Nor would I have him till I do deserve him;
Yet never know how that desert should be.
I know I love in vain, strive against hope;
Yet in this captious and intenible sieve
I still pour in the waters of my love,
And lack not to lose still: thus, Indian-like,
Religious in mine error, I adore
The sun, that looks upon his worshipper,
But knows of him no more. My dearest madam,
Let not your hate encounter with my love,
For loving where you do: but, if yourself,
Whose aged honour cites a virtuous youth,
Did ever, in so true a flame of liking,
Wish chastely, and love dearly, that your Dian
Was both herself and Love; O, then, give pity
To her, whose state is such, that cannot choose
But lend and give, where she is sure to lose;
That seeks not to find that her search implies,
But, riddle-like, lives sweetly where she dies!

COUNTESS.
Had you not lately an intent,—speak truly,—
To go to Paris?

HELENA.
Madam, I had.

COUNTESS.
Wherefore?
Tell true.

HELENA.
I will tell truth; by grace itself, I swear.
You know my father left me some prescriptions
Of rare and proved effects, such as his reading
And manifest experience had collected
For general sovereignty; and that he will'd me
In heedfull'st reservation to bestow them,
As notes, whose faculties inclusive were,
More than they were in note: amongst the rest,
There is a remedy, approved, set down,
To cure the desperate languishings whereof
The king is render'd lost.

COUNTESS.
This was your motive
For Paris, was it? speak.

HELENA.
My lord your son made me to think of this;
Else Paris, and the medicine, and the king,
Had from the conversation of my thoughts
Haply been absent then.

COUNTESS.
But think you, Helen,
If you should tender your supposed aid,
He would receive it? he and his physicians
Are of a mind; he, that they cannot help him;
They, that they cannot help: how shall they credit
A poor unlearned virgin, when the schools,
Embowell'd of their doctrine, have left off
The danger to itself?

HELENA.
There's something hints,
More than my father's skill, which was the greatest
Of his profession, that his good receipt
Shall, for my legacy, be sanctified
By th'luckiest stars in heaven: and, would your honour
But give me leave to try success, I'ld venture
This well-lost life of mine on his Grace's cure
By such a day and hour.

COUNTESS.
Dost thou believe't?

HELENA.
Ay, madam, knowingly.

COUNTESS.

Why, Helen, thou shalt have my leave, and love,
Means, and attendants, and my loving greetings
To those of mine in court: I'll stay at home,
And pray God's blessing into thy attempt:
Be gone to-morrow; and be sure of this,
What I can help thee to, thou shalt not miss.
[*Exeunt.*

ACT II. SCENE I.

Paris. A room in the KING'S *palace.*

Enter the KING, *with divers young* LORDS, *taking leave for the Florentine war;* BERTRAM, PAROLLES, *and* ATTENDANTS. *Flourish of cornets.*

KING.

FAREWELL, young lords; these warlike principles
Do not throw from you: and you, my lords, farewell:
Share the advice betwixt you; if both gain, all
The gift doth stretch itself as 'tis received,
And is enough for both.

FIRST LORD.

'Tis our hope, sir,
After well-enter'd soldiers, to return
And find your Grace in health.

KING.

No, no, it cannot be; and yet my heart
Will not confess he owes the malady
That doth my life besiege. Farewell, young lords;
Whether I live or die, be you the sons
Of worthy Frenchmen: let higher Italy—
Those lated that inherit but the fall
Of the last monarchy—see that you come
Not to woo honour, but to wed it; when
The bravest questant shrinks, find what you seek,
That fame may cry you loud: I say, farewell.

SECOND LORD.

Health, at your bidding, serve your majesty!

KING.

Those girls of Italy, take heed of them:
They say, our French lack language to deny,
If they demand: beware of being captives,
Before you serve.

BOTH LORDS.

Our hearts receive your warnings.

KING.

Farewell.—Come hither to me. [*Exit, attended.*

FIRST LORD.

O my sweet lord, that you will stay behind us!

PAROLLES.

'Tis not his fault, the spark.

SECOND LORD.

O, 'tis brave wars!

PAROLLES.

Most admirable: I have seen those wars.

BERTRAM.

I am commanded here, and kept a coil with
'Too young,' and 'the next year,' and ''tis too early.'

PAROLLES.

An thy mind stand to't, boy, steal away bravely.

BERTRAM.

I shall stay here the forehorse to a smock,
Creaking my shoes on the plain masonry,
Till honour be bought up, and no sword worn
But one to dance with! By heaven, I'll steal away.

FIRST LORD.

There's honour in the theft.

PAROLLES.

Commit it, count.

SECOND LORD.

I am your accessary; and so, farewell.

BERTRAM.

I grow to you, and our parting is a tortured body.

FIRST LORD.

Farewell, captain.

SECOND LORD.

Sweet Monsieur Parolles!

PAROLLES.

Noble heroes, my sword and yours are kin. Good sparks and lustrous, a word, good metals:—you shall find in the regiment of the Spinii one Captain Spurio, with his cicatrice, an emblem of war, here on his sinister cheek; it was this very sword entrencht it: say to him, I live; and observe his reports for me.

SECOND LORD.

We shall, noble captain.

PAROLLES.

Mars dote on you for his novices!
[*Exeunt* LORDS.
What will ye do?

BERTRAM.

Stay; the king!

Enter KING; BERTRAM *&* PAROLLES *retire.*

PAROLLES.

Use a more spacious ceremony to the noble lords; you have restrain'd yourself within the list of too cold an adieu: be more expressive to them: for they wear themselves in the cap of the time, there do muster true gait, eat, speak, and move under the influence of the most received star; and though the devil lead the measure, such are to be follow'd: after them, and take a more dilated farewell.

BERTRAM.

And I will do so.

PAROLLES.

Worthy fellows; and like to prove most sinewy sword-men. [*Exeunt* BERTRAM *and* PAROLLES.

Enter LAFEU.

LAFEU [*kneeling*].

Pardon, my lord, for me and for my tidings.

KING.

I'll fee thee to stand up.

LAFEU [*rising*].

Then here's a man stands that has brought his pardon.
I would you had kneel'd, my lord, to ask me mercy;
And that, at my bidding, you could so stand up.

KING.

I would I had; so I had broke thy pate,
And askt thee mercy for't.

LAFEU.

Good faith, across: but, my good lord, 'tis thus;
Will you be cured of your infirmity?

KING.

No.

LAFEU.

O, will you eat no grapes, my royal fox?
Yes, but you will my noble grapes, an if
My royal fox could reach them: I have seen a medicine
That's able to breathe life into a stone,
Quicken a rock, and make you dance canary
With sprightly fire and motion; whose simple touch
Is powerful to araise King Pepin, nay,
To give great Charlemain a pen in's hand,
And write to her a love-line.

KING.

What 'her' is this?

LAFEU.

Why, doctor she: my lord, there's one arrived,
If you will see her:—now, by my faith and honour,
If seriously I may convey my thoughts
In this my light deliverance, I have spoke
With one that, in her sex, her years, profession,
Wisdom, and constancy, hath amazed me more
Than I dare blame my weakness: will you see her,—
For that is her demand,—and know her business?
That done, laugh well at me.

KING.

Now, good Lafeu,
Bring in the admiration; that we with thee
May spend our wonder too, or take off thine
By wondering how thou took'st it.

LAFEU.

Nay, I'll fit you,
And not be all day neither. [*Exit.*

KING.

Thus he his special nothing ever prologues.

Enter LAFEU, *with* HELENA.

LAFEU.

Nay, come your ways.

KING.

This haste hath wings indeed.

LAFEU.

Nay, come your ways;
This is his majesty, say your mind to him:
A traitor you do look like; but such traitors
His majesty seldom fears: I am Cressid's uncle,
That dare leave two together; fare you well.
[*Exit.*

KING.

Now, fair one, does your business follow us?

HELENA.

Ay, my good lord.
Gerard de Narbon was my father; one,
In what he did profess, well found.

KING.

I knew him.

HELENA.

The rather will I spare my praises towards him;
Knowing him is enough. On's bed of death
Many receipts he gave me; chiefly one,
Which, as the dearest issue of his practice,
And of his old experience th'only darling,
He bade me store up, as a triple eye,
Safer than mine own two, more dear: I have so:
And, hearing your high majesty is toucht
With that malignant cause, wherein the honour
Of my dear father's gift stands chief in power,
I come to tender it, and my appliance,
With all bound humbleness.

KING.

We thank you, maiden;
But may not be so credulous of cure,
When our most learned doctors leave us, and
The congregated college have concluded
That labouring art can never ransom nature
From her inaidable state,—I say we must not
So stain our judgement, or corrupt our hope,
To prostitute our past-cure malady
To empirics; or to dissever so
Our great self and our credit, to esteem
A senseless help, when help past sense we deem.

HELENA.

My duty, then, shall pay me for my pains:
I will no more enforce mine office on you;
Humbly entreating from your royal thoughts
A modest one, to bear me back again.

KING.

I cannot give thee less, to be call'd grateful:
Thou thought'st to help me; and such thanks I give
As one near death to those that wish him live:
But, what at full I know, thou know'st no part;
I knowing all my peril, thou no art.

HELENA.

What I can do can do no hurt to try,
Since you set up your rest 'gainst remedy.
He that of greatest works is finisher,
Oft does them by the weakest minister:
So holy writ in babes hath judgement shown,
When judges have been babes; great floods have flown
From simple sources; and great seas have dried,
When miracles have by the greatest been denied.
Oft expectation fails, and most oft there
Where most it promises; and oft it hits
Where hope is coldest, and despair most fits.

KING.

I must not hear thee; fare thee well, kind maid;
Thy pains, not used, must by thyself be paid:
Proffers not took reap thanks for their reward.

HELENA.

Inspired merit so by breath is barr'd:
It is not so with Him that all things knows,
As 'tis with us that square our guess by shows;
But most it is presumption in us when
The help of heaven we count the act of men.
Dear sir, to my endeavours give consent;
Of heaven, not me, make an experiment.
I am not an impostor, that proclaim
Myself against the level of mine aim;
But know I think, and think I know most sure,
My art is not past power, nor you past cure.

KING.

Art thou so confident? within what space
Hopest thou my cure?

HELENA.

The great'st grace lending grace,
Ere twice the horses of the sun shall bring
Their fiery torcher his diurnal ring;
Ere twice in murk and occidental damp
Moist Hesperus hath quencht his sleepy lamp;
Or four and twenty times the pilot's glass
Hath told the thievish minutes how they pass;
What is infirm from your sound parts shall fly,
Health shall live free, and sickness freely die.

KING.

Upon thy certainty and confidence
What darest thou venture?

HELENA.

Tax of impudence,—
A strumpet's boldness, a divulged shame,—
Traduced by odious ballads; my maiden's name
Sear'd otherwise; nay, worse, if worse, extended
With vilest torture let my life be ended.

KING.

Methinks in thee some blessed spirit doth speak,
His powerful sound within an organ weak:
And what impossibility would slay
In common sense, sense saves another way.
Thy life is dear; for all, that life can rate
Worth name of life, in thee hath estimate,—
Youth, beauty, wisdom, courage, all
That happiness and prime can happy call:
Thou this to hazard, needs must intimate
Skill infinite or monstrous desperate.
Sweet practiser, thy physic I will try,
That ministers thine own death, if I die.

HELENA.

If I break time, or flinch in property
Of what I spoke, unpitied let me die,
And well deserved: not helping, death's my fee;
But, if I help, what do you promise me?

KING.

Make thy demand.

HELENA.

But will you make it even?

KING.

Ay, by my sceptre and my hopes of heaven.

HELENA.

Then shalt thou give me with thy kingly hand
What husband in thy power I will command:
Exempted be from me the arrogance
To choose from forth the royal blood of France,
My low and humble name to propagate
With any branch or image of thy state;
But such a one, thy vassal, whom I know
Is free for me to ask, thee to bestow.

KING.

Here is my hand; the premises observed,
Thy will by my performance shall be served:
So make the choice of thy own time; for I,
Thy resolved patient, on thee still rely.
More should I question thee, and more I must,—
Though more to know could not be more to trust,—
From whence thou camest, how tended on: but rest
Unquestion'd welcome, and undoubted blest.—
Give me some help here, ho!—If thou proceed
As high as word, my deed shall match thy deed.
[*Flourish. Exeunt.*

SCENE II.

Rousillon. A room in the house of the COUNTESS.

Enter COUNTESS *and* CLOWN.

COUNTESS.

COME on, sir; I shall now put you to the height of your breeding.

CLOWN.

I will show myself highly fed and lowly taught: I know my business is but to the court.

COUNTESS.

To the court! why, what place make you special, when you put off that with such contempt? But to the court!

CLOWN.

Truly, madam, if God have lent a man any manners, he may easily put it off at court: he that cannot make a leg, put off's cap, kiss his hand, and say nothing, has neither leg, hands, lip, nor cap; and, indeed, such a fellow, to say precisely, were not for the court: but, for me, I have an answer will serve all men.

COUNTESS.

Marry, that's a bountiful answer that fits all questions.

CLOWN.

It is like a barber's chair, that fits all buttocks,—the pin-buttock, the quatch-buttock, the brawn-buttock, or any buttock.

COUNTESS.

Will your answer serve fit to all questions?

CLOWN.

As fit as ten groats is for the hand of an attorney, as your French crown for your taffeta punk, as Tib's rush for Tom's forefinger, as a pancake for Shrove-Tuesday, a morris for May-day, as the nail to his hole, the cuckold to his horn, as a scolding quean to a wrangling knave, as the nun's lip to the friar's mouth, nay, as the pudding to his skin.

COUNTESS.

Have you, I say, an answer of such fitness for all questions?

CLOWN.

From below your duke to beneath your constable, it will fit any question.

COUNTESS.

It must be an answer of most monstrous size that must fit all demands.

CLOWN.

But a trifle neither, in good faith, if the learned should speak truth of it: here it is, and all that belongs to't. Ask me if I am a courtier: it shall do you no harm to learn.

COUNTESS.

To be young again, if we could:—I will be a fool in question, hoping to be the wiser by your answer. I pray you, sir, are you a courtier?

CLOWN.

'O Lord, sir!'—there's a simple putting off.—More, more, a hundred of them.

COUNTESS.

Sir, I am a poor friend of yours that loves you.

CLOWN.

'O Lord, sir!'—Thick, thick, spare not me.

COUNTESS.

I think, sir, you can eat none of this homely meat.

CLOWN.

'O Lord, sir!'—Nay, put me to't, I warrant you.

COUNTESS.

You were lately whipt, sir, as I think.

CLOWN.

'O Lord, sir!'—Spare not me.

COUNTESS.

Do you cry, 'O Lord, sir!' at your whipping, and 'Spare me not'? Indeed, your 'O Lord, sir!' is very sequent to your whipping: you would answer very well to a whipping, if you were but bound to't.

CLOWN.

I ne'er had worse luck in my life in my 'O Lord, sir!' I see things may serve long, but not serve ever.

COUNTESS.

I play the noble housewife with the time,
To entertain it so merrily with a fool.

CLOWN.

'O Lord, sir!'—why, there't serves well again.

COUNTESS.

An end, sir: to your business. Give Helen this,
And urge her to a present answer back:
Commend me to my kinsmen and my son:
This is not much.

CLOWN.

Not much commendation to them.

COUNTESS.

Not much employment for you: you understand me?

CLOWN.

Most fruitfully: I am there before my legs.

COUNTESS.

Haste you again. [*Exeunt severally.*

SCENE III.

Paris. A room in the KING'S *palace.*

Enter LAFEU *and* PAROLLES.

LAFEU.

THEY say miracles are past; and we have our philosophical persons, to make modern and familiar, things supernatural and causeless. Hence is it that we make trifles of terrors; ensconcing ourselves into seeming knowledge, when we should submit ourselves to an unknown fear. Why, 'tis the rarest argument of wonder that hath shot out in our latter times.

PAROLLES.

And so 'tis.

LAFEU.

To be relinquisht of the artists,—

PAROLLES.

So I say.

LAFEU.

Both of Galen and Paracelsus, of all the learned and authentic fellows,—

PAROLLES.

Right; so I say.

LAFEU.

That gave him out incurable,—

PAROLLES.

Why, there 'tis; so say I too.

LAFEU.

Not to be helpt,—

PAROLLES.

Right; as 'twere, a man assured of a—

LAFEU.

Uncertain life, and sure death.

PAROLLES.

Just, you say well; so would I have said.

LAFEU.

I may truly say, it is a novelty to the world.

PAROLLES.

It is, indeed: if you will have it in showing, you shall read it in—What do ye call there?—

LAFEU.

A showing of a heavenly effect in an earthly actor.

PAROLLES.

That's it I would have said, the very same.

LAFEU.

Why, your dolphin is not lustier: 'fore me, I speak in respect—

PAROLLES.

Nay, 'tis strange, 'tis very strange, that is the brief and the tedious of it; and he's of a most facinerious spirit that will not acknowledge it to be the—

LAFEU.

Very hand of heaven—

PAROLLES.

Ay, so I say.

LAFEU.

In a most weak and debile minister great power, great transcendence: which should, indeed, give us a further use to be made than alone the recovery of the king.

PAROLLES.

As to be—

LAFEU.

Generally thankful.

PAROLLES.

I would have said it; you say well.—Here comes the king.

Enter KING, HELENA, *and* ATTENDANTS.

LAFEU.

Lustig, as the Dutchman says: I'll like a maid the better, whilst I have a tooth in my head: why, he's able to lead her a coranto.

PAROLLES.

Mort du vinaigre! is not this Helen?

LAFEU.

'Fore God, I think so.

KING.

Go, call before me all the lords in court.—
[*Exit an* ATTENDANT.
Sit, my preserver, by thy patient's side;
And with this healthful hand, whose banisht sense
Thou hast repeal'd, a second time receive
The confirmation of my promised gift,
Which but attends thy naming.

Enter three or four LORDS *and* BERTRAM.

Fair maid, send forth thine eye: this youthful parcel
Of noble bachelors stand at my bestowing,
O'er whom both sovereign power and father's voice
I have to use: thy frank election make;
Thou hast power to choose, and they none to forsake.

HELENA.

To each of you one fair and virtuous mistress
Fall, when Love please!—marry, to each, but one!

LAFEU.

I'ld give bay curtal and his furniture,
My mouth no more were broken than these boys',
And writ as little beard.

KING.
Peruse them well:
Not one of these but had a noble father.

HELENA.
Gentlemen,
Heaven hath, through me, restored the king to health.

ALL.
We understand it, and thank heaven for you.

HELENA.
I am a simple maid; and therein wealthiest,
That I protest I simply am a maid.—
Please it your majesty, I have done already:
The blushes in my cheeks thus whisper me,
'We blush that thou shouldst choose; but, be refused,
Let the white death sit on thy cheek for ever;
We'll ne'er come there again.'

KING.
Make choice; and, see,
Who shuns thy love shuns all his love in me.

HELENA.
Now, Dian, from thy altar do I fly;
And to imperial Love, that god most high,
Do my sighs stream.—[*to* FIRST LORD] Sir, will you hear my suit?

FIRST LORD.
And grant it.

HELENA.
Thanks, sir; all the rest is mute.

LAFEU.
I had rather be in this choice than throw ames-ace for my life.

HELENA [*to* SECOND LORD].
The honour, sir, that flames in your fair eyes,
Before I speak, too threateningly replies:
Love make your fortunes twenty times above
Her that so wishes and her humble love!

SECOND LORD.
No better, if you please.

HELENA.
My wish receive,
Which great Love grant! and so, I take my leave.

LAFEU.
Do all they deny her? An they were sons of mine, I'ld have them whipt; or I would send them to the Turk, to make eunuchs of.

HELENA [*to* THIRD LORD].
Be not afraid that I your hand should take;
I'll never do you wrong for your own sake:
Blessing upon your vows! and in your bed
Find fairer fortune, if you ever wed!

LAFEU.
These boys are boys of ice, they'll none have her: sure, they are bastards to the English; the French ne'er got 'em.

HELENA [*to* FOURTH LORD].
You are too young, too happy, and too good,
To make yourself a son out of my blood.

FOURTH LORD.
Fair one, I think not so.

LAFEU.
There's one grape yet,—I am sure thy father drunk wine:—but if thou be'st not an ass, I am a youth of fourteen; I have known thee already.

HELENA [*to* BERTRAM].
I dare not say I take you; but I give
Me and my service, ever whilst I live,
Into your guiding power.—This is the man.

KING.
Why, then, young Bertram, take her; she's thy wife.

BERTRAM.
My wife, my liege! I shall beseech your highness,
In such a business give me leave to use
The help of mine own eyes.

KING.
Know'st thou not, Bertram,
What she has done for me?

BERTRAM.
Yes, my good lord;
But never hope to know why I should marry her.

KING.
Thou know'st she has raised me from my sickly bed.

BERTRAM.
But follows it, my lord, to bring me down
Must answer for your raising? I know her well:
She had her breeding at my father's charge.
A poor physician's daughter my wife!—Disdain
Rather corrupt me ever!

KING.
'Tis only title thou disdain'st in her, the which
I can build up. Strange is it that our bloods,
Of colour, weight, and heat, pour'd all together,
Would quite confound distinction, yet stand off
In differences so mighty. If she be
All that is virtuous,—save what thou dislikest,
A poor physician's daughter,—thou dislikest
Of virtue for the name: but do not so:
From lowest place when virtuous things proceed,
The place is dignified by th'doer's deed:
Where great additions swell's, and virtue none,
It is a dropsied honour: good alone
Is good without a name; vileness is so:
The property by what it is should go,
Not by the title. She is young, wise, fair;
In these to nature she's immediate heir;
And these breed honour: that is honour's scorn,
Which challenges itself as honour's born,
And is not like the sire: honours thrive,
When rather from our acts we them derive
Than our foregoers: the mere word's a slave,
Debosht on every tomb, on every grave
A lying trophy; and as oft is dumb
Where dust and damn'd oblivion is the tomb
Of honour'd bones indeed. What should be said?
If thou canst like this creature as a maid,
I can create the rest: virtue and she
Is her own dower; honour and wealth from me.

BERTRAM.
I cannot love her, nor will strive to do't.

KING.
Thou wrong'st thyself, if thou shouldst strive to choose.

HELENA.
That you are well restored, my lord, I'm glad:
Let the rest go.

KING.
My honour's at the stake; which to defeat,
I must produce my power. Here, take her hand,
Proud scornful boy, unworthy this good gift;

That dost in vile misprision shackle up
My love and her desert; that canst not dream,
We, poising us in her defective scale,
Shall weigh thee to the beam; that wilt not know,
It is in us to plant thine honour where
We please to have it grow. Check thy contempt:
Obey our will, which travails in thy good:
Believe not thy disdain, but presently
Do thine own fortunes that obedient right
Which both thy duty owes and our power claims;
Or I will throw thee from my care for ever
Into the staggers and the careless lapse
Of youth and ignorance; both my revenge and hate
Loosing upon thee, in the name of justice,
Without all terms of pity. Speak; thine answer.

BERTRAM.

Pardon, my gracious lord; for I submit
My fancy to your eyes: when I consider
What great creation and what dole of honour
Flies where you bid it, I find that she, which late
Was in my nobler thoughts most base, is now
The praised of the king; who, so ennobled,
Is, as 'twere, born so.

KING.

Take her by the hand,
And tell her she is thine: to whom I promise
A counterpoise; if not to thy estate,
A balance more replete.

BERTRAM.

I take her hand.

KING.

Good fortune and the favour of the king
Smile upon this contract; whose ceremony
Shall seem expedient on the now-born brief,
And be perform'd to-night: the solemn feast
Shall more attend upon the coming space,
Expecting absent friends. As thou lovest her,
Thy love's to me religious; else, does err.

[*Exeunt all but* LAFEU *and* PAROLLES.

LAFEU.

Do you hear, monsieur? a word with you.

PAROLLES.

Your pleasure, sir?

LAFEU.

Your lord and master did well to make his recantation.

PAROLLES.

Recantation!—My lord! my master!

LAFEU.

Ay; is it not a language I speak?

PAROLLES.

A most harsh one, and not to be understood without bloody succeeding. My master!

LAFEU.

Are you companion to the Count Rousillon?

PAROLLES.

To any count,—to all counts,—to what is man.

LAFEU.

To what is count's man: count's master is of another style.

PAROLLES.

You are too old, sir; let it satisfy you, you are too old.

LAFEU.

I must tell thee, sirrah, I write man; to which title age cannot bring thee.

PAROLLES.

What I dare too well do, I dare not do.

LAFEU.

I did think thee, for two ordinaries, to be a pretty wise fellow; thou didst make tolerable vent of thy travel; it might pass: yet the scarfs and the bannerets about thee did manifoldly dissuade me from believing thee a vessel of too great a burthen. I have now found thee; when I lose thee again, I care not: yet art thou good for nothing but taking up; and that thou'rt scarce worth.

PAROLLES.

Hadst thou not the privilege of antiquity upon thee,—

LAFEU.

Do not plunge thyself too far in anger, lest thou hasten thy trial; which if—Lord have mercy on thee for a hen! So, my good window of lattice, fare thee well: thy casement I need not open, for I look through thee. Give me thy hand.

PAROLLES.

My lord, you give me most egregious indignity.

LAFEU.

Ay, with all my heart; and thou art worthy of it.

PAROLLES.

I have not, my lord, deserved it.

LAFEU.

Yes, good faith, every dram of it; and I will not bate thee a scruple.

PAROLLES.

Well, I shall be wiser—

LAFEU.

Ev'n as soon as thou canst, for thou hast to pull at a smack o'th'contrary. If ever thou be'st bound in thy scarf and beaten, thou shalt find what it is to be proud of thy bondage. I have a desire to hold my acquaintance with thee, or rather my knowledge, that I may say, in the default, he is a man I know.

PAROLLES.

My lord, you do me most insupportable vexation.

LAFEU.

I would it were hell-pains for thy sake, and my poor doing eternal: for doing I am past; as I will by thee, in what motion age will give me leave.

[*Exit.*

PAROLLES.

Well, thou hast a son shall take this disgrace off me; scurvy, old, filthy, scurvy lord!—Well, I must be patient; there is no fettering of authority. I'll beat him, by my life, if I can meet him with any convenience, an he were double and double a lord. I'll have no more pity of his age than I would have of—I'll beat him, an if I could but meet him again.

Enter LAFEU.

LAFEU.

Sirrah, your lord and master's married; there's news for you: you have a new mistress.

PAROLLES.

I most unfeignedly beseech your lordship to make some reservation of your wrongs: he is my good lord; whom I serve above is my master.

LAFEU.

Who? God?

PAROLLES.

Ay, sir.

LAFEU.

The devil it is that's thy master. Why dost thou garter up thy arms o' this fashion? dost make hose of thy sleeves? do other servants so? Thou wert best set thy lower part where thy nose stands. By mine honour, if I were but two hours younger, I'ld beat thee: methinks't, thou art a general offence, and every man should beat thee: I think thou wast created for men to breathe themselves upon thee.

PAROLLES.

This is hard and undeserved measure, my lord.

LAFEU.

Go to, sir; you were beaten in Italy for picking a kernel out of a pomegranate; you are a vagabond, and no true traveller: you are more saucy with lords and honourable personages than the heraldry of your birth and virtue gives you commission. You are not worth another word, else I'ld call you knave. I leave you. [*Exit.*

PAROLLES.

Good, very good; it is so then:—good, very good; let it be conceal'd awhile.

Enter BERTRAM.

BERTRAM.

Undone, and forfeited to cares for ever!

PAROLLES.

What's the matter, sweet-heart?

BERTRAM.

Although before the solemn priest I have sworn,
I will not bed her.

PAROLLES.

What, what, sweet-heart?

BERTRAM.

O, my Parolles, they have married me!—
I'll to the Tuscan wars, and never bed her.

PAROLLES.

France is a dog-hole, and it no more merits
The tread of a man's foot: to th'wars!

BERTRAM.

There's letters from my mother: what th'import is, I know not yet.

PAROLLES.

Ay, that would be known. To th'wars, my boy,
to th'wars!
He wears his honour in a box unseen,
That hugs his kicky-wicky here at home,
Spending his manly marrow in her arms,
Which should sustain the bound and high curvet
Of Mars's fiery steed. To other regions!
France is a stable; we that dwell in't jades;
Therefore, to th'wars!

BERTRAM.

It shall be so: I'll send her to my house,
Acquaint my mother with my hate to her,
And wherefore I am fled; write to the king
That which I durst not speak: his present gift
Shall furnish me to those Italian fields,
Where noble fellows strike: war is no strife
To the dark house and the detested wife.

PAROLLES.

Will this capriccio hold in thee, art sure?

BERTRAM.

Go with me to my chamber, and advise me.
I'll send her straight away: to-morrow
I'll to the wars, she to her single sorrow.

PAROLLES.

Why, these balls bound; there's noise in it.—
'Tis hard:
A young man married is a man that's marr'd:
Therefore, away, and leave her; bravely go:
The king has done you wrong; but, hush, 'tis so.
[*Exeunt.*

SCENE IV.

Paris. The KING'S *palace.*

Enter HELENA *and* CLOWN.

HELENA.

My mother greets me kindly: is she well?

CLOWN.

She is not well; but yet she has her health: she's very merry; but yet she is not well: but thanks be given, she's very well, and wants nothing i'th' world; but yet she is not well.

HELENA.

If she be very well, what does she ail, that she's not very well?

CLOWN.

Truly, she's very well indeed, but for two things.

HELENA.

What two things?

CLOWN.

One, that she's not in heaven, whither God send her quickly! the other, that she's in earth, from whence God send her quickly!

Enter PAROLLES.

PAROLLES.

Bless you, my fortunate lady!

HELENA.

I hope, sir, I have your good will to have mine own good fortunes.

PAROLLES.

You had my prayers to lead them on; and to keep them on, have them still.—O, my knave,—how does my old lady?

CLOWN.

So that you had her wrinkles, and I her money, I would she did as you say.

PAROLLES.

Why, I say nothing.

CLOWN.

Marry, you are the wiser man; for many a man's tongue shakes out his master's undoing: to say nothing, to do nothing, to know nothing, and to have nothing, is to be a great part of your title; which is within a very little of nothing.

PAROLLES.

Away! th'art a knave.

CLOWN.

You should have said, sir, before a knave th'art a knave; that's, before me th'art a knave: this had been truth, sir.

PAROLLES.

Go to, thou art a witty fool; I have found thee.

CLOWN.

Did you find me in yourself, sir? or were you taught to find me? The search, sir, was profitable; and much fool may you find in you, even to the world's pleasure, and the increase of laughter.

PAROLLES.
A good knave, i'faith, and well fed.—
Madam, my lord will go away to-night;
A very serious business calls on him.
The great prerogative and rite of love,
Which, as your due, time claims, he does acknowledge;
But puts it off by a compell'd restraint;
Whose want, and whose delay, is strew'd with sweets,
Which they distil now in the curbed time,
To make the coming hour o'erflow with joy,
And pleasure drown the brim.

HELENA.
What's his will else?

PAROLLES.
That you will take your instant leave o'th'king,
And make this haste as your own good proceeding,
Strengthen'd with what apology you think
May make it probable need.

HELENA.
What more commands he?

PAROLLES.
That, having this obtain'd, you presently
Attend his further pleasure.

HELENA.
In every thing I wait upon his will.

PAROLLES.
I shall report it so.

HELENA.
I pray you. [*Exit* PAROLLES.]
Come, sirrah. [*Exeunt.*

SCENE V.

Paris. The KING'S *palace.*

Enter LAFEU *and* BERTRAM.

LAFEU.
BUT I hope your lordship thinks not him a soldier.

BERTRAM.
Yes, my lord, and of very valiant approof.

LAFEU.
You have it from his own deliverance.

BERTRAM.
And by other warranted testimony.

LAFEU.
Then my dial goes not true: I took this lark for a bunting.

BERTRAM.
I do assure you, my lord, he is very great in knowledge, and accordingly valiant.

LAFEU.
I have, then, sinn'd against his experience, and transgrest against his valour; and my state that way is dangerous, since I cannot yet find in my heart to repent. Here he comes: I pray you, make us friends; I will pursue the amity.

Enter PAROLLES.

PAROLLES [*to* BERTRAM].
These things shall be done, sir.

LAFEU.
Pray you, sir, who's his tailor?

PAROLLES.
Sir?

LAFEU.
O, I know him well, I, sir; he, sir, 's a good workman, a very good tailor.

BERTRAM [*aside to* PAROLLES].
Is she gone to the king?

PAROLLES [*aside to* BERTRAM].
She is.

BERTRAM [*aside to* PAROLLES].
Will she away to-night?

PAROLLES [*aside to* BERTRAM].
As you'll have her.

BERTRAM [*aside to* PAROLLES].
I've writ my letters, casketed my treasure,
Given order for our horses; and to-night,
When I should take possession of the bride,
End ere I do begin.

LAFEU.
A good traveller is something at the latter end of a dinner; but one that lies three-thirds, and uses a known truth to pass a thousand nothings with, should be once heard, and thrice beaten.—God save you, captain.

BERTRAM.
Is there any unkindness between my lord and you, monsieur?

PAROLLES.
I know not how I have deserved to run into my lord's displeasure.

LAFEU.
You have made shift to run into't, boots and spurs and all, like him that leapt into the custard; and out of it you'll run again, rather than suffer question for your residence.

BERTRAM.
It may be you have mistaken him, my lord.

LAFEU.
And shall do so ever, though I took him at's prayers. Fare you well, my lord; and believe this of me, there can be no kernel in this light nut; the soul of this man is his clothes: trust him not in matter of heavy consequence; I have kept of them tame, and know their natures.—Farewell, monsieur: I have spoken better of you than you have worth or wit to deserve at my hand; but we must do good against evil. [*Exit.*

PAROLLES.
An idle lord, I swear.

BERTRAM.
I think so.

PAROLLES.
Why, do you not know him?

BERTRAM.
Yes, I do know him well; and common speech
Gives him a worthy pass.—Here comes my clog.

Enter HELENA.

HELENA.
I have, sir, as I was commanded from you,
Spoke with the king, and have procured his leave
For present parting; only, he desires
Some private speech with you.

BERTRAM.
I shall obey his will.
You must not marvel, Helen, at my course,
Which holds not colour with the time, nor does
The ministration and required office
On my particular. Prepared I was not

For such a business; therefore am I found
So much unsettled: this drives me to entreat you,
That presently you take your way for home,
And rather muse than ask why I entreat you;
For my respects are better than they seem,
And my appointments have in them a need
Greater than shows itself, at the first view,
To you that know them not. This to my mother:
[*Giving a letter.*
'Twill be two days ere I shall see you; so,
I leave you to your wisdom.

HELENA.

Sir, I can nothing say,
But that I am your most obedient servant.

BERTRAM.

Come, come, no more of that.

HELENA.

And ever shall
With true observance seek to eke out that
Wherein toward me my homely stars have fail'd
To equal my good fortune.

BERTRAM.

Let that go:
My haste is very great: farewell, hie home.

HELENA.

Pray, sir, your pardon.

BERTRAM.

Well, what would you say?

HELENA.

I am not worthy of the wealth I owe;
Nor dare I say 'tis mine,—and yet it is;
But, like a timorous thief, most fain would steal
What law does vouch mine own.

BERTRAM.

What would you have?

HELENA.

Something; and scarce so much:—nothing, indeed.—
I would not tell you what I would, my lord:—
Faith, yes;—
Strangers and foes do sunder, and not kiss.

BERTRAM.

I pray you, stay not, but in haste to horse.

HELENA.

I shall not break your bidding, good my lord.

BERTRAM.

Where are my other men, monsieur?—Farewell.
[*Exit* HELENA.
Go thou toward home; where I will never come,
Whilst I can shake my sword, or hear the drum.—
Away, and for our flight.

PAROLLES.

Bravely, coragio!
[*Exeunt.*

ACT III. SCENE I.

Florence. A room in the DUKE'S *palace.*

Flourish. Enter the DUKE OF FLORENCE, *two French* LORDS *and a troop of* SOLDIERS.

DUKE.

So that, from point to point, now have you heard
The fundamental reasons of this war;
Whose great decision hath much blood let forth,
And more thirsts after.

FIRST LORD.

Holy seems the quarrel
Upon your Grace's part; black and fearful
On the opposer.

DUKE.

Therefore we marvel much our cousin France
Would, in so just a business, shut his bosom
Against our borrowing prayers.

SECOND LORD.

Good my lord,
The reasons of our state I cannot yield,
But like a common and an outward man,
That the great figure of a council frames
By self-unable motion: therefore dare not
Say what I think of it, since I have found
Myself in my incertain grounds to fail
As often as I guest.

DUKE.

Be it his pleasure.

SECOND LORD.

But I am sure the younger of our nation,
That surfeit on their ease, will day by day
Come here for physic.

DUKE.

Welcome shall they be;
And all the honours that can fly from us
Shall on them settle. You know your places well;
When better fall, for your avails they fell:
To-morrow to the field. [*Flourish. Exeunt.*

SCENE II.

Rousillon. A room in the house of the COUNTESS.

Enter COUNTESS *and* CLOWN.

COUNTESS.

It hath happen'd all as I would have had it, save that he comes not along with her.

CLOWN.

By my troth, I take my young lord to be a very melancholy man.

COUNTESS.

By what observance, I pray you?

CLOWN.

Why, he will look upon his boot, and sing; mend the ruff, and sing; ask questions, and sing; pick his teeth, and sing. I know a man that had this trick of melancholy sold a goodly manor for a song.

COUNTESS.

Let me see what he writes, and when he means to come. [*Opening a letter.*

CLOWN.

I have no mind to Isbel, since I was at court: our old ling and our Isbels o'th'country are nothing like your old ling and your Isbels o'th'court: the brains of my Cupid's knockt out; and I begin to love, as an old man loves money, with no stomach.

COUNTESS.

What have we here?

CLOWN.

E'en that you have there. [*Exit.*

COUNTESS [*reads*].

I have sent you a daughter-in-law: she hath recover'd the king, and undone me. I have wedded her, not bedded her; and sworn to make the 'not' eternal. You shall hear I am run away: know it before the report come. If there be breadth enough in the world, I will hold a long distance. My duty to you. Your unfortunate son,

BERTRAM.

This is not well, rash and unbridled boy,
To fly the favours of so good a king;
To pluck his indignation on thy head
By the misprising of a maid too virtuous
For the contempt of empire.

Enter CLOWN.

CLOWN.

O madam, yonder is heavy news within between two soldiers and my young lady!

COUNTESS.

What is the matter?

CLOWN.

Nay, there is some comfort in the news, some comfort; your son will not be kill'd so soon as I thought he would.

COUNTESS.

Why should he be kill'd?

CLOWN.

So say I, madam, if he run away, as I hear he does: the danger is in standing to't; that's the loss of men, though it be the getting of children. Here they come will tell you more: for my part, I only hear your son was run away. [*Exit.*

Enter HELENA *and two* GENTLEMEN.

FIRST GENTLEMAN.

Save you, good madam.

HELENA.

Madam, my lord is gone, for ever gone.

SECOND GENTLEMAN.

Do not say so.

COUNTESS.

Think upon patience.—Pray you, gentlemen,—
I have felt so many quirks of joy and grief,
That the first face of neither, on the start,
Can woman me unto't:—where is my son, I pray you?

SECOND GENTLEMAN.

Madam, he's gone to serve the Duke of Florence:
We met him thitherward; for thence we came,
And, after some dispatch in hand at court,
Thither we bend again.

HELENA.

Look on his letter, madam; here's my passport.
[*Reads*] When thou canst get the ring upon my finger which never shall come off, and show me a child begotten of thy body that I am father to, then call me husband: but in such a 'then' I write a 'never.'
This is a dreadful sentence.

COUNTESS.

Brought you this letter, gentlemen?

FIRST GENTLEMAN.

Ay, madam;
And, for the contents' sake, are sorry for our pains.

COUNTESS.

I prithee, lady, have a better cheer;
If thou engrossest all the griefs are thine,
Thou robb'st me of a moiety: he was my son;
But I do wash his name out of my blood,
And thou art all my child.—Towards Florence is he?

SECOND GENTLEMAN.

Ay, madam.

COUNTESS.

And to be a soldier?

SECOND GENTLEMAN.

Such is his noble purpose: and, believe't,
The duke will lay upon him all the honour
That good convenience claims.

COUNTESS.

Return you thither?

FIRST GENTLEMAN.

Ay, madam, with the swiftest wing of speed.

HELENA [*reads*].

'Till I have no wife, I have nothing in France.'
'Tis bitter.

COUNTESS.

Find you that there?

HELENA.

Ay, madam.

FIRST GENTLEMAN.

'Tis but the boldness of his hand, haply, which his heart was not consenting to.

COUNTESS.

Nothing in France, until he have no wife!
There's nothing here that is too good for him,
But only she; and she deserves a lord,
That twenty such rude boys might tend upon,
And call her hourly mistress.—Who was with him?

FIRST GENTLEMAN.

A servant only, and a gentleman
Which I have sometime known.

COUNTESS.

Parolles, was't not?

FIRST GENTLEMAN.

Ay, my good lady, he.

COUNTESS.

A very tainted fellow, and full of wickedness.
My son corrupts a well-derived nature
With his inducement.

FIRST GENTLEMAN.

Indeed, good lady,
The fellow has a deal of that too much,
Which holds him much to have.

COUNTESS.

Y'are welcome, gentlemen.
I will entreat you, when you see my son,
To tell him that his sword can never win
The honour that he loses: more I'll entreat you
Written to bear along.

SECOND GENTLEMAN.

We serve you, madam,
In that and all your worthiest affairs.

COUNTESS.

Not so, but as we change our courtesies.
Will you draw near?

[*Exeunt* COUNTESS *and* GENTLEMEN.

HELENA.

'Till I have no wife, I have nothing in France.'
Nothing in France, until he has no wife!
Thou shalt have none, Rousillon, none in France;
Then hast thou all again. Poor lord! is't I
That chase thee from thy country, and expose
Those tender limbs of thine to the event
Of the none-sparing war? and is it I
That drive thee from the sportive court, where thou

Wast shot at with fair eyes, to be the mark
Of smoky muskets? O you leaden messengers,
That ride upon the violent speed of fire,
Fly with false aim; move the still-piecing air,
That sings with piercing; do not touch my lord!
Whoever shoots at him, I set him there;
Whoever charges on his forward breast,
I am the caitiff that do hold him to't;
And, though I kill him not, I am the cause
His death was so effected: better 'twere
I met the ravin lion when he roar'd
With sharp constraint of hunger; better 'twere
That all the miseries which nature owes
Were mine at once. No, come thou home, Rousillon,
Whence honour but of danger wins a scar,
As oft it loses all: I will be gone;
My being here it is that holds thee hence:
Shall I stay here to do't? no, no, although
The air of paradise did fan the house,
The angels officed all: I will be gone,
That pitiful rumour may report my flight,
To consolate thine ear. Come, night; end, day!
For with the dark, poor thief, I'll steal away.
[*Exit.*

SCENE III.

Florence. Before the DUKE'S *palace.*

Flourish. Enter the DUKE OF FLORENCE, BERTRAM, PAROLLES, SOLDIERS, *Drum, and Trumpets.*

DUKE.

THE general of our horse thou art; and we,
Great in our hope, lay our best love and credence
Upon thy promising fortune.

BERTRAM.

Sir, it is
A charge too heavy for my strength; but yet
We'll strive to bear it, for your worthy sake,
To th'extreme edge of hazard.

DUKE.

Then go thou forth;
And Fortune play upon thy prosperous helm,
As thy auspicious mistress!

BERTRAM.

This very day,
Great Mars, I put myself into thy file:
Make me but like my thoughts, and I shall prove
A lover of thy drum, hater of love. [*Exeunt.*

SCENE IV.

Rousillon. A room in the house of the COUNTESS.

Enter COUNTESS *and* STEWARD.

COUNTESS.

ALAS! and would you take the letter of her?
Might you not know she would do as she has done,
By sending me a letter? Read it again.

STEWARD [*reads*].

I am Saint Jaques' pilgrim, thither gone:
Ambitious love hath so in me offended,
That barefoot plod I the cold ground upon,
With sainted vow my faults to have amended.
Write, write, that from the bloody course of war
My dearest master, your dear son, may hie:
Bless him at home in peace, whilst I from far
His name with zealous fervour sanctify:
His taken labours bid him me forgive;
I, his despiteful Juno, sent him forth
From courtly friends, with camping foes to live,
Where death and danger dogs the heels of worth:
He is too good and fair for death and me;
Whom I myself embrace, to set him free.

COUNTESS.

Ah, what sharp stings are in her mildest words!—
Rinaldo, you did never lack advice so much,
As letting her pass so: had I spoke with her,
I could have well diverted her intents,
Which thus she hath prevented.

STEWARD.

Pardon me, madam:
If I had given you this at over-night,
She might have been o'erta'en; and yet she writes,
Pursuit would be but vain.

COUNTESS.

What angel shall
Bless this unworthy husband? he cannot thrive,
Unless her prayers, whom heaven delights to hear,
And loves to grant, reprieve him from the wrath
Of greatest justice.—Write, write, Rinaldo,
To this unworthy husband of his wife;
Let every word weigh heavy of her worth,
That he does weigh too light: my greatest grief,
Though little he do feel it, set down sharply.
Dispatch the most convenient messenger:—
When haply he shall hear that she is gone,
He will return; and hope I may that she,
Hearing so much, will speed her foot again,
Led hither by pure love: which of them both
Is dearest to me, I have no skill in sense
To make distinction:—provide this messenger:—
My heart is heavy and mine age is weak:
Grief would have tears, and sorrow bids me speak.
[*Exeunt.*

SCENE V.

Without the walls of Florence. A tucket afar off.

Enter an old WIDOW *of Florence,* DIANA, VIOLENTA, MARIANA, *with other* CITIZENS.

WIDOW.

NAY, come; for if they do approach the city, we shall lose all the sight.

DIANA.

They say the French count has done most honourable service.

WIDOW.

It is reported that he has taken their greatest commander; and that with his own hand he slew the duke's brother. [*Tucket.*] We have lost our labour; they are gone a contrary way: hark! you may know by their trumpets.

MARIANA.

Come, let's return again, and suffice ourselves with the report of it. Well, Diana, take heed of this French earl: the honour of a maid is her name; and no legacy is so rich as honesty.

WIDOW.

I have told my neighbour how you have been solicited by a gentleman his companion.

MARIANA.

I know that knave; hang him! one Parolles: a filthy officer he is in those suggestions for the young earl.—Beware of them, Diana; their promises, enticements, oaths, tokens, and all these engines of lust, are not the things they go under: many a maid hath been seduced by them; and the misery is, example, that so terrible shows in the wrack of maidenhood, cannot for all that dissuade succession, but that they are limed with the twigs that threaten them. I hope I need not to advise you further; but I hope your own grace will keep you where you are, though there were no further danger known but the modesty which is so lost.

DIANA.

You shall not need to fear me.

WIDOW.

I hope so.—Look, here comes a pilgrim: I know she will lie at my house; thither they send one another: I'll question her.

Enter HELENA, *in the dress of a pilgrim.*

God save you, pilgrim! whither are you bound?

HELENA.

To Saint Jaques le Grand.
Where do the palmers lodge, I do beseech you?

WIDOW.

At the Saint Francis here, beside the port.

HELENA.

Is this the way?

WIDOW.

Ay, marry, is't.—Hark you! they come this way.— [*A march afar off.*
If you will tarry, holy pilgrim,
But till the troops come by,
I will conduct you where you shall be lodged;
The rather, for I think I know your hostess
As ample as myself.

HELENA.

Is it yourself?

WIDOW.

If you shall please so, pilgrim.

HELENA.

I thank you, and will stay upon your leisure.

WIDOW.

You came, I think, from France?

HELENA.

I did so.

WIDOW.

Here you shall see a countryman of yours
That has done worthy service.

HELENA.

His name, I pray you.

DIANA.

The Count Rousillon: know you such a one?

HELENA.

But by the ear, that hears most nobly of him:
His face I know not.

DIANA.

Whatsome'er he is,
He's bravely taken here. He stole from France,
As 'tis reported, for the king had married him
Against his liking: think you it is so?

HELENA.

Ay, surely, mere the truth: I know his lady.

DIANA.

There is a gentleman that serves the count
Reports but coarsely of her.

HELENA.

What's his name?

DIANA.

Monsieur Parolles.

HELENA.

O, I believe with him,
In argument of praise, or to the worth
Of the great count himself, she is too mean
To have her name repeated: all her deserving
Is a reserved honesty, and that
I have not heard examined.

DIANA.

Alas, poor lady!
'Tis a hard bondage to become the wife
Of a detesting lord.

WIDOW.

I write good creature; wheresoe'er she is,
Her heart weighs sadly: this young maid might do her
A shrewd turn, if she pleased.

HELENA.

How do you mean?
May be the amorous count solicits her
In the unlawful purpose.

WIDOW.

He does indeed;
And brokes with all that can in such a suit
Corrupt the tender honour of a maid:
But she is arm'd for him, and keeps her guard
In honestest defence.

MARIANA.

The gods forbid else!

WIDOW.

So, now they come:—

Drum and Colours.

Enter BERTRAM, PAROLLES, *and the whole army.*

That is Antonio, the duke's eldest son;
That, Escalus.

HELENA.

Which is the Frenchman?

DIANA.

He;
That with the plume: 'tis a most gallant fellow.
I would he loved his wife: if he were honester,
He were much goodlier: is't not a handsome gentleman?

HELENA.

I like him well.

DIANA.

'Tis pity he is not honest: yond's that same knave
That leads him to these passes: were I his lady,
I would poison that vile rascal.

HELENA.

Which is he?

DIANA.

That jack-an-apes with scarfs: why is he melancholy?

HELENA.

Perchance he's hurt i'the battle.

PAROLLES.

Lose our drum! well.

MARIANA.

He's shrewdly vext at something: look, he has spied us.

WIDOW.

Marry, hang you!

MARIANA.

And your courtesy, for a ring-carrier!

[*Exeunt* BERTRAM, PAROLLES, *&c.*

WIDOW.

The troop is past. Come pilgrim, I will bring you
Where you shall host: of enjoin'd penitents
There's four or five, to Great Saint Jaques bound,
Already at my house.

HELENA.

I humbly thank you:
Please it this matron and this gentle maid
To eat with us to-night, the charge and thanking
Shall be for me; and, to requite you further,
I will bestow some precepts of this virgin
Worthy the note.

BOTH.

We'll take your offer kindly. [*Exeunt.*

SCENE VI.

Camp before Florence.

Enter BERTRAM *and the two French* LORDS.

FIRST LORD.

NAY, good my lord, put him to't; let him have his way.

SECOND LORD.

If your lordship find him not a hilding, hold me no more in your respect.

FIRST LORD.

On my life, my lord, a bubble.

BERTRAM.

Do you think I am so far deceived in him?

FIRST LORD.

Believe it, my lord, in mine own direct knowledge, without any malice, but to speak of him as my kinsman, he's a most notable coward, an infinite and endless liar, an hourly promise-breaker, the owner of no one good quality worthy your lordship's entertainment.

SECOND LORD.

It were fit you knew him; lest, reposing too far in his virtue, which he hath not, he might at some great and trusty business, in a main danger, fail you.

BERTRAM.

I would I knew in what particular action to try him.

SECOND LORD.

None better than to let him fetch off his drum, which you hear him so confidently undertake to do.

FIRST LORD.

I, with a troop of Florentines, will suddenly surprise him; such I will have, whom, I am sure, he knows not from the enemy: we will bind and hoodwink him so, that he shall suppose no other but that he is carried into the leaguer of the adversaries, when we bring him to our own tents. Be but your lordship present at his examination: if he do not, for the promise of his life, and in the highest compulsion of base fear, offer to betray you, and deliver all the intelligence in his power against you, and that with the divine forfeit of his soul upon oath, never trust my judgement in any thing.

SECOND LORD.

O, for the love of laughter, let him fetch off his drum; he says he has a stratagem for't: when your lordship sees the bottom of his success in't, and to what metal this counterfeit lump of ore will be melted, if you give him not John Drum's entertainment, your inclining cannot be removed.—Here he comes.

FIRST LORD.

O, for the love of laughter, hinder not the humour of his design: let him fetch off his drum in any hand.

Enter PAROLLES.

BERTRAM.

How now, monsieur! this drum sticks sorely in your disposition.

SECOND LORD.

A pox on't, let it go; 'tis but a drum.

PAROLLES.

But a drum! is't but a drum? A drum so lost!—There was excellent command,—to charge in with our horse upon our own wings, and to rend our own soldiers!

SECOND LORD.

That was not to be blamed in the command of the service: it was a disaster of war that Cæsar himself could not have prevented, if he had been there to command.

BERTRAM.

Well, we cannot greatly condemn our success: some dishonour we had in the loss of that drum; but it is not to be recover'd.

PAROLLES.

It might have been recover'd.

BERTRAM.

It might; but it is not now.

PAROLLES.

It is to be recover'd: but that the merit of service is seldom attributed to the true and exact performer, I would have that drum or another, or *hic jacet.*

BERTRAM.

Why, if you have a stomach, to't: monsieur, if you think your mystery in stratagem can bring this instrument of honour again into his native quarter, be magnanimous in the enterprise, and go on; I will grace the attempt for a worthy exploit: if you speed well in it, the duke shall both speak of it, and extend to you what further becomes his greatness, even to the utmost syllable of your worthiness.

PAROLLES.

By the hand of a soldier, I will undertake it.

BERTRAM.

But you must not now slumber in it.

PAROLLES.

I'll about it this evening: and I will presently pen down my dilemmas, encourage myself in my certainty, put myself in my mortal preparation; and, by midnight, look to hear further from me.

BERTRAM.

May I be bold to acquaint his Grace you are gone about it?

PAROLLES.

I know not what the success will be, my lord; but the attempt I vow.

BERTRAM.

I know th'art valiant; and, to the possibility of thy soldiership, will subscribe for thee. Farewell.

PAROLLES.

I love not many words. [*Exit.*

FIRST LORD.

No more than a fish loves water.—Is not this a strange fellow, my lord, that so confidently seems to undertake this business, which he knows is not to be done; damns himself to do, and dares better be damn'd than to do't?

SECOND LORD.

You do not know him, my lord, as we do: certain it is, that he will steal himself into a man's favour, and for a week escape a great deal of discoveries; but when you find him out, you have him ever after.

BERTRAM.

Why, do you think he will make no deed at all of this, that so seriously he does address himself unto?

FIRST LORD.

None in the world; but return with an invention, and clap upon you two or thee probable lies: but we have almost embost him,—you shall see his fall to-night; for indeed he is not for your lordship's respect.

SECOND LORD.

We'll make you some sport with the fox, ere we case him. He was first smoked by the old Lord Lafeu: when his disguise and he is parted, tell me what a sprat you shall find him: which you shall see this very night.

FIRST LORD.

I must go look my twigs: he shall be caught.

BERTRAM.

Your brother, he shall go along with me.

FIRST LORD.

As't please your lordship: I'll leave you [*Exit.*

BERTRAM.

Now will I lead you to the house, and show you
The lass I spoke of.

SECOND LORD.

But you say she's honest.

BERTRAM.

That's all the fault: I spoke with her but once,
And found her wondrous cold; but I sent to her,
By this same coxcomb that we have i'the wind,
Tokens and letters which she did re-send;
And this is all I have done. She's a fair creature:
Will you go see her?

SECOND LORD.

With all my heart, my lord.
[*Exeunt.*

SCENE VII.

Florence. A room in the WIDOW'S *house.*

Enter HELENA *and* WIDOW.

HELENA.

IF you misdoubt me that I am not she,
I know not how I shall assure you further,
But I shall lose the grounds I work upon.

WIDOW.

Though my estate be fall'n, I was well born,
Nothing acquainted with these businesses;
And would not put my reputation now
In any staining act.

HELENA.

Nor would I wish you.
First, give me trust, the count he is my husband,
And what to your sworn counsel I have spoken
Is so from word to word; and then you cannot,
By the good aid that I of you shall borrow,
Err in bestowing it.

WIDOW.

I should believe you;
For you have show'd me that which well approves
Y'are great in fortune.

HELENA.

Take this purse of gold,
And let me buy your friendly help thus far,
Which I will over-pay and pay again,
When I have found it. The count he woos your daughter,
Lays down his wanton siege before her beauty,
Resolved to carry her: let her, in fine, consent,
As we'll direct her how 'tis best to bear it;
Now his impatient blood will naught deny
That she'll demand: a ring the county wears,
That downward hath succeeded in his house
From son to son, some four or five descents
Since the first father wore it: this ring he holds
In most rich choice; yet, in his idle fire,
To buy his will, it would not seem too dear,
Howe'er repented after.

WIDOW.

Now I see
The bottom of your purpose.

HELENA.

You see it lawful, then: it is no more,
But that your daughter, ere she seems as won,
Desires this ring; appoints him an encounter;
In fine, delivers me to fill the time,
Herself most chastely absent: after this,
To marry her, I'll add three thousand crowns
To what is past already.

WIDOW.

I have yielded:
Instruct my daughter how she shall persever,
That time and place with this deceit so lawful
May prove coherent. Every night he comes
With music of all sorts, and songs composed
To her unworthiness: it nothing steads us
To chide him from our eaves; for he persists,
As if his life lay on't.

HELENA.

Why, then, to-night
Let us assay our plot; which, if it speed,
Is wicked meaning in a lawful deed,
And lawful meaning in unlawful act;
Where both not sin, and yet a sinful fact:
But let's about it. [*Exeunt.*

ACT IV. SCENE I.

Without the Florentine camp.

Enter First French LORD, *with five or six other* SOLDIERS, *in ambush.*

FIRST LORD.

HE can come no other way but by this hedge-corner. When you sally upon him, speak what terrible language you will,—though you understand it not yourselves, no matter; for we must not seem to understand him, unless some one among us, whom we must produce for an interpreter.

FIRST SOLDIER.

Good captain, let me be th'interpreter.

FIRST LORD.

Art not acquainted with him? knows he not thy voice?

FIRST SOLDIER.

No, sir, I warrant you.

FIRST LORD.

But what linsey-woolsey hast thou to speak to us again?

FIRST SOLDIER.

E'en such as you speak to me.

FIRST LORD.

He must think us some band of strangers i'the adversary's entertainment. Now, he hath a smack of all neighbouring languages; therefore we must every one be a man of his own fancy, not to know what we speak one to another; so we seem to know, is to know straight our purpose: choughs' language, gabble enough, and good enough. As for you, interpreter, you must seem very politic. —But couch, ho! here he comes,—to beguile two hours in a sleep, and then to return and swear the lies he forges.

Enter PAROLLES.

PAROLLES.

Ten o'clock: within these three hours 'twill be time enough to go home. What shall I say I have done? It must be a very plausive invention that carries it: they begin to smoke me; and disgraces have of late knockt too often at my door. I find my tongue is too foolhardy; but my heart hath the fear of Mars before it and of his creatures, not daring the reports of my tongue.

FIRST LORD [*aside*].

This is the first truth that e'er thine own tongue was guilty of.

PAROLLES.

What the devil should move me to undertake the recovery of this drum, being not ignorant of the impossibility, and knowing I had no such purpose? I must give myself some hurts, and say I got them in exploit: yet slight ones will not carry it; they will say, 'Came you off with so little?' and great ones I dare not give. Wherefore, what's the instance? Tongue, I must put you into a butter-woman's mouth, and buy myself another of Bajazet's mule, if you prattle me into these perils.

FIRST LORD [*aside*].

Is it possible he should know what he is, and be that he is?

PAROLLES.

I would the cutting of my garments would serve the turn, or the breaking of my Spanish sword.

FIRST LORD [*aside*].

We cannot afford you so.

PAROLLES.

Or the baring of my beard; and to say it was in stratagem.

FIRST LORD [*aside*].

'Twould not do.

PRAOLLES.

Or to drown my clothes, and say I was stript—

FIRST LORD [*aside*].

Hardly serve.

PAROLLES.

Though I swore I leapt from the window of the citadel—

FIRST LORD [*aside*].

How deep?

PAROLLES.

Thirty fadom.

FIRST LORD [*aside*].

Three great oaths would scarce make that be believed.

PAROLLES.

I would I had any drum of the enemy's: I would swear I recover'd it.

FIRST LORD [*aside*].

You shall hear one anon. [*Alarum within.*

PAROLLES.

A drum now of the enemy's!

FIRST LORD.

Throca movousus, cargo, cargo, cargo.

ALL.

Cargo, cargo, cargo, villianda par corbo, cargo.

PAROLLES.

O, ransom, ransom!—do not hide mine eyes.
[*They seize and blindfold him.*

FIRST SOLDIER.

Boskos thromuldo boskos.

PAROLLES.

I know you are the Muskos' regiment;
And I shall lose my life for want of language:
If there be here German, or Dane, low Dutch,
Italian, or French, let him speak to me; I'll
Discover that which shall undo the Florentine.

FIRST SOLDIER.

Boskos vauvado:—
I understand thee, and can speak thy tongue:—
Kerelybonto:—sir,
Betake thee to thy faith, for seventeen poniards
Are at thy bosom.

PAROLLES.

O!

FIRST SOLDIER.

O, pray, pray, pray!—
Manka revania dulche.

FIRST LORD.

Oscorbidulchos volivorco.

FIRST SOLDIER.

The general is content to spare thee yet;
And, hoodwinkt as thou art, will lead thee on
To gather from thee: haply thou mayst inform
Something to save thy life.

PAROLLES.

O, let me live!
And all the secrets of our camp I'll show,
Their force, their purposes; nay, I'll speak that
Which you will wonder at.

FIRST SOLDIER.

But wilt thou faithfully?

PAROLLES.

If I do not, damn me.

FIRST SOLDIER.

Acordo linta:—
Come on; thou art granted space.
[*Exit, with* PAROLLES *guarded. A short alarum within.*

FIRST LORD.

Go, tell the Count Rousillon, and my brother,
We have caught the woodcock, and will keep him muffled
Till we do hear from them.

SECOND SOLDIER.

Captain, I will.

FIRST LORD.

A' will betray us all unto ourselves:—
Inform 'em that.

SECOND SOLDIER.

So I will, sir.

FIRST LORD.

Till then I'll keep him dark and safely lockt.
[*Exeunt.*

SCENE II.

Florence. A room in the WIDOW'S *house.*

Enter BERTRAM *and* DIANA.

BERTRAM.

THEY told me that your name was Fontibell.

DIANA.

No, my good lord, Diana.

BERTRAM.

Titled goddess;
And worth it, with addition! But, fair soul,
In your fine frame hath love no quality?
If the quick fire of youth light not your mind,
You are no maiden, but a monument:
When you are dead, you should be such a one
As you are now, for you are cold and stern;
And now you should be as your mother was
When your sweet self was got.

DIANA.

She then was honest.

BERTRAM.

So should you be.

DIANA.

No:
My mother did but duty; such, my lord,
As you owe to your wife.

BERTRAM.

No more o'that,—
I prithee, do not strive against my vows:
I was compell'd to her; but I love thee
By love's own sweet constraint, and will for ever
Do thee all rights of service.

DIANA.

Ay, so you serve us
Till we serve you; but when you have our roses,
You barely leave our thorns to prick ourselves,
And mock us with our bareness.

BERTRAM.

How have I sworn!

DIANA.

'Tis not the many oaths that makes the truth,
But the plain single vow that is vow'd true.
What is not holy, that we swear not by,
But take the High'st to witness: then, pray you, tell me,
If I should swear by Jove's great attributes,
I loved you dearly, would you believe my oaths,
When I did love you ill? this has no holding,
To swear by him whom I protest to love,
That I will work against him. Therefore your oaths
Are words and poor conditions; but unseal'd;
At least in my opinion.

BERTRAM.

Change it, change it;
Be not so holy-cruel: love is holy;
And my integrity ne'er knew the crafts
That you do charge men with. Stand no more off,
But give thyself unto my sick desires,
Who then recover: say thou art mine, and ever
My love as it begins shall so persever.

DIANA.

I see that men make ropes in such a scarr,
That we'll forsake ourselves. Give me that ring.

BERTRAM.

I'll lend it thee, my dear; but have no power
To give it from me.

DIANA.

Will you not, my lord?

BERTRAM.

It is an honour 'longing to our house,
Bequeathed down from many ancestors;
Which were the greatest obloquy i'the world
In me to lose.

DIANA.

Mine honour's such a ring:
My chastity's the jewel of our house,
Bequeathed down from many ancestors;
Which were the greatest obloquy i'the world
In me to lose: thus your own proper wisdom
Brings in the champion honour on my part,
Against your vain assault.

BERTRAM.

Here, take my ring:
My house, mine honour, yea, my life, be thine,
And I'll be bid by thee.

DIANA.

When midnight comes, knock at my chamber-window:
I'll order take my mother shall not hear.
Now will I charge you in the band of truth,
When you have conquer'd my yet maiden bed,
Remain there but an hour, nor speak to me:
My reasons are most strong; and you shall know them
When back again this ring shall be deliver'd:
And on your finger, in the night, I'll put
Another ring, that what in time proceeds
May token to the future our past deeds.
Adieu, till then; then fail not. You have won
A wife of me, though there my hope be done.

BERTRAM.

A heaven on earth I have won by wooing thee.
[*Exit.*

DIANA.

For which live long to thank both heaven and me!
You may so in the end.—
My mother told me just how he would woo,
As if she sat in's heart; she says all men
Have the like oaths: he has sworn to marry me
When his wife's dead; therefore I'll lie with him
When I am buried. Since Frenchmen are so braid,
Marry that will, I live and die a maid:
Only, in this disguise, I think't no sin
To cozen him that would unjustly win. [*Exit.*

SCENE III.

The Florentine camp.

Enter the two French LORDS *and some two or three* SOLDIERS.

FIRST LORD.

YOU have not given him his mother's letter?

SECOND LORD.

I have deliver'd it an hour since: there is something in't that stings his nature; for, on the reading it, he changed almost into another man.

FIRST LORD.

He has much worthy blame laid upon him for shaking off so good a wife and so sweet a lady.

SECOND LORD.

Especially he hath incurr'd the everlasting displeasure of the king, who had even tuned his bounty to sing happiness to him. I will tell you a thing, but you shall let it dwell darkly with you.

FIRST LORD.

When you have spoken it, 'tis dead, and I am the grave of it.

SECOND LORD.

He hath perverted a young gentlewoman here in Florence, of a most chaste renown; and this night he fleshes his will in the spoil of her honour: he hath given her his monumental ring, and thinks himself made in the unchaste composition.

FIRST LORD.

Now, God delay our rebellion! as we are ourselves, what things are we!

SECOND LORD.

Merely our own traitors. And as in the common course of all treasons, we still see them reveal themselves, till they attain to their abhorr'd ends, so he that in this action contrives against his own nobility, in his proper stream o'erflows himself.

FIRST LORD.

Is it not meant damnable in us, to be trumpeters of our unlawful intents? We shall not, then, have his company to-night?

SECOND LORD.

Not till after midnight; for he is dieted to his hour.

FIRST LORD.

That approaches apace: I would gladly have him see his company anatomized, that he might take a measure of his own judgements, wherein so curiously he had set this counterfeit.

SECOND LORD.

We will not meddle with him till he come; for his presence must be the whip of the other.

FIRST LORD.

In the mean time, what hear you of these wars?

SECOND LORD.

I hear there is an overture of peace.

FIRST LORD.

Nay, I assure you, a peace concluded.

SECOND LORD.

What will Count Rousillon do then? will he travel higher, or return again into France?

FIRST LORD.

I perceive, by this demand, you are not altogether of his council.

SECOND LORD.

Let it be forbid, sir! so should I be a great deal of his act.

FIRST LORD.

Sir, his wife, some two months since, fled from his house; her pretence is a pilgrimage to Saint Jaques le Grand; which holy undertaking, with most austere sanctimony, she accomplisht; and, there residing, the tenderness of her nature became as a prey to her grief; in fine, made a groan of her last breath; and now she sings in heaven.

SECOND LORD.

How is this justified?

FIRST LORD.

The stronger part of it by her own letters, which make her story true, even to the point of her death: her death itself, which could not be her office to say is come, was faithfully confirm'd by the rector of the place.

SECOND LORD.

Hath the count all this intelligence?

FIRST LORD.

Ay, and the particular confirmations, point from point, to the full arming of the verity.

SECOND LORD.

I am heartily sorry that he'll be glad of this.

FIRST LORD.

How mightily sometimes we make us comforts of our losses!

SECOND LORD.

And how mightily some other times we drown our gain in tears! The great dignity that his valour hath here acquired for him shall at home be encounter'd with a shame as ample.

FIRST LORD.

The web of our life is of a mingled yarn, good and ill together: our virtues would be proud, if our faults whipt them not: and our crimes would despair, if they were not cherisht by our virtues.

Enter a MESSENGER.

How now! where's your master?

MESSENGER.

He met the duke in the street, sir, of whom he hath taken a solemn leave: his lordship will next morning for France. The duke hath offer'd him letters of commendations to the king. [*Exit.*

SECOND LORD.

They shall be no more than needful there, if they were more than they can commend.

FIRST LORD.

They cannot be too sweet for the king's tartness. Here's his lordship now.

Enter BERTRAM.

How now, my lord! is't not after midnight?

BERTRAM.

I have to-night dispatcht sixteen businesses, a month's length a-piece, by an abstract of success: I have congied with the duke, done my adieu with his nearest; buried a wife, mourn'd for her; writ to my lady mother I am returning; entertain'd my convoy; and between these main parcels of dispatch, effected many nicer needs: the last was the greatest, but that I have not ended yet.

SECOND LORD.

If the business be of any difficulty, and this morning your departure hence, it requires haste of your lordship.

BERTRAM.
I mean, the business is not ended, as fearing to hear of it hereafter. But shall we have this dialogue between the fool and the soldier?—Come, bring forth this counterfeit module, has deceived me, like a double-meaning prophesier.

SECOND LORD.
Bring him forth [*Exeunt* SOLDIERS]:—has sat i'the stocks all night, poor gallant knave.

BERTRAM.
No matter; his heels have deserved it, in usurping his spurs so long. How does he carry himself?

SECOND LORD.
I have told your lordship already,—the stocks carry him. But, to answer you as you would be understood; he weeps like a wench that had shed her milk: he hath confest himself to Morgan, whom he supposes to be a friar, from the time of his remembrance to this very instant disaster of his setting i'the stocks: and what think you he hath confest?

BERTRAM.
Nothing of me, has a'?

SECOND LORD.
His confession is taken, and it shall be read to his face: if your lordship be in't, as I believe you are, you must have the patience to hear it.

Enter SOLDIERS *with* PAROLLES *muffled.*

BERTRAM.
A plague upon him! muffled! he can say nothing of me.

FIRST LORD.
Hush, hush! Hoodman comes.—*Portotartarossa.*

FIRST SOLDIER.
He calls for the tortures: what will you say without 'em?

PAROLLES.
I will confess what I know without constraint: if ye pinch me like a pasty, I can say no more.

FIRST SOLDIER.
Bosko chimurcho.

FIRST LORD.
Boblibindo chicurmurco.

FIRST SOLDIER.
You are a merciful general.—Our general bids you answer to what I shall ask you out of a note.

PAROLLES.
And truly, as I hope to live.

FIRST SOLDIER [*reads*].
'First demand of him how many horse the duke is strong.' What say you to that?

PAROLLES.
Five or six thousand; but very weak and unserviceable: the troops are all scatter'd, and the commanders very poor rogues, upon my reputation and credit, and as I hope to live.

FIRST SOLDIER.
Shall I set down your answer so?

PAROLLES.
Do: I'll take the sacrament on't, how and which way you will.

BERTRAM.
All's one to him. What a past-saving slave is this!

FIRST LORD.
Y'are deceived, my lord: this is Monsieur Parolles, the gallant militarist,—that was his own phrase,—that had the whole theoric of war in the knot of his scarf, and the practice in the chape of his dagger.

SECOND LORD.
I will never trust a man again for keeping his sword clean; nor believe he can have every thing in him by wearing his apparel neatly.

FIRST SOLDIER.
Well, that's set down.

PAROLLES.
Five or six thousand horse, I said,—I will say true,—or thereabouts, set down,—for I'll speak truth.

FIRST LORD.
He's very near the truth in this.

BERTRAM.
But I con him no thanks for't, in the nature he delivers it.

PAROLLES.
Poor rogues, I pray you, say.

FIRST SOLDIER.
Well, that's set down.

PAROLLES.
I humbly thank you, sir. A truth's a truth,—the rogues are marvellous poor.

FIRST SOLDIER [*reads*].
'Demand of him, of what strength they are a-foot.' What say you to that?

PAROLLES.
By my troth, sir, if I were to live but this present hour, I will tell true. Let me see: Spurio, a hundred and fifty; Sebastian, so many; Corambus, so many; Jaques, so many; Guiltian, Cosmo, Lodowick, and Gratii, two hundred fifty each; mine own company, Chitopher, Vaumond, Bentii, two hundred fifty each: so that the muster-file, rotten and sound, upon my life, amounts not to fifteen thousand poll; half of the which dare not shake the snow from off their cassocks, lest they shake themselves to pieces.

BERTRAM.
What shall be done to him?

FIRST LORD.
Nothing, but let him have thanks.—Demand of him my condition, and what credit I have with the duke.

FIRST SOLDIER.
Well, that's set down. [*Reads*] 'You shall demand of him, whether one Captain Dumain be i'the camp, a Frenchman; what his reputation is with the duke; what his valour, honesty, and expertness in wars; or whether he thinks it were not possible, with well-weighing sums of gold, to corrupt him to a revolt.' What say you to this? what do you know of it?

PAROLLES.
I beseech you, let me answer to the particular of the inter'gatories: demand them singly.

FIRST SOLDIER.
Do you know this Captain Dumain?

PAROLLES.
I know him: a' was a botcher's 'prentice in Paris, from whence he was whipt for getting the shrieve's fool with child,—a dumb innocent, that could not say him nay.

[FIRST LORD *lifts up his hand in anger.*

BERTRAM.

Nay, by your leave, hold your hands; though I know his brains are forfeit to the next tile that falls.

FIRST SOLDIER.

Well, is this captain in the Duke of Florence's camp?

PAROLLES.

Upon my knowledge, he is, and lousy.

FIRST LORD.

Nay, look not so upon me; we shall hear of your lordship anon.

FIRST SOLDIER.

What is his reputation with the duke?

PAROLLES.

The duke knows him for no other but a poor officer of mine; and writ to me this other day to turn him out o'the band: I think I have his letter in my pocket.

FIRST SOLDIER.

Marry, we'll search.

PAROLLES.

In good sadness, I do not know; either it is there, or it is upon a file, with the duke's other letters, in my tent.

FIRST SOLDIER.

Here 'tis; here's a paper: shall I read it to you?

PAROLLES.

I do not know if it be it or no.

BERTRAM.

Our interpreter does it well.

FIRST LORD.

Excellently.

FIRST SOLDIER [*reads*].

Dian, the count's a fool, and full of gold,—

PAROLLES.

That is not the duke's letter, sir; that is an advertisement to a proper maid in Florence, one Diana, to take heed of the allurement of one Count Rousillon, a foolish idle boy, but, for all that, very ruttish: I pray you, sir, put it up again.

FIRST SOLDIER.

Nay, I'll read it first, by your favour.

PAROLLES.

My meaning in't, I protest, was very honest in the behalf of the maid; for I knew the young count to be a dangerous and lascivious boy, who is a whale to virginity, and devours up all the fry it finds.

BERTRAM.

Damnable both-sides rogue!

FIRST SOLDIER [*reads*].

When he swears oaths, bid him drop gold, and take it;
After he scores, he never pays the score:
Half won is match well made; match, and well make it;
He ne'er pays after-debts, take it before;
And say a soldier, Dian, told thee this,
Men are to mell with, boys are but to kiss:
For count of this, the count's a fool, I know it,
Who pays before, but not when he does owe it.

Thine, as he vow'd to thee in thine ear,
PAROLLES.

BERTRAM.

He shall be whipt through the army, with this rime in's forehead.

SECOND LORD.

This is your devoted friend, sir, the manifold linguist and the armipotent soldier.

BERTRAM.

I could endure any thing before but a cat, and now he's a cat to me.

FIRST SOLDIER.

I perceive, sir, by our general's looks, we shall be fain to hang you.

PAROLLES.

My life, sir, in any case: not that I am afraid to die; but that, my offences being many, I would repent out the remainder of nature: let me live, sir, in a dungeon, i'the stocks, or any where, so I may live.

FIRST SOLDIER.

We'll see what may be done, so you confess freely; therefore, once more to this Captain Dumain: you have answer'd to his reputation with the duke, and to his valour: what is his honesty?

PAROLLES.

He will steal, sir, an egg out of a cloister: for rapes and ravishments he parallels Nessus: he professes not keeping of oaths; in breaking 'em he is stronger than Hercules: he will lie, sir, with such volubility, that you would think truth were a fool: drunkenness is his best virtue, for he will be swine-drunk; and in his sleep he does little harm, save to his bed-clothes about him; but they know his conditions, and lay him in straw. I have but little more to say, sir, of his honesty: he has every thing that an honest man should not have; what an honest man should have, he has nothing.

FIRST LORD.

I begin to love him for this.

BERTRAM.

For this description of thine honesty? A pox upon him for me, he's more and more a cat.

FIRST SOLDIER.

What say you to his expertness in war?

PAROLLES.

Faith, sir, has led the drum before the English tragedians,—to belie him, I will not,—and more of his soldiership I know not; except, in that country he had the honour to be the officer at a place there called Mile-end, to instruct for the doubling of files: I would do the man what honour I can, but of this I am not certain.

FIRST LORD.

He hath out-villain'd villainy so far, that the rarity redeems him.

BERTRAM.

A pox on him, he's a cat still.

FIRST SOLDIER.

His qualities being at this poor price, I need not to ask you if gold will corrupt him to revolt.

PAROLLES.

Sir, for a cardecu he will sell the fee-simple of his salvation, the inheritance of it; and cut th'entail from all remainders, and a perpetual succession for it perpetually.

FIRST SOLDIER.

What's his brother, the other Captain Dumain?

SECOND LORD.

Why does he ask him of me?

FIRST SOLDIER.

What's he?

PAROLLES.

E'en a crow o'the same nest; not altogether so great as the first in goodness, but greater a great deal in evil: he excels his brother for a coward, yet his brother is reputed one of the best that is: in a retreat he outruns any lackey; marry, in coming on he has the cramp.

FIRST SOLDIER.

If your life be saved, will you undertake to betray the Florentine?

PAROLLES.

Ay, and the captain of his horse, Count Rousillon.

FIRST SOLDIER.

I'll whisper with the general, and know his pleasure.

PAROLLES [*aside*].

I'll no more drumming; a plague of all drums! Only to seem to deserve well, and to beguile the supposition of that lascivious young boy the count, have I run into this danger: yet who would have suspected an ambush where I was taken?

FIRST SOLDIER.

There is no remedy, sir, but you must die: the general says, you that have so traitorously discover'd the secrets of your army, and made such pestiferous reports of men very nobly held, can serve the world for no honest use; therefore you must die.—Come, headsman, off with his head.

PAROLLES.

O Lord, sir, let me live, or let me see my death!

FIRST SOLDIER.

That shall you, and take your leave of all your friends. [*Unmuffling him.*
So, look about you: know you any here?

BERTRAM.

Good morrow, noble captain.

SECOND LORD.

God bless you, Captain Parolles.

FIRST LORD.

God save you, noble captain.

SECOND LORD.

Captain, what greeting will you to my Lord Lafeu? I am for France.

FIRST LORD.

Good captain, will you give me a copy of the sonnet you writ to Diana in behalf of the Count Rousillon? an I were not a very coward, I'ld compel it of you; but fare you well.

[*Exeunt* BERTRAM *and* LORDS.

FIRST SOLDIER.

You are undone, captain; all but your scarf, that has a knot on't yet.

PAROLLES.

Who cannot be crusht with a plot?

FIRST SOLDIER.

If you could find out a country where but women were that had received so much shame, you might begin an impudent nation. Fare ye well, sir; I am for France too: we shall speak of you there.

[*Exit with* SOLDIERS.

PAROLLES.

Yet am I thankful: if my heart were great,
'Twould burst at this. Captain I'll be no more;
But I will eat and drink, and sleep as soft
As captain shall: simply the thing I am
Shall make me live. Who knows himself a braggart,
Let him fear this; for it will come to pass,
That every braggart shall be found an ass.
Rust, sword! cool, blushes! and, Parolles, live
Safest in shame! being fool'd, by foolery thrive!
There's place and means for every man alive.
I'll after them. [*Exit.*

SCENE IV.

Florence. A room in the WIDOW'S *house.*

Enter HELENA, WIDOW, *and* DIANA.

HELENA.

THAT you may well perceive I have not wrong'd you,
One of the greatest in the Christian world
Shall be my surety; 'fore whose throne 'tis needful,
Ere I can perfect mine intents, to kneel:
Time was, I did him a desired office,
Dear almost as his life; which gratitude
Through flinty Tartar's bosom would peep forth,
And answer, thanks: I duly am inform'd
His Grace is at Marseilles; to which place
We have convenient convoy. You must know,
I am supposed dead: the army breaking,
My husband hies him home; where, heaven aiding,
And by the leave of my good lord the king,
We'll be before our welcome.

WIDOW.

Gentle madam,
You never had a servant to whose trust
Your business was more welcome.

HELENA.

Nor you, mistress,
Ever a friend whose thoughts more truly labour
To recompense your love: doubt not but heaven
Hath brought me up to be your daughter's dower,
As it hath fated her to be my motive
And helper to a husband. But, O strange men!
That can such sweet use make of what they hate,
When saucy trusting of the cozen'd thoughts
Defiles the pitchy night! so lust doth play
With what it loathes, for that which is away:
But more of this hereafter.—You, Diana,
Under my poor instructions yet must suffer
Something in my behalf.

DIANA.

Let death and honesty
Go with your impositions, I am yours
Upon your will to suffer.

HELENA.

Yet, I pray you:
But, with the word, the time will bring on summer,
When briers shall have leaves as well as thorns,
And be as sweet as sharp. We must away;
Our wagon is prepared, and time revives us:
All's Well that Ends Well: still the fine's the crown;
Whate'er the course, the end is the renown.
[*Exeunt.*

SCENE V.

Rousillon. A room in the house of the COUNTESS.

Enter COUNTESS, LAFEU, *and* CLOWN.

LAFEU.

NO, no, no, your son was misled with a snipt-taffeta fellow there, whose villainous saffron would have made all the unbaked and doughy youth of a nation in his colour: your daughter-in-law had been alive at this hour, and your son here at home, more advanced by the king than by that red-tail'd humble-bee I speak of.

COUNTESS.

I would he had not known him! it was the death of the most virtuous gentlewoman that ever nature had praise for creating: if she had partaken of my flesh, and cost me the dearest groans of a mother, I could not have owed her a more rooted love.

LAFEU.

'Twas a good lady, 'twas a good lady: we may pick a thousand sallets ere we light on such another herb.

CLOWN.

Indeed, sir, she was the sweet marjoram of the sallèt, or rather, the herb of grace.

LAFEU.

They are not sallet-herbs, you knave; they are nose-herbs.

CLOWN.

I am no great Nebuchadnezzar, sir; I have not much skill in grass.

LAFEU.

Whether dost thou profess thyself,—a knave or a fool?

CLOWN.

A fool, sir, at a woman's service, and a knave at a man's.

LAFEU.

Your distinction?

CLOWN.

I would cozen the man of his wife, and do his service.

LAFEU.

So you were a knave at his service, indeed.

CLOWN.

And I would give his wife my bauble, sir, to do her service.

LAFEU.

I will subscribe for thee, thou art both knave and fool.

CLOWN.

At your service.

LAFEU.

No, no, no.

CLOWN.

Why, sir, if I cannot serve you, I can serve as great a prince as you are.

LAFEU.

Who's that? a Frenchman?

CLOWN.

Faith, sir, a' has an English name; but his phisnomy is more hotter in France than there.

LAFEU.

What prince is that?

CLOWN.

The black prince, sir; *alias*, the prince of darkness; *alias*, the devil.

LAFEU.

Hold thee, there's my purse: I give thee not this to suggest thee from thy master thou talk'st of; serve him still.

CLOWN.

I am a woodland fellow, sir, that always loved a great fire; and the master I speak of ever keeps a good fire. But, sure, he is the prince of the world; let his nobility remain in's court. I am for the house with the narrow gate, which I take to be too little for pomp to enter: some that humble themselves may; but the many will be too chill and tender, and they'll be for the flowery way that leads to the broad gate and the great fire.

LAFEU.

Go thy ways, I begin to be a-weary of thee; and I tell thee so before, because I would not fall out with thee. Go thy ways: let my horses be well lookt to, without any tricks.

CLOWN.

If I put any tricks upon 'em, sir, they shall be jades' tricks; which are their own right by the law of nature. [*Exit.*

LAFEU.

A shrewd knave and an unhappy.

COUNTESS.

So he is. My lord that's gone made himself much sport out of him: by his authority he remains here, which he thinks is a patent for his sauciness; and, indeed, he has no pace, but runs where he will.

LAFEU.

I like him well; 'tis not amiss. And I was about to tell you, since I heard of the good lady's death, and that my lord your son was upon his return home, I moved the king my master to speak in the behalf of my daughter; which, in the minority of them both, his majesty, out of a self-gracious remembrance, did first propose; his highness hath promised me to do it: and, to stop up the displeasure he hath conceived against your son, there is no fitter matter. How does your ladyship like it?

COUNTESS.

With very much content, my lord; and I wish it happily effected.

LAFEU.

His highness comes post from Marseilles, of as able body as when he number'd thirty: he will be here to-morrow, or I am deceived by him that in such intelligence hath seldom fail'd.

COUNTESS.

It rejoices me, that I hope I shall see him ere I die. I have letters that my son will be here to-night: I shall beseech your lordship to remain with me till they meet together.

LAFEU.

Madam, I was thinking with what manners I might safely be admitted.

COUNTESS.

You need but plead your honourable privilege.

LAFEU.

Lady, of that I have made a bold charter; but, I thank my God, it holds yet.

Enter CLOWN.

CLOWN.

O madam, yonder's my lord your son with a patch of velvet on's face: whether there be a scar under't or no, the velvet knows: but 'tis a goodly patch of velvet: his left cheek is a cheek of two pile and a half, but his right cheek is worn bare.

LAFEU.

A scar nobly got, or a noble scar, is a good livery of honour; so belike is that.

CLOWN.

But it is your carbonadoed face.

LAFEU.

Let us go see your son, I pray you: I long to talk with the young noble soldier.

CLOWN.

Faith, there's a dozen of 'em, with delicate fine hats, and most courteous feathers, which bow the head and nod at every man. [*Exeunt.*

ACT V. SCENE I.

Marseilles. A street.

Enter HELENA, WIDOW, *and* DIANA, *with two* ATTENDANTS.

HELENA.

BUT this exceeding posting day and night
Must wear your spirits low; we cannot help it:
But, since you have made the days and nights as one,
To wear your gentle limbs in my affairs,
Be bold you do so grow in my requital
As nothing can unroot you.—In happy time;—

Enter a GENTLE ASTRINGER.

This man may help me to his majesty's ear,
If he would spend his power.—God save you, sir.

GENTLE ASTRINGER.

And you.

HELENA.

Sir, I have seen you in the court of France.

GENTLE ASTRINGER.

I have been sometimes there.

HELENA.

I do presume, sir, that you are not fall'n
From the report that goes upon your goodness;
And therefore, goaded with most sharp occasions,
Which lay nice manners by, I put you to
The use of your own virtues; for the which
I shall continue thankful.

GENTLE ASTRINGER.

What's your will?

HELENA.

That it will please you
To give this poor petition to the king;
And aid me with that store of power you have
To come into his presence.

GENTLE ASTRINGER.

The king's not here.

HELENA.

Not here, sir!

GENTLE ASTRINGER.

Not, indeed:
He hence removed last night, and with more haste
Than is his use.

WIDOW.

Lord, how we lose our pains!

HELENA.

All's Well that Ends Well yet,
Though time seem so adverse and means unfit.—
I do beseech you, whither is he gone?

GENTLE ASTRINGER.

Marry, as I take it, to Rousillon;
Whither I am going.

HELENA.

I do beseech you, sir,
Since you are like to see the king before me,
Commend the paper to his gracious hand;
Which, I presume, shall render you no blame,
But rather make you thank your pains for it.
I will come after you with what good speed
Our means will make us means.

GENTLE ASTRINGER.

This I'll do for you.

HELENA.

And you shall find yourself to be well thankt,
Whate'er falls more.—We must to horse again:—
Go, go, provide. [*Exeunt.*

SCENE II.

Rousillon. Before the house of the COUNTESS.

Enter CLOWN *and* PAROLLES.

PAROLLES.

GOOD Monsieur Lavache, give my Lord Lafeu this letter: I have ere now, sir, been better known to you, when I have held familiarity with fresher clothes; but I am now, sir, muddied in Fortune's mood, and smell somewhat strong of her strong displeasure.

CLOWN.

Truly, Fortune's displeasure is but sluttish, if it smell so strongly as thou speak'st of: I will henceforth eat no fish of Fortune's buttering. Prithee, allow the wind.

PAROLLES.

Nay, you need not to stop your nose, sir; I spake but by a metaphor.

CLOWN.

Indeed, sir, if your metaphor stink, I will stop my nose; or against any man's metaphor. Prithee, get thee further.

PAROLLES.

Pray you, sir, deliver me this paper.

CLOWN.

Foh, prithee, stand away: a paper from Fortune's close-stool to give to a nobleman! Look, here he comes himself.

Enter LAFEU.

Here is a pur of Fortune's, sir, or of Fortune's cat,—but not a musk-cat,—that has fall'n into the unclean fishpond of her displeasure, and, as he says, is muddied withal: pray you, sir, use the carp as you may: for he looks like a poor, decay'd, ingenious, foolish, rascally knave. I do pity his distress in my similes of comfort, and leave him to your lordship. [*Exit.*

PAROLLES.

My lord, I am a man whom Fortune hath cruelly scratcht.

LAFEU.

And what would you have me to do? 'tis too late to pare her nails now. Wherein have you play'd the knave with Fortune, that she should scratch you, who of herself is a good lady, and would not have knaves thrive long under her? There's a cardecu for you: let the justices make you and Fortune friends; I am for other business.

PAROLLES.

I beseech your honour to hear me one single word.

LAFEU.

You beg a single penny more: come, you shall ha't; save your word.

PAROLLES.

My name, my good lord, is Parolles.

LAFEU.

You beg more than 'word,' then.—Cox my passion! give me your hand:—how does your drum?

PAROLLES.

O my good lord, you were the first that found me!

LAFEU.

Was I, in sooth? and I was the first that lost thee.

PAROLLES.

It lies in you, my lord, to bring me in some grace, for you did bring me out.

LAFEU.

Out upon thee, knave! dost thou put upon me at once both the office of God and the devil? one brings thee in grace, and the other brings thee out. [*Trumpets sound.*] The king's coming; I know by his trumpets.—Sirrah, inquire further after me; I had talk of you last night: though you are a fool and a knave, you shall eat; go to, follow.

PAROLLES.

I praise God for you. [*Exeunt.*

SCENE III.

The same. A room in the house of the COUNTESS.

Flourish. Enter KING, COUNTESS, LAFEU, *the two French* LORDS, GENTLEMEN, GUARDS, *&c.*

KING.

WE lost a jewel of her; and our esteem
Was made much poorer by it: but your son,
As mad in folly, lackt the sense to know
Her estimation home.

COUNTESS.

'Tis past, my liege;
And I beseech your majesty to make it
Natural rebellion, done i'the blaze of youth;
When oil and fire, too strong for reason's force,
O'erbears it, and burns on.

KING.

My honour'd lady,
I have forgiven and forgotten all;
Though my revenges were high-bent upon him,
And watcht the time to shoot.

LAFEU.

This I must say,—
But first I beg my pardon,—the young lord
Did to his majesty, his mother, and his lady,
Offence of mighty note: but to himself
The greatest wrong of all: he lost a wife,
Whose beauty did astonish the survey
Of richest eyes; whose words all ears took captive;
Whose dear perfection hearts that scorn'd to serve
Humbly call'd mistress.

KING.

Praising what is lost
Makes the remembrance dear. Well, call him hither;
We are reconciled, and the first view shall kill
All repetition:—let him not ask our pardon;
The nature of his great offence is dead,
And deeper than oblivion we do bury
Th'incensing reliques of it: let him approach,
A stranger, no offender; and inform him
So 'tis our will he should.

FIRST GENTLEMAN.

I shall, my liege. [*Exit.*

KING.

What says he to your daughter? have you spoke?

LAFEU.

All that he is hath reference to your highness.

KING.

Then shall we have a match. I have letters sent me
That sets him high in fame.

Enter BERTRAM, *with* FIRST GENTLEMAN.

LAFEU.

He looks well on't.

KING.

I am not a day of season,
For thou mayst see a sunshine and a hail
In me at once: but to the brightest beams
Distracted clouds give way; so stand thou forth,
The time is fair again.

BERTRAM.

My high-repented blames,
Dear sovereign, pardon to me.

KING.

All is whole;
Not one word more of the consumed time.
Let's take the instant by the forward top;
For we are old, and on our quick'st decrees
Th'inaudible and noiseless foot of Time
Steals ere we can effect them. You remember
The daughter of this lord?

BERTRAM.

Admiringly, my liege: at first
I stuck my choice upon her, ere my heart
Durst make too bold a herald of my tongue:
Where the impression of mine eye infixing,
Contempt his scornful perspective did lend me,
Which warpt the line of every other favour;
Scorn'd a fair colour, or exprest it stol'n;
Extended or contracted all proportions
To a most hideous object: thence it came
That she whom all men praised, and whom myself,
Since I have lost, have loved, was in mine eye
The dust that did offend it.

KING.

Well excused:
That thou didst love her, strikes some scores away
From the great compt: but love that comes too late,
Like a remorseful pardon slowly carried,
To the great sender turns a sour offence,
Crying, 'That's good that's gone.' Our rasher faults
Make trivial price of serious things we have,

Not knowing them until we know their grave:
Oft our displeasures, to ourselves unjust,
Destroy our friends, and after weep their dust:
Our old love waking cries to see what's done;
While shameful hate sleeps out the afternoon.
Be this sweet Helen's knell, and now forget her.
Send forth your amorous token for fair Maudlin:
The main consents are had; and here we'll stay
To see our widower's second marriage-day.

COUNTESS.

Which better than the first, O dear heaven, bless!
Or, ere they meet, in me, O nature, cesse!

LAFEU.

Come on, my son, in whom my house's name
Must be digested, give a favour from you,
To sparkle in the spirits of my daughter,
That she may quickly come.—

[BERTRAM *gives a ring to* LAFEU.

By my old beard,
And every hair that's on't, Helen, that's dead,
Was a sweet creature: such a ring as this,
The last that e'er I took her leave at court,
I saw upon her finger.

BERTRAM.

Hers it was not.

KING.

Now, pray you, let me see it; for mine eye,
While I was speaking, oft was fasten'd to't.—
This ring was mine, and when I gave it Helen,
I bade her, if her fortunes ever stood
Necessitied to help, that by this token
I would relieve her. Had you that craft, to reave her
Of what should stead her most?

BERTRAM.

My gracious sovereign,
Howe'er it pleases you to take it so,
The ring was never hers.

COUNTESS.

Son, on my life,
I have seen her wear it; and she reckon'd it
At her life's rate.

LAFEU.

I am sure I saw her wear it.

BERTRAM.

You are deceived, my lord; she never saw it:
In Florence was it from a casement thrown me,
Wrapt in a paper, which contain'd the name
Of her that threw it: noble she was, and thought
I stood engaged: but when I had subscribed
To mine own fortune, and inform'd her fully
I could not answer in that course of honour
As she had made the overture, she ceased
In heavy satisfaction, and would never
Receive the ring again.

KING.

Plutus himself,
That knows the tinct and multiplying medicine,
Hath not in nature's mystery more science
Than I have in this ring: 'twas mine, 'twas Helen's,
Whoever gave it you. Then, if you know
That you are well acquainted with yourself,
Confess 'twas hers, and by what rough enforcement
You got it from her: she call'd the saints to surety
That she would never put it from her finger,
Unless she gave it to yourself in bed,—
Where you have never come,—or sent it us
Upon her great disaster.

BERTRAM.

She never saw it.

KING.

Thou speak'st it falsely, as I love mine honour;
And makest conjectural fears to come into me,
Which I would fain shut out. If it should prove
That thou art so inhuman,—'twill not prove so;—
And yet I know not:—thou didst hate her deadly,
And she is dead, which nothing, but to close
Her eyes myself, could win me to believe,
More than to see this ring.—Take him away.—

[*Guards seize* BERTRAM.

My fore-past proofs, howe'er the matter fall,
Shall tax my fears of little vanity,
Having vainly fear'd too little.—Away with him!—
We'll sift this matter further.

BERTRAM.

If you shall prove
This ring was ever hers, you shall as easy
Prove that I husbanded her bed in Florence,
Where yet she never was. [*Exit, guarded.*

KING.

I am wrapt in dismal thinkings.

Enter a GENTLE ASTRINGER.

GENTLE ASTRINGER.

Gracious sovereign,
Whether I have been to blame or no, I know not:
Here's a petition from a Florentine,
Who hath for four or five removes come short
To tender it herself. I undertook it,
Vanquisht thereto by the fair grace and speech
Of the poor suppliant, who by this, I know,
Is here attending: her business looks in her
With an importing visage; and she told me,
In a sweet verbal brief, it did concern
Your highness with herself.

KING [*reads*].

Upon his many protestations to marry me when his wife was dead, I blush to say it, he won me. Now is the Count Rousillon a widower: his vows are forfeited to me, and my honour's paid to him. He stole from Florence, taking no leave, and I follow him to his country for justice: grant it me, O king! in you it best lies; otherwise a seducer flourishes, and a poor maid is undone.

DIANA CAPULET.

LAFEU.

I will buy me a son-in-law in a fair, and toll: for this, I'll none of him.

KING.

The heavens have thought well on thee, Lafeu,
To bring forth this discov'ry.—Seek these suitors.—
Go speedily and bring again the count.

[*Exeunt* GENTLEMAN *and some* ATTENDANTS.

I am afeared the life of Helen, lady,
Was foully snatcht.

COUNTESS.

Now, justice on the doers!

Enter BERTRAM, *guarded.*

KING.

I wonder, sir, sith wives are monsters to you,
And that you fly them as you swear them lordship,
Yet you desire to marry.

Enter GENTLEMAN, *with* WIDOW *and* DIANA.

What woman's that?

DIANA.

I am, my lord, a wretched Florentine,
Derived from the ancient Capulet:
My suit, as I do understand, you know,
And therefore know how far I may be pitied.

WIDOW.

I am her mother, sir, whose age and honour
Both suffer under this complaint we bring;
And both shall cease, without your remedy.

KING.

Come hither, count: do you know these women?

BERTRAM.

My lord, I neither can nor will deny
But that I know them: do they charge me further?

DIANA.

Why do you look so strange upon your wife?

BERTRAM.

She's none of mine, my lord.

DIANA.

If you shall marry,
You give away this hand, and that is mine;
You give away heaven's vows, and those are mine;
You give away myself, which is known mine;
For I by vow am so embodied yours,
That she which marries you must marry me,—
Either both or none.

LAFEU [*to* BERTRAM].

Your reputation comes too short for my daughter; you are no husband for her.

BERTRAM.

My lord, this is a fond and desperate creature,
Whom sometime I have laught with: let your highness
Lay a more noble thought upon mine honour
Than for to think that I would sink it here.

KING.

Sir, for my thoughts, you have them ill to friend
Till your deeds gain them: fairer prove your honour
Than in my thought it lies!

DIANA.

Good my lord,
Ask him upon his oath, if he does think
He had not my virginity.

KING.

What say'st thou to her?

BERTRAM.

She's impudent, my lord,
And was a common gamester to the camp.

DIANA.

He does me wrong, my lord; if I were so,
He might have bought me at a common price:
Do not believe him: O, behold this ring,
Whose high respect and rich validity
Did lack a parallel; yet, for all that,
He gave it to a commoner o'the camp,
If I be one.

COUNTESS.

He blushes, and 'tis his:
Of six preceding ancestors, that gem,
Conferr'd by testament to the sequent issue,
Hath it been owed and worn. This is his wife;
That ring's a thousand proofs.

KING.

Methought you said
You saw one here in court could witness it.

DIANA.

I did, my lord, but loth am to produce
So bad an instrument: his name's Parolles.

LAFEU.

I saw the man to-day, if man he be.

KING.

Find him, and bring him hither.

[*Exit an* ATTENDANT.

BERTRAM.

What of him?
He's quoted for a most perfidious slave,
With all the spots o'the world taxt and debosht;
Whose nature sickens but to speak a truth.
Am I or that or this for what he'll utter,
That will speak any thing?

KING.

She hath that ring of yours.

BERTRAM.

I think she has: certain it is I liked her,
And boarded her i'the wanton way of youth:
She knew her distance, and did angle for me,
Madding my eagerness with her restraint,
As all impediments in fancy's course
Are motives of more fancy; and, in fine,
Her infinite cunning, with her modern grace,
Subdued me to her rate: she got the ring;
And I had that which any inferior might
At market-price have bought.

DIANA.

I must be patient:
You, that turn'd off a first so noble wife,
May justly diet me. I pray you yet,—
Since you lack virtue, I will lose a husband,—
Send for your ring, I will return it home,
And give me mine again.

BERTRAM.

I have it not.

KING.

What ring was yours, I pray you?

DIANA.

Sir, much like
The same upon your finger.

KING.

Know you this ring? this ring was his of late.

DIANA.

And this was it I gave him, being a-bed.

KING.

The story, then, goes false, you threw it him
Out of a casement.

DIANA.

I have spoke the truth.

BERTRAM.

My lord, I do confess the ring was hers.

KING.

You boggle shrewdly, every feather starts you.—

Enter PAROLLES, *with* ATTENDANT.

Is this the man you speak of?

DIANA.

Ay, my lord.

KING.

Tell me, sirrah,—but tell me true, I charge you,
Not fearing the displeasure of your master,

Which, on your just proceeding, I'll keep off,—
By him and by this woman here what know you?

PAROLLES.

So please your majesty, my master hath been an honourable gentleman: tricks he hath had in him, which gentlemen have.

KING.

Come, come, to the purpose: did he love this woman?

PAROLLES.

Faith, sir, he did love her; but how?

KING.

How, I pray you?

PAROLLES.

He did love her, sir, as a gentleman loves a woman.

KING.

How is that?

PAROLLES.

He loved her, sir, and loved her not.

KING.

As thou art a knave, and no knave.—What an equivocal companion is this!

PAROLLES.

I am a poor man, and at your majesty's command.

LAFEU.

He's a good drum, my lord, but a naughty orator.

DIANA.

Do you know he promised me marriage?

PAROLLES.

Faith, I know more than I'll speak.

KING.

But wilt thou not speak all thou know'st?

PAROLLES.

Yes, so please your majesty. I did go between them, as I said; but more than that, he loved her, —for, indeed, he was mad for her, and talkt of Satan, and of Limbo, and of Furies, and I know not what: yet I was in that credit with them at that time, that I knew of their going to bed; and of other motions, as promising her marriage, and things which would derive me ill will to speak of; therefore I will not speak what I know.

KING.

Thou hast spoken all already, unless thou canst say they are married; but thou art too fine in thy evidence; therefore stand aside.—
This ring, you say, was yours?

DIANA.

Ay, my good lord.

KING.

Where did you buy it? or who gave it you?

DIANA.

It was not given me, not I did not buy it.

KING.

Who lent it you?

DIANA.

It was not lent me neither.

KING.

Where did you find it, then?

DIANA.

I found it not.

KING.

If it were yours by none of all these ways,
How could you give it him?

DIANA.

I never gave it him.

LAFEU.

This woman's an easy glove, my lord; she goes off and on at pleasure.

KING.

This ring was mine; I gave it his first wife.

DIANA.

It might be yours or hers, for aught I know.

KING.

Take her away; I do not like her now;
To prison with her: and away with him.—
Unless thou tell'st me where thou hadst this ring,
Thou diest within this hour.

DIANA.

I'll never tell you.

KING.

Take her away.

DIANA.

I'll put in bail, my liege.

KING.

I think thee now some common customer.

DIANA.

By Jove, if ever I knew man, 'twas you.

KING.

Wherefore hast thou accused him all this while?

DIANA.

Because he's guilty, and he is not guilty:
He knows I am no maid, and he'll swear to't;
I'll swear I am a maid, and he knows not.
Great king, I am no strumpet, by my life;
I'm either maid, or else this old man's wife.
[*Pointing to* LAFEU.

KING.

She does abuse our ears: to prison with her.

DIANA.

Good mother, fetch my bail.—Stay, royal sir:
[*Exit* WIDOW.
The jeweller that owes the ring is sent for,
And he shall surety me. But for this lord,
Who hath abused me, as he knows himself,
Though yet he never harm'd me, here I quit him:
He knows himself my bed he hath defiled;
And at that time he got his wife with child:
Dead though she be, she feels her young one kick:
So there's my riddle,—One that's dead is quick:
And now behold the meaning.

Enter WIDOW, *with* HELENA.

KING.

Is there no exorcist
Beguiles the truer office of mine eyes?
Is't real that I see?

HELENA.

No, my good lord;
'Tis but the shadow of a wife you see,
The name, and not the thing.

BERTRAM.

Both, both:—O, pardon!

HELENA.

O my good lord, when I was like this maid,
I found you wondrous kind. There is your ring;
And, look you, here's your letter; this it says:
'When from my finger you can get this ring,
And are by me with child, &c.' This is done:
Will you be mine, now you are doubly won?

BERTRAM.

If, she, my liege, can make me know this clearly,
I'll love her dearly, ever, ever dearly.

HELENA.

If it appear not plain, and prove untrue,
Deadly divorce step between me and you!—
O my dear mother, do I see you living?

LAFEU.

Mine eyes smell onions; I shall weep anon:—
[*to* PAROLLES] Good Tom Drum, lend me a handkercher: so, I thank thee: wait on me home, I'll make sport with thee: let thy courtesies alone, they are scurvy ones.

KING.

Let us from point to point this story know,
To make the even truth in pleasure flow.—
[*to* DIANA] If thou be'st yet a fresh uncropped flower,
Choose thou thy husband, and I'll pay thy dower;
For I can guess that, by thy honest aid,
Thou kept'st a wife herself, thyself a maid.—
Of that, and all the progress, more and less,
Resolvedly more leisure shall express:
All yet seems well; and if it end so meet,
The bitter past, more welcome is the sweet.
[*Flourish.*

EPILOGUE.

Spoken by the KING.

The king's a beggar, now the play is done:
All is well ended, if this suit be won,
That you express content; which we will pay,
With strife to please you, day exceeding day:
Ours be your patience then, and yours our parts;
Your gentle hands lend us, and take our hearts.
[*Exeunt.*

PERICLES

DRAMATIS PERSONAE

ANTIOCHUS, *King of Antioch.*
PERICLES, *Prince of Tyre.*
HELICANUS, } *two lords of Tyre.*
ESCANES, }
SIMONIDES, *King of Pentapolis.*
CLEON, *governor of Tarsus.*
LYSIMACHUS, *governor of Mytilene.*
CERIMON, *a lord of Ephesus.*
THALIARD, *a lord of Antioch.*
PHILEMON, *servant to Cerimon.*
LEONINE, *servant to Dionyza.*
MARSHALL.
A PANDAR.
BOULT, *his servant.*

THE DAUGHTER OF ANTIOCHUS.
DIONYZA, *wife to Cleon.*
THAISA, *daughter to Simonides.*
MARINA, *daughter to Pericles and Thaisa.*
LYCHORIDA, *nurse to Marina.*
A BAWD.

LORDS, LADIES, KNIGHTS, GENTLEMEN, SAILORS, PIRATES, FISHERMEN, *and* MESSENGERS.

DIANA.

GOWER, *as* CHORUS.

SCENE—*Dispersedly in various countries.*

ACT I.

Enter GOWER.

Before the palace of Antioch.

GOWER.

To sing a song that old was sung,
From ashes ancient Gower is come,
Assuming man's infirmities,
To glad your ear and please your eyes.
It hath been sung at festivals,
On ember-eves and holy-ales;
And lords and ladies in their lives
Have read it for restoratives:
The purchase is to make men glorious;
Et bonum quo antiquius, eo melius.
If you, born in these latter times,
When wit's more ripe, accept my rimes,
And that to hear an old man sing
May to your wishes pleasure bring,
I life would wish, and that I might
Waste it for you, like taper-light.—
This Antioch, then, Antiochus the Great
Built up, this city, for his chiefest seat;
The fairest in all Syria,—
I tell you what mine authors say:
This king unto him took a fere,
Who died and left a female heir,
So buxom, blithe, and full of face,
As heaven had lent her all his grace;
With whom the father liking took,
And her to incest did provoke:—
Bad child; worse father! to entice his own
To evil should be done by none:
But custom what they did begin
Was with long use account no sin.
The beauty of this sinful dame
Made many princes thither frame,
To seek her as a bed-fellow,
In marriage-pleasures play-fellow:
Which to prevent he made a law,—
To keep her still, and men in awe,—
That whoso askt her for his wife,
His riddle told not, lost his life:
So for her many a wight did die,
As yon grim looks do testify.
What now ensues, to the judgement of your eye
I give, my cause who best can justify. [*Exit.*

SCENE I.

Antioch. A room in the palace.

Enter ANTIOCHUS, PERICLES, *and* FOLLOWERS.

ANTIOCHUS.

Young prince of Tyre, you have at large received
The danger of the task you undertake.

PERICLES.

I have, Antiochus, and, with a soul
Embolden'd with the glory of her praise,
Think death no hazard in this enterprise.

ANTIOCHUS.

Bring in our daughter, clothed like a bride,
For the embracements even of Jove himself;
At whose conception, till Lucina reign'd,
Nature this dowry gave, to glad her presence,
The senate-house of planets all did sit,
To knit in her their best perfections.

Music. Enter ANTIOCHUS' DAUGHTER.

PERICLES.

See where she comes, apparell'd like the spring,
Graces her subjects, and her thoughts the king
Of every virtue gives renown to men!
Her face the book of praises, where is read
Nothing but curious pleasures, as from thence
Sorrow were ever razed, and testy wrath
Could never be her mild companion.
You gods that made me man, and sway in love,
That have inflamed desire in my breast
To taste the fruit of yon celestial tree,
Or die in the adventure, be my helps,
As I am son and servant to your will,
To compass such a boundless happiness!

ANTIOCHUS.

Prince Pericles,—

PERICLES.

That would be son to great Antiochus.

ANTIOCHUS.

Before thee stands this fair Hesperides,
With golden fruit, but dangerous to be toucht;
For death-like dragons here affright thee hard:
Her face, like heaven, enticeth thee to view
Her countless glory, which desert must gain;
And which, without desert, because thine eye
Presumes to reach, all thy whole heap must die.
Yon sometimes famous princes, like thyself,
Drawn by report, adventurous by desire,
Tell thee, with speechless tongues and semblance pale,
That, without covering, save yon field of stars,
Here they stand martyrs, slain in Cupid's wars;
And with dead cheeks advise thee to desist
For going on death's net, whom none resist.

PERICLES.

Antiochus, I thank thee, who hath taught
My frail mortality to know itself,
And by those fearful objects to prepare
This body, like to them, to what I must;
For death remember'd should be like a mirror,
Who tells us life's but breath, to trust it error.
I'll make my will, then; and, as sick men do,
Who know the world, see heaven, but, feeling woe,
Gripe not at earthly joys, as erst they did;
So I bequeath a happy peace to you
And all good men, as every prince should do;
My riches to the earth from whence they came;—
But my unspotted fire of love to you.

[*To the* DAUGHTER *of* ANTIOCHUS.

Thus ready for the way of life or death,
I wait the sharpest blow.

ANTIOCHUS.

Scorning advice,—read the conclusion, then:
Which read and not expounded, 'tis decreed,
As these before thee, thou thyself shalt bleed.

DAUGHTER OF ANTIOCHUS.

Of all 'say'd yet, mayst thou prove prosperous!
Of all 'say'd yet, I wish thee happiness!

PERICLES.

Like a bold champion, I assume the lists,
Nor ask advice of any other thought
But faithfulness and courage. [*Reads the riddle.*

> I am no viper, yet I feed
> On mother's flesh which did me breed.
> I sought a husband, in which labour
> I found that kindness in a father:
> He's father, son, and husband mild;
> I mother, wife, and yet his child.
> How they may be, and yet in two,
> As you will live, resolve it you.

Sharp physic is the last: but, O you powers
That give heaven countless eyes to view men's acts,
Why cloud they not their sights perpetually,
If this be true, which makes me pale to read it?—
Fair glass of light, I loved you, and could still,

[*Takes hold of the hand of the* PRINCESS.

Were not this glorious casket stored with ill:
But I must tell you,—now my thoughts revolt;
For he's no man on whom perfections wait
That, knowing sin within, will touch the gate.
You are a fair viol, and your sense the strings;
Who, finger'd to make man his lawful music,
Would draw heaven down, and all the gods, to hearken;
But being play'd upon before your time,
Hell only danceth at so harsh a chime.
Good sooth, I care not for you.

ANTIOCHUS.

Prince Pericles, touch not, upon thy life,
For that's an article within our law,
As dangerous as the rest. Your time's expired:
Either expound now, or receive your sentence.

PERICLES.

Great king,
Few love to hear the sins they love to act;
'Twould braid yourself too near for me to tell it.
Who has a book of all that monarchs do,
He's more secure to keep it shut than shown:
For vice repeated is like the wandering wind,
Blows dust in others' eyes, to spread itself;
And yet the end of all is bought thus dear,
The breath is gone, and the sore eyes see clear
To stop the air would hurt them. The blind mole casts
Copt hills towards heaven, to tell the earth is throng'd
By man's oppression; and the poor worm doth die for't.
Kings are earth's gods; in vice their law's their will;
And if Jove stray, who dares say Jove doth ill?
It is enough you know; and it is fit,
What being more known grows worse, to smother it.
All love the womb that their first being bred,
Then give my tongue like leave to love my head.

ANTIOCHUS [*aside*].

Heaven, that I had thy head! he has found the meaning:
But I will gloze with him.—Young prince of Tyre,
Though by the tenour of our strict edict,
Your exposition misinterpreting,
We might proceed to cancel of your days;
Yet hope, succeeding from so fair a tree
As your fair self, doth tune us otherwise:
Forty days longer we do respite you;
If by which time our secret be undone,
This mercy shows we'll joy in such a son:
And until then your entertain shall be,
As doth befit our honour, and your worth.

[*Exeunt all but* PERICLES.

PERICLES.

How courtesy would seem to cover sin,
When what is done is like an hypocrite,
The which is good in nothing but in sight!
If it be true that I interpret false,
Then were it certain you were not so bad
As with foul incest to abuse your soul;
Where now you're both a father and a son
By your untimely claspings with your child,—
Which pleasure fits a husband, not a father;
And she an eater of her mother's flesh
By the defiling of her parent's bed;
And both like serpents are, who though they feed
On sweetest flowers, yet they poison breed.
Antioch, farewell! for wisdom sees, those men
Blush not in actions blacker than the night,
Will shun no course to keep them from the light.
One sin, I know, another doth provoke;

Murder's as near to lust as flame to smoke:
Poison and treason are the hands of sin,
Ay, and the targets, to put off the shame:
Then, lest my life be cropt to keep you clear,
By flight I'll shun the danger which I fear. [*Exit.*

Enter ANTIOCHUS.

ANTIOCHUS.

He hath found the meaning, for the which we mean
To have his head.
He must not live to trumpet forth my infamy,
Nor tell the world Antiochus doth sin
In such a loathed manner;
And therefore instantly this prince must die;
For by his fall my honour must keep high.—
Who attends us there?

Enter THALIARD.

THALIARD.

Doth your highness call?

ANTIOCHUS.

Thaliard,
You are of our chamber, and our mind partakes
Her private actions to your secrecy:
And for your faithfulness we will advance you.
Thaliard, behold, here's poison, and here's gold;
We hate the prince of Tyre, and thou must kill him:
It fits thee not to ask the reason why,
Because we bid it. Say, is it done?

THALIARD.

My lord,
'Tis done.

ANTIOCHUS.

Enough.

Enter a MESSENGER.

Let your breath cool yourself, telling your haste.

MESSENGER.

My lord, Prince Pericles is fled. [*Exit.*

ANTIOCHUS.

As thou
Wilt live, fly after; and, like an arrow shot
From a well-experienced archer, hits the mark
His eye doth level at, so thou ne'er return
Unless thou say 'Prince Pericles is dead.'

THALIARD.

My lord,
If I can get him within my pistol's length,
I'll make him sure enough: so, farewell to your highness.

ANTIOCHUS.

Thaliard, adieu! [*Exit* THALIARD] Till Pericles be dead
My heart can lend no succour to my head. [*Exit.*

SCENE II.

Tyre. A room in the palace.

Enter PERICLES.

PERICLES [*to* LORDS *without*].

LET none disturb us.—Why should this charge of thoughts,
The sad companion, dull-eyed melancholy,
Be my so-used a guest as not an hour,
In the day's glorious walk or peaceful night,
The tomb where grief should sleep, can breed me quiet?
Here pleasures court mine eyes, and mine eyes shun them,
And danger, which I fear'd, is at Antioch,
Whose arm seems far too short to hit me here:
Yet neither pleasure's art can joy my spirits,
Nor yet the other's distance comfort me.
Then it is thus: the passions of the mind,
That have their first conception by mis-dread,
Have after-nourishment and life by care;
And what was first but fear what might be done,
Grows elder now, and cares it be not done.
And so with me:—the great Antiochus—
'Gainst whom I am too little to contend,
Since he's so great can make his will his act—
Will think me speaking, though I swear to silence;
Nor boots it me to say I honour him,
If he suspect I may dishonour him:
And what may make him blush in being known,
He'll stop the course by which it might be known;
With hostile forces he'll o'erspread the land,
And with th'ostent of war will look so huge,
Amazement shall drive courage from the state;
Our men be vanquisht ere they do resist,
And subjects punisht that ne'er thought offence:
Which care of them, not pity of myself,
Who am no more but as the tops of trees,
Which fence the roots they grow by and defend them,
Makes both my body pine and soul to languish,
And punish that before that he would punish.

Enter HELICANUS *and other* LORDS.

FIRST LORD.

Joy and all comfort in your sacred breast!

SECOND LORD.

And keep your mind, till you return to us,
Peaceful and comfortable!

HELICANUS.

Peace, peace, and give experience tongue.
They do abuse the king that flatter him:
For flattery is the bellows blows up sin;
The thing the which is flatter'd, but a spark,
To which that blast gives heat and stronger glowing;
Whereas reproof, obedient, and in order,
Fits kings, as they are men, for they may err.
When Signior Sooth here does proclaim a peace,
He flatters you, makes war upon your life.
Prince, pardon me, or strike me, if you please;
I cannot be much lower than my knees.

PERICLES.

All leave us else; but let your cares o'erlook
What shipping and what lading's in our haven,
And then return to us. [*Exeunt* LORDS.] Helicanus, thou
Hast moved us: what seest thou in our looks?

HELICANUS.

An angry brow, dread lord.

PERICLES.

If there be such a dart in princes' frowns,
How durst thy tongue move anger to our face?

HELICANUS.

How dare the plants look up to heaven, from whence
They have their nourishment?

PERICLES.

Thou know'st I have power
To take thy life from thee.

HELICANUS [*kneeling*].
I have ground the axe myself;
Do you but strike the blow.

PERICLES.
Rise, prithee, rise.
Sit down: thou art no flatterer:
I thank thee for it; and heaven forbid
That kings should let their ears hear their faults chid!
Fit counsellor and servant for a prince,
Who by thy wisdom makest a prince thy servant,
What wouldst thou have me do?

HELICANUS.
To bear with patience
Such griefs as you yourself do lay upon yourself.

PERICLES.
Thou speak'st like a physician, Helicanus,
That minister'st a potion unto me
That thou wouldst tremble to receive thyself.
Attend me, then: I went to Antioch,
Where, as thou know'st, against the face of death,
I sought the purchase of a glorious beauty,
From whence an issue I might propagate,
Are arms to princes, and bring joys to subjects.
Her face was to mine eye beyond all wonder;
The rest—hark in thine ear—as black as incest:
Which by my knowledge found, the sinful father
Seem'd not to strike, but smooth: but thou know'st this,
'Tis time to fear when tyrants seem to kiss.
Which fear so grew in me, I hither fled,
Under the covering of a careful night,
Who seem'd my good protector; and, being here,
Bethought me what was past, what might succeed.
I knew him tyrannous; and tyrants' fears
Decrease not, but grow faster than the years:
And should he doubt it,—as no doubt he doth,—
That I should open to the listening air
How many worthy princes' bloods were shed,
To keep his bed of blackness unlaid ope,—
To lop that doubt, he'll fill this land with arms,
And make pretence of wrong that I have done him;
When all, for mine, if I may call offence,
Must feel war's blow, who spares not innocence:
Which love to all,—of which thyself art one,
Who now reprovest me for't,—

HELICANUS.
Alas, sir!

PERICLES.
Drew sleep out of mine eyes, blood from my cheeks,
Musings into my mind, with thousand doubts
How I might stop this tempest, ere it came;
And finding little comfort to relieve them,
I thought it princely charity to grieve them.

HELICANUS.
Well, my lord, since you have given me leave to speak,
Freely will I speak. Antiochus you fear,
And justly too, I think, you fear the tyrant,
Who either by public war or private treason
Will take away your life.
Therefore, my lord, go travel for a while,
Till that his rage and anger be forgot,
Or till the Destinies do cut his thread of life.
Your rule direct to any; if to me,
Day serves not light more faithful than I'll be.

PERICLES.
I do not doubt thy faith;
But should he wrong my liberties in my absence?

HELICANUS.
We'll mingle our bloods together in the earth,
From whence we had our being and our birth.

PERICLES.
Tyre, I now look from thee, then, and to Tarsus
Intend my travel, where I'll hear from thee;
And by whose letters I'll dispose myself.
The care I had and have of subjects' good
On thee I lay, whose wisdom's strength can bear it.
I'll take thy word for faith, not ask thine oath:
Who shuns not to break one will sure crack both:
But in our orbs we'll live so round and safe,
That time of both this truth shall ne'er convince,
Thou show'dst a subject's shine, I a true prince.
[*Exeunt.*

SCENE III.

Tyre. An ante-chamber in the palace.

Enter THALIARD.

THALIARD.
So, this is Tyre, and this the court. Here must I kill King Pericles; and if I do it not, I am sure to be hang'd at home: 'tis dangerous.—Well, I perceive he was a wise fellow and had good discretion, that, being bid to ask what he would of the king, desired he might know none of his secrets: now do I see he had some reason for't; for if a king bid a man be a villain, he's bound by the indenture of his oath to be one.—Hush! here come the lords of Tyre.

Enter HELICANUS *and* ESCANES, *with other* LORDS.

HELICANUS.
You shall not need, my fellow peers of Tyre,
Further to question me of your king's departure:
His seal'd commission, left in trust with me,
Doth speak sufficiently he's gone to travel.

THALIARD [*aside*].
How! the king gone!

HELICANUS.
If further yet you will be satisfied,
Why, as it were unlicensed of your loves,
He would depart, I'll give some light unto you.
Being at Antioch,—

THALIARD [*aside*].
What from Antioch?

HELICANUS.
Royal Antiochus—on what cause I know not—
Took some displeasure at him,—at least he judged so;
And doubting lest that he had err'd or sinn'd,
To show his sorrow, he'ld correct himself;
So puts himself unto the shipman's toil,
With whom each minute threatens life or death.

THALIARD [*aside*].
Well, I perceive I shall not be hang'd now, although I would; but since he's gone, the king's seas must please,—he scaped the land, to perish at the sea. I'll present myself.—Peace to the lords of Tyre!

HELICANUS.
Lord Thaliard from Antiochus is welcome.

THALIARD.

From him I come
With message unto princely Pericles;
But since my landing I have understood
Your lord has betook himself to unknown travels,
My message must return from whence it came.

HELICANUS.

We have no reason to desire it,
Commended to our master, not to us:
Yet, ere you shall depart, this we desire,—
As friends to Antioch, we may feast in Tyre.

[*Exeunt.*

SCENE IV.

Tarsus. A room in the GOVERNOR'S *house.*

Enter CLEON *the Governor of Tarsus, with his Wife* DIONYZA, *and others.*

CLEON.

My Dionyza, shall we rest us here,
And by relating tales of others' griefs,
See if 'twill teach us to forget our own?

DIONYZA.

That were to blow at fire in hope to quench it;
For who digs hills because they do aspire
Throws down one mountain to cast up a higher.
O my distressed lord, even such our griefs are;
Here they are but felt, and seen with mischief's eyes,
But like to groves, being topt, they higher rise.

CLEON.

O Dionyza,
Who wanteth food, and will not say he wants it,
Or can conceal his hunger till he famish?
Our tongues and sorrows do sound deep our woes
Into the air; our eyes do weep, till tongues
Fetch breath that may proclaim them louder; that,
If heaven slumber while their creatures want,
They may awake their helps to comfort them.
I'll, then, discourse our woes, felt several years,
And, wanting breath to speak, help me with tears.

DIONYZA.

I'll do my best, sir.

CLEON.

This Tarsus, o'er which I have the government,
A city on whom Plenty held full hand,
For Riches strew'd herself even in the streets;
Whose towers bore heads so high they kist the clouds,
And strangers ne'er beheld but wonder'd at;
Whose men and dames so jetted and adorn'd,
Like one another's glass to trim them by:
Their tables were stored full, to glad the sight,
And not so much to feed on as delight;
All poverty was scorn'd, and pride so great,
The name of help grew odious to repeat.

DIONYZA.

O, 'tis too true.

CLEON.

But see what heaven can do! By this our change,
These mouths who but of late earth, sea, and air,
Were all too little to content and please,
Although they gave their creatures in abundance,
As houses are defiled for want of use,
They are now starved for want of exercise:
Those palates who, not yet two summers younger,
Must have inventions to delight the taste,
Would now be glad of bread, and beg for it:
Those mothers who, to nousle up their babes,
Thought naught too curious, are ready now
To eat those little darlings whom they loved.
So sharp are hunger's teeth, that man and wife
Draw lots who first shall die to lengthen life:
Here stands a lord, and there a lady weeping;
Here many sink, yet those which see them fall
Have scarce strength left to give them burial.
Is not this true?

DIONYZA.

Our cheeks and hollow eyes do witness it,

CLEON.

O, let those cities that of Plenty's cup
And her prosperities so largely taste,
With their superfluous riots, hear these tears!
The misery of Tarsus may be theirs.

Enter a LORD.

LORD.

Where's the lord governor?

CLEON.

Here.
Speak out thy sorrows which thou bring'st in haste,
For comfort is too far for us to expect.

LORD.

We have descried, upon our neighbouring shore,
A portly sail of ships make hitherward.

CLEON.

I thought as much.
One sorrow never comes but brings an heir,
That may succeed as his inheritor;
And so in ours: some neighbouring nation,
Taking advantage of our misery,
Hath stuft these hollow vessels with their power,
To beat us down, the which are down already;
And make a conquest of unhappy me,
Whereas no glory's got to overcome.

LORD.

That's the least fear; for, by the semblance
Of their white flags display'd, they bring us peace
And come to us as favourers, not as foes.

CLEON.

Thou speak'st like him's untutor'd to repeat:
Who makes the fairest show means most deceit.
But bring they what they will and what they can,
What need we fear?
The ground's the lowest, and we are half-way there.
Go tell their general we attend him here,
To know for what he comes, and whence he comes,
And what he craves.

LORD.

I go, my lord. [*Exit.*

CLEON.

Welcome is peace, if he on peace consist;
If wars, we are unable to resist.

Enter PERICLES *with* ATTENDANTS.

PERICLES.

Lord Governor, for so we hear you are,
Let not our ships and number of our men
Be, like a beacon fired, t'amaze your eyes.
We have heard your miseries as far as Tyre,
And seen the desolation of your streets:

Nor come we to add sorrow to your tears,
But to relieve them of their heavy load;
And these our ships, you happily may think
Are like the Trojan horse was stuft within
With bloody veins, expecting overthrow,
Are stored with corn to make your needy bread,
And give them life whom hunger starved half dead.

ALL.

The gods of Greece protect you!
And we'll pray for you.

PERICLES.

Arise, I pray you, rise:
We do not look for reverence, but for love,
And harbourage for ourself, our ships, and men.

CLEON.

The which when any shall not gratify,
Or pay you with unthankfulness in thought,
Be it our wives, our children, or ourselves,
The curse of heaven and men succeed their evils!
Till when,—the which I hope shall ne'er be seen,—
Your Grace is welcome to our town and us.

PERICLES.

Which welcome we'll accept; feast here awhile,
Until our stars that frown lend us a smile.
[*Exeunt.*

ACT II.

Enter GOWER.

GOWER.

HERE have you seen a mighty king
His child, I wis, to incest bring;
A better prince, and benign lord,
That will prove awful both in deed and word.
Be quiet, then, as men should be,
Till he hath past necessity.
I'll show you those in troubles reign,
Losing a mite, a mountain gain.
The good in conversation—
To whom I give my benison—
Is still at Tarsus, where each man
Thinks all is writ he speken can;
And, to remember what he does,
Build his statue to make him glorious:
But tidings to the contrary
Are brought your eyes; what need speak I?

DUMB-SHOW.

Enter, at one door, PERICLES, *talking with* CLEON, *all the* TRAIN *with them. Enter, at another door, a* GENTLEMAN, *with a letter to* PERICLES; PERICLES *shows the letter to* CLEON; *gives the* MESSENGER *a reward, and knights him. Exit* PERICLES *at one door, and* CLEON *at another.*

Good Helicane, that stay'd at home,
Not to eat honey like a drone
From others' labours; for though he strive
To killen bad, keep good alive;
And to fulfil his prince' desire,
Sends word of all that haps in Tyre:
How Thaliard came full bent with sin
And hid intent to murder him;
And that in Tarsus was not best
Longer for him to make his rest.
He, doing so, put forth to seas,
Where when men been, there's seldom ease;
For now the wind begins to blow;
Thunder above, and deeps below,
Make such unquiet, that the ship
Should house him safe is wrackt and split;
And he, good prince, having all lost,
By waves from coast to coast is tost:
All perishen of man, of pelf,
Ne aught escapen but himself;
Till fortune, tired with doing bad,
Threw him ashore, to give him glad:
And here he comes. What shall be next,
Pardon old Gower,—this longs the text. [*Exit.*

SCENE I.

Pentapolis. An open place by the sea-side.

Enter PERICLES, *wet.*

PERICLES.

YET cease your ire, you angry stars of heaven!
Wind, rain, and thunder, remember, earthly man
Is but a substance that must yield to you;
And I, as fits my nature, do obey you:
Alas, the sea hath cast me on the rocks,
Washt me from shore to shore, and left me breath
Nothing to think on but ensuing death:
Let it suffice the greatness of your powers
To have bereft a prince of all his fortunes;
And having thrown him from your watery grave,
Here to have death in peace is all he'll crave.

Enter three FISHERMEN.

FIRST FISHERMAN.

What, ho, Pilch!

SECOND FISHERMAN.

Ha, come and bring away the nets!

FIRST FISHERMAN.

What, Patch-breech, I say!

THIRD FISHERMAN.

What say you, master?

FIRST FISHERMAN.

Look how thou stirr'st now! come away, or I'll fetch thee with a wanion.

THIRD FISHERMAN.

Faith, master, I am thinking of the poor men that were cast away before us even now.

FIRST FISHERMAN.

Alas, poor souls, it grieved my heart to hear what pitiful cries they made to us to help them, when, well-a-day, we could scarce help ourselves.

THIRD FISHERMAN.

Nay, master, said not I as much when I saw the porpus, how he bounced and tumbled? they say they're half-fish, half-flesh: a plague on them, they ne'er come but I look to be washt. Master, I marvel how the fishes live in the sea.

FIRST FISHERMAN.

Why, as men do a-land,—the great ones eat up the little ones: I can compare our rich misers to nothing so fitly as to a whale; a' plays and tumbles, driving the poor fry before him,and at last devours them all at a mouthful: such whales have I heard on o'the land, who never leave gaping till they've swallow'd the whole parish, church, steeple, bells, and all.

PERICLES [*aside*].

A pretty moral.

THIRD FISHERMAN.

But, master, if I had been the sexton, I would have been that day in the belfry.

SECOND FISHERMAN.

Why, man?

THIRD FISHERMAN.

Because he should have swallow'd me too: and when I had been in his belly, I would have kept such a jangling of the bells, that he should never have left, till he cast bells, steeple, church, and parish, up again. But if the good King Simonides were of my mind,—

PERICLES [*aside*].

Simonides!

THIRD FISHERMAN.

We would purge the land of these drones, that rob the bee of her honey.

PERICLES [*aside*].

How from the finny subject of the sea
These fishers tell the infirmities of men;
And from their watery empire recollect
All that may men approve or men detect!—
Peace be at your labour, honest fishermen.

SECOND FISHERMAN.

Honest! good fellow, what's that? If it be a day fits you, search out of the calendar, and nobody look after it.

PERICLES.

May see the sea hath cast upon your coast.

SECOND FISHERMAN.

What a drunken knave was the sea to cast thee in our way!

PERICLES.

A man whom both the waters and the wind,
In that vast tennis-court, have made the ball
For them to play upon, entreats you pity him;
He asks of you, that never used to beg.

FIRST FISHERMAN.

No, friend, cannot you beg? Here's them in our country of Greece gets more with begging than we can do with working.

SECOND FISHERMAN.

Canst thou catch any fishes, then?

PERICLES.

I never practised it.

SECOND FISHERMAN.

Nay, then thou wilt starve, sure; for here's nothing to be got now-a-days, unless thou canst fish for't.

PERICLES.

What I have been I have forgot to know;
But what I am, want teaches me to think on:
A man throng'd up with cold: my veins are chill,
And have no more of life than may suffice
To give my tongue that heat to ask your help;
Which if you shall refuse, when I am dead,
For that I am a man, pray see me buried.

FIRST FISHERMAN.

Die quoth-a? Now gods forbid't! And I have a gown here; come, put it on; keep thee warm. Now, afore me, a handsome fellow! Come, thou shalt go home, and we'll have flesh for holidays, fish for fasting-days, and moreo'er puddings and flap-jacks; and thou shalt be welcome.

PERICLES.

I thank you, sir.

SECOND FISHERMAN.

Hark you, my friend,—you said you could not beg.

PERICLES.

I did but crave.

SECOND FISHERMAN.

But crave! Then I'll turn craver too, and so I shall scape whipping.

PERICLES.

Why, are all your beggars whipt, then?

SECOND FISHERMAN.

O, not all, my friend, not all; for if all your beggars were whipt, I would wish no better office than to be beadle.—But, master, I'll go draw up the net.

[*Exit with* THIRD FISHERMAN.

PERICLES [*aside*].

How well this honest mirth becomes their labour!

FIRST FISHERMAN.

Hark you, sir,—do you know where ye are?

PERICLES.

Not well.

FIRST FISHERMAN.

Why, I'll tell you: this is call'd Pentapolis, and our king the good Simonides.

PERICLES.

The good Simonides, do you call him?

FIRST FISHERMAN.

Ay, sir; and he deserves so to be call'd for his peaceable reign and good government.

PERICLES.

He is a happy king, since he gains from his subjects the name of good by his government. How far is his court distant from this shore?

FIRST FISHERMAN.

Marry, sir, half a day's journey: and I'll tell you, he hath a fair daughter, and to-morrow is her birth-day; and there are princes and knights come from all parts of the world to just and tourney for her love.

PERICLES.

Were my fortunes equal to my desires, I could wish to make one there.

FIRST FISHERMAN.

O, sir, things must be as they may; and what a man cannot get, he may lawfully deal for—his wife's soul.

Enter SECOND *and* THIRD FISHERMEN, *drawing up a net.*

SECOND FISHERMAN.

Help, master, help! here's a fish hangs in the net, like a poor man's right in the law; 'twill hardly come out. Ha! bots on't, 'tis come at last, and 'tis turn'd to a rusty armour.

PERICLES.

An armour, friends! I pray you, let me see it.—
Thanks, fortune, yet, that, after all thy crosses,
Thou givest me somewhat to repair myself;
And though it was mine own, part of my heritage,
Which my dead father did bequeath to me,
With this strict charge, even as he left his life,
'Keep it, my Pericles; it hath been a shield
'Twixt me and death;'—and pointed to this brace;
'For that it saved me, keep it; in like necessity—
The which the gods protect thee from!—may defend thee.'
It kept where I kept, I so dearly loved it;

Till the rough seas, that spare not any man,
Took it in rage, though calm'd have given't again:
I thank thee for't; my shipwrack now's no ill,
Since I have here my father's gift in's will.

FIRST FISHERMAN.

What mean you, sir?

PERICLES.

To beg of you, kind friends, this coat of worth,
For it was sometime target to a king;
I know it by this mark. He loved me dearly,
And for his sake I wish the having of it;
And that you'ld guide me to your sovereign's court,
Where with it I may appear a gentleman;
And if that ever my low fortunes better,
I'll pay your bounties; till then rest your debtor.

FIRST FISHERMAN.

Why, wilt thou tourney for the lady?

PERICLES.

I'll show the virtue I have borne in arms.

FIRST FISHERMAN.

Why, do'e take it, and the gods give thee good on't!

SECOND FISHERMAN.

Ay, but hark you, my friend; 'twas we that made up this garment through the rough seams of the waters: there are certain condolements, certain vails. I hope, sir, if you thrive, you'll remember from whence you had them.

PERICLES.

Believe't, I will.
By your furtherance I am clothed in steel;
And, spite of all the rapture of the sea,
This jewel holds his building on my arm:
Unto thy value I will mount myself
Upon a courser, whose delightful steps
Shall make the gazer joy to see him tread.—
Only, my friends, I yet am unprovided
Of a pair of bases.

SECOND FISHERMAN.

We'll sure provide: thou shalt have my best gown to make thee a pair: and I'll bring thee to the court myself.

PERICLES.

Then honour be but egal to my will,
This day I'll rise, or else add ill to ill. [*Exeunt.*

SCENE II.

The same. A public way or platform leading to the lists. A pavilion by the side of it for the reception of the KING, PRINCESS, LORDS, *&c.*

Enter SIMONIDES, THAISA, LORDS, *and* ATTENDANTS.

SIMONIDES.

ARE the knights ready to begin the triumph?

FIRST LORD.

They are, my liege;
And stay your coming to present themselves.

SIMONIDES.

Return them, we are ready; and our daughter,
In honour of whose birth these triumphs are,
Sits here, like beauty's child, whom nature gat
For men to see, and seeing wonder at.
[*Exit a* LORD.

THAISA.

It pleaseth you, my royal father, to express
My commendations great, whose merit's less.

SIMONIDES.

It's fit it should be so; for princes are
A model, which heaven makes like to itself:
As jewels lose their glory if neglected,
So princes their renown if not respected.
'Tis now your honour, daughter, to explain
The labour of each knight in his device.

THAISA.

Which, to preserve mine honour, I'll perform.

The FIRST KNIGHT *passes by, and his* SQUIRE *presents his shield to the* PRINCESS.

SIMONIDES.

Who is the first that doth prefer himself?

THAISA.

A knight of Sparta, my renowned father;
And the device he bears upon his shield
Is a black Aethiop reaching at the sun;
The word, *Lux tua vita mihi.*

SIMONIDES.

He loves you well that holds his life of you.
[*The* SECOND KNIGHT *passes.*
Who is the second that presents himself?

THAISA.

A prince of Macedon, my royal father;
And the device he bears upon his shield
Is an arm'd knight that's conquer'd by a lady;
The motto thus in Spanish, *Piu por dulzura que por fuerza.* [*The* THIRD KNIGHT *passes.*

SIMONIDES.

And what's the third?

THAISA.

The third of Antioch;
And his device, a wreath of chivalry;
The word, *Me pompæ provexit apex.*
[*The* FOURTH KNIGHT *passes.*

SIMONIDES.

What is the fourth?

THAISA.

A burning torch that's turned upside down;
The word, *Quod me alit, me extinguit.*

SIMONIDES.

Which shows that beauty hath his power and will,
Which can as well inflame as it can kill.
[*The* FIFTH KNIGHT *passes.*

THAISA.

The fifth, an hand environed with clouds,
Holding out gold that's by the touchstone tried;
The motto thus, *Sic spectanda fides.*
[*The* SIXTH KNIGHT *passes.*

SIMONIDES.

And what's
The sixth and last, the which the knight himself
With such a graceful courtesy deliver'd?

THAISA.

He seems to be a stranger; but his present is
A wither'd branch, that's only green at top;
The motto, *In hac spe vivo.*

SIMONIDES.

A pretty moral;
From the dejected state wherein he is,
He hopes by you his fortunes yet may flourish.

FIRST LORD.
He had need mean better than his outward show
Can any way speak in his just commend;
For, by his rusty outside, he appears
To have practised more the whipstock than the lance.

SECOND LORD.
He well may be a stranger, for he comes
To an honour'd triumph strangely furnished.

THIRD LORD.
And on set purpose let his armour rust
Until this day, to scour it in the dust.

SIMONIDES.
Opinion's but a fool, that makes us scan
The outward habit by the inward man.
But stay, the knights are coming: we'll withdraw
Into the gallery. [*Exeunt.*
[*Great shouts, and all cry* 'The mean knight!'

SCENE III.

The same. A hall of state; a banquet prepared.

Enter SIMONIDES, THAISA, LADIES, LORDS, *and* KNIGHTS, *from tilting.*

SIMONIDES.
KNIGHTS,
To say you're welcome were superfluous.
To place upon the volume of your deeds,
As in a title-page, your worth in arms,
Were more than you expect, or more than's fit,
Since every worth in show commends itself.
Prepare for mirth, for mirth becomes a feast:
You are princes and my guests.

THAISA.
But you, my knight and guest;
To whom this wreath of victory I give,
And crown you king of this day's happiness.

PERICLES.
'Tis more by fortune, lady, than my merit.

SIMONIDES.
Call it by what you will, the day is yours;
And here, I hope, is none that envies it.
In framing an artist, art hath thus decreed,
To make some good, but others to exceed;
And you are her labour'd scholar.—Come, queen o'the feast,—
For, daughter, so you are,—here take your place:
Marshal the rest, as they deserve their grace.

KNIGHTS.
We are honour'd much by good Simonides.

SIMONIDES.
Your presence glads our days: honour we love;
For who hates honour hates the gods above.

MARSHAL.
Sir, yonder is your place.

PERICLES.
Some other is more fit.

FIRST KNIGHT.
Contend not, sir; for we are gentlemen
That neither in our hearts nor outward eyes
Envy the great nor do the low despise.

PERICLES.
You are right courteous knights.

SIMONIDES.
Sit, sir, sit.—
By Jove, I wonder, that is king of thoughts,
These cates resist me, he not thought upon.

THAISA [*aside*].
By Juno, that is queen of marriage,
All viands that I eat do seem unsavoury,
Wishing him my meat.—Sure, he's a gallant gentleman.

SIMONIDES.
He's but a country gentleman;
Has done no more than other knights have done;
Has broken a staff or so; so let it pass.

THAISA [*aside*].
To me he seems like diamond to glass.

PERICLES [*aside*].
Yon king's to me like to my father's picture,
Which tells me in that glory once he was;
Had princes sit, like stars, about his throne,
And he the sun, for them to reverence;
None that beheld him, but, like lesser lights,
Did vail their crowns to his supremacy:
Where now his son like a glow-worm in the night,
The which hath fire in darkness, none in light:
Whereby I see that Time's the king of men,
For he's their parent, and he is their grave,
And gives them what he will, not what they crave.

SIMONIDES.
What, are you merry, knights?

FIRST KNIGHT.
Who can be other in this royal presence?

SIMONIDES.
Here, with a cup that's stored unto the brim,—
As you do love, fill to your mistress' lips,—
We drink this health to you.

KNIGHTS.
We thank your Grace.

SIMONIDES.
Yet pause awhile:
Yon knight doth sit too melancholy,
As if the entertainment in our court
Had not a show might countervail his worth.
Note it not you, Thaisa?

THAISA.
What is it
To me, my father?

SIMONIDES.
O, attend, my daughter:
Princes, in this, should live like gods above,
Who freely give to every one that comes
To honour them:
And princes not doing so are like to gnats,
Which make a sound, but kill'd are wonder'd at.
Therefore to make his entertain more sweet,
Here, say we drink this standing-bowl of wine to him.

THAISA.
Alas, my father, it befits not me
Unto a stranger knight to be so bold:
He may my proffer take for an offence,
Since men take women's gifts for impudence.

SIMONIDES.
How!
Do as I bid you, or you'll move me else.

THAISA [*aside*].
Now, by the gods, he could not please me better.
SIMONIDES.
And furthermore tell him, we desire to know of him,
Of whence he is, his name and parentage.
THAISA
The king my father, sir, has drunk to you.
PERICLES.
I thank him.
THAISA.
Wishing it so much blood unto your life.
PERICLES.
I thank both him and you, and pledge him freely.
THAISA.
And further he desires to know of you,
Of whence you are, your name and parentage.
PERICLES.
A gentleman of Tyre,—my name, Pericles;
My education been in arts and arms;—
Who, looking for adventures in the world,
Was by the rough seas reft of ships and men,
And, after shipwrack, driven upon this shore.
THAISA.
He thanks your Grace; names himself Pericles,
A gentleman of Tyre,
Who only by misfortune of the seas
Bereft of ships and men, cast on this shore.
SIMONIDES.
Now, by the gods, I pity his misfortune,
And will awake him from his melancholy.—
Come, gentlemen, we sit too long on trifles,
And waste the time, which looks for other revels.
Even in your armours, as you are addrest,
Will very well become a soldier's dance.
I will not have excuse, with saying this
Loud music is too harsh for ladies' heads,
Since they love men in arms as well as beds.
[*The* KNIGHTS *dance.*
So, this was well askt, 'twas so well perform'd.—
Come, sir;
Here is a lady that wants breathing too:
And I have heard, you knights of Tyre
Are excellent in making ladies trip;
And that their measures are as excellent.
PERICLES.
In those that practise them they are, my lord.
SIMONIDES.
O, that's as much as you would be denied
Of your fair courtesy.
[*The* KNIGHTS *and* LADIES *dance.*
Unclasp, unclasp:
Thanks, gentlemen, to all; all have done well,
[*to* PERICLES] But you the best.—Pages and lights, to conduct
These knights unto their several lodgings!—[*to* PERICLES] Yours, sir.
We have given order to be next our own.
PERICLES.
I am at your Grace's pleasure.
SIMONIDES.
Princes, it is too late to talk of love;
And that's the mark I know you level at:
Therefore each one betake him to his rest;
To-morrow all for speeding do their best.
[*Exeunt.*

SCENE IV.

Tyre. A room in the GOVERNOR'S *house.*

Enter HELICANUS *and* ESCANES.

HELICANUS.
No, Escanes; know this of me,—
Antiochus from incest lived not free:
For which, the most high gods not minding longer
To withhold the vengeance that they had in store,
Due to this heinous capital offence,
Even in the height and pride of all his glory,
When he was seated in a chariot
Of an inestimable value, and his daughter with him,
A fire from heaven came, and shrivell'd up
Their bodies, even to loathing; for they so stunk,
That all those eyes adored them ere their fall
Scorn now their hand should give them burial.
ESCANES.
'Twas very strange.
HELICANUS.
And yet but justice; for though
This king were great, his greatness was no guard
To bar heaven's shaft, but sin had his reward.
ESCANES.
'Tis very true.
Enter two or three LORDS.
FIRST LORD.
See, not a man in private conference
Or council has respect with him but he.
SECOND LORD.
It shall no longer grieve without reproof.
THIRD LORD.
And curst be he that will not second it.
FIRST LORD.
Follow me, then.—Lord Helicane, a word.
HELICANUS.
With me? and welcome:—happy day, my lords.
FIRST LORD.
Know that our griefs are risen to the top,
And now at length they overflow their banks.
HELICANUS.
Your griefs! for what? wrong not the prince you love.
FIRST LORD.
Wrong not yourself, then, noble Helicane;
But if the prince do live, let us salute him,
Or know what ground's made happy by his breath.
If in the world he live, we'll seek him out;
If in his grave he rest, we'll find him there;
And be resolved he lives to govern us,
Or dead, give's cause to mourn his funeral,
And leave us to our free election.
SECOND LORD.
Whose death's indeed the strongest in our censure:
And knowing this kingdom is without a head,—
Like goodly buildings left without a roof,
Soon fall to ruin,—your noble self,
That best know how to rule and how to reign,
We thus submit unto, our sovereign.
ALL.
Live, noble Helicane!
HELICANUS.
For honour's cause, forbear your suffrages:
If that you love Prince Pericles, forbear.

Take I your wish, I leap into the seas,
Where's hourly trouble for a minute's ease.
A twelvemonth longer, let me entreat you
To forbear the absence of your king;
If in which time expired, he not return,
I shall with aged patience bear your yoke.
But if I cannot win you to this love,
Go search like nobles, like noble subjects,
And in your search spend your adventurous worth;
Whom if you find, and win unto return,
You shall like diamonds sit about his crown.

FIRST LORD.
To wisdom he's a fool that will not yield;
And since Lord Helicane enjoineth us,
We with our travels will endeavour it.

HELICANUS.
Then you love us, we you, and we'll clasp hands:
When peers thus knit, a kingdom ever stands.
[*Exeunt.*

SCENE V.

Pentapolis. A room in the palace.

Enter SIMONIDES, *reading of a letter, at one door: the* KNIGHTS *meet him.*

FIRST KNIGHT.
GOOD morrow to the good Simonides.

SIMONIDES.
Knights, from my daughter this I let you know,
That for this twelvemonth she'll not undertake
A married life.
Her reason to herself is only known,
Which yet from her by no means can I get.

SECOND KNIGHT.
May we not get access to her, my lord?

SIMONIDES.
Faith, by no means; she hath so strictly
Tied her to her chamber, that 'tis impossible.
One twelve moons more she'll wear Diana's livery;
This by the eye of Cynthia hath she vow'd,
And on her virgin honour will not break it.

THIRD KNIGHT.
Loth to bid farewell, we take our leaves.
[*Exeunt* KNIGHTS.

SIMONIDES.
So,
They are well dispatcht; now to my daughter's letter:
She tells me here, she'll wed the stranger knight,
Or never more to view nor day nor light.
'Tis well, mistress; your choice agrees with mine;
I like that well:—nay, how absolute she's in't,
Not minding whether I dislike or no!
Well, I do commend her choice;
And will no longer have it be delay'd.—
Soft! here he comes: I must dissemble it.

Enter PERICLES.

PERICLES.
All fortune to the good Simonides!

SIMONIDES.
To you as much, sir! I am beholding to you
For your sweet music this last night: I do
Protest my ears were never better fed
With such delightful pleasing harmony.

PERICLES.
It is your Grace's pleasure to commend;
Not my desert.

SIMONIDES.
Sir, you are music's master.

PERICLES.
The worst of all her scholars, my good lord.

SIMONIDES.
Let me ask you one thing:
What do you think of my daughter, sir?

PERICLES.
A most virtuous princess.

SIMONIDES.
And she is fair too, is she not?

PERICLES.
As a fair day in summer,—wondrous fair.

SIMONIDES.
Sir, my daughter thinks very well of you;
Ay, so well, that you must be her master,
And she will be your scholar: therefore look to it.

PERICLES.
I am unworthy for her schoolmaster.

SIMONIDES.
She thinks not so; peruse this writing else.

PERICLES [*aside*].
What's here?
A letter, that she loves the knight of Tyre!
'Tis the king's subtilty to have my life.—
O, seek not to entrap me, gracious lord,
A stranger and distressed gentleman,
That never aim'd so high to love your daughter,
But bent all offices to honour her.

SIMONIDES.
Thou hast bewitcht my daughter, and thou art
A villain.

PERICLES.
By the gods, I have not:
Never did thought of mine levy offence;
Nor never did my actions yet commence
A deed might gain her love or your displeasure.

SIMONIDES.
Traitor, thou liest.

PERICLES.
Traitor!

SIMONIDES.
Ay, traitor.

PERICLES.
Even in his throat—unless it be the king—
That calls me traitor, I return the lie.

SIMONIDES [*aside*].
Now, by the gods, I do applaud his courage.

PERICLES.
My actions are as noble as my thoughts,
That never relisht of a base descent.
I came unto your court for honour's cause,
And not to be a rebel to her state;
And he that otherwise accounts of me,
This sword shall prove he's honour's enemy.

SIMONIDES.
No?
Here comes my daughter, she can witness it.

Enter THAISA.

PERICLES.
Then, as you are as virtuous as fair,
Resolve your angry father, if my tongue

Did e'er solicit, or my hand subscribe
To any syllable that made love to you.

THAISA.

Why, sir, say if you had,
Who takes offence at that would make me glad?

SIMONIDES.

Yea, mistress, are you so peremptory?—
[*aside*] I am glad on't with all my heart.—
I'll tame you; I'll bring you in subjection.
Will you, not having my consent,
Bestow your love and your affections
Upon a stranger?—[*aside*] who, for aught I know,
May be—nor can I think the contrary—
As great in blood as I myself.—
Therefore hear you, mistress; either frame
Your will to mine,—and you, sir, hear you,
Either be ruled by me, or I'll make you—
Man and wife:
Nay, come, your hands and lips must seal it too;
And being join'd, I'll thus your hopes destroy;—
And for a further grief,—God give you joy!—
What, are you both pleased?

THAISA.

Yes,—if you love me, sir,

PERICLES.

Even as my life, or blood that fosters it.

SIMONIDES.

What, are you both agreed?

BOTH.

Yes, if't please your majesty.

SIMONIDES.

It pleaseth me so well, that I will see you wed;
And then with what haste you can get you to bed.
[*Exeunt.*

ACT III.

Enter GOWER.

GOWER.

NOW sleep yslaked hath the rout;
No din but snores the house about,
Made louder by the o'er-fed breast
Of this most pompous marriage-feast.
The cat, with eyne of burning coal,
Now couches fore the mouse's hole;
And crickets sing at the oven's mouth,
Aye the blither for their drouth.
Hymen hath brought the bride to bed,
Where, by the loss of maidenhead,
A babe is moulded.—Be attent,
And time that is so briefly spent
With your fine fancies quaintly eche:
What's dumb in show I'll plain with speech.

DUMB-SHOW.

Enter PERICLES *and* SIMONIDES, *at one door, with* ATTENDANTS; *a* MESSENGER *meets them, kneels, and gives* PERICLES *a letter:* PERICLES *shows it* SIMONIDES; *the* LORDS *kneel to* PERICLES. *Then enter* THAISA *with child, with* LYCHORIDA, *a nurse: the* KING *shows her the letter; she rejoices: she and* PERICLES *take leave of her father, and depart with* LYCHORIDA *and their* ATTENDANTS. *Then exeunt* SIMONIDES *and the rest.*

By many a dern and painful perch
Of Pericles the careful search,
By the four opposing coigns
Which the world together joins,
Is made with all due diligence
That horse and sail and high expense
Can stead the quest. At last from Tyre—
Fame answering the most strange inquire—
To th'court of King Simonides
Are letters brought, the tenour these:—
Antiochus and his daughter dead;
The men of Tyrus on the head
Of Helicanus would set on
The crown of Tyre, but he will none:
The mutiny he there hastes t'oppress;
Says to 'em, if King Pericles
Come not home in twice six moons,
He, obedient to their dooms,
Will take the crown. The sum of this,
Brought hither to Pentapolis,
Yravished the regions round,
And every one with claps can sound,
'Our heir-apparent is a king!
Who dreamt, who thought of such a thing?'
Brief, he must hence depart to Tyre:
His queen with child makes her desire—
Which who shall cross?—along to go:—
Omit we all their dole and woe:—
Lychorida, her nurse, she takes,
And so to sea. Their vessel shakes
On Neptune's billow; half the flood
Hath their keel cut: but fortune's mood
Varies again; the grisled north
Disgorges such a tempest forth,
That, as a duck for life that dives,
So up and down the poor ship drives:
The lady shrieks, and, well-a-near,
Does fall in travail with her fear:
And what ensues in this fell storm
Shall for itself itself perform.
I nill relate, action may
Conveniently the rest convey;
Which might not what by me is told.
In your imagination hold
This stage the ship, upon whose deck
The sea-tost Pericles appears to speak. [*Exit.*

SCENE I.

Enter PERICLES, *a-shipboard.*

PERICLES.

THOU god of this great vast, rebuke these surges,
Which wash both heaven and hell; and thou, that hast
Upon the winds command, bind them in brass,
Having call'd them from the deep! O, still
Thy deafening, dreadful thunders; gently quench
Thy nimble, sulphurous flashes!—O, how, Lychorida,
How does my queen?—Thou stormest venomously;
Wilt thou spit all thyself?—The seaman's whistle
Is as a whisper in the ears of death,
Unheard.—Lychorida!—Lucina, O
Divinest patroness, and midwife gentle
To those that cry by night, convey thy deity

Aboard our dancing boat; make swift the pangs
Of my queen's travails!

Enter LYCHORIDA, *with an* INFANT.

Now, Lychorida!

LYCHORIDA.

Here is a thing too young for such a place,
Who, if it had conceit, would die, as I
Am like to do: take in your arms this piece
Of your dead queen.

PERICLES.

How, how, Lychorida!

LYCHORIDA.

Patience, good sir; do not assist the storm.
Here's all that is left living of your queen,—
A little daughter: for the sake of it,
Be manly, and take comfort.

PERICLES.

O you gods!
Why do you make us love your goodly gifts,
And snatch them straight away? We here below
Recall not what we give, and therein may
Vie honour with you.

LYCHORIDA.

Patience, good sir,
Even for this charge.

PERICLES.

Now, mild may be thy life!
For a more blusterous birth had never babe:
Quiet and gentle thy conditions! for
Thou art the rudeliest welcome to this world
That ever was prince's child. Happy what follows!
Thou hast as chiding a nativity
As fire, air, water, earth, and heaven can make,
To herald thee from the womb: even at the first
Thy loss is more than can thy portage quit,
With all thou canst find here.—Now, the good gods
Throw their best eyes upon't!

Enter two SAILORS.

FIRST SAILOR.

What courage, sir? God save you!

PERICLES.

Courage enough: I do not fear the flaw;
It hath done to me the worst. Yet, for the love
Of this poor infant, this fresh-new seafarer,
I would it would be quiet.

FIRST SAILOR.

Slack the bolins there!—Thou wilt not, wilt thou?
Blow, and split thyself.

SECOND SAILOR.

But sea-room, an the brine and cloudy billow kiss the moon, I care not.

FIRST SAILOR.

Sir, your queen must overboard: the sea works high, the wind is loud, and will not lie till the ship be clear'd of the dead.

PERICLES.

That's your superstition.

FIRST SAILOR.

Pardon us, sir; with us at sea it hath been still observed; and we are strong in custom. Therefore briefly yield her; for she must overboard straight.

PERICLES.

As you think meet.—Most wretched queen!

LYCHORIDA.

Here she lies, sir.

PERICLES.

A terrible childbed hast thou had, my dear;
No light, no fire: th'unfriendly elements
Forgot thee utterly; nor have I time
To give thee hallow'd to thy grave, but straight
Must cast thee, scarcely coffin'd, in the ooze;
Where, for a monument upon thy bones,
And aye-remaining lamps, the belching whale
And humming water must o'erwhelm thy corpse,
Lying with simple shells.—O Lychorida,
Bid Nestor bring me spices, ink and paper,
My casket and my jewels; and bid Nicander
Bring me the satin coffer: lay the babe
Upon the pillow: hie thee, whiles I say
A priestly farewell to her: suddenly, woman.

[*Exit* LYCHORIDA.

SECOND SAILOR.

Sir, we have a chest beneath the hatches, caulkt and bitumed ready.

PERICLES.

I thank thee.—Mariner, say what coast is this?

SECOND SAILOR.

We are near Tarsus.

PERICLES.

Thither, gentle mariner,
Alter thy course for Tyre. When canst thou reach it?

SECOND SAILOR.

By break of day, if the wind cease.

PERICLES.

O, make for Tarsus!—
There will I visit Cleon, for the babe
Cannot hold out to Tyrus: there I'll leave it
At careful nursing.—Go thy ways, good mariner:
I'll bring the body presently. [*Exeunt.*

SCENE II.

Ephesus. A room in CERIMON'S *house.*

Enter CERIMON, *a* SERVANT, *and some* PERSONS *who have been shipwrackt.*

CERIMON.

PHILEMON, ho!

Enter PHILEMON.

PHILEMON.

Doth my lord call?

CERIMON.

Get fire and meat for these poor men:
'T has been a turbulent and stormy night.

SERVANT.

I have been in many; but such a night as this,
Till now, I ne'er endured.

CERIMON.

Your master will be dead ere you return;
There's nothing can be minister'd to nature
That can recover him.—[*to* PHILEMON] Give this to the pothecary,
And tell me how it works.

[*Exeunt all but* CERIMON.

Enter two GENTLEMEN.

FIRST GENTLEMAN.

Good morrow.

SECOND GENTLEMAN.

Good morrow to your lordship.

CERIMON.
Gentlemen,
Why do you stir so early?

FIRST GENTLEMAN.
Sir,
Our lodgings, standing bleak upon the sea,
Shook as the earth did quake;
The very principals did seem to rend,
And all-to topple: pure surprise and fear
Made me to quit the house.

SECOND GENTLEMAN.
That is the cause we trouble you so early;
'Tis not our husbandry.

CERIMON.
O, you say well.

FIRST GENTLEMAN.
But I much marvel that your lordship, having
Rich tire about you, should at these early hours
Shake off the golden slumber of repose.
'Tis most strange,
Nature should be so conversant with pain,
Being thereto not compell'd.

CERIMON.
I hold it ever,
Virtue and cunning were endowments greater
Than nobleness and riches: careless heirs
May the two latter darken and expend;
But immortality attends the former,
Making a man a god. 'Tis known, I ever
Have studied physic, through which secret art,
By turning o'er authorities, I have—
Together with my practice—made familiar
To me and to my aid the blest infusions
That dwell in vegetives, in metals, stones;
And I can speak of the disturbances
That nature works, and of her cures; which doth give me
A more content in course of true delight
Than to be thirsty after tottering honour,
Or tie my treasure up in silken bags,
To please the fool and death.

SECOND GENTLEMAN.
Your honour has through Ephesus pour'd forth
Your charity, and hundreds call themselves
Your creatures, who by you have been restored:
And not your knowledge, your personal pain, but even
Your purse, still open, hath built Lord Cerimon
Such strong renown as time shall never—

Enter two or three SERVANTS *with a chest.*

FIRST SERVANT.
So; lift there.

CERIMON.
What is that?

FIRST SERVANT.
Sir, even now
Did the sea toss upon our shore this chest:
'Tis of some wrack.

CERIMON.
Set't down, let's look upon't.

SECOND GENTLEMAN.
'Tis like a coffin, sir.

CERIMON.
Whate'er it be,
'Tis wondrous heavy. Wrench it open straight:
If the sea's stomach be o'ercharged with gold,
'Tis a good constraint of fortune it belches upon us.

SECOND GENTLEMAN.
'Tis so, my lord.

CERIMON.
How close 'tis caulkt and bitumed!—
Did the sea cast it up?

FIRST SERVANT.
I never saw so huge a billow, sir,
As tost it upon shore.

CERIMON.
Wrench it open;
Soft!—it smells most sweetly in my sense.

SECOND GENTLEMAN.
A delicate odour.

CERIMON.
As ever hit my nostril.—So, up with it.—
O you most potent gods! what's here? a corse!

FIRST GENTLEMAN.
Most strange!

CERIMON.
Shrouded in cloth of state; balm'd and entreasured with full bags of spices! A passport too!—Apollo, perfect me in the characters! [*Reads from a scroll.*
Here I give to understand,—
If e'er this coffin drive a-land,—
I, King Pericles, have lost
This queen, worth all our mundane cost.
Who finds her, give her burying;
She was the daughter of a king:
Besides this treasure for a fee,
The gods requite his charity!
If thou livest, Pericles, thou hast a heart
That even cracks for woe!—This chanced to-night.

SECOND GENTLEMAN.
Most likely, sir.

CERIMON.
Nay, certainly to-night;
For look how fresh she looks!—They were too rough
That threw her in the sea.—Make a fire within:
Fetch hither all my boxes in my closet.—
[*Exit a* SERVANT.
Death may usurp on nature many hours,
And yet the fire of life kindle again
The o'erprest spirits. I heard of an Egyptian
That had nine hours lien dead,
Who was by good appliance recovered.

Enter a SERVANT, *with boxes, napkins, and fire.*

Well said, well said; the fire and cloths.—
The rough and woeful music that we have,
Cause it to sound, beseech you.
The viol once more:—how thou stirr'st, thou block!—
The music there!—I pray you, give her air.—
Gentlemen, this queen will live: nature awakes;
A warmth breathes out of her: she hath not been
Entranced above five hours: see how she gins
To blow into life's flower again!

FIRST GENTLEMAN.
The heavens,
Through you, increase our wonder, and set up
Your fame for ever.

CERIMON.
She is alive; behold,
Her eyelids, cases to those heavenly jewels

Which Pericles hath lost, begin to part
Their fringes of bright gold; the diamonds
Of a most praised water do appear,
To make the world twice rich.—Live,
And make us weep to hear your fate, fair creature,
Rare as you seem to be! [*She moves.*

THAISA.

O dear Diana,
Where am I? Where's my lord? What world is this?

SECOND GENTLEMAN.

Is not this strange?

FIRST GENTLEMAN.

Most rare.

CERIMON.

Hush, my gentle neighbours!
Lend me your hands; to the next chamber bear her.
Get linen: now this matter must be lookt to,
For her relapse is mortal. Come, come;
And Aesculapius guide us!

[*Exeunt, carrying out* THAISA.

SCENE III.

Tarsus. A room in the GOVERNOR'S *house.*

Enter PERICLES, CLEON, DIONYZA, *and* LYCHORIDA *with* MARINA *in her arms.*

PERICLES.

MOST honour'd Cleon, I must needs be gone;
My twelve months are expired, and Tyrus stands
In a litigious peace. You, and your lady,
Take from my heart all thankfulness! The gods
Make up the rest upon you!

CLEON.

Your shafts of fortune, though they hurt you mortally,
Yet glance full wanderingly on us.

DIONYZA.

O your sweet queen!
That the strict Fates had pleased you had brought her hither,
To have blest mine eyes with her!

PERICLES.

We cannot but obey
The powers above us. Could I rage and roar
As doth the sea she lies in, yet the end
Must be as 'tis. My gentle babe Marina,—whom,
For she was born at sea, I have named so,—here
I charge your charity withal, leaving her
The infant of your care; beseeching you
To give her princely training, that she may be
Manner'd as she is born.

CLEON.

Fear not, my lord, but think
Your grace, that fed my country with your corn,—
For which the people's prayers still fall upon you,—
Must in your child be thought on. If neglection
Should therein make me vile, the common body,
By you relieved, would force me to my duty:
But if to that my nature need a spur,
The gods revenge it upon me and mine,
To the end of generation!

PERICLES.

I believe you;
Your honour and your goodness teach me to't,
Without your vows.—Till she be married, madam,
By bright Diana, whom we honour, all
Unscissar'd shall this hair of mine remain,
Though I show ill in't. So I take my leave.
Good madam, make me blessed in your care
In bringing up my child.

DIONYZA.

I have one myself,
Who shall not be more dear to my respect
Than yours, my lord.

PERICLES.

Madam, my thanks and prayers.

CLEON.

We'll bring your Grace e'en to the edge o'th'shore,
Then give you up to the meek'st Neptune and
The gentlest winds of heaven.

PERICLES.

I will embrace
Your offer. Come, dearest madam.—O, no tears,
Lychorida, no tears:
Look to your little mistress, on whose grace
You may depend hereafter.—Come, my lord.

[*Exeunt.*

SCENE IV.

Ephesus. A room in CERIMON'S *house.*

Enter CERIMON *and* THAISA.

CERIMON.

MADAM, this letter, and some certain jewels,
Lay with you in your coffer: which are
At your command. Know you the character?

THAISA.

It is my lord's.
That I was shipt at sea, I well remember,
Even on my eaning time; but whether there
Delivered, by the holy gods,
I cannot rightly say. But since King Pericles,
My wedded lord, I ne'er shall see again,
A vestal livery will I take me to,
And never more have joy.

CERIMON.

Madam, if this you purpose as ye speak,
Diana's temple is not distant far,
Where you may abide till your date expire.
Moreover, if you please, a niece of mine
Shall there attend you.

THAISA.

My recompense is thanks, that's all;
Yet my good will is great, though the gift small.

[*Exeunt.*

ACT IV.

Enter GOWER.

GOWER.

IMAGINE Pericles arrived at Tyre,
Welcomed and settled to his own desire.
His woeful queen we leave at Ephesus,
Unto Diana there's a votaress.
Now to Marina bend your mind,
Whom our fast-growing scene must find
At Tarsus, and by Cleon train'd

In music, letters; who hath gain'd
Of education all the grace,
Which makes her both the heart and place
Of general wonder. But, alack,
That monster envy, oft the wrack
Of earned praise, Marina's life
Seeks to take off by treason's knife.
And in this kind hath our Cleon
One daughter, and a wench full grown,
Even ripe for marriage-rite; this maid
Hight Philoten: and it is said
For certain in our story, she
Would ever with Marina be:
Be't when she weaved the sleided silk
With fingers long, small, white as milk;
Or when she would with sharp needle wound
The cambric, which she made more sound
By hurting it; or when to the lute
She sung, and made the night-bird mute,
That still records with moan; or when
She would with rich and constant pen
Vail to her mistress Dian; still
This Philoten contends in skill
With absolute Marina: so
With the dove of Paphos might the crow
Vie feathers white. Marina gets
All praises, which are paid as debts,
And not as given. This so darks
In Philoten all graceful marks,
That Cleon's wife, with envy rare,
A present murderer does prepare
For good Marina, that her daughter
Might stand peerless by this slaughter.
The sooner her vile thoughts to stead,
Lychorida, our nurse, is dead:
And cursed Dionyza hath
The pregnant instrument of wrath
Prest for this blow. The unborn event
I do commend to your content:
Only I carry winged time
Post on the lame feet of my rime;
Which never could I so convey,
Unless your thoughts went on my way.—
Dionyza does appear,
With Leonine, a murderer. [*Exit.*

SCENE I.

Tarsus. An open place near the sea-shore.

Enter DIONYZA *and* LEONINE.

DIONYZA.

THY oath remember; thou hast sworn to do't:
'Tis but a blow, which never shall be known.
Thou canst not do a thing in the world so soon,
To yield thee so much profit. Let not conscience,
Which is but cold, inflame love in thy bosom,
Inflame too nicely; nor let pity, which
Even women have cast off, melt thee, but be
A soldier to thy purpose.

LEONINE.

I'll do't; but yet she is a goodly creature.

DIONYZA.

The fitter, then, the gods should have her.—Here
She comes weeping for her only nurse's death.—
Thou art resolved?

LEONINE.

I am resolved.

Enter MARINA, *with a basket of flowers.*

MARINA.

No, I will rob Tellus of her weed,
To strew thy green with flowers; the yellows, blues,
The purple violets, and marigolds,
Shall, as a carpet, hang upon thy grave,
While summer-days do last.—Ay me! poor maid,
Born in a tempest, when my mother died,
This world to me is like a lasting storm,
Whirring me from my friends.

DIONYZA.

How now, Marina! why do you keep alone?
How chance my daughter is not with you? Do not
Consume your blood with sorrowing: you have
A nurse of me. Lord, how your favour's changed
With this unprofitable woe! Come,
Give me your flowers, ere the sea mar it.
Walk with Leonine; the air is quick there,
And it pierces and sharpens the stomach.—Come,
Leonine, take her by the arm, walk with her.

MARINA.

No, I pray you;
I'll not bereave you of your servant.

DIONYZA.

Come, come;
I love the king your father, and yourself,
With more than foreign heart. We every day
Expect him here: when he shall come, and find
Our paragon to all reports thus blasted,
He will repent the breadth of his great voyage;
Blame both my lord and me, that we have taken
No care to your best courses. Go, I pray you,
Walk, and be cheerful once again; reserve
That excellent complexion, which did steal
The eyes of young and old. Care not for me;
I can go home alone.

MARINA.

Well, I will go;
But yet I have no desire to it.

DIONYZA.

Come, come,
I know 'tis good for you.—
Walk half an hour, Leonine, at the least:
Remember what I have said.

LEONINE.

I warrant you, madam.

DIONYZA.

I'll leave you, my sweet lady, for a while:
Pray, walk softly, do not heat your blood:
What! I must have care of you.

MARINA.

My thanks, sweet madam.—
[*Exit* DIONYZA.
Is this wind westerly that blows?

LEONINE.

South-west.

MARINA.

When I was born, the wind was north.

LEONINE.

Was't so?

MARINA.

My father, as nurse said, did never fear,
But cried 'Good seamen!' to the sailors, galling

His kingly hands, haling ropes;
And, clasping to the mast, endured a sea
That almost burst the deck.

LEONINE.

When was this?

MARINA.

When I was born:
Never was waves nor wind more violent;
And from the ladder-tackle washes off
A canvas-climber. 'Ha!' says one, 'wilt out?'
And with a dropping industry they skip
From stem to stern: the boatswain whistles, and
The master calls, and trebles their confusion.

LEONINE.

Come, say your prayers.

MARINA.

What mean you?

LEONINE.

If you require a little space for prayer,
I grant it: pray; but be not tedious, for
The gods are quick of ear, and I am sworn
To do my work with haste.

MARINA.

Why will you kill me?

LEONINE.

To satisfy my lady.

MARINA.

Why would she have me kill'd?
Now, as I can remember, by my troth,
I never did her hurt in all my life:
I never spake bad word, nor did ill turn
To any living creature: believe me, la,
I never kill'd a mouse, nor hurt a fly:
I trod upon a worm once 'gainst my will,
But I wept for it. How have I offended,
Wherein my death might yield her any profit,
Or my life imply her any danger?

LEONINE.

My commission
Is not to reason of the deed, but do't.

MARINA.

You will not do't for all the world, I hope.
You are well-favour'd, and your looks foreshow
You have a gentle heart. I saw you lately,
When you caught hurt in parting two that fought:
Good sooth, it show'd well in you: do so now:
Your lady seeks my life; come you between,
And save poor me, the weaker.

LEONINE.

I am sworn,
And will dispatch.

Enter PIRATES.

FIRST PIRATE.

Hold, villain! [LEONINE *runs away.*

SECOND PIRATE.

A prize! a prize!

THIRD PIRATE.

Half-part, mates, half-part. Come, let's have her aboard suddenly.

[*Exeunt* PIRATES *with* MARINA.

Enter LEONINE.

LEONINE.

These roguing thieves serve the great pirate Valdes;
And they have seized Marina. Let her go:
There's no hope she will return. I'll swear she's dead,
And thrown into the sea.—But I'll see further:
Perhaps they will but please themselves upon her,
Not carry her aboard. If she remain,
Whom they have ravisht must by me be slain.

[*Exit.*

SCENE II.

Mytilene. A room in a brothel.

Enter PANDAR, BAWD, *and* BOULT.

PANDAR.

Boult,—

BOULT.

Sir?

PANDAR.

Search the market narrowly; Mytilene is full of gallants. We lost too much money this mart by being too wenchless.

BAWD.

We were never so much out of creatures. We have but poor three, and they can do no more than they can do; and they with continual action are even as good as rotten.

PANDAR.

Therefore let's have fresh ones, whate'er we pay for them. If there be not a conscience to be used in every trade, we shall never prosper.

BAWD.

Thou sayest true: 'tis not our bringing up of poor bastards,—as, I think, I have brought up some eleven,—

BOULT.

Ay, to eleven; and brought them down again.—But shall I search the market?

BAWD.

What else, man? The stuff we have, a strong wind will blow it to pieces, they are so pitifully sodden.

PANDAR.

Thou sayest true: they're too unwholesome, o' conscience. The poor Transylvanian is dead, that lay with the little baggage.

BOULT.

Ay, she quickly poopt him; she made him roast-meat for worms.—But I'll go search the market.

[*Exit.*

PANDAR.

Three or four thousand chequins were as pretty a proportion to live quietly, and so give over.

BAWD.

Why to give over, I pray you? is it a shame to get when we are old?

PANDAR.

O, our credit comes not in like the commodity, nor the commodity wages not with the danger: therefore, if in our youths we could pick up some pretty estate, 'twere not amiss to keep our door hatcht. Besides, the sore terms we stand upon with the gods will be strong with us for giving o'er.

BAWD.

Come, other sorts offend as well as we.

PANDAR.

As well as we! ay, and better too; we offend worse. Neither is our profession any trade; it's no calling.—But here comes Boult.

Enter BOULT, *with the* PIRATES *and* MARINA.

BOULT [*to* MARINA].

Come your ways.—My masters, you say she's a virgin?

FIRST PIRATE.

O, sir, we doubt it not.

BOULT.

Master, I have gone through for this piece, you see: if you like her, so; if not, I have lost my earnest.

BAWD.

Boult, has she any qualities?

BOULT.

She has a good face, speaks well, and has excellent good clothes: there's no further necessity of qualities can make her be refused.

BAWD.

What's her price, Boult?

BOULT.

I cannot be bated one doit of a thousand pieces.

PANDAR.

Well, follow me, my masters, you shall have your money presently.—Wife, take her in; instruct her what she has to do, that she may not be raw in her entertainment. [*Exeunt* PANDAR *and* PIRATES.

BAWD.

Boult, take you the marks of her,—the colour of her hair, complexion, height, her age, with warrant of her virginity; and cry, 'He that will give most shall have her first.' Such a maidenhead were no cheap thing, if men were as they have been. Get this done as I command you.

BOULT.

Performance shall follow [*Exit.*

MARINA.

Alack that Leonine was so slack, so slow!
He should have struck, not spoke; or that these pirates—
Not enough barbarous—had not o'erboard thrown me
For to seek my mother!

BAWD.

Why lament you, pretty one?

MARINA.

That I am pretty.

BAWD.

Come, the gods have done their part in you.

MARINA.

I accuse them not.

BAWD.

You are light into my hands, where you are like to live.

MARINA.

The more my fault
To scape his hands where I was like to die.

BAWD.

Ay, and you shall live in pleasure.

MARINA.

No.

BAWD.

Yes, indeed shall you, and taste gentlemen of all fashions: you shall fare well; you shall have the difference of all complexions. What! do you stop your ears?

MARINA.

Are you a woman?

BAWD.

What would you have me be, an I be not a woman?

MARINA.

An honest woman, or not a woman.

BAWD.

Marry, whip thee, gosling: I think I shall have something to do with you. Come, you're a young foolish sapling, and must be bow'd as I would have you.

MARINA.

The gods defend me!

BAWD.

If it please the gods to defend you by men, then men must comfort you, men must feed you, men must stir you up.—Boult's return'd.

Enter BOULT.

Now, sir, hast thou cried her through the market?

BOULT.

I have cried her almost to the number of her hairs; I have drawn her picture with my voice.

BAWD.

And I prithee tell me, how dost thou find the inclination of the people, especially of the younger sort?

BOULT.

Faith, they listen'd to me as they would have hearken'd to their father's testament. There was a Spaniard's mouth so water'd, that he went to bed to her very description.

BAWD.

We shall have him here to-morrow with his best ruff on.

BOULT.

To-night, to-night. But, mistress, do you know the French knight that cowers i'the hams?

BAWD.

Who, Monsieur Veroles?

BOULT.

Ay, he: he offer'd to cut a caper at the proclamation; but he made a groan at it, and swore he would see her to-morrow.

BAWD.

Well, well; as for him, he brought his disease hither: here he does but repair it. I know he will come in our shadow, to scatter his crowns in the sun.

BOULT.

Well, if we had of every nation a traveller, we should lodge them with this sign.

BAWD [*to* MARINA].

Pray you, come hither awhile. You have fortunes coming upon you. Mark me: you must seem to do that fearfully which you commit willingly, despise profit where you have most gain. To weep that you live as ye do makes pity in your lovers: seldom but that pity begets you a good opinion, and that opinion a mere profit.

MARINA.

I understand you not.

BOULT.

O, take her home, mistress, take her home: these blushes of hers must be quencht with some present practice.

BAWD.

Thou sayest true, i'faith, so they must; for your bride goes to that with shame which is her way to go with warrant.

BOULT.

Faith, some do, and some do not. But, mistress, if I have bargain'd for the joint,—

BAWD.

Thou mayst cut a morsel off the spit.

BOULT.

I may so.

BAWD.

Who should deny it?—Come, young one, I like the manner of your garments well.

BOULT.

Ay, by my faith, they shall not be changed yet.

BAWD.

Boult, spend thou that in the town: report what a sojourner we have; you'll lose nothing by custom. When nature framed this piece, she meant thee a good turn; therefore say what a paragon she is, and thou hast the harvest out of thine own report.

BOULT.

I warrant you, mistress, thunder shall not so awake the beds of eels as my giving out her beauty stir up the lewdly-inclined. I'll bring home some to-night.

BAWD.

Come your ways; follow me.

MARINA.

If fires be hot, knives sharp, or waters deep,
Untied I still my virgin knot will keep.
Diana, aid my purpose!

BAWD.

What have we to do with Diana? Pray you, will you go with us? [*Exeunt.*

SCENE III.

Tarsus. A room in the GOVERNOR'S *house.*

Enter CLEON *and* DIONYZA.

DIONYZA.

WHY, are you foolish? Can it be undone?

CLEON.

O Dionyza, such a piece of slaughter
The sun and moon ne'er lookt upon!

DIONYZA.

I think
You'll turn a child again.

CLEON.

Were I chief lord of all this spacious world,
I'ld give it to undo the deed.—O lady,
Much less in blood than virtue, yet a princess
To equal any single crown o'the earth
I'the justice of compare!—O villain Leonine!
Whom thou hast poison'd too:
If thou hadst drunk to him, 't had been a kindness
Becoming well thy fact: what canst thou say
When noble Pericles shall demand his child?

DIONYZA.

That she is dead. Nurses are not the Fates,
To foster it, nor ever to preserve.
She died at night; I'll say so. Who can cross it?
Unless you play the pious innocent,
And for an honest attribute cry out
'She died by foul play.'

CLEON.

O, go to. Well, well,
Of all the faults beneath the heavens, the gods
Do like this worst.

DIONYZA.

Be one of those that think
The petty wrens of Tarsus will fly hence,
And open this to Pericles. I do shame
To think of what a noble strain you are,
And of how coward a spirit.

CLEON.

To such proceeding
Who ever but his approbation added,
Though not his prime consent, he did not flow
From honourable sources.

DIONYZA.

Be it so, then:
Yet none does know, but you, how she came dead,
Nor none can know, Leonine being gone.
She did distain my child, and stood between
Her and her fortunes: none would look on her,
But cast their gazes on Marina's face;
Whilst ours was blurted at, and held a malkin,
Not worth the time of day. It pierced me thorough;
And though you call my course unnatural,
You not your child well loving, yet I find
It greets me as an enterprise of kindness
Perform'd to our sole daughter.

CLEON.

Heavens forgive it!

DIONYZA.

And as for Pericles,
What should he say? We wept after her hearse,
And yet we mourn: her monument
Is almost finisht, and her epitaphs
In glittering golden characters express
A general praise to her, and care in us
At whose expense 'tis done.

CLEON.

Thou art like the harpy,
Which, to betray, dost, with thine angel's face,
Seize with thine eagle's talons.

DIONYZA.

You are like one that superstitiously
Doth swear to the gods that winter kills the flies:
But yet I know you'll do as I advise. [*Exeunt.*

Enter GOWER, *before the monument of* MARINA *at Tarsus.*

GOWER.

Thus time we waste, and longest leagues make short;
Sail seas in cockles, have and wish but for't;
Making—to take your imagination—
From bourn to bourn, region to region.
By you being pardon'd, we commit no crime
To use one language in each several clime
Where our scenes seem to live. I do beseech you
To learn of me, who stand i'th'gaps to teach you,
The stages of our story. Pericles
Is now again thwarting the wayward seas,
Attended on by many a lord and knight,
To see his daughter, all his life's delight.
Old Helicanus goes along: behind
Is left to govern it, you bear in mind,
Old Escanes, whom Helicanus late

Advanced in time to great and high estate.
Well-sailing ships and bounteous winds have brought
This king to Tarsus—think his pilot thought;
So with his steerage shall your thoughts grow on—
To fetch his daughter home, who first is gone.
Like motes and shadows see them move awhile;
Your ears unto your eyes I'll reconcile.

DUMB-SHOW.

Enter PERICLES, *at one door, with all his Train;* CLEON *and* DIONYZA *at the other.* CLEON *shows* PERICLES *the tomb; whereat* PERICLES *makes lamentation, puts on sackcloth, and in a mighty passion departs. Then exeunt* CLEON, DIONYZA, *and the rest.*

See how belief may suffer by foul show!
This borrow'd passion stands for true old woe;
And Pericles, in sorrow all devour'd,
With sighs shot through and biggest tears o'er-shower'd,
Leaves Tarsus, and again embarks. He swears
Never to wash his face, nor cut his hairs:
He puts on sackcloth, and to sea. He bears
A tempest, which his mortal vessel tears,
And yet he rides it out. Now please you wit
The epitaph is for Marina writ
By wicked Dionyza.

[*Reads the inscription on* MARINA'S *monument.*

'The fairest, sweet'st, and best lies here,
Who wither'd in her spring of year.
She was of Tyrus the king's daughter,
On whom foul death hath made this slaughter;
Marina was she call'd; and at her birth,
Thetis, being proud, swallow'd some part o'th' earth:
Therefore the earth, fearing to be o'erflow'd,
Hath Thetis' birth-child on the heavens bestow'd:
Wherefore she does—and swears she'll never stint—
Make raging battery upon shores of flint.'
No visor doth become black villainy
So well as soft and tender flattery.
Let Pericles believe his daughter's dead,
And bear his courses to be ordered
By Lady Fortune; while our scene must play
His daughter's woe and heavy well-a-day
In her unholy service. Patience, then,
And think you now are all in Mytilen. [*Exit.*

SCENE IV.

Mytilene. A street before the brothel.

Enter, from the brothel, two GENTLEMEN.

FIRST GENTLEMAN.

DID you ever hear the like?

SECOND GENTLEMAN.

No, nor never shall do in such a place as this, she being once gone.

FIRST GENTLEMAN.

But to have divinity preacht there! did you ever dream of such a thing?

SECOND GENTLEMAN.

No, no. Come, I am for no more bawdy-houses:—shall's go hear the vestals sing?

FIRST GENTLEMAN.

I'll do any thing now that is virtuous; but I am out of the road of rutting for ever. [*Exeunt.*

SCENE V.

The same. A room in the brothel.

Enter PANDAR, BAWD, *and* BOULT.

PANDAR.

WELL, I had rather than twice the worth of her she had ne'er come here.

BAWD.

Fie, fie upon her! she's able to freeze the god Priapus, and undo a whole generation. We must either get her ravisht, or be rid of her. When she should do for clients her fitment, and do me the kindness of our profession, she has me her quirks, her reasons, her master reasons, her prayers, her knees; that she would make a puritan of the devil, if he should cheapen a kiss of her.

BOULT.

Faith, I must ravish her, or she'll disfurnish us of all our cavaliers, and make all our swearers priests.

PANDAR.

Now, the pox upon her green-sickness for me!

BAWD.

Faith, there's no way to be rid on't but by the way to the pox.—Here comes the Lord Lysimachus disguised.

BOULT.

We should have both lord and lown, if the peevish baggage would but give way to customers.

Enter LYSIMACHUS.

LYSIMACHUS.

How now! How a dozen of virginities?

BAWD.

Now, the gods to-bless your honour!

BOULT.

I am glad to see your honour in good health.

LYSIMACHUS.

You may so; 'tis the better for you that your resorters stand upon sound legs. How now, wholesome iniquity! Have you that a man may deal withal, and defy the surgeon?

BAWD.

We have here one, sir, if she would—but there never came her like in Mytilene.

LYSIMACHUS.

If she'd do the deed of darkness, thou wouldst say.

BAWD.

Your honour knows what 'tis to say well enough.

LYSIMACHUS.

Well, call forth, call forth.

BOULT.

For flesh and blood, sir, white and red, you shall see a rose; and she were a rose indeed, if she had but—

LYSIMACHUS.

What, prithee?

BOULT.

O, sir, I can be modest.

LYSIMACHUS.

That dignifies the renown of a bawd, no less than it gives a good report to a member to be chaste. [*Exit* BOULT.

BAWD.

Here comes that which grows to the stalk,—never pluckt yet, I can assure you.

Enter BOULT *with* MARINA.

Is she not a fair creature?

LYSIMACHUS.

Faith, she would serve after a long voyage at sea. Well, there's for you:—leave us.

BAWD.

I beseech your honour, give me leave: a word, and I'll have done presently.

LYSIMACHUS.

I beseech you, do.

BAWD [*to* MARINA].

First, I would have you note, this is an honourable man.

MARINA.

I desire to find him so, that I may worthily note him.

BAWD.

Next, he's the governor of this country, and a man whom I am bound to.

MARINA.

If he govern the country, you are bound to him indeed; but how honourable he is in that, I know not.

BAWD.

Pray you, without any more virginal fencing, will you use him kindly? He will line your apron with gold.

MARINA.

What he will do graciously, I will thankfully receive.

LYSIMACHUS.

Ha' you done?

BAWD.

My lord, she's not paced yet: you must take some pains to work her to your manage.—Come, we will leave his honour and her together.—Go thy ways. [*Exeunt* BAWD, PANDAR, *and* BOULT.

LYSIMACHUS.

Now, pretty one, how long have you been at this trade?

MARINA.

What trade, sir?

LYSIMACHUS.

Why, I cannot name't but I shall offend.

MARINA.

I cannot be offended with my trade. Please you to name it.

LYSIMACHUS.

How long have you been of this profession?

MARINA.

E'er since I can remember.

LYSIMACHUS.

Did you go to't so young? Were you a gamester at five or at seven?

MARINA.

Earlier too, sir, if now I be one.

LYSIMACHUS.

Why, the house you dwell in proclaims you to be a creature of sale.

MARINA.

Do you know this house to be a place of such resort, and will come into't? I hear say you are of honourable parts, and are the governor of this place.

LYSIMACHUS.

Why, hath your principal made known unto you who I am?

MARINA.

Who is my principal?

LYSIMACHUS.

Why, your herb-woman; she that sets seeds and roots of shame and iniquity. O, you have heard something of my power, and so stand aloof for more serious wooing. But I protest to thee, pretty one, my authority shall not see thee, or else look friendly upon thee. Come, bring me to some private place: come, come.

MARINA.

If you were born to honour, show it now;
If put upon you, make the judgement good
That thought you worthy of it.

LYSIMACHUS.

How's this? how's this?—Some more;—be sage.

MARINA.

For me,
That am a maid, though most ungentle fortune
Have placed me in this sty, where, since I came,
Diseases have been sold dearer than physic,—
O, that the gods
Would set me free from this unhallow'd place,
Though they did change me to the meanest bird
That flies i'the purer air!

LYSIMACHUS.

I did not think
Thou couldst have spoke so well; ne'er dreamt thou couldst.
Had I brought hither a corrupted mind,
Thy speech had alter'd it. Hold, here's gold for thee:
Persever in that clear way thou goest,
And the gods strengthen thee!

MARINA.

The good gods preserve you!

LYSIMACHUS.

For me, be you thoughten
That I came with no ill intent; for to me
The very doors and windows savour vilely.
Fare thee well. Thou art a piece of virtue, and
I doubt not but thy training hath been noble.—
Hold, here's more gold for thee.—
A curse upon him, die he like a thief,
That robs thee of thy goodness! If thou dost
Hear from me, it shall be for thy good.

Enter BOULT.

BOULT.

I beseech your honour, one piece for me.

LYSIMACHUS.

Avaunt, thou damned doorkeeper!
Your house, but for this virgin that doth prop it,
Would sink, and overwhelm you. Away! [*Exit.*

BOULT.

How's this? We must take another course with you. If your peevish chastity, which is not worth a breakfast in the cheapest country under the cope, shall undo a whole household, let me be gelded like a spaniel. Come your ways.

MARINA.

Whither would you have me?

BOULT.

I must have your maidenhead taken off, or the common hangman shall execute it. Come your ways. We'll have no more gentlemen driven away. Come your ways, I say.

Enter BAWD.

BAWD.

How now! what's the matter?

BOULT.

Worse and worse, mistress; she has here spoken holy words to the Lord Lysimachus.

BAWD.

O abominable!

BOULT.

She makes our profession as it were to stink afore the face of the gods.

BAWD

Marry, hang her up for ever!

BOULT.

The nobleman would have dealt with her like a nobleman, and she sent him away as cold as a snowball; saying his prayers too.

BAWD.

Boult, take her away; use her at thy pleasure: crack the glass of her virginity, and make the rest malleable.

BOULT.

An if she were a thornier piece of ground than she is, she shall be plough'd.

MARINA.

Hark, hark, you gods!

BAWD.

She conjures: away with her! Would she had never come within my doors!—Marry, hang you!—She's born to undo us.—Will you not go the way of women-kind? Marry, come up, my dish of chastity with rosemary and bays! [*Exit.*

BOULT.

Come, mistress; come your ways with me.

MARINA.

Whither wilt thou have me?

BOULT.

To take from you the jewel you hold so dear.

MARINA.

Prithee, tell me one thing first.

BOULT.

Come now, your one thing.

MARINA.

What canst thou wish thine enemy to be?

BOULT.

Why, I could wish him to be my master, or rather, my mistress.

MARINA.

Neither of these are so bad as thou art,
Since they do better thee in their command.
Thou hold'st a place, for which the pained'st fiend
Of hell would not in reputation change:
Thou art the damned doorkeeper to every
Coistrel that comes inquiring for his Tib;
To the choleric fisting of every rogue
Thy ear is liable; thy food is such
As hath been belcht on by infected lungs.

BOULT.

What would you have me do? go to the wars, would you? where a man may serve seven years for the loss of a leg, and have not money enough in the end to buy him a wooden one?

MARINA.

Do anything but this thou doest. Empty
Old receptacles, or common shores, of filth;
Serve by indenture to the common hangman:
Any of these ways are yet better than this;
For what thou professest, a baboon, could he speak,
Would own a name too dear.—O, that the gods
Would safely deliver me from this place!—
Here, here's gold for thee.
If that thy master would gain by me,
Proclaim that I can sing, weave, sew, and dance,
With other virtues, which I'll keep from boast;
And I will undertake all these to teach.
I doubt not but this populous city will
Yield many scholars.

BOULT.

But can you teach all this you speak of?

MARINA.

Prove that I cannot, take me home again,
And prostitute me to the basest groom
That doth frequent your house.

BOULT.

Well, I will see what I can do for thee: if I can place thee, I will.

MARINA.

But amongst honest women.

BOULT.

Faith, my acquaintance lies little amongst them. But since my master and mistress have bought you, there's no going but by their consent: therefore I will make them acquainted with your purpose, and I doubt not but I shall find them tractable enough. Come, I'll do for thee what I can; come your ways. [*Exeunt.*

ACT V.

Enter GOWER.

GOWER.

MARINA thus the brothel scapes, and chances
Into an honest house, our story says.
She sings like one immortal, and she dances
As goddess-like to her admired lays;
Deep clerks she dumbs; and with her needle composes
Nature's own shape, of bud, bird, branch, or berry,
That even her art sisters the natural roses;
Her inkle, silk, twin with the rubied cherry:
That pupils lacks she none of noble race,
Who pour their bounty on her; and her gain
She gives the cursed bawd. Here we her place;
And to her father turn our thoughts again,
Where we left him, on the sea. We there him lost:
Whence, driven before the winds, he is arrived
Here where his daughter dwells; and on this coast
Suppose him now at anchor. The city strived
God Neptune's annual feast to keep: from whence
Lysimachus our Tyrian ship espies,
His banners sable, trimm'd with rich expense;
And to him in his barge with fervour hies.

In your supposing once more put your sight
Of heavy Pericles; think this his bark:
Where what is done in action, more, if might,
Shall be discover'd; please you, sit, and hark.
[*Exit.*

SCENE I.

On board PERICLES' *ship, off Mytilene. A pavilion on deck, with a curtain before it;* PERICLES *within it, reclined on a couch. A barge lying beside the Tyrian vessel.*

Enter two SAILORS, *one belonging to the Tyrian vessel, the other to the barge; to them* HELICANUS.

TYRIAN SAILOR [*to the* SAILOR *of Mytilene*].

WHERE is Lord Helicanus? he can resolve you. O, here he is.—Sir, there is a barge put off from Mytilene, and in it is Lysimachus the governor, who craves to come aboard. What is your will?

HELICANUS.

That he have his. Call up some gentlemen.

TYRIAN SAILOR.

Ho, gentlemen! my lord calls.

Enter two or three GENTLEMEN.

FIRST GENTLEMAN.

Doth your lordship call?

HELICANUS.

Gentlemen, there is some of worth would come aboard: I pray, greet him fairly.

[*The* GENTLEMEN *and the two* SAILORS *descend, and go on board the barge.*

Enter, from thence, LYSIMACHUS *and* LORDS, *with the* GENTLEMEN *and the two* SAILORS.

TYRIAN SAILOR.

Sir, this is the man that can, in aught you would, resolve you.

LYSIMACHUS.

Hail, reverend sir! the gods preserve you!

HELICANUS.

And you, sir, to outlive the age I am,
And die as I would do.

LYSIMACHUS.

You wish me well.
Being on shore, honouring of Neptune's triumphs,
Seeing this goodly vessel ride before us,
I made to it, to know of whence you are.

HELICANUS.

First, what is your place?

LYSIMACHUS.

I am the governor
Of this place you lie before.

HELICANUS.

Sir,
Our vessel is of Tyre, in it the king;
A man who for this three months hath not spoken
To any one, nor taken sustenance
But to prorogue his grief.

LYSIMACHUS.

Upon what ground is his distemperature?

HELICANUS.

'Twould be too tedious to repeat;
But the main grief springs from the loss
Of a beloved daughter and a wife.

LYSIMACHUS.

May we not see him?

HELICANUS.

You may;
But bootless is your sight,—he will not speak
To any.

LYSIMACHUS.

Yet let me obtain my wish.

HELICANUS.

Behold him. [*Draws the curtains, and discovers* PERICLES.] This was a goodly person,
Till the disaster that, one mortal night,
Drove him to this.

LYSIMACHUS.

Sir king, all hail! the gods preserve you!
Hail, royal sir!

HELICANUS.

It is in vain; he will not speak to you.

FIRST LORD.

Sir,
We have a maid in Mytilen, I durst wager,
Would win some words of him.

LYSIMACHUS.

'Tis well bethought.
She, questionless, with her sweet harmony
And other chosen attractions, would allure,
And make a battery through his deafen'd parts,
Which now are midway stopt:
She is all happy as the fairest of all,
And, with her fellow maids, is now upon
The leafy shelter that abuts against
The island's side.

[*Whispers* FIRST LORD; *who goes off in the barge of* LYSIMACHUS.

HELICANUS.

Sure, all's effectless; yet nothing we'll omit
That bears recovery's name. But, since your kindness
We have stretcht thus far, let us beseech you
That for our gold we may provisiòn have,
Wherein we are not destitute for want,
But weary for the staleness.

LYSIMACHUS.

O, sir, a courtesy
Which if we should deny, the most just gods
For every graff would send a caterpillar,
And so inflict our province.—Yet once more
Let me entreat to know at large the cause
Of your king's sorrow.

HELICANUS.

Sit, sir: I will recount it to you:—
But, see, I am prevented.

Enter, from the barge, FIRST LORD, *with* MARINA *and a young* LADY.

LYSIMACHUS.

O, here is
The lady that I sent for.—Welcome, fair one!—
Is't not a goodly presence?

HELICANUS.

She's a gallant lady.

LYSIMACHUS.

She's such a one, that, were I well assured
Came of a gentle kind and noble stock,
I'ld wish no better choice, and think me rarely wed.—
Fair one, all goodness that consists in bounty
Expect even here, where is a kingly patient:
If that thy prosperous and artificial feat

Can draw him but to answer thee in aught,
Thy sacred physic shall receive such pay
As thy desires can wish.

MARINA.

Sir, I will use
My utmost skill in his recovery,
Provided
That none but I and my companion maid
Be suffer'd to come near him.

LYSIMACHUS.

Come, let's leave her;
And the gods make her prosperous!

[MARINA *sings.*

LYSIMACHUS.

Markt he your music?

MARINA.

No, nor lookt on us.

LYSIMACHUS.

See, she will speak to him.

MARINA.

Hail, sir! my lord, lend ear.

PERICLES.

Hum, ha!

MARINA.

I am a maid,
My lord, that ne'er before invited eyes,
But have been gazed on like a comet: she speaks,
My lord, that, may be, hath endured a grief
Might equal yours, if both were justly weigh'd.
Though wayward fortune did malign my state,
My derivation was from ancestors
Who stood equivalent with mighty kings:
But time hath rooted out my parentage,
And to the world and awkward casualties
Bound me in servitude.—[*aside*] I will desist;
But there is something glows upon my cheek,
And whispers in mine ear, 'Go not till he speak.'

PERICLES.

My fortunes—parentage—good parentage—
To equal mine!—was it not thus? what say you?

MARINA.

I said, my lord, if you did know my parentage,
You would not do me violence.

PERICLES.

I do think so.—Pray you, turn your eyes upon
me.
You are like something that—What country-
woman?
Here of these shores?

MARINA.

No, nor of any shores:
Yet I was mortally brought forth, and am
No other than I appear.

PERICLES.

I am great with woe, and shall deliver weeping.
My dearest wife was like this maid, and such a
one
My daughter might have been: my queen's square
brows;
Her stature to an inch; as wand-like straight;
As silver-voiced; her eyes as jewel-like,
And cased as richly; in pace another Juno;
Who starves the ears she feeds, and makes them
hungry,
The more she gives them speech.—Where do you
live?

MARINA.

Where I am but a stranger: from the deck
You may discern the place.

PERICLES.

Where were you bred?
And how achieved you these endowments, which
You make more rich to owe?

MARINA.

If I should tell my history, it would seem
Like lies disdain'd in the reporting.

PERICLES.

Prithee, speak:
Falseness cannot come from thee; for thou look'st
Modest as Justice, and thou seem'st a palace
For the crown'd Truth to dwell in: I will believe
thee,
And make my senses credit thy relation
To points that seem impossible; for thou look'st
Like one I loved indeed. What were thy friends?
Didst thou not say, when I did push thee back,—
Which was when I perceived thee,—that thou
camest
From good descending?

MARINA.

So indeed I did.

PERICLES.

Report thy parentage. I think thou said'st
Thou hadst been tost from wrong to injury,
And that thou thought'st thy griefs might equal
mine,
If both were open'd.

MARINA.

Some such thing
I said, and said no more but what my thoughts
Did warrant me was likely.

PERICLES.

Tell thy story;
If thine consider'd prove the thousandth part
Of my endurance, thou art a man, and I
Have suffer'd like a girl: yet thou dost look
Like Patience gazing on kings' graves, and smil-
ing
Extremity out of act. What were thy friends?
How lost thou them? Thy name, my most kind
virgin?
Recount, I do beseech thee: come, sit by me.

MARINA.

My name is Marina.

PERICLES.

O, I am mockt,
And thou by some incensed god sent hither
To make the world to laugh at me.

MARINA.

Patience, good sir,
Or here I'll cease.

PERICLES.

Nay, I'll be patient,
Thou little know'st how thou dost startle me,
To call thyself Marina.

MARINA.

The name
Was given me by one that had some power,—
My father, and a king.

PERICLES.

How! a king's daughter?
And call'd Marina?

MARINA.

You said you would believe me;
But, not to be a troubler of your peace,
I will end here.

PERICLES.

But are you flesh and blood?
Have you a working pulse? and are no fairy?
Motion!—Well; speak on. Where were you born?
And wherefore call'd Marina?

MARINA.

Call'd Marina
For I was born at sea.

PERICLES.

At sea! what mother?

MARINA.

My mother was the daughter of a king;
Who died the minute I was born,
As my good nurse Lychorida hath oft
Deliver'd weeping.

PERICLES.

O, stop there a little!—
[*aside*] This is the rarest dream that e'er dull sleep
Did mock sad fools withal: this cannot be:
My daughter's buried.—Well:—where were you bred?
I'll hear you more, to the bottom of your story,
And never interrupt you.

MARINA.

You scorn: believe me, 'twere best I did give o'er.

PERICLES.

I will believe you by the syllable
Of what you shall deliver. Yet, give me leave:—
How came you in these parts? where were you bred?

MARINA.

The king my father did in Tarsus leave me;
Till cruel Cleon, with his wicked wife,
Did seek to murder me: and having woo'd
A villain to attempt it, who having drawn to do't,
A crew of pirates came and rescued me;
Brought me to Mytilene. But, good sir,
Whither will you have me? Why do you weep? It may be
You think me an impostor: no, good faith;
I am the daughter to King Pericles,
If good King Pericles be.

PERICLES.

Ho, Helicanus!

HELICANUS.

Calls my lord?

PERICLES.

Thou art a grave and noble counsellor,
Most wise in general: tell me, if thou canst,
What this maid is, or what is like to be,
That thus hath made me weep?

HELICANUS.

I know not; but
Here is the regent, sir, of Mytilene
Speaks nobly of her.

LYSIMACHUS.

She never would tell
Her parentage; being demanded that,
She would sit still and weep.

PERICLES.

O Helicanus, strike me, honour'd sir;
Give me a gash, put me to present pain;
Lest this great sea of joys rushing upon me
O'erbear the shores of my mortality,
And drown me with their sweetness.—O, come hither,
Thou that begett'st him that did thee beget;
Thou that wast born at sea, buried at Tarsus,
And found at sea again!—O Helicanus,
Down on thy knees, thank the holy gods as loud
As thunder threatens us: this is Marina.—
What was thy mother's name? tell me but that,
For truth can never be confirm'd enough,
Though doubts did ever sleep.

MARINA.

First, sir, I pray,
What is your title?

PERICLES.

I am Pericles of Tyre: but tell me now
My drown'd queen's name, as in the rest you said
Thou hast been godlike perfect:
Be heir of kingdoms, and another life
To Pericles thy father.

MARINA.

Is it no more to be your daughter than
To say my mother's name was Thaisa?
Thaisa was my mother, who did end
The minute I began.

PERICLES.

Now, blessing on thee! rise; thou art my child.—
Give me fresh garments.—Mine own, Helicanus,—
She is not dead at Tarsus, as she should have been,
By savage Cleon: she shall tell thee all;
When thou shalt kneel, and justify in knowledge
She is thy very princess.—Who is this?

HELICANUS.

Sir, 'tis the governor of Mytilene,
Who, hearing of your melancholy state,
Did come to see you.

PERICLES.

I embrace you.
Give me my robes.—I am wild in my beholding.—
O heavens bless my girl!—But, hark, what music?—
Tell Helicanus, my Marina, tell him
O'er, point by point, for yet he seems to doubt,
How sure you are my daughter.—But, what music?

HELICANUS.

My lord, I hear none.

PERICLES.

None!
The music of the spheres!—List, my Marina.

LYSIMACHUS.

It is not good to cross him; give him way.

PERICLES.

Rarest sounds! Do ye not hear?

LYSIMACHUS.

My lord, I hear. [*Music.*

PERICLES.

Most heavenly music!
It nips me unto listening, and thick slumber
Hangs upon mine eyes: let me rest. [*Sleeps.*

LYSIMACHUS.

A pillow for his head:—
So, leave him all.—Well, my companion friends,

If this but answer to my just belief,
I'll well remember you.
[*Exeunt all but* PERICLES.

DIANA *appears.*

DIANA.

My temple stands in Ephesus: hie thee thither,
And do upon mine altar sacrifice.
There, when my maiden priests are met together,
Before the people all,
Reveal how thou at sea didst lose thy wife:
To mourn thy crosses, with thy daughter's, call,
And give them repetition to the life.
Or perform my bidding, or thou livest in woe;
Do it, and happy; by my silver bow!
Awake, and tell thy dream. [*Disappears.*

PERICLES.

Celestial Dian, goddess argentine,
I will obey thee.—Helicanus!

Enter HELICANUS, LYSIMACHUS, MARINA, *&c.*

HELICANUS.

Sir?

PERICLES.

My purpose was for Tarsus, there to strike
The inhospitable Cleon; but I am
For other service first: toward Ephesus
Turn our blown sails; eftsoons I'll tell thee why.—
[*to* LYSIMACHUS] Shall we refresh us, sir, upon your shore,
And give you gold for such provision
As our intents will need?

LYSIMACHUS.

Sir,
With all my heart; and, when you come ashore,
I have another suit.

PERICLES.

You shall prevail,
Were it to woo my daughter; for it seems
You have been noble towards her.

LYSIMACHUS.

Sir, lend me your arm.

PERICLES.

Come, my Marina. [*Exeunt.*

Enter GOWER, *before the temple of* DIANA *at Ephesus.*

GOWER.

Now our sands are almost run;
More a little, and then dumb.
This, my last boon, give me,—
For such kindness must relieve me,
That you aptly will suppose
What pageantry, what feats, what shows,
What minstrelsy, and pretty din,
The regent made in Mytilin,
To greet the king. So he thrived,
That he is promised to be wived
To fair Marina; but in no wise
Till he had done his sacrifice,
As Dian bade: whereto being bound,
The interim, pray you, all confound.
In feather'd briefness sails are fill'd,
And wishes fall out as they're will'd.
At Ephesus, the temple see,
Our king, and all his company.
That he can hither come so soon,
Is by your fancies' thankful doom. [*Exit.*

SCENE II.

The temple of DIANA *at Ephesus;* THAISA *standing near the altar, as high priestess; a number of* VIRGINS *on each side;* CERIMON *and other* INHABITANTS *of Ephesus attending.*

Enter PERICLES, *with his Train;* LYSIMACHUS, HELICANUS, MARINA, *and a* LADY.

PERICLES.

HAIL, Dian! to perform thy just command,
I here confess myself the king of Tyre;
Who, frighted from my country, did wed
At Pentapolis the fair Thaisa.
At sea in childbed died she, but brought forth
A maid-child call'd Marina; who, O goddess,
Wears yet thy silver livery. She at Tarsus
Was nurst with Cleon; who at fourteen years
He sought to murder: but her better stars
Brought her to Mytilene; 'gainst whose shore
Riding, her fortunes brought the maid aboard us,
Where, by her own most clear remembrance, she
Made known herself my daughter.

THAISA.

Voice and favour!—
You are, you are—O royal Pericles!— [*Faints.*

PERICLES.

What means the nun? she dies! help, gentlemen!

CERIMON.

Noble sir,
If you have told Diana's altar true,
This is your wife.

PERICLES.

Reverend appearer, no;
I threw her overboard with these very arms.

CERIMON.

Upon this coast, I warrant you.

PERICLES.

'Tis most certain.

CERIMON.

Look to the lady;—O, she's but overjoy'd.—
Early one blustering morn this lady was
Thrown upon this shore. I oped the coffin,
Found there rich jewels; recover'd her, and placed her
Here in Diana's temple.

PERICLES.

May we see them?

CERIMON.

Great sir, they shall be brought you to my house,
Whither I invite you.—Look, Thaisa is
Recover'd.

THAISA.

O, let me look!
If he be none of mine, my sanctity
Will to my sense bend no licentious ear,
But curb it, spite of seeing.—O, my lord,
Are you not Pericles? Like him you speak,
Like him you are: did you not name a tempest,
A birth, and death?

PERICLES.

The voice of dead Thaisa!

THAISA.

That Thaisa am I, supposed dead
And drown'd.

PERICLES.

Immortal Dian!

THAISA.

Now I know you better.—
When we with tears parted Pentapolis,
The king my father gave you such a ring.

[*Shows a ring.*

PERICLES.

This, this: no more, you gods! your present kindness
Makes my past miseries sport: you shall do well,
That on the touching of her lips I may
Melt, and no more be seen.—O, come, be buried
A second time within these arms.

MARINA.

My heart
Leaps to be gone into my mother's bosom.

[*Kneels to* THAISA.

PERICLES.

Look, who kneels here! Flesh of thy flesh, Thaisa;
Thy burden at the sea, and call'd Marina
For she was yielded there.

THAISA.

Blest, and mine own!

HELICANUS.

Hail, madam, and my queen!

THAISA.

I know you not.

PERICLES.

You have heard me say, when I did fly from Tyre,
I left behind an ancient substitute:
Can you remember what I call'd the man?
I have named him oft.

THAISA.

'Twas Helicanus, then.

PERICLES.

Still confirmation:
Embrace him, dear Thaisa; this is he.
Now do I long to hear how you were found;
How possibly preserved; and who to thank,
Besides the gods, for this great miracle.

THAISA.

Lord Cerimon, my lord; this is the man,
Through whom the gods have shown their power, that can
From first to last resolve you.

PERICLES.

Reverend sir,
The gods can have no mortal officer
More like a god than you. Will you deliver
How this dead queen re-lives?

CERIMON.

I will, my lord.
Beseech you, first go with me to my house,
Where shall be shown you all was found with her;
How she came placed here in the temple;
No needful thing omitted.

PERICLES.

Pure Dian, bless thee for thy vision! I
Will offer night-oblations to thee,—Thaisa,
This prince, the fair-betrothed of your daughter,
Shall marry her at Pentapolis.—And now,
This ornament
Makes me look dismal will I clip to form;
And what this fourteen years no razor toucht,
To grace thy marriage-day, I'll beautify.

THAISA.

Lord Cerimon hath letters of good credit, sir,
My father's dead.

PERICLES.

Heavens make a star of him! Yet there, my queen,
We'll celebrate their nuptials, and ourselves
Will in that kingdom spend our following days:
Our son and daughter shall in Tyrus reign.—
Lord Cerimon, we do our longing stay
To hear the rest untold: sir, lead's the way.

[*Exeunt.*

Enter GOWER.

GOWER.

In Antiochus and his daughter you have heard
Of monstrous lust the due and just reward:
In Pericles, his queen and daughter, seen,
Although assail'd with fortune fierce and keen,
Virtue preserved from fell destruction's blast,
Led on by heaven, and crown'd with joy at last:
In Helicanus may you well descry
A figure of truth, of faith, of loyalty:
In reverend Cerimon there well appears
The worth that learned charity aye wears:
For wicked Cleon and his wife, when fame
Had spread their cursed deed, and honour'd name
Of Pericles, to rage the city turn,
That him and his they in his palace burn;
The gods for murder seemed so content
To punish them,—although not done, but meant.
So, on your patience evermore attending,
New joy wait on you! Here our play has ending.

[*Exit.*

CYMBELINE

DRAMATIS PERSONAE

CYMBELINE, *King of Britain.*
CLOTEN, *son to the Queen by a former husband.*
POSTHUMUS LEONATUS, *a gentleman, husband to Imogen.*
BELARIUS, *a banisht lord, disguised under the name of Morgan.*
GUIDERIUS, ARVIRAGUS, *sons to Cymbeline, disguised under the names of Polydore and Cadwal, supposed sons of Belarius.*
PHILARIO, *friend to Posthumus,* IACHIMO, *friend to Philario,* *Italians.*
A FRENCH GENTLEMAN, *friend to Philario.*
CAIUS LUCIUS, *general of the Roman forces.*
A ROMAN CAPTAIN.
TWO BRITISH CAPTAINS.
PISANIO, *servant to Posthumus.*
CORNELIUS, *a physician.*
TWO LORDS *of Cymbeline's court.*
TWO GENTLEMEN *of the same.*
TWO GAOLERS.

QUEEN, *wife to Cymbeline.*
IMOGEN, *daughter to Cymbeline by a former Queen.*
HELEN, *woman to Imogen.*

LORDS, LADIES, ROMAN SENATORS, TRIBUNES, *a* SOOTHSAYER, *a* DUTCH GENTLEMAN, *a* SPANISH GENTLEMAN, MUSICIANS, OFFICERS, CAPTAINS, SOLDIERS, MESSENGERS, *and* ATTENDANTS.

APPARITIONS.

SCENE—*Sometimes in Britain, sometimes in Italy.*

ACT I. SCENE I.

Britain. The garden of CYMBELINE'S *palace.*

Enter two GENTLEMEN.

FIRST GENTLEMAN.
YOU do not meet a man but frowns: our bloods
No more obey the heavens than our courtiers
Still seem as does the king.

SECOND GENTLEMAN.
But what's the matter?

FIRST GENTLEMAN.
His daughter, and the heir of's kingdom, whom
He purposed to his wife's sole son—a widow
That late he married—hath referr'd herself
Unto a poor but worthy gentleman: she's wedded;
Her husband banisht; she imprison'd: all
Is outward sorrow; though, I think, the king
Be toucht at very heart.

SECOND GENTLEMAN.
None but the king?

FIRST GENTLEMAN.
He that hath lost her too: so is the queen,
That most desired the match: but not a courtier,
Although they wear their faces to the bent
Of the king's looks, hath a heart that is not
Glad at the thing they scowl at.

SECOND GENTLEMAN.
And why so?

FIRST GENTLEMAN.
He that hath mist the princess is a thing
Too bad for bad report: and he that hath her—
I mean, that married her, alack, good man!
And therefore banisht—is a creature such
As, to seek through the regions of the earth
For one his like, there would be something failing
In him that should compare:—I do not think
So fair an outward, and such stuff within,
Endows a man but he.

SECOND GENTLEMAN.
You speak him far.

FIRST GENTLEMAN.
I do extend him, sir, within himself;
Crush him together, rather than unfold
His measure duly.

SECOND GENTLEMAN.
What's his name and birth?

FIRST GENTLEMAN.
I cannot delve him to the root: his father
Was call'd Sicilius, who did join his honour
Against the Romans with Cassibelan,
But had his titles by Tenantius, whom
He served with glory and admired success,—
So gain'd the sur-addition Leonatus:
And had, besides this gentleman in question,
Two other sons, who, in the wars o'the time,
Died with their swords in hand; for which their father,
Then old and fond of issue, took such sorrow,
That he quit being; and his gentle lady,
Big of this gentleman our theme, deceased
As he was born. The king he takes the babe
To his protection; calls him Posthumus Leonatus;
Breeds him, and makes him of his bed-chamber;
Puts to him all the learnings that his time
Could make him the receiver of; which he took,
As we do air, fast as 'twas minister'd;
And in's spring became a harvest; lived in court—
Which rare it is to do—most praised, most loved;
A sample to the youngest; to the more mature
A glass that feated them; and to the graver
A child that guided dotards: to his mistress,
For whom he now is banisht,—her own price
Proclaims how she esteem'd him and his virtue;
By her election may be truly read
What kind of man he is.

SECOND GENTLEMAN.
I honour him
Even out of your report. But, pray you, tell me,
Is she sole child to the king?

FIRST GENTLEMAN.
His only child.
He had two sons,—if this be worth your hearing,
Mark it,—the eldest of them at three years old,
I'the swathing-clothes the other, from their nursery
Were stoln; and to this hour no guess in knowledge
Which way they went.

SECOND GENTLEMAN.
How long is this ago?
FIRST GENTLEMAN.
Some twenty years.
SECOND GENTLEMAN.
That a king's children should be so convey'd!
So slackly guarded! and the search so slow,
That could not trace them!
FIRST GENTLEMAN.
Howsoe'er 'tis strange,
Or that the negligence may well be laught at,
Yet is it true, sir.
SECOND GENTLEMAN.
I do well believe you.
FIRST GENTLEMAN.
We must forbear: here comes the gentleman,
The queen, and princess. [*Exeunt.*
Enter the QUEEN, POSTHUMUS, *and* IMOGEN.
QUEEN.
No, be assured you shall not find me, daughter,
After the slander of most stepmothers,
Evil-eyed unto you: you're my prisoner, but
Your gaoler shall deliver you the keys
That lock up your restraint.—For you, Posthumus,
So soon as I can win the offended king,
I will be known your advocate: marry, yet
The fire of rage is in him; and 'twere good
You lean'd unto his sentence with what patience
Your wisdom may inform you.
POSTHUMUS LEONATUS.
Please your highness,
I will from hence to-day.
QUEEN.
You know the peril.—
I'll fetch a turn about the garden, pitying
The pangs of barr'd affections; though the king
Hath charged you should not speak together.
[*Exit.*
IMOGEN.
O
Dissembling courtesy! How fine this tyrant
Can tickle where she wounds!—My dearest husband,
I something fear my father's wrath; but nothing—
Always reserved my holy duty—what
His rage can do on me: you must be gone;
And I shall here abide the hourly shot
Of angry eyes; not comforted to live,
But that there is this jewel in the world,
That I may see again.
POSTHUMUS LEONATUS.
My queen! my mistress!
O lady, weep no more, lest I give cause
To be suspected of more tenderness
Than doth become a man! I will remain
The loyal'st husband that did e'er plight troth:
My residence in Rome at one Philario's;
Who to my father was a friend, to me
Known but by letter: thither write, my queen,
And with mine eyes I'll drink the words you send,
Though ink be made of gall.
Enter QUEEN.
QUEEN.
Be brief, I pray you:
If the king come, I shall incur I know not
How much of his displeasure.—[*aside*] Yet I'll move him
To walk this way: I never do him wrong,
But he does buy my injuries, to be friends;
Pays dear for my offences. [*Exit.*
POSTHUMUS LEONATUS.
Should we be taking leave
As long a term as yet we have to live,
The loathness to depart would grow. Adieu!
IMOGEN.
Nay, stay a little:
Were you but riding forth to air yourself,
Such parting were too petty. Look here, love;
This diamond was my mother's: take it, heart;
But keep it till you woo another wife,
When Imogen is dead.
POSTHUMUS LEONATUS.
How, how! another?—
You gentle gods, give me but this I have,
And sear up my embracements from a next
With bonds of death!—Remain, remain thou here
[*Putting on the ring.*
While sense can keep it on! And, sweetest, fairest,
As I my poor self did exchange for you,
To your so infinite loss; so in our trifles
I still win of you: for my sake wear this;
It is a manacle of love; I'll place it
Upon this fairest prisoner.
[*Putting a bracelet upon her arm.*
IMOGEN.
O the gods!
When shall we see again?
POSTHUMUS LEONATUS.
Alack, the king!
Enter CYMBELINE *and* LORDS.
CYMBELINE.
Thou basest thing, avoid! hence, from my sight!
If after this command thou fraught the court
With thy unworthiness, thou diest: away!
Thou'rt poison to my blood.
POSTHUMUS LEONATUS.
The gods protect you!
And bless the good remainders of the court!
I am gone. [*Exit.*
IMOGEN.
There cannot be a pinch in death
More sharp than this is.
CYMBELINE.
O disloyal thing,
That shouldst repair my youth, thou heap'st
A year's age on me!
IMOGEN.
I beseech you, sir,
Harm not yourself with your vexation:
I am senseless of your wrath; a touch more rare
Subdues all pangs, all fears.
CYMBELINE.
Past grace? obedience?
IMOGEN.
Past hope, and in despair; that way, past grace.
CYMBELINE.
That mightst have had the sole son of my queen!
IMOGEN.
O blest, that I might not! I chose an eagle,
And did avoid a puttock.

CYMBELINE.

Thou took'st a beggar; wouldst have made my throne
A seat for baseness.

IMOGEN.

No; I rather added
A lustre to it.

CYMBELINE.

O thou vile one!

IMOGEN.

Sir,
It is your fault that I have loved Posthumus:
You bred him as my playfellow; and he is
A man worth any woman; overbuys me
Almost the sum he pays.

CYMBELINE.

What, art thou mad!

IMOGEN.

Almost, sir: heaven restore me!—Would I were
A neat-herd's daughter, and my Leonatus
Our neighbour shepherd's son!

CYMBELINE.

Thou foolish thing!—

Enter QUEEN.

They were again together: you have done
Not after our command. Away with her,
And pen her up.

QUEEN.

Beseech your patience.—Peace,
Dear lady daughter, peace!—Sweet sovereign,
Leave us to ourselves; and make yourself some comfort
Out of your best advice.

CYMBELINE.

Nay, let her languish
A drop of blood a day; and, being aged,
Die of this folly!

[*Exeunt* CYMBELINE *and* LORDS.

QUEEN.

Fie! you must give way.

Enter PISANIO.

Here is your servant.—How now, sir! What news?

PISANIO.

My lord your son drew on my master.

QUEEN.

Ha!
No harm, I trust, is done?

PISANIO.

There might have been,
But that my master rather play'd than fought,
And had no help of anger: they were parted
By gentlemen at hand.

QUEEN.

I am very glad on't.

IMOGEN.

Your son's my father's friend; he takes his part.—
To draw upon an exile!—O brave sir!—
I would they were in Afric both together;
Myself by with a needle, that I might prick
The goer-back.—Why came you from your master?

PISANIO.

On his command: he would not suffer me
To bring him to the haven; left these notes
Of what commands I should be subject to,
When't pleased you to employ me.

QUEEN.

This hath been
Your faithful servant: I dare lay mine honour
He will remain so.

PISANIO.

I humbly thank your highness.

QUEEN.

Pray, walk awhile.

IMOGEN.

About some half-hour hence,
I pray you, speak with me: you shall at least
Go see my lord aboard: for this time leave me.

[*Exeunt.*

SCENE II.

The same. A public place.

Enter CLOTEN *and two* LORDS.

FIRST LORD.

SIR, I would advise you to shift a shirt; the violence of action hath made you reek as a sacrifice: where air comes out, air comes in: there's none abroad so wholesome as that you vent.

CLOTEN.

If my shirt were bloody, then to shift it.—Have I hurt him?

SECOND LORD [*aside*].

No, faith; not so much as his patience.

FIRST LORD.

Hurt him! his body's a passable carcass, if he be not hurt: it is a thoroughfare for steel, if it be not hurt.

SECOND LORD [*aside*].

His steel was in debt; it went o'the backside the town.

CLOTEN.

The villain would not stand me.

SECOND LORD [*aside*].

No; but he fled forward still, toward your face.

FIRST LORD.

Stand you! You have land enough of your own: but he added to your having; gave you some ground.

SECOND LORD [*aside*].

As many inches as you have oceans.—Puppies!

CLOTEN.

I would they had not come between us.

SECOND LORD [*aside*].

So would I, till you had measured how long a fool you were upon the ground.

CLOTEN.

And that she should love this fellow, and refuse me!

SECOND LORD [*aside*].

If it be a sin to make a true election, she is damn'd.

FIRST LORD.

Sir, as I told you always, her beauty and her brain go not together: she's a good sign, but I have seen small reflection of her wit.

SECOND LORD [*aside*].

She shines not upon fools, lest the reflection should hurt her.

CLOTEN.

Come, I'll to my chamber. Would there had been some hurt done!

SECOND LORD [*aside*].

I wish not so; unless it had been the fall of an ass, which is no great hurt.

CLOTEN.

You'll go with us?

SECOND LORD.

I'll attend your lordship.

CLOTEN.

Nay, come, let's go together.

SECOND LORD.

Well, my lord. [*Exeunt.*

SCENE III.

A room in CYMBELINE'S *palace.*

Enter IMOGEN *and* PISANIO.

IMOGEN.

I WOULD thou grew'st unto the shores o'the haven,
And question'dst every sail: if he should write,
And I not have it, 'twere a paper lost,
As offer'd mercy is. What was the last
That he spake to thee?

PISANIO.

It was, 'His queen, his queen!'

IMOGEN.

Then waved his handkerchief?

PISANIO.

And kist it, madam.

IMOGEN.

Senseless linen! happier therein than I!—
And that was all?

PISANIO.

No, madam; for so long
As he could make me with this eye or ear
Distinguish him from others, he did keep
The deck, with glove, or hat, or handkerchief,
Still waving, as the fits and stirs of's mind
Could best express how slow his soul sail'd on,
How swift his ship.

IMOGEN.

Thou shouldst have made him
As little as a crow, or less, ere left
To after-eye him.

PISANIO.

Madam, so I did.

IMOGEN.

I would have broke mine eye-strings; crackt them, but
To look upon him; till the diminution
Of space had pointed him sharp as my needle;
Nay, follow'd him, till he had melted from
The smallness of a gnat to air; and then
Have turn'd mine eye, and wept.—But, good Pisanio,
When shall we hear from him?

PISANIO.

Be assured, madam,
With his next vantage.

IMOGEN.

I did not take my leave of him, but had
Most pretty things to say: ere I could tell him
How I would think on him, at certain hours,
Such thoughts and such; or I could make him swear
The shes of Italy should not betray
Mine interest and his honour; or have charged him,
At the sixth hour of morn, at noon, at midnight,
T'encounter me with orisons, for then
I am in heaven for him; or ere I could
Give him that parting kiss which I had set
Betwixt two charming words, comes in my father,
And, like the tyrannous breathing of the north,
Shakes all our buds from growing.

Enter a LADY.

LADY.

The queen, madam,
Desires you highness' company.

IMOGEN.

Those things I bid you do, get them dispatcht.—
I will attend the queen.

PISANIO.

Madam, I shall. [*Exeunt.*

SCENE IV.

Rome. PHILARIO'S *house.*

Enter PHILARIO, IACHIMO, *a* FRENCHMAN, *a* DUTCHMAN, *and a* SPANIARD.

IACHIMO.

BELIEVE it, sir, I have seen him in Britain: he was then of a crescent note; expected to prove so worthy as since he hath been allow'd the name of: but I could then have lookt on him without the help of admiration, though the catalogue of his endowments had been tabled by his side, and I to peruse him by items.

PHILARIO.

You speak of him when he was less furnisht than now he is with that which makes him both without and within.

FRENCHMAN.

I have seen him in France: we had very many there could behold the sun with as firm eyes as he.

IACHIMO.

This matter of marrying his king's daughter—wherein he must be weigh'd rather by her value than his own—words him, I doubt not, a great deal from the matter.

FRENCHMAN.

And then his banishment,—

IACHIMO.

Ay, and the approbation of those that weep this lamentable divorce under her colours are wonderfully to extend him; be it but to fortify her judgement, which else an easy battery might lay flat, for taking a beggar without less quality. But how comes it he is to sojourn with you? how creeps acquaintance?

PHILARIO.

His father and I were soldiers together; to whom I have been often bound for no less than my life.
—Here comes the Briton: let him be so entertain'd amongst you as suits, with gentlemen of your knowing, to a stranger of his quality.

Enter POSTHUMUS.

I beseech you all, be better known to this gentleman; whom I commend to you as a noble friend of mine: how worthy he is I will leave to appear hereafter, rather than story him in his own hearing.

FRENCHMAN.

Sir, we have known together in Orleans.

POSTHUMUS LEONATUS.

Since when I have been debtor to you for courtesies, which I will be ever to pay, and yet pay still.

FRENCHMAN.

Sir, you o'er-rate my poor kindness: I was glad I did atone my countryman and you; it had been pity you should have been put together with so mortal a purpose as then each bore, upon importance of so slight and trivial a nature.

POSTHUMUS LEONATUS.

By your pardon, sir, I was then a young traveller; rather shunn'd to go even with what I heard than in my every action to be guided by others' experiences: but, upon my mended judgement,—if I offend not to say it is mended,—my quarrel was not altogether slight.

FRENCHMAN.

Faith, yes, to be put to the arbitrement of swords; and by such two that would, by all likelihood, have confounded one the other, or have faln both.

IACHIMO.

Can we, with manners, ask what was the difference?

FRENCHMAN.

Safely, I think: 'twas a contention in public, which may, without contradiction, suffer the report. It was much like an argument that fell out last night, where each of us fell in praise of our country mistresses; this gentleman at that time vouching, and upon warrant of bloody affirmation, his to be more fair, virtuous, wise, chaste, constant-qualified, and less attemptable, than any the rarest of our ladies in France.

IACHIMO.

That lady is not now living; or this gentleman's opinion, by this, worn out.

POSTHUMUS LEONATUS.

She holds her virtue still, and I my mind.

IACHIMO.

You must not so far prefer her 'fore ours of Italy.

POSTHUMUS LEONATUS.

Being so far provoked as I was in France, I would abate her nothing; though I profess myself her adorer, not her friend.

IACHIMO.

As fair and as good—a kind of hand-in-hand comparison—had been something too fair and too good for any lady in Britany. If she went before others I have seen, as that diamond of yours outlustres many I have beheld, I could not but believe she excell'd many: but I have not seen the most precious diamond that is, nor you the lady.

POSTHUMUS LEONATUS.

I praised her as I rated her: so do I my stone.

IACHIMO.

What do you esteem it at?

POSTHUMUS LEONATUS.

More than the world enjoys.

IACHIMO.

Either your unparagon'd mistress is dead, or she's outprized by a trifle.

POSTHUMUS LEONATUS.

You are mistaken: the one may be sold, or given, or if there were wealth enough for the purchase, or merit for the gift: the other is not a thing for sale, and only the gift of the gods.

IACHIMO.

Which the gods have given you?

POSTHUMUS LEONATUS.

Which, by their graces, I will keep.

IACHIMO.

You may wear her in title yours: but, you know, strange fowl light upon neighbouring ponds. Your ring may be stoln too: so, your brace of unprizable estimations, the one is but frail, and the other casual; a cunning thief, or a that-way-accomplisht courtier, would hazard the winning both of first and last.

POSTHUMUS LEONATUS.

Your Italy contains none so accomplisht a courtier to convince the honour of my mistress; if, in the holding or loss of that, you term her frail. I do nothing doubt you have store of thieves; notwithstanding, I fear not my ring.

PHILARIO.

Let us leave here, gentlemen.

POSTHUMUS LEONATUS.

Sir, with all my heart. This worthy signior, I thank him, makes no stranger of me; we are familiar at first.

IACHIMO.

With five times so much conversation, I should get ground of your fair mistress; make her go back, even to the yielding, had I admittance, and opportunity to friend.

POSTHUMUS LEONATUS.

No, no.

IACHIMO.

I dare thereupon pawn the moiety of my estate to your ring; which, in my opinion, o'ervalues it something: but I make my wager rather against your confidence than her reputation; and, to bar your offence herein too, I durst attempt it against any lady in the world.

POSTHUMUS LEONATUS.

You are a great deal abused in too bold a persuasion; and I doubt not you sustain what y'are worthy of by your attempt.

IACHIMO.

What's that?

POSTHUMUS LEONATUS.

A repulse: though your attempt, as you call it, deserve more,—a punishment too.

PHILARIO.

Gentlemen, enough of this: it came in too suddenly; let it die as it was born, and, I pray you, be better acquainted.

IACHIMO.

Would I had put my estate and my neighbour's on the approbation of what I have spoke!

POSTHUMUS LEONATUS.

What lady would you choose to assail?

IACHIMO.

Yours; whom in constancy you think stands so safe. I will lay you ten thousand ducats to your ring, that, commend me to the court where your lady is, with no more advantage than the opportunity of a second conference, and I will bring from thence that honour of hers which you imagine so reserved.

POSTHUMUS LEONATUS.

I will wage against your gold, gold to it: my ring I hold dear as my finger; 'tis part of it.

IACHIMO.

You are afraid, and therein the wiser. If you buy ladies' flesh at a million a dram, you cannot preserve it from tainting: but I see you have some religion in you, that you fear.

POSTHUMUS LEONATUS.

This is but a custom in your tongue; you bear a graver purpose, I hope.

IACHIMO.

I am the master of my speeches; and would undergo what's spoken, I swear.

POSTHUMUS LEONATUS.

Will you?—I shall but lend my diamond till your return:—let there be covenants drawn between's: my mistress exceeds in goodness the hugeness of your unworthy thinking: I dare you to this match: here's my ring.

PHILARIO.

I will have it no lay.

IACHIMO.

By the gods, it is one.—If I bring you no sufficient testimony that I have enjoy'd the dearest bodily part of your mistress, my ten thousand ducats are yours; so is your diamond too: if I come off, and leave her in such honour as you have trust in, she your jewel, this your jewel, and my gold are yours; provided I have your commendation for my more free entertainment.

POSTHUMUS LEONATUS.

I embrace these conditions; let us have articles betwixt us.—Only, thus far you shall answer: if you make your voyage upon her, and give me directly to understand you have prevail'd, I am no further your enemy; she is not worth our debate: if she remain unseduced,—you not making it appear otherwise,—for your ill opinion, and the assault you have made to her chastity, you shall answer me with your sword.

IACHIMO.

Your hand,—a covenant: we will have these things set down by lawful counsel, and straight away for Britain, lest the bargain should catch cold and starve: I will fetch my gold, and have our two wagers recorded.

POSTHUMOUS LEONATUS.

Agreed. [*Exeunt* POSTHUMUS *and* IACHIMO.

FRENCHMAN.

Will this hold, think you?

PHILARIO.

Signior Iachimo will not from it. Pray, let us follow 'em. [*Exeunt.*

SCENE V.

Britain. *A room in* CYMBELINE'S *palace.*

Enter QUEEN, LADIES, *and* CORNELIUS.

QUEEN.

WHILES yet the dew's on ground, gather those flowers;
Make haste: who has the note of them?

FIRST LADY.

I, madam.

QUEEN.

Dispatch.— [*Exeunt* LADIES.
Now, master doctor, have you brought those drugs?

CORNELIUS.

Pleaseth your highness, ay: here they are, madam: [*Presenting a small box.*
But I beseech your Grace, without offence,—
My conscience bids me ask,—wherefore you have
Commanded of me these most poisonous compounds,
Which are the movers of a languishing death;
But, though slow, deadly?

QUEEN.

I wonder, doctor,
Thou ask'st me such a question. Have I not been
Thy pupil long? Hast thou not learn'd me how
To make perfumes? distil? preserve? yea, so
That our great king himself doth woo me oft
For my confections? Having thus far proceeded,
Unless thou think'st me devilish,—is't not meet
That I did amplify my judgement in
Other conclusions? I will try the forces
Of these thy compounds on such creatures as
We count not worth the hanging,—but none human,—
To try the vigour of them, and apply
Allayments to their act; and by them gather
Their several virtues and effects.

CORNELIUS.

Your highness
Shall from this practice but make hard your heart:
Besides, the seeing these effects will be
Both noisome and infectious.

QUEEN.

O, content thee.—
[*aside*] Here comes a flattering rascal; upon him
Will I first work: he's for his master,
And enemy to my son.—

Enter PISANIO.

How now, Pisanio!—
Doctor, your service for this time is ended;
Take your own way.

CORNELIUS [*aside*].

I do suspect you, madam;
But you shall do no harm.

QUEEN [*to* PISANIO].

Hark thee, a word.

CORNELIUS [*aside*].

I do not like her. She doth think she has
Strange lingering poisons: I do know her spirit,
And will not trust one of her malice with
A drug of such damn'd nature. Those she has
Will stupefy and dull the sense awhile;
Which first, perchance, she'll prove on cats and dogs,
Then afterward up higher: but there is
No danger in what show of death it makes,
More than the locking-up the spirits a time,
To be more fresh, reviving. She is fool'd
With a most false effect; and I the truer,
So to be false with her.

QUEEN.

No further service, doctor,
Until I send for thee.

CORNELIUS.

I humbly take my leave. [*Exit.*

QUEEN.

Weeps she still, say'st thou? Dost thou think in time
She will not quench, and let instructions enter
Where folly now possesses? Do thou work:
When thou shalt bring me word she loves my son,
I'll tell thee on the instant thou art then
As great as is thy master; greater,—for
His fortunes all lie speechless, and his name
Is at last gasp: return he cannot, nor
Continue where he is: to shift his being
Is to exchange one misery with another;
And every day that comes comes to decay
A day's work in him. What shalt thou expect,
To be depender on a thing that leans,—
Who cannot be new built, nor has no friends,
[*The* QUEEN *drops the box:* PISANIO *takes it up.*
So much as but to prop him?—Thou takest up
Thou know'st not what; but take it for thy labour:
It is a thing I made, which hath the king
Five times redeem'd from death: I do not know
What is more cordial:—nay, I prithee, take it;
It is an earnest of a further good
That I mean to thee. Tell thy mistress how
The case stands with her; do't as from thyself.
Think what a chance thou chancest on; but think
Thou hast thy mistress still,—to boot, my son,
Who shall take notice of thee: I'll move the king
To any shape of thy preferment, such
As thou'lt desire; and then myself, I chiefly,
That set thee on to this desert, am bound
To load thy merit richly. Call my women:
Think on my words. [*Exit* PISANIO.
A sly and constant knave;
Not to be shaked; the agent for his master;
And the remembrancer of her to hold
The hand-fast to her lord.—I have given him that,
Which, if he take, shall quite unpeople her
Of liegers for her sweet; and which she after,
Except she bend her humour, shall be assured
To taste of too.

Enter PISANIO *and* LADIES.

So, so;—well done, well done:
The violets, cowslips, and the primroses,
Bear to my closet.—Fare thee well, Pisanio;
Think on my words.
[*Exeunt* QUEEN *and* LADIES.

PISANIO.

And shall do:
But when to my good lord I prove untrue,
I'll choke myself: there's all I'll do for you. [*Exit.*

SCENE VI.

Another room in the palace.

Enter IMOGEN.

IMOGEN.

A FATHER cruel, and a step-dame false;
A foolish suitor to a wedded lady,
That hath her husband banisht;—O, that husband!
My supreme crown of grief! and those repeated
Vexations of it! Had I been thief-stoln,
As my two brothers, happy! but most miserable
Is the desire that's glorious: blest be those,
How mean soe'er, that have their honest wills,
Which seasons comfort.—Who may this be? Fie!

Enter PISANIO *and* IACHIMO.

PISANIO.

Madam, a noble gentleman of Rome
Comes from my lord with letters.

IACHIMO.

Change you, madam?
The worthy Leonatus is in safety,
And greets your highness dearly.
[*Presents a letter.*

IMOGEN.

Thanks, good sir:
You're kindly welcome.

IACHIMO [*aside*].

All of her that is out of door most rich!
If she be furnisht with a mind so rare,
She is alone the Arabian bird; and I
Have lost the wager. Boldness be my friend!
Arm me, audacity, from head to foot!
Or, like the Parthian, I shall flying fight;
Rather, directly fly.

IMOGEN [*reads*].

He is one of the noblest note, to whose kindnesses I am most infinitely tied. Reflect upon him accordingly, as you value your trust—LEONATUS.

So far I read aloud:
But even the very middle of my heart
Is warm'd by the rest, and takes it thankfully.—
You are as welcome, worthy sir, as I
Have words to bid you; and shall find it so,
In all that I can do.

IACHIMO.

Thanks, fairest lady.—
What, are men mad? Hath nature given them eyes
To see this vaulted arch, and the rich crop
Of sea and land, which can distinguish 'twixt
The fiery orbs above, and the twinn'd stones
Upon the unnumber'd beach? and can we not
Partition make with spectacles so precious
'Twixt fair and foul?

IMOGEN.

What makes your admiration?

IACHIMO.

It cannot be i'the eye; for apes and monkeys,
'Twixt two such shes, would chatter this way, and
Contemn with mows the other: nor i'the judgement;
For idiots, in this case of favour, would
Be wisely definite: nor i'the appetite;
Sluttery, to such neat excellence opposed,
Should make desire vomit emptiness,
Not so allured to feed.

IMOGEN.

What is the matter, trow?

IACHIMO.

The cloyed will,—
That satiate yet unsatisfied desire, that tub
Both fill'd and running,—ravening first the lamb,
Longs after for the garbage.

IMOGEN.

What, dear sir,
Thus raps you? Are you well?

IACHIMO.

Thanks, madam; well.—[*to* PISANIO] Beseech you, sir,

Desire my man's abode where I did leave him:
He's strange and peevish.

PISANIO.

I was going, sir,
To give him welcome. [*Exit.*

IMOGEN.

Continues well my lord? His health, beseech you?

IACHIMO.

Well, madam.

IMOGEN.

Is he disposed to mirth? I hope he is.

IACHIMO.

Exceeding pleasant; none a stranger there
So merry and so gamesome: he is call'd
The Briton reveller.

IMOGEN.

When he was here
He did incline to sadness, and oft-times
Not knowing why.

IACHIMO.

I never saw him sad.
There is a Frenchman his companion, one
An eminent monsieur, that, it seems, much loves
A Gallian girl at home; he furnaces
The thick sighs from him; whiles the jolly Briton—
Your lord, I mean—laughs from's free lungs, cries 'O,
Can my sides hold, to think that man—who knows
By history, report, or his own proof,
What woman is, yea, what she cannot choose
But must be—will his free hours languish for
Assured bondage?'

IMOGEN.

Will my lord say so?

IACHIMO.

Ay, madam; with his eyes in flood with laughter:
It is a recreation to be by,
And hear him mock the Frenchman. But, heavens know,
Some men are much to blame.

IMOGEN.

Not he, I hope.

IACHIMO.

Not he: but yet heaven's bounty towards him might
Be used more thankfully. In himself, 'tis much;
In you, which I account his, beyond all talents.
Whilst I am bound to wonder, I am bound
To pity too.

IMOGEN.

What do you pity, sir?

IACHIMO.

Two creatures heartily.

IMOGEN.

Am I one, sir?
You look on me: what wrack discern you in me
Deserves your pity?

IACHIMO.

Lamentable! What,
To hide me from the radiant sun, and solace
I'the dungeon by a snuff?

IMOGEN.

I pray you, sir,
Deliver with more openness your answers
To my demands. Why do you pity me?

IACHIMO.

That others do—
I was about to say—enjoy your—But
It is an office of the gods to venge it,
Not mine to speak on't.

IMOGEN.

You do seem to know
Something of me, or what concerns me: pray you—
Since doubting things go ill often hurts more
Than to be sure they do; for certainties
Either are past remedies, or, timely knowing,
The remedy then born—discover to me
What both you spur and stop.

IACHIMO.

Had I this cheek
To bathe my lips upon; this hand, whose touch,
Whose every touch, would force the feeler's soul
To the oath of loyalty; this object, which
Takes prisoner the wild motion of mine eye,
Fixing it only here;—should I—damn'd then—
Slaver with lips as common as the stairs
That mount the Capitol; join gripes with hands
Made hard with hourly falsehood—falsehood, as
With labour; then by-peeping in an eye
Base and illustrous as the smoky light
That's fed with stinking tallow;—it were fit
That all the plagues of hell should at one time
Encounter such revolt.

IMOGEN.

My lord, I fear,
Has forgot Britain.

IACHIMO.

And himself. Not I,
Inclined to this intelligence, pronounce
The beggary of his change; but 'tis your graces
That from my mutest conscience to my tongue
Charms this report out.

IMOGEN.

Let me hear no more.

IACHIMO.

O dearest soul, your cause doth strike my heart
With pity, that doth make me sick! A lady
So fair, and fasten'd to an empery
Would make the great'st king double, to be partner'd
With tomboys, hired with that self-exhibition
Which your own coffers yield! with diseased ventures
That play with all infirmities for gold
Which rottenness can lend nature! such boil'd stuff
As well might poison poison! Be revenged;
Or she that bore you was no queen, and you
Recoil from your great stock.

IMOGEN.

Revenged!
How should I be revenged? If this be true,—
As I have such a heart that both mine ears
Must not in haste abuse,—if it be true,
How should I be revenged?

IACHIMO.

Should he make me
Live, like Diana's priest, betwixt cold sheets,
Whiles he is vaulting variable ramps,
In your despite, upon your purse? Revenge it.

I dedicate myself to your sweet pleasure;
More noble than that runagate to your bed;
And will continue fast to your affection,
Still close as sure.

IMOGEN.

What ho, Pisanio!

IACHIMO.

Let me my service tender on your lips.

IMOGEN.

Away!—I do condemn mine ears that have
So long attended thee.—If thou wert honourable,
Thou wouldst have told this tale for virtue, not
For such an end thou seek'st,—as base as strange.
Thou wrong'st a gentleman who is as far
From thy report as thou from honour; and
Solicit'st here a lady that disdains
Thee and the devil alike.—What ho, Pisanio!—
The king my father shall be made acquainted
Of thy assault: if he shall think it fit,
A saucy stranger, in his court, to mart
As in a Romish stew, and to expound
His beastly mind to us,—he hath a court
He little cares for, and a daughter who
He not respects at all.—What ho, Pisanio!—

IACHIMO.

O happy Leonatus! I may say:
The credit that thy lady hath of thee
Deserves thy trust; and thy most perfect goodness
Her assured credit.—Blessed live you long!
A lady to the worthiest sir that ever
Country call'd his! and you his mistress, only
For the most worthiest fit! Give me your pardon.
I have spoke this, to know if your affiance
Were deeply rooted; and shall make your lord,
That which he is, new o'er: and he is one
The truest manner'd; such a holy witch,
That he enchants societies into him;
Half all men's hearts are his.

IMOGEN.

You make amends.

IACHIMO.

He sits 'mongst men like a descended god:
He hath a kind of honour sets him off,
More than a mortal seeming. Be not angry,
Most mighty princess, that I have adventured
To try your taking of a false report; which hath
Honour'd with confirmation your great judgement
In the election of a sir so rare,
Which you know cannot err: the love I bear him
Made me to fan you thus; but the gods made
you,
Unlike all others, chaffless. Pray, your pardon.

IMOGEN.

All's well, sir: take my power i'the court for yours.

IACHIMO.

My humble thanks. I had almost forgot
T'entreat your Grace but in a small request,
And yet of moment too, for it concerns
Your lord, myself, and other noble friends,
Are partners in the business.

IMOGEN.

Pray, what is't?

IACHIMO.

Some dozen Romans of us, and your lord—
The best feather of our wing—have mingled
sums
To buy a present for the emperor;
Which I, the factor for the rest, have done
In France: 'tis plate of rare device, and jewels
Of rich and exquisite form; their values great;
And I am something curious, being strange,
To have them in safe stowage: may it please you
To take them in protection?

IMOGEN.

Willingly;
And pawn mine honour for their safety: since
My lord hath interest in them, I will keep them
In my bedchamber.

IACHIMO.

They are in a trunk,
Attended by my men: I will make bold
To send them to you, only for this night;
I must aboard to-morrow.

IMOGEN.

O, no, no.

IACHIMO.

Yes, I beseech; or I shall short my word
By lengthening my return. From Gallia
I crost the seas on purpose and on promise
To see your Grace.

IMOGEN.

I thank you for your pains:
But not away to-morrow!

IACHIMO.

O, I must, madam:
Therefore I shall beseech you, if you please
To greet your lord with writing, do't to-night:
I have outstood my time; which is material
To the tender of our present.

IMOGEN.

I will write.
Send your trunk to me; it shall safe be kept,
And truly yielded you. You're very welcome.

[*Exeunt.*

ACT II. SCENE I.

Britain. Before CYMBELINE'S *palace.*

Enter CLOTEN *and two* LORDS.

CLOTEN.

WAS there ever man had such luck! when I kist the jack, upon an up-cast to be hit away! I had a hundred pound on't: and then a whoreson jackanapes must take me up for swearing; as if I borrow'd mine oaths of him, and might not spend them at my pleasure.

FIRST LORD.

What got he by that? You have broke his pate with your bowl.

SECOND LORD [*aside*].

If his wit had been like him that broke it, it would have run all out.

CLOTEN.

When a gentleman is disposed to swear, it is not for any standers-by to curtail his oaths, ha?

SECOND LORD.

No, my lord; [*aside*] nor crop the ears of them.

CLOTEN.

Whoreson dog! I give him satisfaction? Would he had been one of my rank!

SECOND LORD [*aside*].

To have smelt like a fool.

CLOTEN.

I am not vext more at any thing in the earth: a pox on't! I had rather not be so noble as I am; they dare not fight with me, because of the queen my mother: every Jack-slave hath his bellyful of fighting, and I must go up and down like a cock that nobody can match.

SECOND LORD [*aside*].

You are cock and capon too; and you crow, cock, with your comb on.

CLOTEN.

Sayest thou?

SECOND LORD.

It is not fit your lordship should undertake every companion that you give offence to.

CLOTEN.

No, I know that: but it is fit I should commit offence to my inferiors.

SECOND LORD.

Ay, it is fit for your lordship only.

CLOTEN.

Why, so I say.

FIRST LORD.

Did you hear of a stranger that's come to court to-night?

CLOTEN.

A stranger, and I not know on't!

SECOND LORD [*aside*].

He's a strange fellow himself, and knows it not.

FIRST LORD.

There's an Italian come; and, 'tis thought, one of Leonatus' friends.

CLOTEN.

Leonatus! a banisht rascal; and he's another, whatsoever he be. Who told you of this stranger?

FIRST LORD.

One of your lordship's pages.

CLOTEN.

Is it fit I went to look upon him? is there no derogation in't?

SECOND LORD.

You cannot derogate, my lord.

CLOTEN.

Not easily, I think.

SECOND LORD [*aside*].

You are a fool granted; therefore your issues, being foolish, do not derogate.

CLOTEN.

Come, I'll go see this Italian: what I have lost to-day at bowls I'll win to-night of him. Come, go.

SECOND LORD.

I'll attend your lordship.

[*Exeunt* CLOTEN *and* FIRST LORD.

That such a crafty devil as is his mother
Should yield the world this ass! a woman that
Bears all down with her brain; and this her son
Cannot take two from twenty, for his heart,
And leave eighteen. Alas, poor princess,
Thou divine Imogen, what thou endurest,
Betwixt a father by thy step-dame govern'd,
A mother hourly coining plots, a wooer
More hateful than the foul expulsion is
Of thy dear husband, than that horrid act
Of the divorce he'ld make! The heavens hold
  firm
The walls of thy dear honour; keep unshaked
That temple, thy fair mind; that thou mayst
  stand,
T'enjoy thy banisht lord and this great land!

[*Exit.*

SCENE II.

IMOGEN'S *bedchamber: a trunk in one corner of it.*

Enter IMOGEN *in her bed, and a* LADY.

IMOGEN.

WHO'S there? my woman Helen?

LADY.

Please you, madam.

IMOGEN.

What hour is it?

LADY.

Almost midnight, madam.

IMOGEN.

I have read three hours, then: mine eyes are weak:
Fold down the leaf where I have left: to bed:
Take not away the taper, leave it burning;
And if thou canst awake by four o'the clock,
I prithee, call me. Sleep hath seized me wholly.

[*Exit* LADY.

To your protection I commend me, gods!
From fairies, and the tempters of the night,
Guard me, beseech ye!

[*Sleeps.* IACHIMO *comes from the trunk.*

IACHIMO.

The crickets sing, and man's o'er-labour'd sense
Repairs itself by rest. Our Tarquin thus
Did softly press the rushes, ere he waken'd
The chastity he wounded.—Cytherea,
How bravely thou becomest thy bed! fresh lily!
And whiter than the sheets! That I might touch!
But kiss; one kiss!—Rubies unparagon'd,
How dearly they do't!—'Tis her breathing that
Perfumes the chamber thus: the flame o'the taper
Bows towards her; and would under-peep her lids,
To see the enclosed lights, now canopied
Under these windows, white and azure, laced
With blue of heaven's own tinct.—But my design
To note the chamber: I will write all down:—
Such and such pictures;—there the window;—
  such
The adornment of her bed;—the arras, figures,
Why, such and such;—and the contents o'the
  story,—
Ah, but some natural notes about her body,
Above ten thousand meaner movables
Would testify, t'enrich mine inventory:—
O sleep, thou ape of death, lie dull upon her!
And be her sense but as a monument,
Thus in a chapel lying!—Come off, come off;—

[*Taking off her bracelet.*

As slippery as the Gordian knot was hard!—
'Tis mine; and this will witness outwardly,
As strongly as the conscience does within,
To the madding of her lord.—On her left breast
A mole cinque-spotted, like the crimson drops
I'the bottom of a cowslip: here's a voucher,
Stronger than ever law could make: this secret
Will force him think I have pickt the lock, and
  ta'en
The treasure of her honour. No more. To what
  end?

Why should I write this down, that's riveted,
Screw'd to my memory?—She hath been reading late
The tale of Tereus: here the leaf's turn'd down
Where Philomel gave up.—I have enough:
To the trunk again, and shut the spring of it.—
Swift, swift, you dragons of the night, that dawning
May bare the raven's eye! I lodge in fear;
Though this a heavenly angel, hell is here.
[*Clock strikes.*
One, two, three,—Time, time!
[*Goes into the trunk. Scene closes.*

SCENE III.

An ante-chamber adjoining IMOGEN'S *apartments.*

Enter CLOTEN *and* LORDS.

FIRST LORD.
YOUR lordship is the most patient man in loss, the most coldest that ever turn'd up ace.

CLOTEN.
It would make any man cold to lose.

FIRST LORD.
But not every man patient after the noble temper of your lordship. You are most hot and furious when you win.

CLOTEN.
Winning will put any man into courage. If I could get this foolish Imogen, I should have gold enough. It's almost morning, is't not?

FIRST LORD.
Day, my lord.

CLOTEN.
I would this music would come: I am advised to give her music o'mornings; they say it will penetrate.—

Enter MUSICIANS.

Come on; tune: if you can penetrate her with your fingering, so; we'll try with tongue too: if none will do, let her remain; but I'll never give o'er. First, a very excellent good-conceited thing; after, a wonderful sweet air, with admirable rich words to it,—and then let her consider.

Song.

Hark, hark! the lark at heaven's gate sings,
And Phœbus gins arise,
His steeds to water at those springs
On chaliced flowers that lies;
And winking Mary-buds begin
To ope their golden eyes:
With every thing that pretty is,
My lady sweet, arise;
Arise, arise!

CLOTEN.
So, get you gone. If this penetrate, I will consider your music the better: if it do not, it is a vice in her ears, which horse-hairs and calves'-guts, nor the voice of unpaved eunuch to boot, can never amend. [*Exeunt* MUSICIANS.

SECOND LORD.
Here comes the king.

CLOTEN.
I am glad I was up so late; for that's the reason I was up so early; he cannot choose but take this service I have done fatherly.

Enter CYMBELINE *and* QUEEN.

Good morrow to your majesty and to my gracious mother.

CYMBELINE.
Attend you here the door of our stern daughter?
Will she not forth?

CLOTEN.
I have assail'd her with musics; but she vouchsafes no notice.

CYMBELINE.
The exile of her minion is too new;
She hath not yet forgot him: some more time
Must wear the print of his remembrance out,
And then she's yours.

QUEEN.
You are most bound to the king,
Who lets go by no vantages that may
Prefer you to his daughter. Frame yourself
To orderly solicits, and be friended
With aptness of the season; make denials
Increase your services; so seem as if
You were inspired to do those duties which
You tender to her; that you in all obey her,
Save when command to your dismission tends,
And therein you are senseless.

CLOTEN.
Senseless! not so.

Enter a MESSENGER.

MESSENGER.
So like you, sir, ambassadors from Rome;
The one is Caius Lucius.

CYMBELINE.
A worthy fellow,
Albeit he comes on angry purpose now;
But that's no fault of his: we must receive him
According to the honour of his sender;
And towards himself, his goodness forespent on us,
We must extend our notice.—Our dear son,
When you have given good morning to your mistress,
Attend the queen and us; we shall have need
T'employ you towards this Roman.—Come, our queen. [*Exeunt all but* CLOTEN.

CLOTEN.
If she be up, I'll speak with her; if not,
Let her lie still and dream.—By your leave, ho!—
[*Knocks.*
I know her women are about her: what
If I do line one of their hands? 'Tis gold
Which buys admittance; oft it doth; yea, and makes
Diana's rangers false themselves, yield up
Their deer to the stand o'the stealer; and 'tis gold
Which makes the true man kill'd, and saves the thief;
Nay, sometime hangs both thief and true man: what
Can it not do and undo? I will make
One of her women lawyer to me; for
I yet not understand the case myself.—
By your leave. [*Knocks.*

Enter a LADY.

LADY.

Who's there that knocks?

CLOTEN.

A gentleman.

LADY.

No more?

CLOTEN.

Yes, and a gentlewoman's son.

LADY.

That's more
Than some, whose tailors are as dear as yours,
Can justly boast of. What's your lordship's pleasure?

CLOTEN.

Your lady's person: is she ready?

LADY.

Ay,
To keep her chamber.

CLOTEN.

There is gold for you;
Sell me your good report.

LADY.

How! my good name? or to report of you
What I shall think is good?—The princess!

Enter IMOGEN.

CLOTEN.

Good morrow, fairest: sister, your sweet hand.

[*Exit* LADY.

IMOGEN.

Good morrow, sir. You lay out too much pains
For purchasing but trouble: the thanks I give
Is telling you that I am poor of thanks,
And scarce can spare them.

CLOTEN.

Still, I swear I love you.

IMOGEN.

If you but said so, 'twere as deep with me:
If you swear still, your recompense is still
That I regard it not.

CLOTEN.

This is no answer.

IMOGEN.

But that you shall not say, I yield being silent,
I would not speak. I pray you, spare me: faith,
I shall unfold equal discourtesy
To your best kindness: one of your great knowing
Should learn, being taught, forbearance.

CLOTEN.

To leave you in your madness, 'twere my sin:
I will not.

IMOGEN.

Fools are not mad folks.

CLOTEN.

Do you call me fool?

IMOGEN.

As I am mad, I do:
If you'll be patient, I'll no more be mad;
That cures us both. I am much sorry, sir,
You put me to forget a lady's manners,
By being so verbal: and learn now, for all,
That I, which know my heart, do here pronounce,
By the very truth of it, I care not for you;
And am so near the lack of charity,—
To accuse myself,—I hate you; which I had rather
You felt than make't my boast.

CLOTEN.

You sin against
Obedience, which you owe your father. For
The contract you pretend with that base wretch,—
One bred of alms, and foster'd with cold dishes,
With scraps o'the court,—it is no contract, none:
And though it be allow'd in meaner parties—
Yet who than he more mean?—to knit their souls—
On whom there is no more dependency
But brats and beggary—in self-figured knot;
Yet you are curb'd from that enlargement by
The consequence o'the crown; and must not foil
The precious note of it with a base slave,
A hilding for a livery, a squire's cloth,
A pantler, not so eminent.

IMOGEN.

Profane fellow!
Wert thou the son of Jupiter, and no more
But what thou art besides, thou wert too base
To be his groom: thou wert dignified enough,
Even to the point of envy, if 'twere made
Comparative for your virtues, to be styled
The under-hangman of his kingdom; and hated
For being preferr'd so well.

CLOTEN.

The south-fog rot him!

IMOGEN.

He never can meet more mischance than come
To be but named of thee. His meanest garment,
That ever hath but clipt his body, is dearer
In my respect than all the hairs above thee,
Were they all made such men.

Enter PISANIO.

How now, Pisanio!

CLOTEN.

'His garment'! Now, the devil—

IMOGEN.

To Dorothy my woman hie thee presently—

CLOTEN.

'His garment'!

IMOGEN.

I am sprited with a fool;
Frighted, and anger'd worse:—go bid my woman
Search for a jewel that too casually
Hath left mine arm: it was thy master's; shrew me,
If I would lose it for a revenue
Of any king's in Europe. I do think
I saw't this morning: confident I am
Last night 'twas on mine arm; I kist it:
I hope it be not gone to tell my lord
That I kiss aught but he.

PISANIO.

'Twill not be lost.

IMOGEN.

I hope so: go and search. [*Exit* PISANIO.

CLOTEN.

You have abused me:—
'His meanest garment'!

IMOGEN.

Ay, I said so, sir:
If you will make't an action, call witness to't.

CLOTEN.

I will inform your father.

IMOGEN.

Your mother too:
She's my good lady; and will conceive, I hope,
But the worst of me. So, I leave you, sir,
To the worst of discontent. [*Exit.*

CLOTEN.

I'll be revenged:—
'His meanest garment'!—Well. [*Exit.*

SCENE IV.

Rome. PHILARIO'S *house.*

Enter POSTHUMUS *and* PHILARIO.

POSTHUMUS LEONATUS.

FEAR it not, sir: I would I were so sure
To win the king, as I am bold her honour
Will remain hers.

PHILARIO.

What means do you make to him?

POSTHUMUS LEONATUS.

Not any; but abide the change of time;
Quake in the present winter's state, and wish
That warmer days would come: in these fear'd [hopes,
I barely gratify your love; they failing,
I must die much your debtor.

PHILARIO.

Your very goodness and your company
O'erpays all I can do. By this, your king
Hath heard of great Augustus: Caius Lucius
Will do's commission throughly: and I think
He'll grant the tribute, send the arrearages,
Or look upon our Romans, whose remembrance
Is yet fresh in their grief.

POSTHUMUS LEONATUS.

I do believe—
Statist though I am none, nor like to be—
That this will prove a war; and you shall hear
The legions now in Gallia sooner landed
In our not-fearing Britain than have tidings
Of any penny tribute paid. Our countrymen
Are men more order'd than when Julius Cæsar
Smiled at their lack of skill, but found their courage
Worthy his frowning at: their discipline
Now mingled with their courages will make known
To their approvers they are people such
That mend upon the world.

PHILARIO.

See! Iachimo!

Enter IACHIMO.

POSTHUMUS LEONATUS.

The swiftest harts have posted you by land;
And winds of all the corners kist your sails,
To make your vessel nimble.

PHILARIO.

Welcome, sir.

POSTHUMUS LEONATUS.

I hope the briefness of your answer made
The speediness of your return.

IACHIMO.

Your lady
Is one of the fairest that I have lookt upon.

POSTHUMUS LEONATUS.

And therewithal the best; or let her beauty
Look through a casement to allure false hearts,
And be false with them.

IACHIMO.

Here are letters for you.

POSTHUMUS LEONATUS.

Their tenour good, I trust.

IACHIMO.

'Tis very like.

PHILARIO.

Was Caius Lucius in the Britain court
When you were there?

IACHIMO.

He was expected then,
But not approacht.

POSTHUMUS LEONATUS.

All is well yet.—
Sparkles this stone as it was wont? or is't not
Too dull for your good wearing?

IACHIMO.

If I had lost it,
I should have lost the worth of it in gold.
I'll make a journey twice as far, t'enjoy
A second night of such sweet shortness which
Was mine in Britain; for the ring is won.

POSTHUMUS LEONATUS.

The stone's too hard to come by.

IACHIMO.

Not a whit,
Your lady being so easy.

POSTHUMUS LEONATUS.

Make not, sir,
Your loss your sport: I hope you know that we
Must not continue friends.

IACHIMO.

Good sir, we must,
If you keep covenant. Had I not brought
The knowledge of your mistress home, I grant
We were to question further: but I now
Profess myself the winner of her honour,
Together with your ring; and not the wronger
Of her or you, having proceeded but
By both your wills.

POSTHUMUS LEONATUS.

If you can make't apparent
That you have tasted her in bed, my hand
And ring is yours: if not, the foul opinion
You had of her pure honour gains or loses
Your sword or mine, or masterless leaves both
To who shall find them.

IACHIMO.

Sir, my circumstances,
Being so near the truth as I will make them,
Must first induce you to believe: whose strength
I will confirm with oath; which, I doubt not,
You'll give me leave to spare, when you shall find
You need it not.

POSTHUMUS LEONATUS.

Proceed.

IACHIMO.

First, her bedchamber,—
Where, I confess, I slept not; but profess
Had that was well worth watching,—it was hang'd
With tapestry of silk and silver; the story
Proud Cleopatra, when she met her Roman,
And Cydnus swell'd above the banks, or for
The press of boats or pride: a piece of work
So bravely done, so rich, that it did strive
In workmanship and value; which I wonder'd

Could be so rarely and exactly wrought,
Since the true life on't was—

POSTHUMUS LEONATUS.

This is true;
And this you might have heard of here, by me
Or by some other.

IACHIMO.

More particulars
Must justify my knowledge.

POSTHUMUS LEONATUS.

So they must,
Or do your honour injury.

IACHIMO.

The chimney
Is south the chamber; and the chimney-piece
Chaste Dian bathing: never saw I figures
So lively to report themselves: the cutter
Was as another nature, dumb; outwent her,
Motion and breath left out.

POSTHUMUS LEONATUS.

This is a thing
Which you might from relation likewise reap,
Being, as it is, much spoke of.

IACHIMO.

The roof o'the chamber
With golden cherubins is fretted: her andirons—
I had forgot them—were two winking Cupids
Of silver, each on one foot standing, nicely
Depending on their brands.

POSTHUMUS LEONATUS.

This is her honour!—
Let it be granted you have seen all this,—and praise
Be given to your remembrance,—the description
Of what is in her chamber nothing saves
The wager you have laid.

IACHIMO.

Then, if you can,
[*Pulling out the bracelet.*
Be pale: I beg but leave to air this jewel; see!—
And now 'tis up again: it must be married
To that your diamond; I'll keep them.

POSTHUMUS LEONATUS.

Jove!—
Once more let me behold it: is it that
Which I left with her?

IACHIMO.

Sir,—I thank her,—that:
She stript it from her arm; I see her yet;
Her pretty action did outsell her gift,
And yet enricht it too: she gave it me, and said
She prized it once.

POSTHUMUS LEONATUS.

May be she pluckt it off
To send it me.

IACHIMO.

She writes so to you, doth she?

POSTHUMUS LEONATUS.

O, no, no, no! 'tis true. Here, take this too;
[*Gives the ring*
It is a basilisk unto mine eye,
Kills me to look on't.—Let there be no honour
Where there is beauty; truth, where semblance; love,
Where there's another man: the vows of women
Of no more bondage be to where they are made
Than they are to their virtues; which is nothing.—
O, above measure false!

PHILARIO.

Have patience, sir,
And take your ring again; 'tis not yet won:
It may be probable she lost it; or
Who knows if one of her women, being corrupted,
Hath stoln it from her?

POSTHUMUS LEONATUS.

Very true;
And so, I hope, he came by't.—Back my ring:
Render to me some corporal sign about her,
More evident than this; for this was stoln.

IACHIMO.

By Jupiter, I had it from her arm.

POSTHUMUS LEONATUS.

Hark you, he swears; by Jupiter he swears.
'Tis true,—nay, keep the ring,—'tis true: I am sure
She would not lose it: her attendants are
All sworn and honourable:—they induced to steal it!
And by a stranger!—No, he hath enjoy'd her:
The cognizance of her incontinency
Is this,—she hath bought the name of whore thus dearly.—
There, take thy hire; and all the fiends of hell
Divide themselves between you!

PHILARIO.

Sir, be patient:
This is not strong enough to be believed
Of one persuaded well of—

POSTHUMUS LEONATUS.

Never talk on't;
She hath been colted by him.

IACHIMO.

If you seek
For further satisfying, under her breast—
Worthy the pressing—lies a mole, right proud
Of that most delicate lodging: by my life,
I kist it; and it gave me present hunger
To feed again, though full. You do remember
This stain upon her?

POSTHUMUS LEONATUS.

Ay, and it doth confirm
Another stain, as big as hell can hold,
Were there no more but it.

IACHIMO.

Will you hear more?

POSTHUMUS LEONATUS.

Spare your arithmetic: never count the turns;
Once, and a million!

IACHIMO.

I'll be sworn—

POSTHUMUS LEONATUS.

No swearing.
If you will swear you have not done't, you lie;
And I will kill thee, if thou dost deny
Thou'st made me cuckold.

IACHIMO.

I'll deny nothing.

POSTHUMUS LEONATUS.

O, that I had her here, to tear her limb-meal!
I will go there and do't; i'the court; before
Her father:—I'll do something— [*Exit.*

PHILARIO.

Quite besides
The government of patience!—You have won:
Let's follow him, and pervert the present wrath
He hath against himself.

IACHIMO.

With all my heart. [*Exeunt.*

SCENE V.

Another room in PHILARIO'S *house.*

Enter POSTHUMUS.

POSTHUMUS LEONATUS.

IS there no way for men to be, but women
Must be half-workers? We are all bastards:
And that most venerable man which I
Did call my father, was I know not where
When I was stampt; some coiner with his tools
Made me a counterfeit: yet my mother seem'd
The Dian of that time: so doth my wife
The nonpareil of this.—O, vengeance, vengeance!
Me of my lawful pleasure she restrain'd,
And pray'd me oft forbearance; did it with
A pudency so rosy, the sweet view on't
Might well have warm'd old Saturn; that I thought her
As chaste as unsunn'd snow:—O, all the devils!—
This yellow Iachimo, in an hour,—was't not?—
Or less,—at first?—perchance he spoke not, but,
Like a full-acorn'd boar, a German one,
Cried 'O!' and mounted; found no opposition
But what he lookt for should oppose, and she
Should from encounter guard.—Could I find out
The woman's part in me! For there's no motion
That tends to vice in man, but I affirm
It is the woman's part: be it lying, note it,
The woman's; flattering, hers; deceiving, hers;
Lust and rank thoughts, hers, hers; revenges, hers;
Ambitions, covetings, change of prides, disdain,
Nice longing, slanders, mutability,
All faults that may be named, nay, that hell knows,
Why, hers, in part or all; but rather, all;
For even to vice
They are not constant, but are changing still
One vice, but of a minute old, for one
Not half so old as that. I'll write against them,
Detest them, curse them:—yet 'tis greater skill
In a true hate, to pray they have their will:
The very devils cannot plague them better. [*Exit.*

ACT III. SCENE I.

Britain. A room of state in CYMBELINE'S *palace.*

Enter in state CYMBELINE, QUEEN, CLOTEN, *and* LORDS *at one door, and at another* CAIUS LUCIUS *and* ATTENDANTS.

CYMBELINE.

NOW say, what would Augustus Cæsar with us?

CAIUS LUCIUS.

When Julius Cæsar, whose remembrance yet
Lives in men's eyes and will to ears and tongues
Be theme and hearing ever, was in this Britain
And conquer'd it, Cassibelan, thine uncle,—
Famous in Cæsar's praises, no whit less
Than in his feats deserving it,—for him
And his succession granted Rome a tribute,
Yearly three thousand pounds; which by thee lately
Is left untender'd.

QUEEN.

And, to kill the marvel,
Shall be so ever.

CLOTEN.

There be many Cæsars,
Ere such another Julius. Britain is
A world by itself; and we will nothing pay
For wearing our own noses.

QUEEN.

That opportunity,
Which then they had to take from's, to resume
We have again.—Remember, sir, my liege,
The kings your ancestors, together with
The natural bravery of your isle, which stands
As Neptune's park, ribbed and paled in
With rocks unscalable and roaring waters;
With sands that will not bear your enemies' boats,
But suck them up to the topmast. A kind of conquest
Cæsar made here; but made not here his brag
Of 'Came, and saw, and overcame:' with shame—
The first that ever toucht him—he was carried
From off our coast, twice beaten; and his shipping—
Poor ignorant baubles!—on our terrible seas,
Like egg-shells moved upon their surges, crackt
As easily 'gainst our rocks: for joy whereof
The famed Cassibelan, who was once at point—
O giglot Fortune!—to master Cæsar's sword,
Made Lud's-town with rejoicing fires bright,
And Britons strut with courage.

CLOTEN.

Come, there's no more tribute to be paid: our kingdom is stronger than it was at that time; and, as I said, there is no moe such Cæsars: other of them may have crookt noses; but to owe such straight arms, none.

CYMBELINE.

Son, let your mother end.

CLOTEN.

We have yet many among us can gripe as hard as Cassibelan: I do not say I am one; but I have a hand.—Why tribute? why should we pay tribute? If Cæsar can hide the sun from us with a blanket, or put the moon in his pocket, we will pay him tribute for light; else, sir, no more tribute, pray you now.

CYMBELINE.

You must know,
Till the injurious Romans did extort
This tribute from's, we were free: Cæsar's ambition,—
Which swell'd so much, that it did almost stretch
The sides o'the world,—against all colour, here
Did put the yoke upon's; which to shake off
Becomes a warlike people, whom we reckon
Ourselves to be. We do say, then, to Cæsar,
Our ancestor was that Mulmutius which

Ordain'd our laws,—whose use the sword of Cæsar
Hath too much mangled; whose repair and franchise
Shall, by the power we hold, be our good deed,
Though Rome be therefore angry;—Mulmutius made our laws,
Who was the first of Britain which did put
His brows within a golden crown, and call'd
Himself a king.

CAIUS LUCIUS.

I am sorry, Cymbeline,
That I am to pronounce Augustus Cæsar—
Cæsar, that hath moe kings his servants than
Thyself domestic officers—thine enemy:
Receive it from me, then:—war and confusion
In Cæsar's name pronounce I 'gainst thee: look
For fury not to be resisted.—Thus defied,
I thank thee for myself.

CYMBELINE.

Thou art welcome, Caius.
Thy Cæsar knighted me; my youth I spent
Much under him; of him I gather'd honour;
Which he to seek of me again, perforce,
Behoves me keep at utterance. I am perfect
That the Pannonians and Dalmatians for
Their liberties are now in arms,—a precedent
Which not to read would show the Britons cold:
So Cæsar shall not find them.

CAIUS LUCIUS.

Let proof speak.

CLOTEN.

His majesty bids you welcome. Make pastime with us a day or two, or longer: if you seek us afterwards in other terms, you shall find us in our salt-water girdle: if you beat us out of it, it is yours; if you fall in the adventure, our crows shall fare the better for you; and there's an end.

CAIUS LUCIUS.

So, sir.

CYMBELINE.

I know your master's pleasure, and he mine:
All the remain is 'Welcome.' [*Exeunt.*

SCENE II.

Another room in the palace.

Enter PISANIO, *with a letter.*

PISANIO.

HOW! of adultery? Wherefore write you not
What monster's her accuser? Leonatus!
O master! what a strange infection
Is faln into thy ear! What false Italian,
As poisonous-tongued as handed, hath prevail'd
On thy too ready hearing? Disloyal! No:
She's punisht for her truth; and undergoes,
More goddess-like than wife-like, such assaults
As would take in some virtue. O my master!
Thy mind to her is now as low as were
Thy fortunes. How! that I should murder her?
Upon the love, and truth, and vows, which I
Have made to thy command? I, her? her blood?
If it be so to do good service, never
Let me be counted serviceable. How look I,
That I should seem to lack humanity
So much as this fact comes to? [*reading*] 'Do't: the letter
That I have sent her, by her own command
Shall give thee opportunity:'—O damn'd paper!
Black as the ink that's on thee! Senseless bauble,
Art thou a feodary for this act, and look'st
So virgin-like without?—Lo, here she comes.—
I am ignorant in what I am commanded.

Enter IMOGEN.

IMOGEN.

How now, Pisanio!

PISANIO.

Madam, here is a letter from my lord.

IMOGEN.

Who? thy lord? that is my lord,—Leonatus?
O, learn'd indeed were that astronomer
That knew the stars as I his characters;
He'ld lay the future open. You good gods,
Let what is here contain'd relish of love,
Of my lord's health, of his content,—yet not
That we two are asunder; let that grieve him:
Some griefs are medicinable; that is one of them,
For it doth physic love;—of his content
All but in that!—Good wax, thy leave: blest be
You bees that make these locks of counsel! Lovers,
And men in dangerous bonds, pray not alike:
Though forfeiters you cast in prison, yet
You clasp young Cupid's tables.—Good news, gods! [*Reads.*

Justice, and your father's wrath, should he take me in his dominion, could not be so cruel to me, as you, O the dearest of creatures, would even renew me with your eyes. Take notice that I am in Cambria, at Milford-Haven: what your own love will, out of this, advise you, follow. So, he wishes you all happiness, that remains loyal to his vow, and your, increasing in love,

LEONATUS POSTHUMUS.

O, for a horse with wings! Hear'st thou, Pisanio?
He is at Milford-Haven: read, and tell me
How far 'tis thither. If one of mean affairs
May plod it in a week, why may not I
Glide thither in a day? Then, true Pisanio,—
Who long'st, like me, to see thy lord; who long'st,—
O, let me bate,—but not like me;—yet long'st,
But in a fainter kind;—O, not like me;
For mine's beyond beyond,—say, and speak thick,—
Love's counsellor should fill the bores of hearing,
To the smothering of the sense,—how far it is
To this same blessed Milford: and, by the way,
Tell me how Wales was made so happy as
T'inherit such a haven: but, first of all,
How we may steal from hence; and for the gap
That we shall make in time, from our hence-going
And our return, to excuse:—but first, how get hence:
Why should excuse be born or e'er begot?
We'll talk of that hereafter. Prithee, speak,
How many score of miles may we well ride
'Twixt hour and hour?

PISANIO.

One score 'twixt sun and sun,
Madam, 's enough for you, and too much too.

IMOGEN.

Why, one that rode to's execution, man,
Could never go so slow: I have heard of riding
wagers,
Where horses have been nimbler than the sands
That run i'the clock's behalf:—but this is foolery:—
Go bid my woman feign a sickness; say
She'll home to her father: and provide me presently
A riding-suit, no costlier than would fit
A franklin's housewife.

PISANIO.

Madam, you're best consider.

IMOGEN.

I see before me, man: nor here, nor here,
Nor what ensues, but have a fog in them,
That I cannot look through. Away, I prithee;
Do as I bid thee: there's no more to say;
Accessible is none but Milford way. [*Exeunt.*

SCENE III.

Wales: a mountainous country with a cave.

Enter BELARIUS, GUIDERIUS, *and* ARVIRAGUS.

BELARIUS.

A GOODLY day not to keep house, with such
Whose roof's as low as ours! Stoop, boys: this
gate
Instructs you how t'adore the heavens, and bows
you
To morning's holy office: the gates of monarchs
Are archt so high, that giants may jet through
And keep their impious turbans on, without
Good morrow to the sun.—Hail, thou fair heaven!
We house i'the rock, yet use thee not so hardly
As prouder livers do.

GUIDERIUS.

Hail, heaven!

ARVIRAGUS.

Hail, heaven!

BELARIUS.

Now for our mountain sport: up to yond hill,
Your legs are young; I'll tread these flats. Consider,
When you above perceive me like a crow,
That it is place which lessens and sets off;
And you may then revolve what tales I have told
you
Of courts, of princes, of the tricks in war:
This service is not service, so being done,
But being so allow'd: to apprehend thus,
Draws us a profit from all things we see;
And often, to our comfort, shall we find
The sharded beetle in a safer hold
Than is the full-wing'd eagle. O, this life
Is nobler than attending for a check,
Richer than doing nothing for a bribe,
Prouder than rustling in unpaid-for silk:
Such gain the cap of him that makes 'em fine,
Yet keeps his book uncrost: no life to ours.

GUIDERIUS.

Out of your proof you speak: we, poor unfledged,
Have never wing'd from view o'the nest, nor know
not
What air's from home. Haply this life is best,
If quiet life be best; sweeter to you
That have a sharper known; well corresponding
With your stiff age: but unto us it is
A cell of ignorance; travelling a-bed;
A prison for a debtor, that not dares
To stride a limit.

ARVIRAGUS.

What should we speak of
When we are old as you? when we shall hear
The rain and wind beat dark December, how,
In this our pinching cave, shall we discourse
The freezing hours away? We have seen nothing:
We are beastly; subtle as the fox for prey;
Like warlike as the wolf for what we eat:
Our valour is to chase what flies; our cage
We make a quire, as doth the prison'd bird,
And sing our bondage freely.

BELARIUS.

How you speak!
Did you but know the city's usuries,
And felt them knowingly: the art o'the court,
As hard to leave as keep; whose top to climb
Is certain falling, or so slippery that
The fear's as bad as falling: the toil o'the war,
A pain that only seems to seek out danger
I'the name of fame and honour; which dies i'the
search;
And hath as oft a slanderous epitaph
As record of fair act; nay, many times
Doth ill deserve by doing well; what's worse,
Must court'sy at the censure:—O boys, this story
The world may read in me: my body's markt
With Roman swords; and my report was once
First with the best of note: Cymbeline loved me;
And when a soldier was the theme, my name
Was not far off: then was I as a tree
Whose boughs did bend with fruit: but in one
night,
A storm or robbery, call it what you will,
Shook down my mellow hangings, nay, my leaves,
And left me bare to weather.

GUIDERIUS.

Uncertain favour!

BELARIUS.

My fault being nothing,—as I have told you oft,—
But that two villains, whose false oaths prevail'd
Before my perfect honour, swore to Cymbeline
I was confederate with the Romans: so,
Follow'd my banishment; and, this twenty years,
This rock and these demesnes have been my world:
Where I have lived at honest freedom; paid
More pious debts to heaven than in all
The fore-end of my time.—But, up to the mountains!
This is not hunters' language:—he that strikes
The venison first shall be the lord o'the feast;
To him the other two shall minister;
And we will fear no poison, which attends
In place of greater state. I'll meet you in the
valleys. [*Exeunt* GUIDERIUS *and* ARVIRAGUS.
How hard it is to hide the sparks of nature!
These boys know little they are sons to the king;
Nor Cymbeline dreams that they are alive.
They think they are mine; and, though train'd up
thus meanly
I'the cave wherein they bow, their thoughts do hit

The roofs of palaces; and nature prompts them,
In simple and low things, to prince it much
Beyond the trick of others. This Polydore,—
The heir of Cymbeline and Britain, who
The king his father call'd Guiderius,—Jove!
When on my three-foot stool I sit, and tell
The warlike feats I have done, his spirits fly out
Into my story: say, 'Thus mine enemy fell,
And thus I set my foot on's neck;' even then
The princely blood flows in his cheek, he sweats,
Strains his young nerves, and puts himself in posture
That acts my words. The younger brother, Cadwal,—
Once Arviragus,—in as like a figure,
Strikes life into my speech, and shows much more
His own conceiving.—Hark, the game is roused!—
O Cymbeline! heaven and my conscience knows
Thou didst unjustly banish me: whereon,
At three and two years old, I stole these babes;
Thinking to bar thee of succession, as
Thou reft'st me of my lands. Euriphile,
Thou wast their nurse; they took thee for their mother,
And every day do honour to her grave:
Myself, Belarius, that am Morgan call'd,
They take for natural father.—The game is up.
[*Exit.*

SCENE IV.

Near Milford-Haven.

Enter PISANIO *and* IMOGEN.

IMOGEN.

THOU told'st me, when we came from horse, the place
Was near at hand:—ne'er long'd my mother so
To see me first, as I have now:—Pisanio! man!
Where is Posthumus? What is in thy mind,
That makes thee stare thus? Wherefore breaks that sigh
From th'inward of thee? One, but painted thus,
Would be interpreted a thing perplext
Beyond self-explication: put thyself
Into a haviour of less fear, ere wildness
Vanquish my staider senses. What's the matter?
Why tender'st thou that paper to me, with
A look untender? If't be summer news,
Smile to't before; if winterly, thou need'st
But keep that countenance still.—My husband's hand!
That drug-damn'd Italy hath out-crafted him,
And he's at some hard point.—Speak, man: thy tongue
May take off some extremity, which to read
Would be even mortal to me.

PISANIO.

Please you, read;
And you shall find me, wretched man, a thing
The most disdain'd of fortune.

IMOGEN.

IMOGEN [*reads*].

Thy mistress, Pisanio, hath play'd the strumpet in my bed; the testimonies whereof lie bleeding in me. I speak not out of weak surmises; but from proof as strong as my grief, and as certain as I expect my revenge. That part thou, Pisanio, must act for me, if thy faith be not tainted with the breach of hers. Let thine own hands take away her life: I shall give thee opportunity at Milford-Haven: she hath my letter for the purpose: where, if thou fear to strike, and to make me certain it is done, thou art the pandar to her dishonour, and equally to me disloyal.

PISANIO.

What shall I need to draw my sword? the paper
Hath cut her throat already.—No, 'tis slander;
Whose edge is sharper than the sword; whose tongue
Outvenoms all the worms of Nile; whose breath
Rides on the posting winds, and doth belie
All corners of the world: kings, queens, and states,
Maids, matrons, nay, the secrets of the grave
This viperous slander enters.—What cheer, madam?

IMOGEN.

False to his bed! What is it to be false?
To lie in watch there, and to think on him?
To weep 'twixt clock and clock? if sleep charge nature,
To break it with a fearful dream of him,
And cry myself awake! that's false to's bed, is it?

PISANIO.

Alas, good lady!

IMOGEN.

I false! Thy conscience witness:—Iachimo,
Thou didst accuse him of incontinency;
Thou then look'dst like a villain; now, methinks,
Thy favour's good enough.—Some jay of Italy,
Whose mother was her painting, hath betray'd him:
Poor I am stale, a garment out of fashion;
And, for I am richer than to hang by the walls,
I must be ript:—to pieces with me!—O,
Men's vows are women's traitors! All good seeming,
By thy revolt, O husband, shall be thought
Put on for villainy; not born where't grows,
But worn a bait for ladies.

PISANIO.

Good madam, hear me.

IMOGEN.

True honest men being heard, like false Aeneas,
Were, in his time, thought false; and Sinon's weeping
Did scandal many a holy tear, took pity
From most true wretchedness: so thou, Posthumus,
Wilt lay the leaven on all proper men;
Goodly and gallant shall be false and perjured
From thy great fail.—Come, fellow, be thou honest:
Do thou thy master's bidding: when thou see'st him,
A little witness my obedience: look!
I draw the sword myself: take it, and hit
The innocent mansion of my love, my heart:
Fear not; 'tis empty of all things but grief:
Thy master is not there; who was, indeed,
The riches of it: do his bidding; strike.
Thou mayst be valiant in a better cause;
But now thou seem'st a coward.

PISANIO.

Hence, vile instrument!
Thou shalt not damn my hand.

IMOGEN.

Why, I must die;
And if I do not by thy hand, thou art
No servant of thy master's: 'gainst self-slaughter
There is a prohibition so divine
That cravens my weak hand. Come, here's my heart:—
Something's afore't: soft, soft! we'll no defence;—
Obedient as the scabbard. What is here?
The scriptures of the loyal Leonatus
All turn'd to heresy? Away, away,
Corrupters of my faith! you shall no more
Be stomachers to my heart. Thus may poor fools
Believe false teachers: though those that are betray'd
Do feel the treason sharply, yet the traitor
Stands in worse case of woe.
And thou, Posthumus, thou that didst set up
My disobedience 'gainst the king my father,
And make me put into contempt the suits
Of princely fellows, shalt hereafter find
It is no act of common passage, but
A strain of rareness: and I grieve myself
To think, when thou shalt be disedged by her
That now thou tirest on, how thy memory
Will then be pang'd by me.—Prithee, dispatch:
The lamb entreats the butcher: where's thy knife?
Thou art too slow to do thy master's bidding,
When I desire it too.

PISANIO.

O gracious lady,
Since I received command to do this business
I have not slept one wink.

IMOGEN.

Do't and to bed then.

PISANIO.

I'll wake mine eyeballs out first.

IMOGEN.

Wherefore, then,
Didst undertake it? Why hast thou abused
So many miles with a pretence? this place?
Mine action, and thine own? our horses' labour?
The time inviting thee? the perturb'd court
For my being absent, whereunto I never
Purpose return? Why hast thou gone so far,
To be unbent when thou hast ta'en thy stand,
Th'elected deer before thee?

PISANIO.

But to win time
To lose so bad employment; in the which
I have consider'd of a course. Good lady,
Hear me with patience.

IMOGEN.

Talk thy tongue weary; speak:
I have heard I am a strumpet; and mine ear,
Therein false struck, can take no greater wound,
Nor tent to bottom that. But speak.

PISANIO.

Then, madam,
I thought you would not back again.

IMOGEN.

Most like,
Bringing me here to kill me.

PISANIO.

Not so, neither:
But if I were as wise as honest, then
My purpose would prove well. It cannot be
But that my master is abused:
Some villain, ay, and singular in his art,
Hath done you both this cursed injury.

IMOGEN.

Some Roman courtezan.

PISANIO.

No, on my life.
I'll give but notice you are dead, and send him
Some bloody sign of it; for 'tis commanded
I should do so: you shall be mist at court,
And that will well confirm it.

IMOGEN.

Why, good fellow,
What shall I do the while? where bide? how live?
Or in my life what comfort, when I am
Dead to my husband?

PISANIO.

If you'll back to the court,—

IMOGEN.

No court, no father; nor no more ado
With that harsh, noble, simple nothing,—
That Cloten, whose love-suit hath been to me
As fearful as a siege.

PISANIO.

If not at court,
Then not in Britain must you bide.

IMOGEN.

Where then?
Hath Britain all the sun that shines? Day, night,
Are they not but in Britain? I'the world's volume
Our Britain seems as of it, but not in't;
In a great pool a swan's nest: prithee, think
There's livers out of Britain.

PISANIO.

I am most glad
You think of other place. Th'ambassador,
Lucius the Roman, comes to Milford-Haven
To-morrow: now, if you could wear a mind
Dark as your fortune is, and but disguise
That which, t'appear itself, must not yet be
But by self-danger, you should tread a course
Pretty and full of view; yea, happily, near
The residence of Posthumus,—so nigh at least
That though his actions were not visible, yet
Report should render him hourly to your ear
As truly as he moves.

IMOGEN.

O, for such means!
Though peril to my modesty, not death on't,
I would adventure.

PISANIO.

Well, then, here's the point:
You must forget to be a woman; change
Command into obedience; fear and niceness—
The handmaids of all women, or, more truly,
Woman it pretty self—into a waggish courage;
Ready in gibes, quick-answer'd, saucy, and
As quarrelous as the weasel; nay, you must
Forget that rarest treasure of your cheek,
Exposing it—but, O, the harder heart!
Alack, no remedy!—to the greedy touch
Of common-kissing Titan; and forget

Your laboursome and dainty trims, wherein
You made great Juno angry.

IMOGEN.

Nay, be brief:
I see into thy end, and am almost
A man already.

PISANIO.

First, make yourself but like one.
Fore-thinking this, I have already fit—
'Tis in my cloak-bag—doublet, hat, hose, all
That answer to them: would you, in their serving,
And with what imitation you can borrow
From youth of such a season, fore noble Lucius
Present yourself, desire his service, tell him
Wherein you're happy,—which you'll make him know,
If that his head have ear in music,—doubtless
With joy he will embrace you; for he's honourable,
And, doubling that, most holy. Your means abroad,
You have me, rich; and I will never fail
Beginning nor supplyment.

IMOGEN.

Thou art all the comfort
The gods will diet me with. Prithee, away:
There's more to be consider'd; but we'll even
All that good time will give us: this attempt
I am soldier to, and will abide it with
A prince's courage. Away, I prithee.

PISANIO.

Well, madam, we must take a short farewell,
Lest, being mist, I be suspected of
Your carriage from the court. My noble mistress,
Here is a box; I had it from the queen:
What's in't is precious; if you are sick at sea,
Or stomach-qualm'd at land, a dram of this
Will drive away distemper. To some shade,
And fit you to your manhood: may the gods
Direct you to the best!

IMOGEN.

Amen: I thank thee. [*Exeunt.*

SCENE V.

A room in CYMBELINE'S *palace.*

Enter CYMBELINE, QUEEN, CLOTEN, LUCIUS, *and* LORDS.

CYMBELINE.

THUS far; and so, farewell.

LUCIUS.

Thanks, royal sir.
My emperor hath wrote; I must from hence;
And am right sorry that I must report ye
My master's enemy.

CYMBELINE.

Our subjects, sir,
Will not endure his yoke; and for ourself
To show less sovereignty than they, must needs
Appear unkinglike.

LUCIUS.

So, sir, I desire of you
A conduct overland to Milford-Haven.—
Madam, all joy befall your Grace, and you!

CYMBELINE.

My lords, you are appointed for that office;
The due of honour in no point omit.—
So, farewell, noble Lucius.

LUCIUS.

Your hand, my lord.

CLOTEN.

Receive it friendly; but from this time forth
I wear it as your enemy.

LUCIUS.

Sir, the event
Is yet to name the winner: fare you well.

CYMBELINE.

Leave not the worthy Lucius, good my lords,
Till he have crost the Severn.—Happiness!

[*Exeunt* LUCIUS *and* LORDS.

QUEEN.

He goes hence frowning: but it honours us
That we have given him cause.

CLOTEN.

'Tis all the better;
Your valiant Britons have their wishes in it.

CYMBELINE.

Lucius hath wrote already to the emperor
How it goes here. It fits us therefore ripely
Our chariots and our horsemen be in readiness:
The powers that he already hath in Gallia
Will soon be drawn to head, from whence he moves
His war for Britain.

QUEEN.

'Tis not sleepy business;
But must be lookt to speedily and strongly.

CYMBELINE.

Our expectation that it would be thus
Hath made us forward. But, my gentle queen,
Where is our daughter? She hath not appear'd
Before the Roman, nor to us hath tender'd
The duty of the day: she looks us like
A thing more made of malice than of duty:
We have noted it.—Call her before us; for
We have been too slight in sufferance.

[*Exit an* ATTENDANT.

QUEEN.

Royal sir,
Since the exile of Posthumus, most retired
Hath her life been; the cure whereof, my lord,
'Tis time must do. Beseech your majesty,
Forbear sharp speeches to her: she's a lady
So tender of rebukes, that words are strokes,
And strokes death to her.

Enter ATTENDANT.

CYMBELINE.

Where is she, sir? How
Can her contempt be answer'd?

ATTENDANT.

Please you, sir,
Her chambers are all lockt; and there's no answer
That will be given to the loud'st of noise we make.

QUEEN.

My lord, when last I went to visit her,
She pray'd me to excuse her keeping close;
Whereto constrain'd by her infirmity,
She should that duty leave unpaid to you,
Which daily she was bound to proffer: this
She wisht me to make known; but our great court
Made me to blame in memory.

CYMBELINE.

Her doors lockt?
Not seen of late? Grant, heavens, that which I fear
Prove false! [*Exit.*

QUEEN.

Son, I say, follow the king.

CLOTEN.

That man of hers, Pisanio, her old servant,
I have not seen these two days.

QUEEN.

Go, look after. [*Exit* CLOTEN.
Pisanio, thou that stand'st so for Posthumus!—
He hath a drug of mine; I pray his absence
Proceed by swallowing that; for he believes
It is a thing most precious. But for her,
Where is she gone? Haply, despair hath seized her;
Or, wing'd with fervour of her love, she's flown
To her desired Posthumus: gone she is
To death or to dishonour; and my end
Can make good use of either: she being down,
I have the placing of the British crown.

Enter CLOTEN.

How now, my son!

CLOTEN.

'Tis certain she is fled.
Go in and cheer the king: he rages; none
Dare come about him.

QUEEN [*aside*]

All the better: may
This night forestall him of the coming day! [*Exit.*

CLOTEN.

I love and hate her: for she's fair and royal,
And that she hath all courtly parts more exquisite
Than lady, ladies, woman; from every one
The best she hath, and she, of all compounded,
Outsells them all,—I love her therefore: but,
Disdaining me, and throwing favours on
The low Posthumus, slanders so her judgement,
That what's else rare is choked; and in that point
I will conclude to hate her, nay, indeed,
To be revenged upon her. For, when fools
Shall—

Enter PISANIO.

Who is here? What, are you packing, sirrah?
Come hither: ah, you precious pandar! Villain,
Where is thy lady? In a word; or else
Thou art straightway with the fiends.

PISANIO.

O, good my lord!—

CLOTEN.

Where is thy lady? or, by Jupiter—
I will not ask again. Close villain,
I'll have this secret from thy heart, or rip
Thy heart to find it. Is she with Posthumus?
From whose so many weights of baseness cannot
A dram of worth be drawn.

PISANIO.

Alas, my lord,
How can she be with him? When was she mist?
He is in Rome.

CLOTEN.

Where is she, sir? Come nearer;
No further halting: satisfy me home
What is become of her.

PISANIO.

O, my all-worthy lord!—

CLOTEN.

All-worthy villain!
Discover where thy mistress is at once,
At the next word,—no more of 'worthy lord;'
Speak, or thy silence on the instant is
Thy condemnation and thy death.

PISANIO.

Then, sir,
This paper is the history of my knowledge
Touching her flight. [*Presenting a letter.*

CLOTEN.

Let's see't.—I will pursue her
Even to Augustus' throne.

PISANIO [*aside*].

Or this, or perish.
She's far enough; and what he learns by this
May prove his travel, not her danger.

CLOTEN.

Hum!

PISANIO [*aside*].

I'll write to my lord she's dead. O Imogen,
Safe mayst thou wander, safe return agen!

CLOTEN.

Sirrah, is this letter true?

PISANIO.

Sir, as I think.

CLOTEN.

It is Posthumus' hand; I know't.—Sirrah, if thou wouldst not be a villain, but do me true service, undergo those employments wherein I should have cause to use thee with a serious industry,—that is, what villainy soe'er I bid thee do, to perform it directly and truly,—I would think thee an honest man: thou shouldst neither want my means for thy relief, nor my voice for thy preferment.

PISANIO.

Well, my good lord.

CLOTEN.

Wilt thou serve me?—for since patiently and constantly thou hast stuck to the bare fortune of that beggar Posthumus, thou canst not, in the course of gratitude, but be a diligent follower of mine,—wilt thou serve me?

PISANIO.

Sir, I will.

CLOTEN.

Give me thy hand; here's my purse. Hast any of thy late master's garments in thy possession?

PISANIO.

I have, my lord, at my lodging, the same suit he wore when he took leave of my lady and mistress.

CLOTEN.

The first service thou dost me, fetch that suit hither: let it be thy first service; go.

PISANIO.

I shall, my lord. [*Exit.*

CLOTEN.

Meet thee at Milford-Haven!—I forgot to ask him one thing; I'll remember't anon:—even there, thou villain Posthumus, will I kill thee.—I would these garments were come. She said upon a time —the bitterness of it I now belch from my heart— that she held the very garment of Posthumus in more respect than my noble and natural person, together with the adornment of my qualities. With that suit upon my back, will I ravish her: first kill him, and in her eyes, there shall she see my valour, which will then be a torment to her contempt. He on the ground, my speech of insultment ended on his dead body, and when my lust hath dined,—

which, as I say, to vex her I will execute in the clothes that she so praised,—to the court I'll knock her back, foot her home again. She hath despised me rejoicingly, and I'll be merry in my revenge.

Enter PISANIO, *with the clothes.*

Be those the garments?

PISANIO.

Ay, my noble lord.

CLOTEN.

How long is't since she went to Milford-Haven?

PISANIO.

She can scarce be there yet.

CLOTEN.

Bring this apparel to my chamber; that is the second thing that I have commanded thee: the third is, that thou wilt be a voluntary mute to my design. Be but duteous and true, preferment shall tender itself to thee.—My revenge is now at Milford: would I had wings to follow it!—Come, and be true. [*Exit.*

PISANIO.

Thou bidd'st me to my loss: for, true to thee
Were to prove false, which I will never be,
To him that is most true.—To Milford go,
And find not her whom thou pursuest.—Flow, flow,
You heavenly blessings, on her!—This fool's speed
Be crost with slowness; labour be his meed! [*Exit.*

SCENE VI.

Wales: before the cave of BELARIUS.

Enter IMOGEN, *in boy's clothes.*

IMOGEN.

I SEE a man's life is a tedious one:
I have tired myself; and for two nights together
Have made the ground my bed. I should be sick,
But that my resolution helps me.—Milford,
When from the mountain-top Pisanio show'd thee,
Thou wast within a ken: O Jove! I think
Foundations fly the wretched; such, I mean,
Where they should be relieved. Two beggars told me
I could not miss my way: will poor folks lie,
That have afflictions on them, knowing 'tis
A punishment or trial? Yes; no wonder,
When rich ones scarce tell true: to lapse in fullness
Is sorer than to lie for need; and falsehood
Is worse in kings than beggars.—My dear lord!
Thou art one o'the false ones: now I think on thee
My hunger's gone; but even before, I was
At point to sink for food.—But what is this?
Here is a path to't: 'tis some savage hold:
I were best not call; I dare not call: yet famine,
Ere clean it o'erthrow nature, makes it valiant.
Plenty and peace breeds cowards; hardness ever
Of hardiness is mother.—Ho! who's here?
If any thing that's civil, speak; if savage,
Take or lend. Ho!—No answer? then I'll enter.
Best draw my sword; and if mine enemy
But fear the sword like me, he'll scarcely look on't.
Such a foe, good heavens! [*Exit into the cave.*

Enter BELARIUS, GUIDERIUS, *and* ARVIRAGUS.

BELARIUS.

You, Polydore, have proved best woodman, and
Are master of the feast: Cadwal and I
Will play the cook and servant; 'tis our match:
The sweat of industry would dry and die,
But for the end it works to. Come; our stomachs
Will make what's homely savoury: weariness
Can snore upon the flint, when resty sloth
Finds the down-pillow hard.—Now, peace be here,
Poor house, that keep'st thyself!

GUIDERIUS.

I am throughly weary.

ARVIRAGUS.

I am weak with toil, yet strong in appetite.

GUIDERIUS.

There is cold meat i'the cave; we'll browse on that,
Whilst what we have kill'd be cookt.

BELARIUS.

Stay; come not in.
[*Looking into the cave.*
But that it eats our victuals, I should think
Here were a fairy.

GUIDERIUS.

What's the matter, sir?

BELARIUS.

By Jupiter, an angel! or, if not,
An earthly paragon!—Behold divineness
No elder than a boy!

Enter IMOGEN.

IMOGEN.

Good masters, harm me not:
Before I enter'd here, I call'd; and thought
To have begg'd or bought what I have took: good troth,
I have stoln naught; nor would not, though I had found
Gold strew'd i'the floor. Here's money for my meat:
I would have left it on the board, so soon
As I had made my meal; and parted
With prayers for the provider.

GUIDERIUS.

Money, youth?

ARVIRAGUS.

All gold and silver rather turn to dirt!
And 'tis no better reckon'd, but of those
Who worship dirty gods.

IMOGEN.

I see you're angry:
Know, if you kill me for my fault, I should
Have died had I not made it.

BELARIUS.

Whither bound?

IMOGEN.

To Milford-Haven.

BELARIUS.

What's your name?

IMOGEN.

Fidele, sir. I have a kinsman who
Is bound for Italy; he embarkt at Milford;

To whom being going, almost spent with hunger,
I am faln in this offence.

BELARIUS.

Prithee, fair youth,
Think us no churls, nor measure our good minds
By this rude place we live in. Well encounter'd!
'Tis almost night: you shall have better cheer
Ere you depart; and thanks to stay and eat it.—
Boys, bid him welcome.

GUIDERIUS.

Were you a woman, youth,
I should woo hard but be your groom:—in honesty,
I bid for you as I do buy.

ARVIRAGUS.

I'll make't my comfort
He is a man: I'll love him as my brother:—
And such a welcome as I'ld give to him
After long absence, such is yours: most welcome!
Be sprightly, for you fall 'mongst friends.

IMOGEN.

'Mongst friends,
If brothers.—[*aside*] Would it had been so, that they
Had been my father's sons! then had my prize
Been less; and so more equal ballasting
To thee, Posthumus.

BELARIUS.

He wrings at some distress.

GUIDERIUS.

Would I could free't!

ARVIRAGUS.

Or I; whate'er it be,
What pain it cost, what danger! Gods!

BELARIUS.

Hark, boys. [*Whispering.*

IMOGEN.

Great men,
That had a court no bigger than this cave,
That did attend themselves, and had the virtue
Which their own conscience seal'd them,—laying by
That nothing-gift of differing multitudes,—
Could not out-peer these twain. Pardon me, gods!
I'ld change my sex to be companion with them,
Since Leonatus' false.

BELARIUS.

It shall be so.
Boys, we'll go dress our hunt.—Fair youth, come in:
Discourse is heavy, fasting; when we have supt,
We'll mannerly demand thee of thy story,
So far as thou wilt speak it.

GUIDERIUS.

Pray, draw near.

ARVIRAGUS.

The night to the owl, and morn to the lark, less welcome.

IMOGEN.

Thanks, sir.

ARVIRAGUS.

I pray, draw near. [*Exeunt.*

SCENE VII.

Rome. A public place.

Enter two SENATORS *and* TRIBUNES.

FIRST SENATOR.

THIS is the tenour of the emperor's writ,—
That since the common men are now in action
'Gainst the Pannonians and Dalmatians;
And that the legions now in Gallia are
Full weak to undertake our wars against
The faln-off Britons; that we do incite
The gentry to this business. He creates
Lucius pro-consul: and to you the tribunes,
For this immediate levy, he commends
His absolute commission. Long live Cæsar!

FIRST TRIBUNE.

Is Lucius general of the forces?

SECOND SENATOR.

Ay.

FIRST TRIBUNE.

Remaining now in Gallia?

FIRST SENATOR.

With those legions
Which I have spoke of, whereunto your levy
Must be supplyant: the words of your commission
Will tie you to the numbers, and the time
Of their dispatch.

FIRST TRIBUNE.

We will discharge our duty.
[*Exeunt.*

ACT IV. SCENE I.

Wales: the forest near the cave of BELARIUS.

Enter CLOTEN.

CLOTEN.

I AM near to the place where they should meet, if Pisanio have mapt it truly. How fit his garments serve me! Why should his mistress, who was made by him that made the tailor, not be fit too? the rather—saving reverence of the word—for 'tis said a woman's fitness comes by fits. Therein I must play the workman. I dare speak it to myself,—for it is not vainglory for a man and his glass to confer; in his own chamber, I mean,—the lines of my body are as well drawn as his; no less young, more strong, not beneath him in fortunes, beyond him in the advantage of the time, above him in birth, alike conversant in general services, and more remarkable in single oppositions: yet this imperceiverant thing loves him in my despite. What mortality is! Posthumus, thy head, which now is growing upon thy shoulders, shall within this hour be off; thy mistress enforced; thy garments cut to pieces before her face: and all this done, spurn her home to her father; who may happily be a little angry for my so rough usage; but my mother, having power of his testiness, shall turn all into my commendations. My horse is tied up safe: out, sword, and to a sore purpose! Fortune, put them into my hand! This is the very description of their meeting-place; and the fellow dares not deceive me. [*Exit.*

SCENE II.

Before the cave of BELARIUS.

Enter BELARIUS, GUIDERIUS, ARVIRAGUS, *and* IMOGEN *from the cave.*

BELARIUS [*to* IMOGEN].

YOU are not well: remain here in the cave;
We'll come to you after hunting.

ARVIRAGUS [*to* IMOGEN].

Brother, stay here:
Are we not brothers?

IMOGEN.

So man and man should be;
But clay and clay differs in dignity,
Whose dust is both alike. I am very sick.

GUIDERIUS.

Go you to hunting; I'll abide with him.

IMOGEN.

So sick I am not,—yet I am not well;
But not so citizen a wanton as
To seem to die ere sick: so please you, leave me;
Stick to your journal course: the breach of custom
Is breach of all. I am ill; but your being by me
Cannot amend me; society is no comfort
To one not sociable: I am not very sick,
Since I can reason of it. Pray you, trust me here:
I'll rob none but myself; and let me die,
Stealing so poorly.

GUIDERIUS.

I love thee; I have spoke it:
How much the quantity, the weight as much,
As I do love my father.

BELARIUS.

What? how! how!

ARVIRAGUS.

If it be sin to say so, sir, I yoke me
In my good brother's fault: I know not why
I love this youth; and I have heard you say,
Love's reason's without reason: the bier at door,
And a demand who is't shall die, I'ld say,
'My father, not this youth.'

BELARIUS [*aside*].

O noble strain!
O worthiness of nature! breed of greatness!
Cowards father cowards, and base things sire base:
Nature hath meal and bran, contempt and grace.
I'm not their father; yet who this should be,
Doth miracle itself, loved before me.—
'Tis the ninth hour o'the morn.

ARVIRAGUS.

Brother, farewell.

IMOGEN.

I wish ye sport.

ARVIRAGUS.

You health.—So please you, sir.

IMOGEN [*aside*].

These are kind creatures. Gods, what lies I have heard!
Our courtiers say all's savage but at court:
Experience, O, thou disprovest report!
Th'imperious seas breed monsters; for the dish
Poor tributary rivers as sweet fish.
I am sick still; heart-sick:—Pisanio,
I'll now taste of thy drug.

GUIDERIUS.

I could not stir him:
He said he was gentle, but unfortunate;
Dishonestly afflicted, but yet honest.

ARVIRAGUS.

Thus did he answer me: yet said, hereafter
I might know more.

BELARIUS.

To the field, to the field!—
We'll leave you for this time: go in and rest.

ARVIRAGUS.

We'll not be long away.

BELARIUS.

Pray, be not sick,
For you must be our housewife.

IMOGEN.

Well or ill,
I am bound to you.

BELARIUS.

And shalt be ever.

[*Exit* IMOGEN *into the cave.*

This youth, howe'er distrest, appears he hath had
Good ancestors.

ARVIRAGUS.

How angel-like he sings!

GUIDERIUS.

But his neat cookery! he cuts our roots in characters;
And sauced our broths, as Juno had been sick,
And he her dieter.

ARVIRAGUS.

Nobly he yokes
A smiling with a sigh,—as if the sigh
Was that it was for not being such a smile;
The smile mocking the sigh, that it would fly
From so divine a temple, to commix
With winds that sailors rail at.

GUIDERIUS.

I do note
That grief and patience, rooted in him both,
Mingle their spurs together.

ARVIRAGUS.

Grow, patience!
And let the stinking elder, grief, untwine
His perishing root with the increasing vine!

BELARIUS.

It is great morning. Come, away!—Who's there?

Enter CLOTEN.

CLOTEN.

I cannot find those runagates; that villain
Hath mockt me:—I am faint.

BELARIUS.

'Those runagates'!
Means he not us? I partly know him; 'tis
Cloten, the son o'the queen. I fear some ambush.
I saw him not these many years, and yet
I know 'tis he.—We are held as outlaws: hence!

GUIDERIUS.

He is but one: you and my brother search
What companies are near: pray you, away;
Let me alone with him.

[*Exeunt* BELARIUS *and* ARVIRAGUS.

CLOTEN.

Soft!—What are you
That fly me thus? some villain mountaineers?
I have heard of such.—What slave art thou?

GUIDERIUS.

A thing
More slavish did I ne'er than answering
A slave without a knock.

CLOTEN.

Thou art a robber,
A law-breaker, a villain: yield thee thief.

GUIDERIUS.

To who? to thee? What art thou? Have not I
An arm as big as thine? a heart as big?
Thy words, I grant, are bigger; for I wear not
My dagger in my mouth. Say what thou art,
Why I should yield to thee.

CLOTEN.

Thou villain base,
Know'st me not by my clothes?

GUIDERIUS.

No, nor thy tailor, rascal,
Who is thy grandfather: he made those clothes,
Which, as it seems, make thee.

CLOTEN.

Thou precious varlet,
My tailor made them not.

GUIDERIUS.

Hence, then, and thank
The man that gave them thee. Thou art some fool;
I am loth to beat thee.

CLOTEN.

Thou injurious thief,
Hear but my name, and tremble.

GUIDERIUS.

What's thy name?

CLOTEN.

Cloten, thou villain.

GUIDERIUS.

Cloten, thou double villain, be thy name,
I cannot tremble at it: were it Toad, or Adder, Spider,
'Twould move me sooner.

CLOTEN.

To thy further fear,
Nay, to thy mere confusion, thou shalt know
I am son to the queen.

GUIDERIUS.

I am sorry for't; not seeming
So worthy as thy birth.

CLOTEN.

Art not afeard?

GUIDERIUS.

Those that I reverence, those I fear,—the wise:
At fools I laugh, not fear them.

CLOTEN.

Die the death:
When I have slain thee with my proper hand,
I'll follow those that even now fled hence,
And on the gates of Lud's-town set your heads:
Yield, rustic mountaineer. [*Exeunt, fighting.*

Enter BELARIUS *and* ARVIRAGUS.

BELARIUS.

No company's abroad.

ARVIRAGUS.

None in the world: you did mistake him, sure.

BELARIUS.

I cannot tell:—long is it since I saw him,
But time hath nothing blurr'd those lines of favour
Which then he wore; the snatches in his voice,
And burst of speaking, were as his: I am absolute
'Twas very Cloten.

ARVIRAGUS.

In this place we left them:
I wish my brother make good time with him,
You say he is so fell.

BELARIUS.

Being scarce made up,
I mean, to man, he had not apprehension
Of roaring terrors; for defect of judgement
Is oft the cure of fear.—But, see, thy brother.

Enter GUIDERIUS *with* CLOTEN'S *head.*

GUIDERIUS.

This Cloten was a fool, an empty purse,—
There was no money in't: not Hercules
Could have knockt out his brains, for he had none:
Yet I not doing this, the fool had borne
My head as I do his.

BELARIUS.

What hast thou done?

GUIDERIUS.

I am perfect what: cut off one Cloten's head,
Son to the queen, after his own report;
Who call'd me traitor, mountaineer; and swore
With his own single hand he'ld take us in,
Displace our heads where—thank the gods!—they grow,
And set them on Lud's-town.

BELARIUS.

We are all undone.

GUIDERIUS.

Why, worthy father, what have we to lose
But that he swore to take our lives? The law
Protects not us: then why should we be tender
To let an arrogant piece of flesh threat us,
Play judge and executioner all himself,
For we do fear the law? What company
Discover you abroad?

BELARIUS.

No single soul
Can we set eye on; but in all safe reason
He must have some attendants. Though his humour
Was nothing but mutation,—ay, and that
From one bad thing to worse; not frenzy, not
Absolute madness could so far have raved,
To bring him here alone: although, perhaps,
It may be heard at court, that such as we
Cave here, hunt here, are outlaws, and in time
May make some stronger head; the which he hearing—
As it is like him—might break out, and swear
He'ld fetch us in; yet is't not probable
To come alone, either he so undertaking,
Or they so suffering: then on good ground we fear,
If we do fear this body hath a tail,
More perilous than the head.

ARVIRAGUS.

Let ordinance
Come as the gods foresay it: howsoe'er,
My brother hath done well.

BELARIUS.

I had no mind
To hunt this day: the boy Fidele's sickness
Did make my way long forth.

GUIDERIUS.

With his own sword,
Which he did wave against my throat, I have ta'en
His head from him: I'll throw't into the creek
Behind our rock; and let it to the sea,
And tell the fishes he's the queen's son, Cloten:
That's all I reck. [*Exit.*

BELARIUS.

I fear 'twill be revenged:
Would, Polydore, thou hadst not done 't! though valour
Becomes thee well enough.

ARVIRAGUS.

Would I had done't,
So the revenge alone pursued me!—Polydore,
I love thee brotherly; but envy much
Thou hast robb'd me of this deed: I would revenges,
That possible strength might meet, would seek us through,
And put us to our answer.

BELARIUS.

Well, 'tis done:—
We'll hunt no more to-day, nor seek for danger
Where there's no profit. I prithee, to our rock;
You and Fidele play the cooks: I'll stay
Till hasty Polydore return, and bring him
To dinner presently.

ARVIRAGUS.

Poor sick Fidele!
I'll willingly to him: to gain his colour
I'ld let a parish of such Clotens blood,
And praise myself for charity. [*Exit.*

BELARIUS.

O thou goddess,
Thou divine Nature, how thyself thou blazon'st
In these two princely boys! They are as gentle
As zephyrs, blowing below the violet,
Not wagging his sweet head; and yet as rough,
Their royal blood enchafed, as the rudest wind,
That by the top doth take the mountain pine,
And make him stoop to the vale. 'Tis wonder
That an invisible instinct should frame them
To royalty unlearn'd; honour untaught;
Civility not seen from other; valour,
That wildly grows in them, but yields a crop
As if it had been sow'd. Yet still it's strange
What Cloten's being here to us portends,
Or what his death will bring us.

Enter GUIDERIUS.

GUIDERIUS.

Where's my brother?
I have sent Cloten's clotpoll down the stream,
In embassy to his mother: his body's hostage
For his return. [*Solemn music.*

BELARIUS.

My ingenious instrument!
Hark, Polydore, it sounds! But what occasion
Hath Cadwal now to give it motion? Hark!

GUIDERIUS.

Is he at home?

BELARIUS.

He went hence even now.

GUIDERIUS.

What does he mean? since death of my dear'st mother
It did not speak before. All solemn things
Should answer solemn accidents. The matter?
Triumphs for nothing, and lamenting toys,
Is jollity for apes, and grief for boys.
Is Cadwal mad?

BELARIUS.

Look, here he comes,
And brings the dire occasion in his arms
Of what we blame him for!

Enter ARVIRAGUS, *with* IMOGEN *as dead, bearing her in his arms.*

ARVIRAGUS.

The bird is dead
That we have made so much on. I had rather
Have skipt from sixteen years of age to sixty,
To have turn'd my leaping-time into a crutch,
Than have seen this.

GUIDERIUS.

O sweetest, fairest lily!
My brother wears thee not the one half so well
As when thou grew'st thyself.

BELARIUS.

O melancholy!
Who ever yet could sound thy bottom? find
The ooze, to show what coast thy sluggish crare
Might easiliest harbour in?—Thou blessed thing!
Jove knows what man thou mightst have made; but I,
Thou diedst, a most rare boy, of melancholy!—
How found you him?

ARVIRAGUS.

Stark, as you see:
Thus smiling, as some fly had tickled slumber,
Not as death's dart, being laught at; his right cheek
Reposing on a cushion.

GUIDERIUS.

Where?

ARVIRAGUS.

O'the floor;
His arms thus leagued: I thought he slept; and put
My clouted brogues from off my feet, whose rudeness
Answer'd my steps too loud.

GUIDERIUS.

Why, he but sleeps:
If he be gone, he'll make his grave a bed;
With female fairies will his tomb be haunted,
And worms will not come to't.

ARVIRAGUS.

With fairest flowers,
Whilst summer lasts, and I live here, Fidele,
I'll sweeten thy sad grave: thou shalt not lack
The flower that's like thy face, pale primrose; nor
The azured harebell, like thy veins; no, nor
The leaf of eglantine, whom not to slander,
Out-sweeten'd not thy breath: the ruddock would,
With charitable bill,—O bill, sore-shaming
Those rich-left heirs that let their fathers lie
Without a monument!—bring thee all this;
Yea, and furr'd moss besides, when flowers are none,
To winter-ground thy corse.

GUIDERIUS.

Prithee, have done;
And do not play in wench-like words with that

Which is so serious. Let us bury him,
And not protract with admiration what
Is now due debt.—To the grave!

ARVIRAGUS.

Say, where shall's lay him?

GUIDERIUS.

By good Euriphile, our mother.

ARVIRAGUS.

Be't so:
And let us, Polydore, though now our voices
Have got the mannish crack, sing him to the ground,
As once our mother; use like note and words,
Save that Euriphile must be Fidele.

GUIDERIUS.

Cadwal,
I cannot sing: I'll weep, and word it with thee;
For notes of sorrow out of tune are worse
Than priests and fanes that lie.

ARVIRAGUS.

We'll speak it, then.

BELARIUS.

Great griefs, I see, medicine the less; for Cloten
Is quite forgot. He was a queen's son, boys:
And, though he came our enemy, remember
He was paid for that: though mean and mighty rotting
Together have one dust, yet reverence—
That angel of the world—doth make distinction
Of place 'tween high and low. Our foe was princely;
And though you took his life as being our foe,
Yet bury him as a prince.

GUIDERIUS.

Pray you, fetch him hither.
Thersites' body is as good as Ajax',
When neither are alive.

ARVIRAGUS.

If you'll go fetch him,
We'll say our song the whilst.—Brother, begin.

[*Exit* BELARIUS.

GUIDERIUS.

Nay, Cadwal, we must lay his head to th'east;
My father hath a reason for't.

ARVIRAGUS.

'Tis true.

GUIDERIUS.

Come on, then, and remove him.

ARVIRAGUS.

So.—Begin.

Song.

GUIDERIUS.

Fear no more the heat o'the sun,
Nor the furious winter's rages;
Thou thy worldly task hast done,
Home art gone, and ta'en thy wages:
Golden lads and girls all must,
As chimney-sweepers, come to dust.

ARVIRAGUS.

Fear no more the frown o'the great,
Thou art past the tyrant's stroke;
Care no more to clothe and eat;
To thee the reed is as the oak:
The sceptre, learning, physic, must
All follow this, and come to dust.

GUIDERIUS.

Fear no more the lightning-flash,

ARVIRAGUS.

Nor th'all-dreaded thunder-stone;

GUIDERIUS.

Fear not slander, censure rash;

ARVIRAGUS.

Thou hast finisht joy and moan:

BOTH.

All lovers young, all lovers must,
Consign to thee, and come to dust.

GUIDERIUS.

No exorciser harm thee!

ARVIRAGUS.

Nor no witchcraft charm thee!

GUIDERIUS.

Ghost unlaid forbear thee!

ARVIRAGUS.

Nothing ill come near thee!

BOTH.

Quiet consummation have;
And renowned be thy grave!

Enter BELARIUS *with the body of* CLOTEN.

GUIDERIUS.

We have done our obsequies: come, lay him down.

BELARIUS.

Here's a few flowers; but 'bout midnight, more:
The herbs that have on them cold dew o'the night
Are strewings fitt'st for graves.—Upon their faces.—
You were as flowers, now wither'd: even so
These herblets shall, which we upon you strow.—
Come on, away: apart upon our knees.
The ground that gave them first has them again:
Their pleasures here are past, so is their pain.

[*Exeunt* BELARIUS, GUIDERIUS, *and* ARVIRAGUS.

IMOGEN [*awaking*].

Yes, sir, to Milford-Haven; which is the way?—
I thank you.—By yond bush?—Pray, how far thither?
'Ods pittikins! can it be six mile yet?—
I have gone all night:—faith, I'll lie down and sleep.
But, soft! no bedfellow:—O gods and goddesses!

[*Seeing the body of* CLOTEN.

These flowers are like the pleasures of the world;
This bloody man, the care on't.—I hope I dream;
For so I thought I was a cave-keeper,
And cook to honest creatures: but 'tis not so;
'Twas but a bolt of nothing, shot at nothing,
Which the brain makes of fumes: our very eyes
Are sometimes like our judgements, blind. Good faith,
I tremble still with fear: but if there be
Yet left in heaven as small a drop of pity
As a wren's eye, fear'd gods, a part of it!
The dream's here still: even when I wake, it is
Without me, as within me; not imagined, felt.
A headless man!—The garments of Posthumus!
I know the shape of's leg: this is his hand;
His foot Mercurial; his Martial thigh;
The brawns of Hercules: but his Jovial face—
Murder in heaven?—How!—'Tis gone.—Pisanio,

All curses madded Hecuba gave the Greeks,
And mine to boot, be darted on thee! Thou,
Conspired with that irregulous devil, Cloten,
Hast here cut off my lord.—To write and read
Be henceforth treacherous!—Damn'd Pisanio
Hath with his forged letters,—damn'd Pisanio—
From this most bravest vessel of the world
Struck the main-top!—O Posthumus! alas,
Where is thy head? where's that? Ay me! where's that?
Pisanio might have kill'd thee at the heart,
And left thy head on.—How should this be? Pisanio?
'Tis he and Cloten: malice and lucre in them
Have laid this woe here. O, 'tis pregnant, pregnant!
The drug he gave me, which he said was precious
And cordial to me, have I not found it
Murderous to the senses? That confirms it home:
This is Pisanio's deed and Cloten's: O!—
Give colour to my pale cheek with thy blood,
That we the horrider may seem to those
Which chance to find us: O, my lord, my lord!
[*Throws herself on the body.*

Enter LUCIUS, CAPTAINS, *and a* SOOTHSAYER.

CAPTAIN.
To them the legions garrison'd in Gallia,
After your will, have crost the sea; attending
You here at Milford-Haven with your ships:
They are in readiness.

CAIUS LUCIUS.
But what from Rome?

CAPTAIN.
The senate hath stirr'd up the confiners
And gentlemen of Italy; most willing spirits,
That promise noble service: and they come
Under the conduct of bold Iachimo,
Sienna's brother.

CAIUS LUCIUS.
When expect you them?

CAPTAIN.
With the next benefit o'the wind.

CAIUS LUCIUS.
This forwardness
Makes our hopes fair. Command our present numbers
Be muster'd; bid the captains look to't.—Now, sir,
What have you dream'd of late of this war's purpose?

SOOTHSAYER.
Last night the very gods show'd me a vision,—
I fast and pray'd for their intelligence,—thus:
I saw Jove's bird, the Roman eagle, wing'd
From the spongy south to this part of the west,
There vanisht in the sunbeams: which portends—
Unless my sins abuse my divination—
Success to the Roman host.

CAIUS LUCIUS.
Dream often so,
And never false.—Soft, ho! what trunk is here
Without his top? The ruin speaks that sometime
It was a worthy building.—How! a page!—
Or dead, or sleeping on him? But dead, rather;
For nature doth abhor to make his bed
With the defunct, or sleep upon the dead.—
Let's see the boy's face.

CAPTAIN.
He's alive, my lord.

CAIUS LUCIUS.
He'll, then, instruct us of this body.—Young one,
Inform us of thy fortunes; for it seems
They crave to be demanded. Who is this
Thou makest thy bloody pillow? Or who was he
That, otherwise than noble nature did,
Hath alter'd that good picture? What's thy interest
In this sad wrack? How came it? Who is it?
What art thou?

IMOGEN.
I am nothing; or if not,
Nothing to be were better. This was my master,
A very valiant Briton and a good,
That here by mountaineers lies slain:—alas!
There is no more such masters: I may wander
From east to occident, cry out for service,
Try many, all good, serve truly, never
Find such another master.

CAIUS LUCIUS.
'Lack, good youth!
Thou movest no less with thy complaining than
Thy master in bleeding: say his name, good friend.

IMOGEN.
Richard du Champ.—[*aside*] If I do lie, and do
No harm by it, though the gods hear, I hope
They'll pardon it.—Say you, sir?

CAIUS LUCIUS.
Thy name?

IMOGEN.
Fidele, sir.

CAIUS LUCIUS.
Thou dost approve thyself the very same:
Thy name well fits thy faith, thy faith thy name.
Wilt take thy chance with me? I will not say
Thou shalt be so well master'd; but, be sure,
No less beloved. The Roman emperor's letters,
Sent by a consul to me, should not sooner
Than thine own worth prefer thee: go with me.

IMOGEN.
I'll follow, sir. But first, an't please the gods,
I'll hide my master from the flies, as deep
As these poor pickaxes can dig: and when
With wild wood-leaves and weeds I ha' strew'd his grave,
And on it said a century of prayers,
Such as I can, twice o'er, I'll weep and sigh;
And leaving so his service, follow you,
So please you entertain me.

CAIUS LUCIUS.
Ay, good youth;
And rather father thee than master thee.—
My friends,
The boy hath taught us manly duties: let us
Find out the prettiest daisied plot we can,
And make him with our pikes and partisans
A grave: come, arm him.—Boy, he is preferr'd
By thee to us; and he shall be interr'd
As soldiers can. Be cheerful; wipe thine eyes:
Some falls are means the happier to arise.
[*Exeunt.*

SCENE III.

A room in CYMBELINE'S *palace.*

Enter CYMBELINE, LORDS, PISANIO, *and* ATTENDANTS.

CYMBELINE.

AGAIN; and bring me word how 'tis with her.
A fever with the absence of her son;
[*Exit an* ATTENDANT.
A madness, of which her life's in danger,—Heavens,
How deeply you at once do touch me! Imogen,
The great part of my comfort, gone; my queen
Upon a desperate bed, and in a time
When fearful wars point at me; her son gone,
So needful for this present: it strikes me, past
The hope of comfort.—But for thee, fellow,
Who needs must know of her departure, and
Dost seem so ignorant, we'll enforce it from thee
By a sharp torture.

PISANIO.

Sir, my life is yours,
I humbly set it at your will: but, for my mistress,
I nothing know where she remains, why gone,
Nor when she purposes return. Beseech your highness
Hold me your loyal servant.

FIRST LORD.

Good my liege,
The day that she was missing he was here:
I dare be bound he's true, and shall perform
All parts of his subjection loyally. For Cloten,
There wants no diligence in seeking him,
And will, no doubt, be found.

CYMBELINE.

The time is troublesome.—
[*to* PISANIO] We'll slip you for a season; but our jealousy
Does yet depend.

FIRST LORD.

So please your majesty,
The Roman legions, all from Gallia drawn,
Are landed on your coast; with a supply
Of Roman gentlemen, by the senate sent.

CYMBELINE.

Now for the counsel of my son and queen!—
I am amazed with matter.

FIRST LORD.

Good my liege,
Your preparation can affront no less
Than what you hear of: come more, for more you're ready:
The want is, but to put those powers in motion
That long to move.

CYMBELINE.

I thank you. Let's withdraw;
And meet the time as it seeks us. We fear not
What can from Italy annoy us; but
We grieve at chances here.—Away!
[*Exeunt all but* PISANIO.

PISANIO.

I heard no letter from my master since
I wrote him Imogen was slain: 'tis strange:
Nor hear I from my mistress, who did promise
To yield me often tidings; neither know I
What is betid to Cloten; but remain
Perplext in all:—the heavens still must work.
Wherein I am false I am honest: not true, to be true:
These present wars shall find I love my country,
Even to the note o'the king, or I'll fall in them.
All other doubts, by time let them be clear'd:
Fortune brings in some boats that are not steer'd.
[*Exit.*

SCENE IV.

Wales: before the cave of BELARIUS.

Enter BELARIUS, GUIDERIUS, *and* ARVIRAGUS.

GUIDERIUS.

THE noise is round about us.

BELARIUS.

Let us from it.

ARVIRAGUS.

What pleasure, sir, find we in life, to lock it
From action and adventure?

GUIDERIUS.

Nay, what hope
Have we in hiding us? This way, the Romans
Must or for Britons slay us, or receive us
For barbarous and unnatural revolts
During their use, and slay us after.

BELARIUS.

Sons,
We'll higher to the mountains; there secure us.
To the king's party there's no going: newness
Of Cloten's death—we being not known, not muster'd
Among the bands—may drive us to a render
Where we have lived; and so extort from's that
Which we have done, whose answer would be death
Drawn on with torture.

GUIDERIUS.

This is, sir, a doubt
In such a time nothing becoming you,
Nor satisfying us.

ARVIRAGUS.

It is not likely
That when they hear the Roman horses neigh,
Behold their quarter'd fires, have both their eyes
And ears so cloy'd importantly as now,
That they will waste their time upon our note,
To know from whence we are.

BELARIUS.

O, I am known
Of many in the army: many years,
Though Cloten then but young, you see, not wore him
From my remembrance. And, besides, the king
Hath not deserved my service nor your loves;
Who find in my exile the want of breeding,
The certainty of this hard life; aye hopeless
To have the courtesy your cradle promised,
But to be still hot summer's tanlings, and
The shrinking slaves of winter.

GUIDERIUS.

Than be so,
Better to cease to be. Pray, sir, to the army:
I and my brother are not known; yourself
So out of thought, and thereto so o'ergrown,
Cannot be question'd.

ARVIRAGUS.

By this sun that shines,
I'll thither: what thing is it that I never
Did see man die! scarce ever lookt on blood,
But that of coward hares, hot goats, and venison!
Never bestrid a horse, save one that had
A rider like myself, who ne'er wore rowel
Nor iron on his heel! I am ashamed
To look upon the holy sun, to have
The benefit of his blest beams, remaining
So long a poor unknown.

GUIDERIUS.

By heavens, I'll go:
If you will bless me, sir, and give me leave,
I'll take the better care; but if you will not,
The hazard therefore due fall on me by
The hands of Romans!

ARVIRAGUS.

So say I,—Amen.

BELARIUS.

No reason I, since of your lives you set
So slight a valuation, should reserve
My crackt one to more care. Have with you, boys!
If in your country wars you chance to die,
That is my bed too, lads, and there I'll lie:
Lead, lead.—[*aside*] The time seems long; their blood thinks scorn,
Till it fly out, and show them princes born.
[*Exeunt.*

ACT V. SCENE I.

Britain. The Roman camp.

Enter POSTHUMUS *with a bloody handkerchief.*

POSTHUMUS LEONATUS.

YEA, bloody cloth, I'll keep thee; for I wisht
Thou shouldst be colour'd thus. You married ones,
If each of you should take this course, how many
Must murder wives much better than themselves
For wrying but a little!—O Pisanio!
Every good servant does not all commands:
No bond but to do just ones.—Gods! if you
Should have ta'en vengeance on my faults, I never
Had lived to put on this: so had you saved
The noble Imogen to repent; and struck
Me, wretch more worth your vengeance. But, [alack,
You snatch some hence for little faults; that's love,
To have them fall no more: you some permit
To second ills with ills, each elder worse,
And make them dread it, to the doers' thrift.
But Imogen is your own: do your best wills,
And make me blest to obey!—I am brought hither
Among the Italian gentry, and to fight
Against my lady's kingdom: 'tis enough
That, Britain, I have kill'd thy mistress; peace!
I'll give no wound to thee. Therefore, good heavens,
Hear patiently my purpose:—I'll disrobe me
Of these Italian weeds, and suit myself
As does a Briton peasant: so I'll fight
Against the part I come with; so I'll die
For thee, O Imogen, even for whom my life
Is, every breath, a death: and thus, unknown,
Pitied nor hated, to the face of peril
Myself I'll dedicate. Let me make men know
More valour in me than my habits show.
Gods, put the strength o'the Leonati in me!
To shame the guise o'the world, I will begin
The fashion,—less without and more within.
[*Exit.*

SCENE II.

A field between the British and Roman camps.

Enter LUCIUS, IACHIMO, IMOGEN, *and the* ROMAN ARMY *at one door, and the* BRITON ARMY *at another;* LEONATUS POSTHUMUS *following, like a poor soldier. They march over and go out. Then enter again, in skirmish,* IACHIMO *and* POSTHUMUS: *he vanquisheth and disarmeth* IACHIMO, *and then leaves him.*

IACHIMO.

THE heaviness and guilt within my bosom
Takes off my manhood: I have belied a lady,
The princess of this country, and the air on't
Revengingly enfeebles me; or could this carl,
A very drudge of nature's, have subdued me
In my profession? Knighthoods and honours, borne
As I wear mine, are titles but of scorn.
If that thy gentry, Britain, go before
This lout as he exceeds our lords, the odds
Is that we scarce are men, and you are gods. [*Exit.*

The battle continues; the BRITONS *fly;* CYMBELINE *is taken: then enter, to his rescue,* BELARIUS, GUIDERIUS, *and* ARVIRAGUS.

BELARIUS.

Stand, stand! We have the advantage of the ground;
The lane is guarded: nothing routs us but
The villainy of our fears.

GUIDERIUS *and* ARVIRAGUS.

Stand, stand, and fight!

Enter POSTHUMUS, *and seconds the* BRITONS: *they rescue* CYMBELINE, *and all exeunt. Then enter* LUCIUS, IACHIMO, *and* IMOGEN.

CAIUS LUCIUS.

Away, boy, from the troops, and save thyself;
For friends kill friends, and the disorder's such
As war were hoodwinkt.

IACHIMO.

'Tis their fresh supplies.

CAIUS LUCIUS.

It is a day turn'd strangely: or betimes
Let's re-inforce, or fly. [*Exeunt.*

SCENE III.

Another part of the field.

Enter POSTHUMUS *and a Briton* LORD.

LORD.

CAMEST thou from where they made the stand?

POSTHUMUS LEONATUS.

I did:
Though you, it seems, come from the fliers.

LORD.

I did.

POSTHUMUS LEONATUS.

No blame be to you, sir; for all was lost,
But that the heavens fought: the king himself
Of his wings destitute, the army broken,

And but the backs of Britons seen, all flying
Through a strait lane; the enemy full-hearted.
Lolling the tongue with slaughtering, having work
More plentiful than tools to do't, struck down
Some mortally, some slightly toucht, some falling
Merely through fear; that the strait pass was damm'd
With dead men hurt behind, and cowards living
To die with lengthen'd shame.

LORD.

Where was this lane?

POSTHUMUS LEONATUS.

Close by the battle, ditcht, and wall'd with turf;
Which gave advantage to an ancient soldier,—
An honest one, I warrant; who deserved
So long a breeding as his white beard came to,
In doing this for's country:—athwart the lane,
He, with two striplings,—lads more like to run
The country base than to commit such slaughter;
With faces fit for masks, or rather fairer
Than those for preservation cased or shame,—
Made good the passage; cried to those that fled,
'Our Britain's harts die flying, not our men:
To darkness fleet, souls that fly backwards! Stand;
Or we are Romans, and will give you that
Like beasts, which you shun beastly, and may save,
But to look back in frown: stand, stand!'—These three,
Three thousand confident, in act as many,—
For three performers are the file when all
The rest do nothing,—with this word, 'Stand, stand,'
Accommodated by the place, more charming
With their own nobleness,—which could have turn'd
A distaff to a lance,—gilded pale looks,
Part shame, part spirit renew'd; that some, turn'd coward
But by example,—O, a sin in war,
Damn'd in the first beginners!—gan to look
The way that they did, and to grin like lions
Upon the pikes o'the hunters. Then began
A stop i'the chaser, a retire; anon
A rout, confusion-thick: forthwith they fly
Chickens, the way which they stoopt eagles; slaves,
The strides they victors made: and now our cowards—
Like fragments in hard voyages—became
The life o'the need: having found the back-door open
Of the unguarded hearts, heavens, how they wound!
Some slain before; some dying; some their friends
O'er-borne i'the former wave: ten, chased by one,
Are now each one the slaughter-man of twenty:
Those that would die or e'er resist are grown
The mortal bugs o'the field.

LORD.

This was strange chance,—
A narrow lane, an old man, and two boys!

POSTHUMUS LEONATUS.

Nay, do not wonder at it: you are made
Rather to wonder at the things you hear
Than to work any. Will you rime upon't,
And vent it for a mockery? Here is one:
'Two boys, an old man twice a boy, a lane,
Preserved the Britons, was the Romans' bane.'

LORD.

Nay, be not angry, sir.

POSTHUMUS LEONATUS.

'Lack, to what end?
Who dares not stand his foe, I'll be his friend;
For if he'll do as he is made to do,
I know he'll quickly fly my friendship too.
You have put me into rime.

LORD.

Farewell; you're angry.

POSTHUMUS LEONATUS.

Still going? [*Exit* Lord.
This is a lord! O noble misery!
To be i'the field, and ask, what news, of me!
To-day how many would have given their honours
To have saved their carcasses! took heel to do't,
And yet died too! I, in mine own woe charm'd,
Could not find death where I did hear him groan,
Nor feel him where he struck: being an ugly monster,
'Tis strange he hides him in fresh cups, soft beds,
Sweet words; or hath moe ministers than we
That draw his knives i'the war. Well, I will find him:
For being now a favourer to the Briton,
No more a Briton, I have resumed again
The part I came in: fight I will no more,
But yield me to the veriest hind that shall
Once touch my shoulder. Great the slaughter is
Here made by the Roman; great the answer be
Britons must take: for me, my ransom's death;
On either side I come to spend my breath;
Which neither here I'll keep nor bear agen,
But end it by some means for Imogen.

Enter two Briton CAPTAINS *and* SOLDIERS.

FIRST CAPTAIN.

Great Jupiter be praised! Lucius is taken:
'Tis thought the old man and his sons were angels.

SECOND CAPTAIN.

There was a fourth man, in a silly habit,
That gave the affront with them.

FIRST CAPTAIN.

So 'tis reported:
But none of 'em can be found.—Stand! who's there?

POSTHUMUS LEONATUS.

A Roman;
Who had not now been drooping here, if seconds
Had answer'd him.

SECOND CAPTAIN.

Lay hands on him; a dog!—
A leg of Rome shall not return to tell
What crows have peckt them here:—he brags his service
As if he were of note: bring him to the king.

Enter CYMBELINE, BELARIUS, GUIDERIUS, ARVIRAGUS, PISANIO, *and Roman* CAPTIVES. *The* CAPTAINS *present* POSTHUMUS *to* CYMBELINE, *who delivers him over to a* GAOLER: *then exeunt omnes.*

SCENE IV.

A prison.

Enter POSTHUMUS *and two* GAOLERS.

FIRST GAOLER.

You shall not now be stoln, you have locks upon you;
So graze as you find pasture.

SECOND GAOLER.

Ay, or a stomach. [*Exeunt* GAOLERS.

POSTHUMUS LEONATUS.

Most welcome, bondage! for thou art a way,
I think, to liberty: yet am I better
Than one that's sick o'the gout; since he had rather
Groan so in perpetuity than be cured
By the sure physician, death; who is the key
T'unbar these locks. My conscience, thou art fetter'd
More than my shanks and wrists: you good gods, give me
The penitent instrument to pick that bolt,
Then free for ever! Is't enough I am sorry?
So children temporal fathers do appease;
Gods are more full of mercy. Must I repent?
I cannot do it better than in gyves,
Desired more than constrain'd: to satisfy,
If of my freedom 'tis the main part, take
No stricter render of me than my all.
I know you are more clement than vile men,
Who of their broken debtors take a third,
A sixth, a tenth, letting them thrive again
On their abatement: that's not my desire:
For Imogen's dear life take mine; and though
'Tis not so dear, yet 'tis a life; you coin'd it:
'Tween man and man they weigh not every stamp;
Though light, take pieces for the figure's sake:
You rather mine, being yours: and so, great powers,
If you will take this audit, take this life,
And cancel these cold bonds.—O Imogen!
I'll speak to thee in silence. [*Sleeps.*

Solemn music. Enter, as in an apparition, SICILIUS LEONATUS, *father to* POSTHUMUS, *an old man, attired like a warrior; leading in his hand an ancient matron, his wife, and mother to* POSTHUMUS, *with music before them: then, after other music, follows the two young* LEONATI, *brothers to* POSTHUMUS, *with wounds as they died in the wars. They circle* POSTHUMUS *round, as he lies sleeping.*

SICILIUS LEONATUS.

No more, thou thunder-master, show
Thy spite on mortal flies:
With Mars fall out, with Juno chide,
That thy adulteries
Rates and revenges.
Hath my poor boy done aught but well,
Whose face I never saw?
I died whilst in the womb he stay'd
Attending nature's law:
Whose father then, as men report
Thou orphans' father art,
Thou shouldst have been, and shielded him
From this earth-vexing smart.

MOTHER.

Lucina lent not me her aid,
But took me in my throes;
That from me was Posthumus ript,
Came crying 'mongst his foes,
A thing of pity!

SICILIUS LEONATUS.

Great nature, like his ancestry,
Moulded the stuff so fair,
That he deserved the praise o'the world,
As great Sicilius' heir.

FIRST BROTHER.

When once he was mature for man,
In Britain where was he
That could stand up his parallel;
Or fruitful object be
In eye of Imogen, that best
Could deem his dignity?

MOTHER.

With marriage wherefore was he mockt,
To be exiled, and thrown
From Leonati seat, and cast
From her his dearest one,
Sweet Imogen?

SICILIUS LEONATUS.

Why did you suffer Iachimo,
Slight thing of Italy,
To taint his nobler heart and brain
With needless jealousy;
And to become the geck and scorn
O'the other's villainy?

SECOND BROTHER.

For this, from stiller seats we came,
Our parents, and us twain,
That, striking in our country's cause,
Fell bravely, and were slain;
Our fealty and Tenantius' right
With honour to maintain.

FIRST BROTHER.

Like hardiment Posthumus hath
To Cymbeline perform'd:
Then, Jupiter, thou king of gods,
Why hast thou thus adjourn'd
The graces for his merits due;
Being all to dolours turn'd?

SICILIUS LEONATUS.

Thy crystal window ope; look out;
No longer exercise
Upon a valiant race thy harsh
And potent injuries.

MOTHER.

Since, Jupiter, our son is good,
Take off his miseries.

SICILIUS LEONATUS.

Peep through thy marble mansion; help;
Or we poor ghosts will cry
To the shining synod of the rest
Against thy deity.

BOTH BROTHERS.

Help, Jupiter; or we appeal,
And from thy justice fly.

JUPITER *descends in thunder and lightning, sitting upon an eagle: he throws a thunderbolt. The* GHOSTS *fall on their knees.*

JUPITER.

No more, you petty spirits of region low,
Offend our hearing; hush! How dare you ghosts
Accuse the thunderer, whose bolt, you know,
Sky-planted, batters all rebelling coasts?

Poor shadows of Elysium, hence; and rest
Upon your never-withering banks of flowers:
Be not with mortal accidents opprest;
No care of yours it is; you know 'tis ours.
Whom best I love I cross; to make my gift,
The more delay'd, delighted. Be content;
Your low-laid son our godhead will uplift:
His comforts thrive, his trials well are spent.
Our Jovial star reign'd at his birth, and in
Our temple was he married.—Rise, and fade!—
He shall be lord of lady Imogen,
And happier much by his affliction made.
This tablet lay upon his breast; wherein
Our pleasure his full fortune doth confine:
And so, away! no further with your din
Express impatience, lest you stir up mine.—
Mount, eagle, to my palace crystalline.
[*Ascends.*

SICILIUS LEONATUS.

He came in thunder; his celestial breath
Was sulphurous to smell: the holy eagle
Stoopt, as to foot us: his ascension is
More sweet than our blest fields: his royal bird
Prunes the immortal wing, and cloys his beak,
As when his god is pleased.

ALL.

Thanks, Jupiter!

SICILIUS LEONATUS.

The marble pavement closes, he is enter'd
His radiant roof.—Away! and, to be blest,
Let us with care perform his great behest.
[*The* GHOSTS *vanish.*

POSTHUMUS LEONATUS [*waking*].

Sleep, thou hast been a grandsire, and begot
A father to me; and thou hast created
A mother and two brothers: but—O scorn!—
Gone! they went hence so soon as they were born:
And so I am awake.—Poor wretches that depend
On greatness' favour dream as I have done;
Wake, and find nothing.—But, alas, I swerve:
Many dream not to find, neither deserve,
And yet are steept in favours; so am I,
That have this golden chance, and know not why.
What fairies haunt this ground? A book? O rare one!
Be not, as is our fangled world, a garment
Nobler than that it covers: let thy effects
So follow, to be most unlike our courtiers,
As good as promise. [*Reads.*
Whenas a lion's whelp shall, to himself unknown, without seeking find, and be embraced by a piece of tender air; and when from a stately cedar shall be lopt branches, which, being dead many years, shall after revive, be jointed to the old stock, and freshly grow; then shall Posthumus end his miseries, Britain be fortunate, and flourish in peace and plenty.
'Tis still a dream; or else such stuff as madmen
Tongue, and brain not: either both, or nothing:
Or senseless speaking, or a speaking such
As sense cannot untie. Be what it is,
The action of my life is like it, which
I'll keep, if but for sympathy.

Enter FIRST GAOLER.

FIRST GAOLER.

Come, sir, are you ready for death?

POSTHUMUS LEONATUS.

Over-roasted rather; ready long ago.

FIRST GAOLER.

Hanging is the word, sir: if you be ready for that, you are well cookt.

POSTHUMUS LEONATUS.

So, if I prove a good repast to the spectators, the dish pays the shot.

FIRST GAOLER.

A heavy reckoning for you, sir. But the comfort is, you shall be call'd to no more payments, fear no more tavern-bills; which are often the sadness of parting, as the procuring of mirth: you come in faint for want of meat, depart reeling with too much drink; sorry that you have paid too much, and sorry that you are paid too much; purse and brain both empty,—the brain the heavier for being too light, the purse too light being drawn of heaviness: of this contradiction you shall now be quit.—O, the charity of a penny cord! it sums up thousands in a trice: you have no true debitor and creditor but it; of what's past, is, and to come, the discharge:—your neck, sir, is pen, book, and counters; so the acquittance follows.

POSTHUMUS LEONATUS.

I am merrier to die than thou art to live.

FIRST GAOLER.

Indeed, sir, he that sleeps feels not the toothache: but a man that were to sleep your sleep, and a hangman to help him to bed, I think he would change places with his officer; for, look you, sir, you know not which way you shall go.

POSTHUMUS LEONATUS.

Yes, indeed do I, fellow.

FIRST GAOLER.

Your death has eyes in's head, then; I have not seen him so pictured: you must either be directed by some that take upon them to know, or to take upon yourself that which I am sure you do not know; or jump the after-inquiry on your own peril: and how you shall speed in your journey's end, I think you'll never return to tell one.

POSTHUMUS LEONATUS.

I tell thee, fellow, there are none want eyes to direct them the way I am going, but such as wink and will not use them.

FIRST GAOLER.

What an infinite mock is this, that a man should have the best use of eyes to see the way of blindness! I am sure hanging's the way of winking.

Enter a MESSENGER.

MESSENGER.

Knock off his manacles; bring your prisoner to the king.

POSTHUMUS LEONATUS.

Thou bring'st good news,—I am call'd to be made free.

FIRST GAOLER.

I'll be hang'd, then.

POSTHUMUS LEONATUS.

Thou shalt be then freer than a gaoler; no bolts for the dead.
[*Exeunt* POSTHUMUS *and* MESSENGER.

FIRST GAOLER.

Unless a man would marry a gallows, and beget young gibbets, I never saw one so prone. Yet, on my conscience, there are verier knaves desire to live, for all he be a Roman: and there be some of them too that die against their wills; so should I, if I were one. I would we were all of one mind, and one mind good; O, there were desolation of gaolers and gallowses! I speak against my present profit; but my wish hath a preferment in't.

[*Exit.*

SCENE V.

CYMBELINE'S *tent.*

Enter CYMBELINE, BELARIUS, GUIDERIUS, ARVIRAGUS, PISANIO, LORDS, OFFICERS, *and* ATTENDANTS.

CYMBELINE.

STAND by my side, you whom the gods have made
Preservers of my throne. Woe is my heart
That the poor soldier, that so richly fought,
Whose rags shamed gilded arms, whose naked breast
Stept before targes of proof, cannot be found:
He shall be happy that can find him, if
Our grace can make him so.

BELARIUS.

I never saw
Such noble fury in so poor a thing;
Such precious deeds in one that promised naught
But beggary and poor looks.

CYMBELINE.

No tidings of him?

PISANIO.

He hath been searcht among the dead and living,
But no trace of him.

CYMBELINE.

To my grief, I am
The heir of his reward; which I will add
To you, the liver, heart, and brain of Britain,
[*To* BELARIUS, GUIDERIUS, *and* ARVIRAGUS.
By whom I grant she lives. 'Tis now the time
To ask of whence you are:—report it.

BELARIUS.

Sir,
In Cambria are we born, and gentlemen:
Further to boast were neither true nor modest,
Unless I add we are honest.

CYMBELINE.

Bow your knees.
Arise my knights o'the battle; I create you
Companions to our person, and will fit you
With dignities becoming your estates.

Enter CORNELIUS *and* LADIES.

There's business in these faces.—Why so sadly
Greet you our victory? you look like Romans,
And not o'the court of Britain.

CORNELIUS.

Hail, great king!
To sour your happiness, I must report
The queen is dead.

CYMBELINE.

Who worse than a physician
Would this report become? But I consider
By medicine life may be prolong'd, yet death
Will seize the doctor too.—How ended she?

CORNELIUS.

With horror, madly dying, like her life;
Which, being cruel to the world, concluded
Most cruel to herself. What she confest
I will report, so please you: these her women
Can trip me, if I err; who with wet cheeks
Were present when she finisht.

CYMBELINE.

Prithee, say.

CORNELIUS.

First, she confest she never loved you; only
Affected greatness got by you, not you:
Married your royalty, was wife to your place;
Abhorr'd your person.

CYMBELINE.

She alone knew this;
And, but she spoke it dying, I would not
Believe her lips in opening it. Proceed.

CORNELIUS.

Your daughter, whom she bore in hand to love
With such integrity, she did confess
Was as a scorpion to her sight; whose life,
But that her flight prevented it, she had
Ta'en off by poison.

CYMBELINE.

O most delicate fiend!
Who is't can read a woman?—Is there more?

CORNELIUS.

More, sir, and worse. She did confess she had
For you a mortal mineral; which, being took,
Should by the minute feed on life, and, lingering,
By inches waste you: in which time she purposed,
By watching, weeping, tendance, kissing, to
O'ercome you with her show; yes, and in time,
When she had fitted you with her craft, to work
Her son into the adoption of the crown:
But, failing of her end by his strange absence,
Grew shameless-desperate; open'd, in despite
Of heaven and men, her purposes; repented
The evils she hatcht were not effected; so,
Despairing, died.

CYMBELINE.

Heard you all this, her women?

LADIES.

We did, so please your highness.

CYMBELINE.

Mine eyes
Were not in fault, for she was beautiful;
Mine ears, that heard her flattery; nor my heart,
That thought her like her seeming; it had been vicious
To have mistrusted her: yet, O my daughter!
That it was folly in me, thou mayst say,
And prove it in thy feeling. Heaven mend all!

Enter LUCIUS, IACHIMO, *the* SOOTHSAYER, *and other Roman* PRISONERS, *guarded;* POSTHUMUS *behind, and* IMOGEN.

Thou comest not, Caius, now for tribute; that
The Britons have razed out, though with the loss
Of many a bold one; whose kinsmen have made suit
That their good souls may be appeased with slaughter

Of you their captives, which ourself have granted:
So think of your estate.

LUCIUS.

Consider, sir, the chance of war: the day
Was yours by accident; had it gone with us,
We should not, when the blood was cool, have threaten'd
Our prisoners with the sword. But since the gods
Will have it thus, that nothing but our lives
May be call'd ransom, let it come: sufficeth
A Roman with a Roman's heart can suffer:
Augustus lives to think on't: and so much
For my peculiar care. This one thing only
I will entreat; my boy, a Briton born,
Let him be ransom'd: never master had
A page so kind, so duteous-diligent,
So tender over his occasions, true,
So feat, so nurse-like: let his virtue join
With my request, which I'll make bold your highness
Cannot deny; he hath done no Briton harm,
Though he have served a Roman: save him, sir,
And spare no blood beside.

CYMBELINE.

I have surely seen him:
His favour is familiar to me.—
Boy, thou hast lookt thyself into my grace,
And art mine own.—I know not why, nor wherefore,
To say, 'Live, boy:' ne'er thank thy master; live:
And ask of Cymbeline what boon thou wilt,
Fitting my bounty and thy state, I'll give it;
Yea, though thou do demand a prisoner,
The noblest ta'en.

IMOGEN.

I humbly thank your highness.

LUCIUS.

I do not bid thee beg my life, good lad;
And yet I know thou wilt.

IMOGEN.

No, no: alack,
There's other work in hand: I see a thing
Bitter to me as death: your life, good master,
Must shuffle for itself.

LUCIUS.

The boy disdains me,
He leaves me, scorns me: briefly die their joys
That place them on the truth of girls and boys.—
Why stands he so perplext?

CYMBELINE.

What wouldst thou, boy?
I love thee more and more: think more and more
What's best to ask. Know'st him thou look'st on? speak,
Wilt have him live? Is he thy kin? thy friend?

IMOGEN.

He is a Roman; no more kin to me
Than I to your highness; who, being born your vassal,
Am something nearer.

CYMBELINE.

Wherefore eyest him so?

IMOGEN.

I'll tell you, sir, in private, if you please
To give me hearing.

CYMBELINE.

Ay, with all my heart,
And lend my best attention. What's thy name?

IMOGEN.

Fidele, sir.

CYMBELINE.

Thou'rt my good youth, my page;
I'll be thy master: walk with me; speak freely.

[CYMBELINE *and* IMOGEN *converse apart.*

BELARIUS.

Is not this boy revived from death?

ARVIRAGUS.

One sand another
Not more resembles that sweet rosy lad
Who died, and was Fidele.—What think you?

GUIDERIUS.

The same dead thing alive.

BELARIUS.

Peace, peace! see further; he eyes us not; forbear;
Creatures may be alike: were't he, I am sure
He would have spoke to us.

GUIDERIUS.

But we saw him dead.

BELARIUS.

Be silent; let's see further.

PISANIO [*aside*].

It is my mistress:
Since she is living, let the time run on
To good or bad.

[CYMBELINE *and* IMOGEN *come forward.*

CYMBELINE.

Come, stand thou by our side;
Make thy demand aloud.—[*to* IACHIMO] Sir, step you forth;
Give answer to this boy, and do it freely;
Or, by our greatness, and the grace of it,
Which is our honour, bitter torture shall
Winnow the truth from falsehood.—On, speak to him.

IMOGEN.

My boon is, that this gentleman may render
Of whom he had this ring.

POSTHUMUS LEONATUS [*aside*].

What's that to him?

CYMBELINE.

That diamond upon your finger, say
How came it yours?

IACHIMO.

Thou'lt torture me to leave unspoken that
Which, to be spoke, would torture thee.

CYMBELINE.

How! me?

IACHIMO.

I am glad to be constrain'd to utter that
Which torments me to conceal. By villainy
I got this ring: 'twas Leonatus' jewel;
Whom thou didst banish; and—which more may grieve thee,
As it doth me—a nobler sir ne'er lived
'Twixt sky and ground. Wilt thou hear more, my lord?

CYMBELINE.

All that belongs to this.

IACHIMO.

That paragon, thy daughter,—
For whom my heart drops blood, and my false spirits
Quail to remember—Give me leave; I faint.

CYMBELINE.

My daughter! what of her? Renew thy strength:
I had rather thou shouldst live while nature will
Than die ere I hear more: strive, man, and speak.

IACHIMO.

Upon a time,—unhappy was the clock
That struck the hour!—it was in Rome,—accurst
The mansion where!—'twas at a feast,—O, would
Our viands had been poison'd, or at least
Those which I heaved to head!—the good Posthumus—
What should I say? he was too good to be
Where ill men were; and was the best of all
Amongst the rarest of good ones—sitting sadly,
Hearing us praise our loves of Italy
For beauty that made barren the swell'd boast
Of him that best could speak; for feature, laming
The shrine of Venus, or straight-pight Minerva,
Postures beyond brief nature; for condition,
A shop of all the qualities that man
Loves woman for; besides, that hook of wiving,
Fairness which strikes the eye,—

CYMBELINE.

I stand on fire:
Come to the matter.

IACHIMO.

All too soon I shall,
Unless thou wouldst grieve quickly.—This Posthumus,
Most like a noble lord in love, and one
That had a royal lover, took his hint;
And, not dispraising whom we praised,—therein
He was as calm as virtue,—he began
His mistress' picture; which by his tongue being made,
And then a mind put in't, either our brags
Were crackt of kitchen-trulls, or his description
Proved us unspeaking sots.

CYMBELINE.

Nay, nay, to the purpose.

IACHIMO.

Your daughter's chastity—there it begins.
He spake of her, as Dian had hot dreams,
And she alone were cold: whereat I, wretch,
Made scruple of his praise; and wager'd with him
Pieces of gold 'gainst this which then he wore
Upon his honour'd finger, to attain
In suit the place of 's bed, and win this ring
By hers and mine adultery. He, true knight,
No lesser of her honour confident
Than I did truly find her, stakes this ring;
And would so, had it been a carbuncle
Of Phœbus' wheel; and might so safely, had it
Been all the worth of's car. Away to Britain
Post I in this design:—well may you, sir,
Remember me at court; where I was taught
Of your chaste daughter the wide difference
'Twixt amorous and villainous. Being thus quencht
Of hope, not longing, mine Italian brain
Gan in your duller Britain operate
Most vilely; for my vantage, excellent:
And, to be brief, my practice so prevail'd
That I return'd with simular proof enough
To make the noble Leonatus mad,
By wounding his belief in her renown
With tokens thus and thus; averring notes
Of chamber-hanging, pictures, this her bracelet,—
O cunning, how I got it!—nay, some marks
Of secret on her person, that he could not
But think her bond of chastity quite crackt,
I having ta'en the forfeit. Whereupon—
Methinks, I see him now—

POSTHUMUS LEONATUS [*coming forward*].

Ay, so thou dost,
Italian fiend!—Ay me, most credulous fool,
Egregious murderer, thief, any thing
That's due to all the villains past, in being,
To come!—O, give me cord, or knife, or poison,
Some upright justicer! Thou, king, send out
For torturers ingenious: it is I
That all the abhorred things o'the earth amend
By being worse than they. I am Posthumus,
That kill'd thy daughter:—villain-like, I lie;
That caused a lesser villain than myself,
A sacrilegious thief, to do't:—the temple
Of virtue was she; yea, and she herself.
Spit, and throw stones, cast mire upon me, set
The dogs o'the street to bay me: every villain
Be call'd Posthumus Leonatus; and
Be villainy less than 'twas!—O Imogen!
My queen, my life, my wife! O Imogen,
Imogen, Imogen!

IMOGEN.

Peace, my lord; hear, hear—

POSTHUMUS LEONATUS.

Shall's have a play of this? Thou scornful page,
There lie thy part. [*Striking her: she falls.*

PISANIO.

O, gentlemen, help!
Mine and your mistress!—O, my lord Posthumus!
You ne'er kill'd Imogen till now.—Help, help!—
Mine honour'd lady!

CYMBELINE.

Does the world go round?

POSTHUMUS LEONATUS.

How comes these staggers on me?

PISANIO.

Wake, my mistress!

CYMBELINE.

If this be so, the gods do mean to strike me
To death with mortal joy.

PISANIO.

How fares my mistress?

IMOGEN.

O, get thee from my sight;
Thou gavest me poison: dangerous fellow, hence!
Breathe not where princes are.

CYMBELINE.

The tune of Imogen!

PISANIO.

Lady,
The gods throw stones of sulphur on me, if
That box I gave you was not thought by me
A precious thing; I had it from the queen.

CYMBELINE.

New matter still?

IMOGEN.

It poison'd me.

CORNELIUS.
O gods!—
I left out one thing which the queen confest,
Which must approve thee honest: 'If Pisanio
Have,' said she, 'given his mistress that confection
Which I gave him for cordial, she is served
As I would serve a rat.'

CYMBELINE.
What's this, Cornelius?

CORNELIUS.
The queen, sir, very oft importuned me
To temper poisons for her; still pretending
The satisfaction of her knowledge only
In killing creatures vile, as cats and dogs,
Of no esteem: I, dreading that her purpose
Was of more danger, did compound for her
A certain stuff, which, being ta'en, would cease
The present power of life; but in short time
All offices of nature should again
Do their due functions.—Have you ta'en of it?

IMOGEN.
Most like I did, for I was dead.

BELARIUS.
My boys,
There was our error.

GUIDERIUS.
This is, sure, Fidele.

IMOGEN.
Why did you throw your wedded lady from you?
Think that you are upon a lock; and now
Throw me again. [*Embracing him.*

POSTHUMUS LEONATUS.
Hang there like fruit, my soul,
Till the tree die!

CYMBELINE.
How now, my flesh, my child!
What, makest thou me a dullard in this act?
Wilt thou not speak to me?

IMOGEN.
Your blessing, sir.
[*Kneeling.*

BELARIUS.
Though you did love this youth, I blame ye not;
You had a motive for't.
[*To* GUIDERIUS *and* ARVIRAGUS.

CYMBELINE.
My tears that fall
Prove holy water on thee! Imogen,
Thy mother's dead.

IMOGEN.
I am sorry for't, my lord.

CYMBELINE.
O, she was naught: and long of her it was
That we meet here so strangely: but her son
Is gone, we know not how nor where.

PISANIO.
My lord,
Now fear is from me, I'll speak troth. Lord Cloten,
Upon my lady's missing, came to me
With his sword drawn; foam'd at the mouth, and swore,
If I discover'd not which way she was gone,
It was my instant death. By accident,
I had a feigned letter of my master's
Then in my pocket; which directed him
To seek her on the mountains near to Milford;
Where, in a frenzy, in my master's garments,
Which he enforced from me, away he posts
With unchaste purpose, and with oath to violate
My lady's honour: what became of him
I further know not.

GUIDERIUS.
Let me end the story:
I slew him there.

CYMBELINE.
Marry, the gods forfend!
I would not thy good deeds should from my lips
Pluck a hard sentence: prithee, valiant youth,
Deny't again.

GUIDERIUS.
I have spoke it, and I did it.

CYMBELINE.
He was a prince.

GUIDERIUS.
A most incivil one: the wrongs he did me
Were nothing prince-like; for he did provoke me
With language that would make me spurn the sea,
If it could so roar to me: I cut off's head;
And am right glad he is not standing here
To tell this tale of mine.

CYMBELINE.
I am sorry for thee:
By thine own tongue thou art condemn'd, and must
Endure our law: thou'rt dead.

IMOGEN.
That headless man
I thought had been my lord.

CYMBELINE.
Bind the offender,
And take him from our presence.

BELARIUS.
Stay, sir king:
This man is better than the man he slew,
As well descended as thyself; and hath
More of thee merited than a band of Clotens
Had ever scar for.—[*to the* GUARD] Let his arms alone:
They were not born for bondage.

CYMBELINE.
Why, old soldier
Wilt thou undo the worth thou art unpaid for,
By tasting of our wrath? How of descent
As good as we?

ARVIRAGUS.
In that he spake too far.

CYMBELINE.
And thou shalt die for't.

BELARIUS.
We will die all three:
But I will prove that two on's are as good
As I have given out him.—My sons, I must,
For mine own part, unfold a dangerous speech,
Though, haply, well for you.

ARVIRAGUS.
Your danger's ours.

GUIDERIUS.
And our good his.

BELARIUS.
Have at it, then!—
By leave,—thou hadst, great king, a subject who
Was call'd Belarius.

CYMBELINE.
What of him? he is
A banisht traitor.

BELARIUS.
He it is that hath
Assumed this age: indeed, a banisht man;
I know not how a traitor.

CYMBELINE.
Take him hence:
The whole world shall not save him.

BELARIUS.
Not too hot:
First pay me for the nursing of thy sons;
And let it be confiscate all, so soon
As I have received it.

CYMBELINE.
Nursing of my sons!

BELARIUS.
I am too blunt and saucy: here's my knee:
Ere I arise, I will prefer my sons;
Then spare not the old father. Mighty sir,
These two young gentlemen, that call me father,
And think they are my sons, are none of mine;
They are the issue of your loins, my liege,
And blood of your begetting.

CYMBELINE.
How! my issue!

BELARIUS.
So sure as you your father's. I, old Morgan,
Am that Belarius whom you sometime banisht:
Your pleasure was my mere offence, my punishment
Itself, and all my treason; that I suffer'd
Was all the harm I did. These gentle princes—
For such and so they are—these twenty years
Have I train'd up: those arts they have as I
Could put into them; my breeding was, sir, as
Your highness knows. Their nurse, Euriphile,
Whom for the theft I wedded, stole these children
Upon my banishment: I moved her to't;
Having received the punishment before,
For that which I did then: beaten for loyalty
Excited me to treason: their dear loss,
The more of you 'twas felt, the more it shaped
Unto my end of stealing them. But, gracious sir,
Here are your sons again; and I must lose
Two of the swect'st companions in the world.
The benediction of these covering heavens
Fall on their heads like dew! for they are worthy
To inlay heaven with stars.

CYMBELINE.
Thou weep'st, and speak'st.
The service that you three have done is more
Unlike than this thou tell'st. I lost my children:
If these be they, I know not how to wish
A pair of worthier sons.

BELARIUS.
Be pleased awhile.—
This gentleman, whom I call Polydore,
Most worthy prince, as yours, is true Guiderius:
This gentleman, my Cadwal, Arviragus,
Your younger princely son: he, sir, was lapt
In a most curious mantle, wrought by the hand
Of his queen-mother, which, for more probation,
I can with ease produce.

CYMBELINE.
Guiderius had
Upon his neck a mole, a sanguine star;
It was a mark of wonder.

BELARIUS.
This is he;
Who hath upon him still that natural stamp:
It was wise nature's end in the donation,
To be his evidence now.

CYMBELINE.
O, what, am I
A mother to the birth of three? Ne'er mother
Rejoiced deliverance more.—Blest pray you be,
That, after this strange starting from your orbs,
You may reign in them now!—O Imogen,
Thou hast lost by this a kingdom.

IMOGEN.
No, my lord;
I have got two worlds by't.—O my gentle brothers,
Have we thus met? O, never say hereafter
But I am truest speaker: you call'd me brother,
When I was but your sister; I you brothers,
When ye were so indeed.

CYMBELINE.
Did you e'er meet?

ARVIRAGUS.
Ay, my good lord.

GUIDERIUS.
And at first meeting loved;
Continued so, until we thought he died.

CORNELIUS.
By the queen's dram she swallow'd.

CYMBELINE.
O rare instinct!
When shall I hear all through? This fierce abridgement
Hath to it circumstantial branches, which
Distinction should be rich in.—Where? how lived you?
And when came you to serve our Roman captive?
How parted with your brothers? how first met them?
Why fled you from the court? and whither? These,
And your three motives to the battle, with
I know not how much more, should be demanded;
And all the other by-dependances,
From chance to chance: but nor the time nor place
Will serve our long inter'gatories. See,
Posthumus anchors upon Imogen;
And she, like harmless lightning, throws her eye
On him, her brothers, me, her master, hitting
Each object with a joy: the counterchange
Is severally in all. Let's quit this ground,
And smoke the temple with our sacrifices.—
[*to* BELARIUS] Thou art my brother; so we'll hold thee ever.

IMOGEN.
You are my father too; and did relieve me,
To see this gracious season.

CYMBELINE.
All o'erjoy'd,
Save these in bonds: let them be joyful too,
For they shall taste our comfort.

IMOGEN.
My good master,
I will yet do you service.

CAIUS LUCIUS.
Happy be you!

CYMBELINE.
The forlorn soldier, that so nobly fought,
He would have well becomed this place, and graced
The thankings of a king.

POSTHUMUS LEONATUS.
I am, sir,
The soldier that did company these three
In poor beseeming; 'twas a fitment for
The purpose I then follow'd.—That I was he,
Speak, Iachimo: I had you down, and might
Have made you finish.

IACHIMO.
I am down again:
[*Kneeling.*
But now my heavy conscience sinks my knee,
As then your force did. Take that life, beseech you,
Which I so often owe: but your ring first;
And here the bracelet of the truest princess
That ever swore her faith.

POSTHUMUS LEONATUS.
Kneel not to me:
The power that I have on you is to spare you;
The malice towards you to forgive you: live,
And deal with others better.

CYMBELINE.
Nobly doom'd!
We'll learn our freeness of a son-in-law;
Pardon's the word to all.

ARVIRAGUS.
You holp us, sir,
As you did mean indeed to be our brother;
Joy'd are we that you are.

POSTHUMUS LEONATUS.
Your servant, princes.—Good my lord of Rome,
Call forth your soothsayer: as I slept, methought
Great Jupiter, upon his eagle backt,
Appear'd to me, with other spritely shows
Of mine own kindred: when I waked, I found
This label on my bosom; whose containing
Is so from sense in hardness, that I can
Make no collection of it: let him show
His skill in the construction.

CAIUS LUCIUS.
Philarmonus,—

SOOTHSAYER.
Here, my good lord.

CAIUS LUCIUS.
Read, and declare the meaning.

SOOTHSAYER [*reads*].
Whenas a lion's whelp shall, to himself unknown, without seeking find, and be embraced by a piece of tender air; and when from a stately cedar shall be lopt branches, which, being dead many years, shall after revive, be jointed to the old stock, and freshly grow; then shall Posthumus end his miseries, Britain be fortunate, and flourish in peace and plenty.
Thou, Leonatus, art the lion's whelp:
The fit and apt construction of thy name,
Being Leo-natus, doth import so much:
[*to* CYMBELINE] The piece of tender air, thy virtuous daughter,
Which we call *mollis aer*; and *mollis aer*
We term it *mulier*: [*to* POSTHUMUS] which *mulier* I divine
Is thy most constant wife; who, even now,
Answering the letter of the oracle,
Unknown to you, unsought, were clipt about
With this most tender air.

CYMBELINE.
This hath some seeming.

SOOTHSAYER.
The lofty cedar, royal Cymbeline,
Personates thee: and thy lopt branches point
Thy two sons forth; who, by Belarius stoln,
For many years thought dead, are now revived,
To the majestic cedar join'd; whose issue
Promises Britain peace and plenty.

CYMBELINE.
Well,
My peace we will begin:—and, Caius Lucius,
Although the victor, we submit to Cæsar,
And to the Roman empire; promising
To pay our wonted tribute, from the which
We were dissuaded by our wicked queen;
Whom heavens, in justice, both on her and hers,
Have laid most heavy hand.

SOOTHSAYER.
The fingers of the powers above do tune
The harmony of this peace. The vision
Which I made known to Lucius, ere the stroke
Of this yet scarce-cold battle, at this instant
Is full accomplisht; for the Roman eagle,
From south to west on wing soaring aloft,
Lessen'd herself, and in the beams o'the sun
So vanisht; which foreshow'd our princely eagle,
Th'imperial Cæsar, should again unite
His favour with the radiant Cymbeline,
Which shines here in the west.

CYMBELINE.
Laud we the gods;
And let our crooked smokes climb to their nostrils
From our blest altars. Publish we this peace
To all our subjects. Set we forward: let
A Roman and a British ensign wave
Friendly together: so through Lud's-town march:
And in the temple of great Jupiter
Our peace we'll ratify; seal it with feasts.—
Set on there!—Never was a war did cease,
Ere bloody hands were washt, with such a peace.
[*Exeunt.*

THE WINTER'S TALE

DRAMATIS PERSONAE

LEONTES, *king of Sicilia.*
MAMILLIUS, *young prince of Sicilia.*
CAMILLO, ANTIGONUS, CLEOMENES, DION, *four lords of Sicilia.*
POLIXENES, *king of Bohemia.*
FLORIZEL, *prince of Bohemia.*
ARCHIDAMUS, *a lord of Bohemia.*
OLD SHEPHERD, *reputed father of Perdita.*
CLOWN, *his son.*
AUTOLYCUS, *a rogue.*
A MARINER.
GAOLER.

HERMIONE, *queen to Leontes.*
PERDITA, *daughter to Leontes and Hermione.*
PAULINA, *wife to Antigonus.*
EMILIA, *a lady attending on Hermione.*
MOPSA, DORCAS, *Shepherdesses.*

Other LORDS *and* GENTLEMEN, LADIES, OFFICERS, *and* SERVANTS, SHEPHERDS *and* SHEPHERDESSES.

TIME, *as* CHORUS.

SCENE—*Sometimes in Sicilia, sometimes in Bohemia.*

ACT I. SCENE I.

Sicilia. Antechamber in LEONTES' *palace.*

Enter CAMILLO *and* ARCHIDAMUS.

ARCHIDAMUS.

IF you shall chance, Camillo, to visit Bohemia, on the like occasion whereon my services are now on foot, you shall see, as I have said, great difference betwixt our Bohemia and your Sicilia.

CAMILLO.

I think, this coming summer, the King of Sicilia means to pay Bohemia the visitation which he justly owes him.

ARCHIDAMUS.

Wherein our entertainment shall shame us we will be justified in our loves; for, indeed,—

CAMILLO.

Beseech you,—

ARCHIDAMUS.

Verily, I speak it in the freedom of my knowledge· we cannot with such magnificence—in so rare—I know not what to say.—We will give you sleepy drinks, that your senses, unintelligent of our insufficience, may, though they cannot praise us, as little accuse us.

CAMILLO.

You pay a great deal too dear for what's given freely.

ARCHIDAMUS.

Believe me, I speak as my understanding instructs me, and as mine honesty puts it to utterance.

CAMILLO.

Sicilia cannot show himself over-kind to Bohemia. They were train'd together in their childhoods; and there rooted betwixt them such an affection, which cannot choose but branch now. Since their more mature dignities and royal necessities made separation of their society, their encounters, though not personal, hath been royally attorney'd with interchange of gifts, letters, loving embassies; that they have seem'd to be together, though absent; shook hands, as over a vast; and embraced, as it were, from the ends of opposed winds. The heavens continue their loves!

ARCHIDAMUS.

I think there is not in the world either malice or matter to alter it. You have an unspeakable comfort of your young prince Mamillius: it is a gentleman of the greatest promise that ever came into my note.

CAMILLO.

I very well agree with you in the hopes of him: it is a gallant child; one that, indeed, physics the subject, makes old hearts fresh: they that went on crutches ere he was born desire yet their life to see him a man.

ARCHIDAMUS.

Would they else be content to die?

CAMILLO.

Yes; if there were no other excuse why they should desire to live.

ARCHIDAMUS.

If the king had no son, they would desire to live on crutches till he had one. [*Exeunt.*

SCENE II.

A room of state in the same.

Enter LEONTES, POLIXENES, HERMIONE, MAMILLIUS, CAMILLO, *and* ATTENDANTS.

POLIXENES.

NINE changes of the watery star hath been
The shepherd's note since we have left our throne
Without a burden: time as long again
Would be fill'd up, my brother, with our thanks;
And yet we should, for perpetuity,
Go hence in debt: and therefore, like a cipher,
Yet standing in rich place, I multiply
With one we-thank-you many thousands moe
That go before it.

LEONTES.

Stay your thanks awhile,
And pay them when you part.

POLIXENES.

Sir, that's to-morrow.
I am question'd by my fears, of what may chance
Or breed upon our absence: that may blow

No sneaping winds at home, to make us say,
'This is put forth too truly!' Besides, I have stay'd
To tire your royalty.

LEONTES.
We are tougher, brother,
Than you can put us to't.

POLIXENES.
No longer stay.

LEONTES.
One seven-night longer.

POLIXENES.
Very sooth, to-morrow.

LEONTES.
We'll part the time between's, then: and in that
I'll no gainsaying.

POLIXENES.
Press me not, beseech you, so.
There is no tongue that moves, none, none i'the world,
So soon as yours, could win me: so it should now,
Were there necessity in your request, although
'Twere needful I denied it. My affairs
Do even drag me homeward: which to hinder,
Were, in your love, a whip to me; my stay,
To you a charge and trouble: to save both,
Farewell, our brother.

LEONTES.
Tongue-tied, our queen? speak you.

HERMIONE.
I had thought, sir, to have held my peace until
You had drawn oaths from him not to stay. You, sir,
Charge him too coldly. Tell him, you are sure
All in Bohemia's well; this satisfaction
The by-gone day proclaim'd: say this to him,
He's beat from his best ward.

LEONTES.
Well said, Hermione.

HERMIONE.
To tell, he longs to see his son, were strong:
But let him say so then, and let him go;
But let him swear so, and he shall not stay,
We'll thwack him hence with distaffs.—
Yet of your royal presence I'll adventure
The borrow of a week. When at Bohemia
You take my lord, I'll give you my commission
To let him there a month behind the gest
Prefixt for's parting:—yet, good deed, Leontes,
I love thee not a jar o'the clock behind
What lady she her lord.—You'll stay?

POLIXENES.
No, madam.

HERMIONE.
Nay, but you will?

POLIXENES.
I may not, verily.

HERMIONE.
Verily!
You put me off with limber vows; but I,
Though you would seek t'unsphere the stars with oaths,
Should yet say, 'Sir, no going.' Verily,
You shall not go: a lady's 'verily' is
As potent as a lord's. Will you go yet?
Force me to keep you as a prisoner,
Not like a guest; so you shall pay your fees
When you depart, and save your thanks. How say you?
My prisoner, or my guest? by your dread 'verily,'
One of them you shall be.

POLIXENES.
Your guest, then, madam:
To be your prisoner should import offending;
Which is for me less easy to commit
Than you to punish.

HERMIONE.
Not your gaoler, then,
But your kind hostess. Come, I'll question you
Of my lord's tricks and yours when you were boys:
You were pretty lordings then?

POLIXENES.
We were, fair queen,
Two lads that thought there was no more behind
But such a day to-morrow as to-day,
And to be boy eternal.

HERMIONE.
Was not my lord the verier wag o'the two?

POLIXENES.
We were as twinn'd lambs that did frisk i'the sun,
And bleat the one at the other: what we changed
Was innocence for innocence; we knew not
The doctrine of ill-doing, no, nor dream'd
That any did. Had we pursued that life,
And our weak spirits ne'er been higher rear'd
With stronger blood, we should have answer'd heaven
Boldly, 'Not guilty;' the imposition clear'd
Hereditary ours.

HERMIONE.
By this we gather
You have tript since.

POLIXENES.
O my most sacred lady,
Temptations have since then been born to's; for
In those unfledged days was my wife a girl;
Your precious self had then not crost the eyes
Of my young playfellow.

HERMIONE.
Grace to boot!
Of this make no conclusion, lest you say
Your queen and I are devils: yet, go on;
Th'offences we have made you do, we'll answer;
If you first sinn'd with us, and that with us
You did continue fault, and that you slipt not
With any but with us.

LEONTES.
Is he won yet?

HERMIONE.
He'll stay, my lord.

LEONTES.
At my request he would not.
Hermione, my dear'st, thou never spokest
To better purpose.

HERMIONE.
Never?

LEONTES.
Never, but once.

HERMIONE.
What! have I twice said well? when was't before?
I prithee tell me; cram's with praise, and make's

As fat as tame things: one good deed dying tongueless
Slaughters a thousand waiting upon that.
Our praises are our wages: you may ride's
With one soft kiss a thousand furlongs, ere
With spur we heat an acre. But to the goal:—
My last good deed was to entreat his stay:
What was my first? it has an elder sister,
Or I mistake you: O, would her name were Grace!
But once before I spoke to the purpose: when?
Nay, let me have't; I long.

LEONTES.

Why, that was when
Three crabbed months had sour'd themselves to death,
Ere I could make thee open thy white hand,
And clap thyself my love: then didst thou utter,
'I am yours for ever.'

HERMIONE.

'Tis Grace indeed.—
Why, lo you now, I have spoke to the purpose twice:
The one for ever earn'd a royal husband;
Th'other for some while a friend.

[*Giving her hand to* POLIXENES.

LEONTES [*aside*].

Too hot, too hot!
To mingle friendship far, is mingling bloods.
I have *tremor cordis* on me,—my heart dances;
But not for joy,—not joy.—This entertainment
May a free face put on; derive a liberty
From heartiness, from bounty's fertile bosom,
And well become the agent; 't may, I grant:
But to be paddling palms and pinching fingers,
As now they are; and making practised smiles,
As in a looking-glass; and then to sigh, as 'twere
The mort o'the deer; O, that is entertainment
My bosom likes not, nor my brows!—Mamillius,
Art thou my boy?

MAMILLIUS.

Ay, my good lord.

LEONTES.

I'fecks!
Why, that's my bawcock. What, hast smutcht thy nose?—
They say it is a copy out of mine. Come, captain,
We must be neat;—not neat, but cleanly, captain:
And yet the steer, the heifer, and the calf,
Are all call'd neat.—Still virginalling
Upon his palm?—How now, you wanton calf!
Art thou my calf?

MAMILLIUS.

Yes, if you will, my lord.

LEONTES.

Thou want'st a rough pash, and the shoots that I have,
To be full like me:—yet they say we are
Almost as like as eggs; women say so,
That will say any thing: but were they false
As o'er-dyed blacks, as wind, as waters,—false
As dice are to be wisht by one that fixes
No bourn 'twixt his and mine; yet were it true
To say this boy were like me.—Come, sir page,
Look on me with your welkin eye: sweet villain!
Most dear'st! my collop!—Can thy dam?—may't be?—
Affection! thy intention stabs the centre:
Thou dost make possible things not so held,
Communicatest with dreams;—how can this be?—
With what's unreal thou coactive art,
And fellow'st nothing: then 'tis very credent
Thou mayst co-join with something; and thou dost,
And that beyond commission, and I find it,—
And that to the infection of my brains
And hardening of my brows.

POLIXENES.

What means Sicilia?

HERMIONE.

He something seems unsettled.

POLIXENES.

How, my lord!
What cheer? how is't with you, best brother?

HERMIONE.

You look
As if you held a brow of much distraction:
Are you moved, my lord?

LEONTES.

No, in good earnest.—
How sometimes nature will betray its folly,
Its tenderness, and make itself a pastime
To harder bosoms!—Looking on the lines
Of my boy's face, methoughts I did recoil
Twenty-three years; and saw myself unbreecht,
In my green velvet coat; my dagger muzzled,
Lest it should bite its master, and so prove,
As ornaments oft do, too dangerous:
How like, methought, I then was to this kernel,
This squash, this gentleman.—Mine honest friend,
Will you take eggs for money?

MAMILLIUS.

No, my lord, I'll fight.

LEONTES.

You will? why, happy man be's dole!—My brother,
Are you so fond of your young prince as we
Do seem to be of ours?

POLIXENES.

If at home, sir,
He's all my exercise, my mirth, my matter:
Now my sworn friend, and then mine enemy;
My parasite, my soldier, statesman, all:
He makes a July's day short as December;
And with his varying childness cures in me
Thoughts that would thick my blood.

LEONTES.

So stands this squire
Officed with me. We two will walk, my lord,
And leave you to your graver steps.—Hermione,
How thou lovest us, show in our brother's welcome;
Let what is dear in Sicily be cheap:
Next to thyself and my young rover, he's
Apparent to my heart.

HERMIONE.

If you would seek us,
We are yours i'the garden: shall's attend you there?

LEONTES.

To your own bents dispose you: you'll be found,
Be you beneath the sky.—[*aside*] I am angling now,

Though you perceive me not how I give line.
Go to, go to!
How she holds up the neb, the bill to him!
And arms her with the boldness of a wife
To her allowing husband!
[*Exeunt* POLIXENES, HERMIONE, *and* ATTENDANTS.
Gone already!
Inch-thick, knee-deep, o'er head and ears a forkt one!
Go, play, boy, play: thy mother plays, and I
Play too; but so disgraced a part, whose issue
Will hiss me to my grave: contempt and clamour
Will be my knell.—Go, play, boy, play.—There have been,
Or I am much deceived, cuckolds ere now;
And many a man there is, even at this present,
Now while I speak this, holds his wife by th'arm,
That little thinks she has been sluiced in's absence,
And his pond fisht by his next neighbour, by
Sir Smile, his neighbour: nay, there's comfort in't,
Whiles other men have gates, and those gates open'd,
As mine, against their will: should all despair
That have revolted wives, the tenth of mankind
Would hang themselves. Physic for't there's none;
It is a bawdy planet, that will strike
Where 'tis predominant; and 'tis powerful, think it,
From east, west, north, and south: be it concluded,
No barricado for a belly; know't;
It will let in and out the enemy
With bag and baggage: many thousand on's
Have the disease, and feel't not.—How now, boy!

MAMILLIUS.
I am like you, they say.

LEONTES.
Why, that's some comfort.
What, Camillo there?

CAMILLO.
Ay, my good lord.

LEONTES.
Go, play, Mamillius; thou'rt an honest man.
[*Exit* MAMILLIUS.
Camillo, this great sir will yet stay longer.

CAMILLO.
You had much ado to make his anchor hold:
When you cast out, it still came home.

LEONTES.
Didst note it?

CAMILLO.
He would not stay at your petitions; made
His business more material.

LEONTES.
Didst perceive it?—
[*aside*] They're here with me already; whispering, rounding,
'Sicilia is a—so-forth:' 'tis far gone,
When I shall gust it last.—How came't, Camillo,
That he did stay?

CAMILLO.
At the good queen's entreaty.

LEONTES.
At the queen's be't: 'good' should be pertinent;
But, so it is, it is not. Was this taken
By any understanding pate but thine?
For thy conceit is soaking, will draw in
More than the common blocks:—not noted, is't,
But of the finer natures? by some severals
Of head-piece extraordinary? lower messes
Perchance are to this business purblind? say.

CAMILLO.
Business, my lord! I think most understand
Bohemia stays here longer.

LEONTES.
Ha!

CAMILLO.
Stays here longer.

LEONTES.
Ay, but why?

CAMILLO.
To satisfy your highness, and the entreaties
Of our most gracious mistress.

LEONTES.
Satisfy
Th'entreaties of your mistress!—satisfy!—
Let that suffice. I have trusted thee, Camillo,
With all the nearest things to my heart, as well
My chamber-councils; wherein, priest-like, thou
Hast cleansed my bosom,—I from thee departed
Thy penitent reform'd: but we have been
Deceived in thy integrity, deceived
In that which seems so.

CAMILLO.
Be it forbid, my lord!

LEONTES.
To bide upon't,—thou art not honest; or,
If thou inclinest that way, thou art a coward,
Which hoxes honesty behind, restraining
From course required; or else thou must be counted
A servant grafted in my serious trust,
And therein negligent; or else a fool
That seest a game play'd home, the rich stake drawn,
And takest it all for jest.

CAMILLO.
My gracious lord,
I may be negligent, foolish, and fearful;
In every one of these no man is free,
But that his negligence, his folly, fear,
Among the infinite doings of the world,
Sometime puts forth. In your affairs, my lord,
If ever I were wilful-negligent,
It was my folly; if industriously
I play'd the fool, it was my negligence,
Not weighing well the end; if ever fearful
To do a thing, where I the issue doubted,
Whereof the execution did cry out
Against the non-performance, 'twas a fear
Which oft infects the wisest: these, my lord,
Are such allow'd infirmities that honesty
Is never free of. But, beseech your Grace,
Be plainer with me; let me know my trespass
By its own visage: if I then deny it,
'Tis none of mine.

LEONTES.
Ha'not you seen, Camillo,—
But that's past doubt, you have, or your eye-glass
Is thicker than a cuckold's horn,—or heard,—
For, to a vision so apparent, rumour

Cannot be mute,—or thought,—for cogitation
Resides not in that man that does not think,—
My wife is slippery? If thou wilt confess,—
Or else be impudently negative,
To have nor eyes nor ears nor thought,—then say
My wife's a hobby-horse; deserves a name
As rank as any flax-wench that puts-to
Before her troth-plight: say't, and justify't.

CAMILLO.

I would not be a stander-by to hear
My sovereign mistress clouded so, without
My present vengeance taken: 'shrew my heart,
You never spoke what did become you less
Than this; which to reiterate were sin
As deep as that, though true.

LEONTES.

Is whispering nothing?
Is leaning cheek to cheek? is meeting noses?
Kissing with inside lip? stopping the career
Of laughter with a sigh?—a note infallible
Of breaking honesty;—horsing foot on foot?
Skulking in corners? wishing clocks more swift?
Hours, minutes? noon, midnight? and all eyes
Blind with the pin-and-web, but theirs, theirs only,
That would unseen be wicked? is this nothing?
Why, then the world and all that's in't is nothing;
The covering sky is nothing; Bohemia nothing;
My wife is nothing; nor nothing have these nothings,
If this be nothing.

CAMILLO.

Good my lord, be cured
Of this diseased opinion, and betimes;
For 'tis most dangerous.

LEONTES.

Say it be, 'tis true.

CAMILLO.

No, no, my lord.

LEONTES.

It is; you lie, you lie:
I say thou liest, Camillo, and I hate thee;
Pronounce thee a gross lout, a mindless slave;
Or else a hovering temporizer, that
Canst with thine eyes at once see good and evil,
Inclining to them both; were my wife's liver
Infected as her life, she would not live
The running of one glass.

CAMILLO.

Who does infect her?

LEONTES.

Why, he that wears her like his medal, hanging
About his neck, Bohemia: who—if I
Had servants true about me, that bare eyes
To see alike mine honour as their profits,
Their own particular thrifts,—they would do that
Which should undo more doing: ay, and thou,
His cupbearer,—whom I from meaner form
Have bencht, and rear'd to worship; who mayst see
Plainly, as heaven sees earth, and earth sees heaven,
How I am gall'd,—mightst bespice a cup,
To give mine enemy a lasting wink;
Which draught to me were cordial.

CAMILLO.

Sir, my lord,
I could do this, and that with no rash potion,
But with a lingering dram, that should not work
Maliciously like poison: but I cannot
Believe this crack to be in my dread mistress,
So sovereignly being honourable.
I have loved thee,—

LEONTES.

Make that thy question, and go rot!
Dost think I am so muddy, so unsettled,
To appoint myself in this vexation; sully
The purity and whiteness of my sheets,—
Which to preserve is sleep, which being spotted
Is goads, thorns, nettles, tails of wasps;
Give scandal to the blood o'the prince my son,—
Who I do think is mine, and love as mine,—
Without ripe moving to't? Would I do this?
Could man so blench?

CAMILLO.

I must believe you, sir:
I do; and will fetch off Bohemia for't;
Provided that, when he's removed, your highness
Will take again your queen as yours at first,
Even for your son's sake; and thereby for sealing
The injury of tongues in courts and kingdoms
Known and allied to yours.

LEONTES.

Thou dost advise me
Even so as I mine own course have set down:
I'll give no blemish to her honour, none.

CAMILLO.

My lord,
Go then; and with a countenance as clear
As friendship wears at feasts, keep with Bohemia
And with your queen. I am his cupbearer:
If from me he have wholesome beverage,
Account me not your servant.

LEONTES.

This is all:—
Do't, and thou hast the one half of my heart;
Do't not, thou splitt'st thine own.

CAMILLO.

I'll do't, my lord.

LEONTES.

I will seem friendly, as thou hast advised me. [*Exit.*

CAMILLO.

O miserable lady!—But, for me,
What case stand I in? I must be the poisoner
Of good Polixenes: and my ground to do't
Is the obedience to a master; one
Who, in rebellion with himself, will have
All that are his so too.—To do this deed,
Promotion follows: if I could find example
Of thousands that had struck anointed kings,
And flourisht after, I'ld not do't; but since
Nor brass nor stone nor parchment bears not one,
Let villainy itself forswear't. I must
Forsake the court: to do't, or no, is certain
To me a break-neck.—Happy star reign now!
Here comes Bohemia.

Enter POLIXENES.

POLIXENES.

This is strange: methinks
My favour here begins to warp. Not speak?—
Good day, Camillo.

CAMILLO.
Hail, most royal sir!

POLIXENES.
What is the news i'the court?

CAMILLO.
None rare, my lord.

POLIXENES.
The king hath on him such a countenance
As he had lost some province, and a region
Loved as he loves himself: even now I met him
With customary compliment; when he,
Wafting his eyes to the contrary, and falling
A lip of much contempt, speeds from me; and
So leaves me, to consider what is breeding
That changes thus his manners.

CAMILLO.
I dare not know, my lord.

POLIXENES.
How! dare not! do not. Do you know, and dare not?
Be intelligent to me: 'tis thereabouts;
For, to yourself, what you do know, you must,
And cannot say you dare not. Good Camillo,
Your changed complexions are to me a mirror,
Which shows me mine changed too; for I must be
A party in this alteration, finding
Myself thus alter'd with't.

CAMILLO.
There is a sickness
Which puts some of us in distemper; but
I cannot name the disease; and it is caught
Of you that yet are well.

POLIXENES.
How! caught of me!
Make me not sighted like the basilisk:
I have lookt on thousands, who have sped the better
By my regard, but kill'd none so. Camillo,—
As you are certainly a gentleman; thereto
Clerk-like experienced, which no less adorns
Our gentry than our parents' noble names,
In whose success we are gentle,—I beseech you,
If you know aught which does behove my knowledge
Thereof to be inform'd, imprison't not
In ignorant concealment.

CAMILLO.
I may not answer.

POLIXENES.
A sickness caught of me, and yet I well!
I must be answer'd.—Dost thou hear, Camillo,
I conjure thee, by all the parts of man
Which honour does acknowledge,—whereof the least
Is not this suit of mine,—that thou declare
What incidency thou dost guess of harm
Is creeping toward me: how far off, how near;
Which way to be prevented, if to be;
If not, how best to bear it.

CAMILLO.
Sir, I will tell you;
Since I am charged in honour, and by him
That I think honourable: therefore mark my counsel,
Which must be even as swiftly follow'd as
I mean to utter it, or both yourself and me
Cry 'lost,' and so good night!

POLIXENES.
On, good Camillo.

CAMILLO.
I am appointed him to murder you.

POLIXENES.
By whom, Camillo?

CAMILLO.
By the king.

POLIXENES.
For what?

CAMILLO.
He thinks, nay, with all confidence he swears,
As he had seen't, or been an instrument
To vice you to't, that you have toucht his queen
Forbiddenly.

POLIXENES.
O, then my best blood turn
To an infected jelly, and my name
Be yoked with his that did betray the Best!
Turn then my freshest reputation to
A savour that may strike the dullest nostril
Where I arrive, and my approach be shunn'd,
Nay, hated too, worse than the great'st infection
That e'er was heard or read!

CAMILLO.
Swear his thought over
By each particular star in heaven and
By all their influences, you may as well
Forbid the sea for to obey the moon,
As or by oath remove, or counsel shake
The fabric of his folly, whose foundation
Is piled upon his faith, and will continue
The standing of his body.

POLIXENES.
How should this grow?

CAMILLO.
I know not: but I am sure 'tis safer to
Avoid what's grown than question how 'tis born.
If, therefore, you dare trust my honesty,
That lies enclosed in this trunk, which you
Shall bear along impawn'd,—away to-night!
Your followers I will whisper to the business;
And will, by twos and threes, at several posterns,
Clear them o'the city: for myself, I'll put
My fortunes to your service, which are here
By this discovery lost. Be not uncertain;
For, by the honour of my parents, I
Have utter'd truth: which if you seek to prove,
I dare not stand by; nor shall you be safer
Than one condemn'd by the king's own mouth, thereon
His execution sworn.

POLIXENES.
I do believe thee:
I saw his heart in's face. Give me thy hand:
Be pilot to me, and thy places shall
Still neighbour mine. My ships are ready, and
My people did expect my hence-departure
Two days ago.—This jealousy
Is for a precious creature: as she's rare,
Must it be great; and, as his person's mighty,
Must it be violent; and as he does conceive
He is dishonour'd by a man which ever
Profest to him, why, his revenges must
In that be made more bitter. Fear o'ershades me:
Good expedition be my friend, and comfort

The gracious queen, part of his theme, but nothing
Of his ill-ta'en suspicion! Come, Camillo;
I will respect thee as a father, if
Thou bear'st my life off hence: let us avoid.

CAMILLO.

It is in mine authority to command
The keys of all the posterns: please your highness
To take the urgent hour: come, sir, away.
[*Exeunt.*

ACT II. SCENE I.

Sicilia. LEONTES' *palace.*

Enter HERMIONE, MAMILLIUS, *and* LADIES.

HERMIONE.

TAKE the boy to you: he so troubles me,
'Tis past enduring.

FIRST LADY.

Come, my gracious lord,
Shall I be your playfellow?

MAMILLIUS.

No, I'll none of you.

FIRST LADY.

Why, my sweet lord?

MAMILLIUS.

You'll kiss me hard, and speak to me as if
I were a baby still.—I love you better.

SECOND LADY.

And why so, my lord?

MAMILLIUS.

Not for because
Your brows are blacker, yet black brows, they say,
Become some women best, so that there be not
Too much hair there, but in a semicircle,
Or a half-moon made with a pen.

SECOND LADY.

Who taught ye this?

MAMILLIUS.

I learn'd it out of women's faces.—Pray now,
What colour are your eyebrows?

FIRST LADY.

Blue, my lord.

MAMILLIUS.

Nay, that's a mock: I have seen a lady's nose
That has been blue, but not her eyebrows.

FIRST LADY.

Hark ye;
The queen your mother rounds apace: we shall
Present our services to a fine new prince
One of these days; and then you'ld wanton with us,
If we would have you.

SECOND LADY.

She is spread of late
Into a goodly bulk; good time encounter her!

HERMIONE.

What wisdom stirs amongst you? Come, sir, now
I am for you again: pray you, sit by us,
And tell's a tale.

MAMILLIUS.

Merry or sad shall't be?

HERMIONE.

As merry as you will.

MAMILLIUS.

A sad tale's best for winter: I have one
Of sprites and goblins.

HERMIONE.

Let's have that, good sir.
Come on, sit down:—come on, and do your best
To fright me with your sprites; you're powerful at it.

MAMILLIUS.

There was a man,—

HERMIONE.

Nay, come, sit down; then on.

MAMILLIUS.

Dwelt by a churchyard:—I will tell it softly;
Yond crickets shall not hear it.

HERMIONE.

Come on, then,
And give't me in mine ear.

Enter LEONTES, ANTIGONUS, LORDS, *and* GUARDS.

LEONTES.

Was he met there? his train? Camillo with him?

FIRST LORD.

Behind the tuft of pines I met them; never
Saw I men scour so on their way: I eyed them
Even to their ships.

LEONTES.

How blest am I
In my just censure, in my true opinion!—
Alack, for lesser knowledge! how accurst
In being so blest!—There may be in the cup
A spider steept, and one may drink, depart,
And yet partake no venom; for his knowledge
Is not infected: but if one present
Th'abhorr'd ingredient to his eye, make known
How he hath drunk, he cracks his gorge, his sides,
With violent hefts:—I have drunk, and seen the spider.
Camillo was his help in this, his pandar:—
There is a plot against my life, my crown;
All's true that is mistrusted:—that false villain,
Whom I employ'd, was pre-employ'd by him:
He has discover'd my design, and I
Remain a pincht thing: yea, a very trick
For them to play at will.—How came the posterns
So easily open?

FIRST LORD.

By his great authority;
Which often hath no less prevail'd than so,
On your command.

LEONTES.

I know't too well.—
Give me the boy:—I am glad you did not nurse him:
Though he does bear some signs of me, yet you
Have too much blood in him.

HERMIONE.

What is this? sport?

LEONTES.

Bear the boy hence; he shall not come about her;
Away with him!—and let her sport herself
[*Exit* MAMILLIUS *with some of the* GUARDS.
With that she's big with;—for 'tis Polixenes
Has made thee swell thus.

HERMIONE.

But I'ld say he had not,
And I'll be sworn you would believe my saying,
Howe'er you lean to the nayward.

LEONTES.

You, my lords,
Look on her, mark her well; be but about
To say, 'She is a goodly lady,' and
The justice of your hearts will thereto add,
''Tis pity she's not honest, honourable:'
Praise her but for this her without-door form,—
Which, on my faith, deserves high speech,—and straight
The shrug, the hum, or ha,—these petty brands
That calumny doth use:—O, I am out,
That mercy does; for calumny will sear
Virtue itself:—these shrugs, these hums and ha's,
When you have said 'she's goodly,' come between
Ere you can say 'she's honest:' but be't known,
From him that has most cause to grieve it should be,
She's an adultress.

HERMIONE.

Should a villain say so,
The most replenisht villain in the world,
He were as much more villain: you, my lord,
Do but mistake.

LEONTES.

You have mistook, my lady,
Polixenes for Leontes: O thou thing!
Which I'll not call a creature of thy place,
Lest barbarism, making me the precedent,
Should a like language use to all degrees,
And mannerly distinguishment leave out
Betwixt the prince and beggar!—I have said
She's an adultress; I have said with whom:
More, she's a traitor; and Camillo is
A feoderary with her; and one that knows,
What she should shame to know herself
But with her most vile principal, that she's
A bed-swerver, even as bad as those
That vulgars give bold'st titles; ay, and privy
To this their late escape.

HERMIONE.

No, by my life,
Privy to none of this. How will this grieve you,
When you shall come to clearer knowledge, that
You thus have publisht me! Gentle my lord,
You scarce can right me throughly then, to say
You did mistake.

LEONTES.

No; if I mistake
In those foundations which I build upon,
The centre is not big enough to bear
A schoolboy's top.—Away with her to prison!
He who shall speak for her is afar off guilty
But that he speaks.

HERMIONE.

There's some ill planet reigns:
I must be patient till the heavens look
With an aspect more favourable. Good my lords,
I am not prone to weeping, as our sex
Commonly are; the want of which vain dew
Perchance shall dry your pities; but I have
That honourable grief lodged here which burns
Worse than tears drown: beseech you all, my lords,
With thoughts so qualified as your charities
Shall best instruct you, measure me; and so
The king's will be perform'd!

LEONTES [*to the* GUARDS].

Shall I be heard?

HERMIONE.

Who is't that goes with me? Beseech your highness
My women may be with me; for, you see,
My plight requires it. Do not weep, good fools;
There is no cause: when you shall know your mistress
Has deserved prison, then abound in tears
As I come out: this action I now go on
Is for my better grace. Adieu, my lord:
I never wisht to see you sorry; now
I trust I shall.—My women, come; you have leave.

LEONTES.

Go, do our bidding; hence!

[*Exeunt* HERMIONE *and* LADIES, *with* GUARDS.

FIRST LORD.

Beseech your highness, call the queen again.

ANTIGONUS.

Be certain what you do, sir, lest your justice
Prove violence; in the which three great ones suffer,
Yourself, your queen, your son.

FIRST LORD.

For her, my lord,
I dare my life lay down, and will do't, sir,
Please you t'accept it, that the queen is spotless
I'the eyes of heaven and to you; I mean,
In this which you accuse her.

ANTIGONUS.

If it prove
She's otherwise, I'll keep my stables where
I lodge my wife; I'll go in couples with her;
Than when I feel and see her no further trust her;
For every inch of woman in the world,
Ay, every dram of woman's flesh, is false,
If she be.

LEONTES.

Hold your peaces.

FIRST LORD.

Good my lord,—

ANTIGONUS.

It is for you we speak, not for ourselves:
You are abused, and by some putter-on,
That will be damn'd for't; would I knew the villain,
I would land-damn him. Be she honour-flaw'd,—
I have three daughters; the eldest is eleven;
The second and the third, nine and some five;
If this prove true, they'll pay for't: by mine honour,
I'll geld 'em all; fourteen they shall not see,
To bring false generations: they are co-heirs;
And I had rather glib myself than they
Should not produce fair issue.

LEONTES.

Cease; no more.
You smell this business with a sense as cold
As is a dead man's nose: but I do see't and feel't,
As you feel doing thus; and see withal
The instruments that feel.

ANTIGONUS.

If it be so,
We need no grave to bury honesty:
There's not a grain of it the face to sweeten
Of the whole dungy earth.

LEONTES.

What! lack I credit?

FIRST LORD.

I had rather you did lack than I, my lord,
Upon this ground; and more it would content me
To have her honour true than your suspicion,
Be blamed for't how you might.

LEONTES.

Why, what need we
Commune with you of this, but rather follow
Our forceful instigation? Our prerogative
Calls not your counsels; but our natural goodness
Imparts this: which, if you—or stupefied,
Or seeming so in skill—cannot or will not
Relish a truth, like us, inform yourselves
We need no more of your advice: the matter,
The loss, the gain, the ordering on't, is all
Properly ours.

ANTIGONUS.

And I wish, my liege,
You had only in your silent judgement tried it,
Without more overture.

LEONTES.

How could that be?
Either thou art most ignorant by age,
Or thou wert born a fool. Camillo's flight,
Added to their familiarity,—
Which was as gross as ever toucht conjecture,
That lackt sight only, naught for approbation
But only seeing, all other circumstances
Made up to the deed,—doth push on this proceeding:
Yet, for a greater confirmation,—
For, in an act of this importance 'twere
Most piteous to be wild,—I have dispatcht in post
To sacred Delphos, to Apollo's temple,
Cleomenes and Dion, whom you know
Of stuft sufficiency: now, from the oracle
They will bring all; whose spiritual counsel had,
Shall stop or spur me. Have I done well?

FIRST LORD.

Well done, my lord.

LEONTES.

Though I am satisfied, and need no more
Than what I know, yet shall the oracle
Give rest to the minds of others; such as he
Whose ignorant credulity will not
Come up to the truth. So have we thought it good
From our free person she should be confined,
Lest that the treachery of the two fled hence
Be left her to perform. Come, follow us;
We are to speak in public; for this business
Will raise us all.

ANTIGONUS [*aside*].

To laughter, as I take it,
If the good truth were known. [*Exeunt.*

SCENE II.

A prison.

Enter PAULINA *and* ATTENDANTS.

PAULINA.

THE keeper of the prison,—call to him;
Let him have knowledge who I am.
[*Exit an* ATTENDANT.
Good lady!
No court in Europe is too good for thee;
What dost thou, then, in prison?

Enter ATTENDANT, *with the* GAOLER.

Now, good sir,
You know me, do you not?

GAOLER.

For a worthy lady,
And one who much I honour.

PAULINA.

Pray you, then,
Conduct me to the queen.

GAOLER.

I may not, madam: to the contrary
I have express commandment.

PAULINA.

Here's ado,
To lock up honesty and honour from
Th'access of gentle visitors!—Is't lawful, pray you,
To see her women? any of them? Emilia?

GAOLER.

So please you, madam,
To put apart these your attendants, I
Shall bring Emilia forth.

PAULINA.

I pray now, call her.—
Withdraw yourselves. [*Exeunt* ATTENDANTS.

GOALER.

And, madam,
I must be present at your conference.

PAULINA.

Well, be't so, prithee. [*Exit* GAOLER.
Here's such ado to make no stain a stain,
As passes colouring.

Enter GAOLER, *with* EMILIA.

Dear gentlewoman,
How fares our gracious lady?

EMILIA.

As well as one so great and so forlorn
May hold together: on her frights and griefs,—
Which never tender lady hath borne greater,—
She is something before her time deliver'd.

PAULINA.

A boy?

EMILIA.

A daughter; and a goodly babe,
Lusty, and like to live: the queen receives
Much comfort in't; says, 'My poor prisoner,
I am innocent as you.'

PAULINA.

I dare be sworn:—
These dangerous unsafe lunes i'the king, beshrew them!
He must be told on't, and he shall: the office
Becomes a woman best; I'll take't upon me:
If I prove honey-mouth'd, let my tongue blister,
And never to my red-lookt anger be

The trumpet any more.—Pray you, Emilia,
Commend my best obedience to the queen:
If she dares trust me with her little babe,
I'll show't the king, and undertake to be
Her advocate to the loud'st. We do not know
How he may soften at the sight o'the child:
The silence often of pure innocence
Persuades, when speaking fails.

EMILIA.

Most worthy madam,
Your honour and your goodness is so evident,
That your free undertaking cannot miss
A thriving issue: there is no lady living
So meet for this great errand. Please your ladyship
To visit the next room, I'll presently
Acquaint the queen of your most noble offer;
Who but to-day hammer'd of this design,
But durst not tempt a minister of honour,
Lest she should be denied.

PAULINA.

Tell her, Emilia,
I'll use that tongue I have: if wit flow from't,
As boldness from my bosom, let't not be doubted
I shall do good.

EMILIA.

Now be you blest for it!
I'll to the queen: please you, come something nearer.

GAOLER.

Madam, if't please the queen to send the babe,
I know not what I shall incur to pass it,
Having no warrant.

PAULINA.

You need not fear it, sir:
The child was prisoner to the womb, and is,
By law and process of great nature, thence
Freed and enfranchised; not a party to
The anger of the king, nor guilty of,
If any be, the trespass of the queen.

GAOLER.

I do believe it.

PAULINA.

Do not you fear: upon mine honour, I
Will stand betwixt you and danger. [*Exeunt.*

SCENE III.

LEONTES' *palace.*

Enter LEONTES, ANTIGONUS, LORDS, *and* ATTENDANTS.

LEONTES.

Nor night nor day no rest: it is but weakness
To bear the matter thus,—mere weakness. If
The cause were not in being,—part o'the cause,
She, the adultress; for the harlot king
Is quite beyond mine arm, out of the blank
And level of my brain, plot-proof; but she
I can hook to me:—say that she were gone,
Given to the fire, a moiety of my rest
Might come to me again.—Who's there?

FIRST ATTENDANT [*advancing*].

My lord?

LEONTES.

How does the boy?

FIRST ATTENDANT.

He took good rest to-night;
'Tis hoped his sickness is discharged.

LEONTES.

To see his nobleness!
Conceiving the dishonour of his mother,
He straight declined, droopt, took it deeply,
Fasten'd and fixt the shame on't in himself,
Threw off his spirit, his appetite, his sleep,
And downright languisht.—Leave me solely:—go,
See how he fares. [*Exit* FIRST ATTENDANT.]—Fie, fie! no thought of him;—
The very thought of my revenges that way
Recoil upon me: in himself too mighty,
And in his parties, his alliance; let him be,
Until a time may serve: for present vengeance,
Take it on her. Camillo and Polixenes
Laugh at me, make their pastime at my sorrow:
They should not laugh, if I could reach them; nor
Shall she, within my power.

Enter PAULINA, *with a Child.*

FIRST LORD.

You must not enter.

PAULINA.

Nay, rather, good my lords, be second to me:
Fear you his tyrannous passion more, alas,
Than the queen's life? a gracious innocent soul,
More free than he is jealous.

ANTIGONUS.

That's enough.

SECOND ATTENDANT.

Madam, he hath not slept to-night; commanded
None should come at him.

PAULINA.

Not so hot, good sir:
I come to bring him sleep. 'Tis such as you,—
That creep like shadows by him, and do sigh
At each his needless heavings,—such as you
Nourish the cause of his awaking: I
Do come, with words as medicinal as true,
Honest as either, to purge him of that humour
That presses him from sleep.

LEONTES.

What noise there, ho?

PAULINA.

No noise, my lord; but needful conference
About some gossips for your highness.

LEONTES.

How!—
Away with that audacious lady!—Antigonus,
I charged thee that she should not come about me:
I knew she would.

ANTIGONUS.

I told her so, my lord,
On your displeasure's peril and on mine,
She should not visit you.

LEONTES.

What, canst not rule her?

PAULINA.

From all dishonesty he can: in this,—
Unless he take the course that you have done,
Commit me for committing honour,—trust it,
He shall not rule me.

ANTIGONUS.
La you now, you hear:
When she will take the rein, I let her run;
But she'll not stumble.

PAULINA.
Good my liege, I come,—
And, I beseech you, hear me, who profess
Myself your loyal servant, your physician,
Your most obedient counsellor; yet that dares
Less appear so, in comforting your evils,
Than such as most seem yours:—I say, I come
From your good queen.

LEONTES.
Good queen!

PAULINA.
Good queen, my lord, good queen; I say good queen;
And would by combat make her good, so were I
A man, the worst about you.

LEONTES.
Force her hence.

PAULINA.
Let him that makes but trifles of his eyes
First hand me: on mine own accord I'll off;
But first I'll do my errand.—The good queen—
For she is good—hath brought you forth a daughter;
Here 'tis; commends it to your blessing.
[*Laying down the Child.*

LEONTES.
Out!
A mankind witch! Hence with her, out o'door,—
A most intelligencing bawd!

PAULINA.
Not so:
I am as ignorant in that as you
In so entitling me; and no less honest
Than you are mad; which is enough, I'll warrant,
As this world goes, to pass for honest.

LEONTES.
Traitors!
Will you not push her out?—Give her the bastard:—
[*to* ANTIGONUS] Thou dotard, thou art woman-tired, unroosted
By thy Dame Partlet here:—take up the bastard;
Take't up, I say; give't to thy crone.

PAULINA.
For ever
Unvenerable be thy hands, if thou
Takest up the princess by that forced baseness
Which he has put upon't!

LEONTES.
He dreads his wife.

PAULINA.
So I would you did; then 'twere past all doubt
You'ld call your children yours.

LEONTES.
A nest of traitors!

ANTIGONUS.
I am none, by this good light.

PAULINA.
Nor I; nor any,
But one, that's here, and that's himself; for he
The sacred honour of himself, his queen's,
His hopeful son's, his babe's, betrays to slander,
Whose sting is sharper than the sword's; and will not—
For, as the case now stands, it is a curse;
He cannot be compell'd to't—once remove
The root of his opinion, which is rotten
As ever oak or stone was sound.

LEONTES.
A callet
Of boundless tongue, who late hath beat her husband,
And now baits me!—This brat is none of mine;
It is the issue of Polixenes:
Hence with it, and together with the dam
Commit them to the fire!

PAULINA.
It is yours;
And, might we lay the old proverb to your charge,
So like you, 'tis the worse.—Behold, my lords,
Although the print be little, the whole matter
And copy of the father,—eye, nose, lip;
The trick of's frown; his forehead; nay, the valley,
The pretty dimples of his chin and cheek; his smiles;
The very mould and frame of hand, nail, finger:—
And thou, good goddess Nature, which hast made it
So like to him that got it, if thou hast
The ordering of the mind too, 'mongst all colours
No yellow in't, lest she suspect, as he does,
Her children not her husband's!

LEONTES.
A gross hag!—
And, losel, thou art worthy to he hang'd,
That wilt not stay her tongue.

ANTIGONUS.
Hang all the husbands
That cannot do that feat, you'll leave yourself
Hardly one subject.

LEONTES.
Once more, take her hence.

PAULINA.
A most unworthy and unnatural lord
Can do no more.

LEONTES.
I'll ha'thee burnt.

PAULINA.
I care not:
It is an heretic that makes the fire,
Not she which burns in't. I'll not call you tyrant;
But this most cruel usage of your queen—
Not able to produce more accusation
Than your own weak-hinged fancy—something savours
Of tyranny, and will ignoble make you,
Yea, scandalous to the world.

LEONTES.
On your allegiance
Out of the chamber with her! Were I a tyrant,
Where were her life? she durst not call me so,
If she did know me one. Away with her!

PAULINA.
I pray you do not push me; I'll be gone.—
Look to your babe, my lord; 'tis yours: Jove send her
A better-guiding spirit!—What needs these hands?
You, that are thus so tender o'er his follies,

Will never do him good, not one of you.
So, so:—farewell; we are gone. [*Exit.*

LEONTES.

Thou, traitor, has set on thy wife to this.—
My child? away with't!—even thou, that hast
A heart so tender o'er it, take it hence,
And see it instantly consumed with fire;
Even thou, and none but thou. Take it up straight.
Within this hour bring me word 'tis done,
And by good testimony; or I'll seize thy life,
With what thou else call'st thine. If thou refuse,
And wilt encounter with my wrath, say so;
The bastard-brains with these my proper hands
Shall I dash out. Go, take it to the fire;
For thou sett'st on thy wife.

ANTIGONUS.

I did not, sir:
These lords, my noble fellows, if they please,
Can clear me in't.

LORDS.

We can:—my royal liege,
He is not guilty of her coming hither.

LEONTES.

You're all liars.

FIRST LORD.

Beseech your highness, give us better credit:
We have always truly served you; and beseech
So to esteem of us: and on our knees we beg,
As recompense of our dear services
Past and to come, that you do change this purpose,
Which being so horrible, so bloody, must
Lead on to some foul issue: we all kneel.

LEONTES.

I am a feather for each wind that blows:
Shall I live on, to see this bastard kneel
And call me father? better burn it now
Than curse it then. But be it; let it live.
It shall not neither.—You, sir, come you hither;
[*to* ANTIGONUS.
You that have been so tenderly officious
With Lady Margery, your midwife, there,
To save this bastard's life,—for 'tis a bastard,
So sure as this beard's gray,—what will you adventure
To save this brat's life?

ANTIGONUS.

Any thing, my lord,
That my ability may undergo,
And nobleness impose: at least, thus much,—
I'll pawn the little blood which I have left
To save the innocent:—any thing possible.

LEONTES.

It shall be possible. Swear by this sword
Thou wilt perform my bidding.

ANTIGONUS.

I will, my lord.

LEONTES.

Mark, and perform it; seest thou? for the fail
Of any point in't shall not only be
Death to thyself, but to thy lewd-tongued wife,
Whom for this time we pardon. We enjoin thee,
As thou art liegeman to us, that thou carry
This female bastard hence; and that thou bear it
To some remote and desert place, quite out
Of our dominions; and that there thou leave it,
Without more mercy, to it own protection
And favour of the climate. As by strange fortune
It came to us, I do in justice charge thee,
On thy soul's peril and thy body's torture,
That thou commend it strangely to some place
Where chance may nurse or end it. Take it up.

ANTIGONUS.

I swear to do this, though a present death
Had been more merciful.—Come on, poor babe:
Some powerful spirit instruct the kites and ravens
To be thy nurses! Wolves and bears, they say,
Casting their savageness aside, have done
Like offices of pity.—Sir, be prosperous
In more than this deed does require!—and blessing,
Against this cruelty, fight on thy side,
Poor thing, condemn'd to loss! [*Exit with the Child.*

LEONTES.

No, I'll not rear
Another's issue.

Enter a SERVANT.

SERVANT.

Please your highness, posts
From those you sent to the oracle are come
An hour since: Cleomenes and Dion,
Being well arrived from Delphos, are both landed
Hasting to the court.

FIRST LORD.

So please you, sir, their speed
Hath been beyond account.

LEONTES.

Twenty-three days
They have been absent: 'tis good speed; foretells
The great Apollo suddenly will have
The truth of this appear. Prepare you, lords;
Summon a session, that we may arraign
Our most disloyal lady; for, as she hath
Been publicly accused, so shall she have
A just and open trial. While she lives,
My heart will be a burden to me. Leave me;
And think upon my bidding. [*Exeunt.*

ACT III. SCENE I.

Sicilia. A street in some town.

Enter CLEOMENES *and* DION.

CLEOMENES.

THE climate's delicate; the air most sweet;
Fertile the isle; the temple much surpassing
The common praise it bears.

DION.

I shall report,
For most it caught me, the celestial habits—
Methinks I so should term them—and the reverence
Of the grave wearers. O, the sacrifice!
How ceremonious, solemn, and unearthly
It was i'the offering!

CLEOMENES.

But, of all, the burst
And the ear-deafening voice o'the oracle,
Kin to Jove's thunder, so surprised my sense,
That I was nothing.

DION.

If the event o'the journey
Prove as successful to the queen,—O, be't so!—

As it has been to us rare, pleasant, speedy,
The time is worth the use on't.

CLEOMENES.
Great Apollo
Turn all to the best! These proclamations,
So forcing faults upon Hermione,
I little like.

DION.
The violent carriage of it
Will clear or end the business: when the oracle—
Thus by Apollo's great divine seal'd up—
Shall the contents discover, something rare
Even then will rush to knowledge.—Go; fresh horses!
And gracious be the issue! [*Exeunt.*

SCENE II.

A Court of Justice.

Enter LEONTES, LORDS, *and* OFFICERS.

LEONTES.
THIS sessions—to our great grief, we pronounce—
Even pushes 'gainst our heart; the party tried,
The daughter of a king, our wife, and one
Of us too much beloved. Let us be clear'd
Of being tyrannous, since we so openly
Proceed in justice; which shall have due course,
Even to the guilt or the purgation.—
Produce the prisoner.

FIRST OFFICER.
It is his highness' pleasure that the queen
Appear in person here in court. Silence!

HERMIONE *is brought in guarded;* PAULINA *and* LADIES *attending.*

LEONTES.
Read the indictment.

FIRST OFFICER [*reads*].
Hermione, queen to the worthy Leontes, king of Sicilia, thou art here accused and arraign'd of high treason, in committing adultery with Polixenes, king of Bohemia, and conspiring with Camillo to take away the life of our sovereign lord the king, thy royal husband: the pretence whereof being by circumstances partly laid open, thou, Hermione, contrary to the faith and allegiance of a true subject, didst counsel and aid them, for their better safety, to fly away by night.

HERMIONE.
Since what I am to say must be but that
Which contradicts my accusation, and
The testimony on my part no other
But what comes from myself, it shall scarce boot me
To say, 'Not guilty:' mine integrity
Being counted falsehood, shall, as I express it,
Be so received. But thus: if powers divine
Behold our human actions, as they do,
I doubt not, then, but innocence shall make
False accusation blush, and tyranny
Tremble at patience. You, my lord, best know,
Who least will seem to do so, my past life
Hath been as continent, as chaste, as true,
As I am now unhappy: which is more
Than history can pattern, though devised
And play'd to take spectators; for, behold me,—
A fellow of the royal bed, which owe
A moiety of the throne, a great king's daughter,
The mother to a hopeful prince,—here standing
To prate and talk for life and honour 'fore
Who please to come and hear. For life, I prize it
As I weigh grief, which I would spare: for honour,
'Tis a derivative from me to mine,
And only that I stand for. I appeal
To your own conscience, sir, before Polixenes
Came to your court, how I was in your grace,
How merited to be so; since he came,
With what encounter so uncurrent I
Have strain'd, t'appear thus: if one jot beyond
The bound of honour, or in act or will
That way inclining, harden'd be the hearts
Of all that hear me, and my near'st of kin
Cry 'Fie' upon my grave!

LEONTES.
I ne'er heard yet
That any of these bolder vices wanted
Less impudence to gainsay what they did
Than to perform it first.

HERMIONE.
That's true enough;
Though 'tis a saying, sir, not due to me.

LEONTES.
You will not own it.

HERMIONE.
More than mistress of
Which comes to me in name of fault, I must not
At all acknowledge. For Polixenes,—
With whom I am accused,—I do confess
I loved him, as in honour he required;
With such a kind of love as might become
A lady like me; with a love even such,
So and no other, as yourself commanded:
Which not to have done, I think had been in me
Both disobedience and ingratitude
To you and toward your friend; whose love had spoke,
Even since it could speak, from an infant, freely,
That it was yours. Now, for conspiracy,
I know not how it tastes; though it be disht
For me to try how: all I know of it
Is, that Camillo was an honest man;
And why he left your court, the gods themselves,
Wotting no more than I, are ignorant.

LEONTES.
You knew of his departure, as you know
What you have underta'en to do in's absence.

HERMIONE.
Sir,
You speak a language that I understand not:
My life stands in the level of your dreams,
Which I'll lay down.

LEONTES.
Your actions are my dreams;
You had a bastard by Polixenes,
And I but dream'd it: as you were past all shame,—
Those of your fact are so,—so past all truth:
Which to deny concerns more than avails; for as
Thy brat hath been cast out, like to itself,
No father owning it,—which is, indeed,
More criminal in thee than it,—so thou
Shalt feel our justice; in whose easiest passage
Look for no less than death.

HERMIONE.
Sir, spare your threats:
The bug which you would fright me with I seek.
To me can life be no commodity:
The crown and comfort of my life, your favour,
I do give lost; for I do feel it gone,
But know not how it went: my second joy
And first-fruits of my body, from his presence
I am barr'd, like one infectious: my third comfort,
Starr'd most unluckily, is from my breast,
The innocent milk in it most innocent mouth,
Haled out to murder: myself on every post
Proclaimed a strumpet; with immodest hatred
The child-bed privilege denied, which 'longs
To women of all fashion; lastly, hurried
Here to this place, i'the open air, before
I have got strength of limit. Now, my liege,
Tell me what blessings I have here alive,
That I should fear to die? Therefore, proceed.
But yet hear this; mistake me not:—for life,
I prize it not a straw; but for mine honour,
Which I would free, if I shall be condemn'd
Upon surmises, all proofs sleeping else,
But what your jealousies awake,—I tell you,
'Tis rigour, and not law.—Your honours all,
I do refer me to the oracle:
Apollo be my judge!

FIRST LORD.
This your request
Is altogether just:—therefore, bring forth,
And in Apollo's name, his oracle,
[*Exeunt certain* OFFICERS.

HERMIONE.
The Emperor of Russia was my father:
O, that he were alive, and here beholding
His daughter's trial! that he did but see
The flatness of my misery,—yet with eyes
Of pity, not revenge!

Enter OFFICERS, *with* CLEOMENES *and* DION.

FIRST OFFICER.
You here shall swear upon this sword of justice,
That you, Cleomenes and Dion, have
Been both at Delphos; and from thence have brought
This seal'd-up oracle, by the hand deliver'd
Of great Apollo's priest; and that, since then,
You have not dared to break the holy seal,
Nor read the secrets in't.

CLEOMENES *and* DION.
All this we swear.

LEONTES.
Break up the seals, and read.

FIRST OFFICER [*reads*].
Hermione is chaste; Polixenes blameless; Camillo a true subject; Leontes a jealous tyrant; his innocent babe truly begotten; and the king shall live without an heir, if that which is lost be not found.

LORDS.
Now blessed be the great Apollo!

HERMIONE.
Praised!

LEONTES.
Hast thou read truth?

FIRST OFFICER.
Ay, my lord; even so
As it is here set down.

LEONTES.
There is no truth at all i'the oracle:
The sessions shall proceed: this is mere falsehood.

Enter an ATTENDANT *hastily.*

ATTENDANT.
My lord the king, the king!

LEONTES.
What is the business?

ATTENDANT.
O sir, I shall be hated to report it!
The prince your son, with mere conceit and fear
Of the queen's speed, is gone.

LEONTES.
How! gone!

ATTENDANT.
Is dead.

LEONTES.
Apollo's angry; and the heavens themselves
Do strike at my injustice. [HERMIONE *faints.*]
How now, there!

PAULINA.
This news is mortal to the queen:—look down,
And see what death is doing.

LEONTES.
Take her hence:
Her heart is but o'ercharged; she will recover:—
I have too much believed mine own suspicion:—
Beseech you, tenderly apply to her
Some remedies for life.
[*Exeunt* PAULINA *and* LADIES, *with* HERMIONE.
Apollo, pardon
My great profaneness 'gainst thine oracle!
I'll reconcile me to Polixenes;
New woo my queen; recall the good Camillo,
Whom I proclaim a man of truth, of mercy;
For, being transported by my jealousies
To bloody thoughts and to revenge, I chose
Camillo for the minister, to poison
My friend Polixenes: which had been done,
But that the good mind of Camillo tardied
My swift command, though I with death and with
Reward did threaten and encourage him,
Not doing it and being done: he, most humane,
And fill'd with honour, to my kingly guest
Unclaspt my practice; quit his fortunes here,
Which you knew great; and to the certain hazard
Of all incertainties himself commended,
No richer than his honour:—how he glisters
Thorough my rust! and how his piety
Does my deeds make the blacker!

Enter PAULINA.

PAULINA.
Woe, the while!
O, cut my lace, lest my heart, cracking it,
Break too!

FIRST LORD.
What fit is this, good lady?

PAULINA.
What studied torments, tyrant, hast for me?
What wheels? racks? fires? what flaying? boiling?
In leads or oils? what old or newer torture
Must I receive, whose every word deserves
To taste of thy most worst? Thy tyranny
Together working with thy jealousies,—
Fancies too weak for boys, too green and idle

For girls of nine,—O, think what they have done,
And then run mad indeed,—stark mad! for all
Thy by-gone fooleries were but spices of it.
That thou betray'dst Polixenes, 'twas nothing,—
That did but show thee, of a fool, inconstant,
And damnable ingrateful; not was't much,
Thou wouldst have poison'd good Camillo's honour,
To have him kill a king;—poor trespasses,
More monstrous standing by: whereof I reckon
The casting forth to crows thy baby daughter,
To be or none, or little,—though a devil
Would have shed water out of fire ere done't;
Nor is't directly laid to thee, the death
Of the young prince, whose honourable thoughts—
Thoughts high for one so tender—cleft the heart
That could conceive a gross and foolish sire
Blemisht his gracious dam: this is not, no,
Laid to thy answer: but the last,—O lords,
When I have said, cry, 'Woe,'—the queen, the queen,
The sweet'st, dear'st creature's dead; and vengeance for't
Not dropt down yet.

FIRST LORD.

The higher powers forbid!

PAULINA.

I say she's dead; I'll swear't. If word nor oath
Prevail not, go and see: if you can bring
Tincture or lustre in her lip, her eye,
Heat outwardly or breath within, I'll serve you
As I would do the gods.—But, O thou tyrant!
Do not repent these things; for they are heavier
Than all thy woes can stir: therefore betake thee
To nothing but despair. A thousand knees
Ten thousand years together, naked, fasting,
Upon a barren mountain, and still winter
In storm perpetual, could not move the gods
To look that way thou wert.

LEONTES.

Go on, go on:
Thou canst not speak too much; I have deserved
All tongues to talk their bitterest.

FIRST LORD.

Say no more:
Howe'er the business goes, you have made fault
I'the boldness of your speech.

PAULINA.

I am sorry for't:
All faults I make, when I shall come to know them,
I do repent. Alas, I have show'd too much
The rashness of a woman! he is toucht
To the noble heart.—What's gone, and what's past help,
Should be past grief: do not receive affliction
At my petition; I beseech you, rather
Let me be punisht, that have minded you
Of what you should forget. Now, good my liege,
Sir, royal sir, forgive a foolish woman:
The love I bore your queen,—lo, fool again!—
I'll speak of her no more, nor of your children;
I'll not remember you of my own lord,
Who is lost too: take your patience to you,
And I'll say nothing.

LEONTES.

Thou didst speak but well,
When most the truth; which I receive much better
Than to be pitied of thee. Prithee, bring me
To the dead bodies of my queen and son:
One grave shall be for both; upon them shall
The causes of their death appear, unto
Our shame perpetual. Once a day I'll visit
The chapel where they lie; and tears shed there
Shall be my recreation: so long as nature
Will bear up with this exercise, so long
I daily vow to use it. Come, and lead me
To these sorrows. [*Exeunt.*

SCENE III.

Bohemia. A desert country near the sea.

Enter ANTIGONUS *with the Child, and a* MARINER.

ANTIGONUS.

THOU art perfect, then, our ship hath toucht upon
The deserts of Bohemia?

MARINER.

Ay, my lord; and fear
We have landed in ill time: the skies look grimly,
And threaten present blusters. In my conscience,
The heavens with that we have in hand are angry,
And frown upon's.

ANTIGONUS.

Their sacred wills be done!—Go, get aboard;
Look to thy bark: I'll not be long before
I call upon thee.

MARINER.

Make your best haste; and go not
Too far i'the land: 'tis like to be loud weather;
Besides, this place is famous for the creatures
Of prey that keep upon't.

ANTIGONUS.

Go thou away:
I'll follow instantly.

MARINER.

I am glad at heart
To be rid so o'the business. [*Exit.*

ANTIGONUS.

Come, poor babe:—
I have heard,—but not believed,—the spirits o'the dead
May walk again: if such thing be, thy mother
Appear'd to me last night; for ne'er was dream
So like a waking. To me comes a creature,
Sometimes her head on one side, some another;
I never saw a vessel of like sorrow,
So fill'd and so becoming: in pure white robes,
Like very sanctity, she did approach
My cabin where I lay; thrice bow'd before me;
And, gasping to begin some speech, her eyes
Became two spouts: the fury spent, anon
Did this break from her: 'Good Antigonus,
Since fate, against thy better disposition,
Hath made thy person for the thrower-out
Of my poor babe, according to thine oath,—
Places remote enough are in Bohemia,
There weep, and leave it crying; and, for the babe
Is counted lost for ever, Perdita,

I prithee, call't. For this ungentle business,
Put on thee by my lord, thou ne'er shalt see
Thy wife Paulina more:'—and so, with shrieks,
She melted into air. Affrighted much,
I did in time collect myself; and thought
This was so, and no slumber. Dreams are toys:
Yet, for this once, yea, superstitiously,
I will be squared by this. I do believe
Hermione hath suffer'd death; and that
Apollo would, this being indeed the issue
Of king Polixenes, it should here be laid,
Either for life or death, upon the earth
Of its right father.—Blossom, speed thee well!
[*Laying down the* CHILD, *with a scroll.*
There lie; and there thy character: there these;
[*Laying down a bundle.*
Which may, if fortune please, both breed thee, pretty,
And still rest thine.—The storm begins:—poor wretch, [*Thunder.*
That, for thy mother's fault, art thus exposed
To loss and what may follow!—Weep I cannot,
But my heart bleeds: and most accurst am I
To be by oath enjoin'd to this.—Farewell!—
The day frowns more and more:—thou'rt like to have
A lullaby too rough:—I never saw
The heavens so dim by day.—A savage clamour!—
[*Noise of hunters, dogs, and bears within.*
Well may I get aboard!—This is the chase:
I am gone for ever. [*Exit, pursued by a bear.*

Enter an old SHEPHERD.

SHEPHERD.

I would there were no age between ten and three-and-twenty, or that youth would sleep out the rest; for there is nothing in the between but getting wenches with child, wronging the ancientry, stealing, fighting—Hark you now!—Would any but these boil'd brains of nineteen and two-and-twenty hunt this weather? They have scared away two of my best sheep, which I fear the wolf will sooner find than the master: if any where I have them, 'tis by the sea-side, browzing of ivy. Good luck, an't be thy will! what have we here? [*Seeing the* CHILD.] Mercy on's, a barne; a very pretty barne! A boy or a child, I wonder? A pretty one; a very pretty one: sure, some scape: though I am not bookish, yet I can read waiting-gentlewoman in the scape. This has been some stair-work, some trunk-work, some behind-door-work: they were warmer that got this than the poor thing is here. I'll take it up for pity: yet I'll tarry till my son come; he hallooed but even now.—Whoa, ho, hoa!

CLOWN [*within*].

Hilloa, loa!

SHEPHERD.

What, art so near? If thou'lt see a thing to talk on when thou art dead and rotten, come hither.

Enter CLOWN.

What ail'st thou, man?

CLOWN.

I have seen two such sights, by sea and by land!—but I am not to say it is a sea, for it is now the sky: betwixt the firmament and it you cannot thrust a bodkin's point.

SHEPHERD.

Why, boy, how is it?

CLOWN.

I would you did but see how it chafes, how it rages, how it takes up the shore!—but that's not to the point. O, the most piteous cry of the poor souls! sometimes to see 'em, and not to see 'em; now the ship boring the moon with her main-mast, and anon swallow'd with yest and froth, as you'ld thrust a cork into a hogshead. And then for the land-service,—to see how the bear tore out his shoulder-bone; how he cried to me for help, and said his name was Antigonus, a nobleman:—but to make an end of the ship,—to see how the sea flap-dragon'd it:—but, first, how the poor souls roar'd, and the sea mockt them;—and how the poor gentleman roar'd, and the bear mockt him, both roaring louder than the sea or weather.

SHEPHERD.

Name of mercy, when was this, boy?

CLOWN.

Now, now; I have not winkt since I saw these sights: the men are not yet cold under water, nor the bear half dined on the gentleman,—he's at it now.

SHEPHERD.

Would I had been by, to have helpt the nobleman!

CLOWN.

I would you had been by the ship-side, to have helpt her: there your charity would have lackt footing.

SHEPHERD.

Heavy matters! heavy matters! but look thee here, boy. Now bless thyself: thou met'st with things dying, I with things new-born. Here's a sight for thee; look thee, a bearing-cloth for a squire's child! look thee here; take up, take up, boy; open't. So, let's see: it was told me I should be rich by the fairies; this is some changeling: open't. What's within, boy?

CLOWN.

You're a made old man: if the sins of your youth are forgiven you, you're well to live. Gold! all gold!

SHEPHERD.

This is fairy gold, boy, and 'twill prove so; up with't, keep it close: home, home, the next way. We are lucky, boy; and to be so still, requires nothing but secrecy.—Let my sheep go:—come, good boy, the next way home.

CLOWN.

Go you the next way with your findings. I'll go see if the bear be gone from the gentleman, and how much he hath eaten: they are never curst, but when they are hungry: if there be any of him left, I'll bury it.

SHEPHERD.

That's a good deed. If thou mayst discern by that which is left of him what he is, fetch me to the sight of him.

CLOWN.

Marry, will I; and you shall help to put him i'the ground.

SHEPHERD.

'Tis a lucky day, boy, and we'll do good deeds on't. [*Exeunt.*

ACT IV.

Enter TIME, *the* CHORUS.

TIME.

I,—that please some, try all; both joy and terror
Of good and bad; that masks and unfolds error,—
Now take upon me, in the name of Time,
To use my wings. Impute it not a crime
To me or my swift passage, that I slide
O'er sixteen years, and leave the growth untried
Of that wide gap; since it is in my power
To o'erthrow law, and in one self-born hour
To plant and o'erwhelm custom. Let me pass
The same I am, ere ancient'st order was,
Or what is now received: I witness to
The times that brought them in; so shall I do
To the freshest things now reigning, and make stale
The glistering of this present, as my tale
Now seems to it. Your patience this allowing,
I turn my glass, and give my scene such growing
As you had slept between. Leontes leaving,
The effects of his fond jealousies so grieving
That he shuts up himself,—imagine me,
Gentle spectators, that I now may be
In fair Bohemia; and remember well,
I mention'd a son o'the king's, which Florizel
I now name to you; and with speed so pace
To speak of Perdita, now grown in grace
Equal with wond'ring: what of her ensues,
I list not prophesy; but let Time's news
Be known when 'tis brought forth:—a shepherd's daughter,
And what to her adheres, which follows after,
Is the argument of Time. Of this allow,
If ever you have spent time worse ere now;
If never, yet that Time himself doth say
He wishes earnestly you never may. [*Exit.*

SCENE I.

Bohemia. POLIXENES' *palace.*

Enter POLIXENES *and* CAMILLO.

POLIXENES.

I PRAY thee, good Camillo, be no more importunate: 'tis a sickness denying thee any thing; a death to grant this.

CAMILLO.

It is fifteen years since I saw my country: though I have, for the most part, been air'd abroad, I desire to lay my bones there. Besides, the penitent king, my master, hath sent for me; to whose feeling sorrows I might be some allay, or I o'erween to think so,—which is another spur to my departure.

POLIXENES.

As thou lovest me, Camillo, wipe not out the rest of thy services by leaving me now: the need I have of thee, thine own goodness hath made; better not to have had thee than thus to want thee: thou, having made me businesses which none without thee can sufficiently manage, must either stay to execute them thyself, or take away with thee the very services thou hast done; which if I have not enough consider'd,—as too much I cannot,—to be more thankful to thee shall be my study; and my profit therein, the heaping friendships. Of that fatal country Sicilia, prithee speak no more; whose very naming punishes me with the remembrance of that penitent, as thou call'st him, and reconciled king, my brother; whose loss of his most precious queen and children are even now to be afresh lamented. Say to me, when saw'st thou the Prince Florizel, my son? Kings are no less unhappy, their issue not being gracious, than they are in losing them when they have approved their virtues.

CAMILLO.

Sir, it is three days since I saw the prince. What his happier affairs may be, are to me unknown: but I have missingly noted, he is of late much retired from court, and is less frequent to his princely exercises than formerly he hath appear'd.

POLIXENES.

I have consider'd so much, Camillo, and with some care; so far, that I have eyes under my service which look upon his removedness; from whom I have this intelligence:—that he is seldom from the house of a most homely shepherd; a man, they say, that from very nothing, and beyond the imagination of his neighbours, is grown into an unspeakable estate.

CAMILLO.

I have heard, sir, of such a man, who hath a daughter of most rare note: the report of her is extended more than can be thought to begin from such a cottage.

POLIXENES.

That's likewise part of my intelligence; but I fear the angle that plucks our son thither. Thou shalt accompany us to the place; where we will, not appearing what we are, have some question with the shepherd; from whose simplicity I think it not uneasy to get the cause of my son's resort thither. Prithee, be my present partner in this business, and lay aside the thoughts of Sicilia.

CAMILLO.

I willingly obey your command.

POLIXENES.

My best Camillo!—We must disguise ourselves. [*Exeunt.*

SCENE II.

A road near the SHEPHERD'S *cottage.*

Enter AUTOLYCUS, *singing.*

WHEN daffodils begin to peer,
With hey! the doxy over the dale,
Why, then comes in the sweet o'the year;
For the red blood reigns in the winter's pale.

The white sheet bleaching on the hedge,
With hey! the sweet birds, O, how they sing!
Doth set my pugging tooth on edge;
For a quart of ale is a dish for a king.

The lark, that tirra-lirra chants,
With hey! with hey! the thrush and the jay,
Are summer songs for me and my aunts,
While we lie tumbling in the hay.

I have served Prince Florizel, and, in my time, wore three-pile; but now I am out of service:

But shall I go mourn for that, my dear?
  The pale moon shines by night:
And when I wander here and there,
  I then do most go right.

If tinkers may have leave to live,
  And bear the sow-skin budget,
Then my account I well may give,
  And in the stocks avouch it.

My traffic is sheets; when the kite builds, look to lesser linen. My father named me Autolycus; who being, as I am, litter'd under Mercury, was likewise a snapper-up of unconsider'd trifles. With die and drab I purchased this caparison; and my revenue is the silly cheat: gallows and knock are too powerful on the highway; beating and hanging are terrors to me; for the life to come, I sleep out the thought of it.—A prize! a prize!

Enter CLOWN.

CLOWN.

Let me see:—every 'leven wether tods; every tod yields pound and odd shilling: fifteen hundred shorn, what comes the wool to?

AUTOLYCUS [*aside*].

If the springe hold, the cock's mine.

CLOWN.

I cannot do't without counters.—Let me see; what am I to buy for our sheep-shearing feast? Three pound of sugar; five pound of currants; rice—what will this sister of mine do with rice? But my father hath made her mistress of the feast, and she lays it on. She hath made me four-and-twenty nosegays for the shearers,—three-man songmen all, and very good ones; but they are most of them means and bases; but one puritan amongst them, and he sings psalms to hornpipes. I must have saffron, to colour the warden-pies; mace; dates,—none, that's out of my note; nutmegs, seven; a race or two of ginger,—but that I may beg; four pound of prunes, and as many of raisins o'the sun.

AUTOLYCUS.

O, that ever I was born!

[*Grovelling on the ground.*

CLOWN.

I'the name of me,—

AUTOLYCUS.

O, help me, help me! pluck but off these rags; and then, death, death!

CLOWN.

Alack, poor soul! thou hast need of more rags to lay on thee, rather than have these off.

AUTOLYCUS.

O sir, the loathsomeness of them offend me more than the stripes I have received, which are mighty ones and millions.

CLOWN.

Alas, poor man! a million of beating may come to a great matter.

AUTOLYCUS.

I am robb'd, sir, and beaten; my money and apparel ta'en from me, and these detestable things put upon me.

CLOWN.

What, by a horseman or a footman?

AUTOLYCUS.

A footman, sweet sir, a footman.

CLOWN.

Indeed, he should be a footman by the garments he has left with thee: if this be a horseman's coat, it hath seen very hot service. Lend me thy hand, I'll help thee: come, lend me thy hand.

[*Helping him up.*

AUTOLYCUS.

O, good sir, tenderly, O!

CLOWN.

Alas, poor soul!

AUTOLYCUS.

O, good sir, softly, good sir! I fear, sir, my shoulder-blade is out.

CLOWN.

How now! canst stand?

AUTOLYCUS.

Softly, dear sir [*picks his pocket*]; good sir, softly. You ha'done me a charitable office.

CLOWN.

Dost lack any money? I have a little money for thee.

AUTOLYCUS.

No, good sweet sir; no, I beseech you, sir: I have a kinsman not past three quarters of a mile hence, unto whom I was going; I shall there have money, or any thing I want: offer me no money, I pray you,—that kills my heart.

CLOWN.

What manner of fellow was he that robb'd you?

AUTOLYCUS.

A fellow, sir, that I have known to go about with troll-my-dames: I knew him once a servant of the prince: I cannot tell, good sir, for which of his virtues it was, but he was certainly whipt out of the court.

CLOWN.

His vices, you would say; there's no virtue whipt out of the court: they cherish it, to make it stay there; and yet it will no more but abide.

AUTOLYCUS.

Vices, I would say, sir. I know this man well: he hath been since an ape-bearer; then a process-server,—a bailiff; then he compast a motion of the Prodigal Son, and married a tinker's wife within a mile where my land and living lies; and, having flown over many knavish professions, he settled only in rogue: some call him Autolycus.

CLOWN.

Out upon him! prig, for my life, prig: he haunts wakes, fairs, and bear-baitings.

AUTOLYCUS.

Very true, sir; he, sir, he; that's the rogue that put me into this apparel.

CLOWN.

Not a more cowardly rogue in all Bohemia; if you had but lookt big and spit at him, he'ld have run.

AUTOLYCUS.

I must confess to you, sir, I am no fighter; I am false of heart that way; and that he knew, I warrant him.

CLOWN.

How do you now?

AUTOLYCUS.
Sweet sir, much better than I was; I can stand and walk: I will even take my leave of you, and pace softly towards my kinsman's.

CLOWN.
Shall I bring thee on the way?

AUTOLYCUS.
No, good-faced sir; no, sweet sir.

CLOWN.
Then fare thee well: I must go buy spices for our sheep-shearing.

AUTOLYCUS.
Prosper you, sweet sir! [*Exit* CLOWN.] Your purse is not hot enough to purchase your spice. I'll be with you at your sheep-shearing too: if I make not this cheat bring out another, and the shearers prove sheep, let me be unroll'd, and my name put in the book of virtue! [*Sings.*

Jog on, jog on, the footpath way,
And merrily hent the stile-a:
A merry heart goes all the day,
Your sad tires in a mile-a. [*Exit.*

SCENE III.

Before the SHEPHERD'S *cottage.*

Enter FLORIZEL *and* PERDITA.

FLORIZEL.
THESE your unusual weeds to each part of you
Do give a life: no shepherdess; but Flora
Peering in April's front. This your sheep-shearing
Is as a meeting of the petty gods,
And you the queen on't.

PERDITA.
Sir, my gracious lord,
To chide at your extremes, it not becomes me,—
O, pardon that I name them!—your high self,
The gracious mark o'the land, you have obscured
With a swain's wearing; and me, poor lowly maid,
Most goddess-like prankt up: but that our feasts
In every mess have folly, and the feeders
Digest it with a custom, I should blush
To see you so attired; swoon, I think,
To show myself a glass.

FLORIZEL.
I bless the time
When my good falcon made her flight across
Thy father's ground.

PERDITA.
Now Jove afford you cause!
To me the difference forges dread; your greatness
Hath not been used to fear. Even now I tremble
To think your father, by some accident,
Should pass this way, as you did: O, the Fates!
How would he look, to see his work, so noble,
Vilely bound up? What would he say? Or how
Should I, in these my borrow'd flaunts, behold
The sternness of his presence?

FLORIZEL.
Apprehend
Nothing but jollity. The gods themselves,
Humbling their deities to love, have taken
The shapes of beasts upon them: Jupiter
Became a bull, and bellow'd; the green Neptune
A ram, and bleated; and the fire-robed god,
Golden Apollo, a poor humble swain,
As I seem now:—their transformations
Were never for a piece of beauty rarer,—
Nor in a way so chaste, since my desires
Run not before mine honour, nor my lusts
Burn hotter than my faith.

PERDITA.
O, but, sir,
Your resolution cannot hold, when 'tis
Opposed, as it must be, by the power of the king:
One of these two must be necessities.
Which then will speak,—that you must change this purpose,
Or I my life.

FLORIZEL.
Thou dearest Perdita,
With these forced thoughts, I prithee, darken not
The mirth o'the feast: or I'll be thine, my fair,
Or not my father's; for I cannot be
Mine own, nor any thing to any, if
I be not thine: to this I am most constant,
Though destiny say no. Be merry, gentle;
Strangle such thoughts as these with any thing
That you behold the while. Your guests are coming:
Lift up your countenance, as it were the day
Of celebration of that nuptial which
We two have sworn shall come.

PERDITA.
O Lady Fortune,
Stand you auspicious!

FLORIZEL.
See, your guests approach:
Address yourself to entertain them sprightly,
And let's be red with mirth.

Enter SHEPHERD, *with* POLIXENES *and* CAMILLO *disguised;* CLOWN, MOPSA, DORCAS, *and other* SHEPHERDS *and* SHEPHERDESSES.

SHEPHERD.
Fie, daughter! when my old wife lived, upon
This day she was both pantler, butler, cook;
Both dame and servant; welcomed all; served all;
Would sing her song and dance her turn; now here,
At upper end o'the table, now i'the middle;
On his shoulder, and his; her face o'fire
With labour, and the thing she took to quench it,
She would to each one sip. You are retired,
As if you were a feasted one, and not
The hostess of the meeting: pray you, bid
These unknown friends to's welcome; for it is
A way to make us better friends, more known.
Come, quench your blushes, and present yourself
That which you are, mistress o'the feast: come on,
And bid us welcome to your sheep-shearing,
As your good flock shall prosper.

PERDITA [*to* POLIXENES].
Sir, welcome:—
It is my father's will I should take on me
The hostess-ship o'the day.—[*to* CAMILLO]
You're welcome, sir.—
Give me those flowers there, Dorcas.—Reverend sirs,
For you there's rosemary and rue; these keep
Seeming and savour all the winter long:

Grace and remembrance be to you both,
And welcome to our shearing!

POLIXENES.

Shepherdess,—
A fair one are you,—well you fit our ages
With flowers of winter.

PERDITA.

Sir, the year growing ancient,—
Not yet on summer's death, nor on the birth
Of trembling winter,—the fairest flowers o'the season
Are our carnations, and streakt gillyvors,
Which some call nature's bastards: of that kind
Our rustic garden's barren; and I care not
To get slips of them.

POLIXENES.

Wherefore, gentle maiden,
Do you neglect them?

PERDITA.

For I have heard it said,
There is an art which, in their piedness, shares
With great creating nature.

POLIXENES.

Say there be;
Yet nature is made better by no mean,
But nature makes that mean: so, over that art
Which you say adds to nature, is an art
That nature makes. You see, sweet maid, we marry
A gentler scion to the wildest stock,
And make conceive a bark of baser kind
By bud of nobler race: this is an art
Which does mend nature,—change it rather; but
The art itself is nature.

PERDITA.

So it is.

POLIXENES.

Then make your garden rich in gillyvors,
And do not call them bastards.

PERDITA.

I'll not put
The dibble in earth to set one slip of them;
No more than, were I painted, I would wish
This youth should say, 'twere well, and only therefore
Desire to breed by me.—Here's flowers for you;
Hot lavender, mints, savory, marjoram;
The marigold, that goes to bed wi'the sun,
And with him rises weeping: these are flowers
Of middle summer, and, I think, they are given
To men of middle age. Y'are very welcome.

CAMILLO.

I should leave grazing, were I of your flock,
And only live by gazing.

PERDITA.

Out, alas!
You'ld be so lean, that blasts of January
Would blow you through and through.—Now, my fair'st friend,
I would I had some flowers o'the spring that might
Become your time of day;—and yours, and yours,
That wear upon your virgin branches yet
Your maidenheads growing:—O Proserpina,
For the flowers now, that, frighted, thou lett'st fall
From Dis's wagon! daffodils,
That come before the swallow dares, and take
The winds of March with beauty; violets dim,
But sweeter than the lids of Juno's eyes
Or Cytherea's breath; pale primroses,
That die unmarried, ere they can behold
Bright Phœbus in his strength,—a malady
Most incident to maids; bold oxlips and
The crown-imperial; lilies of all kinds,
The flower-de-luce being one! O, these I lack,
To make you garlands of; and my sweet friend,
To strew him o'er and o'er!

FLORIZEL.

What, like a corse?

PERDITA.

No, like a bank for love to lie and play on;
Not like a corse; or if,—not to be buried,
But quick, and in mine arms.—Come, take your flowers:
Methinks I play as I have seen them do
In Whitsun pastorals: sure, this robe of mine
Does change my disposition.

FLORIZEL.

What you do
Still betters what is done. When you speak, sweet,
I'ld have you do it ever: when you sing,
I'ld have you buy and sell so; so give alms;
Pray so; and, for the ord'ring your affairs,
To sing them too: when you do dance, I wish you
A wave o'the sea, that you might ever do
Nothing but that; move still, still so,
And own no other function: each your doing,
So singular in each particular,
Crowns what you are doing in the present deeds,
That all your acts are queens.

PERDITA.

O Doricles,
Your praises are too large: but that your youth,
And the true blood which peeps fairly through't,
Do plainly give you out an unstain'd shepherd,
With wisdom I might fear, my Doricles,
You woo'd me the false way.

FLORIZEL.

I think you have
As little skill to fear as I have purpose
To put you to't.—But, come; our dance, I pray:
Your hand, my Perdita: so turtles pair,
That never mean to part.

PERDITA.

I'll swear for 'em.

POLIXENES.

This is the prettiest low-born lass that ever
Ran on the green-sward: nothing she does or seems
But smacks of something greater than herself,
Too noble for this place.

CAMILLO.

He tells her something
That makes her blood look out: good sooth, she is
The queen of curds and cream.

CLOWN.

Come on, strike up!

DORCAS.

Mopsa must be your mistress: marry, garlic,
To mend her kissing with!

MOPSA.

Now, in good time!

CLOWN.

Not a word, a word; we stand upon our manners.—
Come, strike up!

[*Music. Here a dance of Shepherds and Shepherdesses.*

POLIXENES.

Pray, good shepherd, what fair swain is this
Which dances with your daughter?

SHEPHERD.

They call him Doricles; and boasts himself
To have a worthy feeding: I but have it
Upon his own report, and I believe it;
He looks like sooth. He says he loves my daughter:
I think so too; for never gazed the moon
Upon the water, as he'll stand, and read,
As 'twere, my daughter's eyes: and, to be plain,
I think there is not half a kiss to choose
Who loves another best.

POLIXENES.

She dances featly.

SHEPHERD.

So she does any thing; though I report it,
That should be silent: if young Doricles
Do light upon her, she shall bring him that
Which he not dreams of.

Enter a SERVANT.

SERVANT.

O master, if you did but hear the pedlar at the door, you would never dance again after a tabor and pipe; no, the bagpipe could not move you: he sings several tunes faster than you'll tell money; he utters them as he had eaten ballads, and all men's ears grew to his tunes.

CLOWN.

He could never come better; he shall come in: I love a ballad but even too well, if it be doleful matter merrily set down, or a very pleasant thing indeed and sung lamentably.

SERVANT.

He hath songs for man or woman, of all sizes,—no milliner can so fit his customers with gloves: he has the prettiest love-songs for maids; so without bawdry, which is strange; with such delicate burdens of 'dildos' and 'fadings,' 'jump her and thump her;' and where some stretch-mouth'd rascal would, as it were, mean mischief, and break a foul jape into the matter, he makes the maid to answer, 'Whoop, do me no harm, good man;' puts him off, slights him, with 'Whoop, do me no harm, good man.'

POLIXENES.

This is a brave fellow.

CLOWN.

Believe me, thou talkest of an admirable-conceited fellow. Has he any unbraided wares?

SERVANT.

He hath ribands of all the colours i'the rainbow; points more than all the lawyers in Bohemia can learnedly handle, though they come to him by the gross; inkles, caddisses, cambrics, lawns: why, he sings 'em over, as they were gods or goddesses; you would think a smock were a she-angel, he so chants to the sleeve-hand, and the work about the square on't.

CLOWN.

Prithee, bring him in; and let him approach singing.

PERDITA.

Forewarn him that he use no scurrilous words in's tunes. [*Exit* SERVANT.

CLOWN.

You have of these pedlars, that have more in them than you'ld think, sister.

PERDITA.

Ay, good brother, or go about to think.

Enter AUTOLYCUS, *singing.*

Lawn as white as driven snow;
Cyprus black as e'er was crow;
Gloves as sweet as damask roses;
Masks for faces and for noses;
Bugle-bracelet, necklace-amber,
Perfume for a lady's chamber;
Golden quoifs and stomachers,
For my lads to give their dears;
Pins and poking-sticks of steel,
What maids lack from head to heel:
Come buy of me, come; come buy, come buy;
Buy, lads, or else your lasses cry:
Come buy.

CLOWN.

If I were not in love with Mopsa, thou shouldst take no money of me; but being enthrall'd as I am, it will also be the bondage of certain ribands and gloves.

MOPSA.

I was promised them against the feast; but they come not too late now.

DORCAS.

He hath promised you more than that, or there be liars.

MOPSA.

He hath paid you all he promised you: may be, he has paid you more,—which will shame you to give him again.

CLOWN.

Is there no manners left among maids? will they wear their plackets where they should bear their faces? Is there not milking-time, when you are going to bed, or kiln-hole, to whistle-off these secrets, but you must be tittle-tattling before all our guests? 'tis well they are whispering. Clamour your tongues, and not a word more.

MOPSA.

I have done. Come, you promised me a tawdry-lace and a pair of sweet gloves.

CLOWN.

Have I not told thee how I was cozen'd by the way, and lost all my money?

AUTOLYCUS.

And, indeed, sir, there are cozeners abroad; therefore it behoves men to be wary.

CLOWN.

Fear not thou, man, thou shalt lose nothing here.

AUTOLYCUS.

I hope so, sir; for I have about me many parcels of charge.

CLOWN.

What hast here? ballads?

MOPSA.

Pray now, buy some: I love a ballet in print a-life, for then we are sure they are true.

AUTOLYCUS.

Here's one to a very doleful tune, How a usurer's wife was brought to bed of twenty money-bags at a burden, and how she long'd to eat adders' heads and toads carbonadoed.

MOPSA.

Is it true, think you?

AUTOLYCUS.

Very true; and but a month old.

DORCAS.

Bless me from marrying a usurer!

AUTOLYCUS.

Here's the midwife's name to't, one Mistress Taleporter, and five or six honest wives that were present. Why should I carry lies abroad?

MOPSA.

Pray you now, buy it.

CLOWN.

Come on, lay it by: and let's first see moe ballads; we'll buy the other things anon.

AUTOLYCUS.

Here's another ballad, Of a fish, that appear'd upon the coast on Wednesday the fourscore of April, forty thousand fadom above water, and sung this ballad against the hard hearts of maids: it was thought she was a woman, and was turn'd into a cold fish for she would not exchange flesh with one that loved her: the ballad is very pitiful, and as true.

DORCAS.

Is it true too, think you?

AUTOLYCUS.

Five justices' hands at it, and witnesses more than my pack will hold.

CLOWN.

Lay it by too: another.

AUTOLYCUS.

This is a merry ballad, but a very pretty one.

MOPSA.

Let's have some merry ones.

AUTOLYCUS.

Why, this is a passing merry one, and goes to the tune of, 'Two maids wooing a man:' there's scarce a maid westward but she sings it; 'tis in request, I can tell you.

MOPSA.

We can both sing it: if thou'lt bear a part, thou shalt hear; 'tis in three parts.

DORCAS.

We had the tune on't a month ago.

AUTOLYCUS.

I can bear my part; you must know 'tis my occupation: have at it with you!

Song.

AUTOLYCUS.

Get you hence, for I must go;
Where, it fits not you to know.

DORCAS.

Whither?

MOPSA.

O, whither?

DORCAS.

Whither?

MOPSA.

It becomes thy oath full well,
Thou to me thy secrets tell:

DORCAS.

Me too, let me go thither.

MOPSA.

Or thou go'st to the grange or mill:

DORCAS.

If to either, thou dost ill.

AUTOLYCUS.

Neither.

DORCAS.

What, neither?

AUTOLYCUS.

Neither.

DORCAS.

Thou hast sworn my love to be;

MOPSA.

Thou hast sworn it more to me:
Then, whither go'st? say, whither?

CLOWN.

We'll have this song out anon by ourselves: my father and the gentlemen are in sad talk, and we'll not trouble them.—Come, bring away thy pack after me.—Wenches, I'll buy for you both.—Pedlar, let's have the first choice.—Follow me, girls. [*Exit with* DORCAS *and* MOPSA.

AUTOLYCUS.

And you shall pay well for 'em.— [*Singing.*

Will you buy any tape,
Or lace for your cape,
My dainty duck, my dear-a?
Any silk, any thread,
Any toys for your head,
Of the new'st and fin'st, fin'st wear-a?
Come to the pedlar;
Money's a meddler,
That doth utter all men's ware-a. [*Exit.*

Enter SERVANT.

SERVANT.

Master, there is three carters, three shepherds, three neat-herds, three swine-herds, that have made themselves all men of hair,—they call themselves Saltiers: and they have a dance which the wenches say is a gallimaufry of gambols, because they are not in't; but they themselves are o'the mind,—if it be not too rough for some that know little but bowling,—it will please plentifully.

SHEPHERD.

Away! we'll none on't: here has been too much homely foolery already.—I know, sir, we weary you.

POLIXENES.

You weary those that refresh us: pray, let's see these four threes of herdsmen.

SERVANT.

One three of them, by their own report, sir, hath danced before the king; and not the worst of the three but jumps twelve foot and a half by the squier.

SHEPHERD.

Leave your prating: since these good men are pleased, let them come in; but quickly now.

SERVANT.

Why, they stay at door, sir. [*Exit.*

Here a dance of twelve Satyrs.

POLIXENES.

O, father, you'll know more of that hereafter.—
[*to* CAMILLO] Is it not too far gone? 'Tis time to part them.
He's simple and tells much.—How now, fair shepherd!
Your heart is full of something that does take
Your mind from feasting. Sooth, when I was young,
And handed love as you do, I was wont
To load my she with knacks: I would have ransackt
The pedlar's silken treasury, and have pour'd it
To her acceptance; you have let him go,
And nothing marted with him. If your lass
Interpretation should abuse, and call this
Your lack of love or bounty, you were straited
For a reply, at least if you make care
Of happy holding her.

FLORIZEL.

Old sir, I know
She prizes not such trifles as these are:
The gifts she looks from me are packt and lockt
Up in my heart; which I have given already,
But not deliver'd.—O, hear me breathe my life
Before this ancient sir, who, it should seem,
Hath sometime loved! I take thy hand,—this hand,
As soft as dove's down and as white as it,
Or Ethiopian's tooth, or the fann'd snow that's bolted
By the northern blasts twice o'er.

POLIXENES.

What follows this?—
How prettily the young swain seems to wash
The hand was fair before!—I have put you out:—
But to your protestation; let me hear
What you profess.

FLORIZEL.

Do, and be witness to't.

POLIXENES.

And this my neighbour too?

FLORIZEL.

And he, and more
Than he, and men, the earth, the heavens, and all:—
That, were I crown'd the most imperial monarch,
Thereof most worthy; were I the fairest youth
That ever made eye swerve; had force and knowledge
More than was ever man's,—I would not prize them
Without her love; for her employ them all;
Commend them, and condemn them, to her service,
Or to their own perdition.

POLIXENES.

Fairly offer'd.

CAMILLO.

This shows a sound affection.

SHEPHERD.

But, my daughter,
Say you the like to him?

PERDITA.

I cannot speak
So well, nothing so well; no, nor mean better:
By the pattern of mine own thoughts I cut out
The purity of his.

SHEPHERD.

Take hands, a bargain!—
And, friends unknown, you shall bear witness to't:
I give my daughter to him, and will make
Her portion equal his.

FLORIZEL.

O, that must be
I'the virtue of your daughter: one being dead,
I shall have more than you can dream of yet:
Enough then for your wonder. But, come on,
Contract us 'fore these witnesses.

SHEPHERD.

Come, your hand;—
And, daughter, yours.

POLIXENES.

Soft, swain, awhile, beseech you;
Have you a father?

FLORIZEL.

I have: but what of him?

POLIXENES.

Knows he of this?

FLORIZEL.

He neither does nor shall.

POLIXENES.

Methinks a father
Is, at the nuptial of his son, a guest
That best becomes the table. Pray you, once more;
Is not your father grown incapable
Of reasonable affairs? is he not stupid
With age and alt'ring rheums? can he speak? hear?
Know man from man? dispute his own estate?
Lies he not bed-rid? and again does nothing
But what he did being childish?

FLORIZEL.

No, good sir;
He has his health, and ampler strength indeed
Than most have of his age.

POLIXENES.

By my white beard,
You offer him, if this be so, a wrong
Something unfilial: reason my son
Should choose himself a wife; but as good reason
The father,—all whose joy is nothing else
But fair posterity,—should hold some counsel
In such a business.

FLORIZEL.

I yield all this;
But, for some other reasons, my grave sir,
Which 'tis not fit you know, I not acquaint
My father of this business.

POLIXENES.

Let him know't.

FLORIZEL.

He shall not.

POLIXENES.

Prithee, let him.

FLORIZEL.

No, he must not.

SHEPHERD.

Let him, my son; he shall not need to grieve
At knowing of thy choice.

FLORIZEL.

Come, come, he must not.—
Mark our contract.

POLIXENES.

Mark your divorce, young sir, [*Discovering himself*.
Whom son I dare not call; thou art too base
To be acknowledged: thou a sceptre's heir,
That thus affects a sheep-hook!—Thou old traitor,
I am sorry that, by hanging thee, I can but
Shorten thy life one week.—And thou, fresh piece
Of excellent witchcraft, who, of force, must know
The royal fool thou copest with,—

SHEPHERD.

O, my heart!

POLIXENES.

I'll have thy beauty scratcht with briers, and made
More homely than thy state.—For thee, fond boy,
If I may ever know thou dost but sigh
That thou no more shalt see this knack,—as never
I mean thou shalt,—we'll bar thee from succession;
Not hold thee of our blood, no, not our kin,
Far' than Deucalion off:—mark thou my words:—
Follow us to the court.—Thou churl, for this time,
Though full of our displeasure, yet we free thee
From the dead blow of it.—And you, enchantment,
Worthy enough a herdsman; yea, him too
That makes himself, but for our honour therein,
Unworthy thee,—if ever henceforth thou
These rural latches to his entrance open,
Or hoop his body more with thy embraces,
I will devise a death as cruel for thee
As thou art tender to't. [*Exit*.

PERDITA.

Even here undone!
I was not much afeard; for once or twice
I was about to speak, and tell him plainly,
The selfsame sun that shines upon his court
Hides not his visage from our cottage, but
Looks on alike. [*to* FLORIZEL] Will't please you, sir, be gone?
I told you what would come of this: beseech you,
Of your own state take care: this dream of mine,—
Being now awake, I'll queen it no inch further,
But milk my ewes and weep.

CAMILLO.

Why, how now, father!
Speak ere thou diest.

SHEPHERD.

I cannot speak, nor think,
Nor dare to know that which I know.—[*to* FLORIZEL] O sir,
You have undone a man of fourscore three,
That thought to fill his grave in quiet,—yea,
To die upon the bed my father died,
To lie close by his honest bones! but now
Some hangman must put on my shroud, and lay me
Where no priest shovels-in dust.—[*to* PERDITA] O cursed wretch,
That knew'st this was the prince, and wouldst adventure
To mingle faith with him!—Undone! undone!
If I might die within this hour, I have lived
To die when I desire. [*Exit*.

FLORIZEL.

Why look you so upon me?
I am but sorry, not afeard; delay'd,
But nothing alter'd: what I was, I am;
More straining on for plucking back; not following
My leash unwillingly.

CAMILLO.

Gracious my lord,
You know your father's temper: at this time
He will allow no speech,—which I do guess
You do not purpose to him;—and as hardly
Will he endure your sight as yet, I fear:
Then, till the fury of his highness settle,
Come not before him.

FLORIZEL.

I not purpose it.
I think Camillo?

CAMILLO.

Even he, my lord.

PERDITA.

How often have I told you 'twould be thus!
How often said my dignity would last
But till 'twere known!

FLORIZEL.

It cannot fail but by
The violation of my faith; and then
Let nature crush the sides o'the earth together,
And mar the seeds within!—Lift up thy looks:—
From my succession wipe me, father! I
Am heir to my affection.

CAMILLO.

Be advised.

FLORIZEL.

I am,—and by my fancy: if my reason
Will thereto be obedient, I have reason;
If not, my senses, better pleased with madness,
Do bid it welcome.

CAMILLO.

This is desperate, sir.

FLORIZEL.

So call it: but it does fulfil my vow;
I needs must think it honesty. Camillo,
Not for Bohemia, nor the pomp that may
Be thereat glean'd; for all the sun sees, or
The close earth wombs, or the profound seas hide
In unknown fadoms, will I break my oath
To this my fair beloved: therefore, I pray you,
As you have ever been my father's honour'd friend,
When he shall miss me,—as, in faith, I mean not
To see him any more,—cast your good counsels
Upon his passion: let myself and fortune
Tug for the time to come. This you may know,
And so deliver,—I am put to sea
With her who here I cannot hold on shore;
And, most opportune to her need, I have
A vessel rides fast by, but not prepared
For this design. What course I mean to hold
Shall nothing benefit your knowledge, nor
Concern me the reporting.

CAMILLO.

O my lord,
I would your spirit were easier for advice,
Or stronger for your need!

FLORIZEL.
Hark, Perdita.—[*Taking her aside.*
[*to* CAMILLO] I'll hear you by and by.

CAMILLO.
He's irremovable,
Resolved for flight. Now were I happy, if
His going I could frame to serve my turn;
Save him from danger, do him love and honour;
Purchase the sight again of dear Sicilia,
And that unhappy king my master, whom
I so much thirst to see.

FLORIZEL.
Now, good Camillo,
I am so fraught with curious business, that
I leave out ceremony.

CAMILLO.
Sir, I think
You have heard of my poor services, i'the love
That I have borne your father?

FLORIZEL.
Very nobly
Have you deserved: it is my father's music
To speak your deeds; not little of his care
To have them recompensed as thought on.

CAMILLO.
Well, my lord,
If you may please to think I love the king,
And, through him, what's nearest to him, which is
Your gracious self, embrace but my direction,—
If your more ponderous and settled project
May suffer alteration,—on mine honour
I'll point you where you shall have such receiving
As shall become your highness; where you may
Enjoy your mistress,—from the whom, I see,
There's no disjunction to be made, but by,
As heavens forfend! your ruin;—marry her;
And—with my best endeavours in your absence—
Your discontenting father strive to qualify,
And bring him up to liking.

FLORIZEL.
How, Camillo,
May this, almost a miracle, be done?
That I may call thee something more than man,
And, after that, trust to thee.

CAMILLO.
Have you thought on
A place whereto you'll go?

FLORIZEL.
Not any yet:
But as the unthought-on accident is guilty
To what we wildly do, so we profess
Ourselves to be the slaves of chance, and flies
Of every wind that blows.

CAMILLO.
Then list to me:
This follows,—if you will not change your purpose,
But undergo this flight,—make for Sicilia;
And there present yourself and your fair princess—
For so I see she must be—'fore Leontes:
She shall be habited as it becomes
The partner of your bed. Methinks I see
Leontes opening his free arms, and weeping
His welcomes forth; asks thee, the son, forgiveness,
As 'twere i'the father's person; kisses the hands
Of your fresh princess; o'er and o'er divides him
'Twixt his unkindness and his kindness,—the one
He chides to hell, and bids the other grow
Faster than thought or time.

FLORIZEL.
Worthy Camillo,
What colour for my visitation shall I
Hold up before him?

CAMILLO.
Sent by the king your father
To greet him and to give him comforts. Sir,
The manner of your bearing towards him, with
What you, as from your father, shall deliver,
Things known betwixt us three, I'll write you down:
The which shall point you forth at every sitting
What you must say; that he shall not perceive
But that you have your father's bosom there,
And speak his very heart.

FLORIZEL.
I am bound to you:
There is some sap in this.

CAMILLO.
A course more promising
Than a wild dedication of yourselves
To unpath'd waters, undream'd shores, most certain
To miseries enough: no hope to help you;
But, as you shake off one, to take another:
Nothing so certain as your anchors; who
Do their best office, if they can but stay you
Where you'll be loth to be: besides, you know
Prosperity's the very bond of love,
Whose fresh complexion and whose heart together
Affliction alters.

PERDITA.
One of these is true:
I think affliction may subdue the cheek,
But not take in the mind.

CAMILLO.
Yea, say you so?
There shall not, at your father's house, these seven years
Be born another such.

FLORIZEL.
My good Camillo,
She's as forward of her breeding as she is
I'the rear o'her birth.

CAMILLO.
I cannot say 'tis pity
She lacks instructions, for she seems a mistress
To most that teach.

PERDITA.
Your pardon, sir, for this;
I'll blush you thanks.

FLORIZEL.
My prettiest Perdita!—
But, O, the thorns we stand upon!—Camillo,—
Preserver of my father, now of me,
The medicine of our house!—how shall we do?
We are not furnisht like Bohemia's son,
Nor shall appear in Sicilia.

CAMILLO.
My lord,
Fear none of this: I think you know my fortunes

Do all lie there: it shall be so my care
To have you royally appointed as if
The scene you play were mine. For instance, sir,
That you may know you shall not want,—one
word. [*They talk aside.*

Enter AUTOLYCUS.

AUTOLYCUS.

Ha, ha! what a fool Honesty is! and Trust, his sworn brother, a very simple gentleman! I have sold all my trumpery; not a counterfeit stone, not a riband, glass, pomander, brooch, table-book, ballad, knife, tape, glove, shoe-tie, bracelet, horn-ring, to keep my pack from fasting: they throng who should buy first, as if my trinkets had been hallow'd, and brought a benediction to the buyer: by which means I saw whose purse was best in picture; and what I saw, to my good use I remember'd. My clown—who wants but something to be a reasonable man—grew so in love with the wenches' song, that he would not stir his pettitoes till he had both tune and words; which so drew the rest of the herd to me, that all their other senses stuck in ears: you might have pincht a placket,—it was senseless; 'twas nothing to geld a codpiece of a purse,—I would have filed keys off that hung in chains: no hearing, no feeling, but my sir's song, and admiring the nothing of it. So that, in this time of lethargy, I pickt and cut most of their festival purses; and had not the old man come in with a whoobub against his daughter and the king's son, and scared my choughs from the chaff, I had not left a purse alive in the whole army.

[CAMILLO, FLORIZEL, *and* PERDITA *come forward.*

CAMILLO.

Nay, but my letters, by this means being there
So soon as you arrive, shall clear that doubt.

FLORIZEL.

And those that you'll procure from King Leontes,—

CAMILLO.

Shall satisfy your father.

PERDITA.

Happy be you!
All that you speak shows fair.

CAMILLO.

Who have we here?
[*Seeing* AUTOLYCUS.
We'll make an instrument of this; omit
Nothing may give us aid.

AUTOLYCUS [*aside*].

If they have overheard me now,—why, hanging.

CAMILLO.

How now, good fellow! why shakest thou so? Fear not, man; here's no harm intended to thee.

AUTOLYCUS.

I am a poor fellow, sir.

CAMILLO.

Why, be so still; here's nobody will steal that from thee: yet, for the outside of thy poverty, we must make an exchange; therefore discase thee instantly,—thou must think there's a necessity in't,—and change garments with this gentleman though the pennyworth on his side be the worst, yet hold thee, there's some boot. [*Giving money.*

AUTOLYCUS.

I am a poor fellow, sir.—[*aside*] I know ye well enough.

CAMILLO.

Nay, prithee, dispatch: the gentleman is half flay'd already.

AUTOLYCUS.

Are you in earnest, sir?—[*aside*] I smell the trick on't.

FLORIZEL.

Dispatch, I prithee.

AUTOLYCUS.

Indeed, I have had earnest; but I cannot with conscience take it.

CAMILLO.

Unbuckle, unbuckle.—
[FLORIZEL *and* AUTOLYCUS *exchange garments.*
Fortunate mistress,—let my prophecy
Come home to ye!—you must retire yourself
Into some covert: take your sweetheart's hat,
And pluck it o'er your brows; muffle your face;
Dismantle you; and, as you can, disliken
The truth of your own seeming; that you may—
For I do fear eyes over—to shipboard
Get undescried.

PERDITA.

I see the play so lies
That I must bear a part.

CAMILLO.

No remedy.—
Have you done there?

FLORIZEL.

Should I now meet my father,
He would not call me son.

CAMILLO.

Nay, you shall have no hat,—
[*Giving it to* PERDITA.
Come, lady, come.—Farewell, my friend.

AUTOLYCUS.

Adieu, sir.

FLORIZEL.

O Perdita, what have we twain forgot!
Pray you, a word. [*They converse apart.*

CAMILLO [*aside*].

What I do next, shall be to tell the king
Of this escape, and whither they are bound;
Wherein, my hope is, I shall so prevail
To force him after: in whose company
I shall review Sicilia, for whose sight
I have a woman's longing.

FLORIZEL.

Fortune speed us!—
Thus we set on, Camillo, to the sea-side.

CAMILLO.

The swifter speed the better.
[*Exeunt* FLORIZEL, PERDITA, *and* CAMILLO.

AUTOLYCUS.

I understand the business, I hear it: to have an open ear, a quick eye, and a nimble hand, is necessary for a cut-purse; a good nose is requisite also, to smell out work for the other senses. I see this is the time that the unjust man doth thrive. What an exchange had this been without boot! what a boot is here with this exchange! Sure, the gods do this year connive at us, and we may do any thing extempore. The prince himself is about a piece of iniquity,—stealing away from his father with his clog at his heels: if I thought it were not a piece of honesty to acquaint the king withal, I would do't: I hold it the more knavery to conceal it; and therein am I constant to my profession.

Enter CLOWN *and* SHEPHERD.

Aside, aside;—here is more matter for a hot brain: every lane's end, every shop, church, session, hanging, yields a careful man work.

CLOWN.

See, see; what a man you are now! There is no other way but to tell the king she's a changeling, and none of your flesh and blood.

SHEPHERD.

Nay, but hear me.

CLOWN.

Nay, but hear me.

SHEPHERD.

Go to, then.

CLOWN.

She being none of your flesh and blood, your flesh and blood has not offended the king; and so your flesh and blood is not to be punisht by him. Show those things you found about her; those secret things, all but what she has with her: this being done, let the law go whistle; I warrant you.

SHEPHERD.

I will tell the king all, every word, yea, and his son's pranks too,—who, I may say, is no honest man neither to his father nor to me, to go about to make me the king's brother-in-law.

CLOWN.

Indeed, brother-in-law was the furthest off you could have been to him; and then your blood had been the dearer by I know not how much an ounce.

AUTOLYCUS [*aside*].

Very wisely, puppies!

SHEPHERD.

Well, let us to the king: there is that in this fardel will make him scratch his beard.

AUTOLYCUS [*aside*].

I know not what impediment this complaint may be to the flight of my master.

CLOWN.

Pray heartily he be at palace.

AUTOLYCUS [*aside*].

Though I am not naturally honest, I am so sometimes by chance:—let me pocket up my pedlar's excrement. [*Takes off his false beard.*]—How now, rustics! whither are you bound?

SHEPHERD.

To the palace, an it like your worship.

AUTOLYCUS.

Your affairs there? what? with whom? the condition of that fardel, the place of your dwelling, your names, your ages, of what having, breeding, and any thing that is fitting to be known, discover.

CLOWN.

We are but plain fellows, sir.

AUTOLYCUS.

A lie; you are rough and hairy. Let me have no lying: it becomes none but tradesmen, and they often give us soldiers the lie: but we pay them for it with stampt coin, not stabbing steel; therefore they do not give us the lie.

CLOWN.

Your worship had like to have given us one, if you had not taken yourself with the manner.

SHEPHERD.

Are you a courtier, an't like you, sir?

AUTOLYCUS.

Whether it like me or no, I am a courtier. See'st thou not the air of the court in these enfoldings? hath not my gait in it the measure of the court? receives not thy nose court-odour from me? reflect I not on thy baseness court-contempt? Think'st thou, for that I insinuate, or toaze from thee thy business, I am therefore no courtier? I am courtier cap-a-pe; and one that will either push on or pluck back thy business there: whereupon I command thee to open thy affair.

SHEPHERD.

My business, sir, is to the king.

AUTOLYCUS.

What advocate hast thou to him?

SHEPHERD.

I know not, an't like you.

CLOWN [*aside to* SHEPHERD].

Advocate's the court-word for a pheasant: say you have none.

SHEPHERD.

None, sir; I have no pheasant, cock nor hen.

AUTOLYCUS.

How blest are we that are not simple men!
Yet nature might have made me as these are,
Therefore I will not disdain.

CLOWN [*aside to* SHEPHERD].

This cannot be but a great courtier.

SHEPHERD [*aside to* CLOWN].

His garments are rich, but he wears them not handsomely.

CLOWN [*aside to* SHEPHERD].

He seems to be the more noble in being fantastical: a great man, I'll warrant; I know by the picking on's teeth.

AUTOLYCUS

The fardel there? what's i'the fardel? Wherefore that box?

SHEPHERD.

Sir, there lies such secrets in this fardel and box, which none must know but the king; and which he shall know within this hour, if I may come to the speech of him.

AUTOLYCUS.

Age, thou hast lost thy labour.

SHEPHERD.

Why, sir?

AUTOLYCUS.

The king is not at the palace; he is gone aboard a new ship to purge melancholy and air himself: for, if thou be'st capable of things serious, thou must know the king is full of grief.

SHEPHERD.

So 'tis said, sir,—about his son, that should have married a shepherd's daughter.

AUTOLYCUS.

If that shepherd be not in hand-fast, let him fly: the curses he shall have, the tortures he shall feel, will break the back of man, the heart of monster.

CLOWN.

Think you so, sir?

AUTOLYCUS.

Not he alone shall suffer what wit can make heavy and vengeance bitter; but those that are germane to him, though removed fifty times, shall all come under the hangman: which though it be great pity, yet it is necessary. An old sheep-whistling rogue, a ram-tender, to offer to have his daughter come into grace! Some say he shall be stoned; but that death is too soft for him, say I: draw our throne into a sheep-cote! all deaths are too few, the sharpest too easy.

CLOWN.

Has the old man e'er a son, sir, do you hear, an't like you, sir?

AUTOLYCUS.

He has a son,—who shall be flay'd alive; then, 'nointed over with honey, set on the head of a wasps' nest; then stand till he be three quarters and a dram dead; then recover'd again with aqua-vitæ or some other hot infusion; then, raw as he is, and in the hottest day prognostication proclaims, shall he be set against a brick-wall, the sun looking with a southward eye upon him,—where he is to behold him with flies blown to death. But what talk we of these traitorly rascals, whose miseries are to be smiled at, their offences being so capital? Tell me—for you seem to be honest plain men—what you have to the king: being something gently consider'd, I'll bring you where he is aboard, tender your persons to his presence, whisper him in your behalfs; and if it be in man besides the king to effect your suits, here is man shall do it.

CLOWN [*aside to* SHEPHERD].

He seems to be of great authority: close with him; give him gold: and though authority be a stubborn bear, yet he is oft led by the nose with gold: show the inside of your purse to the outside of his hand, and no more ado. Remember,—stoned, and flay'd alive.

SHEPHERD.

An't please you, sir, to undertake the business for us, here is that gold I have: I'll make it as much more, and leave this young man in pawn till I bring it you.

AUTOLYCUS.

After I have done what I promised?

SHEPHERD.

Ay, sir.

AUTOLYCUS.

Well, give me the moiety.—Are you a party in this business?

CLOWN.

In some sort, sir: but though my case be a pitiful one, I hope I shall not be flay'd out of it.

AUTOLYCUS.

O, that's the case of the shepherd's son:—hang him, he'll be made an example.

CLOWN [*aside to* SHEPHERD].

Comfort, good comfort! We must to the king, and show our strange sights: he must know 'tis none of your daughter nor my sister; we are gone else.—Sir, I will give you as much as this old man does, when the business is perform'd; and remain, as he says, your pawn till it be brought you.

AUTOLYCUS.

I will trust you. Walk before toward the sea-side; go on the right hand: I will but look upon the hedge, and follow you.

CLOWN [*aside to* SHEPHERD].

We are blest in this man, as I may say, even blest.

SHEPHERD [*aside to* CLOWN].

Let's before, as he bids us: he was provided to do us good. [*Exeunt* SHEPHERD *and* CLOWN.

AUTOLYCUS.

If I had a mind to be honest, I see Fortune would not suffer me: she drops booties in my mouth. I am courted now with a double occasion,—gold, and a means to do the prince my master good; which who knows how that may turn back to my advancement? I will bring these two moles, these blind ones, aboard him: if he think it fit to shore them again, and that the complaint they have to the king concerns him nothing, let him call me rogue for being so far officious; for I am proof against that title, and what shame else belongs to't. To him will I present them: there may be matter in it. [*Exit.*

ACT V. SCENE I.

Sicilia. LEONTES' *palace.*

Enter LEONTES, CLEOMENES, DION, PAULINA, *and others.*

CLEOMENES.

SIR, you have done enough, and have perform'd
A saint-like sorrow: no fault could you make,
Which you have not redeem'd; indeed, paid down
More penitence than done trespass: at the last,
Do as the heavens have done, forget your evil;
With them, forgive yourself.

LEONTES.

Whilst I remember
Her and her virtues, I cannot forget
My blemishes in them; and so still think of
The wrong I did myself: which was so much,
That heirless it hath made my kingdom; and
Destroy'd the sweet'st companion that e'er man
Bred his hopes out of.

PAULINA.

True, too true, my lord:
If, one by one, you wedded all the world,
Or from the all that are took something good,
To make a perfect woman, she you kill'd
Would be unparallel'd.

LEONTES.

I think so. Kill'd!
She I kill'd! I did so: but thou strikest me
Sorely, to say I did; it is as bitter
Upon thy tongue as in my thought: now, good now,
Say so but seldom.

CLEOMENES.

Not at all, good lady:
You might have spoken a thousand things that would

Have done the time more benefit, and graced
Your kindness better.

PAULINA.

You are one of those
Would have him wed again.

DION.

If you would not so,
You pity not the state, nor the remembrance
Of his most sovereign name; consider little
What dangers, by his highness' fail of issue,
May drop upon his kingdom, and devour
Incertain lookers-on. What were more holy
Than to rejoice the former queen is well?
What holier than,—for royalty's repair,
For present comfort, and for future good,—
To bless the bed of majesty again
With a sweet fellow to't?

PAULINA.

There is none worthy,
Respecting her that's gone. Besides, the gods
Will have fulfill'd their secret purposes;
For has not the divine Apollo said,
Is't not the tenour of his oracle,
That King Leontes shall not have an heir
Till his lost child be found? which that it shall,
Is all as monstrous to our human reason
As my Antigonus to break his grave
And come again to me; who, on my life,
Did perish with the infant. 'Tis your counsel
My lord should to the heavens be contrary,
Oppose against their wills.—[*to* LEONTES] Care not for issue;
The crown will find an heir: great Alexander
Left his to the worthiest; so his successor
Was like to be the best.

LEONTES.

Good Paulina,
Who hast the memory of Hermione,
I know, in honour,—O, that ever I
Had squared me to thy counsel!—then, even now,
I might have lookt upon my queen's full eyes;
Have taken treasure from her lips,—

PAULINA.

And left them
More rich for what they yielded.

LEONTES.

Thou speak'st truth.
No more such wives; therefore, no wife: one worse,
And better used, would make her sainted spirit
Again possess her corpse, and on this stage—
Where we offend her now—appear soul-vext,
And begin, 'Why to me?'

PAULINA.

Had she such power
She had just cause.

LEONTES.

She had; and would incense me
To murder her I married.

PAULINA.

I should so.
Were I the ghost that walkt, I'ld bid you mark
Her eye, and tell me for what dull part in't
You chose her; then I'ld shriek, that even your ears
Should rift to hear me; and the words that follow'd
Should be, 'Remember mine.'

LEONTES.

Stars, stars,
And all eyes else dead coals!—fear thou no wife;
I'll have no wife, Paulina.

PAULINA.

Will you swear
Never to marry but by my free leave?

LEONTES.

Never, Paulina; so be blest my spirit!

PAULINA.

Then, good my lords, bear witness to his oath.

CLEOMENES.

You tempt him over-much.

PAULINA.

Unless another,
As like Hermione as is her picture,
Affront his eye.

CLEOMENES.

Good madam,—

PAULINA.

I have done.
Yet, if my lord will marry,—if you will, sir,
No remedy, but you will,—give me the office
To choose you a queen: she shall not be so young
As was your former; but she shall be such
As, walkt your first queen's ghost, it should take joy
To see her in your arms.

LEONTES.

My true Paulina,
We shall not marry till thou bidd'st us.

PAULINA.

That
Shall be when your first queen's again in breath;
Never till then.

Enter a GENTLEMAN.

GENTLEMAN.

One that gives out himself Prince Florizel,
Son of Polixenes, with his princess,—she
The fairest I have yet beheld,—desires access
To your high presence.

LEONTES.

What with him? he comes not
Like to his father's greatness: his approach,
So out of circumstance and sudden, tells us
'Tis not a visitation framed, but forced
By need and accident. What train?

GENTLEMAN.

But few,
And those but mean.

LEONTES.

His princess, say you, with him?

GENTLEMAN.

Ay, the most peerless piece of earth, I think,
That e'er the sun shone bright on.

PAULINA.

O Hermione,
As every present time doth boast itself
Above a better gone, so must thy grave
Give way to what's seen now! Sir, you yourself
Have said and writ so; but your writing now
Is colder than that theme, 'She had not been,
Nor was not to be equall'd;'—thus your verse
Flow'd with her beauty once: 'tis shrewdly ebb'd
To say you have seen a better.

GENTLEMAN.

Pardon, madam:
The one I have almost forgot,—your pardon;

The other, when she has obtain'd your eye,
Will have your tongue too. This is a creature,
Would she begin a sect, might quench the zeal
Of all professors else; make proselytes
Of who she but bid follow.

PAULINA.

How! not women?

GENTLEMAN.

Women will love her, that she is a woman
More worth than any man; men, that she is
The rarest of all women.

LEONTES.

Go, Cleomenes;
Yourself, assisted with your honour'd friends,
Bring them to our embracement.

[*Exeunt* CLEOMENES *and others.*

Still, 'tis strange
He thus should steal upon us.

PAULINA.

Had our prince,
Jewel of children, seen this hour, he had pair'd
Well with this lord: there was not full a month
Between their births.

LEONTES

Prithee, no more; cease; thou know'st
He dies to me again when talkt of: sure,
When I shall see this gentleman, thy speeches
Will bring me to consider that which may
Unfurnish me of reason.—They are come.

Enter CLEOMENES *and others, with* FLORIZEL *and* PERDITA.

Your mother was most true to wedlock, prince;
For she did print your royal father off,
Conceiving you: were I but twenty-one,
Your father's image is so hit in you,
His very air, that I should call you brother,
As I did him, and speak of something wildly
By us perform'd before. Most dearly welcome!
And your fair princess-goddess!—O, alas,
I lost a couple, that 'twixt heaven and earth
Might thus have stood, begetting wonder, as
You, gracious couple, do! and then I lost—
All mine own folly—the society,
Amity too, of your brave father, whom,
Though bearing misery, I desire my life
Once more to look on him.

FLORIZEL.

By his command
Have I here toucht Sicilia, and from him
Give you all greetings, that a king, at friend,
Can send his brother; and, but infirmity—
Which waits upon worn times—hath something seized
His wisht ability, he had himself
The lands and waters 'twixt your throne and his
Measured to look upon you; whom he loves—
He bade me say so—more than all the sceptres,
And those that bear them, living.

LEONTES.

O my brother,
Good gentleman, the wrongs I have done thee stir
Afresh within me; and these thy offices,
So rarely kind, are as interpreters
Of my behindhand slackness!—Welcome hither,
As is the spring to the earth. And hath he too
Exposed this paragon to the fearful usage—
At least ungentle—of the dreadful Neptune,
To greet a man not worth her pains, much less
The adventure of her person?

FLORIZEL.

Good my lord,
She came from Libya.

LEONTES.

Where the warlike Smalus,
That noble honour'd lord, is fear'd and loved?

FLORIZEL.

Most royal sir, from thence; from him, whose daughter
His tears proclaim'd his, parting with her: thence,
A prosperous south-wind friendly, we have crost
To execute the charge my father gave me,
For visiting your highness: my best train
I have from your Sicilian shores dismist;
Who for Bohemia bend, to signify
Not only my success in Libya, sir,
But my arrival, and my wife's, in safety
Here where we are.

LEONTES.

The blessed gods
Purge all infection from our air whilst you
Do climate here! You have a holy father,
A graceful gentleman; against whose person,
So sacred as it is, I have done sin:
For which the heavens, taking angry note,
Have left me issueless; and your father's blest,
As he from heaven merits it, with you,
Worthy his goodness. What might I have been,
Might I a son and daughter now have lookt on,
Such goodly things as you!

Enter a LORD.

LORD.

Most noble sir,
That which I shall report will bear no credit,
Were not the proof so nigh. Please you, great sir,
Bohemia greets you from himself by me;
Desires you to attach his son, who has—
His dignity and duty both cast off—
Fled from his father, from his hopes, and with
A shepherd's daughter.

LEONTES.

Where's Bohemia? speak.

LORD.

Here in your city; I now came from him:
I speak amazedly; and it becomes
My marvel and my message. To your court
Whiles he was hastening,—in the chase, it seems,
Of this fair couple,—meets he on the way
The father of this seeming lady, and
Her brother, having both their country quitted
With this young prince.

FLORIZEL.

Camillo has betray'd me;
Whose honour and whose honesty till now
Endured all weathers.

LORD.

Lay't so to his charge:
He's with the king your father.

LEONTES.

Who? Camillo?

LORD.

Camillo, sir; I spake with him; who now
Has these poor men in question. Never saw I

Wretches so quake: they kneel, they kiss the earth;
Forswear themselves as often as they speak:
Bohemia stops his ears, and threatens them
With divers deaths in death.

PERDITA.

O my poor father!
The heaven set spies upon us, will not have
Our contract celebrated.

LEONTES.

You are married?

FLORIZEL.

We are not, sir, nor are we like to be;
The stars, I see, will kiss the valleys first:—
The odds for high and low's alike.

LEONTES.

My lord,
Is this the daughter of a king?

FLORIZEL.

She is,
When once she is my wife.

LEONTES.

That 'once,' I see by your good father's speed,
Will come on very slowly. I am sorry,
Most sorry, you have broken from his liking,
Where you were tied in duty; and as sorry
Your choice is not so rich in worth as beauty,
That you might well enjoy her.

FLORIZEL.

Dear, look up:
Though Fortune, visible an enemy,
Should chase us, with my father, power no jot
Hath she to change our loves.—Beseech you, sir,
Remember since you owed no more to time
Than I do now: with thought of such affections,
Step forth mine advocate; at your request
My father will grant precious things as trifles.

LEONTES.

Would he do so, I'ld beg your precious mistress,
Which he counts but a trifle.

PAULINA.

Sir, my liege,
Your eye hath too much youth in't: not a month
'Fore your queen died, she was more worth such gazes
Than what you look on now.

LEONTES.

I thought of her,
Even in these looks I made.—[*to* FLORIZEL] But your petition
Is yet unanswer'd. I will to your father:
Your honour not o'erthrown by your desires,
I am friend to them and you: upon which errand
I now go toward him; therefore follow me,
And make what way I make: come, good my lord.
[*Exeunt.*

SCENE II.

Before LEONTES' *palace.*

Enter AUTOLYCUS *and a* GENTLEMAN.

AUTOLYCUS.

BESEECH you sir, were you present at this relation?

FIRST GENTLEMAN.

I was by at the opening of the fardel, heard the old shepherd deliver the manner how he found it: whereupon, after a little amazedness, we were all commanded out of the chamber; only this, methought I heard the shepherd say he found the child.

AUTOLYCUS.

I would most gladly know the issue of it.

FIRST GENTLEMAN.

I make a broken delivery of the business;—but the changes I perceived in the king and Camillo were very notes of admiration: they seem'd almost, with staring on one another, to tear the cases of their eyes; there was speech in their dumbness, language in their very gesture; they lookt as they had heard of a world ransom'd, or one destroy'd: a notable passion of wonder appear'd in them; but the wisest beholder, that knew no more but seeing, could not say if the importance were joy or sorrow,—but in the extremity of the one, it must needs be.—Here comes a gentleman that happily knows more.

Enter another GENTLEMAN.

The news, Rogero?

SECOND GENTLEMAN.

Nothing but bonfires: the oracle is fulfill'd; the king's daughter is found: such a deal of wonder is broken out within this hour, that ballad-makers cannot be able to express it.—Here comes the Lady Paulina's steward: he can deliver you more.

Enter a third GENTLEMAN.

How goes it now, sir? this news, which is call'd true, is so like an old tale, that the verity of it is in strong suspicion: has the king found his heir?

THIRD GENTLEMAN.

Most true, if ever truth were pregnant by circumstance: that which you hear you'll swear you see, there is such unity in the proofs. The mantle of Queen Hermione's; her jewel about the neck of it; the letters of Antigonus, found with it, which they know to be his character; the majesty of the creature, in resemblance of the mother; the affection of nobleness, which nature shows above her breeding; and many other evidences,—proclaim her with all certainty to be the king's daughter. Did you see the meeting of the two kings?

SECOND GENTLEMAN.

No.

THIRD GENTLEMAN.

Then have you lost a sight, which was to be seen, cannot be spoken of. There might you have beheld one joy crown another, so and in such manner, that it seem'd sorrow wept to take leave of them,—for their joy waded in tears. There was casting up of eyes, holding up of hands, with countenance of such distraction, that they were to be known by garment, not by favour. Our king, being ready to leap out of himself for joy of his found daughter, as if that joy were now become a loss, cries, 'O, thy mother, thy mother!' then asks Bohemia forgiveness; then embraces his son-in-law; then again worries he his daughter with clipping her, now he thanks the old shepherd, which stands by like a weather-bitten conduit of many kings' reigns. I never heard of such another encounter, which lames report to follow it, and undoes description to do it.

SECOND GENTLEMAN.

What, pray you, became of Antigonus, that carried hence the child?

THIRD GENTLEMAN.

Like an old tale still, which will have matter to rehearse, though credit be asleep, and not an ear open. He was torn to pieces with a bear: this avouches the shepherd's son; who has not only his innocence, which seems much, to justify him, but a handkerchief and rings of his, that Paulina knows.

FIRST GENTLEMAN.

What became of his bark and his followers?

THIRD GENTLEMAN.

Wrackt the same instant of their master's death, and in view of the shepherd: so that all the instruments which aided to expose the child were even then lost when it was found. But, O, the noble combat that, 'twixt joy and sorrow, was fought in Paulina! She had one eye declined for the loss of her husband, another elevated that the oracle was fulfill'd: she lifted the princess from the earth; and so locks her in embracing, as if she would pin her to her heart, that she might no more be in danger of losing.

FIRST GENTLEMAN.

The dignity of this act was worth the audience of kings and princes, for by such was it acted.

THIRD GENTLEMAN.

One of the prettiest touches of all, and that which angled for mine eyes—caught the water, though not the fish—was when, at the relation of the queen's death, with the manner how she came to't,—bravely confest and lamented by the king,—how attentiveness wounded his daughter; till, from one sign of dolour to another, she did, with an 'Alas,' I would fain say, bleed tears; for I am sure my heart wept blood. Who was most marble there changed colour; some swownded, all sorrow'd: if all the world could have seen't, the woe had been universal.

FIRST GENTLEMAN.

Are they return'd to the court?

THIRD GENTLEMAN.

No: the princess hearing of her mother's statue, which is in the keeping of Paulina,—a piece many years in doing, and now newly perform'd by that rare Italian master, Julio Romano, who, had he himself eternity, and could put breath into his work, would beguile Nature of her custom, so perfectly he is her ape: he so near to Hermione hath done Hermione, that they say one would speak to her, and stand in hope of answer:—thither with all greediness of affection are they gone; and there they intend to sup.

SECOND GENTLEMAN.

I thought she had some great matter there in hand; for she hath privately twice or thrice a day, ever since the death of Hermione, visited that removed house. Shall we thither, and with our company piece the rejoicing?

FIRST GENTLEMAN.

Who would be thence that has the benefit of access? every wink of an eye, some new grace will be born: our absence makes us unthrifty to our knowledge. Let's along. [*Exeunt* GENTLEMEN.

AUTOLYCUS.

Now, had I not the dash of my former life in me, would preferment drop on my head. I brought the old man and his son aboard the prince; told him I heard them talk of a fardel, and I know not what: but he at that time, overfond of the shepherd's daughter,—so he then took her to be,—who began to be much sea-sick, and himself little better, extremity of weather continuing, this mystery remain'd undiscover'd. But 'tis all one to me; for had I been the finder-out of this secret, it would not have relisht among my other discredits.—Here come those I have done good to against my will, and already appearing in the blossoms of their fortune.

Enter SHEPHERD *and* CLOWN.

SHEPHERD.

Come, boy; I am past moe children, but thy sons and daughters will be all gentlemen born.

CLOWN.

You are well met, sir. You denied to fight with me this other day, because I was no gentleman born. See you these clothes? say you see them not, and think me still no gentleman born: you were best say these robes are not gentlemen born: give me the lie, do; and try whether I am not now a gentleman born.

AUTOLYCUS.

I know you are now, sir, a gentleman born.

CLOWN.

Ay, and have I been so any time these four hours.

SHEPHERD.

And so have I, boy.

CLOWN.

So you have:—but I was a gentleman born before my father; for the king's son took me by the hand, and call'd me brother; and then the two kings call'd my father brother; and then the prince my brother and the princess my sister call'd my father father; and so we wept,—and there was the first gentleman-like tears that ever we shed.

SHEPHERD.

We may live, son, to shed many more.

CLOWN.

Ay; or else 'twere hard luck, being in so preposterous estate as we are.

AUTOLYCUS.

I humbly beseech you, sir, to pardon me all the faults I have committed to your worship, and to give me your good report to the prince my master.

SHEPHERD.

Prithee, son, do; for we must be gentle, now we are gentlemen.

CLOWN.

Thou wilt amend thy life?

AUTOLYCUS.

Ay, an it like your good worship.

CLOWN.

Give me thy hand: I will swear to the prince thou art as honest a true fellow as any is in Bohemia.

SHEPHERD.

You may say it, but not swear it.

CLOWN.

Not swear it, now I am a gentleman? Let boors and franklins say it, I'll swear it.

SHEPHERD.

How if it be false, son?

CLOWN.

If it be ne'er so false, a true gentleman may swear it in the behalf of his friend:—and I'll swear to the prince thou art a tall fellow of thy hands, and that thou wilt not be drunk; but I know thou art no tall fellow of thy hands, and that thou wilt be drunk: but I'll swear it; and I would thou wouldst be a tall fellow of thy hands.

AUTOLYCUS.

I will prove so, sir, to my power.

CLOWN.

Ay, by any means prove a tall fellow: if I do not wonder how thou darest venture to be drunk, not being a tall fellow, trust me not.—[*Trumpets within.*] Hark! the kings and the princes, our kindred, are going to see the queen's picture. Come, follow us: we'll be thy good masters. [*Exeunt.*

SCENE III.

A chapel in PAULINA'S *house.*

Enter LEONTES, POLIXENES, FLORIZEL, PERDITA, CAMILLO, PAULINA, LORDS, *and* ATTENDANTS.

LEONTES.

O GRAVE and good Paulina, the great comfort
That I have had of thee!

PAULINA.

What, sovereign sir,
I did not well, I meant well. All my services
You have paid home: but that you have vouchsafed
With your crown'd brother and these your contracted
Heirs of your kingdoms my poor house to visit,
It is a surplus of your grace, which never
My life may last to answer.

LEONTES.

O, Paulina,
We honour you with trouble:—but we came
To see the statue of our queen· your gallery
Have we past through, not without much content
In many singularities; but we saw not
That which my daughter came to look upon,
The statue of her mother.

PAULINA.

As she lived peerless,
So her dead likeness, I do well believe,
Excels whatever yet you lookt upon,
Or hand of man hath done; therefore I keep it
Lonely, apart. But here it is: prepare
To see the life as lively mockt as ever
Still sleep mockt death: behold, and say 'tis well.

[PAULINA *draws back a curtain, and discovers* HERMIONE *standing as a statue.*

I like your silence,—it the more shows off
Your wonder: but yet speak;—first, you, my liege:
Comes it not something near?

LEONTES.

Her natural posture!—
Chide me, dear stone, that I may say indeed
Thou art Hermione; or rather, thou art she
In thy not chiding, for she was as tender
As infancy and grace.—But yet, Paulina,
Hermione was not so much wrinkled, nothing
So aged as this seems.

POLIXENES.

O, not by much.

PAULINA.

So much the more our carver's excellence;
Which lets go by some sixteen years, and makes her
As she lived now.

LEONTES.

As now she might have done,
So much to my good comfort, as it is
Now piercing to my soul. O, thus she stood,
Even with such life of majesty,—warm life,
As now it coldly stands,—when first I woo'd her!
I am ashamed: does not the stone rebuke me
For being more stone than it?—O royal piece,
There's magic in thy majesty; which has
My evils conjured to remembrance, and
From thy admiring daughter took the spirits,
Standing like stone with thee!

PERDITA.

And give me leave,
And do not say 'tis superstition that
I kneel, and then implore her blessing.—Lady,
Dear queen, that ended when I but began,
Give me that hand of yours to kiss.

PAULINA.

O, patience!
The statue is but newly fixt, the colour's
Not dry.

CAMILLO.

My lord, your sorrow was too sore laid on,
Which sixteen winters cannot blow away,
So many summers dry: scarce any joy
Did ever so long live; no sorrow
But kill'd itself much sooner.

POLIXENES.

Dear my brother,
Let him that was the cause of this have power
To take off so much grief from you as he
Will piece up in himself.

PAULINA.

Indeed, my lord,
If I had thought the sight of my poor image
Would thus have wrought you,—for the stone is mine,—
I'ld not have show'd it.

LEONTES.

Do not draw the curtain.

PAULINA.

No longer shall you gaze on't, lest your fancy
May think anon it moves.

LEONTES.

Let be, let be.—
Would I were dead, but that, methinks, already—
What was he that did make it?—See, my lord,
Would you not deem it breathed? and that those veins
Did verily bear blood?

POLIXENES.

Masterly done:
The very life seems warm upon her lip.

LEONTES.

The fixture of her eye has motion in't,
As we are mockt with art.

PAULINA.

I'll draw the curtain:
My lord's almost so far transported, that
He'll think anon it lives.

LEONTES.
O sweet Paulina.
Make me to think so twenty years together!
No settled senses of the world can match
The pleasure of that madness. Let't alone.

PAULINA.
I am sorry sir, I have thus far stirr'd you; but
I could afflict you further.

LEONTES.
Do, Paulina;
For this affliction has a taste as sweet
As any cordial comfort.—Still, methinks,
There is an air comes from her: what fine chisel
Could ever yet cut breath? Let no man mock me,
For I will kiss her.

PAULINA.
Good my lord, forbear:
The ruddiness upon her lip is wet;
You'll mar it, if you kiss it; stain your own
With oily painting. Shall I draw the curtain?

LEONTES.
No, not these twenty years.

PERDITA.
So long could I
Stand by, a looker-on.

PAULINA.
Either forbear,
Quit presently the chapel, or resolve you
For more amazement. If you can behold it,
I'll make the statue move indeed, descend
And take you by the hand: but then you'll think,—
Which I protest against,— I am assisted
By wicked powers.

LEONTES.
What you can make her do,
I am content to look on; what to speak,
I am content to hear; for 'tis as easy
To make her speak as move.

PAULINA.
It is required
You do awake your faith. Then all stand still;
Or those that think it is unlawful business
I am about, let them depart.

LEONTES.
Proceed:
No foot shall stir.

PAULINA.
Music, awake her; strike!—[*Music.*
'Tis time; descend; be stone no more; approach;
Strike all that look upon with marvel. Come;
I'll fill your grave up: stir; nay, come away;
Bequeath to death your numbness, for from him
Dear life redeems you.—You perceive she stirs:
[HERMIONE *comes down from the pedestal.*
Start not; her actions shall be holy as
You hear my spell is lawful: do not shun her,
Until you see her die again; for then
You kill her double. Nay, present your hand:
When she was young, you woo'd her; now in age
Is she become the suitor.

LEONTES.
O, she's warm! [*Embracing her.*
If this be magic, let it be an art
Lawful as eating.

POLIXENES.
She embraces him.

CAMILLO.
She hangs about his neck:
If she pertain to life, let her speak too.

POLIXENES.
Ay, and make't manifest where she has lived,
Or how stolen from the dead.

PAULINA.
That she is living,
Were it but told you, should be hooted at
Like an old tale: but it appears she lives,
Though yet she speak not. Mark a little while.—
Please you to interpose, fair madam; kneel,
And pray your mother's blessing.—Turn, good lady;
Our Perdita is found.
[*Presenting Perdita, who kneels to* HERMIONE.

HERMIONE.
You gods, look down,
And from your sacred vials pour your graces
Upon my daughter's head!— Tell me, mine own,
Where hast thou been preserved? where lived? how found
Thy father's court? for thou shalt hear that I,—
Knowing by Paulina that the oracle
Gave hope thou wast in being,—have preserved
Myself to see the issue.

PAULINA.
There's time enough for that:
Lest they desire, upon this push, to trouble
Your joys with like relation.—Go together,
You precious winners all; your exultation
Partake to every one. I, an old turtle,
Will wing me to some wither'd bough, and there
My mate, that's never to be found again,
Lament till I am lost.

LEONTES.
O, peace, Paulina!
Thou shouldst a husband take by my consent,
As I by thine a wife: this is a match,
And made between's by vows. Thou hast found mine;
But how, is to be question'd; for I saw her,
As I thought, dead; and have, in vain, said many
A prayer upon her grave. I'll not seek far,—
For him, I partly know his mind,—to find thee
An honourable husband. Come, Camillo,
And take her by the hand; whose worth and honesty
Is richly noted; and here justified
By us, a pair of kings.—Let's from this place.—
What! look upon my brother:—both your pardons,
That e'er I put between your holy looks
My ill suspicions.—This your son-in-law,
And son unto the king, whom heavens directing,
Is troth-plight to your daughter.—Good Paulina,
Lead us from hence; where we may leisurely
Each one demand, and answer to his part
Perform'd in this wide gap of time, since first
We were dissever'd; hastily lead away. [*Exeunt.*

THE TEMPEST

DRAMATIS PERSONAE

ALONSO, *King of Naples.*
SEBASTIAN, *his brother.*
PROSPERO, *the right Duke of Milan.*
ANTONIO, *his brother, the usurping Duke of Milan.*
FERDINAND, *son to the King of Naples.*
GONZALO, *an honest old counsellor.*
ADRIAN, } *lords.*
FRANCISCO, }
CALIBAN, *a savage and deformed slave.*
TRINCULO, *a jester.*
STEPHANO, *a drunken butler.*
MASTER OF A SHIP, BOATSWAIN, *and* MARINERS.

MIRANDA, *daughter to Prospero.*

ARIEL, *an airy spirit.*
IRIS, }
CERES, }
JUNO, } *presented by spirits.*
NYMPHS, }
REAPERS, }

OTHER SPIRITS ATTENDING ON PROSPERO.

SCENE—*A ship at sea; afterwards an island.*

ACT I. SCENE I.

A ship at sea: a tempestuous noise of thunder and lightning heard.

Enter a SHIP-MASTER *and a* BOATSWAIN.

SHIP-MASTER.
BOATSWAIN!

BOATSWAIN.
Here, master: what cheer?

SHIP-MASTER.
Good, speak to the mariners: fall to't yarely, or we run ourselves a-ground: bestir, bestir. [*Exit.*

Enter MARINERS.

BOATSWAIN.
Heigh, my hearts! cheerly, cheerly, my hearts! yare, yare! Take in the topsail! Tend to the master's whistle! [*Exeunt* MARINERS.]—Blow, till thou burst thy wind, if room enough!

Enter ALONSO, SEBASTIAN, ANTONIO, FERDINAND, GONZALO, *and others.*

ALONSO.
Good boatswain, have care. Where's the master? Play the men.

BOATSWAIN.
I pray now, keep below.

ANTONIO.
Where is the master, boatswain?

BOATSWAIN.
Do you not hear him? You mar our labour: keep your cabins: you do assist the storm.

GONZALO.
Nay, good, be patient.

BOATSWAIN.
When the sea is. Hence! What cares these roarers for the name of king? To cabin: silence! trouble us not.

GONZALO.
Good, yet remember whom thou hast aboard.

BOATSWAIN.
None that I more love than myself. You are a counsellor; if you can command these elements to silence, and work the peace of the present, we will not hand a rope more; use your authority: if you cannot, give thanks you have lived so long, and make yourself ready in your cabin for the mischance of the hour, if it so hap.—Cheerly, good hearts!—Out of our way, I say. [*Exit.*

GONZALO.
I have great comfort from this fellow: methinks he hath no drowning-mark upon him; his complexion is perfect gallows. Stand fast, good Fate, to his hanging! make the rope of his destiny our cable, for our own doth little advantage! If he be not born to be hang'd, our case is miserable. [*Exeunt.*

Enter BOATSWAIN.

BOATSWAIN.
Down with the topmast! yare; lower, lower! Bring her to try with main-course! [*A cry within.*] A plague upon this howling! they are louder than the weather or our office.

Enter SEBASTIAN, ANTONIO, *and* GONZALO.

Yet again! what do you here? Shall we give o'er, and drown? Have you a mind to sink?

SEBASTIAN.
A pox o'your throat, you bawling, blasphemous, incharitable dog!

BOATSWAIN.
Work you, then.

ANTONIO.
Hang, cur, hang! you whoreson, insolent noisemaker, we are less afraid to be drown'd than thou art.

GONZALO.
I'll warrant him for drowning; though the ship were no stronger than a nutshell, and as leaky as an unstanch'd wench.

BOATSWAIN.
Lay her a-hold, a-hold! set her two courses off to sea again: lay her off!

Enter MARINERS *wet.*

MARINERS.
All lost! to prayers, to prayers! all lost!

BOATSWAIN.
What, must our mouths be cold?

GONZALO.
The king and prince at prayers! let's assist them,
For our case is as theirs.

SEBASTIAN.
I'm out of patience.

ANTONIO.
We are merely cheated of our lives by drunkards:
This wide-chopt rascal,—would thou mightst lie
The washing of ten tides! [drowning,

GONZALO.

He'll be hang'd yet,
Though every drop of water swear against it,
And gape at widest to glut him.

[*A confused noise within,*—'Mercy on us!'—
'We split, we split!—'Farewell, my wife and children!'—
'Farewell, brother!'—'We split, we split, we split!']

ANTONIO.

Let's all sink with the king.

SEBASTIAN.

Let's take leave of him.

[*Exeunt* ANTONIO *and* SEBASTIAN.

GONZALO.

Now would I give a thousand furlongs of sea for an acre of barren ground,—long heath, broom, furze, anything. The wills above be done! but I would fain die a dry death. [*Exeunt.*

SCENE II.

The island: before PROSPERO'S *cell.*

Enter PROSPERO *and* MIRANDA.

MIRANDA.

IF by your art, my dearest father, you have
Put the wild waters in this roar, allay them.
The sky, it seems, would pour down stinking pitch,
But that the sea, mounting to the welkin's cheek,
Dashes the fire out. O, I have suffer'd
With those that I saw suffer! a brave vessel,
Who had, no doubt, some noble creature in her,
Dash'd all to pieces. O, the cry did knock
Against my very heart! Poor souls, they perish'd!
Had I been any god of power, I would
Have sunk the sea within the earth, or ere
It should the good ship so have swallow'd, and
The fraughting souls within her.

PROSPERO.

Be collected;
No more amazement: tell your piteous heart
There's no harm done.

MIRANDA.

O, woe the day!

PROSPERO.

No harm.
I have done nothing but in care of thee,
Of thee, my dear one, thee, my daughter, who
Art ignorant of what thou art, naught knowing
Of whence I am, nor that I am more better
Than Prospero, master of a full poor cell,
And thy no greater father.

MIRANDA.

More to know
Did never meddle with my thoughts.

PROSPERO.

'Tis time
I should inform thee further. Lend thy hand,
And pluck my magic garment from me. So:

[*Lays down his mantle.*

Lie there, my art. Wipe thou thine eyes; have comfort.
The direful spectacle of the wrack, which touch'd
The very virtue of compassion in thee,
I have with such provision in mine art
So safely order'd, that there is no soul—
No, not so much perdition as an hair
Betid to any creature in the vessel
Which thou heard'st cry, which thou saw'st sink. Sit down;
For thou must now know further.

MIRANDA.

You have often
Begun to tell me what I am; but stopt,
And left me to a bootless inquisition,
Concluding, 'Stay, not yet.'

PROSPERO.

The hour's now come;
The very minute bids thee ope thine ear:
Obey, and be attentive. Canst thou remember
A time before we came unto this cell?
I do not think thou canst, for then thou wast not
Out three years old.

MIRANDA.

Certainly, sir, I can.

PROSPERO.

By what? by any other house or person?
Of any thing the image tell me that
Hath kept with thy remembrance.

MIRANDA.

'Tis far off,
And rather like a dream than an assurance
That my remembrance warrants. Had I not
Four or five women once that tended me?

PROSPERO.

Thou hadst, and more, Miranda. But how is it
That this lives in thy mind? What see'st thou else
In the dark backward and abysm of time?
If thou remember'st aught ere thou camest here,
How thou camest here thou mayst.

MIRANDA.

But that I do not.

PROSPERO.

Twelve year since, Miranda, twelve year since,
Thy father was the Duke of Milan, and
A prince of power.

MIRANDA.

Sir, are not you my father?

PROSPERO.

Thy mother was a piece of virtue, and
She said thou wast my daughter; and thy father
Was Duke of Milan; thou his only heir,
And princess, no worse issued.

MIRANDA.

O the heavens!
What foul play had we, that we came from thence?
Or blessed was't we did?

PROSPERO.

Both, both, my girl:
By foul play, as thou say'st, were we heaved thence;
But blessedly holp hither.

MIRANDA.

O, my heart bleeds
To think o'the teen that I have turn'd you to,
Which is from my remembrance! Please you, further.

PROSPERO.

My brother, and thy uncle, call'd Antonio,—
I pray thee, mark me,—that a brother should
Be so perfidious!—he whom, next thyself,

Of all the world I loved, and to him put
The manage of my state; as, at that time,
Through all the signiories it was the first,
And Prospero the prime duke, being so reputed
In dignity, and for the liberal arts
Without a parallel: those being all my study,
The government I cast upon my brother,
And to my state grew stranger, being transported
And rapt in secret studies. Thy false uncle—
Dost thou attend me?

MIRANDA.

Sir, most heedfully,

PROSPERO.

Being once perfected how to grant suits,
How to deny them, who t'advance, and who
To trash for over-topping, new created
The creatures that were mine, I say, or changed 'em,
Or else new-form'd 'em; having both the key
Of officer and office, set all hearts i'the state
To what tune pleased his ear; that now he was
The ivy which had hid my princely trunk,
And suck'd my verdure out on't. Thou attend'st not.

MIRANDA.

O, good sir, I do.

PROSPERO.

I pray thee, mark me.
I, thus neglecting worldly ends, all dedicate
To closeness, and the bettering of my mind
With that which, but by being so retired,
O'er-prized all popular rate, in my false brother
Awaked an evil nature; and my trust,
Like a good parent, did beget of him
A falsehood, in its contrary as great
As my trust was; which had indeed no limit,
A confidence sans bound. He being thus lorded,
Not only with what my revenue yielded,
But what my power might else exact, like one
Who having into truth, by telling of it,
Made such a sinner of his memory,
To credit his own lie, he did believe
He was indeed the duke; out o'the substitution,
And executing the outward face of royalty,
With all prerogative:—hence his ambition growing,—
Dost thou hear?

MIRANDA.

Your tale, sir, would cure deafness.

PROSPERO.

To have no screen between this part he play'd
And him he play'd it for, he needs will be
Absolute Milan. Me, poor man, my library
Was dukedom large enough: of temporal royalties
He thinks me now incapable; confederates—
So dry he was for sway—with the King of Naples
To give him annual tribute, do him homage,
Subject his coronet to his crown, and bend
The dukedom, yet unbow'd,—alas, poor Milan!—
To most ignoble stooping.

MIRANDA.

O the heavens!

PROSPERO.

Mark his condition, and the event; then tell me
If this might be a brother.

MIRANDA.

I should sin
To think but nobly of my grandmother:
Good wombs have borne bad sons.

PROSPERO.

Now the condition.
This King of Naples, being an enemy
To me inveterate, hearkens my brother's suit;
Which was, that he, in lieu o'the premises,—
Of homage, and I know not how much tribute,—
Should presently extirpate me and mine
Out of the dukedom, and confer fair Milan,
With all the honours, on my brother: whereon,
A treacherous army levied, one midnight
Fated to the purpose, did Antonio open
The gates of Milan; and, i'the dead of darkness,
The ministers for the purpose hurried thence
Me and thy crying self.

MIRANDA.

Alack, for pity!
I, not rememb'ring how I cried out then,
Will cry it o'er again: it is a hint
That wrings mine eyes to't.

PROSPERO.

Hear a little further,
And then I'll bring thee to the present business
Which now's upon's; without the which this story
Were most impertinent.

MIRANDA.

Wherefore did they not
That hour destroy us?

PROSPERO.

Well demanded, wench:
My tale provokes that question. Dear, they durst not,
So dear the love my people bore me, nor set
A mark so bloody on the business; but
With colours fairer painted their foul ends.
In few, they hurried us aboard a bark,
Bore us some leagues to sea; where they prepared
A rotten carcass of a butt, not rigg'd,
Nor tackle, sail, nor mast; the very rats
Instinctively have quit it: there they hoist us,
To cry to the sea that roar'd to us; to sigh
To the winds, whose pity, sighing back again,
Did us but loving wrong.

MIRANDA.

Alack, what trouble
Was I then to you!

PROSPERO.

O, a cherubin
Thou wast that did preserve me! Thou didst smile,
Infused with a fortitude from heaven,
When I have deck'd the sea with drops full salt,
Under my burden groan'd; which raised in me
An undergoing stomach, to bear up
Against what should ensue.

MIRANDA.

How came we ashore?

PROSPERO.

By Providence divine.
Some food we had, and some fresh water, that
A noble Neapolitan, Gonzalo,
Out of his charity (who being then appointed
Master of this design), did give us, with

Rich garments, linens, stuffs, and necessaries,
Which since have steaded much; so, of his gentleness,
Knowing I loved my books, he furnish'd me,
From mine own library, with volumes that
I prize above my dukedom.

MIRANDA.

Would I might
But ever see that man!

PROSPERO.

Now I arise:
[*Resuming his mantle.*
Sit still, and hear the last of our sea-sorrow.
Here in this island we arrived; and here
Have I, thy schoolmaster, made thee more profit
Than other princess' can, that have more time
For vainer hours, and tutors not so careful.

MIRANDA.

Heavens thank you for't! And now, I pray you, sir,
For still 'tis beating in my mind, your reason
For raising this sea-storm?

PROSPERO.

Know thus far forth.
By accident most strange, bountiful Fortune,
Now my dear lady, hath mine enemies
Brought to this shore; and by my prescience
I find my zenith doth depend upon
A most auspicious star, whose influence
If now I court not, but omit, my fortunes
Will ever after droop. Here cease more questions:
Thou art inclined to sleep; 'tis a good dulness,
And give it way: I know thou canst not chuse.—
[MIRANDA *sleeps.*
Come away, servant, come! I am ready now:
Approach, my Ariel; come!

Enter ARIEL.

ARIEL.

All hail, great master! grave sir, hail! I come
To answer thy best pleasure; be't to fly,
To swim, to dive into the fire, to ride
On the curl'd clouds,—to thy strong bidding task
Ariel and all his quality.

PROSPERO.

Hast thou, spirit,
Perform'd to point the tempest that I bade thee?

ARIEL.

To every article.
I boarded the king's ship; now on the beak,
Now in the waist, the deck, in every cabin,
I flamed amazement: sometime I'ld divide,
And burn in many places; on the topmast,
The yards, and bowsprit, would I flame distinctly,
Then meet, and join. Jove's lightnings, the precursors
O'the dreadful thunder-claps, more momentary
And sight-outrunning were not: the fire, and cracks
Of sulphurous roaring, the most mighty Neptune
Seem to besiege, and make his bold waves tremble,
Yea, his dread trident shake.

PROSPERO.

My brave spirit!
Who was so firm, so constant, that this coil
Would not infect his reason?

ARIEL.

Not a soul
But felt a fever of the mad, and play'd
Some tricks of desperation. All but mariners
Plunged in the foaming brine, and quit the vessel,
Then all a-fire with me: the king's son, Ferdinand,
With hair up-staring,—then like reeds, not hair,—
Was the first man that leapt; cried, 'Hell is empty,
And all the devils are here.'

PROSPERO.

Why, that's my spirit!
But was not this nigh shore?

ARIEL.

Close by, my master.

PROSPERO.

But are they, Ariel, safe?

ARIEL.

Not a hair perish'd;
On their sustaining garments not a blemish,
But fresher than before: and, as thou bad'st me,
In troops I have dispersed them 'bout the isle.
The king's son have I landed by himself;
Whom I left cooling of the air with sighs
In an odd angle of the isle, and sitting,
His arms in this sad knot.

PROSPERO.

Of the king's ship
The mariners, say how thou hast disposed,
And all the rest o'the fleet.

ARIEL.

Safely in harbour
Is the king's ship; in the deep nook, where once
Thou call'dst me up at midnight to fetch dew
From the still-vext Bermoothes, there she's hid:
The mariners all under hatches stow'd;
Who, with a charm join'd to their suffer'd labour,
I have left asleep: and for the rest o'the fleet,
Which I dispersed, they all have met again,
And are upon the Mediterranean flote,
Bound sadly home for Naples,
Supposing that they saw the king's ship wrackt,
And his great person perish.

PROSPERO.

Ariel, thy charge
Exactly is perform'd; but there's more work.
What is the time o'the day?

ARIEL.

Past the mid season.

PROSPERO.

At least two glasses. The time 'twixt six and now
Must by us both be spent most preciously.

ARIEL.

Is there more toil? Since thou dost give me pains,
Let me remember thee what thou hast promised,
Which is not yet perform'd me.

PROSPERO.

How now? moody?
What is't thou canst demand?

ARIEL.

My liberty.

PROSPERO.

Before the time be out? no more!

ARIEL.

I prithee,
Remember I have done thee worthy service;

Told thee no lies, made thee no mistakings, served
Without or grudge or grumblings; thou did promise
To bate me a full year.

PROSPERO.

Dost thou forget
From what a torment I did free thee?

ARIEL.

No.

PROSPERO.

Thou dost; and think'st it much to tread the ooze
Of the salt deep,
To run upon the sharp wind of the north,
To do me business in the veins o'the earth
When it is baked with frost.

ARIEL.

I do not, sir.

PROSPERO.

Thou liest, malignant thing! Hast thou forgot
The foul witch Sycorax, who with age and envy
Was grown into a hoop? hast thou forgot her?

ARIEL.

No, sir.

PROSPERO.

Thou hast. Where was she born? speak; tell me.

ARIEL.

Sir, in Argier.

PROSPERO.

O, was she so? I must
Once in a month recount what thou hast been,
Which thou forgett'st. This damn'd witch Sycorax,
For mischiefs manifold, and sorceries terrible
To enter human hearing, from Argier,
Thou know'st, was banish'd: for one thing she did
They would not take her life. Is not this true?

ARIEL.

Ay, sir.

PROSPERO.

This blue-eyed hag was hither brought with child,
And here was left by the sailors. Thou, my slave,
As thou report'st thyself, was then her servant;
And, for thou wast a spirit too delicate
To act her earthy and abhorr'd commands,
Refusing her grand hests, she did confine thee,
By help of her more potent ministers,
And in her most unmitigable rage,
Into a cloven pine; within which rift
Imprison'd, thou didst painfully remain
A dozen years; within which space she died,
And left thee there; where thou didst vent thy groans
As fast as mill-wheels strike. Then was this island—
Save for the son that she did litter here,
A freckled whelp hag-born—not honour'd with
A human shape.

ARIEL.

Yes, Caliban, her son.

PROSPERO.

Dull thing, I say so; he, that Caliban,
Whom now I keep in service. Thou best know'st
What torment I did find thee in; thy groans
Did make wolves howl, and penetrate the breasts
Of ever-angry bears: it was a torment
To lay upon the damn'd, which Sycorax
Could not again undo: it was mine art,
When I arrived and heard thee, that made gape
The pine, and let thee out.

ARIEL.

I thank thee, master.

PROSPERO.

If thou more murmur'st, I will rend an oak,
And peg thee in his knotty entrails, till
Thou'st howl'd away twelve winters.

ARIEL.

Pardon, master:
I will be correspondent to command,
And do my spriting gently.

PROSPERO.

Do so; and after two days
I will discharge thee.

ARIEL.

That's my noble master!
What shall I do? say what; what shall I do?

PROSPERO.

Go make thyself like a nymph o'the sea: be subject
To no sight but thine and mine: invisible
To every eyeball else. Go take this shape,
And hither come in't: go; hence with diligence!
[*Exit* ARIEL.
Awake, dear heart, awake! thou hast slept well;
Awake!

MIRANDA [*waking*].

The strangeness of your story put
Heaviness in me.

PROSPERO.

Shake it off. Come on;
We'll visit Caliban my slave, who never
Yields us kind answer.

MIRANDA.

'Tis a villain, sir,
I do not love to look on.

PROSPERO.

But, as 'tis,
We cannot miss him: he does make our fire,
Fetch in our wood; and serves in offices
That profit us.—What, ho! slave! Caliban!
Thou earth, thou! speak.

CALIBAN [*within*].

There's wood enough within.

PROSPERO.

Come forth, I say! there's other business for thee:
Come, thou tortoise, when?

Enter ARIEL *like a water-nymph.*

Fine apparition! My quaint Ariel,
Hark in thine ear.

ARIEL.

My lord, it shall be done. [*Exit.*

PROSPERO.

Thou poisonous slave, got by the devil himself
Upon thy wicked dam, come forth!

Enter CALIBAN.

CALIBAN.

As wicked dew as e'er my mother brush'd
With raven's feather from unwholesome fen
Drop on you both! a south-west blow on ye,
And blister you all o'er!

PROSPERO.

For this, be sure, to-night thou shalt have cramps,
Side-stitches that shall pen thy breath up; urchins
Shall, for that vast of night that they may work,
All exercise on thee; thou shalt be pinch'd
As thick as honeycomb, each pinch more stinging
Than bees that made 'em.

CALIBAN.

I must eat my dinner.
This island's mine, by Sycorax my mother,
Which thou takest from me. When thou camest first,
Thou strokedst me, and made much of me; wouldst give me
Water with berries in't; and teach me how
To name the bigger light, and how the less,
That burn by day and night: and then I loved thee,
And show'd thee all the qualities o'the isle,
The fresh springs, brine-pits, barren place and fertile:
Cursed be I that did so! All the charms
Of Sycorax, toads, beetles, bats, light on you!
For I am all the subjects that you have,
Which first was mine own king: and here you sty me
In this hard rock, whiles you do keep from me
The rest o'the island.

PROSPERO.

Thou most lying slave,
Whom stripes may move, not kindness! I have used thee,
Filth as thou art, with human care, and lodged thee
In mine own cell, till thou didst seek to violate
The honour of my child.

CALIBAN.

O ho, O ho! would't had been done!
Thou didst prevent me; I had peopled else
This isle with Calibans.

PROSPERO.

Abhorred slave,
Which any print of goodness wilt not take,
Being capable of all ill! I pitied thee,
Took pains to make thee speak, taught thee each hour
One thing or other: when thou didst not, savage,
Know thine own meaning, but wouldst gabble like
A thing most brutish, I endow'd thy purposes
With words that made them known. But thy vile race,
Though thou didst learn, had that in't which good natures
Could not abide to be with; therefore wast thou
Deservedly confined into this rock,
Who hadst deserved more than a prison.

CALIBAN.

You taught me language; and my profit on't
Is, I know how to curse. The red plague rid you
For learning me your language!

PROSPERO.

Hag-seed, hence!
Fetch us in fuel; and be quick, thou'rt best,
To answer other business. Shrugg'st thou, malice?
If thou neglect'st, or dost unwillingly
What I command, I'll rack thee with old cramps,
Fill all thy bones with aches, make thee roar,
That beasts shall tremble at thy din.

CALIBAN.

No, 'pray thee.—
[*aside*] I must obey: his art is of such power,
It would control my dam's god, Setebos,
And make a vassal of him.

PROSPERO.

So, slave; hence! [*Exit* CALIBAN.

Enter ARIEL, *invisible, playing and singing;* FERDINAND *following.*

ARIEL'S *song.*

Come unto these yellow sands,
And then take hands:
Court'sied when you have and kist,—
The wild waves whist,—
Foot it featly here and there;
And, sweet sprites, the burden bear.
Hark, hark!
[*Burden, dispersedly, within.* Bow, wow.]
The watch-dogs bark:
[*Burden, dispersedly, within.* Bow, wow.]
Hark, hark! I hear
The strain of strutting chanticleer.
[*Cry:* Cock-a-diddle-dow.]

FERDINAND.

Where should this music be? i'the air or the earth?
It sounds no more:—and, sure, it waits upon
Some god o'the island. Sitting on a bank,
Weeping again the king my father's wrack,
This music crept by me upon the waters,
Allaying both their fury and my passion
With its sweet air: thence I have follow'd it,
Or it hath drawn me rather:—but 'tis gone.
No, it begins again.

ARIEL *sings.*

Full fadom five thy father lies;
Of his bones are coral made;
Those are pearls that were his eyes;
Nothing of him that doth fade
But doth suffer a sea-change
Into something rich and strange.
Sea-nymphs hourly ring his knell:
[*Burden within.* Ding-dong.]
Hark! now I hear them,—Ding-dong, bell.

FERDINAND.

The ditty does remember my drown'd father:—
This is no mortal business, nor no sound
That the earth owes:—I hear it now above me.

PROSPERO.

The fringed curtains of thine eye advance,
And say what thou see'st yond.

MIRANDA.

What is't? a spirit?
Lord, how it looks about! Believe me, sir,
It carries a brave form:—but 'tis a spirit.

PROSPERO.

No, wench; it eats, and sleeps, and hath such senses
As we have, such. This gallant which thou see'st
Was in the wrack; and, but he's something stain'd
With grief, that's beauty's canker, thou mightst call him

A goodly person: he hath lost his fellows,
And strays about to find 'em.

MIRANDA.

I might call him
A thing divine; for nothing natural
I ever saw so noble.

PROSPERO [*aside*].

It goes on, I see,
As my soul prompts it.—Spirit, fine spirit! I'll free thee
Within two days for this.

FERDINAND.

Most sure, the goddess
On whom these airs attend!—Vouchsafe my prayer
May know if you remain upon this island;
And that you will some good instruction give
How I may bear me here: my prime request,
Which I do last pronounce, is, O you wonder!
If you be maid or no?

MIRANDA.

No wonder, sir;
But certainly a maid.

FERDINAND.

My language! heavens!
I am the best of them that speak this speech,
Were I but where 'tis spoken.

PROSPERO.

How! the best!
What wert thou, if the King of Naples heard thee?

FERDINAND.

A single thing, as I am now, that wonders
To hear thee speak of Naples. He does hear me;
And that he does I weep: myself am Naples;
Who with mine eyes, never since at ebb, beheld
The king my father wrackt.

MIRANDA.

Alack! for mercy!

FERDINAND.

Yes, faith, and all his lords: the Duke of Milan
And his brave son being twain.

PROSPERO [*aside*].

The Duke of Milan
And his more braver daughter could control thee,
If now 'twere fit to do't. At the first sight
They have changed eyes. Delicate Ariel,
I'll set thee free for this!—A word, good sir;
I fear you have done yourself some wrong: a word.

MIRANDA.

Why speaks my father so ungently? This
Is the third man that e'er I saw; the first
That e'er I sigh'd for: pity move my father
To be inclined my way!

FERDINAND.

O, if a virgin,
And your affection not gone forth, I'll make you
The queen of Naples.

PROSPERO.

Soft, sir! one word more.—
[*aside*] They are both in either's powers: but this swift business
I must uneasy make, lest too light winning
Make the prize light.—One word more; I charge thee
That thou attend me: thou dost here usurp
The name thou owest not; and hast put thyself
Upon this island as a spy, to win it
From me, the lord on't.

FERDINAND.

No, as I am a man.

MIRANDA.

There's nothing ill can dwell in such a temple:
If the ill spirit have so fair a house,
Good things will strive to dwell with't.

PROSPERO.

Follow me.
Speak not you for him; he's a traitor. Come;
I'll manacle thy neck and feet together:
Sea-water shalt thou drink; thy food shall be
The fresh-brook mussels, wither'd roots, and husks
Wherein the acorn cradled. Follow.

FERDINAND.

No;
I will resist such entertainment till
Mine enemy has more power.
[*Draws, and is charm'd from moving.*

MIRANDA.

O dear father,
Make not too rash a trial of him, for
He's gentle, and not fearful.

PROSPERO.

What, I say,
My foot my tutor! Put thy sword up, traitor;
Who makest a show, but darest not strike, thy conscience
Is so possest with guilt: come from thy ward;
For I can here disarm thee with this stick,
And make thy weapon drop.

MIRANDA.

Beseech you, father!—

PROSPERO.

Hence! hang not on my garments.

MIRANDA.

Sir, have pity;
I'll be his surety.

PROSPERO.

Silence! one word more
Shall make me chide thee, if not hate thee. What,
An advocate for an impostor! hush!
Thou think'st there are no more such shapes as he,
Having seen but him and Caliban: foolish wench!
To the most of men this is a Caliban,
And they to him are angels.

MIRANDA.

My affections
Are, then, most humble; I have no ambition
To see a goodlier man.

PROSPERO.

Come on; obey:
Thy nerves are in their infancy again,
And have no vigour in them.

FERDINAND.

So they are:
My spirits, as in a dream, are all bound up.
My father's loss, the weakness which I feel,
The wrack of all my friends, nor this man's threats
To whom I am subdued, are but light to me,
Might I but through my prison once a day
Behold this maid: all corners else o'the earth
Let liberty make use of; space enough
Have I in such a prison.

PROSPERO [*aside*].

It works.—Come on.— [*To* FERDINAND.
Thou hast done well, fine Ariel!—Follow me.—
[*To* FERDINAND.
Hark what thou else shalt do me. [*To* ARIEL.

MIRANDA.

Be of comfort;
My father's of a better nature, sir,
Than he appears by speech: this is unwonted
Which now came from him.

PROSPERO.

Thou shalt be as free
As mountain winds: but then exactly do
All points of my command.

ARIEL.

To the syllable.

PROSPERO.

Come, follow.—Speak not for him. [*Exeunt.*

ACT II. SCENE I.

Another part of the island.

Enter ALONSO, SEBASTIAN, ANTONIO, GONZALO, ADRIAN, FRANCISCO, *and others.*

GONZALO.

BESEECH you, sir, be merry; you have cause,
So have we all, of joy; for our escape
Is much beyond our loss. Our hint of woe
Is common; every day some sailor's wife,
The masters of some merchant, and the merchant,
Have just our theme of woe; but for the miracle,
I mean our preservation, few in millions
Can speak like us: then wisely, good sir, weigh
Our sorrow with our comfort.

ALONSO.

Prithee, peace.

SEBASTIAN.

He receives comfort like cold porridge.

ANTONIO.

The visitor will not give him o'er so.

SEBASTIAN.

Look, he's winding up the watch of his wit; by and by it will strike.

GONZALO.

Sir,—

SEBASTIAN.

One: tell.

GONZALO.

When every grief is entertain'd that's offer'd,
Comes to the entertainer—

SEBASTIAN.

A dollar.

GONZALO.

Dolour comes to him, indeed; you have spoken truer than you purposed.

SEBASTIAN.

You have taken it wiselier than I meant you should.

GONZALO.

Therefore, my lord,—

ANTONIO.

Fie, what a spendthrift is he of his tongue!

ALONSO.

I prithee, spare.

GONZALO.

Well, I have done: but yet,—

SEBASTIAN.

He will be talking.

ANTONIO.

Which, of he or Adrian, for a good wager, first begins to crow?

SEBASTIAN.

The old cock.

ANTONIO.

The cockerel.

SEBASTIAN.

Done! The wager?

ANTONIO.

A laughter.

SEBASTIAN.

A match!

ADRIAN.

Though this island seem to be desert,—

SEBASTIAN.

Ha, ha, ha!

ANTONIO.

So: you've paid.

ADRIAN.

Uninhabitable, and almost inaccessible,—

SEBASTIAN.

Yet,—

ADRIAN.

Yet,—

ANTONIO.

He could not miss't.

ADRIAN.

It must needs be of subtle, tender, and delicate temperance.

ANTONIO.

Temperance was a delicate wench.

SEBASTIAN.

Ay, and a subtle; as he most learnedly deliver'd.

ADRIAN.

The air breathes upon us here most sweetly.

SEBASTIAN.

As if it had lungs, and rotten ones.

ANTONIO.

Or as 'twere perfumed by a fen.

GONZALO.

Here is everything advantageous to life.

ANTONIO.

True; save means to live.

SEBASTIAN.

Of that there's none, or little.

GONZALO.

How lush and lusty the grass looks! how green!

ANTONIO.

The ground, indeed, is tawny.

SEBASTIAN.

With an eye of green in't.

ANTONIO.

He misses not much.

SEBASTIAN.

No; he doth but mistake the truth totally.

GONZALO.

But the rariety of it is,—which is indeed almost beyond credit,—

SEBASTIAN.

As many voucht rarieties are.

GONZALO.
That our garments, being, as they were, drencht in the sea, hold, notwithstanding, their freshness and glosses, being rather new-dyed than stain'd with salt water.

ANTONIO.
If but one of his pockets could speak, would it not say he lies?

SEBASTIAN.
Ay, or very falsely pocket up his report.

GONZALO.
Methinks our garments are now as fresh as when we put them on first in Afric, at the marriage of the king's fair daughter Claribel to the King of Tunis.

SEBASTIAN.
'Twas a sweet marriage, and we prosper well in our return.

ADRIAN.
Tunis was never graced before with such a paragon to their queen.

GONZALO.
Not since widow Dido's time.

ANTONIO.
Widow! a pox o'that! How came that widow in? widow Dido!

SEBASTIAN.
What if he had said 'widower Aeneas' too? Good Lord, how you take it!

ADRIAN.
Widow Dido, said you? you make me study of that: she was of Carthage, not of Tunis.

GONZALO.
This Tunis, sir, was Carthage.

ADRIAN.
Carthage!

GONZALO.
I assure you, Carthage.

ANTONIO.
His word is more than the miraculous harp.

SEBASTIAN.
He hath raised the wall, and houses too.

ANTONIO.
What impossible matter will he make easy next?

SEBASTIAN.
I think he will carry this island home in his pocket, and give it his son for an apple.

ANTONIO.
And, sowing the kernels of it in the sea, bring forth more islands.

GONZALO.
Ay.

ANTONIO.
Why, in good time.

GONZALO.
Sir, we were talking that our garments seem now as fresh as when we were at Tunis at the marriage of your daughter, who is now queen.

ANTONIO.
And the rarest that e'er came there.

SEBASTIAN.
Bate, I beseech you, widow Dido.

ANTONIO.
O, widow Dido: ay, widow Dido.

GONZALO.
Is not, sir, my doublet as fresh as the first day I wore it? I mean, in a sort.

ANTONIO.
That sort was well fish'd for.

GONZALO.
When I wore it at your daughter's marriage?

ALONSO.
You cram these words into mine ears against
The stomach of my sense. Would I had never
Married my daughter there! for, coming thence,
My son is lost; and, in my rate, she too,
Who is so far from Italy removed,
I ne'er again shall see her. O thou mine heir
Of Naples and of Milan, what strange fish
Hath made his meal on thee?

FRANCISCO.
Sir, he may live:
I saw him beat the surges under him,
And ride upon their backs; he trod the water,
Whose enmity he flung aside, and breasted
The surge most swoln that met him; his bold head
'Bove the contentious waves he kept, and oar'd
Himself with his good arms in lusty stroke
To the shore, that o'er his wave-worn basis bow'd,
As stooping to relieve him: I not doubt
He came alive to land.

ALONSO.
No, no, he's gone.

SEBASTIAN.
Sir, you may thank yourself for this great loss,
That would not bless our Europe with your daughter,
But rather lose her to an African;
Where she, at least, is banish'd from your eye,
Who hath cause to wet the grief on't.

ALONSO.
Prithee, peace.

SEBASTIAN.
You were kneel'd to, and importuned otherwise,
By all of us; and the fair soul herself
Weigh'd, between loathness and obedience, at
Which end o'the beam should bow. We have lost your son,
I fear, for ever: Milan and Naples have
Moe widows in them of this business' making
Than we bring men to comfort them:
The fault's your own.

ALONSO.
So is the dear'st o'the loss.

GONZALO.
My lord Sebastian,
The truth you speak doth lack some gentleness,
And time to speak it in: you rub the sore,
When you should bring the plaster.

SEBASTIAN.
Very well

ANTONIO.
And most chirurgeonly.

GONZALO.
It is foul weather in us all, good sir,
When you are cloudy.

SEBASTIAN.
Foul weather!

ANTONIO.
Very foul.

GONZALO.
Had I plantation of this isle, my lord,—

ANTONIO.

He'd sow't with nettle-seed.

SEBASTIAN.

Or docks, or mallows.

GONZALO.

And were the king on't, what would I do?

SEBASTIAN.

Scape being drunk for want of wine.

GONZALO.

I'the commonwealth I would by contraries
Execute all things; for no kind of traffic
Would I admit; no name of magistrate;
Letters should not be known; riches, poverty,
And use of service, none; contract, succession,
Bourn, bound of land, tilth, vineyard, none;
No use of metal, corn, or wine, or oil;
No occupation; all men idle, all;
And women too,—but innocent and pure;
No sovereignty,—

SEBASTIAN.

Yet he would be king on't.

ANTONIO

The latter end of his commonwealth forgets the beginning.

GONZALO.

All things in common nature should produce
Without sweat or endeavour: treason, felony,
Sword, pike, knife, gun, or need of any engine,
Would I not have, but nature should bring forth,
Of it own kind, all foison, all abundance,
To feed my innocent people.

SEBASTIAN.

No marrying 'mong his subjects?

ANTONIO.

None, man; all idle; whores and knaves.

GONZALO.

I would with such perfection govern, sir,
T'excel the golden age.

SEBASTIAN.

'Save his majesty!

ANTONIO.

Long live Gonzalo!

GONZALO.

And,—do you mark me, sir?—

ALONSO.

Prithee, no more: thou dost talk nothing to me.

GONZALO.

I do well believe your highness; and did it to minister occasion to these gentlemen, who are of such sensible and nimble lungs that they always use to laugh at nothing.

ANTONIO

'Twas you we laugh'd at.

GONZALO.

Who in this kind of merry fooling am nothing to you: so you may continue, and laugh at nothing still.

ANTONIO.

What a blow was there given!

SEBASTIAN.

An it had not fallen flat-long.

GONZALO.

You are gentlemen of brave mettle; you would lift the moon out of her sphere, if she would continue in it five weeks without changing.

Enter ARIEL, *invisible, playing solemn music.*

SEBASTIAN.

We would so, and then go a bat-fowling.

ANTONIO.

Nay, good my lord, be not angry.

GONZALO.

No, I warrant you; I will not adventure my discretion so weakly. Will you laugh me asleep, for I am very heavy?

ANTONIO.

Go sleep, and hear us.

[*All sleep except* ALONSO, SEBASTIAN, *and* ANTONIO.

ALONSO.

What, all so soon asleep! I wish mine eyes
Would, with themselves, shut up my thoughts: I find
They are inclined to do so.

SEBASTIAN.

Please you, sir,
Do not omit the heavy offer of it:
It seldom visits sorrow; when it doth,
It is a comforter.

ANTONIO.

We two, my lord,
Will guard your person while you take your rest,
And watch your safety.

ALONSO.

Thank you.—Wondrous heavy.

[ALONSO *sleeps. Exit* ARIEL.

SEBASTIAN.

What a strange drowsiness possesses them!

ANTONIO.

It is the quality o'the climate.

SEBASTIAN.

Why
Doth it not, then, our eyelids sink? I find not
Myself disposed to sleep.

ANTONIO.

Nor I; my spirits are nimble.
They fell together all, as by consent;
They dropt, as by a thunder-stroke. What might,
Worthy Sebastian, O, what might?—No more:—
And yet methinks I see it in thy face,
What thou shouldst be: the occasion speaks thee; and
My strong imagination sees a crown
Dropping upon thy head.

SEBASTIAN.

What, art thou waking?

ANTONIO.

Do you not hear me speak?

SEBASTIAN.

I do; and surely
It is a sleepy language, and thou speak'st
Out of thy sleep. What is it thou didst say?
This is a strange repose, to be asleep
With eyes wide open; standing, speaking, moving,
And yet so fast asleep.

ANTONIO.

Noble Sebastian,
Thou lett'st thy fortune sleep,—die, rather; wink'st
Whiles thou art waking.

SEBASTIAN.

Thou dost snore distinctly;
There's meaning in thy snores.

ANTONIO.
I am more serious than my custom: you
Must be so too, if heed me; which to do
Trebles thee o'er.

SEBASTIAN.
Well, I am standing water.

ANTONIO.
I'll teach you how to flow.

SEBASTIAN.
Do so: to ebb
Hereditary sloth instructs me.

ANTONIO.
O,
If you but knew how you the purpose cherish
Whiles thus you mock it! how, in stripping it,
You more invest it! Ebbing men, indeed,
Most often do so near the bottom run
By their own fear or sloth.

SEBASTIAN.
Prithee, say on:
The setting of thine eye and cheek proclaim
A matter from thee; and a birth, indeed,
Which throes thee much to yield.

ANTONIO.
Thus, sir:
Although this lord of weak remembrance, this,
Who shall be of as little memory
When he is earth'd, hath here almost persuaded,—
For he's a spirit of persuasion, only
Professes to persuade,—the king his son's alive,
'Tis as impossible that he's undrown'd
As he that sleeps here swims.

SEBASTIAN.
I have no hope
That he's undrown'd.

ANTONIO.
O, out of that 'no hope'
What great hope have you! no hope, that way, is
Another way so high a hope that even
Ambition cannot pierce a wink beyond,
But doubts discovery there. Will you grant with me
That Ferdinand is drown'd?

SEBASTIAN.
He's gone.

ANTONIO.
Then, tell me,
Who's the next heir of Naples?

SEBASTIAN.
Claribel.

ANTONIO.
She that is queen of Tunis; she that dwells
Ten leagues beyond man's life; she that from Naples
Can have no note, unless the sun were post,—
The man-i'the-moon's too slow,—till new-born chins
Be rough and razorable; she that—from whom
We all were sea-swallow'd, though some cast again;
And, by that destiny, to perform an act
Whereof what's past is prologue; what to come,
In yours and my discharge.

SEBASTIAN.
What stuff is this!—How say you?
'Tis true, my brother's daughter's queen of Tunis;
So is she heir of Naples; 'twixt which regions
There is some space.

ANTONIO.
A space whose every cubit
Seems to cry out, 'How shall that Claribel
Measure us back to Naples? Keep in Tunis,
And let Sebastian wake!'—Say, this were death
That now hath seized them; why, they were no worse
Than now they are. There be that can rule Naples
As well as he that sleeps; lords that can prate
As amply and unnecessarily
As this Gonzalo; I myself could make
A chough of as deep chat. O, that you bore
The mind that I do! what a sleep were this
For your advancement! Do you understand me?

SEBASTIAN.
Methinks I do.

ANTONIO.
And how does your content
Tender your own good fortune?

SEBASTIAN.
I remember
You did supplant your brother Prospero.

ANTONIO.
True:
And look how well my garments sit upon me;
Much feater than before: my brother's servants
Were then my fellows; now they are my men.

SEBASTIAN.
But, for your conscience,—

ANTONIO.
Ay, sir; where lies that? if 'twere a kibe,
'Twould put me to my slipper: but I feel not
This deity in my bosom: twenty consciences,
That stand 'twixt me and Milan, candied be they,
And melt, ere they molest! Here lies your brother,
No better than the earth he lies upon,
If he were that which now he's like, that's dead;
Whom I, with this obedient steel, three inches of it,
Can lay to bed for ever; whiles you, doing thus,
To the perpetual wink for aye might put
This ancient morsel, this Sir Prudence, who
Should not upbraid our course. For all the rest,
They'll take suggestion as a cat laps milk;
They'll tell the clock to any business that
We say befits the hour.

SEBASTIAN.
Thy case, dear friend,
Shall be my precedent; as thou gott'st Milan,
I'll come by Naples. Draw thy sword: one stroke
Shall free thee from the tribute which thou pay'st
And I the king shall love thee.

ANTONIO.
Draw together;
And when I rear my hand, do you the like,
To fall it on Gonzalo.

SEBASTIAN.
O, but one word.

Enter ARIEL, *invisible, with music and song.*

ARIEL.
My master through his art foresees the danger
That you, his friend, are in; and sends me forth,—
For else his project dies,—to keep them living.
[*Sings in* GONZALO'S *ear.*

While you here do snoring lie,
Open-eyed conspiracy
His time doth take.
If of life you keep a care,
Shake off slumber, and beware:
Awake, awake!

ANTONIO.

Then let us both be sudden.

GONZALO [*waking*].

Now, good angels
Preserve the king! Why, how now? ho, awake!
Why are you drawn? wherefore this ghastly looking?

ALONSO [*waking*].

What's the matter?

SEBASTIAN.

Whiles we stood here securing your repose,
Even now, we heard a hollow burst of bellowing
Like bulls, or rather lions: did't not wake you?
It struck mine ear most terribly.

ALONSO.

I heard nothing.

ANTONIO.

O, 'twas a din to fright a monster's ear,
To make an earthquake! sure, it was the roar
Of a whole herd of lions.

ALONSO.

Heard you this, Gonzalo?

GONZALO.

Upon mine honour, sir, I heard a humming,
And that a strange one too, which did awake me:
I shaked you, sir, and cried: as mine eyes open'd,
I saw their weapons drawn:—there was a noise,
That's verily. 'Tis best we stand upon our guard,
Or that we quit this place: let's draw our weapons.

ALONSO.

Lead off this ground; and let's make further search
For my poor son.

GONZALO.

Heavens keep him from these beasts!
For he is, sure, i'the island.

ALONSO.

Lead away.

ARIEL.

Prospero my lord shall know what I have done:—
So, king, go safely on to seek thy son. [*Exeunt.*

SCENE II.

Another part of the island.

Enter CALIBAN *with a burden of wood. A noise of thunder heard.*

CALIBAN.

ALL the infections that the sun sucks up
From bogs, fens, flats, on Prosper fall, and make him
By inch-meal a disease! His spirits hear me,
And yet I needs must curse. But they'll nor pinch,
Fright me with urchin-shows, pitch me i'the mire,
Nor lead me, like a firebrand, in the dark
Out of my way, unless he bid 'em: but
For every trifle are they set upon me;
Sometime like apes, that mow and chatter at me,
And after bite me; then like hedgehogs, which
Lie tumbling in my barefoot way, and mount
Their pricks at my footfall; sometime am I
All wound with adders, who with cloven tongues
Do hiss me into madness. Lo, now, lo!
Here comes a spirit of his; and to torment me
For bringing wood in slowly. I'll fall flat;
Perchance he will not mind me.

Enter TRINCULO.

TRINCULO.

Here's neither bush nor shrub, to bear off any weather at all, and another storm brewing; I hear it sing i' the wind: yond same black cloud, yond huge one, looks like a foul bombard that would shed his liquor. If it should thunder as it did before, I know not where to hide my head: yond same cloud cannot choose but fall by pailfuls.—What have we here? a man or a fish? dead or alive? A fish: he smells like a fish; a very ancient and fish-like smell; a kind of, not of the newest, Poor-John. A strange fish! Were I in England now, as once I was, and had but this fish painted, not a holiday fool there but would give a piece of silver: there would this monster make a man; any strange beast there makes a man: when they will not give a doit to relieve a lame beggar, they will lay out ten to see a dead Indian. Legg'd like a man! and his fins like arms! Warm, o' my troth! I do now let loose my opinion, hold it no longer,—this is no fish, but an islander, that hath lately suffer'd by a thunderbolt. [*Thunder.*] Alas, the storm is come again! my best way is to creep under his gaberdine; there is no other shelter hereabout: misery acquaints a man with strange bedfellows. I will here shroud till the dregs of the storm be past.

[*Creeps under* CALIBAN'S *gaberdine.*

Enter STEPHANO, *singing; a bottle in his hand.*

STEPHANO.

I shall no more to sea, to sea,
Here shall I die ashore,—

This is a very scurvy tune to sing at a man's funeral: well, here's my comfort. [*Drinks.*

The master, the swabber, the boatswain, and I,
The gunner, and his mate,
Loved Mall, Meg, and Marian, and Margery,
But none of us cared for Kate;
For she had a tongue with a tang,
Would cry to a sailor, Go hang!
She loved not the savour of tar nor of pitch;
Yet a tailor might scratch her where'er she did itch.
Then, to sea, boys, and let her go hang!

This is a scurvy tune too: but here's my comfort. [*Drinks.*

CALIBAN.

Do not torment me:—O!

STEPHANO.

What's the matter? Have we devils here? Do you put tricks upon's with salvages and men of Inde? ha! I have not scaped drowning, to be afeard now of your four legs; for it hath been said, As proper a man as ever went on four legs cannot make him give ground; and it shall be said so again, while Stephano breathes at nostrils.

CALIBAN.

The spirit torments me:—O!

STEPHANO.

This is some monster of the isle with four legs, who hath got, as I take it, an ague. Where the devil should he learn our language? I will give him some relief, if it be but for that. If I can recover him, and keep him tame, and get to Naples with him, he's a present for any emperor that ever trod on neat's-leather.

CALIBAN.

Do not torment me, prithee; I'll bring my wood home faster.

STEPHANO.

He's in his fit now, and does not talk after the wisest. He shall taste of my bottle: if he have never drunk wine afore, it will go near to remove his fit. If I can recover him, and keep him tame, I will not take too much for him; he shall pay for him that hath him, and that soundly.

CALIBAN.

Thou dost me yet but little hurt; thou wilt anon, I know it by thy trembling: now Prosper works upon thee.

STEPHANO.

Come on your ways; open your mouth; here is that which will give language to you, cat: open your mouth; this will shake your shaking, I can tell you, and that soundly: you cannot tell who's your friend: open your chaps again.

TRINCULO.

I should know that voice: it should be—but he is drown'd; and these are devils:—O, defend me!

STEPHANO.

Four legs and two voices,—a most delicate monster! His forward voice, now, is to speak well of his friend; his backward voice is to utter foul speeches and to detract. If all the wine in my bottle will recover him, I will help his ague. —Come,—Amen! I will pour some in thy other mouth.

TRINCULO.

Stephano!—

STEPHANO.

Doth thy other mouth call me?—Mercy, mercy! This is a devil, and no monster: I will leave him; I have no long spoon.

TRINCULO.

Stephano!—if thou be'st Stephano, touch me, and speak to me; for I am Trinculo,—be not afeard,—thy good friend, Trinculo.

STEPHANO.

If thou be'st Trinculo, come forth: I'll pull thee by the lesser legs: if any be Trinculo's legs, these are they. [*Draws* TRINCULO *out by the legs.*]—Thou art very Trinculo indeed! How camest thou to be the siege of this moon-calf? can he vent Trinculos?

TRINCULO.

I took him to be kill'd with a thunder-stroke.—But art thou not drown'd, Stephano? I hope, now, thou art not drown'd. Is the storm overblown? I hid me under the dead moon-calf's gaberdine for fear of the storm. And art thou living, Stephano? O Stephano, two Neapolitans scaped!

STEPHANO.

Prithee, do not turn me about; my stomach is not constant.

CALIBAN [*aside*].

These be fine things, an if they be not sprites.
That's a brave god, and bears celestial liquor:
I will kneel to him.

STEPHANO.

How didst thou scape? How camest thou hither? swear, by this bottle, how thou camest hither. I escaped upon a butt of sack, which the sailors heaved o'erboard, by this bottle! which I made of the bark of a tree with mine own hands, since I was cast ashore.

CALIBAN.

I'll swear, upon that bottle, to be thy true subject; for the liquor is not earthly.

STEPHANO.

Here; swear, then, how thou escapedst.

TRINCULO.

Swum ashore, man, like a duck: I can swim like a duck, I'll be sworn.

STEPHANO.

Here, kiss the book. Though thou canst swim like a duck, thou art made like a goose.

TRINCULO.

O Stephano, hast any more of this?

STEPHANO.

The whole butt, man: my cellar is in a rock by the sea-side, where my wine is hid.—How now, moon-calf! how does thine ague?

CALIBAN.

Hast thou not dropt from heaven?

STEPHANO.

Out o'the moon, I do assure thee: I was the man-i'-the-moon when time was.

CALIBAN.

I have seen thee in her, and I do adore thee: my mistress show'd me thee, and thy dog, and thy bush.

STEPHANO.

Come, swear to that; kiss the book:—I will furnish it anon with new contents:—swear.

TRINCULO.

By this good light, this is a very shallow monster!—I afeard of him!—a very weak monster:—the man-i'the-moon!—a most poor credulous monster!—Well drawn, monster, in good sooth.

CALIBAN.

I'll show thee every fertile inch o'the island; and I will kiss thy foot: I prithee, be my god.

TRINCULO.

By this light, a most perfidious and drunken monster! when's god's asleep, he'll rob his bottle.

CALIBAN.

I'll kiss thy foot; I'll swear myself thy subject.

STEPHANO.

Come on, then; down, and swear.

TRINCULO.

I shall laugh myself to death at this puppy-headed monster: a most scurvy monster! I could find in my heart to beat him,—

STEPHANO.

Come, kiss.

TRINCULO.

But that the poor monster's in drink: an abominable monster!

CALIBAN.

I'll show thee the best springs; I'll pluck thee berries;
I'll fish for thee, and get thee wood enough.
A plague upon the tyrant that I serve!
I'll bear him no more sticks, but follow thee,
Thou wondrous man.

TRINCULO.

A most ridiculous monster, to make a wonder of a poor drunkard!

CALIBAN.

I prithee, let me bring thee where crabs grow;
And I with my long nails will dig thee pig-nuts;
Show thee a jay's nest, and instruct thee how
To snare the nimble marmoset; I'll bring thee
To clustering filberts, and sometimes I'll get thee
Young scamels from the rock. Wilt thou go with me?

STEPHANO.

I prithee now, lead the way, without any more talking.—Trinculo, the king and all our company else being drown'd, we will inherit here. Here, bear my bottle: fellow Trinculo, we'll fill him by and by again.

CALIBAN [*sings drunkenly*].

Farewell, master; farewell, farewell!

TRINCULO.

A howling monster; a drunken monster!

CALIBAN.

No more dams I'll make for fish;
Nor fetch in firing
At requiring;
Nor scrape trenchering, nor wash dish:
'Ban, 'Ban, Ca-Caliban
Has a new master: get a new man.

Freedom, high-day! high-day, freedom! freedom, high-day, freedom!

STEPHANO.

O brave monster! lead the way. [*Exeunt.*

ACT III. SCENE I.

Before PROSPERO'S *cell.*

Enter FERDINAND, *bearing a log.*

FERDINAND.

THERE be some sports are painful, and their labour
Delight in them sets off: some kinds of baseness
Are nobly undergone; and most poor matters
Point to rich ends. This my mean task
Would be as heavy to me as odious, but
The mistress which I serve quickens what's dead,
And makes my labours pleasures: O, she is
Ten times more gentle than her father's crabb'd;
And he's composed of harshness. I must remove
Some thousands of these logs, and pile them up,
Upon a sore injunction: my sweet mistress
Weeps when she sees me work; and says such baseness
Had never like executor. I forget:
But these sweet thoughts do even refresh my labour;
Most busiless when I do it.

Enter MIRANDA; *and* PROSPERO *behind.*

MIRANDA.

Alas, now, pray you,
Work not so hard: I would the lightning had
Burnt up those logs that you are enjoin'd to pile!
Pray, set it down, and rest you: when this burns,
'Twill weep for having wearied you. My father
Is hard at study; pray, now, rest yourself:
He's safe for these three hours.

FERDINAND.

O most dear mistress,
The sun will set before I shall discharge
What I must strive to do.

MIRANDA.

If you'll sit down,
I'll bear your logs the while: pray, give me that;
I'll carry it to the pile.

FERDINAND.

No, precious creature;
I had rather crack my sinews, break my back,
Than you should such dishonour undergo,
While I sit lazy by.

MIRANDA.

It would become me
As well as it does you: and I should do it
With much more ease; for my good will is to it,
And yours it is against.

PROSPERO [*aside*].

Poor worm, thou art infected!
This visitation shows it.

MIRANDA.

You look wearily.

FERDINAND.

No, noble mistress; 'tis fresh morning with me
When you are by at night. I do beseech you,—
Chiefly that I might set it in my prayers,—
What is your name?

MIRANDA.

Miranda:—O my father,
I've broke your hest to say so!

FERDINAND.

Admired Miranda!
Indeed the top of admiration; worth
What's dearest to the world! Full many a lady
I have eyed with best regard; and many a time
The harmony of their tongues hath into bondage
Brought my too diligent ear: for several virtues
Have I liked several women; never any
With so full soul, but some defect in her
Did quarrel with the noblest grace she owed,
And put it to the foil: but you, O you,
So perfect and so peerless, are created
Of every creature's best!

MIRANDA.

I do not know
One of my sex; no woman's face remember,
Save, from my glass, mine own; nor have I seen
More that I may call men, than you, good friend,
And my dear father: how features are abroad,
I'm skilless of; but, by my modesty,—
The jewel in my dower,—I would not wish
Any companion in the world but you;

Nor can imagination form a shape,
Besides yourself, to like of. But I prattle
Something too wildly, and my father's precepts
I therein do forget.

FERDINAND.

I am, in my condition,
A prince, Miranda; I do think, a king,—
I would not so!—and would no more endure
This wooden slavery than to suffer
The flesh-fly blow my mouth. Hear my soul speak:
The very instant that I saw you, did
My heart fly to your service; there resides
To make me slave to it; and for your sake
Am I this patient log-man.

MIRANDA.

Do you love me?

FERDINAND.

O heaven, O earth, bear witness to this sound,
And crown what I profess with kind event,
If I speak true! if hollowly, invert
What best is boded me to mischief! I,
Beyond all limit of what else i'the world,
Do love, prize, honour you.

MIRANDA.

I am a fool
To weep at what I am glad of.

PROSPERO [*aside*].

Fair encounter
Of two most rare affections! Heavens rain grace
On that which breeds between 'em!

FERDINAND.

Wherefore weep you?

MIRANDA.

At mine unworthiness, that dare not offer
What I desire to give; and much less take
What I shall die to want. But this is trifling;
And all the more it seeks to hide itself,
The bigger bulk it shows. Hence, bashful cunning!
And prompt me, plain and holy innocence!
I am your wife, if you will marry me;
If not, I'll die your maid: to be your fellow
You may deny me; but I'll be your servant,
Whether you will or no.

FERDINAND.

My mistress, dearest;
And I thus humble ever.

MIRANDA.

My husband, then?

FERDINAND.

Ay, with a heart as willing
As bondage e'er of freedom: here's my hand.

MIRANDA.

And mine, with my heart in't: and now farewell
Till half an hour hence.

FERDINAND.

A thousand thousand!

[*Exeunt* FERDINAND *and* MIRANDA *severally*.

PROSPERO.

So glad of this as they I cannot be,
Who are surprised withal; but my rejoicing
At nothing can be more. I'll to my book;
For yet, ere supper-time, must I perform
Much business appertaining. [*Exit.*

SCENE II.

Another part of the island.

Enter CALIBAN, STEPHANO, *and* TRINCULO.

STEPHANO.

TELL not me; when the butt is out, we will drink water; not a drop before: therefore bear up, and board 'em. Servant-monster, drink to me.

TRINCULO.

Servant-monster! the folly of this island! They say there's but five upon this isle: we are three of them; if the other two be brain'd like us, the state totters.

STEPHANO.

Drink, servant-monster, when I bid thee: thy eyes are almost set in thy head.

TRINCULO.

Where should they be set else? he were a brave monster indeed, if they were set in his tail.

STEPHANO.

My man-monster hath drown'd his tongue in sack: for my part, the sea cannot drown me; I swam, ere I could recover the shore, five-and-thirty leagues off and on, by this light.—Thou shalt be my lieutenant, monster, or my standard.

TRINCULO.

Your lieutenant, if you list; he's no standard.

STEPHANO.

We'll not run, Monsieur Monster.

TRINCULO.

Nor go neither: but you'll lie, like dogs; and yet say nothing neither.

STEPHANO.

Moon-calf, speak once in thy life, if thou be'st a good moon-calf.

CALIBAN.

How does thy honour? Let me lick thy shoe. I'll not serve him, he is not valiant.

TRINCULO.

Thou liest, most ignorant monster: I am in case to justle a constable. Why, thou debosh'd fish, thou, was there ever man a coward that hath drunk so much sack as I to-day? Wilt thou tell a monstrous lie, being but half a fish and half a monster?

CALIBAN.

Lo, how he mocks me! wilt thou let him, my lord?

TRINCULO.

'Lord,' quoth he!—that a monster should be such a natural!

CALIBAN.

Lo, lo, again! bite him to death, I prithee.

STEPHANO.

Trinculo, keep a good tongue in your head: if you prove a mutineer, the next tree! The poor monster's my subject, and he shall not suffer indignity.

CALIBAN.

I thank my noble lord. Wilt thou be pleased to hearken once again to the suit I made to thee?

STEPHANO.

Marry, will I: kneel and repeat it; I will stand, and so shall Trinculo.

Enter ARIEL [*invisible*].

CALIBAN.

As I told thee before, I am subject to a tyrant,—a sorcerer, that by his cunning hath cheated me of the island.

ARIEL.

Thou liest.

CALIBAN.

Thou liest, thou jesting monkey, thou:
I would my valiant master would destroy thee!
I do not lie.

STEPHANO.

Trinculo, if you trouble him any more in's tale, by this hand, I will supplant some of your teeth.

TRINCULO.

Why, I said nothing.

STEPHANO.

Mum, then, and no more.—Proceed.

CALIBAN.

I say, by sorcery, he got this isle;
From me he got it. If thy greatness will,
Revenge it on him, for I know thou darest,
But this thing dare not,—

STEPHANO.

That's most certain.

CALIBAN.

Thou shalt be lord of it, and I'll serve thee.

STEPHANO.

How now shall this be compast? Canst thou bring me to the party?

CALIBAN.

Yea, yea, my lord: I'll yield him thee asleep,
Where thou mayst knock a nail into his head.

ARIEL.

Thou liest; thou canst not.

CALIBAN.

What a pied ninny's this! Thou scurvy patch!
I do beseech thy greatness, give him blows,
And take his bottle from him: when that's gone,
He shall drink naught but brine; for I'll not show him
Where the quick freshes are.

STEPHANO.

Trinculo, run into no further danger: interrupt the monster one word further, and, by this hand I'll turn my mercy out o'doors, and make a stock-fish of thee.

TRINCULO.

Why, what did I? I did nothing. I'll go further off.

STEPHANO.

Didst thou not say he lied?

ARIEL.

Thou liest.

STEPHANO.

Do I so? take thou that [*Strikes* TRINCULO]. As you like this, give me the lie another time.

TRINCULO.

I did not give the lie.—Out o'your wits, and hearing too?—A pox o' your bottle! this can sack and drinking do—A murrain on your monster, and the devil take your fingers!

CALIBAN.

Ha, ha, ha!

STEPHANO.

Now, forward with your tale.—Prithee, stand further off.

CALIBAN.

Beat him enough: after a little time,
I'll beat him too.

STEPHANO.

Stand further.—Come, proceed.

CALIBAN.

Why, as I told thee, 'tis a custom with him
I'the afternoon to sleep: then thou mayst brain him,
Having first seized his books; or with a log
Batter his skull, or paunch him with a stake,
Or cut his wesand with thy knife: remember,
First to possess his books; for without them
He's but a sot, as I am, nor hath not
One spirit to command: they all do hate him
As rootedly as I:—burn but his books.
He has brave utensils,—for so he calls them,—
Which, when he has a house, he'll deck withal:
And that most deeply to consider is
The beauty of his daughter; he himself
Calls her a nonpareil: I never saw a woman,
But only Sycorax my dam and she;
But she as far surpasseth Sycorax
As great'st does least.

STEPHANO.

Is it so brave a lass?

CALIBAN.

Ay, lord; she will become thy bed, I warrant,
And bring thee forth brave brood.

STEPHANO.

Monster, I will kill this man: his daughter and I will be king and queen,—save our graces!—and Trinculo and thyself shall be viceroys.—Dost thou like the plot, Trinculo?

TRINCULO.

Excellent.

STEPHANO.

Give me thy hand: I am sorry I beat thee, but, while thou livest, keep a good tongue in thy head.

CALIBAN.

Within this half hour will he be asleep:
Wilt thou destroy him then?

STEPHANO.

Ay, on mine honour.

ARIEL.

This will I tell my master.

CALIBAN.

Thou makest me merry; I am full of pleasure:
Let us be jocund: will you troll the catch
You taught me but while-ere?

STEPHANO.

At thy request, monster, I will do reason, any reason.—Come on, Trinculo, let us sing. [*Sings.*

'Flout 'em and scout 'em, and scout 'em
and flout 'em;
Thought is free.'

CALIBAN.

That's not the tune.

[ARIEL *plays a tune on a tabor and pipe.*

STEPHANO.

What is this same?

TRINCULO.

This is the tune of our catch, played by the picture of Nobody.

STEPHANO.

If thou be'st a man, show thyself in thy likeness: if thou be'st a devil, take't as thou list.

TRINCULO.
O, forgive me my sins!

STEPHANO.
He that dies pays all debts: I defy thee.—Mercy upon us!

CALIBAN.
Art thou afeard?

STEPHANO.
No, monster, not I.

CALIBAN.
Be not afeard; the isle is full of noises,
Sounds, and sweet airs, that give delight, and hurt not.
Sometimes a thousand twangling instruments
Will hum about mine ears; and sometime voices,
That, if I then had waked after long sleep,
Will make me sleep again: and then, in dreaming,
The clouds methought would open, and show riches
Ready to drop upon me; that, when I waked,
I cried to dream again.

STEPHANO.
This will prove a brave kingdom to me, where I shall have my music for nothing.

CALIBAN.
When Prospero is destroy'd.

STEPHANO.
That shall be by and by: I remember the story.

TRINCULO.
The sound is going away; let's follow it, and after do our work.

STEPHANO.
Lead, monster; we'll follow.—I would I could see this taborer! he lays it on.

TRINCULO.
Wilt come? I'll follow, Stephano. [*Exeunt.*

SCENE III.

Another part of the island.

Enter ALONSO, SEBASTIAN, ANTONIO, GONZALO, ADRIAN, FRANCISCO, *and others.*

GONZALO.
BY'R lakin, I can go no further, sir;
My old bones ache! here's a maze trod, indeed,
Through forth-rights and meanders! by your patience,
I needs must rest me.

ALONSO.
Old lord, I cannot blame thee,
Who am myself attach'd with weariness,
To the dulling of my spirits: sit down, and rest.
Even here I will put off my hope, and keep it
No longer for my flatterer: he is drown'd
Whom thus we stray to find; and the sea mocks
Our frustrate search on land. Well, let him go.

ANTONIO [*aside to* SEBASTIAN].
I am right glad that he's so out of hope.
Do not, for one repulse, forgo the purpose
That you resolved t'effect.

SEBASTIAN [*aside to* ANTONIO].
The next advantage
Will we take throughly.

ANTONIO [*aside to* SEBASTIAN].
Let it be to-night;
For, now they are oppress'd with travel, they
Will not, nor cannot, use such vigilance
As when they are fresh.

SEBASTIAN [*aside to* ANTONIO].
I say, to-night: no more.
[*Solemn and strange music.*

ALONSO.
What harmony is this?—My good friends, hark!

GONZALO.
Marvellous sweet music!

Enter PROSPERO, *above, invisible. Enter, below, several strange Shapes, bringing in a banquet: they dance about it with gentle actions of salutation; and, inviting the King, &c., to eat, they depart.*

ALONSO.
Give us kind keepers, heavens!—What were these?

SEBASTIAN.
A living drollery. Now I will believe
That there are unicorns; that in Arabia
There is one tree, the phœnix' throne; one phœnix
At this hour reigning there.

ANTONIO.
I'll believe both;
And what does else want credit, come to me,
And I'll be sworn 'tis true: travellers ne'er did lie,
Though fools at home condemn 'em.

GONZALO.
If in Naples
I should report this now, would they believe me?
If I should say, I saw such islanders,—
For, certes, these are people of the island,—
Who, though they are of monstrous shape, yet, note,
Their manners are more gentle-kind than of
Our human generation you shall find
Many, nay, almost any.

PROSPERO [*aside*].
Honest lord,
Thou hast said well; for some of you there present
Are worse than devils.

ALONSO.
I cannot too much muse
Such shapes, such gesture, and such sound, expressing—
Although they want the use of tongue—a kind
Of excellent dumb discourse.

PROSPERO [*aside*].
Praise in departing.

FRANCISCO.
They vanish'd strangely.

SEBASTIAN.
No matter, since
They have left their viands behind; for we have stomachs.—
Will't please you taste of what is here?

ALONSO.
Not I.

GONZALO.
Faith, sir, you need not fear. When we were boys,
Who would believe that there were mountaineers
Dew-lapp'd like bulls, whose throats had hanging at 'em
Wallets of flesh? or that there were such men

Whose heads stood in their breasts? which now
  we find
Each putter-out of five for one will bring us
Good warrant of.

ALONSO.

I will stand to, and feed,
Although my last: no matter, since I feel
The best is past.—Brother, my lord the duke,
Stand to, and do as we.

Thunder and lightning. Enter ARIEL, *like a harpy; claps his wings upon the table; and, with a quaint device, the banquet vanishes.*

ARIEL.

You are three men of sin, whom Destiny,—
That hath to instrument this lower world
And what is in't,—the never-surfeited sea
Hath caused to belch up you; and on this island,
Where man doth not inhabit,—you 'mongst men
Being most unfit to live. I have made you mad;
And even with such-like valour men hang and
  drown
Their proper selves. [*They draw their swords.*
You fools! I and my fellows
Are ministers of Fate: the elements,
Of whom your swords are temper'd, may as well
Wound the loud winds, or with bemock'd-at stabs
Kill the still-closing waters, as diminish
One dowle that's in my plume: my fellow-ministers
Are like invulnerable. If you could hurt,
Your swords are now too massy for your strengths,
And will not be uplifted. But remember,—
For that's my business to you,—that you three
From Milan did supplant good Prospero;
Exposed unto the sea, which hath requit it,
Him and his innocent child: for which foul deed
The powers, delaying, not forgetting, have
Incensed the seas and shores, yea, all the creatures,
Against your peace. Thee of thy son, Alonso,
They have bereft; and do pronounce, by me,
Lingering perdition—worse than any death
Can be at once—shall step by step attend
You and your ways; whose wraths to guard you
  from,—
Which here, in this most desolate isle, else falls
Upon your heads,—is nothing but heart's sorrow
And a clear life ensuing.

He vanishes in thunder; then, to soft music, enter the Shapes again, and dance, with mocks and mows, and carrying out the table.

PROSPERO [*aside*].

Bravely the figure of this harpy hast thou
Perform'd, my Ariel; a grace it had, devouring:
Of my instruction hast thou nothing bated
In what thou hadst to say: so, with good life
And observation strange, my meaner ministers
Their several kinds have done. My high charms
  work,
And these, mine enemies, are all knit up
In their distractions: they now are in my power;
And in these fits I leave them, while I visit
Young Ferdinand,—whom they suppose is
  drown'd,—
And his and mine loved darling. [*Exit above.*

GONZALO.

I'the name of something holy, sir, why stand you
In this strange stare?

ALONSO.

O, it is monstrous, monstrous!
Methought the billows spoke, and told me of it;
The winds did sing it to me; and the thunder,
That deep and dreadful organ-pipe, pronounced
The name of Prosper: it did bass my trespass.
Therefore my son i'the ooze is bedded; and
I'll seek him deeper than e'er plummet sounded,
And with him there lie mudded. [*Exit.*

SEBASTIAN.

But one fiend at a time,
I'll fight their legions o'er.

ANTONIO.

I'll be thy second.
[*Exeunt* SEBASTIAN *and* ANTONIO.

GONZALO.

All three of them are desperate: their great guilt,
Like poison given to work a great time after,
Now 'gins to bite the spirits.—I do beseech you,
That are of suppler joints, follow them swiftly,
And hinder them from what this ecstasy
May now provoke them to.

ADRIAN.

Follow, I pray you. [*Exeunt.*

ACT IV. SCENE I.

Before PROSPERO'S *cell.*

Enter PROSPERO, FERDINAND, *and* MIRANDA.

PROSPERO.

If I have too austerely punish'd you,
Your compensation makes amends; for I
Have given you here a thread of mine own life,
Or that for which I live: who once again
I tender to thy hand: all thy vexations
Were but my trials of thy love, and thou
Hast strangely stood the test: here, afore Heaven,
I ratify this my rich gift. O Ferdinand,
Do not smile at me that I boast her off,
For thou shalt find she will outstrip all praise,
And make it halt behind her.

FERDINAND.

I do believe it
Against an oracle.

PROSPERO.

Then, as my gift, and thine own acquisition
Worthily purchased, take my daughter: but
If thou dost break her virgin-knot before
All sanctimonious ceremonies may
With full and holy rite be minister'd,
No sweet aspersion shall the heavens let fall
To make this contract grow; but barren hate,
Sour-eyed disdain, and discord, shall bestrew
The union of your bed with weeds so loathly
That you shall hate it both: therefore take heed,
As Hymen's lamps shall light you.

FERDINAND.

As I hope
For quiet days, fair issue, and long life,
With such love as 'tis now,—the murkiest den,
The most opportune place, the strong'st sugges-
  tion
Our worser Genius can, shall never melt
Mine honour into lust; to take away
The edge of that day's celebration,

When I shall think, or Phœbus' steeds are founder'd,
Or Night kept chain'd below.

PROSPERO.

Fairly spoke.
Sit, then, and talk with her; she is thine own.—
What, Ariel! my industrious servant, Ariel!

Enter ARIEL.

ARIEL.

What would my potent master? here I am.

PROSPERO.

Thou and thy meaner fellows your last service
Did worthily perform; and I must use you
In such another trick. Go bring the rabble,
O'er whom I give thee power, here, to this place:
Incite them to quick motion; for I must
Bestow upon the eyes of this young couple
Some vanity of mine art: it is my promise,
And they expect it from me.

ARIEL.

Presently?

PROSPERO.

Ay, with a twink.

ARIEL.

Before you can say, 'Come,' and 'Go,'
And breathe twice, and cry, 'So, so,'
Each one, tripping on his toe,
Will be here with mop and mow.
Do you love me, master? no?

PROSPERO.

Dearly, my delicate Ariel. Do not approach
Till thou dost hear me call

ARIEL.

Well, I conceive. [*Exit.*

PROSPERO.

Look thou be true; do not give dalliance
Too much the rein; the strongest oaths are straw
To the fire i'the blood: be more abstemious,
Or else good night your vow!

FERDINAND.

I warrant you, sir;
The white-cold virgin snow upon my heart
Abates the ardour of my liver.

PROSPERO.

Well.—
Now come, my Ariel! bring a corollary,
Rather than want a spirit: appear, and pertly!
No tongue; all eyes; be silent. [*Soft music.*

Enter IRIS.

IRIS.

Ceres, most bounteous lady, thy rich leas
Of wheat, rye, barley, vetches, oats, and pease;
Thy turfy mountains, where live nibbling sheep,
And flat meads thatch'd with stover, them to keep;
Thy banks with pioned and twilled brims,
Which spongy April at thy hest betrims,
To make cold nymphs chaste crowns; and thy broom-groves,
Whose shadow the dismissed bachelor loves,
Being lass-lorn; thy pole-clipt vineyard;
And thy sea-marge, sterile and rocky-hard,
Where thou thyself dost air;—the queen o' the sky,
Whose watery arch and messenger am I,
Bids thee leave these; and with her sovereign grace,
Here on this grass-plot, in this very place,
To come and sport:—her peacocks fly amain:
Approach, rich Ceres, her to entertain.

Enter CERES.

CERES.

Hail, many-colour'd messenger, that ne'er
Dost disobey the wife of Jupiter;
Who, with thy saffron wings, upon my flowers
Diffusest honey-drops, refreshing showers;
And with each end of thy blue bow dost crown
My bosky acres and my unshrubb'd down,
Rich scarf to my proud earth;—why hath thy queen
Summon'd me hither, to this short-grass'd green?

IRIS.

A contract of true love to celebrate;
And some donation freely to estate
On the bless'd lovers.

CERES.

Tell me, heavenly bow,
If Venus or her son, as thou dost know,
Do now attend the queen? Since they did plot
The means that dusky Dis my daughter got,
Her and her blind boy's scandall'd company
I have forsworn.

IRIS.

Of her society
Be not afraid: I met her deity
Cutting the clouds towards Paphos, and her son
Dove-drawn with her. Here thought they to have done
Some wanton charm upon this man and maid,
Whose vows are, that no bed-rite shall be paid
Till Hymen's torch be lighted: but in vain;
Mars's hot minion is return'd again;
Her waspish-headed son has broke his arrows,
Swears he will shoot no more, but play with sparrows,
And be a boy right out.

CERES.

Highest queen of state,
Great Juno, comes; I know her by her gait.

Enter JUNO.

JUNO.

How does my bounteous sister? Go with me
To bless this twain, that they may prosperous be,
And honour'd in their issue.

Song.

JUNO.

Honour, riches, marriage-blessing,
Long continuance, and increasing,
Hourly joys be still upon you!
Juno sings her blessings on you.

CERES.

Earth's increase, foison plenty,
Barns and garners never empty;
Vines with clustering bunches growing;
Plants with goodly burden bowing,
Spring come to you at the farthest
In the very end of harvest!
Scarcity and want shall shun you;
Ceres' blessing so is on you.

FERDINAND.

This is a most majestic vision, and
Harmonious charmingly. May I be bold
To think these spirits?

PROSPERO.

Spirits, which by mine art
I have from their confines call'd to enact
My present fancies.

FERDINAND.

Let me live here ever;
So rare a wonder'd father, and a wife,
Makes this place Paradise.

[*JUNO and CERES whisper, and send IRIS on employment.*

PROSPERO.

Sweet, now, silence!
Juno and Ceres whisper seriously;
There's something else to do; hush, and be mute,
Or else our spell is marr'd.

IRIS.

You nymphs, call'd Naiades, of the windring brooks,
With your sedged crowns and ever-harmless looks,
Leave your crisp channels, and on this green land
Answer your summons; Juno does command:
Come, temperate nymphs, and help to celebrate
A contract of true love; be not too late.

Enter certain NYMPHS.

You sunburn'd sicklemen, of August weary,
Come hither from the furrow, and be merry:
Make holiday; your rye-straw hats put on,
And these fresh nymphs encounter every one
In country footing.

Enter certain REAPERS, *properly habited: they join with the* NYMPHS *in a graceful dance; towards the end whereof* PROSPERO *starts suddenly, and speaks; after which, to a strange, hollow, and confused noise, they heavily vanish.*

PROSPERO [*aside*].

I had forgot that foul conspiracy
Of the beast Caliban and his confederates
Against my life: the minute of their plot
Is almost come.—[*to the* SPIRITS] Well done;—avoid,—no more.

FERDINAND.

This is strange: your father's in some passion
That works him strongly.

MIRANDA.

Never till this day
Saw I him touch'd with anger so distemper'd.

PROSPERO.

You do look, my son, in a moved sort,
As if you were dismay'd: be cheerful, sir.
Our revels now are ended. These our actors,
As I foretold you, were all spirits, and
Are melted into air, into thin air:
And, like the baseless fabric of this vision,
The cloud-capp'd towers, the gorgeous palaces,
The solemn temples, the great globe itself,
Yea, all which it inherit, shall dissolve,
And, like this insubstantial pageant faded,
Leave not a rack behind. We are such stuff
As dreams are made on; and our little life
Is rounded with a sleep.—Sir, I am vext;
Bear with my weakness; my old brain is troubled:
Be not disturb'd with my infirmity:
If you be pleased, retire into my cell,
And there repose: a turn or two I'll walk,
To still my beating mind.

FERDINAND *and* MIRANDA.

We wish your peace. [*Exeunt.*

PROSPERO [*to* ARIEL].

Come with a thought!—I thank thee, Ariel, come!

Enter ARIEL.

ARIEL.

Thy thoughts I cleave to. What's thy pleasure?

PROSPERO.

Spirit,
We must prepare to meet with Caliban.

ARIEL.

Ay, my commander: when I presented Ceres,
I thought to have told thee of it; but I fear'd
Lest I might anger thee.

PROSPERO.

Say again, where didst thou leave these varlets?

ARIEL.

I told you, sir, they were red-hot with drinking;
So full of valour that they smote the air
For breathing in their faces; beat the ground
For kissing of their feet; yet always bending
Towards their project. Then I beat my tabor;
At which, like unback'd colts, they prick'd their ears,
Advanced their eyelids, lifted up their noses
As they smelt music: so I charm'd their ears,
That, calf-like, they my lowing follow'd through
Tooth'd briers, sharp furzes, pricking goss, and thorns,
Which enter'd their frail shins: at last I left them
I'the filthy-mantled pool beyond your cell,
There dancing up to the chins, that the foul lake
O'erstunk their feet.

PROSPERO.

This was well done, my bird.
Thy shape invisible retain thou still:
The trumpery in my house, go bring it hither,
For stale to catch these thieves.

ARIEL.

I go, I go. [*Exit.*

PROSPERO.

A devil, a born devil, on whose nature
Nurture can never stick; on whom my pains,
Humanely taken, all, all lost, quite lost;
And as with age his body uglier grows,
So his mind cankers. I will plague them all,
Even to roaring.

Enter ARIEL, *loaden with glistering apparel, &c.*

Come, hang them on this line.

PROSPERO *and* ARIEL *remain, invisible. Enter* CALIBAN, STEPHANO, *and* TRINCULO, *all wet.*

CALIBAN.

Pray you, tread softly, that the blind mole may not
Hear a foot fall: we now are near his cell.

STEPHANO.

Monster, your fairy, which you say is a harmless fairy, has done little better than play'd the Jack with us.

TRINCULO.

Monster, I do smell all horse-piss; at which my nose is in great indignation.

STEPHANO.

So is mine.—Do you hear, monster? If I should take a displeasure against you, look you,—

TRINCULO.

Thou wert but a lost monster.

CALIBAN.

Good my lord, give me thy favour still.
Be patient, for the prize I'll bring thee to
Shall hoodwink this mischance: therefore speak softly;—
All's hush'd as midnight yet.

TRINCULO.

Ay, but to lose our bottles in the pool,—

STEPHANO.

There is not only disgrace and dishonour in that, monster, but an infinite loss.

TRINCULO.

That's more to me than my wetting: yet this is your harmless fairy, monster.

STEPHANO.

I will fetch off my bottle, though I be o'er ears for my labour.

CALIBAN.

Prithee, my king, be quiet. See'st thou here,
This is the mouth o'the cell: no noise, and enter.
Do that good mischief which may make this island
Thine own for ever, and I, thy Caliban,
For aye thy foot-licker.

STEPHANO.

Give me thy hand. I do begin to have bloody thoughts.

TRINCULO.

O King Stephano! O peer! O worthy Stephano! look what a wardrobe here is for thee!

CALIBAN.

Let it alone, thou fool; it is but trash.

TRINCULO.

O, ho, monster! we know what belongs to a frippery.—O King Stephano!

STEPHANO.

Put off that gown, Trinculo: by this hand, I'll have that gown.

TRINCULO.

Thy grace shall have it.

CALIBAN.

The dropsy drown this fool! what do you mean
To dote thus on such luggage? Let's along,
And do the murder first: if he awake,
From toe to crown he'll fill our skins with pinches,
Make us strange stuff.

STEPHANO.

Be you quiet, monster.—Mistress line, is not this my jerkin? Now is the jerkin under the line: now, jerkin, you are like to lose your hair, and prove a bald jerkin.

TRINCULO.

Do, do: we steal by line and level, an't like your grace.

STEPHANO.

I thank thee for that jest; here's a garment for't: wit shall not go unrewarded while I am king of this country. 'Steal by line and level' is an excellent pass of pate; there's another garment for't.

TRINCULO.

Monster, come, put some lime upon your fingers, and away with the rest.

CALIBAN.

I will have none on't: we shall lose our time,
And all be turn'd to barnacles, or to apes
With foreheads villainous low.

STEPHANO.

Monster, lay-to your fingers: help to bear this away where my hogshead of wine is, or I'll turn you out of my kingdom: go to, carry this.

TRINCULO.

And this.

STEPHANO.

Ay, and this.

A noise of hunters heard. Enter divers SPIRITS, *in shape of dogs and hounds, hunting them about;* PROSPERO *and* ARIEL *setting them on.*

PROSPERO.

Hey, Mountain, hey!

ARIEL.

Silver! there it goes, Silver!

PROSPERO.

Fury, Fury! there, Tyrant, there! hark, hark!

[CALIBAN, STEPHANO, *and* TRINCULO *are driven out.*

Go charge my goblins that they grind their joints
With dry convulsions; shorten up their sinews
With aged cramps; and more pinch-spotted make them
Than pard or cat-o'-mountain.

ARIEL.

Hark, they roar!

PROSPERO.

Let them be hunted soundly. At this hour
Lie at my mercy all mine enemies:
Shortly shall all my labours end, and thou
Shalt have the air at freedom: for a little
Follow, and do me service. [*Exeunt.*

ACT V. SCENE I.

Before the cell of PROSPERO.

Enter PROSPERO *in his magic robes, and* ARIEL.

PROSPERO.

Now does my project gather to a head:
My charms crack not; my spirits obey; and Time
Goes upright with his carriage. How's the day?

ARIEL.

On the sixth hour; at which time, my lord,
You said our work should cease.

PROSPERO.

I did say so,
When first I raised the tempest. Say, my spirit,
How fares the king and's followers?

ARIEL.

Confined together
In the same fashion as you gave in charge,
Just as you left them; all prisoners, sir,
In the line-grove which weather-fends your cell;
They cannot budge till your release. The king,
His brother, and yours, abide all three distracted;
And the remainder mourning over them,
Brimful of sorrow and dismay; but chiefly
Him that you term'd, sir, 'The good old lord, Gonzalo';
His tears run down his beard, like winter's drops
From eaves of reeds. Your charm so strongly works 'em,
That if you now beheld them, your affections
Would become tender.

PROSPERO.

Dost thou think so, spirit?

ARIEL.

Mine would, sir, were I human.

PROSPERO.

And mine shall.
Hast thou, which art but air, a touch, a feeling
Of their afflictions, and shall not myself,
One of their kind, that relish all as sharply,
Passion as they, be kindlier moved than thou art?
Though with their high wrongs I am struck to the quick,
Yet, with my nobler reason, 'gainst my fury
Do I take part: the rarer action is
In virtue than in vengeance: they being penitent,
The sole drift of my purpose doth extend
Not a frown further. Go release them, Ariel:
My charms I'll break, their senses I'll restore,
And they shall be themselves.

ARIEL.

I'll fetch them, sir. [*Exit.*

PROSPERO.

Ye elves of hills, brooks, standing lakes, and groves;
And ye that on the sands with printless foot
Do chase the ebbing Neptune, and do fly him
When he comes back; you demi-puppets that
By moonshine do the green sour ringlets make,
Whereof the ewe not bites; and you whose pastime
Is to make midnight mushrumps, that rejoice
To hear the solemn curfew; by whose aid—
Weak masters though ye be—I have bedimm'd
The noontide sun, call'd forth the mutinous winds,
And 'twixt the green sea and the azured vault
Set roaring war: to the dread-rattling thunder
Have I given fire, and rifted Jove's stout oak
With his own bolt: the strong-based promontory
Have I made shake; and by the spurs pluck'd up
The pine and cedar: graves at my command
Have waked their sleepers, oped, and let 'em forth
By my so potent art. But this rough magic
I here abjure; and, when I have required
Some heavenly music,—which even now I do,—
To work mine end upon their senses that
This airy charm is for, I'll break my staff,
Bury it certain fadoms in the earth,
And deeper than did ever plummet sound
I'll drown my book. [*Solemn music.*

Here enters ARIEL *before: then* ALONSO, *with a frantic gesture, attended by* GONZALO; SEBASTIAN *and* ANTONIO *in like manner, attended by* ADRIAN *and* FRANCISCO: *they all enter the circle which* PROSPERO *had made, and there stand charm'd; which* PROSPERO *observing, speaks.*

A solemn air, and the best comforter
To an unsettled fancy, cure thy brains,
Now useless, boil'd within thy skull! There stand,
For you are spell-stopt.
Holy Gonzalo, honourable man,
Mine eyes, even sociable to the show of thine,
Fall fellowly drops. The charm dissolves apace;
And as the morning steals upon the night,
Melting the darkness, so their rising senses
Begin to chase the ignorant fumes that mantle
Their clearer reason. O good Gonzalo,
My true preserver, and a loyal sir
To him thou follow'st! I will pay thy graces
Home both in word and deed. Most cruelly
Didst thou, Alonso, use me and my daughter:
Thy brother was a furtherer in the act;
Thou art pinch'd for't now, Sebastian. Flesh and blood,
You, brother mine, that entertain'd ambition,
Expell'd remorse and nature; who, with Sebastian,—
Whose inward pinches therefore are most strong,—
Would here have kill'd your king; I do forgive thee,
Unnatural though thou art.—Their understanding
Begins to swell; and the approaching tide
Will shortly fill the reasonable shore,
That now lies foul and muddy. Not one of them
That yet looks on me, or would know me:—Ariel,
Fetch me the hat and rapier in my cell:—
I will discase me, and myself present
As I was sometime Milan:—quickly, spirit;
Thou shalt ere long be free.

ARIEL *sings and helps to attire him.*

Where the bee sucks, there suck I:
In a cowslip's bell I lie;
There I couch when owls do cry.
On the bat's back I do fly
After summer merrily.
Merrily, merrily shall I live now
Under the blossom that hangs on the bough.

PROSPERO.

Why, that's my dainty Ariel! I shall miss thee;
But yet thou shalt have freedom:—so, so, so.—
To the king's ship, invisible as thou art:
There shalt thou find the mariners asleep
Under the hatches; the master and the boatswain
Being awake, enforce them to this place,
And presently, I prithee.

ARIEL.

I drink the air before me, and return
Or e'er your pulse twice beat. [*Exit.*

GONZALO.

All torment, trouble, wonder, and amazement,
Inhabit here: some heavenly power guide us
Out of this fearful country!

PROSPERO.

Behold, sir king,
The wronged Duke of Milan, Prospero:
For more assurance that a living prince
Does now speak to thee, I embrace thy body;
And to thee and thy company I bid
A hearty welcome.

ALONSO.

Whe'r thou be'st he or no,
Or some enchanted trifle to abuse me,
As late I have been, I not know: thy pulse
Beats, as of flesh and blood; and, since I saw thee,
The affliction of my mind amends, with which,
I fear, a madness held me: this must crave
(An if this be at all) a most strange story.
Thy dukedom I resign, and do entreat
Thou pardon me my wrongs.—But how should Prospero
Be living and be here?

PROSPERO.
First, noble friend,
Let me embrace thine age, whose honour cannot
Be measured or confined.

GONZALO.
Whether this be
Or be not, I'll not swear.

PROSPERO.
You do yet taste
Some subtilties o'the isle, that will not let you
Believe things certain.—Welcome, my friends all:—
[aside to SEBASTIAN *and* ANTONIO] But you, my brace of lords, were I so minded,
I here could pluck his highness' frown upon you,
And justify you traitors: at this time
I will tell no tales.

SEBASTIAN *[aside]*.
The devil speaks in him.

PROSPERO.
No.—
For you, most wicked sir, whom to call brother
Would even infect my mouth, I do forgive
Thy rankest fault,—all of them; and require
My dukedom of thee, which perforce, I know,
Thou must restore.

ALONSO.
If thou be'st Prospero,
Give us particulars of thy preservation;
How thou hast met us here, who three hours since
Were wrack'd upon this shore; where I have lost—
How sharp the point of this remembrance is!—
My dear son Ferdinand.

PROSPERO.
I'm woe for't, sir.

ALONSO.
Irreparable is the loss; and patience
Says it is past her cure.

PROSPERO.
I rather think
You have not sought her help; of whose soft grace,
For the like loss I have her sovereign aid,
And rest myself content.

ALONSO.
You the like loss!

PROSPERO.
As great to me as late; and, supportable
To make the dear loss, have I means much weaker
Than you may call to comfort you; for I
Have lost my daughter.

ALONSO.
A daughter!
O heavens, that they were living both in Naples,
The king and queen there! that they were, I wish
Myself were mudded in that oozy bed
Where my son lies. When did you lose your daughter?

PROSPERO.
In this last tempest. I perceive, these lords
At this encounter do so much admire,
That they devour their reason, and scarce think
Their eyes do offices of truth, their words
Are natural breath: but, howsoe'er you have
Been justled from your senses, know for certain
That I am Prospero, and that very duke
Which was thrust forth of Milan; who most strangely
Upon this shore, where you were wrack'd, was landed,
To be the lord on't. No more yet of this;
For 'tis a chronicle of day by day,
Not a relation for a breakfast, nor
Befitting this first meeting. Welcome, sir;
This cell's my court: here have I few attendants,
And subjects none abroad: pray you, look in.
My dukedom since you have given me again,
I will requite you with as good a thing;
At least bring forth a wonder, to content ye
As much as me my dukedom.

Here PROSPERO *discovers* FERDINAND *and* MIRANDA *playing at chess.*

MIRANDA.
Sweet lord, you play me false.

FERDINAND.
No, my dearest love,
I would not for the world.

MIRANDA.
Yes, for a score of kingdoms you should wrangle,
And I would call it fair play.

ALONSO.
If this prove
A vision of the island, one dear son
Shall I twice lose.

SEBASTIAN.
A most high miracle!

FERDINAND.
Though the seas threaten, they are merciful:
I have cursed them without cause.
[Kneels to ALONSO.

ALONSO.
Now all the blessings
Of a glad father compass thee about!
Arise, and say how thou camest here.

MIRANDA.
O, wonder!
How many goodly creatures are there here!
How beauteous mankind is! O brave new world,
That has such people in't!

PROSPERO.
'Tis new to thee.

ALONSO.
What is this maid with whom thou wast at play?
Your eld'st acquaintance cannot be three hours:
Is she the goddess that hath sever'd us,
And brought us thus together?

FERDINAND.
Sir, she's mortal;
But by immortal Providence she's mine:
I chose her when I could not ask my father
For his advice, nor thought I had one. She
Is daughter to this famous Duke of Milan,
Of whom so often I have heard renown,
But never saw before; of whom I have
Received a second life; and second father
This lady makes him to me.

ALONSO.
I am hers:
But, O, how oddly will it sound that I
Must ask my child forgiveness!

PROSPERO.
There, sir, stop:
Let us not burden our remembrances
With a heaviness that's gone.

GONZALO.

I have inly wept,
Or should have spoke ere this.—Look down, you gods,
And on this couple drop a blessed crown!
For it is you that have chalk'd forth the way
Which brought us hither.

ALONSO.

I say, Amen, Gonzalo!

GONZALO.

Was Milan thrust from Milan, that his issue
Should become kings of Naples? O, rejoice
Beyond a common joy! and set it down
With gold on lasting pillars,—In one voyage
Did Claribel her husband find at Tunis;
And Ferdinand, her brother, found a wife
Where he himself was lost; Prospero, his dukedom
In a poor isle; and all of us, ourselves
When no man was his own.

ALONSO [*to* FERDINAND *and* MIRANDA].

Give me your hands:
Let grief and sorrow still embrace his heart
That doth not wish you joy!

GONZALO.

Be it so! Amen!

Enter ARIEL, *with the* MASTER *and* BOATSWAIN *amazedly following.*

O, look, sir, look, sir! here is more of us:
I prophesied, if a gallows were on land,
This fellow could not drown.—Now, blasphemy,
That swear'st grace o'erboard, not an oath on shore?
Hast thou no mouth by land? What is the news?

BOATSWAIN.

The best news is, that we have safely found
Our king and company; the next, our ship—
Which, but three glasses since, we gave out split—
Is tight, and yare, and bravely rigg'd, as when
We first put out to sea.

ARIEL [*aside to* PROSPERO.]

Sir, all this service
Have I done since I went.

PROSPERO [*aside to* ARIEL].

My tricksy spirit!

ALONSO.

These are not natural events; they strengthen
From strange to stranger.—Say, how came you hither?

BOATSWAIN.

If I did think, sir, I were well awake,
I'ld strive to tell you. We were dead of sleep,
And—how we know not—all clapt under hatches;
Where, but even now, with strange and several noises
Of roaring, shrieking, howling, jingling chains,
And more diversity of sounds, all horrible,
We were awaked; straightway, at liberty:
Where we, in all her trim, freshly beheld
Our royal, good, and gallant ship; our master
Capering to eye her: on a trice, so please you,
Even in a dream, were we divided from them,
And were brought moping hither.

ARIEL [*aside to* PROSPERO].

Was't well done?

PROSPERO [*aside to* ARIEL].

Bravely, my diligence. Thou shalt be free.

ALONSO.

This is as strange a maze as e'er men trod;
And there is in this business more than nature
Was ever conduct of: some oracle
Must rectify our knowledge.

PROSPERO.

Sir, my liege,
Do not infest your mind with beating on
The strangeness of this business; at pick'd leisure,
Which shall be shortly, single I'll resolve you—
Which to you shall seem probable—of every
These happen'd accidents: till when, be cheerful,
And think of each thing well.—[*aside to* ARIEL]
Come hither, spirit:
Set Caliban and his companions free;
Untie the spell. [*Exit* ARIEL.]—How fares my gracious sir?
There are yet missing of your company
Some few odd lads that you remember not.

Enter ARIEL, *driving in* CALIBAN, STEPHANO, *and* TRINCULO, *in their stolen apparel.*

STEPHANO.

Every man shift for all the rest, and let no man take care for himself; for all is but fortune.—Coragio, bully-monster, coragio!

TRINCULO.

If these be true spies which I wear in my head, here's a goodly sight.

CALIBAN.

O Setebos, these be brave spirits indeed!
How fine my master is! I am afraid
He will chastise me.

SEBASTIAN.

Ha, ha!
What things are these, my lord Antonio?
Will money buy 'em?

ANTONIO.

Very like; one of them
Is a plain fish, and, no doubt, marketable.

PROSPERO.

Mark but the badges of these men, my lords,
Then say if they be true.—This mis-shapen knave,—
His mother was a witch; and one so strong
That could control the moon, make flows and ebbs,
And deal in her command, without her power.
These three have robb'd me; and this demi-devil—
For he's a bastard one—had plotted with them
To take my life: two of these fellows you
Must know and own; this thing of darkness I
Acknowledge mine.

CALIBAN.

I shall be pinch'd to death.

ALONSO.

Is not this Stephano, my drunken butler?

SEBASTIAN.

He is drunk now: where had he wine?

ALONSO.

And Trinculo is reeling ripe: where should they
Find this grand liquor that hath gilded 'em?—
How camest thou in this pickle?

TRINCULO.

I have been in such a pickle, since I saw you last, that, I fear me, will never out of my bones: I shall not fear fly-blowing.

SEBASTIAN.

Why, how now, Stephano!

STEPHANO.

O, touch me not:—I am not Stephano, but a cramp.

PROSPERO.

You'ld be king o'the isle, sirrah?

STEPHANO.

I should have been a sore one, then.

ALONSO.

This is a strange thing as e'er I look'd on.

[*Pointing to* CALIBAN.

PROSPERO.

He is as disproportion'd in his manners
As in his shape.—Go, sirrah, to my cell;
Take with you your companions; as you look
To have my pardon, trim it handsomely.

CALIBAN.

Ay, that I will; and I'll be wise hereafter,
And seek for grace. What a thrice-double ass
Was I, to take this drunkard for a god,
And worship this dull fool!

PROSPERO.

Go to; away!

ALONSO.

Hence, and bestow your luggage where you found it.

SEBASTIAN.

Or stole it, rather.

[*Exeunt* CALIBAN, STEPHANO, *and* TRINCULO.

PROSPERO.

Sir, I invite your highness and your train
To my poor cell, where you shall take your rest
For this one night; which, part of it, I'll waste
With such discourse as, I doubt not, shall make it
Go quick away; the story of my life,
And the particular accidents gone by
Since I came to this isle: and in the morn
I'll bring you to your ship, and so to Naples,
Where I have hope to see the nuptial
Of these our dear-beloved solemnized;
And thence retire me to my Milan, where
Every third thought shall be my grave.

ALONSO.

I long
To hear the story of your life, which must
Take the ear strangely.

PROSPERO.

I'll deliver all;
And promise you calm seas, auspicious gales,
And sail so expeditious, that shall catch
Your royal fleet far off.—[*aside to* ARIEL] My Ariel,—chick,—
That is thy charge: then to the elements
Be free, and fare thou well!—Please you, draw near.

[*Exeunt.*

EPILOGUE.

SPOKEN BY PROSPERO.

NOW my charms are all o'erthrown,
And what strength I have's mine own,—
Which is most faint: now, 'tis true,
I must be here confined by you,
Or sent to Naples. Let me not,
Since I have my dukedom got,
And pardon'd the deceiver, dwell
In this bare island by your spell;
But release me from my bands
With the help of your good hands:
Gentle breath of yours my sails
Must fill, or else my project fails,
Which was to please: now I want
Spirits to enforce, art to enchant;
And my ending is despair,
Unless I be relieved by prayer,
Which pierces so, that it assaults
Mercy itself, and frees all faults.
As you from crimes would pardon'd be,
Let your indulgence set me free.

THE TWO NOBLE KINSMEN

DRAMATIS PERSONAE

THESEUS, *Duke of Athens.*
PIRITHOUS, *friend to Theseus.*
ARTESIUS, *an Athenian.*
PALAMON, ARCITE } *kinsmen, nephews to Creon, King of Thebes.*
VALERIUS, *a Theban.*
SIX KNIGHTS.
JAILER.
WOOER *to the Jailer's daughter.*
DOCTOR.
BROTHER *to the Jailer.*
TWO FRIENDS *to the Jailer.*
SCHOOLMASTER.
HERALD, MESSENGERS, COUNTRYMEN, HYMEN, BOY, EXECUTIONER, GUARD, TABORER, BAVIAN *or* FOOL, LORDS *and* ATTENDANTS.
HIPPOLYTA, *an Amazon, bride to Theseus.*
EMILIA, *her sister.*
THREE QUEENS.
DAUGHTER *of the Jailer.*
WAITING-WOMAN *to Emilia.*
MAIDS, COUNTRY WENCHES *and* NYMPHS.

SCENE
Athens and the country nearby; and Thebes.

PROLOGUE.

Flourish.

New plays and maidenheads are near akin:
Much followed both, for both much money gi'en,
If they stand sound and well. And a good play –
Whose modest scenes blush on his marriage day,
And shake to lose his honour – is like her
That after holy tie and first night's stir
Yet still is modesty, and still retains
More of the maid to sight than husband's pains.
We pray our play may be so, for I am sure
It has a noble breeder, and a pure,
A learned, and a poet never went
More famous yet 'twixt Po and silver Trent.
Chaucer, of all admired, the story gives:
There constant to eternity it lives.
If we let fall the nobleness of this,
And the first sound this child hear be a hiss,
How will it shake the bones of that good man,
And make him cry from under ground, 'O fan
From me the witless chaff of such a writer
That blasts my bays, and my famed works makes lighter
Than Robin Hood!' This is the fear we bring;
For, to say truth, it were an endless thing,
And too ambitious, to aspire to him.
Weak as we are, and almost breathless swim
In this deep water, do but you hold out
Your helping hands, and we shall tack about,
And something do to save us. You shall hear
Scenes, though below his art, may yet appear
Worth two hours' travail. To his bones sweet sleep;
Content to you. If this play do not keep
A little dull time from us, we perceive
Our losses fall so thick we must needs leave.
[*Flourish.*

ACT I. SCENE I.

Athens. Before a temple.

Enter HYMEN *with a torch burning; a boy in a white robe before, singing and strewing flowers; after* HYMEN, *a* NYMPH *encompassed in her tresses, bearing a wheaten garland; then* THESEUS *between two other nymphs with wheaten chaplets on their heads; then* HIPPOLYTA *the bride, led by* PIRITHOUS, *and another holding a garland over her head, her tresses likewise hanging; after her,* EMILIA *holding up her train;* ARTESIUS *and* ATTENDANTS. *Music.*

The Song.

Roses, their sharp spines being gone,
Not royal in their smells alone,
But in their hue;
Maiden pinks, of odour faint,
Daisies smell-less, yet most quaint,
And sweet thyme true;

Primrose, first-born child of Ver,
Merry springtime's harbinger,
With harebells dim;
Oxlips, in their cradles growing,
Marigolds, on deathbeds blowing,
Lark's-heels trim;

All dear Nature's children sweet
Lie 'fore bride and bridegroom's feet,
[*Strew flowers.*]
Blessing their sense;
Not an angel of the air,
Bird melodious, or bird fair,
Is absent hence;

The crow, the sland'rous cuckoo, nor
The boding raven, nor chough hoar,
Nor chatt'ring pie,
May on our bridehouse perch or sing,
Or with them any discord bring,
But from it fly.

Enter three QUEENS *in black, with veils stained, with imperial crowns. The first* QUEEN *falls down at the foot of* THESEUS; *the second falls down at the foot of* HIPPOLYTA; *the third before* EMILIA.

FIRST QUEEN.
For pity's sake and true gentility's,

Hear and respect me.

SECOND QUEEN.

For your mother's sake,
And as you wish your womb may thrive with fair ones,
Hear and respect me.

THIRD QUEEN.

Now for the love of him whom Jove hath marked
The honour of your bed, and for the sake
Of clear virginity, be advocate
For us, and our distresses. This good deed
Shall raze you out o' th' Book of Trespasses
All you are set down there.

THESEUS.

Sad lady, rise.

HIPPOLYTA.

Stand up.

EMILIA.

No knees to me.
What woman I may stead that is distressed
Does bind me to her.

THESEUS.

What's your request? Deliver you for all.

FIRST QUEEN.

We are three queens, whose sovereigns fell before
The wrath of cruel Creon; who endured
The beaks of ravens, talons of the kites,
And pecks of crows, in the foul fields of Thebes.
He will not suffer us to burn their bones,
To urn their ashes, nor to take th' offence
Of mortal loathsomeness from the blest eye
Of holy Phoebus, but infects the winds
With stench of our slain lords. O pity, duke,
Thou purger of the earth, draw thy feared sword
That does good turns to th' world; give us the bones
Of our dead kings, that we may chapel them;
And of thy boundless goodness take some note
That for our crowned heads we have no roof,
Save this which is the lion's and the bear's,
And vault to everything.

THESEUS.

Pray you kneel not.
I was transported with your speech, and suffered
Your knees to wrong themselves. I have heard the fortunes
Of your dead lords, which gives me such lamenting
As wakes my vengeance and revenge for 'em.
King Capaneus was your lord. The day
That he should marry you, at such a season
As now it is with me, I met your groom.
By Mars's altar, you were that time fair:
Not Juna's mantle fairer than your tresses,
Nor in more bounty spread her; your wheaten wreath
Was then nor threshed nor blasted; Fortune at you
Dimpled her cheek with smiles. Hercules our kinsman,
Then weaker than your eyes, laid by his club:
He tumbled down upon his Nemean hide
And swore his sinews thawed. O grief and time,
Fearful consumers, you wilt all devour.

FIRST QUEEN.

O I hope some god,
Some god hath put his mercy in your manhood,
Whereto he'll infuse pow'r, and press you forth
Our undertaker.

THESEUS.

O no knees, none, widow,
Unto the helmeted Bellona use them,
And pray for me your soldier.
Troubled I am. [*Turns away. The Queens rise.*]

SECOND QUEEN.

Honoured Hippolyta,
Most dreaded Amazonian, that hast slain
The scythe-tusked boar, that with thy arm as strong
As it is white, wast near to make the male
To thy sex captive, but that this thy lord,
Born to uphold creation in that honour
First Nature 'stilled it in, shrunk thee into
The bound thou wast o'erflowing, at once subduing
Thy force and thy affection; soldieress,
That equally canst poise sternness with pity,
Whom now I know hast much more power on him
Than ever he had on thee, who ow'st his strength
And his love too, who is a servant for
The tenor of thy speech; dear glass of ladies,
Bid him that we whom flaming war doth scorch
Under the shadow of his sword may cool us;
Require him he advance it o'er our heads;
Speak't in a woman's key, like such a woman
As any of us three; weep ere you fail;
Lend us a knee;
But touch the ground for us no longer time
Than a dove's motion when the head's plucked off;
Tell him if he i' th' blood-sized field lay swoll'n,
Showing the sun his teeth, grinning at the moon,
What you would do.

HIPPOLYTA.

Poor lady, say no more.
I had as lief trace this good action with you
As that whereto I am going, and never yet
Went I so willing way. My lord is taken
Heart-deep with your distress. Let him consider.
I'll speak anon.

THIRD QUEEN.

[*Kneels to Emilia.*]
O my petition was
Set down in ice, which by hot grief uncandied
Melts into drops, so sorrow wanting form
Is pressed with deeper matter.

EMILIA.

Pray stand up,
Your grief is written in your cheek.

THIRD QUEEN.

O woe,
You cannot read it there; there through my tears,
Like wrinkled pebbles in a glassy stream
You may behold 'em. Lady, lady, alack!
He that will all the treasure know o' th' earth
Must know the centre too; he that will fish
For my least minnow, let him lead his line
To catch one at my heart. O pardon me,
Extremity that sharpens sundry wits
Makes me a fool. [*She rises.*]

EMILIA.

Pray you say nothing, pray you.
Who cannot feel nor see the rain, being in't,
Knows neither wet nor dry. If that you were
The ground-piece of some painter, I would buy you
T' instruct me 'gainst a capital grief indeed
Such heart-pierced demonstration. But alas,

Being a natural sister of our sex,
Your sorrow beats so ardently upon me
That it shall make a counter-reflect 'gainst
My brother's heart, and warm it to some pity
Though it were made of stone. Pray have good
comfort.

THESEUS.

Forward to th' temple, leave not out a jot
O' th' sacred ceremony.

FIRST QUEEN.

O this celebration
Will long last, and be more costly than
Your suppliants' war. Remember that your fame
Knolls in the ear o' th' world; what you do quickly
Is not done rashly; your first thought is more
Than others' laboured meditance, your
premeditating
More than their actions. But O Jove, your actions,
Soon as they move, as ospreys do the fish,
Subdue before they touch. Think, dear duke,
think
What beds our slain kings have.

SECOND QUEEN.

What griefs our beds
That our dear lords have none.

THIRD QUEEN.

None fit for th' dead.
Those that with cords, knives, drams' precipitance,
Weary of this world's light, have to themselves
Been death's most horrid agents, human grace
Affords them dust and shadow.

FIRST QUEEN.

But our lords
Lie blist'ring 'fore the visitating sun,
And were good kings when living.

THESEUS.

It is true,
And I will give you comfort, to give your dead
lords graves.
The which to do, must make some work with Creon.

FIRST QUEEN.

And that work presents itself to th' doing.
Now 'twill take form, the heats are gone tomorrow.
Then bootless toil must recompense itself
With its own sweat. Now he's secure,
Not dreams we stand before your puissance,
Rinsing our holy begging in our eyes
To make petition clear.

SECOND QUEEN.

Now you may take him,
Drunk with his victory.

THIRD QUEEN.

And his army full
Of bread' and sloth.

THESEUS.

Artesius, that best knowest
How to draw out fit to this enterprise
The prim'st for this proceeding, and the number
To carry such a business, forth and levy
Our worthiest instruments, whilst we dispatch
This grand act of our life, this daring deed
Of fate in wedlock.

FIRST QUEEN.

Dowagers, take hands,
Let us be widows to our woes, delay
Commends us to a famishing hope.

ALL QUEENS.

Farewell.

SECOND QUEEN.

We come unseasonably, but when could grief
Cull forth, as unpanged judgement can, fitt'st time
For best solicitation?

THESEUS.

Why, Good ladies.
This is a service whereto I am going
Greater than any was; it more imports me
Than all the actions that I have foregone
Or futurely can cope.

FIRST QUEEN.

The more proclaiming
Our suit shall be neglected. When her arms,
Able to lock Jove from a synod, shall
By warranting moonlight corslet thee, O when
Her twining cherries shall their sweetness fall
Upon thy tasteful lips, what wilt thou think
Of rotten kings or blubbered queens, what care
For what thou feel'st not, what thou feel'st
being able
To make Mars spurn his drum? O if thou couch
But one night with her, every hour in't will
Take hostage of thee for a hundred, and
Thou shalt remember nothing more than what
That banquet bids thee to.

HIPPOLYTA.

[*Kneels.*] Though much unlike
You should be so transported, as much sorry
I should be such a suitor; yet I think,
Did I not by th' abstaining of my joy,
Which breeds a deeper longing, cure their
surfeit
That craves a present med'cine, I should pluck
All ladies' scandal on me. Therefore, sir,
As I shall here make trial of my pray'rs,
Either presuming them to have some force
Or sentencing for aye their vigour dumb,
Prorogue this business we are going about, and
hang
Your shield afore your heart, about that neck
Which is my fee, and which I freely lend
To do these poor queens service.

ALL QUEENS.

[*To Emilia*] O help now,
Our cause cries for your knee.

EMILIA.

[*Kneels*] If you grant not
My sister her petition in that force,
With that celerity and nature which
She makes it in, from henceforth I'll not dare
To ask you anything, nor be so hardy
Ever to take a husband.

THESEUS.

Pray stand up.
[*Hippolyta and Emilia rise.*]
I am entreating of myself to do
That which you kneel to have me. Pirithous,
Lead on the bride; get you and pray the gods
For success, and return; omit not anything
In the pretended celebration. Queens,
Follow your soldier, as before. [*To Artesius.*] Hence
you,
And at the banks of Aulis meet us with
The forces you can raise, where we shall find

The moiety of a number for a business
More bigger-looked. [*Exit* ARTESIUS.
Since that our theme is haste,
I stamp this kiss upon thy current lip.
Sweet, keep it as my token. [*Kisses* HIPPOLYTA.] Set you forward,
For I will see you gone.

HIPPOLYTA, EMILIA, PIRITHOUS *and* ATTENDANTS *begin to move towards the temple.*

Farewell, my beauteous sister. Pirithous,
Keep the feast full, bate not an hour on't.

PIRITHOUS.

Sir,
I'll follow you at heels. The feast's solemnity
Shall want till your return.

THESEUS.

Cousin, I charge you
Budge not from Athens. We shall be returning
Ere you can end this feast, of which I pray you
Make no abatement. Once more, farewell all.
[*The procession enters the temple.*]

FIRST QUEEN.

Thus dost thou still make good the tongue o' th' world.

SECOND QUEEN.

And earn'st a deity equal with Mars.

THIRD QUEEN.

If not above him, for
Thou being but mortal makest affections bend
To godlike honours. They themselves, some say,
Groan under such a mast'ry.

THESEUS.

As we are men,
Thus should we do. Being sensually subdued,
We lose our human title. Good cheer, ladies.
Now turn we towards your comforts.
Flourish. [*Exeunt.*

ACT I. SCENE II.

Thebes.

Enter PALAMON *and* ARCITE.

ARCITE.

Dear Palamon, dearer in love than blood
And our prime cousin, yet unhardened in
The crimes of nature, let us leave the city
Thebes, and the temptings in't, before we further
Sully our gloss of youth;
And here to keep in abstinence we shame
As in incontinence: for not to swim
I' th' aid o' th' current were almost to sink,
At least to frustrate striving; and to follow
The common stream, 'twould bring us to an eddy
Where we should turn or drown; if labour through,
Our gain but life and weakness.

PALAMON.

Your advice
Is cried up with example: what strange ruins
Since first we went to school may we perceive
Walking in Thebes? Scars and bare weeds
The gain o' th' Martialist, who did propound
To his bold ends honour and golden ingots,
Which though he won he had not, and now flirted
By peace for whom he fought: who then shall offer
To Mars's so scorned altar? I do bleed
When such I meet, and wish great Juno would
Resume her ancient fit of jealousy
To get the soldier work, that peace might purge
For her repletion, and retain anew
Her charitable heart, now hard and harsher
Than strife or war could be.

ARCITE.

Are you not out?
Meet you no ruin but the soldier in
The cranks and turns of Thebes? You did begin
As if you met decays of many kinds.
Perceive you none that do arouse your pity
But th' unconsidered soldier?

PALAMON.

Yes, I pity
Decays where'er I find them, but such most
That sweating in an honourable toil
Are paid with ice to cool 'em.

ARCITE.

'Tis not this
I did begin to speak of: this is virtue
Of no respect in Thebes. I spake of Thebes,
How dangerous if we will keep our honours
It is for our residing, where every evil
Hath a good colour, where every seeming good's
A certain evil, where not to be ev'n jump
As they are, here were to be strangers, and
Such things to be, mere monsters.

PALAMON

'Tis in our power
(Unless we fear that apes can tutor 's) to
Be masters of our manners. What need I
Affect another's gait, which is not catching
Where there is faith, or to be fond upon
Another's way of speech, when by mine own
I may be reasonably conceived – saved too,
Speaking it truly? Why am I bound
By any generous bond to follow him
Follows his tailor, haply so long until
The followed make pursuit? Or let me know
Why mine own barber is unblest, with him
My poor chin too, for 'tis not scissored just
To such a favourite's glass. What canon is there
That does command my rapier from my hip
To dangle't in my hand, or to go tiptoe
Before the street be foul? Either I am
The fore-horse in the team, or I am none
That draw i' th' sequent trace. These poor slight sores
Need not a plantain. That which rips my bosom
Almost to th' heart's –

ARCITE.

Our uncle Creon.

PALAMON.

He,
A most unbounded tyrant, whose successes
Makes heaven unfeared, and villainy assured
Beyond its power there's nothing; almost puts
Faith in a fever, and deifies alone
Voluble chance; who only attributes
The faculties of other instruments
To his own nerves and act; commands men service,
And what they win in't, boot and glory; one
That fears not to do harm; good, dares not. Let
The blood of mine that's sib to him be sucked
From me with leeches, let them break and fall
Off me with that corruption.

ARCITE.

Clear-spirited cousin,
Let's leave his court, that we may nothing share
Of his loud infamy; for our milk
Will relish of the pasture, and we must
Be vile or disobedient, not his kinsmen
In blood unless in quality.

PALAMON.

Nothing truer.
I think the echoes of his shames have deafed
The ears of heav'nly justice: widows' cries
Descend again into their throats, and have not
Due audience of the gods.

Enter VALERIUS.

Valerius!

VALERIUS.

The king calls for you; yet be leaden-footed
Till his great rage be off him. Phoebus, when
He broke his whipstock and exclaimed against
The horses of the sun, but whispered to
The loudness of his fury.

PALAMON.

Small winds shake him
But what's the matter?

VALERIUS.

Theseus, who where he threats appalls, hath sent
Deadly defiance to him and pronounces
Ruin to Thebes, who is at hand to seal
The promise of his wrath.

ARCITE.

Let him approach.
But that we fear the gods in him, he brings not
A jot of terror to us. Yet what man
Thirds his own worth (the case is each of ours)
When that his action's dregged, with mind assured
'Tis bad he goes about.

PALAMON.

Leave that unreasoned.
Our services stand now for Thebes, not Creon.
Yet to be neutral to him were dishonour,
Rebellious to oppose: therefore we must
With him stand to the mercy of our Fate,
Who hath bounded our last minute.

ARCITE.

So we must.
Is't said this war's afoot, or it shall be
On fail of some condition?

VALERIUS.

'Tis in motion:
The intelligence of state came in the instant
With the defier.

PALAMON.

Let's to the king, who were he
A quarter carrier of that honour which
His enemy come in, the blood we venture
Should be as for our health, which were not spent,
Rather laid out for purchase. But alas,
Our hands advanced before our hearts, what will
The fall o' th' stroke do damage?

ARCITE.

Let th' event,
That never erring arbitrator, tell us
When we know all ourselves, and let us follow
The becking of our chance. [*Exeunt.*

ACT I. SCENE III.

Athens.

Enter PIRITHOUS, HIPPOLYTA, EMILIA.

PIRITHOUS.

No further.

HIPPOLYTA.

Sir, farewell. Repeat my wishes
To our great lord, of whose success I dare not
Make any timorous question, yet I wish him
Excess and overflow of power, and 't might be
To dure ill-dealing Fortune. Speed to him:
Store never hurts good governors.

PIRITHOUS.

Though I know
His ocean needs not my poor drops, yet they
Must yield their tribute there. [*To Emilia.*] My precious maid,
Those best affections that the heavens infuse
In their best-tempered pieces, keep enthroned
In your dear heart.

EMILIA.

Thanks, sir. Remember me
To our all-royal brother, for whose speed
The great Bellona I'll solicit; and
Since in our terrene state petitions are not
Without gifts understood, I'll offer to her
What I shall be advised she likes: our hearts
Are in his army, in his tent.

HIPPOLYTA.

In 's bosom.
We have been soldiers, and we cannot weep
When our friends don their helms, or put to sea,
Or tell of babes broached on the lance, or women
That have sod their infants in – and after eat them –
The brine they wept at killing 'em. Then if
You stay to see of us such spinsters, we
Should hold you here for ever.

PIRITHOUS.

Peace be to you
As I pursue this war, which shall be then
Beyond further requiring. [*Exit* PIRITHOUS.

EMILIA.

How his longing
Follows his friend! Since his depart, his sports,
Though craving seriousness and skill, passed slightly
His careless execution, where nor gain
Made him regard, or loss consider, but
Playing one business in his hand, another
Directing in his head – his mind nurse equal
To these so diff'ring twins. Have you observed him,
Since our great lord departed?

HIPPOLYTA.

With much labour;
And I did love him for't. They two have cabined
In many as dangerous as poor a corner,
Peril and want contending. They have skiffed
Torrents whose roaring tyranny and power
I' th' least of these was dreadful; and they have
Fought out together where Death's self was lodged,
Yet Fate hath brought them off. Their knot of love,
Tied, weaved, entangled, with so true, so long,
And with a finger of so deep a cunning,
May be outworn, never undone. I think
Theseus cannot be umpire to himself,
Cleaving his conscience into twain and doing
Each side like justice, which he loves best.

EMILIA.

Doubtless
There is a best, and Reason has no manners
To say it is not you. I was acquainted
Once with a time when I enjoyed a playfellow.
You were at wars, when she the grave enriched
Who made too proud the bed, took leave o' th' moon
(Which then looked pale at parting) when our count
Was each eleven.

HIPPOLYTA.

'Twas Flavina

EMILIA.

Yes.
You talk of Pirithous' and Theseus' love.
Theirs has more ground, is more maturely seasoned,
More buckled with strong judgement, and their needs
The one of th' other may be said to water
Their intertangled roots of love. But I
And she I sigh and spoke of were things innocent,
Loved for we did, and like the elements
That know not what, nor why, yet do effect
Rare issues by their operance, our souls
Did so to one another: what she liked
Was then of me approved, what not condemned –
No more arraignment; the flow'r that I would pluck
And put between my breasts, O then but beginning
To swell about the blossom, she would long
Till she had such another, and commit it
To the like innocent cradle, where phoenix-like
They died in perfume; on my head no toy
But was her pattern; her affections – pretty
Though happily her careless were – I followed
For my most serious decking; had mine ear
Stol'n some new air, or at adventure hummed on
From musical coinage, why, it was a note
Whereon her spirits would sojourn, rather dwell on,
And sing it in her slumbers. This rehearsal,
Which – every innocent wots well – comes in
Like old importment's bastard, has this end
That the true love 'tween maid and maid may be
More than in sex dividual.

HIPPOLYTA.

Y' are out of breath,
And this high-speeded pace is but to say
That you shall never, like the maid Flavina,
Love any that's called man.

EMILIA.

I am sure I shall not.

HIPPOLYTA.

Now alack, weak sister,
I must no more believe thee in this point,
Though in't I know thou dost believe thyself,
Than I will trust a sickly appetite
That loathes even as it longs. But sure, my sister,
If I were ripe for your persuasion, you
Have said enough to shake me from the arm
Of the all-noble Theseus, for whose fortunes
I will now in and kneel, with great assurance
That we, more than his Pirithous, possess
The high throne in his heart.

EMILIA.

I am not against
Your faith, yet I continue mine. [*Exeunt.*

ACT I. SCENE IV.

Thebes.

Cornets. A battle struck within. Then a retreat. Flourish. Then enter THESEUS *(victor) with a* HERALD, LORDS *and* ATTENDANTS *and with* PALAMON *and* ARCITE *carried on hearses. The three* QUEENS *meet him, and fall on their faces before him.*

FIRST QUEEN.

To thee no star be dark!

SECOND QUEEN.

Both heaven and earth
Friend thee for ever!

THIRD QUEEN.

All the good that may
Be wished upon thy head, I cry 'amen' to't!

THESEUS.

Th' impartial gods, who from the mounted heavens
View us their mortal herd, behold who err
And in their time chastise. Go and find out
The bones of your dead lords, and honour them
With treble ceremony; rather than a gap
Should be in their dear rites, we would supply't.
But those we will depute which shall invest
You in your dignities, and even each thing
Our haste does leave imperfect. So adieu,
And heaven's good eyes look on you.

[*Exeunt* QUEENS.

What are those?

HERALD.

Men of great quality, as may be judged
By their appointment. Some of Thebes have told's
They are sisters' children, nephews to the king.

THESEUS.

By th' helm of Mars, I saw them in the war,
Like to a pair of lions smeared with prey,
Make lanes in troops aghast. I fixed my note
Constantly on them, for they were a mark
Worth a god's view. What prisoner was't that told me
When I enquired their names?

HERALD.

We 'lieve they're called
Arcite and Palamon.

THESEUS.

'Tis right: those, those;
They are not dead?

HERALD.

Nor in a state of life: had they been taken
When their last hurts were given, 'twas possible
They might have been recovered. Yet they breathe
And have the name of men.

THESEUS.

Then like men use 'em.
The very lees of such – millions of rates –
Exceed the wine of others. All our surgeons
Convent in their behoof, our richest balms,
Rather than niggard, waste. Their lives concern us
Much more than Thebes is worth. Rather than have 'em
Freed of this plight and in their morning state,
Sound and at liberty, I would 'em dead,
But forty-thousandfold we had rather have 'em
Prisoners to us than Death. Bear 'em speedily
From our kind air, to them unkind, and minister
What man to man may do – for our sake more,
Since I have known frights, fury, friends' behests,
Love's provocations, zeal, a mistress' task,

Desire of liberty, a fever, madness,
Hath set a mark which Nature could not reach to
Without some imposition – sickness in will
O'er-wrestling strength in reason. For our love
And great Apollo's mercy, all our best
Their best skill tender. Lead into the city,
Where, having bound things scattered, we win post
To Athens 'fore our army. [*Flourish. Exeunt.*

ACT I. SCENE V.

Thebes.

Music. Enter the QUEENS *with the hearses of their knights, in a funeral solemnity, etc.*

Song

Urns and odours bring away,
Vapours, sighs, darken the day;
Our dole more deadly looks than dying:
Balms and gums and heavy cheers,
Sacred vials filled with tears,
And clamours through the wild air flying.

Come, all sad and solemn shows
That are quick-eyed Pleasure's foes:
We convent nought else but woes,
We convent, etc.

THIRD QUEEN.
[*To Second Queen.*]
This funeral path brings to your household's grave.
Joy seize on you again. Peace sleep with him.

SECOND QUEEN.
[*To First Queen.*]
And this to yours.

FIRST QUEEN.
[*To Third Queen.*]
Yours this way. Heavens lend
A thousand differing ways to one sure end.

THIRD QUEEN.
This world's a city full of straying streets,
And death's the market place where each one meets.
[*Exeunt severally.*

ACT II. SCENE I.

Athens. A garden with a room in a prison above.
Enter JAILER *and* WOOER.

JAILER.
I may depart with little while I live: something I may cast to you, not much. Alas, the prison I keep, though it be for great ones, yet they seldom come. Before one salmon you shall take a number of minnows. I am given out to be better lined than it can appear to me report is a true speaker. I would I were really that I am delivered to be. Marry, what I have, be it what it will, I will assure upon my daughter at the day of my death.

WOOER.
Sir, I demand no more than your own offer, and I will estate your daughter in what I have promised.

JAILER.
Well, we will talk more of this when the solemnity is passed. But have you a full promise of her?

Enter DAUGHTER.

When that shall be seen, I tender my consent.

WOOER.
I have, sir. Here she comes.

JAILER.
Your friend and I have chanced to name you here, upon the old business; but no more of that now. So soon as the court-hurry is over, we will have an end of it. I' th' meantime look tenderly to the two prisoners. I can tell you they are princes.

DAUGHTER.
These strewings are for their chamber. 'Tis pity they are in prison, and 'twere pity they should be out. I do think they have patience to make any adversity ashamed: the prison itself is proud of 'em, and they have all the world in their chamber.

JAILER.
They are famed to be a pair of absolute men.

DAUGHTER.
By my troth, I think Fame but stammers 'em: they stand a grize above the reach of report.

JAILER.
I heard them reported in the battle to be the only doers.

DAUGHTER.
Nay, most likely, for they are noble suff'rers. I marvel how they would have looked had they been victors, that with such a constant nobility enforce a freedom out of bondage, making misery their mirth, and affliction a toy to jest at.

JAILER.
Do they so?

DAUGHTER.
It seems to me they have no more sense of their captivity than I of ruling Athens. They eat well, look merrily, discourse of many things, but nothing of their own restraint and disasters. Yet sometime a divided sigh, martyred as 'twere i' th' deliverance, will break from one of them – when the other presently gives it so sweet a rebuke that I could wish myself a sigh to be so chid, or at least a sigher to be comforted.

WOOER.
I never saw 'em.

JAILER.
The duke himself came privately in the night, and so did they: what the reason of it is I know not.

Enter PALAMON *and* ARCITE *above.*

Look, yonder they are. That's Arcite looks out.

DAUGHTER.
No, sir, no! That's Palamon! Arcite is the lower of the twain. You may perceive a part of him.

JAILER.
Go to, leave your pointing. They would not make us their object. Out of their sight!

DAUGHTER.
It is a holiday to look on them. Lord, the diff'rence of men!
[*Exeunt* JAILER, WOOER, DAUGHTER.

PALAMON.
How do you, noble cousin?

ARCITE.
How do you, sir?

PALAMON.
Why, strong enough to laugh at misery,

And bear the chance of war. Yet we are prisoners
I fear for ever, cousin.

ARCITE.

I believe it,
And to that destiny have patiently
Laid up my hour to come.

PALAMON.

O cousin Arcite,
Where is Thebes now? Where is our noble country?
Where are our friends, and kindreds? Never more
Must we behold those comforts, never see
The hardy youths strive for the games of honour,
Hung with the painted favours of their ladies,
Like tall ships under sail; then start amongst 'em
And as an east wind leave 'em all behind us,
Like lazy clouds, whilst Palamon and Arcite,
Even in the wagging of a wanton leg,
Outstripped the people's praises, won the garlands
Ere they have time to wish 'em ours. O never
Shall we two exercise, like twins of Honour,
Our arms again, and feel our fiery horses
Like proud seas under us! Our good swords now –
Better the red-eyed god of war ne'er wore! –
Ravished our sides, like age must run to rust
And deck the temples of those gods that hate us.
These hands shall never draw 'em out like lightning
To blast whole armies more.

ARCITE.

No, Palamon,
Those hopes are prisoners with us: here we are
And here the graces of our youths must wither
Like a too timely spring; here age must find us,
And which is heaviest, Palamon, unmarried;
The sweet embraces of a loving wife,
Loaden with kisses, armed with thousand Cupids,
Shall never clasp our necks, no issue know us,
No figures of ourselves shall we e'er see,
To glad our age, and like young eagles teach 'em
Boldly to gaze against bright arms, and say:
'Remember what your fathers were, and conquer.'
The fair-eyed maids shall weep our banishments,
And in their songs curse ever-blinded Fortune
Till she for shame see what a wrong she has done
To youth and nature. This is all our world:
We shall know nothing here but one another,
Hear nothing but the clock that tells our woes.
The vine shall grow, but we shall never see it;
Summer shall come, and with her all delights;
But dead-cold winter must inhabit here still.

PALAMON.

'Tis too true, Arcite. To our Theban hounds,
That shook the aged forest with their echoes,
No more now must we halloo, no more shake
Our pointed javelins, whilst the angry swine
Flies like a Parthian quiver from our rages,
Struck with our well-steeled darts. All valiant uses,
The food and nourishment of noble minds,
In us two here shall perish. We shall die –
Which is the curse of honour – lastly,
Children of grief and ignorance.

ARCITE.

Yet, cousin,
Even from the bottom of these miseries,
From all that Fortune can inflict upon us,
I see two comforts rising, two mere blessings,
If the gods please: to hold here a brave patience,
And the enjoying of our griefs together.
Whilst Palamon is with me, let me perish
If I think this our prison.

PALAMON.

Certainly,
'Tis a main goodness, cousin, that our fortunes
Were twined together. 'Tis most true, two souls
Put in two noble bodies, let 'em suffer
The gall of hazard, so they grow together,
Will never sink; they must not, say they could.
A willing man dies sleeping, and all's done.

ARCITE.

Shall we make worthy uses of this place
That all men hate so much?

PALAMON.

How, gentle cousin?

ARCITE.

Let's think this prison holy sanctuary,
To keep us from corruption of worse men.
We are young and yet desire the ways of honour
That liberty and common conversation,
The poison of pure spirits, might like women
Woo us to wander from. What worthy blessing
Can be but our imaginations
May make it ours? And here being thus together,
We are an endless mine to one another;
We are one another's wife, ever begetting
New births of love; we are father, friends,
acquaintance;
We are in one another families;
I am your heir, and you are mine. This place
Is our inheritance; no hard oppressor
Dare take this from us; here with a little patience
We shall live long, and loving; no surfeits seek us;
The hand of war hurts none here, nor the seas
Swallow their youth. Were we at liberty,
A wife might part us lawfully, or business,
Quarrels consume us, envy of ill men
Crave our acquaintance. I might sicken, cousin,
Where you should never know it, and so perish
Without your noble hand to close mine eyes,
Or prayers to the gods. A thousand chances,
Were we from hence, would sever us.

PALAMON.

You have made me –
I thank you, cousin Arcite – almost wanton
With my captivity. What a misery
It is to live abroad, and everywhere!
'Tis like a beast, methinks. I find the court here,
I am sure a more content, and all those pleasures
That woo the wills of men to vanity
I see through now, and am sufficient
To tell the world 'tis but a gaudy shadow
That old Time, as he passes by, takes with him.
What had we been old in the court of Creon,
Where sin is justice, lust and ignorance
The virtues of the great ones! Cousin Arcite,
Had not the loving gods found this place for us,
We had died as they do, ill old men, unwept,
And had their epitaphs, the people's curses.
Shall I say more?

ARCITE.

I would hear you still.

PALAMON.

Ye shall.
Is there record of any two that loved

Better than we do, Arcite?

ARCITE.

Sure there cannot.

PALAMON.

I do not think it possible our friendship
Should ever leave us.

ARCITE.

Till our deaths it cannot,

Enter EMILIA *and her* WAITING-WOMAN.

And after death our spirits shall be led
To those that love eternally. Speak on, sir.
[PALAMON *sees* EMILIA.]

EMILIA.

This garden has a world of pleasures in't.
What flow'r is this?

WOMAN.

'Tis called Narcissus, madam.

EMILIA.

That was a fair boy certain, but a fool
To love himself: were there not maids enough?

ARCITE.

Pray, forward.

PALAMON.

Yes.

EMILIA.

Or were they all hard-hearted?

WOMAN.

They could not be to one so fair.

EMILIA.

Thou wouldst not.

WOMAN.

I think I should not, madam.

EMILIA.

That's a good wench;
But take heed to your kindness, though.

WOMAN.

Why, madam?

EMILIA.

Men are mad things.

ARCITE.

Will ye go forward, cousin?

EMILIA.

Canst not thou work such flowers in
silk, wench?

WOMAN.

Yes.

EMILIA.

I'll have a gown full of 'em and of these.
This is a pretty colour, will't not do
Rarely upon a skirt, wench?

WOMAN.

Dainty, madam.

ARCITE.

Cousin, cousin, how do you, sir? Why, Palamon!

PALAMON.

Never till now was I in prison, Arcite.

ARCITE.

Why, what's the matter, man?

PALAMON.

Behold, and wonder.
By heaven, she is a goddess.

ARCITE.

[*Seeing* EMILIA]

Ha!

PALAMON.

Do reverence.
She is a goddess, Arcite.

EMILIA.

Of all flow'rs
Methinks a rose is best.

WOMAN.

Why, gentle madam?

EMILIA.

It is the very emblem of a maid.
For when the west wind courts her gently
How modestly she blows, and paints the sun
With her chaste blushes! When the north comes near her,
Rude and impatient, then like chastity
She locks her beauties in her bud again,
And leaves him to base briers.

WOMAN.

Yet, good madam,
Sometimes her modesty will blow so far
She falls for't: a maid,
If she have any honour, would be loath
To take example by her.

EMILIA.

Thou art wanton.

ARCITE.

She is wondrous fair.

PALAMON.

She is all the beauty extant.

EMILIA.

The sun grows high, let's walk in. Keep these flowers:
We'll see how mere art can come near their colours.
I am wondrous merry-hearted, I could laugh now.

WOMAN.

I could lie down, I am sure.

EMILIA.

And take one with you?

WOMAN.

That's as we bargain, madam.

EMILIA.

Well, agree then.

[*Exeunt* EMILIA *and* WOMAN.

PALAMON.

What think you of this beauty?

ARCITE.

'Tis a rare one.

PALAMON.

Is't but a rare one?

ARCITE.

Yes, a matchless beauty.

PALAMON.

Might not a man well lose himself and love her?

ARCITE.

I cannot tell what you have done. I have.
Beshrew mine eyes for't, now I feel my shackles.

PALAMON.

You love her, then?

ARCITE.

Who would not?

PALAMON.

And desire her?

ARCITE.

Before my liberty.

PALAMON.

I saw her first.

ARCITE.

That's nothing.

PALAMON.
But it shall be.
ARCITE.
I saw her too.
PALAMON.
Yes, but you must not love her.
ARCITE.
I will not as you do, to worship her,
As she is heavenly and a blessed goddess:
I love her as a woman, to enjoy her.
So both may love.
PALAMON.
You shall not love at all.
ARCITE.
Not love at all?
Who shall deny me?
PALAMON.
I that first saw her, I that took possession
First with mine eye of all those beauties
In her revealed to mankind. If thou lov'st her,
Or entertain'st a hope to blast my wishes,
Thou art a traitor, Arcite, and a fellow
False as thy title to her. Friendship, blood
And all the ties between us I disclaim
If thou once think upon her.
ARCITE.
Yes, I love her,
And if the lives of all my name lay on it,
I must do so, I love her with my soul.
If that will lose ye, farewell, Palamon:
I say again, I love, and in loving her maintain
I am as worthy and as free a lover
And have as just a title to her beauty
As any Palamon or any living
That is a man's son.
PALAMON.
Have I called thee friend?
ARCITE.
Yes, and have found me so; why are you moved thus?
Let me deal coldly with you: am not I
Part of your blood, part of your soul? You have told me
That I was Palamon and you were Arcite.
PALAMON.
Yes.
ARCITE.
Am not I liable to those affections,
Those joys, griefs, angers, fears, my friend shall suffer?
PALAMON.
Ye may be.
ARCITE.
Why then would you deal so cunningly,
So strangely, so unlike a noble kinsman,
To love alone? Speak truly, do you think me
Unworthy of her sight?
PALAMON.
No, but unjust,
If thou pursue that sight.
ARCITE.
Because another
First sees the enemy, shall I stand still
And let mine honour down, and never charge?
PALAMON.
Yes, if he be but one.
ARCITE.
But say that one
Had rather combat me?
PALAMON.
Let that one say so,
And use thy freedom; else if thou pursuest her,
Be as that cursed man that hates his country,
A branded villain.
ARCITE.
You are mad.
PALAMON.
I must be,
Till thou art worthy, Arcite: it concerns me.
And in this madness if I hazard thee
And take thy life, I deal but truly.
ARCITE.
Fie, sir.
You play the child extremely. I will love her,
I must, I ought to do so, and I dare,
And all this justly.
PALAMON.
O that now, that now
Thy false self and thy friend had but this fortune
To be one hour at liberty, and grasp
Our good swords in our hands, I would quickly teach thee
What 'twere to filch affection from another.
Thou art baser in it than a cutpurse.
Put but thy head out of this window more,
And as I have a soul, I'll nail thy life to't.
ARCITE.
Thou dar'st not, fool, thou canst not, thou art feeble.
Put my head out? I'll throw my body out,
And leap the garden, when I see her next
Enter JAILER.
And pitch between her arms to anger thee.
PALAMON.
No more; the keeper's coming; I shall live
To knock thy brains out with my shackles.
ARCITE.
Do.
JAILER.
By your leave, gentlemen.
PALAMON.
Now, honest keeper?
JAILER.
Lord Arcite, you must presently to th' duke,
The cause I know not yet.
ARCITE.
I am ready, keeper.
JAILER.
Prince Palamon, I must awhile bereave you
Of your fair cousin's company.
[*Exeunt* ARCITE *and* JAILER.
PALAMON.
And me too,
Even when you please, of life. Why is he sent for?
It may be he shall marry her, he's goodly,
And like enough the duke hath taken notice
Both of his blood and body. But his falsehood –
Why should a friend be treacherous? If that
Get him a wife so noble and so fair,
Let honest men ne'er love again. Once more
I would but see this fair one. Blessed garden,
And fruit, and flowers more blessed that still blossom

As her bright eyes shine on ye! Would I were
For all the fortune of my life hereafter
Yon little tree, yon blooming apricock!
How I would spread, and fling my wanton arms
In at her window! I would bring her fruit
Fit for the gods to feed on; youth and pleasure
Still as she tasted should be doubled on her,
And if she be not heavenly I would make her
So near the gods in nature, they should fear
her.

Enter JAILER *above.*

And then I am sure she would love me. How now,
keeper,
Where's Arcite?

JAILER.

Banished. Prince Pirithous
Obtained his liberty; but never more
Upon his oath and life must he set foot
Upon this kingdom.

PALAMON.

[*Aside.*] He's a blessed man,
He shall see Thebes again, and call to arms
The bold young men, that when he bids 'em charge
Fall on like fire. Arcite shall have a fortune,
If he dare make himself a worthy lover,
Yet in the field to strike a battle for her,
And if he lose her then, he's a cold coward.
How bravely may he bear himself to win her
If he be noble Arcite! Thousand ways.
Were I at liberty, I would do things
Of such a virtuous greatness that this lady,
This blushing virgin, should take manhood to her
And seek to ravish me.

JAILER.

My lord, for you
I have this charge too.

PALAMON.

To discharge my life?

JAILER.

No, but from this place to remove your lordship:
The windows are too open.

PALAMON.

Devils take 'em
That are so envious to me! Prithee kill me.

JAILER.

And hang for't afterward.

PALAMON.

By this good light,
Had I a sword I would kill thee.

JAILER.

Why, my lord?

PALAMON.

Thou bring'st such pelting scurvy news continually
Thou art not worthy life. I will not go.

JAILER.

Indeed you must, my lord.

PALAMON.

May I see the garden?

JAILER.

No.

PALAMON.

Then I am resolved, I will not go.

JAILER.

I must constrain you then; and for you are
dangerous,
I'll clap more irons on you.

PALAMON.

Do, good keeper.
I'll shake 'em so, ye shall not sleep,
I'll make ye a new morris. Must I go?

JAILER.

There is no remedy.

PALAMON.

Farewell, kind window.
May rude wind never hurt thee. O my lady,
If ever thou hast felt what sorrow was,
Dream how I suffer. Come; now bury me.

[*Exeunt* PALAMON *and* JAILER.

ACT II. SCENE II.

The open country.

Enter ARCITE.

ARCITE.

Banished the kingdom! 'Tis a benefit,
A mercy I must thank 'em for; but banished
The free enjoying of that face I die for,
O 'twas a studied punishment, a death
Beyond imagination! Such a vengeance
That, were I old and wicked, all my sins
Could never pluck upon me. Palamon,
Thou has the start now, thou shalt stay and see
Her bright eyes break each morning 'gainst thy
window,
And let in life into thee; thou shalt feed
Upon the sweetness of a noble beauty
That Nature ne'er exceeded, nor ne'er shall.
Good gods! What happiness has Palamon!
Twenty to one, he'll come to speak to her,
And if she be as gentle as she's fair,
I know she's his: he has a tongue will tame
Tempests, and make the wild rocks wanton.
Come what can come,
The worst is death. I will not leave the kingdom.
I know mine own is but a heap of ruins,
And no redress there. If I go, he has her.
I am resolved another shape shall make me,
Or end my fortunes. Either way I am happy:
I'll see her and be near her, or no more.

Enter four COUNTRY PEOPLE, *and one with a garland before them.*

FIRST COUNTRYMAN.

My masters, I'll be there, that's certain.

SECOND COUNTRYMAN.

And I'll be there.

THIRD COUNTRYMAN.

And I.

FOURTH COUNTRYMAN.

Why, then, have with ye, boys. 'Tis but a chiding.
Let the plough play today; I'll tickle't out
Of the jades' tails tomorrow.

FIRST COUNTRYMAN.

I am sure
To have my wife as jealous as a turkey,
But that's all one. I'll go through, let her mumble.

SECOND COUNTRYMAN.

Clap her aboard tomorrow night, and stow her,
And all's made up again.

THIRD COUNTRYMAN.

Aye, do but put
A fescue in her fist, and you shall see her
Take a new lesson out and be a good wench.

Do we all hold, against the Maying?

FOURTH COUNTRYMAN.

Hold?
What should ail us!

THIRD COUNTRYMAN.

Arcas will be there.

SECOND COUNTRYMAN.

And Sennois
And Rycas, and three better lads ne'er danced
Under green tree; and ye know what wenches, ha?
But will the dainty dominie, the schoolmaster,
Keep touch, do you think? For he does all, ye know.

THIRD COUNTRYMAN.

He'll eat a hornbook ere he fail. Go to,
The matter's too far driven between
Him and the tanner's daughter to let slip now,
And she must see the duke, and she must dance too.

FOURTH COUNTRYMAN.

Shall we be lusty!

SECOND COUNTRYMAN.

[*Dances.*] All the boys in Athens
Blow wind i' th' breech on's, and here I'll be
And there I'll be, for our town, and here again
And there again! Ha, boys, hey for the weavers!

FIRST COUNTRYMAN.

This must be done i' th' woods.

FOURTH COUNTRYMAN.

O pardon me.

SECOND COUNTRYMAN.

By any means. Our thing of learning says so,
Where he himself will edify the duke
Most parlously in our behalfs. He's excellent i' th' woods;
Bring him to th' plains, his learning makes no cry.

THIRD COUNTRYMAN.

We'll see the sports, then every man to's tackle.
And, sweet companions, let's rehearse by any means
Before the ladies see us, and do sweetly,
And God knows what may come on't.

FOURTH COUNTRYMAN.

Content;
The sports once ended, we'll perform. Away, boys, and hold!

ARCITE.

[*Comes forward.*] By your leaves, honest friends.
Pray you, whither go you?

FOURTH COUNTRYMAN.

Whither? Why, what a question's that!

ARCITE.

Yes, 'tis a question to me that know not.

THIRD COUNTRYMAN.

To the games, my friend.

SECOND COUNTRYMAN.

Where were you bred you know it not?

ARCITE.

Not far, sir.
Are there such games today?

FIRST COUNTRYMAN.

Yes, marry are there,
And such as you never saw. The duke himself
Will be in person there.

ARCITE.

What pastimes are they?

SECOND COUNTRYMAN.

Wrestling and running.
[*Aside.*] 'Tis a pretty fellow.

THIRD COUNTRYMAN.

Thou wilt not go along?

ARCITE.

Not yet, sir.

FOURTH COUNTRYMAN.

Well, sir,
Take your own time. Come, boys.

FIRST COUNTRYMAN.

My mind misgives me.
This fellow has a vengeance trick o' th' hip:
Mark how his body's made for't.

SECOND COUNTRYMAN.

I'll be hanged, though,
If he dare venture. Hang him! Plum porridge,
He wrestle? He roast eggs! Come, let's be gone, lads.

[*Exeunt the four* COUNTRYMEN.

ARCITE.

This is an offered opportunity
I durst not wish for. Well, I could have wrestled,
The best men called it excellent, and run
Swifter than wind upon a field of corn,
Curling the wealthy ears, never flew. I'll venture,
And in some poor disguise be there. Who knows
Whether my brows may not be girt with garlands,
And happiness prefer me to a place
Where I may ever dwell in sight of her?

[*Exit* ARCITE.

ACT II. SCENE III.

The prison.

Enter JAILER'S DAUGHTER *alone.*

DAUGHTER.

Why should I love this gentleman? 'Tis odds
He never will affect me; I am base,
My father the mean keeper of his prison,
And he a prince; to marry him is hopeless,
To be his whore is witless. Out upon't,
What pushes are we wenches driven to
When fifteen once has found us! First I saw him:
I, seeing, thought he was a goodly man:
He has as much to please a woman in him,
If he please to bestow it so, as ever
These eyes yet looked on. Next, I pitied him,
And so would any young wench o' my conscience
That ever dreamed, or vowed her maidenhead
To a young handsome man. Then I loved him,
Extremely loved him, infinitely loved him.
And yet he had a cousin, fair as he too.
But in my heart was Palamon, and there,
Lord, what a coil he keeps! To hear him
Sing in an evening, what a heaven it is!
And yet his songs are sad ones. Fairer spoken
Was never gentleman. When I come in
To bring him water in a morning, first
He bows his noble body, then salutes me thus:
'Fair, gentle maid, good-morrow, may thy goodness
Get thee a happy husband.' Once he kissed me.
I loved my lips the better ten days after –
Would he would do so ev'ry day! He grieves much,

And me as much to see his misery.
What should I do to make him know I love him,
For I would fain enjoy him? Say I ventured
To set him free? What says the law then? Thus much
For law, or kindred! I will do it,
And this night, or tomorrow, he shall love me.
[*Exit.*

ACT II. SCENE IV.

At the games.
Short flourish of cornets, and shouts within.
Enter THESEUS, HIPPOLYTA, PIRITHOUS, EMILIA *and* ARCITE, *disguised, with a garland, etc.*

THESEUS.
You have done worthily. I have not seen,
Since Hercules, a man of tougher sinews.
Whate'er you are, you run the best and wrestle
That these times can allow.

ARCITE.
I am proud to please you.

THESEUS.
What country bred you?

ARCITE.
This; but far off, prince.

THESEUS.
Are you a gentleman?

ARCITE.
My father said so,
And to those gentle uses gave me life.

THESEUS.
Are you his heir?

ARCITE.
His youngest, sir.

THESEUS.
Your father
Sure is a happy sire, then. What proves you?

ARCITE.
A little of all noble qualities:
I could have kept a hawk, and well have halloo'd
To a deep cry of dogs; I dare not praise
My feat in horsemanship, yet they that knew me
Would say it was my best piece; last, and greatest,
I would be thought a soldier.

THESEUS.
You are perfect.

PIRITHOUS.
Upon my soul, a proper man.

EMILIA.
He is so.

PIRITHOUS.
How do you like him, lady?

HIPPOLYTA.
I admire him:
I have not seen so young a man so noble,
If he say true, of his sort.

EMILIA.
I believe
His mother was a wondrous handsome woman:
His face methinks goes that way.

HIPPOLYTA.
But his body
And fiery mind illustrate a brave father.

PIRITHOUS.
Mark how his virtue, like a hidden sun,
Breaks through his baser garments.

HIPPOLYTA.
He's well got, sure.

THESEUS.
What made you seek this place, sir?

ARCITE.
Noble Theseus,
To purchase name, and do my ablest service
To such a well-found wonder as thy worth,
For only in thy court, of all the world,
Dwells fair-eyed Honour.

PIRITHOUS.
All his words are worthy.

THESEUS.
Sir, we are much indebted to your travel,
Nor shall you lose your wish. Pirithous,
Dispose of this fair gentleman.

PIRITHOUS.
Thanks, Theseus.
[*To Arcite.*] Whate'er you are y' are mine, and I shall give you
To a most noble service, to this lady,
This bright young virgin; pray observe her goodness;
You have honoured her fair birthday with your virtues,
And as your due y' are hers. Kiss her fair hand, sir.

ARCITE.
Sir, y' are a noble giver. Dearest beauty,
Thus let me seal my vowed faith. [*Kisses her hand.*] When your servant,
Your most unworthy creature, but offends you,
Command him die: he shall.

EMILIA.
That were too cruel.
If you deserve well, sir, I shall soon see't.
Y' are mine, and somewhat better than your rank I'll use you.

PIRITHOUS.
I'll see you furnished, and because you say
You are a horseman, I must needs entreat you
This afternoon to ride, but 'tis a rough one.

ARCITE.
I like him better, prince: I shall not then
Freeze in my saddle.

THESEUS.
Sweet, you must be ready,
And you, Emilia, and you, friend, and all,
Tomorrow by the sun to do observance
To flow'ry May in Dian's wood. Wait well, sir,
Upon your mistress. Emily, I hope
He shall not go afoot.

EMILIA.
That were a shame, sir,
While I have horses. [*To Arcite.*] Take your choice, and what
You want at any time, let me but know it.
If you serve faithfully, I dare assure you
You'll find a loving mistress.

ARCITE.
If I do not,
Let me find that my father ever hated,
Disgrace and blows.

THESEUS.
Go, lead the way: you have won it.
It shall be so; you shall receive all dues
Fit for the honour you have won; 'twere wrong else.

Sister, beshrew my heart, you have a servant
That, if I were a woman, would be master.
But you are wise.

EMILIA.

I hope too wise for that, sir.
[*Flourish. Exeunt omnes.*

ACT II. SCENE V.

The prison.
Enter JAILER'S DAUGHTER *alone.*

DAUGHTER.

Let all the dukes, and all the devils, roar:
He is at liberty. I have ventured for him,
And out I have brought him to a little wood
A mile hence. I have sent him where a cedar,
Higher than all the rest, spreads like a plane
Fast by a brook, and there he shall keep close
Till I provide him files and food, for yet
His iron bracelets are not off. O Love,
What a stout-hearted child thou art! My father
Durst better have endured cold iron than done it.
I love him, beyond love and beyond reason,
Or wit, or safety: I have made him know it.
I care not, I am desperate. If the law
Find me, and then condemn me for't, some wenches,
Some honest-hearted maids, will sing my dirge,
And tell to memory my death was noble,
Dying almost a martyr. That way he takes
I purpose is my way too. Sure he cannot
Be so unmanly as to leave me here.
If he do, maids will not so easily
Trust men again. And yet he has not thanked me
For what I have done – no, not so much as kissed me,
And that methinks is not so well. Nor scarcely
Could I persuade him to become a freeman,
He made such scruples of the wrong he did
To me, and to my father. Yet I hope,
When he considers more, this love of mine
Will take more root within him. Let him do
What he will with me, so he use me kindly,
For use me so he shall, or I'll proclaim him,
And to his face, no man. I'll presently
Provide him necessaries, and pack my clothes up,
And where there is a path of ground I'll venture,
So he be with me. By him, like a shadow,
I'll ever dwell. Within this hour the hubbub
Will be all o'er the prison: I am then
Kissing the man they look for. Farewell, father;
Get many more such prisoners, and such daughters,
And shortly you may keep yourself. Now to him.
[*Exit.*

ACT III. SCENE I.

The open country.
Cornets in sundry places. Noise and hallooing as people a-Maying. Enter ARCITE *alone.*

ARCITE.

The duke has lost Hippolyta; each took
A several laund. This is a solemn rite
They owe bloomed May, and the Athenians pay it
To th' heart of ceremony. O Queen Emilia,
Fresher than May, sweeter
Than her gold buttons on the boughs or all
Th' enameled knacks o' th' mead or garden – yea,
We challenge too the bank of any nymph
That makes the stream seem flowers! Thou, O jewel
O' th' wood, o' th' world, hast likewise blest a place
With thy sole presence, in thy rumination,
That I, poor man, might eftsoons come between
And chop on some cold thought. Thrice blessed chance
To drop on such a mistress, expectation
Most guiltless on't! Tell me, O lady Fortune,
Next after Emily my sovereign, how far
I may be proud. She takes strong note of me,
Hath made me near her; and this beauteous morn,
The prim'st of all the year, presents me with
A brace of horses: two such steeds might well
Be by a pair of kings backed, in a field
That their crowns' titles tried. Alas, alas,
Poor cousin Palamon, poor prisoner, thou
So little dream'st upon my fortune that
Thou think'st thyself the happier thing, to be
So near Emilia! Me thou deem'st at Thebes,
And therein wretched, although free. But if
Thou knew'st my mistress breathed on me, and that
I eared her language, lived in her eye – O coz,
What passion would enclose thee!

Enter PALAMON *as out of a bush, with his shackles. He bends his fist at Arcite.*

PALAMON.

Traitor kinsman,
Thou shouldst perceive my passion, if these signs
Of prisonment were off me, and this hand
But owner of a sword. By all oaths in one,
I and the justice of my love would make thee
A confessed traitor, O thou most perfidious
That ever gently looked, the void'st of honour
That e'er bore gentle token! Falsest cousin
That ever blood made kin, call'st thou her thine?
I'll prove it in my shackles, with these hands
Void of appointment, that thou liest, and art
A very thief in love, a chaffy lord,
Nor worth the name of villain – had I a sword,
And these house-clogs away.

ARCITE.

Dear cousin Palamon –

PALAMON.

Cozener Arcite, give me language such
As thou hast showed me feat.

ARCITE.

Not finding in
The circuit of my breast any gross stuff
To form me like your blazon, holds me to
This gentleness of answer: 'tis your passion
That thus mistakes, the which to you being enemy
Cannot to me be kind; honour and honesty
I cherish, and depend on, howsoe'er
You skip them in me, and with them, fair coz,
I'll maintain my proceedings. Pray be pleased
To show in generous terms your griefs, since that
Your question's with your equal, who professes
To clear his own way, with the mind and sword
Of a true gentleman.

PALAMON.
That thou durst, Arcite!
ARCITE.
My coz, my coz, you have been well advertised
How much I dare. Y' have seen me use my sword
Against th' advice of fear. Sure of another
You would not hear me doubted, but your silence
Should break out, though i' th' sanctuary.
PALAMON.
Sir,
I have seen you move in such a place which well
Might justify your manhood: you were called
A good knight and a bold. But the whole week's not fair
If any day it rain. Their valiant temper
Men lose when they incline to treachery,
And then they fight like compelled bears, would fly
Were they not tied.
ARCITE.
Kinsman, you might as well
Speak this and act it in your glass, as to
His ear which now disdains you.
PALAMON.
Come up to me,
Quit me of these cold gyves, give me a sword,
Though it be rusty, and the charity
Of one meal lend me. Come before me then,
A good sword in thy hand, and do but say
That Emily is thine, I will forgive
The trespass thou hast done me, yea my life
If then thou carry't; and brave souls in shades
That have died manly, which will seek of me
Some news from earth, they shall get none but this,
That thou art brave and noble.
ARCITE.
Be content.
Again betake you to your hawthorn house.
With counsel of the night, I will be here
With wholesome viands. These impediments
Will I file off. You shall have garments, and
Perfumes to kill the smell o' th' prison. After,
When you shall stretch yourself and say but, 'Arcite,
I am in plight,' there shall be at your choice
Both sword and armour.
PALAMON.
O you heavens, dares any
So noble bear a guilty business? None
But only Arcite. Therefore none but Arcite
In this kind is so bold.
ARCITE.
Sweet Palamon!
PALAMON.
I do embrace you and your offer. For
Your offer do't I only, sir. Your person
Without hypocrisy I may not wish
[*Wind horns off.*]
More than my sword's edge on't.
ARCITE.
You hear the horns.
Enter your musit lest this match between's
Be crossed ere met. Give me your hand. Farewell.
I'll bring you every needful thing. I pray you
Take comfort and be strong.
PALAMON.
Pray hold your promise,
And do the deed with a bent brow – most certain
You love me not; be rough with me, and pour
This oil out of your language. By this air,
I could for each word give a cuff, my stomach
Not reconciled by reason.
ARCITE.
Plainly spoken,
Yet pardon me hard language. When I spur
[*Wind horns.*]
My horse, I chide him not. Content and anger
In me have but one face. Hark, sir, they call
The scattered to the banquet: you must guess
I have an office there.
PALAMON.
Sir, your attendance
Cannot please heaven, and I know your office
Unjustly is achieved.
ARCITE.
If a good title –
I am persuaded this question, sick between's,
By bleeding must be cured. I am a suitor
That to your sword you will bequeath this plea,
And talk of it no more.
PALAMON.
But this one word:
You are going now to gaze upon my mistress,
For, note you, mine she is.
ARCITE.
Nay, then.
PALAMON.
Nay, pray you,
You talk of feeding me to breed me strength.
You are going now to look upon a sun
That strengthens what it looks on: there you have
A vantage o'er me, but enjoy't till
I may enforce my remedy. Farewell.
[*Exeunt severally.*

ACT III. SCENE II.

The open country.
Enter JAILER'S DAUGHTER *alone.*
DAUGHTER.
He has mistook the brake I meant, is gone
After his fancy. 'Tis now well nigh morning.
No matter, would it were perpetual night,
And darkness lord o' th world. Hark! 'Tis a wolf!
In me hath grief slain fear, and but for one thing
I care for nothing, and that's Palamon.
I reck not if the wolves would jaw me, so
He had this file. What if I halloo'd for him?
I cannot halloo. If I whooped, what then?
If he not answered, I should call a wolf
And do him but that service. I have heard
Strange howls this live-long night: why may't not be
They have made prey of him? He has no weapons,
He cannot run, the jingling of his gyves
Might call fell things to listen, who have in them
A sense to know a man unarmed, and can
Smell where resistance is. I'll set it down
He's torn to pieces: they howled many together
And then they fed on him. So much for that;
Be bold to ring the bell. How stand I then?
All's chared when he is gone. No, no, I lie.
My father's to be hanged for his escape,

Myself to beg, if I prized life so much
As to deny my act, but that I would not,
Should I try death by dozens. I am moped:
Food took I none these two days,
Sipped some water. I have not closed mine eyes
Save when my lids scoured off their brine. Alas,
Dissolve my life, let not my sense unsettle,
Lest I should drown, or stab, or hang myself.
O state of nature, fail together in me,
Since thy best props are warped! So which way now?
The best way is the next way to a grave:
Each errant step beside is torment. Lo,
The moon is down, the crickets chirp, the screech owl
Calls in the dawn. All offices are done
Save what I fail in. But the point is this:
An end, and that is all. [*Exit.*

ACT III. SCENE III.

The open country.

Enter ARCITE, *with meat, wine, and files.*

ARCITE.
I should be near the place. Ho, cousin Palamon!!

Enter PALAMON.

PALAMON.
Arcite?

ARCITE.
The same. I have brought you food and files.
Come forth and fear not; here's no Theseus.

PALAMON.
Nor none so honest, Arcite.

ARCITE.
That's no matter,
We'll argue that hereafter. Come, take courage,
You shall not die thus beastly; here, sir, drink,
I know you are faint; then I'll talk further with you.

PALAMON.
Arcite, thou mightst now poison me.

ARCITE.
I might;
But I must fear you first. Sit down, and good now,
No more of these vain parleys: let us not,
Having our ancient reputation with us,
Make talk for fools and cowards. To your health, etc. [*He drinks.*]

PALAMON.
Do.

ARCITE.
Pray sit down then, and let me entreat you,
By all the honesty and honour in you,
No mention of this woman, 'twill disturb us;
We shall have time enough.

PALAMON.
Well, sir, I'll pledge you.
[*He drinks.*]

ARCITE.
Drink a good hearty draught, it breeds good blood, man.
Do not you feel it thaw you?

PALAMON.
Stay, I'll tell you
After a draught or two more.

ARCITE.
Spare it not,
The duke has more, coz. Eat now.

PALAMON.
Yes. [*He eats.*]

ARCITE.
I am glad
You have so good a stomach.

PALAMON.
I am gladder
I have so good meat to't.

ARCITE.
Is't not mad lodging
Here in the wild woods, cousin?

PALAMON.
Yes for them
That have wild consciences.

ARCITE.
How tastes your victuals?
Your hunger needs no sauce, I see.

PALAMON.
Not much.
But if it did, yours is too tart. Sweet cousin,
What is this?

ARCITE.
Venison.

PALAMON.
'Tis a lusty meat.
Give me more wine. [*Arcite gives him the wine.*]
Here, Arcite, to the wenches
We have known in our days. The Lord Steward's daughter,
Do you remember her? [*He offers the wine to Arcite.*]

ARCITE.
After you, coz.

PALAMON.
She loved a black-haired man.

ARCITE.
She did so. Well, sir?

PALAMON.
And I have heard some call him Arcite, and –

ARCITE.
Out with't, 'faith.

PALAMON.
She met him in an arbor:
What did she there, coz? Play o' th' virginals?

ARCITE.
Something she did, sir.

PALAMON.
Made her groan a month for't;
Or two, or three, or ten.

ARCITE.
The Marshal's sister
Had her share too, as I remember, cousin,
Else there be tales abroad. You'll pledge her?

PALAMON.
Yes. [*He drinks.*]

ARCITE.
A pretty brown wench 'tis. There was a time
When young men went a-hunting – and a wood,
And a broad beech, and thereby hangs a tale.
Heigh ho!

PALAMON.
For Emily, upon my life! Fool,
Away with this strained mirth! I say again
That sigh was breathed for Emily. Base cousin,
Dar'st thou break first?

ARCITE.
You are wide.

PALAMON.
By heaven and earth,
There's nothing in thee honest.

ARCITE.
Then I'll leave you:
You are a beast now.

PALAMON.
As thou mak'st me, traitor.

ARCITE.
There's all things needful: files and shirts and perfumes.
I'll come again some two hours hence, and bring
That that shall quiet all.

PALAMON.
A sword and armour?

ARCITE.
Fear me not; you are now too foul; farewell.
Get off your trinkets, you shall want nought.

PALAMON.
Sirrah –

ARCITE.
I'll hear no more. [*Exit.*

PALAMON.
If he keep touch, he dies for't.
[*Exit.*

ACT III. SCENE IV.

The open country.
Enter JAILER'S DAUGHTER.

DAUGHTER.
I am very cold, and all the stars are out too,
The little stars and all, that look like aglets.
The sun has seen my folly. Palamon!
Alas, no, he's in heaven. Where am I now?
Yonder's the sea, and there's a ship: how't tumbles,
And there's a rock lies watching under water;
Now, now, it beats upon it; now, now, now!
There's a leak sprung, a sound one; how they cry!
Spoon her before the wind, you'll lose all else!
Up with a course or two, and tack about, boys!
Good-night, good-night, y' are gone. I am very hungry.
Would I could find a fine frog; he would tell me
News from all parts o' th' world; then would I make
A carack of a cockleshell, and sail
By east and north-east to the King of Pigmies,
For he tells fortunes rarely. Now my father
Twenty to one is trussed up in a trice
Tomorrow morning. I'll say never a word.

(*Sings*)
For I'll cut my green coat, a foot above my knee,
And I'll clip my yellow locks, an inch below mine eye.
Hey, nonny, nonny, nonny!
He's buy me a white cut, forth for to ride,
And I'll go seek him, through the world that is so wide.
Hey, nonny, nonny, nonny!

O for a prick now like a nightingale,
To put my breast against! I shall sleep like a top else. [*Exit.*

ACT III. SCENE V.

The open country.
Enter a SCHOOLMASTER, *four* COUNTRYMEN *and* BAVIAN, five WENCHES, *with a* TABORER.

SCHOOLMASTER.
Fie, fie,
What tediosity and disensanity
Is here among ye? Have my rudiments
Been laboured so long with ye, milked unto ye,
And, by a figure, even the very plumbroth
And marrow of my understanding laid upon ye?
And do you still cry 'where' and 'how' and 'wherefore'?
You most coarse frieze capacities, ye jean judgments,
Have I said 'thus let be,' and 'there let be,'
And 'then let be,' and no man understand me?
Proh deum, medius fidius, ye are all dunces!
For why, here stand I. Here the duke comes; there are you
Close in the thicket; the duke appears; I meet him
And unto him I utter learned things,
And many figures; he hears, and nods, and hums,
And then cries, 'Rare!', and I go forward; at length
I fling my cap up – mark there – then do you,
As once did Meleager and the boar,
Break comely out before him – like true lovers,
Cast yourselves in a body decently,
And sweetly, by a figure, trace and turn, boys.

FIRST COUNTRYMAN.
And sweetly we will do it, Master Gerald.

SECOND COUNTRYMAN.
Draw up the company. Where's the taborer?

THIRD COUNTRYMAN.
Why, Timothy!

TABORER.
Here, my mad boys, have at ye!

SCHOOLMASTER.
But, I say, where's their women?

FOURTH COUNTRYMAN.
Here's Friz and Maudlin.

SECOND COUNTRYMAN.
And little Luce with the white legs, and bouncing Barbary.

FIRST COUNTRYMAN.
And freckled Nell, that never failed her master.

SCHOOLMASTER.
Where be your ribands, maids? Swim with your bodies,
And carry it sweetly and deliverly,
And now and then a favour, and a frisk.

NELL.
Let us alone, sir.

SCHOOLMASTER.
Where's the rest o' th music?

THIRD COUNTRYMAN.
Dispersed as you commanded.

SCHOOLMASTER.
Couple then,
And see what's wanting. Where's the Bavian?
My friend, carry your tail without offence
Or scandal to the ladies; and be sure
You tumble with audacity, and manhood,
And when you bark do it with judgement.

BAVIAN.
Yes, sir

SCHOOLMASTER.
Quo usque tandem? Here is a woman wanting.

FOURTH COUNTRYMAN.
We may go whistle. All the fat's i' th' fire.

SCHOOLMASTER.
We have,
As learned authors utter, washed a tile,
We have been *fatuus*, and laboured vainly.

SECOND COUNTRYMAN.
This is that scornful piece, that scurvy hilding,
That gave her promise faithfully she would be here,
Cicely the sempster's daughter.
The next gloves that I give her shall be dogskin.
Nay, and she fail me once! You can tell, Arcas,
She swore by wine and bread she would not break.

SCHOOLMASTER.
An eel and woman,
A learnèd poet says, unless by th' tail
And with thy teeth thou hold, will either fail.
In manners this was false position.

FIRST COUNTRYMAN.
A fire ill take her! Does she flinch now?

THIRD COUNTRYMAN.
What
Shall we determine, sir?

SCHOOLMASTER.
Nothing.
Our business is become a nullity,
Yea, and a woeful, and a piteous nullity.

FOURTH COUNTRYMAN.
Now when the credit of our town lay on it,
Now to be frampel, now to piss o' th' nettle!
Go thy ways, I'll remember thee, I'll fit thee!

Enter JAILER'S DAUGHTER.

DAUGHTER.
[*Sings.*]
The George Alow came from the south,
From the coast of Barbary-a,
And there he met with brave gallants of war,
By one, by two, by three-a.
Well hailed, well hailed, you jolly gallants,
And whither now are you bound-a?
O let me have your company
Till we come to the sound-a.

There was three fools fell out about an owlet.

The one said it was an owl;
The other he said nay;
The third he said it was a hawk,
And her bells were cut away.

THIRD COUNTRYMAN.
There's a dainty mad woman, master,
Comes i' th' nick, as mad as a march hare.
If we can get her dance, we are made again:
I warrant her, she'll do the rarest gambols.

FIRST COUNTRYMAN.
A mad woman? We are made, boys.

SCHOOLMASTER.
And are you mad, good woman?

DAUGHTER.
I would be sorry else.
Give me your hand.

SCHOOLMASTER.
Why?

DAUGHTER.
I can tell your fortune.
You are a fool. Tell ten. I have posed him. Buzz.
Friend, you must eat no white bread; if you do,
Your teeth will bleed extremely. Shall we dance, ho?
I know you, y' are a tinker: sirrah tinker,
Stop no more holes but what you should.

SCHOOLMASTER.
Dii boni!
A tinker, damsel?

DAUGHTER.
Or a conjuror.
Raise me a devil now, and let him play
Qui passa, o' th' bells and bones.

SCHOOLMASTER.
Go take her,
And fluently persuade her to a peace.
Et opus exegi, quod nec Iovis ira, nec ignis.
Strike up, and lead her in.

SECOND COUNTRYMAN.
Come, lass, let's trip it.

DAUGHTER.
I'll lead.

THIRD COUNTRYMAN.
Do, do.

SCHOOLMASTER.
Persuasively, and cunningly!
[*Wind horns.*] Away, boys! I hear the horns.
Give me some meditation, and mark your cue.
[*Exeunt all but* SCHOOLMASTER.
Pallas inspire me!

Enter THESEUS, PIRITHOUS, HIPPOLYTA, EMILIA, ARCITE, *and train. A chair and stools are brought out.*

THESEUS.
This way the stag took.

SCHOOLMASTER.
Stay, and edify!

THESEUS.
What have we here?

PIRITHOUS.
Some country sport, upon my life, sir.

THESEUS.
Well, sir, go forward, we will edify.
Ladies, sit down; we'll stay it. [*They sit.*]

SCHOOLMASTER.
Thou doughty duke, all hail! All hail, sweet ladies!

THESEUS.
This is a cold beginning.

SCHOOLMASTER.
If you but favour, our country pastime made is.
We are a few of those collected here
That ruder tongues distinguish villager.
And to say verity, and not to fable,
We are a merry rout, or else a rabble
Or company, or by a figure *Chorus*,
That 'fore thy dignity will dance a morris.
And I that am the rectifier of all,
By title Pedagogus, that let fall
The birch upon the breeches of the small ones,
And humble with a ferula the tall ones,
Do here present this machine, or this frame;

And dainty duke, whose doughty dismal fame
From Dis to Daedalus, from post to pillar
Is blown abroad, help me, thy poor well-willer,
And with thy twinkling eyes look right and straight
Upon this mighty 'Morr', of mickle weight;
'Is' now comes in – which being glued together
Makes 'Morris', and the cause that we came hither,
The body of our sport of no small study.
I first appear, though rude, and raw, and muddy,
To speak before thy noble grace this tenor,
At whose great feet I offer up my penner;
The next the Lord of May, and Lady bright,
The Chambermaid and Servingman by night
That seek out silent hanging; then mine Host
And his fat Spouse, that welcomes to their cost
The gallèd Traveller, and with a beck'ning
Informs the Tapster to inflame the reck'ning;
Then the beest-eating Clown, and next the Fool,
The Bavian with long tail, and eke long tool,
Cum multis aliis that make a dance.
Say 'Aye,' and all shall presently advance.

THESEUS.

Aye, aye, by any means, dear dominie.

PIRITHOUS.

Produce.

SCHOOLMASTER.

Intrate, filii! Come forth and foot it.

Knock. Enter the DANCE. *Music. They dance.*

Ladies, if we have been merry
And have pleased ye with a derry,
And a derry, and a down,
Say the Schoolmaster's no Clown.
Duke, if we have pleased thee too
And have done as good boys should do,
Give us but a tree or twain
For a maypole, and again,
Ere another year run out,
We'll make thee laugh and all this rout.

THESEUS.

Take twenty, dominie. [*To Hippolyta.*] How does my sweetheart?

HIPPOLYTA.

Never so pleased, sir.

EMILIA.

'Twas an excellent dance,
And for a preface I never heard a better.

THESEUS.

Schoolmaster, I thank you. One see 'em all rewarded.

PIRITHOUS.

[*Gives money.*] And here's something to paint your pole withal.

THESEUS.

Now to our sports again.

SCHOOLMASTER.

May the stag thou hunt'st stand long,
And thy dogs be swift and strong,
May they kill him without lets,
And the ladies eat his dowsets! [*Wind horns.*]
[*To the dancers.*] Come, we are all made. *Dii deaeque omnes!*
Ye have danced rarely, wenches. [*Exeunt.*

ACT III. SCENE VI.

The open country.

Enter PALAMON *from the bush.*

PALAMON.

About this hour my cousin gave his faith
To visit me again, and with him bring
Two swords and two good armours: if he fail,
He's neither man nor soldier. When he left me,
I did not think a week could have restored
My lost strength to me, I was grown so low
And crestfall'n with my wants. I thank thee, Arcite,
Thou art yet a fair foe, and I feel myself,
With this refreshing, able once again
To outdure danger. To delay it longer
Would make the world think when it comes to hearing
That I lay fatting like a swine to fight,
And not a soldier. Therefore this blest morning
Shall be the last; and that sword he refuses,
If it but hold, I kill him with: 'tis justice.
So love and Fortune for me!

Enter ARCITE *with armours and swords.*

O good-morrow!

ARCITE.

Good-morrow, noble kinsman.

PALAMON.

I have put you
To too much pains, sir.

ARCITE.

That too much, fair cousin,
Is but a debt to honour, and my duty.

PALAMON.

Would you were so in all, sir! I could wish ye
As kind a kinsman as you force me find
A beneficial foe, that my embraces
Might thank ye, not my blows.

ARCITE.

I shall think either,
Well done, a noble recompense.

PALAMON.

Then I shall quit you.

ARCITE.

Defy me in these fair terms, and you show
More than a mistress to me. No more anger,
As you love anything that's honourable!
We were not bred to talk, man. When we are armed
And both upon our guards, then let our fury,
Like meeting of two tides, fly strongly from us,
And then to whom the birthright of this beauty
Truly pertains – without upbraidings, scorns,
Despisings of our persons, and such poutings
Fitter for girls and schoolboys – will be seen,
And quickly, yours or mine. Will't please you arm, sir?
Or if you feel yourself not fitting yet
And furnished with your old strength, I'll stay, cousin,
And ev'ry day discourse you into health,
As I am spared. Your person I am friends with,
And I could wish I had not said I loved her,
Though I had died. But loving such a lady
And justifying my love, I must not fly from't.

PALAMON.

Arcite, thou art so brave an enemy
That no man but thy cousin's fit to kill thee.

I am well and lusty. Choose your arms.
ARCITE.
Choose you, sir.
PALAMON.
Wilt thou exceed in all, or dost thou do it
To make me spare thee?
ARCITE.
If you think so, cousin,
You are deceived, for as I am a soldier
I will not spare you.
PALAMON.
That's well said.
ARCITE.
You'll find it.
PALAMON.
Then as I am an honest man and love,
With all the justice of affection
I'll pay thee soundly. This I'll take.
[*Chooses an armour.*]
ARCITE.
That's mine then.
[*Takes the other.*]
I'll arm you first.
PALAMON.
Do. [*Arcite arms him.*] Pray
thee tell me, cousin,
Where gott'st thou this good armour?
ARCITE.
'Tis the duke's,
And to say true, I stole it. Do I pinch you?
PALAMON.
No.
ARCITE.
Is't not too heavy?
PALAMON.
I have worn a lighter,
But I shall make it serve.
ARCITE.
I'll buckle't close
PALAMON.
By any means.
ARCITE.
You care not for a grand guard?
PALAMON.
No, no, we'll use no horses. I perceive
You would fain be at that fight.
ARCITE.
I am indifferent.
PALAMON.
'Faith, so am I. Good cousin, thrust the buckle
Through far enough.
ARCITE.
I warrant you.
PALAMON.
My casque now.
ARCITE.
Will you fight bare-armed?
PALAMON.
We shall be the nimbler.
ARCITE.
But use your gauntlets, though. Those are o'th'
least:
Prithee take mine, good cousin.
PALAMON.
Thank you, Arcite.
How do I look, am I fall'n much away?
ARCITE.
'Faith, very little: love has used you kindly.
PALAMON.
I warrant thee, I'll strike home.
ARCITE.
Do, and spare not;
I'll give you cause, sweet cousin.
PALAMON.
Now to you, sir.
[*He arms* ARCITE.] Methinks this armour's very
like that, Arcite,
Thou wor'st that day the three kings fell, but lighter.
ARCITE.
That was a very good one, and that day
I well remember you outdid me, cousin.
I never saw such valour: when you charged
Upon the left wing of the enemy,
I spurred hard to come up, and under me
I had a right good horse.
PALAMON.
You had indeed:
A bright bay, I remember.
ARCITE.
Yes, but all
Was vainly laboured in me: you outwent me,
Nor could my wishes reach you. Yet a little
I did by imitation.
PALAMON.
More by virtue;
You are modest, cousin.
ARCITE.
When I saw you charge first,
Methought I heard a dreadful clap of thunder
Break from the troop.
PALAMON.
But still before that flew
The lightning of your valour. Stay a little,
Is not this piece too strait?
ARCITE.
No, no, 'tis well.
PALAMON.
I would have nothing hurt thee but my sword,
A bruise would be dishonour.
ARCITE.
Now I am perfect.
PALAMON.
Stand off then.
ARCITE.
Take my sword, I hold it better.
PALAMON.
I thank ye. No, keep it, your life lies on it.
Here's one: if it but hold, I ask no more
For all my hopes. My cause and honour guard me!
ARCITE.
And me my love!
[*They bow several ways; then advance and stand.*]
Is there ought else to say?
PALAMON.
This only, and no more. Thou art mine aunt's son,
And that blood we desire to shed is mutual,
In me thine, and in thee mine. My sword
Is in my hand, and if thou kill'st me
The gods and I forgive thee. If there be
A place prepared for those that sleep in honour,
I wish his weary soul that falls may win it.
Fight bravely, cousin. Give me thy noble hand.

ARCITE.

Here, Palamon. [*They take hands.*] This hand shall never more
Come near thee with such friendship.

PALAMON.

I commend thee.

ARCITE.

If I fall, curse me, and say I was a coward,
For none but such dare die in these just trials.
Once more farewell, my cousin.

PALAMON.

Farewell, Arcite.

[*They fight. Horns within; they stand.*]

ARCITE.

Lo, cousin, lo, our folly has undone us.

PALAMON.

Why?

ARCITE.

This is the duke, a-hunting as I told you:
If we be found, we are wretched. O retire
For honour's sake, and safety, presently
Into your bush again. Sir, we shall find
Too many hours to die in, gentle cousin.
If you be seen, you perish instantly
For breaking prison, and I, if you reveal me,
For my contempt; then all the world will scorn us,
And say we had a noble difference,
But base disposers of it.

PALAMON.

No, no, cousin,
I will no more be hidden, nor put off
This great adventure to a second trial.
I know your cunning, and I know your cause.
He that faints now, shame take him: put thyself
Upon thy present guard.

ARCITE.

You are not mad?

PALAMON.

Or I will make th' advantage of this hour
Mine own, and what to come shall threaten me
I fear less than my fortune. Know, weak cousin,
I love Emilia, and in that I'll bury
Thee, and all crosses else.

ARCITE.

Then come what can come,
Thou shalt know, Palamon, I dare as well
Die as discourse or sleep. Only this fears me:
The law will have the honour of our ends.
Have at thy life!

PALAMON.

Look to thine own well, Arcite.

[*They fight again. Horns.*]

Enter THESEUS, HIPPOLYTA, EMILIA, PIRITHOUS *and train.*

THESEUS.

What ignorant and mad malicious traitors
Are you, that 'gainst the tenor of my laws
Are making battle, thus like knights appointed,
Without my leave, and officers of arms?
By Castor, both shall die.

PALAMON.

Hold thy word, Theseus.
We are certainly both traitors, both despisers
Of thee, and of thy goodness. I am Palamon
That cannot love thee, he that broke thy prison:
Think well what that deserves; and this is Arcite:
A bolder traitor never trod thy ground,
A falser ne'er seemed friend. This is the man
Was begged and banished, this is he contemns thee
And what thou dar'st do; and in this disguise
Against thy own edict follows thy sister,
That fortunate bright star, the fair Emilia,
Whose servant – if there be a right in seeing,
And first bequeathing of the soul to – justly
I am, and which is more, dares think her his.
This treachery, like a most trusty lover,
I called him now to answer. If thou be'st
As thou art spoken, great and virtuous,
The true decider of all injuries,
Say, 'Fight again,' and thou shalt see me, Theseus,
Do such a justice thou thyself wilt envy.
Then take me life, I'll woo thee to't.

PIRITHOUS.

O heaven,
What more than man is this!

THESEUS.

I have sworn.

ARCITE.

We seek not
Thy breath of mercy, Theseus: 'tis to me
A thing as soon to die as thee to say it,
And no more moved. Where this man calls me traitor,
Let me say thus much: if in love be treason
In service of so excellent a beauty,
As I love most, and in that faith will perish,
As I have brought my life here to confirm it,
As I have served her truest, worthiest,
As I dare kill this cousin that denies it,
So let me be most traitor, and ye please me.
For scorning thy edict, duke, ask that lady
Why she is fair, and why her eyes command me
Stay here to love her; and if she say 'traitor',
I am a villain fit to lie unburied.

PALAMON.

Thou shalt have pity of us both, O Theseus,
If unto neither thou show mercy. Stop,
As thou art just, thy noble ear against us;
As thou art valiant, for thy cousin's soul
Whose twelve strong labours crown his memory,
Let's die together, at one instant, duke:
Only a little let him fall before me,
That I may tell my soul he shall not have her.

THESEUS.

I grant your wish, for to say true your cousin
Has ten times more offended, for I gave him
More mercy than you found, sir, your offences
Being no more than his. None here speak for 'em,
For ere the sun set both shall sleep forever.

HIPPOLYTA.

Alas the pity! Now or never, sister,
Speak not to be denied: that face of yours
Will bear the curses else of after ages
For these lost cousins.

EMILIA.

In my face, dear sister,
I find no anger to 'em, nor no ruin:
The misadventure of their own eyes kill 'em.
Yet that I will be woman, and have pity,
My knees shall grow to th' ground but I'll get mercy.
Help me, dear sister; in a deed so virtuous

The powers of all women will be with us.
[*They kneel.*]
Most royal brother!

HIPPOLYTA.
Sir, by our tie of marriage!

EMILIA.
By your own spotless honour!

HIPPOLYTA.
By that faith,
That fair hand, and that honest heart you gave me!

EMILIA.
By that you would have pity in another,
By your own virtues infinite!

HIPPOLITA.
By valour,
By all the chaste nights I have ever pleased you!

THESEUS.
These are strange conjurings.

PIRITHOUS.
Nay, then I'll in too:
[*He kneels.*]
By all our friendship, sir, by all our dangers,
By all you love most – wars, and this sweet lady!

EMILIA.
By that you would have trembled to deny
A blushing maid!

HIPPOLYTA.
By your own eyes; by strength,
In which you swore I went beyond all women,
Almost all men, and yet I yielded, Theseus.

PIRITHOUS.
To crown all this: by your most noble soul,
Which cannot want due mercy! I beg first.

HIPPOLYTA.
Next hear my prayers.

EMILIA.
Last let me entreat, sir.

PIRITHOUS.
For mercy!

HIPPOLYTA.
Mercy!

EMILIA.
Mercy on these princes!

THESEUS.
Ye make my faith reel. [*They rise.*] Say I felt
Compassion to 'em both, how would you place it?

EMILIA.
Upon their lives – but with their banishments.

THESEUS.
You are a right woman, sister. You have pity,
But want the understanding where to use it.
If you desire their lives, invent a way
Safer than banishment. Can these two live
And have the agony of love about 'em,
And not kill one another? Every day
They'd fight about you, hourly bring your honour
In public question with their swords. Be wise then,
And here forget 'em. It concerns your credit,
And my oath equally. I have said they die:
Better they fall by th' law than one another.
Bow not my honour.

EMILIA.
O my noble brother,
That oath was rashly made, and in your anger;
Your reason will not hold it. If such vows
Stand for express will, all the world must perish.
Beside, I have another oath, 'gainst yours,
Of more authority, I am sure more love,
Not made in passion neither, but good heed.

THESEUS.
What is it, sister?

PIRITHOUS.
Urge it home, brave lady.

EMILIA.
That you would ne'er deny me anything
Fit for my modest suit, and your free granting.
I tie you to your word now: if ye fall in't,
Think how you maim your honour –
For now I am set a-begging, sir, I am deaf
To all but your compassion – how their lives
Might breed the ruin of my name, opinion.
Shall anything that loves me perish for me?
That were a cruel wisdom. Do men prune
The straight young boughs that blush with thousand blossoms
Because they may be rotten? O duke Theseus,
The goodly mothers that have groaned for these,
And all the longing maids that ever loved,
If your vow stand, shall curse me and my beauty,
And in their funeral songs for these two cousins
Despise my cruelty, and cry woe worth me,
Till I am nothing but the scorn of women.
For heaven's sake save their lives, and banish 'em.

THESEUS.
On what conditions?

EMILIA.
Swear 'em never more
To make me their contention, or to know me,
To tread upon thy dukedom, and to be,
Wherever they shall travel, ever strangers
To one another.

PALAMON.
I'll be cut a-pieces
Before I take this oath: forget I love her?
O all ye gods despise me then! Thy banishment
I not mislike, so we may fairly carry
Our swords and cause along. Else never trifle,
But take our lives, duke: I must love and will,
And for that love must and dare kill this cousin
On any piece the earth has.

THESEUS.
Will you, Arcite,
Take these conditions?

PALAMON.
He's a villain then.

PIRITHOUS.
These are men.

ARCITE.
No, never, duke. 'Tis worse to me than begging
To take my life so basely. Though I think
I never shall enjoy her, yet I'll preserve
The honour of affection, and die for her,
Make death a devil.

THESEUS.
What may be done? For now I feel compassion.

PIRITHOUS.
Let it not fall again, sir.

THESEUS.
Say, Emilia,
If one of them were dead, as one must, are you
Content to take th' other to your husband?

They cannot both enjoy you. They are princes
As goodly as your own eyes, and as noble
As ever Fame yet spoke of. Look upon 'em,
And if you can love, end this difference.
I give consent; are you content too, princes?

BOTH COUSINS.

With all our souls.

THESEUS.

He that she refuses
Must die then.

BOTH COUSINS.

Any death thou canst invent, duke.

PALAMON.

If I fall from that mouth, I fall with favour,
And lovers yet unborn shall bless my ashes.

ARCITE.

If she refuse me, yet my grave will wed me,
And soldiers sing my epitaph.

THESEUS.

Make choice, then.

EMILIA.

I cannot, sir, they are both too excellent:
For me, a hair shall never fall of these men.

HIPPOLYTA.

What will become of 'em?

THESEUS.

Thus I ordain it,
And by mine honour, once again, it stands,
Or both shall die. You shall both to your country,
And each within this month, accompanied
With three fair knights, appear again in this place,
In which I'll plant a pyramid; and whether,
Before us that are here, can force his cousin
By fair and knightly strength to touch the pillar,
He shall enjoy her; the other lose his head,
And all his friends. Nor shall he grudge to fall,
Nor think he dies with interest in this lady.
Will this content ye?

PALAMON.

Yes. Here, cousin Arcite,
I am friends again, till that hour.

ARCITE.

I embrace ye.

THESEUS.

Are you content, sister?

EMILIA.

Yes, I must, sir,
Else both miscarry.

THESEUS.

Come, shake hands again, then,
And take heed, as you are gentlemen, this quarrel
Sleep till the hour prefixed, and hold your course.

PALAMON.

We dare not fail thee, Theseus.

THESEUS.

Come, I'll give ye
Now usage like to princes, and to friends.
When ye return, who wins I'll settle here,
Who loses – yet I'll weep upon his bier.

[*Exeunt.*

ACT IV. SCENE I.

The prison.

Enter JAILER *and his* FRIEND.

JAILER.

Hear you no more, was nothing said of me
Concerning the escape of Palamon?
Good sir, remember.

FRIEND.

Nothing that I heard,
For I came home before the business
Was fully ended. Yet I might perceive,
Ere I departed, a great likelihood
Of both their pardons. For Hippolyta
And fair-eyed Emily upon their knees
Begged with such handsome pity that the duke
Methought stood staggering, whether he
should follow
His rash oath or the sweet compassion
Of those two ladies; and to second them
That truly noble prince Pirithous,
Half his own heart, set in too, that I hope
All shall be well. Neither heard I one question
Of your name, or his 'scape.

Enter SECOND FRIEND.

JAILER.

Pray heaven it hold so.

SECOND FRIEND.

Be of good comfort, man; I bring you news,
Good news.

JAILER.

They are welcome.

SECOND FRIEND.

Palamon has cleared you,
And got your pardon, and discovered how
And by whose means he escaped, which was
your daughter's,
Whose pardon is procured too, and the prisoner,
Not to be held ungrateful to her goodness,
Has given a sum of money to her marriage,
A large one I'll assure you.

JAILER.

Ye are a good man
And ever bring good news.

FIRST FRIEND.

How was it ended?

SECOND FRIEND.

Why, as it should be: they that never begged
But they prevailed had their suits fairly granted.
The prisoners have their lives.

FIRST FRIEND.

I knew 'twould be so.

SECOND FRIEND.

But there be new conditions, which you'll hear of
At better time.

JAILER.

I hope they are good.

SECOND FRIEND.

They are honourable;
How good they'll prove I know not.

Enter WOOER.

FIRST FRIEND.

'Twill be known.

WOOER.

Alas, sir, where's your daughter?

JAILER.

Why do you ask?

WOOER.
O sir, when did you see her?
SECOND FRIEND.
How he looks!
JAILER.
This morning.
WOOER.
Was she well? Was she in health?
Sir, when did she sleep?
FIRST FRIEND.
These are strange questions.
JAILER.
I do not think she was very well, for now
You make me mind her, but this very day
I asked her questions, and she answered me
So far from what she was, so childishly,
So sillily, as if she were a fool,
An innocent, and I was very angry.
But what of her, sir?
WOOER.
Nothing but my pity;
But you must know it, and as good by me
As by another that less loves her.
JAILER.
Well, sir?
FIRST FRIEND.
Not right?
SECOND FRIEND.
Not well?
WOOER.
No, sir, not well.
'Tis too true, she is mad.
FIRST FRIEND.
It cannot be.
WOOER.
Believe you'll find it so.
JAILER.
I half suspected
What you have told me: the gods comfort her!
Either this was her love to Palamon,
Or fear of my miscarrying on his 'scape,
Or both.
WOOER.
'Tis likely.
JAILER.
But why all this haste, sir?
WOOER.
I'll tell you quickly. As I late was angling
In the great lake that lies behind the palace,
From the far shore, thick set with reeds and sedges,
As patiently I was attending sport,
I heard a voice, a shrill one, and attentive
I gave my ear, when I might well perceive
'Twas one that sung, and by the smallness of it
A boy or woman. I then left my angle
To his own skill, came near, but yet perceived not
Who made the sound, the rushes and the reeds
Had so encompassed it. I laid me down
And listened to the words she sung, for then,
Through a small glade cut by the fishermen,
I saw it was your daughter.
JAILER.
Pray go on, sir.
WOOER.
She sung much, but no sense. Only I heard her
Repeat this often: 'Palamon is gone,
Is gone to th' wood to gather mulberries;
I'll find him out tomorrow.'
FIRST FRIEND.
Pretty soul!
WOOER.
'His shackles will betray him, he'll be taken,
And what shall I do then? I'll bring a bevy,
A hundred black-eyed maids, that love as I do,
With chaplets on their heads of daffadillies,
With cherry lips, and cheeks of damask roses,
And all we'll dance an antic 'fore the duke,
And beg his pardon.' Then she talked of you, sir,
That you must lose your head tomorrow morning,
And she must gather flowers to bury you,
And see the house made handsome. Then she sung
Nothing but, 'Willow, willow, willow,' and between
Ever was, 'Palamon, fair Palamon,'
And, 'Palamon was a tall young man.' The place
Was knee-deep where she sat; her careless tresses
A wreath of bulrush rounded; about her stuck
Thousand fresh water flowers of several colours –
That methought she appeared like the fair nymph
That feeds the lake with waters, or as Iris
Newly dropped down from heaven. Rings she made
Of rushes that grew by, and to 'em spoke
The prettiest posies: 'Thus our true love's tied,'
'This you may loose, not me,' and many a one.
And then she wept, and sung again, and sighed,
And with the same breath smiled, and kissed her hand.
SECOND FRIEND.
Alas, what pity it is!
WOOER.
I made in to her.
She saw me, and straight sought the flood; I saved her,
And set her safe to land – when presently
She slipped away, and to the city made,
With such a cry, and swiftness, that believe me
She left me far behind her. Three or four
I saw from far off cross her: one of 'em
I knew to be your brother; where she stayed,
And fell, scarce to be got away. I left them with her,
Enter BROTHER, DAUGHTER *and others.*
And hither came to tell you. Here they are.
DAUGHTER.
[*Sings.*]
May you never more enjoy the light, etc.
Is not this a fine song?
BROTHER.
O, a very fine one.
DAUGHTER.
I can sing twenty more.
BROTHER.
I think you can.
DAUGHTER.
Yes, truly can I. I can sing 'The Broom'
And 'Bonny Robin'. Are not you a tailor?
BROTHER.
Yes.
DAUGHTER.
Where's my wedding gown?
BROTHER.
I'll bring it tomorrow.

DAUGHTER.
Do, very rearly, I must be abroad else
To call the maids, and pay the minstrels,
For I must lose my maidenhead by cocklight:
'Twill never thrive else.
[*Sings.*]
O fair, O sweet, etc.

BROTHER.
You must e'en take it patiently.

JAILER.
'Tis true.

DAUGHTER.
Good-e'en, good men, pray did you ever hear
Of one young Palamon?

JAILER.
Yes, wench, we know him.

DAUGHTER.
Is't not a fine young gentleman?

JAILER.
'Tis, love.

BROTHER.
By no mean cross her, she is then distempered
Far worse than now she shows.

FIRST FRIEND.
Yes, he's a fine man.

DAUGHTER.
O, is he so? You have a sister!

FIRST FRIEND.
Yes.

DAUGHTER.
But she shall never have him, tell her so,
For a trick that I know. Y' had best look to her,
For if she see him once, she's gone, she's done,
And undone in an hour. All the young maids
Of our town are in love with him, but I laugh at 'em
And let 'em all alone. Is't not a wise course?

FIRST FRIEND.
Yes.

DAUGHTER.
There is at least two hundred now with child by him,
There must be four; yet I keep close for all this,
Close as a cockle; and all these must be boys –
He has the trick on't – and at ten years old
They must be all gelt for musicians,
And sing the wars of Theseus.

SECOND FRIEND.
This is strange.

DAUGHTER.
As ever you heard, but say nothing.

FIRST FRIEND.
No.

DAUGHTER.
They come from all parts of the dukedom to him.
I'll warrant ye, he had not so few last night
As twenty to dispatch: he'll tickle 't up
In two hours, if his hand be in.

JAILER.
She's lost
Past all cure.

BROTHER.
Heaven forbid, man.

DAUGHTER.
Come hither, you are a wise man.

FIRST FRIEND.
Does she know him?

SECOND FRIEND.
No, would she did.

DAUGHTER.
You are master of a ship?

JAILER.
Yes.

DAUGHTER.
Where's your compass?

JAILER.
Here.

DAUGHTER.
Set it to th' north.
And now direct your course to th' wood, where Palamon
Lies longing for me. For the tackling let me alone.
Come weigh, my hearts, cheerly all! O, O, O, 'tis up!
The wind's fair: top the bowling! Out with the mainsail!
Where's your whistle, master?

BROTHER.
Let's get her in.

JAILER.
Up to the top, boy!

BROTHER.
Where's the pilot?

FIRST FRIEND.
Here.

DAUGHTER.
What ken'st thou?

SECOND FRIEND.
A fair wood.

DAUGHTER.
Bear for it, master! Tack about!
[*Sings.*]
When Cynthia wlth her borrowed light, etc.
[*Exeunt.*

ACT IV. SCENE II.

The palace of Theseus.
Enter EMILIA *alone, with two pictures.*

EMILIA.
Yet I may bind those wounds up, that must open
And bleed to death for my sake else: I'll choose,
And end their strife. Two such young handsome men
Shall never fall for me; their weeping mothers,
Following the dead cold ashes of their sons,
Shall never curse my cruelty. Good heaven,
What a sweet face has Arcite! If wise Nature
With all her best endowments, all those beauties
She sows into the births of noble bodies,
Were here a mortal woman, and had in her
The coy denials of young maids, yet doubtless
She would run mad for this man. What an eye,
Of what a fiery sparkle, and quick sweetness,
Has this young prince! Here Love himself sits smiling:
Just such another wanton Ganymede
Set Jove a-fire with and enforced the god
Snatch up the goodly boy and set him by him,
A shining constellation. What a brow
Of what a spacious majesty he carries –
Arched like the great-eyed Juno's, but far sweeter,
Smoother than Pelops' shoulder! Fame and Honour

Methinks from hence, as from a promontory
Pointed in heaven, should clap their wings and sing
To all the underworld the loves and fights
Of gods and such men near 'em. Palamon
Is but his foil, to him a mere dull shadow:
He's swarth, and meagre, of an eye as heavy
As if he had lost his mother; a still temper,
No stirring in him, no alacrity,
Of all this spritely sharpness not a smile.
Yet these that we count errors may become him:
Narcissus was a sad boy, but a heavenly.
O who can find the bent of woman's fancy?
I am a fool, my reason is lost in me,
I have no choice, and I have lied so lewdly
That women ought to beat me. On my knees
I ask thy pardon, Palamon: thou art alone,
And only beautiful, and these the eyes,
These the bright lamps of beauty, that command
And threaten Love, and what young maid dare cross 'em?
What a bold gravity, and yet inviting,
Has this brown manly face! O Love, this only
From this hour is complexion. Lie there, Arcite,
Thou art a changeling to him, a mere gypsy,
And this the noble body. I am sotted,
Utterly lost, my virgin's faith has fled me!
For if my brother but even now had asked me
Whether I loved, I had run mad for Arcite;
Now if my sister, more for Palamon.
Stand both together: now come ask me, brother.
Alas, I know not. Ask me now, sweet sister.
I may go look. What a mere child is Fancy,
That having two fair gawds of equal sweetness
Cannot distinguish, but must cry for both!

Enter a GENTLEMAN.

How now, sir?

GENTLEMAN.

From the noble duke your brother,
Madam, I bring you news: the knights are come.

EMILIA.

To end the quarrel?

GENTLEMAN.

Yes.

EMILIA.

Would I might end first!
What sins have I committed, chaste Diana,
That my unspotted youth must now be soiled
With blood of princes, and my chastity
Be made the altar where the lives of lovers,
Two greater and two better never yet
Made mothers joy, must be the sacrifice
To my unhappy beauty?

Enter THESEUS, HIPPOLYTA, PIRITHOUS *and* ATTENDANTS.

THESEUS.

Bring 'em in
Quickly: by any means, I long to see 'em.
Your two contending lovers are returned,
And with them their fair knights. Now, my fair sister,
You must love one of them.

EMILIA.

I had rather both,
So neither for my sake should fall untimely.

Enter a MESSENGER.

THESEUS.

Who saw 'em?

PIRITHOUS.

I a while.

GENTLEMAN.

And I.

THESEUS.

From whence come you, sir?

MESSENGER.

From the knights.

THESEUS.

Pray speak,
You that have seen them, what they are.

MESSENGER.

I will, sir.
And truly what I think. Six braver spirits
Than these they have brought, if we judge by the outside,
I never saw nor read of. He that stands
In the first place with Arcite, by his seeming
Should be a stout man, by his face a prince.
His very looks so say him: his complexion
Nearer a brown than black; stern, and yet noble,
Which shows him hardy, fearless proud of dangers;
The circles of his eyes show fire within him,
And as a heated lion so he looks;
His hair hangs long behind him, black and shining
Like ravens' wings; his shoulders broad and strong,
Armed long and round, and on his thigh a sword
Hung by a curious baldric, when he frowns
To seal his will with: better o' my conscience
Was never soldier's friend.

THESEUS.

Thou hast well described him.

PIRITHOUS.

Yet a great deal short,
Methinks, of him that's first with Palamon.

THESEUS.

Pray speak him, friend.

PIRITHOUS.

I guess he is a prince too,
And if it may be, greater; for his show
Has all the ornament of honour in't.
He's somewhat bigger than the knight he spoke of,
But of a face far sweeter. His complexion
Is, as a ripe grape, ruddy. He has felt
Without doubt what he fights for, and so apter
To make this cause his own. In's face appears
All the fair hopes of what he undertakes,
And when he's angry, then a settled valour,
Not tainted with extremes, runs through his body
And glides his arm to brave things. Fear he cannot,
He shows no such soft temper. His head's yellow,
Hard-haired, and curled, thick twined like ivy tods,
Not to undo with thunder. In his face
The livery of the warlike maid appears,
Pure red and white, for yet no beard has blest him;
And in his rolling eyes sits Victory,
As if she ever meant to court his valour.
His nose stands high, a character of honour;
His red lips, after fights, are fit for ladies.

EMILIA.

Must these men die too?

PIRITHOUS.
When he speaks, his tongue
Sounds like a trumpet. All his lineaments
Are as a man would wish 'em, strong and clean.
He wears a well-steeled axe, the staff of gold.
His age some five and twenty.

MESSENGER.
There's another
A little man, but of a tough soul, seeming
As great as any: fairer promises
In such a body yet I never looked on.

PIRITHOUS.
O, he that's freckle-faced?

MESSENGER.
The same, my lord.
Are they not sweet ones?

PIRITHOUS.
Yes, they are well.

MESSENGER.
Methinks,
Being so few and well disposed, they show
Great and fine art in nature. He's white-haired,
Not wanton white, but such a manly colour
Next to an auburn; tough, and nimble set,
Which shows an active soul. His arms are brawny,
Lined with strong sinews: to the shoulder-piece
Gently they swell, like women new-conceived,
Which speaks him prone to labour, never fainting
Under the weight of arms; stout-hearted, still.
But when he stirs, a tiger. He's grey-eyed,
Which yields compassion where he conquers; sharp
To spy advantages, and where he finds 'em
He's swift to make 'em his. He does no wrongs,
Nor takes none. He's round-faced, and when he smiles
He shows a lover, when he frowns a soldier.
About his head he wears the winner's oak,
And in it stuck the favour of his lady.
His age some six and thirty. In his hand
He bears a charging staff, embossed with silver.

THESEUS.
Are they all thus?

PIRITHOUS.
They are all the sons of Honour.

THESEUS.
Now as I have a soul I long to see 'em!
Lady, you shall see men fight now.

HIPPOLYTA.
I wish it,
But not the cause, my lord. They would show
Bravely about the titles of two kingdoms;
'Tis pity Love should be so tyrannous.
O my soft-hearted sister, what think you?
Weep not till they weep blood. Wench, it must be.

THESEUS.
You have steeled 'em with your beauty. Honoured friend,
To you I give the field: pray order it
Fitting the persons that must use it.

PIRITHOUS.
Yes, sir.

THESEUS.
Come, I'll go visit 'em: I cannot stay,
Their fame has fired me so. Till they appear,
Good friend, be royal.

PIRITHOUS.
There shall want no bravery.

EMILIA.
Poor wench, go weep, for whosoever wins
Loses a noble cousin, for thy sins. [*Exeunt.*

ACT IV. SCENE III.

The prison.

Enter JAILER, WOOER, DOCTOR.

DOCTOR.
Her distraction is more at some time of the moon than at other some, is it not?

JAILER.
She is continually in a harmless distemper, sleeps little, altogether without appetite, save often drinking, dreaming of another world, and a better; and what broken piece of matter soe'er she's about, the name Palamon lards it, that she farces ev'ry business withal, fits it to every question.

Enter DAUGHTER.

Look where she comes, you shall perceive her behaviour.

DAUGHTER.
I have forgot it quite. The burden on't was 'Down-a down-a', and penned by no worse man than Geraldo, Emilia's schoolmaster. He's as fantastical too, as ever he may go upon's legs, for in the next world will Dido see Palamon, and then will she be out of love with Aeneas.

DOCTOR.
What stuffs here? Poor soul!

JAILER.
E'en thus all day long.

DAUGHTER.
Now for this charm that I told you of, you must bring a piece of silver on the tip of your tongue, or no ferry. Then if it be your chance to come where the blessed spirits – as there's a sight now – we maids that have our livers perished, cracked to pieces with love, we shall come there, and do nothing all day long but pick flowers with Proserpine. Then will I make Palamon a nosegay, then let him mark me – then!

DOCTOR.
How prettily she's amiss! Note her a little further.

DAUGHTER.
'Faith, I'll tell you, sometime we go to barley-break, we of the blessed. Alas, 'tis a sore life they have i' th' other place, such burning, frying, boiling, hissing, howling, chatt'ring, cursing – O they have shrewd measure; take heed! If one be mad, or hang or drown themselves, thither they go, Jupiter bless us, and there shall we be put in a cauldron of lead and usurers' grease, amongst a whole million of cut-purses, and there boil like a gammon of bacon that will never be enough. [*Exit.*

DOCTOR.
How her brain coins!

Enter DAUGHTER.

DAUGHTER.
Lords and courtiers, that have got maids with

child, they are in this place, they shall stand in fire up to the navel, and in ice up to th' heart, and there th' offending part burns, and the deceiving part freezes: in troth a very grievous punishment, as one would think, for such a trifle. Believe me, one would marry a leprous witch to be rid on't, I'll assure you.

DOCTOR.

How she continues this fancy! 'Tis not an engraffed madness, but a most thick and profound melancholy.

DAUGHTER.

To hear there a proud lady, and a proud city wife, howl together! I were a beast and I'd call it good sport. One cries, 'O this smoke!' another, 'This fire!' One cries, 'O that ever I did it behind the arras!' and then howls; th' other curses a suing fellow and her garden house.

[*Sings.*]

I will be true, my stars, my fate, etc.

[*Exit* DAUGHTER.

JAILER.

What think you of her, sir?

DOCTOR.

I think she has a perturbed mind, which I cannot minister to.

JAILER.

Alas, what then?

DOCTOR.

Understand you she ever affected any man ere she beheld Palamon?

JAILER.

I was once, sir, in great hope she had fixed her liking on this gentleman my friend.

WOOER.

I did think so too, and would account I had a great penn'orth on't, to give half my 'state that both she and I at this present stood unfeignedly on the same terms.

DOCTOR.

That intemperate surfeit of her eye hath distempered the other senses: they may return and settle again to execute their preordained faculties, but they are now in a most extravagant vagary. This you must do: confine her to a place where the light may rather seem to steal in than be permitted; take upon you, young sir her friend, the name of Palamon; say you come to eat with her, and to commune of love. This will catch her attention, for this her mind beats upon: other objects that are inserted 'tween her mind and eye become the pranks and friskins of her madness. Sing to her such green songs of love as she says Palamon hath sung in prison. Come to her, stuck in as sweet flowers as the season is mistress of, and thereto make an addition of some other compounded odours, which are grateful to the sense. All this shall become Palamon, for Palamon can sing, and Palamon is sweet and ev'ry good thing. Desire to eat with her, carve her, drink to her, and, still among, intermingle your petition of grace and acceptance into her favour. Learn what maids have been her companions and play-feres, and let them repair to her with 'Palamon' in their mouths, and appear with tokens, as if they suggested for him. It is a falsehood she is in, which is with falsehoods to be combated. This may bring her to eat, to sleep, and reduce what's now out of square in her into their former law and regiment. I have seen it approved, how many times I know not, but to make the number more I have great hope in this. I will between the passages of this project come in with my appliance. Let us put it in execution and hasten the success, which doubt not will bring forth comfort. [*Exeunt.*

ACT V. SCENE I.

Before the altars of Mars, Venus and Diana.
Flourish. Enter THESEUS, PIRITHOUS, HIPPOLYTA *and* ATTENDANTS.

THESEUS.

Now let 'em enter, and before the gods
Tender their holy prayers. Let the temples
Burn bright with sacred fires, and the altars
In hallowed clouds commend their swelling incense
To those above us. Let no due be wanting:
They have a noble work in hand, will honour
The very powers that love 'em.

Flourish of cornets. Enter PALAMON *and* ARCITE *and their* KNIGHTS.

PIRITHOUS.

Sir, they enter.

THESEUS.

You valiant and strong-hearted enemies,
You royal german-foes, that this day come
To blow that nearness out that flames between ye,
Lay by your anger for an hour, and dove-like
Before the holy altars of your helpers,
The all-feared gods, bow down your stubborn bodies.
Your ire is more than mortal: so your help be;
And as the gods regard ye, fight with justice.
I'll leave you to your prayers, and betwixt ye
I part my wishes.

PIRITHOUS.

Honour crown the worthiest!

[*Exit* THESEUS *and his train.*

PALAMON.

The glass is running now that cannot finish
Till one of us expire. Think you but thus,
That were there ought in me which strove to show
Mine enemy in this business, were't one eye
Against another, arm oppressed by arm,
I would destroy th' offender, coz, I would
Though parcel of myself. Then from this gather
How I should tender you.

ARCITE.

I am in labour
To push your name, your ancient love, our kindred
Out of my memory, and i' th' self-same place
To seat something I would confound. So hoist we
The sails that must these vessels port even where
The heavenly limiter pleases.

PALAMON.

You speak well.
Before I turn, let me embrace thee, cousin.
[*They embrace.*] This I shall never do again.

ARCITE.

One farewell.

PALAMON.

Why, let it be so; farewell, coz.

[*Exeunt* PALAMON *and his* KNIGHTS.

ARCITE.

Farewell, sir.

Knights, kinsmen, lovers, yea my sacrifices,
True worshippers of Mars – whose spirit in you
Expels the seeds of fear, and th' apprehension,
Which still is farther off it – go with me
Before the god of our profession. There
Require of him the hearts of lions, and
The breath of tigers, yea the fierceness too,
Yea the speed also – to go on, I mean,
Else wish we to be snails. You know my prize
Must be dragged out of blood, force and great feat
Must put my garland on, where she sticks
The queen of flowers: our intercession then
Must be to him that makes the camp a cistern
Brimmed with the blood of men. Give me your aid
And bend your spirits towards him.

[*They prostrate themselves and then kneel before Mars's altar.*]

Thou mighty one, that with thy power hast turned
Green Neptune into purple, whose approach
Comets prewarn, whose havoc in vast field
Unearthed skulls proclaim, whose breath blows down
The teeming Ceres' foison, who dost pluck
With hand armipotent from forth blue clouds
The masoned turrets, that both mak'st and break'st
The stony girths of cities! Me thy pupil,
Youngest follower of thy drum, instruct this day
With military skill, that to thy laud
I may advance my streamer, and by thee
Be styled the lord o' th' day! Give me, great Mars,
Some token of thy pleasure.

[*Here they fall on their faces as formerly, and there is heard clanging of armour, with a short thunder as the burst of a battle, whereupon they all rise and bow to the altar.*]

O great corrector of enormous times,
Shaker of o'er-rank states, thou grand decider
Of dusty and old titles, that heal'st with blood
The earth when it is sick, and cur'st the world
O' th' plurisy of people! I do take
Thy signs auspiciously and, in thy name,
To my design march boldly. Let us go. [*Exeunt.*

Enter PALAMON *and his* KNIGHTS, *with the former observance.*

PALAMON.

Our stars must glister with new fire, or be
Today extinct. Our argument is love,
Which if the goddess of it grant, she gives
Victory too: then blend your spirits with mine,
You whose free nobleness do make my cause
Your personal hazard; to the goddess Venus
Commend we our proceeding, and implore
Her power unto our party.

[*Here they kneel as formerly to Venus's altar.*]

Hail sovereign queen of secrets, who hast power
To call the fiercest tyrant from his rage
And weep unto a girl; that hast the might
Even with an eye-glance to choke Mars's drum
And turn th' alarm to whispers; that canst make
A cripple flourish with his crutch, and cure him
Before Apollo; that may'st force the king
To be his subject's vassal, and induce
Stale Gravity to dance: the polled bachelor
Whose youth like wanton boys through bonfires
Have skipped thy flame, at seventy thou canst catch
And make him, to the scorn of his hoarse throat,
Abuse young lays of love; what godlike power
Hast thou not power upon? To Phoebus thou
Add'st flames, hotter than his; the heavenly fires
Did scorch his mortal son, thine him; the huntress,
All moist and cold, some say began to throw
Her bow away, and sigh. Take to thy grace
Me thy vowed soldier, who do bear thy yoke
As 'twere a wreath of roses, yet is heavier
Than lead itself, stings more than nettles.
I have never been foul-mouthed against thy law,
Ne'er revealed secret, for I knew none; would not,
Had I kenned all that were; I never practised
Upon man's wife, nor would the libels read
Of liberal wits; I never at great feasts
Sought to betray a beauty, but have blushed
At simp'ring sirs that did. I have been harsh
To large confessors, and have hotly asked them
If they had mothers: I had one, a woman,
And women 'twere they wronged. I knew a man
Of eighty winters, this I told them, who
A lass of fourteen brided. 'Twas thy power
To put life into dust: the aged cramp
Had screwed his square foot round,
The gout had knit his fingers into knots,
Torturing convulsions from his globy eyes
Had almost drawn their spheres, that what was life
In him seemed torture. This anatomy
Had by his young fair fere a boy, and I
Believed it was his, for she swore it was,
And who would not believe her? Brief, I am
To those that prate and have done no companion;
To those that boast and have not a defier;
To those that would and cannot a rejoicer.
Yea him I do not love, that tells close offices
The foulest way, nor names concealments in
The boldest language. Such a one I am,
And vow that lover never yet made sigh
Truer than I. O then most soft sweet goddess,
Give me the victory of this question, which
Is true love's merit, and bless me with a sign
Of thy great pleasure.

[*Here music is heard, doves are seen to flutter; they fall again upon their faces, then on their knees.*]

O thou that from eleven to ninety reign'st
In mortal bosoms, whose chase is this world
And we in herds thy game, I give thee thanks
For this fair token, which being laid unto
Mine innocent true heart, arms in assurance
My body to this business. Let us rise
And bow before the goddess.

[*They bow.*] Time comes on.

[*Exeunt.*

Still music of records. Enter EMILIA *in white, her hair about her shoulders, a wheaten wreath; one in white holding up her train, her hair stuck with flowers; one before her carrying a silver hind, in which is conveyed incense and sweet odours, which being set upon the altar of Diana, her maids standing aloof, she sets fire to it; then they curtsy and kneel.*

EMILIA.

O sacred, shadowy, cold and constant queen,
Abandoner of revels, mute contemplative,
Sweet, solitary, white as chaste, and pure
As wind-fanned snow, who to thy female knights
Allow'st no more blood than will make a blush,
Which is their order's robe! I here thy priest
Am humbled 'fore thine altar. O vouchsafe
With that thy rare green eye, which never yet
Beheld thing maculate, look on thy virgin;
And sacred silver mistress, lend thine ear –
Which ne'er heard scurrile term, into whose port
Ne'er entered wanton sound – to my petition
Seasoned with holy fear. This is my last
Of vestal office: I am bride-habited,
But maiden-hearted; a husband I have 'pointed,
But do not know him; out of two I should
Choose one, and pray for his success, but I
Am guiltless of election. Of mine eyes
Were I to lose one, they are equal precious,
I could doom neither: that which perished should
Go to't unsentenced. Therefore, most modest queen,
He of the two pretenders that best loves me
And has the truest title in't, let him
Take off my wheaten garland, or else grant
The file and quality I hold I may
Continue in thy band.
[*Here the hind vanishes under the altar, and in the place ascends a rose tree, having one rose upon it.*]
See what our general of ebbs and flows
Out from the bowels of her holy altar
With sacred act advances: but one rose.
If well inspired, this battle shall confound
Both these brave knights, and I a virgin flow'r
Must grow alone, unplucked.
[*Here is heard a sudden twang of instruments, and the rose falls from the tree.*]
The flow'r is fall'n, the tree descends. O mistress,
Thou here dischargest me, I shall be gathered.
I think so, but I know not thine own will:
Unclasp thy mystery.
I hope she's pleased, her signs were gracious.
[*They curtsy and exeunt.*

ACT V. SCENE II.

The prison.
Enter DOCTOR, JAILER *and* WOOER, *in habit of Palamon.*

DOCTOR.

Has this advice I told you done any good upon her?

WOOER.

O very much. The maids that kept her company
Have half-persuaded her that I am Palamon.
Within this half-hour she came smiling to me,
And asked me what I would eat, and when I would kiss her.
I told her presently, and kissed her twice.

DOCTOR.

'Twas well done. Twenty times had been far better,
For there the cure lies mainly.

WOOER.

Then she told me
She would watch with me tonight, for well she knew
What hour my fit would take me.

DOCTOR.

Let her do so,
And when your fit comes, fit her home, and presently.

WOOER.

She would have me sing.

DOCTOR.

You did so?

WOOER.

No.

DOCTOR.

'Twas very ill done, then:
You should observe her ev'ry way.

WOOER.

Alas,
I have no voice, sir, to confirm her that way.

DOCTOR.

That's all one, if ye make a noise.
If she entreat again, do anything:
Lie with her if she ask you.

JAILER.

Ho there, doctor!

DOCTOR.

Yes, in the way of cure.

JAILER.

But first, by your leave,
I' th' way of honesty.

DOCTOR.

That's but a niceness:
Ne'er cast your child away for honesty;
Cure her first this way, then if she will be honest,
She has the path before her.

JAILER.

Thank ye, doctor.

DOCTOR.

Pray bring her in and let's see how she is.

JAILER.

I will, and tell her her Palamon stays for her.
But, doctor, methinks you are i' th' wrong still.
[*Exit* JAILER.

DOCTOR.

Go, go.
You fathers are fine fools! Her honesty?
And we should give her physic till we find that –

WOOER.

Why, do you think she is not honest, sir?

DOCTOR.

How old is she?

WOOER.

She's eighteen.

DOCTOR.

She may be,
But that's all one, 'tis nothing to our purpose.
Whate'er her father says, if you perceive
Her mood inclining that way that I spoke of,
Videlicet, the way of flesh – you have me?

WOOER.

Yet very well, sir.

DOCTOR.

Please her appetite
And do it home: it cures her *ipso facto*
The melancholy humour that infects her.

WOOER.

I am of your mind, doctor.

Enter JAILER, DAUGHTER, MAID.

DOCTOR.

You'll find it so. She comes: pray humour her.

JAILER.

Come, your love Palamon stays for you, child,
And has done this long hour, to visit you.

DAUGHTER.

I thank him for his gentle patience.
He's a kind gentleman, and I am much bound to him.
Did you ne'er see the horse he gave me?

JAILER.

Yes.

DAUGHTER.

How do you like him?

JAILER.

He's a very fair one.

DAUGHTER.

You never saw him dance?

JAILER.

No.

DAUGHTER.

I have often.
He dances very finely, very comely,
And for a jig – come cut and long tail to him –
He turns ye like a top.

JAILER.

That's fine indeed.

DAUGHTER.

He'll dance the morris twenty mile an hour,
And that will founder the best hobby-horse,
If I have any skill, in all the parish;
And gallops to the tune of 'Light o' Love'.
What think you of this horse?

JAILER.

Having these virtues,
I think he might be brought to play at tennis.

DAUGHTER.

Alas, that's nothing.

JAILER.

Can he write and read too?

DAUGHTER.

A very fair hand, and casts himself th' accounts
Of all his hay and provender: that ostler
Must rise betime that cozens him. You know
The chestnut mare the duke has?

JAILER.

Very well.

DAUGHTER.

She is horribly in love with him, poor beast,
But he is like his master, coy and scornful.

JAILER.

What dowry has she?

DAUGHTER.

Some two hundred bottles,
And twenty strike of oats; but he'll ne'er have her.
He lisps in's neighing able to entice
A miller's mare: he'll be the death of her.

DOCTOR.

What stuff she utters!

JAILER.

Make curtsy, here your love comes.

WOOER.

[*Comes forward.*] Pretty soul,
How do ye? That's a fine maid! There's a curtsy!

DAUGHTER.

Yours to command i' th' way of honesty.
How far is't now to th' end o' th' world, my masters?

DOCTOR.

Why, a day's journey, wench.

DAUGHTER.

[*To Wooer.*] Will you go with me?

WOOER.

What shall we do there, wench?

DAUGHTER.

Why, play at stool-ball.
What is there else to do?

WOOER.

I am content,
If we shall keep our wedding there.

DAUGHTER.

'Tis true,
For there, I will assure you, we shall find
Some blind priest for the purpose, that will venture
To marry us, for here they are nice and foolish.
Besides, my father must be hanged tomorrow,
And that would be a blot i' th' business.
Are not you Palamon?

WOOER.

Do not you know me?

DAUGHTER.

Yes, but you care not for me. I have nothing
But this poor petticoat and two coarse smocks.

WOOER.

That's all one, I will have you.

DAUGHTER.

Will you surely?

WOOER.

Yes, by this fair hand will I. [*Takes her hand.*]

DAUGHTER.

We'll to bed, then.

WOOER.

E'en when you will. [*Kisses her.*]

DAUGHTER.

O sir, you would fain be nibbling

WOOER.

Why do you rub my kiss off?

DAUGHTER.

'Tis a sweet one,
And will perfume me finely against the wedding.
Is not this your cousin Arcite?

DOCTOR.

Yes, sweetheart,
And I am glad my cousin Palamon
Has made so fair a choice.

DAUGHTER.

Do you think he'll have me?

DOCTOR.

Yes, without doubt.

DAUGHTER.

Do you think so too?

JAILER.

Yes.

DAUGHTER.

We shall have many children. [*To the Doctor.*] Lord, how y' are grown!
My Palamon I hope will grow, too, finely
Now he's at liberty. Alas, poor chicken,
He was kept down with hard meat and ill lodging,

But I'll kiss him up again.

Enter a MESSENGER.

MESSENGER.
What do you here? You'll lose the noblest sight
That e'er was seen.

JAILER.
Are they i' th' field?

MESSENGER.
They are.
You bear a charge there, too.

JAILER.
I'll away straight.
I must e'en leave you here.

DOCTOR
Nay, we'll go with you:
I will not lose the fight.

JAILER.
How did you like her?

DOCTOR.
I'll warrant you within these three or four days
I'll make her right again. [*To Wooer.*] You must not from her,
But still preserve her in this way.

WOOER.
I will.

DOCTOR.
Let's get her in.

WOOER.
Come, sweet, we'll go to dinner,
And then we'll play at cards.

DAUGHTER.
And shall we kiss too?

WOOER.
A hundred times.

DAUGHTER.
And twenty?

WOOER.
Aye, and twenty.

DAUGHTER.
And then we'll sleep together?

DOCTOR.
Take her offer.

WOOER.
Yes, marry will we.

DAUGHTER.
But you shall not hurt me.

WOOER.
I will not, sweet.

DAUGHTER.
If you do, love, I'll cry.

[*Exeunt.*

ACT V. SCENE III.

Near the place of the tournament.
Flourish. Enter THESEUS, HIPPOLYTA, EMILIA, PIRITHOUS, *and some* ATTENDANTS.

EMILIA.
I'll no step further.

PIRITHOUS.
Will you lose this sight?

EMILIA.
I had rather see a wren hawk at a fly
Than this decision: ev'ry blow that falls
Threats a brave life, each stroke laments the place
Whereon it falls, and sounds more like a bell
Than blade. I will stay here. It is enough
My hearing shall be punished with what
Shall happen, 'gainst the which there is
No deafing – but to hear, not taint mine eye
With dread sights it may shun.

PIRITHOUS.
Sir, my good lord,
Your sister will no further.

THESEUS.
O she must.
She shall see deeds of honour in their kind,
Which sometime show well, pencilled. Nature now
Shall make and act the story, the belief
Both sealed with eye and ear. [*To Emilia.*] You must be present.
You are the victor's meed, the price, and garland
To crown the question's title.

EMILIA.
Pardon me.
If I were there, I'd wink.

THESEUS.
You must be there:
This trial is as 'twere i' th' night, and you
The only star to shine.

EMILIA.
I am extinct.
There is but envy in that light which shows
The one the other: Darkness, which ever was
The dam of Horror, who does stand accursed
Of many mortal millions, may even now,
By casting her black mantle over both,
That neither could find other, get herself
Some part of a good name, and many a murder
Set off whereto she's guilty.

HIPPOLYTA.
You must go.

EMILIA.
In faith, I will not.

THESEUS.
Why, the knights must kindle
Their valour at your eye. Know of this war
You are the treasure, and must needs be by
To give the service pay.

EMILIA.
Sir, pardon me,
The title of a kingdom may be tried
Out of itself.

THESEUS.
Well, well, then, at your pleasure.
Those that remain with you could wish their office
To any of their enemies.

HIPPOLYTA.
Farewell, sister.
I am like to know your husband 'fore yourself
By some small start of time. He whom the gods
Do of the two know best, I pray them he
Be made your lot.

[*Exeunt* THESEUS, HIPPOLYTA, PIRITHOUS, *&c.*

EMILIA.
Arcite is gently visaged; yet his eye
Is like an engine bent, or a sharp weapon
In a soft sheath: mercy and manly courage
Are bedfellows in his visage. Palamon
Has a most menacing aspect, his brow
Is graved, and seems to bury what it frowns on;

Yet sometime 'tis not so, but alters to
The quality of his thoughts: long time his eye
Will dwell upon his object; melancholy
Becomes him nobly. So does Arcite's mirth,
But Palamon's sadness is a kind of mirth,
So mingled as if mirth did make him sad,
And sadness merry. Those darker humours that
Stick misbecomingly on others, on him
Live in fair dwelling.
[*Cornets. Trumpets sound as to a charge.*]
Hark how yon spurs to spirit do incite
The princes to their proof! Arcite may win me,
And yet may Palamon wound Arcite to
The spoiling of his figure. O what pity
Enough for such a chance? If I were by,
I might do hurt, for they would glance their eyes
Toward my seat, and in that motion might
Omit a ward, or forfeit an offence
Which craved that very time. It is much better
I am not there. O better never born
Than minister to such harm!
[*Cornets. A great cry and noise within, crying 'A Palamon!'*]

Enter a SERVANT.

What is the chance?

SERVANT.

The cry's 'A Palamon!'

EMILIA.

Then he has won: 'twas ever likely.
He looked all grace and success, and he is
Doubtless the prim'st of men. I prithee run
And tell me how it goes.
[*Shout, and cornets. Cries of 'A Palamon!'*]

SERVANT.

Still 'Palamon!'

EMILIA.

Run and inquire. [*Exit* SERVANT.] Poor servant, thou hast lost!
Upon my right side still I wore thy picture,
Palamon's on the left. Why so I know not,
I had no end in't else: chance would have it so.
On the sinister side the heart lies: Palamon
Had the best boding chance.
[*Another cry, and shout within, and cornets.*]
This burst of clamour
Is sure th' end o' th' combat.

Enter SERVANT.

SERVANT.

They said that Palamon had Arcite's body
Within an inch o' th' pyramid, that the cry
Was general 'A Palamon!' But anon
Th' assistants made a brave redemption, and
The two bold titlers at this instant are
Hand-to-hand at it.

EMILIA.

Were they metamorphosed
Both into one! O why? There were no woman
Worth so composed a man: their single share,
Their nobleness peculiar to them, gives
The prejudice of disparity, value's shortness,
To any lady breathing.
[*Cornets. Cry within: 'Arcite! Arcite!'*]
More exulting?
'Palamon' still?

SERVANT.

Nay, now the sound is 'Arcite!'

EMILIA.

I prithee lay attention to the cry.
Set both thine ears to th' business.
[*Cornets. A great shout and cry: 'Arcite! Victory!'*]

SERVANT.

The cry is
'Arcite!' and 'Victory!' Hark! 'Arcite! Victory!'
The combat's consummation is proclaimed
By the wind instruments.

EMILIA.

Half-sights saw
That Arcite was no babe. God's lid, his richness
And costliness of spirit looked through him: it could
No more be hid in him than fire in flax,
Than humble banks can go to law with waters
That drift winds force to raging. I did think
Good Palamon would miscarry, yet I knew not
Why I did think so: our reasons are not prophets
When oft our fancies are. They are coming off.
Alas, poor Palamon!

Cornets. Enter THESEUS, HIPPOLYTA, PIRITHOUS, ARCITE *as victor, and* ATTENDANTS, *&c.*

THESEUS.

Lo, where our sister is in expectation,
Yet quaking and unsettled! Fairest Emily,
The gods by their divine arbitrament
Have given you this knight: he is a good one
As ever struck at head. Give me your hands.
Receive you her, you him; be plighted with
A love that grows as you decay.

ARCITE.

Emily,
To buy you I have lost what's dearest to me
Save what is bought, and yet I purchase cheaply
As I do rate your value.

THESEUS.

O loved sister,
He speaks now of as brave a knight as e'er
Did spur a noble steed. Surely the gods
Would have him die a bachelor, lest his race
Should show i' th' world too godlike! His behaviour
So charmed me that methought Alcides was
To him a sow of lead. If I could praise
Each part of him to th' all I have spoke, your Arcite
Did not lose by't, for he that was thus good
Encount'red yet his better. I have heard
Two emulous Philomels beat the ear o' th' night
With their contentious throats, now one the higher,
Anon the other, then again the first,
And by and by outbreasted, that the sense
Could not be judge between 'em: so it fared
Good space between these kinsmen, till heavens did
Make hardly one the winner. Wear the garland
With joy that you have won. For the subdued,
Give them our present justice, since I know
Their lives but pinch 'em. Let it here be done.
The scene's not for our seeing: go we hence
Right joyful, with some sorrow. [*To Arcite.*] Arm your prize:
I know you will not loose her. Hippolyta,
I see one eye of yours conceives a tear
The which it will deliver. [*Flourish.*]

EMILIA.

Is this winning?
O all you heavenly powers, where is your mercy?

But that your wills have said it must be so,
And charge me live to comfort this unfriended,
This miserable prince, that cuts away
A life more worthy from him than all women,
I should, and would, die too.

HIPPOLYTA.

Infinite pity
That four such eyes should be so fixed on one
That two must needs be blind for't!

THESEUS.

So it is.
[*Exeunt.*

ACT V. SCENE IV

The same.

Enter PALAMON *and his* KNIGHTS *pinioned,* JAILER, EXECUTIONER, *&c.,* GUARD.

PALAMON.

There's many a man alive that hath outlived
The love o' th' people, yea i' th' self-same state
Stands many a father with his child: some comfort
We have by so considering. We expire,
And not without men's pity; to live still
Have their good wishes; we prevent
The loathsome misery of age, beguile
The gout and rheum that in lag hours attend
For grey approachers. We come towards the gods
Young and unwappered, not halting under crimes
Many and stale: that sure shall please the gods
Sooner than such, to give us nectar with 'em,
For we are more clear spirits. My dear kinsmen,
Whose lives for this poor comfort are laid down,
You have sold 'em too too cheap.

FIRST KNIGHT.

What ending could be
Of more content? O'er us the victors have
Fortune, whose title is as momentary
As to us death is certain. A grain of honour
They not o'er-weigh us.

SECOND KNIGHT.

Let us bid farewell,
And with our patience anger tott'ring Fortune,
Who at her certain'st reels.

THIRD KNIGHT.

Come, who begins?

PALAMON.

E'en he that led you to this banquet shall
Taste to you all. [*To Jailer.*] Ah, ha, my friend, my friend,
Your gentle daughter gave me freedom once:
You'll see't done now forever. Pray, how does she?
I heard she was not well. Her kind of ill
Gave me some sorrow.

JAILER.

Sir, she's well restored,
And to be married shortly.

PALAMON.

By my short life,
I am most glad on't: 'tis the latest thing
I shall be glad of, prithee tell her so.
Commend me to her, and to piece her portion
Tender her this. [*Gives him a purse.*]

FIRST KNIGHT.

Nay, let's be offerers all.

SECOND KNIGHT.

Is it a maid?

PALAMON.

Verily I think so,
A right good creature, more to me deserving
Than I can 'quite or speak of.

ALL KNIGHTS.

Commend us to her.
[*They give their purses.*]

JAILER.

The gods requite you all, and make her thankful.

PALAMON.

Adieu; and let my life be now as short
As my leave-taking. [*Lies on the block.*]

FIRST KNIGHT.

Lead, courageous cousin.

SECOND AND THIRD KNIGHTS.

We'll follow cheerfully.

A great noise within, crying 'Run! Save! Hold!'
Enter in haste a MESSENGER.

MESSENGER.

Hold, hold, O hold, hold, hold!

Enter PIRITHOUS *in haste.*

PIRITHOUS.

Hold, ho! It is a cursed haste you made
If you have done so quickly. Noble Palamon,
The gods will show their glory in a life
That thou art yet to lead.

PALAMON.

Can that be,
When Venus I have said is false? How do things fare?

PIRITHOUS.

Arise, great sir, and give the tidings ear
That are most dearly sweet and bitter.

PALAMON.

What
Hath waked us from our dream?

PIRITHOUS.

List then. Your cousin,
Mounted upon a steed that Emily
Did first bestow on him, a black one, owing
Not a hair-worth of white, which some will say
Weakens his price, and many will not buy
His goodness with this note – which superstition
Here finds allowance – on this horse is Arcite
Trotting the stones of Athens, which the calkins
Did rather tell than trample, for the horse
Would make his length a mile, if't pleased his rider
To put pride in him. As he thus went counting
The flinty pavement, dancing as 'twere to th' music
His own hoofs made – for as they say from iron
Came music's origin – what envious flint,
Cold as old Saturn, and like him possessed
With fire malevolent, darted a spark,
Or what fierce sulphur else to this end made,
I comment not: the hot horse, hot as fire,
Took toy at this, and fell to what disorder
His power could give his will, bounds, comes on end,
Forgets school-doing, being therein trained
And of kind manage; pig-like he whines
At the sharp rowel, which he frets at rather
Than any jot obeys; seeks all foul means
Of boist'rous and rough jadery to dis-seat
His lord, that kept it bravely. When nought served,

When neither curb would crack, girth break, nor diff'ring plunges
Dis-root his rider whence he grew, but that
He kept him 'tween his legs, on his hind hoofs
On end he stands,
That Arcite's legs being higher than his head
Seemed with strange art to hang; his victor's wreath
Even then fell off his head; and presently
Backward the jade comes o'er, and his full poise
Becomes the rider's load. Yet is he living,
But such a vessel 'tis that floats but for
The surge that next approaches. He much desires
To have some speech with you. Lo, he appears.

Enter THESEUS, HIPPOLYTA, EMILIA *and* ARCITE *in a chair.*

PALAMON.
O miserable end of our alliance!
The gods are mighty! Arcite, if thy heart,
Thy worthy, manly heart be yet unbroken,
Give me thy last words: I am Palamon,
One that yet loves thee dying.

ARCITE.
Take Emilia,
And with her all the world's joy. Reach thy hand.
Farewell. I have told my last hour. I was false,
Yet never treacherous. Forgive me, cousin.
One kiss from fair Emilia. [*She kisses him.*] 'Tis done.
Take her. I die. [*Dies.*

PALAMON.
Thy brave soul seek Elysium!

EMILIA.
I'll close thine eyes, prince. Blessed souls be with thee!
Thou art a right good man, and while I live
This day I give to tears.

PALAMON.
And I to honour.

THESEUS.
In this place first you fought: e'en very here
I sund'red you. Acknowledge to the gods
Our thanks that you are living.
His part is played, and though it were too short
He did it well. Your day is lengthened, and
The blissful dew of heaven does arrouse you.
The powerful Venus well hath graced her altar,
And given you your love. Our master Mars
Hath vouched his oracle, and to Arcite gave
The grace of the contention. So the deities
Have showed due justice. Bear this hence.

PALAMON.
O cousin,
That we should things desire which do cost us
The loss of our desire! That nought could buy
Dear love but loss of dear love!

THESEUS.
Never Fortune
Did play a subtler game. The conquered triumphs,
The victor has the loss; yet in the passage
The gods have been most equal. Palamon,
Your kinsman hath confessed the right o' th' lady
Did lie in you, for you first saw her, and
Even then proclaimed your fancy. He restored her
As your stol'n jewel, and desired your spirit
To send him hence forgiven. The gods my justice
Take from my hand, and they themselves become
The executioners. Lead your lady off,
And call your lovers from the stage of death,
Whom I adopt my friends. A day or two
Let us look sadly, and give grace unto
The funeral of Arcite, in whose end
The visages of bridegrooms we'll put on
And smile with Palamon; for whom an hour,
But one hour since, I was as dearly sorry
As glad of Arcite; and am now as glad
As for him sorry. O you heavenly charmers,
What things you make of us! For what we lack,
We laugh; for what we have, are sorry; still
Are children in some kind. Let us be thankful
For that which is, and with you leave dispute
That are above our question. Let's go off,
And bear us like the time. [*Flourish. Exeunt.*

EPILOGUE

I would now ask ye how ye like the play,
But, as it is with schoolboys, cannot say.
I am cruel fearful. Pray yet stay awhile,
And let me look upon ye. No man smile?
Then it goes hard, I see. He that has
Loved a young handsome wench, then, show his face –
'Tis strange if none be here – and if he will
Against his conscience, let him hiss, and kill
Our market. 'Tis in vain, I see, to stay ye.
Have at the worst can come, then! Now what say ye?
And yet mistake me not: I am not bold;
We have no such cause. If the tale we have told –
For 'tis no other – any way content ye,
For to that honest purpose it was meant ye,
We have our end; and ye shall have ere long
I dare say many a better, to prolong
Your old loves to us. We, and all our might,
Rest at your service. Gentlemen, good-night.
[*Flourish.*]